W9-BSD-398

For Reference

Not to be taken from this room

ENCYCLOPEDIA OF
SCHOOL
PSYCHOLOGY

This book is dedicated to the memory of my father, Wayne Elbert Lee,
who passed away in January 2004. His forbearance, gentle spirit, and
charity were a model to all who were fortunate enough to know him. He would
have been proud to see this work (as he was of all my work) to completion.

His life was gentle, and the elements
So mix'd in him that Nature might stand up
And say to the world, "This was a man!"

—Shakespeare
from *Julius Caesar*

ENCYCLOPEDIA OF SCHOOL PSYCHOLOGY

EDITOR

STEVEN W. LEE
UNIVERSITY OF KANSAS

A SAGE Reference Publication

SAGE Publications
Thousand Oaks ▪ London ▪ New Delhi

RENFRO LIBRARY
MARS HILL COLLEGE
MARS HILL, N.C. 28754
DISCARD

Copyright © 2005 by Sage Publications, Inc.

All rights reserved. No part of this book may be reproduced or utilized in any form or by any means, electronic or mechanical, including photocopying, recording, or by any information storage and retrieval system, without permission in writing from the publisher.

For information:

Sage Publications, Inc.
2455 Teller Road
Thousand Oaks, California 91320
E-mail: order@sagepub.com

Sage Publications Ltd.
1 Oliver's Yard
55 City Road
London EC1Y 1SP
United Kingdom

Sage Publications India Pvt. Ltd.
B-42, Panchsheel Enclave
Post Box 4109
New Delhi 110 017 India

Printed in the United States of America

Library of Congress Cataloging-in-Publication data

Encyclopedia of school psychology / Steven W. Lee, editor.
     p. cm.
"A Sage reference publication."
Includes bibliographical references and index.
ISBN 0-7619-3080-9 (cloth)
   1. School psychology—Encyclopedias. 2. Educational psychology—Encyclopedias.
3. Child psychology—Encyclopedias. I. Lee, Steven W. (Steven Wayne), 1951-
LB1027.55.E523 2005
370.15—dc22

2004026859

05   06   07   08   09   10   9   8   7   6   5   4   3   2   1

Acquiring Editor:	Jim Brace-Thompson
Editorial Assistant:	Karen Ehrmann
Typesetter:	C&M Digitals (P) Ltd.
Copy Editors:	Freelance Editorial Services
Indexer:	Julie Grayson
Cover Designer:	Michelle Kenny

R
370.15
E563h
2005

NOV 0 9 2006

Contents

Editorial Board *vi*

List of Entries *vii*

Reader's Guide *xi*

About the Editor *xv*

Contributors *xvii*

Acknowledgments *xxv*

Foreword *xxvii*

Preface *xxix*

Entries

A-Z
1-600

Index
601

Associate Editor

Patricia A. Lowe
University of Kansas

Advisory Board Members

Jane Conoley
Texas A & M University

Sandra Christenson
University of Minnesota

Jackie Elliott
Shawnee Heights School District

Stephen Elliott
University of Wisconsin

William Erchul
North Carolina State University

Terry Gutkin
San Francisco State University

Patti Harrison, Ph.D.
University of Alabama

John Hintze
University of Massachusetts at Amherst

Deborah McVey
Lawrence Public Schools

Cecil Reynolds
Texas A & M University

Susan Sheridan
University of Nebraska

Karen Stoiber
University of Wisconsin-Milwaukee

Mark Swerdlik
Illinois State University

Joseph Witt
Louisiana State University

List of Entries

A

Ability Grouping
Abuse and Neglect
Academic Achievement
Accommodation
Adaptive Behavior Assessment
Adjustment Disorder
Aggression in Schools
American Board of Professional Psychology
American Psychological Association
Americans with Disabilities Act
Applied Behavior Analysis
Asthma
Attention
Attention Deficit Hyperactivity Disorder
Authentic Assessment
Autism Spectrum Disorders

B

Behavior
Behavior Contracting
Behavior Intervention
Behavioral Assessment
Behavioral Concepts and Applications
Behavioral Momentum
Bias (Testing)
Biofeedback
Bipolar Disorder (Childhood Onset)
Bullying and Victimization
Buros Mental Measurements Yearbook

C

Cancer
Career Assessment

Careers in School Psychology
Cerebral Palsy
Charter Schools
Cheating
Class Size
Classroom Climate
Classroom Observation
Classwide Peer Tutoring
Cognitive–Behavioral Modification
Cognitive Dissonance
Communication Disorders
Comorbidity
Computer Technology
Conditioning: Classical and Operant
Conduct Disorder
Confidence Interval
Confidentiality
Consultation: Behavioral
Consultation: Conjoint Behavioral
Consultation: Ecobehavioral
Consultation: Mental Health
Cooperative Learning
Corporal Punishment
Council of Directors of School Psychology Programs
Counseling
Crisis Intervention
Criterion-Referenced Assessment
Cross-Cultural Assessment
Cross-Cultural Consultation
Curriculum-Based Assessment

D

DARE Program
Death and Bereavement
Decoding
Defense Mechanisms

Depression
Developmental Milestones
Diagnosis and Labeling
DIBELS
Discipline
Division of School Psychology (Division 16)
Divorce Adjustment
Dropouts
DSM-IV
Due Process
Dyslexia

E

Early Intervention
Eating Disorders
Echolalia
Effect Size
Egocentrism
Encopresis
Enuresis
Erikson's Stages of Psychosocial Development
Ethical Issues in School Psychology
Etiology
Evidence-Based Interventions
Expulsion

F

Facilitated Communication
Family Counseling
Fears
Fetal Alcohol Syndrome
Fluid Intelligence
Formative Evaluation
Fragile X Syndrome
Friendships
Full-Service Schools
Functional Behavioral Assessment
Futures Conference

G

Gangs
Gender
Generalization
Generalized Anxiety Disorder
Gifted Students
Goal Attainment Scaling
Grade Equivalent Scores
Grades

H

Halo Effect
Harassment
Head Start
High School
HIV/AIDS
Homeschooling
Homelessness
Home–School Collaboration
Homework
Hypnosis

I

Individualized Education Plan
Individualized Education Plan Meeting
Individuals With Disabilities Education Act
Individuals With Disabilities Education Act Disability
    Categories–Part B
Infant Assessment
Informed Consent
Intelligence
International School Psychology Association
Intervention
Interviewing

K

Keystone Behaviors
Kohlberg's Stages of Moral Development

L

Latchkey Children
Lead Exposure
Learned Helplessness
Learning
Learning Disabilities
Learning Styles
Least Restrictive Environment
Licensing and Certification in School Psychology

M

Mainstreaming
Manifestation Determination
Mastery Learning
Mathematics Curriculum and Instruction
Mathematics Interventions and Strategies
Media and Children
Memory

Mental Age
Mental Retardation
Mentoring
Middle School
Montessori Schools
Motivation
Motor Assessment
Multicultural Education
Multidisciplinary Teams

N

National Association of School Psychologists
Neuropsychological Assessment
No Child Left Behind Act of 2001, The
Norm-Referenced Tests
Normal Distribution

O

Obesity in Children
Obsessive–Compulsive Disorder
Oppositional Defiant Disorder
Organizational Consultation and Development
Otitis Media
Outcomes-Based Assessment

P

Parent Education and Parent Training
Parent-Teacher Conferences
Parenting
Parents As Teachers
Pedophilia
Peer Mediation
Peer Pressure
Peer Tutoring
Percentile Ranks
Performance-Based Assessment
Perseveration
Personality Assessment
Phenylketonuria
Phonemic Awareness
Pica
Portfolio Assessment
Positive Behavior Support
Posttraumatic Stress Disorder
Prader-Willi Syndrome
Premack Principle
Preschool Assessment
Preschoolers

Prevention
Problem Solving
Program Evaluation
Projective Testing
Psychometric *g*
Psychopathology in Children
Psychotherapy
Psychotropic Medications
Puberty

Q

Qualitative Research

R

Race, Ethnicity, Class, and Gender
Reactive Attachment Disorder of Infancy and
    Early Childhood
Reading Interventions and Strategies
Reciprocal Determinism
Reliability
Reports (Psychological)
Research
Resilience and Protective Factors
Resource Rooms
Responsiveness to Intervention Model
Retention and Promotion

S

Schedules of Reinforcement
School Climate
School Counselors
School–Home Notes
School Psychologist
School Reform
School Refusal
Section 504
Seizure Disorders
Selective Mutism
Self-Concept and Efficacy
Self-Fulfilling Prophecy
Self-Injurious Behavior
Self-Management
Sensorimotor Stage of Development
Separation Anxiety Disorder
Shyness
Single-Case Experimental Design
Single-Parent Families
Smoking (Teenage)

Social Skills
Social Workers (School)
Social–Emotional Assessment
Socioeconomic Status
Sociometric Assessment
Somatoform Disorders
Special Education
Spelling Interventions and Strategies
Standard Deviation
Standard Error of Measurement
Standard Score
Stanines
Statewide Tests
Student Improvement Teams
Study Skills
Stuttering
Substance Abuse
Suicide
Summative Evaluation
Supervision in School Psychology
Suspension

T

Task Analysis
Teacher-Student Relationships
Teen Pregnancy

Theories of Human Development
Time on Task
Time-Out
Token Economy
Tourette's Syndrome
Traumatic Brain Injury
Tutoring

U

U.S. Department of Education

V

Validity
Verbal Praise
Violence in Schools

W

Writing Interventions and Strategies
Written Language Assessment

Z

Zero Tolerance

Reader's Guide

ASSESSMENT

Academic Achievement
Adaptive Behavior Assessment
Applied Behavior Analysis
Authentic Assessment
Behavioral Assessment
Bias (Testing)
Buros Mental Measurements Yearbook
Career Assessment
Classroom Observation
Criterion-Referenced Assessment
Curriculum-Based Assessment
Fluid Intelligence
Functional Behavioral Assessment
Infant Assessment
Intelligence
Interviewing
Mental Age
Motor Assessment
Neuropsychological Assessment
Outcomes-Based Assessment
Performance-Based Assessment
Personality Assessment
Portfolio Assessment
Preschool Assessment
Projective Testing
Psychometric *g*
Reports (Psychological)
Responsiveness to Intervention Model
Social–Emotional Assessment
Sociometric Assessment
Written Language Assessment

BEHAVIOR

Behavior
Behavioral Concepts and Applications

Behavioral Momentum
Conditioning: Classical and Operant
Generalization
Keystone Behaviors
Schedule of Reinforcement

CONSULTATION

Consultation: Behavioral
Consultation: Conjoint Behavioral
Consultation: Ecobehavioral
Consultation: Mental Health
Cross-Cultural Consultation

DEMOGRAPHIC VARIABLES

Race, Ethnicity, Class, and Gender
Socioeconomic Status
Gender

DEVELOPMENT

Developmental Milestones
Egocentrism
Erikson's Stages of Psychosocial Development
Kohlberg's Stages of Moral Development
Perseveration
Preschoolers
Puberty
Sensorimotor Stage of Development
Theories of Human Development

DIAGNOSIS

Comorbidity
Diagnosis and Labeling
Etiology

DISORDERS

Adjustment Disorder
Attention Deficit Hyperactivity Disorder
Autism Spectrum Disorders
Bipolar Disorder (Childhood Onset)
Communication Disorders
Conduct Disorder
Depression
DSM-IV
Dyslexia
Echolalia
Fears
Generalized Anxiety Disorder
Learning Disabilities
Mental Retardation
Obsessive–Compulsive Disorder
Oppositional Defiant Disorder
Pedophilia
Posttraumatic Stress Disorder
Psychopathology in Children
Reactive Attachment Disorder of Infancy and
    Early Childhood
Selective Mutism
Separation Anxiety Disorder
Somatoform Disorders
Stuttering

ETHICAL/LEGAL ISSUES IN SCHOOL PSYCHOLOGY

Confidentiality
Ethical Issues in School Psychology
Informed Consent
Supervision in School Psychology

FAMILY AND PARENTING

Divorce Adjustment
Parent Education and Parent Training
Parenting
Parents As Teachers
Single-Parent Families

INTERVENTIONS

Academic:

Classwide Peer Tutoring
Cooperative Learning
Mathematics Interventions and
    Strategies

Peer Tutoring
Reading Interventions and Strategies
School–Home Notes
Spelling Interventions and Strategies
Study Skills
Time on Task
Tutoring
Writing Interventions and Strategies

Behavioral:

Behavior Contracting
Behavior Intervention
Biofeedback
Corporal Punishment
Positive Behavior Support
Premack Principle
Self-Management
Task Analysis
Time-Out
Token Economy
Verbal Praise

General Terms:

Early Intervention
Intervention
Mathematics Curriculum and Instruction

Other:

Cognitive–Behavioral Modification
Crisis Intervention
Evidence-Based Interventions
Facilitated Communication
Family Counseling
Hypnosis
Mentoring
Psychotherapy
Psychotropic Medications
Student Improvement Teams

Social:

Peer Mediation
Social Skills

ISSUES STUDENTS FACE

Abuse and Neglect
Death and Bereavement

Homelessness
Latchkey Children

LEARNING AND MOTIVATION

Attention
Cognitive Dissonance
Generalization
Learned Helplessness
Learning
Learning Styles
Mastery Learning
Memory
Motivation
Problem Solving
Self-Concept and Efficacy
Self-Fulfilling Prophecy

LEGISLATION

Americans with Disabilities Act
Individuals With Disabilities Education Act
Individuals With Disabilities Education Act
  Disability Categories–Part B
Section 504

MEDICAL CONDITIONS

Asthma
Cancer
Cerebral Palsy
Eating Disorders
Encopresis
Enuresis
Fetal Alcohol Syndrome
Fragile X Syndrome
HIV/AIDS
Lead Exposure
Obesity in Children
Otitis Media
Phenylketonuria
Pica
Prader-Willi Syndrome
Seizure Disorders
Tourette's Syndrome
Traumatic Brain Injury

MULTICULTURAL ISSUES

Cross-Cultural Assessment
Cross-Cultural Consultation
Multicultural Education

PEERS

Friendships
Peer Mediation
Peer Pressure

PREVENTION

DARE Program
Positive Behavior Support
Prevention
Resilience and Protective Factors

READING

Decoding
DIBELS
Phonemic Awareness

RESEARCH

Evidence-Based Interventions
Qualitative Research
Research
Single-Case Experimental Design

SCHOOL ACTIONS

Discipline
Expulsion
Retention and Promotion
Suspension

SCHOOL PERSONNEL

School Counselors
School Psychologist
Social Workers (School)

SCHOOL PSYCHOLOGIST ROLES

Careers in School Psychology
Consultation: Behavioral
Consultation: Conjoint Behavioral
Consultation: Ecobehavioral
Consultation: Mental Health
Counseling
Diagnosis and Labeling
Home–School Collaboration
Multidisciplinary Teams
Parent Education and Parent Training
Program Evaluation

Reports (Psychological)
Research
Responsiveness to Intervention Model
School Reform
(Also, see Assessment)

SCHOOL PSYCHOLOGY ORGANIZATIONS

American Board of Professional Psychology
American Psychological Association
Council of Directors of School Psychology Programs
Division of School Psychology (Division 16)
International School Psychology Association
Licensing and Certification in School Psychology
National Association of School Psychologists

SCHOOL-RELATED TERMS

Ability Grouping
Class Size
Classroom Climate
Grades
Homework
No Child Left Behind Act of 2001, The
Parent-Teacher Conferences
School Climate
Statewide Tests
Teacher-Student Relationships
U.S. Department of Education
Zero Tolerance

SCHOOL TYPES

Charter Schools
Full-Service Schools
Head Start
High School
Homeschooling
Middle School
Montessori Schools

SCHOOLS AS ORGANIZATIONS

Organizational Consultation and Development
Program Evaluation

SPECIAL EDUCATION

Accommodation
Due Process

Gifted Students
Individualized Education Plan
Individualized Education Plan Meeting
Least Restrictive Environment
Mainstreaming
Manifestation Determination
Multidisciplinary Teams
Resource Rooms
Special Education

STATISTICAL AND MEASUREMENT TERMS

Confidence Interval
Effect Size
Formative Evaluation
Goal Attainment Scaling
Grade Equivalent Scores
Halo Effect
Norm-Referenced Tests
Normal Distribution
Percentile Ranks
Reliability
Standard Deviation
Standard Error of Measurement
Standard Score
Stanines
Summative Evaluation
Validity

STUDENT PROBLEMATIC BEHAVIOR

Aggression in Schools
Bullying and Victimization
Cheating
Dropouts
Gangs
Harassment
School Refusal
Self-Injurious Behavior
Shyness
Smoking (Teenage)
Substance Abuse
Suicide
Teen Pregnancy
Violence in Schools

TECHNOLOGY

Computer Technology
Media and Children

About the Editor

Steven W. Lee is an associate professor and director of the School Psychology Program at the University of Kansas. He has been on the faculty at the University of Kansas for 18 years. Dr. Lee is a nationally certified school psychologist and practiced in the Omaha Public Schools and the Department of Pediatrics at the University of Nebraska-Medical Center before coming to Kansas. He has numerous research presentations and publications to his credit. He teaches courses in psychological consultation, counseling, and field experiences in school psychology. His research interests are in child and adolescent anxiety, whole-class assessment systems, and student assistance teams.

Dr. Lee is a member of the American Psychological Association (APA), the National Association of School Psychologists (NASP), and the American Evaluation Association (AEA). He is on the editorial board of *School Psychology Review*. Over the past 12 years, Dr. Lee has been the principal investigator on more than 1.4 million dollars in program evaluation research awards on topics including school reform, school safety, literacy, and economics education. Steven Lee received his bachelor's degree in psychology and his master's degree in educational psychology from the University of Nebraska at Omaha. His Ph.D. is in school psychology from the University of Nebraska–Lincoln.

Contributors

Aaron, P. G.
Indiana State University

Achenbach, Thomas M.
University of Vermont

Adelman, Howard S.
Center for Mental Health in Schools;
University of California, Los Angeles

Alfonso, Vincent C.
Fordham University

Allen, Chiharu
University of Texas at San Antonio

Altschuld, James W.
Ohio State University

Alvermann, Donna E.
University of Georgia

Amaral, Deborah
University of British Columbia

Arbolino, Lauren A.
Syracuse University

Arnold, Wade
University of Florida

Ash, Michael J.
Texas A & M University

Aubrey-Harper, Melissa
University of Utah

Austin, Greg
WestEd

Austin, James T.
Ohio State University

Bainter, Tracey R.
Cartwright School District

Balter, Lawrence
New York University

Barnett, David
University of Cincinnati

Barrett, Rowland P.
Brown Medical School

Barry, Tammy
Texas A & M University

Bass, George M.
College of William and Mary

Bear, George G.
University of Delaware

Beebe, Andrea
Kent State University

Benas, Jessica S.
Rutgers, The State University of
New Jersey

Bieu, Richard P.
University of Hartford

Boehlert, Martha
University of Kansas

Boelter, Eric
The University of Iowa

Bonner, Mike
University of Nebraska at Omaha

Braden, Jeffery P.
North Carolina State University

Bray, Melissa A.
University of Connecticut

Brock, Stephen E.
California State University, Sacramento

Brown, Megan
University of California, Santa Barbara

Brown, Michael B.
East Carolina University

Brown, Ronald T.
Medical University of South Carolina

Brown-Chidsey, Rachel
University of Southern Maine

Busse, R. T.
Chapman University

Caisango, Tommy
Webster University

Callahan, Carolyn M.
University of Virginia

Canivez, Gary L.
Eastern Illinois University

Carey, Karen T.
California State University, Fresno

Carlson, Cindy
University of Texas

Carlson, John S.
Michigan State University

Carlton, Martha
Southern Illinois University, Edwardsville

Christenson, Sandra L.
University of Minnesota

Christiansen, Elizabeth
University of Utah

Cloth, Allison
University of Texas at Austin

Coffman, Diane M.
University of Kansas

Coleman, Tonishea
Baylor University

Conklin, Amy
Northeast Kansas Education Service Center

Cornell, Dewey G.
University of Virginia

Cosden, Merith
University of California, Santa Barbara

Cotnoir, Nicole M.
University of Kansas

Crespi, Tony D.
University of Hartford

Cruise, Tracy K.
Western Illinois University

Cummings, Jack A.
Indiana University

Curtis, Michael J.
University of South Florida

Dalley, Mahlon B.
Eastern Washington University

Daly, Edward J.
University of Nebraska-Lincoln

Davis, Tonya N.
Baylor University

deBoer-Ott, Sonja
University of Kansas

de Moura, Castro Helena
Institute for Community Research; Hartford, CT

Deni, Jim
Appalachian State University

DeRuyck, Kimberly A.
University of Kansas

diSibio, Mary P.
California State University, Hayward

Dolezal, Danielle
The University of Iowa

Downs, Darrell L.
Barry University

Dusek, Jerome B.
Syracuse University

Dye, Gloria A.
Washburn University

Eagle, John W.
University of Nebraska-Lincoln

Ehly, Stewart W.
University of Iowa

Erb, Thomas O.
University of Kansas

Erchul, William P.
North Carolina State University

Fagan, Thomas K.
University of Memphis

Findley, Diane B.
Yale Child Study Center; Yale School of Medicine

Finger, Michael
University of Kansas

Flanagan, Rosemary
Adelphi, University

Flojo, Jonathan R.
Instructional Research Group; Long Beach, CA

Fopiano, Joy E.
Southern Connecticut State University

Ford, Laurie
University of British Columbia

Forman, Susan G.
Rutgers University

Foster, Nancy
Munroe-Meyer Institute;
University of Nebraska Medical Center

Fournier, Constance J.
Texas A & M University

Franz, Carleen
Family Service and Guidance Center and
the University of Kansas

Freeland, Jennifer T.
Indiana State University

Frey, Bruce
University of Kansas

Friedman, Michael A.
Rutgers University

Friman, Patrick C.
Father Flanagan's Boys Home and
the University of Nebraska School of Medicine

Frisby, Craig L.
University of Missouri

Fugate, Mark
Alfred University

Furlong, Michael J.
University of California, Santa Barbara

Gay, A. Susan
University of Kansas

Gentile, J. Ronald
University at Buffalo, State University of New York

Gersten, Russell
Instructional Research Group; Long Beach, CA

Gettinger, Maribeth
University of Wisconsin-Madison

Gilbertson, Donna
Utah State University

Gil-Hernandez, Debby
University of Texas at San Antonio

Gilligan, Tammy D.
James Madison University

Ginsburg-Block, Marika
University of Delaware

Goldstein, Amy B.
University of Pennsylvania School of Medicine and
The Children's Hospital of Philadelphia

Gonzalez, Maricela
Texas A & M University

Gore, Paul A.
ACT, Inc.

Graham, Steve
University of Maryland

Green, Tonika Duren
San Diego State University

Greenfield, Daryl B.
University of Miami

Gregg, Noel
University of Georgia

Greif, Jennifer L.
University of California, Santa Barbara

Haerberli, Frances
University of Wisconsin-Madison

Hamel, Sarah
University of North Carolina at Chapel Hill

Harrison, Kimberly Ann
University of Kansas

Harrison, Patti L.
University of Alabama

Harrison, Richard J.
Emporia State University

Hartwig, Jennifer
University of Georgia

Harvey, Virginia Smith
University of Massachusetts at Boston

Hawken, Leanne S.
University of Utah

Haye, Kisha M.
University of Nebraska-Lincoln

Heeter, Abigeal
University of Kansas

Herrera, Gina Coffee
University of Wisconsin-Madison

Hintze, John M.
University of Massachusetts at Amherst

Hirschstein, Miriam
Committee for Children

Hodapp, Albert F.
Area Education Agency 267; Clear Lake, IA

Hodapp, Joan B.
Area Education Agency 267; Clear Lake, IA

Hoff, Kathryn E.
Illinois State University

Hohn, Robert L.
University of Kansas

Hooper, Stephen R.
University of North Carolina School of Medicine

Howard, Anne M.
Illinois State University

Huberty, Thomas J.
Indiana University

Hughes, Preston
University of Georgia

Ingraham, Colette L.
San Diego State University

Isava, Duane M.
University of Oregon

Jackson, Yo
University of Kansas

Jacob, Susan
Central Michigan University

Jarosewich, Tania
Censeo Group LLC

Jarratt, Kelly Pizzitola
Texas A & M University

Jimerson, Shane R.
University of California, Santa Barbara

Johanning, Mary Lea
University of Kansas

Johnson, David W.
University of Minnesota

Jones, Kevin M.
Miami University

Johnson, Roger T.
University of Minnesota

Kalymon, Kristen
University of Wisconsin-Madison

Kampwirth, Thomas J.
California State University Long Beach

Kaplan, Sebastian G.
University of Virginia

Karcher, Michael J.
University of Texas at San Antonio

Kehle, Thomas J.
University of Connecticut

Ketterlin-Geller, Leanne R.
University of Oregon

Kiekhaefer, Amy
Des Moines Public Schools

Knesting, Kimberly
University of Northern Iowa

Knoff, Howard M.
State of Arkansas Department of Education

Knotek, Steve
University of North Carolina at Chapel Hill

Knox, Pamela L.
Tennessee State University

Kranzler, John H.
University of Florida

Kratochwill, Thomas R.
University of Wisconsin-Madison

Kubick, Robert J.
Akron Public Schools and Kent State University

Kutz, Alexandra
University of Texas at Austin

Landau, Steven
Illinois State University

Lang, Jennifer
University of Kansas

Lange, Jill
University of Kansas

Lapierre, Coady
Tarleton State University

La Rosa, Angela
Medical University of South Carolina

Lauber, Maribel O.
Center for Research on School Safety,
School Climate and Classroom Management;
Georgia State University

Lee, Dong-gwi
Purdue University

Lee, Julie
University of Kansas

Lee, Steven W.
University of Kansas

Leff, Stephen S.
University of Pennsylvania School of Medicine and
The Children's Hospital of Philadelphia

Lehr, Camilla A.
University of Minnesota

Lella, Stacey A.
St. John's University

Lewis, Leon
Appalachian State University

Lewis-Snyder, Gretchen
Eastern Oklahoma University

Lichtenberg, James W.
University of Kansas

Lochman, John E.
University of Alabama

Lopez, Shane J.
University of Kansas

Lowe, Coryn
University of Kansas

Lowe, Patricia A.
University of Kansas

Luhr, Megan E.
University of Kansas

Lundy, Brenda L.
Indiana-Purdue University

Lyon, Mark
University of Denver

Macey, Katherine
Texas A & M University

Macfarlane, Christine
Pacific University

Mahlios, Marc C.
University of Kansas

Manier, Kari L.
Olathe District Schools

Marshall, Megan L.
Center for Research on School Safety, School
Climate and Classroom Management;
Georgia State University

Massengill, Donita
University of Kansas

Mather, Kelli E.
Kansas City, Kansas Public Schools

Mazza, James J.
University of Washington

McCabe, Paul C.
Rochester Institute of Technology

McConaughy, Stephanie H.
University of Vermont

McCoy, Jan D.
University of Oregon

McCurdy, Merilee
University of Nebraska-Lincoln

McKellar, Nancy A.
Wichita State University

Mcloughlin, Caven S.
Kent State University

Medway, Frederic J.
University of South Carolina

Mehaffey, Kerry
Autism Asperger Publishing Company

Mellard, Daryl F.
University of Kansas

Merrell, Kenneth W.
University of Oregon

Metz, A. J.
University of Wisconsin-Milwaukee

Meyers, Joel
Center for Research on School Safety,
School Climate and Classroom Management;
Georgia State University

Miller, Dawn D.
Northeast Kansas Education Service Center

Miller, Michelle A.
University of Wisconsin-Milwaukee

Miller, Rebecca
University of Kansas

Mitchell, Montserrat C.
University of Kansas

Mizerek, Elizabeth A.
University of Minnesota

Moore, James W.
May South

Morrison, Gale M.
University of California, Santa Barbara

Mullis, Cynthia Bainbridge
University of Wisconsin–Whitewater

Murphy, Linda L.
Buros Institute of Mental Measurements;
University of Nebraska-Lincoln

Myles, Brenda Smith
University of Kansas

Nastasi, Bonnie K.
Institute for Community Research; Hartford, CT

Newton, Katherine
Texas A & M University

Northup, John A.
University of Iowa

Oakland, Thomas
University of Florida

O'Farrell, Stacy L.
University of California, Santa Barbara

Oka, Evelyn R.
Michigan State University

Ollendick, Thomas H.
Child Study Center; Virginia Tech

Olmi, D. Joe
The University of Southern Mississippi

Olympia, Daniel E.
University of Utah

Ortiz, Samuel O.
St. John's University

Paige, Leslie Z.
Fort Hays State University

Peerson, Stacey
University of California Davis Medical Center

Perfect, Michelle
University of Texas

Pettersson, Hollie
University of Utah

Peyton, Vicki
University of Kansas

Phelps, LeAdelle
University at Buffalo, State University
of New York

Pianta, Robert C.
University of Virginia

Pickren, Wade E.
American Psychological Association

Poland, Scott
Cypress-Fairbanks ISD; Houston, TX

Powers, Kristin
California State University, Long Beach

Rae, William A.
Texas A & M University

Raffaele Mendez, Linda M.
University of South Florida

Raineri, Gina
University of Alabama

Rasmussen, Heather N.
University of Kansas

Remley, Christine
Lock Haven University of Pennsylvania

Rhoades, Elizabeth Kelley
West Texas A & M University

Riccio, Cynthia A.
Texas A & M University

Richards, Margaret M.
University of Kansas

Ries, Roger R.
College of William and Mary

Ringdahl, Joel
The University of Iowa

Roberts, Michael C.
University of Kansas

Robinson, Cecil D.
University of Alabama

Robinson, Eric
Baylor University

Robinson, Sheri L.
University of Texas at Austin

Rodriguez, Olga
Texas A & M University

Rogers, Karen
University of Kansas

Roodbeen, Paul S.
Warren Consolidated Schools

Rosenthal, Eve
Texas A & M University

Roy-Carlson, Laura
University of Texas at San Antonio

Sailor, Wayne
University of Kansas

Salkind, Neil J.
University of Kansas

Scafidi, Elizabeth C.
Rutgers, The State University of New Jersey

Schaber, Pamela McDonald
University of Texas at Austin

Schensul, Jean J.
*Institute for Community Research;
Hartford, CT*

Semrud-Clikeman, Margaret
University of Texas at Austin

Shaftel, Julia
University of Kansas

Sharkey, Jill D.
University of California, Santa Barbara

Sheridan, Susan M.
University of Nebraska-Lincoln

Shilling, Lilless McPherson
Medical University of South Carolina

Shine, Agnes E.
Barry University

Shriver, Mark
University of Nebraska Medical Center

Siekierski, Becky M.
Texas A & M University

Silver, Cheryl H.
University of Texas Southwestern Medical Center

Simpson, Richard L.
University of Kansas

Skiba, Russell J.
Indiana University

Skorupski, William P.
University of Kansas

Smith, Billy L.
University of Central Arkansas

Smith, Patricia
University of Kansas

Smith, Tom E. C.
University of Arkansas

Snell, Jennie L.
*Private Practice and the University of
Washington in Seattle*

Spies, Robert A.
*Buros Institute of Mental Measurements;
University of Nebraska-Lincoln*

Stamp, Melinda Russell
Northwest Missouri State University

Steege, Mark W.
University of Southern Maine

Steele, Ric G.
University of Kansas

Sterling-Turner, Heather E.
University of Southern Mississippi

Stinnett, Terry A.
Oklahoma State University

Stoiber, Karen C.
University of Wisconsin-Milwaukee

Struckman, Anna
University of Kansas

Stuhlman, Megan W.
University of Virginia/University of Miami

Swanger, Michelle
University of Nebraska-Lincoln

Swanson, H. Lee
University of California, Riverside

Swearer, Susan M.
University of Nebraska-Lincoln

Talbott, Elizabeth
University of Illinois at Chicago

Tarnofsky, Melissa B.
Dumont Public Schools

Tate, Allison L.
Baylor University

Taton, Jonnie
Central Michigan University

Taylor, Linda
Center for Mental Health in Schools;
University of California, Los Angeles

Teitelbaum, Mary Ann
Private Practice

Tharinger, Deborah
University of Texas at Austin

Theodore, Lea A.
Queens College of the City University of New York

Thompson, Rachel H.
University of Kansas

Tindal, Gerald
University of Oregon

Tingstrom, Daniel H.
The University of Southern Mississippi

Tollefson, Nona
University of Kansas

Trapani, Jennifer
University of Texas

Twyman, Todd
University of Oregon

Vacca, John
University of Delaware

Valle, Melisa
Texas A & M University

Vartanian, Lesa Rae
Indiana-Purdue University at Fort Wayne

Veblen-Mortenson, Sara
University of Minnesota

Verhaalen, Susan Elisabeth
Marshall University Graduate College

Vess, Susan M.
The University of Iowa

Wacker, David P.
The University of Iowa

Walkowiak, Jenifer
University of Texas at Austin

Walthall, Keri
University of Kansas

Watson, T. Steuart
Munroe-Meyer Institute, University of Nebraska
Medical Center

Webber, Laura A.
University of Kansas

Webster, Linda
University of the Pacific

Webster, Raymond E.
East Carolina University

Wheeler, Anne Caroline
University of North Carolina at Chapel Hill

Whitaker, Jolyn D.
University of Kansas

Wiethoff, Laure
University of Kansas

Wilkinson, Sloan
University of Alabama

Wilson, Marilyn S.
California State University, Fresno

Witteborg, Kristin
University of Kansas

Woehr, Sarah M.
University of California, Santa Barbara

Yager, Holly
University of Kansas

Acknowledgments

It is not possible to name all of the people that contributed to this volume, so let me first extend thanks to the *ESP* Editorial Advisory Board and the many contributors. Many top-notch scholars in school psychology took time to advise and contribute to this volume, and I owe each of them a large measure of gratitude. This volume would not have been possible if not for Neil Salkind's vision of the *ESP* and his encouragement that helped make it a reality. I would like to thank Jim Brace-Thompson and Karen Ehrmann at Sage for their support and patience during the construction of this volume.

Special thanks go to Patricia Lowe who, as Associate Editor, contributed invaluable content and advice to the volume. Her attention to detail and enthusiasm for the goals of the project were critical in the development of the high quality of the *ESP*. The *ESP* Project Manager, Megan Luhr, showed her unique ability to produce high-quality work from ambiguous directions. Megan never faltered even when the load seemed overwhelming. Thanks, Megan! Finally, my sincere gratitude goes to my wife, Mary, and my family. Without their encouragement and steady support this volume would not have been possible.

Foreword

It is trite, but nonetheless true, to remark upon the information overload that characterizes most of our daily lives. Even highly motivated learners need resources that gather reputable, informative, and important information into formats that are easily accessible and lend themselves to further in-depth exploration. The *Encyclopedia of School Psychology* accomplishes this mission.

While "psychology" is vaguely understood by most people as a career field, the nuances of specialty areas within psychology are not at all available for review outside the purview of the practitioners and researchers in each specialty. The editors of the *Encyclopedia* have gathered an impressive array of information on what school psychology is really about, and regarding what people who are school psychologists really do and know.

The List of Entries is intriguing because of its comprehensiveness, its depth, and ease of study. The list captures the work of school psychologists, who must understand the implications of charter schools (a national educational policy thrust) while being experts in the treatment of a specific pediatric disorder such as echolalia. The Reader's Guide cross-listing is extensive and extremely useful for readers who enter with little prior understanding of how specific (and esoteric) terms such as operant conditioning relate to the daily behavioral assessment practice of school psychologists.

Educators will be interested in entries related to academic success in academics, or programs touted as successful in reducing drug abuse or teenage pregnancy, or strategies to promote schoolwide success. Psychologists will find state of the art information on assessment and interventions across many areas of concern at multiple ecological levels. All will benefit from entries that tackle controversial subjects such as Facilitated Communication; Evidence-Based Intervention; and Race, Ethnicity, Class and Gender.

School psychology is one of psychology's oldest clinical specialties. It is focused on a key facet of human behavior—learning. Positive child and adolescent development, happy family functioning, successful schools, and recovery from debilitating psychological and physical disorders are all influenced by our human capacity to learn.

Diseases, injuries, disorders, poor and dangerous environments, lack of skills and knowledge on the part of caregivers, and poorly considered public policy are all enemies of positive human development. Psychology stands as a field of research and practice that investigates and intervenes at all levels of human experience. School psychologists have focused the formidable power of psychological and educational science toward the experience of children, youth, and families, especially as they relate to schooling and learning in any setting.

The *Encyclopedia* provides both an introduction to the field and a way for experienced practitioners to gain a deeper understanding of how school psychology has progressed to match the demands of the 21st century. I see the volume useful to many public, high school, and university libraries as well as a useful reference for specialists in vocational guidance.

—Jane Close Conoley, Ph.D.
Texas A&M University

Preface

My training in school psychology emphasized that school psychologists should, first and foremost, be consultants. This is, as described by Terry Gutkin and Jane Conoley (1990), the "paradox of school psychology." The paradox is that young school psychology trainees, who are eager to work directly with children through counseling or assessment, find that they may serve children best and most efficiently by changing the behavior of the key adults who are in a position to significantly influence the lives of these children in need. This consultative approach has been embraced by school psychology as an efficient way to deliver services (e.g., through the teacher); and it frees the school psychologist for other assessment, counseling, program development, and prevention activities. However, for some trainees that enter into this paradigm, the notion of working mainly with adults is antithetical to the reasons they entered the field. Others embrace consultation and find that nearly all of their professional encounters are, in fact, consultations. I fall into the latter group and view this volume as a rare opportunity to consult regarding school psychology with you, the reader.

When I mention consultation, the reader is directed to the consultation entries in this volume (as listed under Consultation in the Reader's Guide) written by some of the best-known and most influential scholars in school psychology. The reader will find that consultation has many features, one of which involves providing the consultee (e.g., teacher or parent) with information or content. The *Encyclopedia of School Psychology (ESP)* is designed to provide the depth and breadth of content nonpsychologists need to understand little-known concepts related to psychology in the schools.

The time is right for such a volume. Education is on the forefront of our national thinking, with newspaper headlines covering topics ranging from violence in our schools (e.g., Columbine High School shootings) to identifying schools not making adequate yearly progress under the No Child Left Behind legislation. The public seeks to understand the effectiveness of school alternatives such as homeschooling or charter schools. On a more basic level, parents want to know how their children will fare in school. Will their children make friends? Will they be safe? Will they succeed academically? The goal of this volume is to provide information to attempt to answer these very personal questions while at the same time addressing broad-brush issues in psychology as it intersects with education. Finally, the *ESP* is designed to give the reader a glimpse into the world of a school psychologist and the level of knowledge and skills necessary to negotiate the world of the child and adolescent in schools.

—Steven W. Lee
University of Kansas

REFERENCE

Gutkin, T. B., & Conoley, J. C. (1990). Reconceptualizing school psychology from a service delivery perspective: Implications for practice, training, and research. *Journal of School Psychology, 28,* 203–223.

A

ABILITY GROUPING

Ability grouping is a broad term used to describe a set of educational practices that sort students for instructional purposes based on their perceived learning capacity, as measured by achievement tests, cognitive ability tests, past academic achievement (i.e., grade point average), and teacher recommendations. Historically, ability groups were developed in response to the long-standing belief that the cognitive development of different students occurs at sufficiently different rates to require unique curricula and separate instruction (Oakes & colleagues, 1992). Through these differentiated instructional and curricular conditions, ability groups were originally designed in an attempt to improve instruction for all students based on their diverse capabilities.

Ability grouping is of great interest for school psychologists for a myriad of reasons. Some type of student grouping is present in most schools. However, there are a multitude of claims and questions about the overall effects of ability grouping on student achievement (Kulik & Kulik, 1992; Slavin, 1987, 1990). Ability grouping highlights widespread problems of educational equity among racially and economically diverse student populations. Most important, research and debates about ability grouping have pointed to the promise of providing quality instructional practices to all students—regardless of their perceived ability, ability group, race, or social class—to effectively increase student achievement for all (Loveless, 1999; Ross & Harrison, 1999).

TYPES AND PREVALENCE OF ABILITY GROUPING

The most common forms of ability grouping are within-class and between-class groupings. Within-class grouping occurs when teachers sort students into homogeneous small groups within the same class. A common grouping configuration within a classroom places students who can breeze through a children's novel into one group (e.g., the *redbirds*) and students with limited comprehension skills into the other group (e.g., the *bluebirds*). Between-class grouping, commonly referred to as tracking, occurs when the school sorts students into different classes and/or curricula. Examples of different tracks of classes include advanced placement (AP), honors, regular, and remedial. Examples of different curricular tracks include college preparatory, general, and vocational.

Ability groups are present in virtually all elementary schools (Loveless, 1999). Within-class grouping practices are most prevalent during reading instruction, closely followed by mathematics instruction. While most grouping is within-class, there are limited instances of between-class and across–grade-level groupings.

As students progress through the K–12 curricula, grouping practices begin to shift toward between-class tracking in middle school and become highly pronounced in high school. In middle school, students frequently remain in heterogeneous social studies and science classrooms, but are usually assigned to ability-level classrooms for English and math.

By high school, all students experience a form of tracking. In the past, tracking was typically divided into separate curricular tracks that would either prepare students for college or for the workforce. Today, at least in principle, high schools have moved from static curricular tracks to a flexible multiple pathways model within each discipline, where students are grouped independently in each subject (Loveless, 1999). For example, a student who is weak in social studies, but strong in the sciences can be assigned to general social science courses while advancing to AP physics or chemistry courses. This independent grouping is not without its flaws, however. These flaws are usually the result of scheduling difficulties; a student's placement in one course can and does influence his or her placement into another course. Therefore, a student who is placed in one honors class is likely to be placed in another honors class.

ABILITY GROUPING AND ACHIEVEMENT

The research on ability grouping's effect on achievement is quite extensive, and several meta-analyses have been conducted to synthesize this research. Two prominent researchers who have conducted these analyses are Robert Slavin (1987, 1990), a critic of tracking, and James Kulik (1992), a defender of aspects of tracking and ability grouping.

Slavin and Kulik agree that studies of within-class ability groupings in upper elementary grades, particularly in math and reading, demonstrate grouping is generally effective for all learners, regardless of ability type (high, middle, or low). Each researcher also found that cross-grade ability grouping, commonly referred to as the "Joplin Plan," also raises achievement across ability level in elementary school when compared to heterogeneously grouped students.

In contrast to the within-class practices in elementary schools, research on between-class grouping in middle schools and high schools demonstrates that there are no relative achievement gains in any of the ability groupings when the same curriculum is used across each group. However, most ability groupings do not use the same curriculum across groups. Rather, curricula are adjusted to ability levels of each course. Such curricular adjustments consistently demonstrate positive effects for high-track students. Curricula in the normal and lower tracks demonstrate no effect on student achievement. Because high-ability groups benefit from the instructional changes, and other groups do not, the end result is a widening achievement gap between high- and low-grouped students.

To understand why high-achieving students, but not other groups, benefit from differentiated instruction requires an examination of the instruction in each track.

ABILITY GROUPING AND CLASSROOM INSTRUCTION

Jeannie Oakes and her colleagues (1992) argue there are two issues surrounding ability grouping and classroom instruction: rate of instruction and quality of instruction. Questions surrounding the rate of instruction are most prominent in elementary school where ability groupings usually affect how fast students are exposed to information. Therefore, although the curriculum across ability groups is fairly consistent, the amount of coverage is not. Higher-ability groups move at a quicker pace than lower groups. So, while the research demonstrates that within-classroom ability groups positively affect the achievement of all groups in the classroom when compared to heterogeneously grouped students in the classroom, the distance between the highest- and lowest-achieving groups widens as the higher groups cover more material. As the cumulative effects of this difference grow, the lower-group students fall further and further behind. In this way, ability grouping at the elementary level influences the type of curriculum students experience later in high school.

In high school, and as a result of achievement differences between the highest- and lowest-ability groups of students, instructional focus shifts from rate of instruction to quality of instruction. Lower-track high school courses consistently offer instruction that is not demanding and covers less complex material than high-ability courses. In the lower-ability courses, instruction is often focused on fragmented information, more time is spent in textbooks and completing worksheets, less time is spent on homework, and more time is spent on discipline. In contrast, instruction in high-ability track courses focuses on higher-order thinking skills such as problem solving, comprehension, and application; students are more likely to participate in hands-on learning; and students are assigned greater amounts of homework. In addition to these instructional differences, teachers in high-track classrooms are often the most qualified teachers. These instructional differences may be attributed to the achievement gap between high- and low-track students; but they may have less to do with the institutional structures of tracking, per se, and more to do with the types of instruction students receive. If the focus were to shift to better instruction for all students, this gap could be reduced.

ABILITY GROUPING AND EQUITY

Research indicates ability groups place a disproportionate number of low-income and minority students into lower-ability groups. Thus, ability grouping becomes a sorting mechanism for racial segregation and appears to reinforce inequitable practices and negative stereotypes (Oakes & colleagues, 1992). One reason for the disproportionately high number of minority students in lower groups is consistently lower scores on achievement tests. Although cultural biases on the tests can be questioned, this finding in itself is not problematic. However, when students are placed in lower groups they receive less effective instruction. This serves only to place these students at a greater disadvantage. A second reason is the stereotypical expectations that society and schools have of low-income and minority students. This is consistent with the finding that teachers' perceptions of appropriate student placement into various tracks and ability groups have a small, but significant link to students' race, ethnicity, and social class.

—*Cecil D. Robinson, Gina Raineri,*
Sloan Wilkinson, and Patti L. Harrison

See also Academic Achievement; Classroom Climate; Cooperative Learning; Grades; Learning; Mastery Learning; Math Interventions and Strategies; Reading Interventions and Strategies; Spelling Interventions and Strategies; Writing Interventions and Strategies

REFERENCES AND FURTHER READING

Kulik, J. A., & Kulik, C. C. (1992). Meta-analytic findings on grouping programs. *Gifted Child Quarterly, 36*(2), 73–77.

Loveless, T. (1999). *The tracking wars*. Washington, DC: Brookings Institution Press.

Oakes, J., Gamoran, A., & Page, R. N. (1992). Curriculum differentiation: Opportunities, outcomes and meanings. In P. W. Jackson (Ed.), *Handbook of research on curriculum* (pp. 570–608). Washington, DC: American Educational Research Association.

Ross, C. M., & Harrison, P. L. (1999). Ability grouping. In G. Bear, K. Minke, & A. Thomas (Eds.), *Children's needs II: Development, problems and alternatives*. Washington, DC: National Association of School Psychologists.

Slavin, R. E. (1987). Ability grouping and student achievement in elementary schools: A best-evidence synthesis. *Review of Educational Research, 57*(3), 293–336.

Slavin, R. E. (1990). Achievement effects on ability grouping in secondary schools: A best-evidence synthesis. *Review of Educational Research, 60*(3), 293–336.

ABUSE AND NEGLECT

Child abuse and neglect continue to be serious problems in U.S. society. At some time in their careers, all school personnel are likely to encounter a child who has been maltreated. Through early identification and prevention efforts, educators can play a critical role in helping these children.

PREVALENCE OF CHILD MALTREATMENT

In most instances, acts of child abuse and neglect are initially unknown to anyone except the child and the perpetrator. Given the private nature of these acts, the child's concern about stigmatization and loss, and the offender's fear of criminal prosecution, many instances of abuse and neglect are not reported to authorities. Prevalence rates are hard to ascertain, and are estimated from two sources: reports of substantiated child abuse, and surveys in which adults are asked to recount prior experiences of abuse even if these instances had not been reported when they occurred.

For example, the National Child Abuse and Neglect Data System (NCANDS) is based on state Child Protective Services (CPS) reports. Analysis of the data collected in 2000 found three million referrals to CPS, with 879,000 children identified as maltreated. This is a conservative estimate of the problem, however, as it is based solely on counts of reported and substantiated abuse and neglect. Retrospective adult surveys provide a broader base of information, because they include instances of abuse that were never reported to authorities. Finkelhor (1994) reviewed recent adult surveys and concluded that approximately 20% of women and 5% to 10% of men in the United States had experienced some form of sexual abuse as children, with only one third of those cases reported and substantiated. This estimate did not include instances of physical abuse or neglect.

Despite difficulties inherent in developing prevalence rates of abuse and neglect, estimates indicate that it is a serious national problem. Most importantly, the numbers suggest that most school personnel will encounter children who have been maltreated, although they may not be aware of the identity of these students.

DEFINING ABUSE AND NEGLECT

Abuse and neglect are terms used in everyday discourse, but they have specific and distinct meanings when applied to child maltreatment. Two types of child abuse, physical and sexual, and one type of neglect, physical, are addressed here. Physical abuse is commonly defined as a nonaccidental injury inflicted on a child by another person. Sexual abuse is the sexual assault or exploitation of a child, and can include rape, incest, or other forms of molestation. Either type of abuse can occur as an isolated incident, or frequently over a period of years.

Although it accounts for more than half of CPS reports each year, there has been a neglect of *neglect* in research on child maltreatment. Neglect is defined by the omission of behavior by a parent or caregiver if that omission harms the child, or poses a significant risk of harm to the child. Parents can be willfully neglectful out of hostility, or unintentionally neglectful because of factors such as poverty or depression. To the child, the impact of the neglect is the same regardless of the reasons for it. Thus, definitions of child neglect focus on the unmet needs of the child regardless of parental intent. Physical neglect, including the failure to provide safety from harm or meet the child's basic physical needs, is the most common form of neglect reported. Emotional neglect, defined as an inability to meet the child's needs for connection and support, is more difficult to document, although it can also have serious consequences for the child.

While physical abuse, sexual abuse, and neglect are all forms of child maltreatment, there are several important differences in the circumstances surrounding them. First, sexual and physical abuse may be perpetrated by someone inside or outside the family, while neglect always involves the child's caregivers. It should be noted, however, that in most instances both physical and sexual abuse involve someone known to the child. Second, abuse may focus on one child in a family, while neglect affects all family members. Third, neglect often occurs along with abuse—children who are neglected are also likely to be abused. Abuse, however, commonly occurs without the presence of neglect.

RISK FACTORS FOR CHILD ABUSE AND NEGLECT

There are a number of risk factors associated with maltreatment. Some factors increase the child's vulnerability to abuse outside the home, while others increase the likelihood of familial abuse or neglect. Finkelhor (1994), in a review of studies on child sexual abuse, notes the following risk factors: unavailability of parents, poor parent-child relationships, and parental instability. He also cites a need for caution, however, as some abused children have none of these risks.

Specific risk factors for neglect have also been identified. Peerson (2001) examined differences between neglectful and abusive families and found that neglectful mothers were younger when they had their children, had less education, and had higher levels of depression and parenting stress than the mothers of children who had been abused. In a recent review of the literature, Gaudin and Dubowitz (1996) identified the following risk factors for neglect:

- Maternal age
- Depression
- Passivity
- Poor knowledge of child development
- High stress
- Poor coping skills
- Social isolation
- An underlying deficit in social competence

Poverty is a risk factor common to all types of maltreatment. The association between poverty and maltreatment may be confounded, however, by the access that social service agencies have to poorer families. That is, poverty may be associated with maltreatment because families from middle and upper socioeconomic classes are able to more effectively protect themselves from public scrutiny. Until this issue is addressed, school personnel should not rule out the possibility of abuse or neglect among children with greater financial resources.

Students in special education are at greater risk for maltreatment than are other students. In a study of prevalence rates for abuse within a large, Midwestern city, Sullivan and Knutson (2000) found that children with disabilities were 3.4 times more likely to be maltreated than were their nondisabled peers. Sobsey (2002) identified three ways in which abuse and disability could be associated. First, abuse and neglect may increase the child's need for special education. For example, children who are neglected or abused are likely to miss more school than are other children, and are more likely to have physical and emotional problems that impair their learning. Second, factors such as parental substance abuse, poverty, and violence in the home may increase the risk of both child abuse and having a disability. Finally, the presence of a disability may make children more vulnerable to abuse because they lack the skills to avoid or escape a would-be offender. While a majority of children with disabilities are not abused, educators need to be aware of their vulnerability to maltreatment.

IDENTIFICATION OF CHILD MALTREATMENT

Symptoms of abuse and neglect vary across children. Factors that mediate the severity of symptoms include the nature and duration of the maltreatment, the child's age and stage of development, the support the child receives, and the child's attributions for his or her maltreatment. Some children appear more resilient than others to the effects of abuse for reasons that are not yet understood. At its worst, child abuse and neglect can lead to death or serious injury. A majority of maltreated children present physical and/or psychological symptoms, although no one syndrome has been specifically associated with abuse or neglect. In some instances children indicate no obvious, immediate impact of their maltreatment. However, many investigators believe that that there is a sleeper effect of abuse, and that children are affected in ways that are not evident until they are older.

Although there is no one cluster of symptoms, a number of behavioral problems have been associated with child maltreatment. Table 1 is adapted from two reviews of research on maltreated children (Crosson-Tower, 2002; Veltman & Browne, 2001). The problems noted in Table 1 are not singular to maltreatment and may signal other concerns. Further, while some symptoms are associated with a particular form of maltreatment, many children are exposed to multiple forms of maltreatment and may exhibit an array of these problems. One final caveat is that these behaviors are based on data collected after the identification of abuse or neglect. Thus, these characteristics distinguish maltreated children from nonmaltreated children *after the fact*; but we do not know about differences between these children prior to their abuse or neglect.

Table 1   Characteristics Identified as Possible Signs of Maltreatment

Academic problems
   Delayed/limited language development
   Poor concentration
   Frequent truancy or tardiness

Social or behavioral problems
   Social isolation or aggression
   Frequent misunderstandings of social situations
   Avoidance or clinginess to the teacher
   Psychological distress
   Depression or anxiety
   Low self-esteem

Family problems
   Fear of parents
   Wanting to stay at school; runaway status

Physical signs
   Frequent unexplained bruises
   Unmet physical needs
   Sexual behavior
   Higher levels of sexual knowledge than expected for age
   Sexualized activity or early pregnancy

Adapted from C. Crosson-Tower (2002) and M. Veltman & K. Browne (2001).

As noted in Table 1, maltreated children do not perform as well as their peers academically. As a group, maltreated children tend to have poor language development. Children who have been neglected demonstrate the greatest delays in both receptive and expressive language. These delays are attributed to their social isolation and to the significant role adults play in early language development. Children who have been maltreated, particularly those who have been sexually abused, may also have problems concentrating. Finally, truancy is often noted in children who have been physically abused, particularly when they are trying to hide bruises or other signs of abuse.

Social problems also are evident in this population and may take a number of forms. Children who have been physically abused are more likely to engage in unsolicited aggressive behavior, while children who have been neglected or sexually abused tend toward social isolation. Each of these groups of children demonstrates problems misreading social situations by expecting others to behave toward them in the manner they have been maltreated. Thus, children who have been neglected tend to expect little from others, while those who have experienced physical abuse may behave in an aggressive manner to ward off perceived threats.

Children who have been neglected are likely to have poor attachments to adults, reflecting this through behavior that shows little regard for the teacher or the rules of the classroom. On the other hand, children who have been sexually abused may be too compliant and overly eager to please—behaviors that may not be identified as aberrant because of their positive qualities in the classroom.

The last areas described in Table 1 are behaviors for which the *possibility* of abuse or neglect should be considered. Teachers ought to ask questions of children who are afraid of giving their parents negative feedback even for minor problems. Physical signs of abuse or neglect include unexplained bruises and class absences, poor hygiene, hunger, and chronic tiredness.

Finally, although children with disabilities are more vulnerable than other children to abuse, their symptoms may go unrecognized. When children with disabilities demonstrate withdrawal or aggression, these behaviors are more likely to be interpreted as behavior problems resulting from the disability rather than caused by abuse or neglect. School personnel need to consider the possibility of maltreatment when children with disabilities exhibit problematic behaviors over an extended period of time.

Identification of children who have been abused is a complex and delicate process. As noted, many of the symptoms associated with abuse can reflect other types of problems. However, ignoring the warning signs of abuse can exacerbate the psychological and physical impact of the problem. School personnel need to recognize the symptoms of abuse and understand their obligations to report them.

REPORTING MALTREATMENT

School personnel are required to report the suspicion of child abuse to authorities in charge of child protection. Although abuse typically occurs outside of school, educators are in an important position to recognize and report abuse because of their extensive public contact with children. While school personnel are a primary source of referrals to CPS, studies consistently find that they also tend to underreport their suspicions. Kenny (2001) found that 11% of teachers surveyed admitted to not reporting a suspicion of abuse. Further, when presented with a vignette in which child abuse should have been suspected, only 26% stated that they would report the case to CPS.

There are many perceived barriers to reporting abuse. In a nationwide survey of teachers' reporting practices, Abrahams and colleagues (1992) found that 23% of teachers had reported suspected abuse to CPS. A larger percentage, 74%, indicated that they had suspected abuse at some time, but reported their suspicions to their school administrators rather than the legal authorities. Reasons for not making a formal report included a lack of confidence about their ability to detect abuse, concern about making an inaccurate report, fear of reprisal if the abuse was not substantiated, lack of support from the school, and a belief that child protective services would not be effective.

Before reporting abuse, the educator should talk to the child about his or her concerns. The reporter needs to have sufficient information to confirm his or her suspicion, but does not need the details of the abuse. When interviewing a child about a sensitive topic of this nature, it is important to maintain a calm demeanor and not ask leading questions. It also is critical to be candid with the child about the limits of confidentiality. That is, the child needs to know that any suspicion of abuse will be reported to the legal authorities and school administrators, but that the information can remain confidential from other school personnel, family members, and friends.

Educators need to know the procedures for reporting suspected abuse. The law clearly mandates that school personnel must report their suspicion to the local agency charged with child protection. However, some schools have policies that require anyone who suspects abuse to go through the school's central administration, and this policy is often supported by school personnel who are more comfortable reporting their concerns to the school administration than to CPS. While school policies can be helpful in guiding educators through this process, both legal and ethical problems arise if the school administration decides not to make a report when there is a reasonable suspicion of abuse. School personnel need to be aware that they maintain a legal responsibility to report their suspicions of abuse, whether or not they have the school's support. They are legally protected if the report is unsubstantiated, while failure to report is not only illegal, but is likely to have deleterious effects on the child.

PREVENTION PROGRAMS

School-based abuse-prevention programs have been proliferating since the 1970s. A recent national survey by Finkelhor and Dziuba-Leatherman (1995) found that two thirds of all school children had participated in abuse-prevention programs. However, the extent to which these programs help children to actually prevent abuse is unclear. In 2000 telephone interviews, Finkelhor and Dziuba-Leatherman asked children if they felt that these abuse-prevention programs had helped them to avoid abuse. While program participants were more knowledgeable about abuse and prevention concepts, they did not report fewer incidents of abuse, even when using the strategies, such as yelling or telling someone, that these programs recommend.

The utility of traditional abuse-prevention strategies was also questioned in a study by Ko and Cosden (2001). The surveyed high school students had the opportunity to participate in a school-based prevention program while in elementary or middle school. Students who had attended programs had more specific knowledge about abuse than did those who had not participated. Of the students who participated in these programs, a smaller percentage (15%) reported subsequent abuse than did students who had not participated in a program (24%). However, both groups noted problems in using the strategies taught in these programs. The yell and tell strategies appeared to be more effective with nonfamilial abuse, but most of the abuse they faced was from someone well known to them.

These studies on prevention programs raise the question: What can educators and school psychologists do to help children avoid maltreatment? Prevention programs have traditionally promoted behaviors designed to resist abuse or make it more public. These strategies were developed to help children become more assertive and less compliant with strangers who might play on their fear or passivity. However, these strategies are less effective when the abuse is occurring in the home. In a review of programs for at-risk families, Daro (1993) concluded that effective programs required in-home visitations with modeling and support provided over a period of several years. Thus, while there is a role for school-based prevention programs, there is continued need to monitor for signs of maltreatment, so that relevant community-based programs are made available to intervene within the home and family context.

WORKING WITH MALTREATED CHILDREN

Once maltreatment has been identified, children are likely to receive individual or family counseling outside of school. There has been little research on working with maltreated children in the classroom, although several sources provide guidelines to educators that focus on the child's needs for safety, structure, and support. For example, educators are advised to help these children maintain a routine as this will allow them to feel more secure and clear about expectations. Maintaining confidentiality of the maltreatment—except for those who need to know for legal or treatment purposes—will also increase the child's sense of safety.

Finally, in many instances children who are abused or neglected may find themselves in foster care for varying lengths of time. Maintaining contact with the child's caregivers can help with continuity in academic work. However, children who are separated from their parents are likely to avoid strong attachments with others, regardless of the quality of the care they receive. Thus, educators and other school personnel should not expect students to form strong attachments with them or others. Whatever problems they faced at home, children are likely to be defensive of their parents and mourn their loss.

School personnel are more likely than people in other professions to encounter children who have been abused or neglected. Awareness of the signs of abuse and neglect, and knowledge about how to report and respond to children who have been maltreated, can save lives as well as improve the conditions of these children and their peers both in and out of the classroom.

—*Merith Cosden and Stacey Peerson*

See also Bullying and Victimization; Confidentiality; Crisis Intervention; Ethical Issues in School Psychology; Prevention; Resilience and Protective Factors

REFERENCES AND FURTHER READING

Abrahams, N., Casey, K., & Daro, D. (1992). Teachers' knowledge, attitudes, and beliefs about child abuse and its prevention. *Child Abuse & Neglect, 16*, 229–238.

Children's Bureau Administration on Children Youth & Families. (2002). National child abuse and neglect data system: Summary of key findings from calendar year 2002. Available online at http://nccanch.acf.hhs.gov/pubs/factsheets/fatality.pdf

Crosson-Tower, C. (2002). When children are abused: An educator's guide to intervention. Boston: Allyn & Bacon.

Daro, D. (1993). Child maltreatment research: Implications for program design. In D. Cicchetti and S. I. Toth (Eds.), *Child abuse, child development and social policy* (pp. 331–368). Norwood, NJ: Ablex.

Finkelhor, D. (1994). Current information on the scope and nature of child sexual abuse. *The Future of Children, 4,* 31–54.

Finkelhor, D., & Dziuba-Leatherman, J. (1995). Victimization presentation programs: A national survey of children's exposure and reactions. *Child Abuse & Neglect, 19,* 129–139.

Gaudin, J., & Dubowitz, H. (1996). Family functioning in neglectful families: Recent research. In J. Berrick & N. Barth (Eds.), *Child welfare research review* (Vol. 2). New York: Columbia University Press.

Kenny, M. C. (2001). Child abuse reporting: Teachers' perceived deterrents. *Child Abuse & Neglect, 25,* 81–92.

Ko, S., & Cosden, M. (2001). Do elementary school-based abuse prevention programs work? A high school follow-up. *Psychology in the Schools, 38,* 57–66.

Peerson, S. (2001). *Adding insult to injury: Special needs of families with neglect and abuse.* Unpublished doctoral dissertation, University of California at Santa Barbara.

Sobsey, D. (2002). Exceptionality, education, and maltreatment. *Exceptionality, 10*(1), 29–46.

Sullivan, P. M., & Knutson, J. F. (2000). Maltreatment and disabilities: A population-based epidemiological study. *Child Abuse & Neglect, 24*(10), 1257–1273.

Veltman, M. W. M., & Browne, K. D. (2001). Three decades of child maltreatment research. *Trauma, Violence & Abuse, 2*(3), 215–239.

ACADEMIC ACHIEVEMENT

Academic achievement can be defined as learned proficiency in basic skills and content knowledge. Documentation of achievement is an issue that has seen increasing concern among educators, policy makers, and the general public in recent decades and has been the driving force behind legislative and policy development in education since the turn of the 20th century. Three aspects of academic achievement are addressed in this entry:

1. The format for collecting the observations, typically using academic achievement tests and measures

2. The types of referents or comparisons for making interpretations

3. The purposes of academic achievement testing and the process for making decisions

Each topic is described in detail and related to the larger concern of academic achievement in general using the recently adopted standards for educational and psychological testing promulgated by the American Psychological Association, American Educational Research Association, and the National Council on Measurement in Education.

ITEM FORMAT

In general, tests use either of two format types, depending on how the student is expected to respond. Selected response items present a (question) stem and a set of possible answers from which a response is chosen. In contrast, constructed response items require the student to provide an answer to a given question or prompt without any suggested responses. In *Measurement and Assessment in Teaching*, teachers and researchers believe that both types of items can adequately measure the same content; however, information about student knowledge and/or ability resulting from student responses may be different. For example, selected responses may be more appropriate for understanding the factual knowledge from a student on a unit chapter, whereas a constructed response format is better suited for assessing a student's knowledge of and ability to develop an argument in a debate class. To appropriately influence and direct educational decisions, the intended references and uses of the results must be considered prior to test construction and administration.

Using selected and constructed response items, tests can be designed to measure both declarative knowledge and conditional and procedural skills. The format depends on the nature of the decisions that are to be based on the outcomes. Regardless of format choice, the test items must target the ability of the student (group) and provide enough information to discriminate among different performances to make a valid decision.

Selected Responses

Selected response items provide the test taker with all of the information needed to choose an answer. The item contains a question stem or phrase and a set of possible choices, one of which is correct. Responses include multiple-choice, true/false, and matching questions, and the answers are scored objectively as correct or incorrect using an answer key.

Selection response tests are not limited to measuring factual knowledge, according to most measurement experts. The students' understanding of instructional content and their ability to perform complex analyses—such as judging possible outcomes and interpreting results—can also be measured using selected response items. However, the dependency on reading skills and fixed answer choices may restrict students' responses in a way that limits information for decision making. Apparent correct answers may be the result of guessing by the test taker and can have adverse effects on interpreting a student's actual knowledge and ability. Because of this, positive results obtained from selected response items must be analyzed with caution. With some tests, this type of error is corrected by subtracting an additional fraction of an incorrect response each incorrect response.

Constructed Responses

Test items that use constructed responses ask students to create an answer to a prompting question or issue without any suggested answers provided. Responses may be written, oral, or performance-based. Typical items that require written responses include fill-in-the-blank, short answer, and extended essay. Oral presentations may include speeches and other performances that require demonstration of a physical or motor skill within a specific set of criteria, such as reading fluency within a one-minute time limit. Although most educators believe that responses to these items typically are scored subjectively using a rubric for determining the level of correctness, many performances can actually be scored objectively.

Complex understanding and critical thinking skills can be demonstrated through a variety of production responses. The design of constructed response items enables the student to demonstrate proficiency with skill and content while minimizing the threat of guessing. The format of these items, however, limits the number of opportunities to assess student understanding across broad content areas. Furthermore, reliance on skills of self-expression may interfere with students' ability to demonstrate mastery (e.g., present problems with access skills). Data regarding student knowledge and ability may be further obscured by subjective scoring methods that reduce the repeatability and generalizability of the results.

Summary

Selected and constructed response items allow for the measurement of student academic achievement. Choosing an appropriate test item format depends upon multiple factors. Not only should response type align with the content of the test, but it should also support the decisions to be based on the observed scores.

TEST REFERENTS

Three distinctive types of test referents—norm, criterion, and individual—are available to measure academic achievement. Each uses a different comparative value for interpreting student performance, and each provides different information for educational decisions. Referring to these approaches as "tests," however, connotes a misunderstanding. It is the interpretation of a student's performance rather than the test itself that possesses the characteristic of norm-, criterion-, or individual-reference.

Norm-Referenced

Norm-referenced tests compare students' scores relative to students' scores in another, similar group (a normative sample) on the same items and tasks. Norm-referencing is relative in that the interpretations are quantified with a specific metric that positions the student within a group. A number of different metrics typically are offered, including: (a) ranks in the form of percentile and stanines, all of which provide ordinal outcomes; and (b) scale scores such as z- and t-scores as well as normal curve equivalent scores, all of which provide interval outcomes. For example, a student scoring in the 90th percentile on a given standardized test means that that student scored better than 90% of the students in the normative sample. In contrast, a z-score of −1.0 means that the student performed 1 standard deviation below the average of others in the norm group.

Norm-referenced test interpretations are made primarily when reporting student achievement on widely used standardized academic aptitude or achievement tests. Decisions regarding college admissions, for example, may rely on the SAT (formerly The Scholastic Achievement Test), ACT (formerly The American College Testing Program), or the Graduate Record Examination (GRE). Similarly, most statewide examinations use norm-referenced tests such as the Iowa Test of Basic Skills (ITBS) and the California Achievement Test (CAT).

Criterion-Referenced

Educational decisions based on interpretations of criterion-referenced tests focus on a specific set of items or problems that have been carefully sampled from a well-defined domain to judge student mastery relative to a set of absolute criteria. When states test students to determine if they have met specific standards, they are using criterion-referenced tests. Criterion-referenced interpretations do not depend on how other students performed; rather it is the amount of content or skill mastery that the student possesses that is being measured. For example, teachers typically make criterion-referenced decisions based on chapter tests to rank student performance levels. If a student scores 85% on a chapter test, the teacher can infer that the student possesses 85% mastery of the content or skill tested, from which the teacher can then make qualitative decisions (e.g., grades). Many norm-referenced tests purport to be criterion-referenced by the nature of the alignment with specific objectives. At a national level, the National Assessment of Educational Progress (NAEP) provides explicit skill assessments and specifies certain levels of minimum competency, or criteria, which measure a student's progress toward proficiency in many different subject areas.

Individual-Referenced

A third approach to instructional decision making leads to individual-referenced interpretations. In this case, instructional decisions are made based on data obtained from repeated measures to determine an individual student's improvement over time. Making individual-referenced interpretations requires using several comparable measures to derive different metrics, including changes in:

- Step (spikes in performance because of program introduction)
- Slope (rate of change in performance)
- Variability (inconsistency in performance)
- Overlap (commonalities with other domains)

The best example of this type of test reference is with curriculum-based measures that were developed in the mid-1980s to document student progress in reading, writing, and spelling. Although not formally rendered, teachers focus on change, using the student's previous performance to mark improvement.

In this type of testing, comparable materials are sampled over time (e.g., a reading passage or a list of math problems) and administered to the student. Although a constructed response typically is required, the scoring system is objective (e.g., counting the number of words read or digits computed correctly). The outcomes that are displayed often are graphs showing the changes in the student's performance. To be effective, this system requires that the alternate tests be developed and used to reduce assessment errors associated with familiarity with one repeated test. By equating the tests during development, they can be used to measure the same construct (e.g., reading comprehension) in practice.

Summary

All tests represent a limited sample of behavior from which we can make inferences to larger contexts, generalized situations, or another time following instruction. Norm- and criterion-referenced tests are usually thought of as *summative* assessment techniques that provide a basis for evaluation of student learning gains; whereas individual-referenced tests are *formative* assessments that provide monitoring of student progress over time, thus enabling adjustments in instruction to accommodate individual students. Using individual-referenced assessments, instructional adjustments and academic evaluations can be more timely and accurate. Whether decisions are made summatively or formatively, carefully planned, systematic assessments are critical and must yield data consistent with the instructional purpose for testing.

PURPOSES OF ACADEMIC ACHIEVEMENT TESTING

Edward Haertel (1989), in his article "Validity Arguments for High-Stakes Testing: In Search of the Evidence," suggests that large-scale achievement tests are becoming increasingly commonplace throughout the United States and the developed world, and their primary benefits are that they: "(1) provide information for accountability, evaluation, or comparative purposes; (2) focus public and media attention on educational concerns; and (3) change educational practice by influencing curriculum and instruction or by spurring greater effort on the part of school administrators, teachers, and students" (p. 6). Each of these purposes places differing demands upon an achievement testing system.

Providing Information and Accountability

Often, large-scale testing is used merely to provide a measure of personal academic achievement among students. Test information can be used by individuals or groups (systems) to make decisions, such as:

- Future academic placements (e.g., college admission)
- Whether to promote a student to the next level (grade)
- Whether a student needs special education or Title 1 (of the Elementary and Secondary Education Act of 1965) services
- Whether to assign a student to summer school
- Whether a student needs to participate in tutoring programs

All of these decisions are made using test information, which also can be used to allocate resources for individual students at the systems level. And, increasingly, states are implementing legislation that requires students to pass benchmark or state tests in order to graduate from high school.

Using tests for these purposes often influences public opinion as well as official policy. Results of student achievement measures are commonly reported in local public media alongside the results of these same assessments in comparable or nearby schools and districts. Comparing student achievement data among schools and districts needs to done with caution, because variables such as available classroom resources (both physical and financial), teacher ability, and class size can affect student achievement results. Given the numerous variables that must be taken into consideration when evaluating student achievement measures in the aggregate, it is difficult to draw any indisputable conclusions about the causes of a particular result.

Focusing Public Attention

Aggregate student achievement data are useful for focusing the attention of the public, through media campaigns, on issues of concern in education. Those seeking to influence public perceptions of particular instructional or curricular programs can use achievement data to strengthen their case. This outcome might be useful when attempting, for instance, to increase funding for arts education or to modify the social science curriculum to include more emphasis on geography and map-reading skills. Again, caution is needed as this use typically relies on norm-referenced interpretations.

Changing Educational Practice

The final area of decision making served by testing is school reform, or improvement, where achievement is used to decide which practices are working and which are failing and need to be changed. Two primary areas addressed are curriculum, the content of courses, and instructional practices, the activities in which students and teachers engage. The test scores and evaluations can be used to support the use of a curriculum that is succeeding or to guide staff toward particularly promising practices of a successful instructional model.

SUMMARY

An ongoing and spirited discussion continues among assessment experts, policy makers, legislators, and school staff as to the value and efficacy of current and proposed uses of student achievement testing in decision making. Despite limited research supporting some uses of such outcome measures, continued use of achievement tests in decision making is likely, providing information that allocates resources, evaluates program impact, informs the public, and directs reform in curriculum and instruction. Therefore, a number of considerations must be addressed in making decisions on the basis of student academic achievement, including:

- The suitability of questioning formats in identifying student strengths and weaknesses relative to instructional content
- The appropriate referent for the assessment maximizing information available for decision making
- The potential impact on the student's future educational opportunities from making such decisions

If adequate consideration is given to these issues in developing testing materials and testing students, decisions made based on academic achievement can be relied upon to be as valuable as possible.

—Jan D. McCoy, Todd Twyman,
Leanne R. Ketterlin-Geller, and Gerald Tindal

See also Bias (Testing); Criterion-Referenced Assessment; Grades; Learning Disabilities; Mental Retardation; Normal Distribution; Norm-Referenced Testing; Performance-Based Assessment; Written Language Assessment

REFERENCES AND FURTHER READING

Alexander, P. A., Schallert, D. L., & Hare, V. C. (1989). Coming to terms: How researchers in learning and literacy talk about knowledge. *Review of Educational Research, 61,* 315–343.

American Educational Research Association, American Psychological Association, & National Council on Measurement in Education. (1999). *Standards for Educational and Psychological Testing.* Washington, DC: American Educational Research Association.

Haertel, E. H. (1989). Validity arguments for high-stakes testing: In search of the evidence. *Educational Measurement: Issues and Practice, 13,* 5–9.

Linn, R., & Gronlund, N. (2000). *Measurement and assessment in teaching.* Upper Saddle River, NJ: Merrill.

ACCOMMODATION

Accommodation is the process of changing a current cognitive schema to include new information.

Jean Piaget (1896–1980) proposed that children learn by adaptation, which includes assimilation and accommodation. Assimilation involves bringing new information into the mind. A child knows birds fly. When he or she sees a butterfly, it fits into his or her beliefs regarding things that fly, as it is small and has wings like birds; this is assimilation. However, when a child sees an airplane in the sky, he or she realizes that it is flying, but it is not small and the wings do not move. In order to incorporate airplanes into the child's thinking regarding things that fly, the child must change his or her beliefs to include large machines with motors that can also fly. This is accommodation. Now the child has a broader belief system or schema about things that can fly.

—Marilyn S. Wilson

See also Learning; Preschoolers; Theories of Human Development

ADAPTIVE BEHAVIOR ASSESSMENT

Adaptive behavior includes those skills necessary for personal independence and social responsibility. The criteria for evaluating adaptive behavior vary according to age because those skills expected and needed to be independent and responsible develop as an individual grows. As noted by Sattler (2002), adaptive behavior is most commonly evaluated only when there are questions about an individual's overall functioning and skills. Specifically, adaptive behavior is included as one of the areas requiring documentation for a diagnosis of mental retardation. There are two major diagnostic definitions of mental retardation; both of these include deficits in adaptive behavior as a required component for diagnosis of mental retardation. In addition, cognitive deficits must be present for a diagnosis of mental retardation.

The *Diagnostic and Statistical Manual of Mental Disorders, Fourth Edition-Text Revision* (*DSM-IV-TR*) is published by the American Psychiatric Association (2000) and includes specific domains of adaptive behavior in its definition of mental retardation. According to the *DSM-IV-TR*, mental retardation is characterized in part by "significant limitations in adaptive functioning in at least two of the following skill areas: communication, self-care, home living, social/interpersonal skills, use of community resources, self-direction, functional academic skills, work, leisure, health, and safety." While the *DSM-IV-TR* criteria are designed for use in the diagnostic process, they also provide several domains of functioning typically included in assessment of overall adaptive behavior.

A second conceptualization of adaptive behavior is included the American Association of Mental Retardation (AAMR) (2002). The AAMR wording is more broad and includes three domains of adaptive skills: conceptual, social, and practical. The AAMR definition is accompanied by five major principles for the assessment and understanding of adaptive behavior:

1. Limitations in present functioning must be considered within the context of community environments typical of the individual's age, peers, and culture.

2. Valid assessment considers cultural and linguistic diversity as well as differences in communication, sensory, motor, and behavioral factors.

3. Within an individual, limitations often coexist with strengths.

4. An important purpose of describing limitations is to develop a profile of needed supports.

5. With appropriate personalized supports over a sustained period, the life functioning of the person with mental retardation generally will improve.

An important difference between the definitions of adaptive behavior provided by the *DSM-IV-TR* and by the AAMR is the durability of adaptive behavior limitations. The *DSM-IV-TR* definition is typically interpreted such that adaptive behavior deficits are considered to be permanent characteristics of an individual, and they are not expected to change over time. By contrast, the AAMR definition includes broader terms and is accompanied by a guiding principle (number 5) that acknowledges an individual's adaptive behavior could change over time.

ASSESSMENT OF ADAPTIVE BEHAVIOR

As noted above, assessment of adaptive behavior is commonly done as part of an evaluation for mental retardation. Nonetheless, the specific steps and methods used to conduct adaptive behavior assessments can vary. For adaptive behavior assessments to be useful, three major questions should be asked both before and during the assessment:

1. What type of decision is needed?

2. What adaptive behavior domains need to be evaluated?

3. Can the results be used to inform program planning and monitoring?

First, what is the nature of the decision to be made as a result of the assessment? If it is primarily to determine eligibility for services, then including measures that specifically document how the individual meets the eligibility criteria is important. If the assessment is primarily for program evaluation and planning, then other, more global adaptive skills measures may be more appropriate.

Second, the evaluator should determine which adaptive behaviors need to be assessed. If an individual

has already shown competency in certain adaptive behavior domains, then evaluating those may not be necessary. Instead, the assessment should focus on skills that are less developed or previously identified as deficits. The third step in adaptive behavior assessment is to select measurement tools that can be used to inform program planning and progress monitoring. Regardless of whether the assessment is being conducted for eligibility or program planning reasons, all assessment components should be able to provide information about what types of activities should be included in future programs. Once the purpose, domains, and programming needs of the assessment are identified, the actual assessment of adaptive behavior can begin.

As noted by Salvia and Ysseldyke (2001), many traditional approaches to adaptive behavior assessment have relied heavily on third-party reports. For example, the parents, teachers, or other caregivers of individuals with adaptive behavior impairments fill out ratings scales or are interviewed about an individual's behaviors; this approach to assessment is known as indirect assessment. The limitation of this approach is that it is prone to measurement error in that those who complete the items may have biased or inadequate knowledge about the specific adaptive behaviors being assessed. As a result of the limitations of indirect assessment, direct assessment methods for measuring adaptive behavior skills have been developed. Such direct methods include direct observations and task analysis, as recommended by Browder and Snell (1988).

For adaptive behavior assessments to be considered comprehensive and include the three components described above, it is recommended that they include at least two, and preferably three (depending on the specific needs of the child or the nature of the child's problems), types of data about the individual being assessed. Specifically, a comprehensive adaptive behavior assessment should include information obtained from:

1. Observations of the individual in real-life, everyday situations

2. Performance on tasks taken from the current program

3. Interviews and checklists completed by those who work most closely with the individual on a regular basis

At times it may be necessary to use multiple sets of each type of information so that data from a variety of everyday settings are collected. For example, for a school-age student, observations and task analysis from several different classes, as well as completion of checklists by all current teachers are necessary in order to obtain a complete picture of current adaptive skills.

ADAPTIVE BEHAVIOR INSTRUMENTS

Ideally, the first step in adaptive behavior assessment is to meet the individual being assessed and learn more about the specific behaviors to be evaluated. A logical next step is to observe the individual in natural environments to see how she or he relates and adapts to different settings. As appropriate, performance tasks can be administered to learn how well specific tasks can be done. For example, during or after an observation of a student in a life-skills classroom, the examiner can work one-on-one with the student to evaluate performance on target skills such as meal preparation, dressing, grooming, or academic skills. After the observations and performance assessment, the student's mastery of specific skills can be evaluated using task analysis. This analysis breaks the individual's performance of certain skills down into discrete steps so that progress toward mastery can be measured. Based on the information obtained from both the observations and the direct interactions with the student, the examiner can decide which interview questions or rating scales and checklists are best suited to identify the individual's current adaptive behavior skills.

A number of adaptive behavior instruments and measures have been published. In general, these instruments can be grouped into two categories: norm-referenced and criterion-referenced. Norm-referenced adaptive behavior instruments are those for which normative information from a random sample of individuals has been collected. The performance of the individual being assessed is compared to the national norms to learn his or her relative standing when compared to others of the same age. Criterion-referenced measures include specific behaviors; the individual is measured according to the extent to which these skills (criteria) have been mastered. Norm-referenced measures are better for situations in which the purpose of assessment is eligibility decision making, whereas criterion-based measures are better for situations in which program-planning decisions are the primary purpose for assessment. A brief summary of adaptive behavior instruments is found in Table 1. The table includes examples of both norm-referenced and criterion-referenced instruments.

Table 1   Norm-Referenced and Criterion-Referenced Adaptive Behavior Instruments

Norm-Referenced Instruments	*Criterion-Referenced Instruments*
AAMD* Adaptive Behavior Scales, Second Edition (1993) Residential and Community Scale School Scale	Assessment of Adaptive Areas (1996)
Adaptive Behavior Evaluation Scale, Revised (1995) Home Version School Version	Assessment of Basic Language and Learning Skills (1998)
Adaptive Behavior Inventory (1986)	Checklist of Adaptive Living Skills (1997)
Responsibility and Independence Scale for Adolescents (1990)	Developmental Assessment for Students with Severe Disabilities, Second Edition (1999)
Scales of Independent Behavior, Revised (1996)	Vineland Adaptive Behavior Scale (1984)

*American Association of Mental Deficiency

Several instruments have multiple informant response forms. For example, the Adaptive Behavior Evaluation Scale (ABES) has versions for home and school. The Scales of Independent Behavior, Revised (SIB-R) has only one form, but it can be filled out by multiple informants.

The final step in adaptive behavior assessment is to put together all the collected information to create an adaptive behavior profile. This profile should address the three assessment questions identified earlier (purpose for assessment, domains of skills assessed, and indicators for programming and progress monitoring). Taken together, the information contained in the profile can be used to assist in determining the levels of current adaptive behaviors, whether such behaviors lead to eligibility for special services, what additional programming and services are needed, and how progress toward program goals can be monitored on a regular basis. Below is a brief example of how the above adaptive behavior assessment methods were used to conduct an evaluation of a 10-year-old student.

CASE EXAMPLE

Beth is a 10-year-old girl who has been placed in the fourth grade at her local elementary school. She was diagnosed as having Down syndrome when she was an infant, and, based on that diagnosis, she has been provided with special education and related services since infancy. The purpose of the current evaluation is to determine Beth's progress toward the educational goals included in her Individualized Education Plan (IEP). The target skills to be evaluated are initiating interactions with same-age peers and following one-step directions. First, Beth was observed on three different occasions in her general education classroom. Next, the examiner worked one-on-one with Beth giving one-step directions, including having her say "hello" to a classmate. Based on these data, Beth's parents and teachers completed the Social Skills sections of the Checklist of Adaptive Living Skills (CALS). In addition, Beth's mother and teachers were interviewed to learn whether Beth's demonstrations of the target skills were typical behaviors for her. The information gathered from the observations, task analysis, checklists, and interviews indicated that Beth initiates social interactions with her same-age peers approximately once per day and follows one-step

instructions without prompting approximately three times a day. The information gained from the adaptive behavior assessment can be used to establish new instructional goals for Beth, which can then be monitored each week to learn the rate of her progress toward those goals.

SUMMARY

Adaptive behavior includes skills that allow one to engage in age-appropriate and culturally relevant behaviors for the purpose of everyday functioning. While there are two major conceptualizations of the domains of adaptive behavior, there is agreement that adaptive behaviors are important for participation in the larger society. Assessment of adaptive behavior includes evaluating an individual's skills across several settings and with multiple sources of information to learn the extent to which current behaviors are adequate for optimal functioning. Comprehensive adaptive behavior assessment uses observations, interviews, task analysis, and informant survey responses to develop an adaptive behavior profile that addresses the purpose of the assessment, adaptive behavior domains assessed, and program and progress implications.

—*Rachel Brown-Chidsey and Mark W. Steege*

See also Autism Spectrum Disorders; Individualized Education Plan (IEP); Individuals With Disabilities Education Act; Least Restrictive Environment (LRE); Mental Retardation; Traumatic Brain Injury

REFERENCES AND FURTHER READING

American Association of Mental Retardation (AAMR). (2002). *Mental retardation definition, classification, and systems of supports* (10th ed.). Washington, DC: Author.

American Psychiatric Association. (2000). *Diagnostic and statistical manual of mental disorders* (4th ed., text rev.). Washington, DC: Author.

Browder, D. M., & Snell, M. E. (1988). Assessment of individuals with severe handicaps. In E. S. Shapiro & T. R. Kratochwill (Eds.), *Behavioral assessment in schools*. New York: Guilford.

Bruininks, R. H., & Morreau, L. E. (1995). *Checklist of adaptive living skills*. Itasca, IL: Riverside.

Salvia, J., & Ysseldyke, J. E. (2001). *Assessment* (8th ed.). Boston: Houghton Mifflin.

Sattler, J. M. (2002). *Assessment of children: Behavioral and clinical applications* (4th ed.). San Diego, CA: Jerome M. Sattler.

ADJUSTMENT DISORDER

A normal part of child development involves experiencing events that are unexpected or unpleasant and learning how to overcome these challenges. However, for some individuals, recovery after a stressful event is not so easy and distress appears long after the event is over. Children who exhibit problematic reactions to stressful experiences beyond typical levels may be demonstrating symptoms of an adjustment disorder.

The *Diagnostic and Statistical Manual of Mental Disorders, Fourth Edition-Text Revision* (*DSM-IV-TR*) (American Psychiatric Association, 2000) describes adjustment disorder as a child's response to an identifiable stressor that is much more severe than would be expected. Adjustment disorder also applies when the reaction is expected or typical, but reaches the threshold for an adjustment disorder when that reaction begins to impair the child's social or school functioning. For example, if a child performed poorly on a test, it would not be surprising if, afterwards, the child had some significant anxiety when it was time to take another test. If, however, that anxiety prevented the child from being able to go back to school, the child's overly anxious response would begin to fit the criteria for adjustment disorder.

The duration of the distress and degree of impairment are also important. The diagnosis is not given until the symptoms are present for at least three months since the stress event ended, but not longer than six months. A less-than-six-month period of distress is deemed *acute*. The problem is considered *chronic* when the reaction is in response to a chronic stress event. That is, if the stress event is ongoing (e.g., poverty), the symptoms may persist longer than six months and still meet criteria for a diagnosis of adjustment disorder. However, if the event is not an ongoing event and the symptoms of distress continue past six months, the child may qualify for another disorder (e.g., depression, anxiety). In the latter example, further assessment would likely be needed.

Children with adjustment disorder often feel depressed and anxious. As a result, they often act out against the rules at home and in school. Teachers may notice that some children, who otherwise have been well behaved, may develop serious maladjustment problems after exposure to a stressful event. Other children exposed to the same stressful event may withdraw and become socially isolated. Both the acting out and the withdrawal types of reactions are included in the scope of the adjustment disorder diagnosis. Children in the midst of an adjustment disorder are likely to perform poorly in their schoolwork. Furthermore, they are likely to gather very little support, as their emotional and behavioral difficulties tend to create distance in their family and peer relationships. A key to the diagnosis is the documentation of the change in behavior (both internalizing and externalizing), the duration of the symptoms, and the impairment in functioning.

The distress associated with adjustment disorder can be related to suicide, suicide attempts, substance use, and physical complaints. The combination of an adjustment disorder with a preexisting medical illness may worsen the medical condition. Specifically, the symptoms of adjustment disorder can exacerbate the course of an illness, interfere with adherence to a medical regime, or lengthen a hospital stay. For children with medical conditions, the presence of a co-occurring adjustment disorder may result in increases in time spent outside the classroom and away from peers.

Children diagnosed with adjustment disorder display a range of emotional and behavioral problems. According to the *DSM-IV*, the diagnosis includes several subtypes. Each of the subtypes provides a description of the primary or predominant symptoms demonstrated by the child. For example, Adjustment disorder "with depressed mood" relates to symptoms of hopelessness and tearfulness. Adjustment disorder "with anxiety" refers to symptoms of worry and fear of separation from primary attachment figures. Adjustment disorder "with disturbance of conduct" refers to symptoms indicative of violations of the rights of others or major rule breaking. The *DSM-IV* has two separate subtypes for children who display combinations of the above kinds of symptoms: "with mixed anxiety and depressed mood," and "with mixed disturbance of emotions and conduct." The final subtype is reserved for maladaptive reactions (i.e., physical complaints) that are not classifiable in the other subtype categories. It is important to note that impairment associated with responding to the death of a loved one is not included in the definition of an adjustment disorder.

Overall, it appears that adjustment disorder diagnoses are common; however, the actual prevalence rate is unclear as most findings are based on specific populations (e.g., emergency room admissions). In a child and adolescent community sample, rates between 2% and 8% have been reported. Children of all ages and both females and males are equally likely to be diagnosed with an adjustment disorder.

When behaviors such as rule breaking, acting out, and anxiety are present, it is important to consider if the child's behavior is a part of a maladaptive response to a significant stressful event. Treatment for adjustment disorder involves individual or group therapy, crisis intervention, brief therapy, or education to alleviate the symptoms associated with this disorder. Individual therapy can include efforts to aid the child in reinterpreting the stress event. That is, a cognitive–behavioral approach would assist the child in developing new ways to think about the stress event, while also developing alternative responses to the event and surrounding circumstances. Another individual intervention involves teaching the child relaxation techniques, specifically systematic relaxation and guided imagery, both of which are effective in assisting children with adjustment disorder by increasing their sense of control over their feelings and responses.

Supportive treatment for the anxious or depressed child focuses on identifying the event triggering the adjustment disorder, after which a plan for stress reduction is developed. For children who exhibit the disturbances of conduct as primary symptoms (i.e., externalizing problems), any difficulties occurring in the school or home setting are often resolved by this process of identifying the stress event related to the acting-out and developing a behavioral plan that dictates clear consequences for inappropriate behavior. It is also helpful to have children keep a log of what triggers their stress reactions, how they responded, and what helped to reduce their difficulty in the situation. Children who have experienced the same or a similar stress event (e.g., war, cancer) often benefit from the support of each other within the context of group intervention.

Moreover, monitoring school, home, or social functioning is important to assess progress in treatment. Teachers and parents can work together to track the child's behavior and, for example, rate daily if the child is breaking rules, more or less anxious, or both. Children can also keep a rating sheet to monitor their progress.

—*Yo Jackson*

See also DSM-IV

REFERENCES AND FURTHER READING

American Psychiatric Association. (1994). *The diagnostic and statistical manual of mental disorders*—text revision (4th ed.). Washington, DC: Author.

AFRICAN AMERICAN CHILDREN.

See MULTICULTURAL EDUCATION; RACE, ETHNICITY, CLASS, AND GENDER

AGGRESSION IN SCHOOLS

Although there are many definitions of aggression, most indicate that aggression represents behaviors that are intended to hurt or harm another. Much of the research on aggression has focused primarily upon boys who are physically aggressive (i.e., they physically dominate or intimidate others by hitting, pushing, shoving, kicking, or threatening physical harm). Approximately 10% to 15% of school-age children are the perpetrators of physical aggression.

SUBTYPES OF AGGRESSION

There are a number of different ways to conceptualize subtypes of aggressive behaviors. First, many researchers have subdivided aggression into reactive and proactive subtypes. The reactive subtype is characterized by impulsive aggressive behavior that occurs in retaliation to another's behavior (e.g., a child who is bumped from behind while walking down the hall responds by hitting and punching the child who bumped into him or her). In contrast, the proactive subtype is characterized by aggressive behavior that is enacted in order to achieve a specific goal (e.g., a child pushes another child in order to obtain a desired toy). Children who exhibit reactive aggression have emotional regulation difficulties, inattentive and impulsive behaviors, social skills deficits, and are more disliked than children who frequently exhibit proactive aggression (Bloomquist & Schnell, 2002). On the other hand, children who exhibit high levels of proactive aggressive behavior are typically calm, self-confident, and expect to benefit from the aggressive action (Bloomquist & Schnell, 2002).

Over the past 10 to 15 years, there has been an increasing emphasis on understanding the ways in which boys and girls differently express their anger and aggression toward others. Most researchers agree that boys tend to display anger through direct, physical means, such as hitting, pushing, kicking, and punching. This subtype of aggression has been called *physical* or *overt aggression* and is thought to be related to dominance. However, there is a growing recognition that physical/overt aggression does not adequately capture the means by which girls demonstrate more subtle forms of aggression when angry at others. For instance, some researchers have argued that girls display *indirect aggression*. Indirect aggression is defined as attacking others in a more covert and circuitous manner such as through social manipulation. Others have characterized girls as expressing social aggression, which is described as damaging others' self-esteem, social status, or both, by verbally rejecting them, starting rumors, or expressing displeasure toward another through negative facial and body movements. Finally, the term *relational aggression* is used by an increasing number of researchers to designate the subtype of aggression that involves the harmful manipulation and damage of peer relationships. Relationally aggressive behaviors include starting rumors about others, ignoring peers or threatening to withdraw friendships, and excluding others from a group or activity (Crick & Grotpeter, 1995). Most research suggests that the gender gap in comparing the number of aggressive boys to aggressive girls is considerably lessened when one takes into account the means by which boys and girls aggress. Ongoing research is being conducted to better understand the differences between indirect, social, and relational aggression, and to determine which subtype may be the most meaningful one to contrast with physical/overt aggression.

THE ETIOLOGY OF AGGRESSION

The majority of research has focused upon the etiology of physical aggression, as opposed to relational/social/indirect aggression. The etiology of physical aggression is complex, with theories emanating from both social and natural sciences. While several theories explain the development of aggression, most researchers agree that aggressive behavior is multidetermined, that it begins early in one's life, and can be explained in part by the theories discussed in the following sections.

Biology/Psychobiology

While most research on the role of genetics and the heritability of aggression has ruled out the idea of an aggressive gene (Coie & Dodge, 1998), it is currently thought that one might inherit the biological vulnerability for being aggressive. The current hypothesis is that one's biological/physiological vulnerability (i.e., genotype) may interact with environmental and psychological stressors to cause one to act in aggressive ways (i.e., phenotype).

Aspects of brain functioning have also been linked to aggressive behavior. Quay (1993) hypothesized that aggressive behavior is the result of an imbalance between the different brain systems that are responsible for controlling behavior. Quay posits that aggressive behaviors result when the reward system (REW) of the brain is dominant over the behavioral inhibition system (BIS). The REW causes a person to "go" while the BIS stops behavioral responding. Each system is controlled by different neurotransmitters; dopamine has been linked to REW, whereas ascending noradrenergic fibers have been associated with BIS.

In addition to neurotransmitters, neuroanatomy as a whole has been linked to the development of aggressive behavior. While there is some research suggesting that different areas of the frontal lobe may contribute to emotional, impulsive, and angry outbursts, it is not clear if frontal lobe dysfunction causes violence or vice versa. Other studies have suggested that dysfunction in the left hemisphere is related to violence. Researchers in this area are also testing theories that cortical underarousal is linked to violence, mediated by sensation-seeking behaviors. Finally, sex hormones such as testosterone have also been implicated in aggressive behavior.

Learning/Cognitive Theories

One of the most widely discussed theories of aggressive behavior is Albert Bandura's (1973) social learning theory. According to this theory, children develop repertoires of aggressive behavior by observing and/or imitating aggressive models (e.g., family members and television). Early research conducted by Bandura demonstrated that preschoolers imitated an adult female's aggressive actions toward an inflatable Bobo doll that was decorated as a clown.

Various social information processing models have also been advanced to explain the development and maintenance of aggressive behavior. These theories suggest that how a child processes a series of environmental cues affects whether he or she will behave in a socially appropriate or inappropriate manner. The sequential processing steps are:

1. Encoding relevant cues

2. Interpreting the cues in an accurate manner

3. Accessing potential behavioral responses to the interpreted cues

4. Evaluating and selecting potential responses

5. Enacting a chosen response

It is assumed that these steps happen quickly and at an unconscious level. Physically aggressive children are deficient in each processing step, which is thought to predispose them to react in an impulsive and aggressive manner as compared to their nonaggressive peers. Recent research also suggests that relationally aggressive children are deficient in their interpretation of social cues and in their response enactment decisions (steps 1 and 2). Research has not yet investigated whether relationally aggressive children have processing difficulties in the other three areas (steps 3 through 5).

Ecological Perspectives

In general, studies show that children born into disadvantaged backgrounds are likely to be aggressive later in life. More specifically, researchers find that associations between poverty and low self-esteem, difficulties in peer relationships, and overall adjustment influence later aggressive behavior. It is not clear if poverty has a direct influence on children's behavior, or if its effect is mediated by poverty's influence on a parent's emotional state and stress level.

Developmental psychology research demonstrates that witnessing violence or experiencing abuse and neglect may be related to later aggressive behavior in children. For example, a child's exposure to early abusive experiences may be related to later aggressive behavior; however, the link is not direct and may be mediated by other factors such as life stressors and television viewing. Factors such as prenatal drug exposure or contact with lead are also linked to aggressive behavior.

LONG-TERM EFFECTS OF AGGRESSIVE BEHAVIOR

Research indicates that being the perpetrator of physically aggressive actions toward others in the preschool and elementary age years is associated with academic difficulties, peer relationship problems, emotional arousal deficits, and social cognitive processing deficits in the elementary and middle school years. In addition, for a subset of these youngsters, there seems to be a developmental progression from exhibiting mild aggression (hitting, pushing, and shoving) to displaying more serious aggression during adolescence (delinquency, gang membership, repeated physical fighting), to demonstrating extremely serious violence in late adolescence and adulthood (robbery, rape, and assault). While the long-term effects of relational/social/indirect aggression have not been fully examined, initial evidence suggests that these more subtle forms of aggression in early childhood are associated with peer rejection, physical aggression, and internalizing problems (depression, anxiety, and loneliness) in middle childhood (6 to 12 years of age).

AGGRESSION PREVENTION PROGRAMS

Although there are hundreds of school- and community-based aggression-prevention and social-skills–promotion programs being conducted across the country, only a handful of these programs appear to be effective. For instance, a recent review of school-based aggression-prevention programs for elementary children suggested that there were only five extremely promising programs (Leff & colleagues, 2001). It was suggested that to be effective, programs should define aggression broadly, target multiple forms of aggression (i.e., physical aggression and relational aggression), design and conduct programs in partnership with school staff and community members, improve methodological rigor, and focus upon decreasing aggression in the unstructured school settings, such as on the playground, in the lunchroom, and in the hallways.

—Stephen S. Leff and Amy B. Goldstein

See also Abuse and Neglect; Bullying and Victimization; Conduct Disorder; Discipline; Gangs; Theories of Human Development; Violence in Schools

REFERENCES AND FURTHER READING

Bandura, A. (1973). *Aggression: A social learning analysis.* Englewood Cliffs, NJ: Prentice-Hall.

Bloomquist, M. L., & Schnell, S. V. (2002). *Helping children with aggression and conduct problems: Best practices for intervention.* New York: Guilford.

Coie, J. D., & Dodge, K. A. (1998). Aggression and antisocial behavior. In N. Eisenberg (Ed.), *Handbook of child psychology* (5th ed., Vol. 3, pp. 779–862). New York: Wiley.

Crick, N. R., & Grotpeter, J. K. (1995). Relational aggression, gender, and social-psychological adjustment. *Child Development, 66*, 710–722.

Leff, S. S., Power, T. J., Manz, P. H., Costigan, T. E., & Nabors, L. A. (2001). School-based aggression prevention programs for young children: Current status and implications for violence prevention. *School Psychology Review, 30*, 343–360.

Quay, H. C. (1993). The psychobiology of undersocialized aggressive conduct disorder: A theoretical perspective. *Development and Psychopathology, 5*, 165–180.

AMERICAN BOARD OF PROFESSIONAL PSYCHOLOGY

The American Board of Professional Psychology (ABPP) is an independent credentialing organization that certifies psychologists as having met advanced standards for specialty practice in professional psychology. The ABPP (originally called the American Board of Examiners in Professional Psychology) was developed in 1947 because psychological services were needed for veterans following World War II, and it was thought that some means to indicate to the public which psychologists were qualified as practitioners should be established. Psychological licensure by state psychology boards did not become common until the 1950s and 1960s. Although the ABPP Diploma could have been the credential upon which to base standards for state licensure, it became a credential used to certify psychologists at a high level of practice (Pryzwansky, 1998). The ABPP grants diplomas in 13 areas of practice: Behavioral, Business and Consulting, Clinical, Clinical Child, Clinical Health, Clinical Neuropsychology, Counseling, Family, Forensic, Group, Rehabilitation, Psychoanalysis, and School Psychology. The significance of this credential is that it is the highest credential a practitioner can obtain. All diploma holders meet similar requirements in regard to education and licensure. Diplomate-level psychologists are expected to demonstrate that their practice is

systematic and effective. Common to all ABPP examinations is the requirement that candidates demonstrate they are current and research-based in their practices and provide a rationale for their actions.

THE STRUCTURE OF THE AMERICAN BOARD OF PROFESSIONAL PSYCHOLOGY

The ABPP is composed of a central Board of Trustees with each specialty area represented on the Board. Each specialty area maintains its own examining board, whose charge is to conduct examinations for the ABPP Diploma and carry out administrative functions in the management of the examination process. For school psychology, this group is called the American Board of School Psychology (ABSP). The ABSP is composed of six directors, all of whom possess the ABPP Diploma in School Psychology; some of the ABSP Directors also serve as its officers. Each specialty area has an academy for its diploma recipients; board certified specialists are designated fellows of the respective academies. For school psychology, this is the American Academy of School Psychology (AASP).

THE AMERICAN BOARD OF PROFESSIONAL PSYCHOLOGY PROCESS

The process of becoming an ABPP diplomate involves meeting the application requirements, including:

- A doctorate
- A license to practice from a state psychology board
- A completed application
- A check of one's record to ensure there have been no ethical violations
- Preparation of practice samples illustrating one's professional work
- Passing an oral examination
- Recommendations by two psychologists (who preferably possess the ABPP Diploma)
- Transcripts of graduate study

The primary incentive for becoming a board certified psychologist is intrinsic; one chooses to go through a self-study process that affirms that his or her practice is at the highest level (Flanagan, 2004). Tangible rewards, such as increased remuneration, are limited. The public can be assured of the competency of a board certified psychologist, as the ABPP Diploma is the only credential that specifically attests to one's professional skills. For school psychology, this carries added importance, as state Departments of Education certify psychologists for school-based practice only at the subdoctoral level. The ABPP Diploma signifies that a credentialed school psychologist is practicing at a substantially higher level than the entry level.

—*Rosemary Flanagan*

See also American Psychological Association; National Association of School Psychologists; School Psychologist

REFERENCES AND FURTHER READING

Flanagan, R. (2004). The diplomate in school psychology: Implications for the science and practice of school psychology. *Psychology in the Schools, 41*, 481–489.

Pryzwansky, W. B. (1998). Individual psychologist: Specialty board certification. In A. N. Wiens (Ed.), *Comprehensive clinical psychology* (Vol. 2). New York: Elsevier.

AMERICAN PSYCHOLOGICAL ASSOCIATION

The American Psychological Association (APA), founded in 1892, is a national organization whose primary goal is advancing the science and profession of psychology. The APA has more than 145,000 fellows, members, associates, and affiliates. Fellows and members must hold a doctoral degree in psychology. Affiliate members include Teachers of Psychology in Secondary Schools (TOPSS) and students. APA has members in every state and more than 8,500 members and affiliates in other countries.

APA is a nonprofit organization that is supported by members' dues, sales of publications, investments, and real estate. With nearly 500 central office employees in Washington, DC, and an annual budget exceeding $60 million, APA seeks to serve professional psychologists and the public through outreach, education, and the dissemination of professional psychological information.

APA has three major directorates: Education, Public Interest, and Practice. The Education Directorate includes seven major offices (Table 1) and focuses on learning outcomes at all levels of psychology, from high school to postdoctoral training in psychology. The Office of Program Consultation and Accreditation is located within the Education Directorate and is responsible for the accreditation of training programs in clinical, counseling, and school psychology. The Public Interest Directorate is involved in the dissemination of psychological information and is committed to justice and fair treatment of all members of our society. (Table 1 contains the offices located within the Public Interest Directorate.) The Practice Directorate assists practitioners (clinicians) by promoting legislation and working with divisions within APA and state or local psychology organizations. In this way, the Practice Directorate can provide information needed by clinicians to support their practice.

The APA has 55 divisions, each of which represents a specialty or topical area in psychology. (Table 2 provides a list of the APA divisions.) The divisions of APA represent the diversity within the organization and include topics ranging from the study of animal behavior to social topics such as the media or the study of peace and conflict. School psychology is represented in Division 16 of the APA.

All APA members are bound by the organization's Ethics Code (available online at http://www.apa.org/ethics/). The Ethics Code specifies that professional psychologists have the responsibility to protect the public from unethical practices, such as a psychologist practicing outside his or her area of training.

Table 1 Directorates and Offices With the American Psychological Association

Education Directorate
    Center for Psychology in Schools and Education
    (K–12) Office of Education Public Policy
    Office of Executive Director/Administration, Governance and Communications
    Office of Graduate and Postgraduate Education and Training
    Office of Education in Psychology—Precollege/Undergraduate
    Office of Continuing Education in Psychology
    Office of Program Consultation and Accreditation
Public Interest Directorate
    Office on Aging
    Office on AIDS
    Children, Youth and Families Office
    Disability Issues in Psychology Office
    Office of Ethnic Minority Affairs
    Lesbian, Gay and Bisexual Concerns Office
    Minority Fellowship Program
Public Policy Office—Public Interest Advocacy
    Women's Programs Office
    Work, Stress, and Health Office

Table 2   Divisions (Numbers and Titles) of the American Psychological Association

1. Society for General Psychology	30. Society of Psychological Hypnosis
2. Society for the Teaching of Psychology	31. State Psychological Affairs
3. Experimental Psychology	32. Humanistic Psychology
5. Evaluation, Measurement, and Statistics	33. Mental Retardation and Developmental Disabilities
6. Behavioral Neuroscience and Comparative Psychology	34. Population and Environmental Psychology
7. Developmental Psychology	35. Society for the Psychology of Women
8. Society for Personality and Social Psychology	36. Psychology of Religion
9. Society for the Psychological Study of Social Issues (SPSSI)	37. Child, Youth, and Family Services
10. Society for the Psychology of Aesthetics, Creativity, and the Arts	38. Health Psychology
12. Society of Clinical Psychology	39. Psychoanalysis
13. Society of Consulting Psychology	40. Clinical Neuropsychology
14. Society for Industrial and Organizational Psychology	41. American Psychology-Law Society
15. Educational Psychology	42. Psychologists in Independent Practice
16. School Psychology	43. Family Psychology
17. Society of Counseling Psychology	44. Society for the Psychological Study of Lesbian, Gay, and Bisexual Issues
18. Psychologists in Public Service	45. Society for the Psychological Study of Ethnic Minority Issues
19. Military Psychology	46. Media Psychology
20. Adult Development and Aging	47. Exercise and Sport Psychology
21. Applied Experimental and Engineering Psychology	48. Society for the Study of Peace, Conflict, and Violence: Peace Psychology Division
22. Rehabilitation Psychology	49. Group Psychology and Group Psychotherapy
23. Society for Consumer Psychology	50. Addictions
24. Theoretical and Philosophical Psychology	51. Society for the Psychological Study of Men and Masculinity
25. Behavior Analysis	52. International Psychology
26. Society for the History of Psychology	53. Society of Clinical Child and Adolescent Psychology
27. Society for Community Research and Action: Division of Community Psychology	54. Society of Pediatric Psychology
28. Psychopharmacology and Substance Abuse	55. American Society for the Advancement of Pharmacotherapy
29. Psychotherapy	

The APA is committed to helping the public with programs like the Consumer Help Center and the Disaster Response Network. The Center for Psychology in Schools and Education has mobilized psychologists from many specialties (i.e., clinical psychology, learning, school psychology) to improve learning and behavior of students from early childhood to grade 12.

—*Steven W. Lee*

See also Division of School Psychology (Division 16); National Association of School Psychologists

AMERICANS WITH DISABILITIES ACT

Signed into law in 1990, the Americans with Disabilities Act (ADA), a civil rights statute, prohibits discrimination against qualified persons with disabilities in the areas of employment, telecommunications, and others. Additionally, the ADA reinforces provisions of section 504 of the Rehabilitation Act of 1973, the civil rights law that first recognized persons with disabilities as a protected class. The Civil Rights Act of 1964, which barred discrimination on the basis of race, religion, or national origin, established entitlement to civil rights protections now found in both the ADA and section 504.

Title II of the ADA includes state and local government responsibilities for public education at all levels. Subpart D of section 504 of the Rehabilitation Act of 1973 applies to students with disabilities from preschool through high school; subpart E of section 504 protects students with disabilities attending postsecondary education facilities. The fundamental goal of both the ADA and section 504 is access. Accommodations are often the means through which access is provided to persons with disabilities.

The ADA adopted the definition of disability and the qualified status stipulation found in section 504. To demonstrate that they are members of a protected class, individuals must provide evidence (documentation) that they have a disability that is defined as a physical or mental impairment that substantially limits one or more major life activities, have a record of such impairment, or are regarded as having such impairment. Additionally, to demonstrate their qualified status, they must meet all legitimate standards for participation in educational programs and activities, employment, and so forth, with or without accommodations. In summary, title II of the ADA states that no qualified individual with a disability shall, by reason of such disability, be excluded from participation in or denied the benefits of the services, programs, or activities of a public entity, or be subjected to discrimination by such entity.

—*Susan M. Vess*

See also Individuals With Disabilities Education Act,

ANTECEDENT. *See* BEHAVIOR

APPLIED BEHAVIOR ANALYSIS

Applied behavior analysis (ABA) is the scientific study and application of principles of behavior to improve human behaviors that are recognized as important to society (Baer & colleagues, 1968). The redundancy of the term *behavior* in this definition is purposeful; it reflects the overall emphasis and defining feature of the field. Whereas other psychological models attempt to measure and sometimes change

thoughts, feelings, knowledge, and awareness, behavior is the hallmark of ABA. Behavior is what is measured and behavior is what is changed.

The number and types of behaviors that are significant to society seem almost limitless—a few examples are aberrant behaviors like self-injury, deviant behaviors like stealing, unsafe behaviors like poor driving, and not enough behavior like when a child in a classroom cannot give the right answer to a teacher's question. The list could go on indefinitely. Scientists in the field of ABA (behavior analysts) take their lead from society in terms of which behaviors they study. To behavior analysts, however, there are really only two types of behavior problems—behavioral excesses in which there is too much of a behavior and behavioral deficits in which there is too little of a behavior. Aberrant behaviors, deviant behaviors, and unsafe behaviors are examples of behavioral excesses; not giving the right answer in class is an example of a behavioral deficit.

The techniques studied and used by behavior analysts are defined in terms of how they influence behavior and whether they increase or decrease behavior. These techniques, therefore, have grown out of "principles of behavior." Because society places a high priority on education and pours enormous amounts of money and resources into schools, applied behavior analysts have been systematically studying and refining school-based applications of ABA by applying principles of behavior to school behaviors of students, excesses (e.g., aggression) and deficits (e.g., poor writing) alike.

A key to the study of human behavior is the necessity for an operational definition for measuring behavior. Behavior analysts use an *operational definition* to define a behavior as clearly and precisely as possible so that all observers can agree on what is being measured. For example, on-task behavior may be thought of as "paying attention." However, paying attention is ambiguous and very difficult to measure. When exactly is the child paying attention to the teacher? If we define on-task behavior as a child having his or her eyes focused on the teacher, worksheet, or book, then all observers are more likely to measure the same behavior. Looking at the teacher, worksheet, or book, therefore, becomes the operational definition of on-task behavior.

Another key concept in studying human behavior is the identification of functional relationships between behaviors and events in the environment.

Behavior is purposeful and changes as a function of changes in the environment. A preliminary goal of a behavioral treatment program is to identify these functional relationships between a person's environment and his or her behavior. Next, environmental events are modified in order to change a person's behavior. For example, in the classroom a child may misbehave to gain teacher attention. Teacher attention is a controlling variable (i.e., has a functional relationship with the behavior). By identifying this relationship between child behavior and teacher attention, the way in which the teacher pays attention to the student can be restructured so that the child would be required to engage in positive behaviors to gain teacher attention. If the identification of the controlling variable is correct and the treatment plan directly alters the behavior–environment relationship (i.e., teacher attention controlling student behavior), the student will begin to display more appropriate classroom behavior and less misbehavior.

Identification of functional relationships relies on behavioral processes that govern behavior. These processes have been identified through extensive research over the past century. The most basic principles involve positive reinforcement and punishment. The application of a positive stimulus to increase behavior is positive reinforcement. Punishment is either the application of a negative stimulus to decrease behavior or the withdrawal of a positive stimulus to also decrease behavior. These behavioral processes are used by teachers and parents every day. Giving a child a sticker for completing a math worksheet is an example of reinforcement, while putting a child in time-out for hitting on the playground (i.e., withdrawing the positive stimulus of playing on the playground) is an example of punishment. The procedures are defined in terms of their effect on behavior. If giving a child a sticker for completing s math worksheet does not increase math problems, then it is not a reinforcer. Another common behavior process is *extinction*, which involves the withdrawal of reinforcement for a behavior that has been reinforced in the past. When teachers are told to "ignore" annoying student behaviors, they are putting the student's behaviors on extinction. The immediate result is often an extinction burst, during which the student attempts to gain attention by increasing the frequency, intensity, or duration of the behavior that is being ignored. If the extinction procedure is continued through the extinction burst, the negative behavior will eventually

decrease to acceptable levels. Extinction can be used to reduce many minor negative behaviors such as whining, tattling, begging, yelling, and tantrums.

Combining these basic processes can also have a powerful influence on behavior. When reinforcement is combined with extinction, the resulting process is referred to as *differential reinforcement*. Differential reinforcement procedures require the application of reinforcement that is contingent on positive behaviors and the removal of reinforcement (i.e., extinction) for problem behaviors. The earlier example of manipulating the contingent relationship between teacher attention and student misbehavior involved differential reinforcement. Student misbehavior was placed on extinction through ignoring, while teacher attention (i.e., reinforcement) was given contingent on appropriate classroom behaviors.

There are a number of ways to carry out differential reinforcement (DR). The extinction component is the same in all methods—the teacher does not reinforce inappropriate behavior. It is what is reinforced that differs across the various forms of DR. Variations of DR include:

- Rewarding alternate but functionally equivalent behaviors (differential reinforcement of appropriate behavior [DRA])
- Rewarding other behaviors (differential reinforcement of other behavior [DRO])
- Rewarding incompatible behavior (differential reinforcement of incompatible behavior [DRI])

In the example of student misbehavior, the teacher could use a DRA by reinforcing the student with praise for completing school work. DRO is a trickier concept, and the name is a bit of a misnomer. With the DRO procedure, the teacher reinforces the student for the absence of problem behavior (which means that all other behaviors except the problem behavior are reinforced). To use DRI, the teacher must reinforce the student for a behavior that is physically incompatible with the problem behavior. The idea is that the student cannot engage in problem behavior and the chosen incompatible behavior at the same time. For instance, if calling out in class is a form of misbehavior (e.g., "TEACHER, I DON'T UNDERSTAND THIS STUPID WORK!"), the teacher could reinforce quiet requests for help.

Two additional principles, stimulus control and shaping, are also useful to behavior analysts in understanding how to change behavior. *Stimulus control* is "the control of a stimulus over a behavior as a result of that behavior's having been reinforced in the presence of that stimulus" (Martin & Pear, 1996, p. 105). In other words, a behavior is said to be under stimulus control if that behavior occurs in the presence of a stimulus, signal, or cue. In middle schools, children are prompted by a bell when one class is over and it is time to transition to another class. When the bell rings, the children leave the classroom. Leaving the class is under the stimulus control of the school bell. A teacher may turn the classroom lights on and off to cue the children to be quiet and return to their seats. The students' behavior is under the control of a stimulus, the flickering lights.

In some cases, behavior analysts want to produce behaviors that are not currently being performed. In these situations, reinforcement alone will not work because the desired behavior is not available for reinforcement; the behavior is not occurring at all. *Shaping* is a procedure that can be used to develop behaviors that are not occurring by rewarding successive approximations of the behavior. To use shaping, behavior analysts start by identifying the final desired behavior and a series of intermediate steps or behaviors that can be taught on the way to the desired behavior. The behavior analyst begins with an initial starting behavior that is being performed and that may serve as an approximation of the desired behavior, and uses differential reinforcement to work toward the desired behavior. Reinforcement is provided for occurrences of the initial behavior. When the behavior is occurring reliably, the initial behavior is put on extinction and the next closest approximation of the behavior is reinforced. This process occurs successively until the final behavior is performed under the desired conditions.

Shaping can be used in the classroom to increase work completion in children who are not completing any class work. The final behavior would be for a student to complete an entire math worksheet, and the starting behavior for that goal may be for a student to complete one math problem. As the child completes one problem, a reward such as taking a break or walking to the water fountain is delivered. After the student receives several rewards for completing one problem, the effort required to complete the behavior is increased. In this next step, the student will receive a reward for completing five math problems. Once the student is achieving this

goal, the requirement is increased again. The teacher continues this pattern until the student is completing the entire worksheet.

A number of popular strategies used in the classroom are derived from behavior analytic techniques. Although the names have changed for many of these strategies, the procedures remain essentially the same. For instance, teachers often use *sticker charts* or *star charts* to allow children to earn points for appropriate behavior. Those points can be exchanged for activities, privileges, or things the children like. This popular method of behavior management has its origins in early ABA work and is referred to as a "token economy." When teachers also take away points for misbehavior, this is referred to as "response cost." If the rewards are truly rewarding to the children, these techniques can be very effective for managing children's behavior. The problem is that they are often time-consuming and may add more demands to the teacher's already busy schedule. As the teacher follows through less consistently, results may wane after an initial change in performance (Martens & colleagues, 1999).

Another problem is that these strategies may not address the real reason for the problem. Token economies compete with the reinforcers that are already in place to support problem behavior by offering what the teacher thinks will be a more appealing reinforcer. The original problem, however, does not go away. Therefore, if, for instance, a child acts up in the classroom to gain peer attention—peers laugh and interact with the child for goofing off—getting a special privilege may be less reinforcing than getting the peers' attention. Also, it may be easier to get peer attention, involving less effort on the part of the child. Now, the teacher has extra work (a token economy) and still has the problem behavior because peer attention continues to reinforce the behavior. Fortunately, as behavior analysts have come to understand functional relationships better, they have developed a methodology for identifying and treating the reason for problem behavior. This methodology, called *functional assessment* (FA), is being increasingly applied in schools to resolve students' behavior and learning problems.

Ervin and colleagues (2001) explain that "FA involves relating external conditions to specific behaviors so as to allow those behaviors to be predicted and controlled. FA reveals antecedent variables and consequences that control the behavior of interest, and this information is used to develop interventions that change the behavior in a desired way" (p. 173). In other words, use of FA allows the school practitioner to identify factors (things that precede [antecedents] or follow [consequences] behavior) that control behavior and use that information to develop an intervention that directly counteracts the very reason for the problem. FA is an umbrella term for two categories of methods for investigating causes of behavior excesses and deficits—descriptive analysis and functional analysis.

In a descriptive analysis, the behavior analyst interviews the people who manage the child's problem behavior and conducts structured observations in the setting in which the problem is occurring. Based on observed patterns of antecedents, behaviors, and consequences, the behavior analyst attempts to identify the function of the behavior. For behavior excesses such as acting out, behavior analysts consider a limited number of reasons or functions of behavior. Behavior excesses usually occur so that the individual can (O'Neill & colleagues, 1997):

- Obtain social attention
- Obtain access to tangible objects
- Obtain direct pleasurable effects
- Avoid unpleasant work
- Avoid social attention
- Avoid unpleasant states (like headaches)

These functions are based on the principles of behavior explained earlier in the entry. Once the function of the behavior is identified, an intervention can be chosen that directly relates to the cause of the problem. Martens and colleagues (1999) explain, "Because the reinforcer for problem behavior is known, it can be withheld, contingent on problem behavior (extinction), or presented, contingent on the desired alternative (differential reinforcement)" (p. 647).

Descriptive analysis involves some guesswork on the part of the behavior analyst, and there is no guarantee that the reinforcer for problem behavior has been correctly identified. Functional analysis is a more rigorous methodology for directly verifying the source of reinforcement and developing an intervention. Functional analysis takes the functional assessment a step further by directly manipulating the factors (e.g., obtaining social attention, getting out of work demands) believed to be causing the behavior. Conducting a functional analysis is equivalent to doing an experimental study of the student's problem

behavior using ABA's unique approach to the study of behavior.

In their research and in their clinical work, behavior analysts use single-case experimental designs. In a research study, there is a control group and a treatment group. When a single-case experimental design is used, there is one participant (in this case the student) who serves as both the control group and the treatment group. There are a number of different types of experimental designs that allow the behavior analyst to compare experimental conditions within the person. Because behavior is an individual phenomenon, the best way to study principles of behavior or identify causes for behavior is to examine how the individual responds to all of the experimental conditions. With single-case experimental designs, performance is measured repeatedly and continuously throughout all conditions. Repeated measurement allows the investigator to determine whether there are changes over time as a function of the changes in the environment.

A very common type of single-case experimental design is called the withdrawal design. With this type of design, a student's performance is first repeatedly measured under natural conditions without any kind of intervention. Next, the intervention is introduced. Then, the intervention is withdrawn for a period of time to determine whether the behavior returns to its original state. Finally, the intervention is reinstituted and the level of behavior change is assessed once again. An example can be found in Figure 1, which displays the results of an intervention intended to improve a child's on-task behavior in a classroom during a 30-minute lesson. You will note that on-task, as represented by the data points in the first panel of the graph (baseline), is quite low. The intervention was DRA and involved having the teacher ignore off-task behavior and praise the student for on-task behavior, approximately once every 3 minutes. The results (second panel on the graph) indicate a sharp increase in on-task behavior that is somewhat stable by the end of the intervention phase. The teacher then stopped reinforcing on-task behavior for a few sessions, which led to a precipitous decrease in on-task behavior. When the intervention was put back in place, on-task behavior went back up.

Although it might seem unusual to take a successful intervention away for a period of time, the reason is to be sure that it was the intervention and not something else that is responsible for the change in behavior. If the behavior had failed to return to baseline levels in the example, it would not have been possible

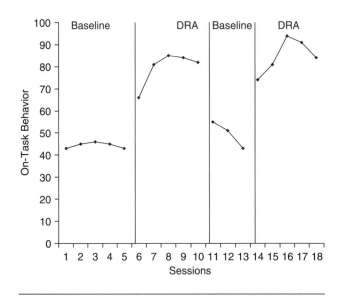

Figure 1   Example of a withdrawal design displaying results of percent on-task during 30-minute lessons for baseline and intervention (DRA) phases.

to be confident that teacher attention was an effective reinforcer for the student. It may be that something else (e.g., the parent threatening the child with severe consequences if misbehavior in the classroom continued) was responsible for the behavior change. Therefore, withdrawing the intervention allows us to identify the true cause of the behavior change. The teacher now knows that he or she is able to exercise control over the behavior to improve the student's ability to function in the classroom. A functional relationship between variables (i.e., the effect of teacher attention on on-task behavior) was demonstrated in this functional analysis.

ABA is a way to bring the scientific method to bear on applied problems in schools. Each case is a new experiment, and principles of behavior can be combined in various ways to identify the best way to meet a student's needs. A real advantage to ABA is that school personnel can directly see the effects of changes and can decide for themselves whether it is their efforts that make a difference or not. In an age of increasing accountability in schools, the ability to show the validity of an intervention plan should be a real asset to educators.

Edward J. Daly III and Merilee McCurdy

See also Behavior; Behavior Intervention; Behavioral Assessment; Cognitive–Behavioral Modification; Consultation: Behavioral

REFERENCES AND FURTHER READING

Baer, D. B., Wolf, M. M., & Risley, T. R. (1968). Some current dimensions of applied behavior analysis. *Journal of Applied Behavior Analysis, 1*, 91–97.

Ervin, R. A., Ehrhardt, K. E., & Poling, A. (2001). Functional assessment: Old wine in new bottles. *School Psychology Review, 30*, 173–179.

Martens, B. K., Witt, J. C., Daly, E. J., III, & Vollmer, T. R. (1999). Behavior analysis: Theory and practice in educational settings. In C. R. Reynolds & T. B. Gutkin (Eds.), *The handbook of school psychology* (3rd ed., pp. 638–663). New York: Wiley.

Martin, G., & Pear, J. (1996). Behavior modification: What it is and how to do it (5th ed.). Upper Saddle River, NJ: Prentice-Hall.

O'Neill, R. E., Horner, R. H., Albin, R. W., Sprague, J. R., Storey, K., & Newton, J. S. (1997). *Functional assessment of problem behavior: A practical assessment guide* (2nd ed.). Pacific Grove, CA: Brooks/Cole.

ASIAN-AMERICAN CHILDREN.

See MULTICULTURAL EDUCATION; RACE, ETHNICITY, CLASS, AND GENDER

ASPERGER'S DISORDER.

See AUTISM SPECTRUM DISORDERS; FACILITATED COMMUNICATION

ASTHMA

Asthma is the most common childhood chronic illness. The Centers for Disease Control and Prevention reported in 1998 that 3.8 million children had at least one asthma attack per year. Asthma is an inflammation of the cells in the bronchial passages, which causes the airways to be hypersensitive to respiratory irritants, such as allergens, exercise, viral infections, and emotional responses (e.g., laughing and crying). When exposed to these irritants, an exaggerated airway response, or "asthma attack," occurs, resulting in the passages narrowing or becoming obstructed from mucus buildup. During this physiological response, the child has rapid shallow breathing, tightness in the chest, and wheezing or coughing. Although physiologically based, asthma is exacerbated by environmental factors (e.g., air pollution and second-hand smoke) and psychological factors (e.g., stress). Sensitivity to these triggers varies as does the frequency and severity of attacks. Therefore, the child's doctor should be consulted before restricting activities and exercise. Asthma medications increase lung capacity and decrease sensitivity to allergens. These treatments include long-term medications to reduce the reactivity and sensitivity of the airways and quick relief medications to control acute attacks.

Compared to their healthy peers, children with asthma at times have problems with decreased adherence to the medication regimen that can further impact the severity of their asthma. Therefore, good control of asthma often requires psychological as well as medical interventions. Psychological interventions for children with asthma typically include disease and treatment education, increasing medication compliance, stress management, and improvement of family interactions. The education component focuses on increasing the child's self-efficacy for controlling the disease and learning how to avoid triggers of attacks. Improved adherence can be achieved by reducing barriers to treatment, clarifying expectations and roles, and behavioral strategies of contracting and reinforcement. Stress management including relaxation therapy can improve the child's physiological response to the symptoms.

Asthma can adversely affect academic functioning directly (e.g., side effects of the medication and increased school absenteeism) and, for some, increase the risk for behavior problems and peer interaction difficulties. Medication side effects should be monitored to balance health benefits with possible negative academic impact. School attendance for children with chronic illnesses is linked to the attitude of the teachers and to the resources provided by the school administration. In response, some schools provide asthma education and training programs for teachers and other school personnel. Additionally, having classmates who are well educated about a peer's condition provides what may be the most effective support and incentive for attending school.

School psychologists may become involved in evaluating academic performance and medication side effects; assisting the child's adjustment or adherence to treatment regimens; and consulting with teachers, staff, and parents. Additionally, they can monitor for the possible development of asthma-related behavior disorders.

—*Montserrat C. Mitchell and Michael C. Roberts*

REFERENCES AND FURTHER READING

McQuaid, E. L., & Walders, N. (2003). Pediatric asthma. In M. C. Roberts (Ed.), *Handbook of pediatric psychology* (3rd ed.). New York: Guilford.

ATTENTION

Attention is a construct for which everyone has an intuitive definition. While most of us believe we know what attention is, it is difficult to operationalize. Because it is a process that is so widely distributed throughout the brain, different networks have been proposed to explain the varying types of attention.

In some ways attention and perception are similar. You need to hear, see, or feel a stimulus to attend to it. But we can also pay attention to internal inputs such as thoughts and ideas. One can be distracted by thoughts that continue to intrude on your mind as well as memories that can be summoned by smells or songs on a radio. In this manner, perception and attention become separate but related constructs.

When a stimulus is perceived initially the perception is at the level of the senses. Additional information processing then occurs where a link for encoding is established in order for the information to be further processed. At this level, the processing is purely perceptual. Once analysis and encoding of the stimulus takes place, higher stages of information processing are used and attention comes into play. Generally stimuli that are salient and being attended to are processed and, subsequently, the person becomes aware of the stimulus.

Generally the most salient information of a stimulus is selectively attended to while irrelevant information is discarded. In this manner stimuli is selected to be attended to so that a person will not become overwhelmed by too much stimulation. At times, however, unattended information that was not completely deleted from conscious awareness is perceived by the person. If this information is important enough, it may become attended to and selected for further processing. This selection allows for previously irrelevant stimuli to become relevant when attention processes switch from attended input to unattended input (Broadbent, 1970; Treisman, 1969).

Woldoroff and Hillyard (1991) studied the responses of attending to one ear while ignoring input to the other ear. Findings indicated that brain activity showed a larger response to the attended stimuli compared to the unattended one. Neuroimaging techniques can trace brain activity level to specific locations. The attention control systems have been found to affect how neurons interpret the features of the attended or unattended stimuli. In other words, attention directs which neurons fire in response to a perceptual input. For example, when a student attends to a teacher presenting in the classroom, neurons in the auditory comprehension and language areas of the brain become active while those in the motor or sensory areas of the brain are not activated. By having specific areas of the brain energized for selected types of tasks, the person is able to focus attention on those aspects and ignore extraneous noises and sensory input.

A MODEL OF ATTENTION

Posner and Raichle (1994) proposed a model of attention that involves three networks, with specific brain areas implicated for each network. The type of network activated depends upon how much conscious awareness is required for the particular attention task. The first network consists of the right frontal portion of the brain and a system that runs through the brainstem that permits the maintenance of alertness and vigilance. This system is the most basic network for attention and allows a person to attend to the environment. The second network includes the posterior portion of the brain and structures in the center of the brain that are instrumental in the disengagement and orientation of attention to a new stimulus object or location. The third network, which is the most complex, consists of deep central structures and the front part of the brain, all of which have been implicated in the executive network of attention. This executive network plans and organizes the attended information after it has been brought into conscious awareness. According to Posner (1994), three stages are necessary for an individual to pay attention to a stimulus. First, the person must disengage attention from the current focus. Second, the person must shift or move attention to the new stimulus. Third, the person must engage attention onto the new stimulus. People who have attention difficulties (ADHD, particular brain lesions, etc.) may encounter problems at any of these three stages.

TYPES OF ATTENTION

The types of attention required for learning and memory are selective, sustained, divided, and alternated. Selective and sustained attention types are important for orienting and vigilance to the intended stimulus. Selective attention enables a person to overcome other inputs from the environment (e.g., noise) and concentrate on the signal of interest, with structures deep in the brain that help filter environmental distractions. If these structures are disabled, the person has difficulty filtering out irrelevant material and may become overwhelmed by too much input. Additionally, the frontal lobe is involved in the inhibition of unattended or extraneous environmental information and, therefore, plays a critical role in how information is selected.

Divided and alternating attention types are more complex, though it should be noted that selective and sustained attention types are still required for understanding the material. Divided attention occurs when an individual does two things simultaneously, such as taking notes and listening to the teacher. Alternating attention is when you need to shift your attention from one thing to another, such as when you are driving and you check your rear view mirror and then look at the road ahead. These types of attention require executive functioning of the frontal lobes and possibly the region of the brain that coordinates attention (anterior cingulate), which lies in the center of the brain and extends from the frontal lobes to the back of the brain.

Generally speaking, alternating attention is less difficult than divided attention. The key to alternating attention involves smoothly transitioning through Posner's three stages of attention as the person switches between two tasks. Attention problems at any of these three stages would make alternating attention most difficult. Additionally, the material currently not being actively attended to, analyzed, manipulated, and so forth, must be efficiently stored in working memory. Otherwise, the person would be starting anew on the task each time he or she redirected attention to the other task, as is required in alternating attention tasks. Divided attention is a much more difficult task because it entails attending to two different tasks simultaneously. This process can lead to a cognitive bottleneck in the brain of available resources given that selective and sustained attention as well as working memory (the central executive and executive attention) would be required to keep the two relevant *data sets* available for simultaneous use.

INHIBITION AND FILTERING

The ability (or inability) for people to filter incoming information affects how they attend to information as well what information they attend to (relevant versus irrelevant stimuli). When participants are asked to attend to only one ear and ignore input to the other in a listening experiment, healthy participants show more response on electroencephalogram (EEG) recordings to the attended ear. This difference is absent in people with brain injury in the frontal lobe (Knight & Grabowecky, 1995). Inhibition of the unattended stimuli must occur to avoid overwhelming an individual with too much information. When inhibition does not occur, difficulties are frequently present in memory because the information has flooded the resources of the brain.

For people unable to filter information, all information becomes important and the person can easily be overwhelmed. In the case of a loss of filtering (or inhibition), information pours into the frontal lobe and the person can be quite vulnerable to such an overload. For people with this difficulty, basic cognitive skills are generally found to be intact (normal IQ), but the person has a very difficult time navigating through life and maintaining focus on the task at hand.

WORKING MEMORY

Attention has a limited capacity. Therefore the flow of information needs to be modulated so that it becomes manageable. Here is where filtering and inhibition operate as particularly important constructs. Working memory has been conceptualized as a temporary and limited capacity network that sustains the current contents of information processing. In other words, it allows us to remember an item while we think of it. For example, when looking up a phone number we rehearse the number in working memory until we use the number. To keep the information in working memory long enough to hold it or manipulate it, one must selectively attend to the desired information while filtering out irrelevant input. If interrupted on our way to the telephone, we will lose the number.

Additionally, one must keep the attention sustained on the material to manipulate or process it; otherwise the shift in attention will cause new items to be placed

in working memory that displace the earlier items in storage. Working memory can decay relatively rapidly. In order for the material to become transferred into the long-term memory systems, the person needs to spend additional time attending to the information, such as through active studying and rehearsal (which require selective and sustained attention).

DEVELOPMENT OF ATTENTION

Attention is a process that improves with age. In infancy and young childhood there is rapid development in many areas, including attention. Infants and young children learn to remember information and will consciously try to attend to tasks, particularly if they are novel in nature. Wellman (1988) hypothesizes that preschool children remember information because they attend to a repeated stimulus over time, and strategies are developing during this time. Divided attention begins emerging at around 2 to 4 years of age and improves drastically by age 7 (Teeter, 1998). In kindergarten, children learn how to selectively attend and focus attention on relevant versus irrelevant material. Although strategies are not developed by this time, involuntary attention heuristics are being developed.

Children in middle childhood, ages 6 to 12 years, begin to learn that attention strategies are needed to study and learn a particular task or to solve a problem (Berk, 1989). Attention becomes more under the child's control and can be sustained as well as planned. In addition, children learn how to adapt attentional processes to cope with environmental demands (Teeter, 1998).

Older children work at ignoring irrelevant details and distractions when learning. Thus they become more attentive and are more successful in focusing attention. The ability to use alternating attentional skills improves during early adolescence and depends on task demands—as tasks become more demanding, these skills are less effective (Teeter, 1998). During late elementary and early middle school years, attention becomes more deliberate, planned, and adaptive.

In adolescence, attention becomes more focused while at the same time diversifying into improvement in divided and alternating skills. Adolescents must learn how to take notes as well as to pay attention to classroom presentations. They also must improve their ability to focus on important aspects of life while attempting to control their attention to salient aspects of the environment (i.e., the opposite sex). Meanwhile, the ability to understand learning and analyzing their own performance is also important and develops rapidly during this phase of life and into adulthood. These skills are very important not only for cognitive development but also for success in interpersonal relationships. Some of the skills in attention and insight continue to improve through the third decade of life coinciding with increased differentiation of the frontal part of the brain.

In adulthood, attention continues to improve through the twenties. The ability to analyze one's behavior and change accordingly is an important related skill and crucial for coping with life. In people as they age, the ability to attend to more than one aspect of the environment at a time decreases; however, focused (sustained) or selective attention continues to be good as a person ages (until an elderly age, which varies with the individual).

MEMORY AND ATTENTION

Learning and memory are also related. Learning is how we acquire new information, while memory has to do with storage and the ability to retrieve this information (Squire, 1987). Distractibility and inattention can negatively impact our ability to remember things. For this reason, people with attentional difficulties are frequently also thought to have memory problems. For something to be remembered, it must be attended to first! Ultimately, the attention processes lead to the learning of the information that, in turn, leads to memory formation. Some types of memories require more overt attentional processes, such as knowledge of facts for both storage and retrieval processes. Other types of memories—such as procedural memories (tying a shoe)—may require selective and sustained attention for storage but do not require intentional attentional resources for retrieval.

CHALLENGES IN ATTENTION

Children with attentional difficulties frequently experience problems in school and with peers. In school they may have difficulty completing assignments, following directions, and following through on requirements. They may be seen as flighty, disorganized, and irresponsible. Many times these same children are frustrated when they cannot complete assignments and are confused as to "why the teacher is mad at me." Children with significant difficulties in this area may be diagnosed with attention deficit hyperactivity disorder (ADHD). This disorder is characterized by problems in attention, impulse control, and sometimes with activity level.

Many people may have difficulty with attention but do not qualify for a diagnosis of ADHD. It is likely that attentional skills lie along a continuum. Because attentional abilities can differ among children, even those without ADHD, providing assistance for these attentional skills in the classroom is an important function of teachers. Providing frequent breaks, allowing the child to break tasks into smaller parts, teaching the child how to budget and manage time, and providing reminders and support are techniques that assist children with attentional difficulty. Visual cues are particularly helpful for children and people with attentional difficulty. Children with attentional difficulties who participate in classrooms that allow for cooperative learning and provide hands-on or visual support are often more successful.

Attentional difficulties, at times, result from medical problems. Severe traumatic brain injury frequently occurs with attentional problems, particularly when severe. Children with attention problems have also been found to have a higher incidence of head injury, possibly caused by poor impulse control. Treatments for leukemia and childhood cancer may also result in difficulty with attention. Individuals with emotional problems such as anxiety and/or depression also have concomitant attentional problems.

Attention is not an all-or-none skill, and it is affected by task demands. A person may do well on tasks that require sustained attention but have significant difficulty on tasks that require divided or alternating attention. Developing coping skills for these tasks is particularly helpful for children and adults. For example, audiotaping a lecture for a college student can help provide additional notes that may have been missed when first listening to the lecture. Providing a lecture outline also can help to focus attention on salient points. For adults, the use of an organizer or a personal digital assistant (PDA) device also provides assistance.

Thus, attention is a skill that develops over the life span and assists one in regulating behavior as well as adapting to changing environmental demands. Attention is intimately entwined with perception, memory, emotion, and learning.

—*Margaret Semrud-Clikeman and Alexandra Kutz*

See also Attention Deficit Hyperactivity Disorder; Time on Task

REFERENCES AND FURTHER READING

Berk, L. E. (1989). *Child development*. Boston: Allyn & Bacon.

Broadbent, D. A. (1970). Stimulus set and response set: Two kinds of selective attention. In D. I. Motofsky (Ed.), *Attention: Contemporary theory and analysis* (pp. 51–60). New York: Appleton-Century-Crofts.

Damasio, A. R. (1994). *Descartes' error: Emotion, reason, and the human brain*. New York: Harcourt Brace.

Damasio, A. R. (1999). *The feeling of what happens: Body and emotion in the making of consciousness*. New York: Harcourt Brace.

Knight, R. T., & Grabowecky, M. (1995). Escape from linear time: Prefrontal cortex and conscious experience. In M. S. Gazzaniga (Ed.), *The cognitive neurosciences* (pp. 1357–1371). Cambridge, MA: MIT Press.

Posner, M. I. (1994). Attention: The mechanisms of consciousness. *Proceedings of the National Academy of Sciences, USA, 91*, 7398–7403.

Posner, M. I., & Raichle, M. E. (1994). *Images of mind*. New York: W. H. Freeman.

Squire, L. R. (1987). *Memory and brain*. New York: Oxford University Press.

Teeter, P. A. (1998). *Interventions for ADHD*. New York: Guilford.

Treisman, A. M. (1969). Strategies and models of selective attention. *Psychological Review, 76*, 282–299.

Wellman, H. M. (1988). The early development of memory strategies. In F. E. Weinert and M. Perlmutter (Eds.), *Memory development: Universal changes and individual differences*. Hillsdale, NJ: Erlbaum.

Woldoroff, M. G., & Hillyard, S. A. (1991). Modulation of early auditory processing during selective listening to rapidly presented tones. *Electroencephalogy and Clinical Neurophysiology, 79*, 170–191.

ATTENTION DEFICIT HYPERACTIVITY DISORDER

Attention deficit hyperactivity disorder (ADHD) is one of the most common types of childhood disorders. Individuals with ADHD exhibit attention problems as well as hyperactive and impulsive behaviors. Children and adolescents with ADHD may have difficulty sitting still, listening to instructions or classroom lectures, organizing materials, completing schoolwork or homework, or playing or engaging in activities quietly. These individuals frequently make careless mistakes in their schoolwork or they may forget or lose things.

According to the *Diagnostic and Statistical Manual of Mental Disorders, Fourth Edition-Text Revision* (*DSM-IV-TR*) (American Psychiatric Association, 2000), there are three subtypes of ADHD:

1. ADHD, Predominantly Inattentive Type

2. ADHD, Predominantly Hyperactive-Impulsive Type

3. ADHD, Combined Type

The ADHD, Combined Type is the most common, and individuals with this subtype exhibit inattentive and hyperactive-impulsive behaviors. To meet the diagnostic criteria for this subtype, individuals must exhibit both of the following:

- At least six of the nine inattentive symptoms (fails to attend to details, does not seem to listen, has difficulty sustaining attention in tasks and play activities, does not follow through on instructions, has difficulty organizing tasks and activities, avoids tasks requiring sustained mental effort, often loses necessary things, is easily distracted, and is often forgetful in daily activities)

- At least six of the nine hyperactive-impulsive symptoms (e.g., often fidgets with hands or feet, often leaves seat in the classroom, often runs about or climbs excessively, has difficulty playing or engaging in leisure activities, acts if "on the go" or "driven by a motor," interrupts others, has difficulty awaiting turn, blurts out responses, and talks excessively)

Inattentiveness characterizes the ADHD, Predominantly Inattentive Type. Individuals with this subtype must exhibit at least six inattentive symptoms and fewer than six hyperactive-impulsive symptoms. In contrast, the symptoms of motor excess and impulsive responding characterize individuals with ADHD, Predominantly Hyperactive-Impulsive Type. Individuals with this subtype must exhibit six or more hyperactive-impulsive symptoms and fewer than six inattentive symptoms. For all three subtypes, the symptoms must be present for at least six months and some of the symptoms must have appeared before seven years of age. Impairment associated with these symptoms is exhibited in at least two settings (e.g., home and school), and the impairment affects social or academic functioning and is clinically significant.

As with other disorders, the prevalence of ADHD among children and adolescents has been difficult to ascertain. Prevalence estimates have ranged from 1% to 14%, with 3% to 7% as the most common prevalence estimates reported in recent years. ADHD is reported to be more common in males than in females, with male-to-female ratios ranging from 2:1 to 9:1 (American Psychiatric Association, 2000).

Children and adolescents with ADHD are at risk for developing comorbid disorders. More than 50% of these individuals are reported to have one or more co-occurring disorders (Barkley, 1998), with the most prevalent co-occurring disorders being oppositional defiant disorders, conduct disorders, mood disorders (i.e., bipolar disorders and unipolar depression), anxiety disorders, learning disorders, and communication disorders. Of these disorders, the disruptive behavior disorders (i.e., oppositional defiant disorders and conduct disorders) are the most common comorbid conditions (American Psychiatric Association, 2000).

Many elementary and secondary students with ADHD experience cognitive, academic, and social problems. Students with ADHD are more likely to be behind their peers in intellectual development. There is evidence to suggest that these students may score an average of 7.5 to 15 points below their classmates on standardized intelligence tests (Hoff & colleagues, 2002). Along with cognitive difficulties, these individuals are at risk for academic problems. Many students with ADHD experience academic difficulties in reading, mathematics, and spelling and may qualify for special education services under the specific learning disability of the Individuals With Disabilities Education Act (IDEA), the major special education law in the United States. These individuals may also qualify for special education services under the other health impairment (OHI) category of IDEA, or they may qualify for accommodations in the regular education classroom under section 504 of the Rehabilitation Act of 1973, a federal law that protects the rights of individuals with disabilities. Because of the academic and cognitive difficulties, some students with ADHD experience failure in school (Hoff & colleagues, 2002) and eventually drop out. Besides experiencing academic and cognitive difficulties, these students are more likely to demonstrate disruptive, intrusive, and off-task behaviors in the classroom, which interferes with their learning and possibly other students' learning, and may make these students less popular with their classmates. In addition to having behavioral, academic, and cognitive difficulties, many students with ADHD experience significant social impairments. These individuals may

have poor peer and adult relationships because they are bossy, impulsive, and easily frustrated in their interactions with their peers. These negative behaviors may lead to peer and adult rejection, which puts these individuals at further risk for subsequent behavioral, emotional, and social problems.

There are a host of plausible explanations for the occurrence of ADHD, with neurological and genetic factors receiving substantial support. ADHD tends to run in families and so, hereditary factors are thought to play a role in this disorder. Possible neurological etiologies include prenatal and perinatal complications; abnormalities in brain structure, function, or chemistry; exposure to environmental toxins; and infections. Barkley (1997) contends that a neurological impairment in the behavioral inhibition system is central to this disorder and provides an explanation for the problems these individuals have (i.e., regulating their behavior to situational demands). Environmental factors have also been suggested as possible explanations for this disorder, including certain parenting styles and parenting characteristics, chaotic home environments, and poverty. However, there is little empirical evidence to support these factors as causes of ADHD (Anastopoulos & colleagues, 2001).

To assess children and adolescents with ADHD, a multimethod assessment approach is strongly recommended. A multimethod assessment approach involves using different measures, informants (parent, teacher, student, peers), and settings (home, school) to glean information about the areas of concern; and then using this information to develop intervention strategies to address the areas of concern. In a clinical setting, a comprehensive evaluation is conducted and typically includes one or more clinical interviews with the parent(s) and child or adolescent, a medical examination, and completion of behavioral rating scales. Intelligence tests, academic achievement tests, neuropsychological tests, personality and/or projective tests, and observations may also be included in the assessment battery to aid in differential diagnosis or to assess the severity of collateral impairments that may occur with this disorder (Gordon & Barkley, 1998). In a school setting, the assessment of students with ADHD may be conducted within a problem-solving model, a model used to identify and resolve problems that a student may be experiencing. Parent, teacher, child, and possibly peer interviews, direct observations (in and outside the classroom), and behavioral ratings scales make up the core of the assessment battery used in the schools and within this model. In recent years, other techniques such as functional behavioral assessment—used to identify the function of a behavior—and curriculum-based measures— used to assess students' fluency in basic skills (e.g., reading and math)—have also been used in the assessment of some students with ADHD who exhibit behavioral or academic difficulties, respectively. If interventions selected and implemented based on the assessment results from the previously administered instruments do not produce positive change in the area(s) of concern, a comprehensive evaluation is likely to follow and may include intelligence tests, academic achievement tests, and other measures, depending on the area or areas of concern. Based on the assessment results of this comprehensive evaluation and discussion among school personnel and the parent(s) and possibly the child or adolescent, placement in special education or implementation of a 504 plan (i.e., accommodations in the regular education classroom) may result.

A variety of strategies have been used in the treatment of children and adolescents with ADHD. Evidence suggests that a multimodal approach, where two or more strategies are combined—such as medication and behavioral modification techniques (e.g., methods used to change behavior by rewarding appropriate behavior and ignoring or punishing inappropriate behavior)—may be more effective in the treatment of ADHD than the use of medication alone.

Stimulant medication such as Ritalin or Concerta is the most common type of medication used to treat children and adolescents with ADHD. Tricyclic antidepressant medications have also been used, especially if a tic disorder (i.e., repetitive motor movements and/or vocalizations) such as Tourette's syndrome is present. Psychostimulant medication tends to increase tic behavior when children and adolescents have both of these disorders. When monitored effectively by school personnel and physicians, stimulant medication is effective, in the short-run, in reducing inattentiveness and decreasing disruptive behaviors, as well as facilitating learning and social functioning. However, there are some significant concerns associated with the use of stimulant medication with these children and adolescents, including:

- Medication costs
- Stigmatization associated with taking the medication

- Adherence to medication regimen
- Dosage levels that are either too high or too low
- Quick-fix approach rather than the selection of intervention strategies to change behavior on a permanent basis
- Short-term side effects (e.g., stomach aches, weight loss, appetite suppression, sleep problems)
- Long-term side effects (e.g., depression, sleep difficulties, height and weight suppression, increased blood pressure)

A variety of nonpharmacological interventions (e.g., environmental modifications, behavior modification techniques, parent training, social skills training, self-monitoring, peer strategies, and home–school notes) have been used with children and adolescents with ADHD, either alone or in combination with medication. The nonpharmacological interventions selected and implemented will depend on a number of factors such as the problem being addressed, age of the individual, severity of the problem, time needed to implement the strategy or strategies, and individuals who will be responsible for implementing the intervention(s).

Environmental or task modifications involve changing the environment or the task in order to obtain the desired outcome. Examples of environmental or task modifications include moving the student's desk closer to the teacher's desk in order to increase on-task behavior or assigning shorter assignments in order to increase completion of schoolwork and/or homework. Behavior modification strategies are interventions used to change behavior by rewarding appropriate behavior and ignoring or punishing inappropriate behavior. The use of verbal praise or the administration of a tangible reinforcer (e.g., a sticker) to a student for sitting in his or her seat during independent seatwork would be an example of a behavior modification strategy in which appropriate behavior (sitting in one's seat) is rewarded. The act of ignoring a student blurting out answers in class where the classroom rule is for students to raise their hands and to wait to be called on by the teacher is another example of a behavior modification strategy; in this case, the strategy (teacher not paying attention to the undesirable behavior) is used to decrease inappropriate behavior (i.e., blurting out answers).

Parent training involves training parents in behavior modification techniques to reduce noncompliant and other inappropriate behaviors found in many children and adolescents with ADHD. In parent training, a mental health professional such as a school psychologist works with parents to teach them behavior modification techniques, such as making a request of their child or adolescent and the child or adolescent responding in an appropriate manner to the parent's request in a short period of time. Parents can also be trained to use behavior modification strategies to increase the frequency of appropriate behavior demonstrated by their child or adolescent. Another strategy to increase the frequency of appropriate behavior, including attending behavior, is self-monitoring.

Self-monitoring is a cognitive–behavioral approach (i.e., a technique used to change behavior by changing one's cognitions). In self-monitoring, students with ADHD monitor their own behavior (e.g., their own attending behavior) to increase the frequency of that behavior. Although self-monitoring is an attractive strategy to parents and teachers, because it is implemented by the child or adolescent and does not require the adult's time, there is some evidence to suggest that this strategy is not effective in changing the individual's behavior.

A strategy used to promote positive peer and adult interactions for some students with ADHD is social skills training. Social skills training involves a mental health professional working with children or adolescents either individually or in groups. The children or adolescents learn skills to interact successfully with peers and adults or learn to perform these skills more frequently or less awkwardly. Skills learned may include how to manage one's anger, how to deal with teasing, how to begin a conversation, or how to join a group of peers.

Other strategies to promote positive peer interactions and to increase the academic performance of students with ADHD are peer strategies, including peer tutoring and classwide peer tutoring. In peer tutoring and classwide peer tutoring, students with ADHD are paired with other students, preferably good role models, in the classroom; the students with ADHD are tutored by the other students (peer tutoring), or the students in the entire class take turns tutoring each other (classwide peer tutoring). Another popular intervention strategy is home–school notes, which are used to address a number of behaviors such as off-task behavior and incomplete assignments. The strategy requires a note or daily report card, evaluating the student's performance or behavior in the classroom to be completed by the student's teacher. Then the student carries the note home where it is reviewed and signed by the student's parents, and consequences are delivered to the student by the parent for his or her performance or behavior demonstrated at school that day. The student returns the signed note to the school the next day. Home–school notes can be effective in addressing problematic behaviors experienced by many children and adolescents with ADHD as long as collaboration exists between the home and the school in the implementation of this intervention strategy.

—Patricia A. Lowe
and Kristin Powers

See also Attention; Behavior Intervention; Conduct Disorder; Diagnosis and Labeling; Individuals With Disabilities Education Act; Learning Disabilities; Psychotropic Medications

REFERENCES AND FURTHER READING

American Psychiatric Association. (2000). *Diagnostic and statistical manual of mental disorders* (4th ed., text rev.). Washington, DC: Author.

Anastopoulos, A. D., Klinger, E. E., & Temple, E. P. (2001). Treating children and adolescents with attention-deficit/hyperactivity disorder. In J. N. Hughes, A. M. La Greca, & J. C. Conoley (Eds.), *Handbook of psychological services for children and adolescents* (pp. 245–265). New York: Oxford University Press.

Barkley, R. A. (1997). *ADHD and the nature of self-control.* New York: Guilford.

Barkley, R. A. (1998). *Attention-deficit hyperactivity disorder.* New York: Guilford.

Gordon, M., & Barkley, R. A. (1998). Tests and observational measures. In R. A. Barkley (Ed.), *Attention-deficit hyperactivity disorder* (pp. 345–372). New York: Guilford.

Hoff, K. E, Doepka, K., & Landau, S. (2002). Best practice in the assessment of children with attention deficit/hyperactivity disorder. In A. Thomas & J. Grimes (Eds.), *Best practices in school psychology* (Vol. 4, pp. 1129–1146). Washington, DC: National Association of School Psychologists.

AUTHENTIC ASSESSMENT

Authentic assessment requires the respondent to construct, rather than select, a response to academic stimuli (e.g., tests, papers) (Salvia & Ysseldyke, 2001). A rubric, based on set criteria, is used to evaluate and assign a number or proficiency level

Table 1   Examples of Authentic Assessments

Assessment	Possible Candidate
Write a response to the story starter, "The best day of my life was. . . ."	Second-grade student
Given four different liquids, design and execute a study to determine which liquid nourishes a bean seedling the best. Record your observations and conclusions in you lab journal.	Fourth-grade student
In a group, research and write a proposal for implementing an efficient, renewable energy source and present it to the board of the local power company.	Sixth-grade student
Build a model of a suspension bridge that would allow pedestrians to cross the Mississippi taking into account potential traffic flow and the impact of natural phenomena like wind.	Tenth-grade student
Using public transportation, go to a local grocery store and complete the shopping for the week, including foods from all four food groups, toiletries, and cleaning supplies.	Twelfth-grade student with cognitive disabilities

to the response. Authentic assessments are typically performance or portfolio assessments designed to measure complex skills such as synthesis, analysis, and collaboration (Vanderwood & Powers, 2002). For example, an authentic assessment may require a group of students to collaborate on analyzing and synthesizing disparate information on a country in order to formulate international policy for that country to be delivered in a mock United Nations address. Table 1 provides additional examples of authentic assessments.

Authentic assessments generally measure skills rather than traits. They are a more direct measure of a skill than tests of cognitive or psychological processing, which require a greater level of inference to draw conclusions about the trait being measured (Salvia & Yesseldyke, 2001). Authentic assessment tasks are designed to support and even enhance the curriculum as well as to assess whether specific instructional objectives are met, whereas traditional psychoeducational assessments attempt to measure more global or innate skills such as intelligence. Accordingly, authentic assessments provide information that is more relevant to the curriculum and instruction of a student than that offered by traditional psychoeducational assessments. For this reason, authentic assessments are more useful in planning instructional programs than for determining eligibility for special education (although a response-to-intervention model for determining special education

eligibility could employ authentic assessments to monitor a student's progress).

Authentic assessments have long been the preferred method of assessing the progress of students with low incidence disabilities (e.g., severe mental retardation, deaf-blindness, etc.) (Coutinho & Malouf, 1993). They gained popularity in general education as dissatisfaction with multiple-choice achievement tests grew (Salvia & Ysseldyke, 2001). During the 1980s large-scale minimum competency testing was widespread, and detractors of these programs argued that these multiple-choice tests failed to assess important "real-life" or authentic skills. In other words, life is not a series of multiple-choice problems; rather, students must be prepared to respond in thoughtful and meaningful ways to complex problems.

Authentic assessments are designed to assess students' procedural knowledge as well as their content or declarative knowledge (Mehrens, 1992). Authentic assessments often provide a multitude of ways for a student to arrive at an answer and contain a record of the student's thought processes (e.g., logs, outlines). By examining how students construct their responses, teachers are better able to identify and correct errors in logic or applications of a new skill. An added benefit of authentic assessments is that they are often much more engaging to students than traditional multiple-choice exams.

Authentic assessments also have limitations, including (Mehrens, 1992):

- Subjectivity in scoring
- Costs associated with administering and scoring
- Potential for assessing a wide breadth of knowledge and depth of knowledge

Because of these limitations, authentic assessment may be augmented by multiple-choice tests. For example, the behind-the-wheel portion of a drivers test provides in-depth and authentic information about how well an individual can drive a car given the particular demands of the course (e.g., terrain, time of day) but a multiple-choice test is the most expedient way to assess the driver's knowledge about all other conditions related to driving that did not occur during the behind-the-wheel test. As the example illustrates, both types of assessments are useful and complementary. School psychologists should consider using authentic assessments when they wish to assess a student's skill in context rather than isolation, and when they desire information that is relevant to the student's curriculum, instruction, and future life-skills.

—*Kristin Powers*

See also Academic Achievement; Criterion-Referenced Assessment; Curriculum-Based Assessment; Outcomes-Based Assessment; Performance-Based Assessment; Portfolio Assessment

REFERENCES AND FURTHER READING

Coutinho, M., & Malouf, D. (1993). Performance assessment and children with disabilities: Issues and possibilities. *Teaching Exceptional Children, 25*(4), 63–67.

Mehrens, W. A., (1992, Spring). Using performance assessment for accountability purposes. *Educational Measurement: Issues and Practice*, 3–20.

Salvia, J., & Ysseldyke, J. E. (2001). *Assessment* (8th ed.). New York: Houghton Mifflin.

Vanderwood, M., & Powers, K. (2002). Standards-based district-wide assessment. In A. Thomas & J. Grimes (Eds.), *Best practices in school psychology* (4th ed., pp. 255–263). Bethesda, MD: National Association of School Psychologists.

AUTISM SPECTRUM DISORDERS

Autism spectrum disorders are a group of separate syndromes with overlapping characteristics, most notably in the areas of social interaction, communication, and distinctive behavioral characteristics.

In the classification scheme of the *Diagnostic and Statistical Manual of Mental Disorders, Fourth Edition (DSM-IV)* of the American Psychiatric Association (1994), the disorders are classified under the umbrella term, *pervasive developmental disorders*. This review examines the disorders as described in the *DSM-IV*. The disorders reviewed are:

- Autism
- Asperger's disorder
- Rett's disorder
- Childhood disintegrative disorder
- Pervasive developmental disorder-not otherwise specified

A brief description is provided for each of these disorders along with the possible etiology , diagnostic criteria, assessment techniques, current treatment options, and prognosis.

AUTISM

Autism is a disorder that is first diagnosed in childhood. Children with autism demonstrate qualitative deficits in their social interaction with others—in communication and play skills—and demonstrate restricted or stereotyped interests and behaviors. In 1943, Kanner was the first to describe the characteristics of children with autism, based on a sample of 11 children he saw in his office with a similar constellation of symptoms (Kanner, 1943). Although the defining characteristics of autism have been refined over the years, the essential cluster of social interaction, communication, and restrictive behaviors/interests have remained. Initially considered to be a relatively rare disorder, recent studies indicate that autism may be more prevalent than previously recognized. The *DSM-IV* indicates a prevalence rate of 2 to 5 cases per 10,000 individuals. More recent studies suggest that the prevalence rate may be as high as 1 case per 1,000 individuals (Gillberg & Coleman, 2000). Likewise, the incidence of autism appears to be increasing, although reasons for this remain unclear; it may be related to increased public and health provider awareness and more effective differential diagnostic assessment. There is approximately a boy-to-girl ratio of 4:1 with a diagnosis of autism. There are no differences in prevalence rate in terms of socioeconomic class, culture, race, or ethnicity.

Table 1   Some Common Autism Myths and Facts

"Cold" parenting causes autism.	There are no known types of parenting practices that cause autism. Autism is most likely caused by multiple genetic and environmental variables, and there may be more than one cause for autism.
Autism is seen primarily in families of high socioeconomic status.	Autism is found across all levels of socioeconomic status equally and across all cultures, races, and ethnicities.
Individuals with autism often have exceptional specialized abilities such as adding or memorizing geography.	Although some individuals with autism may have specific exceptional abilities, this is uncommon and not a distinguishing characteristic of autism.
Individuals with autism typically spend their time alone, spinning objects or engaged in other maladaptive behavior such as self-injury or having tantrums.	Autism is not characterized by maladaptive behavior, but largely by impairment in social and communication functioning. Restricted or stereotyped behaviors and interests are only part of the picture and may present in many.
Children with autism do not hug and do not seek social interaction.	Although there is qualitative impairment in social interaction, this may present itself in many different ways for the individual. Some children with autism do not seek social attention, but other children with autism may seek hugs and social attention and interaction and be affectionate, albeit atypical in their demonstration of these social behaviors.
Autism is not treatable.	Treatment of autism is largely symptomatic, but effective interventions to successfully teach important social and communication skills and reduce maladaptive behaviors are available based on research in applied behavior analysis.

The causes of autism are:
    Immunizations (MMR)
    Gastrointestinal disorders
    Mercury or lead poisoning
    Vitamin deficiencies
	There is not a specific identifiable cause for autism at this time. Most likely the cause is multiply determined and includes genetic and environmental variables.

The etiology of autism is unknown. There were early misconceptions that it was caused by poor or inadequate parenting (Table 1). This viewpoint has largely been discredited. More likely, autism is the result of a confluence of environmental and genetic variables. Scientific inquiry at this time is focused on identifying genetic variables and neurological variables common in children with autism. There are some medical conditions that have a higher rate of autism associated with them—such as tuberous sclerosis, fragile X syndrome, or maternal rubella—and the autism characteristics are likely related to the neurological deficits associated with the medical condition.

There is not a specific medical test available for diagnosing autism. It is diagnosed based on observation and report of behavioral characteristics particular to the child and consistent with diagnostic criteria.

The *DSM-IV* includes three primary areas in the diagnostic scheme, which are:

1. Qualitative impairment in social interaction

2. Qualitative impairment in communication

3. Restrictive, repetitive, or stereotyped patterns of behavior or interests

There are specific behavioral characteristics listed for each of these areas in the *DSM-IV*. Often, when people think of autism, they may think of a child sitting alone and spinning objects or of a character such as played by Dustin Hoffman in the movie *Rain Man*. However, the emphasis in diagnosing autism is on the qualitative impairments in social interaction and communication, not necessarily the atypical behavior patterns. Qualitative differences refer to differences in how a child expresses or demonstrates behavior. Children with autism are impaired in how they interact and communicate, not necessarily in the level of skills they have to interact or communicate. The impairments in social interaction, communication, and restricted behavior and interests typically cause significant impairments in social, occupational, or other (e.g., school performance) areas of functioning.

Because the diagnostic criteria consist of behavioral characteristics, assessment for a diagnosis of autism consists largely of behavioral assessment and includes (Shriver & colleagues, 1999):

- A parent interview
- Review of medical records
- An interview with the child, if possible
- Behavior rating forms (e.g., Childhood Autism Rating Scale, Gilliam Autism Rating Scale, Autism Behavior Checklist)
- Direct interaction with the child
- Observation of the child interacting with parents, teachers, and peers

Following observations, interviews, record reviews, and scoring of autism screening forms, if a child is demonstrating characteristics consistent with the *DSM-IV* classification scheme, and there is not another diagnosis that better explains current functioning, then a diagnosis of autism may be made.

There is no known cure for autism, but there are interventions available that can help children with autism develop the skills they need to function more successfully. These interventions are based on applied behavior analysis (Maurice & colleagues, 1996). Children with autism can learn social and communication skills to function more effectively in their environment. As of 1996, there were more than 500 studies demonstrating the application of applied behavior analysis in the effective treatment of children with autism (Matson & colleagues, 1996). To date, no other treatment methodology has approached this level of demonstrated empirical support for effective intervention for children with autism. Other treatment approaches may be attempted, such as sensory integration or megavitamin therapies or dietary management, but these have not garnered empirical evidence for successful treatment (Smith, 1996). Likewise, there are no known medical or pharmacological treatment approaches demonstrated to be effective in treating autism, although medications may be attempted to assist in managing maladaptive behavior.

Autism is considered a lifetime disorder. The effects on an individual child may vary on a continuum from mild to severe. Children or adults with mild characteristics of autism may function successfully in their families, schools, and even in society; but they need support from others to understand social cues and communicate effectively. A child or adult with severe characteristics of autism may not be able to communicate orally, may not demonstrate awareness of others or of his or her environment, and may engage in significant maladaptive behavior (tantrums, self-injurious behavior). Likewise, mental retardation is often a comorbid disability with autism and will affect the individual's successful functioning. Children with autism who have access to intensive applied behavior analytic treatment approaches, mild mental retardation or higher cognitive functioning, and development of effective communication skills at younger ages tend to have better prognoses than children without these supports and characteristics.

ASPERGER'S DISORDER

Controversy surrounds Asperger's disorder, as many question whether this disorder represents a milder form of autism, a separate disorder similar to autism, or an entirely different disorder that does not even belong under the same umbrella of disorders as autism. Currently, Asperger's disorder is found under the umbrella of pervasive developmental disorders and is defined separately from autism. A physician in Germany named Hans Asperger (1906–1980) was the first to describe the constellation of characteristics that comprise what is now called Asperger's disorder in a paper published in 1944. It was not until the early 1980s, however, that this article was translated to English and became more widely known (Cumine & colleagues, 1998). Studies have been unclear in determining a prevalence rate for Asperger's disorder. It appears to affect more males than females; however, exact ratios have not been identified. There are no known differences related to socioeconomic status, culture, race, or ethnicity.

The diagnostic criteria in the *DSM-IV* for Asperger's disorder emphasize a qualitative impairment in social interaction (e.g., marked impairment in nonverbal behaviors such as eye-to-eye gaze, lack of social or emotional reciprocity) and restrictive, repetitive, stereotyped behaviors and interests (e.g., preoccupation with particular topic of interest, stereotyped and repetitive motor mannerisms). There must be a clinically significant impairment in social, occupational, or other (e.g., school performance) areas of functioning. Asperger's disorder differs from autism in that there are not impairments in communication, or significant delays in cognitive functioning or adaptive behavior, such as self-help skills.

Because there are fewer areas of impairment relative to children with autism, children with Asperger's disorder are often not identified until entering school. It is at this point that impairments in social interaction become more noticeable. Similar to autism, however, the assessment for diagnosis of Asperger's disorder is largely behavioral and includes review of medical history, parent interview, child interview, observations of the child in social situations and/or interacting with parents, and behavior rating forms. A cognitive test, such as the Wechsler Intelligence Scale for Children-4th Edition, may be given to rule out significant cognitive delay or mental retardation. In addition, speech/language testing may be conducted to rule out speech or language delays. Finally, an adaptive behavior measure, such as the Vineland Adaptive Behavior Scales, may be administered to rule out adaptive behavior delays, except in the area of social interaction.

The etiology of Asperger's disorder has not been identified. It does appear to occur more frequently within families with a relative identified with the disease, suggesting a possible genetic link. Similar to autism, it appears that Asperger's disorder may have different causes relative to individual cases and is most likely related to a confluence of environmental and genetic variables.

The behavioral characteristics of Asperger's disorder are amenable to treatment approaches from an applied behavior analytic perspective. Interventions that are effective for children with autism will generally be effective for children with Asperger's disorder. In essence, children with Asperger benefit from behavioral treatments designed to teach effective social interaction and daily functioning and to remediate behavioral difficulties. Similar to autism, other treatment approaches such as sensory integration, vitamin therapy, and diet management have not been found effective for treating characteristics of Asperger's disorder. Medication may be helpful in assisting with managing some of the maladaptive behaviors an individual with Asperger's disorder may exhibit.

Given the normal development of language and cognitive functioning, the prognosis for a child with Asperger's disorder is better than for a child with autism; however, children with the former may experience other mental health difficulties, such as depression or anxiety, as they come to realize differences in their relationships with others. Asperger's disorder is considered a lifetime disorder; but, with effective supports to assist with teaching social skills and socially adaptive functioning, individuals with the disease can lead independent and successful lives.

RETT'S DISORDER

Although Rett's disorder (also called Rett syndrome) has some characteristics similar to autism, there are clear differences as well, and more is known regarding possible causes. Rett's disorder is a developmental disorder that is genetic in origin. It was first described by Dr. Andreas Rett in 1966 based on his observations of girls in his medical clinic. The girls had similar developmental courses including impairment in motor development and language and characteristic hand-wringing. It was not until the mid 1970s and early 1980s that descriptions of the disorder were published in English language medical journals and the disorder was given a name (International Rett Syndrome Association Web site, 2002). Rett's disorder primarily affects females (Gillberg & Coleman, 2000; Pevsner, 2001), with prevalence estimated to be between 1 in 15,000 to 1 in 20,000 females (Gillberg & Coleman, 2000; Pevsner, 2001). There are no differences in prevalence rates across socioeconomic status, culture, race, or ethnicity. Rett's disorder is characterized by early normal development with regression in development apparent starting at approximately 6 to 18 months of age.

It is estimated that approximately 70% to 90% of girls affected by Rett's disorder have a mutation of the MeCP2 gene on the X chromosome (Amir & colleagues, 1999; Gillberg & Coleman, 2000; Pevsner, 2001). For individuals that have characteristics of Rett's disorder, but do not have a mutation of this particular gene, it may be that there are other genes involved or other regions of this particular gene that have not yet been identified in the expression of Rett's disorder characteristics.

Based on the diagnostic criteria of the *DSM-IV*, the following characteristics are required for a diagnosis of Rett's disorder:

- Apparently normal prenatal and perinatal development
- Apparently normal psychomotor development through the first five months after birth
- Normal head circumference at birth

After a period of normal development, *DSM-IV* criteria include documentation of:

- Deceleration of head growth between ages 5 and 48 months
- Loss of previously acquired purposeful hand skills between ages 5 and 30 months, with subsequent development of stereotyped hand movements (e.g., hand-wringing or hand washing)
- Loss of social engagement early in the course, appearance of poorly coordinated gait or trunk movements, and severely impaired expressive and receptive language development with severe psychomotor retardation

The assessment for Rett's disorder is based on the medical documentation of developmental regression and characteristics described above. With the identification of specific gene involvement since the development of the *DSM-IV* criteria, current assessment also includes genetic testing. However, even if genetic testing is negative, if the child meets all the criteria above, she could still be diagnosed with Rett's disorder.

Although highly variable for each individual, as a group children with Rett's disorder follow a similar course of development throughout their lifetime. This course is divided into four stages. Stage I generally encompasses the age range of 6 to 18 months and includes deceleration of head growth, disinterest in play activity, hypotonia, and developmental stagnation. Stage II encompasses the age range of 1 to 3 years and includes rapid regression, irritability, loss of hand use, development of hand stereotypies, and presence of autistic-like characteristics (e.g., social and communication deficits). Stage III encompasses the age range of 2 to 10 years and includes mental retardation, seizures, breathing irregularities, teeth grinding, language deficits, and motor delays. There may be an improvement in social interaction at this stage. Stage IV encompasses the age range of 10 years and beyond and includes progressive scoliosis, muscle wasting and rigidity, and decreased mobility. There may be improved eye contact but

there is limited expressive and receptive language (Gillberg & Colman, 2000; Pevsner, 2001).

There is no known treatment or cure for Rett's disorder. Treatment provided is specific to address the symptoms expressed by the individual with the disease. Physical and occupational therapy, augmentative communication, medical treatment for physical problems associated with the condition, and ongoing educational services are some of the treatment approaches beneficial for improving functioning and quality of life for children with Rett's disorder.

CHILDHOOD DISINTEGRATIVE DISORDER

Childhood disintegrative disorder (also known as Heller syndrome) is characterized primarily by a regression in development starting after the child is two years of age. This regression follows a period of seeming normal development and may result in many of the characteristics of autism, except that it occurs later in development. Seizures appear to be more common in children with childhood disintegrative disorder. It is a rare disorder, but current estimates are of a prevalence rate of 0.11 in 10,000 children (Gillberg & Coleman, 2000). There may be more males identified than females.

The etiology of childhood disintegrative disorder is unknown. It is most likely genetic in origin given the characteristic regression following an at least two-year period of normal development. Diagnosis is based on documentation of specific characteristics. As described in the *DSM-IV*, specific criteria include normal development for at least two years after birth. After 2 years of age, but before 10 years of age, there is significant loss in at least two areas of development such as expressive or receptive language, social skills or adaptive behavior, bowel or bladder control, play, and motor skills. In addition, similar to autism, there are abnormalities in two areas of functioning such as qualitative impairment in social interaction and communication and restricted patterns of behavior or interests. Given the developmental regression, mental retardation is often a comorbid diagnosis with childhood disintegrative disorder.

Assessment is based on documentation of the normal period of development as well as documentation of the regression in skills. Medical records, parent interviews, observations of the child, as well as direct testing with the child (e.g., developmental or intelligence testing) are some components of the assessment process. There is some evidence that the regression in skills plateaus over time, but little evidence of improvement of symptoms. Treatment is symptomatic and may include medication for maladaptive behaviors, physical therapy, occupational therapy, ongoing educational services, speech and language therapy, as well as behavioral treatments to facilitate daily functioning.

PERVASIVE DEVELOPMENTAL DISORDER-NOT OTHERWISE SPECIFIED

Pervasive developmental disorder-not otherwise specified (PDD-NOS) is most similar to autism. This diagnostic category is used for children who exhibit characteristics similar to the other pervasive developmental disorders, but not enough of the characteristics to diagnose a specific one of them. Children who demonstrate qualitative impairment in social interaction, or in communication, or restricted or stereotyped behavior and interests may be included in this category. This differs from autism in that impairment in only one of these areas is required for diagnosis, not all three. If a child exhibits impairment in all three areas, but the number of symptoms present is low, or age of onset is later than typical, then the child may be diagnosed with PDD-NOS rather than autism.

Given the similarities to autism, PDD-NOS may be assumed to also have similar etiology—most likely a combination of genetic and environmental factors. Likewise, there may be multiple causes for PDD-NOS. The assessment of PDD-NOS includes the same process and methods as for autism. Likewise, treatment based on applied behavior analysis is most effective for treatment of specific symptoms or characteristics of PDD-NOS. The prognosis is highly variable and dependent upon the severity of symptoms present, but, given the typical subthreshold symptomatology, individuals with PDD-NOS typically will function more successfully in society and be more amenable to treatment.

SUMMARY

The various disorders that comprise the pervasive developmental disorders or autism spectrum disorders vary substantially in terms of specific characteristics. However, there is some overlap in areas of impairment, specifically those related to social interaction, communication, and restricted or stereotyped behaviors. As research continues for each disorder, it is difficult to predict if they will remain within the same umbrella of disorders. It appears that a genetic component underlies all of the disorders, but there are probably multiple causes (genetic and environmental) across and within each of the autism spectrum disorders. Treatment across the disorders is typically symptomatic and includes behavioral as well as medical and educational approaches.

Children with autism spectrum disorders will receive much of their educational and treatment services within schools. School psychologists are particularly well suited to assist with the diagnosis and educational/treatment planning for children with autism spectrum disorders, as school psychologists typically have training in educational and psychological assessment and treatment approaches often needed by these children (Shriver & colleagues, 1999). Children with autism spectrum disorders can be eligible to receive special education services as defined by the Individuals With Disabilities Education Act (1997) or receive accommodations under section 504 of the Americans With Disabilities Act. School psychologists assist with observations of classroom behavior, social interaction, academic and cognitive assessment, administration of behavior rating forms, student interviews, and interviews with teachers and parents to provide information useful in educational programming. School psychologists work with other disciplines (i.e., speech/language therapists, occupational therapists) and the student's parents on multidisciplinary teams within the school to develop individual goals and objectives for educational programming for students with autism spectrum disorders. Effective educational programming through the work of the multidisciplinary team is a key factor in improving the outcomes for children with autism spectrum disorders.

—*Mark Shriver*

See also Echolalia; Etiology; Preschool Assessment; Self-Management; Social Skills

REFERENCES AND FURTHER READING

American Psychiatric Association. (1994). *Diagnostic and statistical manual of mental disorders, fourth edition (DSM-IV)*. Washington, DC: Author.

Amir, R. E., Van den Veyver, I. B., Wan, M., Tran, C. Q., Francke, U., & Zoghbi, H. Y. (1999). Rett syndrome is caused by mutations in X-linked MECP2, encoding methyl-CpG-binding protein 2. *Nature Genetics, 23*, 1185–1188.

Cumine, V., Leach, J., & Stevenson, G. (1998). *Asperger syndrome: A practical guide for teachers*. London: David Fulton.

Kanner, L. (1943). Autistic disturbances of affective contact. *Nervous Child, 2,* 217–250.

Gillberg, C., & Coleman, M. (2000). *The biology of the autistic syndromes* (3rd ed.). London: Mac Keith Press.

International Rett Syndrome Association. (n.d.). Available online at http://www.rettsyndrome.org

Matson, J. L., Benavidez, D. A., Compton, L. S., Paclawskyj, T., & Baglio, C. (1996). Behavioral treatment of autistic persons: A review of research from 1980 to the present. *Research in Developmental Disabilities, 17,* 433–465.

Maurice, C., Green, G., & Luce, S. C. (1996). *Behavioral interventions for young children with autism: A manual for parents and professionals*. Austin, TX: Pro-Ed.

Pevsner, J. (2001). Rett syndrome 101. Available online at http://www.rettsyndrome.org

Shriver, M. D., Allen, K. D., & Mathews, J. R. (1999). Effective assessment of the shared and unique characteristics of children with autism. *School Psychology Review, 28,* 538–558.

Smith, T. (1996). Are other treatments effective? In C. Maurice, G. Green, & S. C. Luce (Eds.), *Behavioral interventions for young children with autism: A manual for parents and professionals* (pp. 45–59). Austin, TX: Pro-Ed.

AVERSIVE STIMULUS. *See* BEHAVIOR, FUNCTIONAL BEHAVIORAL ASSESSMENT

AVOIDANCE. *See* BEHAVIOR, FUNCTIONAL BEHAVIORAL ASSESSMENT

B

BEHAVIOR

Typically, the definition of behavior can be divided into two categories: observable and unobservable. Observable behavior constitutes anything that an individual does that can be measured by another individual. For example, eating, running, and reading aloud are all types of observable behaviors. The observer watches and records the occurrence of each targeted behavior of the person being observed (e.g., the number of times a student raises his or her hand), thus providing measurements of the observable behavior. Examples of unobservable behaviors are thinking, imagining, learning, reading silently, and analyzing; all of which cannot be accurately recorded and measured because they are internal events. To determine if an unobservable behavior is occurring or has occurred, individuals such as educators and psychologists often devise tests and subjective questionnaires that can measure and quantify the behavior. These tests and questions are attempts at making the unobservable, in fact, observable.

Labels such as autism, schizophrenia, learning disability, and attention deficit disorder are names given to a group of observable behaviors that generally aid in describing individuals and their characteristics. For example, if a child is labeled autistic then one expects to see particular behaviors such as mimicking others' statements and engaging in stereotypies or repetitive behaviors (e.g., rocking back and forth, hand-flapping, and finger-waving). Furthermore, a label of autism would signify behaviors such as a lack of social response, moving away from others when touched, poor performance on verbal tests, and an absence of self-care skills.

THE ORIGINS OF BEHAVIOR

The occurrence of a behavior is generally attributed to biology or environment. However, it is generally accepted that most behavior can be ascribed to both. Developmental psychologists have demonstrated that humans follow a sequential occurrence of behavior, particularly during infancy and early childhood. For example, most human beings roll over before they crawl or walk. These developmental sequences appear to be heavily influenced by biology, but can be manipulated by the environment as well. Learning theorists have shown that many academic behaviors are influenced by environment, although biology also plays an important role (e.g., an individual with retardation may learn more slowly than an individual without retardation). Determining the initial source (nature or nurture) of a behavior is unproductive in the manipulation of behavior, because the exact source of a behavior is almost always a complex relation between both nature and nurture. Also, similar manipulative techniques will be employed regardless of whether the behavior is rooted in nature or nurture.

Traumatic events, both biological and environmental, can have lasting effects on behavior. In fact, some antisocial behaviors can be attributed to reoccurring traumatic experiences. Many behavioral and cognitive therapies focus on trying to help individuals resolve these traumatic experiences and reverse unproductive patterns of behavior so that they can continue or initiate productive lives. They do this by trying to change contingencies as well as helping individuals understand why they behave in the manner that they do. This understanding can often help the individuals change their environment and their reaction to such behavioral historical stimuli so that they can behave in a more appropriate manner.

MEASURING AND ANALYZING BEHAVIOR

The first step in measuring and analyzing behavior is to define the targeted behavior. Behavioral definitions should be written down in objective and observable terms. Behaviors such as *respect* are often difficult to define in observable terms; thus such terminology should be avoided when choosing behaviors to observe. Other behaviors—such as *profanity*, *yelling*, and *noncompliance*—are more readily observable and therefore easier to define than, say, *respect*. The effectiveness of a definition can be tested by having a different individual use the definition and attempt to collect behavioral data with it. If the observing individual accurately records behavior, as deemed by the original writer of the definition, then the definition has merit and could be used again. By devising a sound and coherent behavioral definition, issues of reliability and validity can be addressed.

After constructing the behavioral definition, recording of the behavior can begin. Most behavior is recorded as a frequency (the number of times the behavior occurs) or a duration (the length of time the behavior is demonstrated). Some behaviors are measured by counting the product of the behavior, such as the number of assignments completed or the number of cigarettes smoked in a day. These behavioral products can be counted at the end of any given period of time, so that the information is useful to others who are also analyzing the data. All measured behavior should be put into the context of time. Instead of graphing the raw frequency, duration, or behavioral product data, a more appropriate method is to graph the behavior as a rate—number of student hand raises per 10-minute period—or a percentage—the percentage of time a student was on task during a 10-minute period.

Because of the difficulty of observing every occurrence of a behavior, interval systems are commonly used to record data. A typical interval system is one in which the observer observes for 10 seconds and then records for 5 seconds. In an interval system, the observer does not count the number of occurrences of the behavior; behavior is tabulated only if it occurs at least once in the previous 10-second time period. Data can be graphed by percentage of intervals that the behavior occurred. With the prevalence of computers and electronic handheld devices, software exists that allows individuals to collect and tabulate data more easily and quickly. TimeWands, laptop computers, and personal digital assistants (PDAs) are all currently being used to collect behavioral data.

Graphing data allows for a variety of individuals, beyond the observer, to analyze the picture of the recorded behavior. This analysis should result in determining the importance of the behavior as well as the possible functions of the behavior. Determining the function(s) of a behavior will help in constructing a successful intervention to reduce or increase the behavior observed. For example, if it is determined that an individual is hitting in order to communicate the desire for food, then an intervention can be agreed upon that will include teaching more appropriate communication skills to address the original function of the behavior.

Understanding the origin and complexity of behavior is a phenomenon that will likely continue in order to help people lead more satisfactory lives. However, in this pursuit of behavioral information, it is important to understand the nature and origin of the behavior, the function of the behavior, and the most appropriate and accurate method for measuring and analyzing behavioral data.

—*Richard J. Harrison and Kimberly Ann Harrison*

See also Adaptive Behavior Assessment; Applied Behavior Analysis; Behavior Intervention; Behavioral Assessment; Cognitive–Behavioral Modification; Functional Behavior Assessment; Premack Principle; Self-Injurious Behavior

REFERENCES AND FURTHER READING

Martin, G., & Pear, J. (2002). *Behavior modification: What it is and how to do it* (7th ed.). Upper Saddle River, NJ: Prentice-Hall.

BEHAVIOR CONTRACTING

Contracts are a familiar and accepted part of everyday life, and vary from formal employment agreements (describing job responsibilities, compensation, and even access to performance bonuses/goals) to sales contracts (for buying a house or a car). Behavior contracts (also known as "contingency" contracts) are written documents describing a relationship between the completion of a specific behavior and access to a reward (Heward, 1987; Jenson & Reavis, 1996). Behavior contracts can effectively improve student motivation and academic performance, school attendance, classroom behavior, compliance, adherence to classroom rules, and many other behaviors (Besalel-Azrin and colleagues, 1977).

There are several reasons why behavior contracts are effective. In addition to generally accepted principles of reinforcement, contracts have been described as a type of rule-governed behavior, where the contract serves as a cue to perform a specific behavior, allowing the individual access to a contingent reward, or reinforcer. Contracts also allow for the use of a wider range of effective reinforcers, which may be too delayed in and of themselves (e.g., attending a movie on the weekend with a peer) to immediately reinforce the desired behavior (e.g., satisfactory behavior in school). Behavior contracts also require public commitments, where the individual must perform a behavior simply to avoid guilt or embarrassment for failing to follow through on a task that he or she publicly committed to do.

Good behavior contracts contain several important features that enhance their effectiveness. The contract must be *negotiated* to determine the consequences and specific behaviors to be performed. The negotiated aspect of a contract is one of its most critical features, particularly with adolescents. The contract must be *formalized* as a written document (Figure 1) to indicate that performing a specific behavior results in a positive reward. The desired behavior should also be described in both *positive* and *specific* terms (e.g., complete 90% of assigned seatwork with 80% accuracy or better; keep talking out to three or less per day). It is good practice to ask students initially for their impressions of an attainable goal and to negotiate further refinements in the desired behavior.

The motivational aspect of the contract is contained in the *reward*. Without reinforcement that is truly motivating and attainable, contracts will often fail. Rewards also need to be proportional to the task required. Effective reinforcers for a student can be determined by asking what types of activities, tangible goods, or privileges are motivating to the student. Using a menu of available reinforcers or allowing the

student to choose from a box of items is especially advisable when the *contract* goes beyond one week. Individuals also differ with respect to the frequency or how often they need reinforcement, as well as how quickly they may become bored with a reinforcer. With younger children and students who have behavior problems, it may be necessary to begin with frequent reinforcers and gradually reduce the number of reinforcers as improved behavior becomes more consistent (Anderson, 2002).

Rewards also require someone to judge whether a behavior is performed, a time frame indicating when the reward will be provided, and how much reward will be available after the behavior is performed. Rewards should never be given before the behavior is completed or the terms of the contract are met. Behavior contracts may also contain penalty clauses for behaviors not performed within a certain time frame. Although failure to fulfill a contract is often followed by natural consequences (i.e., receiving a zero for missing homework or not receiving a promised incentive), some situations may require an explicit negative consequence as well. This is particularly true for behaviors that pose a safety risk to self or others, such as physical aggression toward peers or other types of self-damaging or risk-taking behaviors.

An effective enhancement to any behavior contract is the use of a bonus clause with additional opportunities for reinforcement for behaviors that are accomplished at or above a specified level (e.g., perfect performance or completion of a task under more difficult conditions). Contracts can also incorporate a record of task completion, record progress, and provide intermediate rewards if included in the terms of the contract. Some contracts can be implemented for a week or a month; others are open-ended and remain in force until the defined objective is met. In all cases, a predetermined timeline and plan for evaluation should be in place. For lengthy contracts, frequent checkpoints allow for adjustments, if needed. When the student reaches a specific goal, it is essential to provide both recognition and reinforcement, and move on to the next behavior target or continue the existing contract.

While behavior contracting has several advantages and may work well, especially with older students, problems do occur. Sometimes students can be highly motivated initially but then lose interest. In this situation, the reward is frequently perceived as too far removed from the behavior it is intended to reinforce.

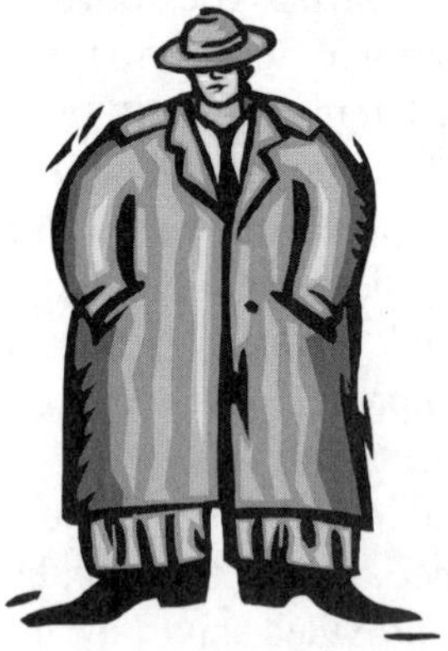

Task Record

M	T	W	Th	F

"An *OFFER* You Can't Refuse"

_______________'s Contract

I agree to: ______________________________
____

If I meet these conditions by __________ (date), I earn the following privilege(s)______________________________
____
____

Contract default penalties: ______________________________
____
____

Perfect score/exceptional work bonus: ______________________________
____

Signed: __________ Witness: __________

Parent/Teacher: __________ Date: __________
____

Figure 1 Sample behavior contract

Consequently, the time requirements for delivery of the reinforcer may need to be adjusted or shortened. This is especially important for younger children. Another potential problem is that students can appear confused or fail to understand expectations. This may be related to poorly defined target behaviors or requiring too much of the desired behavior before rewards become available. Role playing or modeling expected behaviors and adjusting target levels of behaviors can improve a child's response to behavior contracting. Occasionally, children who fail to respond to these adjustments may benefit from a mild "penalty clause" to promote more active participation. An additional potential problem with behavior contracts occurs when they include a requirement for consecutive days/periods of demonstrating or performing the specified behavior. When several days of a specific behavior are required to earn a reward, a cumulative approach is more successful, such as performing the specific behavior two out of three days instead of three consecutive days. A cumulative approach allows the student to have an occasional "bad day" and prevents premature discouragement.

—Daniel E. Olympia, Hollie Pettersson, and Elizabeth Christiansen

See also Behavior; Behavior Intervention; Self-Management

REFERENCES AND FURTHER READING

Anderson, J. (2002). Individualized behavior contracts. *Intervention in School & Clinic, 37*(3), 168–175.

Besalel-Azrin, V., Azrin, N. H., & Armstrong, D. M. (1977). The student-oriented classroom: A method of improving student conduct and satisfaction. *Behavior Therapy, 8*, 193–204.

Heward, W. (1987). Contingency contracting. In J. O. Cooper, T. J. Heron, & W. J. Heward (Eds.), *Applied behavior analysis.* Columbus, OH: Merrill.

Jenson, W. R., & Reavis, H. K. (1996). Contracting to enhance motivation. In H. K. Reavis, S. J. Kukic, W. R. Jenson, D. P. Morgan, D. J. Andrews, & S. Fister (Eds.) *Best practices: Behavioral and educational strategies for teachers.* Longmont, CO: Sopris West.

BEHAVIOR INTERVENTION

Behavior intervention refers to actions taken by school personnel, parents, and/or agency personnel to improve the behavior of school children. The focus of the interventions is limited to what are commonly referred to as behavior problems (or challenges) that are social, interpersonal, and emotional in their nature and effects; it does not address behaviors associated with poor achievement, such as reading, math or writing problems.

Developing, conducting, and monitoring behavior interventions with students (and their caretakers) are important activities for (at the very least) the following reasons:

1. Disruptive behavior is an impediment to the effective management of learning environments.

2. Student engagement in disruptive, unproductive behaviors often reduces the individual's educational progress and the progress of other students who are affected by these behaviors.

3. Students who do not learn positive social behaviors while in school tend to continue their inappropriate behavior in their adult years, resulting in immense costs to themselves and all other citizens.

Society in general governs the behavior of its citizens through regulations encoded in each state's guidelines for civil behavior. In the schools, the behavior of students is governed by regulations established in each state's Education Code, as well as in federal regulations pertaining to students with disabilities (Individuals With Disabilities Education Act [IDEA], 1997). In addition, all school districts have codes of conduct that specify interventions (usually punitive and restrictive) to be taken in cases of serious behavioral transgressions by students. Finally, at the classroom level, everyone recognizes the need for structure, behavioral expectations (usually established as "classroom rules"), and methods for ensuring a peaceful, harmonious atmosphere in all school environments.

The federal government does not establish any specific guidelines in regard to the management of student behavior problems for students in general education classes. However, in the case of students who have been found or are suspected as being eligible for special education and related services (IDEA, 1997), or for those eligible for accommodations through section 504 of the Rehabilitation Act of 1973, the federal government has specified requirements, although not specific guidance, as to how to carry out these requirements. The final regulations governing IDEA, which were established in 1999, specify very little in terms of assessments or interventions, except to note that district personnel must conduct a "Functional Behavioral Assessment (FBA)" and, if appropriate, develop a "Positive Behavioral Intervention (PBI) Plan" for students whose behaviors impede their learning or the learning of others. Section 504 also requires accommodations (intervenions), but indicates no specific guidelines as to the nature or intensity of these accommodations.

The FBA is used as the basis for the development of a PBI. The purpose of the FBA is to gather information about the targeted behavior (type of behavior, intensity, duration, antecedents, etc.) and the (presumed) reason(s) the student engages in the behavior. Put briefly, the reasons are to get something (material objects, power, attention, revenge, etc.) or to avoid something (responsibility, blame, expectations, other people who are disliked or feared, etc.). Although IDEA specifies these activities only for students who are identified or suspected of having disabilities, school personnel may choose to use these or other approaches for nonidentified students.

Generally, both the existence of a behavior problem and the intervention that will be used are determined by the student's teacher, hopefully with the assistance of school psychologists, school counselors, and administrators. In some states (e.g., California), districts are required to have identified individuals who serve as Behavior Intervention Case Managers for students with disabilities. Their responsibilities are to conduct an assessment of the problem (e.g., an FBA) and to assist in the development, monitoring, and evaluation of PBI plans, which are designed to assist teachers and others in managing the behavior problems of students identified as having disabilities.

THREE LEVELS OF INTERVENTION

There are three levels of intervention for dealing with problem behavior: primary, secondary, and tertiary. Primary intervention has as its goal the prevention of problems. Teachers know if they implement certain tactics in the classroom they are likely to experience fewer behavior management problems. The establishment of rules, the development of an appropriate curriculum, and the physical arrangement of the classroom are three examples of these preventive (primary intervention) tactics. At the secondary level are interventions designed to deal with behavior problems that have surfaced. Secondary interventions target a wide range of issues, from those primarily characterized by students wanting to be sociable with each other (talking, passing notes, harmless horseplay) to others that might lead to more serious problems (verbal disagreements, harassment, physical altercations, etc.). The tertiary level is for behaviors that are ongoing and threaten the welfare, safety, or security of others or of property, including major disruptions of the educational process, serious fighting, vandalism, and severe harassment. It is an unfortunate reality that much more time and energy are spent on matters of secondary and tertiary intervention than on primary interventions. However, school psychology is addressing primary prevention at an increasing rate.

THEORETICAL APPROACHES TO BEHAVIOR INTERVENTIONS

A theory is a plausible principle or a set of ideas that helps explain and predict behavior. School psychologists tend to be primarily oriented to, or influenced by, three competing theoretical positions: ecobehavioral, psychodynamic, and biological/neurological. D'Amato and Rothlisberg (1992) have presented a case study approach for interpreting problem behavior from different theoretical stances, each of which can be subsumed under the three positions indicated above.

Ecobehavioral approaches, which include cognitive behavioral and rational–emotive behavioral, have been in the ascendancy in America for at least 50 years. They are based primarily on theories of learning, with roots going back to Watson (1913) and Skinner (1953). In this approach, the primary interest is in analyzing the contingencies of reinforcement; namely, the influences that antecedents and consequences have on a person's actions or thoughts.

Antecedents include:

- Proximal events (something that happened very near in time to the behavior under study that seems to have prompted the behavior)
- Distal events (events that happened previously, including child-rearing history)
- Classroom realities
- Self-talk

Consequent events that follow the behavior of concern may be positive, negative (aversive), or neutral. Positive or aversive events may vary in intensity. In a practical sense, behaviorists try to indirectly influence a student's behavior by directly modifying the behavior of the adults and peers who are in contact with the student. A behaviorist will suggest ways the teacher or parent can modify the antecedents and consequences and then study the effects these changes have on the student's behavior.

Applied behavior analysis (ABA) is a method used by ecobehaviorists to carefully analyze the effects of changes in antecedents and consequences. The ABA process, which is carried out on a case-by-case basis, attempts to isolate all variables except the one under study (e.g., a change in the way a teacher gives directions; a change in one aspect of a reinforcer) and to note what effect this change has on the target behavior. As data are plotted in the course of this procedure, they are compared to a baseline of data that was established prior to the intervention. Changes in the intervention can then be based on real data as opposed to an individual's subjective opinions about the frequency or intensity of the behavior over time.

Psychodynamic approaches vary in their roots from psychoanalytic (characterized by an interest in instinctual urges; repressed feelings; and struggles between ego, id, and superego; etc.) to intrapsychic (characterized by the study of thoughts that interfere with an objective analysis of events in life). A student's history–including traumatic events, how caretakers interpreted the world, and how peer and other socializing agents have modeled reaction patterns–may cause him or her to develop a positive, accepting, realistic view of life; or a hostile, negative view. A student's view of the world colors his or her perceptions and leads to behaviors that may be regarded as inappropriate and self-defeating, or appropriate and self-nurturing. The psychodynamically oriented psychologist relies on a combination of talk and activity (e.g., play, drama, art) therapies to assist the student in understanding his or her own dynamics and in the development of more appropriate response patterns. A recent trend in the psychodynamic approach is the reliance on relatively brief forms of therapy that can easily be carried out in public school settings.

Biological/neurological influences are considered primarily by professionals who put a strong emphasis on the organic aspects of behavior. From this point of view, disruptive behaviors are regarded as biologically based, and are best dealt with through a medical approach, including prescription drugs, diet, and, possibly, vitamins and herbal supplements.

The following is an example of how individuals oriented toward these three approaches (ecobehavioral, psychodynamic, and biological/neurological) might deal with a student whose primary behavior of concern is hyperactivity. From a behavioral point of view, a psychologist would set up a contingency management program that would manipulate the antecedents (e.g., seating arrangements, verbal or nonverbal prompts, curricular adjustments, rules, modeling) and the consequences (e.g., ignoring the target behavior, giving positive or negative reinforcers, or delivering aversive stimuli). As time goes by, the psychologist charts the changes observed in the rate or intensity of the student's hyperactivity.

The psychodynamically oriented clinician would be primarily interested in "getting inside the student's head" by talking with the student about his or her world view, feelings, and thoughts about school and the classroom dynamics, and his or her own perceptions of the reported hyperactivity. The goals would be to get the student to self-reflect on the meaning of this behavior, to self-monitor the hyperactivity, and to attempt to replace this behavior with a more calm approach to school work and social interactions. The clinician would look to the role of anxiety, anger, fear, or other disruptive, negative emotions as being possibly causative in the observed symptom of hyperactivity, and would try to get the student to deal with these destructive emotions, assuming that a reduction in these emotions will be followed by a reduction in the hyperactivity that indicated their presence.

Clinicians adopting a biological/neurological stance would administer various tests to see if they could isolate a biological cause for the hyperactivity. These may include an electroencephalogram (EEG), various imaging techniques, visual and auditory vigilance tasks, and other tests that may indicate the presence of *soft signs* of neurological impairment. Because of these results, or interviews with adults who know the student well, a physician may institute a regimen of drugs designed to control the hyperactivity. Physicians or other health care providers may also try diet, vitamin, or herbal treatments. The purpose of these treatments is to see if any of these biological alterations will influence the rate or severity of the hyperactivity.

SPECIFIC BEHAVIORAL INTERVENTIONS

Most of the interventions listed below can be used with either individual students or with groups of students. They are organized according to five major categories of interventions. Some of the interventions could be classified under two or more of the five categories.

Category 1: Prevention

Prevention involves interventions designed to prevent problems that might occur in the classroom, such as:

- Classroom rules: As discussed earlier, every classroom needs rules. Whether the teacher simply announces them on the first day, or engages the students in discussion that will lead to the development of rules, the important point is that the students accept them as being in the best interests of themselves and the effective management of the classroom. Alberto and Troutman (1999) specify the following "rules about rules":

  Be specific about what is expected.

  Make as few rules as possible.

  Be explicit about the relationship between rules and consequences.

- Curricular and/or methods planning: A major determinant in the rate and severity of student misbehavior is the effectiveness of the teacher in the act of teaching. Ysseldyke and Christenson (2002) have developed the *Functional Assessment of Academic Behavior (FAAB)*, a workbook designed to assist school psychologists in observing classroom interactions between teachers and students. Many school psychologists spend as much time, or more, observing teacher behavior as they do observing a referred student's behavior, because they know that influencing a teacher to alter their curriculum or methods can eliminate present and future behavioral challenges from students.

- Procedural practice: Rathvon (1999) gives a number of suggestions for having students practice engaging in classroom procedures such as raising hands and waiting to be called on, moving from one activity to the next, ending an assignment and going to a free-time activity, and others. One of these activities is called "beat the buzzer." Here the teacher encourages speedy transitions by setting a timer and having the students practice a transition activity within a predetermined time span.

- Encouraging home support for learning: Most students behave better if they know their parents communicate with and support their teachers. Teachers make efforts to get parents to influence their students' classroom behavior, and often use parents as sources of positive reinforcement at home for good classroom behavior. Again, Ysseldyke and Christenson's *FAAB* (2002) has useful information about solidifying these home–school bonds.

Category 2: Communication Methods

With communication, the teacher isn't concerned with a contingency- or reward-based system, but rather wishes to get closer to the thinking and motivations of targeted students by talking with them and the class about their behavior. Students are often referred to counselors for exactly this reason. While teachers often resort to threats about what will happen if a student's behavior doesn't improve, counselors tend to adopt a more accepting, encouraging tone, and apply the psychodynamic techniques mentioned previously.

Category 3: Contingency-Based Approaches

Contingency-based approaches are primarily based on behavioral methods. The teacher:

- Identifies targeted behavior
- Establishes baseline information about the behavior's type, frequency, duration, and other salient features
- Designs an intervention plan for the identified behavior

- Implements the plan
- Monitors the plan's effects
- Changes the plan as appropriate

The usual plan has both positive and negative contingencies attached to it; the student can earn something deemed positive by exhibiting appropriate behavior, and may suffer aversive consequences when engaging in the deviant target behavior. Negative consequences are not generally recommended by behaviorists, although teachers often believe they afford them greater control over eliminating undesirable behaviors. For example, a teacher may establish rules and then find that selected students don't heed them. The teacher may then talk to the offending students about their behavior. If this method doesn't seem to work, the teacher may then conduct a functional behavioral assessment (FBA) and develop a Positive Behavioral Intervention (PBI) Plan based on positive contingencies only. If this plan doesn't have the desired effect, even after repeated adjustments to the plan, the teacher may decide to introduce additional contingencies, which may include aversive consequences.

If *aversive consequences* are to be used, it is important that teachers and others develop a rational sequence of possible interventions that range in severity from mild through serious. Sprick and Howard (1995) list various levels of interventions for each of 100 target behaviors. Kampwirth (2003) describes the BEST system and gives examples of each:

- *B* stands for *Basic* interventions, those actions teachers often take at the onset of disruptive behaviors. For example, the teacher may ignore the behavior, or may give "the look," an obvious cue for the student to desist from the targeted behavior. Other teachers may stop instruction and wait patiently for the student to redirect his or her attention to the lesson, may establish proximity to the student, or may announce the student's name and ask for cooperation.

- *E* refers to *Elaborated* interventions. Here the teacher employs two or more of the basic interventions, directly asks the student to desist, issues a reminder of class rules and possible consequences for rule violation, or asks the student to move from one area of the class to another. The teacher may tell the student to see the teacher at recess time or after school for a discussion of the student's behavior; this is an example of communication-as-intervention method.

- *S* represents *Serious* interventions. Here the teacher may develop a contract with the student, usually with the assistance of the school counselor or school psychologist. The contract specifies both a requirement to reduce targeted (unwanted) behaviors and a requirement to increase more appropriate behaviors. Parental and administrative involvement may be necessary at this level. At the most serious level, the student may be suspended for a period of time, either to home or to some area of the school reserved for in-school suspension purposes.

- *T* refers to *Total* school interventions. When school personnel sense that certain behavior problems are becoming widespread among their students, they may wish to generate programs that are implemented consistently by all teachers in all grades. An example of this that is used in a district's special education program for students with emotional and behavioral disorders is the Franklin-Jefferson Program (Schloss & colleagues, 1988). Some components of this program include a school note, a record-keeping system designed to keep track of awarded and docked points, relaxation training, social skills and aggression management training, and a levels system of reinforcement.

Some teachers find it useful to establish a *structured positive reinforcement* system as a way of awarding points, tokens, chips, or other tangible indicators to students contingent on their good performance, either behavioral or academic. Three examples are:

1. Canter and Canter (1992) recommend the use of a "marble jar," into which the teacher puts marbles when the class members are doing well. When the marble jar gets filled, the whole class is entitled to some special event (party, extra recess time, homework-free weekend, etc.).

2. A variation on the whole-class reinforcer idea consists of establishing teams in the classroom that essentially compete against each other for positive reinforcers. Teams are changed based on criteria related to the teacher's issues, and may include the opportunity to earn reinforcement for either appropriate behavior or academic achievement. Teams may consist of boys versus girls, brown-eyed students versus others, taller students versus shorter students, left side of the room versus right side, and so forth. This idea was presented originally by Barrish & colleagues (1969), and is called *The Good Behavior Game.* Rathvon (1999) discusses numerous variations on this approach.

3. Bear and Richards (1980) used a stopwatch as a signaling device to prompt independent small-group work at the elementary level. When students were off-task the teacher stopped the stopwatch until students were back on task. The longer they were off task, the less free time they earned.

Behavioral contracting with students is a method of establishing a formal statement of behavioral expectations and possible reinforcers for meeting those expectations. The formalization of expectations often has a positive effect on students' willingness to follow through with behavioral expectations. Hall and Hall (1999) and Lassman and colleagues (1999) give specific suggestions for developing behavioral contracts.

Category 4: Social Competency Training

Many students who present with challenging behaviors do so for a combination of the following reasons:

- They have adopted an approach to needs attainment that is not compatible with the value system of the teacher.
- They have not developed positive social skills.
- They let anger dominate their reactions to others.
- They do not have a useful set of conflict reduction techniques that they know and/or practice.
- They have adopted an antiauthority stance that predisposes them to negative reactions to most adults.

Some of these behaviors may be associated with accepted categories of disability (e.g., emotional disturbance), but often they are the hallmarks of students who may be socially maladjusted but not emotionally disturbed. In any event, school personnel recognize these reasons for poor behavior and, increasingly, are developing programs for assisting students who need social competency training in any of the three areas of social skills, anger management, and conflict management:

1. Social skills training involves giving students techniques for initiating and maintaining positive social interactions with others. From learning to say "hello" to accepting a compliment, skills that will enable students to negotiate the sometimes confusing array of social expectations are directly taught, practiced, and then reinforced. Elliott and Gresham (1992) and Goldstein (1999) provide exemplary programs that focus on social skills.

2. Anger management programs focus on giving students the skills to recognize anger in themselves and others as well as tools to deal with this destructive emotion. The Anger Coping Program (Lochman & Wells, 1996) and the Think First program (Larson & McBride, 1990) are typical of these curricular guides.

3. Conflict management is usually encompassed by either social skills or anger management programs, but there have been separate programs developed just for this skill. Bodine and Crawford (1999) describe three forms of conflict resolution programming: Process Curriculum, where problem-solving skills are studied; Peaceable Classroom, where these skills are infused into classroom subject lessons; and Mediation Programs, where teachers and/or students are taught to be mediators who assist others in solving their problems.

Category 5: Medical/Biochemical

Students with behavioral problems are often referred to medical practitioners as a form of intervention. When a medical intervention is attempted, the responsibilities of school personnel are to monitor the effects of the intervention and to give feedback to the medical practitioner regarding the effects of the intervention. It is often the case that a student will be on a behavioral contract at school and at home and be taking some form of stimulant or tricyclic medication at the same time. It is sometimes difficult to know what effect either approach is having when treatments are confounded like this. Often, a combination of medication and behavioral interventions have better effects than just one or the other treatment (Barkley, 1998).

—*Thomas J. Kampwirth*

See also Adaptive Behavior Assessment; Behavioral Assessment; Cognitive–Behavioral Modification; Consultation: Behavioral; Functional Behavioral Assessment

REFERENCES AND FURTHER READING

Alberto, P., & Troutman, A. (1999). *Applied behavior analysis for teachers* (5th ed.). Upper Saddle River, NJ: Prentice-Hall/Merrill.

Bear, G., & Richards, H. (1980). An interdependent group-oriented contingency system for improving academic performance. *School Psychology Review, 9,* 190–193.

Barkley, R. (1998). *Attention-deficit hyperactivity disorder: A handbook for diagnosis and treatment* (2nd ed.) New York: Guilford.

Barrish, H., Saunders, M., & Wolf, M. (1969). Good behavior game: Effects on individual contingencies for group consequences on disruptive behavior in a classroom. *Journal of Applied Behavioral Analysis, 2,* 119–124.

Bodine, R., & Crawford, D. (1999). *Developing emotional intelligence.* Champaign, IL: Research Press.

Canter, L., & Canter, M. (1992). *Assertive discipline: Positive behavior management for today's classrooms* (2nd ed.). Santa Monica, CA: Lee Canter.

D'Amato, R., & Rothlisberg, B. (1992). *Psychological perspectives on intervention.* New York: Longman.

Elliott, S., & Gresham, F. (1992). *Social skills intervention guide.* Circle Pines, MN: American Guidance Service.

Goldstein, A. (1999). *The prepare curriculum.* Champaign, IL: Research Press.

Hall, R., & Hall, M. (1999). *How to negotiate a behavioral contract* (2nd ed.). Austin, TX: Pro-Ed.

Individuals with Disabilities Education Act (IDEA), Amendments of 1997, P.L. 105–17, 105th Cong. 1st session (1997).

Kampwirth, T. (2003). *Collaborative consultation in the schools* (2nd ed.). Upper Saddle River, NJ: Prentice-Hall/Merrill.

Larson, J., & McBride, S. (1990). *Think first: Anger and aggression management for secondary level students* (VHS Tape). Milwaukee, WI: Milwaukee Board of School Directors.

Lassman, K., Jolivette, K., & Wehby, J. (1999). Using collaborative behavioral contracting. *Teaching Exceptional Children, 31*(4), 12–18.

Lochman, J., & Wells, K. (1996). A social-cognitive intervention with aggressive children: Prevention effects and contextual implementation issues. In R. Peters and R. McMahon (Eds.), *Preventing childhood disorders, substance abuse and delinquency* (pp. 111–143). Thousand Oaks, CA: Sage.

Rathvon, N. (1999). *Effective school interventions.* New York: Guilford.

Schloss, P., Holt, J., Mulvaney, M., & Green, J. (1988). The Franklin-Jefferson Program: Demonstration of an integrated social learning approach to education services for behaviorally disordered students. *Teaching Behaviorally Disordered Youth, 4,* 7–15.

Skinner, B. (1953). *Science and human behavior.* New York: Macmillan.

Sprick, R., & Howard, L. (1995). *The teacher's encyclopedia of behavior management.* Longmont, CO: Sopris West.

Watson, J. (1913). Psychology as the behaviorist views it. *Psychological Review, 20,* 158–177.

Ysseldyke, J., & Christenson, (2002). *Functional assessment of academic behavior.* Longmont, CO: Sopris West.

BEHAVIORAL ASSESSMENT

Behavioral assessment is defined as an assessment process that seeks to understand behavior and critical environmental variables that increase or decrease the likelihood of its occurrence. In contrast to traditional assessment procedures, behavioral assessment relies on low-inference, idiographic (comparisons to that individual's previous level of behavior) procedures, and has as its primary objectives the development and evaluation of appropriate treatments and interventions to ameliorate presenting problems.

In addition to the above characteristics (i.e., idiographic, low-inference, and treatment-driven), there are other defining characteristics of behavioral assessment. One is the assessment of situational–environmental variables influencing behavior, including information about events that occur right before the problem behavior (antecedents) and events that occur right after the problem behavior (consequences). Another characteristic of behavioral assessment is the use of multiple methods (e.g., interviews, observations across settings, rating scales) and multiple informants (e.g., parents, teachers, and the child). Using multiple methods and multiple informants is essential for obtaining information that is thorough enough to result in suitable treatment decisions.

Behavioral assessment is an ongoing process requiring repeated measurements. The assessment procedures are used not only to guide intervention development, but also to monitor all phases of an intervention. Prior to intervention development, a baseline of target behaviors is measured to assist in the development of an appropriate intervention plan and to set a criterion against which intervention effects are compared. Once the intervention, or treatment program, is implemented, frequent measures of behavior continue in order to evaluate the intervention. Appropriate intervention evaluation includes data collection throughout treatment leading to a decision of whether or not a desired behavior change resulted from the intervention.

The process of behavioral assessment has been viewed as analogous to the problem-solving process made popular in the school psychology and behavioral consultation literature. The problem-solving process can be defined as a number of phases that incorporate assessment and treatment. Most problem-solving models include four phases: problem identification and analysis, intervention design, intervention implementation, and intervention evaluation/follow-up.

The problem identification and analysis phase involves defining the nature and scope of the problem behavior. During this phase, information is gathered using multiple methods and informants to determine whether problem behaviors are in excess or deficit. If a behavior is in excess, analysis of the antecedents and consequences maintaining the behavior is conducted. If the behavior is a deficit, an analysis of whether the behavior is an acquisition deficit (i.e., the child does not have the skill to demonstrate the behavior) or performance deficit (i.e., the child possesses the skill, but is not demonstrating the behavior) is conducted. Once the problem has been identified, an appropriate intervention is designed to target the problem behavior. It is important to design an intervention that is individualized to the child and based on empirically validated treatments. Once the appropriate intervention is determined, it is implemented as designed. Assessment continues through frequent measures of the behaviors identified in the first phase of the process. In the final stage, the intervention is evaluated and decisions are made as to whether to continue the intervention as designed, to modify the intervention, or to select another one entirely. In this phase, follow-up measures are also taken to assess the effectiveness of the intervention over time.

The school psychologist, behavior therapist, or other assessment specialist is free to use any number of assessment procedures in either phase of the problem-solving or behavioral assessment process and is not restricted to prescribed procedures. In fact, many assessment procedures employed in behavioral assessment have their roots in traditional assessment. An early conceptual framework for the process of behavioral assessment was offered by Cone (1978) in his behavioral assessment grid (BAG). An extension of Cone's model, offered by Gresham and Lambros (1998), focuses on six major components of behavioral assessment:

1. Examining the type of behavior problem (i.e., excess, deficit, situational inappropriateness)

2. Identifying the dimensions of the behavior (i.e., frequency, temporality, intensity, permanent products)

3. Assessing the system used to demonstrate behaviors (i.e., verbal, motoric, emotional)

4. Assessing the methods used to assess the topography, frequency, severity of the behavior (e.g., direct observations, rating scales)

5. Determining the quality of data collected, or, in other words, the reliability (i.e., observer or instrument agreement), the validity (i.e., how well information gathered in assessment adds to positive outcomes in treatment), generalizability, and accuracy of data

6. Assessing the social validity, including consumer satisfaction of the treatment process (e.g., opinions before and after treatment), how well the intervention was implemented as designed, and the social importance of the treatment effects.

In conducting a behavioral assessment, various methods are used that range from direct techniques to indirect techniques. A frequently used direct procedure in behavioral assessment is naturalistic observation, which involves observing an individual in a setting that is part of his or her regular routine. School psychologists may directly observe a child in the classroom, or a parent or teacher may be asked to record the child's behavior during a certain period of time.

Direct observations may be conducted using a variety of techniques. Anecdotal observations are techniques that involve a written description or narrative that details a child's behavior at a particular time and setting. The narrative can be recorded during or after an event and can provide information pertinent to the beginning stages of the problem-solving process. Some disadvantages of anecdotal observations are that the information provided is recorded from the perspective of the observer, it is not systematic or structured, and the process can be time-consuming.

Another observational technique is time/event sampling procedures. An example of an event sampling procedure is one in which the observer records specific behaviors as well as the antecedents and consequences of the behaviors (i.e., antecedent-behavior-consequence [A-B-C]). During A-B-C observations, information is recorded as it occurs, and these observations provide information crucial in identifying the problem behaviors in the first step

of the problem-solving process. One disadvantage of A-B-C observations is that some behaviors may not be seen while the observer is recording behaviors.

Other examples of time- or event-sampling procedures include continuous recording (behavior recorded upon each occurrence)—during which the behavior frequency, duration, and latency (time between event and behavior) can be recorded—and interval recording—during which the occurrence or nonoccurrence of the behavior is recorded in time intervals throughout the observation. Interval recording can be conducted using one of the following time-sampling methods:

- Partial interval, in which the observer records the behavior if it occurs at any point during the interval
- Whole interval, in which the behavior is recorded only if it occurs throughout the entire interval
- Momentary time sampling, in which the behavior is only recorded if it occurs at the start of the time interval

One disadvantage to using interval recording systems is that the percentage of intervals of problem behavior recorded may be an overestimate (partial interval) or an underestimate (whole interval) of the occurrence of the problem behavior. Of the interval recording techniques briefly described here, momentary time sampling typically provides the most accurate measure of occurrence of behaviors.

Another observation technique in behavioral assessment involves the use of systematic observational instruments that focus on specific behaviors. For example, the State-Event Classroom Observation System (SECOS) is used to observe several different behaviors within the classroom setting (Saudargas & Lentz, 1986). Another example is the Behavioral Observation of Students in Schools (BOSS) (Shapiro, 1996). This observation system uses a momentary time-sampling procedure to record student's on-task behavior, off-task behavior, and teacher instruction. Although systematic instruments such as SECOS and BOSS are practical and useful tools, it is important that observers are appropriately trained in their use.

Direct methods are typically more accurate than indirect methods. In other words, direct methods result in less inference of behavior than indirect methods because they do not rely on recollection of past experiences and observations of the target child. Such methods are typically more accurate because the professional (e.g., school psychologist, teacher) is trained to observe particular target behaviors and record their occurrences when exhibited. A disadvantage of such techniques is that measures must be continuous and observer training is often time-consuming.

Some indirect procedures used in the process of behavioral assessment include interviews, rating scales, self-report measures, and permanent products. Behavioral interviews are a widely used tool in the assessment process and can take the form of an informal (unstructured) question-and-answer session or a more formal (semistructured) standardized protocol (e.g., Semistructured Clinical Interview for Children and Adolescents). One system often used in behavioral assessment is the behavioral consultation model developed by Bergan and Kratochwill (1990). This system offers a systematic format to guide the interviewee through the problem-solving process. Another system used is Sheridan and colleagues' (1996) conjoint behavioral consultation process, which involves guiding both the parent and teacher of the targeted individual in the problem-solving process using an interview format.

Other indirect procedures used in behavioral assessment include self-report measures and rating scales from other informants. Self-report measures provide information about behavior that transpired at another time and/or place. They can be obtained through verbal means or through the use of behavior checklists or rating scales. In addition, other informants such as the individual's parents or teachers may be asked to rate the individual's behavior based on past observation and past experience with the individual. One commonly used example of a behavior rating scale is the Child Behavior Checklist (CBCL) (Achenbach, 1991). This scale is used to assess several different behavior problems in children. Finally, another indirect procedure that can be used in behavioral assessment is permanent products. This method can be used when a behavior results in a certain outcome that can be evaluated. For example, a teacher could collect daily math quiz grades as an indication of how a child is performing on a particular math skill.

An advantage of indirect procedures is that they can be used to gather a large amount of information, both general and specific. For example, an advantage of interviews is that follow-up questions can be asked to clarify and provide further information deemed important to defining the problem behaviors. Further, rating scales are useful in gaining pertinent information from teachers and parents, not only about the problem behavior (or referral concern) but also about other behaviors that may be a concern. Rating scales are generally cost- and time-effective, can provide a useful way to classify behaviors, and can provide useful pre- and postmeasurements to evaluate treatment. The major disadvantage of indirect assessment procedures is that the information gathered from such methods is based on an informant's observation or past experience with an individual. This type of information can be subjective, biased, and may not provide accurate information related to the problem behavior.

As mentioned previously, the behavioral assessment process may include a host of possible procedures that can be used by a school psychologist or behavior therapist that range from direct to indirect procedures. Many of these procedures have their beginnings in traditional assessment, yet the objectives of behavioral assessment are very different from traditional assessment. The primary purpose of behavioral assessment is to determine the environmental variables contributing to or maintaining behavior and to design appropriate treatments and interventions, whereas the primary objective of traditional assessment is to diagnose and label. Further strengthening the link between behavioral assessment and appropriately designed treatment is the functional assessment and analysis methodology.

Functional assessment is a broad term referring to a set of procedures designed to determine environmental variables contributing to or maintaining behavior. These variables may be close in time or temporally distant. The procedures used in such an assessment typically include a functional assessment interview and direct observation to develop hypotheses regarding the function of behavior. Such an assessment may then result in an intervention that is directly or *functionally* related to the hypothesized function of the assessed behavior. A functional analysis can be considered one approach to functional assessment. It involves the systematic or experimental manipulation of variables or conditions that occasion behavior or the absence of behavior and results in treatment and intervention based on the information gained during the manipulation.

As in all behavioral assessment, functional behavior assessment can be described in terms of a problem-solving process (i.e., problem identification, intervention design, intervention implementation, and intervention evaluation and possible modification). For example, if Billy, a third grader, is referred by his teacher for having a high frequency of problem behaviors, then the first step in the problem-solving process would be to define and analyze the target problem behaviors. In this phase, an interview with Billy's teacher would be conducted to determine the situational variables, antecedents, and consequences of the problem behaviors. Additionally, direct behavioral observations would be conducted by the school psychologist and/or the teacher to further assess the antecedents, consequences, frequency, and intensity of the behavior (i.e., problem identification). Based on information gathered, it could be determined that specifically Billy does not comply with teacher-presented directives. In other words, when instructed to cease or initiate a behavior by his teacher, Billy ignores the teacher or openly refuses to comply with the instruction. These behaviors typically occurred during large- and small-group instruction and are typically followed by reprimand, redirection, or individualized attention from Billy's teacher. Therefore, in this particular case the hypothesized function of Billy's noncompliant behavior is access to teacher attention.

The next step in the functional assessment process would be to design an appropriate intervention to increase compliance in the classroom or to teach and reinforce an acceptable alternative behavior in Billy that would serve the same hypothesized function as his inappropriate behavior. For example, the long-term goal for this particular student may be that he will comply with teacher directives 90% of the time. Short-term goals should also be established to work toward the long-term goal (e.g., child will comply with directives 70% of the time after undergoing two weeks of intervention).

In Billy's case, an intervention program involving differential reinforcement using teacher attention in response to compliant behavior coupled with a program whereby Billy loses access to a preferred activity for noncompliance could be a preferred intervention approach. Another evidence-based intervention that could be implemented in Billy's case is a daily report card or school–home note paired with a home-based contingency. In such a procedure, baseline or pretreatment data are gathered, specific point-based behavioral objectives are established, and home- and/or school-based contingencies are applied based on Billy's success or failure in meeting

his stated objectives. This procedure demands home–school collaboration and parent involvement in the intervention effort, and it has proved to be an effective approach to behavior problems such as those presented by Billy. Throughout such intervention efforts, behavioral data are continually gathered to assist in evaluating the efficacy of the intervention.

During this point in the intervention process, one of several decisions will be made. If the intervention was successful and behavior change was observed, the intervention should be continued. If the intervention was not successful, decisions for modifications to the intervention could be made. Additionally, it may be necessary to go back to the first step in the problem-solving process and assess whether the appropriate behaviors were targeted for change or whether the targeted behavior for change was appropriately defined. Throughout the functional assessment process it is critical that the school psychologist has the skills to guide the problem-solving process from the data-gathering phase to the intervention evaluation phase, aiding all those involved in the process (e.g., training the teacher how to appropriately implement the intervention). O'Neill and colleagues (1990) provide a more complete guide to functional assessment and analysis.

In summary, behavioral assessment offers the practitioner the opportunity to directly link the assessment and intervention design processes. Without such an approach, the school psychologist or behavior specialist would be less precise in developing potential solutions to problems experienced by children in the educational setting. Without such a process, teachers, parents, and children would experience ongoing problems that would have debilitating effects on the learning process.

—*D. Joe Olmi and Elizabeth Lyons*

See also Adaptive Behavior Assessment; Applied Behavior Analysis; Classroom Observation; Functional Behavior Assessment; Interviewing

REFERENCES AND FURTHER READING

Achenbach, T. M. (1991). *Integrative guide for the 1991 Child Behavior Checklist/4–18, Youth Self-Report Form, and Teacher Report Form Profiles.* Burlington, VT: Department of Psychiatry, University of Vermont.

Bergan, J. R., & Kratochwill, T. R. (1990). *Behavioral consultation and therapy.* New York: Plenum.

Cone, J. D. (1978). The behavioral assessment grid (BAG): A conceptual framework and a taxonomy. *Behavior Therapy*, 9, 882–888.

Gresham, F. M., & Lambros, K. M. (1998). Behavioral and functional assessment. In T. S. Watson & F. M. Gresham (Eds.), *Handbook of child behavior therapy* (pp. 3–22). New York: Plenum.

O'Neill, R. E., Horner, R. H., Albin, R. W., Storey, K., & Sprague, J. R. (1990). *Functional analysis of problem behavior: A practical assessment guide*. Sycamore, IL: Sycamore.

Saudargas, R. A., & Lentz, F. E. (1986). Estimating percent of time and rate via discrete observation: A suggested observational procedure and format. *School Psychology Review*, 15, 36–48.

Shapiro, E. S. (1996). *Direct observation manual for the behavioral observation of students in schools (B.O.S.S.), in academic skills problem workbook*. New York: Guilford.

Sheridan, S. M., Kratochwill, T. R., & Bergan, J. R. (1996). *Conjoint behavioral consultation: A procedural manual*. New York: Plenum.

BEHAVIORAL CONCEPTS AND APPLICATIONS

The behavioral approach views behavior as being responsive to the environment. In the most general sense, the environment consists of the antecedents that occur prior to a behavior (e.g., settings, tasks, presence of people, instructions, prompts) and the consequences that follow a behavior (e.g., reinforcers or punishers after a behavior occurs). Antecedents and consequences that are discriminated by a student define the behavioral context, and behavior is considered to be related to the context or situation within which it occurs. Thus, to understand why a behavior is occurring or not occurring, the behavior is evaluated within specific contexts and is often described as being a function of the antecedents and consequences that surround it.

Behavioral models have been used successfully with a wide range of appropriate and inappropriate behaviors in school settings. Here we focus on applications for inappropriate behaviors, especially those that are the most challenging, because of the growing current interest in reducing severe problem behaviors in school settings. These behaviors include self-injurious, aggressive, disruptive, noncompliant, and off-task behaviors exhibited by students with cognitive, physical, and emotional/behavioral disabilities.

Addressing challenging behaviors through a function-based behavioral model has been especially useful. This approach begins with a functional assessment, which has become the current *state-of-the-art* assessment for problem behaviors. The Individuals With Disabilities Education Act (IDEA) Amendments of 1997 (Public Law 105–17) mandate that functional behavior assessment and function-based treatment must be conducted in an attempt to maintain students in the least restrictive educational environment. This environment is defined as the educational setting that imposes the fewest restrictions possible for the student while providing those services the student needs for optimal growth and development.

ASSESSMENT APPROACHES

The main goal of behavioral assessment is to document how antecedents and consequences guide and maintain behavior. Although several types of assessment can fulfill this goal, the most researched approach is called a functional analysis, which identifies reinforcers that maintain an individual's problem behavior by systematically evaluating the effects of different consequences on problem behavior within a single-case experimental design. Typically, this assessment is conducted under tightly controlled conditions to limit potential confounds. The benefit of this procedure is that it provides a well-controlled demonstration of response–reinforcer relations and thus reduces ambiguity in results. The drawback of the functional analysis is that it can be difficult to conduct in typical classrooms because of the degree of control needed over the delivery of consequences.

An alternative approach is to conduct a more descriptive assessment of problem behavior in which the consequences of problem behavior are not systematically manipulated by the teacher or school psychologist. Instead, data are collected as the target behavior occurs on the behavior itself as well as the various antecedents and consequences that are correlated with the behavior. Because behavior (B) is recorded with its antecedents (A) and consequences (C), this approach is sometimes called an A-B-C assessment. One advantage of an A-B-C assessment is that data are collected without interrupting a student's schedule, removing the student from the educational environment, or explicitly reinforcing problem behavior. The data can then be analyzed to determine the probability that the behavior will occur following specific antecedents (e.g., demands) and be followed by specific consequences (e.g., laughter from peers). Consequences that have a high probability of occurring in close temporal proximity to the problem behavior are identified as possible reinforcers. Thus, descriptive assessments provide information regarding potential response–reinforcer relations but lack the experimental (causal) control of a functional analysis. The results of descriptive assessments can also be confusing because numerous antecedents and consequences can occur in close proximity to a behavior.

Combining brief versions of descriptive and functional analyses is one way to overcome the limitations of each type of assessment. For example, a descriptive assessment might be conducted to generate hypotheses regarding a student's problem behavior in order to reduce the number of antecedents and consequences that need to be tested. Following this hypothesis-generation phase, a brief functional analysis might be conducted to test the most likely hypothesis.

Case Example

A third-grade boy, Quincy, who was diagnosed with attention deficit hyperactivity disorder (ADHD), was referred for an evaluation because he was hitting classmates daily during unstructured play and group work activities. The school psychologist conducted an A-B-C assessment over a period of three days and found that the most likely antecedents to Quincy's behavior were a preferred item being in the possession of a peer and the teacher's attention being diverted to other students. The most likely consequences for Quincy's behavior were access to the preferred item and to the teacher's attention in the form of reprimands. Thus, both tangible items and the teacher's attention were likely reinforcers for aggression. A brief 90-minute functional analysis was then conducted in which Quincy had access to teacher attention continuously during the first 30 minutes of the assessment, but had access to preferred items only 50% of this time. If a problem behavior occurred, he received the preferred item. No problem behavior occurred, appearing to rule out the preferred items as reinforcers for aggression. During the second 30 minutes of the assessment, Quincy was given preferred items, but teacher attention was not provided unless he became aggressive. He became increasingly aggressive over the 30-minute period, suggesting that teacher attention was the consequence that maintained

Quincy's aggression. To confirm this result, we used a single-case reversal design in which intervention was sequentially applied (B) and withdrawn (A) in an ABAB format to evaluate the effects of the behavioral intervention. Thus, Quincy again received continuous teacher attention for 30 minutes and no aggression occurred, even when he was denied access to preferred items.

TREATMENT STRATEGIES

The applied benefit of a functional assessment, whether conducted formally as a functional analysis or more descriptively as an A-B-C assessment, is that the identified functions of behavior can be used to design interventions that are matched to functions in two ways: (1) the reinforcers maintaining problem behavior are reduced or discontinued, and (2) the same reinforcers are provided for a more appropriate response. Both intervention goals can be accomplished using three behavioral strategies, either individually or in combination.

The first strategy is to change the antecedents that appear to trigger a student's problem behavior. For example, if the assessment shows that Quincy's problem behavior is most likely to occur when the teacher's attention is diverted, intervention might allow access to the teacher's attention on a response-independent schedule of reinforcement, known as noncontingent reinforcement (NCR), a schedule in which reinforcement is delivered independent of behavior. If the teacher notices that Quincy's problem behavior occurs after 10 minutes without her attention, she might attend to Quincy approximately every 5 minutes during intervention to reduce the probability that the problem behavior will occur. NCR as an intervention has the advantage of being easy to implement because there is no need to monitor the occurrence or nonoccurrence of any particular behavior. In addition, this intervention ensures that the student will gain access to the reinforcer, thereby reducing the student's motivation for attention. The major drawback to NCR is that some behavior cannot be ignored, and NCR does not specifically teach the student an alternative, more socially desirable behavior.

A second intervention strategy is to implement reinforcers contingent on appropriate behaviors, with the goal being that these appropriate behaviors will replace inappropriate behaviors. Perhaps the best example of this approach is functional communication

(Text continues on page 66)

Table 1   Behavioral Mechanisms

Behavioral Concepts	Definition	Example
General behavioral terms and procedures		
Operant behaviorism	The scientific analysis of intents, motivations, goals, and purposes of human behavior. An operant response is one that can be modified by its consequences.	
Applied behavior analysis	Changing socially important behavior via the systematic application of behavioral principles (Alberto & Troutman, 2003).	
Functional relationship	When changes in a dependent variable systematically correspond to changes in the independent variable (Alberto & Troutman, 2003).	
Functional assessment	Gathering information to develop hypotheses regarding the variables that occasion or maintain behavior (e.g., interview, checklist, direct observation) Alberto & Troutman, 2003).	Observing a child across the school day to identify the antecedent and consequence conditions in which problem behavior most often occurs.
Functional analysis	Procedures that test hypotheses by systematically altering variables thought to trigger or maintain behavior in an attempt to verify a functional relationship (Alberto & Troutman, 2003).	Most functional analyses are based on procedures developed by Iwata et al. (1982/1994) and involve the contingent positive and negative reinforcement of problem behavior within single-case designs. Elevations in problem behavior identify a functional relationship between problem behavior and a specific class of reinforcement.
Function-based treatment	Intervention is matched to the reinforcers maintaining target behavior. For problem behavior, treatment is based on the results of a functional assessment or functional analysis.	For noncompliance maintained by negative reinforcement, breaks from nonpreferred tasks are provided for appropriate behavior. For noncompliance maintained by teacher attention, praise from the teacher is provided for appropriate behavior.
Stimulus–response model	A conceptual model explaining how the environment influences the behavior of an organism. This model is composed of a stimulus (environmental event) that prompts or elicits a response (behavior) that is then followed by some type of consequence (see Consequence in Behavioral Concepts column, p. 63). This model is often referred to as the "three-term contingency."	A teacher asks his class, "Who knows the answer?" (stimulus); a child raises her hand (response); the teacher calls on the child (consequence).
Target behavior	Behavior that is the focus of a behavioral analysis or intervention.	Compliance is the target behavior when an intervention is developed specifically to increase that behavior.

(Continued)

Table 1 (Continued)

Behavioral Concepts	Definition	Example
Aversive stimulus	When presented as a consequence, can decrease the future probability of a behavior. When removed, contingent on a response can increase the future probability of a behavior. When presented as an antecedent, can suppress operant behavior sensitive to positive reinforcement (Catania, 1998).	A difficult homework assignment.
Antecedent terms and teaching procedures		
Antecedent stimulus	A stimulus that precedes a response (Alberto & Troutman, 2003).	The teacher asks a question (antecedent), and this signals the student to raise her hand (response) to answer the question.
Establishing operation (EO)	Environmental event or stimulus that momentarily alters the reinforcing value of another event or stimulus and increases behavioral responses that have resulted in that reinforcer in the past (Michael, 1982). In many cases, an EO involves deprivation or satiation of a reinforcer.	A student will work consistently on classroom assignments when completion of the assignment produces praise from the teacher and the student has not received substantial amounts of praise just before being given the assignment. However, the same student will not work consistently if he has recently received substantial amounts of adult attention.
Discriminative stimulus (S^D)	Stimulus that sets the occasion for a particular behavior being followed by a particular consequence (Catania, 1998).	A student knows that if she completes an assignment given by Mr. Green, he will be allowed to play on the computer. However, he is not allowed to play on the computer when Ms. White gives assignments. If the student completes assignments only for Mr. Green, then Mr. Green has become an S^D for positive reinforcement (access to the computer) contingent on task completion.
Stimulus control	A behavior that occurs reliably in the presence of an S^D and does not occur in the absence of the S^D is said to be under stimulus control.	A student completes his assignments only when given by Mr. Green so that he can gain access to the computer.
Generalization	Expansion of a specific response beyond those conditions under which it was first observed (Alberto & Troutman, 2003).	A student who is taught to use a multiplication table in math class uses the same table to complete science homework.
Forward chaining	An instructional procedure to teach complex behaviors by reinforcing individual responses in sequence, beginning with the first step of the chain and proceeding forward (Alberto & Troutman, 2003).	When teaching a student to clean her desk, put on her jacket, and line up by the door, you first reward a clean desk, then putting on her jacket, and so forth, until all task steps are completed in the designated sequence.

Behavioral Concepts	Definition	Example
Backward chaining	An instructional procedure to teach complex behaviors by reinforcing individual responses in sequence, beginning with the last step of the chain and proceeding backward (Alberto & Troutman, 2003).	Reversing the process of forward chaining by first reinforcing the last step in the sequence and moving backward.
Shaping	Teaching new behaviors by reinforcing successive approximations of the target behavior (Alberto & Troutman, 2003).	Teaching a child to return to his chair by first reinforcing the child if he is standing next to his chair, then reinforcing only for standing in front of his chair, and finally only for sitting in his chair. Most chaining involves shaping.
Fading	The gradual removal of prompts until the desired environmental stimuli become independent S^Ds (Alberto & Troutman, 2003)	Slowly removing the teacher's verbal prompts to begin working until the presentation of a worksheet alone cues a child to begin working.
Reinforcement terms and teaching procedures		
Consequence	Event occurring subsequent to a response that delivers or removes a stimulus. Can be reinforcing (i.e., increase the future likelihood of the response), punishing (i.e., decrease the future likelihood of the response), or neutral (i.e., have no effect on the future likelihood of the response).	Providing praise following completion of nonpreferred homework.
Escape	Termination of an aversive stimulus following a response; a form of negative reinforcement.	When a child who is presented with a nonpreferred homework assignment begins to yell, the assignment is removed.
Contingency	The condition under which a response produces a consequence (Catania, 1998).	A student receives praise for answering questions when asked by the teacher, but not for yelling out the answer at other times.
Social reinforcement	Reinforcers whose delivery is controlled by other individuals in the environment (e.g., access to attention or preferred items, or escape/avoidance of aversive situations).	Access to attention may positively reinforce a child's tantrum behavior.
Differential reinforcement	Reinforcement that is provided contingent on one or some behavior(s) but not on others.	Teacher provides enthusiastic attention when a student raises her hand in class but withholds attention when she shouts the teacher's name.
Noncontingent reinforcement (NCR)	A schedule of reinforcement delivery that is response independent (usually based on time intervals; Catania, 1998).	Providing a child with praise every 5 minutes, regardless of the behavior of the child.
Maintenance	A response occurring over time under the same or similar stimulus conditions (Catania, 1998).	A student continues to raise his hand in class as long as intermittent attention continues to occur.

(Continued)

Table 1 (Continued)

Behavioral Concepts	Definition	Example
Positive reinforcement	The contingent presentation of a stimulus following a response, increasing the probability that the response will occur in the future (Alberto & Troutman, 2003).	The student turns in her homework to receive both good grades and praise from her teacher.
Negative reinforcement	The contingent removal of an aversive stimulus following a response, increasing the future probability of the response.	The student finishes his work in class to avoid having to stay after school.
Automatic reinforcement	Reinforcement that is delivered by the response itself (Catania, 1998).	A child eats a candy bar because the response of eating the candy is reinforcing in and of itself. Individuals may engage in various forms of self-injury (e.g., hand biting, eye poking) because of the stimulation provided by these behaviors.
Satiation	Reduction in the reinforcing value of a stimulus because of previous exposure to the stimulus.	A student who enjoys computer games may complete homework to gain access to this positive reinforcer. However, if the student has just played 3 hours of computer games, he may no longer complete homework if computer games are presented as the reward.
Deprivation	Increase in the reinforcing value of a stimulus because of lack of exposure to the stimulus.	A student who has not had access to the computer for several hours may quickly complete his homework if he is provided access to computer games when the work is completed.
Imitation	Behavior that replicates certain aspects of a modeled behavior (Catania, 1998).	Child A observes child B playing a video game. When child A plays the same game, she uses the same strategies that child B demonstrated.
Avoidance	The prevention of an aversive stimulus by a response (behavior) that delays or keeps the response from occurring (Catania, 1998).	The boys stop their rough play at recess to avoid being taken to the principal's office.
Habit reversal	A treatment package developed by Azrin and Nunn (1973) used for habitual behavior (e.g., nervous habits and tics) consisting of awareness training, competing response training, motivation procedures, and generalization procedures (Miltenberger, 1998).	A student engages in continuous fingernail biting, so the teacher cues the student every time this behavior occurs, prompts the student to chew a piece of gum, and provides positive reinforcement contingent on the absence of fingernail biting.
Functional communication training (FCT)	Training procedure that provides the same reinforcer that maintains problem behavior contingent on an appropriate communicative response (Alberto & Troutman, 2003).	A child is taught to say "please" to receive attention from his teacher rather than throwing his pencil to receive attention.

Behavioral Concepts	Definition	Example
Reductive techniques		
Punishment	The contingent presentation or removal of a stimulus following a response, which decreases the probability of a response occurring in the future (Catania, 1998).	A student is reprimanded by the teacher and loses points on her exam for copying answers from another student's exam.
Time-out	The temporary, contingent removal of reinforcers following a response.	A child is removed from a preferred play activity for 2 minutes because he hit another student.
Overcorrection	A procedure using exaggerated practice of appropriate behaviors implemented to reduce the occurrence of an inappropriate behavior (Alberto & Troutman, 2003).	A student who writes on the wall is made to clean all pen marks off of the walls in the hallway.
Response cost	A procedure used to reduce behavior by withdrawal of a reinforcer in specific amounts, contingent on the occurrence of inappropriate behavior (Alberto & Troutman, 2003).	When the student throws her pencil, the teacher takes away 10 points.
Extinction	Reinforcement is withheld or terminated for a previously reinforced response in order to reduce the occurrence of the response (Catania, 1998).	The teacher ignores the student whenever he yells the teacher's name during class discussions.
Recovery	Recovery occurs when responding returns to an earlier level following reductions in the response through extinction or punishment (Catania, 1998).	A student who has not thrown her pencil in weeks following extinction suddenly throws her pencil several times before discontinuing this behavior.
Habituation	Reductions in respondent behavior that occur because of repeated presentations of the corresponding stimulus (Catania, 1998).	A father playing peek-a-boo with his young child jumps out from behind a door and yells "Peek-a-boo!" The first time the father jumps out, the child is startled; however, after several exposures to peek-a-boo, the child no longer becomes startled.
Design/interventions terms		
Single-case design	Experimental design in which each participant serves as his own control (Alberto & Troutman, 2003). Control is shown when improvement in behavior occurs with treatment relative to baseline, or with one treatment versus another.	Two treatment interventions to increase compliance with math tasks are implemented on alternate days with one student for 2 weeks to determine which intervention is more effective.
Baseline	Within an experimental design, data that are taken prior to the implementation of treatment procedures (Alberto & Troutman, 2003) or as a comparison to treatment.	Data collected on a student's compliance with task requests prior to the implementation of an intervention.

(Continued)

Table 1 (Continued)

Behavioral Concepts	Definition	Example
Treatment	Manipulation of antecedent or consequence variables with the intent of altering (i.e., increase or decrease) a target behavior (Alberto & Troutman, 2003).	Making a child's access to preferred activities contingent on the completion of a task increases the child's compliance.
Social validity	Identification of significant problems targeted for behavior change that are important socially as well as theoretically (Baer, & colleagues, 1968).	The teacher targets increasing the student's compliance on math worksheets because the student needs to learn math to be successful in school.
Treatment integrity	The degree to which the components of a particular treatment are implemented correctly.	The teacher conducts frequent preference assessments with the student to make sure that compliance is followed by preferred activities.
Practice effects	Changes in performance that are related to multiple exposures to a task (Sattler, 2001).	A student's accuracy on math tasks increases because of practice on the math task and not because of positive reinforcement that is provided contingent on completion of the task.

training (FCT), in which the student is taught a communicative response that results in access to the same reinforcers that maintained problem behavior. This contingency (reinforcer delivery following communication) is then provided across situations that were correlated with problem behavior. For example, if assessment indicates that problem behavior is maintained by escape from nonpreferred activities (i.e., negative reinforcement), the student might be taught to signal to the teacher to briefly stop a nonpreferred activity. One benefit to this approach is that an appropriate behavior is taught specifically to replace a problem behavior in the context in which the problem behavior occurs. One drawback to FCT is that the intervention might be time-consuming to implement, at least initially, if the student constantly requests access to the reinforcer.

A third intervention strategy, which should be used only in combination with NCR or FCT, is termed a reductive strategy. Reductive strategies, such as extinction and punishment, are so named because their goal is to reduce problem behavior. For example, when FCT is combined with extinction, the identified reinforcer (teacher attention or breaks) is available only for an appropriate communicative response. Occurrences of problem behavior are ignored, meaning that they no longer result in reinforcement. When

FCT is combined with punishment strategies, access to reinforcement is removed following occurrences of problem behavior. For example, if problem behavior is shown to be maintained by access to preferred items (i.e., a tangible positive reinforcement function), appropriate communication results in access to the items, but problem behavior results in either removal of the items or removal of the student from the context (time-out). Reductive procedures can help to augment reinforcement strategies but are seldom used as the sole approach to intervention.

Case Example

The teacher decided to combine all three intervention strategies to reduce Quincy's aggression. She briefly attended to him every five minutes or so while he was playing or working with peers. She taught him to raise his hand when he wanted her attention and tried to respond each time he raised his hand. She placed him in 5 to 10 minutes of time-out for aggression.

SUMMARY

A function-based approach to assessment and intervention focuses on antecedents that lead to behavior and consequences that maintain behavior.

Interventions that are matched to the results of functional assessments have been shown across diverse groups and settings to be effective in reducing problem behavior and increasing adaptive behavior. Table 1 gives examples of behavioral terms and concepts.

—David P. Wacker, Joel Ringdahl, Danielle Dolezal, and Eric Boelter

See also Applied Behavior Analysis; Behavior Intervention; Behavioral Assessment; Behavioral Momentum; Consultation: Behavioral; Functional Behavior Assessment; Least Restrictive Environment (LRE); Positive Behavior Support

REFERENCES AND FURTHER READING

Alberto, P. A., & Troutman, A. C. (2003). *Applied behavior analysis for teachers* (6th ed.). Upper Saddle River, NJ: Pearson Education.

Azrin, N. H., & Nunn, R. G. (1973). Habit reversal: A method of eliminating nervous habits and tics. *Behaviour Research and Therapy, 11,* 619–628.

Baer, D. M., Wolf, M. M., & Risley, T. R. (1968). Some current dimensions of applied behavior analysis. *Journal of Applied Behavior Analysis, 1,* 91–97.

Catania, C. A. (1998). *Learning* (4th ed.). Upper Saddle River, NJ: Prentice-Hall.

Iwata, B. A., Dorsey, M. F., Slifer, K. J., Bauman, K. E., & Richman, G. S. (1994). Toward a functional analysis of self-injury. *Journal of Applied Behavior Analysis, 27,* 197–209.

Michael, J. (1982). Distinguishing between discriminative and motivational functions of stimuli. *Journal of Experimental Analysis of Behavior, 37,* 149–155.

Miltenberger, R. G., Fuqua, R. W., & Woods, D. W. (1998). Applying behavior analysis to clinic problems: Review and analysis of habit reversal. *Journal of Applied Behavior Analysis, 31,* 447–469.

Sattler, J. M. (2001). *Assessment of children: Cognitive applications* (4th ed.). San Diego, CA: Jerome M. Sattler.

BEHAVIORAL MOMENTUM

Behavioral momentum is a technique used to increase a child's compliance with requests. To apply this technique, the child is first asked to complete multiple tasks that he or she would naturally agree to do. Then, the child is asked to perform a disagreeable task or a task that the child is less likely to complete. Once momentum is established with the agreeable requests, the child is more likely to comply with subsequent requests. For example, John refuses to comply when his teacher asks him to clean his desk. His teacher decides to use behavioral momentum to increase John's compliance. The teacher first determines three simple tasks that are agreeable to John. These tasks include handing out papers, feeding the class's goldfish, and erasing the board. One by one, the teacher asks John to complete each of the agreeable tasks and praises him after their completion. Then, the teacher immediately asks John to clean his desk. Because the momentum of completing tasks has been established, it is more likely that John will comply and perform the disagreeable request.

—Kristin Witteborg

See also Behavior; Behavior Intervention; Self-Management

REFERENCES AND FURTHER READING

Rhode, G., Jenson, W. R., & Reavis, H. K. (1992). *The tough kid book: Practical classroom management strategies.* Longmont, CO: Sopris West.

BIAS (TESTING)

Bias in testing is a concern of psychologists, sociologists, and the general public; but the word *bias* has numerous meanings. Much of the controversy regarding bias in testing is reflected in what might be considered racial or ethnic bias. For the general public and sometimes with other groups, simple group differences in test performance are often interpreted as evidence of bias in the test (e.g., white versus African American intelligence quotient [IQ] scores). This assertion makes an assumption that there can be no group differences in test performance, lest the test be biased against the lower-performing group. This position may be the result of confusing two issues that should be kept separate: test bias and etiology of group differences (Reynolds & colleagues, 1999). Most often, bias in testing is focused on intelligence tests or other aptitude measures, but any psychological test (achievement, personality, psychopathology, perceptual-motor, etc.) can (and should) be the focus of bias investigation.

Bias in psychological testing has been a factor in several notable court cases. According to Reschly and Bersoff (1999), the first two class action law suits that directly challenged the use of IQ tests were *Diana v. State Board of Education* and *Guadalupe v. Tempe Elementary School District No. 3.* Both cases were concerned with the overrepresentation of Hispanic children (and also Native American children in *Guadalupe)* in public education programs for the mentally retarded, and such overrepresentation was a violation of the principle of equal protection. It was also argued that identification and placement of children were made using verbally loaded tests that were unfair for limited English proficient (LEP) children. These two cases were resolved by consent decrees that specified, among other things, that children with LEP would be assessed using nonverbal measures or with measures that were in the child's primary language (Reschly & Bersoff, 1999).

Larry P. v. Riles was a class action lawsuit supported by the Bay Area Association of Black Psychologists on behalf of African American children who were overrepresented in public education programs for the mentally retarded (Reschly & Bersoff, 1999). Judge Peckham ruled that IQ tests used to classify children as mentally retarded and subsequent placement in special education programs were biased against African American children. In his opinion, a test that showed simple mean differences between groups was in and of itself evidence of bias. The ruling banned the use of IQ tests with African American students for consideration of a mental retardation classification and placement into special education classes (Reschly & Bersoff, 1999). This ruling was upheld in the Ninth Circuit Court of Appeals in 1984. In 1986, Judge Peckham approved a settlement that prohibited administration of IQ tests to African American students for any special education purpose. Finally, in *Crawford et al. v. Honig,* a class action case where African American parents who *wanted* their children to receive IQ testing for possible diagnosis of a specific learning disability (SLD), Judge Peckham rescinded the 1986 ruling of *Larry P.* and returned to the original 1979 ruling prohibiting the use of IQ tests with African American children for classification and placement for mental retardation (Reschly & Bersoff, 1999).

Another class action lawsuit pertaining to African American students was *Parents in Action on Special Education (PASE) v. Joseph P. Hannon,* which, like the *Larry P.* case, argued that IQ tests were biased against African American children and resulted in misclassification of such children as mentally retarded. Judge Grady's ruling in federal court was exactly the opposite of Judge Peckham's ruling in the *Larry P.* case. Judge Grady ruled that IQ tests were *not* culturally biased against African American children.

Bias in psychological testing is concerned with the extent to which there is systematic error in test scores as a function of a particular group membership (race, ethnicity, sex, geography, socioeconomic status, etc.). Such a definition allows for empirical investigation of bias in testing. Bias in psychological testing has been examined using several different methods. The trinitarian model of validity (content validity, criterion-related validity, and construct validity) has been used to provide a framework to investigate bias in tests.

Research investigating content validity bias is concerned with the test items and the extent to which individual test items are biased against a particular group. If an item is biased against a particular group, then it should be found to be more difficult for that group. Differential item functioning (DIE) is a statistical method used to identify items that work differently depending on the group. A logical analysis of the item content is made after identifying the different functioning items. Item response theory (IRT) methods are also used, and these methods produce item characteristic curves (ICCs). The ICCs and various statistical tests can determine if there are group differences at the item level. When ICCs differ significantly, the item may be eliminated or modified in the test construction process in an attempt to eliminate item bias.

Research investigating criterion-related validity bias is concerned with differential predictive validity of a test that might indicate bias against a particular group. Many tests (particularly IQ, ability, and aptitude measures) are constructed to make predictions of performance on other relevant measures or future outcomes. Predictive validity for ability tests may be considered the most important type of validity with respect to bias. In this case, a test is examined to determine if it predicts an outcome equally well for various groups. A test that predicts the outcome less well for certain groups might be considered less valid for that group. One way to assess predictive validity is to compare correlation coefficients between various groups that indicate whether the test had greater predictive validity for groups with the higher coefficient. This approach, however, pertains only to the *slope* of the line of predicted scores, which is the most problematic type of "bias."

Research investigating construct validity bias is typically concerned with the differential factor structure of a test that might indicate bias against a particular group. Many tests are constructed to measure more than one construct, trait, or factor; and items are assigned to factors based on their relationships (correlations) with other similar items and their lack of relationships (correlations) with dissimilar items. Other tests contain multiple subtests that are grouped together based on their relationships (correlations) with each other and lack of relationships (correlations) with other different subtests. In this case, groups of subtests together measure a common or similar dimension and represent a composite or global factor or construct. If a test measures a different number of factors for the various groups, it would have a different factor structure depending on the group; and the interpretation of the test scores would not be the same for the different groups. Another problem is if subtests (or items) do not "load" (associate) with the same dimensions or factors. Subtests or items that do not "load" on the same factors might be measuring different characteristics in the different groups.

It is expected that the components (factors) of a test should be similar with respect to different populations (or subgroups within a population), a result that is frequently obtained in the empirical literature.

—*Gary L. Canivez*

REFERENCES AND FURTHER READING

Reschly, D. J., & Bersoff, D. N. (1999). Law and school psychology. In C. R. Reynolds & T. B Gutkin (Eds.), *The handbook of school psychology* (pp. 1077–1112). New York: Wiley.

Reynolds, C. R., Lowe, P. A., & Saenz, A. L. (1999). The problem of bias in psychological assessment. In C. R. Reynolds and T. B Gutkin (Eds.), *The handbook of school psychology* (pp. 549–595). New York: Wiley.

BIOFEEDBACK

Research over the past 30 years has shown a distinct connection between the mind and body. Therefore, a person's thoughts and feelings are viewed as interacting with their physiological state and vice versa. Modern biofeedback grew out of the behavioral movement of the mid-1950s (Schwartz & Andrasik, 2003). In biofeedback, physiological responses (e.g., heart and respiration rate, skin temperature, muscle tension) are amplified from sensors attached to the body and fed back to the individual through a computer in the form of sounds, visuals, or both. This information can be used by the person to consciously control the measured bodily processes. With increased awareness of physiological responses, the person can learn to control his or her bodily reaction to environmental events. There are various types of biofeedback modalities used. Table 1 shows the most frequently used biofeedback modalities.

Reactions to stressful events are mediated by the autonomic (i.e., automatic) nervous system (ANS). There are two antagonistic branches of the ANS: the sympathetic nervous system (SNS) and the parasympathetic nervous system (PNS). The SNS stimulates the body's reaction (e.g., heart rate, breathing, pupil dilation) to stressful events by preparing the person to act quickly to respond to an event. Activation of the SNS causes stress to the body, and prolonged activation can lead to organ damage and a reduction in the capability of the body's immune defenses to ward off disease. In some cases, simply the perception (real or imagined) of physiological arousal itself can trigger worry or fear, further exacerbating the physiological response. The PNS is associated with relaxation, control, and improved health status. Increases in PNS activation lead to lowered heart rate; slower, deeper breathing; and improved blood flow.

Hans Selye (1976) proposed the general adaptation syndrome (GAS) as a way of explaining the relationship between stressful events and physiological reactions to them. In the GAS, a person experiences the initial shock of a stressor that activates the SNS. In some people, this SNS arousal may diminish quickly after the stressor remits, but for others the individual remains chronically aroused (e.g., continued SNS activation), resulting in organ damage and illness. The ability of the person to cope with the stressful events and induce PNS activation leads to reduced vulnerability to disease.

Biofeedback provides individuals with direct information on SNS–PNS activation, or their level of physiological arousal. Psychologists can use this information to assist children and adolescents to learn to cope with stressful events through a variety of therapeutic techniques. The general treatment plan for using biofeedback is to help a child or adolescent to:

Table 1   Types of Biofeedback Modalities

- **Electroencephalography (EEG):** EEG measures brainwave activity through sensors placed on the scalp. Children can learn to emit different types of brainwaves to help them to attend or to relax.
- **Breathing (Respiration [RSP]):** RSP measures breathing rate, location, and volume through a strain gauge worn around the chest. RSP data help the person to detect and change rapid or shallow breathing patterns that are associated with fear.
- **Electrodermal (EDA):** EDA biofeedback measures sweat activity through sensors usually placed on the palm or fingers. Through the use of EDA, the person can become more aware and reduce sweat activity, such as clammy hands, often associated with stressful events when speaking in front of groups or meeting new people.
- **Electromyography (EMG):** EMG sensors placed over a muscle group measure muscle tension by detecting the electrical activity within the muscle fibers. Children and adolescents that experience chronic muscle tension (e.g., headaches) can use EMG feedback to become aware of the muscle group that is contributing to the problem and learn to relax (control) the muscle(s).
- **Heart Rate (HR):** HR is usually measured through sensors placed on the wrist or finger. Stressful events can cause the heart to race or pound. Through HR feedback the person becomes aware of their heart rate when under stress or relaxed. Then through the use of HR feedback, the individual learns to control or maintain a lower heart rate in the face of stressful events.
- **Skin Temperature (ST):** ST measures the skin surface temperature, which is a good indicator of peripheral blood flow. ST is usually measured by a sensor placed on the fingertip. Constriction of the smooth muscles surrounding the blood vessels is an indication of tension resulting in reduced blood flow to the extremities and the feeling of cold hands. The sensitivity of the ST instrument allows the detection of small changes in skin temperature and helps the person to use coping strategies designed to reduce unnecessary physiological arousal.

- Become aware of physiological changes that occur when under stress and when relaxed
- Learn to control the physiological modality in which he or she is most responsive
- Generalize the learned skill so that it can be performed anywhere but especially when the child encounters stressful events

There are numerous therapeutic techniques that are used with biofeedback to assist a child or adolescent in reducing the effects of stressful events. These techniques include:

- Cognitive Behavior Therapy (CBT)—The assumption is that thoughts influence a person's ability to cope with stress. CBT techniques are designed to increase awareness of damaging or disruptive thoughts and to replace them with thoughts that reduce negatively arousing feelings and behavior. When CBT is used with biofeedback, the person becomes immediately aware of the physiological effect of better or more adaptive thoughts.
- Relaxation Training—In relaxation training, the person is taught to deeply and progressively relax muscle groups. The goal of relaxation training is to help the person to achieve relaxation and reduce SNS arousal even in the face of

stressful events. When used with biofeedback, the child or adolescent uses physiological feedback to rapidly learn strategies that lead to more complete relaxation.
- Autogenics—Autogenics are self-statements designed to enhance a therapeutic response. Self-statements like "I feel better now" help induce a more relaxed state or help the person to stay focused on their goal.
- Breathing—Lower abdominal or diaphragmatic breathing is linked to PNS activation and increased oxygenation of the blood. In addition, slower and deeper breathing promotes relaxation and reduces physiological arousal. Respiratory biofeedback provides information on the success of the person in achieving deeper and slower rates of breathing needed to stimulate a PNS response.

Modern biofeedback instruments capitalize on children's and adolescent's interest in video technology by providing interesting audio and video feedback. For example, children may watch the computer progressively color a black and white forest scene as they maintain a low level of physiological arousal. The use of thermometer visuals or playing popular music when criterion levels of relaxation are attained is also frequently used.

Research on the effectiveness of biofeedback with children is in its early stages. A definitive statement about the effectiveness of biofeedback cannot be made at this time. This is true in part because few studies have researched biofeedback alone as a treatment and few well-controlled studies exist. Of the studies that do exist, biofeedback treatment holds promise for the treatment of migraine and tension headaches, pain and anxiety management, sleeping problems, enuresis (e.g., bed or pants wetting), encopresis (e.g., soiling clothes), attention deficit hyperactivity disorder (ADHD), and impulse control difficulties (Culbert & colleagues, 1996).

—*Steven W. Lee*

See also Attention Deficit Hyperactivity Disorder; Behavior Intervention; Generalized Anxiety Disorder; Self-Management

REFERENCES AND FURTHER READING

Culbert, T. P., Kajander, R. L., & Reaney, J. B. (1996). Biofeedback with children and adolescents: Clinical observations and patient perspectives. *Developmental and Behavioral Pediatrics, 17,* 342–350.

Schwartz, M. S., & Andrasik, F. (Eds.). (2003). *Biofeedback: A practitioner's guide* (3rd ed.). New York: Guilford.

Selye, H. (1976). *The stress of life.* New York: McGraw-Hill.

BIPOLAR DISORDER (CHILDHOOD ONSET)

Bipolar disorder (BD), or what historically was called manic-depressive disorder, has long been identified as an adult disorder. BD is characterized by extreme shifts in mood, energy, and behavior that significantly impair an individual's functioning. In adults, it is characterized by cycles of depression alternating with either mania (i.e., feelings of elation, inflated self-esteem, excessive talking, flight of ideas, increased goal-directed and risk-taking behavior, and agitation) or hypomania (manic-like symptoms but less severe and shorter in duration); each component of the cycle lasts at least 4 days. With children, it has been suggested that the components of the cycle can be very short (i.e., rapid or ultrarapid cycling) (Papolos & Papolos, 1999). Furthermore, in children, the depression may manifest as irritability, low motivation, poor concentration, and loss of interest.

BD is believed to be neurological in origin and related to poor regulation of various neurotransmitters (i.e., chemicals) in the brain. The predisposition for this regulatory problem is believed to be inherited. As with other disorders, it is most likely that more than one gene is involved in the familial transmission, with risk increasing for all mood disorders (i.e., depression) when BD is present in the family history.

Characteristics of childhood BD include the worsening of disruptive behavior, hyperactivity, irritability, impulsive behavior, explosive rages and tantrums, difficulty sleeping at night, and difficulty concentrating. Additionally, rapid speech, racing thoughts, grandiose delusions, increased physical and mental activity, separation anxiety, and inappropriate sexual behaviors have been described. In children, it has been suggested that the presentation is more a combination of mania, depression, and irritability. In addition, early onset presentation may include subclinical levels of hypomania, depression, and mixed affective states with episodic aggression (Carlson, 1990). Notably, the two symptoms that are specific to BD in adults, euphoria or elated mood and grandiosity, occur rarely in children with bipolar disorder (Carlson, 1990); in place of the euphoria, irritability is seen as the key symptom in children.

The manifestation of the actual disorder can occur any time from infancy through older adulthood; however, BD has not been diagnosed traditionally until adolescence or early adulthood, with a peak in diagnosis between 14 and 18 years of age. It is estimated that for adults and adolescents, it occurs in 1% to 2% of the population. Research regarding the prevalence of BD in children is limited, with estimates as low as 0.3% and as high as 16%. Prevalence rates for adolescents (ages 14 to 18) with BD have been reported to be 1%, while prevalence rates for adolescents with mania varies from 0.6% to 13.3% (Lewinsohn & colleagues, 1995). No race or ethnic differences exist in the diagnosis of BD (i.e., involving a manic or mixed episode), and research indicates few gender differences with regard to the prevalence of the disorder in adolescents (Lewinsohn & colleagues, 1995).

Not only do some of the behaviors associated with BD occur in the course of normal development, but diagnosis of BD in children often can cause a dilemma because of the degree of symptom overlap between BD and other disorders. Disorders that may mask or mimic BD include attention deficit hyperactivity disorder (ADHD), unipolar depression (e.g., major depressive disorder), conduct disorder (CD), and schizophrenia. Clearly, diagnosis of any one or more of these disorders (e.g., BD, ADHD, CD, depression, or schizophrenia) will result in very different interventions as well as anticipated prognosis and outcome.

It has been suggested that 20% to 40% of children who are initially diagnosed with depression are later diagnosed with bipolar disorder. Children diagnosed with early onset depression may be diagnosed as an adult with later onset BD. Based on retrospective data, many individuals with bipolar disorder first experience depressive episodes.

TREATMENTS FOR CHILDREN WITH BIPOLAR DISORDER

Treatments for children with BD include medication and psychosocial interventions. These treatments are discussed below.

Psychopharmacology

The first line of intervention for adults with BD has been the medications lithium, anticonvulsants, and neuroleptics. Just as the criteria of adults are being projected onto children, so are the treatment approaches. However, little is known about the impact of these medications on learning and memory in children, or the developing brain.

Psychosocial Interventions

Kupfer and colleagues (2002) believe that psychosocial interventions are critical to children with BD. In fact, children with BD evidence greater impairment in social and peer relationships and relationships with parents and adults as compared to other clinical groups. Additional intervention approaches include the use of family-focused therapy and cognitive–behavioral therapy. The family-focused approach tends to emphasize the family relations and emotional expression (Kupfer and colleagues, 2002). Notably, there are no efficacy studies on cognitive–behavioral approaches or family therapy for children with bipolar disorder.

Best Practice

In the absence of a clear, empirically supported treatment for BD, a combination of approaches with careful monitoring of effectiveness on a case-by-case basis constitutes best practice. As with any treatment, it is important that all individuals involved with the child, as well as the child, understand the nature of the disorder and the intent of the interventions being implemented. If an intervention is not proving to be effective or if side effects of the intervention become evident, then intervention development needs to be recycled with an emphasis on the primary problem behaviors that interfere with overall functioning.

ROLE OF SCHOOL PSYCHOLOGISTS IN WORKING WITH CHILDREN DIAGNOSED WITH BIPOLAR DISORDER

Most likely, children with BD will meet one or more of the criteria for emotional disturbance (ED):

- Inability to build or maintain satisfactory interpersonal relationships with peers and teachers
- Inappropriate types of behavior or feelings under normal circumstances
- A general pervasive mood of unhappiness or depression

Whatever the symptom(s), there must be evidence that the child's disorder is adversely affecting school performance. In some cases, children may be served under section 504 of the Rehabilitation Act of 1973 since accommodations in the regular education classroom, and not a special placement, may be the focus of intervention. In severe cases (e.g., with psychotic features), a child's behavior may necessitate hospitalization. After hospitalization, transitioning back into the school setting may be stressful not only for the student, but for teachers and staff in that setting.

For children with BD, increased knowledge and understanding of the disorder and the potential impact of the disorder on learning are important. For this reason, in-service education for teachers who work with these children is needed.

—Michael J. Ash, Cynthia Riccio, Maricela Gonzalez, Eve Rosenthal, and Katherine Macey

See also DSM-IV; Individuals With Disabilities Education Act; Personality Assessment

REFERENCES AND FURTHER READING

Carlson, G. A. (1990). Bipolar disorder in children and adolescents. In B. D. Garfinkel, G. A. Carlson & E. B. Weller (Eds.), *Psychiatric disorders in children and adolescents*. Philadelphia: W. B. Saunders.

Kupfer, D. J., Findling, R. L., Geller, B., & Ghaemi, S. N. (2002). Treatment of bipolar disorder during childhood, adolescent, and young adult years. *Journal of Clinical Psychiatry, 5*(5), 1–18.

Lewinsohn, P. M., Klein D. N., & Seeley, J. R. (1995). Bipolar disorder in a community sample of older adolescents. Prevalence, phenomenology, comorbidity, and course. *Journal of the American Academy of Child and Adolescent Psychiatry, 34,* 454–463.

Papolos, D. F., & Papolos, J. (1999). *The bipolar child.* New York: Broadway Books.

BULLYING AND VICTIMIZATION

Bullying in schools is a serious and prevalent problem. Research conducted around the world has established the negative impact of bullying on both children who are bullied and those who bully others. Until recently, research on bullying in American schools lagged behind work done in other countries. However, increasing attention and concern has put the problem of bullying at the center of public policy. State legislatures have recently begun to mandate that schools take active steps to reduce bullying. Here we summarize the research literature on bullying, including its prevalence and impacts, and features of effective school-based interventions.

DEFINITION OF BULLYING

Discriminating bullying from other types of aggression and from rough play can be challenging. Experts in the field identify three distinguishing features of bullying (Olweus, 1993):

1. It has a power imbalance in which the child doing the bullying has more power because of factors such as age, size, support of a peer group, or higher status.

2. It is carried out with the intent of harming the targeted child.

3. It is usually an activity in which a particular child is singled out repeatedly.

Bullying behaviors can include verbal aggression, physical aggression, and relationship-damaging behaviors. An example of the latter would be using gossip to systematically exclude a child from a peer group. Bullying also may have sexual content, particularly in later elementary years and among older youth. Typically, a distinction is made between direct and indirect bullying to distinguish behaviors that are expressed overtly from those expressed covertly.

Direct bullying is characterized by open physical or verbal attacks on the targeted child. In cases of direct bullying, the child and, often, others within the school know the identity of the person(s) doing the bullying. Direct bullying is easier to recognize because the behaviors are readily observable and the impact is immediate. In contrast, indirect bullying includes covert, harmful behaviors directed toward another child (Olweus, 1993). Indirect bullying can be more difficult to recognize because the person being bullied may not be present when the bullying occurs. Examples of indirect bullying include spreading rumors, writing mean graffiti about a child, and encouraging others to leave a child out. There exists evidence suggesting girls are more likely to engage in indirect forms of bullying, whereas boys are more prone to direct bullying.

PREVALENCE

Most of the information regarding the prevalence of bullying is based on children's self-reports. In a large Norwegian sample, approximately 7% of students reported regularly bullying others, while 9% reported frequent victimization (Olweus, 1993). Self-report data obtained by researchers in Europe, North America, Japan, Australia, and New Zealand have revealed rates of bullying comparable to or higher than the Norwegian sample (Smith & colleagues, 1999). A large-scale, nationally representative sample of 6th through 10th graders in the United States revealed that 13% of the sample regularly bullied others, 11% of the sample were regularly victimized, and 6% of the sample were involved in high levels of both bullying and victimization (Nansel & colleagues, 2001). U.S. studies of children in the middle-to-late elementary years show rates of frequent victimization ranging from 10% to 18% (Pellegrini & colleagues, 1999).

IMPACT OF INVOLVEMENT IN BULLYING

Peer victimization is associated with short- and long-term negative effects on academic, social, and emotional functioning. Children who are bullied may develop negative attitudes about school as early as kindergarten. They also tend to view their school environment as unsupportive and report wanting to stay home from school due to bullying. A relationship between peer victimization and emotional problems has been documented for children as young as preschool and kindergarten. Emotional problems commonly associated with being bullied include lowered self-esteem and increased depression, loneliness, and anxiety. Rigby and Slee (1999) found higher rates of suicidal ideation in children who were bullied. Longitudinal research has established that the harmful emotional consequences of bullying can extend into adulthood (Olweus, 1993).

Bullying others is associated with increased risk of involvement in a wide variety of negative behaviors, including fighting, smoking, and poor academic achievement (Nansel & colleagues, 2001). For boys, childhood physical aggression and bullying have been shown to predict involvement in criminal behavior in adolescence and adulthood. Olweus (1991) found that 60% of boys identified as having serious bullying problems between sixth and ninth grades had at least one criminal conviction by age 24, and 40% of them had three or more arrests. Finally, children who are involved in both bullying and victimization may be at the greatest risk for concurrent and future emotional and behavioral problems (Pellegrini & colleagues, 1999).

CHALLENGES TO SCHOOL-BASED BULLYING PREVENTION

A major obstacle to effective prevention is lack of adult awareness and intervention in relation to bullying problems. Children report that adults rarely intervene in bullying problems and that when they do intervene, they respond poorly, and observational research confirms low rates of adult intervention (Craig & colleagues, 2000). To compound the problem, bullying tends to occur in undersupervised areas of a school such as the playground, bus, and corridors; and many students do not report being bullied to adults.

In addition to the need for effective adult monitoring and intervention, children need assistance coping with the social and emotional challenges posed by bullying. Experts in the field suggest that teaching specific social–emotional skills to support healthy peer relationships and effective responding to problems may be important in preventing bullying. Children with at least one friend are less likely to be bullied, and friendship can function generally as a protective factor. Moreover, learning strategies to

manage emotions and respond assertively may assist children who are bullied. Children who cry or anger easily are likely to be rejected as the school year progresses, putting them at risk for victimization. These findings suggest that providing all children with the social skills to form and maintain friendships contributes to bullying reduction in the long run.

Approaching bullying by solely trying to change the behavior of individual children, however, does not address the role of peer processes. Bullying generally takes place within the context of ongoing dynamics within a group of children who know each other. Consequently, many experts in the field strongly recommend that bullying prevention programs also address peer group attitudes, behaviors, and norms around bullying as well as social skills training.

Finally, effective bullying prevention requires a sustained, consistent schoolwide coordination of effort. A high level of school commitment requires the buy-in of administrative and teaching staff, as well as students, and the resources to develop and support bullying prevention efforts over time. Effective interventions require sustained and coordinated schoolwide effort, increased adult effectiveness in dealing with bullying, and a focus on teaching children the social–emotional skills to support healthy peer networks.

SCHOOL-BASED INTERVENTIONS

Much of the research on bullying prevention program effectiveness emerged from campaigns to reduce school bullying in other nations (e.g., Olweus, 1991; Smith & Brain, 2000; Smith & Sharp, 1994). These programs emphasize a "whole school" approach to bullying prevention. Goals common to a whole school approach include developing effective schoolwide policies and rules related to bullying, increasing staff awareness and responsiveness, surveying students about their experiences, and increasing parental awareness of bullying problems.

Use of such programs has been associated with reductions in student reports of bullying, improved classroom discipline, more positive student attitudes toward school, and increases in students' willingness to seek assistance with bullying. Specifically, two bullying prevention programs have effectively reduced school bullying. Olweus's (1991) school-based program led to a 50% reduction in student-reported bullying, as well as improved classroom atmosphere, when implemented with 2,500 fourth- to seventh-grade Norwegian students. A similar school-based intervention supported by the Department of Education in England showed a significant decrease in bullying and increased willingness on the part of students to seek help with bullying problems (Smith & Sharp, 1994).

A growing body of research findings coupled with increased concern about the problem of bullying in American schools has led to development of new programs that show promise. *Steps to Respect* (Committee for Children, 2001) is one elementary school program designed to reduce bullying and promote healthy peer relationships. A universal prevention program, *Steps to Respect* is comprised of a school-wide implementation manual, staff training, and student lessons for grades three through six. The staff training consists of a core training session for all school staff and two in-depth training sessions intended for teachers, school psychologists, counselors, and administrators. *Steps to Respect* student lessons, taught by classroom teachers over a 12- to 14-week period, emphasize student social–emotional skills related to friendship, coping with bullying, and emotion management. A longitudinal evaluation study of *Steps to Respect* is currently underway.

CONCLUSION

Correcting the power imbalance that characterizes bullying requires school-level changes and coordinated adult involvement. Comprehensive approaches to bullying prevention have demonstrated efficacy. Bullying prevention approaches that promote a coordinated effort between the adults and children in a school community show the most promise for addressing this difficult problem. In leading such an effort, educators hope to decrease the suffering of victimized children and promote the development of a responsible, respectful school community.

—*Jennie L. Snell and Miriam Hirschstein*

See also Aggression in Schools; Behavior Intervention; Corporal Punishment; Parenting

REFERENCES AND FURTHER READING

Committee for Children (2001). *Steps to Respect: A bullying prevention program.* Seattle, WA: Author.

Craig, W. M., Pepler, D. J., & Atlas, R. S. (2000). Observations of bullying on the playground and in the classroom. *School Psychology International, 21,* 22–36.

Nansel, T. R., Overpeck, M., Pilla, R. S., Ruan, W. J., Simons-Mortin, B., & Scheidt, P. (2001). Bullying behaviors among US youth. *Journal of the American Medical Association, 285,* 2094–2100.

Olweus, D. (1991). Bully/victim problems among schoolchildren: Basic facts and effects of a school-based intervention program. In D. Pepler & K. Rubin (Eds.), *The development and treatment of childhood aggression* (pp. 411–448). Hillsdale, NJ: Erlbaum.

Olweus, D. (1993). *Bullying at school.* Cambridge, MA: Blackwell.

Pellegrini, A. D., Bartini, M., & Brooks, F. (1999). School bullies, victims, and aggressive victims: Factors relating to group affiliation and victimization in early adolescence. *Journal of Educational Psychology, 91,* 216–224.

Rigby, K., & Slee, P. T. (1999). Suicidal ideation among adolescent schoolchildren, involvement in bully/victim problems, and perceived low social support. *Suicide and Life-Threatening Behavior, 29,* 119–130.

Smith, P. K., & Brain, P. (2000). Bullying in schools: Lessons from two decades of research. *Aggressive Behavior, 26,* 1–9.

Smith, P., Morita, Y., Junger-Tas, J., Olweus, D., Catalano, R., & Slee, P. (1999). *The nature of school bullying: A cross-national perspective.* New York: Routledge.

Smith, P. K., & Sharp, S. (1994). *School bullying: Insights and perspectives.* New York: Routledge.

BUROS MENTAL MEASUREMENTS YEARBOOK

As a young professor at Rutgers University in the 1930s, Oscar Krisen Buros was alarmed by many of the practices being used to develop and market tests. Buros believed that tests should be supported by firm foundations of statistical methodologies (referred to as reliability and validity) and by appropriate norming procedures that matched the specific population being tested. In an effort to improve the overall quality of tests and testing practices, Buros conceived of a publication series (*The Mental Measurements Yearbook*) that would offer "frankly critical test reviews" of new and recently revised tests written by experienced professionals (Buros, 1938, p. xiii). To supplement this book, Buros also published a comprehensive text, *Tests in Print,* designed to guide users seeking specific data on tests and to provide a current listing of all commercially available tests published in the English language.

Although both *The Mental Measurements Yearbook* and the *Tests in Print* series provide users with a reference to essential testing information

TIMELINE

1938—*The 1938 Mental Measurements Yearbook*; Oscar K. Buros (Ed.).

1940—*The 1940 Mental Measurements Yearbook*; Oscar K. Buros (Ed.).

1949 to 1978—*The Third* through *Eighth Mental Measurements Yearbooks, Tests in Print*, and *Tests in Print II*; Oscar K. Buros (Ed.).

1978—Oscar K. Buros passes away. Luella Gubrud Buros relocates the Buros Institute of Mental Measurements to the University of Nebraska-Lincoln.

1983 to 1985—*Tests in Print III* and *The Ninth Mental Measurements Yearbook*; James V. Mitchell, Jr. (Ed.).

1989—*The Tenth Mental Measurements Yearbook*; Jane Close Conoley & Jack J. Kramer (Eds.).

1992—*The Eleventh Mental Measurements Yearbook*; Jack J. Kramer & Jane Close Conoley (Eds.).

1994—*Tests in Print IV*; Linda L. Murphy, Jane Close Conoley, & James C. Impara (Eds.).

1995—*The Twelfth Mental Measurements Yearbook*; Jane Close Conoley & James C. Impara (Eds.).

1998—*The Thirteenth Mental Measurements Yearbook*; James C. Impara & Barbara S. Plake (Eds.).

1999—*Tests in Print V*; Linda L. Murphy, James C. Impara, & Barbara S. Plake (Eds.).

2001—*The Fourteenth Mental Measurements Yearbook*; Barbara S. Plake & James C. Impara (Eds.). Test Reviews Online (a collection of more than 2,000 recent test descriptions and reviews from *The Mental Measurements Yearbook* and *Tests in Print* series) becomes available via the Internet.

2002—*Tests in Print VI*; Linda L. Murphy, Barbara S. Plake, James C. Impara, & Robert A. Spies (Eds.)

2003—*The Fifteenth Mental Measurements Yearbook*; Barbara S. Plake, James C. Impara, & Robert A. Spies (Eds.), with subsequent editions to be completed at 18-month intervals.

(e.g., test purpose, publisher), the reviews found in *The Mental Measurements Yearbook* series also allow users to make reasoned judgments on whether a test is appropriate for its intended use. To find specific information on tests in these books, users should start with *Tests in Print*. All tests are listed alphabetically. If a review is available for a specific test, the cross-reference section will list the number of that test in *The Mental Measurements Yearbook* (e.g., 14:415 refers *to The Fourteenth Mental Measurements Yearbook*, Test Number 415). Tests without specific reviews either will not have a cross-reference section or that section will contain only a listing with a T number (for a prior edition of *Tests in Print*).

In order to make information on tests increasingly efficient and more widely available to the public, the Buros Institute of Mental Measurements has developed an Internet Web site that allows users instant access to large amounts of the content from its publications. Test descriptions may be searched via keywords, alphabet, or within 18 separate categories. For a modest fee, test reviews are immediately displayed. In addition, articles on current testing practices, frequently asked questions on psychological tests, and current competency standards are among the articles available on the Web site.

The Buros Institute continues the pioneering work begun by Oscar K. Buros more than 65 years ago with continued publication of *The Mental Measurements Yearbook* and *Tests in Print* series. Significant events in the history of the Buros Institute are listed in the accompanying timeline.

—*Robert A. Spies and Linda L. Murphy*

REFERENCES AND FURTHER READING

Buros, O. K. (Ed). (1938). *The nineteen thirty eight mental measurements yearbook.* New Brunswick, NJ: Rutgers University Press.

Test Reviews Online. Available from http://www.unl.edu/buros

CANCER

Cancer is a general term that describes many different diseases; however, the initial development of all cancers is the same. All cancers begin when abnormal cells grow out of control within an individual's body. Normal, healthy cells grow, divide, and then die. Cancer cells also grow and divide, but they do not die. Cancer cells outlive the normal cells, and the cancer cells continue to produce additional abnormal cells. Cancers develop as a result of damaged DNA (the carrier of genetic information) that cannot be repaired by the body. Individuals can inherit damaged DNA or an individual's DNA may become damaged from exposure to something in the environment such as smoke or the sun. Cancer frequently develops as a tumor, but there are some cancers, such as leukemia, that do not develop as tumors. Cancer is named for the part of the body where it first begins, but it often spreads to other areas of the body where it starts growing and replacing the normal, healthy cells (American Cancer Society, 2004).

PREVALENCE

The American Cancer Society predicted in 2004 that 9,200 children and adolescents in the United States younger than 15 years of age would be diagnosed with cancer that year. Because of advances in cancer treatments, approximately 77% of these children and adolescents would survive; nevertheless it is estimated that 1,510 children and adolescents would die in 2004. Cancer is the leading cause of death from disease in people younger than 15 years of age, and, in most age groups, it is the second most frequent cause of death.

COMMON TYPES OF CHILDHOOD CANCER

Leukemia

Leukemia is a cancer involving the blood-forming cells. It typically affects the white blood cells, but it can also affect other types of blood cells (i.e., red blood cells or platelets). Leukemia initially develops in the bone marrow (i.e., the inner part of the bones where blood cells are produced) and then spreads to the blood. Once in the blood, the leukemia can spread to the lymph nodes, the central nervous system (i.e., the brain and spinal cord), or other organs. Symptoms of leukemia include fatigue, pale skin, infection, easy bleeding or bruising, bone pain, swelling of the abdomen, swollen lymph nodes, swollen thymus gland, headaches, seizures, vomiting, rashes, gum disease, and extreme weakness (American Cancer Society, 2004).

Leukemia is identified as being either acute (growing quickly) or chronic (growing slowly). Children with leukemia are typically diagnosed with an acute form of the disease. Acute leukemia is divided into two types, (1) acute lymphocytic leukemia (ALL), also known as acute lymphoblastic leukemia; (2) and acute myelogenous leukemia (AML), also known as acute myeloid leukemia, acute myelocytic leukemia, and acute nonlymphocytic leukemia. ALL is a cancer of the lymphoblasts (cells that help form an individual's immune system). AML is a cancer type that affects immature bone marrow cells (American Cancer Society, 2004).

Overall, leukemia is the most common type of cancer diagnosed in children and adolescents. In 2004, it was estimated that 3,700 children and adolescents under the age of 19 years would develop leukemia. ALL accounts for approximately 75% of the leukemia diagnoses (approximately 2,800 cases). For most cases of leukemia, the exact cause of the disease is unknown; however, research has indicated that mutations in an individual's DNA can lead to the development of leukemia (American Cancer Society, 2004).

Treatment for leukemia includes supportive care for associated conditions, radiation therapy if the leukemia is located in the membranes that cover the brain or in the testes, and chemotherapy (anticancer drugs).

Brain and Spinal Cord Cancers

Brain and spinal cord tumors are the second most common childhood cancer, accounting for 21% of all childhood cancers (American Cancer Society, 2004). Brain tumors involve the brain structures either by growing on or in a structure, or by causing pressure on brain tissues (Armstrong & colleagues, 1999).

Possible symptoms of brain tumors include epileptic seizures and pressure within the skull, which may result in headaches, nausea, vomiting, or blurred vision. Some children experience crossed eyes and double vision as a result of the pressure, and some children lose their vision totally. Symptoms of skull pressure in school-age children include decreased school performance, fatigue, personality changes, and headaches. In younger children, symptoms include irritability, decreased appetite, developmental delays, and losing previously acquired intellectual and motor skills; infant symptoms include increased head size, vomiting, and failure to thrive. Possible symptoms of spinal cord tumors include numbness or weakness of the legs and abnormal movements and positioning of the body (American Cancer Society, 2004).

The causes of most brain tumors are unknown, but ionizing radiation (high-energy radiation) is a known risk factor. Other possible risk factors include exposure to vinyl chloride, aspartame, and electromagnetic fields, as well as family history. Treatments for brain and spinal cord tumors include surgery to remove the tumor, surgery to place a shunt (a tube used to drain cerebrospinal fluid), radiation therapy, and chemotherapy (American Cancer Society, 2004).

Other Childhood Cancers

In addition to leukemia, brain tumors, and spinal cord tumors, there are several other childhood cancers including lymphomas, bone cancers, soft tissue sarcomas, kidney cancers, eye cancers, and cancers of the adrenal glands (American Cancer Society, 2004).

LONG-TERM OUTCOMES

As mentioned previously, because of advances in treatment, 77% of children will live five years or more after being diagnosed with cancer; these treatments, however—specifically chemotherapy and radiation therapy—can have long-term effects on the child. Because treatments for cancer vary among children, the long-term effects also will vary. Chemotherapy and radiation therapy can result in cognitive impairments, causing difficulties in overall ability and academic achievement. A child may also have problems with visual motor skills, memory, and attention. If a child had a tumor that was on or near the eye, blurred vision, double vision, or glaucoma could occur as a result of treatment. Other body parts and functions such as hearing, growth and development, sexual development, reproduction, heart and cardiovascular system, respiratory system, muscles and bones, and teeth can also be affected by cancer treatment. In addition, childhood cancer survivors have a slightly increased risk of developing a second cancer later in life.

EDUCATIONAL IMPLICATIONS

There is evidence suggesting that children diagnosed with cancer should return to school as soon as possible. Returning to school and resuming a routine helps children regain some sense of control over their lives and allows them to feel some sense of normalcy (Sexson & Madan-Swain, 1995). Before a student returns to school, however, there needs to be communication between the parents, school, and medical professionals. To help with the student's transition back to school, a liaison, such as a school psychologist, should be designated to coordinate the communication between all the individuals responsible for the student.

The liaison can inform the student's teachers about the type of cancer the student has; the treatment the child is undergoing; possible side effects; and any possible effects on the student's stamina, appearance, and behavior. The teachers should also be made aware of any upcoming hospitalizations or appointments that will result in absences from school. Teachers also need to know how much information the student has been given about his or her prognosis so they do not go beyond what the parents or medical professionals have shared. It is important that all teachers who work directly with the student understand his or her physical needs (i.e., working for shorter periods of time and taking breaks) and psychological needs (i.e., wearing a hat to cover lost hair) to help prevent uncomfortable situations for the student. In addition, it is important for the liaison to encourage the student's parents to maintain ongoing communication with the school's staff to keep them updated on the student's condition and needs (Spinelli, 2004).

In addition to preparing the student's teachers for his or her return to school, it is also important to prepare the student's classmates. The student should be consulted to find out what information he or she (in consultation with parents) would like shared with the class, after which the teacher or school nurse can develop a developmentally appropriate presentation about cancer, cancer treatments, and possible side effects (Spinelli, 2004).

Besides preparing teachers and classmates, it is important to prepare the student for his or her return to the classroom. The student can be asked what fears or concerns he or she has about returning to school. The student can go over with his or her parents potential questions that teachers or classmates may ask to help alleviate any potential stress they may cause. It is important to try and anticipate as many potentially stressful situations as possible and help prepare the student to deal with them (Spinelli, 2004).

Finally, before returning to school, a student should be assessed to determine whether any accommodations or modifications to the curriculum will be necessary. If the student's educational performance is negatively impacted as a result of the cancer, then the student would be eligible for certain special education services under the Individuals With Disabilities Education Act (IDEA).

An Individualized Education Plan (IEP) can be developed to specify what special education services the student will receive. If the cancer does not negatively affect the student's educational performance, then he or she would not qualify for special education services under IDEA, but he or she would still be protected under section 504 of the Rehabilitation Act of 1973 and the American Disabilities Act (ADA) (Prevatt & colleagues, 1999).

Cancer was once considered an automatic death sentence for a child, but advances in cancer treatments now mean the majority of children and adolescents will survive. Because a majority of children with cancer return to school, it is important to assess their needs and concerns and try to plan ways to make the transition back to school as smooth as possible.

—*Megan E. Luhr*

REFERENCES AND FURTHER READING

American Cancer Society. (2004). *Children and cancer: Information and resources.* Retrieved September 7, 2004, from http://www.cancer.org/docroot/CRI/CRI_2_6x_Children_and_Cancer.asp

Armstrong, F. D., Blumberg, M. J., & Toledano, S. R. (1999). Neurobehavioral issues in childhood cancer. *The School Psychology Review, 28*(2), 194–203.

Prevatt, F. F., Heffer, R. W., & Lowe, P. A. (2000). A review of school reintegration programs for children with cancer. *Journal of School Psychology, 38,* 447–467.

Sexson, S., & Madan-Swain, A. (1995). The chronically ill child in the school. *School Psychology Quarterly, 10,* 359–368.

Spinelli, C. G. (2004). Dealing with cancer in the classroom. The teacher's role and responsibilities. *Teaching Exceptional Children, 36*(4), 14–21.

CAREER ASSESSMENT

Career assessment involves systematic appraisal for the purpose of assisting an individual in the career exploration, career development, or decision-making process. It may include, but is not limited to, assessing an individual's academic and work history, interests, skills, learning styles, personality, needs, and self-efficacy beliefs. Career assessment may be conducted in a formal manner using norm-referenced paper-and-pencil inventories; or it may be conducted less formally using counseling interview techniques, card-sort procedures, or behavioral observation. Optimally, career assessment is just one component of a larger and more comprehensive career guidance process that includes individual or group career guidance and the exploration of career and/or educational information.

THE GOALS OF CAREER ASSESSMENT

In educational settings, career assessment is designed to help students and their parents understand career preferences and skills and to assist them in educational and career planning and in goal setting. Developmentally appropriate career assessment activities in the schools vary depending upon the needs of the individual or the school system; hence, the uses of these assessments vary. For example, some assessment instruments are group administered and interpreted in a classroom setting. One purpose of these assessments is to promote career exploration through self-awareness. In contrast, individualized career assessment might be used to aid in an educational transition or for the purposes of developing an Individualized Education Plan (IEP) for a student with a disability.

Career assessment in the schools is based on the career development tasks that are considered appropriate for a particular age group or grade level. In elementary school, for example, students begin to articulate their preferences and skills, develop a positive attitude toward work, and learn about the relationships between school and work. Middle school students may learn how to use systems for classifying occupations and develop an understanding of their interests and skills. At the high school level, part-time employment opportunities may provide students with an understanding of the role that work values play in career satisfaction. High school students are also more likely to develop a more realistic understanding of their potential in various fields. As they approach graduation, these students face important career decisions and come to assume more responsibility for their career development.

Although career assessment and counseling have historically targeted students in high school and college, a number of authors address the importance of helping elementary and middle school students develop a foundation for later career development tasks (Herring, 1998).

METHODS OF CAREER ASSESSMENT

Herring (1998) notes that career guidance programs in schools often include processes such as classroom instruction, counseling, paper-and-pencil career assessment, career information, placement, consultation, and referral. Counselors promoting the career development of school-aged children should be trained to administer and interpret career assessment instruments and should have training in career development theory and assessment. Further, they should be aware of the potential cultural, gender, and socioeconomic influences that can impact a student's assessment performance.

As an alternative to standardized paper-and-pencil instruments, career assessment is increasingly offered on the computer and the Internet in the form of comprehensive computer-assisted career guidance programs that provide students with formal career assessment, educational and occupational information, job search strategies, and educational planning opportunities. Two popular software or Internet programs are ACT's DISCOVER and Educational Testing Service's (ETS) SIGI PLUS. Finally, many counselors use less formal practices such as behavioral observations, academic and work histories, classroom performance, or in-session exercises to collect information similar in nature to that elicited by standardized assessment.

CAREER ASSESSMENT INSTRUMENTS

Although formal career assessment is not common in elementary schools, assessments such as the Wide Range Interest–Opinion Test or the Career Awareness Inventory are occasionally used at the elementary level to help to foster students' self-awareness and promote broad occupational considerations. Informal assessment and experiential activities that promote self-efficacy beliefs, combat gender-role stereotyping, and encourage understanding of the relations between school and work are appropriate for use with younger students.

The career development of middle school students is especially critical. Students at this age are able to more fully articulate personal characteristics such as interests, skills, and values. Not surprisingly, there are a large number of career assessment instruments available to help middle school students. Assessment systems such the Harrington-O'Shea Career Decision-Making System–Revised (CDM-R) provide middle school students with valuable information about their academic and career-related interests, abilities, and values. The CDM-R makes use of a well-established and empirically supported typology of career interests and abilities (Holland, 1997). Another commonly used instrument is the

Self-Directed Search Career Explorer. Computerized guidance programs such as ACT's DISCOVER for middle school students integrate formal career assessment with academic and career exploration activities.

High school is a time when most students grapple with educational and/or career decisions. Students in 8th through 10th grades may be asked to choose from among math or science electives—choices that may profoundly affect later career opportunities. Upperclassmen face decisions such as whether to pursue further education, enter the workforce, or enlist in the armed services. Standardized instruments such as the Kuder Career Search, the Strong Interest Inventory, and the Campbell Interest and Skills Survey are used to assess students' interests and self-efficacy beliefs. These measures also provide students with a profile of how their personal characteristics match those of individuals employed in a range of occupations. Measures such as the Minnesota Importance Questionnaire are available to assess a student's pattern of work-related needs and values. Students are often introduced to the role that personality characteristics play in making academic or career decisions through the use of instruments such as the Myers-Briggs Type Indicator (MBTI).

As the world of work becomes more complex, individuals will require more comprehensive knowledge of their career options and how to match their personal characteristics to the needs of work environments. Students who are aware of their interests, work values, skills, and other personal characteristics are better prepared to critically evaluate their career alternatives. Career assessment can play an important role in helping students to make more informed and sound career decisions.

—*Paul A. Gore, Jr., and A. J. Metz*

See also Behavioral Assessment; Bias (Testing); Criterion-Referenced Assessment; Performance-Based Assessment; School Psychologist

REFERENCES AND FURTHER READING

Herring, R. (1998). *Career counseling in schools: Multicultural and developmental perspectives.* Alexandria, VA: American Counseling Association.

Holland, J. L. (1997). *Making vocational choices: A theory of vocational personalities and work environments* (3rd ed.). Odessa, FL: Psychological Assessment Resources.

CAREERS IN SCHOOL PSYCHOLOGY

Among the most important events in the history of school psychology is that early psychological practitioners chose to be full-time employees in public school settings. In addition to the many professional and political implications of that event, it also signaled the founding of a profession of psychologists whose principal identity would be the locus of their employment, elementary and secondary schools. Since the time the term *school psychologist* gained identity, the vast majority of persons trained to be school psychologists have held employment in school settings (Fagan & Wise, 2000). Currently, approximately 80% of practitioners work in public school settings, usually under school-year (9 or 10 months) contracts, and have a median salary of approximately $50,000. Starting salaries vary widely, but the range is probably from $25,000 to $55,000. School psychologists are spread across urban, suburban, and rural school districts, with most serving in urban and suburban settings. The field has attracted women throughout its history and women currently make up approximately 70% of practicing school psychologists. A comprehensive overview of demographics and future expectations appears in Reschly (2000) and Curtis and colleagues (2002).

In the school setting, school psychologists typically work in a ratio of one practitioner for every 1,800 to 2,000 school children. They spend at least half of their time in psychoeducational assessment activities, usually related to student eligibility for special education programs. This includes administering tests of ability, school achievement, personality and behavior, motor skills, and so forth. Approximately 20% of their time is spent in interventions such as counseling and behavior management programs with students individually or in groups. For example, the school psychologist might work with a group of students to help them to control their anger. Consultation work with parents and educators accounts for approximately another 20% of their time. In this role, the school psychologist might work with a teacher to develop methods that will result in improved classroom behavior. The remainder of their time is devoted to administrative, in-service education, and research activities. Here, school psychologists might maintain case study records, speak to groups of parents about school readiness, or evaluate a new reading program. More comprehensive descriptions of services appear in Fagan & Wise (2000).

Although the vast majority of school psychologists work in public school districts, 15% to 20% work in other settings. These include private schools, correctional schools, preschools, and postsecondary schools such as colleges and universities. Some work in medical settings, mental health centers, and in private practice independently or in collaboration with other health service providers (e.g., clinical and counseling psychologists, social workers, and physicians). Only 1% to 2% work full time in private practice. Approximately 6% to 7% work as faculty in institutions of higher education, usually associated with training programs for school psychologists.

Students are trained in graduate programs specifically to prepare for being school psychologists, which are accredited by state education agencies, the American Psychological Association (APA), and the National Council for the Accreditation of Teacher Education (NCATE). The National Association of School Psychologists (NASP) accredits graduate programs according to its own training guidelines through a collaborative relationship with NCATE. Training is provided at the doctoral and nondoctoral levels. Doctoral programs culminate in a Doctor of Philosophy (PhD), Doctor of Education (EdD), or Doctor of Psychology (PsyD) degree. Nondoctoral programs culminate in a Master of Arts (MA), Master of Science (MS), Master of Education (MEd), or Educational Specialist (EdS) degree. Master's degrees are usually 32 to 36 semester hours beyond the bachelor's degree, the EdS degree is usually at least 30 semester hours beyond the master's degree, and doctoral degrees are typically a total of 90 to 125 graduate semester hours beyond the bachelor's degree. Although most training programs and practitioners are geared to comprehensive functioning as a general practitioner of school psychology, there is a cluster of officially recognized subspecializations along the lines of practice (e.g., early childhood, neuropsychology) and setting (e.g., rural, urban). Subspecializations are typically available only in doctoral programs. Training program directories are available from the APA and the NASP.

Following training, school psychologists must receive credentials to practice in their state. In most states, school psychologists receive a credential from the State Department of Education to practice in the

school districts and facilities under its jurisdiction. This credential requires a master's or higher degree, or an educational specialist degree level of training. To obtain a credential for nonschool practice, most states require a doctoral degree, and other experiences to obtain a credential from the state board of examiners in psychology. Several states have nonschool practice credentials for nondoctoral-level persons. Directories of credentialing requirements are available from the NASP and the Association of State and Provincial Psychology Boards.

Two sources for exploring the array of practice in nonschool settings are Pfeiffer and Dean (1988) and a special issue of the *School Psychology Review* (1988, Volume 17, No. 3). The American Psychological Association publishes a booklet on careers, accompanied by a videotape, entitled *Psychology: Careers for the Twenty-First Century* (1996), which is for high school and early college-age groups.

Perhaps, with the exception of the Great Depression, there has never been a period when the supply of school psychologists nationwide was sufficient to meet the demand for services. The shortage of personnel has been a subject of considerable concern for the past decade. Since the enactment of federal legislation in the early 1970s, local school districts have been required to have psychological services available to students, and psychological evaluations have been a necessary part of determining eligibility for special education services. Most school districts have responded to these mandates by employing full-time practitioners who are graduates of recognized school psychology training programs. The field has grown from 5,000 members in 1970 to 25,000 at present. The employment outlook for the future appears to be strong and is reflected in a recent *U.S. News and World Report* discussion of careers (Mulrine, 2002).

—*Thomas K. Fagan*

See also American Psychological Association; Division of School Psychology (Division 16); Licensing and Certification in School Psychology; National Association of School Psychologists; School Psychologist

REFERENCES AND FURTHER READING

American Psychological Association. (1996). *Psychology: Careers for the twenty-first century,* Washington, DC: Author.

Curtis, M. J., Grier, J. E. C., Abshier, D. W., Sutton, N. T., & Hunley, S. (2002, June). School psychology: Turning the corner into the twenty-first century. *Communique, 30*(8), 1, 5–6.

Fagan, T. K., & Wise, P. S. (2000). *School psychology: Past, present, and future.* Bethesda, MD: National Association of School Psychologists.

Mulrine, A. (2002, February 18). School psychologist: A balm for the blackboard jungle. *U.S. News and World Report,* 50.

Pfeiffer, S. I., & Dean, R. S. (1988). School psychology in evolution. *School Psychology Review, 17*(3), 388–390.

Reschly, D. J. (2000). The present and future status of school psychology in the United States. *School Psychology Review, 29*(4), 507–522.

CHARACTER EDUCATION.
See MEDIA AND CHILDREN; PARENTING

CEREBRAL PALSY

Cerebral palsy is a condition caused by injury to parts of the brain before, during, or after birth, which results in impaired muscle control and affects a person's ability to move and maintain balance and posture. Cerebral palsy is considered to be a static disorder that will not get progressively worse as time goes on; it is characterized by damage to the brain during early periods of development, usually up to six years of age.

Individuals with cerebral palsy may have varying difficulties with movement, muscle tone, and posture. This condition affects muscle movement in four distinct patterns:

1. Spastic (high tone)—This, the most common type, is present in approximately 70% to 80% of individuals with cerebral palsy (Turnbull & colleagues, 2002). It is characterized by muscle tightness, or hypertonia, which results in stiff or restricted movements.

2. Athetoid (low tone)—This type includes abrupt, involuntary movements of the head, neck, face, and extremities, resulting in difficulties with controlling movement and maintaining posture.

3. Ataxic—This is characterized by unsteadiness, lack of coordination and balance, and difficulties with standing and walking.

4. Mixed—This form of cerebral palsy is a combination of high (spastic) and low (athetoid) muscle tone, resulting in stiff and involuntary movements from muscles that are either too tight or too loose. This type of cerebral palsy is often the result of injury to more than one area of the brain, and commonly leads to quadriplegia.

Cerebral palsy is also classified by the parts of body that are affected, including monoplegia (one limb), paraplegia (legs only), hemiplegia (one half of the body), triplegia (three limbs), quadriplegia (all four limbs), diplegia (more affected in the legs than the arms), and double hemiplegia (arms more involved than the legs).

Approximately 500,000 people in the United States have some form of cerebral palsy. In addition, 8,000 infants and 1,500 preschoolers are diagnosed with this condition each year (National Dissemination Center for Children with Disabilities [NICHCY], 2003). A number of prenatal factors may contribute to the occurrence of cerebral palsy, including genetic disorders, intrauterine infections, exposure to toxins, brain malformations, birth complications, and abnormal blood flow to the brain (Myers & Shapiro, 1999). Numerous perinatal (during or shortly after birth) factors such as lack of oxygen, brain hemorrhage, or jaundice may also cause cerebral palsy. In addition, factors such as traumatic brain injury, brain infection, and cardiac arrest that occur after birth may contribute to its occurrence. However, both perinatal and postnatal causes are rare, occurring in less than 10% of cases.

Children with cerebral palsy may face many challenges in school. Impairments in muscle movement, posture, and balance may require the use of assistive devices such as wheelchairs, scooters, or braces. In addition, language and articulation difficulties may result from limited muscle movement around the mouth and throat. Communication devices such as communication boards, photograph albums, or computerized talkers can help children with cerebral palsy to "talk" with others in the hopes of gaining the social, emotional, and academic benefits that often accompany communication. Because the disease is a result of injury to the brain, mental retardation often occurs. Approximately 66% of people with cerebral palsy have some degree of mental retardation. This has significant impacts on a child's ability to function in daily life and to learn in the academic environment.

By law, schools are required to provide services to children with disabilities in order to meet their needs and allow them to benefit from their educational experience. Up to the age of three years, these services are provided through an early intervention program and are laid out in an Individualized Family Services Plan (IFSP). An Individualized Education Program (IEP) is often developed for school-age children with disabilities in order to meet their needs in the classroom. Special education and related services are typically provided to children with cerebral palsy and may include components such as physical therapy, occupational therapy, and speech–language pathology services. It is very important to build on the strengths of individuals with cerebral palsy. Despite significant physical and mental challenges, these individuals have the potential to learn and become enabled, functioning adults if provided services and the opportunity to do so.

—Abigeal Heeter

REFERENCES AND FURTHER READING

Myers, S., & Shapiro, B. (1999). Origins and causes of cerebral palsy: Symptoms and diagnosis. *The Exceptional Parent, 29*(4), 28–31.

National Dissemination Center for Children with Disabilities (NICHCY). (2003). *NICHCY disability fact sheet: Cerebral palsy.* Retrieved October 23, 2003, from http://www.nichcy.org/pubs/factshe/fs2.pdf

Turnbull, R., Turnbull, A., Shank, M., Smith, S., & Leal, D. (2002). Physical disabilities. In A. C. Davis, G. Marsella, & S. Langner (Eds.), *Exceptional lives: Special education in today's schools* (pp. 406–437). Upper Saddle River, NJ: Person Education.

CHARTER SCHOOLS

Charter schools are independent public schools. As opposed to traditional public schools, which are operated by a local school district with oversight from the state education agency, charter schools are created and supervised by a group of founders. Founders can include parents, community leaders, and/or for-profit managers. The school's charter documents how the school will be operated; it includes the school's mission, philosophy, program and curriculum goals, assessment methods, and standards of performance.

The *charter* is provided to the founders according to state-specified guidelines. The state may authorize universities, local school boards, or a chartering board to issue charters. Charter schools typically receive funds in the same manner as traditional public schools, although they frequently have broader flexibility in overall management. For example, states often allow charter schools independence in matters related to budgetary and fiscal management, curriculum development and implementation, teacher credentialing and staffing, and measurement of outcomes. Standards for academic performance are usually negotiated and included in the charter before the school's opening.

Like traditional public schools, charter schools are held accountable for achieving performance standards; however, charter schools are often exempt from many of the restrictions that impact traditional public schools. Charter schools generally have an overall smaller census and class size than their public counterparts, and may even have nontraditional grade arrangements. The two most common characteristics shared by all charter schools are that they are free from significant state oversight and they have a different means of resolving administrative appeals. The methods for evaluating the effectiveness of charter schools vary across states.

There are two basic types of charter schools—conversion schools and newly created schools. Conversion schools are those that once were public or private schools but have been converted to charter schools. Newly created schools are developed in facilities that had no previous educational history.

Charter schools have grown rapidly since they were first established in 1992. By February 2004, there were approximately 3,000 charter schools in 40 states and the District of Columbia; however, most of the nation's current charter schools are concentrated in five states—California (500 schools), Arizona (491), Florida (258), Texas (241), and Michigan (210)—with no other state having more than 150 schools. Ten states do not have any charter schools (Alabama, Kentucky, Maine, Montana, Nebraska, North Dakota, South Dakota, Vermont, Virginia, Washington, and West Virginia).

Even with these considerable numbers, only approximately 1% of all U.S. school children attend a charter school. It appears likely that charter schools will continue to grow in number and variety in the coming years, increasingly making this an option for parents and families of school-aged children.

STUDENTS IN CHARTER SCHOOLS

Like all publicly funded schools, charter schools must remain nondiscriminatory in their admission practices. The schools cannot exclude specific populations of students, nor can they charge tuition. Because many charter schools have a higher demand for admission than their capacity, they may admit students on a first-come, first-accepted basis, or use a lottery system. Charter schools typically have no requirements for admission beyond those that are present in traditional public schools (e.g., proof of the student's age, immunization record, and emergency contact data).

Although charter schools are open to all students, their founders often target a population of students they would like to serve. This frequently includes students who have been underserved by traditional schools such as students with poor academic performance; students from underprivileged families and/or communities; those with specific gifts, talents, or interests, or students with special educational needs. Other charter schools attempt to recruit students who are at risk for school failure and/or have histories of serious behavioral problems. In some cases, charter schools may be composed largely of students with a common heritage (e.g., a charter school with an Afro-centric curriculum).

CHALLENGES FOR CHARTER SCHOOLS

Many research studies of charter schools report significant academic improvement for enrolled students, regardless of race, gender, age, income level, or special needs. However, the apparent success in delivering educational services via an alternative model has not been without substantial obstacles.

Founders often have difficulty securing adequate facilities for charter schools. In many instances, previously unused school buildings may be rented from a traditional school district or other educational agency. Because of their prior vacancy, many of these sites require substantial renovations prior to occupancy. It can be challenging to reopen such buildings, as their closure may often be caused by health code violations, problems with accessibility for students with disabilities, and even concerns about safety and security that are attributable to building characteristics, the surrounding community, or both.

Charter schools may also have difficulty recruiting and retaining teachers and other professional staff. Because they are typically much smaller than the traditional school districts in their communities, charter schools often have far less financial resources from which to compensate staff members. Many charter schools do not offer employment inducements that are present in traditional school districts (e.g., tenure, seniority status).

Although they have been relatively independent of micromanagement by governmental entities, charter schools (like all public schools that receive federal funding) are subject to the requirements of the No Child Left Behind Act of 2001 (NCLB). This act contains a number of mandates that may be particularly challenging for charter schools to meet. For example, the Act requires that all teachers in public schools meet specific credentialing standards and be qualified in the specific subject they teach by the 2005–2006 school year. This mandate, which may appear valid and reasonable to many in education, has not been readily accomplished in many charter schools. NCLB provisions ultimately may eliminate many of the disparities between traditional public schools and charter schools because of the specific nature of new requirements (e.g., teacher qualifications, accountability for student outcomes).

Point Versus Counterpoint: Charter Schools

The case for:

Because student enrollment in charter schools typically is smaller (approximately 250 students in a school) than traditional public schools, there is greater opportunity for creative and innovative approaches with teaching strategies, grade placements, curriculum initiatives, and staffing patterns. Classroom enrollment also tends to be smaller in charter schools, and students can receive more individualized instruction and attention in these settings.

(Continued)

(Continued)

Charter schools often endorse a particular educational philosophy that can be attractive in recruiting students and staff. Different educational models can be promoted. On-site governance of the school reduces the micromanaging and regulation of the school by external forces that are removed from the daily operation of the institution. Charter schools often are led by business-minded individuals with experience in supervising organizations that use financial and human resources efficiently.

Supporters note the benefits of parents and families having a democratic choice of schools and healthy educational competition within communities. Indeed, charter school advocates maintain that their schools not only benefit their own enrollees, but also the students in traditional public schools (whose schools are thought to be enhanced by competition).

The case against:

Critics of the charter movement argue that such schools lack the safeguards for accountability found in traditional public schools. As a direct result, detractors maintain, charter schools are not competing on a "level playing field." Because of their less-stringent oversight, some charter schools may fall short of meeting broader educational standards of student performance.

Teacher quality in charter schools is another shortcoming. Many charter schools are exempt from state requirements for licensing teachers and, as a result, some charter schools employ teachers and other staff who have little or no training or credentials in the subjects they teach. Charter schools often proclaim pride in their teachers' independence from burdensome external regulation from governmental agencies, but their opponents question the quality of an education provided by staff with limited training in teaching content or methodology. For example, in some chartered religious schools, the simple affirmation of certain religious beliefs is sufficient to be considered a qualified teacher.

In a climate of ongoing efforts at public school reforms nationwide, charter school detractors voice serious concerns about these schools redirecting funds away from traditional public schools at a time when these resources are already stretched.

—*Caven S. Mcloughlin and Robert J. Kubick Jr.*

See also Montessori Schools; School Reform; U.S. Department of Education

REFERENCES AND FURTHER READING

Mcloughlin, C. S., & Chambers, H. (2004). A parent's guide to home schooling. In A. Canter, S. Carroll, L. Paige & I. Romero (Eds.), *Helping children at home and school* (2nd ed.). Bethesda, MD: National Association of School Psychologists.

Mcloughlin, C. S., Lewis, M., & Hutchinson, C. (2002). Charter schools, school psychologists, and the potential for best practice implementation. In A. Thomas & J. Grimes (Eds.), *Best practices in school psychology* (4th ed.). Washington, DC: National Association of School Psychologists.

CHEATING

In the schools, cheating can be defined as any means by which a student breaks rules in order to gain an unfair advantage over classmates on an assignment or exam. The literature has demonstrated that cheating is widespread and increasing in its prevalence (Schab, 1991). For example, Schab found a large increase of endorsements on a measure of cheating given over three decades that included questions such as, "Have you used a cheat sheet on a test?" Among other research, such findings suggest that cheating has become an accepted behavior among students.

Within a developmental framework, cheating behavior can be understood through Lawrence Kohlberg's model of moral reasoning (Powers & Powers, 1997). According to this model, motivation for learning changes from obeying authority in early childhood to valuing knowledge in early adulthood. Youths at higher levels of moral reasoning are less likely to report that they would cheat. However, research demonstrates that youths at all ages are equally likely to engage in cheating behavior. A possible explanation is that at middle stages of moral reasoning, adolescents may more easily rationalize cheating.

Students who report cheating express being more extrinsically driven and less intrinsically motivated than those who report not cheating (Anderman & colleagues, 1998). Thus, environmental factors such as teacher monitoring may better prevent cheating behavior than targeting internal factors such as moral reasoning. In some cases, children may not understand what defines cheating. For example, expectations for work to be completed independently may increase from grade to grade (Powers & Powers, 1997). Similarly, students may have different perceptions than teachers as to what is cheating. For example, one study found that students were unclear that providing test answers to another student constitutes cheating (Evans & Craig, 1990). In these cases, direct teaching of what constitutes cheating is an appropriate intervention.

Research has found that students are most likely to cheat when rewards are high and consequences low (Powers & Powers, 1997). Teaching styles that promote cheating include covering too much material on a single examination, grading on a curve, and using few tests to determine a final grade. In one study, students who reported cheating in school stated they received extrinsic rewards for their performance (e.g., good grades, less homework) (Anderman and colleagues, 1998). Additionally, the quality of the teacher–student relationship and the level of respect for the teacher have been found to be negatively associated with the likelihood of cheating (Murdock & colleagues, 2001).

Motivation research suggests that classrooms that emphasize task mastery over grades are less likely to produce cheating behavior (Anderman and colleagues, 1998). A key to decreasing cheating behaviors is to indoctrinate students with the belief that learning, rather than good grades, is necessary for success (Schab, 1991). Teachers and administrators must model honest behaviors. In addition, teachers can attend to students' sense of moral and civic duties. Instilling an honor system rather than increasing teacher monitoring allows students to take ownership of their behavior rather than feel distrusted. Extrinsic strategies, such as test supervision, widely spaced seating, and clear consequences are important prevention techniques. However, punishments should not be made so severe as to deter students from reporting their peers or admitting to their own cheating (Powers & Powers, 1997). Maintaining flexibility in determining consequences in a democratic approach may help students take responsibility for not cheating (Powers & Powers).

School psychologists should examine motivations for cheating, considering both individual and environmental variables. For example, children with learning difficulties may cheat in order to keep up with the fast pace of the class (Powers & Powers, 1997). When parental pressure to excel contributes to cheating, family interventions are warranted. When students cheat to assuage peer pressure, social skills training is beneficial. Understanding a student's motivation for cheating provides information necessary to form an appropriate intervention strategy.

—*Jill D. Sharkey and Stacy L. O'Farrell*

See also Grades; Peer Pressure; Study Skills

REFERENCES AND FURTHER READING

Anderman, E. M., Griesinger, T., & Westerfield, G. (1998). Motivation and cheating during early adolescence. *Journal of Educational Psychology, 90*(1), 84–93.

Evans, E. D., & Craig, D. (1990). Teacher and student perceptions of academic cheating in middle and senior high schools. *Journal of Educational Research, 84*, 44–52.

Murdock, T. B., Hale, N. M.,& Weber, M. J. (2001). Predictors of cheating among early adolescents: Academic and social motivations. *Contemporary Educational Psychology, 26*, 96-115.

Powers, F. C., & Powers, A. M. R. (1997). Cheating. In G. G. Bear, K. M. Minke, & A. Thomas (Eds.), *Children's needs II: Development, problems, and alternatives.* Bethesda, MD: National Association of School Psychologists.

Schab, F. (1991). Schooling without learning: Thirty years of cheating in high school. *Adolescence, 26*(104), 839–847.

CLASS SIZE

Class size is a different concept than teacher–pupil ratio (i.e., the ratio of the number of students per teacher); it is defined by the number of students who are educated in a single classroom. Although there is no research that suggests an optimum class size, there is research that identifies potential benefits for classes of fewer than 20 children in kindergarten through third grade.

In the 1980s and 1990s, several states initiated Class Size Reduction (CSR) programs, which produced a variety of program evaluation data (e.g.,

Project STAR/Tennessee; Project Sage/Wisconsin; the California CSR program; Project Prime Time/Indiana; Burke County Schools/North Carolina). Typically, CSR occurred in the primary grades (K–3). Overall, the information gained from these projects suggests that class size of fewer than 20 (i.e., 13 to 17) students is associated with modest achievement advantages as measured by standardized achievement tests when compared with students educated in classrooms with more than 20 students. These advantages were most pronounced for low-income and minority children. The effect appeared to be accumulative; the achievement advantage was greater for students who spent more years with small class sizes when compared to students who spent fewer years in such classrooms. There may also be long-term effects of small classes related to higher educational aspirations, higher class rank, fewer classroom disruptions, fewer students retained, and a reduced dropout rate in high school.

The results of the California CSR project suggest that class size alone does not account for the successes of these classes. Initial implementation of CSR in California was hindered by a lack of qualified teachers and building space for additional classrooms. As a result, CSR in California did not lead to the same level of improved achievement as was observed in other CSR projects. It is clear that class size alone does not account for the achievement gains that have been attributed to CSR.

When compared to teachers who have larger classes, teachers of small classes spend more time in direct instruction and less time on classroom management. In addition, teachers tend to use more hands-on instruction, give more feedback, and interact more with individual students. In response, students in small classes appear to be more academically engaged and participate at higher levels. These elements also improve learning in a variety of instructional settings. In addition to these instructional variables, reduced class size may facilitate the development of a learning community within the classroom. Small class size may also increase student perceptions of responsibility for learning.

There are costs associated with the development and maintenance of classes with fewer students. First, there may be additional costs for building construction or renovation that may be necessary to provide a physical plant that will support additional classrooms. In addition, there is the cost associated with hiring additional teachers and training teachers in instructional practices best suited for smaller classes. One approach that has been used to offset these additional expenses has been to replace teacher aides with new teachers given that teachers in smaller classes require less paraprofessional assistance. Another method for controlling costs might be to target schools that might benefit most from small class sizes (e.g., schools with a high number of low socioeconomic status [SES] students).

While the modest benefits of small classes have been consistently demonstrated across a variety of settings, there is still much about class size that is unknown. Projects implementing CSR have generally maintained class sizes of between 13 and 17 students. Unfortunately, there are no data to support the ultimate value of this targeted number. There is no research on the differential effectiveness of class sizes of 10, 15, or 20 students. Also, the value of small class size beyond the primary grades has not been investigated. Finally, the instructional practices that lead to gains in achievement associated with CSR need further study.

—*Mark Fugate*

See also Academic Achievement; School Reform

REFERENCES AND FURTHER READING

Finn, J. D. (2002). Small classes in American schools: Research, practice, and politics. *Phi Delta Kappan, 83,* 551–560.

Nye, B., Hedges, L. V., & Konstantopoulos, S. (2002). Do low achieving students benefit more from small classes? Evidence from the Tennessee class size experiment. *Educational Evaluation and Policy Analysis, 24,* 201–217.

CLASSICAL CONDITIONING.

See BEHAVIOR; BEHAVIOR
ASSESSMENT; BEHAVIOR INTERVENTION;
CONDITIONING: CLASSICAL AND OPERANT

CLASSROOM CLIMATE

Classroom climate sometimes is referred to as the learning environment, as well as by terms such as atmosphere, ambience, ecology, and milieu. The impact of classroom climate on students and staff can be beneficial for or a barrier to learning.

DEFINITIONAL CONSIDERATIONS

Classroom climate is a perceived quality of the setting. It emerges in a somewhat fluid state from the complex transaction of many immediate environmental factors (e.g., physical, material, organizational, operational, and social variables). The climates of both the classroom and the school reflect the influence of a school's culture, which is a stable quality emerging from underlying, institutionalized values and belief systems, norms, ideologies, rituals, and traditions. And, of course, classroom climate and culture both are shaped by the school's surrounding and embedded political, social, cultural, and economic contexts (e.g., home, neighborhood, city, state, country).

Key concepts related to understanding classroom climate include:

- Social system organization
- Social attitudes
- Staff and student morale
- Power, control, guidance, support, and evaluation structures
- Curricular and instructional practices
- Communicated expectations
- Efficacy
- Accountability demands
- Cohesion
- Competition
- The "fit" between key learner and classroom variables
- System maintenance, growth, and change
- Orderliness
- Safety

Rudolph Moos (1979) groups such concepts into three dimensions for classifying human environments and has used them to develop measures of school and classroom climate. Moos's three dimensions are:

1. Relationship—the nature and intensity of personal relationships within the environment; the extent to which people are involved in the environment and support and help each other.

2. Personal development—basic directions along which personal growth and self-enhancement tend to occur.

3. System maintenance and change—the extent to which the environment is orderly, clear in expectations, maintains control, and is responsive to change.

The concept of classroom climate implies the intent to establish and maintain a positive context that facilitates classroom learning, but in practice, classroom climates range from hostile or toxic to welcoming and supportive and can fluctuate daily and over the school year. Moreover, because the concept is a social psychological construct, different observers may have different perceptions of the climate in a given classroom. Therefore, for purposes of his early research, Moos (1979) measured classroom environment in terms of the shared perceptions of those in the classroom. Prevailing approaches to measuring classroom climate use teacher and student perceptions; external observer's ratings and systematic coding; and/or naturalistic inquiry, ethnography, case study, and interpretative assessment techniques (Fraser, 1998; Freiberg, 1999).

IMPORTANCE OF CLASSROOM CLIMATE

Classroom climate is seen as a major determiner of classroom behavior and learning. Understanding how to establish and maintain a positive classroom climate is seen as basic to improving schools.

Research suggests significant relationships between classroom climate and such matters as student engagement, behavior, self-efficacy, achievement, social and emotional development, principal leadership style, stages of educational reform, teacher burnout, and overall quality of school life (Fraser, 1998; Freiberg, 1999). For example, studies report strong associations between achievement levels and classrooms that are perceived as having greater cohesion and goal direction and less disorganization and conflict. Research also suggests that the impact of classroom climate may be greater on students from low-income homes and groups that often are discriminated against.

Given the nature of classroom climate research, cause and effect interpretations remain speculative. The broader body of research on organizational climate does suggest that increasing demands for higher achievement test scores and reliance on social and tangible rewards to control behavior and motivate performance contribute to a classroom climate that is reactive and over-controlling (Mahony & Hextall, 2000).

PROMOTING A POSITIVE CLASSROOM CLIMATE

A proactive approach to developing a positive classroom climate requires careful attention to enhancing the quality of life in the classroom for students and staff; pursuing a curriculum that promotes not only academic, but also social and emotional learning; enabling teachers to be effective with a wide range of students; and fostering intrinsic motivation for classroom learning and teaching. With respect to all this, the literature advocates:

- Creating a welcoming, caring, and hopeful atmosphere
- Providing social support mechanisms for students and staff
- Providing an array of options for pursuing goals
- Encouraging meaningful participation by students and staff in decision making
- Transforming a big classroom into a set of smaller units that maximize intrinsic motivation for learning and are not based on ability or problem-oriented grouping
- Providing instruction and responding to problems in a personalized way
- Using a variety of strategies for preventing and addressing problems as soon as they arise
- Creating a healthy and attractive physical environment that is conducive to learning and teaching

ROLE OF THE SCHOOL PSYCHOLOGIST

Given the importance of classroom climate, the establishment and maintenance of a positive climate in every classroom must be a central focus of all school staff. School psychologists can play an increasing role by taking every available opportunity to work with teachers in their classrooms to increase teacher competence and provide collegial support. This means going beyond traditional consultation about classroom management strategies and how to work with individuals manifesting behavior, learning, and emotional problems. School psychologists can be invited to spend increasing amounts of time in classrooms teaming with teachers to enhance classroom climate.

In addition, school psychologists can work with other student support staff to improve classroom climate by establishing and maintaining a positive school climate that promotes well-being and addresses barriers to teaching and learning (Adelman & Taylor, 1997). A major focus of this should be on developing schoolwide programs that:

- Assist students and families as they negotiate the many school-related transitions
- Increase home involvement with schools
- Respond to, and, where feasible, prevent crises
- Increase community involvement and support
- Facilitate student and family access to specialized services when necessary

CONCLUSION

Classroom climate plays a major role in shaping the quality of school life and learning. Research indicates a range of strategies for enhancing a positive climate. School psychologists can play a major role in ensuring schools strive to create such a climate.

—*Howard S. Adelman and Linda Taylor*

See also Academic Achievement; Discipline; Motivation

REFERENCES AND FURTHER READING

Adelman, H. S., & Taylor, L. (1997). Addressing barriers to learning: Beyond school-linked services and full service schools. *American Journal of Orthopsychiatry, 67,* 408–421.

Fraser, B. J. (1998). Classroom environment instruments: Development, validity, and applications. *Learning Environments Research, 1,* 7–33.

Freiberg, H. J. (Ed.). (1999). *School climate: Measuring, improving, and sustaining healthy learning environments.* London: Falmer.

Mahony, P., & Hextall, I. (2000). *Reconstructing teaching: Standards, performance and accountability.* New York: Routledge Falmer.

Moos, R. H. (1979). *Evaluating educational environments.* San Francisco: Jossey-Bass.

CLASSROOM MANAGEMENT.

See CLASSROOM CLIMATE

CLASSROOM OBSERVATION

Classroom observation is a term used to describe when an individual (school psychologist, principal, counselor, etc.) sits in a room of students and a teacher and examines the behaviors of students or a student. There are several common observation approaches that are used in classrooms.

TYPES OF OBSERVATIONS AND RECORDING TECHNIQUES

One of the most common ways to observe and record a behavior is to use a frequency count, which is when the observer counts the number of times the behavior occurs over a period of time. Counting the number of times a student speaks without raising his or her hand is an example of a frequency count. Duration recording, another type of observation technique, is when the observer determines the amount of time an event lasts. For example, how long a student is out of his or her seat. When an observer wants to determine how long it takes for a student to complete a task that was assigned, he or she would use a latency recording technique. An example of this form of observation is documenting how long it takes a student to begin an assignment once it is given in class. In addition, there are occasions when the best way to evaluate behavior is to determine its level or intensity. For example, a student might consistently have a tantrum that lasts four to five minutes each day, but the level (or intensity) of the tantrum may vary. Intensity recording is the type of observation strategy used in this situation. The observer typically makes a judgment about the intensity of the behavior based on a scale that may range from 1 to 10 or 1 to 100, depending on the observer's choice. Therefore, after observing a behavior (in this example, a tantrum), the observer rates the intensity as a "2" if the level was low or an "8" if the level was high. These judgments are made by the observer and should be coupled with written examples of the behaviors in order to contextualize the rating score. It is important to note that intensity recording is usually completed by the teacher because most "strong" behaviors, such as a tantrum or a fight, are few in number, and, therefore, are difficult for an observer to notice in a single sitting. Thus, a school psychologist typically assists the teacher in creating the rating scale and the teacher completes the observation.

Anecdotal recording, one of the more common observation approaches used by teachers in schools, is a technique where the observer writes a description of the behaviors of interest. This scripted documentation is typically completed after observing a student misbehave. For example, if a student being observed walks across the classroom and knocks another student's books off of his or her desk, the observer would write this out in sentence form and document the time and date. As noted, anecdotal recording is commonly used by teachers who will document the behavior after it has occurred as part of their daily activities.

A-B-C observation (also known as antecedent-behavior-consequence observation) is also a popular approach to use when viewing student behavior. The observer typically uses a sheet of paper where lines are drawn to separate the paper into three equal columns. The left column is for the antecedents, the middle is for behavior, and the right is for consequences. The observer watches the target student, documents behaviors of interest (usually a misbehavior), and then documents what happens right before the behavior occurs (antecedent) and what happens right after the behavior occurs (consequence). For example, an observer in a fourth-grade classroom noticed when the teacher announced it was time for the students to put their books away and sit quietly, a student responded, "Great! It's time for lunch!" which was followed by laughter from other students. Using the A-B-C observation strategy, the teacher's comments would be described as the antecedent (A), the student statement, "Great! It's time for lunch!" is the behavior (B), and the student laughter is the consequence of the statement (C). Continuing with this scenario, the teacher may respond to the "Great! It's time for lunch" comment by saying, "Tommy! Don't talk out in class!" which is followed by Tommy responding, "It wasn't me!" Thus, the teacher's comment would be both the consequence (C), because it followed the behavior and the antecedent (A) for the next student statement (It wasn't me), which is the next behavior (B). The A-B-C approach is a preferable strategy to use when attempting to find a pattern of behavior that occurs in relation to either an antecedent or a consequence.

Momentary time sampling (MTS) is an approach to use when the behavior occurs at a high rate. Instead of counting the number of times a behavior occurs (frequency count), the observer notes if the behavior occurs during a specific moment in time. Typically the MTS is set up for the observer to watch the target student every 30th or 60th second and to document whether the student displayed the target behavior during that moment in time. For example, if a student was reported to talk a lot in class, the observer, using the 30-second MTS, would watch the target student on every 30th second and report (usually with a mark of "O" for on-task–not talking, or "X" for off-task–talking) whether the student was talking. Note that with MTS, the observer does not mark that the behavior occurred during the 30 seconds, just on the 30th second (or at that *moment* in time). The observer would continue to observe every 30th second for a set amount of time.

While this approach might seem unlikely to capture the behavior, MTS is a commonly used strategy when the behavior is occurring at a high rate because it offers several advantages over other approaches. First, it allows the observer to note other behaviors in the classroom because the observer focuses on the target behavior for only 2 seconds out of each minute (the 30th and 60th seconds). Second, this approach allows the observer to take notes—anecdotal recording—on classroom processes such as teacher–student interactions and/or student–student interactions. Another advantage of MTS is that it allows the observer to watch a comparison student, which is another student in the classroom that is typically well-behaved. This type of observation is called a "yoked observation" because two students are observed. This comparison may be important when reporting the results to a school preintervention team or parent, because it communicates that the target student's behavior is very different from other students in the classroom. The comparison student is observed at the moment right after the target student. In other words, the comparison student would be observed on the 31st, 61st, 91st, and so forth seconds (while observing the target student on the 30th, 60th, 90th, etc. seconds).

The data gathered from the MTS should be presented as percentages of time observed. This is accomplished by taking the total number of on-task moments and dividing it by the total number of moments observed. For example, if a student was on task 10 out of the 20 times observed, the student was on task 50% of the time observed. This is another advantage of the MTS approach in that it provides *user-friendly* data to discuss with teachers and parents. Extending this approach further, it is easy for parents and teachers to notice the differences between the target and comparison student by presenting results in percentage form. In other words, it may be important in a parent meeting to report the fact that their child was on task 30% of the time observed, while the comparison student was on task 85% of the time observed. By presenting the target and comparison data in percentage form, it is easier for parents and teachers to understand how the target behavior is viewed in class. It is very important to note that the MTS approach to observation should be used only when the target behavior occurs at a very high rate, because one might miss the behavior otherwise.

WHY OBSERVE STUDENTS IN THE CLASSROOM?

Classroom observations are done for a variety of reasons. The most common reason is when a student is disrupting the classroom and documentation of the problem behavior is needed. Part of the assessment process of students who are being evaluated for special education services includes observations. If the problem is thought to be a result of a learning disability (LD), a school psychologist would observe the student in the classroom in an attempt to monitor the student's approach to learning tasks, level of frustration with tasks, and general behavior. For students who are suspected of having an emotional or behavioral problem, the observer would look for examples of inappropriate behavior with peers and/or teachers. Classroom observations are also done as a part of a consultation program with a teacher. Through consultation between a school psychologist and teacher, it might be important to observe general classroom behaviors to determine key interactions that might be leading to management problems for the teacher. While not observing any student specifically, this observation may focus on classwide behaviors and teacher–student interactions.

An increasingly popular reason to observe students in a classroom is as part of an attention deficit hyperactivity disorder (ADHD) assessment, where the observer (often the school psychologist) monitors student behavior including time-on-task, impulsive actions (such as blurting out answers without raising one's hand or without teacher request), and interpersonal skills. Observations of this type complement other sources of information gathered in the ADHD assessment process. Additionally, when a student is diagnosed with ADHD, an intervention program is usually created (either medical, behavioral, or a combination of both), and classroom observations should be completed to monitor the student's behavior during the program to determine its effectiveness. This information is especially valuable when there is prediagnosis observation data—the student's behavior before and after the intervention can be compared to see if there is any change. An applied behavior analysis (ABA) uses classroom observations of student behavior before, during, and after treatment. In this way, if there are changes in observed behaviors, they can be attributed to the treatment.

—Eric Robinson

See also Applied Behavior Analysis; Behavioral Assessment; Time on Task

CLASSWIDE PEER TUTORING

Classwide Peer Tutoring (CWPT) is an instructional strategy focused on increasing active responding, improving academic achievement, and enhancing interpersonal relationships in the classroom. Research suggests that CWPT is an effective form of tutoring, especially with diverse populations, including students who have learning difficulties (i.e., learning disabilities, mental retardation), have limited English proficiency, or are economically disadvantaged. The core components of CWPT include content development, weekly assessments, training teachers and students, peer pairing (pairing of students), individual and group contingencies (rewards provided to an individual student or group of students for their work effort), and structured tutoring sessions.

In CWPT, the teacher organizes materials for classroom instruction into daily and weekly units based on the current curriculum. The amount of material assigned should be set so that each student can practice all of the material twice. While the focus of CWPT is on curriculum for the entire classroom, material can be individualized for students who have varying needs. Careful organization of materials ensures that a match between student ability and instructional material is created.

Teachers are trained to develop pretests and posttests to monitor the difficulty level of the materials, as well as student progress on those materials. Pretests can be used to confirm that the material is at an appropriate level of difficulty for next week's tutoring sessions. If the class mean or average is higher than 40% correct on the pretest, it is likely that the material is too easy, and the teacher is advised to replace the easy with more difficult material. The posttest data are used to assess the mastery of the material tutored that week; an 80% accuracy rate demonstrates mastery.

Because CWPT requires structure and careful selection of materials, teachers and students should be trained. Teachers can use a manual that describes CWPT procedures, such as how to pair students, how to organize materials, and how to use pretests and posttests to make decisions. Because students play more directive roles in CWPT, they are also trained in the procedures. This training typically consists of modeling by the teacher, student practice, and student feedback.

In CWPT, the teacher sorts class members into pairs, either randomly or by ability level, depending on the instructional goals and the subjects being tutored. Partner pairs should be changed weekly. In subjects like math, spelling, and vocabulary, random assignment is appropriate because answers are provided. In subjects where correct answers may not be available, pairing by ability should be used. In situations where students who have limited English proficiency are tutored, it may be useful to pair a student who is less proficient with a student who speaks the same language as the student, but who is more proficient in English. Students who participate in CWPT receive individual contingencies (i.e., students are rewarded for their own efforts) and group contingencies (i.e., rewards are given to groups for their performance). Each pair of students is randomly placed on one of two competing teams. This game-like format encourages students to perform roles appropriately and to work collaboratively with their partners to learn the material. The cooperative and competitive aspects of CWPT also help keep students motivated and on task. In carrying out their roles, students earn points for their team. Tutors earn points for keeping tutees engaged, correcting errors, and giving feedback and reinforcement. Tutees earn points for answering questions accurately and correcting wrong answers. Teams earning the most points are identified daily and weekly. The team that earns the most points at the end of the week is applauded and receives social reinforcement (e.g., praise) plus a certificate of achievement or a special privilege in the classroom. The team with fewer points is also applauded for their hard work and sportsmanship and receives encouragement for continued work effort.

CWPT lasts approximately 30 minutes for most subject areas, but 45 minutes should be allotted for reading lessons. CWPT is most effective if implemented four to five days per week for the specified period of time. These sessions should be structured according to the CWPT model. The following example illustrates the use of CWPT for spelling. At the beginning of spelling, the teacher briefly introduces the material and then announces new partner and team assignments for the week. Students transition into tutoring partnerships, and the teacher hands out tutoring materials. For the first 10 minutes, one partner (the tutor) presents tasks orally (there may be a visual presentation for some subjects). The tutee responds in written and oral forms. If the tutee is correct, the tutor awards two points. If the tutee makes an error, the tutor stops the tutee and states the correct response. The tutee then practices the correct response by writing and verbalizing it three times. For correcting the error, the tutee earns one point. The tutor also has opportunities to earn points for his or her team by demonstrating appropriate tutoring behaviors. These behaviors include presenting items clearly; awarding points based on correct responses; conducting the correction procedure precisely; and providing praise, feedback, and reinforcement to tutees. After 10 minutes, the partners switch roles, and the tutoring resumes for an additional 10 minutes. Throughout the tutoring session, the teacher monitors the tutoring process and awards points to tutors. After the 20 minutes expire, students total their daily points and record them on a chart. The team with the most points is applauded, and the classmates transition back to their desks.

RESEARCH ON CLASSWIDE PEER TUTORING

Since its development in the 1980s, many studies have examined the effects of CWPT in diverse classrooms. Many of these studies have found that CWPT is more effective than traditional teacher-directed instruction with Hispanic, bilingual students with academic delays. Similarly, CWPT is effective with students with mild disabilities at the high school level (Maheady & colleagues, 1988), students with

moderate and severe disabilities in middle school (McDonnell & colleagues, 2001), students with mild mental retardation in inclusive classroom settings (Mortweet & colleagues, 1999), and students with ADHD (DuPaul & colleagues, 1998). Kamps and colleagues (1994) also found that CWPT is effective with students with autism.

Research indicates that CWPT leads to improvement in spelling accuracy, completion of math problems (Harper and colleagues, 1990), and oral reading rates (Mathes and colleagues, 1994).

In a 12-year experimental longitudinal study comparing at-risk students receiving CWPT in grades 1 through 4 to at-risk and nonrisk students who did not receive CWPT, students who received the strategy performed significantly better on state standardized assessments. CWPT has also increased student engagement during instruction (Greenwood, 1991), increased student achievement (Greenwood, 1991; Greenwood & colleagues, 1989; Greenwood & colleagues, 1993), reduced the number of students needing special education services by 7th grade (Greenwood & colleagues, 1993), and reduced the number of dropouts by 12th grade.

CLASSWIDE PEER TUTORING VERSUS INDIVIDUAL PEER TUTORING

While CWPT and individualized tutoring are based on the same premise of using students as teachers, increasing academic engagement and active responding, and providing individualized instruction, tutoring programs vary on a number of factors. The first variable is the usefulness of peer tutors. In traditional peer tutoring programs, tutors are no longer needed once the tutee has mastered the material. Because CWPT focuses on changing academic content on a weekly basis, tutoring is an ongoing process where tutors can always help their tutee to understand new material.

Another difference between individual peer tutoring and CWPT involves the requirements for individuals to be tutors. Because material is designed to be at the instructional level for the entire class, all students are tutors and tutees in CWPT. This is not always the case in individual peer tutoring where one student is often seen as the expert and material covered is the material that one student is struggling with. One type of peer tutoring, cross-age tutoring, uses older students for tutoring, and tutoring may occur in the classroom or elsewhere. In CWPT, the tutor is always a classmate, the process occurs in the classroom, and the entire class is simultaneously engaged in the process.

In individual peer tutoring programs, training can range from no training to structured training in the presentation of materials; correction of errors; and provision of feedback, praise, and reinforcement. In CWPT, all students receive training and are given opportunities to practice and receive feedback on their skills.

The arrangement of tutoring groups also varies across tutoring programs. In CWPT, students are divided into dyads and these dyads are randomly assigned to a team. In individual peer tutoring, the group may contain one or two tutees and it is unlikely that teams are formed.

Although individual peer tutoring can be used for a variety of subjects, materials are often presented as flashcards or passages from the curricular reading book. In CWPT, information may be presented orally and/or visually and the tutee must respond verbally and in writing. In some individual peer tutoring programs, responding in two modes may not be required.

In CWPT, material difficulty and student progress is monitored and used to make decisions about instructional methods and the content to be used. While most tutoring programs promote the use of progress monitoring, the method for collecting the data may vary across tutoring programs.

—*Anna Struckman*

See also Classroom Climate; Peer Tutoring; Study Skills

REFERENCES AND FURTHER READING

DuPaul, G. J., Ervin, R. A., Hook, C. L., & McGoey, K. E. (1998). Peer tutoring for children with attention deficit hyperactivity disorder: Effects on classroom behavior and academic performance. *Journal of Applied Behavior Analysis, 31*(4), 579–592.

Greenwood, C. R. (1991). Longitudinal analysis of time, engagement, and achievement of at-risk versus no-risk students. *Exceptional Children, 57*(6), 521–535.

Greenwood, C. R., Delquadri, J., & Hall, R. V. (1989). Longitudinal effects of classwide peer tutoring. *Journal of Educational Psychology, 81*, 371–383.

Greenwood, C. R., Terry, B., Utley, C. A., Montagna, D., & Walker, D. (1993). Achievement, placement, and services: Middle school benefits of classwide peer tutoring used at the elementary school. *School Psychology Review, 22*(3), 497–516.

Harper, G. F., Mallette, B., Maheady, L., & Clifton, R. (1990). Responsive research: Applications of peer tutoring to arithmetic and spelling. *Direct Instruction News, 9*, 34–38.

Kamps, D., Barbetta, P. M., Leonard, B. R., & Delquadri, J. (1994). Classwide peer tutoring: An integration strategy to improve reading skills and promote peer interactions among students with autism and general education peers. *Journal of Applied Behavior Analysis, 27*, 49–61.

Maheady, L., Sacca, M. K., & Harper, G. F. (1988). Classwide peer tutoring with mildly handicapped high school students. *Exceptional Children, 55*(1), 52–60.

Mathes, P. G., Fuchs, D., Fuchs, L. S., Henley, A. M., & Sanders, M. (1994). Increasing strategic reading practice with Peabody classwide peer tutoring. *Learning Disabilities Research & Practice, 9*(1), 44–48.

McDonnell, J., Mathot-Buckner, C., Thorson, N., & Fister, S. (2001). Supporting the inclusion of students with moderate and severe disabilities in junior high school general education classes: The effects of classwide peer tutoring, multi-curriculum, and accommodations. *Education and Treatment of Children, 24*(2), 141–160.

Mortweet, S. L., Utley, C. A., Dawson, H., Delquadri, J. C., Reddy, S. S., Greenwood, C. R., et al. (1999). Classwide peer tutoring: Teaching students with mild mental retardation in inclusive classrooms. *Exceptional Children, 65*(4), 524–536.

COGNITIVE–BEHAVIORAL MODIFICATION

Cognitive–behavioral interventions integrate thoughts and behaviors into problem-assessment approaches, conceptualization, and intervention. The cognitive–behavioral approach views problems as resulting from both environmental and cognitive antecedents, and combines what has typically been called the behavioral or learning approach with the cognitive or semantic approach. Cognitions are seen as necessary concerns for treatment of mental or behavioral problems in children and adolescents. Cognitions are viewed as mediators of behavior and learning. Learning-based methods that have been used to alter overt behaviors are also used to alter cognitions. The cognitive–behavioral therapist works to alter the individual's internal dialogue and images and external context to produce behavior change.

In 1971, Meichenbaum and Goodman published the first study of the use of the cognitive–behavioral approach with children. They reported on the use of self-instructional training to alter problematic thoughts of behaviorally impulsive youngsters. The focus of this program was on teaching the children to generate guiding verbal self-commands that would bring their behavior under their own control.

The cognitive factors related to the problems of children and adolescents have been described as cognitive distortions and cognitive deficiencies. When cognitive distortion occurs, situations are misinterpreted; cognitive deficiency results in actions that have not been thought out. When using the cognitive–behavioral approach, the therapist guides the child in learning new cognitive, behavioral, interpersonal, and emotional skills. The child is helped to understand how thoughts affect emotions and behavior, and is helped to construct a coping template, which is a strategy and structure for thinking about interactions with others and life events.

TECHNIQUES

Several different cognitive and behavioral techniques are used in cognitive–behavioral interventions. According to Henin and colleagues (2002) these include:

- Education about emotions (affective education)
- Relaxation training
- Social problem solving
- Cognitive restructuring/attribution retraining
- Contingent reinforcement
- Modeling
- Role-play

The techniques used with a particular child or adolescent are linked to the specific problems of that individual. The child and the therapist are seen as collaborators in identifying the problem. The child is taught to identify situations and feelings that lead to problems and then to control his or her cognitive, physiological, and behavioral reactions to these situations.

Relaxation may be used as a means of helping children and adolescents control their physiological responses in difficult situations and reduce their anxiety or other type of physiological overarousal once it occurs. According to Forman (1993), deep muscle relaxation training, imagery-based procedures, and deep breathing are typically used to teach children and adolescents how to relax. Deep muscle relaxation training involves a series of tension–release cycles in which the child is directed to:

- Tense the muscle(s)
- Hold the tension for a few seconds while focusing on the tense feelings
- Relax the muscle(s)

- Notice the difference between the feelings of tension and relaxation
- Focus on the pleasant feelings of relaxation

Imagery procedures, such as having the child contrast acting like a "robot" and then a "rag doll," have also been used to help children achieve a relaxed state. Deep breathing procedures call for the child to take a deep breath, hold it, exhale slowly, and, while exhaling, relax the whole body and concentrate on a cue word such as "relax."

Social problem-solving interventions, such as those developed by Shure and Spivack (1988), teach a systematic means of dealing with social problem situations through a structured sequence. Most social problem-solving programs include six steps, which enable the practitioner to change behavior and to resolve problems:

1. Identifying the problem
2. Determining the goals
3. Generating alternative solutions
4. Examining consequences
5. Choosing the solution
6. Evaluating the outcome

Cognitive restructuring can help children and adolescents become aware of their thoughts and feelings and realize that their irrational thoughts are not facts and may not be constructive. The child is taught to use a series of questions to identify thoughts and then is assisted in evaluating the thoughts logically with the goal of changing to more appropriate behavior. A variety of methods have been used in cognitive restructuring interventions.

The principles and procedures of rational–emotive therapy are frequently used in cognitive restructuring efforts. Rational–emotive therapy identifies a number of beliefs commonly held in our culture that lead to problem emotions and behavior, disputes these beliefs, and provides alternative rational ways of thinking. Ellis (1980) indicated that major irrational beliefs include:

- "I must do well and win approval or else I am a rotten person."
- "Others must treat me the way I want them to or else they should be punished."
- "I must get everything I want quickly and easily."

Scripts containing rational thoughts and/or positive self-statements are developed for the child to practice and use in stressful and potentially problematic situations.

Anger control training, another variant of cognitive restructuring, focuses on teaching children and adolescents to guide their behavior through the use of internal dialogue. Potentially provocative experiences are viewed through a sequence of stages:

- Preparing for the provocation ("Here comes Greg.")
- Impact and confrontation ("Keep cool. I don't need to get mad.")
- Coping with arousal ("OK, relax. Take a deep breath.")
- Subsequent reflection ("I handled that one." Or "I blew it this time, but I'll try again.")

The objective is to develop a set of internal controls that permits the child to prepare for a possible anger-provoking event and to deal effectively with it.

Attribution retraining is a procedure that focuses on beliefs about the causes of success and failure. This procedure attempts to increase the success of children in dealing with academic and social tasks by using instruction and feedback regarding their causal beliefs. When this procedure is used, children are encouraged to talk to themselves aloud using statements that attribute outcome to effort and that are self-encouraging.

Contingent reinforcement, modeling, and role-play are behavioral procedures that are used to assist in the process of learning new ways of thinking and acting and to ensure that these become part of the individual's everyday repertoire. In interventions that use a cognitive–behavioral approach, models of use of appropriate cognitions and behavior are typically provided, and the child or adolescent practices new skills through role-play. Reinforcement for use of new skills may be provided externally by the therapist, teacher, or parent, or internally through use of self-management procedures.

RESEARCH REVIEW

Cognitive–behavioral interventions are effective treatments for anxiety disorders in children and adolescents. For example, Kendall (1994) reported on randomized clinical trials in which young people received cognitive–behavioral treatment with four components:

1. Recognizing anxious feelings and physical reactions

2. Identifying and modifying negative self-statements

3. Generating strategies to cope effectively in anxiety-provoking situations

4. Rating and rewarding attempts at coping behavior

Significant reductions in anxiety were found for the treated children compared to the wait-list controls. A significant proportion of the treated children no longer met the criteria for an anxiety disorder, and the gains were maintained at follow-up of up to five years.

A cognitive–behavioral prevention program, the Coping with Stress Course, developed by Clarke and colleagues (1995), is also effective in preventing depression in adolescents at risk for depressive episodes. The course consists of group sessions that focus on identifying and challenging negative, irrational thinking.

Results of studies evaluating the effectiveness of cognitive–behavioral procedures with aggressive or disruptive children have been less conclusive. Although a number of individual studies have shown positive effects from cognitive–behavioral treatment, an analysis of 99 studies that used interventions to decrease disruptive classroom behavior in public education settings by Stage and Quiroz (1997) found that group contingencies, self-management strategies, and differential reinforcement techniques were more effective than cognitive–behavioral interventions. A broad-based treatment strategy in which cognitive–behavioral interventions are used as part of a multi-faceted approach within family, peer, school, and community contexts may be necessary for more positive and lasting treatment effects with problems of aggression.

Cognitive–behavioral interventions provide an effective means for addressing emotional and social problems of students. This approach is effective with anxiety-related problems and depression in children and adolescents. There is also some evidence that it is effective with aggression and disruptive behaviors, especially when used as part of a broad-based treatment strategy and/or as a preventive approach. These interventions have been designed with appropriate attention to the developmental level of the child; and many of the cognitive–behavioral prevention programs provide effective ways of involving teachers, as well as other school personnel, in program implementation, making this intervention approach cost-effective as well as ecologically sound.

—Susan G. Forman

See also Behavior Intervention; Learning; Study Skills; Self-Management; Problem Solving

REFERENCES AND FURTHER READING

Clarke, G. N., Hawkins, W., Murphy, M., Sheeber, L. B., Lewinsohn, P. M., & Seeley, J. R. (1995). Targeted prevention of unipolar depressive disorder in an at-risk sample of high school adolescents: A randomized trial of a group cognitive intervention. *Journal of American Academy of Child Adolescent Psychiatry, 34,* 312–321.

Ellis, A. (1980). An overview of the clinical theory of rational-emotive therapy. In R. Grieger & J. Boyd (Eds.), *Rational-emotive therapy: A skills-based approach* (pp. 1–31). New York: Van Nostrand Reinhold.

Forman, S. G. (1993). *Coping skills interventions for children and adolescents.* San Francisco: Jossey-Bass.

Henin, A., Warman, M., & Kendall, P. C. (2002). *Cognitive behavioural therapy with children and adolescents* (pp. 275–313). In G. Simos (Ed.), *Cognitive behaviour therapy.* New York: Taylor & Francis.

Kendall, P. C. (1994). Treating anxiety disorders in children: Results of a randomized clinical trial. *Journal of Consulting and Clinical Psychology, 62,* 100–110.

Meichenbaum, D. H., & Goodman, J. (1971). Training impulsive children to talk to themselves. *Journal of Abnormal Psychology, 77,* 115–126.

Shure, M. B., & Spivack, G. (1988). Interpersonal cognitive problem solving. In R. H. Price, E. L. Cowen, R. P. Lovan, & J. Ramos-McKay (Eds.), *Fourteen ounces of prevention: A casebook for practitioners* (pp. 64–82). Washington, DC: American Psychological Association.

Stage, S. A., & Quiroz, D. B. (1997). A meta-analysis of interventions to decrease disruptive classroom behavior in public education settings. *School Psychology Review, 26,* 333–368.

COGNITIVE DISSONANCE

Leon Festinger's cognitive dissonance theory (1957) holds that two beliefs are dissonant with one another if the opposite of one would follow from the other. For example: "I dislike the president," but "I voted for the president." Being psychologically uncomfortable, dissonance will motivate the individual to reduce it and achieve a consonant set of beliefs. When that occurs, attitude change can occur.

Dissonance can be reduced by:

- Changing one of the discrepant beliefs ("Maybe I actually like the president.")
- Qualifying the belief ("The reason I don't like the president is his environmental policies, but I like his other policies.")
- Downgrading the belief ("I dislike all presidents once they are in office.")
- Altering one's behavior ("I'll never vote for him again.")

For educational purposes, the theory suggests that forcing individuals to take action in regard to dissonant beliefs, such as role-playing or debating one of the conflicting positions, may lead to attitude change.

—Robert L. Hohn

REFERENCES AND FURTHER READING

Festinger, L. (1957). *A theory of cognitive dissonance.* Evanston, IL: Row, Peterson.

COMMUNICATION DISORDERS

Communication disorders may be characterized as deficits or impairments in speech, language, and hearing. Communication is central to the transmission of ideas and thought. It directly impacts people's ability to express themselves, exchange ideas, and interact with others in their environment. Further, in the process of communication, learning takes place. Language is fundamental to a child's overall development, which includes growth in social, emotional, and behavioral functioning. Conversely, impairment in a child's speech and/or language is associated with behavior problems, academic achievement, and emotional and psychiatric problems.

This article provides an overview of communication disorders. More specifically, definitions of language, speech, and hearing disorders, as well as etiology, assessment methodology, and intervention strategies are provided.

LANGUAGE DISORDERS

Language disorders consist of expressive, receptive, or mixed expressive–receptive impairments. A disorder in expressive language is the inability to effectively communicate one's thoughts verbally or in writing. A disorder in receptive language is the inability to comprehend spoken or written material. Children with a mixed receptive–expressive language disorder have difficulty not only expressing themselves, but also comprehending spoken or written material. It has been estimated that approximately 3% to 5% of children are diagnosed with an expressive language disorder and 3% of students are affected by a mixed expressive–receptive language impairment.

Language-Learning Disability

Approximately 40% to 60% of students with a learning disability have also been diagnosed with a language-learning disability. Students with language impairments struggle with academics because learning is demonstrated through a process of reading, writing, and speaking. Potential indicators of language impairment during preschool and kindergarten include difficulty listening to a story, difficulty following directions, immature speech, word-finding difficulties, and poor play skills. During the elementary school years, signs of a language disability include difficulty understanding text, misunderstanding directions, difficulty synthesizing words with more than one syllable, and poor social skills. In high school, adolescents with a language disability struggle with processing complex, higher-order verbal information. Specifically, note taking, written expression, test taking, and poor organizational skills are all areas that may be affected by a language disorder.

Assessment of Language

Based upon suggestions for assessment of a child's language skills, the following methodology and test batteries are recommended for school psychologists in uncovering any deficits a child may have in language:

- A developmental history obtained via a parental interview ascertains the child's milestones as well as academic and medical familial issues.
- Behavioral data in the form of observations in various contexts and rating scales such as the Behavior Assessment System for Children (BASC) yield valuable information regarding behavior in different settings.
- Assessment of a child's adaptive functioning across domains provides information regarding skills that the child has incorporated into his or her repertoire.
- Evaluation of a child's ability to effectively employ spoken language in a given social situation or context (pragmatic language) may be assessed.

The school psychologist may also administer intellectual tests such as the Wechsler Intelligence Scale for Children-Fourth Edition (WISC-IV) to determine whether global cognitive abilities are associated with an impairment in language. However, it should not be the sole instrument used in the assessment process. Language tests typically administered by speech and language pathologists include the Clinical Evaluation of Language Fundamentals–3, the Peabody Picture Vocabulary Test-Revised, Test for Auditory Comprehension of Language-Revised, and the Test of Language Development.

Treatment

School psychologists may help the student with a language disorder by designing opportunities within the classroom to incorporate communication skills and addressing social skills problems by teaching children how to interact with others, take turns, and make friends. Language production may be improved by engaging in role-play and storytelling activities in which the child tells a story about a picture and/or names objects. Comprehension may be enhanced by minimizing classroom distractions, obtaining the child's full attention, having the student repeat directions, and, finally, cueing the child to improve listening.

Allowing more time between asking a question and expecting an answer (wait time) gives the student the opportunity to process the information and formulate his or her thoughts and ideas. Also, scripts that delineate a course of events, different roles, and new language have also been suggested, along with modeling and imitation.

With respect to written expression, brainstorming helps the student create various ideas and vocabulary to be used in his or her writing. In addition, mapping the ideas that were generated during the brainstorming phase aids in organizing thoughts for the written product. Also, students should be encouraged to use word processing programs when completing written assignments. That is, word processing programs allow the student to revise and edit the manuscript, produce a well-organized and neat document, check for spelling errors, and assist with grammar. The advantages afforded by these programs are numerous and provide real individualized assistance in helping students write.

DISORDERS SPEECH

Speech disorders are impairments in the verbal production of speech. Within the domain of speech, disorders include articulation (phonological), stuttering (fluency), and voice.

Phonological Disorder

A phonological or articulation disorder is defined in the *DSM-IV* as "a failure to use developmentally expected speech sounds that are appropriate for the individual's age and dialect. This may involve errors in sound production, use, representation, or organization such as, but not limited to, substitutions of one sound for another or omissions of sounds" (*DSM-IV*, APA, 1994, p. 61). Approximately 50% to 70% of individuals diagnosed with a phonological disorder will experience academic difficulty.

Etiology. Phonological disorder is present in approximately 2% to 3% of first- and second-grade children. The severity of this disorder ranges from mild to severe, with greater frequency for a mild form of the disorder. Impairments in articulation are more common in males.

Assessment. Phonology may be evaluated formally or informally. Formal measures include standardized tests such as the Goldman-Fristoe Test of Articulation–2. This measure is composed of three subtests that assess articulation of speech sounds, the ability to retell a story read by the examiner and depicted with pictures, and the ability to discern phonemes that are mispronounced.

Treatment. Interventions include improving phonemic awareness, teaching students to hear the differences in sounds, and rewarding accurate articulation.

Stuttering

Stuttering, also known as a fluency disorder, "is characterized by frequent repetitions or prolongations of sounds or syllables" that culminate in a lack of fluency in speech (*DSM-IV*, APA, 1994, p. 63). Stuttering affects approximately 1% of individuals, with males being three times more at risk than females. Although early intervention is recommended for individuals who stutter, more than 50% of these individuals recover without any treatment by adulthood. Family history of expressive language impairment, articulation disorder, or stuttering results in a greater risk of stuttering. In addition, increased stuttering is associated with anxiety, depression, and lowered self-esteem, which in turn may impact the student's social communication and academic achievement.

Etiology. Research substantiates a genetic component in individuals who stutter. Onset is typically gradual and is noted to occur between two and seven years of age. Features include a lack of fluency in speech that includes repetitions that become more frequent over time. Notably, language disorders have been shown to be connected to the etiology of stuttering.

Assessment. Evaluation may include a familial history that includes the child's development, a structured speech sample, and observations of the student in various settings. Since children who stutter may experience emotional and academic difficulties, these areas should be monitored.

Treatment. Treatment of fluency disorders includes ignoring speech that is not fluent, speaking slowly, avoiding statements instructing the student to "slow down," refraining from assisting the student to complete a sentence, positively reinforcing speech that is fluent (no stuttering), and allowing the student more time to answer questions. It is important to note that stuttering is less pronounced and sometimes not evident when these students speak with their friends or participate in activities such as choral reading or whispering.

Voice Disorders

Voice disorders include deficits relative to atypical loudness, pitch, duration, and resonance. The speech and language pathologist usually provides services for these students.

HEARING DISORDERS

Hearing impairments may be defined as damage to an individual's hearing that results in hearing that is deficient but functional. This term has been used to describe a wide range of hearing loss. Impairments in hearing do not affect an individual's intellect. However, hearing loss does negatively affect the academic achievement of these students in that instruction generally depends upon verbal instruction. Consequently, students with hearing impairments may be delayed as compared to their peers. Hearing impairments have also been noted to affect a child's social and emotional development. The social use of language as well as conversational skills of children with a hearing impairment are often deficient. An audiologist and/or speech-language pathologist typically conduct the assessment. With respect to treatment, the school psychologist may provide social skills training that focuses on conversational skills, turn taking, initiation of activities, and decision making.

Children with central auditory processing disorder (CAPD) evidence difficulty processing information that is presented orally despite normal hearing. The speech-language pathologist and an audiologist typically conduct the assessment and provide treatment strategies. However, children with CAPD often exhibit symptoms similar to attention deficit hyperactivity disorder (ADHD). That is, children with CAPD are often inattentive, distractible, have difficulty following directions, exhibit behavior problems, and demonstrate poor auditory attention and memory. In light of the behavioral manifestations and similarities between ADHD and CAPD, collaboration with the school psychologist for differential diagnosis is recommended.

SUMMARY

Communication is fundamental to all aspects of functioning, including learning and interacting with others. Communication disorders adversely affect academic achievement and socialization and are associated with emotional and behavioral problems. Thus, impairments in communication may be considered pervasive in that they impact academic, behavioral, social, and emotional functioning. In light of the adverse implications stemming from communication disorders, school psychologists, parents, and teachers need to work together toward the goal of expanding upon the language, academic, social–emotional, and behavioral presentation of students with communication disorders. Certainly, this would assist with social interaction as well as academics. This is particularly important as children with communication disorders tend to isolate themselves from social and educational environments. School psychologists are in the unique position to provide assessment, consultation, and intervention services to these students. Through the school psychologist's knowledge of empirically validated interventions, consultative services may provide teachers efficient and effective methods to facilitate communication within the classroom. Such services are designed to maximize students' academic potential and enhance their emotional well-being.

—*Lea A. Theodore, Melissa A. Bray, and Thomas J. Kehle*

See also Adaptive Behavior Assessment; Autism Spectrum Disorders; *DSM-IV*; Echolalia; Facilitated Communication; Selective Mutism; Stuttering

REFERENCES AND FURTHER READING

American Speech-Language-Hearing Association. (1993). Definitions for communicative disorders and differences. *ASHA, 24,* 949–950.

Bray, M. A., Kehle, T. J., & Theodore, L. A. (2002). Best practices in the school psychologist's role in the assessment and treatment of students with communication disorders. In A. Thomas & J. Grimes (Eds.), *Best practices in school psychology* (Vol. 2). Bethesda, MD: The National Association of School Psychologists.

American Psychiatric Association. (1994). *Diagnostic and statistical manual of mental disorders* (4th ed.) (*DSM-IV*). Washington, DC: Author.

Mercer, C. D. (1997). *Students with learning disabilities* (5th ed.). Englewood Cliffs, NJ: Prentice-Hall.

COMORBIDITY

Comorbidity is described as a situation where two or more psychological or educational disorders or syndromes occur together. The exact nature of the relationship between comorbid conditions is a matter of some debate in the research literature. It is particularly difficult to determine whether one condition causes or is simply related to another.

It is important for school psychologists to understand the nature of comorbidity. This will better enable them to conduct a thorough evaluation, develop a treatment plan, and recommend appropriate interventions. When disorders covary in children, the school psychologist can address the specific needs of each disorder.

A large body of studies supports a comorbid relationship, as high as 70%, between learning disabilities and attention deficit disorder (ADD) (with or without hyperactivity). Children diagnosed with a specific learning disability and attention deficit hyperactivity disorder (ADHD) exhibit common characteristics such as difficulty attending to a task, distractibility, unevenness in their learning and thinking abilities, and social immaturity. Equipped with this information, the school psychologist will be able to develop an intervention plan that meets the specific needs of the child. Understanding why different disorders co-occur may provide important opportunities for prevention and intervention.

—*Tommy Caisango*

See also DSM-IV

REFERENCES AND FURTHER READING

Wilens, T. E., Biederman, J., Brown, S., Tanguay, S., Monuteaux, M. C., & Blake, C., et al. (2002). Psychiatric comorbidity and functioning in clinically referred preschool and school-age youths with ADHD (Statistical Data Included). *Journal of the American Academy of Child and Adolescent Psychiatry, 41,* 262–268.

COMPUTER TECHNOLOGY

A computer is a programmable machine with two specific characteristics; it responds to a specific set of instructions in a well-defined manner, and it can execute a prerecorded list of instructions, known as a program. Personal computers were first introduced into the schools in the early 1980s, and since that time computer-related activity in education has penetrated nearly every component of the national educational scene—as demonstrated by the rapid surge in the number of computers found in schools today (Geisert & Futrell, 2000). The modern personal computer, also referred to as a microcomputer or PC1, is electronic and digital. The actual machinery—wires, transistors, and circuits—is called the hardware;

and the instructions, programs, and data are called software. Hardware also refers to additional peripheral devices such as scanners, printers, speakers, microphones, headsets, and gaming devices that are plugged into the computer machine. However, the instructions that make each peripheral device work efficiently are software.

SOFTWARE

The software can be loaded onto the microcomputer using a CD-ROM (Compact Disc-Read-Only Memory) or a floppy disk. Floppy disks (often called floppies or diskettes) are portable and most commonly seen today in a 3½-inch rigid encasement. Much of the multimedia software used with computers in the early 21st century requires more than the 1.44 megabytes (MB) of data available on a single floppy disk; a single CD-ROM has the storage capacity of more than 500 floppy disks, or approximately 650 MB. Since the mid 1990s, many computers come equipped with DVD (Digital Versatile Disc or Digital Video Disc) players. A DVD is a type of optical disk technology similar to the CD-ROM; it holds a minimum of 4.7 gigabytes (GB) of data, enough for a full-length movie. DVDs are commonly used as a medium for digital representation of movies and other multimedia presentations that combine sound with graphics (Jupitermedia Corporation, 2004).

HARDWARE

In the United States, the most popular educational computer systems are supplied by either Apple Computer (Mac) or by the many makers of computers that are based on Intel Corporation's microprocessors (Windows) (Poole, 1997). Operating systems provide a software platform on top of which other programs, called application programs, can run. Most software produced today is compatible with both Windows and Mac operating systems; to date, the sharing of software and data between these platforms has improved, but it is still not flawless (Schwartz & Beichner, 1999).

More recently, other computer devices such as handheld computers (also called personal digital assistants [PDAs]) have made an impact on student learning. Handheld devices are rapidly becoming a common technology in schools. The Palm, Handspring, and other handheld devices share the same operating system, the Palm OS. Because they are inexpensive when compared to laptop computers, many schools are finding that a mixture of desktop, laptop, and handheld devices can be used to meet a variety of educational needs (Lamb, 2004).

INTERNET

The Internet is a network of computer networks that stretches around the globe connecting millions of computers together. The Internet forms a network in which any computer can communicate with any other computer as long as they are both connected to the Internet. The Internet and the World Wide Web are two separate but related things. The World Wide Web is a way of accessing information over the Internet. It is an information-sharing model that is built on top of the Internet. The Web also uses browsers, such as Internet Explorer or Netscape, to access Web documents, called Web pages, that are linked to each other via hyperlinks. (Jupitermedia Corporation, 2004). The Internet is commonly accessible through school networks that are wired together, known as a LAN (Local Area Network). In some instances, wireless technology allows computers and handheld devices to access the Internet using radio waves.

APPLICATION IN INSTRUCTION

Multiple software applications with a wide range of features are available to support teachers and students in the classroom, with the most widely used being word processing, spreadsheet, and database programs. Software support tools can offer a variety of benefits including improved productivity, appearance, and accuracy (Geisert & Futrell, 2000; Roblyer & Edwards, 2000). Students and teachers are more productive and engaged in their work when technology-based tools and strategies are used effectively in the classroom. For example, research shows that although word processing alone cannot improve the quality of students' writing, it can help them make corrections more efficiently; this can motivate students to write more and take more interest in improving their written work (Roblyer & Edwards, 2000).

Instructional software, sometimes referred to as courseware, varies in quality and price. Choosing courseware based on a clearly articulated instructional goal can help teachers choose the most effective

instructional software for their needs (Poole, 1997). There are many types of courseware:

- Tutorial courseware uses the computer to deliver an entire instructional sequence by presenting the information and individually guiding students' learning (Roblyer & Edwards, 2000).
- Drill and practice courseware provides opportunities, usually one at a time, for students to engage in activities that drill factual memorization and practice the skill to develop fluency. The programs vary in sophistication, but all offer students immediate feedback to reinforce learning (Roblyer & Edwards, 2000).
- A simulation is a computerized model of a real or imaginary system. The learner can control a number of key factors to manipulate the system and determine the outcomes. Simulations are designed to promote problem-solving skills by demonstrating the steps in a process (Roblyer & Edwards, 2000).
- Instructional games, in many cases, are some version of tutorials or drill and practice. The difference is that the instructional game motivates the learner by adding specific game rules and an opportunity to win—the emphasis is on competition and entertainment. Typically, the games offer a higher quality of animation, graphics, and sound (Newby & colleagues, 2000).
- Problem-solving courseware is designed to foster students' problem-solving skills, often by focusing on a specific problem type. It is designed to meet students' higher-order thinking skills such as logic, reasoning, pattern recognition, and strategies (Newby & colleagues, 2000). Although many problem-solving programs focus on mathematical concepts (e.g., special reasoning, mathematical patterns, sequencing), some are designed to help the learner remember instructions and follow directions (Newby & colleagues, 2000; Roblyer & Edwards, 2000).

The applications on PDAs allow students to use their handheld devices as a graphing calculator, word processor, database, test prep tool, and reference resource. Teachers and administrators are using handheld devices for recordkeeping, scheduling, and other administrative as well as teaching applications. Additional devices, including science probes, digital cameras, digital audio recorders, keyboards, and

Global Positioning System (GPS) devices, can expand the hardware even further (Lamb, 2004).

The Internet and the World Wide Web provide innumerable opportunities for instruction, learning, and assessment. There are numerous Web sites that offer free games, quizzes, and interactive projects that students can safely use in the classroom. Many Web-based activities can be brought together in an instructional strategy called a *WebQuest*. A WebQuest is an inquiry-oriented activity in which some or all of the information that students interact with comes from the Internet (Geisert, 2000; Norton & Wiburg, 1998). WebQuest activities can be done individually or in small groups and often focus on a single discipline or topic.

The microcomputer offers some alternatives to the chapter test presented in many textbooks. Teacher utility programs are available to maintain the classroom grade book, generate games and puzzles, present classroom materials, and create tests. Database programs allow the teacher to store, review, analyze, revise, and score any number of test questions. But the use of microcomputers can go far beyond the traditional concept of instruction and assessment; the microcomputer also can be used to assess students' work in an ongoing manner. Students' work and evaluation can be personalized based on their performance. For example, instead of teaching a unit for a defined period of time, testing students, and then moving to the next unit, teachers can free students to work varied amounts of time within each of the many units in a course. After studying a given unit, a student who feels ready to demonstrate his or her understanding of the objectives could go to the computer and take the unit test (Geisert & Futrell, 2000). This kind of individualized teaching allows the teacher to guide students through the learning process focusing on individual needs.

APPLICATIONS FOR SCHOOL PSYCHOLOGISTS

Electronic technology has impacted areas of professional practice, ranging from the assessment of individual students to communication with peers to systemwide data collection. School psychologists routinely use specially designed software for word processing, report writing, data collection, and the computerized scoring of assessments. The Internet and the World Wide Web offer fast and efficient means to communicate with colleagues, join list

serves, and find information related to intervention and practice.

Report Writing and Scoring

Many of the most popular assessment batteries (i.e., the Wechsler Intelligence Scale for Children and Woodcock-Johnson Tests of Achievement) have electronic programs that assist with scoring, interpretation, and report writing. These programs reduce the likelihood of scoring errors, provide interpretations that are consistent with the theoretical underpinnings of the assessment battery, collect data across students, and have report writers that may speed writing. Special care must be taken to ensure that data are kept confidential, that the generalized interpretations presented for individual students are carefully considered along with other data sources, and that the student's data are correctly entered.

Internet and the World Wide Web

Communicative technology allows the school psychologist to move past often isolated working conditions and to easily communicate with colleagues within his or her building, district, or state. E-mail enables psychologists to easily schedule meetings with multiple participants, to request information from teachers and parents, and to circulate drafts of materials.

An emerging trend is for e-mail to support online consultation, supervision, and professional development. Psychologists can maintain ongoing conversations with teachers and parents about the status of interventions (i.e., treatments). Treatment implementation and fidelity may be increased as service providers are able to communicate with psychologists about the progress of an intervention. Supervisees can e-mail questions or request assistance outside of regularly scheduled meetings. For example, a student may use e-mail to jointly ask both his or her campus and field supervisors for an opinion about an assessment result.

The World Wide Web gives psychologists across the nation access to current information from assessment publishers, government agencies, and universities and professional organizations. Practitioners can visit publishers' Web sites to read about changes in scoring tables or other recent issues and make appropriate changes to their use of assessment instruments. Organizations such as the National Association of School Psychologists maintain comprehensive Web sites that are regularly updated to provide school psychologists with current legal, ethical, and technical information. These sites cover topics ranging from attention deficit hyperactivity disorder (ADHD) to crisis intervention. List serves support *communities of learners* for professionals with similar interests or who are engaging in online professional development.

Users of the Internet and e-mail must ensure confidentiality and evaluate the veracity of information obtained online. E-mail communications about sensitive topics or confidential materials should be securely sent or be void of identifiable names or references. Information downloaded from the Web must be evaluated for reliability and validity.

—*Christine Remley, Steve Knotek, and Sarah Hamel*

See also Communication Disorders; Learning; Study Skills

REFERENCES AND FURTHER READING

Geisert, P. G., & Futrell, M. K. (2000). *Teachers, computers, and curriculum: Microcomputers in the classroom* (3rd ed.). Needham Heights, MA: Allyn & Bacon.

Jupitermedia Corporation. (2004). *Webopedia: Online computer dictionary for computer and Internet terms and definitions*. Available online at http://www.webopedia.com

Lamb, A. (2004). *The teacher tap: Handheld devices in the classroom*. EduScapes. Available online at http://eduscapes.com

Newby, T. J., Stepich, D. A., Lehman, J. D., & Russell, J. D. (2000). *Instructional technology for teaching and learning—Designing instruction, integrating computers, and using media* (2nd ed.). Upper Saddle River, NJ: Merrill/Prentice-Hall.

Norton, P., & Wiburg, K. M. (1998). *Teaching with technology*. Orlando, FL: Harcourt Brace.

Poole, B. J. (1997). *Education for an information age. Teaching in the computerized classroom* (2nd ed.). Boston: McGraw-Hill College.

Roblyer, M. D., & Edwards, J. (2000). *Integrating educational technology into teaching* (2nd ed.). Upper Saddle River, NJ: Merrill/Prentice-Hall.

Schwartz, J. E., & Beichner, R. J. (1999). *Essentials of educational technology*. Needham Heights, MA: Allyn & Bacon.

CONDITIONING: CLASSICAL AND OPERANT

Classical conditioning, also known as respondent conditioning, is defined as a procedure in which a previously neutral stimulus comes to elicit a response after it is paired with a stimulus that automatically elicits that response (Martin & Pear, 2003). The principle of classical conditioning is based on the fact that certain stimuli (unconditioned stimuli) automatically elicit certain responses without learning (unconditioned responses). Humans exhibit many reflexes that are not learned behaviors. For example, when exposed to our favorite foods, we salivate and when exposed to high temperatures, we sweat. These are natural, unconditioned responses to natural, unconditioned stimuli found in the environment. However, when these unconditioned stimuli are paired with neutral stimuli, the neutral stimuli will begin to elicit the same response as the unconditioned stimuli and will become conditioned stimuli. This sounds confusing, but a review of the most recognized classical conditioning experiment, Ivan Pavlov's study that employed a dog and a bell, will help. Pavlov found that a dog would naturally salivate when exposed to meat powder. The meat powder was the unconditioned stimuli, and the resulting salivation was the unconditioned response. To condition the ringing of the bell to elicit salivation, Pavlov began ringing the bell as the dog was exposed to the meat powder. The result of this pairing was that the dog began to salivate upon hearing the ringing bell, even when not exposed to the meat powder. The ringing bell had become a conditioned stimuli that evoked the same response (salivation) as the exposure to the meat powder (unconditioned stimuli).

With operant conditioning, behavior is modified by environmental consequences, such as peer attention, removal of aversive stimuli, and punishment. Behaviors operate on the environment to generate consequences and, in turn, are controlled by those consequences. Behaviors can be reinforced or punished, which will result in the repetition of the behaviors or in the termination of behaviors, respectively. If reinforcement is delivered following a behavior, the behavior is more likely to be repeated. However, if punishment is delivered following a behavior, the behavior is not likely to be repeated. An example of operant conditioning is putting gas into a car. When an individual does not put gas in his or her car, the consequence is that the individual's car runs out of gas and the car stops. Therefore, the individual's behavior is controlled by the consequence—next time the individual's car is low on gas, the person will fill the gas tank. When environmental consequences are manipulated, behaviors in the environment are also modified to respond to the contingencies (Miltenberger, 2001).

If a child misbehaves at home, he or she knows punishment will follow. However, at school, the negative behaviors are rewarded by peer attention and approval. This child will behave differently in these two environments based on the consequences available in each.

When contrasting classical and operant conditioning, it is clear that both approaches are distinct and allude to different types of learning. There are three main distinctions between classical and operant conditioning—the procedure, the behavioral response, and the amount of control issued during the procedure (Malott & Trojan Suarez, 2004).

First, both conditioning procedures involve a type of pairing. In classical conditioning, behaviors are exhibited by pairing a neutral stimulus with an unconditioned stimulus; whereas in operant conditioning, behavior is controlled by pairing a behavior and a consequence. For example, in classical conditioning, antecedent events are environmental influences that occur before a behavior is exhibited, and the result is the development of a conditioned stimulus from a newly acquired stimulus, such as in the example of Pavlov's study. In contrast, behavior is controlled by consequences (reinforcers and punishers) in operant conditioning. For example, if a child is reinforced for raising his hand in class, he will repeat that behavior. However, if a child is ignored or punished for raising her hand, she will be less likely to repeat that behavior.

Second, exhibition of the behavioral response prior to conditioning is not required in each conditioning procedure. In classical conditioning, the behavior does not have to exist prior to the conditioning procedure. However, in operant conditioning, the behavioral response must occur to experience the consequence and allow for conditioning. Many people are not afraid of small white animals. Neither was "Little Albert" until John Watson classically conditioned a fear of white mice by pairing his reaching for the animal with a loud, startling noise. In this situation, fear of small white animals was not required prior to the conditioning procedures. Instead, the procedure (e.g., loud noise) elicited the behavior (i.e., fear). However, if a fear response was to be operantly conditioned, it would have to be exhibited prior to the conditioning procedures. Using operant procedures, fear would occur first and then the procedures of reinforcement or punishment would be used to maintain the behavior.

Finally, traditional psychologists have said that classical conditioning generally is *involuntary* while operant conditioning involves more *voluntary* learning.

For example, in classical conditioning, unconditioned responses are typically reflexive behaviors such as salivating, sneezing, sweating, and coughing. However, in operant conditioning, behaviors are controlled by consequences and involve behaviors such as running, walking, or talking.

In our daily lives, many examples of classical and operant conditioning are at work. Food aversions and fears may be learned through classical conditioning. Additionally, these conditioned behaviors can be operantly maintained. As an example, consider children responding to a teacher turning on and off the classroom lights. The students learn that the flickering lights are a cue to get in their seats, sit down, and be quiet. How did they learn this behavior and how is this behavior maintained over time? Initially, the behaviors were classically conditioned. The first time the teacher turned the lights on and off she paired this neutral stimulus with an unconditioned stimulus. The unconditioned stimulus was probably a verbal command to "get in your seat and be quiet." Following several of these pairings between the unconditioned stimulus and the neutral stimulus, the teacher no longer had to give the verbal command and instead could flicker the lights. The children immediately walked to their seats and sat quietly. Although these classroom behaviors were initially classically conditioned, they may require operant conditioning to be maintained. Using consequences such as reinforcement or punishment would ensure that the children continued to follow the classroom rule. Following operant conditioning principles, the teacher could use a reward chart. After the lights are turned on and off, the children are required to get to their seats and sit quietly within 10 seconds. Children in their seat at the 10-second mark would receive a sticker or other reward. Those children compliant with the classroom rule are reinforced for their behavior and, therefore, this positive behavior will be expected to occur in the future.

—*Merilee McCurdy and Michelle Swanger*

See also Behavior; Behavior Intervention; Learning

REFERENCES AND FURTHER READING

Malott, R. W., & Trojan Suarez, E. A. (2004). *Principles of behavior*. Upper Saddle River, NJ: Pearson Education.

Martin, G., & Pear, J. (2003). *Behavior modification: What it is and how to do it* (7th ed.). Upper Saddle River, NJ: Prentice-Hall.

Miltenberger, R.G. (2001). *Behavior modification: Principles and procedures* (3rd ed.). Pacific Grove, CA: Wadsworth.

CONDUCT DISORDER

Conduct disorder (CD) is defined in the *Diagnostic and Statistical Manual of Mental Disorders, Fourth Edition-Text Revision* (*DSM-IV-TR*) as "a repetitive and persistent pattern of behavior in which the basic rights of others or major age-appropriate societal norms or rules are violated" (American Psychiatric Association, 2000, p. 93). Patterns of behavior associated with CD fall into four main categories (American Psychiatric Association, 2000, p. 94):

1. "Aggressive conduct that causes or threatens physical harm to other people or animals"

2. "Nonaggressive conduct that causes property loss or damage"

3. "Deceitfulness or theft"

4. "Serious violations of rules"

Conduct disorder may have its onset in childhood or in adolescence; prevalence estimates of CD in the population of youth range from 1% to more than 10% (American Psychiatric Association, 2000).

Researchers have found that the causes of childhood-onset CD are multiple and interactive; biological risks (e.g, verbal IQ, executive cognitive functioning) interact with environmental risks (from family, peer, and school contexts) to increase children's chances of developing CD.

The social contexts of family, peers, and school interact with the child's biology over the course of a child's development. Certain children are apparently born with biological predispositions (e.g., neuropsychological deficits) that make them vulnerable to developing conduct problems. In the family context, maintaining a balance of warmth and control has long been considered a hallmark of effective parenting. Children who develop CD are more likely to experience parenting strategies that are harsh and ineffective (Patterson, 1982). Through these strategies, children learn to use coercive behavior (e.g., temper tantrums, whining) to get what they want. Parents, in turn, learn to escape the coercive behavior of their children by failing to discipline and monitor them (Patterson, 1982). Ironically, parents of children with conduct disorder may actually monitor their children less closely than do parents of children without CD to avoid highly aversive conflicts with them. As a result, a child is free to affiliate with deviant peers and fails

to learn effective strategies for managing the adolescent world (Dodge & Pettit, 2003).

Peers can play a substantial role in the development and maintenance of CD. When children enter elementary school, they may continue on the trajectory of CD if their academic and social readiness skills fall short of their nonaggressive peers and they are ridiculed and rejected by them (Dodge & Pettit, 2003; Patterson & colleagues, 1992). The support of aggressive peers for the continuing development of CD cannot be overestimated; aggressive children affiliate together in school and support one another in bullying, fighting, and getting in trouble (Cairns & Cairns, 1994). From childhood through adolescence, youth with CD are likely to associate with one another and together participate in aggressive and delinquent activities (Cairns & Cairns, 1994; Moffitt, 1993; Patterson & colleagues, 1992).

The role of peers for youth with adolescent-onset conduct disorder is particularly critical. Moffitt (1993) has theorized that youth with childhood-onset CD provide the model for those for whom aggressive and antisocial acts begin during adolescence. Behaviors associated with CD take a different form during adolescence—they include covert activities such as lying, stealing, vandalism, and drug and alcohol use. Nearly all adolescents engage in some form of these activities (Moffitt, 1993), thus making it a challenge to distinguish youth with adolescent-onset CD from those for whom participation is experimental.

The role of the school context ranges from perpetuation to prevention of CD. When low-performing, aggressive students are grouped together in classrooms, they can refine their aggressive tendencies and share low expectations for achievement (Cairns & Cairns, 1994). By grouping these youth together, schools can actually contribute to disproportionately high dropout rates among youth with patterns of aggressive behavior and low achievement. Alternatively, relationships in the school context can be critical for keeping youth in school; for example, among urban youth, feeling committed to school in early adolescence is one factor that has been associated with reduced rates of later substance abuse, delinquency, teen pregnancy, and participation in violence.

Patterns associated with CD differ for boys and girls. Boys are more likely to be identified with childhood-onset CD than girls (American Psychiatric Association, 2000). Loeber and colleagues (1993) identified three antisocial pathways followed by boys from childhood to adolescence:

1. An authority conflict pathway, characterized in childhood by stubborn behavior and in adolescence by defiance and avoidance of authority

2. A covert pathway, characterized in childhood by minor covert behavior such as lying and shoplifting, and followed by property damage in late childhood and adolescence

3. An overt pathway, characterized by aggressive acts in childhood, such as annoying and bullying, and followed by physical fighting and violence in late childhood and adolescence.

Girls are more likely to be identified with adolescent-onset rather than childhood-onset CD; they are identified during adolescence with nearly the same frequency as boys (American Psychiatric Association, 2000). However, girls' pathways to antisocial behavior are not as clear, in part because of a decline in their participation in physical aggression during adolescence (Cairns & Cairns, 1994) and an increase in frequency of depression. Complicating this picture is a simultaneous increase in girls' participation in episodes of social aggression during adolescence (i.e., gossip, verbal aggression, and social exclusion). Social aggression may appear to be less harmful than physical aggression, but can provide the fuel for larger disputes and provoke episodes of physical violence in schools.

Conditions comorbid with CD include, in probable order of onset, attention deficit hyperactivity disorder, anxiety, depression, substance use, and somatic complaints (Loeber & Keenan, 1994). The presence of CD can make one vulnerable to developing comorbid problems, particularly during adolescence (Loeber & Keenan, 1994). Although girls have a lower prevalence of CD than boys, once they qualify for this disorder, they have a higher probability of developing comorbid problems (Loeber & Keenan, 1994). Furthermore, the majority of children and adolescents who attempt suicide have a history of aggressive, assaultive, or violent behavior, with females more likely than males to try and kill themselves (Cairns & Cairns, 1994).

Because of the intractable and challenging nature of CD (it persists across social contexts and across development), prevention is an essential goal for treatment. Assessment and treatment for CD must consider the diverse contexts (family, peer, and school) in which the disorder develops and is maintained. The Conduct Problems Prevention Research Group (CPPRG) has intervened with young children at risk for developing CD in the family, school, and peer contexts. CPPRG developed Fast Track, a program designed initially for

kindergartners in four communities and carried out with those kindergartners over the course of six years. Fast Track staff trained parents, visited homes, worked to enhance parent–child relationships, taught social–cognitive skills, and supported academic achievement and peer relationships for these children. CPPRG found a significant reduction in aggression and improved classroom behavior among students who participated in Fast Track, according to reports from teachers, peers, and classroom observers.

Similarly, Patterson and colleagues (1982) reduced aggressive behavior among boys in middle childhood (6 to 12 years of age) by working with families first—using behavioral interventions—then carrying out the same approach with teachers and peers at school. They measured their success at reducing aggression via reports from family members, school personnel, and youth themselves as well as from observations of youth at home and at school. In adolescence, helping parents monitor their children's whereabouts and increasing youth bonding or connection to school is critical to preventing adolescent-onset CD.

Both Patterson's and CPPRG's results confirm the need for pervasive, long-term interventions to prevent and treat CD. Such interventions should consist of:

- Universal social–emotional curricula for all youth (primarily involving school contexts)
- Targeted interventions for at-risk youth (involving family and school contexts)
- Intensive interventions for youth with identified CD (involving the family, school, peer, and community contexts)

School psychologists must be ready to assess children at risk for developing CD, as well as work with students who have already been identified. Family, peer, and classroom contexts become the settings for intervention. Early childhood is the ideal developmental period for preventing childhood-onset CD; early adolescence is prime developmental time for preventing adolescent-onset CD. Psychologists can identify young children at risk using parent and teacher reports and observation data; young adolescents may be identified using parent, teacher, peer, and self-reports, as well as archival data (e.g., disciplinary records, grades, test scores).

—*Elizabeth Talbott*

See also Aggression in Schools; Attention Deficit Hyperactivity Disorder; *DSM-IV*; Gangs; Oppositional Defiant Disorder

REFERENCES AND FURTHER READING

American Psychiatric Association. (2000). *Diagnostic and Statistical Manual of Mental Disorders* (4th ed., text rev.). Washington, DC: Author.

Cairns, R. B., & Cairns, B. D. (1994). *Lifelines and risks: Pathways of youth in our time.* Cambridge, U.K.: Cambridge University Press.

Dodge, K. A., & Pettit, G. S. (2003). A biopsychosocial model of the development of chronic conduct problems in adolescence. *Developmental Psychology, 39,* 349–371.

Loeber, R., & Keenan, K. (1994). Interaction between conduct disorder and its comorbid conditions: Effects of age and gender. *Clinical Psychology Review, 14,* 497–523.

Loeber, R., Wung, P., Keenan, K., Giroux, B., Stouthamer-Loeber, M., Van Kammen, W. B., et al. (1993). Developmental pathways in disruptive child behavior. *Development and Psychopathology, 5,* 103–133.

Moffitt, T. E. (1993). Adolescent-limited and life-course-persistent antisocial behavior: A developmental taxonomy. *Psychological Review, 100,* 674–701.

Patterson, G. R. (1982). *A social learning approach: Vol. 3. Coercive family processes.* Eugene, OR: Castalia.

Patterson, G. R., Reid, J. B., & Dishion, T. J. (1992). *A social learning approach: Vol. 4. Antisocial boys.* Eugene, OR: Castalia Press.

CONFIDENCE INTERVAL

A confidence interval (CI) is an estimated range of values expected in the population but calculated from a sample. One common use of CIs is in the reporting of standardized test results, such as from the Iowa Test of Basic Skills (ITBS) (Hoover & colleagues, 1993). A student who takes the ITBS receives an overall score on the mathematics subtest. Because the observed test score is an imperfect reflection of the test-taker's *true* mathematical ability, a test-taker's true (or *error-free*) score will differ by some amount from the *observed* test score. As such, a value is added or subtracted from the test score to form a plausible range on which a person's true test score may lie. The interval width indicates the degree of uncertainty in the accuracy of the observed score as a reflection of the test-taker's true score; the wider the interval, the greater the uncertainty. CIs are also available for other types of statistics, such as group means and percentages, to indicate the degree of error in the observed value of the statistic.

—*Michael Finger*

See also Norm-Referenced Testing; Reliability; Standard Error of Measurement

REFERENCES AND FURTHER READING

Hoover, H., Hieronymus, A., Frisbie, D., & Dunbar, S. (1993). *Iowa Test of Basic Skills.* Chicago: Riverside.

CONFIDENTIALITY

Confidentiality is an ethical practice that applies to professional psychologists, including school psychologists. Confidentiality refers to a decision made by a professional psychologist "not to reveal what is learned in a professional relationship" (Hummel & colleagues, 1985, p. 54). Confidentiality applies to students, parents, and teachers who reveal information to a school psychologist as they receive services (e.g., counseling or consultation). Confidentiality is an ethical standard, and a school psychologist is held to this ethical standard by ethics codes of the National Association of School Psychologists—*Principles for Professional Ethics* (2000)—and the American Psychological Association—*Principles of Psychologists and Code of Conduct* (2002).

Keeping information confidential requires careful attention and diligence on the part of the school psychologist. The school psychologist should not seek to obtain information from parents, teachers, or students that is not needed for the provision of services. Psychological reports should not contain information that is not relevant to the identified problem or the services needed. Regardless of the method of communication, school psychologists should be sure that the information shared is limited to what is required, and only shared with people who need that information. They must resist the temptation to give in to social pressures to "gossip" about children in a teachers' lounge or with others who do not need the information.

There are a few situations when confidentiality must be breached. One situation is when information is revealed in a professional relationship that abuse occurred or is suspected. In this situation, a school psychologist is both ethically and legally required to break confidentiality and report the abuse to the appropriate authorities. State laws and school policies vary about reporting procedures; however, a school psychologist should refer to these sources to determine the appropriate course of action to take.

Another situation when a school psychologist must break confidentiality is when information is revealed indicating that a student intends to harm others. In a school setting, this could be especially critical because the school psychologist is ethically required to protect all of the students in the building. The school psychologist must inform the intended victims, depending on their age, intended victims' parents, the parents of the student who is intending to do the harm, and other relevant people such as the principal and local law enforcement agency.

A third situation in which confidentiality must be breached is when information is revealed indicating that a student intends to harm him- or herself. Under this circumstance, a school psychologist is required to break confidentiality in order to inform the parents (if the student is a minor) and obtain help for the client, such as hospitalization.

In contrast, privileged communication is a right that belongs to a client, or parents of a client if the client is a minor, and is used to prevent the disclosure of confidential information obtained in a special relationship (i.e., psychologist–client relationship) in legal proceedings. Privilege status is available in some states but not others. However, if the parent waives the right to privilege in a legal proceeding, the school psychologist must then reveal the information. The judge might also waive privilege to ensure that justice is being served. Privilege varies from state to state, so school psychologists must be aware of local laws governing privileged communication.

Most students/clients served by school psychologists are minors, according to the law. Therefore parents, and not students, have the right to receive information about services provided, including information that the child or adolescent would prefer to keep confidential. This can be problematic for the school psychologist, who needs to maintain a trusting relationship with the student, while keeping the parents informed. One solution is to discuss the importance of confidentiality with the parents at the outset of services, and then keep them updated with brief, global summaries of what was covered or discussed with the student to protect the student's privacy. For example, a school psychologist might tell a parent after an individual counseling session, "Today we worked on self-esteem," instead of giving the parent specifics about what the student said during the session.

It is important for a school psychologist to discuss the limits of confidentiality at the outset of services and to continue to discuss them with the client whenever it is warranted to do so. A school psychologist should also make an effort to discuss foreseeable uses of information provided by the client. A school psychologist needs to use age-appropriate language to explain confidentiality and its limits to children and adults. In addition, the school psychologist should explain confidentiality to school building administrators to protect teachers who seek consultation services from the professional. The school psychologist should be extremely clear about what type of information will be shared with administrators and what will remain confidential before any consultation with teachers or other staff begins.

When it is necessary to break confidentiality, it is important to explain to the client the need for disclosure of the information. The school psychologist should use the opportunity to explore with the client how the disclosure of the information might affect the relationship between the client and the psychologist. Finally, the client and the psychologist should discuss how to proceed in order to minimize the negative consequences of the disclosure. For example, if the psychologist needs to disclose information to the client's parents, the client might choose whether or not he or she wants to be in the room when that disclosure is made.

Protecting the confidentiality of clients is important in the delivery of school psychological services. This ethical standard allows students, parents, and teachers to speak more freely when working with a school psychologist, and thus the school psychologist is provided with information that will help in his or her work with the student.

—*Keri Walthall*

See also Counseling; Ethical Issues in School Psychology; Interviewing

REFERENCES AND FURTHER READING

American Psychological Association. (2002). *Ethical principles of psychologists and codes of conduct.* Washington, DC: Author.

Jacob, S., & Hartshone, T. S. (2003). *Ethics and law for school psychologists* (4th ed.). Hoboken, NJ: Wiley.

Hummel, D. L., Talbutt, L .C., & Alexander, M. D. (1985). *Law and ethics in counseling.* New York: Van Nostrand-Reinhold.

National Association of School Psychologists. (2000). *Principles for professional ethics and guidelines for provision of school psychological services.* Bethesda, MD: Author.

CONSEQUENCE. *See* BEHAVIOR; BEHAVIORAL CONCEPTS AND APPLICATIONS

CONSTRUCTIVISM. *See* LEARNING

CONSULTATION: BEHAVIORAL

Behavioral consultation (BC), most commonly associated with John Bergan and Thomas Kratochwill, is an indirect service provided to a client (e.g., child, parent, teacher, patient) by a consultant who works directly with a consultee (e.g., parent, teacher, administrator, medical doctor) to define a problem and develop and evaluate an intervention. The consultee then provides direct services to the client.

Because BC is based upon behavioral theory and procedures that have been effective in teaching new skills and reducing learning and behavior problems, it has become particularly popular in school settings. In comparison to other models of consultation, BC emphasizes direct observations of client behavior, implementation of empirically validated interventions, and systematic evaluation of interventions to guide decisions and determine efficacy.

BC is a four-stage problem-solving model used to design, implement, and evaluate interventions. The four stages of the model are conducted in three separate interviews with the consultee. These stages are:

1. Problem identification (where problems are clearly defined and prioritized)

2. Problem analysis (where goals are established and intervention is designed and implemented)

3. Treatment implementation (where intervention is monitored and changes are made if necessary)

4. Treatment evaluation (where plan effectiveness is evaluated, future plans are determined)

The role of the consultant in BC is to provide information and resources to the consultee based on empirical evidence. The consultant helps the consultee identify the problem and develop a plan to make positive changes in the client's environment. This may or may not include changing the consultee's behavior as well. One aspect that has been highlighted in BC is emphasizing communication and relationship skills of the consultant.

As the mediator between the consultant and the client, the consultee's primary role is to be an active participant in the problem-solving process. This includes acting as information provider and decision maker to design and implement interventions, and as evaluator to determine the efficacy of interventions in changing client behavior.

Although each participant has a specific role, the success of the behavioral consultation process is considered to be a function of the interdependent contribution between consultant and consultee. The consultee is free to reject consultant recommendations at any point in the problem-solving process.

Researchers have examined different facets of BC including changes in clients (most often children and adolescents), consultees (teachers, parents, etc), consultants, and the system. Although not exhaustive, outcome data have included a variety of measures, including:

- Changes in perceptions of problem behaviors resulting in consultation referrals
- Consultee preferences for conducting consultations in different ways (e.g., expert versus collaborative models of consultation)
- Effects of different consultation training procedures
- Effects of different methods of communicating with consultees (i.e., verbalizations)
- Actual consultee and client behavioral change

Researchers also have looked at the efficacy of BC by examining outcome data across published research articles. In general, two main types of studies have appeared in the literature that compare outcomes across studies: the *voting method* and the *meta-analysis*. The voting method occurs when researchers collect available published studies in a particular area (in this case, BC) and report percentages of positive outcomes. For example, in 1979, Fredric Medway found that 84% of consultation studies resulted in positive changes for both consultees and clients. Of the reviewed models of consultation, BC was found to be the most effective in producing changes in clients and consultees. Susan Sheridan and her colleagues conducted a review of consultation research from 1985 to 1995 and found that the majority of reviewed studies (76%) resulted in positive outcomes; whereas 33% reported no or mixed changes, and 4% resulted in negative changes. When examining those studies using BC only, 89% of the reviewed studies had positive results; whereas 11% were neutral, and none had negative outcomes. Sheridan also reported that BC was the most commonly employed model of consultation across reviewed studies (46%).

A second type of efficacy study, the meta-analysis, is a statistical means of evaluating research outcomes across studies. In 1982, Medway and Updyke conducted a meta-analysis on consultation studies published from 1972 to 1979. They reported that both consultees and clients showed improvements when compared to no-treatment groups; however, they found no differences when comparing the efficacy of BC to any other model of consultation. It must be noted, however, that the outcome measures used in the majority of investigations were mainly self-report and attitudinal data, rather than actual measures of behavior change.

The following is an example of a typical school-based problem that would be appropriate for BC. Mrs. Johnson, a third-grade teacher, contacts her school psychologist because she has concerns about a student in her class, John, who is behaving inappropriately during reading class. In the *problem identification* stage, the school psychologist helps Mrs. Johnson accurately define the problem behavior of concern. Through interviewing, it is determined that the primary problem is that John often talks out of turn. The school psychologist asks Mrs. Johnson to monitor and collect data on John's reading group for the next week. In the following interview (*problem analysis*), Mrs. Johnson and the school psychologist review the data and find that John talked out of turn, on average, six times per reading period compared to other students in the class who spoke out, on average, two times per class period. John's talking out was always followed by peer attention. Based on these data, it was determined that a reasonable goal would be to reduce John's talking out to no more than two instances per reading period. Because it appeared that John's talking was reinforced by peers, they decide to design an intervention in which John was moved away from peers he was most likely to talk to. In addition, if John did not display more than two instances of talking out during reading, then he was allowed to have "visiting time" with a peer of his choice for five minutes after reading. The teacher was asked to continue to collect data on John's reading group over the next week. During *treatment implementation*, the school psychologist called Mrs. Johnson on two occasions to determine if the intervention was effective. Mrs. Johnson reported that John's behavior had changed in the desired direction. After three weeks of intervention, Mrs. Johnson

and the school psychologist meet for a *treatment evaluation* interview. Mrs. Johnson reported no further problem from John since treatment implementation and consultation was terminated.

—Heather E. Sterling-Turner and Sheri L. Robinson

See also Consultation: Conjoint Behavioral; Consultation: Ecobehavioral; Consultation: Mental Health; Ethical Issues in School Psychology; Prevention

REFERENCES AND FURTHER READING

Bergan, J. R., & Kratochwill, T. R. (1990). *Behavioral consultation and therapy.* New York, NY: Plenum.

Medway, F. J. (1979). How effective is school consultation? A review of recent research. *Journal of School Psychology, 17,* 275–282.

Medway, F. J., & Updyke, J. F. (1985). Meta-analysis of consultation outcome studies. *American Journal of Community Psychology, 13,* 489–505.

Sheridan, S. M., Welch, M., & Orme, S. F. (1996). Is consultation effective? A review of outcome research. *Remedial and Special Education, 17,* 341–354.

CONSULTATION: CONJOINT BEHAVIORAL

Conjoint behavioral consultation (CBC) is defined as a "structured, indirect form of service delivery in which parents and teachers are joined together to address the academic, social, or behavioral needs of an individual" (Sheridan & Kratochwill, 1992, p. 122). CBC incorporates a data-based, behavioral approach to supporting children's needs in naturalistic settings within an ecological–systems theoretical framework. CBC is a process that is guided by a consultant (e.g., school psychologist, special educator, or other team member) who facilitates a problem-solving process through the use of technical and interpersonal skills (Christenson & Sheridan, 2001). The foci of CBC are remediating and preventing problems and developing home–school partnerships.

There are several differences and similarities between CBC and other forms of consultation. CBC uses the problem-solving model of behavioral consultation (Sheridan & colleagues, 1996), which consists of four stages: problem identification, problem analysis, treatment implementation, and treatment evaluation. Similar to ecobehavioral consultation, CBC is founded upon an ecological–systems perspective that stresses the importance of the entire system surrounding a child, as well as interactions within the system. However, unlike behavioral and ecobehavioral consultation, CBC endorses conjoint (parent and teacher together), not parallel (i.e., parent-only or teacher-only) forms of interaction. In a collaborative fashion, a consultant, parents, and teachers participate in all aspects of the CBC problem-solving process.

CBC can be used as a service delivery model for a variety of concerns. However, it appears to be most beneficial when used to address concerns that exist both at home and at school. First, CBC provides services to parents and teachers simultaneously. Second, information is gathered and expertise is shared across primary caregivers in different settings. Thus, the knowledge and perspectives of parents and teachers can be exchanged across systems. Third, CBC uses ecological assessment and intervention to increase the generalization and maintenance of treatment gains across home and school contexts. By developing consistent intervention procedures across settings, the child is more likely to receive consistent feedback and assistance in developing appropriate skills. Fourth, CBC emphasizes the establishment of a home–school partnership, in which families and schools have a shared responsibility throughout all phases of the consultation process. Thus, parents and teachers are more likely to continue to work collaboratively on immediate and future concerns.

There is an extensive and growing body of empirical research that has demonstrated the effectiveness of CBC. A large-scale study (Sheridan & colleagues, 2001) found CBC to be an acceptable and effective mode of treatment for children's academic, social, and behavioral difficulties in naturalistic environments. This four-year longitudinal study reported positive, moderate-to-large effect sizes across home and school settings. Additionally, experimental small n-studies (e.g., studies done with one or few subjects) and case studies demonstrate that CBC is successful in treating children with irrational fears, increasing social initiation behaviors of socially withdrawn children, increasing positive social interactions of children with attention deficit hyperactivity disorder (ADHD), and improving academic performance. Finally, CBC has been found to be a more acceptable model than teacher-only consultation (Freer & Watson, 1999).

—*John W. Eagle and Susan M. Sheridan*

See also Consultation: Behavioral; Consultation: Ecobehavioral; Parenting

REFERENCES AND FURTHER READING

Christenson, S. L., & Sheridan, S. M. (2001). *Schools and families: Creating essential connections for learning.* New York: Guilford.

Freer, P., & Watson, T. S. (1999). A comparison of parent and teacher acceptability ratings of behavior and conjoint behavioral consultation. *School Psychology Review, 28,* 672–684.

Sheridan, S. M., Eagle, J. W., Cowan, R. J., & Mickelson, W. (2001). The effects of conjoint behavioral consultation: Results of a 4-year investigation. *Journal of School Psychology, 39,* 361–385.

Sheridan, S. M., Kratochwill, T. R., & Bergan, J. R. (1996). *Conjoint behavioral consultation: A procedural manual.* New York: Plenum.

Sheridan, S. M., & Kratochwill, T. R. (1992). Behavioral parent-teacher consultation: Conceptual and research considerations. *Journal of School Psychology, 30,* 117–139.

CONSULTATION: ECOBEHAVIORAL

Ecobehavioral consultation refers to an approach to consultation guided by an integration of behavioral theory and ecological theory with the problem-solving process common to all models of consultation. Consultation is a method of providing indirect psychological services to children. Instead of offering counseling directly to the student, for instance, the psychologist offers professional expertise to one or more adults (e.g., teacher, parent) in a manner that is helpful to resolving concerns associated with the child. The term ecobehavioral consultation was first coined by Gutkin (1993), but has been described by others (e.g., Conoley & Conoley, 1992; Kantor, 1924).

All psychologists, and thus all psychological consultants, are guided by theories when attempting to understand human behavior. Behavioral theory has a long history of explaining human behavior and guiding psychological interventions (Skinner, 1953; Watson, 1924). An ecological theory of human behavior borrows the concept of an ecological system from the biological sciences and applies it to the understanding of human behavior (Barker, 1978; Brofenbrenner, 1979; von Bertalanffy, 1968). In biological sciences, ecology is defined as a system made up of interdependent parts that interact with and influence each other. The integration of behavior theory and ecological systems theory defines the guiding orientation of an ecobehavioral consultant.

AN ECOBEHAVIORAL VIEW OF HUMAN BEHAVIOR

Behavioral theory, or behaviorism, explains human behavior as occurring in direct relation to environmental antecedents and consequences. *Antecedents* are factors present in an environment that precede a behavior of interest and that give rise to, or stimulate, the occurrence of the behavior. These are things such as how a classroom is arranged, how a teacher presents instructions, or how a parent states a request for compliance. Some antecedents can occur outside of the immediate situation and are called setting events. *Setting events* are events that occur separate in time or place, yet can have an influence on behavior in subsequent situations. For example, if a student experiences teasing on the bus ride to school, the teasing may adversely affect the student's attitude or performance in class that day. Although important to consider, in behavioral psychology research, setting events tend to receive less attention than immediate antecedents. *Consequences* are events in an environment that directly follow a targeted behavior and have a reinforcing or punishing effect, thus making the behavior more (if reinforced) or less (if punished) likely to occur. For example, if a teacher praises a child for trying a difficult problem and the teacher's praise serves as a reinforcing event, then the student is more likely to put forth effort in the future when faced with challenging work. It is important to note that reinforcing consequences serve to create learning of new behavior, but punishing consequences only serve to limit the display of already learned behavior. This is why it is important for people to experience high amounts of reinforcement when learning new skills or behaviors.

Ecological theory, or systems theory, attempts to explain how factors associated with various social systems (ecologies) influence human behavior. An individual child is a part of many different social systems such as family, friends, school, church, and other important systems. Each of these individual systems has interdependent components (i.e., a family can be comprised of parents, siblings, and extended family members) and is also part of larger systems such as neighborhoods, school districts, and political entities. Nonsocial factors are present in a child's ecology as well. For example, a child's behavior can be influenced by the physical location, size, and characteristics of his or her home. While these nonsocial factors may merit some attention in ecobehavioral consultation, the major focus is on the interaction of human elements within and between various ecological systems. An important aspect of ecological theory is that attitudes and cognitions are an important part of the ecology, not just observable behavior.

The integration of behavioral theory and ecological theory provides a comprehensive and highly useful basis for improving student behavior or helping a student to learn through consultation. The use of behavior theory allows the consultant to carefully analyze the immediate environment to help adults maximize the positive effect of antecedent and consequence factors. Adding ecological systems theory expands the universe of possibilities for providing psychological assistance. The task for the ecobehavioral consultant becomes one of analyzing the dynamics of the various interdependent parts within the various systems in which the child resides. The theory suggests that changes made in part of an ecological system will potentially affect the other parts, including other systems. The key is to fully analyze the relationships so a *ripple effect* of change will occur.

APPLYING ECOBEHAVIORAL CONSULTATION

Applying this theory to the process of providing help to children has a long-standing history in school psychology (Minor, 1972). When a school psychologist who is operating from an ecobehavioral orientation approaches a problem situation associated with a child, the problem symptoms are seen as indicators of a mismatch between the child and the ecology where the problem is occurring. Additionally, the other ecological systems where the child resides are seen as potential resources to understanding and improving the problem situation.

To illustrate the application of ecobehavioral consultation, consider the following example of a child experiencing an academic problem. When presented with a primarily academic problem, understanding the child's specific skill levels through direct behavioral assessment techniques (e.g., classroom observations) is important, and it also fits within the ecobehavioral consultation model. This approach is also consistent with behavioral consultation. What distinguishes ecobehavioral consultation is the broader analysis in which the school psychologist engages. In addition to the typical analysis of how the curriculum instructional techniques match the child's learning strengths, the consultant assesses whether there is a mismatch between the child's abilities and expectations. In this regard, it is important for the psychologist to understand the attitudes and expectations of adults toward the child's learning. This would include attitudes and expectations of parents, siblings, and even peers. Examining how the other important people in the child's life view schooling and his or her academic problems is important for the ecobehavioral consultant to note and understand. As a result, any of these areas serve as potential places to intervene, and potential interventions include:

- Adjusting curriculum
- Adjusting expectations, attitudes, instruction
- Adjusting the kind of support offered in each setting

Often the ecologically oriented consultant tries to intervene in multiple areas, thereby increasing the likelihood of achieving positive change.

Similarly, when presented with a child who is exhibiting behavioral problems in the one setting, one solution may be to adjust parenting or teacher discipline tactics to better match the child's temperament. Another possibility may be to introduce routines and stories about those routines to add more predictability for the child. Of course, an ecobehavioral consultant also looks at the child's academic performance to determine if the child's performance in the classroom is associated with the child's problematic behavior. Thus, an ecobehavioral consultant seeks to change specific characteristics associated with the child by creating change in another part of the system or another system to better support the child's development.

—*Mike Bonner*

See also Consultation: Behavioral; Consultation: Conjoint Behavioral; Consultation: Mental Health

REFERENCES AND FURTHER READING

Barker, R. G. (1978). *Habitats, environments, and human behavior.* San Francisco: Jossey-Bass.

Brofenbrenner, U. (1979). *The ecology of human development.* Cambridge, MA: Harvard University Press.

Conoley, J. C., & Conoley, C. W. (1992). *School consultation: Practice and training* (2nd ed.). New York: Macmillan.

Gutkin, T. B. (1993). Moving from behavioral to ecobehavioral consultation: What's in a name? *Journal of Educational and Psychological Consultation, 4,* 95–99.

Kantor, J. R. (1924). *Principles of psychology* (Vol. 1). Bloomington, IN: Principia Press.

Minor, M. W. (1972). Systems analysis and school psychology. *Journal of School Psychology, 10,* 227–232.

Skinner, B. F. (1953). *Science and human behavior.* New York: Free Press.

von Bertalanffy, L. (1968). *A systems view of man.* Boulder CO: Westview.

Watson, J. B. (1924/1970). *Behaviorism.* New York: Norton.

CONSULTATION: MENTAL HEALTH

Consultation is a method of providing preventively oriented psychoeducational services in which a consultant (e.g., school psychologist) and consultee (e.g., teacher) develop a cooperative partnership and engage in a systematic problem-solving process. The goal is to enhance and empower consultee systems, so as to promote client (e.g., student) adjustment and academic performance. With regard to models for practice, behavioral consultation, mental health consultation, and organizational development consultation are the three major human services models of consultation within school psychology. Erchul and Schulte (1993) further note that mental health consultation distinguishes itself through its conceptual bases in psychodynamic and systems-level thinking, a population-oriented preventive model of psychiatry, crisis theory and intervention, and support systems.

ORIGINS

In 1949, psychiatrist Gerald Caplan and his small clinical staff were given the difficult task of addressing the mental health needs of 16,000 adolescent immigrants in Israel (Caplan & Caplan, 1999). In response, Caplan developed a new approach to service delivery, which he originally termed "counseling the counselors." Rather than meet with individual clients at a central clinic location, Caplan and his coworkers traveled to the many residential institutions to meet with the caregivers of the referred teenagers. Supportive, collegial discussions with the caregivers about their clients often resulted in a return to work with enlightened perspectives that produced more effective management of client problems. According to Erchul and Schulte, the contemporary practice of mental health consultation emerged from this approach, which developed further during Caplan's 1953–1977 tenure at Harvard University.

THE CONSULTANT/ CONSULTEE RELATIONSHIP

Caplan and Caplan (1993/1999) outline the unique features of the consultant/consultee relationship found in mental health consultation (MHC). Although also underlying other models of consultation, these features distinguish MHC from other professional relationships such as supervision, teaching, and psychotherapy. They include:

- The consultation relationship is triadic, involving a consultant, consultee(s), and client(s). Consultees typically lack the training and experience that consultants have, although they are still legitimately considered professionals.
- The desired working relationship in MHC is seen as coordinating and nonhierarchical; ideally no power differential should exist between consultant and consultee.
- Consultee work-related problems rather than personal problems form the basis for consultative discussion.
- Because the consultant has no administrative responsibility for or formal authority over the consultee, the final professional responsibility for client outcomes rests with the consultee.
- The consultee's participation in MHC is considered voluntary because he or she has the freedom to accept or reject whatever guidance the consultant may offer.
- Conversations between consultant and consultee are regarded as confidential, unless the consultant believes someone will be harmed if silence is maintained.
- MHC has two purposes: (1) to assist the consultee with a current professional problem and (2) to arm the consultee with additional insights and skills that will allow him or her to deal effectively with similar future problems, preferably without the consultant's continued help.

THE FOUR TYPES OF MENTAL HEALTH CONSULTATION

Caplan and Caplan (1993/1999) delineate four types of MHC, which are based on two major considerations: whether the content focus is on a client concern or an administrative concern, and whether the primary goal is to provide information drawn from the consultant's area of expertise or to improve the problem-solving capacity of the consultee.

Client-centered case consultation perhaps is the most frequent type of consultation conducted by school psychologists. For example, a teacher who is encountering difficulty with a student may contact a psychologist who then assesses the student, formulates a diagnosis, and provides recommendations about how the teacher might work more effectively with the student. The primary goal here is to devise a plan for handling a client's difficulties; consultee education or skill development is secondary.

Consultee-centered case consultation focuses on the difficulties a consultee faces with a particular client. Gutkin and Curtis (1999) note that this is the type of MHC most closely associated with Caplan. The primary goal of consultee-centered case consultation is to address the deficits in the consultee's functioning that create problems in handling the present case; client improvement is secondary.

Program-centered administrative consultation is similar to client-centered case consultation, except that a program is under consideration. Here, the consultant considers the range of issues surrounding the development of a new program or other aspects of organizational functioning.

Consultee-centered administrative consultation has the goal of improving the professional functioning of staff members, and is generally based on a more broadly defined role for the consultant. For example, the consultant may not limit his or her purview to consultee-generated issues, but rather may be active in evaluating many different organizational problems.

ADDRESSING CONSULTEE DIFFICULTIES

Especially when engaged in consultee-centered MHC, a consultant must determine the likely cause(s) of consultee difficulty. These include lack of knowledge, lack of skill, lack of self-confidence, and lack of objectivity. The first three mentioned are relatively straightforward, but lack of objectivity appears more complicated. Lack of objectivity occurs when a consultee loses his or her usual professional distance when working with a client, and consequently is unable to apply established skills effectively to resolve a current work problem. In an interview, Caplan stated that, when supervisory and administrative systems are functioning well (and lack of knowledge and lack of skill thus can be eliminated as causes), most displays of consultee ineffectiveness are caused by a lack of objectivity.

Caplan and Caplan point to five types of consultee lack of objectivity:

1. Direct personal involvement
2. Simple identification
3. Transference
4. Characterological distortion
5. Theme interference

To address problems surrounding consultee objectivity, they recommend several indirect, psychodynamic techniques (e.g., theme interference reduction, verbal focus on the client, parable, nonverbal focus on the client, nonverbal focus on the consultation relationship).

WHEN TO USE MENTAL HEALTH CONSULTATION

According to Brown and colleagues (2001), many consultants are left to their general theoretical and personal biases rather than any solid empirical findings when deciding which consultation model to use. Nonetheless, Erchul and Martens (2002) indicate that MHC provides a useful framework for understanding consultee relationship and systems-level issues within consultation. (In a complementary manner, behavior analytic principles embedded in behavioral consultation supply a solid basis for selecting client interventions.) Whether MHC can reach the standard of an "evidence-based intervention," a key contemporary concept promoted by Kratochwill and Stoiber (2000), remains to be seen.

In conclusion, MHC developed after World War II in Israel as a pragmatic response to a difficult set of mental health care circumstances. It is a conceptually rich model of consultation that seems particularly relevant when consultee and organizational setting issues are relevant to understanding problems within the context of consultation.

—*William P. Erchul*

See also Academic Achievement; Learning

REFERENCES AND FURTHER READING

Brown, D., Pryzwansky, W. B., & Schulte, A. C. (2001). *Psychological consultation: Introduction to theory and practice* (5th ed.). Boston: Allyn & Bacon.

Caplan, G., & Caplan, R. B. (1999). *Mental health consultation and collaboration* Prospect Heights, IL: Waveland. (Original work published 1993).

Erchul, W. P. (1993). Reflections on mental health consultation: An interview with Gerald Caplan. In W. P. Erchul (Ed.), *Consultation in community, school, and organizational practice: Gerald Caplan's contributions to professional psychology* (pp. 57–72). Washington, DC: Taylor and Francis.

Erchul, W. P., & Martens, B. K. (2002). *School consultation: Conceptual and empirical bases of practice.* New York: Kluwer Academic/Plenum.

Erchul, W. P., & Schulte, A. C. (1993). Gerald Caplan's contributions to professional psychology: Conceptual underpinnings. In W. P. Erchul (Ed.), *Consultation in community, school, and organizational practice: Gerald Caplan's contributions to professional psychology* (pp. 3–40). Washington, DC: Taylor and Francis.

Gutkin, T. B. & Curtis, M. J. (1999). School-based consultation theory and practice: The art and science of indirect service delivery. In C. R. Reynolds & T. B. Gutkin (Eds.), *Handbook of school psychology* (3rd ed., pp. 598–637). New York: Wiley.

Kratochwill, T. R., & Stoiber, K. C. (2000). Empirically supported interventions and school psychology: Conceptual and practice issues–Part II. *School Psychology Quarterly, 15,* 233–253.

CONTINGENCY. *See*
APPLIED BEHAVIOR ANALYSIS; BEHAVIOR; BEHAVIOR INTERVENTION; BEHAVIOR ASSESSMENT

COOPERATIVE LEARNING

Cooperative learning is the instructional use of small groups such that students work together to maximize their own and each other's learning. In cooperative learning situations, there is a positive interdependence among students' goal attainments; students perceive that they can reach their learning goals if and only if the other students in the learning group also reach their goals (Deutsch, 1962; Johnson & Johnson, 1989). Cooperative learning is usually contrasted with competitive learning (students working to achieve goals that only a few can attain; students can succeed if and only if other students in the class fail to obtain their goals) and individualistic learning (students working alone on goals independent from the goals of others).

There are three types of cooperative learning (Johnson & colleagues, 1998a, 1998b; Johnson & Johnson, 1999): formal cooperative learning, informal cooperative learning, and cooperative base groups. Formal cooperative learning involves students working together, for one class period to several weeks, to achieve shared learning goals and complete jointly specific tasks and assignments such as decision-making or problem-solving tasks, writing a report, conducting a survey or experiment, reading a chapter or reference book. Any course requirement or assignment may be reformulated to be cooperative. In formal cooperative learning groups teachers make a number of preinstructional decisions (teachers have to decide on the objectives of the lesson, size of groups, the method of assigning students to groups, the roles students will be assigned, the materials needed to conduct the lesson, and the way the room will be arranged). Teachers then have to explain the task and the cooperative structure to the class. Teachers explain the academic task, teach the required concepts and strategies, specify the positive goal interdependence and individual accountability, give the criteria for success, and explain the expected social skills to be engaged in. Teachers monitor students' learning and, when it is needed, intervene in the groups to provide assistance. Finally, teachers assess the quality of students' learning and help students process how well their groups functioned and members worked together.

Informal cooperative learning consists of having students work together to achieve a joint learning goal in temporary, ad-hoc groups that last from a few minutes to one class period (Johnson & colleagues, 1998b; Johnson & Johnson, 1999). During direct teaching (a lecture, demonstration, or film) informal cooperative learning groups may be used to have students engage in 3-to-5-minute focused discussions before and after the direct teaching, and 2-to-3-minute turn-to-your-partner discussions interspersed every 15 minutes or so throughout the direct teaching.

Cooperative base groups are long-term, heterogeneous cooperative learning groups with stable membership (Johnson & colleagues, 1998b; Johnson & Johnson, 1999). The purposes of the base group are to give the support, help, encouragement, and assistance each member needs to make academic progress (attend class, complete all assignments, learn) and to develop cognitively and socially in healthy ways.

EXAMPLE OF CLASSROOM USE OF COOPERATIVE LEARNING

An example of the use of the cooperative learning procedures is as follows. Students arrive at class and meet in their base groups (i.e., their cooperative learning groups) to welcome each other, check each others' homework, and make sure each member is prepared for class. The teacher then begins a lesson on the limitations of being human. Informal cooperative learning is used to help students cognitively organize in advance what they know about the advantages and disadvantages of being human. The teacher asks students to form pairs and ponder for 2 minutes the limitations of being human. In the next few minutes, the teacher explains that humans, like all other organisms, have very specific limitations. We cannot see bacteria in a drop of water, hear as well as a deer, or fly like an eagle, but we have invented microscopes, telescopes, and our own wings. The teacher then instructs students to discuss for 3 minutes in their pairs, "What have we invented to overcome the limitations you identified, and what other human limitations might we be able to overcome?"

Formal cooperative learning is used next in the classroom. The teacher randomly assigns students to groups of four. The task is to design a "Being" that overcomes the human limitations thought of by the class and draw a diagram of it. Each member is assigned a role: encourager of participation, summarizer, recorder, and comprehension checker. Each group is to make one drawing (positive goal interdependence) that all members have contributed to and can explain. The criterion for success is to complete the diagram in 30 minutes. The teacher establishes individual accountability by observing each group and, when needed, intervening to provide academic assistance and help in working together effectively. At the end of the lesson, the groups hand in their diagrams to be assessed. Group members then process how well they worked together by identifying actions each member engaged in that helped the group succeed and one thing that could be added to improve their group effectiveness next time.

The teacher next uses informal cooperative learning to provide closure to the lesson by explaining more about the strengths and limitations of humans. Students are asked to meet in pairs and write out six conclusions about the limitations of human beings and what humans have done to overcome the limitations. At the end of the class session, the cooperative base groups meet to review what students have learned and the homework assignment.

KEY ELEMENTS OF COOPERATIVE LEARNING

For cooperative learning to be effective, five key elements must be structured into the learning situation (Johnson & Johnson, 1989, 1999). The heart of cooperation is positive interdependence, which is established through mutual goals, joint rewards, divided resources, complementary roles, and a team identity. Individual accountability is established by assessing the performance of each individual member and giving the results to group members to compare against a standard of performance. Group members know that they cannot "hitchhike" or receive a "free ride" on the work of others. Promotive interaction occurs as group members encourage and facilitate each other's efforts to contribute to the accomplishment of the group's goals. Group members give and receive help, exchange resources, give and receive feedback, challenge each other's reasoning, advocate increased effort to achieve, and mutually influence each other. The appropriate use of social skills (leadership, decision making, trust building, communication, and conflict management) is essential for effective group work. These social skills have to be taught just as purposefully and precisely as task-related skills. Group processing occurs when members discuss how well they are achieving their goals and maintaining effective working relationships among members. To continuously improve, group members need to describe what member actions are helpful and unhelpful and make decisions about what behaviors to continue or change.

RESEARCH ON COOPERATIVE LEARNING

During the past 110 years, more than 550 experimental and 100 correlational studies have been conducted by a wide variety of researchers in different decades with diverse participants, in different subject areas, and in different settings (Johnson & Johnson, 1989, 1999). The research on cooperation, therefore, has a validity and a generalizability rarely found in the educational literature.

Working together to achieve mutual goals can have profound effects on the individuals involved (Johnson & Johnson, 1989), which may be subsumed within three interrelated categories:

1. Effort exerted to achieve (higher achievement and greater productivity, more frequent use of higher-level reasoning, more frequent generation of new ideas and solutions, greater intrinsic and achievement motivation, greater long-term retention, more on-task behavior, and greater transfer of what is learned within one situation to another)

2. Quality of relationships among participants (greater interpersonal attraction, liking, cohesion, valuing of heterogeneity, and social support)

3. Psychological adjustment (greater psychological health, social competencies, self-esteem, self-efficacy, shared identity, and ability to cope with stress and adversity)

GOALS OF COOPERATIVE LEARNING

Cooperative learning is used to achieve a wide variety of goals connected with its documented outcomes (Johnson & Johnson, 1989, 1999). It ensures that all students are:

- Meaningfully and actively involved in learning (thereby reducing disruptive, off-task behavior)
- Achieving up to their potential (thereby experiencing psychological success and being less at risk for psychological withdrawal and dropping out)
- Developing caring and committed relationships (thereby being less isolated or alienated from their peers)

Cooperative groups provide an arena in which students develop the interpersonal and small-group skills needed to work effectively with diverse schoolmates and to engage in personal discussions in which problems are shared and solved (thereby increasing their resilience and ability to cope with adversity). Helping one's group mates promotes a sense of meaning, pride, and esteem. The systematic use of cooperative learning provides the context for resolving conflicts in constructive ways.

—*David W. Johnson and Roger T. Johnson*

See also Ability Grouping; Academic Achievement; Learning

REFERENCES AND FURTHER READING

Deutsch, M. (1962). Cooperation and trust: Some theoretical notes. In M. R. Jones (Ed.), *Nebraska symposium on motivation* (pp. 275–319). Lincoln, NE: University of Nebraska Press.

Johnson, D. W., & Johnson, R. (1989). *Cooperation and competition: Theory and research.* Edina, MN: Interaction Book.

Johnson, D. W., & Johnson, R. (1999). *Learning together and alone: Cooperative, competitive, and individualistic learning* (5th ed.). Boston: Allyn & Bacon

Johnson, D. W., Johnson, R., & Holubec, E. (1998a). *Cooperation in the classroom* (7th ed.). Edina, MN: Interaction Book.

Johnson, D. W., Johnson, R., & Holubec, E. (1998b). *Advanced cooperative learning* (3rd ed.). Edina, MN: Interaction Book.

CORPORAL PUNISHMENT

Historically, corporal punishment (CP) has been defined as the infliction of pain, loss, or confinement of the human body—as distinguished from financial consequence—as a penalty for some offense. In the past, it was a common civil penalty used on citizens, slaves, sailors, and school children. Parental spanking, in contemporary times, is defined as the use of physical force with the intention of causing a child to experience pain but not injury, for purposes of correction or control of the child's behavior (Straus, 1994).

In contemporary educational settings, CP is generally synonymous with paddling for breaking a school rule. However, because of case law, the definition has expanded to include any punishment that includes the infliction of pain that results in unreasonable discomfort (Hyman, 1997). CP includes excessive physical drills, shaking, making students stand for long periods in uncomfortable positions, excessive time in time-out rooms, tying students in time-out chairs, not allowing use of bathroom facilities for unreasonable periods of time, and forcing children to ingest obnoxious substances. In school settings, the legal definition of corporal punishment does not cover the use of force or restraint to protect one's self, another, and property; to obtain weapons; or to prevent students from harming themselves.

INCIDENCE OF CORPORAL PUNISHMENT

A study by Burns (1992) found that 85% of the American population approved of corporal punishment, compared to 64% of Austrians and 37% of Swedes. Straus and Kantor (1994) examined the reported use of corporal punishment and found that more than 90% of Americans used corporal punishment, and 84% found spanking to be necessary and harmless.

Currently, the United States is one of few western democracies in which the use of CP in the schools is still legal. Internationally, most industrialized, European democracies eliminated the use of corporal punishment by the end of the 20th century. In 1967, New Jersey became the first state to legislatively ban corporal punishment in schools, followed in 1972 by Massachusetts.

As of 2004, the following 28 states have banned corporal punishment in the schools: Alaska (1989), California (1986), Connecticut (1989), Delaware (2003), Hawaii (1973), Illinois (1993), Iowa (1989), Maine (1975), Maryland (1993), Massachusetts (1971), Michigan (1989), Minnesota (1989), Montana (1991), Nebraska (1988), Nevada (1993), New Hampshire (1983), New Jersey (1967), New York (1985), North Dakota (1989), Oregon (1989), Rhode Island (all local boards have banned), South Dakota (1990), Utah (1992), Vermont (1985), Virginia (1989), Washington (1993), West Virginia (1994), Wisconsin (1988). In addition, Pennsylvania is close to passing a CP ban.

In addition to statewide bans on corporal punishment, most major cities and affluent suburbs have banned it. Research, especially data collected in biannual Office of Civil Rights (OCR) surveys, suggests that most legal use of corporal punishment occurs in rural areas and in schools in the South and Southwest. Data from the first OCR survey in 1976 suggested at that time there were at least two to three million incidents in all of the schools in America (Hyman, 1997). This is in comparison to the last survey available from the U.S. Department of Education, in which 365,058 public school paddlings occurred in the 1997–1998 academic year (U.S. Department of Education, 2000). Since most parochial schools forbid the use of corporal punishment, the remainder of incidents occur in various religious schools and academies that adhere to literal interpretations of the Bible as a guide for discipline (Hyman, 1997).

While legislation regarding corporal punishment initially focused on schools, recent efforts have been made internationally to ban the use of corporal punishment by parents. Sweden has banned parental use of corporal punishment since 1979, being the first country in the world to do so (Hyman & colleagues,

2002). Ten other countries have since enacted similar laws, with Iceland being the most recent to do so in 2003. Eventually, because of actions of the European Convention on Human Rights, it may be that all European signatory states eventually ban parental spanking.

LEGAL ISSUES

Legal arguments against the use of corporal punishment include Constitutional and emotional or physical damage claims. In the 1974 case of *Ingraham v. Wright* (Hyman & colleagues, 2002; Hyman & Wise, 1979) the U.S. Supreme Court ruled that students are not entitled to Eighth Amendment protections against cruel and unusual punishment or the Fifth Amendment guarantees of procedural due process. They did not rule on the issue of substantive due process (i.e., the deprivation of personal liberty), which involves the invasion of the physical and psychological integrity of the student. Federal district courts have given differing opinions about what level of force denies a student substantive due-process rights.

In the 1987 case of *Garcia v. Miera,* the Tenth Circuit Court of Appeals ruled that the school had used excessive force and violated the victim's federal Constitutional right of substantive due process. In this case, which involved a student in New Mexico, the court allowed the plaintiff to sue the defendant school for relief, based on the substantive due-process guarantees of the Constitution. However, in a completely contrary opinion in 1988, the Fifth Circuit Court decided in *Cunningham v. Beavers,* that corporal punishment in Texas may be administered up to the point "of deadly force" (Hyman & colleagues, 2002).

Even though students or their parents may be entitled to sue under the Fifth Amendment, many states have passed strong immunity laws that protect public officials and employees from being sued for performing their duties in a "reasonable " manner. In order to sue for damages to a child who has been severely hit by a school official, the parents must convince the court that the official's action would "shock the conscience" of most people (Hyman & colleagues, 2002). This has become increasingly difficult to demonstrate, especially in states where CP is popular. But successful litigation against schools is still possible by proving that the CP caused such emotional damage that the student developed severe emotional reactions such as posttraumatic stress disorder (PTSD) (Hyman, 1997).

EFFECTS OF CORPORAL PUNISHMENT

Most research indicates that children who are spanked are more aggressive and view physical force as an appropriate means of dealing with conflict (Straus, 1994). CP can lead to multiple physical injuries including bruises, broken bones, and internal injuries. One national study of newspaper accounts found a high incidence of reported cases of death occurred because of intentionally nonabusive use of CP escalating (Hyman, 1997).

Research indicates that the use of corporal punishment on children may result in increases in vandalism, truancy, pupil violence, and higher school dropout rates as well as increased cheating, lying, bullying, and disobedience. While many claim that CP is *only* used as a last resort, unfortunately, CP is often a first resort for even minor misbehaviors (Hyman, 1997). Beatings for minor infractions can cause children to suffer stress symptoms, destroying their self-esteem and setting the stage for future emotional problems, including feelings of helplessness and rejection (Hyman, 1997). Hitting children, especially in school, can also lead to delinquency, sexual acting-out behavior, increased anxiety, sleeping difficulties, enuresis, and violent acting out if it is accompanied by other acts that alienate the students (Hyman, 1997; Hyman & colleagues, 2002).

As the frequency of CP administered to a child is increased, so too are the negative effects, including an increased probability of alcohol abuse, as well as children repressing feelings of anger, resentment, and humiliation, resulting in them becoming especially prone to suicidal thoughts, suicide, and depression (Straus & Kantor, 1994).

Research has also revealed that increases in CP were associated with decreases in cognitive ability (Hyman, 1997). Finally, Straus and Donnelly (1993) concluded that CP of adolescents is particularly harmful and should not be used because it is associated with an increased probability of violence, crime, and depression, as well as adult behavior problems such as physical assault on a spouse, physical abuse of children, alienation, and masochistic sex.

PREVENTION TECHNIQUES

Extensive literature reviews suggest that, while pain can cause immediate cessation of misbehavior, praise, reward, encouragement, and preventive techniques are far superior in changing children's behavior (American Academy of Pediatrics, 1998). Effective prevention methods include:

- Consistently enforcing realistic rules
- Providing firm limits and structure
- Speaking and teaching at a level children understand
- Allowing children to have their voices heard while making rules
- Making it clear and known to children what behaviors are and are not acceptable

Further recommendations include parents removing their children from potential misbehaviors when possible. For example, keeping their children away from breakable objects or childproofing their house are effective preventive strategies. Finally, it is suggested that parents model appropriate behavior and catch their children being good as this praise will reinforce their appropriate behavior (Hyman, 1997).

ALTERNATIVES TO CORPORAL PUNISHMENT

If punishment appears necessary, use withdrawal of favored objects, use time-out, and make consequences relate to the misbehavior. For example, if children make a mess, they should clean it up. When possible, teach children acceptable behavior rather than punish them as this is more effective in preventing further misbehavior. Finally, infants and toddlers should be redirected when engaging in inappropriate behavior as they do not yet understand right from wrong. Overall, nearly 100% of pediatricians surveyed believe using alternative disciplinary measures, such as removal of privileges and time-out, are more effective than hitting children (American Academy of Pediatrics, 1998).

—*Theresa A. Erbacher and Irwin A. Hyman*

See also Discipline; Due Process

REFERENCES AND FURTHER READING

American Academy of Pediatrics. (1998). Policy statement: Guidance for effective discipline. *Pediatrics* [Online], *101*(4), 723–728. Available online at http://silcon.com/~ptave/aap.htm

Burns, N. (1992, September 1). *Legislative and attitudinal comparison of western countries on corporal punishment.* Paper presented at the International Society for the Prevention of Child Abuse (ISPCAN) Conference in Chicago, IL.

Hyman, I. A. (1997). *The case against spanking: How to discipline your child without hitting.* San Francisco, CA: Jossey-Bass.

Hyman, I., Cohen, I., & Mahon, M. (2003) Student alienation syndrome: A paradigm for understanding the relation between school trauma and school violence. *The California School Psychologist, 8,* 73–86.

Hyman, I, Stefkovich, J., & Taich, S. (2002). Paddling and pro-paddling polemics: Refuting nineteenth century pedagogy. *Journal of Law and Education, 31*(1), 74–84.

Hyman, I., & Wise, J. (Eds.). (1979). *Corporal punishment in American education.* Philadelphia: Temple University Press.

Straus, M. A. (1994). *Beating the devil out of them: CP in American families.* New York: Lexington Books.

Straus, M., & Donnelly, D. (1993). Corporal punishment of adolescents by American parents. *Youth and Society, 24,* 419-442.

Straus, M. A., & Kantor, G. K. (1994). Corporal punishment of adolescents by parents: A risk factor in the epidemiology of depression, suicide, alcohol abuse, child abuse, and wife beating. *Adolescence, 29*(115), 543-561.

U.S. Department of Education (2000). *Fall 1998 elementary and secondary school civil rights compliance report.* Washington, DC: U.S. Department of Education.

COUNCIL OF DIRECTORS OF SCHOOL PSYCHOLOGY PROGRAMS

Council of Directors of School Psychology Programs (CDSPP) was formed in 1977 to coincide with similar leadership groups representing clinical psychology (Council of University Directors of Clinical Psychology [CUDCP]), counseling psychology (Council of Counseling Psychology Training Programs [CCPTP]), professional schools (National Council of Schools of Professional Psychology [NCSPP]), and internship organizations (Association of Psychology Postdoctoral and Internship Centers [APPIC]). The mission of the CDSPP is to assist doctoral-level school psychology program directors by:

- Providing a forum for discussion and dissemination of relevant materials
- Promoting and advocating for doctoral-level school psychology training and practice
- Communicating with school psychology organizations such as Division 16 (School Psychology) of the American Psychological Association

(APA) and the National Association of School Psychologists (NASP)

- Participating in meetings such as the Council of Chairs of Training Councils (CCTC) and the APA Board of Educational Affairs (BEA).

Membership in the CDSPP has grown from 35 membership institutions in 1978 to 103 in 2004. For most of the organization's history, annual meetings were held during the APA annual convention. Under the leadership of LeAdelle Phelps (Chair) and Elaine Clark (Secretary/Treasurer), the CDSPP embarked on a yearly midwinter meeting with the first conference held in Fort Lauderdale, Florida, on January 31 to February 2, 1997. The midwinter meetings have been highly successful and have been held the last week in January since 1997.

—*LeAdelle Phelps*

See also American Psychological Association; National Association of School Psychologists; School Psychologist

COUNSELING

Counseling can be defined as a human service that enhances personal and interpersonal functioning across the life span and addresses emotional, social, vocational, educational, health-related, developmental, and organizational concerns. The focus is typically on healthy aspects of the client, personal and environmental characteristics (including culture, ethnicity, gender, sexual orientation, socioeconomic status, and physical ability), and the role of career on individual development and functioning. A brief description of the historical foundations of the counseling profession follows.

The industrial revolution (early 1900s) created a large number of jobs, and it became clear that young people had more career choices than their predecessors. Frank Parsons was a social reformer who identified the need to help people learn how to make these new career choices. He opened a career counseling service in 1908, and his work spurred the vocational guidance movement. This movement continued to flourish during the two World Wars because of the need for occupational classification of the men who were part of the military campaigns (Gelso & Fretz, 2001).

A second historical development that influenced the emergence of counseling was the psychometric movement. Psychometrics is essentially the science of measuring human behaviors and psychological processes. This movement began in the mid-to-late 1800s with Sir Francis Galton, who was interested in trying to understand differences between people by using mathematics. Alfred Binet, along with colleague Theodore Simon, published the first intelligence test in 1905. This further legitimized the measurement of individual differences. The psychometric movement also equipped vocational guidance counselors with the tools needed to gather information about individual aptitudes, abilities, and interests.

Counseling also has its roots in E. G. Williamson's goal-oriented counseling approach to help students adjust in large universities. Also, Carl Rogers created the client-centered approach to counseling that emphasized counseling and growth of individuals (rather than the diagnosis and assessment of psychopathology). Both of these developments occurred in the late 1930s and early 1940s and shifted the focus of treatments from long-term therapy, emphasizing diagnosis and remediation, to more short-term counseling focused on growth.

LONG-STANDING AND EMERGING THEMES

Developmental Emphasis

Counselors focus on healthy development across the life span. They use human development theories and models to inform their practice. With knowledge of and focus on normal development, counselors can enhance the lives of those they serve by helping teachers, parents, and others create growth-promoting environments. In addition, they can teach individuals skills to deal with everyday problems. For example, counselors in a high school setting could develop training programs to enhance study skills or create workshops on career choice and development for students, both of which are developmentally appropriate issues for youth. These interventions foster the students' skills and personal development, rather than simply remedying deficient behaviors.

Brief Individual and Group Counseling

The counseling process unfolds fairly systematically over the course of time-limited sessions (i.e., 50 minutes for individual sessions, 90 minutes for group sessions; school counseling sessions may be shorter). First, counselors work to establish rapport with clients and develop a sound therapeutic relationship (characterized by genuineness and trust). Within the context of that relationship, the counselor and client define the focus of their work. Goal setting often serves to create markers of progress over the course of sessions. Well-conceptualized interventions are then used by counselors to address psychological concerns or to equip clients with skills or resources. When counseling goals are met, the counselor facilitates termination and then arranges for follow-up.

Counselors work with both individuals and groups. Like individual counseling, group counseling is usually brief (12 to 15 sessions). Certain concerns can be more effectively treated in a group-counseling format than in individual counseling. For example, if an adolescent is having difficulties interacting with peers, a group setting can provide an arena for the person to practice interpersonal skills. Groups allow individuals to give and get feedback and empathy from other group members. This form of counseling also provides individuals with a re-creation of everyday life because group members get to interact with and affect others (Corey & Corey, 1997). Not all issues and people are amenable to group work. Some people may be too vulnerable to the influence of group members or, conversely, may be too suspicious of others to gain anything from the group process. Thus, counselors must consider the impact each individual will have on the group, as well as whether the individual might benefit from group counseling.

Multicultural Perspective

Cultural diversity in the United States necessitates that counselors develop culturally sensitive and culturally competent practice techniques. Understanding cultural differences in normal behavior and values is required when a counselor works with a client from another background. In addition, putting psychological concerns and strengths in a multicultural context may contribute to positive counseling outcomes.

Counselors and the American Counseling Association have led other human service professions in the development of standards that guide culturally competent practice. These standards can be distilled by determining:

- The source of a client's identity (within self and within the family/community)
- The client's orientation toward verbal expressiveness, emotional openness, and disclosure
- The client's willingness to be introspective as opposed to taking action on the external problem

By discussing the client's worldview, a strong therapeutic relationship can be formed and appropriate therapeutic goals can be set.

DISTINGUISHING COUNSELING FROM OTHER HUMAN SERVICES

Counseling Versus Psychotherapy

Gelso and Fretz (2001) suggest that the primary difference between counseling and psychotherapy is length of the process. In counseling, the emphasis is on relatively brief interventions or approximately 12 to 15 sessions. Psychotherapy interventions typically go beyond that number of sessions and generally are not considered short-term services. Also, counselors generally are supportive and seek to educate, with a focus on problem solving at the conscious level with intact individuals; whereas, psychotherapy interventions are conducted to attempt to reconstruct personalities and focus on subconscious processes with more troubled individuals (Brammer & colleagues, 1993).

Counseling Versus Consultation

Counseling is a direct helping relationship in which the client actively pursues change. This relationship typically is characterized by emotional depth. Successful consultation also requires a sound working relationship between professional and another adult (e.g., parent, teacher) that works with the target student; however, the relationship is not as psychologically intimate and the services are indirectly provided. (A mental health consultation may provide a classroom teacher with the skills needed to work with a student with anxiety and discipline problems, but does not work with the student directly.)

COUNSELING THEORIES, MODELS, AND TECHNIQUES

Diversity of Approaches

Counselors work in schools and various community settings and serve clientele from all walks of life.

Serving people of all ages and cultures with a broad range of needs requires counselors to draw from various counseling theories to guide their work. Personal values and beliefs may lead counselors to develop unique, flexible philosophies about the process of change, but most professionals acknowledge that they subscribe to particular theories that influence their provision of services. There are no shortages of these influential theories. Indeed, there are more than 400 counseling theories ranging from Freud's famous psychoanalytic theory to relatively new theories such as William Glasser's choice theory. Given that there are an abundance of theories and no valid means of identifying the most important ones, a range of theories and related techniques are discussed below under the nonmutually exclusive headings of Affective Approaches, Behavioral Approaches, Cognitive Approaches, Systemic Approaches, and Eclectic Approaches.

Affective Approaches

A diverse set of theories and techniques are included in the category of affective approaches. Indeed, entire schools of therapeutic thought (e.g., person-centered, gestalt, psychodynamic, experiential) could be described as "affective" because their focus is primarily on eliciting, understanding, and responding to feelings and emotions.

Behavioral Approaches

Behaviorism has produced many theories that influence today's counseling practice. Most notable are theories of classical and operant conditioning. Change strategies flow logically from behavioral theories as learned maladaptive behavior is modified or replaced. Counseling goals are typically framed as overt behavior changes, rather than changes in perspective or emotion. Behavioral strategies that are commonly used today stem from social learning theory, multimodel therapy, and behavior therapy.

Cognitive Approaches

Counselors who use cognitive approaches to psychological change tend to emphasize the intricate connection between thought, feelings, and behavior. By focusing on beliefs and attitudes, counselors attempt to achieve emotional and behavioral change.

Aaron Beck's development of cognitive therapy for depression helped to establish that thinking differently actually results in mood changes. Albert Ellis's work on Rational Emotional Therapy, which involves the development of rational behavior, also demonstrated that irrational thoughts can have deleterious effects on mood. Today, cognitive and behavioral strategies often are used in tandem.

Systemic Approaches

Systemic (or interactional) theories of change focus on relationship patterns and how they affect well-being. Family systems theory and interpersonal theory of depression are two good examples of systemic theories that have numerous associated change strategies.

Eclectic Approaches

The most popular approach to counseling is a combined, or eclectic approach. Most counselors acknowledge that they subscribe to several theories of change and/or they practice technical eclecticism (i.e., they select change strategies that are best suited for the particular practice situation). Counselors adopting eclecticism typically are strategic in their work and flexible in their selection of techniques.

COUNSELING PROCESS AND OUTCOME

Counseling Process

In counseling, we can analyze counseling processes in small units. Process variables often researched include verbal behavior, counselor intentions, content of discussions, interpersonal manner of participants, nature of strategies, and working alliance. These process variables are studied to better understand how techniques affect counseling outcomes. Hence, counselors often discuss the counseling process with clients and supervisors to get a sense of what is appropriate and what works.

Counseling Outcome

Counselors are committed to the enhancement of their clients' well-being. However, historically outcome research has rarely focused on health; rather the amelioration of illness is often the focus of counseling efforts. Hence, the robust finding that counseling works needs to be clarified. Indeed, it is known that counseling works to remove and lessen the severity of negative psychological symptoms and concerns.

Some outcome research focuses on variables other than general treatment outcome. Session outcome needs to be monitored because the result of each session may determine how counseling progresses. Furthermore, immediate change induced by specific interventions needs to be considered; examining what works and what doesn't work in the course of a session could yield feedback that will benefit the counseling process and outcome.

COUNSELING EFFECTIVENESS

Effectiveness research and consumer satisfaction studies (e.g., Seligman, 1995) indicate that counseling is generally an effective treatment for psychological concerns. Furthermore, Whiston and Sexton (1998) demonstrated that school counseling is beneficial to students and school communities. Empirically supported or "validated" treatments of particular disorders also have been identified, yet the debate regarding the reasons some counseling approaches are effective lingers.

Explaining Counseling Outcomes: Common Factors and Specific Effectiveness

The general effectiveness of counseling has been well-established by numerous researchers (e.g., Smith & Glass, 1977; Wampold & colleagues, 1997). Yet, there is disagreement as to what makes counseling effective—common or specific factors. Common factors are those ingredients that are common across theories and models of counseling. Frank (1982) identified the following as factors common to all approaches to counseling:

- An emotionally charged, confiding relationship exists with a helping professional.
- The relationship takes place in a healing setting.
- A rationale exists that provides a plausible explanation for the client's symptoms and a procedure to resolve these symptoms.
- The procedure requires the active participation of both the client and therapist.

Others (e.g., Wampold, 2001) have identified additional common components such as the opportunity to express emotions and the possibility of insight. Thus, proponents of the "common factors" argument assert that the theoretical model a counselor chooses when working with a client is not the most relevant variable; rather, what increases the effectiveness is ensuring the existence of the basic elements common across approaches and the belief (by both the counselor and client) that counseling will help resolve the client's concerns.

Others believe that the specific components of the different counseling approaches are responsible for the benefits of counseling. Proponents of this view assert that a client presents to a counselor with a specific problem and that a psychological explanation exists for the problem. From this psychological explanation, specific types of counseling interventions are created and administered to the client. Thus, different approaches to counseling (e.g., affective, behavioral, cognitive, systems) may look very different from one another and employ different strategies to help a client resolve his or her difficulties. It is believed that these different strategies are responsible for the benefits of counseling. For example, a counselor using a behavioral approach may educate parents about behavior modification as a way to enhance their parenting skills. A proponent of the specific-factors view of counseling effectiveness would emphasize that teaching parents the behavior modification techniques is responsible for benefits observed from the counseling. Those arguing for common factors would claim that the relationship between the counselor and the parents, as well as the belief that the behavior modification would help resolve the parents' issues (component common to all approaches), is responsible for the effectiveness of counseling.

Counseling is a word that is often used to describe when a professional listens to a person's story and then offers feedback on the client's experience of the world. Counseling professionals conduct helping exchanges in the context of sound therapeutic relationships. While the philosophies that underpin counseling efforts differ, outcome research findings do not; counseling is generally effective.

—*Shane J. Lopez and Heather N. Rasmussen*

See also Behavior Intervention; Cognitive–Behavioral Modification; Etiology; Psychotherapy; Substance Abuse

REFERENCES AND FURTHER READING

Brammer, L. M., Abrego, P. J., & Showstrom, E. L. (1993). *Therapeutic counseling and psychotherapy* (6th ed.). Englewood Cliffs, NJ: Prentice-Hall.

Corey, M. S., & Corey, G. (1997). *Groups: Process and practice* (5th ed.). Pacific Grove, CA: Brooks/Cole.

Frank, J. D. (1982). Therapeutic components shared by all psychotherapies. In J. Harvey & M. Parks (Eds.), *Psychotherapy research and behavior change* (pp. 9–37). Washington, DC: American Psychological Association.

Gelso, C., & Fretz, B. (2001). *Counseling psychology* (2nd ed.). New York: Harcourt College.

Seligman, M. E. P. (1995). The effectiveness of psychotherapy: The Consumer Reports study. *American Psychologist, 50,* 965–974

Smith, M. & Glass, G. (1977). Meta-analysis of psychotherapy outcome studies. *American Psychologist, 50,* 995–1002.

Wampold, B. E. (2001). *The great psychotherapy debate.* Mahwah, NJ: Erlbaum.

Wampold, B. E, Mondin, G. W., Moody, M., Stich, F., Benson, K., & Ahn, H. (1997). A meta-analysis of outcome studies comparing bona fide psychotherapies: Empiricially, "all must have prizes." *Psychological Bulletin, 122,* 203–215.

Whiston, S. C., & Sexton, T. L. (1998). A review of school counseling outcome research: Implications for practice. *Journal of Counseling and Development, 76,* 412–426.

CRISIS INTERVENTION

Many questions have been raised about the role of school psychologists in crisis intervention (i.e., strategies to use in a crisis) over the last two decades. Poland and Pitcher (1992) emphasized the need for schools to be prepared for violence that might come from outside the school, such as a violent act committed by a disturbed adult. The highly publicized school shootings that occurred in the mid-to-late 1990s, including the mass murders at Columbine High School, highlight the fact that school safety is an inside job requiring a commitment first of all from students, as the majority of the recent violent acts at schools have been committed by student perpetrators. There has been an increased level of emphasis on crisis training for school psychologists in recent years (Poland & colleagues, 2002) and the National Association of School Psychologists (NASP) has provided leadership at both the state and national level.

NASP formed the National Emergency Assistance Team (NEAT) in 1996 with an emphasis on advocacy, training, and emergency mobile response. The team received a great deal of publicity for providing on-site assistance following school shootings in locations such as Paducah, Jonesboro, Littleton, Springfield, and El Cajon.

NASP also formed very strong alliances with the National Organization for Victim Assistance (NOVA) and the U.S. Department of Education. NOVA is best known for its Community Response Teams that are sent when requested to communities that have experienced a crisis, whether it is the result of a violent act or a natural disaster.

Many workshops have been conducted at both the state and national levels to increase both the skills and confidence of school psychologists to respond to a crisis. A number of state school psychology associations (e.g., Florida, Georgia, Colorado, and California) have formed their own crisis teams. NASP is also currently working on training standards for crisis intervention.

After Columbine the U.S. Department of Education developed Project SERV (School Emergency Response to Violence). Project SERV has provided both short- and long-term assistance to schools after a crisis, including sending members of the NEAT for initial assistance as well as providing funds through grants to hire additional counselors and to create prevention programs.

School psychologists are skilled in conducting processing sessions or debriefing for faculty and students after a tragedy. Poland and colleagues (2002) emphasized the importance of these skills for school psychologists and the reality that one processing model will not fit every situation; therefore, adaptations often need to be made. There have been a number of research studies on the effectiveness of processing interventions, and, although participants overwhelmingly reported that they were beneficial, the research has not consistently demonstrated benefits.

STATISTICS AND SCHOOL CRISES

The final report of the Safe School Initiative from the U.S. Secret Service and the Department of Education (Vossekuil & colleagues, 2002), emphasized that:

- The number of violent deaths on school grounds has decreased, and the average for the past 10 years has been 33 deaths per year.
- Schools are the safest place for children.
- More than 99% of youth homicides occur in the home, neighborhood, or community.

- Profiles of school shooters do not exist other than they are almost always male. However, prevention efforts must reduce bullying in the schools and detect suicidal students, as the majority of school shooters were suicidal and victims of bullying.
- The majority of school shootings committed by student perpetrators were motivated by revenge and planned over a long period of time, and friends were told of the school shooters' homicidal plans.

CRISIS PLANNING

The September 11, 2001, attacks also have many significant implications for crisis planning in the schools. School administrators have made significant improvements in crisis planning in recent years and there is a wealth of materials available to assist them.

School Psychologist's Role in Crisis Planning

School psychologists can play a key role in crisis planning to not only assist schools to manage the waves of emotionality following a crisis but also the police, medical workers, media personnel, and parents who rush to a school after a crisis. Poland and McCormick (2000) outlined roles for support personnel that vary from architect of the crisis plan to consultant, and from direct service provider to those directly affected. They also indicated that prevention programs should reduce bullying and increase student reporting of weapons and violent threats on campus.

A THEORETICAL FRAMEWORK FOR CRISIS PLANNING

School crisis planning is a broad area, and starting with a theoretical model is essential. Caplan (1964) developed a well-known model that emphasizes three levels of crisis intervention. This framework has been expanded with regard to the schools and encompasses all areas of crisis planning (Pitcher & Poland, 1992). Schools must develop crisis plans at all three of the following levels:

1. *Primary prevention* consists of activities devoted to preventing a crisis from occurring. A few examples are conflict resolution, gun safety, safe driving, suicide prevention programs, and training school personnel in first aid and CPR.

School psychologists are in a key position to initiate prevention programs that reduce leading causes of death.

2. *Secondary intervention* includes steps taken in the immediate aftermath of a crisis to minimize effects and escalation. Examples are evacuating students to a safe place away from danger and reopening the school as quickly as possible after a crisis.

3. *Tertiary intervention* involves providing long-term follow-up assistance to those who have experienced a severe crisis. Examples are monitoring and supporting the friends of a suicide victim for a year after the suicide and adding support personnel such as counselors after a school shooting. Research has clarified that adolescents in particular who have been traumatized are increasingly at risk for substance abuse, reckless behavior, and suicide.

School personnel often view crisis intervention as having only one level, secondary intervention. For example, at a high school tragedy in which an assistant principal was shot by a student during lunch in the cafeteria, students and staff members described in great detail their thoughts and actions in the immediate aftermath of the shooting. However, the critical need for additional assistance for faculty and students, and the importance of prevention activities designed to reduce the incidence of weapons at school were initially met with some resistance. The crisis had presented an excellent opportunity to create prevention programs and develop crisis teams designed to improve the school's ability to respond to such events. All schools experience some type of crisis event. When a crisis occurs at a school, the school administrators should review with a critical eye how the event was handled, carefully noting what worked and what did not work. Schools should anticipate any additional types of crises that might occur and formulate plans to deal with them, and it is especially important today that schools not be left out of homeland security planning. Schools must work closely with local and state authorities and must take added security measures when the national threat level increases.

ORGANIZING CRISIS TEAMS

Schools must look at their own resources and then use one of the following three options as teams are organized:

1. A building team in which every member works in the same building. The advantages are that team members are acquainted with each other and they can easily meet to review crisis plans. This approach works well when a school is large enough to have campus personnel in key positions (e.g., nurse, counselor, psychologist, and security).

2. A district team in which all members are employed by the school district, but they are located in various buildings throughout the district. This arrangement makes communication and crisis planning more difficult than in a building approach. A counselor or nurse may need to cover several locations, and the psychologist may need to be called from the central office. It is important that the team include a representative from each high school, because statistics clearly indicate that after a crisis, high school students are more at risk for violent, suicidal, and accidental deaths.

3. A combination district and community team in which some team members are district employees and others (e.g., medical personnel, mental health workers, or police officers) are employed by community agencies. This format is more difficult to organize, but it is essential in many small and rural school districts in order to develop a comprehensive plan. A school district should never be in the position of establishing relations with outside agencies *after* a crisis has occurred.

Planning meetings should be scheduled and should include representatives from all the agencies that will be involved. Some schools have been frustrated by a lack of response from community agencies; however, it is important to note that involvement in the planning process between local and state agencies and schools has improved since 9/11/2001. Brock and Poland (2002) discussed the difference between a centralized and an on-site team. School or building teams are in the best position to work on prevention, and centralized or district teams can assist with intervention after a crisis has occurred.

Crisis Team Size and Membership

The purpose of a crisis team is to incorporate sufficient staff to delegate duties because it is impossible

for one administrator to do everything that is needed in the aftermath of a crisis. There are school districts with 20-member teams and 200-page crisis plans. But, plans that are so lengthy that school personnel will not review them on a regular basis are virtually useless. The question of team size is an administrative as well as commonsense one. Pitcher and Poland (1992) recommended a team size of five to eight that includes:

1. Medical liaison

2. Security liaison

3. Parent liaison

4. Counseling liaison

5. Administrative liaison

This would result in a team of five, and these liaisons could designate additional school staff members to assist them. The addition of a media liaison and a campus or staff liaison would be useful, but the building principal may prefer to carry out these duties rather than delegate them to someone else.

COPING WITH A DEATH OR TRAGEDY

Poland and McCormick (1999) cited governmental figures that indicate that the number of deaths for young people is at or near an all-time high. The leading causes of death for children are, in order, accident, homicide, and suicide. School personnel, especially counselors, need to be aware of the developmental stages of understanding death. The principal must verify the death has occurred and then notify the faculty through either a calling tree or faculty meeting, keeping in mind the importance of giving school personnel the opportunity to work through their own issues about death and loss before having to assist their students. If it is not possible to use either of these notification methods, then the teachers should be given hand-delivered memorandums that include specific information as well as ideas about how to assist their students. Teachers often appreciate having an actual script written out for them, and Poland and Poland (2004) developed a lesson plan that can be used after a crisis. Pitcher and Poland (1992) developed a tip sheet for teachers dealing with death. They recommend an in-service training session designed to empower teachers to help students by supporting the expression of a range of emotions. Teachers can provide various beneficial classroom activities for expressing emotions such as talking, writing, artwork, music, and ceremonies or activities to assist the family of the deceased. Having students make a list of all the good things and positive memories of the deceased, and preparing students for funeral attendance are additional positive activities. Zenere (2004) discussed the Israeli model of crisis intervention, which helps determine who is at risk:

- Geographic proximity, which is based on physical distance of a person in relation to a tragedy
- Social proximity, which is the degree of relationship one has to the victim
- Population factors, which relate to the crisis history of each individual and whether each individual has experienced losses of significant others in his or her life
- Psychological proximity, which is the degree of identification an individual has to the crisis incident or victim

School personnel, and especially teachers, need to be informed about the circles of vulnerability as well as the common reactions that children have to a tragedy or crisis. Common reactions appear below:

- Fears and worry about the future
- Regression academically and behaviorally
- Nightmares and sleeping difficulties
- Vulnerability to depression, substance abuse, reckless behavior, and suicide, particularly in adolescents

SUICIDE INTERVENTION

National interest in youth suicide prevention has escalated as a result of the Surgeon General's Call to Action to Prevent Suicide (U.S. Public Health Service, 1999), and national suicide prevention strategies have been developed that are to be implemented by 2005. The Call to Action stressed three key components of the study of the problem of suicide: awareness, intervention, and methodology.

Suicide remains very rare for elementary children, but suicidal thoughts and actions are very common for adolescents. Bearman and Moody (2004) reported the following for adolescents:

- 4% attempted suicide last year (2003).
- 20% knew a friend who attempted suicide last year.

- 60% reported knowing an adolescent who attempted suicide previously.
- Social networks exert powerful influences on adolescents; isolated adolescents who experience peer conflict and lack of connection to school are most at risk.

Recent research emphasizes that the suicide rate for 10- to 14-year-old students has increased more than 100% in the last decade, with the suicide rate for older adolescents remaining more constant.

Schools have been slow in addressing the problem of youth suicide, and a national grassroots parent effort is helping schools and communities to increase prevention efforts. One organization that is making a difference is Yellow Ribbon, founded by suicide survivors. Poland and McCormick (1999) documented that few schools have training in suicide prevention or a plan in place, and they cited a growing number of cases in which schools have been subjected to lawsuits after the suicide of a student. The key issue is not whether the school somehow caused the suicide, but whether the school failed to take reasonable steps to prevent it. Schools have a responsibility to have prevention programs in place, to foresee that a student who is threatening suicide is at risk, to take steps to supervise that student, and to obtain counseling assistance. School personnel must also notify parents whenever they have reason to believe that a student is suicidal.

All school personnel who interact with students must be taught the warning signs of suicide and empowered to follow procedures to alert the appropriate personnel and get assistance for a suicidal student. School psychologists and counselors are the logical personnel to assess the severity level. It is very important that these personnel receive training on how to interact with suicidal students and what questions to ask. No-harm contracts have been found to be a promising intervention in the schools. School psychologists are encouraged to have students sign such a contract, which provides suicidal students with an alternative to suicide and stresses the importance of getting adult help and using local crisis hotlines. The assessment of suicidal severity can be compressed to three levels after direct inquiry.

1. *Low risk*: A student with suicidal thoughts but no plan now to die by suicide, and with no history of a suicide attempt.

2. *Medium risk*: A student with a history of a suicide attempt but no plan now, or a student with

a plan to die by suicide now but no history of a previous attempt.

3. *High risk*: A student with a history of a suicide attempt and a plan to die by suicide. A student assessed at this level should be supervised constantly, until he or she is turned over to parents or authorities.

Regardless of a student's level of severity, the student's parents must be notified, unless there is a history of parental neglect, in which case protective services would be called.

Parents have occasionally been uncooperative and minimized the suicidal ideation or actions of their child. In this situation, school personnel must be firm in their insistence that counseling assistance is necessary. Parents have become angry with school personnel during this notification process and have tried to forbid them from interacting with their child again. This situation is covered in Texas by legislation stating that under the circumstance of suicide, personnel such as physicians, psychologists, and counselors need not obtain parental permission to work with a minor. When parents refuse to get emotional assistance for a suicidal child, a referral should be made to the local child protective services agency. It is absolutely essential that the appropriate school personnel follow up and provide emotional support, regardless of what the parents do. Parents should be asked to sign an emergency notification form that indicates they were informed of the suicidal ideation and or actions of their child.

The most common factors in youth suicide are depression, substance abuse, conduct problems, recklessness, and gun availability. Young people almost always tell their friends about their suicidal plans, and, unfortunately, their friends do not always take their threats seriously or solicit assistance from adults. Because 60% of male and 47% of female youth suicides involve guns (Poland and Lieberman, 2002), many professionals believe that reducing gun access to troubled youth is the single most critical factor to reducing youth suicides. A number of schools have started to screen depressed and suicidal students. The Signs of Suicide (SOS) program, sponsored by NASP and the National Association of Secondary School Principals, has two primary components. The first is a 30-minute video that students view to increase their awareness of suicide warning signs and to empower students to prevent suicide through notification to adults and local and national crisis hot lines when they or their friends are suicidal. The second component involves having students and or their parents fill out a short questionnaire designed to assess depression and suicide. Poland and Lieberman (2004) emphasized that the SOS program has been used in some form in more than 1,500 schools with students in the 8th through 12th grades, with very promising results. It is particularly noteworthy that the SOS program has been found to increase adult help-seeking behavior. This promising program needs to be used by more schools, but there still is much denial of the problem of youth suicide; many schools do not want to take the time away from academics to implement the program, and there is also a modest cost involved.

Schools must have carefully developed postvention plans in place for use after a suicide occurs. These guidelines are very important to prevent suicide contagion because adolescents are particularly susceptible. Poland and Lieberman (2004) summarized the literature about suicide contagion, which particularly emphasizes that sensationalized media coverage contributes to the contagion. They defined contagion as more suicides than are to be expected in a specific geographical location. The American Association of Suicidology (AAS) published (1998) school postvention guidelines that include the following:

- Don't dismiss school or encourage funeral attendance during school hours.
- Don't hold a large-scale school assembly or dedicate a memorial to the deceased.
- Do provide individual and group counseling.
- Do verify the facts and treat the death as a suicide, and do contact the family of the deceased.
- Do emphasize that no one is to blame for the suicide.
- Do emphasize that help is available, that suicide is preventable, and that everyone has a role to play in prevention.

The AAS postvention guidelines also include recommendations that encourage the media not to dramatize the suicide:

- Don't make the suicide front-page news or print a picture of the deceased.
- Avoid details about the method.
- Don't report that the suicide is the result of simplistic, romantic, or mystic factors.
- Do emphasize that there are alternatives to suicide, and publicize where to get assistance.

NATIONAL TRAGEDIES

Many children in America viewed the extensive and graphic television news coverage of shocking school shootings, such as that at Columbine and the 9/11/2001 attack. School officials should anticipate increases in feelings of fear for student safety in their school subsequent to such an event. Such incidents can present a "teachable moment" because students are more open to discussion about the incidents and are more open to constructive input from adults. The following are key points:

- Conduct faculty meetings to prepare for discussion of the tragedy with students.
- Make sure classroom discussions are focused on how to make schools safer rather than on glamorizing the perpetrators.
- The 9/11/01 attack especially demonstrated the necessity of classroom discussions on diversity so that all Arab-Americans and Muslims were not blamed.
- Young children should view very little, if any, television coverage, and it should be emphasized that the tragedy is far away, when that is the case. Secondary students could view the coverage but not constantly, and the most important point is for the teacher to turn off the coverage and lead classroom activities to process the event.
- Recognize that children of different ages are at different developmental levels, with elementary children in particular needing reassurance of their personal safety. Middle and high school students will have strong opinions about the tragedy, a greater understanding of the finality of death, and concrete suggestions about what needs to be done.
- Children look to adults to see how they are responding. Adults should remain calm and let students know that they have permission for a range of emotions. Poland and Poland (2004) stressed the importance of helping parents and teachers cope first so they will be better able to assist children. Younger children especially need to express emotions though play and artwork.
- Children's questions should be addressed, and they should be told the truth in age-appropriate terms. Adults should avoid overwhelming students with more information than is requested, and they should avoid statements such as, "Our world will never be the same" when referring to 9/11/2001.
- A key concept in psychology is the term resiliency, which means the ability to bounce back and deal effectively with adversity. Research has found post-9/11/01 that those Americans that have done the best have been surrounded by caring family and friends, have been comfortable venting strong emotions, and have maintained an optimistic view of the future.

School crisis literature can be divided into the periods before and after the shooting at Columbine High School on April 20, 1999. There is no doubt that school crisis planning has improved post-Columbine, with dramatic improvements in school and police cooperation and a greater presence of police at school. Additional developments have been the implementation of zero tolerance policies for weapons and violence in almost all schools, and many schools have developed threat assessment teams that often involve school psychologists. School psychologists are increasingly asked to make an assessment of whether or not a particular student is capable of violence, but many school psychologists have not been trained to make such an assessment. Poland and McCormick (1999) outlined the following important crisis lessons for school personnel:

- Recognize that it could happen to you.
- What you learn in one crisis situation will help you in the next situation, although no two crisis situations are alike.
- Crisis plans must be updated annually and crisis team members must understand their duties.
- The identification of students who are at risk for violence is complex and should include fascination with media violence, fascination with guns and bombs, lack of remorse, cruelty to others (especially animals), lack of connections to adults and school, and fire setting. The more of these behaviors a student has, the more we should be concerned. It is important that school personnel know each student well.
- Everyone must be alert for crises and crisis prevention is an "inside job" that involves a prepared staff, student body, and community.
- School crisis planning must include a variety of crisis situations and cannot concentrate only on school shootings.

Crisis planning in schools has perhaps never been so important as today in the aftermath of 9/11/2001. All schools need a carefully developed crisis plan and a commitment from both staff and students. School administrators need to coordinate their crisis planning efforts with local, state, and national homeland security initiatives and must carefully review the excellent body of literature available on the topic of school crisis. School psychologists need to be represented in all areas of crisis planning, including prevention activities.

—Scott Poland

See also Aggression in Schools; Bullying and Victimization; Counseling; Death and Bereavement; Depression; Prevention; Violence in Schools

REFERENCES AND FURTHER READING

American Association of Suicidology. (1998). *Suicide postvention guidelines: Suggestions for dealing with the aftermath of suicide in the schools.* Washington, DC: Author.

Bearman, P. S., & Moody, J. (2004, January). Suicide friendships among American adolescents. *American Journal of Public Health, 94*(1), 10–14.

Brock, S., & Poland, S. (2002). School crisis preparedness. In S. Brock, P. Lazarus, & S. Jimerson (Eds.), *Best practices in school crisis prevention and intervention* (pp. 273–289). Bethesda, MD: National Association of School Psychologists.

Caplan, G. (1964). *Principles of preventative psychiatry.* New York: Basic Books.

Pitcher, G., & Poland, S. (1992). *Crisis intervention in the schools.* New York: Guilford.

Poland, S. (1989). *Suicide intervention in the schools.* New York: Guilford.

Poland, S., & Lieberman, R. (2002). Best practices in suicide intervention. In A. Thomas & J. Grimes (Eds.), *Best practices in school psychology* (Vol. 3, pp. 1151–1166). Bethesda, MD: National Association of School Psychologists.

Poland S., & Lieberman, R. (2004, June). NEAT supports Nebraska schools following suicide cluster. *NASP Communiqué, 32*(8), 21–22.

Poland, S., & McCormick, J. (1999). *Coping with crisis: Lessons learned.* Longmont, CO: Sopris West.

Poland, S., & McCormick, J. (2000). *Coping with crisis: Quick reference guide.* Longmont, CO: Sopris West.

Poland, S., Pitcher, G., & Lazarus, P. (2002). Best practices in crisis intervention & management. In A. Thomas & J. Grimes (Eds.), *Best practices in school psychology* (Vol. 3, pp. 1057–1080). Bethesda, MD: National Association of School Psychologists.

Poland, S., & Poland D. (2004, April). Dealing with death at school. *Principal Leadership, 4*(8), 8–12.

U.S. Public Health Service. (1999). *The Surgeon General's call to action to prevent suicide.* Washington, DC: Author.

Vossekuil, B., Fein, R., Reddy, M., Borum, R., & Modzeleski, W. (2002). *The final report of the Safe School Initiative: Implications for the prevention of school attacks in the United States.* Washington, DC: U.S. Secret Service & U.S. Department of Education.

Zenere, F. (2004, June). Living and learning in the shadow of threat. *NASP Communiqué, 32*(8), 38.

CRITERION-REFERENCED ASSESSMENT

Criterion-referenced assessment is designed to measure how well a student has learned a specific domain of knowledge and skills. Students are assessed on the basis of their performance relative to a specific, predetermined criterion or standard. For example, in order to obtain a driver's license, a person must successfully pass both a paper-and-pencil test and an on-the-road driving test. Both of these tests are criterion-referenced tests. Passing is determined by an applicant's ability to demonstrate the knowledge and skills necessary for proficient and safe driving. In criterion-referenced assessment, it is possible that all, or none, of the examinees will pass or show proficiency.

WHAT IS CRITERION-REFERENCED ASSESSMENT?

Although criterion-referenced testing is the term most commonly used, educators do not agree that it is the best term to describe the assessment method in which score interpretation is based on a predetermined, set criterian of performance. During the past 30 years, terms such as competency tests, mastery tests, domain-referenced measurement, objectives-referenced assessment, curriculum-based assessment, and performance or direct assessment have been used in place of criterion-referenced assessment. More recently, as states and school systems have adopted learning and curriculum standards that describe what students should know and be able to do in core subjects at each grade level, they have developed a variation of criterion-referenced assessment referred to as "standards-referenced testing" or "standards-based assessment." Furthermore, the broader term *assessment* seems to be replacing the term *testing*.

CRITERION- AND NORM-REFERENCED TESTING (ASSESSMENT)

As originally defined by Glaser (1963) in *American Psychologist*, criterion-referenced tests "depend upon an absolute standard of quality," while norm-referenced tests "depend upon a relative standard." Since Glaser's original article, it has become common to label tests as criterion-referenced or norm-referenced. However, these labels actually apply to the interpretation of the examinee's performance as expressed through test scores rather than the testing instruments themselves.

This shift in emphasis from test type to test score interpretation is captured by Popham in his 2002 edition of *Classroom Assessment: What Teachers Need to Know*, in which he says " . . . a criterion-referenced interpretation is an absolute interpretation because it hinges on the extent to which the criterion assessment domain represented by the test is actually possessed by the student. Once an assessment domain is defined, the student's test performance can be interpreted according to the degree to which the domain has been mastered" (p. 111).

Linn and Gronlund (2000) propose that criterion-referenced and norm-referenced assessments should be "viewed as ends of a continuum, rather than as a clear-cut dichotomy" (p. 44). Typically, criterion-referenced tests focus on a delimited and clearly specified achievement domain (i.e., objectives and/or learning standards) and emphasize what learning tasks students can and cannot perform. In developing criterion-referenced tests, a large pool of test items are constructed or selected that match the learning task. Their level of difficulty is determined by the difficulty of the task. Test items are eliminated only from the pool of items if they are judged not to measure the learning task or objective.

An important consideration in test item selection for published norm-referenced tests is the statistical properties of the individual items. Items of moderate difficulty and high discriminating power are most likely to be included because they will yield distributions of test scores that enable educators to distinguish performances among individuals. To interpret a person's performance, the performance is compared to the performance of other examinees with similar characteristics.

Recently, educators and test publishers have collaborated to take advantage of the unique benefits of both types of tests in assessing achievement. Publishers of norm-referenced tests are using more detailed tables of specification (test blueprints) with clear and specific statements of objectives that identify the specific knowledge and skills the test measures. Norm-referenced interpretations have been added to tests designed for criterion-referenced interpretation.

CRITERION-REFERENCED ASSESSMENT IN THE CLASSROOM

Criterion-referenced assessment has a primary role in instructional decision making. Most, if not all, instructional decisions are informed by information provided through criterion-referenced assessment. In most instances, criterion-referenced test scores tell teachers, parents, and students whether specific instructional objectives have been achieved.

Criterion-referenced assessment also can help teachers determine if their students have the prerequisite knowledge and skills necessary to achieve the defined learning outcomes of a lesson or curricular unit. It allows teachers to monitor student learning, and, if necessary, modify instruction. Since criterion-referenced assessment identifies what students can and cannot do, teachers can pinpoint areas of difficulty and can help students to discover flaws and inconsistencies in their own thinking, thereby helping them identify gaps in their understanding.

CURRENT USE OF CRITERION-REFERENCED TESTS

Arguably the most important use of criterion-referenced tests at the beginning of the 21st century has been in the widespread compulsory testing of public school students. In their 1999–2000 annual survey of state assessment programs, the Council of Chief State School Officers reported that 48 states described their mandatory K–12 statewide assessment programs. Twenty-one states indicated a use of both norm-referenced tests and criterion-referenced tests. For the remaining states, 18 used only criterion-referenced tests and 9 used only norm-referenced tests. Most states identified multiple-choice and extended-constructed (i.e., medium-to-long answer items) response items as their exam format, regardless of whether they were using criterion-referenced or norm-referenced tests. Short-constructed response items (i.e., short-answer items) were used by 66% of the criterion-referenced–testing-only states compared to just one of the nine norm-referenced–testing-only states. These data again emphasize how often criterion-referenced test items may look like norm-referenced test items. However, the use of short-answer items on standardized state assessment tests appears to be a more typical characteristic of a criterion-referenced approach.

CONTINUING ISSUES: DEFINING THE DOMAIN

Because the essence of criterion-referenced assessment is its ability to duplicate the criterion tasks of interest, it is critical that the test developers define explicitly what skills or knowledge are being measured. In the late 1970s and early 1980s, many states developed criterion-referenced minimum competency tests. These tests were meant to verify that students had achieved the "basics" in reading, writing, and arithmetic. Because they were focused on lower-level academic skills, test developers were able to identify domains of specific language arts skills and mathematical skills that were consider requisites of "minimum competency." Criterion-referenced tests to measure these domains were constructed without much controversy. While educators and their critics might argue about the level of students' "minimum competency" necessary to graduate from high school, few argued that these tests did not assess students' ability to do mathematical computations, recognize standard English grammar, and read with comprehension.

In the 1990s, states expanded their criterion-referenced tests to assess students' learning with respect to more rigorous state, national, and international academic standards. The emphasis was now on higher-level cognitive skills such as solving real life problems or interpreting historical events. Developing criterion-referenced tests to measure more complicated knowledge and skills is much harder than developing those to measure minimum competency skills. James Popham, speaking at a 1993 symposium on a 30-year retrospective of criterion-referenced measurement, said, "the more lofty the assessment target, the tougher it is to spell out succinctly what is to be measured."

CONTINUING ISSUES: SETTING THE STANDARDS

Because criterion-referenced tests aim to be authentic measures of particular skills or domains of knowledge, it is common to set a single score to determine an individual student's proficiency or deficiency. While these tests do not require "cut scores" for determining who passes or fails the test, they are often used that way. Typically, the state-mandated criterion-referenced tests have a specific score that determines which students pass or fail the test. The percentage of students who pass the test can then be used for "high stakes" decisions on school accreditation, program evaluation, improvement of instruction, or even student promotion.

It is important to ask how carefully these standards have been set. The more important the decision being made with criterion-referenced assessment, the more important it is that the assessment have high reliability and validity. For example, have cut scores (criterion level of performance on a test) been set by experts using their best judgment of what constitutes inadequate, solid, or advanced student performance? How does the standard error of measurement of the assessment affect strict adherence to a single cut-score value? Have cut scores been set to attain a predetermined number of successful applicants? Have developers established the predictive validity of their assessments through empirical research on the relationship between criterion-referenced assessments and other authentic measures of success and failure? Table 1 contains a list of important questions for any consumer of criterion-referenced assessment.

Criterion-referenced assessment was originally conceived as a way to map knowledge acquisition along a continuum of no proficiency to consummate performance. Since its inception almost four decades ago, criterion-referenced testing has emphasized measurement of absolute performance rather than comparisons with others. Its essence is that it provides accurate inferences about students' cognitive activity and skill performance, not just relative comparisons to other norm groups. It is critically important that judgments made from criterion-referenced assessment data give valid and practical insights into students' understandings and skills, especially when high stakes decisions result.

—*Roger R. Ries and George M. Bass*

See also Academic Achievement; Norm-Referenced Testing; Reliability; Retention and Promotion; Standard Error of Measurement; Statewide Tests

Table 1   Top Ten Questions to Ask about Criterion-Referenced Assessment

1. How clearly does the developer state the purpose and reasons for designing the criterion-referenced assessment?

2. How well does the criterion-referenced assessment constructor understand the mental and physical operations behind the criterion tasks?

3. How well can the continuum of performance on the criterion task be described and represented as tested skills and knowledge?

4. How have the reliability and validity of the criterion-referenced assessments been determined and how are these technical test characteristics reported to the public?

5. How were the "cut scores" to determine "pass/fail" or "competency-incompetency" determined—by expert judgment or by empirical verification?

6. How well does the original purpose for developing the criterion-referenced assessment match the way it is being used?

7. How much does the criterion-referenced assessment score improve the decision-making process?

8. How confident are you that the criterion-referenced test performance is a good predictor of the real life criterion task performance?

9. What are the personal and social consequences of using the "cut scores" to make educational and employment decisions?

10. Was the criterion-referenced test in fact designed as a criterion-referenced test, or is it really a norm-referenced test used for a different purpose?

REFERENCES AND FURTHER READING

Glaser, R. (1963). Instructional technology and the measurement of learning outcomes. *American Psychologist, 18,* 519–521.

Linn, R. L., & Gronlund, N. E. (2000). *Measurement and assessment in teaching* (8th ed.). Upper Saddle River, NJ: Prentice-Hall

Popham, J. W. (1994). The instructional consequences of criterion-referenced clarity. *Educational measurement: Issues and practice, 13,* 15–18, 30.

Popham, J. W. (2002). *Classroom assessment: What teachers need to know* (3rd ed.). Boston: Allyn & Bacon.

CROSS-CULTURAL ASSESSMENT

As the population of the United States becomes more diverse, the need for school psychologists to be competent in assessing individuals from cultures other than the U.S. mainstream has progressively intensified. *Assessment* is a broad term encompassing many different kinds of procedures and techniques. Cross-cultural testing is the use of standardized tests of intelligence and cognitive abilities with individuals who are culturally different and often linguistically different as well.

The term *culture*, as Matsumoto (1994) defines it, refers to the collection of values, attitudes, traditions, behaviors, and language that are specific to a particular group of individuals who purposely transmit those characteristics from one generation to the next. Therefore, the term *culturally different* can refer not only to those individuals who come from a culture other than the United States, but also to those who may be a member of a particular U.S. subculture (e.g., those who live in poverty, the deaf community, Greek Americans, etc.).

With respect to cross-cultural testing, there are four main issues with which school psychologists should be knowledgeable:

1. The cultural loading and linguistic demands of standardized, norm-referenced ability tests

2. Norm sample representation and stratification of different cultural groups

3. Effects of cultural differences on performance on tests

4. Cross-cultural dynamics involving the examiner and the examinee

CULTURAL LOADING AND LINGUISTIC DEMANDS OF ABILITY TESTS

Intelligence and cognitive ability tests have long been criticized as unfair, inappropriate, and invalid for the purpose of assessing individuals who are culturally different. In general, they have been attacked as being culturally *biased*. In general, cultural bias has been defined historically as being psychometrically based. Such bias, therefore, has been sought with regard to item content, test sequence or difficulty, factor structure, prediction, and indices of reliability. For example, bias in item content might exist if tests that require knowledge of U.S. mainstream culture place culturally different individuals at a disadvantage because they have not been raised in the majority culture. Essentially, any aspect of the test that results in systematic differences in performance between one group and another, except for the actual ability being measured, could be construed as evidence of bias. Yet, when defined from the psychometric perspective, very few tests have ever shown evidence of bias. The reason may be that cultural differences in and of themselves simply do not alter the basic psychometric properties of a test, particularly not those related to reliability. However, the same cannot be said with respect to issues of validity.

Well-developed, modern tests of intelligence and cognitive ability may well be free of the types of psychometric-based cultural bias defined above; however, it cannot be disputed that such tests remain invariably loaded with cultural content and also require some type of linguistic or communicative ability. That is, all tests are a reflection of the very culture that gave rise to them and, by definition, will sample to varying degrees the knowledge and familiarity of that same culture possessed by any given individual. Test developers have long sought culture-free or culture-fair tests that eliminate cultural bias, but even tests that purportedly meet this goal contain elements with which individuals from some cultures would likely not be familiar (e.g., blocks and puzzles). Likewise, even so-called "nonverbal" tests require some form of linguistic or meta-linguistic communication and comprehension by the individual taking the test, albeit it may not require oral or spoken language. These factors are undeniably and inextricably linked to tests of ability developed in any country, and such tests are, therefore, inherently culturally loaded and linguistically demanding. If cross-cultural testing is to achieve a greater degree of fairness, it must come in the form of understanding the manner in which cultural loading, not cultural bias, affects test performance.

Recently, Flanagan and Ortiz (2001) provided classifications of tests along the dimensions of cultural loading and linguistic demand that assist psychologists in selecting and interpreting tests that may be more appropriate for a given individual relative to his or her background. By viewing tests first from the perspective of cultural loading and linguistic demand, the basic question regarding whether performance is related more to differences in cultural or linguistic experiences versus differences in actual ability can be answered. That is, the validity of the obtained results can be directly evaluated, offering psychologists a systematic method for reducing the potential discriminatory aspects of cross-cultural testing with respect to issues of validity that ultimately underlie the fairness and equity of interpretations and conclusions.

NORM-SAMPLE REPRESENTATION

Norm-referenced measures are used to evaluate an individual's performance relative to other people (i.e., the norm sample). To make such comparisons, test developers strive to obtain a norm sample that is as representative of the general population as possible with respect to important variables that generally are associated with performance—age, grade, geographic location, socioeconomic status, and so forth. Whenever comparisons are made, it is assumed that the individual being tested is comparable or very similar to those in the norm sample in terms of his or her background experiences, particularly acculturation and language development. Salvia and Ysseldyke (1991) describe the underlying assumption of comparability relative to acculturation as the collection of background experiences; and formal and informal learning opportunities that involve familial, social, educational, cultural, and linguistic experiences. Only when an individual's background experiences are comparable, not necessarily identical, to the background experiences of the individuals who comprise the norm sample can it be said that comparisons regarding performance are valid.

It has long been the practice of test developers to include a heterogeneous mix of races in their norm sample development and routinely provide representation of the various major racial/ethnic groups that exist in the United States according to their proportion in the general population. Although this makes some sense on the surface, it begs the question regarding whether differences in ability actually exist as a function of race or ethnicity. But test developers tend to defend inclusion of different racial and ethnic groups primarily as a way of controlling for the effect of culture on test performance. Unfortunately, race and ethnicity are not the same thing as culture. They are related, of course, but to equate them is a mistake and does little to directly address the variable that actually affects test performance—background experiences. People from different races and ethnicities may or may not share a common culture. For example, Puerto Ricans have a mixed racial heritage that includes native origins (the Taìno), African origins (from the slave trade), and Anglo-European origins (Portugal, Spain, and France). Thus, to equate culture with race or ethnicity misses the point because it is not race or ethnicity that results in group differences in performance, but rather the extent to which the acculturation and background experiences of the individual taking the test are similar to that of the individuals included in the norm sample. The validity of results obtained from the use of tests with culturally different individuals is, therefore, questionable, as it may likely be more a reflection of the extent to which the individual has learned information pertinent to U.S. mainstream culture rather than actual intelligence or ability.

Because acculturation varies directly and proportionally according to an individual's length of experience and exposure to U.S. mainstream culture, use of standardized, norm-referenced tests with culturally different individuals may become more an exercise in evaluation of acculturation than intelligence or ability. This is true even with tests that include norms sampled from other countries, because diverse individuals in the United States have backgrounds that are bicultural and bilingual compared to the monocultural and monolingual experiences of individuals raised and educated in their native countries.

EFFECTS OF CULTURAL DIFFERENCE ON TEST PERFORMANCE

Culture may interact with test performance indirectly through acculturation and linguistic variables as described or it can directly affect test performance. Huerta-Macias (1995) provides an example wherein she notes that her daughter had a negative reaction to "none of the above" as a response choice in a fourth-grade multiple-choice test. Her daughter's lack of familiarity with the concept of "none of the above" illustrates that seemingly innocuous content may well carry implicit cultural expectations—in this case, the learning of particular test-taking strategies. Individuals may well know the concepts being tested but be unfamiliar or uncomfortable with the manner in which they are being measured, which adversely affects their performance. Children from culturally and linguistically diverse backgrounds may have difficulty with test taking because of a lack of exposure to the culture and testing situation as well as a lack of understanding of the importance of the test and the lack of practice or preparation. Similar limitations in exposure or experience with materials, content, or language (as a function of differences in cultural experiences) can also affect an individual's ability to answer questions or complete tasks that currently exist on tests of intelligence or cognitive ability. For example, Native American children are often taught to value reflective thought and deliberation as well as group harmony and a pluralistic community philosophy. This contrasts with some of the cultural implications of tests that tend to rely on speed of processing and responding, and individual excellence and competition. Western European cultural variables that tend to emphasize academic or intellectual achievement and individuality may create significant difficulties for individuals from diverse cultural backgrounds who have not been so inculcated or who, for whatever reasons, are simply disinclined to adopt such values. In general, individuals who are unfamiliar with and have had limited exposure to the mainstream U.S. society, the public education system, and the embedded cultural values therein are likely to be less adept when being tested than students who have been raised and indoctrinated in the mainstream U.S. culture.

CROSS-CULTURAL DYNAMICS BETWEEN EXAMINER AND EXAMINEE

The vast majority of research involving examiner–examinee effects in testing has relied upon racial differences between the two. Again, this is quite distinct from the dynamics that might result as a function of difference in culture, such as might occur with a Mexican examiner and a Cuban child—both possess an Hispanic ethnic heritage but have different cultural backgrounds. In general, when examiner–examinee effects have been studied with respect to racial difference, very little evidence has been uncovered to suggest that performance is significantly or adversely affected. Perhaps the reason for such findings relates again to the manner in which such effects were defined (i.e., racially instead of culturally). Variables that relate to cultural differences such as examiner's perceptions, prejudices, and stereotypic beliefs about the examinee's race can have a negative effect on rapport with the student, and subsequent performance on tests, particularly if the cultural difference is linked to a racial difference.

Management of potential bias related to examiner–examinee effects rests primarily on securing training, education, and experience in serving diverse cultural populations. Although the opportunity to obtain such experiences may be rather limited, psychologists nonetheless must possess specific skills and knowledge that help to guard against the more egregious forms of errors in assessment that can stem from preconceived notions, racial bias, or cultural stereotypes. Such qualifications should include competence in selecting and using tests appropriate for the individual, knowledge of and sensitivity toward the examinee's culture and its effect on establishing rapport and the subsequent test performance, and knowledge of first and second language acquisition and their relationship to cognitive and academic development. In addition, where feasible, the ability to assess the individual in his or her native language is extremely valuable.

SUMMARY

The preceding discussed the primary issues relevant to the practice of cross-cultural testing. Modern, well-developed tests of intelligence and cognitive ability are rarely biased from a psychometric point of view, but remain potentially discriminatory and unfair for several reasons. Tests developed and normed in the United States will always be imbued with content and concepts that reflect mainstream U.S. values. Moreover, the degree to which an individual is expected to possess these values or be familiar with such content is a function of the length of time spent living and being exposed to that culture and language. Thus, individuals whose cultural and linguistic backgrounds and experiences differ significantly from those of the individuals on whom the test was normed will necessarily perform at a lower level than age- or grade-related peers directly in proportion to the degree of difference. The more *different*

an individual is with respect to cultural experiences (or linguistic experiences), the more his or her performance on tests of intelligence or cognitive ability will be compromised.

To mitigate the potential biasing effects that can arise in cross-cultural assessment, it is necessary for psychologists to understand the assumption of comparability and the inherent dangers of comparing the performance of culturally different individuals with those on whom the test was normed. In addition, psychologists should be knowledgeable regarding several background and experiential issues of the individuals they seek to test, including:

- Their level of acculturation and knowledge of culture-based information
- Their exposure to and familiarity with testing situations
- The implied concepts required by specific tests and tasks
- Culture-specific values that may affect aspects of response style, speed, or even motivation

Psychologists should also seek to develop the qualifications required for conducting competent cross-cultural assessments including skill in using less biased or nondiscriminatory methods, as well as an awareness of how their own beliefs and prejudices may affect the testing situation and examinee performance. Professional ethics mandate that psychologists be cognizant of when an assessment or evaluation may be beyond their level or scope of competence and know when to elicit the supervision of a more experienced or qualified professional.

—*Samuel O. Ortiz and Stacey A. Lella*

See also Academic Achievement; Bias (Testing); Intelligence; Multicultural Education; Race, Ethnicity, Class, and Gender; Reliability

REFERENCES AND FURTHER READING

Flanagan, D. P., & Ortiz, S. (2001). *Essentials of cross-battery assessment.* New York: Wiley.

Huerta-Macias, A. (1995). Alternative assessment: Responses to commonly asked questions. *TESOL Journal, 5,* 8–11.

Matsumoto, D. (1994). *Cultural influences on research methods and statistics.* Pacific Grove, CA: Brooks/Cole.

Salvia, J., & Ysseldyke, J. E. (1991). *Assessment* (5th ed.). Boston: Houghton Mifflin.

CROSS-CULTURAL CONSULTATION

Cross-cultural consultation is of a type of problem-solving consultation that attends to the diverse values, perspectives, styles of communication, and cultural contexts prevalent in today's multicultural schools. It helps consultants bridge across the different cultures and perspectives among members of the consultation system (consultant, consultee, and client). Culture is complex and may be influenced by a wide range of factors such as familial values, ethnicity, race, religion, geographic location, education, level of acculturation, status within larger society, and identity within a minority group. School psychologists skilled in cross-cultural consultation help develop shared understandings of the problems and ways to resolve them.

Cross-cultural consultation is an approach that brings cultural issues to the forefront and adjusts the consultation services to address the needs and culture of the consultee and/or client (Ingraham, 2000; Tarver Behring & Ingraham, 1998). The psychologist guides the consultation process with a consultee (often a teacher or parent) who is concerned about one or more students or clients. Thus, consultation is a triadic relationship involving at least three different people in a consultation system.

Within the fields of counseling and psychology, there is growing awareness of the Eurocentric sociopolitical values embedded in the theories and research. Similarly, a Eurocentric view influences many consultation theories, representing the mainstream and neglecting the diversity of cultures and languages represented in today's communities (Ingraham, 2000; Ingraham & Meyers, 2000; Tarver Behring & Ingraham, 1998). Traditional consultation theories emphasize egalitarian and collaborative relationships, orientation to the problem behavior, and values consistent with the dominant culture, sometimes conflicting with the norms of diverse or minority groups within schools.

Psychologists can take several steps to broaden their perspective and enhance effectiveness with students, parents, and staff in our increasing pluralistic schools. The fields of psychology (American Psychological Association, 1993), multicultural counseling (Arredondo & colleagues, 1996), and multicultural school psychology (Rogers & colleagues, 1999) created national guidelines for specific knowledge and skills for culturally competent practice. Shari

Tarver Behring and Colette Ingraham (1998), among others, critiqued the consultation literature for its Eurocentric perspective; called for culture to become a central component of consultation theories, research, and practice; and proposed multicultural consultation approaches and competencies. Consultants need to know their own culture and its relations with other cultures, respect and understand the cultures of others, and use specific communication and interpersonal skills to build bridges between members of differing cultural backgrounds. The first step is to understand that all people do not share the same worldview and ways of understanding and resolving problems. One's cultural context can influence the patterns of thinking, behaving, and relating to others. The effective cross-cultural consultant is respectful of cultural differences and develops ways to educate and connect members who are of differing perspectives and cultures.

Rogerio Pinto proposed a model of cross-cultural consultation to guide people working in organizations and institutional development across cultures. Consultants need to be aware of and sensitive to the variations of their own values compared with those of others. Pinto's model laid the foundation for concepts that were expanded by later scholars, many of whom are authors, in a special journal issue on multicultural and cross-cultural consultation (Ingraham & Meyers, 2000).

In one approach (Ingraham, 2000), the consultant considers ways to support the consultee's development of knowledge, skill, perspective, and/or confidence. With the cultural and linguistic diversity that students bring to today's schools, it is likely that school personnel lack knowledge about each of the home cultures of their students. Consultants can:

- Guide school professionals in learning more about their students' cultural contexts and family histories, and how these may influence learning and behaviors at school
- Support consultees by modeling ways to learn about new cultures, describing their own learning process, and balancing emotional support with the introduction of new information

When consulting with families who are culturally different from the cultures of school personnel, consultants can modify their approaches to increase compatibility with the families' specific culture (Brown, 1997; Tarver Behring & colleagues, 2000). Cultural values can influence:

- Trust of school personnel
- Comfort in communicating with school members
- Preferences for home versus school meetings
- Expectations for consultants and teachers

Consultants can mediate between home and school cultures, coordinating development of a shared understanding and intervention.

Multicultural school consultation (MSC) is a framework developed to guide research and practice in consultation (Ingraham, 2000). It is used to teach effective cross-cultural consultation and in research that analyzes actual consultation sessions with teachers. MSC includes five components:

1. Consultant learning and development

2. Consultee learning and development

3. Cultural diversity in consultation constellations

4. Contextual and power influences

5. Methods to support consultee and client success

The model details five ways, shown in Figure 1, that cultural variations can occur within the triadic consultation system: consultant–consultee similarity, consultant–client similarity, consultee–client similarity, three-way diversity, and cultural similarity within a different cultural context. For each of these variations, there are unique processes and strategies consultants can use to promote understanding and successful outcomes. For example, when the consultant and family share the same culture but the teacher is culturally different from both (as in diagram *b* in Fig. 1), the consultant can help educate the teacher about the family's culture to improve the teacher/family communication and understanding. This can take pressure off the family to teach the teacher about their family traditions and values. In this case, the teacher may project onto the consultant certain stereotypes about the family's culture, and the consultant can address these with the teacher in ways that build greater teacher understanding and reduce potential bias. When the consultant and teacher are culturally different from the family's culture (as in diagram *a*), the consultant can model methods of cultural learning and educate the teacher by showing how to learn about the family's culture and values in ways that respect the family and lead to culturally compatible interventions. In diagram *c*, the teacher and family are culturally similar and the consultant is culturally different from both of them. In this situation the teacher may overidentify with the family's culture and think he or she completely understands the family's perspective. The consultant, as a third party, can ask how the family feels about the problem situation and its potential solutions; thereby drawing attention to the unique circumstances of this case, rather than cultural generalities, and giving the family more voice and input into the interventions.

In these ways, the consultant can act as a coach or educator to help the teacher learn about the family's culture and to help the family learn how to communicate with the teacher and navigate within the teacher's and/or school's culture. Even a consultant who does not know about a particular family's culture or the teacher's can use cultural learning strategies to increase their learning and can use communication styles and concepts that are compatible with those of the other members of the consultation triad. MSC offers consultants tools to improve their practice and support the learning and development of all members in the consultation system, resulting in successful outcomes for students, teachers, parents, and others.

Other works focus on cross-cultural consultation with specific populations or contexts, such as consultation across languages using interpreters, culturally diverse families (Brown, 1997; Lynch & Hanson, 1998), and specific racial or cultural groups. Cross-cultural consultation is informed by literature in several disciplines, including intergroup communications, multicultural counseling, cross-cultural psychology, and international school psychology.

Consultants can engage in cross-cultural consultation when one or more members of the consultation system holds values, perspectives, or cultural practices that diverge from others in the work context. For example, a consultant to a minority family can use cross-cultural consultation to enhance positive home–school relationships and understandings. Families of some cultural traditions prefer a relational style where they to get to know the consultant as a person before jumping into the problem-solving agenda; whereas other families prefer a more direct and formal interaction that gets right to the problems. When teachers are culturally different from their students, cross-cultural consultation helps them learn methods to build positive student–teacher relationships and to understand student behaviors within the context of students' home cultures. Finally, when consultants are culturally different from teachers or parents, cross-cultural consultation approaches help

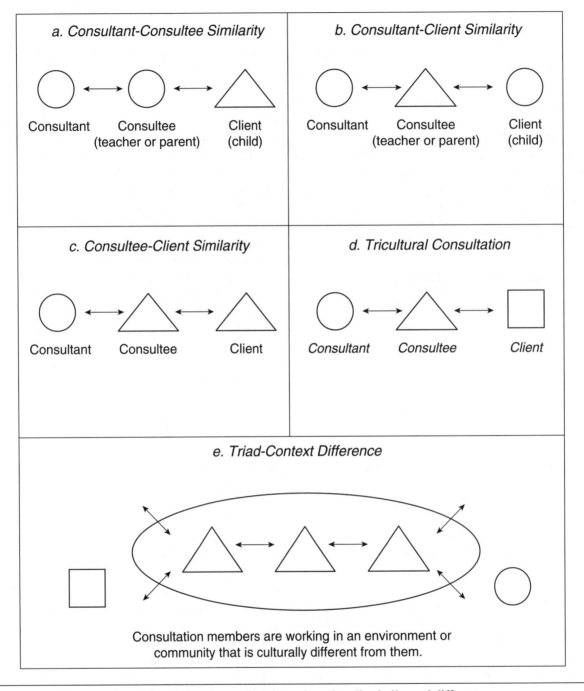

Figure 1   Five ways the triadic parties of consultation can be culturally similar and different.

them navigate the variety of complex issues that can arise. For example, if the consultee projects stereotypes about a given culture onto the consultant, the consultant's nonthreatening use of self-disclosure can help the consultee see the situation from a different perspective without defensiveness.

Case studies offer detailed descriptions of effective cross-cultural consultation (e.g., Ingraham, 2003; Tarver Behring & Ingraham, 1998; Tarver Behring & colleagues, 2000). In one case, a European-American teacher of mostly Spanish-speaking English learners was concerned about one student's lack of progress, participation, and peer relationships. The consultant used cross-cultural consultation to broaden the teacher's perspective and develop a new conceptualization about her work with this Vietnamese immigrant. As a result, the teacher, student, and classmates all benefited. Outcomes included the student's improved class participation and peer relationships, peer learning about the boy's culture, and teacher development of a new conceptualization of the problem, leading her to use different teaching strategies and regain a sense of confidence and competence (see Ingraham, 2003).

—Colette L. Ingraham

See also Consultation: Behavioral; Consultation: Conjoint Behavioral; Consultation: Ecobehavioral; Consultation: Mental Health; Multicultural Education; Race, Ethnicity, Class and Gender

REFERENCES AND FURTHER READING

American Psychological Association. (1993). Guidelines for providers of psychological services to ethnic, linguistic and culturally diverse populations. *American Psychologist, 48,* 45–48.

Arredondo, P., Toporek, R., Brown, S. P., Jones, J., Locke, D. C., Sanchez, J., et al. (1996). Operationalization of the multicultural counseling competencies. *Journal of Multicultural Counseling and Development, 24,* 42–78.

Brown, D. (1997). Implications of cultural values for cross-cultural consultation with families. *Journal of Counseling & Development, 76,* 29–35.

Ingraham, C. L. (2000). Consultation through a multicultural lens: Multicultural and cross-cultural consultation in schools. *School Psychology Review, 29*(3), 320–343.

Ingraham, C. L. (2003). Multicultural consultee-centered consultation: When novice consultants explore cultural hypotheses with experienced teacher consultees. *Journal of Educational and Psychological Consultation, 14*(3, 4), 329–362.

Ingraham, C. L., & Meyers, J. (Guest Eds.) (2000). Multicultural and cross-cultural Consultation in schools: Cultural diversity issues in school consultation [Special issue]. *School Psychology Review, 29*(3).

Lynch, E. W., & Hanson, N. J. (Eds.). (1998). *Developing cross-cultural competence: A guide for working with children and their families* (2nd ed.). Baltimore: Paul H. Brookes.

Rogers, M. R., Ingraham, C. L., Bursztyn, A., Cajigas-Segredo, N., Esquivel, G., Hess, R., et al. (1999). Providing psychological services to racially, ethnically, culturally, and linguistically diverse individuals in the schools: Recommendations for practice. *School Psychology International Journal, 20,* 243–264.

Tarver Behring, S., Cabello, B., Kushida, D., & Murguia, A. (2000). Cultural modifications to current school-based consultation approaches reported by culturally diverse beginning consultants. *School Psychology Review, 29*(3), 354–367.

Tarver Behring, S., & Ingraham, C. L. (1998). Culture as a central component to consultation: A call to the field. *Journal of Educational and Psychological Consultation, 9,* 57–72.

CURRICULUM-BASED ASSESSMENT

Curriculum-based assessment (CBA) can be defined as any set of measurement procedures that use "direct observation and recording of a student's performance in the local curriculum as a basis for gathering information to make instructional decisions" (Deno, 1987, p. 41). Although the term CBA increasingly has come into common usage as a methodology, it represents a number of diverse assessment practices. Shinn and colleagues (1989) identified four different models of CBA that have been presented in the professional literature:

1. Curriculum-based assessment for instructional design (CBA-ID)

2. Criterion-referenced curriculum-based assessment (CR-CBA)

3. Curriculum-based evaluation (CBE)

4. Curriculum-based measurement (CBM)

Shapiro (1990) offered another model that integrates aspects of the models listed above in addition to assessing the instructional ecology of the academic environment.

Although the definition of CBA as posed by Deno (1987) is straightforward and clearly establishes the most salient features shared by all forms of CBA, confusion persists regarding the important distinctions among the many variants of CBA. Fuchs and Deno (1991) identified two major models of instructionally relevant measurement into which most forms of CBA can be categorized. The first model, which is highly related to the behaviorally oriented measurement systems of the 1960s, is referred to as *Specific Subskill Mastery Measurement* and is best represented by CBA-ID, CR-CBA, and CBE. This approach breaks down global curriculum outcomes into a set of subskills, which are then ordered as short-term instructional objectives. Specific subskill testing relies on mastery measurement, where small domains of test items and mastery criteria are specified for each subskill. These criterion-referenced items are designed to produce student performance data required for inferring mastery of subtasks embedded in the objectives. The second model, *General Outcome Measurement,* represents a more general approach to instructionally relevant measurement. General outcome measurement was developed to measure general performance outcome indicators, toward which whole instructional programs are directed, rather than short-term mastery of specific objectives. Prescriptive procedures aimed at providing teachers with reliable, valid, and efficient procedures for obtaining student performance data to evaluate their instructional programs with long-range consistency are the distinctive features of general outcome measurement.

Although mastery measurement possesses many advantages over traditional assessment, a number of limitations may limit its usefulness. First, because mastery measurement focuses on skill hierarchies, it is the skill or instructional hierarchy that determines measurement. When the measurement system is embedded in a skill sequence, the assessor cannot use the data to evaluate the effectiveness of alternative skill sequences or of qualitatively different approaches to teaching (Fuchs & Deno, 1991). Thus, within a mastery measurement framework, instruction is viewed essentially as a matter of selecting, teaching, and testing for mastery of a set of specific skills that consist of logically or formally similar subsets of stimuli. These skills are treated as though they represent the only important skills of instruction.

Another concern is that, given the one-to-one correspondence between testing and instructional focus, mastery measurement does not automatically assess retention and generalization of related skills (Fuchs & Deno, 1991). Tying the instructional format too closely to the assessment device in this manner may lead to a restricted instructional focus, which in turn may limit the maintenance and transfer of skills. This close connection between measurement and instruction may create a measurement framework that is limited, resulting in a reduction in the overall validity of the assessment. Because measurement requires constant shifts in measurement focus as skills are mastered, overall progress across skill domains is

difficult to assess. Moreover, because different skills are measured in different points in time and are not of equal difficulty, scores drop each time a new skill is introduced. These shifts in measurement, coupled with limited summaries of generalized learning in many circumstances, reduce the usefulness of mastery measurement. Finally, because these forms of CBA have largely been developed by teachers, the technical adequacy of such measures is questionable. Psychometric characteristics such as the accuracy of the scores and the extent to which the scores represent a child's true skills are uncertain (Shinn & colleagues, 1989). Consequently, the accuracy and meaningfulness of most CBA approaches used in mastery measurement remain largely unknown (Fuchs & Deno, 1991).

As distinguished from the specific subskill mastery measurement model of instructional assessment, the two most prominent features of measuring general outcome indicators are (Fuchs & Deno, 1991):

1. Assessment of proficiency on the global outcomes toward which the entire curriculum is directed

2. Reliance on a standardized, prescriptive measurement methodology that produces critical indicators of performance

Currently, the model most closely associated with general outcome measurement is CBM.

The salient features of the general outcome measurement model parallel and contrast those of mastery measurement (Fuchs & Deno, 1991). First, in contrast to specific subskill mastery measurement, measurement of general outcomes does not require assessors to specify instructional hierarchies prior to assessment. To establish a general outcomes measurement system, assessors must identify the domain they will use to measure student proficiency throughout the year. Such a system of measurement offers a number of advantages. First, instead of focusing on sequential subskills for mastery, general outcome measurement focuses on the broader final task outcome. As such, general outcome measurement attends to long-term goals by measuring the critical outcomes of the curriculum. Second, by focusing measurement on the outcome desired at the end of the year, general outcome measurement avoids the troublesome task of breaking down the curriculum into a sequence of instructional units. By doing this, the assessor protects against specifying instructional units and orderings that eventually may prove difficult to an individual student's learning style.

Third, general outcome measurement does not determine the instructional content and procedures as does mastery measurement. The structure of subskill mastery measurement specifies what will be taught, determines the order in which the content should be presented, and dictates that progress in teaching new skills should not occur until mastery of the current skill has been demonstrated. Consequently, with mastery measurement, instruction and measurement are confounded. By contrast, general outcome measurement and instruction are independent of one another. With general outcome measurement, measurement is not tied to or determined by the current instructional focus or procedures. General outcome measurement permits assessors to experiment with different instructional units, methods, materials, and procedures—while at the same time allowing data to serve as a primary outcome measure for investigating the effectiveness of contrasting instructional approaches. Whereas specific subskill mastery measurement determines the content and sequence of instruction, measures of general outcome are designed deliberately to allow assessors to vary content, sequence, and method freely so that the effectiveness of these instructional variations can be evaluated.

The general outcome measurement system also offers advantages of automatic assessment of retention and generalization of learning, because sampling from such broad domains includes skills representing past and future instructional targets. For example, if a student improves in vowel team (two vowels together in a word) spelling abilities, his or her performance on general outcome measures of spelling is likely to increase—the increased proficiency will most likely enable the student to correctly spell more blends on future assignments or tests. In this manner, a general outcome measurement system produces performance indicators that are sensitive to retention, because it samples skills across the annual curriculum. Conversely, if the student generalizes learning to a new skill where vowel team instruction occurs, the general outcome indicators are again likely to increase, because opportunities for spelling taught words are provided by general outcome measurement tests. In this way, the general outcome measurement model serves as an index of generalization.

The third critical feature of general outcome measurement is that, by definition, it focuses on the broad goals of the curriculum, rather than on a series of short-term objectives. Compared to the specific mastery measurement approach, where assessment focuses on current instruction, general outcome measurement samples the critical behavior and content aggregated across the entire year-long curriculum. Because of this, general outcome measurement is less sensitive to the specific skills taught. However, despite this apparent limitation, general outcome measurement provides a database sensitive to instructional effects, which can be used effectively for instructional decision making. With general outcome measurement, the probability of sampling each curricular skill is proportional to the frequency with which that skill occurs in the curriculum. As such, most skills are included in most tests, and across a small number of tests all skills can be expected to be sampled. Furthermore, because general outcome measurement employs critical behaviors that are broadly indicative of the annual curriculum, the content validity (the extent to which it represents the true desired outcome) and its criterion validity (the extent to which it relates to other socially important indices of achievement) are strong.

With general outcome measurement, assessors can monitor students' development across a school year without any shifts in measurement. Because general outcome measurement samples material across the curriculum, the difficulty of the tests remains constant across the year. This contrasts sharply with mastery measurement, where the measurement domains and the difficulty of testing material continually shift as the instructional content changes. In specific subskill mastery measurement, performance across tasks is not interpretable, because the two tasks are, in fact, two separate entities. By avoiding these shifts in measurement domain, the general outcome measurement model allows for summative descriptions of student performance across time, in addition to evaluative comparisons across:

- Alternative instructional programs implemented during different times of the year
- Rates of learning under different service delivery arrangements
- Program efficiency for different students

Finally, general outcome measurement procedures are both reliable and valid (Shinn, 1989). Once broad domains of curriculum across the school year have been determined, the methodology prescribes what outcome indicators to measure over time and what methods to employ for creating, administrating, scoring, and interpreting resultant data in a meaningful fashion. This standardized, prescriptive measurement approach is directly opposed to the criterion-referenced approach used with specific subskill mastery measurement.

CURRICULUM-BASED ASSESSMENT IN SCHOOL PSYCHOLOGY PRACTICE

For school psychologists, the choice among CBA approaches rests largely on the type of assessment question being asked. If, for example, the assessment question focused on differentiating a student's basic skills from those of his or her peers or on monitoring the progress of a basic skill development over time, CBM as a general outcome indicator might be the best approach. If, on the other hand, the assessment question focused on a diagnostic assessment of a student's mastery of a particular skill or criterion, a specific subskill mastery measurement approach—such as CBE, CR-CBA, or CBA-ID—would provide the criterion-referenced information needed.

In practice, the combination of both approaches would provide the assessor with information regarding both the general level of basic skill development and specific information on patterns of strengths and/or weaknesses within a diagnostic profile. Take, for example, a third-grade student who was referred for an academic assessment by his teacher, who notes concerns in both reading and mathematics. The school psychologist might begin the assessment process using standardized CBM approaches in reading and mathematics to:

- Identify whether a problem in each area is evident
- If a problem is evident, determine the magnitude of the problem

In reading, the school psychologist might administer grade-level CBM oral reading fluency probes and silently read Maze probes to assess the student's general oral reading fluency and comprehension skills. In mathematics, initial CBM assessment might consist of grade-level multiple-skill computational problems and a series of application problems. Once administered, the target student's performance can be compared to grade-level standards to identify whether or not a problem exists. If so, successively easier (lower grade level) CBM materials in both domains could be administered to ascertain at what level the student demonstrated success. The difference between the student's current grade level and his instructional level would define the magnitude of difficulty, as well as provide initial insight into possible intervention and instructional strategies and goals for intervention.

Once initial levels of performance are assessed using CBM, assessment procedures that examine more specific areas of academic performance—CBE, CR-CBA, and/or CBA-ID—may be used to evaluate more specific areas of strength and/or weakness. For example, in the area of reading, word lists of basic sight words or lists of words with specific vowel team combinations might be administered to obtain a more diagnostic appraisal of the student's particular difficulty. Similarly, in mathematics specific types of computational problems could be administered to obtain a more detailed account of the student's difficulties. Once specific areas of weakness are identified, diagnostic prescriptive instructional intervention techniques could be developed based on the assessment information provided by the specific subskill mastery measurement approach. The student's progress toward specific instructional objectives and his response to intervention could be monitored using any one or a combination of approaches. The most comprehensive formative assessment of progress would most likely involve both CBM as a general outcome measure (i.e., to provide information regarding progress toward long-term objectives) and CBE, CR-CBA, or CBA-ID to monitor progress in specific objectives and instructional strategies.

Finally, once instructional intervention strategies are implemented, CBM assessments similar to those used in the initial assessment could be reemployed to assess the student's overall progress toward his long-term objectives and to once again assess whether a basic skill weakness is evident, and, if so, what is his grade-level equivalent.

—*John M. Hintze*

See also Academic Achievement; Authentic Assessment; Behavioral Assessment; Norm-Referenced Testing; Performance-Based Assessment; Written Language Assessment

Point Versus Counterpoint: Curriculum-Based Assessment

The case for:

The CBA model claims several advantages, including:

- Technical or psychometric adequacy as reflected in studies of reliability and validity
- Clear and effective communication of judgments regarding student progress
- Sensitivity to small but important gains in student performance over relatively short periods of time (such as days or weeks)
- Frequent and continuous assessment of achievement without practice effects
- Simplicity in administration and scoring
- Cost-effectiveness with respect to the time required to administer the test and the cost of the materials
- Collection of data essential to general and special education decision making with respect to screening, eligibility, and program evaluation

The case against:

The CBA model's disadvantages include:

- Its focus on basic skills and not higher-order critical thinking skills
- Its use, to date, only at the elementary grades
- Its varying administration and scoring procedures across the different models
- Its recommended continuous data collection, which can be a challenge
- Its overreliance on the use of local norms
- Its (some say in essence) "teaching to the test," which does not reflect "real" learning

REFERENCES AND FURTHER READING

Deno, S. L. (1987). Curriculum-based measurement. *Teaching Exceptional Children, 20,* 41.

Fuchs, L. S., & Deno, S. L. (1991). Paradigmatic distinctions between instructionally relevant measurement models. *Exceptional Children, 57,* 488–500.

Shapiro, E. S. (1990). An integrated model for curriculum-based assessment. *School Psychology Review, 19,* 331–349.

Shinn, M. R. (Ed.). (1989). *Curriculum-based measurement: Assessing special children.* New York: Guilford.

Shinn, M. R., Rosenfield, S., & Knutson, N. (1989). Curriculum-based assessment: A comparison of models. *School Psychology Review, 18,* 299–316.

D

DARE PROGRAM

DARE is an acronym for the Drug Abuse Resistance Education Program and was created in 1983 by Los Angeles Police Chief Daryl Gates. DARE is the most widely used drug use prevention program in the United States, being delivered to 26 million school children in nearly 75% of the nation's school districts, and to 10,000 million in more than 54 countries around the world.

DARE's primary mission is to provide children and adolescents with the information and skills they need to live drug-and-violence-free lives by equipping children and youths with the tools that will enable them to avoid negative influences and, instead, allow them to focus on their strengths and potential. Additionally, the program seeks to establish positive relationships between students and law enforcement, teachers, parents, and other community leaders.

DARE America, the parent organization for the DARE programs, is located in Los Angeles, California. This national nonprofit organization describes its role as serving as a resource to communities, and helping to establish and improve local DARE programs. DARE America also provides police officer training, supports the development and evaluation of the DARE curricula, provides student educational materials, monitors instruction standards and program results, and creates national awareness for DARE.

One of the unique aspects of the DARE curricula is that the programs are designed to be taught by specially trained police officers who then lead a series of classroom lessons that teach children and adolescents from kindergarten through 12th grade. Officers are used to implement the program under the assumption that a curriculum on substance abuse prevention is more effective when the instructors represent legitimate authority figures within the community.

Prior to implementing the elementary and middle/junior high school programs, officers undergo 80 hours of special training in areas such as child development, classroom management, teaching techniques, and communication skills, which also certifies them as School Resource Officers. In addition, 40 hours of training are provided to DARE instructors to prepare them to teach the high school curriculum.

DARE America views the police officer's role in the classroom as an important program component because the program allows young people to begin to relate to officers as people, to see officers in a helping role, not just an enforcement role, opens lines of communication between law enforcement and youths, as well as between the school, police, and parents to deal with other issues. The officer is also viewed as a conduit to provide information beyond drug-related topics.

Programs are offered for kindergarten through second grades (4 sessions) and third through fourth grades (5 sessions), but most students who participate in the elementary school DARE curriculum are fifth and sixth graders. The DARE curriculum, newly revised in 2003, is intended for fifth- and sixth-grade students and consists of 9 lessons with an optional 10th class culmination event. In addition to the elementary curriculum, there is a 10-lesson program designed for middle/junior high school students, also newly revised in 2003, and a 9-session high school curriculum.

The K–12 DARE curricula focus on the following content areas:

- "No use" messages for alcohol, marijuana, and tobacco
- Immediate consequences of use
- Normative beliefs (perceptions about how many people use a specific substance)
- Problem solving and conflict management
- Self-management skills
- Voluntary commitment (to remain substance- and violence-free)
- Character education
- Interactive participatory learning
- Resistance skills
- Alternatives to using substances or participating in violence
- Self-esteem
- Role modeling

There are also two other DARE educational components: parent training and an after-school program called DARE + PLUS (Play and Learn Under Supervision). The parent training program has been introduced in communities throughout the United States. This six-session program is designed to help parents talk with their children and complement in-school DARE programs for students in grades K–12. DARE+PLUS is an on-campus program offering middle school students educational after-school activities. The program combines community volunteers with DARE officers and school staff for the benefits of students on campus immediately after school.

—Sara Veblen-Mortenson

See also Prevention; Substance Abuse

Point Versus Counterpoint: DARE Program

The case for:

DARE provides the answer to the question, "Is DARE effective in reducing drug use and antisocial behavior?" by stating, "While there has been debate in some quarters about DARE's effectiveness, DARE has been clearly shown to make a difference. Evaluations show significant differences between students receiving DARE and those who do not, in terms of their drug use and gang involvement. The DARE curriculum has been shown to improve skills that help students resist risk-taking behaviors and peer influences that might lead to drug use" (DARE America Online, 2004).

DARE states that the program is such a widely used and popular program because it provides unique involvement for a wide range of community leaders, including law enforcement officers, classroom teachers, peer leaders, and parents.

DARE has acknowledged that its program has not been very effective at reducing actual drug use and announced in 2001 that it is redesigning its program in an attempt to make it more effective. The DARE organization is reinventing itself and revising its curricula to reflect the "New DARE." Two of the most significant changes are the implementation of a newly developed elementary curriculum for 5th and 6th graders. Highlights of their new "state-of-the-art" elementary curriculum include shorter sessions (9–10 sessions as opposed to the original 17 sessions), officers using facilitation skills to promote student discussion and learning, and providing more opportunities for students to engage in active student learning. The New DARE middle and/or junior high school curriculum is in its third year of a five-year national research effort to develop, implement, and evaluate the program. Conclusions about the effectiveness of that program are forthcoming.

DARE has succeeded in organizing and implementing an effective dissemination strategy. This has been difficult for many prevention researchers to do in a climate of competitive prevention funding and increasing demands on the students' time in the classroom. With the advent of the newly revised DARE curricula and forthcoming scientific evaluations of those curricula, the prevention community, schools, parents, and local communities will wait to see if DARE can continue to fulfill its intended mission of the "New DARE."

The case against:

While the DARE program is clearly the most widely disseminated prevention program and has great popularity, it has also come under scrutiny by the prevention community and local communities who have questioned the program's effectiveness, content, and cost.

There has been much debate about what aspects of the DARE program make it successful. The scientific and prevention community would argue that the most critical measure of any substance use prevention program's success is whether or not the program affects young people's short- and/or long-term drug use behavior when rigorous scientific evaluation standards are applied.

If the measure of success of DARE is whether or not it is effective in reducing drug use or misuse among young people, the evaluations uniformly conclude it is not effective. DARE is not more effective than any other drug education program, nor more effective than no program at all. Although many evaluations have been conducted, scientific study has not discovered any statistically significant difference in drug usage rates between students who had taken the DARE program and those who had not.

Because the elementary curriculum is the one that is most widely disseminated, it has also been the most widely evaluated DARE curriculum. Numerous studies of the original curriculum have found no long-term effects on actual drug use (Clayton & colleagues, 1996; Dukes & colleagues, 1996; Ennett & colleagues, 1994; Lynam & colleagues, 1999). Several evaluations have reported short-term changes in cigarette smoking among participants that were small in size and much smaller than those associated when compared with other prevention programs (Clayton & colleagues, 1996; Dukes & colleagues, 1996; Ennett & colleagues, 1994, Lynam & colleagues, 1999). One study showed no significant differences in behavior change for alcohol, multidrug, or tobacco use and victimization of the original middle/junior high school curriculum when a group that received the program was compared with a group that did not receive the program.

While scientific program evaluations have not shown significant behavior changes, there still is popular support for the implementation of the DARE program.

If the measure of success of DARE is popularity, then yes, DARE has been enormously effective in attracting widespread popular and financial support, and has achieved a level of visibility unparalleled by any other single drug education program.

Evaluations indicate that the positive reactions to DARE are not tied to people's belief that DARE is effective in preventing alcohol, drug, or tobacco use, but that the program's impact can be seen in improved relationships between the police and the community, with student perceptions of the police, and better police understanding of the students. In addition, some educators recommend the program to other schools and recommend that the program continue in their own schools despite their view of the program. A major national report concluded that, while the DARE program had strong support by the teachers, students, parents, and community members, it had no effect on the students' drug use.

REFERENCES AND FURTHER READING

Clayton, R. C., Catterello, A. N., & Johnstone, B. M. (1996). The effectiveness of Drug Abuse Resistance Education (Project DARE): Five year follow-up results. *Preventive Medicine, 25*, 307–318.

DARE America Online. (n.d.). Retrieved December, 2002, from http://www.dare-america.com/home

Dukes, R. L., Ullman, J. B., Stein, J. A. (1996). A three-year follow-up of Drug Abuse Resistance Education (DARE). *Evaluation Review, 20*, 49–66.

Ennett, S. T., Tobler, N. S., Ringwalt, C. L., Fleweling, R. L. (1994). How effective is Drug Abuse Resistance Education? A meta-analysis of Project DARE outcome evaluations. *American Journal of Public Health, 84*, 1394–1402.

Lynam, D. R., Milich, R., Zimmerman, R., Novak, S. P., Logan, T. K., Martin, C., et al. (1999). Project DARE: No effects at 10-year follow-up. *Journal of Consulting and Clinical Psychology, 4,* 590–593.

DEATH AND BEREAVEMENT

To effectively assist a student in dealing with a death, the school psychologist must have an understanding of the student's developmental level and an understanding of the bereavement process. This article reviews the role of the student's developmental level in coping with grief, the bereavement process, and bereavement programs available within the schools.

CHILDREN'S UNDERSTANDING OF DEATH FROM A DEVELOPMENTAL PERSPECTIVE

Chronological age, cognitive and socioemotional development, culture, and experiences all influence a child's understanding of death. Important concepts in understanding a child's view of death include:

- Universality (All living things die.)
- Irreversibility (A physically dead body cannot live again.)
- Nonfunctionality (All physical functions cease.)
- Causality (There is abstract and realistic understanding of the external and internal events that lead to death.)
- Noncorporeal continuation (Some form of personal continuation exists after death of physical body.)

Early studies indicated younger children (ages 5 and younger) did not understand the finality of death and felt death could be avoided (Nagy, 1948), but children frequently encounter death in nature, such as a dead bird, and can understand the finality of it (Bowlby, 1980). A more mature understanding of death solidifies with the typical 10-year-old child.

Further research into children's understanding of the conceptualization of death has used Piaget's stages of cognitive development. During the concrete operational stage (ages 7 to 10 years) children develop a more adult understanding of death, and by the formal operational stage (beginning at ages 11 to 12 years) they are likely to understand the abstract ideas that characterize death.

CHILDREN'S BEREAVEMENT FROM A DEVELOPMENTAL PERSPECTIVE

Children's understanding of death, family, and cultural influences, family stability, personal characteristics, relationship with the deceased, and the circumstances of the death affect the bereavement process. There is no specific model that targets the bereavement process based on child development, although theories of Freud, Piaget, and Erikson are evident in discussions of a child's ability to grieve, to understand the finality of death, or to create an identity after the death of a parent.

Some question very young children's ability to grieve. Because a child does not understand the finality of death, grieving would not be possible. Most thanatologists (those who engage in the scientific study of death) agree that children can grieve, at least as an experience of separation, as infants or as toddlers (Bowlby, 1980). These grief reactions to loss may not constitute true understanding of death's finality and may not be viewed as true *mourning*—the conscious and unconscious work done in coping with the loss of a loved one and the public expression of that loss.

Little research exists to delineate age-related children's bereavement reactions, although clinical observations suggest that children up to five years of age often show anxiety or aggressive behaviors. Sleep disturbances, temper tantrums, aggressive play, and regression, including elimination problems, may be expected. Elementary school–age children may deny death or the resultant emotions, assume a caretaker role, experience excessive guilt, and develop phobic or somatic symptoms. Adolescents are more likely to become depressed and withdrawn; to escape through acting-out behaviors such as promiscuity, increased chemical use, or risk-taking behaviors; to assume a caretaker role; to struggle with the philosophical meaning of death; or to be preoccupied with guilt. These are possible but not the most likely behaviors exhibited during bereavement. These behaviors are evident as a result of premorbid functioning and the severity of the loss.

Deaths of parents, siblings, and friends can also elicit discrete concerns. Although Fleming and Balmer (1996) report that research indicates increased depression and school-related problems in adolescents who experience the death of a parent, an increased sense of maturity and an opportunity for growth may also follow. Baker and Sedney (1996) note that younger children may have cognitive limitations, which inhibit understanding of the death. Furthermore, identification with the parent and the developmental stage at which the child experiences the death of a parent influences reactions to the death. Because of the special nature of sibling relationships, which are often complex interactions of rivalry as well as companionship and friendship, guilt may predominate emotional experiences when a sibling dies; and a myriad of educational, social, and behavioral complications may be expected, the expression of which may be dependent on the age of the survivor. Also, Oltjenbruns (1996) identifies that the death of a friend in adolescence may challenge a sense of a predictable and safe world. Because many adolescent relationships may be marked by ambivalence or conflict, grieving may be complicated in nature. Some of the many typical grief responses are identified as:

- Denial, panic, anger, guilt, aggression
- Bodily distress, anxiety, clinging
- Preoccupation with the deceased
- Hyperactivity, shortened attention span
- Withdrawal, delayed expressions of grief
- Assumption of mannerisms of the deceased, idealization of the deceased
- Searching, yearning, and pining
- Disorganization, eating disorders, school difficulties

Clinical depression occurred in more than 20% of a sample of grieving children studied by Weller and colleagues (1991).

FACTORS OF THE BEREAVEMENT PROCESS

Early researchers suggested that the bereaved pass through discrete stages and phases of emotions and behaviors. Currently, most thanatologists describe a series of tasks to be completed that focus on acknowledging the reality of death, experiencing the pain, adjusting self-identity and adapting to new life circumstances, finding meaning in the loss, and adapting to the new relationship with the deceased.

During bereavement, emotional expressions are normal and helpful and do not signify weakness or illness. Children benefit from adults who validate feelings of grief in their expressions of mourning. Intense emotional experiences as well as physiological

reactions to the death of a family member or friend are normal. It is when the intensity or duration of the experience hampers normal social or academic development that intervention may be warranted. For example, failing grades, withdrawal from social interactions, increased aggression, suicidal ideation or attempts, chemical use, or promiscuous behaviors should prompt intervention. Early researchers suggested that the bereavement process should be completed within a year, but current thought suggests that the bereavement process continues throughout a life span. Thus, children's grief may exist for several years and may also become more pronounced during life transitions, which Oltjenbruns (2001) describes as a "re-grief" process.

ROLE OF SCHOOL PSYCHOLOGISTS

School psychologists can be instrumental in helping children navigate the tasks of bereavement through the use of systems consultation, program development, and crisis intervention; as well as assessment, counseling, and consultation. School psychologists can help to develop a curriculum addressing death and dying and assist in developing district policy to address crises. They can assist by writing grants to expand bereavement services in the classroom and in small group counseling sessions, which can be cofacilitated by bereavement counselors.

School psychologists can also provide counseling following the death of faculty and/or students. Several models to address these events are described in the literature. Schoolwide, classroom, and individual interventions can be crucial at the time of a tragic event.

Not all children suffering loss will require intervention, although approximately 33% may have sufficient concerns that warrant counseling, and intrusive symptoms may require intervention. Childhood loss can affect psychological development, but not everyone who suffers loss will experience debilitating psychological effects. Even so, parents often request additional help assessing and addressing the needs of their children.

Academic problems and behavioral concerns may surface during bereavement. Assessing the severity of a problem is critical for the initiation of appropriate interventions. Interventions that have been found to be helpful include:

- Play therapy
- Bibliotherapy
- Structured group intervention
- Storytelling, games, writing
- Art therapy

Structured groups often address topics dealing with memories of favorite activities with the deceased, coping with feelings, understanding life cycles, coping specifically with grief, experiencing the rituals of grieving, being aware of one's own body, and developing support systems. Memory books capture important events. Special consideration to the culture of the participants, posttraumatic stress symptoms, anger concerns, and assertiveness may be required in some situations.

Numerous issues may need to be addressed when consulting with families as they grieve. Changes in roles, need for additional supports, recognizing societal influences on grieving, sharing developmental information with parents regarding participation in rituals and cognitive–emotional development are all critical issues facing a bereaved family. Parents may also appreciate referrals to literature and to community resources such as counseling agencies, funeral directors, or bereavement centers that can provide additional support.

—Mary Ann Teitelbaum

See also Crisis Intervention; Defense Mechanisms; Fears; Parenting

REFERENCES AND FURTHER READING

Baker, J., & Sedney, M. (1996). How bereaved children cope with loss: An overview. In C. A. Corr & D. M. Corr (Eds.), *Handbook of childhood death and bereavement* (pp. 109–130). New York: Springer.

Bowlby, J. (1980). *Attachment and loss: Vol. III. Loss: Sadness and depression.* New York: Basic Books.

Fleming, S., & Balmer, L. (1996). Bereavement in adolescence. In C. A. Corr & D. E. Balk, (Eds.), *Handbook of adolescent death and bereavement* (pp. 139–154). New York: Springer.

Nagy, M. H. (1948). The child's theories concerning death. *Journal of Genetic Psychology, 73,* 3–27.

Oltjenbruns, K. A. (1996). Death of a friend during adolescence: Issues and impacts. In C. A. Corr & D. E. Balk (Eds.), *Handbook of adolescent death and bereavement* (pp. 196–215). New York: Springer.

Oltjenbruns, K. A. (2001). Developmental context of childhood: Grief and regrief phenomena. In R. O. Hansson, M. S. Stroebe, W. Stroebe, & H. Schut (Eds.), *Handbook of bereavement research: Consequences, coping, and care* (pp. 169–197). Washington, DC: American Psychological Association.

Weller, E. B., Weller, R. A., Fristad, M. A., & Bowes, J. M. (1991). Depression in recently bereaved prepubertal children. *American Journal of Psychiatry, 148,* 1536–1541.

DECODING

Decoding is the ability to interpret graphic symbols, through the use of letter–sound correspondences, so the message can be understood. Another term for this process is phonological recoding.

The ability to identify and understand words is fundamental to the reading process. There are several strategies readers use to decipher unknown words including decoding, sight, analogy, and context. Decoding plays a fundamental role in students' early reading development because phonological recoding enables a bond, or connection, between letters and sounds to be formed. Reading decoding research shows that once the bond has been established, decoding the word is no longer necessary because the word is recognized in memory and can be read rapidly by sight. Decoding is one of the most important word-recognition strategies because it allows the reader to understand the letter–sound relationship, which provides a mnemonic device for memory and it may be a self-teaching mechanism for unknown words.

—Donita Massengill

See also Reading Interventions and Strategies

DEFENSE MECHANISMS

Defense mechanisms refer to patterns of thinking and behaving as ways to adapt and adjust to difficult life circumstances. Freud (1901) first described these thinking and behavior patterns as being abnormal because he believed that they were ways in which people deluded themselves to deal with conflicts between id impulses and superego constraints and punishments. More recent perspectives suggest that these mechanisms may be viewed as protective in that they develop in response to either perceived or real threats. These threats can arise from how the person interprets reality. Defenses allow the person to cope with these threats. The most common defense mechanisms are:

- Denial
- Repression
- Displacement
- Substitution
- Sublimation
- Projection
- Reaction formation
- Rationalization
- Isolation

In the school setting it is not unusual for teachers to encounter the defense mechanism of projection in aggressive or acting-out students. These students justify their aggression by "projecting" that it was provoked by the teacher because of how the teacher looked at them, or accusing the teacher of talking about them to others.

—*Raymond E. Webster*

REFERENCES AND FURTHER READING

Freud, S. (1901). *The psychopathology of everyday life.* London: Hogarth.

DEPRESSION

Depression, currently the most common psychiatric diagnosis given in the United States, is an illness that involves an individual's cognitive, emotional, and physical functioning. In contrast to the normal feelings of sadness, shifting moods, or loss, depression is persistent and can interfere with the way one eats and sleeps, feels about one's self, and the way one thinks. It can affect people of any age, race, ethnic, or economic group. Depression affects an estimated 9.9% of adults older than 18 years, 8% of adolescents, and 2.5% of children in a given year in the United States. Nearly twice as many females as males are affected with depression each year. Research indicates that depression onset is earlier today than in past decades.

DEPRESSION AND SCHOOL-AGE CHILDREN

Depression in children and adolescents frequently goes undetected. Signs of depression in young people are often seen as normal mood swings typical of a particular developmental stage. Professionals are also often reluctant to prematurely "label" a young person with the diagnosis of depression, but early diagnosis and treatment are crucial to healthy emotional, social, and behavioral development. A longitudinal study published in 1999 found that early onset of depression often persists, recurs, and continues into adulthood and indicates that depression in youths may predict more severe illness in their adult life.

CAUSES OF DEPRESSION

Depression may be a result of physiologically (biochemical) and genetically based causes, and like other illnesses, just happens. It may occur after a divorce in the family, the end of a relationship, the death of a loved one, financial problems, or difficulties at home. Depression in both young people and adults may occur at the same time as anxiety or panic attacks, disruptive behavior, substance abuse disorders, sexual dysfunctions, personality disorders, and with physical illness (e.g., diabetes mellitus).

SYMPTOMS AND TYPES OF DEPRESSION

People react differently when they are depressed. Symptoms of depression include:

- Sadness or crying (that does not always go away)
- Loss of interest or pleasure in once-enjoyed activities (whether work, school, family, or friends)
- Increases or decreases in appetite
- Loss or gain in weight (when not dieting)
- Difficulty sleeping or oversleeping
- Physically slowing down or feeling agitated
- No energy to do things
- Feelings of worthlessness or guilt (without any reason)
- Difficulty thinking or concentrating
- Recurrent thoughts of death or suicide

An individual should be evaluated by a professional if five or more of the above symptoms are present for more than two weeks, or if any of them cause such a change in life that the person cannot keep up his or her usual home, work, or school routine.

There are three types of depressive disorders: *major depressive disorder, dysthymic disorder* (a chronic, mild depression), and *bipolar disorder* (commonly known by the now-obsolete term manic–depressive disorder). Each type varies in the duration, number, and experience of depressive symptoms. In bipolar disorder, which is rare in young children, feeling down alternates with manic behavior. The symptoms of mania include overly inflated self-esteem, decreased need for sleep, increased talkativeness, racing thoughts, distractibility, physical agitation, and excessive risk taking. Bipolar disorder may begin with either manic, depressive, or both manic and depressive symptoms.

SIGNS OF DEPRESSION IN CHILDREN AND ADOLESCENTS

Symptoms of depression in children and adolescents are expressed in a variety of ways based on the individual's developmental stage and ability to express feelings. In other words, instead of talking about feelings, they may act out or be irritable, which may be viewed by others as misbehaving or being disobedient. Signs associated with depression in children and adolescents are:

- Frequent vague, nonspecific physical complaints (such as headaches, muscle aches, stomach aches, or tiredness)
- Lack of interest in playing with friends
- Alcohol or substance abuse
- Social isolation, including poor communication
- Fear of death
- Extreme sensitivity to rejection or failure
- Increased irritability, anger, or hostility
- Frequent absences from school or poor school performance
- Talk of or efforts to run away from home
- Outbursts of shouting, complaining, unexplained irritability, or crying
- Being bored
- Reckless behavior
- Difficulty with relationships

Children who develop major depression are more likely to have a family history of the disorder, often a parent who experiences depression at an early age, more than with individuals who develop depression as adolescents or adults. Adolescents with depression are also likely to have a family history of depression, although the correlation is not as high as with children. Bipolar disorder is more likely to occur in children and adolescents who have parents affected by the disorder. Twenty percent to 40% of adolescents with major depression develop bipolar disorder within five years after the onset of depression. When the onset is before puberty, it is often characterized by a continuous, rapid cycling, irritable, and mixed symptom state that may occur with other disruptive behaviors, particularly attention deficit hyperactivity disorder (ADHD) or conduct disorder (CD). In contrast, in adolescence, the onset of bipolar disorder tends to begin with a manic episode and to be more episodic with relatively stable periods between episodes. There is also less occurrence of ADHD or CD among those with later onset of the illness.

Other risk factors for depression include:

- Stress
- Cigarette smoking
- Loss of parent or loved one
- Breakup in a romantic relationship
- Attention, conduct, or learning disorders
- Chronic illnesses, such a diabetes mellitus
- Abuse or neglect
- Other trauma, including natural disasters

TREATMENT OF CHILDREN AND ADOLESCENTS

Children and adolescents with dysthymic disorder are at risk for developing major depression. Prompt identification and treatment can reduce the duration, severity, and associated impairment of depression. Several screening tools, including the Children's Depression Inventory (CDI) for children and adolescents ages 7 to 17 years, the Beck Depression Inventory (BDI), and the Center for Epidemiologic Studies Depression (CESD) Scale, are useful for diagnosing possible depression with this group. When children and adolescents screen positive on any of these instruments, a comprehensive diagnostic evaluation by a mental health professional, which includes the youth, their parents, and other sources of information such as teachers and friends, is warranted.

Although the scientific literature on treatment of adolescents and children with depression is far less extensive than that concerning adults, a number of studies conducted between 1997 and 2002, have confirmed the short-term efficacy and safety of treatments for depression in youths. Recent research shows that certain types of psychotherapy, particularly cognitive behavior therapy (CBT), can help relieve depression in children and adolescents. CBT is based on the premise that people with depression have cognitive distortions in their views of themselves, the world, and the future. A study supported by the National Institutes of Mental Health (NIMH) compared different types of psychotherapy for major depression in adolescents and found that CBT led to a rapid response and remission in nearly 65% of cases, a higher rate than either supportive therapy or family therapy. Interpersonal psychotherapy (IPT), an approach to therapy that focuses on helping individuals work through personal relationships that may contribute to depression, has been found to be effective for adults. Additional studies are still needed to determine which treatment works best for children and adolescents. Continuing psychotherapy for several months after remission of symptoms may help children, adolescents, and their families internalize the skills learned during the depressive phase, deal with the aftermath of the depression, address the environmental stressors, and understand how the individual's thoughts and behaviors might contribute to a potential relapse.

Although research clearly demonstrates that antidepressant medications, especially when combined with psychotherapy, can be effective treatments for depression in adults, using antidepressant medication for children has been considered controversial. Since 1997, however, researchers have conducted studies that demonstrated some of the newer antidepressant medications, especially the selective serotonin reuptake inhibitors (SSRIs), are safe and efficacious for the short-term treatment of severe and/or persistent depression in children and youths. Available studies do not support the use of tricyclic antidepressants (TCAs) for depression in youths. Medication is the initial treatment that should be considered for children and adolescents with severe symptoms that would prevent effective psychotherapy, for those unable to undergo psychotherapy, for those with psychosis, and for those with chronic recurrent episodes. Following remission of symptoms, continuing medication and/or psychotherapy for at least several months may be recommended given the high risk of relapse and reoccurrence of depression. Discontinuation of medications, when appropriate, should be done gradually over six weeks or longer.

SUICIDE AND DEPRESSION

Most people who are depressed do not commit suicide, but depression increases the risk for suicide or suicide attempts, especially with adolescent boys with conduct disorders and alcohol or other substance abuse problems. In 1997, suicide was the third leading cause of deaths in persons 10 to 24 years old. Adolescents with a major depressive disorder are seven times as likely to commit suicide as young adults in their twenties. Early diagnosis and treatment, accurate evaluation of suicidal thinking by trained professionals, and limiting young people's access to lethal agents, including firearms and medication, may hold the greatest prevention value.

—*Pamela L. Knox and James W. Lichtenberg*

See also Abuse and Neglect; Attention Deficit Hyperactivity Disorder; Bullying and Victimization; Comorbidity; Conduct Disorder; Learned Helplessness; Psychotherapy; Psychotropic Medications; Shyness; Theories of Human Development

REFERENCES AND FURTHER READING

Mazure, C. M., & Bruce, M. L. (2000). Adverse life events and cognitive-personality characteristics in the prediction of major depression and antidepressant response. *American Journal of Psychiatry, 157*(6), 896–903.

National Institute of Mental Health. (2000). Depression in children and adolescents. (NIH Publication No. 00-4744). Available online at http://www.nimh.nih.gov/publicat/depression.cfm

NIMH Genetics Workgroup. (1998). *Genetics and mental disorders.* (NIH Publication No. 98-4268). Rockville, MD: National Institute of Mental Health.

U.S. Department of Health and Human Services. (1999). *Mental Health: A report of the Surgeon General.* Rockville, MD: U. S. Department of Health and Human Services, Substance Abuse and Mental Health Services Administration, Center for Mental Health Services, National Institutes of Health, National Institute of Mental Health.

DEVELOPMENTAL MILESTONES

Developmental milestones are important, measurable indicators of an individual's growth that are evaluated based upon age. Each milestone is associated with a specific age and indicates typical development, although the age at which a typically developing child reaches each of these milestones may vary considerably. The variability in the age that children reach these milestones results from the interaction between

Table 1   Selected Developmental Milestones

Ages	Domains			
	Physical	*Cognitive*	*Language*	*Social*
Birth–2 months	Lifts head for short period Hands remain in fists Grasp reflex evident Kicks legs and flings out arms	Repeated motor movements Visually explores objects in environment	Cries Gurgles Coos (vowel sounds)	Responds to smile with smile or vocalization
2–4 months	Rolls from side to side Lifts head Begins reaching for objects Grasps objects	Follows objects with eyes Looks around Responds to environment (open mouth for nipple)	Coos more frequently Vocalizes to make noise	Smiles at others (social smile) Laughs aloud Makes brief eye contact
4–6 months	Rolls from back to side Places fingers in mouth First teeth emerge Sits with support Grasps and shakes objects	Attention becomes flexible and changes Turns toward sources of noise	Squeals Babbles (vowel/consonant combinations) Repeats syllables Imitates sounds	Vocalizes to get attention Joint attention with parents to label objects
6–9 months	Crawls Pulls self up to stand with support Sits without support Moves objects from hand to hand	Looks toward objects when named Awareness of objects only if in sight Responds to name	Babbles 2 syllables (mama) Creates nonsense syllables	Stranger anxiety (fear of unfamiliar people) Expresses anger more frequently
9–12 months	Steps with support Pincer grasp Stands alone Walks with support (holding furniture) Coordination between two hands Feeds self using fingers	Solves sensorimotor problems by using similar situations from the past Follows 1-word directions Acquires object permanence (searches for objects that are not in sight)	Speaks first words Uses gestures to influence others' behavior (point) Uses nonverbal communication signals (waves bye-bye) Understands meaning of no	Points to objects for others to look at Laughs aloud Imitates actions and facial expressions of others Responds when adult's mood changes
12–18 months	Walks without support Turns pages of a book Scribbles Crawls up and down stairs	Finds objects hidden in several places Categorizes objects Attention improves Delayed imitation	Speaks several words – often nouns Uses up to 20 words Shakes head to indicate "no" Asks for "more" Copies unfamiliar sounds	Engages in turn-taking games (peek-a-boo) Joins in play with familiar people Signs of empathy apparent Imitates adults
18–24 months	Runs Climbs Jumps in place Kicks Pulls and pushes objects	Follows simple directions Identifies own body parts Begins make-believe play	Speaks 2-word combinations Uses 50–200 words Says own name	Parallel play (plays next to a peer) Self-control appears Recognizes emotions in others

Ages	Domains			
	Physical	*Cognitive*	*Language*	*Social*
2–3 years	Fine motor skills improve drastically Begins to draw Feeds self with utensils Alternates feet on stairs	Plays with toys functionally (uses for intended purpose) Plays make believe	Uses 3-word phrases Names body parts Uses up to 500 words Asks simple questions	Demonstrates empathy Difficulty sharing Takes turns in games
3–4 years	Reaches bladder & bowel control Hops Skips	Uses color and shape to sort objects Uses mechanical toys Understands the concept of two	Uses 4- to 5-word sentences Uses up to 1000 words Says name and age	Cooperatively plays with other children Prefers to play with other children
4–5 years	Throws ball overhead Uses scissors Copies shapes	Names colors Recalls story segments Understands same/different concept	Uses 4- to 7-word sentences Tells stories Understands basic grammatical rules	Understands gender constancy Plays creatively Seeks independence
5–6 years	Hand dominance apparent Prints letters Catches a ball appropriately	Counts to 10 or higher Names several colors	Uses 5- to 8-word sentences Asks meaning of words	Wants to be similar to friends Likes to dance and sing

genetic and environmental factors. These developmental indicators are commonly used among infants and young children to assess their growth in a variety of areas. Examples of developmental milestones include children's first steps and words. Parents and professionals may observe these developmental areas to assess for delays, or reaching a milestone at a later-than-expected age. Delays in any area may affect future developmental capabilities, depending on the length and severity of the delay. If a delay is detected in any developmental area, professionals may search for the etiology and encourage early intervention.

Although development is frequently viewed holistically, developmental milestones are often applied to specific domains of development. Some of the most prominent areas in which development is assessed include the physical, cognitive, language, and social domains. Physical development entails all physical growth that changes a child's body, and includes such things as coordination and motor skills. Cognitive development refers to mental processes and includes memory and the ability to learn, among others. Language growth encompasses language acquisition and development and includes babbling and baby talk, as well as more advanced expressive language skills. Social development consists of social indicators that demonstrate adjustment to the social environment and includes emotion and interactions with others.

These developmental areas each possess countless specific milestones that indicate whether typical development is occurring. Although not all children will develop at the same rate in all areas of development, these developmental milestones may be used as a benchmark for typical development. Table 1 includes selected physical, cognitive, language, and social milestones. These developmental milestones are considered to be characteristic of typical development within each domain for the specified ages. For example, a typically developing five-month-old infant will sit with support, turn toward sources of noise, imitate sounds, and vocalize to receive attention. Biological and environmental factors may alter the developmental course for children. Biological factors, such as congenital diseases and genetic contributions, as well as environmental factors, such as cultural differences and socioeconomic status, may affect the age at which children reach these developmental milestones.

—*Kimberly A. DeRuyck*

See also Communication Disorders; Early Intervention; Infant Assessment; Mental Retardation; Preschool Assessment; Theories of Human Development

REFERENCES AND FURTHER READING

Bayley, N. (1993). *Bayley scales of infant development manual.* (2nd ed.). San Antonio: Psychological Corporation.

Berger, K. S. (2000). *The developing person through childhood and adolescence* (5th ed.). New York: Worth.

DIAGNOSIS AND LABELING

A label is simply a word or phrase used to describe or classify a person or group. Classification of individuals into categories by psychologists and psychiatrists is a form of labeling referred to as diagnosis. Psychologists and psychiatrists have a long tradition of labeling people into diagnostic categories as a means to classify and organize psychopathology and to communicate efficiently with other mental health professionals. Diagnosis may be an efficient way to initially provide general information to different professionals who work with the same client. Many times diagnoses are needed to make clients eligible to access educational and mental health services. Diagnoses are also often required so that payment can be received for services that are rendered to clients. Even though all diagnostic systems have some drawbacks, the ones in current use have allowed for advancement of knowledge and understanding of psychological and educational problems (Merrell, 2003).

Modern psychological and psychiatric diagnosis and labeling can be traced to the written recording of case studies and detailed observations of patients in hospital settings. As a result, it has its foundations in the medical model. Study of case records allowed early clinicians to classify on the basis of symptom clusters, an already established technique used by botanical and zoological taxonomists (Millon, 1969). The central idea of this method was that because certain groups of symptoms or behaviors often occurred together, clinicians could use symptom clusters to identify particular disorders.

In 1883, Emil Kraepelin wrote a compendium that linked symptom pictures, patterns of onset, course, and outcomes for mental disorders. Kraepelin's nosology was the framework for the structure that would become the prototype for the most widely used diagnostic system of mental disorders, the *Diagnostic and Statistical Manual of Mental Disorders (DSM)*, now in its fourth edition. School psychologists use two major classification systems, the psychiatrically oriented *DSM* system and a classification system based on federal special education law, the Individuals With Disabilities Education Act (IDEA).

Another diagnostic approach is the empirically based behavioral dimensions taxonomy, but this method is not as commonly used as the *DSM* and IDEA models (Achenbach, 1993, 2002; McDermott, 1993; McDermott & Weiss, 1995; Quay, 1975, 1977; Quay & Peterson, 1967, 1987). This approach has identified dimensions of psychopathology through the use of multivariate statistical methods such as factor analysis (e.g., internalizing-overcontrolled, externalizing-undercontrolled, etc.). One advantage to this method is that because diagnoses are based on norm-referenced scales, clinicians can determine where an individual child falls in relation to others in the population. This can allow for estimates of severity of particular disorders. Although the dimensions have been identified by various independent researchers and appear to be robust, each set of researchers has used different names for the same constructs, which has led to some confusion. Nonetheless, the empirically based behavioral dimensions system shows promise for extending research and practice in the area of diagnosis and psychopathology in children and youths. Psychologists might use the empirically derived diagnostic information to aid in making a *DSM* or IDEA diagnosis. Ultimately, an IDEA diagnosis is required before the child can be determined eligible for special education services in the schools and/or a *DSM* diagnosis is often desired in nonschool settings.

The *Diagnostic and Statistical Manual for Mental Disorders, Fourth Edition-Text Revision (DSM-IV-TR)* (American Psychiatric Association, 2000) is the latest version of the mental disorders classification system. The first version of the *DSM* appeared in 1952. It was then and remains today a categorical approach based on the medical model of psychopathology (i.e., psychological disorders are the result of mental disease and the cause is within the individual). The *DSM-IV* uses a multiaxial diagnostic procedure, which means the client is evaluated on five broad dimensions. Each dimension, or "axis," represents an aspect of the patient's functioning. Axes I and II refer to types of psychological or psychiatric disorders, while Axes III through V represent general medical conditions, psychosocial and environmental problems, and a global assessment of functioning respectively. School psychologists and those who primarily work with

Table 1   *DSM-IV* Disorders Usually First Diagnosed in Infancy, Childhood, or Adolescence

Mental Retardation
  Mild Mental Retardation
  Moderate Mental Retardation
  Severe Mental Retardation
  Profound Mental Retardation
  Mental Retardation, Severity Unspecified
Learning Disorders
  Reading Disorder
  Mathematics Disorder
  Disorder of Written Expression
  Learning Disorder, Not Otherwise Specified
Motor Skills Disorder
Developmental Coordination Disorder
Communication Disorders
  Expressive Language Disorder
  Mixed Expressive–Receptive Language Disorder
  Phonological Disorder
  Stuttering
  Communication Disorder, Not Otherwise Specified
Pervasive Developmental Disorders
  Autistic Disorder
  Rett's Disorder
  Childhood Disintegrative Disorder
  Aspergers Disorder
  Pervasive Developmental Disorder, Not Otherwise
    Specified
Attention Deficit and Disruptive Behavior Disorders
  Attention Deficit Hyperactivity Disorder
    Combined Type
    Predominantly Inattentive Type
    Predominantly Hyperactive-Impulsive type

Attention Deficit Hyperactivity Disorder, Not
  Otherwise Specified
Conduct Disorder
  Childhood-Onset Type
  Adolescent-Onset Type
  Unspecified Onset
Oppositional Defiant Disorder
Disruptive Behavior Disorder, Not Otherwise Specified
Feeding and Eating Disorders of Infancy or Early Childhood
  Pica (eating disorder)
  Rumination Disorder
  Feeding Disorder of Infancy or Early Childhood,
    Not Otherwise Specified
Tic Disorders
  Tourette's Disorder (or syndrome)
  Chronic Motor or Vocal Tic Disorder
  Transient Tic Disorder
  Tic Disorder, Not Otherwise Specified
Elimination Disorders
  Encopresis
    With Constipation and Overflow Incontinence
    Without Constipation and Overflow Incontinence
  Enuresis
Other Disorders of Infancy, Childhood, or Adolescence
  Separation Anxiety Disorder
  Selective Mutism
  Reactive Attachment Disorder of Infancy or
    Early Childhood
  Stereotypic Movement Disorder
  Disorder of Infancy, Childhood, or Adolescence,
    Not Otherwise Specified

children and youths are most likely to use the diagnostic categories in the *Disorders Usually First Diagnosed in Infancy, Childhood, or Adolescence* section of the *DSM-IV* (Table 1).

However, there are many other disorders listed in the *DSM* that can have their onset in childhood or adolescence and would also often be used by school psychologists for diagnostic purposes (e.g., mood, anxiety, and somatoform disorders) (Mash & Dozois, 1996). To make a diagnosis, clinicians examine the list of symptoms associated with the disorder and determine whether a symptom is present or absent. If the required and specified number of symptoms is present, then a diagnosis is rendered on either Axis I or Axis II. This is done usually by a single clinician who may or may not have acquired information using

multiple sources of information and multiple methods of assessment to make the decision. Although the diagnosis criteria are relatively objective, guidelines for assessment are not offered in the *DSM* and a fair degree of subjectivity is involved in the process. The *DSM* has been criticized for reliability and validity problems in the past, particularly for use with children and youths in the schools (Gresham & Gansle, 1992). Gresham (2002) also argues there is little empirical evidence to substantiate the claim that psychiatric diagnoses lead to better treatment outcomes and that they often describe behavior circularly rather than functionally, which makes them less relevant for treatment planning. The *DSM-IV*, however, was revised with specific attention to improving the reliability and validity of the system and incorporating recent advances in the scientific literature related to psychopathology and continues to be the most widely used taxonomic system of psychopathology in existence.

Another important diagnostic system used by school psychologists and educational professionals in the public schools was established with the passing of the *Education for All Handicapped Children Act* also known as Public Law (P.L.) 94–142 (1975) and is now referred to as the Individuals With Disabilities Education Act or IDEA (P.L. 105–117, 1997). IDEA is a comprehensive law that has the intent that all children with disabilities have available to them a free, appropriate public education. A part of the law includes the list of disabilities recognized as eligible to receive special education, the diagnostic criteria for special education eligibility, as well as the required procedures for assessment and placement. Table 2 presents the IDEA special education diagnostic categories. Diagnosis of children and youths with disabilities under IDEA is somewhat different than the process of *DSM* diagnosis. For example, IDEA requires that the evaluation procedures are not racially or culturally discriminatory, that the assessment is done in the child's native language or other mode of communication, and that a variety of assessment tools and strategies are used to gather relevant functional and developmental information about the child. This includes information provided by the parent for the purpose of enabling the child to be involved in and progress in the general curriculum, or to participate in appropriate educational activities. No single evaluation procedure can be the solitary source of information when making the diagnosis. Any test that is used must be valid for the purpose for which it is used. Another requirement is that the child is assessed in all areas related to the suspected disability, including, if appropriate:

- Health
- Vision
- Hearing
- Social and emotional status
- General intelligence
- Academic performance
- Communicative status
- Motor abilities

Another big difference between the *DSM* and IDEA systems is that the diagnostic determination for special education must be made by a multidisciplinary team

Table 2   Individuals With Disabilities Education Act (IDEA) Special Education Diagnostic Categories

Autism
Deaf–Blindness
Deafness
Emotional Disturbance
Hearing Impairment
Mental Retardation
Multiple Disabilities
Orthopedic Impairment
Other Health Impairment*
Specific Learning Disability
Speech or Language Impairment
Traumatic Brain Injury
Visual Impairment including blindness

*Attention deficit hyperactivity disorder falls into this special education category.

and the parent of the child. This team is a group of qualified professionals and at least one member must be an expert in the child's specific area of disability. Even with these procedural differences from the *DSM* system, the IDEA categories are criticized as being ambiguous and subjective. The IDEA categories which reflect mild levels of impairment are unreliable. Furthermore, like the *DSM* system, IDEA diagnoses have also been criticized as having little relevance for the design of appropriate and effective interventions.

A relatively new approach to diagnosis of child psychopathology that shows promise for linking assessment of disorders to treatment is the "Resistance to Intervention" paradigm. In this model a child might be diagnosed as having a behavioral disorder if behavioral excesses, deficits, and/or situationally inappropriate behaviors continue at unacceptable levels after an intervention (Gresham, 1991, 2002; Gresham & colleagues, 2000). Further research is needed to demonstrate the potential of this approach for improving diagnosis and treatment. Resistance to intervention may be a function of a number of contextual factors like severity and chronicity of behavior, teachers' tolerance of behavior, as well as the strength, acceptability, and effectiveness of the intervention.

Over time certain diagnostic labels have made their way into the common vernacular and are used in a derogatory fashion. Terms like feebleminded, idiot, imbecile, and/or moron were once considered formal psychological and educational labels. Do such labels result in differential expectations for those who are labeled? *Pygmalion in the Classroom* (Rosenthal & Jacobson, 1966, 1968) helped to popularize the notion that teacher expectancies for students can actually impact the students' performance and contribute to the students' own self-fulfilling prophecies. This research on bias demonstrated that differential expectations for school-age children can be elicited by presenting observers with various special education and/or psychiatric labels. Frequently more negative attributions are made toward children who are labeled than toward those who are not labeled, even when their behavior is identical (e.g., Crawford & colleagues, 2001; Fairbanks & Stinnett, 1997; Fox & Stinnett, 1996; Johnson & Blankenship, 1984; Stinnett & colleagues, 1999). However, when actual behavior is observed and judged, the effects of labels can be negated or minimized and team decision making can also minimize the negative effects of labels when placement decisions are made. Nevertheless, when written summaries or reports are given to observers who have not made behavior observations, labels are likely to have adverse effects.

Although diagnosis and labeling offer a number of challenges for psychologists, the activity remains a frequent and valued aspect of service delivery. All of the diagnostic systems discussed have continued to evolve and improve over time. Each has helped to further research and practice with children and youths who have psychopathological disorders. No doubt diagnosis will remain an integral part of psychological service delivery in the future.

—*Terry A. Stinnett*

See also DSM-IV; Individuals With Disabilities Education Act; Reports (Psychological); Special Education; Responsiveness to Intervention Model

REFERENCES AND FURTHER READING

Achenbach, T. M. (1993). Empirically based taxonomy: *How to use syndromes and profile types derived from the CBCL/4–18, TRF, and YSR.* Burlington, VT: University of Vermont, Department of Psychiatry.

Achenbach, T. M. (2002). Empirically based assessment and taxonomy across the life span. In J. E. Helzer & J. J. Hudziak (Eds.), *Defining psychopathology in the 21st century: DSM-V and beyond* (pp. 155–168). Washington, DC: American Psychiatric Association.

American Psychiatric Association. (2000). *Diagnostic and statistical manual of mental disorders* (4th ed., text rev.). Washington, DC: Author.

Fairbanks, L. D., & Stinnett, T. A. (1997). Effects of professional group membership, intervention type and diagnostic label on treatment acceptability. *Psychology in the Schools, 34,* 329–335.

Fox, J. D., & Stinnett, T. A. (1996). The effects of labeling bias on prognostic outlook for children as a function of diagnostic label and profession. *Psychology in the Schools, 33,* 143–152.

Gresham, F. M. (1991). Conceptualizing behavior disorders in terms of resistance to intervention. *School Psychology Review, 20,* 23–36.

Gresham, F. M. (2002). Caveat emptor: Considerations before buying into the "new" medical model. *Behavioral Disorders, 27,* 158–167.

Gresham, F. M., & Gansle, K. A. (1992). Misguided assumptions of *DSM-III-R*: Implications for school psychological practice. *School Psychology Quarterly, 7,* 79–95.

Gresham, F. M., Lane, K. L., & Lambros, K. M. (2000). Comorbidity of conduct problems and ADHD: Identification of "fledgling psychopaths". *Journal of Emotional and Behavioral Disorders, 8,* 83–93.

Johnson, L. J., & Blankenship, C. S. (1984). A comparison of label-induced expectancy bias in two preservice teacher education programs. *Behavioral Disorders, 9,* 167–174.

Mash, E. J., & Dozois, D. J. A. (1996). Child psychopathology: A developmental-systems perspective. In E. J. Mash & R. A. Barkley (Eds.), *Child Psychopathology* (pp. 3–60). New York: Guilford.

McDermott, P. A. (1993). National standardization of uniform multisituational measures of child and adolescent behavior pathology. *Psychological Assessment, 5,* 413–424.

McDermott, P. A., & Weiss, R. V. (1995). A normative typology of healthy, subclinical, and clinical behavior styles among American children and adolescents. *Psychological Assessment, 7,* 162–170.

Merrell, K. W. (2003). *Behavioral, social, and emotional assessment of children and adolescents.* Mahwah, NJ: Erlbaum.

Millon, T. (1969). *Modern psychopathology: A biosocial approach to maladaptive learning and functioning.* Philadelphia: Saunders.

Public Law (P.L.) 94–142. Education for All Handicapped Children Act of 1975. (20 U.S.C. and 34 C.F.R.).

Public Law (P.L.) 105–117. Individuals With Disabilities Education Act of 1997.

Quay, H. C. (1975). Classification in the treatment of delinquency and antisocial behavior. In N. Hobbs (Ed.), *Issues in the classification of children* (Vol. 1). San Francisco: Jossey-Bass.

Quay, H. C. (1977). Measuring dimensions of deviant behavior: The behavior problem checklist. *Journal of Abnormal Child Psychology, 5,* 277–289.

Quay, H. C., & Peterson, D. R. (1967). *Manual for the behavior problem checklist.* Coral Gables, FL: Author.

Quay, H. C., & Peterson, D. R. (1987). *Manual for the revised behavior problem checklist.* Coral Gables, FL: Author.

Rosenthal, R., & Jacobson, L. (1966). Teachers' expectancies: Determinants of pupils' IQ gains. *Psychological Reports, 19*, 115–118.

Rosenthal, R., & Jacobson, L. (1968). *Pygmalion in the classroom: Teacher expectation and pupils' intellectual development.* New York: Holt, Rinehart and Winston.

Stinnett, T. A., Bull, K. S., Koonce, D. A., & Aldridge, J. O. (1999). The effects of diagnostic label, race, gender, educational placement, and definitional knowledge on prognostic outlook for children with behavior problems. *Psychology in the Schools, 36*, 51–59.

Stinnett, T. A., Crawford, S. A, Gillespie, M., Cruce, M., & Langford, C. A. (2001). Effects of the ADHD label on judgments of treatment acceptability for psychostimulant medication versus psychoeducational intervention. *Psychology in the Schools, 38*, 585–591.

DIBELS

DIBELS stands for Dynamic Indicators of Basic Early Literacy Skills. DIBELS was designed as a tool for ongoing progress monitoring of the acquisition of reading skills and for early identification of children with reading problems. The original DIBELS included 10 measures assessing sound–symbol relationships (i.e., the student is able to say the sounds that a letter makes), phonemic awareness (i.e., knowledge of the sounds made by each letter and the ability to blend them into a word), language development, and knowledge of print and letter names. Research shows that DIBELS is a reliable and valid measure of the acquisition of early reading skills. School psychologists use DIBELS to detect children who might need additional help in learning to read and to monitor the progress of the special instruction that is implemented.

—*Steven W. Lee*

See also Academic Achievement; Early Intervention

DIFFERENTIAL REINFORCEMENT.

See BEHAVIOR; BEHAVIOR INTERVENTION; DISCIPLINE; BEHAVIORAL CONCEPTS AND APPLICATIONS

DISCIPLINE

In both definition and practice there are two common sides to school discipline. The first side is teaching or training to develop moral character (i.e., *self-discipline*). The second is training or treatment to correct or control behavior. Traditionally, schools have valued both. That is, throughout the history of education in the United States, schools have strived not only to govern students but also to develop the knowledge, values, moral reasoning, and skills that reflect the personal qualities of self-control, responsibility, and autonomy (i.e., *self-regulation*).

Although developing self-discipline and correcting misbehavior comprise the two most traditional components of comprehensive school discipline, two other components are found in most schools: preventing misbehavior with effective classroom management and addressing or remediating chronic and serious behavior problems (Bear, 2005). These four components are closely interrelated. For example, developing self-discipline and preventing misbehavior reduce the need to correct common problematic behaviors and to remediate more serious and chronic behavior problems.

DEVELOPING SELF-DISCIPLINE

Before the early 20th century, it was believed that the best way to develop self-discipline was with the direct teaching of religion and the frequent and harsh use of punishment. The use of these methods of developing self-discipline waned in the 19th century, and by the early 20th century they were largely replaced by the more progressive methods of education commonly found in schools today. For example, during the first half of the 20th century, nearly all schools in the United States instituted comprehensive "character education" programs. Good character was defined as "caring about, and acting upon core ethical values" (Character Education Partnership, 2004)). As is true today, character education programs in the early 20th century were designed to develop values and virtues, including those discussed previously. Chief among them were values believed to be critical to democracy, including self-discipline. However, it is understood that the direct teaching of moral content (e.g., scripture, oaths, pledges, etc.) is insufficient for the development of self-discipline. Thus, emphasis shifted to teaching students how to think. This entailed the teaching of social and moral problem-solving skills such as taking the perspective of others, generating alternative solutions, weighing consequences to self and others, considering issues of fairness, and making the "right" decision. Character education also emphasized that schools are to provide students with multiple experiences in which they can actively learn and practice these skills in real life. Thus, students were encouraged to participate in student government, club activities, and community service. Character education today shares these strategies.

Recently, social and emotional learning (SEL) (Collaborative for Academic, Social, and Emotional Learning [CASEL]) has gained popularity as a term that refers to various programs and approaches, including most character education programs that are designed to develop social and emotional competencies such as self-discipline. SEL is defined as "the process of developing the ability to recognize and manage emotions, develop caring and concern for others, make responsible decisions, establish positive relationships, and handle challenging situations effectively" (CASEL, 2004, p. 1). SEL programs associated with self-discipline focus on the development of:

- Social and moral problem-solving skills (e.g., perspective-taking, goal-setting, moral reasoning)
- Adaptive emotions (e.g., positive attitudes and values, empathy, feelings of pride and responsibility, anger control)
- Behaviors (e.g., prosocial behavior, impulse control, conflict resolution, peer resistance, negotiation)

SEL programs are supported by research, which shows that self-discipline is related to academic achievement, fewer behavior problems, positive relations with peers and teachers, and a positive self-concept. These positive outcomes benefit not only the individual child, but also classmates and society in general.

In helping schools develop self-discipline among students, school psychologists often assist in the development, implementation, and evaluation of programs of demonstrated effectiveness. Programs recognized by both the Character Education Partnership and CASEL for their effectiveness in developing self-discipline are:

- Second Step: A Violence Prevention Curriculum
- Child Development Project
- Responsive Classroom
- Resolving Conflict Creatively Program

PREVENTING MISBEHAVIOR WITH EFFECTIVE CLASSROOM MANAGEMENT

Developing self-discipline is not the only way to help prevent misbehavior. A wealth of research shows that teachers can prevent most behavior problems from occurring by using strategies and techniques of effective classroom management. Classroom management consists of "actions taken to create and maintain a learning environment conducive to successful instruction" (Brophy, 1996, p. 43). The key element of effective classroom management is an emphasis on prevention. Indeed, research shows that it is techniques for prevention of misbehavior, and not for correction, that best differentiate effective and ineffective teachers. Preventive techniques that characterize the most effective classrooms are when teachers (Bear, 2005):

- Demonstrate warmth, respect, and caring toward all students. For example, they demonstrate a sincere interest in the lives of their students; encourage open communication and mutual respect; and display such interpersonal qualities as humor, kindness, self-confidence, empathy, understanding, respect, honesty, and trust.
- Foster social and moral problem-solving skills among students. They teach students to assume responsibility for their own behavior. As such, they directly teach and model social problem-solving and decision-making skills during classroom discussions and disciplinary encounters.
- Understand, and are responsive to, the importance of close home–school relations. That is, they recognize that the motivation, values, attitudes, goals, and behavior of all students are influenced by the families and communities in which they live.
- Provide academic instruction and activities that motivate learning. For example, they ensure high rates of success, especially when new concepts are first taught; provide frequent positive feedback for both effort and achievement; demonstrate their own interest and enthusiasm toward learning; set high, reasonable, and clear expectations and standards; use a variety of challenging and novel materials; hold students accountable for their academic and social behavior; arrange for cooperative learning opportunities; offer students opportunities to participate in decisions

pertaining to academics and class climate; and modify instruction, curriculum, and academic materials, as needed, to meet the individual needs of all students.

- Are aware of the advantages and limitations to the use of praise and rewards. They use these positive techniques in a manner that maximizes their effectiveness in improving behavior while minimizing the risk of diminishing intrinsic motivation. For example, they are sincere when praising students and emphasize that students are responsible for their own behavior, including positive behavior.

- Create a physical classroom environment that is well organized, efficient, attractive, comfortable, and conducive to teaching and learning. For example, they arrange the classroom so they can easily monitor the behavior of all students and in which students can easily participate in instruction.

- Establish fair rules and consequences. Rules are clear, limited in number, discussed with the class, and periodically reviewed. Consequences are fair, reasonable, and imposed in a judicious manner.

- Establish predictable procedures and routines. That is, they set, and discuss with students, the procedures and routines for use of the room and facilities (e.g., use of the bathroom, drinking fountain), for completing seatwork and participating in class activities (e.g., when one can talk to others, how to obtain assistance, what to do when one finishes work early, how to return homework), and how transitions into and out of the classroom should be handled.

- Closely monitor the behavior of students and respond early to signs of misbehavior. Effective teachers are like air traffic controllers in that they constantly scan the classroom while on alert for indicators of potential problems. When potential problems are detected, they respond immediately with such techniques as making eye contact, verbally redirecting students, or moving near students who show the first signs of potentially disruptive behavior.

Each of the above techniques not only prevents misbehavior, but also promotes a positive classroom climate that fosters the development of self-discipline and learning. School psychologists help teachers and schools prevent behavior problems by working collaboratively with teachers, parents, and others in implementing the above strategies of effective classroom management.

CORRECTING MISBEHAVIOR

As noted previously, discipline is defined as the correction of misbehavior. Indeed, it is this aspect of discipline, rather than the development of self-discipline, that is most often associated with the term. Unfortunately, too often correction is equated with the use of punishment. Punishment refers to techniques that decrease the occurrence of a behavior by presenting a student with an aversive or undesirable consequence. This includes the use of corporal punishment, which is now banned in more than half of the states and denounced by most professional organizations in education and psychology. Punishment also includes more common (and more ethical) techniques that nearly all teachers and schools use routinely to reduce the occurrence of a wide range of misbehaviors. For example, for mild behavior problems teachers typically use:

- Physical proximity (moving near the student as soon as the misbehavior begins)
- Redirection (e.g., "Mary, instead of talking, shouldn't you be working on your assignment?")
- Verbal reprimand
- Response cost (e.g., taking away privileges)
- Overcorrection (e.g., having to wash all desks in the room as a consequence of writing on his or her own desk)

For more serious behavior problems teachers and schools are likely to use a contingency contract (in which the student agrees in writing to rewards and/or punishments as a consequence of targeted behaviors), parent conferences, counseling, time-out, suspension, placement in an alternative program, and expulsion.

To be sure, the use of punishment, particularly noncorporal forms, is effective in reducing misbehavior, and most educators believe that it should be one part of a comprehensive school discipline program. However, there are many limitations to punishment that bring into question why it has always remained the most common response to correcting misbehavior. These limitations are (Bear, 2005):

- Punishment teaches students what *not* to do. It does not teach what students should do. Many students need to learn alternatives to their inappropriate behavior.
- Punishment often teaches students to aggress toward or punish others. Children often emulate the behaviors of adults, especially those whom they respect.
- Punishment fails to address the multiple factors that typically contribute to a student's misbehavior. For example, punishment is unlikely to improve behavior when students misbehave because they cannot understand or read the academic material.
- The effects of punishment often are short-term and nonlasting. Because punishment fails to teach replacement behaviors (i.e., more appropriate or socially desirable behaviors) or address the factors contributing to the misbehavior, its effects are short-term.
- Punishment can be reinforcing. That is, although intended to decrease a behavior, a punitive technique may actually increase misbehavior. A classic example of this is the use of out-of-school suspension for students who dislike school.
- Punishment may produce undesirable side effects. These include anger, resentment, revenge, dislike toward the person administering the punishment, poor self-perceptions, and depression.
- Punishment can create a negative classroom climate.

Despite these limitations, it is difficult for teachers to avoid the use of punishment. Most administrators and parents demand it, and perhaps for good reasons. As shown in research, punishment is an effective technique for managing behavior. This is particularly true, however, when it is used in combination with more positive techniques. Thus, teachers should not necessarily avoid the use of punishment, particularly mild forms of punishment, but should limit its use by placing much greater emphasis on techniques for developing self-discipline and for preventing misbehavior. Importantly, this should always include the use of positive techniques that teach and reinforce appropriate behavior. This is consistent with a popular approach called the *positive behavior supports* approach to preventing and correcting misbehavior and establishing positive school climates. This approach emphasizes that the reinforcement of positive behaviors should be the primary means for preventing and correcting behavior problems. Positive behavior supports, defined as strategies for achieving important social and learning outcomes while preventing the problem behavior, have been found be effective in reducing a wide range of behavior problems.

In addition to working on school-based teams that implement programs for preventing and correcting behavior problems, school psychologists provide a wide range of other services to reduce behavior problems. Most common are the assessment of various individual and environmental factors that contribute to behavior problems (often referred to as *functional behavioral assessment*), problem-solving consultations with teachers and parents, implementing behavioral interventions, counseling, and social skills training.

SERIOUS AND CHRONIC BEHAVIOR PROBLEMS

Common strategies and techniques for developing self-discipline and for preventing and correcting misbehavior are sufficient for responding to the behavioral needs of the majority of students. However, most educators recognize that a small percentage of students, varying in number from school to school but generally being less than 5%, require more than what can reasonably be expected of teachers in the regular classroom. These students repeatedly disobey rules and are unresponsive to common classroom techniques for developing self-discipline and for preventing and correcting misbehavior. Their behavior interferes with the learning of others, as well as their own learning. This includes serious acts of misconduct that threaten the safety and welfare of others, such as acts of aggression or violence and the possession of weapons or illegal substances. Many school psychologists devote considerable time delivering services to help these students, as well as to help those who are at risk for serious and chronic behavior problems.

The most common response to chronic and serious misbehavior is suspension, which includes in-school suspension, out-of-school suspension, and expulsion. Approximately 15% of all students are suspended out-of-school for one or more days (U.S. General Accounting Office, 2001), with the length of the suspension depending on the seriousness of the offense. Common reasons for suspension are defiance, disobedience, fighting, smoking, using alcohol, disrupting the classroom, using obscene language, excessive tardiness, skipping class, forging parent signatures, and extortion. Expulsion differs from suspension in that removal from school is for a longer period of time. Typically, the offending student is removed for the remainder of the school year or forever. Expulsion generally applies only to the most serious behavior problems, such as violent or repeated acts of aggression, possession of weapons or drugs, and other criminal acts.

Often, students who are expelled or suspended for a lengthy period of time are also placed in an alternative education program during the period of school removal. This is required in more than half of the states and is a common feature of what is referred to as zero tolerance policies—policies that dictate the automatic removal of students who exhibit serious offenses such as the possession of weapons, illegal substances, or acts of violence. Such policies are intended to protect the safety of all students, as well as to punish students for their misbehavior. Unfortunately, a zero tolerance approach is sometimes applied not only to serious offenses but also to minor misbehavior that does not threaten the safety of others.

The limitations of punishment, as noted previously, apply to the use of suspension and expulsion. An additional limitation, however, is that suspension and expulsion decrease the amount of time the student spends in academic learning (as well as in learning alternatives to the misbehavior). This may actually increase misbehavior in that the student falls behind academically. In light of their limitations, suspension and expulsion should be used only for the most serious and chronic offenses. When feasible, they also should be used only as a last resort—after other interventions have already been attempted.

Perhaps the greatest shortcoming of suspension and expulsion is that they do not address the factors contributing to the behavior that led to removal from school. That is, they do little, if anything, to remediate the problem behavior and prevent it from reoccurring. Effective school programs avoid this shortcoming by making sure that a variety of remedial services are provided during the time of long-term suspension or expulsion. Services are generally provided in either a special education setting (for students with disabilities, including behavioral disorders) or in an alterative educational setting (for all students). School psychologists often work in these settings. To be effective, the services provided must be intensive, comprehensive, and sustained over time; and include a wide range of interventions that target the student's academic, social, and emotional needs. This includes:

- The systematic use of behavioral interventions based on principles of reinforcement and punishment, particularly the former
- The assessment of the individual needs of students
- The teaching of social and moral problem-solving skills (including anger management training, prosocial behavior skills, conflict resolution skills)
- Academic remediation
- Counseling
- Collaborating and supporting parents by providing parent management training and/or family therapy—a key element of effective programs for students with serious and chronic behavior problems

The services should be individualized and provided within the context of a team problem-solving model in which the student, teachers, parents, and support staff work together to help prevent the reoccurrence of the behavior that led to suspension or expulsion. It should be noted that many of these services, as well as the requirement that students who are removed from school continue to receive educational services and positive behavioral supports, are mandated by federal law (Individual With Disabilities Act [IDEA]) for students with disabilities. As a major service provider recognized in IDEA, school psychologists often play key roles in delivering these services for children with serious and chronic behavior problems.

—*George G. Bear*

See also Aggression in Schools; Behavior Intervention; Bullying and Victimization; Classroom Climate; Consultation: Behavioral; Corporal Punishment; Dropouts; Expulsion; Functional Behavioral Assessment; Harassment; Prevention; Social Skills; Suspension; Violence in Schools

REFERENCES AND FURTHER READING

Advancement Project/Civil Rights Project. (2000). *Opportunities suspended: The devastating consequences of zero tolerance and school discipline policies*. Cambridge, MA: Harvard University.

Bear, G. G. (2005). *Developing self-discipline and preventing and correcting misbehavior*. Boston: Allyn & Bacon.

Brophy, J. E. (1996). *Teaching problem students*. New York: Guilford.

The Character Education Partnership (CEP) (2005). *Eleven principles of effective character education*. Retrieved January 24, 2005, from http://www.character.org/principles.

Collaborative for Academic, Social, and Emotional Learning (CASEL). (2004). *Safe and sound: An educational leader's guide to evidence-based social and emotional learning (SEL) programs*. Retrieved April 15, 2004, from http://www.CASEL.org

U.S. General Accounting Office. (2001). *Student discipline: Individuals With Disabilities Education Act*. Report to the Committees on Appropriations, U.S. Senate and House of Representatives. Washington, DC: Author. Available online at http://www.gao.gov

DIVISION OF SCHOOL PSYCHOLOGY (DIVISION 16)

The Division of School Psychologists was one of the original 18 divisions created during the 1945 reorganization of the American Psychological Association (APA). In an effort to be inclusive of university faculty, the title of the Division was subsequently modified to be the Division of School Psychology, and is commonly referred to as Division 16 (see the Division 16 timeline at the end of this entry).

The objectives of Division 16 are:

- To promote and maintain high standards of professional education
- To create scientific and scholarly knowledge
- To promote the practice of psychology within the schools and other settings through collaboration/cooperation with individuals, groups, and organizations
- To support ethical and social responsibilities of the specialty
- To encourage opportunities for ethnic minority participation
- To encourage and effect publications, communications, and conferences regarding the activities, interests, and concerns within the specialty on a regional, national, and international basis

In 1981, the *Specialty Guidelines for the Delivery of Services by School Psychologists* was published in the *American Psychologist*. The guidelines defined the duties of professional school psychologists, school psychological service units, accountability, and environmental considerations. Then in 1997, a revision of the specialty guidelines was developed as a collaborative effort of the Division, with representatives of the National Association of School Psychologists (NASP) and the Council of Directors of School Psychology Programs. This revised description of the specialty, known as the archival description of school psychology, was approved by the APA Commission for the Recognition of Specialties and Proficiencies in Professional Psychology (CRSPPP).

Throughout the history of the Division, the doctoral level of preparation has been advocated. This emphasis, by the APA and the Division, on the doctoral degree as the entry level to the profession of school psychology was a driving force in the formation of NASP. The advocacy of the specialist level of preparation (two years of full-time course work with a one-year internship) has been the source of periodic and recurring tension between the Division and NASP.

Over the course of the last six decades, the Division has been instrumental in the major conferences convened to examine the profession. Starting with the Thayer Conference in 1954 and followed by the Spring Hill Conference in 1979, Olympia Conference in 1981, and the 2002 Conference on the Future of School Psychology, leaders from the Division have contributed to the planning, implementation, and follow-up for gatherings that have helped chart the course of the profession.

In 1986, Thomas R. Kratochwill was the founding editor of the Division's journal, *Professional School Psychology*. In 1990, the journal was renamed *School Psychology Quarterly* to reflect a greater emphasis on empirical research and to increase the scientific understanding of the practice of school psychology. The video *Conversation Series* was initiated by Alex Thomas in 1991 when William Erchul engaged Gerald Caplan in a conversation on consultation.

Division 16 sponsors and the APA publishes the book series, *Applying Psychology to the Schools*. The series integrates theoretical developments and empirical findings on assessment and intervention approaches and thus provides a framework for conceptualizing change processes in school and learning contexts.

Together with the Society for the Study of School Psychology, the Division supported the Evidence-Based Intervention Task Force. The Task Force has developed a coding manual for evaluating intervention research which will serve as a template to judge the merit of prevention and intervention procedures.

—*Jack A. Cummings*

See also American Psychological Association; National Association of School Psychologists; School Psychologist

TIMELINE

1945: American Psychological Association reorganizes and the Division of School Psychologists is founded.

1954: Thayer Conference is held to examine the functions, qualifications, and training of school psychologists.

1963: Division 16 initiated a failed effort for APA to accredit school psychology doctoral programs. (The effort failed.)

1970: APA Committee on Accreditation approved Standards and Criteria for the accreditation of Doctoral Programs in School Psychology.

1971: University of Texas was recognized as the first doctoral program in school psychology accredited by APA.

1979: Spring Hill Symposium on the Future of Psychology in the Schools is held.

1981: Olympia Conference is held.

1981: Division 16 successfully promoted the Specialty Guidelines for the delivery of services by school psychologists.

1986: Division 16 journal, *Professional School Psychology*, is published.

1990: *Professional School Psychology* journal is renamed *School Psychology Quarterly*.

1991: Conversation Series (videotape series) is initiated by Alex Thomas featuring William Erchul engaged in a conversation with Gerald Caplan on consultation.

1997: Archival description of school psychology was approved by the APA Commission for the Recognition of Specialties and Proficiencies in Professional Psychology.

1999: Division 16 and Society for the Study of School Psychology collaborate to form a joint Task Force on Evidence-Based Interventions.

2002: Multisite conference on the Future of School Psychology was convened to examine the response of the profession to school psychologist shortages and to develop an agenda to maximize the benefits to the children and schools.

DIVORCE ADJUSTMENT

Marital conflict, family separations, divorce, and remarriages, although common in the last 30 years, are difficult and often painful challenges for children. Today, approximately 50% of all first-time marriages end in divorce, and this figure has increased approximately 40% from 10 years ago. At any one time nearly 15% of all families will be divorced and in a given year, 17 out of 1,000 children will face a family divorce. Between 40% and 50% of children will experience a family divorce before age 18 years.

Divorce adjustment occurs when children and adolescents cope relatively well with parental divorce and separation provided that other factors such as a decline in parenting or parental psychopathology do not complicate the process, and provided that children receive some support through the transition. A minority of children will actually emerge from the challenges that divorce poses with greater strength, competence, resiliency, and personal enhancement.

Children with divorce adjustment difficulties, estimated at 25% of children in divorcing families, exhibit a variety of behavior problems, including:

- Anxiety
- Attention difficulties
- Impulse control problems
- Depression
- Oppositional and defiant behavior
- Academic difficulties and school drop out
- Eating and sleeping difficulties
- Various physical symptoms
- Social difficulties
- Damaged self-esteem
- Early or inappropriate sexual activity
- Substance abuse

These children are demanding, dependent, or noncompliant with both adults and peers. Approximately 9% of them receive psychological assistance although more could benefit from it. Most children show adequate divorce adjustment within two to three years, although some have difficulties continuing into their adult years. Children living with formerly married mothers also have poorer health, more chronic illnesses, more hospitalizations, and more accidents than children in continuously married families. Nevertheless, it is very difficult to predict which children will exhibit difficulties and what types of problems they will show.

Both researchers and public agree that adjusting to divorce is difficult for children and can cause:

- Loss
- Despair
- Divided loyalties
- Parent absence
- Economic difficulties
- Relocation
- Family reorganization

Divorce is not a singular event but involves a series of multiple transitions and adjustments that both parents and children must make. The transitions involve coping with initial stages of family conflict and impending separation, actual separation and legal divorce, and readjustment to a new lifestyle and family arrangement. Although research has shown that both children and adolescents generally have difficulty adjusting to family divorce and its aftermath, and are at risk for various psychological, social, and educational problems, there is considerable diversity in children's divorce adjustment.

Longitudinal studies show that children's adjustment is poorest in the first year after divorce; by year two, many girls show adequate adjustment, but adjustment declines may occur in adolescence and remarriage is especially challenging for adolescent girls. Compared to girls, boys' adjustment is slower and boys from divorced homes continue to be more withdrawn and act out more than boys from intact families into the adolescent years.

Children's divorce adjustment broadly depends on several interacting factors. The first factor comprises aspects such as personality, age, temperament, intelligence, maturity, resilience, gender, and any preexisting behavioral or cognitive issues they may have had prior to the family disruption. Simply put, well-adjusted and easy-temperament children tend to have less difficulty than children with difficult temperaments, disabilities, self-image problems, or issues such as anxiety, dependence, and noncompliance.

Divorce is particularly difficult for preschool children and early adolescents. Toddlers cannot understand divorce and may react with confusion, clinginess, or regressive behaviors. Children between the ages of 3 and 10 years may react with sadness, anger, and self-blame. Adolescents may show a variety of withdrawn or acting-out behaviors, and also may be at risk for academic problems, substance abuse, and inappropriate sexual behavior.

The second factor influencing divorce adjustment is the nature of predivorce family relationships (e.g., family conflict leading to divorce, parental alcoholism) and how much divorce resolves these family issues. Some children will be surprised and shocked to learn of parental divorce, and will require a great deal of comfort and support. Further, because families in conflict are likely to have serious preexisting communication problems, they may not have communicated together with their children about divorce and this may leave their children with doubts, confusion, and self-blame. Other children have witnessed various forms of family conflict and domestic violence including parent abuse or have been abuse victims themselves. Overall, parental conflict is the strongest predictor of children's divorce adjustment. If divorce or separation ends children's exposure to family violence, the long-term outcomes likely will be positive. On the other hand, many parents continue contentious relationships during the divorcing period and subsequently in custody battles, visitation disagreements, and child support litigation. Children in joint custody arrangements have fewer adjustment problems and better self-esteem than children in sole custody arrangements.

The third factor is the degree of disruption caused by the family breakup, particularly economic changes, relocation, increased custodial parent workload, home absenteeism, school changes, and lack of contact with a biological parent or siblings. Divorced mothers tend to have half the family income of married mothers, are most likely to be on public assistance, and approximately 20% are forced to move in with their parents.

The fourth factor involves parental and parenting changes associated with divorce, remarriage, and stepfamily issues. In the first year following divorce, there is frequently a decrease in parental warmth and increase in authoritarian parenting. This is particularly true in the case of single mothers raising sons and those raising preadolescent daughters seeking their independence. Increased parent depression, which may occur, has serious negative consequences for children.

The fifth factor is the extent to which other social systems such as peers, extended family members, schools, faith organizations, and neighborhood groups support the child's adjustment. For example, maintaining greater closeness to grandparents is associated with fewer adjustment problems.

Any dramatic change in a child's behavior may be a signal that professional help is needed. Specific warnings may include:

- Sadness and withdrawn behavior
- Negative statements made about the self or parent(s)
- Anger and temper tantrums
- Regressive behavior
- Difficulty separating from parents
- Wishes to return to the past family unit
- Concentration difficulties
- School problems
- Guilt

Although many children will exhibit one or more of these behaviors, most can be helped within their families and communities and will not require professional counseling. Their needs can be met by well-functioning parents and caregivers who minimize trauma and keep the home environment consistent and predictable.

In most cases, school psychologists will be called on to provide (a) interventions that ensure that children from divorced families experience school environments that are organized, nurturing, predictable, and in which standards are consistently enforced and (b) parent consultation focusing on the importance of authoritative parenting and stable, positive peer relationships. School psychologists may serve as valuable resources to recommend self-help books on talking to children about divorce and helping them cope with it. They can also conduct workshops for teachers, administrators, and parents on how children deal with divorce and ways to ease this transition.

Schools can offer children counseling and other therapeutic interventions to improve their divorce adjustment. Most school-based divorce interventions involve either just the child or the child and family members. Those focusing only on the child include individual and group therapies, and both are designed to provide support and developmental guidance. Individual therapy approaches provide the child a secure and predictable environment. Children in the early school years often receive play therapy, art and drawing-based therapy, and bibliotherapy (e.g., readings that assist the child to understand and cope with their problems) to aid their adjustment. Because individual therapies are often described in case studies with no evaluation data, their success will most likely depend on particulars of the client–therapist interaction.

Group therapies for children in divorcing families have considerable research support. These groups usually last several weeks and are intended for children in the 6 to 14 year age range. They typically address anxiety, depression, self-esteem, anger management, or feelings about divorce, and have the advantages of allowing children to talk about their feelings in a safe environment by allowing them to hear how other children think and feel. These groups have been found to be particularly effective in reducing children's anxiety and improving self-esteem. One of the most successful programs is Pedro-Carroll, Alpert-Gillis, and Sterling's (1987) *Children of Divorce Intervention Project*. This project is a 12-session school-based cognitive and coping intervention for kindergarten through eighth graders that has been found to increase children's divorce-related problem solving and reduce negative outcomes for up to two years compared to a control group.

Excellent family-focused interventions for children are relatively new. A particularly noteworthy and scientifically tested program is called the *New Beginnings Program* (Lustig & colleagues, 1999). This is an 11-session program focusing on improving parent–child relationships and discipline, and reducing family conflict. It has been found to reduce aggression, mental disorders, and substance use, and improve school grades for up to 6 years after the termination of the program and is successful with high-risk families. Another impressive and successful family intervention for divorce is Lebow's (1997) *Integrative Family Therapy Model*. This program approaches each family as a unique case and combines both individual treatment of family members and family therapy. It addresses parenting, family communication and negotiation, ends blaming, builds parent–child understanding, and coordination with the legal system.

—*Frederic J. Medway*

See also Latchkey Children; Parenting; Resilience and Protective Factors; Single-Parent Families

REFERENCES AND FURTHER READING

Grych, J. H., & Fincham, F. D. (1999). The adjustment of children from divorced families: Implications of empirical research for clinical intervention. In R. M. Galatzer-Levy & L. Kraus (Eds.), *The scientific basis of child custody decisions* (pp. 96–119). New York: Wiley.

Hetherington, E. M., & Kelly, J. (2002). *For better or worse: Divorce reconsidered.* New York: Norton.

Lebow, J. (1997). The integrative revolution in couple and family therapy. *Family Process, 36,* 1–12.

Lustig, J. L., Wolchik, S. A., & Weiss, L. (1999). The New Beginnings parenting program for divorced mothers: Linking theory and intervention. In C.A. Essau & F. Petermann (Eds.), *Depressive disorders in children and adolescents: Epidemiology, risk factors, and treatment* (pp. 361–381). Northvale, NJ: Jason Aronson.

Pedro-Carroll, J. L., Alpert-Gillis, L. J., & Sterling, S. E. (1987). *Children of Divorce Intervention Program: Procedures manual for conducting support groups with 2nd and 3rd grade children.* Rochester, NY: University of Rochester, Center for Community Study.

Teyber, E. (2001). *Helping children cope with divorce.* San Francisco: Jossey-Bass.

Wallerstein, J., Kelly, J. B., & Blakeslee, S. (1996). *Surviving the breakup: How children and parents cope with divorce.* New York: Basic Books.

DOWN SYNDROME.

See MENTAL RETARDATION

DROPOUTS

Although the national dropout rate has declined since the 1970s and remained stable over the past several years, the issue of high school dropouts is still a significant concern for educators and policy makers alike. Concern remains high because students who drop out of school today are entering a more hostile and less supportive society than did students a quarter of a century ago. They face a workplace that puts an ever-increasing emphasis on education, a competitive (and highly skilled) job market, and a culture that considers a high school diploma a necessity for a successful life.

CALCULATING DROPOUT RATES

Accurately estimating dropout rates is difficult for three reasons. One source of confusion is the definition of dropout used. In order to track students, school districts develop codes for describing those who are no longer attending classes. In addition to "dropout," other codes may be "lost—not coming to school," "needed at home," "married," or "cannot adjust." Not all of a district's codes are included in the calculation of its dropout rate, and the codes that are included may vary from district to district, and state to state. Additionally, mandatory attendance laws typically require school attendance until age 16 years. Thus, students who leave school before turning 16 are defined as truants, not dropouts.

A second source of confusion is the use of different formulas to calculate dropout rates. Dropout rates are determined in three ways:

1. Event rate—the proportion of students in a given age range (e.g., 15 to 24 years) who leave school in a single school year

2. Status rate—the proportion of a given age range who have not graduated from high school and are not currently attending school, regardless of when they left

3. Cohort rate—the number of students in a specific grade that drop out over time

In addition to dropout rates, graduation rates are also calculated. The graduation rate is the proportion of a given age range who have earned either a high school diploma or a General Education Development (GED) credential. These different calculations provide different estimates of the number of students who drop out of school.

Finally, the reliability of dropout rates is brought into question because of inaccurate reporting. According to Fossey (1996), embarrassment about their dropout rates, along with pressure from school boards and administrators, may lead school districts to cover up the true number of students who leave each year. He contends that some school districts "may unconsciously be engaging in triage," getting rid of those students with the most severe needs—discipline problems, and learning and emotional difficulties—"to spend more energy on those believed more likely to succeed" (p. 143). This variability in defining dropout and calculating the dropout rate, along with the possibility of inaccurately reported data, makes both understanding the dropout problem and developing prevention programs difficult.

DROPOUT RATES

Despite limitations in determining actual dropout rates, sufficient evidence exists to demonstrate a significant problem. Looking at national event dropout rates, 4.8% of 15-to-24-year-old students in grades 10 through 12 left school between October 1999 and October 2000. The status dropout rate—the number of 16-to-24-year-old persons either not enrolled in school or without a high school diploma—in October 2000, was 10.9%. During the 1970s and 1980s both of these dropout rates showed downward trends, from 6.1% in 1972 to 4.1% in 1987 for the event rate, and from 14.6% in 1972 to 12.7% in 1987 for the status rate. Since the late 1980s, both rates have remained relatively stable (Kaufman & colleagues, 2001).

Because of the decline in dropout rates since the 1970s, it would seem logical to assume that the problem is being adequately addressed. Yet in southern and western states, dropout rates remain higher than in other areas of the country. Students coming from low-income families are still significantly more likely to leave school early. The dropout rates for African American and white youths have decreased, and the gap between the two groups has decreased; yet, among Hispanic youth the number of dropouts is almost twice that of these two groups. Demands for higher academic standards in our high schools, increased competition in the workplace, and an increase in the number of minority students (who are more likely than their peers to drop out) maintain political and societal attention on school dropouts. Thus, understanding why students leave school and determining how to help them stay in school continue to be of critical importance.

FACTORS THAT INFLUENCE DROPPING OUT

Research shows that dropouts more often come from low-income families, are members of ethnic minorities, and receive less educational support at home. According to Eckstrom and colleagues (1986), dropouts have fewer study aids in their homes, have less opportunity for non-school learning, are less likely to have both parents living at home, have mothers who have less formal education and who are more likely to be working, and have parents who are less involved in their child's school experience.

At school, dropouts have lower grades and lower standardized test scores, and they complete less homework than students who graduate. They have more discipline problems as measured by higher suspension rates, more absenteeism, and more tardiness. Students who fail to graduate also feel generally less involved in school and participate less in extracurricular activities. Outside of school, dropouts spend less time talking about school with their parents and less time reading. Dropouts also are more likely to work outside of school and to report enjoying work more than school.

In addition to individual student characteristics, schools themselves play a role in a student's decision to either drop out or persist. Kortering and colleagues (1995) describe how factors such as grade retention, tracking, and the school environment play a significant role in the decision to either stay in or leave school. Student grade retention is associated with continued academic struggles, increased behavioral problems, and dropping out. Students who have been retained are three times as likely to drop out of school, and the likelihood of dropping out increases with multiple retentions.

Educational tracking (grouping students based on academic ability) also influences dropping out. Students placed in low-ability tracks demonstrate lower academic achievement than their peers in higher tracks. They are less likely to take college preparatory classes and more likely to drop out of high school. Finally, the school environment also has a significant influence. For students who are at risk for dropping out, school is often perceived as an unwelcoming place. Teachers are seen as not being interested in their students' welfare and the school's discipline practices are believed unfair. Some students may best be described as "pushouts," encouraged by their school to drop out, rather than dropouts, leaving of their own accord.

CONSEQUENCES OF DROPPING OUT

The consequences of students leaving school before graduation appear to be negative both for the individual student and for society as a whole. Dropouts generally have low-level academic skills, difficulty finding employment and an adequate income, and less chance of receiving additional education that may be necessary to remain competitive in the job market (Rumberger, 1987). They are also less likely to vote and to be socially and politically active (McCaul & colleagues, 1992), and are more likely to live with family or guardians and have little contact with friends or people other than family. Additionally, individuals who drop out of school are more likely to commit a crime and to live in poverty (Blackorby & colleagues, 1991).

DROPOUT PREVENTION

The issue of high dropout rates is complex and multifaceted; therefore, there is not a simple, one-size-fits-all solution. Although the end goal of education is well-established—providing all students with an education that prepares them for life after high school—the means for reaching this goal are not always clear. Researchers are only beginning to understand how to support student persistence. Effective prevention efforts address student needs on a multitude of levels, integrating services in ways that are tailored to individual needs. They seek to make school meaningful and purposeful to students and provide caring and supportive learning environments. Additionally, the following factors are vital to effective prevention programs:

- Addressing individual student academic needs
- Providing counseling to meet students' psychological needs
- Identifying at-risk students early
- Providing early interventions for these identified students

Students are more likely to stay in school if they experience academic success and are reinforced for school attendance. Those who are involved in formal mentoring programs or who have an informal, but significant relationship with an adult at school are also more likely to persist until graduation.

Despite stabilization in the school dropout rate, the number of students who fail to graduate remains unacceptably high to parents, educators, and society as a whole. While there is a growing understanding of both the students who leave school and the schools from which they leave, less is known about how to prevent students from dropping out. What is clear is that as workplace demands and high school graduation standards continue to increase, addressing the issue of school dropouts becomes increasingly urgent.

—*Kimberly Knesting*

See also Academic Achievement; Expulsion; High School; Race, Ethnicity, Class, and Gender; Resilience and Protective Factors; Retention and Promotion; School Refusal; Self-Concept and Efficacy; Substance Abuse; Suspension

REFERENCES AND FURTHER READING

Blackorby, J., Edgar, E., & Kortering, L. J. (1991). A third of our youth? A look at the problem of high school dropout among students with mild handicaps. *The Journal of Special Education, 25*(1), 102–113.

Eckstrom, R. B., Goertz, M. E., Pollack, J. M., & Rock, D. A. (1986). Who drops out of high school and why? Findings from a national study. *Teachers College Record, 87,* 356–373.

Fossey, R. (1996). School dropout rates: Are we sure they are going down? *Phi Delta Kappan, 78*(2), 140–144.

Kaufman, P., Alt, M. N., & Chapman, C. D. (2001). *Dropout rates in the United States, 2000: Statistical analysis* (Report No. NCES-2002–114). Washington, DC: National Center for Education Statistics. (ERIC Document Reproduction Service No. ED460174)

Kortering, L. J., Hess, R. S., & Braziel, P. M. (1995). School dropout. In G. G. Bear, K. M. Minke, & A. Thomas (Eds.), *Children's needs II: Development, problems, and alternatives* (pp. 511–521). Bethesda, MD: The National Association of School Psychologists.

McCaul, E. J., Donaldson, G. A., Coladarci, T., & Davis, W. E. (1992). Consequences of dropping out of school: Findings from high school and beyond. *Journal of Educational Research, 85,* 198–207.

Rumberger, R. W. (1987). High school dropouts: A review of issues and evidence. *Review of Educational Research, 57,* 101–121.

DSM-IV

The *Diagnostic and Statistical Manual of Mental Disorders, Fourth Edition-Text Revision* (*DSM-IV-TR*) (American Psychiatric Association [APA], 2000) is used for clinical, research, and educational purposes. The focus of the manual is on diagnostic codes that are used in medical record keeping and communication of information to governmental agencies, private insurers, and the World Health Organization (APA, 2000). The relative infancy of this classification system warrants skepticism, yet empirical support for diagnostic reliability and validity has evolved significantly since its inception.

The first edition of the *Diagnostic and Statistical Manual of Mental Disorders (DSM-I)* (1952) was recognized as *the* manual of mental health categorization. It was developed as a variant of the "Mental Disorders" section of the sixth edition of the World Health Organization's (WHO, 1949) International Classification of Diseases (ICD). *DSM-I* included one child mental health category (adjustment reactions of childhood and adolescence) as developmental differences between psychopathology in adults and children went unrecognized within the nomenclature. The psychoanalytic term of "reaction" (changes in personality related to psychological, social, and biological factors) found extensively within *DSM-I* was largely excluded from the second edition (*DSM-II*) (APA, 1968). However, few changes were made to improve the specificity of diagnostic definitions as narrative descriptions of symptoms remained. The third edition (*DSM-III,* APA, 1980) paralleled advancements made within the ninth edition of ICD (WHO, 1975), which emphasized diagnostic clarity and improved clinical utility. Specifically, diagnostic criteria were made more explicit, a multiaxial assessment system was included, and greater neutrality in etiological explanations of disorders was evident. The five Axes included in a multiaxial diagnosis are:

1. Axis I: Clinical Disorders and Other Conditions That May Be a Focus of Clinical Attention

2. Axis II: Personality Disorders and Mental Retardation

3. Axis III: General Medical Conditions

4. Axis IV: Psychosocial and Environmental Problems

5. Axis V: Global Assessment of Functioning

This system helps to capture the complexity of mental health conditions and the diversity of contexts and issues surrounding individuals presenting with the same diagnoses (APA, 2000).

Revisions and corrections to the major changes made within *DSM-III* resulted in the publication of *DSM-III-R* (APA, 1987). Because of the extensive research that was generated by the diagnostic criteria used in *DSM-III* and *DSM-III-R,* the fourth edition (*DSM-IV*) (APA, 1994) underwent significant research development, specifically for the childhood categories. A three-stage evidence-based process involving thorough literature reviews, reanalyses of extant data sets, and comprehensive field trials was completed. *DSM-IV* includes 10 categories specific to children

called *Disorders Usually First Diagnosed in Infancy, Childhood, or Adolescence* with criteria available for more than 40 mental health diagnoses. Consistent with the purpose of serving as an educational tool, changes within the text sections of *DSM-IV* were made to reflect new information available since the early 1990s. This resulted in the publication of *DSM-IV-TR* (APA, 2000). No substantive changes in diagnostic criteria were made nor are they anticipated until *DSM-V,* which is scheduled to be published sometime after 2010.

DSM-IV-TR facilitates communication and consultation across multiple settings. Mental health professionals in clinical settings use the manual for diagnostic decision making within a comprehensive evaluation to guide treatment planning and development, to communicate service need to third-party payers like insurance companies, and to improve communication with others who may work with the client such as physicians and teachers. Within school settings, the use of the *DSM-IV-TR* is limited and used in combination with educational categories derived from the Individuals With Disabilities Education Act (IDEA). Eligibility for special educational programming is based on the presence of a special educational classification from IDEA such as "Other Health Impairment" or "Learning Disabilities." For these two examples, one might find comparable symptom profiles within *DSM-IV-TR* under categories termed "Attention Deficit Hyperactivity Disorder" and "Reading Disorder," respectively. The lack of overlapping classifications and incompatible terminology creates difficulties in communication between professionals in the school and community settings that are not easily resolved. School personnel often consult this manual to improve understanding of children's social–emotional behavior in an effort to ultimately create learning environments that meet the child's mental health and academic needs.

Diagnostic definitions and procedures within the manual imply a close examination of biological, psychological, and ecological contributions to mental health functioning. Professionals use a multisource, multimethod assessment framework within this classification system. Specifically, data may be collected from multiple informants and settings to examine academic, social, emotional, and behavioral difficulties. In order to meet diagnostic definitions, symptoms and behaviors must typically persist across time and impair the functioning of the individual. A multiaxial assessment system is used to help gather and organize this data to help make this determination.

The effective use of this manual requires considerable training and experience (APA, 2000). *DSM-IV-TR* will ultimately be improved upon as evidenced by the historical review of this classification system. Currently, the utility and acceptability of *DSM* far exceeds that of other published works in this area.

—*John S. Carlson*

See also Individuals With Disabilities Education Act

REFERENCES AND FURTHER READING

American Psychiatric Association. (1952). *The diagnostic and statistical manual of mental disorders (DSM-I)*. Washington DC: Author.

American Psychiatric Association. (1968). *The diagnostic and statistical manual of mental disorders* (2nd ed.) *(DSM-II)*. Washington DC: Author

American Psychiatric Association. (1980). *The diagnostic and statistical manual of mental disorders* (3rd ed.) *(DSM-III)*. Washington DC: Author.

American Psychiatric Association. (1987). *The diagnostic and statistical manual of mental disorders* (3rd ed., Rev.) *(DSM-III-R)*. Washington DC: Author.

American Psychiatric Association. (1994). *The diagnostic and statistical manual of mental disorders* (4th ed.) *(DSM-IV)*. Washington DC: Author.

American Psychiatric Association. (2000). *The diagnostic and statistical manual of mental disorders* (4th ed., Text rev.) *(DSM-IV-TR)*. Washington DC: Author.

World Health Organization. (1949). *The international classification of diseases* (6th ed.). Geneva, Switzerland: Author.

World Health Organization. (1975). *The international classification of diseases* (9th ed.). Geneva, Switzerland: Author.

DUE PROCESS

DEFINITION

Due process of law refers to the regular administration of a system of laws, which must conform to fundamental and generally accepted legal principles and be applied without favor or prejudice to all citizens. Due process is the fundamental principles of justice as opposed to a specific rule of law.

HOW IS DUE PROCESS APPLIED TO SCHOOL SYSTEMS?

Within the school system, due process is generally seen as the steps and rules established to ensure fairness in providing educational opportunities for all children. With the advent of Public Law (P. L.) 94–142, the Education for All Handicapped Children Act in 1975, to the most current reauthorization of this law called the Individuals With Disabilities Education Act (IDEA), 1997, a specific procedure called an "impartial due-process hearing" has provided parents and schools an avenue for resolving disputes and complaints. This due-process hearing affords the parents and schools the right to present their complaint and is conducted by the state's educational agency or by the local educational agency. A complaint by the parent can relate to the identification, evaluation, educational placement, or the provision of a free appropriate public education (FAPE) of children.

In addition to an impartial due-process hearing, IDEA also established a process called "mediation" to ensure that procedures are established and implemented to allow the parties who are in conflict to resolve such disputes through a mediation process. Mediation is available whenever a hearing is requested. Mediation has to be voluntary on the part of both parties; and it is not to be used to deny or delay a parent's right to a due-process hearing. A qualified and impartial mediator who is trained in effective mediation techniques conducts the mediation. It should be noted that an impartial due-process hearing might occur without mediation.

DESCRIPTION OF INDIVIDUALS THAT TYPICALLY PARTICIPATE IN DUE-PROCESS HEARINGS

Individuals who participate in due-process hearings are most likely the parents of a child with a disability who have a grievance with the school system. During the dispute, a parent advocate or an attorney may accompany the parents. The school district is usually represented by its own counsel, but administrators, school psychologists, counselors, teachers, and other school personnel may be involved most often as expert witnesses, but they could be part of a team that prepares the defense.

COMMON STAGES OF A DUE-PROCESS HEARING

The first stage of a due-process hearing is the complaint regarding the identification, evaluation, or educational placement of the child, or the provision of a free appropriate public education. Whenever a complaint has been received, the parents involved have an opportunity for an impartial due-process hearing or mediation. During the due-process hearing, unless the parents agree otherwise, the child involved in the dispute will remain in his or her current educational placement.

At least five business days prior to a hearing, each party shall disclose to all other parties the evaluations and recommendations that they intend to use at the hearing. Any party to a hearing shall be accorded the right to be accompanied and advised by counsel and by individuals with special knowledge or training with respect to the problems of children with disabilities. Each party has the right to present evidence and confront, cross-examine, and compel the attendance of witnesses. They also have the right to a written or electronic verbatim record of the hearing, and the right to written or electronic findings of fact and decisions. The decision made in a hearing is final, except that any parties involved in such hearings may appeal to the State educational agency. If appealed, this agency will conduct an impartial review of the decision and will make an independent decision. Any party who does not have the right to an appeal and any party aggrieved by the findings and decision has the right to bring a civil action with respect to the complaint presented.

STRATEGIES ON HOW TO AVOID DUE PROCESS

Promoting favorable impressions and good relations with parents and advocates results in fewer conflicts and litigation. School psychologists, school administrators, and special services staff can be instrumental in avoiding due-process hearings by implementing the following suggestions. The first is to design in-service training programs to help staff learn to work more effectively with parents, become less defensive in responding to parental inquiries and complaints, and become more skilled at respecting parents' opinions. Schools should identify, early on, cases in which the relationship with parents is not proceeding amicably, and alert others in the system to potential problems. An important consideration is that staff and administrators should become sensitized to parents' anger and learn not to take parents' anger and frustration personally, and if parents are angry, to include other professionals outside the evaluation team to talk with them. Another suggestion is for staff to spend more

time with parents before educational planning meetings to explain procedures and evaluation results so that parents are prepared for the meetings. When possible, the number of people at meetings should be limited so that parents don't feel overwhelmed (recommend 4–6). Another suggestion is to encourage parents to visit the program for the child so that parents can see more correctly what is being offered. It is also important to follow up with families that do not sign or do not return signed educational plans, and find out why. Finally, it is important for school personnel to use good communication skills prior to and during hearings and present an organized and coherent account of the case.

ROLE OF THE SCHOOL PSYCHOLOGIST IN DUE-PROCESS HEARINGS

The most important role of the school psychologist in due-process hearings is as an expert witness. In preparing for the due-process hearing, the expert witness needs to meet with the lawyer at least 1 week before testimony and ask what the testimony will be about, what questions will be asked, what questions should be asked, and what testimony the other witnesses going to give.

—*Mahlon B. Dalley*

See also Confidentiality; Ethical Issues in School Psychology; Individuals With Disabilities Education Act; Special Education

DYSLEXIA

Dyslexia occurs as a result of deficits in understanding speech sounds, and therefore results in problems with accurate and fluent word recognition, poor spelling, and decoding or understanding the sounds that go with written language (International Dyslexia Association, 2003). The disorder is often characterized by poor reading, but good listening ability. It has been described as "an unexpected difficulty learning to read despite having all the factors necessary to read–good thinking and reasoning skills and the ability to think creatively" (Campbell, 2003, p. 20). These children frequently have aural/oral, cognitive, fine motor, and executive functions that are normally developed. Their cognitive abilities are often in the average to above average range (International Dyslexia Association, 2003). However, children and adults with dyslexia may also have specific impairments in other academic skills like writing and math (Berninger, 2001).

Throughout the life span, dyslexia may be expressed differently. In early grade school, children may have difficulty reading words in isolation, make consistent spelling errors such as letter reversals, rely on guessing to read, have difficulty writing number sequences, and confuse math signs. Another sign includes trouble remembering facts. As students reach middle school, they are often reading below grade level. They may demonstrate difficulties, such as reversing letter sequences; be slow to learn prefixes, suffixes, and root words; may have trouble with word problems in math; and may have difficulties with recall of facts and comprehension. Some signs of the disorder may continue to occur throughout the life span. For example, difficulties with planning and organization can afflict those with dyslexia from elementary school through adulthood. They also experience difficulty with memory and acquiring vocabulary. As children, they may have difficulty acquiring vocabulary, which results in an inadequate vocabulary as they enter high school and go on to college or careers. In middle school, high school, and into adulthood, the person may avoid writing tasks and continue to spell poorly. They also may try to hide their reading disability or avoid written tasks to avoid embarrassment. As adults, people with dyslexia often work well below their intellectual capacity (International Dyslexia Association, 2003).

Currently there is no specific set of criteria for the diagnosis of dyslexia. Therefore it is important to remember that when one refers to dyslexia they may be referring to any degree of reading difficulties. Often a child who has dyslexia and needs special education services will fall under the category of learning disabled or as having a reading disorder.

The neurological origins of dyslexia were first investigated by a French neurologist, Dejerine, in 1891. The use of functional brain imaging investigations has revealed converging data that support the neurological basis of dyslexia, pointing primarily to the failure of left hemisphere posterior brain systems to function properly (Lyon & colleagues, 2003). Genetic research has found a link between dyslexia and Chromosome 6. These biological factors could play a role in differences in how well children may be

able to learn by affecting cognitive, language, and other skills (Berninger, 2001).

A common belief is that people with dyslexia read and write letters backwards. A study investigating letter orientation confusion in children with reading disabilities revealed that children with reading disabilities did confuse the orientation of stimuli more frequently than average readers in reception and production tasks, but this is not the sole problem or determinant of dyslexia (Terepocki & colleagues, 2002).

A language-based learning disability occurs in 15% to 20% of the population. The lack of specific criteria for the diagnosis of dyslexia makes it difficult to determine an exact prevalence of the learning disability (Padget, 1998). Dyslexia occurs fairly equally among males and females, and among different ethnic and socioeconomic backgrounds (International Dyslexia Association, 2003). Children with a phonological disorder have an increased risk of later having a reading disorder (Tunick & Pennington, 2002). Phonological disorders are manifested by errors in sound production, use, representation, or substitutions and omissions of sounds. People who have a phonological disorder or a reading disorder are at an increased risk of having other disorders. For example, approximately 50% of those diagnosed with a learning or reading disorder have also been diagnosed with attention deficit hyperactivity disorder (International Dyslexia Association, 2003).

One fourth of all children with dyslexia have a parent who also has the disability. Children with two parents that have the disability are at a greater risk for dyslexia (Berninger, 2001). Children with dyslexia often experience low self-esteem and a negative self-image. Many times this is a result of the many difficulties and failures children with dyslexia experience, which cause them to doubt their intelligence and motivation (Dyslexia and the Life Course, 2003).

Academic interventions are essential to the success of children with dyslexia and should focus on the student's area of weakness including word recognition, spelling, and decoding. Phonological training should begin while the child is in kindergarten (International Dyslexia Association, 2003). The type of help the child requires to overcome the learning disability will vary based on the individual child's area of need and the extent of the problem. "Keys to success appear to be early intervention, encouragement of talents and hobbies, good family support, and involvement in the search for self-worth. . . . Awareness, sensitivity, and action on the part of the caregiver foster the process of compensation at both functional and psychological levels within the child" (Dyslexia and the Life Course, 2003, pg. 363).

—*Julie Lee*

See also Reading Interventions and Strategies

REFERENCES AND FURTHER READING

Berninger, V. W. (2001). Understanding the 'lexia' in dyslexia: A multidisciplinary team approach to learning disabilities. *Annals of Dyslexia, 51,* 23–48.

Campbell, M. (2003). Dyslexia: Early detection is crucial. *American Teacher, 88*(2), 20.

Dyslexia and the life course. (2003). *Journal of Learning Disabilities, 36*(4), 363–381.

International Dyslexia Association. Retrieved November 16, 2003, from http://www.interdys.org

Lyon, G. R., Shaywitz, S., Shaywitz, B. A. (2003). Defining dyslexia, comorbity, teachers' knowledge of language and reading: A definition of dyslexia. *Annals of Dyslexia, 53,* 1–14.

Padget, S. Y. (1998). Lessons from research on dyslexia: Implications for a classification system for learning disabilities. *Learning Disability Quarterly, 21*(2), 167–178.

Terepocki, M., Kruk, R. S., Willows, D. M. (2002). The incidence and nature of letter orientation errors in reading disability. *Journal of Learning Disabilities, 35*(3), 214–233.

Tunick, R. A., & Pennington, B. F. (2002). The etiological relationship between reading disability and phonological disorder. *Annals of Dyslexia, 52,* 75–97.

E

EARLY INTERVENTION

Early intervention (EI) is best seen as a system of multidisciplinary services designed to support those family interactions that enhance optimal development of children ages birth to three years. The benefits of such a system include remediating existing developmental difficulties, preventing the future effect of these difficulties, alleviating potential delays, limiting the development of additional handicaps, and promoting improved family functioning. These goals are accomplished by providing a wide array of therapeutic and developmental services for children, coupled with instruction and support for families. EI serves children with difficulties deriving from established disabilities (Down syndrome, autism, visual/aural impairments, etc), as well as environmental risks (disadvantaged families, maltreating parents, low-birthweight child).

The history of EI is closely tied to federal legislation for special education services. With the passage of Public Law 94–142, Public Law 99–457, and subsequent legislation, and the implementation of the Individuals With Disabilities Education Act (IDEA), educators were made more aware of the special needs of infants, toddlers, and their families. Part C of IDEA (Program for Infants and Toddlers with Disabilities) is a federal grant program that aids in establishing and overseeing a comprehensive program of EI services for children birth to 36 months of age. Each individual state is responsible for creating a comprehensive early intervention system. One part of this system is the establishment of a comprehensive Child Find System. This system is a continuous process planned to locate, identify, and refer young children with disabilities to intervention services. The system also includes activities to increase public awareness of available services, and screening and evaluation of eligible children.

Originally, all programs were child-centered, with parents only playing peripheral roles. First the child was assessed for specific handicapping conditions, and then assigned to a multidisciplinary team of service providers including, but not limited to educators, social service personnel, speech and language clinicians, occupational and physical therapists, psychologists, and nurses. The parents were responsible for keeping all appointments and for continuing remediation programs within the home. Positive outcomes were seen as the extent to which parents learned and carried out the intervention activities that they were taught.

As a greater understanding was developed between families and service providers, it was realized that the needs of young children could only be truly appreciated in the context of their families. The focus of EI then shifted from the child as a single entity to the child within the family and the family within a total social context. Children's development is now viewed as being closely related to the environment within which the child is developing, namely, the family. As the family influences the development of the child, so does the child shape the development and dynamics of the family. Present models of EI are family-centered with emphasis on the family's strengths rather than deficits.

Cultural traditions play a very strong role in all family interactions; therefore, this role cannot be ignored within the context of the EI program. Cultural views of disabilities are extremely varied, and the parents' view of what constitutes an area that is acceptable for change and what is not can be difficult to understand before first considering cultural views. For example, within the rigid hierarchical structure of some societies, the deference that is paid to experts can easily be mistaken for trust. Parents may acquiesce to the recommendations of experts within the context of the conference, but may not follow through with activities that are dissonant with their cultural beliefs. By understanding the cultural background of the child's family, EI professionals can better design programs that will be helpful and acceptable to both child and family.

From a service provision standpoint, early intervention seeks to integrate a large range of services within a variety of settings and coordinates those services in a way that conflicts are minimized between service providers. Children experiencing difficulties because of poor parent–child interactions may be best helped through a clinic-based system; while children dealing with more environmental difficulties, such as poverty, may be best served by a community-based program. Hospital-based programs usually supervise interventions for children born with severe handicapping conditions. Home-based programs help parents and children through professional visits to the family's home environment.

Programming and services for each individual child are created on a developmental basis. Whether a child is an infant or a toddler, the services are based on the child's developmental needs rather than age level. Services for the family are also based on need rather than age level of the child.

The effectiveness of early intervention programs is a difficult question to answer. According to policy makers and individual parents, a quick consensus can be reached that early intervention does make a difference. Any of these stakeholders can cite particular instances where services have made a world of difference for the families and children involved. From a scientific standpoint, the answer becomes a little less clear. Significant methodological difficulties in many studies that sought to answer this question only pose additional questions. Most studies were completed when early intervention services were first instituted. Children receiving the "new" intervention services were compared to children receiving no services whatever, creating a huge positive effect for the new EI services. While subsequent studies have been mainly focused on one particular area of disability (i.e., hearing impaired), making global conclusion difficult, aggregated results have shown overwhelmingly that EI does make a difference in children's lives.

Early intervention has been seen as the best hope for the future of children facing challenging handicaps to learning. EI programs work with children in the context of their family rather than as a separate entity that needs adjustment, thus helping the family as well as the child. While programs vary greatly in the delivery of services, all programs integrate a variety of professionals in the task of improving the lives of at-risk children and their families. Through EI, the devastating effects of handicapping, or potentially handicapping situations, can be addressed.

—*Martha Carlton*

See also Autism Spectrum Disorders; Head Start

Point Versus Counterpoint: Early Intervention

The case for:

- It targets environmentally vulnerable children.
- It is most promising when programs are based upon structured curriculum and target parents as well as children.
- The focus is on the needs of the entire family.
- It is based in local communities.
- Various agencies successfully plan and coordinate supports and services together.
- It prevents declines in intellectual development for children with developmental delays.

- It may reduce family stress.
- It often lessens the necessity for special education services later in the child's educational future.

The case against:

- Gains made with developmentally delayed children tend to be limited.
- Service providers are more child-centered and find it difficult to work with and through families.
- Most programs do not meet the needs of historically underrepresented populations.
- There is often a lack of coordination of services.
- Some treatments are extremely expensive and time intensive.
- Some well-known therapeutic practices (such as sensory integration and patterning) have not proved to be effective in valid research studies.
- Multiple services often are not integrated and cause conflict or confusion for families.
- Programs focused on case management and parent education were not effective in improving the developmental outcomes of low-income children.

For further information see:

Guralnick, M. J. (1997). *The effectiveness of early intervention.* Baltimore, MD: Paul H. Brookes.

REFERENCES AND FURTHER READING

Bruder, M. B. (2000). Family centered early intervention: Clarifying our values for the new millennium. *Topics in Early Childhood Special Education, 20,* 105–15.

Guralnick, M. J. (2001). A developmental systems model for early intervention. *Infants and Young Children, 14,* 1–18.

Guralnick, M. J. (1997). *The effectiveness of early intervention.* Baltimore, MD: Paul H. Brookes.

Zero to Three. (n.d.). Available online at http://www.zerotothree.org

EATING DISORDERS

Eating disorders are emotional problems characterized by an obsession with food and weight. These disorders start with a preoccupation with food and weight and then escalate into an emotional dysfunction that is characterized by an obsession with food and weight. This obsession first involves secrecy, where the person with the eating disorder tries to hide the problem by possibly avoiding social situations involving food and may eat alone in order to hide the quantity of food eaten. The obsession also involves control. People with eating disorders may feel that they have no control over their life, so they gain control through restriction *of* food. However, this control is short lived because they then lose control *to* food (http://www.nationaleatingdisorders.org). These disorders can result in death if not taken seriously. Eating disorders fit into three categories: anorexia nervosa, bulimia nervosa, and binge eating.

ANOREXIA NERVOSA

Anorexia nervosa is the most serious and life-threatening eating disorder, with an estimated mortality rate of 10%, and affects approximately 1% of all females. The onset of this disorder is usually in adolescence. According to the *Diagnostic and Statistical Manual, Fourth Edition-Text Revision (DSM-IV-TR)* (American Psychiatric Association, 2000), anorexia nervosa is diagnosed if the following characteristics are present:

- A refusal to maintain minimal normal body weight for age
- An intense fear of gaining weight or becoming fat
- Feeling fat even when obviously underweight
- Amenorrhea (i.e., cessation of the menstrual cycle)

The *DSM-IV-TR* distinguishes between two subtypes of anorexia nervosa: the restricting type and the binge eating-purging type. Individuals diagnosed with anorexia nervosa-restricted type limit and/or avoid eating foods (e.g., foods containing fat) and may exercise excessively to lose weight. Those diagnosed with the binge eating-purging type exhibit the same bingeing and purging behaviors as bulimics; they consume large amounts of food in one sitting and then purge to avoid weight gain. These individuals differ from those diagnosed with bulimia nervosa because their initial diagnosis is anorexia nervosa-restricted type.

Health consequences of anorexia nervosa include slow heart rate, osteoporosis, muscle loss and weakness, severe dehydration, kidney failure, excessive weight loss, fainting, fatigue and overall weakness, dry hair and skin, hair loss, and a growth of layer of hair over the body for warmth (Hughes & colleagues, 2001). People with anorexia nervosa may display a depressed mood, somatic dysfunction (i.e., impaired or altered functioning of the body), or sexual dysfunction in which they lose interest in sexual behavior. They may also display guilt or an obsessive and/or anxious, fearful, or dependent personality (Guide to Recovery, 2002).

BULIMIA NERVOSA

Bulimia nervosa may co-occur with anorexia nervosa, but this is not always the case. Thirty to 80% of people with bulimia nervosa have a history of anorexia nervosa. It is often hard to diagnose bulimia nervosa because those with the disorder tend to be normal or slightly overweight (Levine & Smotak, 2002). Bulimia nervosa usually occurs in adolescence or early adulthood. As many as 17% of college-age women engage in bulimic behaviors, which are distinguished in the *DSM-IV-TR* by recurrent episodes of binge eating followed by purging.

People with bulimia nervosa may also engage in recurrent inappropriate compensatory behavior to prevent weight gain. This behavior includes self-induced vomiting; misuse of laxatives, diuretics, enemas, or other medications; fasting; or excessive exercise. To be classified as having bulimia nervosa, binge eating and inappropriate compensatory behavior must occur, on average, two times per week for three months (Hughes & colleagues, 2001). People with bulimia nervosa evaluate themselves based on their body weight and shape. The health consequences of bulimia nervosa are:

- Electrolyte (chemical) imbalances, which can lead to heart failure and irregular heart beat
- Possible rupture of the esophagus
- Constipation
- Tooth decay
- Peptic ulcers and inflammation of the pancreas
- A potential for gastric rupture during bingeing

Associated features of bulimia nervosa include depressed mood, somatic or sexual dysfunction, addiction, and/or disregard for the violation of others' rights (Guide to Recovery, 2002).

BINGE EATING

Binge eating disorder is perhaps the least recognized eating disorder and is listed in the *DSM-IV-TR* as a category requiring further study. This disorder is characterized by eating large quantities of food rapidly within any two-hour period. Bingeing is often done in private and binge eaters often feel a lack of control in their eating, such that they cannot stop eating or control their intake. This disorder affects approximately 2% to 5% of the general population and occurs more often in women than in men. It is estimated that approximately 30% of people with binge eating disorder are participating in medically supervised weight loss programs (Thomas Jefferson University Hospital, 2002). People with binge eating disorder experience feelings of shame, disgust, or guilt after a bingeing episode. The health consequences associated with a binge eating disorder include high blood pressure, high cholesterol levels, heart disease, diabetes, and gallbladder disease (Guide to Recovery, 2002).

FACTORS ASSOCIATED WITH EATING DISORDERS

Eating disorders are most common in industrialized societies such as the United States, Canada, Japan, Australia, and Europe (Davison & Neale, 1998). In the United States, the incidence rate of anorexia nervosa is eight times higher in white women than in nonwhite women. White teenage girls are reported to diet more frequently and are more likely to be dissatisfied with their bodies (Davison & Neale, 1998). Hughes and colleagues (2001) report that overall, eating disorders are most common in Native American cultures, and are found to be more common in white and Hispanic cultures than in Asian and African American cultures.

A variety of etiological factors contribute to eating disorders. These include biological predisposition, personality, family dysfunction, and cultural values with regard to body image. From a biological perspective, female relatives of young women with an eating disorder are five times more likely to have an eating disorder. Davison and Neale (1998) found a 47% concordance rate for monozygotic (identical) twins after combing data from several studies. The sociocultural factors surrounding eating disorders include the "ideal of thinness" shared by most Western nations and the negative view that societies have toward obesity. The media often relay the value that beauty equals thinness (Davison & Neale, 1998).

Gender plays an influential role in the onset of eating disorders. Ninety percent of all eating disorder victims are female. The primary reason for the greater prevalence of eating disorders in women than among men is that women appear to be more heavily influenced by cultural standards (i.e., magazines, advertisements, dolls). In the media, women are often portrayed as thin and being thin is associated with attractiveness. This type of portrayal often leads many (including very young girls) to desire to be thin because it appears to them that being thin is the socially accepted norm. Additionally, the desire to be perceived as attractive and/or socially acceptable influences many women to go to desperate measures to be thin. As authors Davison and Neale (1998) point out, women are more likely to diet, which puts them on a path leading to the possible development of an eating disorder.

There are different personality features associated with eating disorders. Anorexics tend to be shy, compliant, and perfectionists, while bulimics demonstrate mood changes, an outgoing social disposition, and histrionic features (i.e., sexual promiscuity, substance abuse, and a flair for dramatics). Both anorexic and bulimic patients show neurotic features and low self-esteem (Davison & Neale, 1998).

Families unduly influence eating disorders. However, whether the eating disorder precedes the family characteristics or the eating disorder is the cause of family dysfunction is debatable. There are four common patterns found in families of individuals with eating disorders (Davison & Neale, 1998):

1. They are overly enmeshed, meaning they are overinvolved with each other and have little or no boundaries. For example, in an enmeshed family, a parent or parents may speak for their child because they believe they know exactly how their child feels.

2. They are overprotective of each other, demonstrating an extreme level of concern for each other's welfare.

3. They have a tendency to try to maintain the status quo and avoid change at all costs.

4. They exhibit a strong avoidance of conflict or a chronic state of conflict.

The relationship between child abuse and eating disorders is gaining greater attention. Some studies indicate self-reports of childhood sexual, physical, and/or psychological abuse are higher than normal in individuals with eating disorders. Also, abuse at an early age that involves force is related to the later development of an eating disorder (Davison & Neale, 1998).

INTERVENTIONS FOR EATING DISORDERS

A variety of treatment plans are available for individuals with eating disorders. Many hospitals and eating disorder clinics offer support groups for friends and families, as well as group therapy for clients. Individual and family therapy approaches may consist of behavioral, cognitive, cognitive–behavioral, and psychodynamic techniques (Davison & Neale, 1998). Behavioral counseling may involve reinforcing good eating habits. Generally, a reward system is used as an incentive to encourage healthier eating habits (Davison & Neale, 1998). Psychodynamic approaches may look at possible family antecedents from early childhood that may be linked to the onset of the disorder. Cognitive therapies are used to reframe negative misconceptions and false irrational beliefs. Other areas of treatment for eating disorders include nutritional counseling and dental work.

A school psychologist can help protect students by providing information to parents, educators, and students about the signs and symptoms of eating disorders; addressing self-esteem through positive body image; addressing sociocultural factors such as media and propaganda awareness; and focusing on nutrition and healthy living. School psychologists can also be instrumental in developing prevention programs in schools that encourage good nutrition and physical fitness, reinforce healthy habits, and empower students to combat the occurrence of eating disorders. School psychologists should be equipped with a list of agencies within the community to consult if students are suspected of having eating disorders. Parents of children with suspected eating disorders should be immediately informed, as early intervention increases the likelihood of successful outcomes.

—Rebecca Miller, Coryn Lowe, and Patricia Smith

See also Etiology; Parenting; Prevention; Puberty

REFERENCES AND FURTHER READING

American Psychiatric Association. (2000). *Diagnostic and statistical manual of mental disorders* (4th ed., text rev.). Washington, DC: Author.

Davison, G. C., & Neale, J. M. (1998). *Abnormal psychology* (7th ed.). New York: Wiley.

Guide to Recovery. (2002). *Online Psychological Services.* Retrieved November 22, 2002 from http://www.psychology net.org

Hughes, J. M., La Greca, A .M., & Conoley, J. C. (2001). *Handbook of psychological services for children and adolescents.* New York: Oxford University Press.

Levine, M., & Smotak, L. (2002). Ten things parents can do to prevent eating disorders. *National Eating Disorders Association.* Retrieved November 22, 2002, from www. nationaleatingdisorders.org

Thomas Jefferson University Hospital. (2002). *Binge eating disorder.* Retrieved December 1, 2002, from http://www. jeffersonhospital.org

ECHOLALIA

Echolalia refers to persistent and inappropriate repetition or echoing of heard speech, either immediately or after a brief delay. The individual may repeat a single word or a phrase. For example, if someone says, "Let's walk over here," a child might echo, "here" or "Let's walk over here." This behavior is usually associated with Tourette's syndrome, schizophrenia, or dementia, but most commonly occurs in children with autism. Echolalia may also be associated with focal brain injury or other developmental or neurological disorders, although this is not typical. While toddlers are notorious for imitating heard speech, this strategy for language acquisition is both purposeful and fleeting. In contrast, echolalia occurs at later stages of development, including adulthood, and may be involuntary. Use of this term indicates that the speaker's facility with language is limited; echolalic speech may be irrelevant to the situation and is often characterized by unusual intonation (e.g., wooden or sing song) and inappropriate effect.

Earlier approaches to language assessment assumed that echolalic speech was random and meaningless. Recent approaches by people who work with autistic children take a different view, which is that interactive echolalic utterances may facilitate naming object, taking turns, or initiating requests; whereas noninteractive echolalia may help the autistic child regulate his or her behavior. Thus, echolalic verbalizations may represent a positive strategy that enables autistic children to communicate verbally despite significant deficits in expressive language.

—Cynthia Bainbridge Mullis

EDUCATION OF ALL HANDICAPPED CHILDREN ACT. *See* INDIVIDUALS WITH DISABILITIES EDUCATION ACT; INDIVIDUALIZED EDUCATION PLAN MEETING; SPECIAL EDUCATION

EFFECT SIZE

An effect size refers to the magnitude of the impact of treatment on an outcome measure. There are two broad families of effect size indexes: the standardized mean difference and measures of association (Kline, 2004). Both compare results across different studies or variables measured in different units and each is a first step toward evaluating the practical importance of a research finding.

For example, suppose that the same two treatments are compared in two different studies. The outcome variable in each study reflects the same construct, off-task behavior, but the standard deviation (the square root of the average squared distance of a set of scores from their mean or average [i.e., the sum of all the scores divided by the number of scores in the set]) is 10 in the first study and 50 in the second, and the mean (average) difference between treatments in each study is 5. The first study, therefore, has a larger, more powerful effect than the second study. This is because a mean difference of 5 points corresponds to half of a standard deviation in the first study (5.00/10.00) but to a tenth of a standard deviation in the second (5.00/50.00). These ratios are standardized mean differences, and they express the difference between treatments in a common metric, as the proportion of a standard deviation. Standardized mean differences and other standardized effect size indexes provide a common language for comparing results measured on different scales (Kline, 2004).

A measure of association describes the relationship between the independent and dependent variables. An example of a measure of association is the correlation coefficient, a measure of the extent of the relationship between two variables. Squaring the correlation coefficient provides the proportion of variance in the dependent variable that is explained by the independent variable. The proportion of variance (i.e., variability) can be calculated for each independent variable or can be calculated when all variables are simultaneously accounting for the variance in the dependent variable.

—*Vicki Peyton*

See also Behavior Intervention; Research

REFERENCES AND FURTHER READING

Kline, R. B. (2004). *Beyond significance testing: Reforming data analysis methods in behavioral research*. Washington, DC: American Psychological Association.

EGOCENTRISM

Egocentrism refers to error in differentiating some aspect of self-other relations (i.e., the tendency to view one's environment only from one's own point of view). Piaget saw egocentrism as a common characteristic of young children's thinking. Although it may contribute to selfish attitudes or behavior, *egocentrism* is not synonymous with *selfishness*. Research demonstrates that when minimal demands are placed on the child's perceptual and short-term memory abilities, egocentrism is reduced.

David Elkind's (1967) work yielded the concept of adolescent egocentrism—one of the most well-known and intuitively appealing theories of adolescent development. Adolescents' mistaken belief that others watch and evaluate them includes the creations of an imaginary audience and a personal fable. However, research has not supported the notion that social cognition during adolescence is egocentric. More recent research on the imaginary audience and personal fable constructs seeks to place them in a larger context of adolescent development and adjustment into young adulthood.

—*Lesa Rae Vartanian*

REFERENCES AND FURTHER READING

Elkind, D. (1967). Egocentrism in adolescence. *Child Development, 38,* 1025–1034.

ENCOPRESIS

Encopresis is the leakage of feces in children four years of age or older. This must occur at least once a month for at least three months to make a diagnosis. Children with primary or continuous encopresis have never developed control of their bowel movements. Children with secondary or discontinuous encopresis develop elimination problems after having had bowel control.

BACKGROUND

Encopresis affects 3% to 7% of school-age children and is much more common in boys than girls. Encopresis with constipation and overflow incontinence is the most common type. This type starts when children withhold bowel movements because of previously painful bowel movements, fear of the toilet, or not wanting to stop what they are doing to use the bathroom. Over time, this results in the loss of the urge to defecate and constipation. An overflow of liquid bowel occurs, resulting in soiling of clothing. The child generally doesn't experience the urge to defecate and does not intend to soil. When the child must defecate, the feces are often large and painful to pass. Once this cycle is established, children continue to withhold feces to avoid further painful elimination, and parental attention may reinforce this behavior.

Most children with encopresis do not have significant emotional problems, but do tend to have more social and behavioral problems. Attentional difficulties may be present, and a treatment goal is to help them attend to the internal cues necessary for elimination. Many children with encopresis are not aware of their own soiling, having become accustomed to the odor. They often feel ashamed and embarrassed and fear discovery by peers or parents. Coping strategies include hiding soiled clothing, avoiding peers, and acting indifferently toward the situation.

Some children have the intentional or nonretentive type of encopresis, in which they have entire bowel movements in their clothing and/or in inappropriate places such as a dresser drawer or a closet. This type of encopresis may be associated with oppositional defiant disorder or other emotional issues. Toileting behavior becomes a way for the child to exert control or express anger toward adults. Parents of children with nonretentive encopresis may find discipline and family issues are a challenge.

TREATMENT

Treatment for retentive encopresis is usually multimodal, including medical, dietary, and behavioral interventions. The goal of treatment is to establish regular bowel habits, and effectiveness rates are between 55% and 82%. Medical intervention (enemas or laxatives) to relieve constipation is the typical first step, followed by the use of laxatives or stool softeners and increasing dietary fiber to foster regular bowel movements. To establish regular toileting times the child sits on the toilet twice daily for at least 10 minutes (usually 20 minutes after breakfast and dinner to take advantage of the natural colon reflex after eating). Behavioral interventions include the use of positive reinforcement for appropriate toileting and clean clothing along with overcorrection for soiling (i.e., the child cleans himself and his clothing after soiling). Intentional or nonretentive encopresis may require individual or family therapy to resolve the problems that lead to encopresis. Controlled studies of treatment effectiveness for nonretentive encopresis are lacking.

The role of the school psychologist is to identify students with encopresis and facilitate a referral for treatment. Teacher consultation may help the teacher implement any school-based intervention plans. The school psychologist may provide supportive counseling for the child and parents. Social skills training or friendship groups could be helpful if the child has experienced a disruption in social relationships.

—*Michael B. Brown*

See also DSM-IV; Enuresis

REFERENCES AND FURTHER READING

Brown, M. B. (2004). Encopresis: A guide for parents. In A. Canter, L. Paige, M. Roth, I. Romero, & S. Carroll (Eds.), *Helping children at home and school II* (pp. S6 31–S6 34). Washington, DC: National Association of School Psychologists.

ENURESIS

Enuresis refers to repeatedly urinating in one's clothes or bed after the age of five years that is not the result of an illness or medication. For children with developmental delays, a mental age of five is necessary for a diagnosis of enuresis. In addition, the incontinence (wetting) must occur two times each week for a minimum of three months or cause significant distress. Bedwetting is one of the major reasons that children are referred to psychologists.

The two major types of enuresis are *primary* and *secondary*. Primary enuresis is when the child has never achieved a period of dryness (continence). In secondary enuresis, dryness is established for at least six months, but the child loses continence. There are three subtypes of both primary and secondary enuresis:

1. Nocturnal (nighttime)

2. Diurnal (daytime)

3. Mixed nocturnal and diurnal

Primary nocturnal enuresis is the most common as it accounts for 80% to 90% of all enuresis cases.

Enuresis is more commonly diagnosed in males— approximately 7% of males and 3% of females are enuretic at age five years. The percentage of children with enuresis decreases with age. Family history is one of the best predictors of the disease, as the majority (70%) of enuretic children have two parents who were previously enuretic. Only 15% of children with enuresis do not have a direct blood relative that was enuretic.

It has been suggested that physiological immaturity, decreased bladder capacity, sleep disorders, and psychological problems can cause enuresis. Although there is evidence of a link between physiological immaturity and enuresis, there is little to no evidence that bladder capacity or psychological problems are contributory causes. In addition, enuretic children often urinate more frequently than nonenuretic children despite having the ability to hold the same amount of urine. Although sleep disorders are not direct causes of enuresis, it seems that children with enuresis do sleep more soundly than children without it. The most likely explanation is that children with enuresis have simply failed to learn to voluntarily control their urinary sphincter.

The first step in the treatment of enuresis involves a physical exam to rule out a medical cause such as a urinary tract infection or juvenile diabetes. Because primary nocturnal enuresis is the most common form, treatment has focused on it. The urine alarm is the most successful treatment, with an approximately

75% success rate. The alarm consists of a moisture sensitive snap placed in the child's underwear. Wires travel from the pad to an alarm that fastens to the child's pajamas. When the child urinates, the electrical circuit is completed and an alarm sounds. Initially, the sound of the alarm awakens the child, signaling that the child has already urinated. Eventually, the child learns to prevent waking up by avoiding urination during sleep. An incentive program, combined with the urine alarm, seems to enhance the effectiveness of treatment.

Although a small percentage of children relapse with the use of the alarm, dryness usually returns quickly. One limitation of the urine alarm is the intense time and cooperation required from parents. The alarm is worn nightly for a minimum of three weeks and up to four to six months.

Medication is also a popular treatment for enuresis, especially among pediatricians. The three most commonly used drugs are desmopressin, imipramine, and oxybutynin chloride. Oxybutynin chloride has a reported success rate of 90% for diurnal enuresis. Although desmopressin and imipramine provide moderate success (25% to 50%), incontinence usually returns when children stop taking the drug. In addition, side effects are possible with each drug.

—*T. Steuart Watson and Nancy Foster*

See also DSM-IV; Encopresis

REFERENCES AND FURTHER READING

Friman, P.C., & Jones, K. M. (1998). Elimination disorders in children. In T. S. Watson & F. M. Gresham (Eds.), *Handbook of child behavior therapy* (pp. 239–260). New York: Plenum Press.

ERIKSON'S STAGES OF PSYCHOSOCIAL DEVELOPMENT

Erik Erikson was born in Hamburg, Germany, in 1902 and died in 1994 in Cambridge, Massachusetts. Known as the father of psychosocial development, his perspective on psychological growth grew to be quite different than that of Sigmund Freud, his early teacher. Where Freud believed that the focus of growth and development was in changing sensitive zones of the body, Erikson placed the locus of importance on the social world surrounding the individual.

In addition to this distinction, another important difference was Erikson's concern for psychological development throughout the entire life span, rather than just the years from birth through adolescence. Erikson examined the consequences of early experiences on later life and described the nature of qualitative change during the middle and later years of life.

Erikson's most lasting contribution is his description of psychosocial development, with a psychosocial task or crisis associated with each stage. Here's a brief description of each stage and the social task at hand.

STAGE 1: ORAL–SENSORY

The Psychosocial Task: Trust Versus Distrust

It is during the oral–sensory stage that the infant experiences the first of many interactions with the immediate environment and needs these outside influences to help regulate basic behaviors. The trust–mistrust continuum reflects the value of the child's experiences during the first year of life and how the child feels about interactions with outside forces. Erikson emphasized that it is not just the quantity of trustfulness that is important but the quality as well.

STAGE 2: MUSCULAR–ANAL

The Psychosocial Task: Autonomy Versus Doubt

The muscular–anal stage deals with the child's ability to regulate or control his or her own physical behavior, including the functions associated with toilet training. Erikson notes that control of all the muscles becomes the focus of the child's surplus energy. Not only are children expected to develop control of the muscles that deal with elimination, they are also expected to develop some control of impulses in general. This change leads to a successful feeling of control over one's behavior, as opposed to feelings of less control.

STAGE 3: LOCOMOTOR–GENITAL

The Psychosocial Task: Initiative Versus Guilt

Erikson believed that the locomotor–genital stage is set by social expectations for independent movement and motivation as a result of new-found autonomy and control. The locomotor component of this stage represents the child's movement away from the dependency on parents and toward the ability to meet personal needs. Children become capable of initiating more complex actions on their own, resulting in more gratification than was possible earlier when they were more dependent on parents.

STAGE 4: LATENCY

The Psychosocial Task: Industry Versus Inferiority

Erikson believed that the latency time of development is crucial for the child's sense of industry, which is seen as the ability to master the social skills necessary to compete and function successfully in the society in which the child lives. At this stage of development, cultural expectations take precedence over other needs, and the ability to master certain skills and abilities becomes paramount. For children who are not even given the opportunity to master their own world or who have their efforts blocked, these unsuccessful experiences lead to a sense of inferiority, or lack of worthiness.

STAGE 5: PUBERTY AND ADOLESCENCE

The Psychosocial Task: Identity Versus Role Confusion

Puberty is a time when some of the most drastic changes occur in all spheres of individual development. Up to this time, the child has not experienced such great changes in both physical and psychological capacities and needs. Adolescents are expected to begin defining their interests in terms of career choices, further education, trade skills, and raising a family. Both biologically and culturally, adolescence is considered the end of childhood and the entrance into adulthood. This time is one of great change and excitement, and it is also when the individual develops an identity, or a definition of self.

STAGE 6: YOUNG ADULTHOOD

The Psychosocial Task: Intimacy Versus Isolation

Because Erikson's theory of psychosocial development is based on the notion of stages and what he called the epigenetic process, development will be optimally successful if the crisis associated with each stage is successfully resolved. Stage 6 illustrates how important dependency on earlier stages is. For the first time, new goals and tasks that directly involve other people are placed before individuals, and they are expected not only to develop and meet career goals, but also to begin the developmental process of interacting with others of the same and opposite sex.

STAGE 7: ADULTHOOD

The Psychosocial Task: Generativity Versus Stagnation

One of the important elements of Erikson's theory is that development is a continuous, ongoing process. For the young adult who is well on the way to a successful career and intimate personal relationships, the relevant task is to generate whatever is necessary to define a style or life role. A major component of stage 7 is emphasis on continuity with preceding stages. The sense of generativity that the adult feels comes from efforts to have some part in supporting and encouraging the development of the next generation. Those individuals who cannot lend this continuity to the next generation may become overly absorbed in personal needs, ignore the needs of others, and gradually become stagnated.

STAGE 8: MATURITY

The Psychosocial Task: Ego integrity Versus Despair

Erikson used the term *ego integrity* to describe older people who have come to recognize, after a lifetime of successfully resolving conflicts, that they have led a meaningful, productive, and worthwhile life. Stage 8 has mystical elements, and Erikson stresses the importance of being "one with your past," and creating and feeling a new love for the human ego and not necessarily for oneself. The older person can dispense wisdom to young children. This wisdom has traveled the hard and difficult road from basic trust–mistrust conflict experienced as an infant through this final stage of realization. If development has proceeded successfully through the years, Erikson considered that this stage consists in taking or gaining a perspective on what has occurred.

—Neil J. Salkind

ESCAPE. *See* Behavior; Behavior Intervention

ETHICAL ISSUES IN SCHOOL PSYCHOLOGY

ETHICS

The term *ethics* refers to a system of principles of conduct that guide and limit the behavior of an individual. Ethics is composed of a range of acceptable (or unacceptable) social and personal behaviors, from rules of etiquette to more basic rules of society. Ethics defines both what is good for the individual and society, and the obligations people owe themselves and one another. A system of ethics develops within the context of a society or culture, and may change over time as the society changes.

The terms ethics and morality are often used interchangeably. However, according to philosophers such as Solomon (1984), the term *morality* refers to a subset of ethical rules of special importance. Moral rules can be differentiated from other aspects of ethics in that they are more important, fundamental, universal, rational, and objective. A society's moral rules, if violated, typically result in strong disapproval or punishment.

The term *applied professional ethics* refers to the application of broad ethical principles and specific rules to the problems that arise in professional practice. W. D. Ross, a 20th-century English philosopher, identified a number of principles that provide a foundation for the ethical codes of psychologists and other professionals: nonmaleficence, fidelity, beneficence, justice, and autonomy (Bersoff & Koeppl, 1993).

CODES OF ETHICS

Professional organizations such as the American Psychological Association (APA) and the National Association of School Psychologists (NASP) adopt codes of ethics to protect the welfare of consumers of psychological services and maintain the public trust in psychology. These codes are drafted by committees within professional organizations, and reflect the beliefs of association members about what constitutes appropriate professional conduct. When practitioners violate codes of ethics, they may face sanctions by their professional organization. Adoption of a formal code of ethics also serves to enhance the prestige of the profession, and may reduce the perceived need for external regulation and control.

The NASP's *Professional Conduct Manual* (NASP, 2000) was developed to provide guidelines specifically for school psychologists employed in the schools or in independent practice. The NASP's code focuses on protecting the well-being of the student/client, but also prescribes conduct to protect the rights and welfare of parents, teachers, and other consumers of school psychological services. The code provides guidelines in:

- Professional competence
- Professional relationships with students, parents, the school, the community, other professionals, and trainees and interns
- Advocacy of the rights and welfare of the student/client
- Professional responsibilities in assessment and intervention
- Reporting data and sharing results
- Use of materials and technology
- Research, publication, and presentation
- Professional responsibilities related to independent practice

The APA's *Ethical Principles of Psychologists and Code of Conduct* (2002) consists of general principles and specific ethical standards to protect the welfare of individuals and groups with whom psychologists work. The APA's code differs from the NASP's *Professional Conduct Manual* in that it was developed for psychologists with training in diverse specialty areas (e.g., clinical, industrial-organizational, school), and who work in a number of different settings (private practice, industry, hospitals and clinics, public schools, university teaching, and research). The sections comprising the APA's code are Introduction and Applicability, Preamble, General Principles, and Ethical Standards. The General Principles section includes five broadly worded aspirational goals to be considered by psychologists in ethical decision making:

1. Principle A is Beneficence and Nonmaleficence. In accordance with this principle, psychologists engage in professional actions that are likely to benefit others, or at least do no harm.

2. Principle B is Fidelity and Responsibility. Fidelity refers to a continuing faithfulness to one's professional duties (Bersoff & Koeppl, 1993). Consistent with this principle, school psychologists build and maintain trust by being aware of, and honoring, their professional responsibilities to clients and community.

3. Principle C is Integrity. The principle of Integrity obligates school psychologists to be open and honest in their professional interactions, faithful to the truth, and to guard against unclear or unwise commitments.

4. Principle D is Justice. In accordance with this principle, school psychologists seek to ensure that all persons have access to and can benefit from what school psychology has to offer, and strive for fairness and nondiscrimination in the provision of services.

5. Principle E is Respect for People's Rights and Dignity. It encourages school psychologists to respect the worth of all people, and their rights to privacy, confidentiality, autonomy, and self-determination. Psychologists have an obligation to safeguard the rights of those who cannot make autonomous decisions (e.g., minor clients).

The Ethical Standards section of the 2002 APA Ethics Code sets forth enforceable *rules for conduct.* The standards are organized into six general sections on Resolving Ethical Issues, Competence, Human Relations, Privacy and Confidentiality, Advertising and Other Public Representations, and Record Keeping and Fees. These are followed by sections on Education and Training, Research and Publication, Assessment, and Therapy (APA, 2002).

The ethical codes of both the NASP and the APA provide guidance for the professional in decision making. Ethical conduct, however, involves careful choices based on knowledge of broad principles, ethics codes, and ethical reasoning. In many situations, more than one course of action is acceptable. In some situations, no course of action is completely satisfactory. In all situations, the responsibility for ethical conduct rests with the individual practitioner.

ETHICS AND LAW

Many aspects of school psychological practice are regulated by federal and state laws. Law is a body of rules of conduct prescribed by the state that have binding legal force. Failure to comply with the law can result in legal action against the practitioner (e.g., malpractice suits) or the school, and possible loss of certification or licensure to practice. Although both ethical principles and law guide and regulate behavior, law and ethics are not mutually inclusive. Many acts that would be considered unethical are not prohibited by law, as the law does not simply codify ethical norms.

Both the NASP and the APA codes of ethics require practitioners to know the law. According to Ballantine (1979), ethical behavior must conform with the law, not defy it. Professional codes of ethics are generally viewed as requiring decisions that are "more correct or more stringent" than required by law (Ballantine, 1979, p. 636). If the ethical responsibilities of psychologists conflict with a law, psychologists make known their commitment to their code of ethics and take steps to resolve the conflict in a responsible manner. However, if the conflict continues to be irresolvable via such means, psychologists may adhere to the requirements of the law as long as doing so is in keeping with basic principles of human rights (APA, 2002).

ETHICS TRAINING

Both the NASP and the APA require formal coursework in ethics as a component of graduate training. Growing consensus exists within psychology that ethics education should consist of a planned, multilevel approach that includes formal coursework along with supervised discussion of ethical issues in practicum and internship settings. A number of goals for ethics training have been suggested in the literature. Ideally, as a result of multilevel training in professional ethics, students learn (Jacob & Hartshorne, 2003):

- Sensitivity to the ethical components of daily practice
- A sound working knowledge of the content of ethical codes
- A commitment to a proactive rather than a reactive stance in ethical thinking and conduct
- The ability to analyze the ethical dimensions of a situation and "think through" issues using a problem-solving model
- Sensitivity to the ways in which personal values and standards for behavior may differ for

individuals from diverse cultural and experiential backgrounds

- An awareness of the role of personal feelings and values in ethical decision making
- An appreciation of the complexity of ethical decisions, tolerance for ambiguity and uncertainty, and acceptance that there may be more than one appropriate course of action
- The personal strength to act on decisions made and accept responsibility for actions

ETHICAL DILEMMAS

Most ethically challenging situations encountered by practitioners concern difficult situations rather than clear-cut violations of the specific rules outlined in professional codes of ethics. Ethical dilemmas are created by situations involving competing ethical principles, conflicts between ethics and law, dilemmas inherent in the dual roles of employee and pupil advocate, conflicting interests of multiple clients (e.g., pupil, parents, classmates), and poor educational practices. All of these situations are potentially harmful to students (Jacob & Hartshorne, 2003).

PROBLEM-SOLVING MODELS

Eberlein (1987) suggests that mastery of an explicit decision-making model or procedure may not only help the practitioner make informed, well-reasoned, choices when dilemmas arise in professional practice, but also will allow the practitioner to describe *how* a decision was made. This may afford some protection when difficult decisions come under the scrutiny of others. Furthermore, practitioners may find a systematic decision-making model helpful in anticipating and preventing problems from occurring.

A number of ethical decision-making models have been proposed in the literature (see Cottone & Claus, 2000, for a review). The following eight-step problem-solving model is adapted from Koocher and Keith-Spiegel (1998, pp. 12–15):

1. Describe the situation.

2. Define the potential ethical-legal issues involved.

3. Consult ethical and legal guidelines and district policies that might apply to the resolution of each issue, and consult with colleagues as

needed. Consider the broad ethical principles and specific mandates involved.

4. Evaluate the rights, responsibilities, and welfare of all affected parties, while considering the cultural characteristics of affected parties that may be salient to the decision.

5. Generate a list of alternative decisions possible for each issue.

6. Enumerate and evaluate the short-term, ongoing, and long-term consequences of each possible decision, considering the possible psychological, social, and economic costs to affected parties.

7. Present any evidence that the various consequences or benefits resulting from each decision will actually occur (i.e., a risk–benefit analysis).

8. Make the decision. Consistent with codes of ethics, school psychologists accept responsibility for the decision made and monitor the consequences of the course of action chosen.

ETHICAL ISSUES

The primary ethical obligation of school psychology practitioners is to protect the welfare and rights of schoolchildren. In addition, there are a number of more specific ethical issues that cut across their many job roles. In all roles, school psychologists practice within the boundaries of their competence and accept responsibility for their actions. They are sensitive to and respectful of cultural, individual, and role differences, and knowledgeable of the ways in which diversity factors may influence a student's learning, behavior, and development. In all roles, school psychologists respect people's rights to privacy, confidentiality, and autonomy/self-determination.

Privacy has been defined as "the freedom of individuals to choose for themselves the time and the circumstances under which and the extent to which their beliefs, behaviors, and opinions are to be shared or withheld from others" (Siegel, 1979, p. 251). The school child's right to privacy is a legal and an ethical issue. Statutory and case laws have recognized the need to balance the interest of the state (school) in fulfilling its duty to maintain order, ensure pupil safety, and educate children, with the personal freedoms and rights generally afforded citizens. Consequently, in the school setting, students do not have the full range of privacy rights afforded adult citizens, but they are not without privacy protections. A school child has privacy rights with regard to his or her person (body) and personal possessions (U.S. Constitution); education records (Family Educational Rights and Privacy Act of 1974 [FERPA]); and private thoughts, beliefs, and behaviors (e.g., the Protection of Pupil Rights Act of 1978).

Respect for client privacy is also an ethical mandate. Consistent with the general principle of respect for the dignity of persons and the valuing of autonomy, school psychologists are obligated to respect the pupil's (or other client's) right to self-determine the circumstances under which they disclose private information. Furthermore, every effort is made to minimize intrusions on privacy.

Ethical codes, professional standards, and law are consistent in requiring parental consent (or the consent of an adult student) for school actions that may result in a significant intrusion on personal or family privacy beyond what might be expected in the course of ordinary classroom and school activities. Consequently, with the exception of unusual situations, informed consent is obtained prior to the provision of psychological services. In the delivery of psychological services in the schools, as elsewhere, the three key elements of informed consent are that it must be knowing, competent, and voluntary. Knowing means the individual giving consent has a clear understanding of what it is they are consenting to. Competent means legally competent to give consent. In law, adults are presumed to be competent, while minors are presumed not to be capable of making legally binding decisions; consequently, consent typically is sought from the parent or guardian of a minor child prior to the provision of services. Parental consent may be bypassed in emergency situations (e.g., student is suicidal) and, in some states, minors may self-refer for psychological assistance independent of parental notice or consent. The third element of informed consent is that it must be voluntary; that is, consent is obtained without coercion or undue enticement. Federal education law outlines specific requirements for informed consent for psychological evaluation of students with suspected disabilities and for the release of information from school records.

School psychologists are ethically obligated to respect the confidentiality of information obtained during their professional work. Information is revealed only with the informed consent of the client, or the client's parent or legal guardian, except in those situations in which failure to release information would result in clear danger to the client or others. The interpretation of the principle of confidentiality as it relates to the delivery of psychological services in the school setting is a complicated matter. However, one clear guideline emerges from the literature on confidentiality in the school setting. School psychologists define the parameters of confidentiality at the onset of offering services. The parameters of the promise of confidentiality will vary depending on the nature of the services offered.

In the provision of direct services to the student, there are three situations in which the school psychologist is obligated to share confidential student–client disclosures with others:

1. When the student requests it

2. When there is a situation involving danger to the student or others (e.g., potential suicide, suspected child abuse or neglect, a student who is a danger to others)

3. When there is a legal obligation to testify in a court of law

Thus, for school practitioners, concern for the welfare of schoolchildren is the top priority in-service delivery. In addition, there are also special ethical concerns associated with specific job roles. When practitioners conduct psychological assessments of individual students, ethics codes require that they select assessment instruments that are valid for the purpose of the assessment and for the student being tested, and appropriate to the student's language preference and competence. Failure to do so may result in misdiagnosis, misclassification, miseducation, and possible psychological harm. For example, it would be unethical for a practitioner to give a standard IQ test in English to a student with limited English proficiency and then to interpret the score as a measure of intellectual ability.

When psychologists assist in planning interventions for students with learning difficulties or behavior problems, they are ethically obligated to recommend evidence-based interventions—those techniques that the profession considers to be responsible, research-based practice. They also are obligated to minimize harm. Consistent with these principles, experts in the ethics of applied behavior analysis advise psychologists to select the most positive, least punitive procedures that are likely to be effective when planning interventions. For example, it would be unethical for a psychologist to recommend use of time-out procedures to reduce an undesired student behavior unless differential reinforcement (positive reinforcement for appropriate behavior) had first been tried and found ineffective.

Consultation also can pose special ethical challenges, particularly when there are conflicting interests, values, and beliefs of multiple parties (parent, pupil, school). For example, when providing consultation to a team meeting to determine the placement of a pupil with special education needs, the parents might request full-time placement in regular education so their child can benefit from social interaction with students who are not disabled. The regular classroom teacher might believe part-time placement in a special education classroom is justified on the basis of greater academic benefit. The psychologist is ethically obligated to advocate for what he or she believes is in the best interest of the student, taking into account the mandates of special education law.

There also are special ethical issues associated with supervision of trainees. School psychologists who supervise interns are responsible for the professional practices of the persons being supervised. This may pose a dilemma because, for the supervisee to learn new skills, the supervisor must assign new and challenging tasks; yet he or she must ensure that client welfare is not compromised because of the supervisee's lack of competence. Thus, the supervisor must protect the client from the supervisee's errors by monitoring the supervisee closely enough to ensure the competent delivery of services. Failure to do so is unethical.

UNETHICAL CONDUCT

As noted previously, among the functions of professional associations are to develop and promote standards to enhance the quality of work by its members. By encouraging appropriate professional conduct, associations such as the APA and the NASP strive to ensure that each person served will receive the highest quality of service and thus build and maintain public trust in psychology and psychologists. The APA and the NASP both support a standing ethics committee composed of volunteer members of the professional association. These committees

respond to informal inquiries about ethical issues, investigate complaints about possible code violations by association members, and impose sanctions on violators. Ethics committees only investigate complaints regarding violation of specific ethical standards. While the general ethical principles outlined in ethics codes provide guidance in decision making, they are not the basis for imposing sanctions. Both the NASP and the APA list a number of possible sanctions for ethics code violations, such as requesting that the respondent take corrective measures, issuing an educative letter, censuring or reprimanding the violator, requiring restitution or an apology, imposing a period of probation, or evicting the violator from the organization.

—*Susan Jacob and Jonnie Taton*

See also Confidentiality; Informed Consent

REFERENCES AND FURTHER READING

American Psychological Association. (2002). Ethical principles of psychologists and code of conduct. *American Psychologist, 57,* 1060–1073.

Ballantine, H. T. (1979). The crisis in ethics, anno domini 1979. *New England Journal of Medicine, 301,* 634–638.

Bersoff, D. N., & Koeppl, P. M. (1993). The relation between ethical codes and moral principles. *Ethics and Behavior, 3,* 345–357.

Cottone, R. R., & Claus, R. E. (2000). Ethical decision-making models: A review of the literature. *Journal of Counseling & Development, 78,* 275–283.

Eberlein, L. (1987). Introducing ethics to beginning psychologists: A problem-solving approach. *Professional Psychology: Research and Practice, 18,* 353–359.

Family Educational Rights and Privacy Act of 1974 (part of Pub. L. No 93–380), 20 U.S.C. § 1232g (1974). Regulations appear at 34 C.F.R. § Part 99.

Jacob, S., & Hartshorne, T. S. (2003). *Ethics and law for school psychologists* (4th ed.). Hoboken, NJ: Wiley.

Koocher, G., & Keith-Spiegel, P. (1998). *Ethics in psychology* (2nd ed.). New York: Oxford.

National Association of School Psychologists. (2000). *Professional conduct manual.* Bethesda, MD: Author.

Protection of Pupil Rights Act. A 1978 amendment to the Elementary and Secondary Education Act of 1965. Amended in 1994 by Pub. L. No. 103–227 and in 2001 by Pub. L. No. 107–110.

Siegel, M. (1979). Privacy, ethics, and confidentiality. *Professional Psychology, 10,* 249–258.

Solomon, R. S. (1984). *Ethics: A brief introduction.* New York: McGraw-Hill.

ETIOLOGY

Etiology refers to the presumed cause of an individual's difficulties. Typically with children and adolescents, the range of potential single or multiple causes to explain the difficulties these individuals encounter is often extensive (Kamphaus & Frick, 2002). For example, a host of etiologies have been suggested to explain the occurrence of an attention deficit hyperactivity disorder (ADHD) in children and adolescents, including neurological factors (e.g., prenatal and perinatal complications; abnormalities in brain structure, function, or chemistry; exposure to environmental toxins; and infections), genetic factors, and environmental factors (e.g., certain parenting characteristics and parenting styles, chaotic home environment, and poverty). The etiologies of some difficulties or disorders may be solely biological, psychological, social, or a combination of the three. Knowledge of the etiology is relevant to school psychologists engaged in educational and psychological practice in the schools, because knowledge of the cause will direct intervention efforts and development of prevention programs.

—*Patricia A. Lowe*

See also Diagnosis and Labeling

REFERENCES AND FURTHER READING

Kamphaus, R. W., & Frick, P. J. (2002). *Clinical assessment of child and adolescent personality and behavior* (2nd ed.). Boston, MA: Allyn & Bacon.

EVALUATION. *See* PROGRAM EVALUATION; REPORTS (PSYCHOLOGICAL)

EVIDENCE-BASED INTERVENTIONS

The term *evidence-based* is often in the educational and psychological literature as the level of evidence that supports the efficacy, generality, and use of a practice as indicated by research. The more specific term *evidence-based interventions* (EBIs) refers to intervention or treatment approaches that are supported by sufficient scientific or research evidence. In determining the evidence base of a prevention or intervention approach or program, consideration is given to the level, degree, and/or type of research supporting the conclusion that a prevention/intervention/treatment is effective. An evaluation of the evidence base to support an intervention requires examining whether reliable and valid methods were applied in documenting the effectiveness of prevention and intervention programs. In addition, consideration is given to critical aspects of the intervention, including its:

- Acceptability (degree to which consumers find the intervention procedures and outcomes acceptable in their daily lives)
- Feasibility (degree to which intervention components can be implemented in naturalistic contexts)
- Social validity (relevance of the targeted outcomes to the everyday life of consumers)
- Fidelity or integrity (extent to which an intervention is carried out as intended)
- Sustainability (extent to which the intervention can be maintained without support from external agents)

RELEVANCE OF EVIDENCE-BASED INTERVENTIONS TO SCHOOL PSYCHOLOGY

Most practitioners and researchers agree there is an urgent need for proven practices that improve educational and psychological outcomes. The primary basis for the EBI movement in school psychology is to translate research into effective practices in the hope that such translation efforts will improve the quality of services for children, including those with and without disabilities, and their families. Through an interest in EBIs, the field of school psychology recognizes a need for prevention and intervention practices that improve learning, social–emotional, and behavioral performance outcomes for students. In brief, the EBI movement is consistent with initiatives to promote student success, effective schools, and family well-being.

RATIONALE AND HISTORY OF THE EVIDENCE-BASED MOVEMENT IN SCHOOL PSYCHOLOGY

Educational and psychological practices, including those occurring for prevention and intervention purposes, seldom produce intended effects for all individuals under all conditions (Kratochwill &

Stoiber, 2002). In addition, there are research-supported effective intervention approaches that tend not to be frequently used in typical educational settings. School psychology practitioners and researchers need valid information to guide the application of prevention and intervention methods to the range of school contexts and populations they serve (i.e., there is a need to translate research and scientific-based approaches to diverse settings and problems as well as to specific field-based contexts).

The EBI movement has roots both in psychology and education. Since British psychologist Hans Eysenck (1952) provocatively questioned the effectiveness of psychotherapy, the notion of whether and how psychologists make clinical decisions based on science has remained a hotly debated issue. To counter a non-scientific or "clinical judgment" approach in school psychology, the training approach commonly referred to as the "scientist–practitioner model" (an equal emphasis on learning clinical practice and research skills in a training program) has been widely embraced. Despite widespread endorsement of a scientist–practitioner model at the graduate school psychology training level, many question the degree to which empirical results actually guide the practice of school psychologists. Although little formal documentation exists on the basis of psychologists' clinical decisions, legitimate concerns have been raised regarding the actual use of research knowledge by practitioners (Nathan, 1998).

Perhaps one of the most noteworthy developments to occur within psychology and mental health fields has been the attempt to formalize criteria for evaluating the effectiveness of interventions and to document which approaches or programs show significant, intended results. This development is in direct response to pressure from the managed health care movement (HMOs) and the focus on cost containment in the medical profession. Treatment guidelines based on a patient's diagnosis were developed for medical treatments in efforts to promote cost efficiency. Pressure increased to expand such guidelines to include mental health conditions, and thus the American Psychological Association (APA) formed the Task Force on Psychological Intervention Guidelines (1995). In response to these trends, members of Division 12 (clinical psychology) of the APA and others began the process of identifying criteria by which psychological interventions could be judged (Weisz & Hawley, 1999). It was argued that such efforts would best preserve the ability of

psychology to identify interventions that are of value to clients and eligible for reimbursement by insurance or other third-party payers.

Although the issues surrounding managed health care and third-party reimbursement in psychology are important to understand, school psychologists typically work in educational settings and thus must be responsive to the unique context of schools. When moving research to practice in educational settings, the day-to-day demands and structure of schools, which can be more chaotic and less controlled than clinical settings, must be considered. Thus, school psychologists do not provide *treatments* to students under the same conditions that characterize clinical practice. Whereas in clinical psychology it may prove most useful to prescribe treatments based on what has been found to work or be effective, school psychology has avoided the development of dichotomous lists, where an intervention is judged either to be efficacious or as not meeting established criteria. Rather, the level of evidence is thought to exist along a continuum—knowledge of intervention effects is evolving through the implementation of a variety of research methodologies as opposed to being a static understanding.

PURPOSE AND ORGANIZATION OF THE PROCEDURAL AND CODING MANUAL

A major task undertaken in school psychology has been the construction of a manual titled the *Procedural and Coding Manual for Review of Evidence-Based Interventions* (hereafter called the *Procedural and Coding Manual*). The purpose of the *Procedural and Coding Manual* is to describe the procedures developed by the Task Force on Evidence-Based Interventions in School Psychology (Kratochwill & Stoiber, 2002) to identify, review, and code studies of psychological and educational interventions for a wide variety of academic, social–emotional, and related prevention and intervention programs for school-aged children and their families.

The *Procedural and Coding Manual* attempts to address the diversity apparent in schools as well as new methodological directions in psychological and educational intervention research. It includes technical codes and is intended to provide users with detailed guidelines for how to code the evidence from studies on various interventions.

The general characteristics coding examines the empirical/theoretical basis, general design qualities, and statistical treatment of the prevention/intervention under review. These coding criteria address whether a strong theoretical or empirical basis for conducting the study has been established, the overall quality of the research design, and the use of an appropriate outcome evaluation (i.e., statistical procedures). The second type of criteria, called key evidence components, focuses on the validity criteria of school- or field-based intervention studies. To determine whether interventions are effective, several criteria are invoked, including:

- Outcome measurement procedures that are valid, reliable, multimethod (i.e., different techniques), and multisource (i.e., parent, teacher respondents)
- A comparison group demonstrating the same target problem to test outcome differences when a group design is used (i.e., group equivalence established)
- Key outcomes that are statistically significant
- Equivalent mortality (dropping out of the study) for participants
- Evidence of durability of effects
- Identifiable components indicating what aspects of the intervention produced what outcomes
- Evidence of intervention fidelity/integrity
- Information on replication

Each of these eight key evidence components is evaluated using a "benchmark" or "standards" scoring structure ranging from 0 to 3 (where 3 = strong evidence/support, 2 = promising evidence/support, 1 = weak evidence/support, 0 = no evidence/support). The third type of information addressed within the EBI criteria refers to other dimensions or considerations that consumers may want to consider when evaluating the appropriateness of an intervention for their specific needs. Within the third set of criteria is an examination of external validity indicators (e.g., factors external to the study like treatment interference or experimenter behavior), including descriptive information on participant characteristics and the context within which the intervention occurred.

POTENTIAL ADVANTAGES AND DISADVANTAGES OF EVIDENCE-BASED INTERVENTIONS

From a conceptual perspective, efforts aimed at identifying prevention and intervention strategies that have strong evidence would seem to be applauded by researchers and practitioners. However, several criticisms of the evidence-based movement have been noted, including an overreliance on randomized clinical trials, poor generalization of interventions from research to field-based settings, failure to address the presence of comorbid conditions or complex issues frequently found in real world settings, and the artificial nature of "manualized" interventions. Another possible disadvantage of the EBI effort is that it can narrow the scope of professional practice by creating rigid lists of interventions deemed as "empirically supported" or "evidence-based," which could result in clinicians becoming psychological technicians, mechanistically applying a narrow list of approved interventions. For this reason, the perspective taken in school psychology toward defining and determining EBIs is that no single list of "approved" interventions can adequately address the complexities inherent in educational settings.

One of the most important advantages of identifying EBIs is to enhance the functioning of psychologists as scientist practitioners (e.g., Stoiber & Kratochwill, 2000). At its most fundamental level, the scientist–practitioner model endorses a vision of psychologists who embrace critical, scientific thinking skills in their approach to the unique problems that confront them. This involves a complex array of decision-making processes that consider setting factors (e.g., the situation in which the experiment takes place) as well as the characteristics of the children, teachers, and parents involved.

Given this complex context of effective practice, the rich, descriptive, dimensional approach undertaken in school psychology to determine EBIs should help promote improved intervention planning and implementation by practitioners. By providing relevant and practical information about intervention options to practitioners, an understanding of EBIs should enhance both the flexibility and the rigor of professional problem solving. As such, EBI efforts are viewed as consistent with the core values of the scientist–practitioner, but more importantly, as positive and empowering for school psychologists. The systematic delineation of what types of evidence support which interventions facilitates the important reciprocal relationship between theory and scientific research. In addition, the EBI effort assists researchers in identifying gaps in the scientific literature, thus leading to more strategic investigations of those interventions and demonstrating the greatest potential for effectiveness. Together such efforts will lead to a more credible and accountable approach to intervention planning, monitoring, and implementation, and, ultimately, should improve the quality of school psychology services for children and families.

—Karen C. Stoiber, Gretchen Lewis-Snyder, and Michelle A. Miller

See also Comorbidity; Effect Size; Research

REFERENCES AND FURTHER READING

American Psychological Association. (1995). *Template for developing guidelines: Interventions for mental disorders and psychosocial aspects of physical disorders.* Washington, DC: Author.

Eysenck, H. (1952). The effects of psychotherapy: An evaluation. *Journal of Consulting Psychology, 16,* 319–324.

Kratochwill, T. R., & Stoiber, K. C. (2002). Evidence-based interventions within school psychology: Conceptual foundations of the procedural and coding manual of Division 16 and the Society for the Study of School Psychology Task Force. *School Psychology Quarterly, 17*(4), 341–389.

Nathan, P. E. (1998). Practice guidelines: Not yet ideal. *American Psychologist, 53,* 290–299.

Stoiber, K. C., & Kratochwill, T. R. (2000). Empirically supported interventions and school psychology: Rationale and methodological issues—Part I. *School Psychology Quarterly, 15,* 75–105.

Weisz, J. R., & Hawley, K. (1999). *Procedural and coding manual for identification of beneficial treatments.* Washington, DC: American Psychological Association, Society for Clinical Psychology Division 12 Committee on Science and Practice.

EXPULSION

Expulsion, a punishment technique used to manage serious behavior problems, involves the long-term exclusion of a student from school and school-related activities. Such exclusion occurs following a set of procedures, usually including a formal school board hearing with the student and parent present. Written notification of the hearing and its results are provided. Readmission following expulsion is generally not permissible until the following academic year and after action from the school board.

Expulsion is considered to be the ultimate punishment for serious rules violations in the school. Skiba and Noam (2002) note that, in the aftermath of serious school violence, techniques to prevent violence and to intervene with at-risk children have come to the educational policy forefront. Many schools have adopted zero-tolerance policies, thus leading to increases in the number of students expelled from school and the length of time they are expelled. Typical reasons for expulsion include habitual disruptiveness, severe aggression, unsafe conduct, habitual truancy, drug-related incidents, severe threats (e.g., bomb), illegal behaviors, and carrying of weapons (e.g., knife); whereas carrying a firearm requires a minimum one-year expulsion, based on the Safe Schools Act.

Students at risk for expulsion include those with disruptive behavior problems, such as attention deficit hyperactivity disorder and conduct disorder. Given that these are male-dominated disorders, it is not surprising that boys are twice as likely as girls to be expelled from school, according to the U.S. Department of Education. Research by Morrison and D'Incau (1997) shows that students with a history of special education, including below-average grades and achievement scores, are also at risk, particularly when children exhibit emotional and behavioral risk factors in addition to their disability. A student with a disability is given a manifestation determination hearing following the decision for expulsion, which involves a meeting of the student's Individualized Education Plan (IEP) team. If it is determined that the misconduct resulted from the student's disability or from an inappropriate placement for the disability, then the student cannot be expelled. Although school systems are obligated to provide continuing services to the child with disabilities, they must balance that obligation with their responsibility to all students.

Expelled students are typically offered alternative education programs to either help them graduate or aid in their reintegration to the regular school. According to the U.S. Department of Education, these programs usually have a low student-to-teacher ratio, highly trained staff, and intensive counseling and monitoring, among other key components. Nevertheless, research by the U.S. Department of Education shows a positive association between expulsion and later school dropout. Thus, students, schools, and society may benefit from less severe disciplinary alternatives in the regular school setting, if appropriate. These may include time-out (e.g., sent to a disciplinary room or the principal's office), privilege removal (e.g., not allowed to attend a field trip), in-school suspension, and short-term or long-term out-of-school suspension. Alternatives that focus on teaching and reinforcing appropriate behaviors are particularly appealing, such as those reviewed by Wiseman and Hunt (2001), given that children usually benefit from reinforcement of positive behaviors.

—*Tammy D. Barry and John E. Lochman*

See also Discipline; Due Process; Individualized Education Plan; Manifestation Determination; Special Education; Suspension; Violence in Schools

REFERENCES AND FURTHER READING

Morrison, G. M., & D'Incau, B. (1997). The web of zero-tolerance: Characteristics of students who are recommended for expulsion from school. *Education and Treatment of Children, 20,* 316–335.

Skiba, R. J., & Noam, G. G. (2002). *Zero tolerance: Can suspension and expulsion keep school safe?* San Francisco: Jossey-Bass/Pfeiffer.

Wiseman, D. G., & Hunt, G. H. (2001). *Best practice in motivation and management in the classroom.* Springfield, IL: Charles C Thomas.

U.S. Department of Education. (n.d.). Available online from http://www.ed.gov

EXTINCTION AND RECOVERY. *See* BEHAVIOR; APPLIED BEHAVIOR ANALYSIS

F

FACILITATED COMMUNICATION

Facilitated communication (FC) is an augmentative communication method that purportedly allows persons with severe communication and other disabilities to demonstrate an unanticipated ability to communicate that significantly exceeds the boundaries of their potential abilities. Assisted by hand-over-hand support or other types of physical assistance from an individual without disabilities, individuals with disabilities thought to have limited communication and other abilities purportedly are able to type FC-enhanced thoughts and ideas that are extraordinary. After only minimal experience with FC, individuals with severe disabilities allegedly have communicated that they have normal intelligence and adept social skills and knowledge. Other individuals have revealed that through FC they are for the first time in their lives able to communicate. Others with severe disabilities have allegedly communicated that they are trapped within a body that prohibits them from competently communicating with others because of a condition known as *global apraxia.* Biklen (1992) stated that persons with global apraxia may have normal intelligence and language processing abilities, and when permitted to use FC, these individuals may, indeed, reveal their normal intelligence and good communication abilities.

Rosemary Crossley, an Australian, is acknowledged as the developer of FC. During the 1970s she worked at the St. Nicholas Institution in Melbourne with persons with multiple disabilities, most of whom were thought to have severe and profound retardation.

At St. Nicholas, Crossley became acquainted with a young woman who had athetoid cerebral palsy. This individual was unable to effectively communicate, feed herself, or walk. Although the staff at the institution believed the young woman to have profound retardation, Crossley was convinced that she had more ability than she was given credit. Crossley also considered her capable of communication if given assistance.

By supporting the woman's index finger, Crossley found that she was able to identify many objects by pointing. Using a procedure similar to what is now known as facilitated communication, Crossley was able to assist this young woman to read and write by pointing to letters with facilitation. In 1979, when the woman was 18 years of age, she left the institution to live with Crossley. Crossley and the young woman were instrumental in closing the St. Nicholas institution, based on claims that the staff treated residents in an inhumane fashion.

In 1986 the Dignity through Education and Language Communication Centre (DEAL) opened in Victoria, Australia, to assist persons with severe communication disorders. Crossley introduced facilitated communication to DEAL, because of her belief that clients' physical problems did not permit them to readily use standard augmentative communication devices. Facilitated communication was determined to be an effective communication option for many of DEAL's clients, including those thought to have mental retardation and autism.

Douglas Biklen is given credit for introducing facilitated communication in the United States. He saw FC used at the DEAL Centre, during which individuals with severe disabilities revealed unexpected literacy and abilities. Biklen was impressed by the alleged desire of many of these students to be in normalized educational settings and to be able to use their purported FC-supported skills in general education classrooms. Upon his return to the United States, Biklen introduced FC to the Syracuse, New York, public school system. Based on the remarkable success he purportedly witnessed, Biklen (1990) wrote an article strongly supporting FC.

From that point, word of FC spread throughout the United States. Professionals and parents perceived it to be the breakthrough that ultimately would allow people with severe disabilities to reveal their true abilities. Remarking on the rapid spread of FC information, Rimland (1992b) noted that "facilitated communication workshops spread throughout the country and virtually every major newspaper, news magazine and news show ran stories on facilitated communication" (p. 1). Because of its interactive connection and lack of scientific support, controversy also quickly became an element of FC. Thus, acceptance of FC as a valid method was widely questioned almost from the time the method was first introduced in the United States. The newsletter of the Autism Society of America, Inc., *The Advocate,* observed that "hard evidence for the authenticity of FC [facilitated communication] is nearly nonexistent" (1992–1993, p. 19). Calculator (1992) also noted that "in the absence of empirical evidence, this communication technique [facilitated communication] remains one that is characterized by its ambiguity, mystique, recurring anecdotes, and spiritual underpinnings" (p. 18).

The most prominent issue related to the use of FC as an intervention for persons with disabilities concerns authorship. Scientific FC validation studies have consistently concluded that when facilitators lack the information needed to answer questions correctly, individuals whom these facilitators assist are unable to communicate independently beyond their expected level. However, some advocates contend that FC should not be subjected to robust forms of scientific evaluation, because such objective scientific methods are ineffective in assessing the efficacy of FC. This argument against scientific validation is based on the contention that individuals with severe disabilities, especially autism, resist communication in objective, scientific studies because they resist communicating with more than one facilitator. In addition, proponents have argued that systematic, scientific

validation attempts of FC violate the trust bond between communicator and facilitator by suggesting that the person with a disability is incapable of advanced communication. Because of these factors, Crossley (1988) and others have contended that objective, scientific validation of FC is not recommended.

Not withstanding the arguments against scientific validation of FC by some proponents, the generally agreed-upon issue for the vast majority of professionals and parents is whether or not this controversial method "works." That is, when physically assisted in communicating by a nondisabled individual, can persons with severe disabilities such as autism, communicate independently at a level that is significantly above their estimated cognitive, social, and language abilities?

Researchers have convincingly demonstrated through numerous objective, scientific validation studies that individuals being facilitated are able to respond correctly only to the extent that their facilitators have the information needed to answer questions and otherwise communicate, and that extraordinary communication fails to occur. In contrast, less rigorous studies and those that have used less scientific methodology (e.g., anecdotal reports) have reported more positive results. Accordingly, inconsistent research findings resulting from the use of different research methods and models confront individuals attempting to analyze the efficacy of FC. Nevertheless, there is clear evidence that FC has not been demonstrated to be a reliable and scientifically valid method. In this regard, *scientific and valid* refers to use of systematic, standard methods that assures others that claims of effectiveness are supported by objective observations, and that nonobjective variables are accounted for or controlled. Scientific methodology also relies on measurable outcomes, established research designs, empirical data-collection procedures, and quantitative data analysis. In this regard, Calculator (1992) contended that, in the absence of objective scientific evidence, FC is little more than an "Ouija Board phenomenon."

It is also important to recognize that there have been reports of individuals who have allegedly been harmed by FC. For example, Rimland (1992a) reported that, according to the Australian newspaper, *The Sunday Age,* a 29-year-old woman with retardation was removed from her home after communicating through FC that her family had abused her sexually. According to the article, the woman was removed from her home on two separate occasions after typing, during FC, that she wanted to leave home to escape sexual abuse. However, after being removed from the family she had purportedly asked to escape, the woman was distraught. To establish reliability regarding the reported abuse, the Australian government contracted two facilitators, one of whom was unfamiliar with the woman, to work with the individual. The woman's FC reports of sexual abuse came under serious question when she was unable to answer basic questions, such as her father's name or the name of the family's pet. Moreover, she spelled her own name incorrectly, in spite of otherwise using sophisticated grammar and spelling.

As a means of resolving the issue of who was communicating, the Phillip Institute of Australia conducted a series of tests wherein the staff of the center she attended prepared 40 questions, to which she knew the answers. The facilitator with whom she was accustomed to working taped the questions. This facilitator assisted the woman in answering the 40 questions under four separate conditions:

1. Both the woman and the facilitator were permitted to hear the questions.

2. While wearing earphones the facilitator and the woman heard the same questions.

3. While wearing earphones the facilitator and the woman heard different questions.

4. While wearing earphones the facilitator heard only music while the woman heard the questions.

The study revealed that under condition (1), the woman correctly knew 8 or 9 of the 10 items; under condition (2), she correctly answered 4 of 10 items; under condition (3), she answered her own questions incorrectly, but answered 4 questions correctly that only the facilitator heard; and under condition (4), she answered every question incorrectly. Based on these results the investigators concluded that the woman was unable to communicate independently.

In conclusion, support for FC has primarily come in the form of informal reports and case studies. In contrast, researchers who have relied on objective scientific procedure have consistently come to different conclusions. These more objective efforts have been designed to identify objectively authors of FC-assisted products by posing questions to which facilitators did not know the answers. These scientific validation studies have concluded consistently that when facilitators lacked information needed to answer questions asked of the individuals being facilitated, the latter were unable to communicate independently.

Point Versus Counterpoint: Facilitated Communication

Three points of controversy pervade the literature and research on facilitated communication (FC). Is the participant using FC communicating independently? Are researchers using the appropriate methods to assess and evaluate the effectiveness of FC? How can the unexpected literacy displayed by the users of FC be explained?

There appear to be equal numbers of qualitative and quantitative studies that evaluate FC's effectiveness. The purpose of the qualitative studies has consistently been to identify effective strategies and methods that facilitators use with participants. In contrast, the purpose of the quantitative studies has been to test FC's effectiveness with individuals with autism and related disabilities. These studies have attempted to validate FC by testing facilitator manipulation and ability of the participants to independently communicate. Interestingly, all the qualitative studies accomplished their purpose, namely to validate FC and identify further training techniques; while the vast majority of quantitative studies reported that there is no scientific validity to FC. These two different philosophies and *approaches to validating* FC have led to further controversy surrounding appropriate methods of testing participants and facilitators in the actual *attempts to validate* FC.

FC literature has clearly revealed a split in the research regarding FC practices and effectiveness. Yet, qualitative and quantitative researchers generally agree on one point: there have been and continue to be instances wherein FC-enhanced information that a participant was believed to be communicating was not communicated by that individual. Rather the facilitator manipulated the participant. FC proponents

(Continued)

(Continued)

contend that these occasions are rare and that researchers and observers should be able to easily identify facilitators who manipulate a participant's communication. Opponents, which include traditional researchers, counter that these occasions are the norm and it is an exception to find a participant who is truly communicating using FC.

A review of FC quantitative studies performed with individuals with autism all reveal significant internal and external validity, reliability, and fidelity threats. Most of these studies involve making the facilitator "blind" or "deaf" (using a blindfold, not showing facilitator the materials, and/or using earplugs and headsets) to insure that there is no possibility that the facilitator knows the questions asked or the materials presented to the participant. In this connection FC proponents have argued that such methods are incompatible with FC principles and therefore are not reliable.

Another thread of FC controversy that is found throughout the qualitative and quantitative literature is the unexpected and sudden appearance of participants' literacy skills. How is it possible that an individual is able to locate letters or type words and sentences incorporating spelling, grammar, and organization of words when previously there was no evidence that he or she could read? This is a question that researchers on both sides of the controversy have not been able to conclusively answer. In an attempt to address this question, researchers using qualitative methodology have discussed the individual's previous exposure to literacy, the individual's previous use of echolalia, and the general hyperlexic tendencies seen in many individuals with autism. Quantitative researchers have generally invested less effort in addressing this question; instead, they have contended that this is evidence that the participants' communication is actually that of the facilitator.

Taking into consideration the controversy surrounding the issue of whether the participant or the facilitator is communicating, the appropriate methods of evaluating FC effectiveness, and the inability of researchers to explain participants' unexpected literacy, it is conceivably difficult to validate and recommend the use of FC with individuals with autism.

—*Richard L. Simpson, Brenda Smith Myles, and Sonja deBoer-Ott*

See also Autism Spectrum Disorders; Communication Disorders; Mental Retardation; Sensory Impairments

REFERENCES AND FURTHER READING

Autism Society of America. (1992–1993, Winter). Facilitated communication under the microscope. *Advocate,* 19–20.

Biklen, D. (1990). Communication unbound; Autism and praxis. *Harvard Educational Review, 60*(3), 291–314.

Biklen, D. (1992). Typing to talk: Facilitated communication. *American Journal of Speech and Language Pathology, 1*(2), 15–17.

Calculator, S. N. (1992). Perhaps the emperor has clothes after all: A response to Bilken. *American Journal of Speech and Language Pathology, 1*(2), 18–20.

Crossley, R. (1988, October). *Unexpected communication attainments by persons diagnosed as autistic and intellectually impaired.* Unpublished paper presented at International Society for Augmentative and Alternative Communication, Los Angeles, CA.

Rimland, B. (1992a). A facilitated communication "horror story." *Autism Research Review, 6*(1), 1–7.

Rimland, B. (1992b). Facilitated communication: Problems, puzzles, and paradoxes: Six challenges for researchers. *Autism Research Review, 5*(4), 3.

FADING. *See* BEHAVIOR; BEHAVIOR INTERVENTION

FAMILY COUNSELING

Family counseling is a form of intervention that occurs when the problematic behavior of an individual child is treated therapeutically in the context of the family. Family counseling is a time-limited intervention that includes the assessment of the problem and the development and implementation of strategies to create change not only in the child, but also in the family that has shaped and supported the maladaptive behavior of the child. Family counseling is based on systems theory that views the behavior of family members to be interrelated and to function in reciprocal patterns of response to one another. Unlike individual counseling, which focuses on the child alone, in family counseling, the child's difficulties are viewed as interrelated with family processes.

REASONS FOR SEEKING FAMILY COUNSELING

The symptoms of one member, often the child, usually bring the family into counseling. The child is referred to as the "identified patient," whom the family labels as "having problems" or "being the problem." The full range of child and adolescent problems would be considered appropriate for a referral to family counseling, as the behavior problems presented by any single family member are viewed to require accommodation from other family members. Alternatively, a parent may seek counseling when he or she recognizes that an event has affected the functioning of the family as a whole. Examples include:

- Divorce
- Remarriage
- Death
- Geographical relocation
- Unexpected trauma

Family counselors tend to view the stressors that cause families to benefit from counseling as emanating from two sources:

1. Stressors outside the family may come from the work environment, public schools, social agencies, neighborhood, and extended family. Stressors external to the family may strain the normal capacity of the family to function adequately.

2. Stressors within the family reflect developmental growth and change among family members. Stress is common at developmental transition points, such as the birth of a child, the entry of a first child into school, and a child's move into adolescence. Changes in family composition also create family stress, including the addition of family members as in the birth of a sibling, remarriage, and the removal of family members (e.g., because of imprisonment or military service). The special needs of an individual family member (e.g., serious chronic or acute physical

or mental illness), can also place strain on family functioning.

Families experience difficulty when, in the face of stress, they increase the rigidity of their transactional patterns and avoid or resist the development of new patterns of behavior that would help them adapt to the changing circumstances. An individual child's "problematic" behavior may be a manifestation of stress within the family system. Family counseling can help members develop more adaptive attitudes and behavior patterns for coping with their changing internal and external environment.

SETTINGS FOR FAMILY COUNSELING

Family counseling can occur in a number of settings, including in schools, hospitals, and clinics. Counseling can also occur in the home when, for example, family members cannot physically attend sessions elsewhere. The counseling setting should be comfortable for the family and facilitative of group discussion. It is optimal to include all family members in counseling. Multisystemic family counseling may include adults from systems beyond the family, including teachers, school counselors, and/or social workers.

TYPES OF FAMILY COUNSELING

Theoretical orientations of family counseling are many, but several are most helpful in the school setting based on their short-term and problem-focused approach.

1. *Structural family therapy.* Structural family therapy emphasizes the organization of the family system as it relates to the problem behavior of the child. Children's symptoms are viewed as adaptive responses to the existing organization. Structural family therapists focus on clarity and appropriateness of family roles, power, and hierarchy to meet the developmental stage of the family. The focus of change is twofold: the presenting problem and the organizational context in which the problem is embedded.

2. *Strategic family therapy.* The strategic family therapy approach is brief and focused on solving the specific problem. The strategic family therapist views the problem behavior of the child to

be embedded in the ongoing interaction patterns between and among family members. The intervention is focused on disrupting the maladaptive interaction patterns within the family.

3. *Solution-focused therapy.* The solution-focused approach takes the problem-focused approach of strategic therapy and shifts it to a focus on solutions in assessment and intervention. Solution-focused therapists seek to identify the family behavior patterns that operate when the problem behavior is not enacted. The focus of intervention is highlighting exceptions to the problem, as well as family strengths and resources.

4. *Cognitive–behavioral family therapy.* The basic premise of behavior therapy is that problematic behavior will change when the contingencies that reinforce the behavior are altered. The cognitive–behavioral model also assumes that family members' beliefs, expectancies, and attributions regarding their relationships and the problem child will mediate their behavior toward the child and toward one another. Cognitive–behavioral family counseling includes standard behavioral treatment to modify the behavioral contingencies and cognitive restructuring techniques to modify distorted beliefs, expectancies, and attributions about family relationships.

5. *Multisystemic family therapy.* Multisystemic therapy views the individual child as nested within increasingly complex systems (e.g., family, school, or neighborhood). The child's behavior problem is thought to be maintained by problematic interactions within and across the multiple systems in which the child is embedded. The influence of these interactions on a child's problem behavior may be direct (e.g., negative peer influence) or indirect (e.g., parental work stress impacts parental monitoring of the child). Multisystemic treatment uses behavioral and systems techniques to intervene at the multiple system levels related to the child's problem (e.g., family, school, and/or peer group).

FAMILY VERSUS INDIVIDUAL COUNSELING

Therapists that do individual counseling have always recognized the importance of family life in shaping personality. They assume, however, that family influences are internalized and become the dominant forces controlling behavior. Treatment is thus targeted to the individual personality. Family counselors, in contrast, believe that individual behavior is strongly influenced by their social context, and the family is the most influential context for the development of children. Family counseling, therefore, targets for change the context in which the child's behavior is embedded.

Advantages to the family counseling approach include the probability that behavior change can be lasting because each family member is a part of the change process and continues to exert a reciprocal influence on one another over time. Problems with children are especially suited to family counseling, as the minor child must reside within the family context.

The advantage of individual child therapy is that it is likely to be easier to conduct. Children may be accessible through school for either individual or group therapy. Family counseling, in contrast, requires the participation and cooperation of multiple family members. This presents both a logistical and attitudinal challenge. It can be difficult for family members to coordinate schedules to participate in family counseling, and many parents would prefer that someone else simply "fix" their child without their active involvement.

THE ROLE OF THE SCHOOL PSYCHOLOGIST IN FAMILY COUNSELING

Given the dramatic shifts in the social demographics of the American family, and given that children's problems often persist despite school-based interventions, it behooves the school psychologist to be prepared to facilitate intervention at the family level. This facilitation can occur at several levels, including understanding the role of family dynamics in children's school problems, conducting family–school meetings, providing consultation with parents and families, leading parent and family support groups, and providing family counseling if appropriately trained. School psychologists who lack competencies in family–school practice, including family consultation and family counseling, should obtain needed competencies before taking on this role. Without appropriate training in family counseling theory and techniques, school psychologists should consider providing referrals to appropriate community resources.

School psychologists who choose to intervene with the family and school system also must respect the traditional boundary between home and school. Schools are traditionally viewed to be the domain for education and home the domain for socialization of children's behavior. It is not reasonable to assume that parents of children in public school systems are open to the exploration of family issues when they seek intervention services for their child. Respecting the family's right of privacy should include allowing them to choose the level at which they choose to deal with the identified problem.

Working with the multiple subsystems of families and schools in assessing, planning, and implementing interventions also requires the maintenance of confidential information. Schools have not traditionally placed as strong an emphasis on maintaining confidentiality as do health care systems. School records are accessible to a broad range of professionals and nonprofessionals. It becomes the responsibility of the family counselor operating in the school system to be well informed of the legal regulations and ethical guidelines governing their behavior.

—*Cindy Carlson and Jennifer Trapani*

See also Behavior Intervention; Counseling; Divorce Adjustment; Parenting; Single-Parent Families

FAMILY EDUCATIONAL RIGHTS AND PRIVACY ACT (FERPA).

See AMERICANS WITH DISABILITIES ACT; INDIVIDUALS WITH DISABILITIES EDUCATION ACT; SECTION 504; U.S. DEPARTMENT OF EDUCATION

FEARS

Most children experience fear sometime during their development. In fact, studies show that approximately 75% of normal children between 4 and 12 years of age report being fearful of one thing or another (Ollendick & colleagues, 2002). In general, childhood fears tend to be mild, age-specific, and transitory. For most children, the initial experience of fear occurs during infancy when a loud noise or loss of support produces a startle-like response. Following this, panic-like fear tends to occur in older infants when exposed to new situations, unfamiliar people, or separation from major attachment figures. Later on, children between the ages of 2 and 4 begin to develop fears of imaginary creatures (i.e., ghosts, monsters) as well as animals and the dark. School-related fears tend to appear shortly after this when the child first enters formal schooling. Finally, during later childhood and adolescence, common fears related to social and evaluative anxiety emerge.

These developmental patterns in fear type have been reported in several studies. For example, in an early study, Bauer (1976) showed that 76% of 4- to 6-year-old children reported fears of ghosts and monsters, as compared to 53% of children 6 to 8 years old, and only 5% of 10- to12-year-old children. Conversely, only 11% of the youngest group of children reported fears of bodily injury or physical danger as compared with 53% and 55%, respectfully, of the two older groups of children. Regardless of age, children's most common fears are related to perceived danger and harm.

A major advance in the study of childhood fears occurred with the development of the Fear Survey Schedule for Children-Revised (FSSC-R) (Ollendick, 1983). Numerous studies have used this survey, resulting in a rich body of literature from studies conducted in the United States, as well as in many other countries. These studies have provided information on cultural norms as well as cross-cultural differences in the patterning and expression of fear. Although cultural differences occur, these studies reveal similar findings in these various countries regarding the number and types of fears (Ollendick & colleagues, 2002). In line with the previous description of the developmental patterning of fears, the most frequently endorsed fears in all countries tend to be related to physical harm and dangerous situations at an early age, and fears of social and evaluative concerns in adolescence.

Although most fears are relatively transient and age-specific, for some children these fears persist and evolve into phobias. A specific phobia can be defined as an excessive and persistent fear that results in response to, or anticipation of, an explicitly feared object or situation. A phobia may be expressed through crying, tantrum, freezing, or clinging behaviors. In addition, the feared stimulus is usually avoided or endured with intense anxiety or distress. Finally, in order to separate the typical developmental fears experienced by most children (which tend to dissipate over time), a duration parameter of six months is required for the diagnosis of specific phobias in children. Phobias can be quite problematic for children and professional treatment is frequently called for.

Ollendick and King (1998) identified a number of interventions for effective treatment of children with specific phobias. Among these treatments are participant modeling, reinforced practice, in vivo exposure, and systematic desensitization (SD). One of the main underlying assumptions of SD is reciprocal inhibition or counter-conditioning; that is, pairing an anxiety-provoking stimulus with a response that is incompatible with the phobic response. As described by Wolpe (1958), it is believed that these pairings will inhibit or quell the anxiety response. Relaxation is the most commonly used incompatible response, although others have been employed as well (e.g., eating, singing, or playing games with child clients). The three principal components of SD are:

1. Relaxation training

2. Construction of an anxiety hierarchy

3. SD proper—the systematic pairing of anxiety-provoking stimuli with the incompatible response (i.e., the relaxation response)

Relaxation requires the systematic tension and release of diverse muscle groups. For adolescents, basic relaxation scripts can be used to provide a smooth transition between muscle groups, while for younger children further considerations may be required. For example, Ollendick and Cerny (1981) suggest that simplifying instructions, shortening the duration of training sessions (i.e., 15 minutes), and incorporating "fantasy" into the descriptions (e.g., "Pretend you are a furry, lazy cat. You want to stretch. Stretch your arms out in front of you . . .") can be especially advantageous. In addition, including the parents of younger children in the relaxation training exercises can be useful, so that they may help the child practice outside of therapy sessions. It may also be beneficial to create a relaxation audiotape for the child (and parents) to use when practicing the techniques.

The anxiety hierarchy typically consists of 10 to 12 steps that are graded in the amount of anxiety or avoidance experienced by the child. For example, using DS proper, a young child who has a severe dog phobia might progress as follows:

- Looking at pictures of a dog in a story book
- Looking at a dog out of the office window
- Stepping outside to look at the dog
- Standing 20 feet away from the dog, then 10 feet away, then 5 feet away
- Touching the dog lightly on its back
- Touching the dog on its head
- Kneeling down by the dog and petting it
- Feeding the dog

This approach to the previously feared object can be accomplished either by imaging or in vivo (i.e., in real life). The important therapeutic feature is that the child approaches the dog in a controlled, safe, and predictable way. Under such condition, fear is diminished and the child is said to "habituate" to the previously feared stimulus. As noted by Ollendick and colleagues (2002), considerable support exists for the efficacy of these exposure-based desensitization procedures, especially those that are enacted in real-life settings. With such treatments, the excessive fears of childhood can be managed and effectively eliminated.

—*Thomas H. Ollendick*

See also Behavior Intervention; Bullying and Victimization; Intervention; Posttraumatic Stress Disorder; Resilience and Protective Factors; School Refusal

REFERENCES AND FURTHER READING

Bauer, D. H. (1976). An exploratory study of developmental changes in children's fears. *Journal of Child Psychology & Psychiatry, 17,* 69–74.

Ollendick, T. H. (1983). Reliability and validity of the Revised Fear Survey Schedule for Children (FSSC-R). *Behaviour Research and Therapy, 21,* 685–692.

Ollendick, T. H., & Cerny, J. A. (1981). *Clinical behavior therapy with children.* New York: Plenum.

Ollendick, T. H., & King, N. J. (1998). Empirically supported treatments for children with phobic and anxiety disorders: Current status. *Journal of Clinical Child Psychology, 27,* 156–167.

Ollendick, T. H., King, N. J., & Muris, P. (2002). Fears and phobias in children: Phenomenology, epidemiology, and etiology. *Child and Adolescent Mental Health, 7,* 98–106.

Wolpe, J. (1958). *Psychotherapy by reciprocal inhibition.* Stanford, CA: Stanford University Press.

FETAL ALCOHOL SYNDROME

Fetal alcohol syndrome (FAS) is the result of ingestion of alcohol during pregnancy. Binge drinking and drinking early in the pregnancy may be more detrimental to the developing fetus than moderate drinking and ingesting alcohol on a regular basis during the pregnancy (Maier & West, 2001). Prevalence is approximately one to two per 1,000 live births, with a higher incidence in low socioeconomic status (SES) populations. Individuals with FAS have characteristic facial anomalies (flat upper lip, low nasal bridge, short nose, small head size), retardation of growth, and behavioral (social problems) and cognitive deficits (mental retardation, difficulty learning new material) (Warren & Foudin, 2001). In the past, a diagnosis of fetal alcohol effect (FAE) was made when an individual did not have the characteristic facial anomalies, but had other deficits associated with alcohol exposure; and when maternal drinking was denied or unknown. Alcohol-related birth defects (ARBDs) (congenital defects) and alcohol-related neurodevelopmental disorder (ARND) (behavioral or cognitive deficits) are now used instead of FAE (Warren & Foudin, 2001).

—*Agnes E. Shine and Darrell L. Downs*

See also Substance Abuse; Mental Retardation

REFERENCES AND FURTHER READING

Maier, S. E., & West, J. R. (2001). Drinking patterns and alcohol-related birth defects. *Alcohol Research and Health, 25*(3), 168–174.

Warren, K. R., & Foudin, L. L. (2001). Alcohol-related birth defects: The past, present, and future. *Alcohol Research and Health, 25*(3), 153–158.

FLUID INTELLIGENCE

Fluid intelligence refers to mental operations used when learning new information and dealing with unfamiliar or novel problem-solving situations. The hallmarks of fluid intelligence are inductive and deductive reasoning abilities, cognitive flexibility, and the ability to adapt well to new problem-solving conditions. It includes such cognitive processes as forming and recognizing concepts, identifying and perceiving relationships among patterns, drawing inferences, comprehending implications, novel problem solving, extrapolating, and recognizing or transforming information. Fluid reasoning abilities are less influenced by cultural and educational experiences than are other aspects of cognitive abilities such as crystallized abilities. Originally described by Cattell as one of two components of general cognitive ability (fluid and crystallized), most research indicates that fluid intelligence typically peaks in late adolescence and then declines with age. Considered by many to be at the core of what it means to be "intelligent," fluid intelligence has a strong relationship with higher-level mathematics reasoning and reading comprehension.

—*Laurie Ford and Deborah Amaral*

See also Intelligence

FORMATIVE EVALUATION

Formative evaluation is used to monitor progress and to provide feedback about the progress being made toward a defined goal. In the classroom setting, formative evaluation is used to inform students and teachers about progress during instruction. Formative evaluation is generally used to monitor progress toward a defined goal and is typically not graded. For example, at the end of a lesson, a teacher may ask students to complete a short test or activity whose purpose is to assess whether students have mastered the desired outcomes for the lesson. Students do not earn a grade for the activity. In program evaluation, formative evaluation is typically used to monitor progress toward the goals of the program, and data from formative evaluation may be used to alter or modify the program so that it is more likely that the outcomes of the program will be achieved.

—*Nona Tollefson*

See also Grades; Retention and Promotion; Summative Evaluation; Program Evaluation

FRAGILE X SYNDROME

Fragile X syndrome (FXS), the leading inherited cause of developmental disability, results from an expansion of CGG nucleotide repeats in the fragile X mental retardation gene on the X chromosome. More than 200 repeats are considered a full mutation, which is associated with a reduction of fragile X mental retardation (FMR) protein, known to be essential for normal brain development and function. FXS is associated with mild to moderate cognitive impairment, behavioral difficulties, communication delays, and characteristic physical and behavioral features. Males are affected more severely than females. The estimated prevalence of full-mutation FXS is 1:4000 males and 1:8000 females. During infancy development may appear fairly typical. Moderate to severe delays are observed throughout early to mid childhood and development appears to plateau around adolescence. Although there is significant variability, most children with FXS are placed in special education classrooms and require services that target speech development, sensory issues, motor development, and occupational skills.

—Anne Caroline Wheeler

REFERENCES AND FURTHER READING

Carolina Fragile X Project. Available online at http://www.fpg.unc.edu/~fx

The Fragile X Information Center. Available online at http://www.fpg.unc.edu/~FXIC

FRAXA Research Foundation. Available online at http://www.fraxa.org

Hagerman, R. J., & Hagerman, P. J. (Eds.). (2002). *Fragile X syndrome: Diagnosis, treatment and research* (3rd ed.). Baltimore: Johns Hopkins University.

The National Fragile X Foundation. Available online at http://www.nxfx.org

Overview of genetic component of fragile X syndrome. *Your genes, your health.* Available online at http://www.ygyh.org

FRIENDSHIPS

Ralph Waldo Emerson nicely articulated the reciprocal nature of friendships when he stated, "The only way to have a friend is to be one." Friendships are defined as close relationships between two individuals that involve mutual attraction and reciprocity of social exchanges. Characteristics often associated with friendships include trust, respect, admiration, acceptance, social support, and shared common interests. Within the disciplines of social science, friendship information is usually determined by mutual peer nominations (i.e., whether two children indicate one another as friends). Friendships should not be confused with related, but separate constructs including social status and peer reputation. The former refers to the child's likeability within the peer group; and the latter to the child's particular, salient behavioral characteristics as seen by peers. In addition, the notion of friendship differs from social skills, which pertain to the child's aptitude or capability in peer relations (e.g., knowing how to make friends), and social competence, an evaluative term pertaining to the child's success in performing social skills. The following entry includes an examination of the importance and developmental course of friendships. Additionally, the role of school psychologists in developing and maintaining positive peer relations will be discussed.

IMPORTANCE OF FRIENDSHIPS

Although it is difficult to ascertain the role friendships play in the development of an individual, there is a general consensus among researchers in this field that close, positive relationships are developmentally significant throughout the life span. However, the importance of friendships varies as a function of age as one progresses through major developmental milestones (e.g., toddlers learn to cooperate and play games with their friends, whereas adolescents seek friendship for intimacy and social support). Friendships foster social competence by providing a framework through which children discover and appreciate social skills and concepts. Through interactions with friends, children and adolescents develop empathy, cooperation, reciprocity, conflict resolution, social problem-solving skills, interpersonal skills, and morals. Friendships can alleviate the effects of stress and hardship often associated with school, work, peer relationships, family difficulties, bereavement, and illness. Cross-sectional comparisons of children with friends versus children without friends, such as those conducted by Newcomb and Bagwell (1995), indicate that children with friends tend to be self-confident, cooperative, more sociable, and less lonely. Friendships help to make children and adolescents resilient when challenged by stressors (e.g., the transition from elementary to middle school). Additionally, friendships foster self-esteem and promote well-being and, therefore, serve as a protective factor against future psychopathology and other unfavorable outcomes.

Perhaps the importance of friendships is best illuminated by examining the detrimental effects of having poor quality friendships, as well as the effects of being without friends. Hartup and Stevens (1997) argue that it is not enough to simply have friends to ensure healthy development. What also matters is the qualitative nature of one's friends (i.e., prosocial versus deviant) and quality of these friendship relationships (e.g., reciprocal and supportive). Positive, supportive relationships serve as a constant resource to enhance resilience to vulnerability. Conversely, relationships with deviant peers can escalate problem behaviors and reinforce delinquency, especially during adolescence. In addition, Vitaro and colleagues (2000) determined that having "best friends" who engage in rule- and law-violating behaviors predict adolescents' subsequent delinquent behavior. These findings emphasize the influential role of peers during adolescence, and suggest that careful attention by parents, teachers, and mental health professionals should be paid to youth regarding the nature of their friends. Children without friends lack the opportunity to practice social skills and are, therefore, at risk for many adjustment difficulties. Indeed, the notion of developmental mastery should include consideration of the number of friends and the qualitative nature of friendships.

There are a number of characteristics that may put youths at risk for poor quality friendship development. Mostow and colleagues (2002) identify emotion knowledge (i.e., recognizing and understanding emotions in oneself and others) as an important component to adaptive social behavior, which is crucial for achieving peer acceptance. Children who have difficulties in recognizing social cues and expressing emotions, such as empathy, may struggle to gain peer acceptance. Other cases of social deficits include withdrawn children. A 1999 study by Schneider found that socially withdrawn children can have good quality friendships despite their reserved nature. He infers the dyadic experience of friendships may alleviate the uncomfortable feelings withdrawn children tend to associate with larger groups.

Another study examined dyadic friendships among aggressive and depressed children from both the children's own and the peers' perspective (Brendgen & colleagues, 2002). Interestingly, depressed children reported lower friendship quality with their best friends than did well-adjusted children. However, from the peers' perspective, there were no significant problems in the relationship, and these relationships were reported to be comparable to those of well-adjusted children regarding friendship quality. A negatively biased perspective may put depressed children at further risk for poor friendship development. Aggressive children, on the other hand, perceived their dyadic friendships as positively as well-adjusted children, but contrasting perceptions were reported by their peers (i.e., peers of aggressive children were less positive about the relationship). A positively biased view could serve as a protective factor for aggressive children by encouraging them to establish and maintain close relationships.

Finally, disturbed peer relations are often found among children with learning disabilities, and those with emotional and behavioral problems. Specifically, children with attention deficit hyperactivity disorder (ADHD) commonly have impaired social functioning and disturbed peer relations, which begin in early childhood and persist into adolescence.

DEVELOPMENTAL COURSE

Throughout the life course, having friends serves a socialization function and promotes psychological well-being. Friendships support the individual as new developmental challenges in the social and emotional development of children and adolescents arise. Hartup and Stevens (1997) suggest that to examine the developmental course of friendships, one must distinguish deep structure from surface structure. Deep structure refers to the social meaning of relationships and mainly focuses on reciprocity. This information is determined by asking children the characteristics of a friend or friends. Surface structure refers to the actual social exchanges that occur among friends reflecting developmental tasks. Between the ages of two and six, children emerge from an egocentric infancy and begin to acquire a wide range of social skills as they are introduced into the peer network. Toddlers, who have limited peer interactions, engage in simple cooperative play with siblings, parents, and other adults. A kindergartener, however, is able to gain entry into a play group and differentiate among children regarding their friendliness and likeability. Based on these characteristics, young children select playmates and, in doing so, form friendships. Therefore, the surface structure of kindergarten friends involves reciprocal play and sharing.

During the school-age years, children are faced with the developmental task of mastering the more formal skills of life, such as adjusting to structured rules and greater academic expectations. Friendships become much more sophisticated and important during this preadolescent phase, as evidenced by the large amount of time spent thinking about the formation and maintenance of these relationships. School-age children engage in telephone conversations, participate in "sleepovers," and share common interests and activities with their friends. During this stage, children describe friends as trustworthy, understanding, and faithful, and expect their self-disclosure will be reciprocated (Hartup & Stevens, 1997).

Adolescence is marked by a substantial decrease in the role of parental influence concomitant with an increase in the influential role of friends. The surface structure of adolescent friendships reflects the developmental challenge of identity formation, and the school-age expectations of loyalty, trust, intimacy, and self-disclosure are amplified. Friends help each other navigate through the difficult trials of adolescence as one attempts to gain self-understanding and stabilize his or her identity by aligning with friends who share common interests, talents, and personality characteristics. Friendships can also emerge as a function of shared interests resulting from extracurricular activities, including high school athletics, clubs, and organizations. Unfortunately, the selection of friends can also be influenced by a shared interest in alcohol, marijuana, and other illicit drugs. Finally, increases in intimacy between opposite-gender friends tend to correspond with the onset of puberty.

ROLE OF SCHOOL PSYCHOLOGY

Friendships often originate and thrive in the school setting and are of paramount concern to parents and educators alike. It is imperative to identify children and adolescents who do not have friends, or associate with deviant peers, to prevent negative effects and adverse outcomes. Even though social skills and social competence training programs in schools are designed to provide children with the necessary tools to enhance positive friendships, most research studies indicate they are of limited efficacy. As social scientists, school psychologists must shift the focus beyond the academic domain and achievement status of the child to the child's repertoire of interpersonal skills (e.g., social problem solving and leadership) needed to facilitate friendship acquisition and mental health.

Aside from the daunting task of promoting social competence, school psychologists need to be knowledgeable of the importance of friendships and sensitive to the child in the context of his or her friends and peers. Friendship research delineates the protective nature of close, positive relationships, as well as the detrimental effects of poor quality friendships and the complete absence of friends. Information regarding friends can inform school psychologists about the child's risk status, as quality friendships serve as a predictor of the child's current and future functioning.

—*Anne M. Howard and Steven Landau*

See also Aggression in Schools; Cooperative Learning; Middle School; Prevention; Retention and Promotion; Shyness; Single-Parent Families; Social Skills

REFERENCES AND FURTHER READING

Brendgen, M., Vitaro, F., Turgeon, L., & Poulin, F. (2002). Assessing aggressive and depressed children's social relations with classmates and friends: A matter of perspective. *Journal of Abnormal Child Psychology, 30,* 609–624.

Hartup, W. W., & Stevens, N. (1997). Friendships and adaptation in the life course. *Psychological Bulletin, 121,* 355–370.

Mostow, A. J., Izard, C. E., Fine, S., & Trentacosta, C. J. (2002). Modeling emotional, cognitive, and behavioral predictors of peer acceptance. *Child Development, 73,* 1775–1787.

Newcomb, A. F., & Bagwell, C. L. (1995). Children's friendship relations: A meta-analytic review. *Psychological Bulletin, 117,* 306–347.

Schneider, B. (1999). A multimethod exploration of the friendships of children considered socially withdrawn by their school peers. *Journal of Abnormal Child Psychology, 27,* 115–123.

Vitaro, F., Brendgen, M., & Tremblay, R. (2000). Influence of deviant friends on delinquency: Searching for moderator variables. *Journal of Abnormal Child Psychology, 28,* 313–325.

FULL-SERVICE SCHOOLS

Full-Service Schools are designed to integrate social and mental health/health services with educational programs under one organizational system in order to promote the physical, emotional, social, and academic well-being of children. The Full-Service School (FSS) movement represents a new era in the quest to address the needs of children living in high-risk situations (McMahon, 2000). It is a contemporary response to the awareness that children in high-risk environments are often so overwhelmed with getting their basic needs met that their ability to learn is seriously affected. It is well documented that poverty, abuse, chronic safety concerns, family disruption, poor health, poor mental health, and learning and emotional disabilities can seriously disrupt children's learning processes, resulting in a lasting impact on achievement and development, and thus severely limiting opportunities for educational attainment and occupational success.

Values inherent to the FSS movement (McMahon, 2000) include:

- A recognition of the complex transaction of risk and protective factors in children's lives
- The difficulty disenfranchised families have accessing quality services
- The need to bring a full complement of health, mental health, and human services into the community in accessible ways (i.e., housed in schools)
- The need for interagency coordination and service integration
- The importance of community involvement

The FSS also represents an effort to make human service systems partner with school systems in the delivery of human services and education (Adelman & Taylor, 1999). FSSs are designed to promote the physical, emotional, social, and academic development of children (Dryfoos & Maguire, 2002; Kronick, 2000; McMahon, 2000).

There are many different components to the FSS, and they are generally offered *à la carte*, allowing schools and communities to choose which components are most needed (Dryfoos & Maguire, 2002). Despite the idiosyncrasies, Dryfoos and Maguire outline several commonalities, including case management (assigning an individual to help families qualify for and best utilize services), primary health clinics, youth development programs, family resource centers, early childhood development programs, referrals, and after-school programs. Deciding which components to include in a FSS is based on a needs assessment of the community where service practitioners work together with families to identify needed services for their community, such as after-school care or career services. Services typically reflect the entire continuum, from prevention, to early intervention, to systems of care for children with severe and/or chronic problems. Cultural competence in service delivery reflects the needs of each community.

FSSs provide many benefits to the community. By integrating many distinct services, families and children have easier access to services, increasing the likelihood of use. With the help of case managers, families are able to tap into the resources available to

them. With easier access to services, children and families may benefit in numerous ways, such as increased physical and mental well-being, which may, in turn, enhance each child's ability to learn (Dryfoos & Maguire, 2000), as well as prevent or alleviate juvenile delinquency, school dropouts, and future unemployment (Kronick, 2000).

Challenges to implementation of FSSs are numerous, including issues with creating the model, working through the coordination, obtaining and sustaining funding, addressing complex legal and ethical concerns, and surviving political controversy. Deciding which services to offer and in what order can engender heated debate. It can be very difficult to achieve interagency collaboration and to secure and manage the funding needed in a FSS (Dryfoos & Maguire, 2002; Kronick, 2000). Legal and ethical issues can also arise regarding confidentiality (keeping information private), informed consent (making sure families understand the services offered and their rights before agreeing to them), and professional responsibility (McMahon, 2000). FSSs are not without political controversy, as some view them as eroding the primary mission of public education in the United States, namely, the teaching of academic skills. In addition, opinions can differ in terms of the array of health services that may be offered in FSSs, such as information on contraception.

The uniqueness of each FSS, as well as the complexities of intricate coordination and the value of both micro and macro outcomes, make for challenging research and evaluation efforts. Evaluators stress that the FSSs needs to be viewed as "works in progress." It is heartening that evaluations to date have yielded positive effects in terms of access and utilization, consumer satisfaction (parents, teachers, children), improved academic functioning, decreased absenteeism and mobility, increased participation in after-school activities, enhanced relationships with positive adult role models, decreased depression, enhanced family cohesion, effective parenting practices, effective interface between special education teachers, and awareness of comprehensive services available.

The potential of the FSS programs for enhancing the developmental outcomes of students with disabilities and for interfacing with special education services is only beginning to become apparent. Research is needed to explore how specific features of the FSS models may best serve students with disabilities. Research also needs to address the variety of implementation issues (e.g., funding, forming collaborative partnerships, eligibility for services, and interfacing classroom staff with service providers) that affect delivery of services to children with recognized disabilities. School psychologists, who could be central to the coordination process, typically have played a minor role in FSSs, although specific roles have been proposed that school psychologists would be uniquely prepared to undertake, including team members, coordinators, and consultants (Reeder & Maccow, 1997). School psychologists are encouraged to prepare for and contribute to the FSS movement as it attempts to better serve children at risk.

—*Deborah Tharinger and Pamela McDonald Schaber*

See also School Reform

REFERENCES AND FURTHER READING

Adelman, H. S., & Taylor, L. (1999). Mental health in schools and system restructuring. *Clinical Psychology Review, 19,* 137–163.

Dryfoos, J., & Maguire, S. (2002). *Inside full-service community schools.* Thousand Oaks, CA: Corwin.

Kronick, R. F. (2000). *Human services and the full service school: The need for collaboration.* Springfield, IL: Charles C. Thomas.

McMahon, T. J. (2000). Building full-service schools: Lessons learned in the development of interagency collaboratives. *Journal of Educational and Psychological Consultation, 11*(1), 65–92.

Reeder G. D., & Maccow, G. C. (1997). School psychologists and full-service schools: Partnerships with medical, mental health, and social services. *School Psychology Review, 26*(4), 603–618.

FUNCTION. *See* FUNCTIONAL BEHAVIORAL ASSESSMENT

FUNCTIONAL BEHAVIOR ANALYSIS.
See BEHAVIOR INTERVENTION, APPLIED BEHAVIOR ANALYSIS; FUNCTIONAL BEHAVIORAL ASSESSMENT

FUNCTIONAL BEHAVIORAL ASSESSMENT

Accommodating the special needs of students with severe behavior disorders is a challenge, particularly when administering school discipline policies: How do educators maintain safe and orderly environments while also preserving the rights of all children to a free and appropriate education? Teachers certainly have the authority to discipline students with disabilities, but recent amendments to the Individuals With Disabilities Act (IDEA 1997) require schools to be proactive in addressing behavior problems by developing well-designed positive interventions and conducting a functional behavioral assessment (FBA) when a student's behavior impedes his or her learning or the learning of others. Although IDEA 1997 first introduced the term functional behavioral assessment, its use throughout the statute is consistent with functional assessment practices that have dominated the field of applied behavior analysis for more than 30 years. Functional assessment identifies the function or purpose of behavior, or those environmental events that "turn the behavior on and off, or up and down, at will" (Baer & colleagues, 1968, p. 94). Research demonstrates that a majority of problem behaviors related to self-injury, aggression, habit disorders, fears and/or phobias, noncompliance, and delinquency are controlled by specific environmental events, and identifying the function of problem behavior can lead to a better understanding of these behaviors, and thus, more effective interventions.

THE FUNCTIONS OF BEHAVIOR

A bird that builds its nest too close to the ground or to the trunk of a tree may be easily approached by predators. If the nest is built too far out on the limb, it may be lost in a strong wind. In a similar manner, dimensions of human behavior (rate, duration, intensity) are shaped and maintained by access to favorable consequences or escape from aversive ones. For example, a high school student may develop study habits that result in better grades and hygienic skills that avoid the ridicule of peers. These interactions with the environment are often described in terms of positive or negative reinforcement. Positive reinforcement refers to a desirable event that is presented or made available after a behavior occurs, and strengthens the behavior. Events that commonly function as positive reinforcers include teacher attention, peer attention, tangible items, and preferred activities. Negative reinforcement refers to an aversive event that is avoided or terminated after a behavior occurs, and strengthens the behavior. Events that commonly function as negative reinforcers include the termination or avoidance of social disapproval, demands, and activity restrictions.

For some students with disabilities, problem behaviors occur because their consequences are more immediate, powerful, or reliable than those associated with appropriate skills. For a youth confronted with challenging work, perseverance may result in frustration and failure, while a tantrum creates teacher sympathy and assistance. It is interesting to note that the impact of a school's response to problem behavior may be unintended. Suspending or expelling an antisocial student with serious learning problems, for example, provides escape from aversive academic demands, as well as access to the comforts of home and, possibly, the activities of other antisocial students with serious learning problems who have been removed from school. When routine consequences for problem behavior are ineffective or make things worse, an FBA may assist the teacher in developing alternative, appropriate skills.

STEPS IN A FUNCTIONAL BEHAVIORAL ASSESSMENT

An FBA consists of several coordinated activities that are typically planned and evaluated through consultation among teachers, parents, and other school professionals. First, broad information about the student's skills, interests or preferences, health concerns, educational history, and academic/social goals and expectations is gathered. Second, specific problem behaviors and appropriate replacement skills are defined in observable, measurable terms. This may be a difficult step because teachers and parents often refer to behavior in vague, general terms such as depression, attachment problems, or poor self-control. A more constructive approach, however, is to specify and prioritize the behaviors used to infer these attributes. For example, a child may be described as having poor self-control because he or she yells out in class, touches or plays with objects, or turns in sloppy work. During this step, it is important to label behavior as verbs (i.e., what the child does) rather than nouns (i.e., who the child is or what the child has). A useful definition is one that allows the behavior to be measured repeatedly and conveniently.

The third step in an FBA is to determine the function of the problem behavior, through one or more of the following methods:

- *Indirect assessment* involves the use of structured interviews or rating scales that provide a detailed account of situations in which the problem behavior occurs.
- A *descriptive analysis* involves actually measuring the problem behavior as changes occur in natural classroom conditions, such as when the class moves from one type of instruction to another.
- An *experimental analysis* is the most rigorous method, and involves directly applying and removing the consequences of behavior, such as teacher attention, peer attention, demands, or sensory stimulation, while observing the impact of these changes on problem behavior. This step is completed when the most likely consequences of behavior are identified, as well as antecedent events (e.g., time of day, type of instruction) that may influence their availability or strength.

The fourth and final step is to link prior information to a treatment plan. This plan usually consists of rearranging the child's environment so that sources of positive or negative reinforcement for the problem behavior are eliminated and these same reinforcers are made available for an alternative, appropriate response. The rationale is that if these events strengthened inappropriate behavior, then they will likely strengthen an appropriate, alternative behavior as well.

IMPLICATIONS FOR EDUCATORS

IDEA 1997 requires that an FBA be conducted when:

- A student's problem behavior impedes his or her learning, or the learning of others.
- A student's behavior presents a danger to himself or herself or others.
- A student's suspension or placement in an interim alternative setting approaches 10 cumulative days.

The National Association of State Directors of Special Education (NASDE) (1998), however, recognized the potential value of FBA across a wide range of educational decisions and recommended that a functional assessment be included whenever an individual evaluation of behavior, academic, or adaptive skills is conducted. A broader application of FBA in school policies and practices is also consistent with recent amendments to IDEA 1997 that set new standards for preventing school failure, implementing prereferral interventions, determining special education eligibility, and developing proactive, positive behavioral treatment plans for students with disabilities.

—*Kevin M. Jones*

See also Applied Behavior Analysis; Behavioral Assessment; Expulsion; Individuals With Disabilities Education Act; Manifestation Determination; Suspension

REFERENCES AND FURTHER READING

Baer, D. M., Wolf, M. M., & Risley, T. R. (1968). Some current dimensions of applied behavior analysis. *Journal of Applied Behavior Analysis, 1,* 91–97.

National Association of State Directors of Special Education. (1998). *Functional behavioral assessment: Policy development in light of emerging research and practice.* Alexandria, VA: Author.

FUTURES CONFERENCE

The Futures Conference was a multisite conference held in November, 2002, which provided the profession of school psychology with the opportunity to reflect upon its past, to examine current issues and practices, and to discuss its future. Participants of the conference were academicians, practitioners, and graduate students in school psychology who met at the host site in Indianapolis, Indiana, and 30 remote sites located around the world. Individuals at the 30 remote sites were able to communicate in thoughtful dialogue with participants at the host site through an interactive Web cast. The Futures Conference was sponsored by the:

- National Association of School Psychologists (NASP)
- American Psychological Association (APA)-Division 16 (School Psychology Division)
- American Academy of School Psychology
- American Psychological Association (APA)
- Council of Directors of School Psychology Programs

- International School Psychology Association
- Society for the Science of School Psychology
- Trainers of School Psychologists

The conference was designed to "achieve consensus on current and future demands for school psychologists and our profession's ability to meet those demands, [to] conceptualize the practice of school psychology in the face of diminishing numbers and increasing demand for services, and [to] develop an agenda to use the resources we have to maximize the benefits to the children and schools that we serve" (Harrison & colleagues, 2004, p. 12). Several themes emerged from the conference including:

- Recognition of a shortage of school psychologists, and how the shortage will impact the field and the delivery of school psychological services
- A need to focus on evidence-based interventions (i.e., standardized, manual interventions), indirect psychological services models (i.e., problem-solving models), and prevention and early intervention
- Promotion of home–school partnerships (i.e., promote relationships between the home and school)
- Recognition of the value of action research (i.e., a systematic inquiry process to understand and solve specific problems with the goal of improving practice) and qualitative (i.e., descriptive) inquiry to the field, and to perform this kind of research in the schools in addition to the traditional research methods used
- The importance of technology to disseminate information, facilitate communication among professionals, and to redesign the practice of school psychology
- The importance of collaborating with other educators and professionals in psychology
- Recognition of the importance of diversity and how diversity impacts children and various contexts (e.g., families, schools, communities)
- A need to incorporate a public health approach in the practice of school psychology to make the best use of limited resources
- Inclusion of innovative approaches in the training of school psychology students and professionals to develop the skills needed to practice effectively in school and nonschool settings.

Conference participants suggested strategies to help the profession reach its long-term goals (i.e., improve academic competence and social–emotional functioning of children and adolescents; enhance home–school partnerships and parent involvement in the schools; provide more effective instruction to students; and promote full-service or school-linked services in the schools—that is, physical and mental health services in the schools—and integrate these services with community-based services) to better serve its constituency. Action plans were developed to ensure that the long-term goals set would be actively pursued and that the School Psychology Leadership Roundtable, an advisory council consisting of leaders in the field of school psychology, would implement and monitor the profession's progress in achieving these goals (Dawson & colleagues, 2004).

—*Patricia A. Lowe*

REFERENCES AND FURTHER READING

Dawson, M., Cummings, J. A., Harrison, P. L., Short, R. J., Gorin, S., & Palomares, R. (2004). The 2002 multisite conference on the future of school psychology: Next steps. *School Psychology Review, 33*(1), 115–125.

Harrison, P. L., Cummings, J. A., Dawson, M., Short, R. J., Gorin, S., & Palomares, R. (2004). Responding to the needs of children, families, and schools: The 2002 conference on the future of school psychology. *School Psychology Review, 33*(1), 12–20.

G

GANGS

The proliferation of gangs and gang violence in the United States has led to increased concerns from educators, law enforcement officials, and citizens. The magnitude of this problem has fueled the public's fear and, consequently, has led to an explosion of research conducted in this area. The 2000 National Gang Youth Survey indicated that there are more than 750,000 gang members in more than 24,000 gangs. Gang membership shows no boundaries. It encompasses people of all ages, ethnic backgrounds, gender, and geographic areas. Therefore, examining defining elements of a gang, typical profile characteristics of members, and the risk factors associated with gang membership provide insight into the true nature of gangs.

DEFINITION OF GANGS

There is no consensus about what comprises a gang or being a gang member. Providing a single definition has proved to be difficult because gang activities have shifted and evolved over time. However, most definitions include the following elements:

- An organizational structure—This refers to having some aspect of internal order including participation in regular meetings, having leaders or core gang members, and seeing themselves as a group.
- A group of individuals who share a sense of identity—This involves the use of symbols to create a shared sense of identity. Gangs commonly use symbols such as a name, special clothing or colors, and allegiance to a specified territory.
- Involvement in criminal or antisocial activity— This characteristic is tautological by nature. Most definitions include a reference to delinquent activity, allowing a defining feature to be a possible product of gang activity.

These elements are used to varying degrees depending upon the specific function the definition will serve. Although there is no consensus to what constitutes a gang, there is significant agreement that gangs exist and they disturb the life of their community.

CHARACTERISTICS OF GANG MEMBERS

The typical age for gang members ranges from 12 to 26 years old. However, gang members have been seen as young as 8 years of age and as old as 50, with an average age of 17 to 18 years old. Male gang members outnumber female gang members; however, actual estimates of female gang involvement vary greatly. Law enforcement records indicate that fewer than 10% of gang members are female; nonetheless, self-report studies consistently find rates ranging from 10% to 40%. Females have been found to join gangs later and often leave earlier than males.

Gang activity has been reported in every state. Gangs now inhabit nearly all of our cities and are present in many of our suburbs and rural communities. In large cities with populations exceeding 250,000 people, almost all law enforcement agencies report consistent gang-related activities. In contrast, in cities with populations under 25,000 people, only 13% of law enforcement agencies report gang-related activities. Despite this lower percentage, there has been a proliferation of gangs in smaller cities and rural areas. Additionally, female gangs are more likely to be found in these smaller communities than in major urban centers.

Gangs are often seen as primarily consisting of African American and Hispanic members; however, self-report measures indicate that almost 25% of gang members are white. The 1998 Youth Gang Survey indicated that the ethnicity of the gang members is closely tied to size of their community. In rural communities, whites accounted for almost 33% of gang members, while in urban areas, only 11% of gang members were white. Also, individuals with other backgrounds have been associated with gang membership, including Asian-Americans, Irish-Americans and Russian-Americans.

Members of gangs are more likely than nongang members to participate in violent and criminal activities. Gangs have been found to employ these violent behaviors as a symbol of gang identity and loyalty. Gang members are more involved in property crimes and individual drug sales than in violent crimes and drug distribution. Additionally, gang members are twice as likely to carry a gun and three times more likely to engage in drug sales than nongang members. Delinquency rates of female gang members are lower than those of male gang members but higher than nongang males or females. Generally, female gang members commit fewer violent crimes than male gang members and are more prone to commit property and status offenses.

RISK FACTORS

Much research has been focused on identifying predictors to gang membership. Features associated with participation in gangs can be grouped into four categories of risk factors: community, family, school, and individual or peer. The extent to which these factors influence gang membership varies from individual to individual and, therefore, should be regarded as predictive factors rather indicative of causality.

Some neighborhood or community factors are associated with gang membership include disorganized neighborhoods that are afflicted with social and economic hardship. Additionally, high rates of mobility, availability of drugs and firearms, and living in an area of high gang activity are also predictive of gang membership.

Family composition and performance in school are also linked to gang membership. Individuals with family members in a gang are likely to become involved in gang activity. Furthermore, high family disorganization, low socioeconomic status, and lack of strong familial support are predictive of gang membership. Research suggests that academic failure, dropping out of school, and demonstrating low commitment to school or low educational aspirations are predictive of gang involvement.

Finally, many individual or peer risk factors are associated with joining gangs. Children who display antisocial behaviors at a young age are more likely to join gangs. Similarly, children who show aggressive characteristics are more likely to associate with peers who behave in a similar manner. Additionally, children with low self-esteem and records of prior delinquency have been linked to increased gang activity. A desire for social connectedness also appears to be an important risk factor, especially for females. Alcohol and drug use, peer pressure from delinquent youth or gang members, and modeling or association with current gang members are also cited as prevalent risk factors for gang membership.

*—Maribel O. Lauber, Megan L. Marshall,
and Joel Meyers*

See also Aggression in Schools; Bullying and Victimization; Friendships; High School; Middle School; Race, Ethnicity, Class, and Gender; Peer Pressure; Substance Abuse; Violence in Schools

REFERENCES AND FURTHER READING

Bjerregaard, B. (2002). Self-definitions of gang membership and involvement in delinquent activities. *Youth & Society, 34*(1), 31–54.

Covey, H. C., Menard, S., & Franzese, R. J. (1997). *Juvenile gangs* (2nd ed.). Springfield, IL: Charles C Thomas.

Decker, S. H., & Curry, D. G. (2000). Addressing key features of gang membership: Measuring the involvement of gang members. *Journal of Criminal Justice, 28,* 473–482.

Egley, A., Jr. (2002). *National youth gang survey trends from 1996 to 2000.* Washington, DC: U.S. Department of Justice, Office of Justice Programs, Office of Juvenile Justice and Delinquency Prevention.

Howell, J. C. (1998). *Youth gangs: An overview. Juvenile Justice Bulletin. Youth Gang Series.* Washington, DC: U.S. Department of Justice, Office of Justice Programs, Office of Juvenile Justice and Delinquency Prevention.

GENDER

Gender refers to the social aspects of being male or female. Gender equity refers to actions and assumptions leading to equal opportunities and expectations for all children. While Title IX banned sex discrimination in schools and, therefore, eliminated obvious barriers, girls and boys may have different experiences in school because of more subtle factors. Boys are more likely to repeat a grade, to be disciplined or expelled, and to drop out of school. Females are less likely to receive mentoring or special education services. Biology and culture contribute to these dissimilar pathways. An understanding of these influences is necessary to maximize education and choices for all children.

GENDER AND SCHOOL SUCCESS

Competency in school can be attributed to intrinsic (e.g., innate ability, self-concept) and external influences (e.g., experiences, peers, parental and teacher expectations). Some apparently innate differences in ability were reported by Eleanor Maccoby and Carol Jacklin in their 1974 classic work, *The Psychology of Sex Differences*, including that girls have higher verbal abilities, while boys surpass them in quantitative and spatial reasoning. However, more recent research has found smaller and fewer gender differences and greater differences in ability within each gender than between genders. Researchers now believe that culture, as well as biology, plays a crucial role in how well children succeed in school.

Gender role refers to social expectations regarding how males and females should behave. Parents, teachers, peers, media, and the school curriculum transmit these expectations to children. Boys are encouraged to explore and take things apart, tasks that are prerequisites for science and spatial knowledge. Math and computers are often considered male domains by boys, teachers, and parents. While more girls are now taking higher-level math courses, females still obtain less than 25% of college degrees in math, engineering, and computer science. Girls exhibit desired school behavior (e.g., neatness, compliance) and obtain higher grades throughout school, but without encouragement from teachers and parents many talented young women are reticent to compete in fields where they are a minority. The American

Association of University Women (AAUW) has numerous studies and programs that focus on enhancing education and raising goals for female students.

In their book, *Failing at Fairness,* Myra and David Saedker report boys receive more teacher attention for negative, positive, or even no behavior. Teachers were found to ask boys more questions. Teachers showed boys how to do things; they did them for girls. Teachers waited for boys to respond, implying that boys were capable of giving the correct response. Conversely, teachers often ignored girls or moved on when they did not answer quickly. Minority girls tended to be ignored more by teachers than white females. Girls were praised for the appearance of their work and failure attributed to low ability, while feedback to boys indicated failure was because of lack of effort or task difficulty. These messages of confidence/no confidence are received and internalized by students. By the time they reach upper elementary grades, boys tend to overestimate their academic competencies while girls underestimate theirs. As a result, boys are more likely to persevere, and many girls tend to stop trying.

GENDER AND SCHOOL FAILURE

Students leave school because of academic, social, and economic factors. Males and females drop out of school for different reasons. Male, economically deprived, and minority students are more likely to fail and consequently be retained or diagnosed with learning problems. Retained students (i.e., those held back in school) and those in special education have higher school dropout rates. Students in special education, minority students, and males are more likely to leave school through discipline, suspension, and expulsion. Black males are three times more likely to drop out of school as white males and twice as likely as black girls. Males may drop out to go to work; minority males can be discouraged by perceptions of limited job opportunities regardless of whether they graduate. Career development and vocational training opportunities in schools are limited and may retain vestiges of traditional gender stereotypes.

Females tend to do better in school, but drop out for family reasons, such as pregnancy or to help take care of siblings. The dropout rate for minority females is two to three times as high as for white females. Minority girls are likely to drop out of school because of limited family support for education or feeling estranged from school. Regardless of factors that lead to dropping out of school, the result is apt to be a lifetime of poverty. Gender-fair (or teaching that has no gender bias) and multicultural perspectives need to be an integral part of school climate to reduce school failure.

GENDER AND DISABILITIES

The school experience is further complicated and the future even more uncertain for students with disabilities. Males have higher rates of autism, psychoses, and schizophrenia, as well as attention deficit hyperactivity disorder (ADHD) and learning disabilities. Females are more likely to be diagnosed with depression; however, teenage males are more likely to commit suicide. Female teens are more likely to display eating disorders. Many disorders have a genetic basis; however, social expectations also contribute to gender differences in prevalence.

Russo and Wehmeyer report in their recent book, *Double Jeopardy: Addressing Gender Equity in Special Education,* that the ratio of males to females in special education is 2:1. Students who are referred, assessed, and eventually placed are those who are noticed. It is hypothesized that more boys are referred because they are more likely to display noticeable behavior problems combined with learning problems. Boys are more often referred for services for anger and bullying. Girls often have attention deficits without hyperactivity and internalizing disorders such as anxiety and depression, which are less likely to be detected. As a result, girls often display greater academic deficits by the time they are referred for a special education evaluation.

School is not the same experience for boys and girls. Gender school is a term that was coined by Luria and Herzog (1985) to describe how peers reinforce gender-associated behavior. However, parents begin gender education at birth by their differential treatment of girls and boys. Schools and society promote innate differences by stereotyped curriculum and expectations. Eliminating gender bias will maximize the potential of all boys and girls.

—*Marilyn S. Wilson*

See also Aggression in Schools; Attention Deficit Hyperactivity Disorder; Bullying and Victimization; Depression; Discipline; Dropouts; Eating Disorders; Gangs; Harassment; Puberty; Race, Ethnicity, Class, and Gender; Social Skills

REFERENCES AND FURTHER READING

American Association of University Women. (1998). *Gender gaps: Where our schools still fail our children.* Washington, DC: Author.

Luria, A., & Herzog, E. (1985, April). *Gender segregation across and within settings.* Paper presented at the biennial meeting of the Society for Research in Child Development, Toronto.

Maccoby, E., & Jacklin, C. (1974). *The psychology of sex differences.* Stanford, CA: Stanford University Press.

Rousso, H., & Wehmeyer, M. (2001). *Double jeopardy: Addressing gender equity in special education.* Albany: State University of New York Press.

Saedker, M., & Saedker, D. (1994). *Failing at fairness: How America's schools cheat girls.* New York: Scribners.

GENERALIZATION

Generalization is the transfer of training effects from one situation to another. There are three types of student performance that may be considered evidence of generalization. The first, *stimulus generalization*, occurs when skills taught in one situation transfer to other situations. For example, a student who is taught by his teacher to say "please" when asking for assistance may begin to say "please" at the family dinner table when requesting another serving of food. In this example, the student uses a new skill (saying please) with different individuals (the family) in a new setting (the home) to make a new type of request (food).

A second form of generalization, *response generalization*, occurs when a strategy applied to one type of behavior changes a related behavior to which the strategy was not applied. For example, a program designed to reduce physical aggression in the school may also result in a reduction in other problematic behaviors such as truancy and verbal assaults.

Finally, *maintenance*, a third form of generalization, occurs when trained responses continue to be demonstrated across time after the completion of training. For example, a child who participates in social skills training to improve peer interactions may continue to use the trained skills with peers long after the formal training is terminated.

The goal of education is to teach students skills that will benefit them in other educational environments, in the community, and at home. However, generalization rarely occurs spontaneously. Therefore, it is important for educational experiences to be designed to promote the transfer of training effects.

One strategy for enhancing generalization is to make training conditions as similar as possible to natural conditions. For example, students learning about the value and exchange of money would benefit from classroom activities that simulate those under which money is exchanged and from field trips (e.g., going to the grocery store) with supervised opportunities for money to be exchanged. A similar strategy involves the inclusion of multiple examples in training. For example, when teaching students to label dogs, one might expose children to live dogs, pictures of several breeds of dogs, and abstract representations of dogs. Exposing students to multiple examples increases the likelihood that student performance will generalize to other examples and decreases the likelihood that performance will be limited to the one or two examples presented during training.

Teaching children to self-instruct and self-monitor are other ways to support generalization. For example, teaching children to state rules that describe the desired behavior will increase the probability that those skills will be performed in the teacher's absence. If students in a social studies class are taught the self-instruction, "Take out a sheet of paper and a pencil when the bell rings," they are more likely to state the rule in math class and follow it.

When student performance depends on intensive training or management programs, generalization to nontraining conditions may not occur. To enhance generalization, training programs should be designed so that when the desired behavior is performed, it is reinforced naturally in the environment. For example, a special education student with severely limited communication skills might be taught to operate a voice-output device to request attention from others. Although intensive training may be required to perform the behavior, the natural responses of others may be sufficient to reinforce and maintain the behavior.

It should be noted that some forms of generalization are undesirable, such as the performance of a particular behavior only under certain conditions. For example, students learning the plural form of nouns must learn that an "s" is added only to certain nouns. Exposure to both examples and exceptions during training can facilitate the development of this discrimination.

Given that transfer of training effects is a critical outcome of educational programs, educational research should be designed to evaluate the extent to which training procedures result in generalization. This approach requires measurement of student behavior under a variety of relevant conditions and across time. Results of this research will ultimately assist in the development of procedures that increase the generalization of student behavior.

—*Nicole M. Cotnoir and Rachel H. Thompson*

See also Learning; Research; Single Case Experimental Design

REFERENCES AND FURTHER READING

Alberto, P. A., & Troutman, A. C. (2002). *Applied behavior analysis for teachers*. Upper Saddle River, NJ: Prentice-Hall.

Haring, N. G. (Ed.). (1988). *Generalization for students with severe handicaps*. Seattle, WA: University of Washington Press.

Kazdin, A. E. (2001). *Behavior modification in applied settings*. Belmont, CA: Wadsworth/Thomson Learning.

Stokes, T. F. & Baer, D. M. (1977). An implicit technology of generalization. *Journal of Applied Behavior Analysis, 10*, 349–367.

GENERALIZED ANXIETY DISORDER

Generalized anxiety disorder (GAD) is the presence of worry and anxiety far out of proportion to the feared event. Children and adolescents with GAD may also experience restlessness, fatigue, difficulty concentrating, irritability, and muscle tension in addition to the ever-present worry and anxiety. To make a diagnosis of GAD, the psychologist or psychiatrist would expect the worry and anxiety to have been present for at least six months. Furthermore, the child or adolescent with GAD is likely to be overly concerned about the frequency or intensity of the worrying. Children may feel an inability to control their worrying, which at times interferes with their ability to pay attention in school or at work.

Children and adolescents with GAD tend to worry about their performance in sports and school, their health, or the safety and well-being of others. Perfectionism is frequently present in children and adolescents with GAD. They may not undertake tasks in which there is a risk of imperfect performance. In addition, these children tend to be overcritical of themselves and worry about meeting deadlines and abiding by the rules. Researchers believe that these children have fundamental distortions in threat perception and "have suggested that individuals with anxiety disorders tend to overestimate the likelihood and catastrophize the outcomes of dangerous events" (Flannery-Schroeder, 2004, p. 127).

In schools, children and adolescents with GAD may go unrecognized because the key characteristics (e.g., worry) of the disorder cannot be seen or do not disrupt the classroom. However, the debilitating nature of GAD interferes with learning and socialization. The school psychologist should help parents and teachers understand the behaviors (e.g., verbalizations about perfectionism, worry) that are associated with GAD. A comprehensive, multidisciplinary evaluation, if needed, should focus on the degree to which the symptoms of GAD interfere with school learning.

PREVALENCE RATES AND ASSOCIATED FEATURES

Prevalence estimates for GAD are 2% to 4% of the general population of children and adolescents (Flannery-Schroeder, 2004) and a 5% lifetime prevalence (*DSM-IV-TR*, 2000). GAD is somewhat more prevalent in females than in males. It appears that anxiety-related symptoms are more likely to occur in the children of anxious parents. Moreover, "recent twin studies suggest a genetic contribution to the development of this disorder." (*DSM-IV-TR*, 2000, p. 474).

Comorbidity is a co-occurring disorder or disease that usually worsens the clinical picture. Depression and other anxiety-related disorders are frequent comorbid conditions with GAD. In a related area, the study of temperament in children has revealed that behaviorally inhibited young children (e.g., shy, worrying, fearful, withdrawn) are more likely to manifest GAD symptoms later in life.

INTERVENTIONS

Effective treatments for children and adolescents with GAD mainly fall into two areas, cognitive–behavior therapy (CBT) and pharmacological interventions. CBT involves helping the child to identify anxious thoughts and physiological reactions that are in excess of the stimulus or concern. Next, children are trained to become aware of self-statements they make that exacerbate their feelings of anxiety and worry.

Children are then trained in cognitive techniques (e.g., imagining a road map that signals a different or prescribed way of thinking about events) that assist them in coping with a life event or controlling their worry. Finally, in CBT, children learn to reward themselves for coping or attempting to cope with anxiety-provoking events.

The available research on CBT shows that it is effective in reducing symptoms of GAD. In several studies, symptomatic improvement as a result of CBT was observed by parents and teachers. A study by Kendall and colleagues (1997) showed that 71% of children treated using CBT are not identified as having GAD after treatment. The gains made by these children were still present after one year.

Few controlled studies using pharmacological interventions for the treatment of children and adolescents with GAD have been done. However, studies with adults have shown benzodiazepines (a class of drug that inhibits the firing of neurotransmitters that may affect the behavioral response of anxiety) to be the most effective medication for treating symptoms of GAD (Telch & colleagues, 2002).

THE SCHOOL PSYCHOLOGIST AND GENERALIZED ANXIETY DISORDER

School psychologists' training and experience places them in a position to respond to the needs of children with GAD through screening and prevention, assessment and diagnosis, and intervention or referral. A GAD prevention program that is implemented in the schools may include screening measures completed by parents to assess risk factors, such as parental GAD or other anxiety disorder, parent availability to the child, and child temperament. The collection of this type of information would assist in the development of a GAD prevention program targeted toward children that are at risk for GAD. The GAD prevention program might include parent training in interacting with their child and/or elements of CBT. The child component could include developmentally adjusted strategies for coping with potentially stressful life events using CBT.

When a child or adolescent with GAD has symptoms that interfere with learning, he or she may be referred for a multidisciplinary, comprehensive evaluation. As part of this process, the school psychologist may use behavior observations and personality and behavior assessments to detect the presence and extent of GAD. According to the Individuals With Disabilities Education Act, GAD is not a diagnosable condition for educational purposes. Students with GAD as well as other mental disorders that affect academic performance are grouped together (diagnostically) into a category called serious emotional disturbance (SED) or emotional disturbance (ED). Students are classified as falling within this category if the multidisciplinary team (including the parent) agree that the child:

- Has difficulty learning that cannot be explained by health or sensory factors
- Cannot build satisfactory interpersonal relationships
- Displays inappropriate types of behavior or feelings in normal circumstances
- Has a tendency to develop physical symptoms or fears related to school problems

When the information obtained from a psychoeducational assessment leads to the conclusion that the student's problems with anxiety interfere with learning, the skilled interpretation of the diagnostic information by the school psychologist may lead to targeted interventions. Such interventions might include Kendall's (2000) "Coping Cat" program. This program, which is frequently run in group settings, is designed to increase awareness of the causes of the anxious reaction. Each child and parent explores the physiological symptoms and thoughts that trigger or result from the anxious response. Through role playing and modeling, children are taught thought-stopping techniques as well as ways to inject alternative coping cognitions. In addition, participants are taught problem-solving techniques and are rewarded for successful demonstration of coping thoughts and behaviors. Finally, strategies for maintenance and generalization of what they have learned are planned and implemented.

In severe and debilitating cases of GAD, the school psychologist may make a referral to medical or mental health centers or hospitals for acute care and/or intensive treatment. After treatment has been completed, the school psychologist would work with the mental health staff to plan for a smooth transition back into school.

—*Steven W. Lee*

See also Counseling; *DSM-IV*; Psychopathology in Children; Separation Anxiety Disorder

REFERENCES AND FURTHER READING

American Psychiatric Association. (2000). *Diagnostic and statistical manual of mental disorders* (4th ed., text rev.). Washington, DC: Author.

Flannery-Schroeder, E. C. (2004). Generalized anxiety disorder. In T. L. Morris & J. S. March (Eds.), *Anxiety disorders in children and adolescents* (pp. 125–140). New York: Guilford.

Kendall, P. C. (2000). *Cognitive-behavioral therapy for anxious children: Therapist manual.* (2nd ed.). Ardmore, PA: Workbook.

Kendall, P. C., Flannery-Schroeder, E., Panichelli-Mindel, S. M., Southam-Gerow, M., Henin, A., & Warman, M. (1997). Therapy for youth with anxiety disorders: A second randomized clinical trial. *Journal of Consulting and Clinical Psychology, 65,* 366–380.

Telch, M. J., Smits, J. A., Brown, M., & Beckner, V. (2002). Treatment of anxiety disorders: Implications for medical cost offset. In N. A. Cummings, W. T. O'Donohue, & K. E. Ferguson (Eds.), *The impact of medical cost offset on practice and research: Making it work for you* (pp. 167–200). Reno, Nevada: Context Press.

GIFTED STUDENTS

The U.S. Department of Education defines gifted students as those who demonstrate extraordinary performance or have the potential to demonstrate outstanding performance in the areas of general intellectual ability, specific academic areas, the fine and performing arts, creativity, and leadership. The definition also stipulates that these are students who require services beyond what is offered in the regular school program and curriculum. This definition is the most widely adopted definition at the state and local school division levels. However, in most cases, identification procedures and program implementation limit the scope of the definition to exceptional intellectual ability and/or achievement in the specific discipline areas (e.g., mathematics).

Renzulli and colleagues (1981) offered what has become a very popular alternative definition, which is based on the three characteristics of above-average intelligence, creativity, and task commitment in any specific area of performance (mathematics, verbal ability, etc.). In their definition, above-average intelligence in the specific performance area and creativity are considered consistent characteristics, while lack of commitment is temporal. Thus, they recommend creating a talent pool including the top 20% of the population and then providing high-interest activities to stimulate task commitment. Students who exhibit tasking commitment are provided instruction that leads them to create professional-quality products in the areas of talent they exhibit.

PREVALENCE OF GIFTED STUDENTS

It has been estimated that 3% to 5% of the population are gifted. However, confusion persists over the question of whether that means 3% to 5% in each category or across all categories. The data provided to the Office of Civil Rights indicate that there is great variation across states, with some states identifying more than 13% of their population as gifted, while other states serve only 1%. In many cases, the proportion of identified gifted students reported is determined by state regulations specifying that funding will only be provided for a given percentage of students in a school district.

IDENTIFICATION

Most school districts focus on general intellectual ability (IQ) to determine giftedness, which relies on the results of intelligence and achievement tests, in combination with teacher rating scales and sometimes grades. Reliance on these assessment tools has been criticized on the grounds of narrowness of conception of intellectual abilities and the bias in using these strategies for assessing students from minority groups, low socioeconomic groups, and students for whom English is a second language.

Guidelines offered for the appropriate identification of gifted students to counter these criticisms include:

- Use instruments and procedures that are reliable and measure giftedness according to the definition of giftedness the school has adopted.
- Use separate and appropriate tools to measure different aspects of giftedness (i.e., artistic ability, intelligence tests, creativity).
- Use multiple criteria for the identification of giftedness, not a single test score or rating scale. Do not use matrices for combining scores from different assessment tools.
- Use appropriate measures and criteria for assessing underserved populations, including children from minority groups, low socioeconomic status, and those who may be both gifted and handicapped.

- Consider expanding sources of evidence to multiple sources of information, and include both school and nonschool performance.
- Consider assessments that reflect how students respond to instruction rather than simply snapshots of performance at one period in time (e.g., portfolios [collections of students' work], classroom observations, and responses to high-level instructional activities).

The process of identification should be a process that begins with a Child Find or a nominating process for students who may need special services because of their high ability or achievement. The nomination stage could involve multiple methods for selecting children, including scores on achievement or aptitude measures, nomination by teachers or other school personnel, and any other available valid data regarding talent. A complete profile of each nominated child is then created. A qualified placement team (e.g., a school psychologist, an expert in gifted education, a classroom teacher, an administrator) should then determine whether the profile of the student suggests a need for a different school program and/or curriculum. The identification process should lead to recommendations for placement and curricular modifications that address the identified educational or other needs of the students.

ROLE OF THE SCHOOL PSYCHOLOGIST IN THE IDENTIFICATION AND EDUCATION OF GIFTED STUDENTS

School psychologists play a critical role in the identification of and programming for gifted students—they offer expertise in the areas of assessment, interpretation of the test results, and assessment of critical developmental and adjustment variables that may influence placement or curricular decisions. In the area of assessment, school psychologists can assist school personnel in evaluating the psychometric properties of tools that are being considered for use in the identification process. Second, appropriate interpretation of test scores will enhance appropriate decision making. Finally, school psychologists can be very important sources of information about the many issues surrounding the bias in assessment of minority students and the issues in identifying gifted underachievers and gifted students with handicapping conditions such as learning disabilities. These groups are traditionally underrepresented in programs for the gifted because of the use of inappropriate or sometimes biased instruments and narrow and biased identification procedures.

Finally, the school psychologist should be involved when parents and educators are weighing whether the appropriate placement of a student should be acceleration to another class or grade level or whether or not a student should be placed in a special class or school. Whether the decision focuses on the benefits of going to a more advanced class for math instruction, or to skip one or more grades, or to enter school or college early, school psychologists are best qualified to determine whether the maturity of the child (physically, socially, emotionally) and the child's achievement and cognitive characteristics warrant acceleration. Further, the school psychologist can use knowledge of these same characteristics in helping to determine whether recommendations regarding separation from peers to attend a special school or class is likely to be a positive experience for the gifted child.

—*Carolyn M. Callahan*

See also Ability Grouping; Academic Achievement; Intelligence; Learning

---

Point Versus Counterpoint: Educating Gifted Students in the Regular Classroom

The case for:

- Differentiation in the regular classroom provides opportunities for high end learning that is integrated with the disciplines of the school curriculum.
- The gifted child is not just gifted for some short, specifically designated period of time each day or week. Differentiation in the regular classroom allows for consistency.
- The gifted child is not separated from peers, reducing concerns about elitism.
- Differentiation in the regular classroom may provide opportunities for other students who are highly motivated, very able, but perhaps not yet identified as gifted to share in high end learning experiences that may spark the development of gifted behaviors.

The case against:

- Most classroom teachers have not been provided adequate training or resources in how to differentiate curriculum appropriately for gifted students. Some teachers do not have the skill or will to differentiate. They may believe that gifted students do not have different educational needs and will not differentiate the curriculum, or they do not have sufficiently advanced knowledge and understanding of the content to be able to do so.
- If gifted students are not grouped together within a given classroom, then a teacher is unlikely to invest the time and energy in differentiating units of study.
- Differentiation of curriculum and instructional strategies requires the availability of resources not normally available in the regular classroom (e.g., additional readings at advanced and more complex levels). Providing duplicates of these materials across many classrooms is expensive.

REFERENCES AND FURTHER READING

Callahan, C. M., Tomlinson, C. A., & Pizzat, P. M. (1994). *Context for promise: Noteworthy practices in the identification of gifted students.* Charlottesville, VA: University of Virginia, National Research Center on the Gifted and Talented.

Donovan, M. S., & Christopher C. (Eds.). (2002). National Research Council Committee on Minority Representation in Special Education. *Minority students in special and gifted education.* Washington, DC: National Academy Press.

Renzulli, J. S., & Reis, S. M. (1997). *The schoolwide enrichment model: A how-to guide to education excellence.* Mansfield Center, CT: Creative Learning Press.

Renzulli, J. S., Reis, S. M., & Smith, L. H. (1981). *The revolving door identification model.* Mansfield Center, CT: Creative Learning Press.

GOAL ATTAINMENT SCALING

Goal Attainment Scaling (GAS) is a process of monitoring progress from a list of predetermined goals. Each goal is clearly set, then broken down into five categories that range from much better, to neutral,

Outcome level	Goals		
	Math	Impulse Control	Social Skills
Much less than expected (−2)	Will make no further progress; weekly average class grade is less than 50.	More than 12 referrals to the office per month for class disruptions	Cannot list anyone as a friend or cannot describe a completed activity with someone else.
Less than expected (−1)	Will start failing class; weekly average class grade of 50–60.	6–12 referrals to the office per month for class disruptions	Can list 1 person as friend and can describe an activity completed with that person.
Expected outcome (0)	Will continue to have an average weekly class grade of 60–69.	4–5 referrals to the office per month for class disruptions	Can list 2–3 people as friends and describe two or three activities completed with them.
More than expected (+1)	Will improve to an average class grade of 70–79.	1–3 referrals to the office per month for class disruptions	Can list 4 or more people as friends and can describe more than three activities completed with them.
Much more than expected (+2)	Will make excellent progress; average class grade greater than 80.	No office referrals for one month	Can list 4 or more people as friends and has been invited to an outing or party by others.
Weighting	7	8	5

Figure 1   Goal Attainment Scaling

to much worse outcomes. GAS is tailored to a specific individual and his or her expected progress, and can be adapted to all skill ranges and used to address a large number of issues (Figure 1). GAS is widely used in education, counseling, social work, rehabilitation, medicine, and other areas.

The development of GAS has several steps. To begin, the major problems that need to be addressed are stated. For example, to use GAS with a student, the major issues may be numerous referrals to the office for misbehavior, failing class, or social problems. Next, goals are created to address the major issues. In the creation of goals, it is generally best to state the goals in simple, jargon-free terms. It is also necessary to create a few goals; three is optimal. To continue with the example, three goals are set; the student will pass math class, limit the number of referrals to the office for class disruptions, and improve social skills.

In GAS, goals must be operationally defined. How can these goals be described in a way that could be rated? What behavior (or feeling) can be rated that applies to the goal? In the example, good choices might be average of daily grades in math, number of referrals to the office, and listing of friends and activities successfully completed with peers. While typically only one indicator of progress is used for each goal, it is possible to use more.

The major component of GAS is the addition of expected levels of progress. Where is the student expected to be at the end of the intervention(s)? After a set period of time, what is the expected progress of the student? This progress is typically expressed as a range, so a range of expected progress may be an average weekly class grade of 60 to 69, 4 to 5 office referrals a month, a list 2 to 3 individuals who are friends, and completion of 2 to 3 activities with these friends. Having defined expected progress, GAS then identifies what "slightly better" and "slightly worse" levels of accomplishment would look like. It is important that goal levels are continuous and discrete (i.e., no gaps between two goal levels, and no overlapping goal levels). Having defined slightly better and slightly worse progress, GAS then defines what "much better" and "much worse" progress would look like. While this process represents the basic use of a GAS, it is also possible to give weights to the different goals to indicate the level of importance attached to each one. These weights typically range from 1 (low importance) to 10 (high importance), but other weighting scales can be used.

GAS was first described in 1969 by Thomas Kiresuk and Robert Sherman. GAS was used as a program evaluation tool to study the effectiveness of treatment options and therapists. Kiresuk and

Sherman proposed that goals should be set by a group of therapists who are not involved with the treatment of the individual. They also designed GAS originally to have independent raters to assess the client's level of progress. In this way, both individual therapists and treatment options could be evaluated. More modern uses of GAS have altered the original idea of independent goal setters and evaluators in favor of self-selected goals and evaluation by the client. As a clinical tool, the GAS is ultimately the responsibility of the therapist, but in some cases there may be benefit in collaborating with the client and negotiating the goals. GAS can also be effective when a multidisciplinary team—a decision-making group composed of different professionals such as a regular education teacher, special education teacher, school psychologist, principal, and parents—collaborates to set goals for a student.

—*Coady Lapierre*

See also Behavior Intervention; Criterion-Referenced Assessment

REFERENCES AND FURTHER READING

Kiresuk, T. J., & Sherman, R. E. (1969). Goal Attainment Scaling: A general method for evaluating community mental health programs. *Community Mental Health Journal, 4,* 443–453.

GRADE EQUIVALENT SCORES

Grade equivalent scores are norm-referenced, developmental scores. They are most frequently reported for achievement tests. Grade equivalent scores compare an individual's score to those of a norm group comprised of students attending the same grade in school as the individual whose score is being reported. For example, developmental scores may be expressed as 5.6 or 5–6 and interpreted as the average scores of fifth graders at the sixth month of fifth grade. Some grade equivalent scores are the mean score; others are the median score. The technical manual for the test indicates which measure of central tendency (i.e., mean or median) was used to determine grade equivalent scores reported. Grade equivalent scores are widely used in schools, but they are very difficult to interpret because they do not have good psychometric properties.

There are several guidelines for interpreting grade equivalent scores. Norm-referenced grade equivalent scores should not be confused with standards of acceptable or desirable grade-level performance. Grade equivalent scores are average scores. At any particular grade level, approximately 50% of the students will score above the grade equivalent score and 50% will score below it. For this reason, it is not reasonable for a school district to expect all of its students to be at or above grade level on a norm-referenced score. Norm-referenced scores indicate achievement relative to a particular norm group of students at a particular grade level. They do not indicate the level at which students should be performing.

A grade equivalent is not an estimate of the grade at which the student is working or should be placed. Students complete test items designed for the curriculum taught at the grade level in which they are enrolled. Grade equivalent scores that exceed the grade level of the student indicate that the student knows grade-level material better than most students at the grade level. For instance, the fourth-grade student who earns a grade equivalent score of 7.3 on a reading subtest understands fourth-grade reading material very well. The score does not mean that the student could or should be assigned seventh-grade reading material. The same principle applies to a fourth-grade student who earns a grade equivalent score of 2.1. The student likely has difficulty reading fourth-grade material. The score does not mean the student should be reading third-grade material or that the student can only read third-grade material.

Most nationally norm-standardized achievement tests provide grade equivalent scores for a series of tests. Grade equivalent scores on different subtests of the same test are not comparable because grade equivalent scores do not have equal units of measurement. That is, a grade equivalent score of 5.1 on a social studies subtest is not necessarily higher than a grade equivalent score of 4.2 on a science subtest. If students, teachers, or parents wish to compare scores on different subtests of the same achievement test or the same content areas from different achievement tests, they need to make the comparisons based on percentile ranks or standard scores.

—*Nona Tollefson*

See also Academic Achievement; Intelligence; Percentile Ranks; Stanines

GRADES

Grades consist of numbers, letters, or phrases that indicate a student's school performance during a certain period of time or on a particular assignment. In addition to measuring the quality of a student's work, grades are also an indication of the progress a student has or has not made. Consistently poor grades indicate that a student is not progressing academically. He or she is then placed at a higher risk of being retained the following school year. Consistently high grades indicate that a student is progressing well academically and should be promoted to the next level.

In addition to affecting whether or not a student is retained, grades are also used in academic placements. Students who receive poor grades may be placed in classes that are more tailored to their needs. In these classes, they may receive more individualized attention in an effort to increase their academic success. Students receiving average grades typically remain in regular education classrooms and will continue with the standard curricula. Students receiving very high grades may be placed into accelerated, advanced placement, or gifted and talented classes. In these cases, the students may advance through the curricula at a faster pace or study topics in more depth.

There are many ways in which schools place number grades with corresponding letter grades. This is typically calculated by assigning percentages of the final grade to class assignments and exams. For example, a teacher may count homework assignments as 40% of a final grade and two exams as 30% each—the percentages of the homework and two exams will equal 100%.

The most common system in the United States for assigning number grades with letters is the 10-point system: 90 to 100 = A; 80 to 89 = B; 75 to 79 = C; 70 to 74 = D; 0 to 69 = F. Another widely used system is the 7-point system, which is: 93 to 100 = A; 85 to 92 = B; 75 to 84 = C; 65 to 74 = D; 0 to 64 = F. Additionally, most schools evaluate very young students without number grades. A common grading scale for students in kindergarten through second grade is by giving a child an 'S' for Satisfactory, or a 'U' for Unsatisfactory. This is done because it is very difficult to assess a young student's abilities; the skills being graded are more transitory and are tied to development.

When students reach high school, grades are also used to rank students in relation to one another by calculating the students' grade point averages (GPAs). These GPA rankings are used by the school in determining the order in which students will graduate in relation to their peers. GPAs are also used by colleges and universities in determining which students will be admitted to their school. While the minimum GPAs of accepted students changes from school to school, some states, such as Texas, require all state schools to admit every applicant who graduates in the top 10% of his/her respective high school class.

To determine a student's GPA on the common 4.00 scale, each of the student's individual course grades is assigned a value:

- A equals 4.00.
- B equals 3.00.
- C equals 2.00.
- D equals 1.00.
- F equals 0.00.

Grades received in advanced placement courses may receive one point higher on each grade value. So an 'A' may be given a 5.00 value, and 'B' may be given a 4.00 value, and so on. As a result, it is possible for a student who has received A's in advanced placement courses to have a GPA higher than 4.00. These extra points for advanced placement courses recognize the higher level of difficulty in their coursework. After assigning each course grade a value, the values are added together to form the total number of points a student has received. This total is then divided by the number of courses the student completed. The calculation results in the student's GPA. For example, the calculation of a student's GPA who has taken three courses and received two A's and a B is:

$$4.00 + 4.00 + 3.00 = 11.00 \div 3 = 3.67 \text{ GPA}$$

However, when students get to the college level, courses are given a credit value. Typical academic courses are given three credits, academic courses with an accompanying lab course are typically given four credits, and physical education courses are typically given one credit. When calculating a student's GPA at the college level, the assigned number values corresponding with the letter grades are divided by the number of credits taken by the student. This is done in order to allow certain courses to have a greater or lesser impact on the GPA. For example, the grade a student receives in a science course with a lab will impact the GPA far more than a physical education course.

—*Allison L. Tate*

See also Ability Grouping; Academic Achievement; Criterion-Referenced Tests; Retention and Promotion

H

HALO EFFECT

A halo effect often refers to the tendency to let one characteristic of an individual positively influence the appraisal of other characteristics. For example, individuals often assume that attractive people are more intelligent or that muscular men are aggressive. In both of these examples, we allow one characteristic to positively influence our assessment of other characteristics (intelligence and aggression). The tendency for school staff or students to have a halo bias in rating is of particular concern in school psychology. School officials (teachers, administrators, school psychologists) can develop a positive feeling about a student, a class, or a group of students that may influence how they rate (on a rating scale) or interact with the person. For example, a teacher who feels that students who come from an upper-class, dual-parent home are better behaved as compared to those who come from a single-parent home will probably behave differently toward these groups. Social class, sex, and prior knowledge of an individual are other factors that may influence a teacher's ratings of student performance.

—*Billy L. Smith*

See also Bias (Testing); Race, Ethnicity, Class, and Gender; Reliability

REFERENCES AND FURTHER READING

Thorndike, E. L. (1920). A constant error on psychological rating. *Journal of Applied Psychology, 4,* 25–29.

HARASSMENT

Harassment is a general term used to describe victimization that is characterized by an imbalance of power between the perpetrator and the victim.

Harassment in a school context involves victimization of a peer by a peer. Harassment may also refer to victimization of a child by an adult (and, in rare cases, victimization of an adult perpetrated by a child or adolescent). There are multiple forms of victimization that fall under the general heading of "harassment," with two of the most common types of harassment being bullying and sexual harassment.

Bullying has begun to receive popular attention; however, research on bullying has been only active since the pioneering work of Dan Olweus. Olweus (1993) and others define bullying as aggression that is (a) intentional, (b) repeated over time, and (c) perpetrated by a bully who is more powerful than the victim. These defining characteristics of bullying create a situation in which one student is continually intimidated by another and with diminished ability to defend himself or herself. Bullying behavior may be overt (e.g., physical and verbal harassment) or covert (e.g., spreading rumors, gossiping, and social manipulation).

According to the U.S. Equal Employment Opportunity Commission, "unwelcome sexual advances, requests for sexual favors, and other verbal or physical conduct of a sexual nature constitutes sexual harassment when submission to or rejection of this conduct explicitly or implicitly affects an individual's employment, unreasonably interferes with an individual's work performance or creates an intimidating, hostile or offensive work environment" (Title VII of the Civil Rights Act of 1964—Public Law 88–352). This definition is created to protect adults in a work setting. The equivalency of this law is Title IX of the Education Amendments of 1972, which is under the jurisdiction of the Office of Civil Rights (OCR). This amendment addresses discrimination based on sex. Sexual harassment is carried under this title, and charges of sexual harassment in education are referred to the OCR. The OCR Web site states that:

> Sexual harassment can take two forms: quid pro quo and hostile environment. Quid pro quo harassment occurs when a school employee causes a student to believe that he or she must submit to unwelcome sexual conduct in order to participate in a school program or activity.
>
> Hostile environment harassment occurs when unwelcome conduct of a sexual nature is so severe, persistent, or pervasive that it affects a student's ability to participate in or benefit from an education program or activity, or creates an intimidating, threatening or abusive educational environment.

This statement clearly says that schools are ultimately responsible for ensuring the safety of students and responding to instances of sexual harassment.

The academic literature on bullying and sexual harassment has not been well integrated. There is some debate over whether the term "bullying" is most appropriate to describe all related student experiences. Stein (2003) argues that the term bullying is not "gendered." Much of what educators consider "bullying," Stein says, is actually sexual harassment. One distinction made between bullying and sexual harassment is that repetition is a required component of bullying, but not of sexual harassment (Land, 2003). In addition, some researchers note that physical aggression (more indicative of bullying) seems to be most prevalent among younger students, and it transforms into sexual harassment in adolescence (Land, 2003).

To study students' perceptions of the differences between teasing, bullying, and sexual harassment, Land (2003) asked secondary school students to provide an example of each. She found that almost all students included sexual behaviors in their description of sexual harassment, with some including sexual behaviors in their descriptions of bullying as well. Teasing and bullying descriptions were more likely to be repeated incidences than sexual harassment. In addition, sexual harassment descriptions primarily involved mixed-gender situations, while bullying and teasing were described as both mixed- and same-gender interactions. Land does not recommend using these terms interchangeably and states that their distinctions need to be further clarified.

PREVALENCE

Estimates of the prevalence of harassment vary greatly and seem to largely depend on the types of questions that students are asked, as well as the type of harassment that is assessed. For example, approximately 10% of students will say that they are victims of bullying (Nansel & colleagues, 2001; Solberg & Olweus, 2003). However, when the behaviors are specified and students are asked about experiencing particular types of bullying behaviors, this number increases, with studies showing that a range of 39% to 85% of girls have experienced frequent sexual harassment (Strauss, 2003). A large-scale study completed by the American Association of University Women (AAUW) Educational Foundation found that 81% of students experienced sexual harassment at least once while in school, and 27% of students reported being frequent victims of sexual harassment (AAUW, 2001). A study by Craig and colleagues (2001) indicated that boys experience more same-sex sexual harassment than girls, with both genders endorsing equivalent rates of opposite-sex sexual harassment.

Data on several types of harassment were collected as part of the California Student Survey (CSS), a survey of 7th, 9th, and 11th graders (Table 1). These findings suggest that hitting or shoving behaviors decrease with age, while sexual comments increase, particularly for girls, to the point that more than 40% of 11th grade girls say they have had sexual jokes made about them.

EFFECTS OF HARASSMENT ON YOUTHS

Harassment of all kinds can have a long-standing impact on both victims and perpetrators. The nature of this impact will vary based on:

- The type and duration of harassment experienced
- The stability of harassment across multiple settings in the child's life

Table 1 Percentage of California Student Survey Respondents Harassed in the Past 12 Months

Harassment Experiences at School	7th Grade		9th Grade		11th Grade	
	Males	Females	Males	Females	Males	Females
Pushed, shoved, slapped, hit, or kicked	37.0%	20.1%	23.0%	11.7%	16.1%	6.7%
Threatened or injured by a weapon	5.7%	3.4%	4.7%	2.3%	4.9%	1.7%
Afraid of being beaten up	15.2%	10.2%	10.8%	8.0%	7.4%	3.9%
Had rumors or lies spread about you	21.9%	25.3%	17.7%	24.4%	17.8%	24.9%
Had sexual jokes, comments, or gestures made to you	25.0%	25.6%	24.9%	39.1%	31.5%	43.2%
Made fun of because of your looks or the way you talk	22.9%	24.5%	22.1%	22.7%	21.6%	18.2%
Had property stolen or deliberately damaged	13.7%	9.5%	15.1%	9.0%	13.6%	8.8%

- The child's attitudes about the reason they are being targeted for harassment
- Whether the youth is able to respond and/or stop the harassment

Victims of bullying are at risk for a number of poor social, emotional, and academic outcomes. These include anxiety; depression; posttraumatic stress disorder (PTSD); psychosomatic symptoms; social, emotional, and academic maladjustment; school absenteeism; and negative school attitudes. Solberg and Olweus (2003) found that students who had experienced bullying at least two to three times a month were at a much greater risk for externalizing behavior problems than students who were bullied at a lower frequency. Given that bullying is, by definition, a repeated pattern of interactions rather than a one-time event, Solberg and Olweus suggest that a frequency of two to three times a month is a frequency associated with poor developmental outcomes.

Experiences of sexual harassment are often ambiguous, leading to situations in which the victim may be unsure if he or she actually experienced harassment, possibly resulting in a sense of hopelessness and incompetence (Sabella, 2001). According to the AAUW survey, 47% of students who experienced sexual harassment reported that they felt very or somewhat upset following the incident. Additionally, students reported feeling embarrassed (43%), avoiding the person who perpetrated the harassment (40%), talking less in class (24%), and having trouble paying attention in school (20%).

Perpetrators of bullying and sexual harassment are also likely to experience negative consequences. School discipline may compromise the perpetrator's attendance if they are suspended or expelled (Sabella, 2001). In addition, perpetrators may learn that aggressive behavior is effective in getting them what they want, thus leading to a pattern of reinforcement of perpetration of aggression against weaker parties.

PREVENTION AND INTERVENTION IN THE SCHOOLS

Schools have a legal responsibility to protect their students from harm. Several states have enacted legislation directly or indirectly designed to address bullying and harassment. Zero tolerance policies are common, but are contraindicated by research on their efficacy.

There are several evidence-based bullying prevention programs that schools can select from and modify to meet the needs of the unique school climate and context. Comprehensive programs have been found to be more effective than one-time or fragmented prevention activities. Espelage and Swearer (2003) recommend conceptualizing bullying as a series of social interactions, rather than a one-time event. Conceptualizing bullying as a maladjusted social relationship will inform interventions aimed at altering social interactions, rather than taking a primarily punitive approach. In general, Espelage and Swearer suggest that viewing bullying from a social–ecological perspective will enable more effective interventions. Taking into

Table 2   Percentage of California Student Survey Respondents Harassed or Bullied on School Property for the Following Reasons in the Past 12 Months

Reasons for Harassment at School	7th Grade Males	7th Grade Females	9th Grade Males	9th Grade Females	11th Grade Males	11th Grade Females
Race, ethnicity, or national origin	7.5%	4.1%	9.0%	5.4%	8.3%	4.0%
Religion	4.3%	2.2%	4.7%	2.4%	2.6%	3.0%
Gender	4.1%	4.6%	2.6%	5.1%	2.8%	4.4%
Sexual orientation	5.8%	2.7%	5.4%	3.1%	4.8%	2.1%
Physical or mental disability	2.8%	1.6%	3.6%	1.9%	3.0%	1.1%
Other reasons	12.7%	13.3%	11.5%	12.9%	10.7%	8.2%

account the larger context will facilitate appropriate selection of programs and enable the development of comprehensive interventions.

Several recommendations have been derived for school districts addressing sexual harassment. Strauss (2003) provided a comprehensive list of recommendations, including suggestions that schools:

- Assess the current problem
- Develop a task force to address harassment
- Implement a sexual harassment policy
- Engage in trainings for all school staff
- Incorporate topics related to sexual harassment into class curriculums
- Offer support groups and services to youths at risk for sexual harassment
- Label actions as "sexual harassment," when appropriate
- Ensure that all allegations are taken seriously and investigated by a trained team

Schools that successfully reduce sexual harassment will accurately define the problem, implement model interventions, and monitor their implementation and success.

In general, schools that are effective at reducing harassment will go beyond implementing universal prevention programs focused on character development. Successful schools will clearly define inappropriate behavior and its consequences and go a step farther to make that information known to the entire school community in the form of policies and training. There is a rich literature on the "bystander effect," the passive support of students and teachers who witness harassment but do not intervene. Moving toward a reduction in harassment involves empowering the school community to respond and giving them the means by which to intervene.

FUTURE DIRECTIONS

Harassment is a problem in schools that should be addressed. However, there is groundwork that should be laid before interventions can be effective. Most notably, confusion over definitions of harassment and different forms of harassment has led to inconsistency in measurement and intervention recommendations. For example, several large-scale national studies of bullying have omitted explicit questions about sexual behaviors. Without this information, it is difficult to distinguish between these two forms of harassment.

Often identifying characteristics that differentiate a student from the mainstream (e.g., sexual orientation, ethnicity, and religion) can lead to a student becoming the target of harassment. In the California Student Survey students were asked to indicate the reasons that they had been harassed by others (Table 2). Males reported that they are often harassed because of their race, ethnicity, and/or national origin. Females endorsed these same primary reasons, but also indicated that they were harassed because of their gender.

—*Michael J. Furlong, Jennifer L. Greif, and Greg Austin*

See also Bullying and Victimization; Gender; Multicultural Education; Race, Ethnicity, Class, and Gender

REFERENCES AND FURTHER READING

American Association of University Women. (2001). Hostile hallways: Bullying, teasing, and sexual harassment in school. Retrieved August 23, 2004, from http://www.aauw .org/research.girls_education/hostile.cfm

Craig, W. M., Pepler, D., Connolly, J., & Henderson, K. (2001). Developmental context of peer harassment in early adolescence: The role of puberty and the peer group. In J. Juvonen & S. Graham (Eds.), *Peer harassment in school: The plight of the vulnerable and victimized* (pp. 242–261). New York: Guilford.

Espelage, D. L., & Swearer, S. M. (2003). Research on school bullying and victimization: What have we learned and where do we go from here? *School Psychology Review, 32,* 365–383.

Land, D. (2003). Teasing apart secondary students' conceptualizations of peer teasing, bullying, and sexual harassment. *School Psychology International, 24,* 147–165.

Nansel, T. R., Overpeck, M., Pilla, R. S., Ruan, W. J., Simons-Morton, B., & Scheidt, P. (2001). Bullying behaviors among U.S. youth: Prevalence and association with psychosocial adjustment. *Journal of the American Medical Association, 285,* 2094–2100.

Olweus, D. (1993). *Bullying at school: What we know and what we can do.* Oxford: Blackwell-Science.

Sabella, R. A. (2001). Faces of sexual harassment in schools. In D. S. Sandhu (Ed.), *Faces of violence: Psychological correlates, concepts, and intervention strategies* (pp. 251–265). Hauppauge, NY: Nova Science.

Solberg, M. E., & Olweus, D. (2003). Prevalence estimation of school bullying with the Olweus Bully/Victim Questionnaire. *Aggressive Behavior, 29,* 239–268.

Stein, N. (2003). Bullying or sexual harassment? The missing discourse of rights in an era of zero tolerance. *Arizona Law Review, 45,* 783–799.

Strauss, S. (2003). Sexual harassment in K-12. In M. Paludi & C. A. Pauldi, Jr. (Eds.), *Academic and workplace sexual harassment: A handbook of cultural, social science, management, and legal perspectives* (pp. 105–145). Westport, CT: Praeger & Greenwood.

U.S. Department of Education, Office of Civil Rights. (n.d.). Retrieved April 27, 2004, from http://www.ed.gov/about/ offices/list/ocr/qa-sexharass.html

HEAD START

In the spring of 1965, as part of the *War on Poverty*, President Johnson's administration launched the Head Start program. The White House ceremony had more than 400 guests and widespread news coverage. Hundreds of thousands of citizens signed up as volunteers, and communities across the country submitted applications to sponsor a program. The eight-week summer program served 561,000 preschool children, and in 1966 it was expanded to a school-year-long program. Since its inception, more than 22 million children and families have enrolled. In 1995, children from birth to three years of age began enrolling in the newly created Early Head Start program.

DEFINING HEAD START

Often mistaken as a Department of Education preschool program, Head Start is actually a comprehensive child development program administered by the Department of Health and Human Services through the Head Start Bureau, Administration on Children, Youth and Families, and the Administration for Children and Families. Public and private agencies (e.g., city government, community action agency, school system, Native American tribe, private preschool provider) submit grants to operate Head Start in a community. In addition to preschool education, programs must provide a range of individualized health care services, family social services, and parent involvement components. Head Start programs also work with local school systems to ensure a smooth transition into elementary school. Programs are monitored through an extensive system of performance standards that define the nature and quality of the many services provided to children and families. These standards can be enhanced and modified through Head Start's required periodic reauthorization by the U.S. Congress.

ELIGIBILITY REQUIREMENTS

Head Start and Early Head Start programs serve children from birth to five years of age whose families meet poverty income guidelines based on family size. For example, in 2003, a family of three with an annual income less than $15,260 or a family of four with annual income less than $18,400 qualified. (Alaska and Hawaii had slightly higher values.) In addition, children with disabilities, children from families receiving public assistance such as Temporary Assistance to Needy Families (TANF) and Supplemental Security Income (SSI), and children living in foster care are eligible for Head Start and Early Head Start, regardless of their family's income.

DEMOGRAPHICS OF FAMILIES SERVED

In the 2002–2003 school year, 1,670 Head Start grantees operated 19,200 Head Start Centers containing 47,000 classrooms serving 909,608 children. The majority of children were four (53%) and three (34%) years old. Children five years of age and older upon entry represented 5% of those served, whereas 8% of children were younger than three years of age. African Americans (31.5%), whites (27.6%), and Hispanics (30.6%) were the three major ethnic groups receiving services as well as smaller percentages of Native Americans (3.2%), Asians (1.80%), and Hawaiians/Pacific Islanders (1.1%).

PROGRAM GOALS

The Head Start Planning Committee, a multidisciplinary group representing medicine, health, nursing, social work, education, and psychology, designed the Head Start program to be a multidimensional program focusing on both adult family members and children. The program fosters healthy development in low-income children and their families through the delivery of individualized, comprehensive services in the areas of child development and school readiness, parent involvement, social services, nutrition, and medical, dental, and mental health.

HEAD START RESEARCH AND EVALUATION

In 1968, the government mandated a national evaluation of Head Start, which was conducted by the Westinghouse research group. The planning committee requested a prospective study in which children would be randomly assigned to a Head Start or non-Head Start group before entering the program. The government, however, funded a retrospective study, locating former Head Start participants who were now in first, second, and third grades. A retrospective design had the major problem that the control group, formed years after the program was over, may not be comparable. The main findings showed no differences between Head Start and non-Head Start participants. However, 70% of the Head Start sample had only participated in the eight-week summer program. Positive effects were found for Head Start children who had participated in the full-year program, demonstrating that a summer program is not as effective as a full-year program. Despite these positive findings for full-year participants, greater emphasis was placed on the main findings, which involved the large sample enrolled in the eight-week summer program and which found no differences between Head Start and non-Head Start participants. As a result, the Westinghouse

report was incorrectly viewed at the time as evidence of Head Start's ineffectiveness.

In the period following the Westinghouse report, research was conducted on early intervention programs such as Head Start that clearly showed these programs did work and produced long-term positive effects. Summary reports have been periodically published reviewing this research. Researchers at George Washington University, for example, in 1977 synthesized the results from approximately 150 studies that had previously been conducted on Head Start in a report documenting the program's positive effects on families and communities, as well as on children's health and cognitive development. In 1985, the U.S. Department of Health and Human Services published the *Impact of Head Start on Children, Families and Communities: Head Start Synthesis Project*. This report reviewed more than 1,600 documents and analyzed 210 published and unpublished research reports; it found evidence that former Head Start children were more likely to be promoted to the next grade and less likely to need special education services. Positive effects were also found for families and communities benefiting from having a Head Start program. For example, Head Start families increase their use of health care providers as a result of Head Start programs' effectiveness in linking families with a wide range of health and social services. For communities, positive change is tied to having a highly visible Head Start program. Such change also benefits low-income families not associated with Head Start as community agencies become more aware and responsive to the needs of the poor. However, academic gains shown by former Head Start children in the early grades were no longer present by third grade. Although this lack of a lasting effect has been challenged and debated, a "fade-out effect" became associated with the Head Start program.

Beginning in the 1990s Head Start began research funded by the Head Start Bureau that followed a community-researcher partnership model. This model provides Head Start programs with a joint decision role for participating in the research in ways that promote staff development and ensuring that the research knowledge gained is translated into best practices. Lamb-Parker and colleagues (2000) extensively reviewed Head Start partnership grants funded with this directive and showed the critical importance of this shared decision-making process.

Since 1990, a second major influence on Head Start research has been the focus on school readiness, the first of eight National Educational Goals. An example of these two influences can be seen with Head Start researchers such as Greenfield and colleagues at the University of Miami, who have formed a partnership with the Miami-Dade County Head Start program and the Miami-Dade County Public School System, the fourth largest in the nation. This partnership has conducted research focused on improving Head Start children's school readiness and creating greater continuity in the transition from Head Start to public school. For example, this partnership group served as one of the sites of the National Head Start/ Early Childhood Transition project, evaluating the impact of providing Head-Start–like services through third grade. This project, which has provided extensive data to refute the "fade-out" effect, argued for the importance of continuing strong parent involvement, health care, and family social services into the early elementary grades along with a developmentally appropriate education component. Advocates of this approach argued that low-income children must continue to receive good health care and live in safe and supported homes, with their parents involved in their education, if they are to learn and succeed in public school.

Head Start continues to be involved in national evaluations of its effectiveness. The Head Start Family and Child Experiences Survey (FACES), a longitudinal study begun in 1997 collected data on children, families, and classroom practices from multiple sources and methods during Head Start and kindergarten. The 1997 FACES design included a nationally representative sample of 3,200 children and their families in 40 programs. A second cohort was added to FACES in 2000 that included 2,800 children and their families in 43 different Head Start programs. FACES tracks three- and four-year-old preschool children through one or two years of Head Start experience and follow-up data in kindergarten. Data collection includes direct assessment of children, parents, teachers; staff interviews; and classroom observations. Although there is no non-Head Start comparison group, many of the measures that are being used provide national norms for comparison purposes. Data from FACES show that Head Start is having a positive impact on children. For example, Head Start children show considerable advances in vocabulary, writing skills, and social skills. Children entering the program with high levels of shy, aggressive, and hyperactive behavior had significant reduction in these

behaviors. Observational data indicated that Head Start classrooms were of good quality. Teacher education, knowledge, and positive attitudes also contributed to classroom quality. Congress also included a National Impact Study as part of the 1998 Head Start reauthorization. This study, begun in the fall of 2002 and continuing through 2006, will follow a randomly assigned sample of Head Start and non-Head Start preschoolers through first grade. The National Impact Study has two major goals. The first goal is to evaluate the impact of Head Start on children's school readiness. The second goal is to determine under what conditions and for what groups of children is Head Start most effective. These broad-based questions will be addressed through data collection from multiple domains. These domains include language and literacy, social–emotional development, and characteristics and practices of Head Start staff and families. They are collected from multiple sources including children, staff, and parents. Approximately 75 communities and 5,000 children and families will participate in this study.

ROLE OF THE SCHOOL PSYCHOLOGIST

School psychologists play an important consultative role in the screening, assessment, and identification of school-age children who qualify for special education services. Historically, school systems have used school psychologists for these functions, but the focus of these services has been school-age children. For example, the majority of children who receive disability services in public schools are classified as learning disabled (LD). LD, however, is very difficult to diagnose in the early elementary school years, because in the early grades reading and math are just beginning to be taught and it is nearly impossible for a child to be far enough behind at the beginning of instruction to qualify for an LD diagnosis. As a result, the considerable amount of time that school psychologists spend working with the LD population is work with older children.

In addition, the transition to school is difficult for all children, and varying periods of adjustment to kindergarten are needed. Because the kindergarten child will be in public school for the next 12 years, there is a reluctance to label children as disabled early in their education—such labels can have negative consequences. For these reasons, school psychologists have not traditionally been involved in working extensively with very young children. This emphasis, however, is likely to shift, as there is a growing awareness that the early school years and the transition into public school are critical for the early identification of children who are at high risk for subsequent school failure. Children transitioning from the Head Start program into public school are a group that requires attention. At least 10% of children served in Head Start have disabilities. However, the variations in the types of disabilities typically seen in Head Start versus the public school present school psychologists with many challenges. The majority of children served in Head Start are categorized with a speech or language impairment (SLI). SLI is a much smaller category of children in public school. Research suggests that many of these children with SLI classifications in preschool will qualify for LD services, but not until their later school years when LD classifications typically increase in quantity. In addition to children with disabilities, Head Start serves children raised in poverty, which is a high-risk factor for poor educational outcomes. To meet these growing needs of low-income children transitioning into public school from programs such as Head Start, school psychologists will play a critical role as greater focus on screening, assessment, identification, and services shifts to the early elementary years. This will require better communication between Head Start and public schools that includes valid information on children's strengths and weaknesses as they make this critical transition.

—*Daryl B. Greenfield*

See also Early Intervention; Learning; Preschoolers; Resilience and Protective Factors; U.S. Department of Education

REFERENCES AND FURTHER READING

Fantuzzo, J., Weiss, A., & Coolahan, K. (1998). Community-based partnership-directed research: Actualizing community strengths to treat child victims of physical abuse and neglect. In J. R. Lutzker (Ed.), *Child abuse: A handbook of theory, research, and treatment* (pp. 213–238). New York: Pergamon.

Greenfield, D., & Nicholas, C. (2001). Building statewide partnership capacity to assess school readiness for Florida Head Start children and families. *Dialog 4*(2), 197–209.

Lamb-Parker, F., Greenfield, D., Fantuzzo, J., Clark, C., & Coolahan, K. (2000). Shared decision making in early childhood research: A foundation for successful community-university partnerships. *Dialog 3*(2), 234–257.

Ramey, S., Ramey, C., Philips, M., Lanzi, R., Brezausek, C., Katholi, C., et al. (2000). *Head Start children's entry into public school: A report on the national Head Start/public school early childhood transition demonstration study.* Washington, DC: U.S. Government Printing Office.

U.S. Department of Health and Human Services. (1985). *The impact of Head Start on children, families, and communities: Head Start synthesis project.* Washington, DC: U.S. Government Printing Office.

U.S. Department of Health and Human Services. (2003). *Head Start FACES 2000: A whole-child perspective on program performance.* Washington, DC: U.S. Government Printing Office.

Zigler, E., & Muenchow, S. (1992). *Head Start: The inside story of America's most successful educational experiment.* New York: Basic Books.

HEARING IMPAIRMENT. *See*
OTITIS MEDIA

HIGH SCHOOL

The American high school, an institution with which most adults in the United States have at least a passing familiarity, has existed in largely the same form for the past 150 years, enduring continuing struggles to determine its form and function. Yet, despite such struggles, it goes about its primary duty of educating the young citizens of our nation. Some argue it does not do enough to educate our 14- to 18-year-old students; others say the high school has taken on too much of a burden and needs to scale back its aspirations to the most basic elements. Throughout the argument, the teachers, school psychologists, principals, and other school staff endeavor to do their jobs to guide our youngsters toward adulthood.

The high school first appeared in the United States in 1635 as the Latin Grammar School in Boston, Massachusetts, having been established only five years after that colony itself was founded. It focused on teaching Latin and other subjects considered "classical" in order to prepare a particular segment of our then-U.S. society—namely wealthy, white boys—for college. Subjects included preparing youths to read and speak Latin in verse and prose, to use the Greek language correctly, and to understand "common arithmetic." According to Johnson and colleagues (1985), "within 16 years after the Massachusetts Bay Colony had been founded, seven or eight towns had Latin Grammar schools in operation" (p. 284). The schools were designed similarly to those that had existed in Europe for many years and had as their dual aims the preparation of boys for college and for the service of God.

Within another 100 or so years, Benjamin Franklin established The American Academy in Philadelphia. Franklin believed the Latin Grammar Schools "were not providing the practical secondary education needed by youth" (Johnson & colleagues, 1985, p. 288). His idea for these schools was to prepare youngsters for employment, so the curriculum, philosophy, and methodology of Franklin's Academies focused upon this goal rather than a classical education. Already the underpinnings of some of our current struggles (academic training versus vocational skills) in education were being shaped.

By 1821, the city of Boston opened the English High School, enrolling 100 boys in its first year, under the direction of George B. Emerson. Its curriculum was comprised of three years of English, math, science, and history. Within a few years, more academically oriented courses were added, and the Latin Grammar School was becoming obsolete. The American High School, similar in form to today's schools, had been born (Johnson & colleagues, 1985).

The struggle to determine the goals and, consequently, the curriculum of the high school was emerging in full force. By 1892, the National Education Association (NEA) established the Committee of Ten to study the purpose and function of the high school institution (Willis & colleagues, 1994). They set the following recommendations for secondary schools as the 20th century began:

- Courses shall be arranged sequentially.
- High school should consist of grades 7 through 12.
- Very few electives should be offered to students.
- Carnegie units (measures of how much time a student has studied a subject) should be awarded for each course, provided the course met the time requirements.
- High schools should try to graduate students earlier so that they could attend college sooner.

The first four decades of the past century saw several commissions and committees defining the ultimate aims and objectives of secondary education,

which were to include civic education, vocational training, leisure time pursuits, maintenance of health and physical fitness, preparation for further learning, home membership, and progress in social relations with peers and adults. By 1944, the NEA embraced "every youth in the United States—regardless of sex, economic status, geographic location, or race" in its pursuit of a "broad and balanced education," (Johnson & colleagues, 1985, p. 291).

One of the largest studies of the high school curriculum was undertaken by the Progressive Education Association's Commission on the Relation of School and College in the 1930s (Aikin, 1942). The study was initiated because of a concern that the then-current curriculum was not serving all students well (Kridel & Bullough, 2002). This Eight-Year Study, and its companion work the Follow-up Study, compared the achievements of high school students from schools self-described as progressive versus those who followed a classical college preparatory curriculum. These studies found that students from the experimental progressive schools did much better on measures of "extracurricular achievement" and somewhat better on academic achievement in college than did those students who had come from a more traditional college preparatory curriculum. These studies raised questions about the effectiveness of the classical disciplines as a precollege, high school curriculum.

More fuel was added to the fire of curriculum debate by the Soviet Union's launching of Sputnik in 1957. This scientific and political event raised concern in the minds of Americans that our schools were not rigorous enough in the teaching of math and science to meet the needs of the changing world and to keep America ahead of the Soviet Communist threat (Willis & colleagues, 1994). The comprehensive curriculum was seriously challenged by many (including Rickover, 1963), but defended by Conant (1959). Conant also encouraged the use of ability grouping in subjects, but not tracking of students. Conant advocated that different programs should be offered for vocational proficiency, grading standards should be flexible so that students who were working to capacity would pass, and appropriate remedial support would be provided (Tanner & Tanner, 1995).

During the 1960s and 1970s, the curriculum of secondary schools was broadened to offer a wide variety of courses students could use in life, with less time devoted to basic academic skills and college preparation. Reacting to this, the *Nation at Risk* report

(National Commission on Excellence in Education, 1983) served as a call to the education establishment to put more emphasis on a basic academic curriculum. At the same time, other critics of American high schools argued for fundamental curricular reforms to help high schools better prepare youths for life in the emerging Information Age (Boyer, 1983; Goodlad, 1984; Sizer, 1984). The latter critique of the secondary school curriculum was reinforced by the Secretary of Labor's SCANS (Secretary's Commission on Achieving Necessary Skills) report of the 1990s, which urged better training for technical skills, more focus upon basic academic skills, and increased use of group work to better prepare students for the high-tech world of the 21st century (U.S. Department of Labor, 1991).

Then in 2001 President George W. Bush and the nation's 50 state governors proclaimed the *No Child Left Behind* initiative. This federal mandate, subsequently enacted into law, required that all public schools have their students meet minimum educational standards by specified grade levels in order to be promoted and to graduate. This was to be accomplished by yearly testing of students and ranking of schools according to passing or not-passing criteria. School ranking is being linked to receipt of Title 1 federal funding by the schools.

These continuing concerns over the goals of public high schools are occurring at the same time that schools struggle with:

- An increase in enrollment, especially of minority students (many of whom do not speak English well or fully understand the American culture)
- A rapidly changing workforce for which students need to be prepared
- Severe cuts in state and federal funding
- Ambivalence by parents and many students about the goals and value of a high school education

In an attempt to improve public high schools, the U.S. Department of Education in 2002 defined 11 goals that can help bring about comprehensive school reform when sought as a package, rather than in a piecemeal fashion. These 11 goals include:

- Using effective practices and scientifically based research to teach students and manage the schools

- Integrating all components of the education system
- Furnishing high-quality staff development on a continuous basis
- Having measurable goals for academic achievement and providing markers to show progress in meeting those goals
- Having a unified philosophy and vision that is supported by all school staff and administration
- Creating shared leadership in the schools and then providing support for the staff responsible for implementing the changes
- Encouraging meaningful ways for parents and the community to be involved in planning and implementing school improvement ideas
- Using quality external support organizations that have experience in improving schools
- Developing a written plan for annually evaluating school reform and student results
- Identifying governmental and private resources that are available for assistance in changing schools
- Using a program that has been proven over time and/or with rigorous research practices to effect change in student learning and school functioning (Borman & colleagues, 2003)

Eisner (2003/2004), on the other hand, argued that for schools to truly prepare young people for the future, other features need to be incorporated into the educational process. He advocated including in the curriculum real problems that teach the students to use judgment and ways for students to develop critical thinking so that ideas could be explored and critiqued. Then Eisner would include meaningful uses of literacy that would be explored in a multitude of ways. The schools would promote collaboration of students in many configurations, and finally would use true service opportunities so that students realize how they relate to their community to enrich the lives of others in that community.

Coming from a different perspective, a study by the Horizon research team (Weiss & Pasley, 2004) found that few schools actually provide math and science programs of high quality for all students. While most lessons include content that is worthwhile and accurate in information, and most teachers seem confident in their ability to teach these two subjects, few lessons provided intellectual rigor or helped students in making sense of the broader context of the lesson's material.

They also found a pattern of differing levels of instruction for classes that had various proportions of minority students, classes that had different ability levels, and classes located in rural as opposed to urban or suburban areas. As a result of these findings, in addition to changing the larger school goals, pressure is building to seek improvements in separate content areas.

The struggles of today's public high schools are adding a new dimension to the two-century-old debate about which type of curriculum would best serve high school students: the comprehensive approach predominant in the past century or a more classic disciplines approach that can be traced back to the Latin Grammar Schools.

ROLES AND DUTIES OF SECONDARY SCHOOL PSYCHOLOGISTS

A recurring theme in efforts to seek improvements in secondary schooling has been to relate the curriculum to the needs of individual pupils. The specific duties of school psychologists in assessing and responding to pupil needs in the high school are multifaceted and somewhat dependent in part upon the types of other school support personnel available to serve students in a particular school, workload, and philosophy of the psychologist.

Some schools employ social workers, transition coordinators, and counselors—all of whom assume various duties that might otherwise fall to the school psychologist. Typical duties of a school psychologist may include:

- Evaluating students for inclusion into special education programs
- Reevaluating current special education students for further inclusion or for dismissal from a special education program
- Consulting with regular classroom teachers and other school personnel on behalf of students needing assistance with academic, behavioral, or social matters
- Providing assistance to students in planning for the transition out of high school into the workforce or vocational or college training

They also ensure that special education documents are prepared correctly. School psychologists often work with teachers to modify plans for students who meet the criteria for inclusion under section 504 of the Rehabilitation Act of 1973 and ensure that modifications are being enacted in the classrooms. In addition, they may work with students' families to assist them in making connections to appropriate community services such as therapists and support groups. They may work with students on school and personal issues. In times of crisis, school psychologists may provide counseling to students. School psychologists may conduct research based on local problems, such as attendance, to determine causes and possible solutions to them.

Depending on the types of other personnel available in the school and state regulations concerning student inclusion into special education services, some school psychologists may work mainly with students with exceptionalities, such as students with learning disabilities or behavior disorders or gifted and talented students. Occasionally these school psychologists will work with students not identified as needing special education.

A typical workday for a school psychologist in a high school includes visiting with students, teachers, and school administrators. School psychologists will do required paperwork and meet with school personnel and students' parents to discuss specific students. They will administer tests to students, score the tests, and interpret their results. School psychologists observe students in and out of classrooms to provide a broader perspective on those students. They will see students for individual or group counseling and consult with teachers about classroom and/or individual student problems or concerns and suggest strategies to overcome these problems or concerns. School psychologists also study professional-specific journals and other related materials to remain current in their field. They may visit other community agencies and training programs to find the best matches for their students' interests and abilities for transition into life after high school. They attend scheduled staff meetings and other school functions to build collegiality with school personnel and to gain a better understanding of the culture of their particular high school. In some districts, or school cooperatives, a school psychologist may serve two or more high schools, necessitating travel between school sites.

In sum, a person considering school psychology as a career at the secondary level needs to possess genuine interest in and concern for adolescents, an understanding of the issues facing high schools and their students, and be able to function in a variety of situations and with different people. A future school psychologist should develop good observation recording skills focused on accurate details, but also be able to keep the big picture of schools and adolescence in mind. A school psychologist needs to be able to give various kinds of cognitive, behavioral, and vocational tests and interpret their results, while developing the appropriate connections to community agencies that will assist the students and their families.

—Thomas O. Erb, Marc C. Mahlios,
and Diane M. Coffman

See also Career Assessment; Dropouts

REFERENCES AND FURTHER READING

Aikin, W. M. (1942). *The story of the eight year study.* New York: Harper & Brothers.

Borman, G. D., Hewes, G. M., Overman, L. T., & Brown, S. (2003). Comprehensive school reform and achievement: A meta-analysis. *Review of Educational Research, 73,* 125–230.

Boyer, E. L. (1983). *High school: A report on secondary education in America.* New York: Harper & Row.

Committee of Ten. (1893). *Report of the Committee of Ten on secondary school studies.* Washington, DC: National Education Association.

Conant, J. B. (1959). *The American high school today.* New York: McGraw-Hill.

Eisner, E. W. (2003/2004). Preparing for today and tomorrow. *Educational Leadership, 61*(4), 6–10.

Goodlad, J. I. (1984). *A place called school: Prospects for the future.* New York: McGraw-Hill.

Johnson, J. A., Collins, H. W., Dupuis, V. L., & Johansen, J. H. (1985). *Introduction to the foundations of American education.* Newton, MA: Allyn & Bacon.

Kridel, C., & Bullough, R. V., Jr. (2002). Conceptions and misperceptions of the Eight-Year Study. *Journal of Curriculum and Supervision, 18*(1), 63–82.

National Commission on Excellence in Education. (1983). *A nation at risk: The imperative for educational reform.* Washington, DC: U.S. Government Printing Office.

Rickover, H. G. (1963). *American education: A national failure.* New York: E. P. Dutton.

Sizer, T. (1984). *Horace's compromise: The dilemma of the American high school.* Boston: Houghton Mifflin.

Tanner, D., & Tanner, L. (1995). *Curriculum development: Theory into practice.* Upper Saddle River, NJ: Prentice-Hall.

U. S. Department of Labor. (1991). *What work requires of schools: A SCANS report for America 2000.* Washington, DC: Author.

Weiss, I. R., & Pasley, J. D. (2004). What is high-quality instruction?. *Educational Leadership, 61*(5), 24–28.

Willis, G., Schubert, W. H., Bullough, R. V., Jr., Kridel, C., & Holton, J. (Eds.). (1994). *The American curriculum: A documentary history.* Westport, CT: Praeger.

HIGH STAKES TESTS. *See* ACADEMIC ASSESSMENT; BIAS (TESTING); NORM-REFERENCED TESTS; OUTCOMES-BASED ASSESSMENT

HISPANIC AMERICANS. *See* CROSS-CULTURAL ASSESSMENT; MULTICULTURAL EDUCATION; RACE, ETHNICITY, CLASS, AND GENDER

HIV/AIDS

Human immunodeficiency virus (HIV) is a retrovirus, meaning that once an individual is infected, the virus begins to take over the cells' genetic material and the cells themselves begin to produce more retrovirus. This process of infection may take 8 to 15 years. During this time, the person generally looks and feels perfectly healthy; however, the virus slowly begins to weaken the person's immune system. The individual becomes increasingly vulnerable to a multitude of secondary infections and diseases. Once an individual has a very severely impaired immune system and/or begins to develop a series of illnesses common to people infected with HIV, the person is diagnosed with acquired immune deficiency syndrome (AIDS).

HIV is transmitted only through the exchange of bodily fluids such as blood, semen, vaginal fluids, and breast milk. Any act (vaginal intercourse, anal sex, oral sex, pregnancy and childbirth, consuming breast milk, and receiving blood transfusions or organ donations) involving the transfer of bodily fluids can lead to infection. Unfortunately, there are many common myths that have managed to cloud this clear message. HIV cannot be transmitted by casual contact, by sharing eating utensils, or by donating blood. The most common means of HIV infection worldwide is heterosexual intercourse.

HIV infection has become so widespread throughout the world that it is classified as a pandemic. According to United Nations figures, there were approximately 36.1 million people infected with HIV and AIDS worldwide in 2000, and new infections occurred at a rate of 15,000 per day (Jaffe & Harold, 2001). The majority of these cases were in the developing countries of the world, particularly the sub-Saharan African nations such as South Africa and Botswana. During this same time period, the Centers for Disease Control (CDC) estimated there were 800,000 to 900,000 individuals in the United States infected with HIV and 774,467 diagnosed with AIDS. Many of those infected are young people, and approximately 50% of the individuals infected yearly worldwide are younger than age 25 years.

Adolescents and young adults are particularly vulnerable to infection for a variety of developmental reasons. Nearly all of the risk factors for infection are behaviors that begin during the teen years. Because of youths' imagined invulnerability, most young people do not perceive themselves to be at risk, even when participating in behaviors likely to lead to infection. Sexually active young people often fail to use proven means of protection, such as latex condoms, when engaging in risky behavior. Adolescents who have older sexual partners are at particular risk because these older partners typically have more risk factors for infection, and young people in these relationships tend to rely on the older partner to make decisions and are less likely to use protection. Adolescents have the population's highest infection rate of other sexually transmitted diseases (STDs), and the effects of having another STD make an individual more likely to develop HIV. In addition, the immature reproductive system of adolescent girls makes them more likely to contract HIV. Sexual behavior under the influence of alcohol and recreational drugs is very common in young people. Intoxication greatly increases risk-taking behaviors (i.e., increases the likelihood of sexual activity, increases the number of sexual partners) and greatly reduces protective behaviors (i.e., using a condom).

Primary prevention of HIV infection in young people is a critical need. Research indicates that schools are most effective in providing basic information about HIV/AIDS and that families are most effective in affecting risk behaviors. School-based instruction is either mandatory or suggested in all 50 states. Overall, prevention programs are most effective when they:

- Are sensitive to the culture and current sexual behavior of the youth involved
- Use a social-learning approach

- Deal with social pressures and expectations
- Teach students new skills, giving them the opportunity to observe and practice those skills

Parents who receive information and instruction related to HIV are more likely to talk with their children about the disease.

—Elizabeth Kelley Rhoades
and Susan Elisabeth Verhaalen

See also Confidentiality; Death and Bereavement; Resilience and Protective Factors

REFERENCES AND FURTHER READING

Jaffe, M. D., & Harold, W. (2001). The HIV pandemic: Worldwide perspective and focus on the United States. *HIV InSite*. Available online at http://.hivinsite.ucsf.edu

HOMESCHOOLING

Homeschooling is a type of schooling in which a person is educated outside the school setting, usually at home. Students who are homeschooled are generally taught by one or both of their parents. The act of homeschooling is not a novel concept to our society. Before the public school system became available, education in the home was typical. The recent homeschooling movement began during the 1960s and 1970s when many Americans were questioning the quality of the public education system. The homeschooling movement has continued to grow since this time and laws have been passed allowing parents the right to homeschool their children (Kleist-Tesch, 1998).

PREVALENCE

According to the Home School Legal Defense Association (2004), the number of homeschooled students has been on the rise over the past two decades. In the 2000–2001 school year, an estimated 1.5 to 1.9 million students, grades K–12, were homeschooled. Researchers believe that the numbers have been increasing between 7% and 15% per year. Therefore, it is estimated that 1.7 to 2.2 million students were homeschooled during the 2001–2002 school year. Using a 15% increase per year, an estimated 2.6 to 3.3 million students will be homeschooled in the 2004–2005 school year. To help put things into perspective, there are approximately 49 million students currently enrolled in grades K–12 in the U.S. public school system. In a 2001 study on home-schooling, Bielick and colleagues (2001) found the following demographic information:

- 75.3% of these students were white, non-Hispanic.
- 61.6% of these students were from homes with three or more children in the household.
- 80.4% of these students were from two-parent families.
- 63.6% of these students lived in households with family annual incomes of $50,000 or less.

The researchers also asked the parents why they chose to homeschool their child, and the top three reasons were that the parents felt they could provide their children with a better education at home, religious reasons, and the neighborhood school was a poor learning environment.

CURRENT TRENDS IN HOMESCHOOLING

Different approaches to homeschooling include (Kochenderfer, 2003):

- School-at-home (the most familiar)—The teacher (or parent) orders a curriculum set with all of the materials and supplies included, and follows structured lesson plans.
- Unit studies—The teacher and student find an area of interest for the student and work the area of interest into every subject (e.g., math, reading, science, history).
- "Relaxed" or "eclectic"—This is the most used homeschool method. This approach includes elements of all the other approaches.
- "Unschooling"—Students learn from their own life experiences; they learn by following their interests. They do not follow the typical school schedule, and there are no formal lessons. Students who participate in the unschooling approach do not do as well on formal assessments compared to other students who are homeschooled using a different homeschool approach.

- Online or Internet homeschooling—Home-schooling also appears on the Internet. Online, homeschoolers can find virtual tutors, private distance learning schools, homeschool support academies, Online curriculum programs, and much more.

ADVANTAGES AND DISADVANTAGES OF HOMESCHOOLING

According to the literature, there are advantages and disadvantages associated with homeschooling. Some advantages include:

- Parents are able to spend quality time with their child.
- Parents can control what their child is learning.
- Parents can be more involved in teaching their child their values and ways of life.
- Parents can provide their child with protection from negative social situations.
- Parents can give their child one-on-one attention and extra help in areas that their child may be struggling in.
- Parents can adapt their teaching style to match their child's style of learning, personality, and needs.
- Parents have the pleasure of working with each other to educate their child.

Although there are many advantages to home-schooling, there are also some disadvantages, with the most common disadvantage being financial. Most two-parent families rely on a two-person income; however, because one parent must be home at least part of the day to educate the child, the family suffers a loss of income; also, the homeschooling curricula itself can be expensive. Other disadvantages include (Kochenderfer & Kanna, 2002):

- Parents have to motivate their child to work when the child does not want to and be patient with their child if the child is not learning as fast as he or she should be.
- Families have to defend their choice of home-schooling their child to others.
- Parents often feel inadequate to teach the curriculum.
- Parents must ensure that their child is socializing with other peers.

EDUCATION OUTCOMES AND HOMESCHOOLING

Although a major criticism of homeschooling is that students who are homeschooled are not receiving an appropriate education, the research proves otherwise. According to Ray and Weller (2003), many studies have examined standardized achievement test scores for homeschooled students and regular schooled students. On average, the homeschooled students scored between 15 and 30 percentile points higher than the public school students. In another study, Ray (1997) found that homeschooled students scored between 30 and 37 percentile points higher on a standardized achievement test than students who attended public schools. Public school students had an average score at the 50th percentile, and the homeschooled students had an average score at the 84th percentile. Homeschooled students are also recruited to some of the nation's top colleges and universities because of their academic preparedness, creativity, and maturity (Kochenderfer & Kanna, 2002). However, it is still too early to say whether, on average, homeschooling students are outscoring their public school peers; more research is needed.

SOCIAL OUTCOMES AND HOMESCHOOLING

Another major criticism to homeschooling is that these students do not receive needed social interaction with their peers. In a regular school setting, students interact with same-age peers most of the day for approximately nine months out of the year. Researchers have conducted studies that have examined socialization of homeschooled students. According to Ray (1997), the average homeschooled student is involved in five activities outside of the home. These activities include group sports, music classes, Bible classes, ballet classes, 4-H, volunteer work, scouting programs, organized field trips, and playing with children outside of their family. This list is by no means exhaustive. Teamwork is a necessity to succeed later in life, especially in the workforce. Therefore, according to Bracey (2003), one aspect of homeschooling that needs to be tested is if these students are able to work in groups.

AFFECTIVE OUTCOMES AND HOMESCHOOLING

On measures of adaptive behaviors, homeschooled children reportedly score higher on daily living skills, communication, and social maturity than their peers attending regular school. However, studies comparing homeschooled students' to regular students' self-concepts have either found no difference or only a slight difference favoring homeschooled students between the two groups (Medlin, 2000). Many public school children are exposed to bullying, cruel teasing, and violence on a daily basis while at school; whereas, most homeschooled children are not exposed to these negative acts nearly as often (Kochenderfer & Kanna, 2002).

Homeschooling is a growing trend in the United States. There are many different approaches to homeschooling; the key is for the parents to find the approach and curriculum that matches the strengths and needs of their child. Homeschooling has many advantages and disadvantages. Parents who are considering homeschooling their child or children need to examine both the positives and the negatives associated with homeschooling before making a decision. Overall, homeschooled students perform well academically, and they are socially and emotionally well developed. However, as for whether or not homeschooling works for our nation as a whole, more research is needed (Bracey, 2003).

—*Jolyn D. Whitaker*

See also Career Assessment; Dropouts

REFERENCES AND FURTHER READING

Bielick, S., Chandler, K., & Broughman, S. P. (2001). *Homeschooling in the United States: 1999* (NCES 2001–033). U.S. Department of Education. Washington, DC: National Center for Education Statistics.

Bracey, G. W. (2003). *What you should know about the war against America's public schools.* Boston: Allyn & Bacon.

Home School Legal Defense Association. (2004). *Homeschooling research: Frequently asked questions.* Retrieved May 20, 2004, from http://www.hslda.org/research/faq.asp#1

Kleist-Tesch, J. M. (1998). Home schoolers and the public library. *Journal of Youth Services in Libraries, 11,* 231–241.

Kochenderfer, R. (2003). *Homeschooling approaches.* Retrieved May 20, 2004, from http://www.homeschool.com/Approaches/default.asp

Kochenderfer, R., & Kanna, E. (2002). *Homeschooling for success: How parents can create a superior education for their child.* New York: Warner Bros.

Medlin, R. G. (2000). Homeschooling and the question of socialization. *Peabody Journal of Education, 75,* 107–123.

Ray, B. D. (1997). *Strengths of their own—Home schoolers across America: Family characteristics, student achievement, &*

longitudinal traits. Salem, Oregon: National Home Education Research Institute.

Ray, B. D., & Weller, N. (2003). Homeschooling: An overview and financial implications for public schools. *School Business Affairs, 69,* 22–26.

HOMELESSNESS

During the past decade the numbers of homeless children, youths, and families have increased significantly. It is estimated that 1.35 million children will experience homelessness during the course of a year, representing 39% of the overall homeless population (Urban Institute, 2000). Powers and Jaklitsch (1993) identified two groups of homeless adolescents, runaways and throwaways. Runaways are children who frequently leave home to escape painful and traumatic family situations in search of safety and protection. These youths may or may not return to their family residence. Throwaways are children who have permanently left home or are forced to leave home by parents or guardians. These youths are likely to remain hidden from the public in cities and towns, making their way in illegal trades such as drugs and prostitution. With little hope of locating these youngsters and pulling them into a system of services that could potentially offer them help and support, the literature refers to this runaway group as "throwaway" children. These children are likely to be without skills and education, and no adult to advocate for them to obtain necessary services. Those who do not return home have enormous service needs because of their detachment from family members and support systems. They are often at great risk for exploitation, substance abuse, and delinquency. Nunez and Collignon (1997) reported homeless American children were moving between shelters or placed in overcrowded or inadequate housing. More than 750,000 of the 1.35 million were of school age, with an average age of nine years.

Some families and children are chronically homeless in that they experience homelessness consistently over very long periods of time. Others are transitionally homeless in that they experience homelessness once or a few times and for relatively short periods of time. These families may move from shelter to shelter struggling to sustain any permanent housing. Those who may be transitionally homeless are temporarily without a residence and with support during a homeless period may be successful thereafter in maintaining

their own home. Rafferty and Shinn (1991) in their study of New York City homeless students noted that homeless children were more likely to have been low-birth-weight infants; experienced higher rates of infant mortality than other nonhomeless children; and experienced additional health threats through prenatal drug exposure, AIDS, poor nutrition, lead poisoning, and accidental injury. Educationally, they were more likely to have repeated or be repeating a grade, were performing on achievement tests at a lower level than other students, and appeared to have significantly lower expectations from teachers for long-term educational success than did their peers.

The federal government makes a distinction between a homeless youth and a runaway youth. A runaway is a person younger than the age of 18 who has been away from home or legal residence at least overnight, without the permission of a parent or guardian. The runaway has chosen to leave and has a home to which he or she may return. A homeless youth has no home or shelter and needs services to provide supervision and care. These youth are sometimes referred to as throwaways. Many of these youth leave home because of abusive and violent situations. Studies show that as many as 60% of the youths in shelters experienced abuse before running away. Some studies estimate that as many as two or three million youths between the ages of 10 and 17 years are living on the streets, in abandoned buildings, or in welfare hotels. These numbers are viewed as conservative given that many homeless youths do not use services and may go uncounted by service agencies.

Schools and school personnel may be especially helpful to these children by attending to both their educational and their psychological needs, recognizing the severe stress under which children who are homeless are living. Children residing temporarily in shelters are likely to have moved numerous times before entering a shelter facility. During those transitions, it may be common for basic needs such as food and shelter to have taken priority over educational and psychological needs. Children who have been homeless may experience stress and trauma. They may arrive at school with gaps in their academic knowledge base, communication skills, as well as in their emotional and social skills. These children are unlikely to have experienced the daily consistency of education enjoyed by their same-age peers with homes. School and medical records, perhaps not a priority for parents who have been homeless, may not be readily available. Consequently, school staff must become sensitized to the many special considerations that can be helpful to children and families who are homeless. These considerations include attention to these children's need for specialized services and alternative methods for obtaining documentation and records that may have become difficult to obtain and maintain during multiple moves. Given the instability and uncertainty in their lives, children who are homeless can benefit enormously from being in a welcoming, accepting, and stable school environment.

Toward the goal of inclusion and equal opportunity to education as defined in the 2001 No Child Left Behind Act, the McKinney-Vento Homeless Assistance Act, reauthorized in January 2002, works to protect the rights of children and youths who may suffer homelessness. Under this Act, "all local educational agencies (LEAs) must designate an appropriate staff person, who may also be a coordinator for other federal programs, as a local educational agency liaison for homeless children and youth to perform duties described in paragraph 6(A)[Section 722(g)(1)(J)(ii)]." Further, under this act LEA liaisons must ensure that children who are attending their schools who are homeless be identified by school personnel and that services for them are coordinated with other entities and agencies. Homeless students are to have full and equal opportunity to succeed in the schools of the LEA. As such, it becomes society's responsibility, both legally and ethically, to embrace children who may struggle from their impoverished backgrounds to achieve success in school.

—*Joy E. Fopiano*

See also Dropouts; Homework; School Reform

REFERENCES AND FURTHER READING

Nunez, R., & Collignon, K. (1997). Creating a community of learning for homeless children. *Educational Leadership, 55,* 56–61.

Powers, J. L., & Jaklitsch, B. (1992). Reaching the hard to reach: Educating homeless adolescents in urban settings. *Education & Urban Society, 25,* 394–410.

Rafferty, Y. (1999). Legal issues in educating homeless children: Past accomplishments and future challenges. *Journal for a Just & Caring Education, 5*(1), 19–31.

Urban Institute. (2000, February 1). *A new look at homelessness in America.* Available from the Urban Institute, 2100 M Street, N.W., Washington, DC 20037 or on the Web site at http://www.urban.org

HOME–SCHOOL COLLABORATION

Home–school collaboration, which involves connecting with families at school and at home, can be defined as a partnership between family members and school staff. Building a home–school partnership is a key responsibility for schools in order to promote the highest standards of education. In reaching out to both families and teachers, school psychologists play an important role and have a unique opportunity. The relevance of home–school partnerships has been underscored by the Futures Workgroup of the National Association of School Psychologists (2004), which has named three goals for enhancing these partnerships:

1. Identify evidence-based models of effective family–school partnerships.

2. Engage in activities to change the culture of schooling to ensure that families are integral partners in the educational process of children.

3. Change preservice education and training to infuse a focus on families as integral partners in the educational process.

Home–school collaboration has also become a focus of recent education reform efforts. While family involvement has traditionally been addressed in special education law, Eagle (2004) notes that the relationship between families and schools was also highlighted in two of the eight goals defined by the National Education Goals Panel in 1999. Goal 1 stipulates that parents will help children start school ready to learn, by devoting time each day to working with their preschool children while having access to training and support services, and Goal 8 states that schools will increase parental involvement to promote social, emotional, and academic growth of children. Further, the No Child Left Behind Act of 2001 requires that local education agencies (LEAs) make efforts to establish effective involvement of parents as well as form partnerships between parents, schools, and the community. These agencies must assist school personnel in forming connections with parents, by coordinating parent programs and working with parents as equal partners (Eagle, 2004).

Epstein (2001) outlines six types of involvement for successful school, family, and community alliances, which schools can promote:

1. Parenting—Involves assisting families in establishing supportive home environments, as well as families assisting schools in understanding the home atmosphere. Schools may provide workshops on jointly selected parenting topics that can be held at convenient times and locations.

2. Communicating—Entails talking with parents about school activities and student progress, and promoting effective home-to-school communication as well. Parents and school staff should talk about what forms of communication work best, as well as appropriate times for discussing school issues.

3. Volunteering—Advocates helping parents and teachers work together to support students, and accommodates family schedules to make student events and school programs accessible. Schools should attempt to recruit all parents to let them know their assistance is valued.

4. Learning at home—Involves opportunities for families to become engaged with their students' education at home through homework and other enrichment activities. Teachers can provide assignments for parents and children to do together, as well as inform families about goals and homework policies.

5. Decision making—Entails both families and schools as valued participants in school decisions, as well as family–school organizations and other committees to take action toward shared goals. Schools can promote this involvement by creating leadership positions for family representatives.

6. Collaborating with community—Involves coordinating resources to provide the most effective services for students. Schools can take the lead in identifying accessible resources.

The idea of family–school partnerships is important from both theoretical and empirical perspectives. Ecological systems theory says that children are a part of a social system comprised of several interrelated systems (Bronfenbrenner, 1979). These systems involve reciprocal influences, such as family and school, which are useful in understanding student behavior. Therefore, it is important to recognize each individual system (e.g., home, classroom, school, school district, and culture) and how it relates to the student's overall ecological environment. Greater continuity between home and school systems means a greater chance of student success.

From a research standpoint, the benefits of home–school collaboration are well supported in both academic and social–emotional areas. Forming partnerships with families is associated with increased student achievement, improved attitude toward school, higher attendance rates, and lower dropout rates. Parents and their children become more connected, and families have an improved understanding of schools, better relationships with teachers, and increased self-efficacy. Teacher benefits include more positive associations with families, better teacher performance, and greater job satisfaction.

There are also several barriers to effective home–school collaboration that exist for parents, educators, and the relationship between them. Many attitudinal factors on the part of both families and schools can prevent the development and maintenance of effective partnerships, such as parental resistance, assumptions about others, failure to see differences as strengths, and lack of perspective taking (Christenson & Sheridan, 2001). Hoover-Dempsey and Sandler (1997) also name three sources of influence on parental involvement in school:

1. Parental role construction (i.e., parents' beliefs about how they are involved in their children's education)

2. Parents' sense of efficacy for helping students succeed

3. Parents' perceptions of invitation for involvement in the schools

These three sources of influence can act as potential barriers to successful home–school relationships. Logistical factors can also serve to inhibit these relationships, such as lack of transportation, language differences, and busy work schedules.

School psychologists have the opportunity, knowledge, skills, and responsibility to reach out to families and build effective partnerships between home and school. Using a problem-solving approach to overcome barriers and facilitating mutual trust and respect during collaboration are essential. What parents and schools do is more important than what they are. Building successful relationships takes time and persistence, and must focus on both content (e.g., evidence-based models) and process (e.g., ensuring that families are genuinely involved in the educational process).

Christenson and Sheridan (2001) outlined the four A's as a guide to conceptualize the crucial elements of optimal home–school partnerships: *approach, attitude,* and *atmosphere,* which are prerequisites for successful *action.* Approach, or the general framework for interaction, considers mutual goals, recognition for the value of learning at home and school, and expectations that both families and schools will be involved in making relationships work and are essential for optimal outcomes for children. Attitude, or the perception of value of home–school partnerships, involves a nonblaming atmosphere, an attempt to understand multiple perspectives, and positive thoughts about student strengths. The atmosphere component (i.e., climate of schools) looks at feelings of respect; a welcoming, inclusive environment; and genuine value and solicitation of multiple perspectives. Lastly, examples of actions include two-way communication, creating mutually supportive roles for families and schools, and implementing policies and practices supporting a collaborative approach. These policies and practices should emphasize collective responsibility for educational outcomes (e.g., mutual decision making, contracts, and clarifying roles and responsibilities). Each of these pieces is a necessary condition for successful home–school partnerships. Although schools must take the lead in the collaboration effort to attain the objectives of the Futures Workgroup, the ultimate goal of the home–school partnership is building shared accountability for student success in school.

—*Elizabeth A. Mizerek and Sandra L. Christenson*

See also Homework; Latchkey Children; School–Home Notes; Single-Parent Families

REFERENCES AND FURTHER READING

Bronfenbrenner, U. (1979). *The ecology of human development.* Cambridge, MA: Harvard University Press.

Christenson, S. L., & Sheridan, S. M. (2001). *School and families: Creating essential connections for learning.* New York: Guilford.

Eagle, J. (2004). Why connect family and school contexts? *The School Psychologist, 58*(2), 76–77, 79.

Epstein, J. L. (2001). *School, family, and community partnerships: Preparing educators and improving schools.* Boulder, CO: Westview.

Futures Workgroup. (2004, April). *Home–school partnerships.* Notes presented at the meeting of the Futures Workgroup for Home–School Partnerships at the National Association of School Psychologists Conference, Dallas, TX.

Hoover-Dempsey, K. V., & Sandler, H. M. (1997). Why do parents become involved in their children's education? *Review of Educational Research, 67,* 3–42.

National Education Goals Panel. (1999). *The national education goals report: Building a nation of learners.* Washington, DC: U.S. Government Printing Office. Available online at http://mathforum.org/epigone/k12.ed.math/bixkelpang

HOMEWORK

Cooper (1989) defines homework as "tasks assigned to students by school teachers that are meant to be carried out during nonschool hours"(p. 7). Homework accounts for 20% of the time students spend on academic tasks (Cooper & Nye, 1994; Polloway & colleagues, 1992). Frequency of homework increases across school grades. In high school, a student with four to five teachers may have two to three hours of homework per night. According to proponents of extensive homework assignments, the main reason for homework is that it increases total study time; however, other purposes for homework cited by professional educators include:

- Practice
- Review and enrichment
- Makeup work
- Preparation for future work
- Test preparation
- Communication with parents

Time spent on homework, percentage of tasks solved, and effort put into homework constitutes important facets of homework behavior. In some ways, homework involves the complex interaction of more influences than any other instructional device. For example, factors that affect the nature, quality, and effectiveness of homework include student characteristics, parent involvement and home support (time, space, quiet, materials), characteristics of the assignment (amount, purpose, links to the curriculum, skills needed, student choice and individualization), and feedback and correction provided on the homework product (Cooper, 1989).

HOMEWORK EFFECTS ON ACHIEVEMENT

Given the popular belief that homework has positive effects on students, the research is somewhat contradictory about the specific effects of homework on academic achievement and school performance (Cooper & colleagues, 1998). Such contradictions are likely, in part, because of lack of standard metrics for "homework" (time, amount, design) and student achievement (standardized tests or grades, or both). Larger-scale analyses generally support the relationship between homework and positive student achievement. Cooper (1989) analyzed 17 studies focused on homework assignments and found that in classes where homework was assigned, the academic achievement was higher than in classes where no homework was assigned. However, the effect varied dramatically with grade level. For elementary school students, the effect of homework on achievement was negligible, while junior high students benefited more. For high school students, homework had substantial positive effects. Using a large national database, Keith and colleagues (1993) also found a significant relationship between time spent on homework and standardized achievement scores.

Beyond the assignment of homework and the parallel concepts of amount of homework and time spent on homework, determining the effectiveness of homework as a strategy is a complex task. The impact of homework on academic achievement is mediated by factors such as appropriateness of the design of homework, student learning abilities, student attitudes, and parent and peer support.

ADVANTAGES AND DISADVANTAGES OF HOMEWORK

Aside from the question of the basic effectiveness of homework as a learning strategy, there are both positive and negative potential outcomes or side effects of homework (Cooper & colleagues, 1998). On the positive side, homework is believed to improve learning and achievement through better retention of factual knowledge, increased understanding, and improvements in critical thinking. Homework is also thought to reinforce self-discipline, organizational strategies, and study habits and skills. Homework is sometimes used as a way to get parents involved in their children's schooling. Finally, the longer-term benefits may be a general orientation toward inquisitiveness and positive attitudes toward learning.

On the negative side, if overused, homework may lead to student fatigue and loss of interest in academic material. The pressure accompanying homework completion could lead to cheating. Parental involvement that is based on conflict or that is uninformed or inaccurate is not helpful. Finally, homework may lead to increased inequities in schooling because of the false assumption that all homes will provide an appropriate place, time, and support for homework completion. Families in low socioeconomic conditions may struggle to provide these supports. Language differences between the home and school further complicate parental ability to help with homework when needed (Cosden & colleagues, 2001). Finally, variations in student ability complicate the intended benefits of assigning homework. Approximately 28% of average-achieving students and 56% of students with learning disabilities have problems completing their homework (Polloway & colleagues, 1992).

HOMEWORK INTERVENTIONS

Given the likely positive effects of homework on student achievement, there have been surprisingly few studies that examine the effectiveness of interventions designed to improve homework completion. Studies that have been completed can be characterized by several approaches, including:

- Direct individual student intervention
- Change in teacher practice
- Offering homework support at school
- Change in parent practice

An example of a student-level intervention is teaching self-management (i.e., managing one's own behavior) and organizational skills. Bryan and Sullivan-Burstein (1998) used collaborative student teams to address homework performance. Students were instructed to use self-graphing of their homework completion and homework assignment planners. Real-life assignments were used to help students connect their schoolwork with their home life. Homework planners are particularly effective for students with learning disabilities and average students with homework problems. The planners provide a simple tool that addresses the issue of increased parent communication.

Additionally, the Bryan and Sullivan-Burstein (1998) study provided evidence that working collaboratively with teachers to create and implement homework practices was an effective method of supporting student homework completion. Other effective teacher-directed interventions include methods of individual and group reinforcement, response cost, home notes, cooperative learning, and homework teams.

In an effort to increase the likelihood that students will complete their homework, some schools have offered after-school programs. This approach is thought to be particularly helpful for students who do not have homework support at home. Cosden and colleagues (2001) documented a positive impact of such a program on students who were English language learners in contrast to their English-speaking peers. It is likely that the families who do not speak English are less able to help their children with their schoolwork and have fewer outside resources available to them. While English proficiency is one barrier to parents helping students with their homework, it is not the only one. Others include parent education levels, parent work schedules, space for the student to do homework, and extracurricular activities. Thus, after-school homework programs may help children whose parents cannot or will not help.

Another important finding of the Cosden and colleagues (2001) study was that early homework completion rates and homework session attendance in the fourth grade were predictive of academic outcomes in the sixth grade. It appeared that establishing good homework habits in the fourth grade enabled the students to also establish effective study skills, which supported their academic performance in later elementary school.

After-school programs that allow students to complete homework at school may have the unintended function of taking parents out of the homework equation. Parents in the Cosden and colleagues (2001) study expressed great relief at not having to have the added stress of making sure their children did their homework. However, as homework assignments become more complex and necessitate additional work outside of school, parents whose children attend an after-school homework program may be lulled into a false assumption that their children are completing all of their work at school. Another disadvantage of completing "home" work at school is that the parent–child negotiations surrounding homework do not get established early.

The indications from research are that parent involvement in the homework process positively impacts children's performance in school and attitudes toward school learning. The positive effects seen in research are related to parental communication about schoolwork with their children and their children's teacher, as well as positive attitudes toward the tasks involved in school learning (Epstein & Van Voorhis, 2001; Hoover-Dempsey & colleagues, 2001). Parent involvement in homework provides modeling, reinforcement, and instruction that supports the development of attitudes, knowledge, and behaviors associated with successful school performance (Hoover-Dempsey & colleagues, 2001).

However, it is important to understand what type of involvement is appropriate and helpful. The type of parent involvement in the homework process varies as a function of age (younger children tend to elicit more help than older ones). The types of activities that parents may engage in as part of the homework process include (Hoover-Dempsey & colleagues, 2001):

- Establishing physical and psychological structures for the student's homework performance
- Developing rules and procedures protecting the student from distractions
- Interacting with the student and/or teacher about the homework process
- Engaging in an interactive process supporting the student's understanding of homework

ROLE OF THE SCHOOL PSYCHOLOGIST

One of the goals for school psychologists is to assist with the overall school adjustment of students. A student who is not doing his or her homework is violating one of the main expectations of many schools. Homework is affected by various factors that are not found in school, including family; individual differences in motivation; and specific preferences about when, where, how, and with whom they prefer to do homework. The school psychologist is in an ideal position to take this more "ecological" perspective in helping a student adjust to school and serve as a problem solver, working within and between the contexts of school and home.

At the individual level, school psychologists can assess the difficulties that a student may be experiencing with the homework process (e.g., motivation, organizational skills). The school psychologist is in a unique position to assess the resources that are available to assist the student with homework (e.g., parents, tutors, programs) or to help the student negotiate homework issues with teachers and/or parents. The school psychologist may choose to work individually with students to organize their homework assignments, think about their study habits, and better understand their motivation and preference patterns in homework situations. Small groups organized around these themes is an alternative approach to these issues. The Student Study Team and Individualized Educational Plan team processes provide a forum for discussion of homework habits in relation to a student's performance in school. This forum includes parents, teachers, school psychologists, and potentially the student as well. Finally, at the schoolwide level, the school psychologist can facilitate school staff discussions about homework practice, researching and sharing practices that have been shown to be effective.

It is likely that "homework" as a major educational strategy is here to stay. The school psychologist can play a critical role is helping educators, students, and parents think about homework in a more complex and sophisticated way.

—*Gale M. Morrison and Megan Brown*

See also Academic Achievement; Grades; Learning; Motivation; School–Home Notes; Study Skills

REFERENCES AND FURTHER READING

Bryan, T., & Sullivan-Burstein, K. (1998). Teacher-selected strategies for improving homework completion. *Remedial and Special Education, 19*(5), 263–275.

Cooper, H. (1989). Synthesis of research on homework. *Educational Leadership, 47*(3), 85–91.

Cooper, H., Lindsay, J. J., Nye, B., & Greathouse, S. (1998). Relationships among attitudes about homework, amount of homework assigned and completed, and student achievement. *Journal of Educational Psychology, 90*(1), 70–83.

Cooper, H., & Nye, B. (1994). Homework for students with learning disabilities: The implications of research for policy and practice. *Journal of Learning Disabilities, 27*, 465–536.

Cosden, M., Morrison, G. M., Albanese, A. L., & Macias, S. (2001). When homework is not home work: After-school programs for homework assistance. *Educational Psychologist, 36*(3), 211–221.

Hoover-Dempsey, K. V., Battiato, A. C., Walker, J. M. T., Reed, R. P., Delong, J. M., & Jones, K. P. (2001). Parental involvement in homework. *Educational Psychologist, 36*(3), 195–209.

Keith, T. Z., Keith, P. B., Troutman, G. C., Bickley, P. G., Trivette, P. S., & Singh, K. (1993). Does parental involvement affect eighth-grade student achievement? Structural analysis of national data. *School Psychology Review, 22,* 474–496.

Polloway, E. A., Foley, R. M., & Epstein, M. H. (1992). A comparison of the homework problems of students with learning disabilities and nonhandicapped students. *Learning Disabilities: Research and Practice, 7,* 203–209.

Polloway, E. A., Epstein, M. H., Bursuck, W. D., Jayanthi, M., & Cumblad, C. (1994). Homework practices of general education teachers. *Journal of Learning Disabilities, 27*(8), 500–509.

HYPNOSIS

Hypnosis can be defined as an altered state of consciousness or as a state of mind in which an individual is particularly susceptible to various degrees of suggestibility. Although hypnosis has not been used extensively in educational situations, a review of the literature reveals common, agreed-upon areas of use as an educational instrument. Hypnosis can:

- Reduce test anxiety
- Improve concentration
- Improve memory recall
- Improve self-confidence
- Increase motivation

Most research thus far demonstrates the benefits of hypnosis in laboratory settings rather than a school setting. One of the roadblocks to widespread educational applications is the prevalence of myths that continue to be held by the general population. Most myths center around subjects losing control while in a hypnotic state, thus becoming susceptible to commands to act contrary to their character. Actually, an individual will still maintain essential self-control, although some individuals appear to have more suggestibility than others. Many of the advantages of hypnosis in a laboratory setting are applicable to psychological practice in the schools as well.

—*Jim Deni and Leon Lewis*

See also Ethical Issues in School Psychology; Psychotherapy

I

IMITATION. *See* BEHAVIOR; THEORIES OF HUMAN DEVELOPMENT

IMPULSIVITY. *See* ATTENTION DEFICIT HYPERACTIVITY DISORDER; TIME ON TASK

INDIVIDUALIZED EDUCATION PLAN

The Individualized Education Plan (IEP) is perhaps the most essential document within special education because it formalizes the concept of a free, appropriate public education (FAPE) for a student with disabilities by guiding and regulating all aspects of a student's special education plan. According to Bateman and Linden (1998), there is no document more important from which to monitor and enforce the Individuals With Disabilities Education Act (IDEA) as it applies to special education services. A written instrument, the IEP describes (a) a student's educational needs and the resources that will be used to meet those needs; (b) the goals and objectives that direct the educational program and placement; and (c) the evaluation criteria to be used.

Eight factors must be included in the IEP (Drasgow & colleagues, 2001; IDEA, 1997):

1. Present levels of educational performance

2. Measurable annual goals, including benchmarks and short-term objectives

3. Special education and related services, supplementary aids, and program modifications or supports

4. Participation level with nondisabled peers

5. Participation in statewide and districtwide tests

6. Date and frequency of services and modifications

7. Measurement strategies needed for communication with parents and progress reports

8. Transition services

The IEP sometimes needs to address special factors related to the child's disability, including (Office of Special Education Programs, 2000):

- Strategies to address the child's behavior if it interferes with the child's learning or the learning of others
- Communication modifications, including those related to limited proficiency in English or hearing impairment
- Assistive technology (e.g., hearing aids)
- Instruction in Braille or the use of Braille, if the child is blind or visually impaired

An IEP team is convened after the school's multidisciplinary team (MDT) has determined that a student is eligible for special education services. Specific people must be in attendance at this meeting, including the child's parents/caregivers, a local social service agency representative, and an educational professional who is qualified to explain the instructional implications of the evaluation results. In addition, at least one of the child's general education teachers and a special education teacher or just the student's special education teacher must be in attendance. Other individuals, at the discretion of the parents or school, as well as the student, if appropriate, are also allowed to be included in the IEP process (Drasgow & colleagues, 2001). For example, if the student requires assistive technology (e.g., specialized computer programs, medical equipment) in IEP development, the team may include an individual whose expertise lies in this area.

According to Drasgow and colleagues (2001), the IEP team serves two major purposes during the meeting. First, the team must develop a document based on the student's needs. Second, the team must determine placement using the criterion of least restrictive environment. That is, placement in special education classrooms and schools or other more restrictive settings should occur only when a student cannot receive an appropriate education in the general education classroom, even with the use of additional aids and supports (IDEA, 1997).

HISTORY

As a result of the reauthorization of the Individuals With Disabilities Education Act in 1997 (IDEA, 1997) and the subsequently published U.S. Department of Education regulations (IDEA Regulations, 1999), numerous changes have been made to the IEP process. Specifically, a particular emphasis has been placed on accountability to "hold schools to a higher level of responsibility for developing and implementing valid and beneficial IEPs than in the past" (Drasgow & colleagues, 2001, p. 360).

STRENGTHS

The IEP has several strengths; perhaps most important is the requirement that parents and educators act as partners in formulating IEP objectives. In fact, the law was designed so that all parties who participate in and have a vested interest in the child's education engage in significant dialogue about the needs of the child and have input into the IEP that guides the child's education.

Another major strength of the IEP is the requirement that student progress be continuously evaluated. Thus, appropriate and ongoing data are gathered to evaluate student progress toward stated goals and to

help determine areas to be addressed within the child's school day (Drasgow & colleagues, 2001; IDEA, 1997).

Finally, the IDEA also mandates that the IEP be reviewed annually. This is a tremendous advantage because it allows the IEP team to detect:

- Any lack of progress toward annual goals
- Changes in reevaluation results
- New information about the child as provided by the parents or teachers
- Expected needs of the student
- Any other issues relevant to the student's progress

The law allows for the review to lead to revisions only if necessary (Drasgow & colleagues, 2001). Thus, the annual review provides accountability for educational goals of the student.

WEAKNESSES

Challenges with the IEP process exist within the development of the document itself, and within the IEP team process (Huefner, 2000). Difficulties in developing the IEP document can generally be traced to training and time. That is, some educators have not received adequate training on how to prepare the document—they may not know how to accurately report levels of educational performance and write measurable goals and objectives that are linked to student assessment data. The result is often a lack of appropriate goals, objectives, and evaluation procedures (Huefner, 2000).

Time constraints are also an issue as parents and professionals often find it difficult to meet and coordinate their schedules. Time restraints within schools have frustrated educators who have reported that it is difficult to complete the burdensome paperwork requirements associated with the IEP (Huefner, 2000).

In addition, both parties have identified frustration related to their roles on the team. Specifically, parents often report that they feel that they are not equal members of the team because (Huefner, 2000):

- Educators use unfamiliar jargon in their presence.
- IEP-related process and procedures are never fully explained.
- Legal requirements are often offered only on a "need to know" basis.

Professionals, on the other hand, experience frustration by some parents' lack of knowledge of the IDEA and the IEP process, and a general lack of understanding of what can be accomplished reasonably in a school setting.

ROLE OF THE SCHOOL PSYCHOLOGIST

The school psychologist plays a vital role in the construction, implementation, and monitoring of the IEP. This is especially true when (Nastasi, 2000):

- An individual is initially found to be eligible for special education services.
- Further evaluation information needs to be considered.
- Behavioral, emotional, or placement issues need to be addressed.

Often, the school psychologist is considered the most appropriate member of the IEP team for interpreting and analyzing the evaluation data that are part of the MDT. Given that most parents and many teachers do not have a thorough statistical background, it is very important that the assessment results be explained in terms that are understood by all team members. This facilitates a better understanding of the individual's strengths, weaknesses, and processing abilities, thus allowing the team to develop the most appropriate educational goals for that student (Nastasi, 2000).

Further, when behavioral concerns and/or emotional factors are negatively affecting a student's ability to perform in school, the school psychologist is often called upon to play an active role in the development, implementation, and monitoring of a behavior intervention plan (BIP), which may be included as part of the IEP. The school psychologist's training in the areas of child development, child and adolescent psychopathology, and behavioral psychology offers a unique combination of skills necessary for effectively modifying an individual's behavior in a positive way.

Finally, when the IEP team must consider changing a student's educational placement because of issues regarding least restrictive environment, the school psychologist is often asked to make recommendations. Such recommendations would be based on information gained about the individual through observations, case history, record review, individual assessment, teacher and parent input, as well as the school psychologist's knowledge of how other individuals currently perform in the proposed placement.

—*Brenda S. Myles, Kerry Mehaffey,*
and Paul S. Roodbeen

See also Accommodation; Individuals With Disabilities Education Act; Program Evaluation; Resource Rooms; Special Education

REFERENCES AND FURTHER READING

Bateman, B. D., & Linden, M. A. (1998). *Better IEPs: How to develop legally correct and educationally useful programs* (3rd ed.). Longmont, CO: Sopris West.

Drasgow, E., Yell, M. L., & Robinson, T. R. (2001). Developing legally correct and educationally appropriate IEPs. *Remedial and Special Education, 22,* 359–373.

Education of All Children Handicapped Act 1975. (Public Law No. 94–142), renamed the Individuals With Disabilities Education Act in 1990. 20 U.S.C. Chapter 33.

Huefner, D. S. (2000). The risks and opportunities of the IEP requirements under IDEA 1997. *Exceptional Children, 33,* 195–204.

Individuals With Disabilities Education Act Amendment of 1997 (Public Law 105–17), 20 U.S.C. Chapter 33.

Individuals With Disabilities Education Act Regulations of 1999. 34 C.F.R. Part 300.

Nastasi, B. K. (2000). School psychologists as healthcare providers in the 21st century: Conceptual framework, professional identity, and professional practice. *School Psychology Review, 29,* 540–554.

Office of Special Education Programs. (2000). *A guide to the individualized education plan.* Washington, DC: Author. Available online at http://www.ed.gov/parents/needs/speced/iepguide/index.html

INDIVIDUALIZED EDUCATION PLAN MEETING

The Individualized Education Plan (IEP) is the unique plan for providing special education services to a student who has been determined to have an exceptionality. The IEP is developed after an evaluation or re-evaluation for special education eligibility has occurred. The IEP meeting is required and is designed to discuss the individual and the evaluation results; and to develop, review, and revise the IEP for an individual who qualifies for special education because of the presence of a disability. Each public agency, including public schools, is responsible for initiating and holding IEP meetings. The IEP meeting is an important element in the delivery of special education services, because at the meeting the IEP document is discussed, revised when necessary, finalized, and agreed upon by all team members.

After an IEP meeting, a student's IEP and all of the special education services go into effect or continue to be in effect for the individual (when the IEP meeting occurs after re-evaluation).

General processes of the IEP team members at the meeting include (Küpper, 2000):

- Coming together to pool expertise concerning the child
- Using a problem-solving model to discuss the unique strengths and needs of the child
- Determining the necessary components, including IEP goals and the interventions necessary to achieve these goals
- Working together to improve the educational results of the child by finalizing his or her IEP and creating appropriate interventions for the individual student

The IEP team is typically comprised of the child's parent(s), at least one of the child's regular education teachers, and at least one of the child's special education teachers/providers. In addition, a representative must be present from the public agency or school who is knowledgeable of and is qualified to provide (or provide supervision of) the child's individually designed instruction, is knowledgeable of the general curriculum of the school, and knows the availability of the school's resources. The IEP team also must include an individual who is able to interpret instructional implications of the evaluation results (typically the school psychologist), and, if appropriate, any individual who is knowledgeable or an expert regarding the child, including related services personnel. Finally, the IEP team should include the child when it is deemed appropriate. Transition services must be provided for students in special education when they are beginning to transition out of their current educational setting (i.e. graduation from high school). If transition services are appropriate because of the child's age (generally, 14 years or older), the child must be invited to attend the IEP meeting. If the child does not attend the meeting, the school must take other steps to ensure the student's interest is considered. The IEP team may

also include an interpreter or other such person when needed to ensure the parents understand the proceedings. Teams should be highly individualized and hold expertise concerning the child who is being evaluated (Küpper, 2000).

Parents are a valuable addition to the IEP team because they provide invaluable information concerning the student. Letting parents know they are valuable increases family involvement in the child's education (Comuntzis-Page, 1996). Additionally, parental involvement in their child's education increases student achievement (Turner, 2000).

During the IEP meeting a number of required documents are completed and signed. Forms used generally include an IEP meeting notification, a copy of the Parent's Rights in Special Education, and the draft IEP document; IEP meeting summary; parental consent forms for special education services; and notice/consent of identification, services, and placement.

The IEP team must meet for an initial IEP implementation and again at least once per year to discuss progress toward the goal, at which time any necessary revisions to the IEP should be evaluated and defined. A re-evaluation to determine if the child still has an exceptionality and requires special education services must occur at least every three years. At this time, the entire IEP team must reconvene to collaborate on the progress the student has made on the IEP and plan for the next segment of his or her education (Küpper, 2000).

—*Martha Boehlert*

See also Due Process; Individualized Education Plan; Individuals With Disabilities Education Act; Least Restrictive Environment; Multidisciplinary Teams; Special Education

REFERENCES AND FURTHER READING

Comuntizis-Page, G. (1996). *Critical Issue: Creating the school climate structures to support parent and family involvement.* Naperville, IL: North Central Regional Educational Laboratory. Available online at http://www.ncrel.org/sdrs/areas/issues/envrnmnt/famncomm/pa300.htm

Küpper, L. (Ed.) (2000). *A guide to the individualized education program.* Washington, DC: U.S. Department of Education. Office of Special Education and Rehabilitative Services. Available online at http://www.ed.gov/parents/needs/speced/iepguide/index.html

Turner, J. (2000). Parent involvement: What can we learn from research? *Montessori Life, 12*(2), 37–39.

INDIVIDUALS WITH DISABILITIES EDUCATION ACT

The Individuals With Disabilities Education Act (IDEA) (1990) is the legislation previously known as the Education for All Handicapped Children Act (EAHCA) (1975). Prior to this act, children with disabilities, particularly those with severe disabilities, did not receive a public education. Before IDEA, the main role of a school psychologist was to determine whether a child was eligible for public education or needed to be excluded from the public school because he or she was too difficult to teach. Special education teachers were generally for children with mild mental retardation. Few schools provided services for children with learning disabilities or emotional disturbance.

There is no fundamental right to an education under the U.S. Constitution (Jacob-Timm & Hartshorne, 1998). Education is a property right and states have the responsibility for public education. Following the passage of IDEA, children who had previously not been served were admitted to schools, and programs needed to be developed to meet their needs. Because each state was responsible for determining criteria for admission to programs, services varied depending on the geographic location and the funding criteria set by each state's state department of education (SEA). The federal government basically had oversight for the programs, but the management and direction was seen as a state responsibility.

ASPECTS OF IDEA

Major components of IDEA included concepts formulated in the early 1970s, and they continue to be amended and refined. Child Find, which is part of IDEA, requires schools to proactively identify and evaluate children that are not succeeding in school, potentially because of a disability. IDEA also includes a specific funding formula, which allocates funds to states based on the relative population of children who are of criterion age (3 to 21 years) with additional funding based on the relative population of children who are of criterion age and living in poverty.

There are six major principles of IDEA: zero reject, nondiscriminatory evaluation, free and appropriate public education, the least restrictive environment, procedural due process, and parent–student participation. Zero reject is a mandate to educate every child, regardless of the severity of the disability. This principle of IDEA includes providing for basic skills such as feeding and toileting (Prasse, 1995). Nondiscriminatory evaluation requires unbiased assessments to be conducted to determine if a child needs special education services and to inform placement choice. This mandate attempts to avoid the overidentification of cultural and linguistic minorities to special education. Nondiscriminatory evaluation is a continued concern as many school districts find an overabundance of minority children enrolled in special education. IDEA provides funding to support parent–school involvement and initiate early intervention services to disabled infants, toddlers, and preschoolers and their families. It also mandates compensatory education for young adults up to 21 years of age as well as vocational and transition services (assisting special education students in living and working after formal schooling ends). Procedural due process ensures school adherence to the principles of IDEA, and provides families and schools with legal safeguards for redress of grievances. Parent–student participation mandates the inclusion of parents in educational decision making and goal setting for their disabled children.

Free appropriate public education (FAPE) requires that the Individualized Education Plan (IEP) for disabled students or the Individualized Family Service Plan (IFSP) ensure the appropriateness and benefit of an educational placement, service, and/or setting. This principle has been the basis for much debate in the field and in legal circles. To determine what is appropriate, two key components are used: the least restrictive environment (LRE) and the IEP. The LRE provides disabled students with access to the most independent learning environments and most inclusive peer relations. The goal is to keep the child in the regular classroom for as much of the day as possible. LRE ranges from residential treatment to full inclusion, depending on the child's needs. The IEP is a broad procedure that is more fully discussed in the following section.

INDIVIDUALIZED EDUCATION PLAN

Under IDEA, the school is required to develop a plan that is specific to a particular child's needs. Included in the IEP are the goals, objectives, and timelines for implementation. Also included are an evaluation process to determine a child's progress (in meeting IEP goals and objectives) and a listing of who is responsible for the different components or aspects of the plan. The IEP has been the subject of several legal challenges. In one (*Board v. Rowley*, 1982), the Supreme Court determined that the intent of Congress was not to maximize a child's development but rather to provide a reasonable opportunity to learn. From this decision, the IEP has become important for the implementation of a child's program. If the IEP contains the necessary requirements procedurally mandated by IDEA, it is generally regarded as appropriate. These aspects include the development of an IEP by a group of professionals and parents, and that the IEP provides an individualized program for the child. In *Irving Independent School District v. Tatro* (1984), the court ruled that schools need to provide health-related services for a child's learning. Other related services such as school nursing services are also included.

DISABILITY CATEGORIES

There are several categories of conditions or disorders defined in the IDEA that are deemed appropriate for special education services. These categories are autism, deaf-blind, deaf, hearing impairment, mental retardation, multiple disabilities, orthopedic impairment, other health impairment, serious emotional disturbance, specific learning disability, speech or language impairment, traumatic brain injury, and visual impairment including blindness. The states have established specific criteria for inclusion in special education. These criteria can vary widely between states. The entire IDEA document is available online at http://www.cec.sped.org/law_res/doc/law/index.php.

REAUTHORIZATION OF IDEA

The reauthorization of IDEA is currently taking place and has not been completed. Because of this delay, some provisions may change with the new law but most will be intact (LRE, FAPE, and IEP). Each state needs to develop its own requirements for the new law and these requirements have not been codified as of January, 2005. Basically, the Act supports inclusive education and, additionally, suggests that students with disabilities can be more effectively educated when high expectations are present in the general education curriculum (Gartner & Lipsky, 1998). Moreover, the referral process must consider multiple factors in

addition to the disability that may be affecting a student's performance. This new criterion is particularly important as school psychologists and special educators consider their roles in the assessment process. In addition, a general education teacher is mandated to be on the IEP team. The IEP must now state why a student should be excluded from general education, and a special education student must be taught the general curriculum, not a special education curriculum.

With the reauthorization of IDEA, an emphasis will be placed on student outcomes (Mead, 1997). There will be an improved appeals process, and provisions for discipline problems will be developed. There are plans in the reauthorization to provide schools with more disciplinary authority in the cases of children with disabilities.

Cooney (2001) suggests that schools are not prepared to fulfill the reauthorization's requirements. Inequities in what is expected of children in special education are predicted, with schools and teachers unable and unprepared to meet these needs. Suggestions have been made that schools restructure under the reauthorization requirements to meet the needs of all learners. School psychologists are needed to provide additional support to regular and special education teachers as well as providing systemwide support. Training of teachers is another area that needs to be evaluated in light of the new regulations, and universities may be ill-prepared to provide additional coursework in these areas of need.

CONCLUSION

The reauthorization of IDEA is not complete. Discussion about the appropriate diagnostic procedures for the identification of children with disabilities continues. In addition, there are questions about the roles of specific personnel, such as school psychologists and special education teachers. The roles of both professionals are changing. For example, school psychologists have traditionally been involved in assessment. With changes in IDEA, the emphasis is no longer on assessment but on outcome. The practice of school psychology is now changing to provide training in functional behavioral assessment and to provide parents and teachers with appropriate consultation for students with difficulties. Likewise, the role of the special education teacher is changing from a teacher working in a separate classroom to a teacher providing services through or with a regular education teacher.

Timeline

1954: *Brown v Board of Education*—Right to equal educational opportunities and settings under the law.

1958: P.L. 85–926—Funds granted to train college instructors in teacher training programs for students with special needs.

1964: Title VI of the Civil Rights Act enacted—No public agency may discriminate against participants involved in their programs, services, or activities on the basis of race, color, gender, or nation of origin.

1965: P.L. 89–10, Elementary and Secondary Education Act—Federal financial commitment to the improvement of schools especially for the "educationally disadvantaged."

1968: P.L. 90–583—Services for preschool-age children with disabilities.

1970: Education of the Handicapped Act (EHA) enacted.

1972: *Pennsylvania Association for Retarded Citizens v. Commonwealth of Pennsylvania*—Public schools must provide an education for the severely retarded.

1972: *Mills v. The Board of Education*—Schools must serve all students with disabilities.

1973: *LeBanks v. Spears*—Least Restrictive Environment concept clarified.

1975: P.L. 94–142, The Education for All Handicapped Children Act (EAHCA)—Regulations for the identification, evaluation, and placement of all students with disabilities in public school. The concepts of Free and Appropriate Public Education (FAPE), Least Restrictive Environment (LRE), and the Individualized Education Plan (IEP) are introduced.

1980: Racial, cultural, and socioeconomic bias on intelligence quotient (IQ) and other tests was found to lead to the overrepresentation of minorities in special education.

1982: *Board of Education v. Rowley*—American Sign Language interpreters provided as part of IEP to work with deaf students in their classes.

1983: *Springdale School District v. Grace*—Court rules that appropriate education did not mean "best" education or education supporting maximum development.

1984: *Larry P. v. Riles*—Multiple methods to evaluate a child referred for special education required.

1986: P.L. 99–457, Education of All Handicapped Children Act Amendments Part H—Early interventions are introduced.

1986: P.L. 99–372, The Handicapped Children's Protection Act—Fees for attorneys acting on behalf of parents/ guardians covered if parents/guardians prevail in court.

1986: Courts rule that expulsion of a student with a disability may only be used when exclusion from school is not associated with the student's disability and such action does not eliminate a student's right to services under EAHCA.

1988: "Stay put" provision of EAHCA enacted—A child with a disability stays in current placement and receives services while a due-process dispute takes place.

1990: P.L. 101–336, Americans With Disabilities Act—Prohibits discrimination.

1990: P.L. 94–142, The Individuals With Disabilities Education Act (IDEA) (new name for EAHCA)—Amendments added requiring transition plans for older students with disabilities. Goals 2000 are also adopted.

1990: P.L. 101–476, IDEA expansion of services—Mental health and assistive technology support services added, which provides services to young adults 18 to 21 years of age; introduces new diagnostic categories including traumatic brain injury and autism.

1991: Reauthorization of IDEA—Early intervention services are provided to children birth to five years old and their families through Individualized Family Service Plans (IFSPs).

1994: P.L. 103–239, School-to-Work Opportunities Act.

1997: P.L. 105–17, IDEA amendments—School safety, educational results, and parent–school collaboration promoted.

2001: P.L. 107–110, No Child Left Behind Act of 2001—Reauthorization of the Elementary and Secondary Education Act (ESEA).

2004: P.L. 108–446, Individuals With Disabilities Improvement Act

This is a time of great change and possibilities as all educators become more adept at working with children with all types of abilities and disabilities.

—*Margaret Semrud-Clikeman and Allison Cloth*

See also Diagnosis and Labeling; Due Process; Individualized Education Plan; Least Restrictive Environment; Multidisciplinary Teams; Special Education

REFERENCES AND FURTHER READING

Board of Education of the Hendrick Hudson Central School District v. Rowley, 102 Supreme Court, 3034 (1982).

Cooney, B. (2001, April). *The widening gap of intolerance: An analysis of standards-based reforms and special education in the schools*. Paper presented at the annual meeting of the American Educational Research Association, Seattle, WA.

Education for All Handicapped Children Act of 1975, 20 U.S.C. Section 401 (1975).

Gartner, A., & Lipsky, D. (1998). *The 1997 reauthorization of IDEA*. New York: National Center on Educational Restructuring and Inclusion (NCERI) Bulletin.

IDEA (2000). *22nd Annual Report to Congress on the Implementation of the Individuals With Disabilities Education Act*. Washington, DC: U.S. Department of Education.

Irving Independent School District v. Tatro, 104 Supreme Court, 3371 (1984).

Jacob-Timm, S., & Hartshorne, T. (1998). *Ethics and law for school psychologists* (3rd ed.). New York: Wiley.

Lyon, G. R. (2002). *Why do some children have difficulty learning how to read? What can we do about it?* Paper presented at the 53rd conference of the International Dyslexia Association Conference, Atlanta, GA.

Mead, J. (1997). Wrestling with equity: Reauthorization of IDEA. *School Business Affairs, 63,* 11–15.

Prasse, D. P. (1995). School psychology and the law. In A. Thomas & J. Grimes (Eds.), *Best practices in school psychology* (Vol.3, pp. 41–50). Washington, DC: National Association of School Psychologists.

INDIVIDUALS WITH DISABILITIES EDUCATION ACT DISABILITY CATEGORIES–PART B

Landmark federal legislation—the Individuals With Disabilities Education Act (IDEA)—passed in 1975 (Public Law 94–142) mandated that children with disabilities have access to a free and appropriate public education. Before IDEA became law, an estimated one million children with disabilities were excluded from the public education system. A trend toward increased inclusiveness has occurred as a result of a series of reauthorizations of the original legislation as well as judicial review. Moreover, the zero reject principle requires the identification and education of all children with disabilities regardless of the degree of impairment.

In place at the federal level is a categorically driven service delivery model for special education. Provision of services is contingent upon the child's need, eligibility criteria for a specific disability, and a documented adverse effect on the child's educational performance. Thirteen specific categories, all of which are described in the following sections, are identified in the IDEA.

AUTISM

Core features of autism include deficits in verbal and nonverbal communication as well as impaired social interaction. Atypical characteristics—such as engagement in repetitive behavior, stereotyped movements, resistance to change, and unusual reaction to sensory stimuli—may be present. Features of autism are frequently discernible prior to three years of age; however, establishing a firm diagnosis at an early age is often difficult because limited language, developmental delay, or inattention complicate accurate identification. Autism is described as a "spectrum disorder," meaning the expression of the disorder from one child to another varies in symptoms.

DEAF–BLIND

Precise levels of sensory impairment for deafness and blindness are not specified. Instead, eligibility for these conditions is based upon the presence of both hearing and visual impairments, which results in severe communication and developmental problems. Moreover, it must be established that the child's educational needs cannot be adequately met in a class that focuses on a single sensory deficit.

DEAFNESS

An exact audiologic definition regarding the severity of hearing loss is not specified; rather the degree of hearing loss is determined at the state level. This category applies when a severe hearing impairment interferes with auditory processing of linguistic information. Typically, children included in this category are unable to depend on their hearing to process auditory information.

EMOTIONAL DISTURBANCE

Characteristics of emotional disorders are unusual, because of the intensity and duration of the symptomatology, and negatively affect school performance. Indicators include an unexplained lack of academic progress, interpersonal deficits, inappropriate behaviors or feelings, depressed mood, or development of physical symptoms or fears. Schizophrenia is included in this category. Social maladjustment alone is not sufficient for inclusion, and although maladjustment is not specifically defined, it is generally considered to include the engagement in rule-breaking or oppositional behaviors.

HEARING IMPAIRMENT

Eligibility for the hearing impairment category is based upon the presence of a permanent or fluctuating hearing loss that does not meet the criteria for deafness. Children with a hearing impairment may rely on residual hearing to communicate.

MENTAL RETARDATION

Approximately 10% of children who receive services under IDEA meet criteria for mental retardation. To meet eligibility standards, an individual must exhibit significant subaverage general cognitive functioning in combination with adaptive deficits. Adaptive abilities refer to age-appropriate standards necessary to function successfully in daily life. For example, expectations for young children may include putting away toys, whereas older children may be expected to participate in household tasks such as meal preparation. Evidence of deficits must be present during the developmental period.

MULTIPLE DISABILITIES

Children who exhibit a combination of disabilities, and consequently have severe and unusual needs that cannot be adequately addressed within a single disability category, may be eligible for services under IDEA.

ORTHOPEDIC IMPAIRMENT

Included in the orthopedic impairment category are children with severe physical impairment whose etiology may be either congenital or acquired through disease or trauma.

OTHER HEALTH IMPAIRMENT

Children considered under other health impairment experience "limited strength, vitality or alertness" as a result of chronic or acute illness. Children with attention deficit hyperactivity disorder may be considered under this category if their heightened sensitivity to environmental stimuli results in diminished alertness to educational surroundings (U.S. Department of Education, 2001, p. 12422).

SPECIFIC LEARNING DISABILITY

The majority of children who receive special education assistance under IDEA are identified in the specific learning disability category. Unexpected low academic achievement, despite the provision of appropriate educational experiences, may signal the presence of a disorder in the basic psychological processes. A comprehensive evaluation of cognitive functioning is necessary to discern the child's unique learning profile. Results must support the existence of a disorder in a basic psychological process, which is manifested in at least one of the seven basic skills (see Table 1). Insufficient progress may not be attributable to sensory, motor, cognitive, emotional, or environmental factors.

Since 1977, an ability-achievement discrepancy has been a required marker for identifying a child who has a learning disability (LD). This refers to the comparison of scores obtained on a measure of intellectual functioning (IQ test) to scores of academic achievement. When scores of achievement are significantly below the child's cognitive ability, then an LD may be present. However, controversy exists regarding the ability-achievement model given the lack of scientific rigor and the varied interpretation by states.

SPEECH OR LANGUAGE IMPAIRMENT

Communication disorders are broadly covered in the speech or language impairment category and may include misarticulations, voice problems, and language deficits.

TRAUMATIC BRAIN INJURY

Traumatic brain injury is a loss of functioning caused by an insult to the brain by an external force, which results in a specific deficit (Table 1) and has an adverse consequence upon the ability to function in

Table 1   Individuals With Disabilities Education Act (IDEA) Category Criteria

Category	*Criteria*
Autism	Deficits are evident in verbal and nonverbal communication, and social interaction. Atypical characteristics are repetitive behaviors, stereotyped movements, resistance to change, unusual reaction to sensory stimuli. Features are present before age three.
Deaf-blindness	Hearing and visual impairments are evident. Severe communication and developmental problems are evident. A single category does not meet needs.
Deafness	Severe hearing impairment is evident. There is impaired processing of linguistic information with or without amplification.
Emotional disturbance	Extended duration and extreme intensity of the following are evident: unexplained lack of academic progress, interpersonal deficits, inappropriate behaviors and feelings, pervasive depressed mood, development of physical symptoms and fears.
Hearing impairment	Criteria for deafness is not met. Permanent or fluctuating hearing loss occurs.
Mental retardation	Significant subaverage intellectual functioning and adaptive deficits are evident. Symptoms emerge during the developmental period.
Multiple disabilities	Criteria for inclusion in two or more categories are met. Educational needs are not met under a single category. Deaf-blindness combination is excluded.
Orthopedic impairment	Acquired or congenital severe orthopedic impairment is evident.
Other health impairment	Limited strength, vitality, or alertness as a result of a chronic or acute health problem is evident.
Specific learning disability	Ability/achievement discrepancy in one or more of the following areas is evident: oral expression, listening comprehension, written expression, basic reading skills, reading comprehension, mathematical calculations, or mathematical reasoning. Disorder in a basic psychological process. Not attributable to sensory, cognitive, emotional, or environmental factors.
Speech/language impairment	Communication disorders including voice, articulation, and language impairment.
Traumatic brain injury	Acquired brain injury results in deficits in at least one of the following areas: cognition; language; memory; attention; reasoning; abstract thinking; problem solving; judgment; sensory, perceptual, or motor abilities; psychosocial behavior; physical functioning; information processing; and speech. Brain injury as a result of birth trauma and congenital and degenerative factors are excluded.
Visual impairment including blindness	Includes blindness and partial sight.

Note. Inclusion in a category (or multiple categories) assumes there is an adverse effect upon educational performance.

school. Consideration of services under this category may be extended to children who have undergone aggressive treatment for neurological conditions (e.g., a brain tumor) that result in impairment. Brain injuries that are congenital, degenerative, or the result of birth trauma are excluded.

VISUAL IMPAIRMENT, INCLUDING BLINDNESS

Specific acuity levels for visual impairment are not provided. This category applies when, despite correction, educational performance is compromised because of limited sight or blindness.

—*Andrea Beebe*

See also Diagnosis and Labeling; Individuals With Disabilities Education Act; Learning Disabilities; Mental Retardation; Psychopathology in Children; Traumatic Brain Injury

REFERENCES AND FURTHER READING

Education for All Handicapped Children Act. (1975). PL 94–142. *Federal Register,* Dec. 29, 1977.

Individuals With Disabilities Education Act. (1997). PL 105–17, amendment to IDEA 1990, PL 101–476. *Federal Register,* March 12, 1999.

U. S. Department of Education. (2001). *Twenty-third annual report to Congress on the implementation of the Individuals With Disabilities Education Act.* Washington, DC: U.S. Government Printing Office.

INFANT ASSESSMENT

Roles and responsibilities of school psychologists have changed and expanded to serving not only school-aged children, but also children younger than age five years. This change has come about as scholars in the field recognize that time-efficient assessments and precise diagnoses can be the basis for early intervention before deviations in development become maladaptive patterns of functioning (Zero to Three, National Center for Infants, Toddlers, and Families, 1994). Research on early brain development and its relationship to learning, literacy, school readiness, emotional regulation, and resilience has also been highly publicized. Renowned scholar Jerome Bruner (1980) states, "The importance of early childhood for the intellectual, social, and emotional

growth of human beings is probably . . . one of the most revolutionary discoveries of modern times . . . where emotional and mental growth are concerned; well begun is indeed half done" (p. 3). Additionally, federal law addressing early intervention for infants and young children with special needs has had a major impact on the expansion of the roles and responsibilities of school psychologists. In 1976, the United States Congress passed the Education of All Handicapped Children Act (P.L. 94–142). This law ensured a free and appropriate public education and related services to all students ages 6 to 21 years. The Act was amended in 1986 (P.L. 99–457) and again in 1990 (P.L. 101–476). These amended education laws mandated that a free and appropriate public education be provided for all children from birth to age 21.

As a result of both the federal law and the developing research about the link between early development and later learning, infant assessment has received increased attention. Assessment of infants is different in many ways from the assessment of school-aged children. School psychologists need to understand early development, disabilities in infants and young children, and assessment methods and tools for this age group. In addition, school psychologists have been expected to skillfully interpret assessment information and make recommendations for educating children ages birth to five years.

INFANT ASSESSMENT DEFINED

Assessment in infancy can be defined as a systematic process of gathering information about a very young child and his/her parent(s) that influences the child's development, interests, motivations, and overall daily functioning (McLean & colleagues, 1996). Professionals who routinely work with infants consider observation, parent reports, and clinical judgment (i.e., opinion) to be necessary components of any assessment.

INFANT ASSESSMENT "IS . . ."

Because assessing infants is a unique process, it is important to identify what it is all about. First, infant assessment is nontraditional. Professionals assessing infants cannot use traditional tools or tests that require paper and pencil skills or the ability to answer complex questions. Instead, they use direct assessment methods such as the Bayley Scales of Infant Development-II and the Brazelton Neonatal

Behavioral Assessment Scale, which rely heavily on observations of behavior and general temperament, infant reflexes, overall movement patterns, and information from parents and caregivers. Professionals analyze and interpret the observation data and the parent data, to evaluate where an infant is functioning developmentally and to make recommendations to enhance acquisition of new skills.

Second, infant assessment is complex and highly specialized and requires the evaluating professional to be an astute observer of infant behavior. Further, the professional is required to use observations, parent/caregiver information, and information from direct assessments to make diagnostic decisions about the development, health, and well-being of the infant. A school psychologist's specialized knowledge of the neurobehavioral approach to infant assessment is critical. Neurobehavioral assessment refers to the appraisal of infant behaviors on relevant biobehavioral dimensions (e.g., temperament, conduct, vocal and oral behavior, reflex movements) to provide further evidence about the health of the young child's central nervous system. Within this approach, the psychologist pays special attention to patterns of the infant's arm and leg movements, muscle tone, reflexes, and orientation of the eyes, head, and ears to auditory and visual stimuli (e.g., turning head when a bell is rung, using eyes and head to follow a moving toy).

Third, the changing capabilities of the developing infant require a dynamic approach to assessment. In this case, the term *dynamic* refers to the use of multiple assessment methods that change flexibly depending on the referral problem.

In early intervention, federal law mandates that a team of professionals conduct assessments of infants. Generally, this consists of professionals from psychology, early childhood education, physical and occupational therapy, and speech-language pathology. Key areas of development that are typically assessed include: cognition (or how the mind works), motor skills, communication skills (including speech and language), social skills, and daily living skills. Traditionally, psychologists are charged with the role of evaluating cognitive abilities. This is usually done by observing the infant's movement patterns (e.g., rolling, reaching, crying, smiling) and recording observations on such things as how the infant responds to various stimuli (e.g., ringing of a bell, following a moving object with his or her eyes, reaching in response to a toy that is presented, etc.). These skills (commonly called perceptual-motor skills) are considered to be building blocks for later intelligence, as they are a part of cognitive development.

In early intervention, assessment serves four primary functions: screening, eligibility, program planning, and program monitoring. The event that starts the process in motion is a referral. Typically the parents/caregivers themselves make this referral. For example, parents may notice that their young child is not rolling over to his stomach like other infants they have seen, or their young child is not cooing when she is lying on her baby blanket. With some infants, the referral is made shortly after birth. This is especially true for infants born prematurely (i.e., younger than eight months) or who are born with definite complications caused by heart and lung defects, cerebral palsy (or other syndromes), or physical malformations or medical complications. For the latter situation, these children are already considered to be at risk for future developmental difficulties and can be automatically determined eligible for early intervention services. For infants who had no birth complications but whose parents are concerned about slow development, the process starts at the screening phase. The purpose of screening is to determine whether infants may have disabilities and to refer them for further assessment. The screening process usually lasts from 15 to 20 minutes, and it is conducted by trained professionals. If concerns are present after the screening, a comprehensive evaluation of the child and his or her environment is completed by a multidisciplinary team. The purpose of such an evaluation is to determine the young child's eligibility for early intervention services as specified by state and federal guidelines for infants and toddlers, and to ascertain which intervention approaches might be most effective in accelerating development and learning.

The term *developmental delay* is commonly used as a label to signify the absence of typical development. Other labels that are becoming more common in their application to infants include mental retardation, autism, and multiple disabilities. Each of these labels ensures the provision of appropriate early intervention services. Many question the ability to diagnose such disorders in infants and very young children; yet there is a growing body of research noting that specific behavioral and/or skill deficits occur in infancy that are early signs of disorders such as autism.

Once the infant is determined eligible for early intervention services, the third and fourth critical functions of the assessment process (program planning and program monitoring) play a central role. Assessment data are collected continually to determine what services should be implemented and in what environments (program planning), and to subsequently evaluate the overall effectiveness of the infant's Individualized Family Service Plan or program plan (program monitoring).

Increasingly, school psychologists are called upon to serve preschool-age children or younger. As a result, many school psychologists seek additional coursework and clinical training to be able to provide services, including assessments, to very young children.

School psychologists recognize the role of infant development as building blocks for success in school and life overall in order to help parents and teachers make connections between early learning and later school success.

—*John Vacca*

See also Autism Spectrum Disorders; Cerebral Palsy; Communication Disorders; Early Intervention; Fetal Alcohol Syndrome; Fragile X Syndrome; Individuals With Disabilities Education Act; Motor Assessment; Prevention

REFERENCES AND FURTHER READING

Bagnato, S., & Neisworth, J. (1991). *Assessment for early intervention: Best practices for professionals.* New York: Guilford.

Bruner, J. (1980). *Under five in Britain.* Ypsilanti, MI: High/Scope.

Greenspan, S. (1997). *Infancy and early childhood: The practice of clinical assessment and intervention with emotional and developmental challenges.* Baltimore: Paul H. Brookes.

McLean, M., Bailey, D., & Wolery, M. (1996). *Assessing infants and preschoolers with special needs* (2nd ed.). Englewood Cliffs, NJ: Merrill/Prentice-Hall.

Zero to Three: National center for infants, toddlers, and families. (n.d.). Available online at http://www.zero tothree.org/site_map.html

INFORMED CONSENT

Informed consent is a legal term used to describe how parents and adolescents agree to procedures or processes aimed at improving the child's/adolescent's education. It is a prerequisite to initiating special education decision making, including the development of individualized educational plans. The four essential features of informed consent are competence, disclosure, free will, and accountability. To agree to assessment, consultation, or intervention procedures the parents/ adolescents must be competent or able to understand the service to be provided. Informed consent addresses areas in school psychology ranging from receiving permission (consent) from a parent to assess or intervene with their child to requesting permission to participate in a research project. Specifically, informed consent is a protection of participants that requires that they are not harmed in any way and that they participate only if they freely agree to do so. Additionally, complete and factual knowledge must be given about a procedure in order for one to independently agree to it. Finally, informed consent is documented via a written agreement that indicates compliance with these four features. Obtaining both children's assent and a parent's informed consent is an important ethical consideration when working with school-age populations.

—*John S. Carlson*

INTELLIGENCE

Although there is no universal definition of intelligence, the attributes used to describe it have remained somewhat unchanged over time. The term *intelligence* generally encompasses the ability to adjust or adapt to the environment, the ability to learn, or the ability to perform abstract thinking.

The conceptualization of intelligence can involve multiple perspectives, including biological, cognitive, motivational, and behavioral foci. Biological theorists define intelligence from a structural perspective, linking different parts of the brain to various intellectual functions. Not completely separate from the biological perspective, cognitive perspectives involve not only what is known, but metacognition—knowledge about and control of one's thoughts. Motivational factors are proposed to influence intelligence by determining the level of interest an individual has in learning and in demonstrating what they know. The degree of the individual's motivation is significant to performance and, thus, measured intelligence. Finally, behavioral factors such as what an individual does is believed to influence intelligence. Cognitive, motivational, biological, and behavioral perspectives are not mutually exclusive, but rather are interrelated influences on intelligence. The role of any one or combination of these influences on intelligence varies depending on the theory or model of intelligence considered.

THEORIES OF INTELLIGENCE

Theories of intelligence can generally be divided into those that support a general factor theory of intelligence and those that support a multiple-factor theory of intelligence. Theorists who adhere to a general factor model espouse that intelligence is composed of a general or global ability (g). In contrast, multiple-factor theorists assert that this global ability is comprised of multiple, interrelated, but distinct abilities. Across these models, some theories are hierarchical, while others are not. Regardless of the proposed way in which components are believed to be connected, intelligence is a multifaceted and complex construct.

Alternatively, intelligence can be conceptualized from an information-processing perspective, a psychometric or structural approach, and a cognitive modifiability approach. The oldest and most researched of these is the psychometric approach, which measures and analyzes intellectual performance using quantitative (statistical) methods. In contrast, information-processing models focus on the ways individuals mentally present and manipulate information. Information-processing models see human cognition as similar to the way in which a computer processes information. Cognitive modifiability theories see intelligence as dynamic and modifiable, as opposed to unchanging. Changes that occur result from the individual's interactions with their environment.

The psychometric approach to the conceptualization of intelligence emphasizes the construct of a "general factor" (g) (i.e., global intelligence) and a "specific factor" (i.e., distinct abilities) to account for total intelligence. These two factors account for intelligence to varying degrees. Vernon (1961) also supported a general factor (g) theory of intelligence, followed by major group factors (verbal–educational and spatial–mechanical), as well as minor group factors.

Other models do not include specified hierarchies, but still include multiple components as comprising intelligence or multiple intelligences. Thurstone (1938) used factor analysis, a statistical procedure that examines the intercorrelations, to support the idea that "performance of a task requires a certain number of fundamental or primary abilities" (p. 2). Modern test construction is often based on Thurstone's work.

Thorndike (1997) proposed that intelligence was the result of interrelated intellectual abilities; these abilities form clusters described as social intelligence (dealing with people), concrete intelligence (dealing with things), and abstract intelligence (dealing with verbal and mathematical symbols). Guilford (1967) developed the three-dimensional intellect model:

1. Content—the kind of information (e.g., visual, auditory, symbolic, semantic, or behavioral)

2. Operations—rules of logic or the mental processes that are applied to the content

3. Product—the form that the content or information takes

There are variations in form and processes as there are with content, and the three dimensions are interdependent and can combine in various ways to form 120 possible factors.

Others have examined intelligence as it relates to the type of information processing (e.g., simultaneous, sequential). Simultaneous processing is the ability of the individual to mentally combine information all at once to solve a problem correctly; sequential processing is to the ability of the individual to arrange information in sequential order for problem solving. Based on Luria's (1966) work, an information-processing model of intelligence includes not only simultaneous and success processing, but also attention and planning. Attentional processes allow for focused and sustained cognitive activity, whereas planning involves the ability to think ahead, anticipate consequences, and control and maintain cognitive processes for complex behaviors. Both the two-factor (simultaneous, sequential) and four-factor (simultaneous, sequential, attention, planning) models derived from Luria have been used to develop measures of intelligence.

Sternberg (1997) offered two theories of intelligence, the triarchic theory of intelligence and, its extension, the triarchic model of giftedness. According to the triarchic theory, there are three interacting dimensions of intelligence: componential, experiential, and contextual. The triarchic model of giftedness translates the components of the original model (componential, experiential, and contextual) into analytic, creative, and practical giftedness. From still another perspective, Gardner's (1999) multiple intelligence theory postulates that intelligence can be carried out by 10 distinct competencies: linguistic intelligence, musical intelligence, logical–mathematical intelligence, special intelligence, bodily kinesthetic intelligence, intrapersonal intelligence, interpersonal intelligence, naturalist intelligence, spiritual intelligence, and existential intelligence.

Cattell (1941) proposed two types of intelligence, fluid (Gf) and crystallized (Gc); the theory is often referred to as Gf-Gc theory because of these two major components. Fluid intelligence (Gf) affects all types of problem solving, and it is believed to increase rapidly to approximately age 15 years, regardless of education. In contrast, crystallized intelligence (Gc) refers to a specific ability or expertise that an individual has learned. Horn (1991) expanded on the Gf-Gc model since that time to include 10 types of cognitive ability:

1. Fluid intelligence

2. Crystallized intelligence

3. Short-term memory (retrieval of information recently acquired)

4. Long-term memory (retrieval of information stored in long-term memory)

5. Auditory processing (processing and responding appropriately to information heard)

6. Visual processing (processing and responding appropriately to spatial forms)

7. Processing speed (scanning information quickly)

8. Decision speed (providing answers to tasks quickly)

9. Quantitative knowledge (understanding math concepts)

10. English language, reading, and writing skills

Carroll (1997) extended on previous theories of the structure of cognitive abilities and proposed a three-stratum theory of cognitive abilities. The first, or *narrow*, stratum included various cognitive abilities such as:

- General reasoning
- Oral fluency (the ability to quickly and accurately generate verbal utterances)
- Memory span (ability to attend to and immediately recall sequential information in order)
- Visualization
- Speech sound
- Originality/creativity
- Rate of test taking
- Simple reaction time

The second, or *broad*, stratum included:

- Fluid intelligence
- Crystallized intelligence
- General memory and learning
- Broad visual perception (the ability to accurately perceive and transform stimuli in two- or three-dimensional space)
- Broad auditory perception (the ability to accurately perceive differences in various sounds or to discriminate tones)
- Broad retrieval capacity (the ability to recall and recreate from memory items in a specific category such as foods)
- Broad cognitive speediness (the ability to reproduce simple stimuli rapidly)
- Processing speed (the ability to rapidly scan and react to simple tasks)

By identifying these broad abilities that comprise global intelligence, parts of various intelligence tests can be combined (cross-battery) to provide a wider range and more in-depth assessment of broad abilities. Thus, the work of Catell and Horn, as well as that of Carroll, is key to the application of the Gf-Gc cross-battery approach to the assessment of intelligence.

INTELLIGENCE QUOTIENT TESTS AND THEIR USE IN SCHOOLS

Historically, a child was evaluated whenever he or she experienced difficulty in school or the community. This assessment included some measure or estimate of cognitive ability to determine the extent to which ability factors were related to the referral problem. One rationale for using intelligence tests is to create a profile of strengths and weaknesses, as well as to predict educational achievement. According to some studies, intelligence tests predict success in school better than any other type of measure.

In school settings, assessments may be completed on a variety of students for a myriad of reasons, including intelligence testing that is used to determine eligibility or admittance into gifted and talented programs. Measures of intelligence are included in assessments of children from very young ages up through high school; intelligence measures continue to be used in adulthood and with geriatric populations.

Intelligence tests may be administered to children suspected of (or previously identified as) having a disability, or may be experiencing difficulty in some aspect of school functioning (social, adaptive, academic). The

Table 1   Measures of Intelligence Used for School-Age Children

Test and Publisher	Domains Included
Cognitive Assessment System (CAS) (Das & Naglieri, 1997), Riverside Publishing	Planning, attention, simultaneous, successive; composite (g)*
Differential Ability Scales (DAS) (Elliott, 1990), The Psychological Corporation	Verbal ability, nonverbal reasoning ability, spatial ability; composite (g)
Kaufman Assessment Battery for Children-Second Edition (KABC-II) (Kaufman & Kaufman, 2004), American Guidance Services, Inc.	Simultaneous, sequential, learning, planning, knowledge; nonverbal index, fluid crystallized index, mental processing index (g)
Reynolds Intellectual Assessment Scales (RIAS) (Reynolds & Kamphaus, 2003), Psychological Assessment Resources, Inc.	Verbal Intelligence Index, Nonverbal Intelligence Index, Composite Intelligence Index (g), and Composite Memory Index
Stanford-Binet Intelligence Scale, Fifth Edition (SB-V) (Roid, 2003), Riverside Publishing	Fluid reasoning, knowledge, quantitative reasoning, visual-spatial processing, working memory; full scale IQ (g)
Universal Nonverbal Intelligence Test (UNIT) (Bracken & McCallum, 1998), Riverside Publishing	Reasoning quotient, symbolic quotient, nonsymbolic quotient, memory quotient; full-scale quotient (g)
Wechsler Intelligence Scale for Children, Fourth Edition (WISC-IV) (Wechsler, 2003), The Psychological Corporation	Verbal comprehension, working memory, perceptual reasoning, processing speed; full scale (g)
Woodcock-Johnson III Tests of Cognitive Abilities (WJ-III) (Woodcock, McGrew, & Mather, 2001), Riverside Publishing	Comprehension knowledge, long-term retrieval, visual-spatial thinking, auditory processing, fluid reasoning, processing speed, short-term memory; phonemic awareness, working memory, broad attention, cognitive fluency, executive processes, delayed recall, knowledge; verbal ability, thinking ability, cognitive efficiency; general intellectual ability

Note: This table is not intended to be an exhaustive list of all possible measures of intelligence.

*g refers to the general intelligence factor first described by English psychologist Charles Spearman in 1927.

use of intelligence testing often is conceptualized as most critical in the identification of mental retardation and learning disabilities; the score(s) obtained on measures of intelligence are incorporated into the criteria used for determining eligibility in these classifications.

Intelligence tests differ from academic achievement tests in that the emphasis is not solely on school-based learning. At the same time, however, some measures have been criticized because of their reliance on verbal abilities and school learning, including reading skills (Sternberg & Grigorenko, 2002). Verbal components may include spoken, written, or nonverbal responses. For these tasks, the student may need to manipulate information in memory, process verbal information, comprehend verbal directions, have general knowledge of a topic, or recall learned material and specific knowledge (such as the names of the president) to perform well on the intelligence test. Other tasks require nonverbal responses that include pointing, manipulation, drawing, or marking; some measures eliminate verbal directions as well as verbal responding, and others do not. Nonverbal intelligence measures may be used for non-English speakers and children with hearing or language problems because the measures do not require the use of English to demonstrate their abilities. Intelligence testing is included as one component of information that, in conjunction with achievement and assessment of behavior/personality, is used to make informed decisions and provide an estimate of future performance.

Overall, the use of intelligence tests to obtain an estimate of ability is reliable (i.e., they can be replicated

---

Point Versus Counterpoint: Use of IQ Tests in Determination of Special Education Eligibility

Tests of intelligence frequently are used to make decisions that significantly affect peoples' lives in educational, medical, social, and forensic arenas. The use of these measures in these varied decision-making processes is not without controversy. Specific to the use of measures of intelligence in the determination of special education services, there are multiple issues to consider.

The case for:

- Inclusion of a measure of intelligence provides a better understanding of the child and identifies or eliminates some possible reasons for the child's lack of success.
- The use of standardized measures of intelligence provides an objective component to what otherwise is a highly subjective process.
- Standardized measures of intelligence allow for reliable prediction of achievement and school success.
- Comparing children's performance to other children across the nation facilitates communication across professionals who work with children and the scores are easily understood and translated by differing schools should the child move.

The case against:

- IQ tests contribute minimal information that is useful for planning and do not help to predict how well a given intervention will work for a given child.
- The use of a single score to represent a child's intelligence can result in decreased expectations and altered outcomes for the child.
- It is not the case that all intelligence tests operationally define intelligence in the same way; in fact, results may vary depending on the measure used.
- Results are not consistently analyzed, interpreted, or used in the decision-making process.

---

and are consistent over time) and valid (i.e., the tests measure what they are supposed to measure), but caution should be taken that the test results are not misinterpreted and misused. Consideration of the individual's background is crucial to the estimation of that individual's intelligence. Background is defined as culture and level of acculturation (i.e., the degree to which the individual's cultural orientation has been modified to match the dominant culture), ethnicity, language proficiency, formal and informal training, experience with similar tests, and general health. An individual's personality, motivation, environmental influences, reasons for testing, and random variation (guessing and clerical error) also are variables that affect test scores.

CONTEMPORARY MEASURES OF INTELLIGENCE

Alfred Binet initiated the practice of measuring intelligence with the development of the first test.

His scale was based on having the person complete a number of items of increasing difficulty; the child's intelligence was estimated based on the most difficult items that he or she was able to complete successfully. Binet's conceptualization was that the obtained level of intelligence was not static, but could change with growth. In this respect, Binet is credited with the coupling of ability to age. Eventually, the intelligence quotient (IQ) compared the individual's mental age to his or her chronological age and was growth-referenced. Recently, the score associated with *IQ* is not based on a ratio or quotient, and the term is misleading and inaccurate. Contemporary intelligence tests are norm-referenced as opposed to growth-referenced in that the obtained score is considered within the context of the average or mean score for the individual's age, as well as variability in performance across a large, usually national, sample.

A number of measures to assess intelligence have been developed since Binet's work in 1905; Table 1 lists some current ones. Of these, historically, the Wechsler and Stanford-Binet Intelligence Scales are reported to be used most often in the schools (Stinnet & colleagues, 1994). The number of nonverbal measures has increased in recent years to give greater attention to children whose primary language is not English and who have limited English proficiency. Nonverbal measures may rely on reasoning, memory, and symbolic or nonsymbolic thought rather than on verbal abilities. While most of these measures continue to be norm-referenced, dynamic assessment procedures (methods that take into consideration the child's rate of learning and development) have been reintroduced and reflect back to Binet's original concept of growth-referenced assessment. Regardless of the measures, however, Sternberg and Grigorenko (2002) caution that one cannot assume that any test or method of measurement assesses all that is encompassed by *intelligence*.

—*Cynthia A. Riccio, Olga Rodriguez, and Melisa Valle*

See also Ability Grouping; Bias (Testing); Fluid Intelligence; Mental Age; Mental Retardation; Neuropsychological Assessment; Normal Distribution; Norm-Referenced Testing; Psychometric *g*

REFERENCES AND FURTHER READING

Carroll, J. B. (1997). The three-stratum theory of cognitive abilities. In D. P. Flanagan, J. L. Genshaft, & P. L. Harrison (Eds.), *Contemporary intellectual assessment: Theories, tests, and issues* (pp. 105–121). New York: Guilford.

Cattell, R. B. (1941). Some theoretical issues in adult intelligence. *Psychological Bulletin, 40,* 153–193.

Gardner, H. (1999). *Intelligence reframed: Multiple intelligence for the 21st century.* New York: Basic Books.

Guilford, J. P. (1967). *The nature of human intelligence.* New York: McGraw-Hill.

Horn, J. L. (1991). Measurement of intellectual capabilities: A review of theory. In K. S. McGrew, J. K. Werder, & R. W. Woodcock (Eds.), *WJ-R technical manual.* Chicago: Riverside.

Luria, A. R. (1966). *Higher cortical functions in man.* New York: Basic Books.

Sternberg, R. J. (1997). The triarchic theory of intelligence. In D. P. Flanagan, J. L. Genshaft, & P. L. Harrison (Eds.), *Contemporary intellectual assessment: Theories, tests, and issues* (pp. 92–104). New York: Guilford.

Sternberg, R. J., & Grigorenko, E. L. (2002). Difference scores in the identification of children with learning disabilities: It's time to use a different method. *Journal of School Psychology, 40,* 65–83.

Stinnet, T. A., Harvey, J. M., & Oehler-Stinnet, J. (1994). Current test usage by practicing school psychologists: A national survey. *Journal of Psychoeducational Assessment, 12,* 331–350.

Thorndike, R. M. (1997). The early history of intelligence testing. In D. P. Flanagan, J. L. Genshaft, & P. L. Harrison (Eds.), *Contemporary intellectual assessment: Theories, tests, and issues* (pp. 3–16). New York: Guilford.

Thurstone, L. L. (1938). *Primary mental abilities.* Chicago: University of Chicago Press.

Vernon, P. E. (1961). *The structure of human abilities* (2nd ed.). London: Methuen.

INTERNATIONAL SCHOOL PSYCHOLOGY ASSOCIATION

The International School Psychology Association (ISPA) emerged from efforts by Calvin Catterall and Francis Mullins to broaden the views of school psychologists within the United States to include international perspectives. They initiated the International School Psychology Committee, first within the American Psychological Association's Division of School Psychology and later within the National Association of School Psychologists.

This committee served as a vehicle through which Dr. Catterall established contacts with various school psychologists outside of the United States. This committee sponsored its first international conference in 1975. In 1979, the United Nations (UN)–sponsored International Year of the Child attracted the interests of many school psychologists internationally. Participants recognized the need for an association that would serve ongoing interests of school psychologists internationally. ISPA's constitution and bylaws were adopted in 1982.

ISPA has four major objectives:

1. To foster communication between psychologists in educational settings

2. To encourage the implementation of promising practices in school psychology

3. To raise the effectiveness of education

4. To promote the maximum contribution of psychology to education

Membership approximates 800 and comes from approximately 40 countries. Twenty-two associations of school psychologists are affiliated with ISPA. ISPA sponsors yearly meetings to promote its objectives and to help stimulate the growth of school psychology in a region. ISPA also publishes a newsletter and sponsors a scholarly journal, *School Psychology International.* ISPA has approved three policy statements: an ethics code, a definition of professional practice, and a model professional preparation program. ISPA's international offices are in Copenhagen, Denmark.

—*Thomas Oakland*

See also American Psychological Association; National Association of School Psychologists; School Psychologist

---

INTERNET. *See* COMPUTER TECHNOLOGY; MEDIA AND CHILDREN

INTERVENTION

Interventions are planned strategies or actions designed to improve the academic, behavioral, and social performance of children and adolescents. Intervention is considered a core professional activity of school psychologists and includes an assortment of diverse activities that promote positive change.

School psychologists often work with teams composed of school professionals, parents, and community representatives, when necessary, to identify the significant areas of need of students and school communities. The teams then determine the most appropriate intervention; where the intervention should be implemented (e.g., school, home, and/or community environment); and who should carry out, monitor, and adjust the intervention, if necessary (e.g., special education teacher, school counselor, parent or school psychologist).

Interventions should be chosen with consideration given to certain factors (Rathvon, 1999; Telzrow & Beebe, 2002). These factors can include:

- Techniques that alter significant skills or behaviors
- Techniques that have demonstrated or proven effectiveness

- Techniques that are acceptable to the people involved in the intervention
- Techniques that have a proactive emphasis

—*Tammy D. Gilligan*

See also Behavior Intervention; Counseling; Crisis Intervention; Individualized Education Plan; Prevention; Psychotherapy; Psychotropic Medications

REFERENCES AND FURTHER READING

Rathvon, N. (1999). *Effective school interventions: Strategies for enhancing academic achievement and social competence.* New York: Guilford.

Telzrow, C. F., & Beebe, J. J. (2002). Best practices in facilitating intervention adherence and integrity. In A. Thomas & J. Grimes (Eds.), *Best practices in school psychology* (Vol. 4, pp. 503–516). Bethesda, MD: National Association of School Psychologists.

INTERVIEWING

Clinical interviewing is a widely used assessment method among school psychologists and mental health professionals. Clinical interviewing involves a formally arranged meeting between an interviewer and interviewee to achieve specific goals. Sattler (2001) distinguished between the following four types of interviews (along with the main goal of each):

1. Clinical assessment interview—evaluates an individual's emotional and behavioral functioning and makes recommendations about treatment

2. Psychotherapeutic interview—relieves an individual's emotional stress and fosters change through treatment

3. Forensic interview—investigates specific questions about an individual or family and provides an expert opinion for a legal decision, such as child custody or determination of child maltreatment

4. Survey interview—collects data regarding specific questions or variables of interest to a researcher, such as the prevalence of different disorders or diseases in epidemiological surveys

This discussion focuses on clinical assessment interviews for evaluating the functioning of children and adolescents (for brevity, hereinafter the word *children* includes adolescents). The discussion covers structured diagnostic interviews, semistructured interviews, unstructured interviews with parents and teachers, and clinical interviews as components of multimethod assessment.

STRUCTURED DIAGNOSTIC INTERVIEWS

Structured diagnostic interviews were developed for interviewing parents and children about symptoms and criteria for psychiatric diagnoses. Two examples are the *Diagnostic Interview for Children and Adolescents, Version Four (DICA-IV)* (Reich, 2000) and the National Institute of Mental Health (NIMH) *Diagnostic Interview Schedule for Children, Version Four (DISC-IV)* (Shaffer and colleagues, 2000). To conduct a structured diagnostic interview, the interviewer must follow a set of standard questions and probes geared toward specific response categories. The choice of the next question depends on the interviewee's answer to the previous question. Computer scoring of responses assesses whether the child meets criteria for specific psychiatric diagnoses, such as those in the American Psychiatric Association's (1994) *Diagnostic and Statistical Manual of Mental Disorders, Fourth Edition (DSM-IV)*. Administering the *DISC-IV* or *DICA-IV* generally takes at least an hour and, at times, up to three or more hours.

Research shows that structured diagnostic interviews are more reliable when administered to parents than to children. That is, on two different occasions, parents more often report symptoms for the same diagnoses, whereas children change their answers from one time to the next. The length and rigid format of structured diagnostic interviews can be tedious and, therefore, inappropriate for younger children.

SEMISTRUCTURED INTERVIEWS

Semistructured interviews have a less rigid format than the structured diagnostic interviews. Questions are usually organized by content areas, such as children's school functioning, friends and social relations, and family relations. Some semistructured interviews are designed to produce psychiatric diagnoses. However, as with the *DICA-IV* and *DISC-IV*, reliability of semistructured diagnostic interviews tends to be higher for parents than for children.

The Semistructured Clinical Interview for Children and Adolescents, Second Edition (SCICA)

(McConaughy & Achenbach, 2001) is a clinical assessment interview designed for children ages 6 to 18 years. The SCICA protocol lists a series of open-ended questions that allow a variety of responses rather than "yes" or "no" answers. Table 1 lists samples of SCICA questions in seven topic areas. Interviewers can alter the sequence of questions and topics to follow the child's lead in conversation. This allows more flexibility and a more conversational style than is possible in the structured diagnostic interviews. The SCICA also includes a family drawing for children ages 6 to 11 years.

After interviewers complete the SCICA, they use standardized rating forms to score their observations of children's behavior during the interview and children's own reports of their problems. Interviewer's ratings are then scored on a standardized profile of problem scales. Five scales—anxious, withdrawn/depressed, language/motor problems, attention problems, and self-control problems—include problems observed by the interviewer. Three scales—anxious/depressed, aggressive/rule-breaking, and somatic complaints—include problems reported by the child during the interview (ages 12 to 18 years only). The SCICA profile also provides scores for six scales consistent with *DSM-IV* diagnoses, as well as total observations, total self-reports, internalizing problems (i.e., anxiety, depression, withdrawal) and externalizing problems (i.e., aggressive/rule-breaking behavior, attention problems, and self-control problems). By examining the profile of scores on the various SCICA scales, interviewers can see areas where a child exhibits severe problems compared to clinically referred children, as well as areas where the child has fewer problems than other clinically referred children.

UNSTRUCTURED INTERVIEWS WITH PARENTS AND TEACHERS

As a routine practice, school psychologists and mental health professionals often conduct interviews with parents and teachers that are less structured than the interviews described in the preceding sections. Unstructured clinical interviews with parents can cover the child's presenting problems (referral complaints), developmental and medical history, educational history, family factors and stressors, other possible problem areas, and what interventions (if any) have already been tried at home and at school. Unstructured clinical interviews with teachers can

Table 1   Topic Areas and Sample Questions From the Semistructured Clinical Interview for Children and Adolescents (SCICA)

1. *ACTIVITIES, SCHOOL, JOB*

   What do you like to do in your spare time, like when you are not in school?
   What do you like best in school? What do you like about _____?
   What do you like least in school? What don't you like about _____?
   Do you have a job? (Ages 12–18 years)
   How do you feel about your job/boss? (Ages 12–18 years)

2. *FRIENDS*

   How many friends do you have?
   Tell me about someone you like. What do you like about _____?
   Tell me about someone you don't like. What don't you like about _____?
   Do you ever have problems getting along with other kids?

3. *FAMILY RELATIONS*

   Who are the people in your family? Who lives in your home?
   Who makes the rules in your home?
   What happens when kids break the rules? Do you think the rules are fair or unfair?
   How do your parents get along?

4. *FANTASIES*

   If you had three wishes, what would you wish? Reasons for each?
   If you could change something about yourself, what would it be?

5. *SELF-PERCEPTION, FEELINGS*

   Tell me a little about yourself.
   What makes you happy?
   What makes you sad?
   What makes you mad?
   What makes you scared?
   What do you worry about?

6. *PARENT/TEACHER-REPORTED PROBLEMS*

   I want to talk to you about problems kids sometimes have and hear your opinion about them. Some kids have problems with _____. Is that a problem for you? [The interviewer selects problems of special concern to parents and/or teachers.]

7. *FOR AGES 12–18: SOMATIC COMPLAINTS, ALCOHOL, DRUGS, TROUBLE WITH THE LAW*

   Now I want to ask you about some specific types of problems. Over the past 6 months, have you had _____?
   Aches and pains?
   Headaches?
   Trouble falling asleep?
   Now I want to ask you about some other things. Over the past 6 months, have you _____?
   Drunk beer, wine, or liquor? Been drunk from alcohol?
   Been stoned or high on drugs?
   Used tobacco?
   Been in trouble with the police or law?

Note: From McConaughy, S. H., & Achenbach, T. M. (2001). *Manual for the semistructured clinical interview for children and adolescents* (2nd ed., pp. 9–15). Burlington, VT: University of Vermont, Research Center for Children, Youth, and Families. (Adapted and reprinted with permission.)

Table 2   Sample Questions for Behavioral Interviews With Parents and Teachers

1. *DEFINING THE PROBLEM BEHAVIOR*

   You said you are concerned about Mark's _____.
   What exactly does he do? Describe the problem in observable terms.
   How often does he do _____?
   How long does it last?
   How serious a problem is this?
   Under what circumstances does _____ occur?
   When do you notice that?
   Have you ever noticed that at home (at school)?

2. *ANTECEDENTS (BEFORE THE BEHAVIOR OCCURS)*

   What happens just before _____ occurs?
   What time of day does _____ usually occur?
   Who else was there when _____ occurred?
   What did you want or expect Mark to be doing?

3. *CONSEQUENCES (AFTER THE BEHAVIOR OCCURS)*

   Then what happened? What happened after _____ occurred?
   What did you do? How did you react?
   What did other people do? How did other people react?
   What did Mark do? How did Mark react?

---

address details of the child's current problems in school, relevant educational history, other possible problem areas, and what interventions (if any) have already been tried in the school setting.

School psychologists and mental health practitioners may also conduct *behavioral interviews* with parents and teachers in order to obtain a functional assessment of presenting problems. This involves defining specific problem behavior(s) in observable terms, and then gathering more information about the antecedents (what happened before) and consequences (what happened after) surrounding the specific behavior. Table 2 shows examples of the types of questions that might be asked in behavioral interviews.

The answers to behavioral interview questions can help determine the basic functions of a specific problem behavior, including:

- To increase social attention
- To avoid unpleasant or aversive tasks or situations
- To serve as self-reinforcement (e.g., fun, pleasure, or excitement)

After identifying a specific problem of concern and analyzing the circumstances surrounding the problem, interviewers can ask more questions to develop an intervention plan. For behavioral interventions,

parents and/or teachers may also be asked to collect observational data before implementing an intervention and again during the intervention. The data they and others collect will help to evaluate the effectiveness of an intervention. The entire process of behavioral interviewing (including the intervention phase) can cover several weeks or more and usually requires more than one interview session.

CLINICAL INTERVIEWS AS COMPONENTS OF MULTIMETHOD ASSESSMENT

When adults seek mental health services, they usually refer themselves and can acknowledge in some way why they seek services. Children do not usually refer themselves for assessment or treatment. Instead, knowledgeable adults, such as parents, teachers, guidance counselors, or health care providers, usually refer children for mental health services. In addition, children's behavior often varies from one situation to the next, and different informants can have different perspectives on children's behavior. In fact, research has shown only moderate levels of agreement among different informants reporting on children's behavioral and emotional functioning. For these reasons, no single informant or assessment method should be considered the "gold standard" for assessing children's functioning. Instead, best practice requires a *multimethod* approach to assessment, which involves integrating information from a variety of sources including parents, teachers, and other significant persons, as well as children themselves.

Within the context of multimethod assessment, clinical interviews with children provide opportunities to learn children's own perspectives on their problems, competencies, and life circumstances; and they offer opportunities to observe children's behavior, emotions, and interaction styles. Clinical interviews with children can also help to establish rapport and trust necessary for successful interventions, especially if the interviewer is the same person who will later provide the treatment.

Structured diagnostic interviews with parents can provide information on children's symptoms and criteria for psychiatric diagnoses. Unstructured interviews with parents and teachers can provide information about the children's history and life circumstances, details of presenting problems and surrounding circumstances, and the feasibility of different intervention options.

Besides participating in interviews, parents and teachers can complete standardized rating scales to provide their perspectives on the pattern and severity of children's problems, strengths, and competencies. Older children (usually age 11 years and older) can also complete standardized self-report forms to provide their perspectives on the pattern and severity of their problems and competencies.

The SCICA is an example of a child clinical interview specifically designed to facilitate multimethod assessment. The SCICA is a component of the *Achenbach System of Empirically Based Assessment* (*ASEBA*) (Achenbach & Rescorla, 2001), which consists of an integrated set of standardized rating forms to assess children's competencies and problems. In addition to the information obtained by the SCICA, the *ASEBA* includes rating forms for parents (e.g., Child Behavior Checklist), teachers (e.g., Teacher's Report Form), adolescents' self-reports (e.g., Youth Self-Report), and forms for rating observations of children's behavior in testing sessions and group situations, such as classrooms. (The *ASEBA* also includes rating forms and scoring profiles for assessing preschool children and adults. Using the SCICA along with other *ASEBA* forms, practitioners can easily compare their impressions of the child during the clinical interview with reports from other informants.

CONCLUSION

School psychologists and mental health practitioners often conduct clinical interviews with parents, teachers, and children themselves. Clinical interviewing can serve several clinical or educational purposes, including: (a) providing initial clinical assessments of children's problems; (b) making psychiatric diagnoses; (c) designing mental health treatments and school-based interventions; and (d) evaluating the effectiveness of interventions. School psychologists may also conduct clinical interviews with parents, teachers, and children as components of comprehensive assessments to determine whether a child is eligible for special education services under the Individuals With Disabilities Education Act (IDEA).

—*Stephanie H. McConaughy*

See also Behavioral Assessment; Counseling; Infant Assessment; Personality Assessment; Preschool Assessment; Psychotherapy; Social–Emotional Assessment

REFERENCES AND FURTHER READING

Achenbach, T. M. & Rescorla, L. A. (2001). *Manual for the ASEBA school-age forms & profiles.* Burlington, VT: University of Vermont, Research Center for Children, Youth, and Families.

Achenbach System of Empirically Based Assessment (*ASEBA*) (n.d.). Available online at http://www.ASEBA.org

American Psychiatric Association. (1994). *Diagnostic and statistical manual of mental disorders* (4th ed.). Washington, DC: Author.

Individuals With Disabilities Education Act (IDEA). Public Law 105–17. 20 U.S.C. §1400.

McConaughy, S. H., & Achenbach, T. M. (2001). *Manual for the semistructured clinical interview for children and adolescents* (2nd ed.). Burlington, VT: University of Vermont, Research Center for Children, Youth, and Families.

Reich, W. (2000). Diagnostic interview for children and adolescents. *Journal of the American Academy of Child and Adolescent Psychiatry, 39,* 59–66.

Sattler, J. M. (2001). *Clinical and forensic interviewing of children and families.* San Diego, CA: Jerome M. Sattler.

Shaffer, D., Fisher, P., Lucas, C. P., Dulcan, M., & Schwab-Stone, M. E. (2000). NIMH diagnostic interview schedule for children, Version IV (NIMH DISC-IV): Description, differences form previous versions and reliability of some common diagnoses. *Journal of the American Academy of Child and Adolescent Psychiatry, 39,* 28–38.

IQ. *See* INTELLIGENCE; PSYCHOMETRIC G; FLUID INTELLIGENCE; MENTAL AGE; MENTAL RETARDATION

K

KEYSTONE BEHAVIORS

The analysis of keystone behaviors is a conceptual and research-based target variable selection strategy addressing the question of *what to change* in behavioral problem solving. Keystone behaviors have been defined as:

- Pivotal behaviors associated with response classes of maladaptive behaviors that can positively influence other child behaviors
- Behaviors that result in other beneficial collateral child, peer, and adult outcomes
- Foundation skills necessary for adaptation to present and future environments

Stated differently, keystone variables represent relatively narrow targets for change that have the possibility of widespread benefits to clients. The hypothesized benefits of selecting keystone targets for change include more effective and efficient interventions. Within the context of ecological consultation and systems analysis, the term keystone *variable,* rather than behavior, is suggested because of the broad range of potential targets for efforts at permanent change and to acknowledge that such targets often go beyond presenting child problems.

—David Barnett

See also Behavior Intervention; Behavioral Assessment

KOHLBERG'S STAGES OF MORAL DEVELOPMENT

Lawrence Kohlberg was born in Bronxville, New York, on October 25, 1927, and died on April 15, 1987. His early research was in the area of differences in children's reasoning about moral dilemmas, and this led to a successful career. His work was best known for the influence it had on our understanding of the way children (up through adolescence) think about moral issues. His model of moral development described three distinct levels, and within each of these levels there are two stages.

Kohlberg developed a series of scenarios to determine how children solve moral dilemmas. The child is presented with the dilemma and then asked how he or she would solve it or what action he or she would take. These responses and actions were then judged and categorized, leading to Kohlberg's three-level model.

The three levels are preconventional morality, conventional morality, and postconventional morality. Brief descriptions of these levels as well as the stages within them are given in the following sections.

LEVEL 1: PRECONVENTIONAL MORALITY (EARLY-TO-MIDDLE CHILDHOOD)

At the preconventional level, children make moral judgments solely on the basis of anticipated punishments and rewards—a good or right act is one that is rewarded, while a bad or wrong act is one that is punished. Within this first level are the first two stages of moral development.

Stage 1. Morality focuses on the power and possessions of those in authority and on the necessity for the weak to please the strong in order to avoid punishment. A child does or does not act in order to avoid displeasing those who have power over him or her.

Stage 2. Morality focuses on the pleasure motive. A child does what he or she wants in order to get what he or she wants from others. There is a sense of fair exchange based on purely pragmatic values and of noninterference in the affairs or values of others.

LEVEL II: CONVENTIONAL MORALITY (MIDDLE-TO-LATE CHILDHOOD)

At the conventional level, right behavior is that which is accepted, approved, and praised by other people who are seen as being in positions of authority. Children seek to avoid guilt by behaving in ways that will be approved by the social conventions of their culture. This is broken down into stages 3 and 4 of moral development.

Stage 3. Morality focuses on the approval of those immediately involved in judging one's behavior. Justice at this stage is seen as reciprocity of equality between individuals.

Stage 4. Morality has been called "law and order" morality. The focus is on obeying the rules for their own sake. Justice is seen as the reciprocity between each individual and the social system. Societal order is very important in making judgments at this stage.

LEVEL III: POSTCONVENTIONAL (ADOLESCENCE)

At the postconventional level, people make choices on the basis of principles that they have thought through, accepted, and internalized. Right behavior is the behavior that conforms to these principles, regardless of intermediate social praise or blame. This is broken down into stages 5 and 6 of moral development.

Stage 5. Morality focuses on the social contract and the basic human rights that do not need to be earned. The "law and order" emphasis of stage 4 gives way to a concern for the creation of good laws, which are laws that will maximize the welfare of the individual.

Stage 6. Morality rests upon individual conscience. Right behavior is a product of feeling or being right with oneself; people can obey the law and still feel guilty if they violated their own principles. The rights of humanity, independent of rules of civil society, are acknowledged, and human beings are seen as ends in themselves. At this stage, the individual has achieved the capacity for principled reasoning and it is thus morally mature.

While a major criticism of Kohlberg's work has been its focus on mainly male participants, it has provided a foundation for many other explorations into the moral development of children and adults.

—Neil J. Salkind

REFERENCES AND FURTHER READING

Gibbs, J. C. (2003). Moral development and reality: Beyond the theories of Kohlberg and Hoffman. Thousand Oaks, CA: Sage.

Gilligan, C. (1982). *In a different voice.* Boston: Harvard University Press.

L

LABELING. *See* INDIVIDUALS WITH DISABILITIES EDUCATION ACT; SPECIAL EDUCATION

LATCHKEY CHILDREN

The term "latchkey" originated in the 18th century and referred to lifting the door latch to gain entrance into one's home (Lamorey & colleagues, 1999). Door keys were often worn around their necks on a piece of string. In the 1940s, the term "latchkey children" was used to describe children who took care of themselves while their fathers were away at war and their mothers contributed to the labor force (Lamorey & colleagues, 1999).

After World War II, women did not return to their traditional role as "homemaker," instead they continued to enter the workforce in droves. Between the years of 1940 and 1976, maternal employment increased fivefold. The 1970s saw a trend of separation and divorce that has continued into the 21st century. This trend has forced a growing number of mothers to become the main provider for their families. Among married couples, dual-earner households are now the norm. The shifting gender roles in our society have substantially increased the number of latchkey children (Lamorey & colleagues, 1999). This in turn has created serious concerns for parents, educators, politicians, and communities regarding the well-being of unattended children during after-school hours.

Today, the term latchkey generally refers to children who spend time alone after school. The definition can also be broadened to include children who are cared for by their siblings or provide care for their siblings after school. Many latchkey children spend time in their own homes, while others may be at libraries, after-school programs, parks, or the homes of friends. Some have considerable freedom to roam freely about the community, and others are confined to the walls of their homes (Belle, 1999).

Currently, there are 15 million latchkey children in America. During these after-school hours, the juvenile crime rate triples and these children are more apt to use drugs and/or alcohol, and be victims of accidents and abuse. After-school hours are also the most likely time for adolescents to engage in sexual intercourse, and children ages 10 to 15 years are most at risk of becoming involved with a gang. Furthermore, research indicates that children who return to empty homes are less likely to complete their homework; instead, they spend time doing their preferred activity, watching television.

Latchkey children endure emotional hardships as well. Research shows that latchkey children, particularly those cared for by an older sibling, believe they are significantly less competent in the areas of self-worth, social acceptance, and physical appearance compared to children cared for after school by adults and children in self-care (Belle, 1999).

In the academic arena, studies have produced mixed results. Some studies conclude that latchkey youths earn lower grades and have lower performance scores on standardized tests of achievement. Yet, other studies show no significant difference in academic performance between latchkey and supervised youths (Lamorey & colleagues, 1999).

School officials must be prepared to address the risk factors associated with latchkey children. One possible solution is after-school programming, which is a beneficial way to keep kids safe, help working families, and improve academic achievement. To make more developmentally constructive use of youth's time, it is important that after-school programs engage students in hands-on learning activities that are fun and viewed as separate from the school day. After-school programs should promote learning, while allowing youngsters to explore areas of interest to them. They should also provide students the opportunity to work closely with responsible and caring adults (Bender & colleagues, 2000).

—Coryn Lowe

See also Fears; Parenting

REFERENCES AND FURTHER READING

Belle, D. (1999). *The after-school lives of children: Alone with others while parents work.* Mahwah, NJ: Erlbaum.

Bender, J., Flatter, C. H., & Sorrentino, J. M. (2000). *Half a childhood: Quality programs for out-of-school hours* (2nd ed.). Nashville, TN: School-Age NOTES.

Lamorey, S., Robinson, B. E., Rowland, B. H., & Coleman, M. (1999). *Latchkey kids: Unlocking doors for children and their families* (2nd ed.). Thousand Oaks, CA: Sage.

LEAD EXPOSURE

Although the United States has placed greater restrictions on lead-based products since the 1960s, remaining lead contained in the soil, dust, and paint chips is still a threat for children today. In fact, the U.S. Public of Health Services estimated that one-sixth of children are at risk for lead-related health concerns (Kalat & Wurm, 1999). Children of lower socioeconomic status living in deteriorating homes are the most at risk for lead exposure. Younger children are also susceptible because they are more likely to place objects (e.g., paint chips or toys with lead contaminated dust) in their mouths.

Lead exposure has a wide range of effects on children's development and behavior. Children are especially vulnerable because their bodies are rapidly developing. Lead enters the body through the nose or mouth and remains in the bloodstream until it is absorbed into the bones (U.S. Environmental Protection Agency, 1999). Lead exposure impairs the formation of synapses, interferes with neurotransmitters, damages the covering of motor nerves, and affects metabolism by competing with iron and calcium for absorption (Kalat & Wurm, 1999). At extremely high levels, lead can cause permanent damage to the brain. Yet, evidence doesn't support the long-term neuropsychological effects from mild exposure to lead (Phelps & Nathanson, 1998). Although lead exposure is correlated with impaired motor and visual perceptual skills, poor school performance, absenteeism, deviant behavior, and ADHD, lead can't be identified as a primary cause because of other confounding variables (Kalat & Wurm, 1999). Because the severity and permanency of these effects remain controversial and inconclusive, more research is necessary.

Children who are at risk for lead exposure should undergo a medical evaluation. Children with high levels of lead exposure may require chelation, a medical treatment in which drugs assist in the removal of lead through the urine (Kalat & Wurm, 1999). Chelation is necessary for children with levels of lead exposure greater than 45 µg of lead per dL (Phelps & Nathanson, 1998). In addition to medical treatment, it is important to reduce lead exposure in the child's environment. The following prevention and intervention strategies are recommended by the U.S. Environmental Protection Agency (1999):

- Screening children for lead exposure
- Assessing lead levels in drinking water and determining the presence of decaying lead-based paint in homes
- Hiring a professional to remove contaminated soil and lead-based paint
- Keeping floors, surfaces, and toys clean of lead-based dust and paint
- Increasing iron and calcium in the diet

Children who have been exposed to lead may have learning, behavior, speech, or language problems (U.S. Environmental Protection Agency, 1999). However, many children remain undiagnosed because symptoms aren't always apparent. Therefore, school psychologists play an important role in educating families regarding the risks of lead exposure and encouraging families to have their children screened by a doctor or public health agency.

—Amy Kiekhaefer

REFERENCES AND FURTHER READING

Kalat, J., & Wurm, T. (1999). Implications of recent research in biological research in school psychology. In C. Reynolds & T. Gutkin (Eds.), *The handbook of school psychology* (pp. 271–290). New York: John Wiley.

U.S. Environmental Protection Agency. (1999). *Lead in your home: A parent's reference guide* (EPA Pub. No. 747-B-99–003). Washington, DC: U.S. Government Printing Office.

LEARNED HELPLESSNESS

Learned helplessness is the expectation that one cannot control circumstances and often results in passive acceptance of conditions. This result may lead to decreased motivation and persistence and even depression if individuals sense that they have no control over their lives. Essentially, learned helplessness refers to perceived absence of a relationship between an action and its subsequent outcome, resulting in helpless behavior.

Experimental psychologists introduced the concept of learned helplessness while using classical conditioning to study animal behavior. Dogs were immobilized and exposed to inescapable electric shock. The dogs were again exposed to the electric shock with an escape available. Interestingly, they made no attempt to escape. The researchers proposed that the dogs had learned this helplessness because when initially exposed to the shock, nothing they did improved the aversive condition. Based on this principle, learned helplessness is a response that is learned and able to be modified.

The negative attributions that adults make toward children and academic failure seem to contribute to learned helplessness in the school setting. It is particularly evident in students who have been diagnosed with a learning disability. Students who receive special education services often have a history of poor academic performance. Valas (2001) suggested that academic failure may make these students more susceptible to increased levels of helplessness. In addition to the reduced expectations of themselves, students may feel stigmatized by their label and be held to different standards by peers as well as teachers. This self-defeating process tends to be cyclical and possibly even self-fulfilling. Affected students fail tasks, evaluate themselves negatively, and thus lack the persistence and motivation to engage in similar tasks in the future.

Children's attributions about their behavior also determine how they will act in future situations. Children who believe that academic failure is the result of an ability deficit are unlikely to exert much effort to change this seemingly unavoidable condition. They are more likely to view failure as a permanent, internal, and global condition. Students on the other end of this spectrum attribute academic failure to exerted effort. These students are more likely to try to change this behavior to facilitate academic success.

Many techniques may be useful to counteract learned helplessness. Schools should place students in situations where academic success will be experienced. This may include alternative academic settings until skill levels are commensurate with the expected level. Appropriate and realistic goals must be set—in addition to outlining an explicit plan by which to achieve these goals—to help students realize the distorted thinking that is occurring and recognize that control lies within each individual. Success and failure are based upon individual decisions.

—*Kimberly A. DeRuyck*

See also Bullying and Victimization; Learning

REFERENCES AND FURTHER READING

Garber, J., & Seligman, M. E. P. (Eds.). (1980). *Human helplessness.* New York: Academic Press.

Valas, H. (2001). Learned helplessness and psychological adjustment: Effects of learning disabilities and low achievement. *Scandinavian Journal of Educational Research, 45*(2), 101–114.

LEARNING

Dictionaries typically define learning as the act of acquiring knowledge and skills through observation, study, or instruction, but this definition needs to be clarified to be of use to school psychologists. The process of learning is complex and many factors influence its occurrence. This article will more clearly define the concept of learning, examine the historical development of current theories, consider instructional practices that enhance learning, and describe the importance of understanding learning to school psychology.

It is easy to think of learning as a product or an outcome. When a parent asks Elizabeth what she learned in school that day, the parent is viewing learning as a product. The parent expects Elizabeth to list some specific facts or skills that she acquired. Some theories emphasize observable products. Learning can also be understood as an internal process, not easily observed. Thinking through a problem or figuring out how to follow a procedure also illustrates the learning process.

What we learn is organized according to a network of associations and concepts (often called schema) stored throughout the brain. Much of this information may never be demonstrated, but it has been learned just the same. Elizabeth may have learned all sorts of things in school that day such as how to borrow in two-digit-subtraction problems, that Mrs. Caldwell puts her lipstick on crooked, how to get to Room 113, and that Billy Jones likes her.

The process of learning is continuous, but its products are observable only when directly assessed. Psychologists use the term *performance* to refer to the products of learning that the learner demonstrates.

Performance is the change in behavior that we can observe and from which we infer that learning has occurred. It may be the appearance of a new behavior, or an increase or reduction in a behavior previously learned. For example, as we practice the addition of single-digit numbers, our scores on tests of addition should progressively increase. A teacher would infer that we are learning to add. Here is Ramon's math test scores over five weeks: Week 1 = 13, Week 2 = 17, Week 3 = 16, Week 4 = 19, and Week 5 = 22. Note that the scores did not increase uniformly; they actually decreased on one week's test. Unevenness of performance is common in the learning of most skills. Because we infer learning from performance, it is helpful to have a predetermined standard or criterion in mind when we judge if learning has occurred. Should Ramon's teacher cease providing instruction in adding numbers on the assumption that learning is complete?

To be classified as learning, changes in behavior must occur in relation to practice or experience. Changes in behavior that accompany growth are considered to be products of maturation or development. My six-year-old son once proudly directed me to, "Look at what I learned to do," whereupon he chinned himself on a tree branch. Noting that he had grown three inches in the past few months, I declared "I think you've grown bigger and stronger, too." While this distinction was probably ignored by my son, the incident reminds us that the process of human growth also produces changes in behavior.

Another characteristic of learning is that the change is relatively permanent. Factors such as fatigue, anxiety, illness, the presence of drugs, and lack of motivation may affect performance, but not true learning. Behavioral changes do not have to be maintained for a lifetime; we do forget some facts or skills over time. While no one has established a fixed time period to clarify permanence, failure to perform an act or recall a fact after only a few seconds would suggest that learning has not yet occurred.

SCHOOLS OF THOUGHT ABOUT LEARNING

Speculation about how learning occurs has existed since the early Greek philosophers. Aristotle described laws of association in which certain factors influence memory. For example, the more often events are recalled together, the more likely it is that recall of one will produce recall of the others. It was not until the late 19th century that the study of learning became more theoretical and systematic, however. There were three major schools of thought that spurred research and current learning theories. Figure 1 provides a historical record of these schools.

The first school argued that psychology should be a science, and the learning process could only be understood through experiments following scientific procedures. Early psychologists such as Wundt and Ebbinghaus advocated this position. Ebbinghaus is famous for his studies using nonsense syllables (e.g., *zum–wug*), in which he demonstrated that basic factors of practice and similarity affect memory.

An early theory of learning was classical conditioning (Pavlov and Watson), in which it was demonstrated that stimuli (events such as lights or sounds) could be associated with one another and thus produce similar responses. Remember Pavlov's famous dog salivating at the sound of a bell ringing? It had heard the ringing of the bell at the same time that food was served, thus forming a conditioned stimulus–response bond. Watson demonstrated the same effect with children when he conditioned two-year-old Albert to fear furry objects that had been presented at the same time a loud, scary noise occurred.

The first theory of learning that explained a wide variety of outcomes was instrumental conditioning, developed by Edward Thorndike. One of Thorndike's (1932) important findings is the Law of Effect: "Events

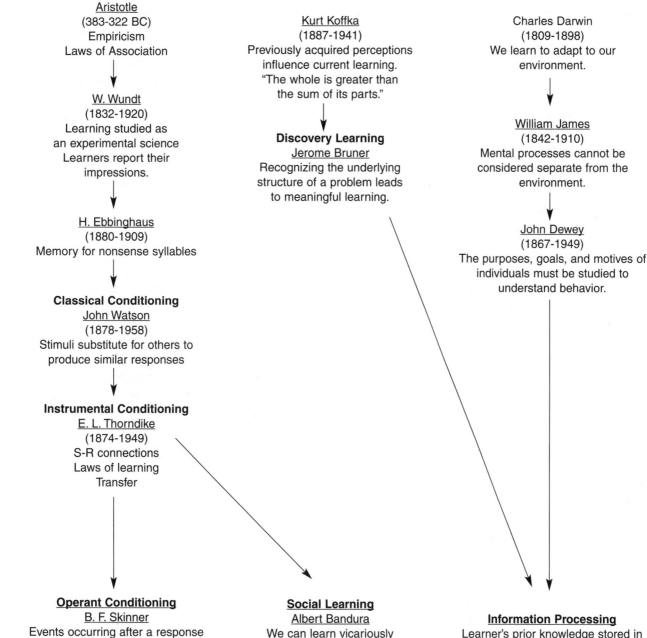

Figure 1   Historical Record of Schools of Thought About Learning

following a response, if pleasant, are likely to stamp in a response, unpleasant events are likely to stamp it out" (p. 34). A second principle is the Law of Exercise: "Every time a connection is made between a stimulus and a response that connection's strength is increased" (p. 46). Thorndike later found this law to depend on feedback from the environment, as well as mere repetition. The Law of Readiness is the third: "When an organism is prepared to act, to do so is satisfying, and not to do so is annoying" (p. 72). This law emphasizes the importance of the learner being physically able to make a particular response, and suggests that the timing of instruction is critical. Teaching a skill before a child is ready, or after he or she has lost interest, may be ineffective or even harmful.

A second school of thought is that of Gestalt psychology. Gestaltist theorists believed that learning is not necessarily incremental; that is, it can occur in sudden spurts or through insights that arise when the learner perceives the underlying structure of a task. The phrase "The whole is greater than the sum of its parts" (Koffka, 1935) describes the Gestalt view that the meaning of an event is more than just an accumulation of facts or responses. This position gave rise to discovery learning (Bruner, 1962), which viewed learners as capable of experimenting with their environment in order to gain greater understanding. Instructors should present information in "nonfinal form" not only to motivate learners, but to help them achieve greater understanding of the subject matter through their own efforts. Current emphasis on "hands-on learning activities" traces its roots to discovery learning.

The third school of thought is derived from the biological evolution theory of Charles Darwin. He believed that people adapt to the demands of their environment. William James and John Dewey extended this view to psychology by arguing that studying an event in isolation ignores its effect on the individual's need to adapt. Without considering the purposes, goals, and motives of the learner, we will not fully understand the learning process. We now turn to more contemporary theories.

OPERANT CONDITIONING

B. F. Skinner's theory of operant conditioning extends the ideas of Thorndike. His concept of reinforcement is fundamental. It is an event that increases the probability of behavior recurring. If I praise Todd, for example, and his studying increases, reinforcement has occurred. The observable behavioral increase is crucial. Likewise, punishment is an event that decreases the probability of a response recurring. If there is not a decrease in behavior, punishment did not occur. Reinforcement can occur in two different ways: by presenting something pleasant such as candy (positive reinforcement) or removing something unpleasant (negative reinforcement). While reinforcement should be applied consistently when the learner is first learning a behavior, it can later be presented following a planned, but less frequent schedule.

Skinner required two processes for learning to occur: (1) the administration of an effective reinforcement schedule and (2) the presentation of material to be learned following a simple-to-complex sequence. By analyzing material into its components, presenting them in sequence, and then providing reinforcement as the learner successively performs each step, teaching is most efficient. This process is called shaping. Skinner insisted that desired learning outcomes be described as specific behavioral objectives with precise criteria. For example, a mathematical objective would be: The learner can multiply single-digit numbers, with no more than 2 errors in 20 problems in 60 seconds.

SOCIAL LEARNING

Another learning theory in the behavioral tradition is social learning (Bandura, 1977). Bandura criticized operant conditioning by insisting that we do not learn only by being directly reinforced ourselves. We can also learn by observing others (models) who are being reinforced for behavior we could have performed. Not everyone is a model, however; we tend to choose those who are similar to us, or who possess competence or perceived status. Thus, our parents and teachers are the most frequent models when we are young, and peers become models for us as we age. Models not only demonstrate new behavior, but may demonstrate that behavior we have already learned will not be reinforced. Parents of adolescents might note the distressing fact that the models their children observe may also be reinforced for behaviors that would be punished at home.

The theory suggests the teaching potential of the media, particularly literature and television. In the classroom, teachers recognize the value of good peer models serving as tutors and mentors to other students. Teachers and peers who demonstrate effective learning strategies ("Class, look how Marianne outlined this chapter.") aid learning. The theory also notes that a student's perception of himself or herself as an effective learner in a specific area (self-efficacy) is influenced by models.

INFORMATION PROCESSING

The most comprehensive of modern learning theories is information processing. It has been influenced by both Gestalt and discovery learning and the biological adaptation views of motivation. The theory emphasizes how information is received, processed, and stored in the brain. Stimuli must be perceived and attended to initially if learning is to occur. Information is further processed into more complex cognitive units in working memory (WM). WM is the thinking phase of the learning process, in which the learner must make sense out of incoming information or encode it. Encoding is based not only on initial input, but also on prior knowledge. When John says "one nation invisible" in reciting the Pledge of Allegiance, he is clearly using past learning to attempt to understand a complex concept. New learning is thus constructed by the individual based on prior knowledge as well as new information.

Information in WM can be transferred to long-term memory (LTM), depending on the efficiency of one's encoding and the motivation to do so. New information is connected in LTM to information already stored. How well it is encoded and connected determines how well it can be recalled and used at a later time. During the phases of attention, WM and LTM, the learner is constantly monitoring the process, called metacognition. We constantly make decisions such as: "Do I need to remember this?" or "Should I write this down?" One form of metacognitive activity is the use of learning strategies that have been useful in the past, such as outlining, note-taking, rereading, and summarizing. Teachers should ensure that students are attending to new stimuli, encoding it correctly, and retrieving information from LTM and using appropriate learning strategies.

CONSTRUCTIVISM

Recent researchers have realized that people are active learners who must discover for themselves the meaning of what the educational environment provides. Meaning is derived as much from one's own experience as from the new content. As a result, learners construct their own knowledge, which is often quite different from what a teacher might anticipate. Consequently, teachers should not serve as a traditional "deliverer" of information but should use materials with which learners become actively involved through manipulation or social interaction. Content should be integrated across different curricular areas so that personal meanings can be constructed in a wider context. For example, constructivist teaching might have students study pumpkins by weighing them

and determining their market price (mathematics), reading about where pumpkins are grown and the kind of soil that is needed (geography), and reviewing how pumpkins were used by early settlers (history).

INSTRUCTIONAL PRACTICES THAT ENHANCE LEARNING

These theories suggest a number of important educational principles and techniques that may be used to enhance learning. From the behavioral point of view, instruction should be sequentially designed, with preliminary learning leading to clear instructional objectives that describe the final goal. Precise criteria should be used to evaluate learning. Reinforcement should be frequent during initial trials, and move to an intermittent schedule as behavior approaches the terminal goal. Responses that are difficult to master should be prompted. For example, a teacher might sing: "Around a tree, around a tree, makes a three" to prompt the learner's writing of the number 3.

Skinner recommends a programmed approach to instruction, in which content is laid out from simple to difficult, and students can work individually at their own pace. Reinforcement is provided through immediate feedback from the materials themselves. Most successful programmed materials are computer-assisted in the form of drill and practice programs. When students practice memorizing facts, dates, definitions, and operations such as addition or verb conjugation, they are learning basic skills through the drill-and-practice method. For the learning of social behavior, behavior modification techniques can also be programmed. A common example is that of token economies, in which students earn stickers or points for demonstrating appropriate behavior, which can be accumulated for more tangible reinforcers such as prizes or preferred activities.

Social learning advocates grouping, in which students can be exposed to positive models. One example is cooperative learning where students of varying ability are all assigned tasks, each of which contributes to a group goal, such as gaining points for one's team, or creating a group project. Advanced students serve as tutors for less-advanced students. Cooperative learning promotes cooperation and respect for others, and it enhances positive feelings of self-efficacy among less-advanced or disabled learners.

The information processing approach has given rise to many classroom instructional techniques that

Table 1   Instructional Techniques to Enhance Information Processing

Technique	Example	Purpose
1. Novel stimuli	"Listen to the words in this song. What do they mean to you?"	Captures attention
2. Mnemonics	"Remember H-O-M-E-S stands for the five Great Lakes: Huron, Ontario, Michigan, Erie, and Superior."	Aids in encoding and retrieval
3. Monitoring and feedback	"Charles, I like the way you carried to the tens place."	Rewards and emphasizes the learner's understanding
4. Advance organizer	"New inventions give rise to new crimes, which result in new methods for controlling them."	Provides general statement to give structure for more-specific content that is coming later
5. Diagrams	The Precipitation Cycle Rain ⟶ evaporation ⟶ cloud formation	Provides visual organization of material
6. Questions	"How might the Confederacy have won the Civil War?"	Encourages students to analyze facts and to solve problems
7. Problem-solving activities	"Go home and measure your bedroom and determine its area in square feet."	Promotes transfer of information to real-life situations
8. Learning strategies	"Ask the questions: Who, what, when, where, and why while reading a mystery story."	Helps students monitor their own understanding

can aid student learning. Their focus is to foster student attention, promote encoding and retrieval of information, and provide examples of learning strategies. Most of the activities are intended to encourage a more personal involvement in learning, reveal subject matter relevance, and stimulate interest and motivation. Table 1 provides a list of activities inspired by the information processing theory, including examples and their purposes.

IMPLICATIONS FOR SCHOOL PSYCHOLOGY

Learning theories have many implications for school psychologists. First, there is no one theory that describes all types and conditions of learning. For example, the behavioral approach seems to apply well to the learning of basic skills for young or disabled learners, while information processing might best fit the secondary school classroom. The school psychologist needs to be aware of contemporary theories and apply them where most appropriate. Moreover, no one theory can account for the extreme diversity we find

among learners. Questions such as how do we find acceptable reinforcers for many children, how do we capture attention and aid encoding for disabled learners, or where do we find appropriate models for disadvantaged learners, challenge the applicability of these theories. They provide us with a way to examine the problems facing all educators.

Second, characteristics of learners interact with instructional processes, so that recommendations for teaching derived from theories must be adapted. Some learners possess unique learning styles or beliefs, preferences, and behaviors used to aid learning.

Some students prefer to learn by themselves, while others find they work best in groups. Other students may possess disabilities that interfere with learning rate, such as those with reading disabilities or attention deficits. These learners cannot process information or maintain attention as efficiently as others. Some may not possess the same motivational level or interests as others. Knowledge of learning theories can provide clues as to how to remediate or bypass these differences.

Third, learning theories emphasize the objective and accurate assessment of learning. It is necessary to employ more than one instrument or method to determine what a student has learned or has the potential to learn. Formal assessment, such as standardized tests, may tell us much about an individual's ability and the general knowledge he or she has accumulated. Learning of specific content and skills, however, may be assessed by curriculum-based methods, which directly tie what is covered in the curriculum to student learning.

Fourth, learning theories emphasize different learning outcomes such as problem solving, critical thinking, creativity, and attitudes as well as memory and understanding. Each type of thinking process requires a different type of test or task to complete for adequate assessment. Learning is displayed in a variety of ways, and good teachers should assess these different types.

Finally, interventions designed to remediate academic or behavioral problems should draw upon learning theories. In many cases, the best interventions draw from a combination of theories. Research demonstrates that interventions that combine behavioral theory (where appropriate behaviors are reinforced), social learning (in which students are taught the basics of self-regulation), and information processing (in which student understanding of the problem is stressed) yield the most success in aiding children. For example, social skills training might include:

- A component stressing reinforcement of appropriate behaviors such as waiting one's turn or raising one's hand
- A social learning component in which peer models are used to demonstrate desired behavior
- An information-processing component in which students discuss and analyze the rationale for various rules designed to encourage social skills

—*Robert L. Hohn*

See also Ability Grouping; Academic Achievement; Cooperative Learning; Curriculum-Based Assessment; Intelligence; Learning Disabilities; Learning Styles; Mastery Learning; Math Interventions and Strategies; Memory; Mental Retardation; Motivation; Reading Interventions and Strategies; Retention and Promotion; Spelling Interventions and Strategies; Study Skills; Writing Interventions and Strategies

REFERENCES AND FURTHER READING

Bandura, A. (1977). *Social learning theory* (2nd ed.). Englewood Cliffs, NJ: Prentice-Hall.

Bruner, J. S. (1962). *The process of education.* Cambridge, MA: Harvard University Press.

Hohn, R. L. (1995). *Classroom learning and teaching.* White Plains, NY: Longman.

Koffka, K. (1935). *Principles of Gestalt psychology.* New York: Harcourt Brace.

Skinner, B. F. (1968). *The technology of teaching.* New York: Appleton-Century-Crofts.

Thorndike, E. L. (1932). *The fundamentals of learning.* New York: Teachers College Press.

LEARNING DISABILITIES

Children and adults classified with learning disabilities (LD) are individuals of normal intelligence, but they suffer with mental information processing difficulties. Several definitions refer to persons with LD as reflecting a heterogeneous group of individuals with intrinsic disorders that are manifested by specific difficulties in the acquisition and use of listening, speaking, reading, writing, reasoning, or mathematical abilities. Most definitions assume that the learning difficulties of such individuals are:

- Not related to inadequate opportunities to learn, general intelligence, or significant physical or emotional disorders. The basic disorders are linked to specific psychological processes (such as remembering the association between sounds and letters).
- Not related to poor instruction, but to specific psychological processing problems. These problems have a neurological, constitutional, and/or biological base.
- Not manifested in all aspects of learning. Such individuals' psychological processing deficits depress only a limited aspect of academic behavior. For example, such individuals may suffer problems in reading, but not arithmetic.

Depending upon the definition, the incidence of children with LD is conservatively estimated to reflect 2% of the public school population. It is also the largest category of children served in special education.

The term *learning disability* was first coined in a speech that Samuel Kirk delivered in 1963 at the Chicago Conference on Children with Perceptual Handicaps. Clinical studies prior to 1963 showed that a group of children who suffered perceptual, memory, and attention difficulties related to their poor academic performance, but who were not intellectually retarded, were not being adequately served in the educational context.

Lee Wiederholt in reviewing the history of the LD field noted that its unique focus was on identifying and remediating specific psychological processing difficulties. Popular intervention approaches during the 1960s and 1970s focused on visual–motor, auditory sequencing, or visual perception training exercises. Several criticisms were directed at these particular interventions on methodological and theoretical grounds.

By the late 1970s, dissatisfaction with a processing orientation to remediation of LDs, as well as the influence of federal regulations (Public Law 94–142), led to remediation programs focused on basic skills such as reading and mathematics. The focus on basic skills rather than psychological processes was referred to as direct instruction. The mid-1980s witnessed a shift from the more remedial-academic approach of teaching to instruction that included both basic skills and cognitive strategies (ways to better learn new information and efficiently access information from long-term memory). Children with LDs were viewed as experiencing difficulty in regulating their learning performance. An instructional emphasis was placed on teaching students to check, plan, monitor, test, revise, and evaluate their learning.

The early 1990s witnessed a resurgence of direct instruction intervention studies, primarily influenced by reading research, which suggested that a primary focus of intervention should be directed to phonological skills. The rationale was that because a large majority of children with LD suffer problems in reading, some of these children's reading problems are exacerbated because of lack of systematic instruction in processes related to phonological awareness (the ability to hear and manipulate sounds in words and understand the sound structure of language). This view gave rise to interventions that focused heavily on phonics instruction, and intense individual one-to-one tutoring to improve children's phonological awareness of word structures and sequences.

Several types of LD have been discussed in the literature. Few of these subtypes have been considered valid because (a) these particular subtypes do not respond differently to instructional programs when compared to other subtypes, and/or (b) the skills deficient in a particular subtype are not relevant to the academic areas important in the school context.

However, there are two subtypes that have been extensively researched and are relevant to the school context: reading disabilities and mathematical disabilities. These subtypes are usually defined by standardized (norm-referenced) and reliable measures of intelligence and achievement. The most commonly used intelligence tests are from the Wechsler series and common achievement tests that include measures of word recognition or identification (Woodcock-Johnson Psychoeducational Battery, Wide Range Achievement Test, Woodcock Reading Mastery Test, Kaufman Test of Educational Achievement, Peabody Individual Achievement Test) and arithmetic calculation (all the aforementioned tests and the Key Math Diagnostic Test). In general, individuals with intelligence quotient (IQ) scores equal to or more than a full-scale IQ score of 85, reading subtest scores equal to or less than the 25th percentile, and/or arithmetic subtest scores equal to or less than the 25th percentile captures two high incidence disorders within LD: reading (word recognition) and arithmetic (computation, written work).

In terms of reading disabilities, Linda Siegel argues that fundamental to evaluating reading disabilities is a focus on word recognition measures, because they capture more basic processes and responses than reading comprehension. She states that the diagnosis of a reading disability should include a reading recognition cutoff score below the 25th percentile. Reading problems are best conceptualized as a continuum with varying degrees of severity. Her research indicates that children with reading disabilities show a remarkable homogeneity in cognitive profiles. That is, she finds that when reading disabilities are defined in terms of word recognition skills that all children with reading problems have deficits in phonological processing, working memory, short-term memory, and syntactic awareness. Her research shows that difficulties in phonological processing are fundamental problems for children with reading disabilities, and this problem continues to adulthood. She also indicates that there is no evidence to suggest that development of decoding skills is a result of specific instruction in grapheme–phoneme conversion rules. Her work and the work of others find three critical processes in the analysis of reading disabilities: those related to phonological processing (ability to segment sounds), syntactical processing (ability to understand grammatical structure), and working memory (combination of transient memory and long-term memory).

In terms of math disabilities, David Geary finds that children with arithmetic disabilities do not necessarily differ from academically normal peers in terms of the types of strategies used to solve simple arithmetic problems. Differences, however, are found in the percentages of retrieval and counting errors. Children with math disabilities have long-term memory representations of addition facts that are not correct. Geary provides a taxonomy of three general subtypes of mathematical disability: those related to procedural errors, those related to semantic memory, and those with visual–spatial difficulties. In the review of literature, an important point he makes is that the defining feature of arithmetic disabilities is an inability to retrieve basic computational facts from long-term memory. When children with arithmetic disabilities retrieve arithmetic facts from long-term memory, they commit more errors than do their academically normal peers and show error and reaction time patterns that often differ from the patterns found with children who are learning the material for the first time.

EFFECTIVE TREATMENTS

In the field of LDs, the term *treatment*, or intervention, is defined as the direct manipulation of variables (e.g., instruction) to assess learning efficiency, accuracy, and understanding. The instructional literature in special education indicates what contributes to good instruction. Several authors, both in mainstream regular and special education, suggest that effective instruction follows the following sequence of events:

- State the learning objectives and orient the students to what they will be learning and what performance will be expected of them.
- Review the skills necessary to understand the concept.
- Present the information, give examples, and demonstrate the concepts/materials.
- Pose questions (probes) to students and assess their level of understanding and correct misconceptions.
- Provide group instruction and independent practice. Give students an opportunity to demonstrate

new skills and learn the new information on their own.
- Assess performance and provide feedback. Review the independent work and give a test. Give feedback for correct answers and re-teach skills if answers are incorrect.
- Provide distributed practice and review.

This sequence of teaching concepts also applies to teaching children with LDs. However, do such children need a greater emphasis on some aspects of the sequence than others? Lee and colleagues provide the most comprehensive analysis of the intervention literature on LDs to date. Interventions were analyzed at three levels: general models of instruction, tactics used to convey information, and components most important in instructional success.

In terms of general models, their synthesis of methodologically sound studies (those studies with well-defined control groups and clearly identified LD samples), found that positive outcomes in remediating academic behaviors (e.g., reading, writing, mathematics) were directly related to a combination of direct and strategy instructional models. These models include a graduated sequence of steps with multiple opportunities for extensive practice and teaching of all component skills to a level that shows mastery. The direct instructional models primarily focus on basic skills, whereas the strategy model includes discussion given to strategy implementation, strategy choice, and self-monitoring. The best of these intervention procedures involve teaching:

- A few concepts extensively
- Students to monitor their performance
- Students when and where to use the strategy in order to enhance generalization
- Strategies as an integrated part of an existing curriculum
- Inclusion of a great deal of supervised student feedback and practice

In terms of tactics, they found that not all tactics used to convey information to children with LDs are necessary to make gains in academic performance. However, some tactics that have been touted to improve academic performance of LD students are:

- Using advance organizers (providing students with a type of mental scaffolding in which to build new understanding, where scaffolding consists of helping students access information already in their minds as well as providing new concepts that can organize this information)

- Organizing information questions directed to encourage students to stop from time to time to assess their understanding
- Elaborating (thinking about the material to be learned in a way that connects the material to information or ideas already in their minds)
- Generative learning (making sense of what they are learning by summarizing the information)
- Applying general study strategies (e.g., underlining, note taking, summarizing, having students generate questions, outlining, and working in pairs to summarize sections of materials)
- Thinking about and controlling one's thinking process (metacognition) and attributions (evaluating the reasons for the effectiveness of a strategy)
- Orienting to critical features

A study by H. Lee Swanson analyzed a number of tactics reported in methodologically rigorous studies. He divided those studies into eight models based on key instruction tactics:

1. Direct instruction (a focus on sequencing and segmentation of skills)

2. Explicit strategy training

3. Monitoring (teaching children strategies)

4. Individualized and remedial tutoring

5. Small interactive group instruction

6. Teacher and indirect instruction (teacher makes use of homework and peers for instruction)

7. Verbal questioning/attribution instruction (asking children key questions during the learning phase and whether they thought what they were learning would transfer)

8. Technology (using computers to present concepts)

The results indicated that explicit strategy instruction (explicit practice, elaboration, strategy cuing) and small-group interactive settings best improved the magnitude of treatment outcomes. Explicit strategy instruction includes two key components. One

component includes strategy cues where teachers verbalize steps or procedures to solve problems and use *think-aloud* models. The other component is elaboration, which includes additional information or explanation about concepts and/or redundant text or repetition within text.

Swanson analyzed interventions at the component level and found that explicit practice—activities related to distributed review and practice, repeated practice, sequenced reviews, daily feedback and/or weekly reviews, and advanced organizers—were effective intervention techniques. Advanced organizers involve statements that:

- Direct children to focus on specific material or information prior to instruction
- Direct children about task concepts or events before beginning
- Give objectives of instruction

Finding that these two components (strategy cues and elaboration) enhance intervention outcomes makes sense from the existing literature. For example, retention of many types of knowledge is increased by practice distributed at different time periods, and the provision of statements about a subject to be learned provides a structure for new information that relates it to information students already possess. Explicit practice is important in several stages of learning. Although intensive practice of newly learned information in the early stages of learning is necessary, the cognitive intervention literature suggests that distributed practice is better for retention. Several studies suggest that long-term retention of all kinds of information and skills is greatly enhanced by distributed practice. Likewise, advanced organizers provide students with a "mental scaffold" with which to build new understandings of information. This scaffolding may consist of helping students access information that is already in their minds to aid in learning new concepts or principles; they can organize the existing information in a form that assists them in new learning.

LEARNING DIASBILITIES AS A CONSTRUCT OF STUDY VERSUS A CONSTRUCT THAT CAN BE ASSESSED AND TREATED

Fundamental problems of definition have severely affected the field of LDs as a discipline. This is because considerable latitude exists among psychologists in defining LD. This latitude is influenced by social/political trends as well as nonoperational definitions of LD. The field of study is further exacerbated because the number of individuals classified with LD has increased dramatically over the last 20 years. Unfortunately, without reliable and valid definitions of LD, very little progress in terms of theory development will emerge.

A related impediment to advances in the field is whether students with LD perform differently than low achievers. Traditionally, studies of children with LD have relied primarily on uncovering a significant discrepancy between achievement in a particular academic domain and general intellectual ability. The implicit assumption for using discrepancy scores is that individuals who experience reading, writing, and/or math difficulties, unaccompanied by a low IQ, are distinct in cognitive processing from slow or low achievers. This assumption is equivocal. A plethora of studies have compared children with discrepancies between IQ and reading with nondiscrepancy-defined poor achievers (i.e., children whose IQ scores are in the same low range as their reading scores) and found that these groups are more similar in processing difficulties than different. As a result, some researchers state that current procedures to identify children with LD are invalid. In the area of reading deficits, some have even suggested dropping the requirement of average intelligence in favor of a view where children with reading problems are best conceptualized as existing at the extreme end of a continuum from poor to good readers. In addition, some researchers have argued that IQ is irrelevant to the definition of reading disabilities and that poor readers share similar cognitive deficits, irrespective of general cognitive abilities.

In contrast to the argument that LD is not a valid area of inquiry, Hoskyn and Swanson (1999) found in a synthesis of the literature that although children with LD in reading and low achievers (LA) share some deficits in phonological processing and automaticity (naming speed), the performance of children with LD was superior to the LA group on measures of syntactical knowledge, lexical knowledge, and spatial ability. Another important finding was that cognitive differences between the two ability groups were more obvious in the earlier grades. Perhaps more importantly, Swanson finds that students with LD and LA differ in their responsiveness to treatment. He finds that students who have low reading scores (25th percentile) but average IQ scores are less responsive to interventions than children whose reading and IQ scores are in the same low range (25th percentile).

One of the major difficulties within the field is that students who are identified by a political notion of LD have very little resemblance to the description offered within the scientific discipline. Thus, in contrast to the above arguments related to the validity of LD as a field, most researchers who study the processing difficulties of children with LD do not use discrepancy criteria. The majority of researchers rely on cutoff scores on standardized measures above a certain criterion of general intelligence measures (e.g., standard score > 85) and cutoff scores below a certain criterion (standard score < 85) on primary academic domains (e.g., reading and mathematics). Researchers distinguish individuals with LD from other general handicapping conditions, such as mental retardation, and visual and/or hearing impairments. Further specification is made that bilingualism, socioeconomic status, and conventional instructional opportunity do not account for depressed achievement scores. Such specification allows the scientist to infer learning problems are intrinsic to the individual. This has also been confirmed with fMRI (functional magnetic resonance imaging) studies. Unfortunately, traditional assessment procedures in the public schools seldom provide information that assesses the stability and/or durability of these intrinsic psychological processing deficits under instructional conditions. If individuals with LD have an inability to remember specific aspects of language (phonological information), then documentation must be provided that they have been systematically exposed to such instruction.

The scientific research shows that children with LD can be assessed, and significant gains can be made in academic performance as a function of treatment. However, there is considerable evidence that some children with normal intelligence when exposed to the best instructional conditions fail to efficiently master skills in reading, mathematics, and/or writing. Some literature suggests that individuals with LD are less responsive to intervention than individuals with similar primary academic levels but without LD, and that these academic problems persist into adulthood. Finally, these difficulties in academic mastery reflect fundamental deficits in phonological process and working memory.

—H. Lee Swanson

See also Academic Achievement; Intelligence; Learning; Learning Styles; Math Interventions and Strategies; Memory; Motivation; Reading Interventions and Strategies; Spelling Interventions and Strategies; Study Skills; Writing Interventions and Strategies

REFERENCES AND FURTHER READING

Geary, D. (1993). Mathematical disabilities: Cognitive, neuropsychological, and genetic components. *Psychological Bulletin, 114,* 345–362.

Hoskyn, M., & Swanson, H. L. (2000). Cognitive processing of low achievers and children with reading disabilities: A selective review of the published literature. *School Psychology Review, 29,* 102–119.

Siegel, L. S. (1992). An evaluation of the discrepancy definition of dyslexia. *Journal of Learning Disabilities, 25*(10), 618–629.

Swanson, H. L. (1989). Operational definition: An overview. *Learning Disability Quarterly, 14,* 242–254.

Swanson, H. L. (in press). *Treatment outcomes as a function of IQ and reading level.* In T. Scruggs & M. Mastropieri (Eds.), *Advances in learning and behavioral disabilities.* New York: Elsevier.

Swanson, H. L., Hoskyn, M., & Lee, C. (1999). *Interventions for students with learning disabilities: A meta-analysis of treatment outcomes.* New York: Guilford.

Weiderholt, L. (1974). Historical perspective on the education of the learning disabled. In L. Mann & D. Sabatino (Eds.), *The second review of special education* (pp. 103–152). Austin, TX: Pro-Ed.

LEARNING STYLES

A "learning style" can be thought of as habitual patterns in how a person learns or in how a person prefers to learn. The manner in which people think, learn, and process information is often influenced by their attitudes, feelings, and preferences. Furthermore, the nature of this influence differs from person to person. Both preservice and in-service teachers are socialized to be sensitive to the unique educational needs of learners for which they have responsibility. Teachers are often encouraged to individualize instruction, as much as possible, within their classrooms. This climate has led to an interest in the learning styles of students.

Education researchers attempt to apply research in learning styles to explanations for academic achievement and school performance. This research activity is typically framed in a general sense as a search for aptitude-treatment interactions (ATIs). ATI theory suggests that optimal learning results when the instruction is exactly matched to the aptitudes, styles, or preferences of the learner. ATI research rests on the hope that some instructional strategies (treatments) are more or less effective for particular individuals, depending upon their specific abilities, cognitive-learning styles, or learning preferences.

HISTORY AND DEFINITIONS

Interest among more contemporary researchers in the concept of *style* arose in part from perceived inadequacies of traditional testing (as most popularly manifested in the intelligence quotient [IQ]). Researchers sought to identify processes that underlie individual differences in task performance, which led to the search for new ways to describe cognitive functioning. Today, much confusion exists in terminology related to the concept of "learning style." Sometimes researchers, working in isolation, define the same concept in different ways. Similarly, different terms are often used interchangeably to refer to the same concepts. For our purposes, learning styles are organized into three styles:

1. Cognition-centered
2. Personality-centered
3. Activity-centered

Cognition-Centered Styles

Cognition-centered styles tend to be closely related to perception and cognitive abilities. They are viewed as having a physiological basis, being relatively fixed at an early age, automatic (not amenable to conscious manipulation), and pervasive. The term *cognitive style* is a generic term that focuses on individual differences in perception, which purportedly provides insight into a person's cognition and how they adapt to the world around them. Many different sources of individual differences in cognitive style have been proposed (see reviews by Riding & Rayner, 1998). These styles are typically assessed through visual/perceptual or object sorting tasks that have been specifically designed to measure individual differences in the style construct. Riding and Cheema (1991) reviewed the literature on cognitive styles, and concluded that they can be grouped into "holistic versus analytic" and "verbal versus imagery" style dimensions.

"Thinking styles" refer to the unique ways in which people use their intelligence and/or knowledge, and reflect how abilities and acquired knowledge are used in day-to-day interactions with the environment. For example, people who enjoy creating their own rules for doing things, prefer tasks that allow them to focus on one aspect of the task until it is completed, and prefer tasks that require abstract thinking would be characterized as having a legislative, monarchic, and global thinking style.

Personality-Centered Styles

Personality-centered styles, as the label suggests, tend to be more closely related to the measurement of personality rather than cognition. Personality-centered models incorporate attitudes, values, and interests as these interact with cognition. Two well-known examples of instruments that measure personality-centered styles are the *Myers-Briggs Type Indicator* (Myers & colleagues, 1998) and the *Gregorc Style Delineator* (Gregorc, 1984). The *Student Styles Questionnaire* (Oakland & colleagues, 1996) is an example of an instrument that is designed to be used with schoolchildren between the ages of 8 to 17 years. Although these instruments are not advertised specifically as "learning style" measures, instrument developers and consumers often argue that personality-centered theory instruments can be used to understand individual differences in learning style.

Activity-Centered Styles

The concept of learning style fits best within this style category. Riding and Rayner (1998) divide learning style models into four categories. First, models based on the learning process describe an individual's approach to learning. For example, Kolb and colleagues (2001) describe two bipolar dimensions that underlie differences in learning style. One bipolar dimension refers to an individual's *mode for "grasping" experience*: concrete experience (i.e., being involved in a new experience) versus abstract conceptualization (i.e., creating theories to explain observations). The other dimension describes individual's *mode for "transforming" experience*: reflective observation (i.e., watching others) versus active experimentation (i.e., using theories to solve problems and make decisions). The theory describes four learning styles based on these two dimensions:

1. Converging (i.e., learners who are motivated by the question "How is this relevant to me?")

2. Diverging (i.e., learners who are motivated by the question "Why is this relevant to me?")

3. Assimilating (i.e., learners who are motivated by the question "What is there to know?")

4. Accommodating (i.e., learners who are motivated by the question "What would happen if I did this?")

A second category of activity-centered learning style models describes differences in college-age students' orientation to studying. For example, Entwistle and Ramsden (1983) devised the Approaches to Studying Inventory (ASI), which was subsequently updated to several versions of the Revised Approaches to Studying Inventory (RASI; Duff, 2000). According to this model, approaches to studying have both "referential" and "relational" components. The referential component refers to the student's intention to focus upon the meaning or upon the structure of the task. The relational component refers to whether the student attempts a "deep, holistic approach" or a "surface, atomistic approach" (Riding & Rayner, 1998, p. 60) to the task.

A third category of learning style models attempts to describe individuals, preferences for a range of environmental or instructional factors affecting their learning behavior. Unlike models of cognitive constructs, these models are more susceptible to fluctuation, hence they are considerably less stable. For example, the Learning Styles Inventory (Dunn & colleagues, 1989) identifies five subcategories of preference variables that supposedly influence learning in school-age students:

1. Environmental stimuli (e.g., light, sound, temperature, classroom design)

2. Emotional stimuli (e.g., need for structure, persistence, motivation, responsibility)

3. Social stimuli (e.g., preferences for learning in proximity to peers, pairs, adults, groups, or alone)

4. Physical stimuli (e.g., perceptual strengths of auditory, visual, tactile, and kinesthetic modalities; mobility; food intake; time of day)

5. Psychological stimuli (e.g., global vs. analytic, impulsive vs. reflective)

A fourth category of models views activity centered learning style as descriptive of strengths and weaknesses in developed cognitive skills. Here, the development of particular cognitive skills is viewed as a prerequisite for effective learning. For example, Letteri (1992) developed the Cognitive Profile Assessment Instrument (CPAI) consisting of the following seven bipolar measures of basic cognitive skills that supposedly predict a student's level of success in academic learning (Chinien & colleagues, 1997, provide a more complete description of these measures):

1. Analytical/global
2. Focus/nonfocus
3. Reflective/impulsive
4. Narrow/broad
5. Complex/simple
6. Sharpener/leveler
7. Tolerant/intolerant

TERMS USED INTERCHANGEABLY WITH LEARNING STYLE

Learning modalities and *learning styles* are terms that are often used interchangeably. A learning modality refers to a perceptual pathway (e.g., visual, verbal, auditory, kinesthetic) through which the individual naturally learns best from the environment. According to Riding and Rayner (1998), *learning strategies* are cognitive tools used by the learner to respond to the demands of a specific learning activity or task. Unlike cognitive styles, learning strategies can be learned and modified. *Learning behaviors* refer to problem-solving strategies or responses to learning situations that can be observed in classroom settings. The Learning Behaviors Scale (LBS; McDermott & colleagues, 1997) is an example of an empirically developed, norm-referenced instrument that measures various aspects of learning behavior in children between the ages of 5 and 17 years. For each of the 29 LBS items, a third party (e.g., teacher) rates the student on the observed frequency of a specific learning or learning-related behavior (e.g., "Is willing to be helped when a task proves too difficult," "Has enterprising ideas that often don't work out," "Carries out tasks according to one's ideas rather than in the accepted way").

INTEGRATING COGNITIVE, LEARNING, AND THINKING STYLES

Individual differences in these various constructs can be manifested in the same learning situation. For example, consider a unit on the Civil War in a typical American high school. Learning style is the construct of interest when Mary prefers to learn about the Civil War through reading, but Tom prefers to learn about the Civil War through listening to lectures. Cognitive style differences are evident if Bill sees each Civil War battle as a distinct entity, but Deborah lumps all battles together as being similar. Finally, thinking styles are evident when Pam prefers to organize the dates and locations of Civil War battles, while Bruce prefers to discuss the role of negotiation in forging peace treaties (Sternberg & Zhang, 2001).

Readers are encouraged to evaluate the learning styles literature with a critical eye. To date, the problematic aspects of learning style theory and research tend to outweigh its benefits.

—Craig L. Frisby

See also Academic Achievement; Learning

Point Versus Counterpoint: Learning Styles

The case for:

- Interest in learning styles is high among professional teaching organizations.
- Interest in learning styles reminds teachers to develop a variety of instructional methods to help diverse students to learn in different ways.
- Empirical evidence supports that there are individual differences in personality traits that may influence learning differences.

- Individual differences in extraversion/introversion personality traits can affect performance on elementary information-processing tasks.
- Some learning styles and learning behavior instruments are being developed with a greater degree of psychometric sophistication, and in some cases are supported by the resources of large testing companies.

The case against:

- Learning style theory ignores results from traditional research in intelligence and its effects on learning and academic achievement; hence failing to persuasively defend its added value in explaining learning problems.
- Distinguishing features that discriminate between learning style models are based more on semantic descriptions, rather than results from empirical investigations.
- Learning style models appear to be "instrument bound" (i.e., do not generalize beyond one or two scales), which limits the generalizability of findings.
- Independent empirical validation for many learning style instruments is poor, and evaluations that are done do not support the reliability (i.e., degree of measurement error), construct validity (i.e., degree to which an instrument measures what it says it measures), or predictive validity (i.e., degree to which it is related to other important measures given at a future time) of these instruments.
- Weaknesses of self-report learning style measures include respondent's inability to accurately or objectively report behavior, and tendency to give responses that promote a favorable impression of oneself.
- Cognitive style measures have shown significant correlations with results from standard intelligence tests, which undermines construct validity (McKenna, 1984).
- Associating differences in learning style with racial, ethnic, and sex differences involves gross stereotyping that misleads educators.
- Given the sheer number of different learning style models and dimensions within models, it is extremely unwieldy to adapt classroom instruction to students' identified learning styles in large classrooms.
- The assumption that students can learn only through their identified learning styles, or that achievement is facilitated if classroom instruction is matched to an individual student's identified learning style, is unsupported by a consistent program of research and in some cases is contradicted by other lines of evidence.

REFERENCES AND FURTHER READING

Chinien, C., Boutin, F., & Letteri, C. (1997). Empowering at-risk students to stay in school using a cognitive based instructional system. *Journal of Industrial Teacher Education, 34*(4), 42–63.

Duff, A. (2000). *Learning styles measurement: The Revised Approaches to Studying Inventory (RASI).* Retrieved July 23, 2004, from http://www.uwe.ac.uk/bbs/trr/Issue3/Is 3–1_5.htm

Dunn, R., Dunn, K., & Price, G. E. (1989). *Learning styles inventory.* Lawrence, KS: Price Systems.

Gregorc, A. F. (1984). *Gregorc style delineator* (Rev. ed.). Columbia, CT: Author.

Kolb, D. A., Boyatzis, R. E., & Mainemelis, C. (2001). Experiential learning theory: Previous research and new directions. In R. J. Sternberg & L. Zhang (Eds.), *Perspectives on thinking, learning, and cognitive styles* (pp. 227–247). Mahwah, NJ: Erlbaum.

Letteri, C. A. (1992). Diagnosing and augmenting basic cognitive skills. In I. W. Keef & H. J. Walberg (Eds.), *Teaching for thinking* (pp. 59–71). Reston, VA: National Association of Secondary School Principals.

McDermott, P. A., Green, L. F., Francis, J. M., & Stott, D. H. (1997). *Learning behaviors scale.* Philadelphia: Edumetric and Clinical Science.

Myers, I. B., McCaulley, M. H., Quenk, N. L., & Hammer, A. L. (1998*). MBTI manual: A guide to the development and use* *of the Myers-Briggs Type Indicator* (3rd ed.). Palo Alto, CA: Consulting Psychologists Press.

Oakland, T., Glutting, J. J., & Horton, C. B. (1996). *Student styles questionnaire manual.* San Antonio, TX: Psychological Corporation.

Riding, R. J., & Cheema, I. (1991). Cognitive styles: An overview and integration. *Educational Psychology, 11,* 193–215.

Riding, R., & Rayner, S. (1998). *Cognitive styles and learning strategies: Understanding style differences in learning and behavior.* London: David Fulton.

Sternberg, R. J., & Zhang, L. (2001). In R. J. Sternberg & L. Zhang (Eds.), *Perspectives on thinking, learning, and cognitive styles* (pp. vii–ix). Mahwah, NJ: Erlbaum.

LEAST RESTRICTIVE ENVIRONMENT

The *Brown v. Board of Education* and *Pennsylvania Assn. for Retarded Children* (*PARC*) cases helped establish the ideals and foundations of educational equity that led to the Individuals with Disabilities Education Act (P.L. 91–230) and the least restrictive environment (LRE) principle. The *Brown* landmark decision held that racial segregation was inherently unequal. Subsequent legal cases (*PARC v. Pennsylvania* and *Mills v. Board of Education*, both of 1972) applied the *Brown* ruling to education and forced the public schools to provide services for children with disabilities. These rulings were then extended to providing services to children in the least restrictive environment and placement in institutions was seen as stigmatizing these children. Thus, children were placed in programs that provided the most interaction with nondisabled peers.

BASIC ASPECTS OF LEAST RESTRICTIVE ENVIRONMENT

LRE provides disabled students access to independent learning environments and inclusive peer relations as much as is possible for them. LRE may range from residential treatment to full inclusion in the regular classroom, depending on an individual child's need. These principles have changed in the past decade or so. Initially the goal was to "mainstream" the child into the regular classroom for as much of the day as possible. In this manner, children were in the regular classroom for many subjects, generally including art, music, physical education, and science/social studies. This practice required the child to go to the special education classroom for individual tutoring and support for the remainder of the school day.

Advocates for disabled students in the 1960s and 1970s promoted physical and social integration of disabled students with nondisabled peers. At that time, educational placements focused on a child's strengths, and a range of placements was developed to decide a disabled child's optimal education setting. Because this regulation was not defined absolutely and words like "mainstreaming" were not used in the law, the definition has been molded by cases in the judicial system over the decades.

In recent years the pendulum has swung to "inclusion." In this case, children are in the regular classroom and the special education teacher comes to them. There are variations on this theme, but generally the child participates in the regular classroom with additional support provided by a paraprofessional aide or a special education teacher.

COURT PRECEDENTS

Many court decisions have supported LRE. *Daniel R.R. v. State Board of Education* (1989) was a two-part test developed to decide whether compliance with LRE was present. First, it must be determined whether the regular classroom can meet the child's needs with additional aides and services provided. Then, if placement outside the classroom is appropriate, the Individualized Education Program (IEP) committee (a team of educators and parents) must decide whether the school has mainstreamed the child to the greatest extent possible (Prasse, 1995). Additional factors that need to be considered are whether the school has tried inclusion, comparing the benefits gained from regular class participation versus special education, and what are the negative effects of the child's inclusion on the other children in the class.

The LRE principle states that unless a regular education setting is in some way prohibitive to the education of the disabled child (or fellow students), they must participate (to some degree) in activities with their nondisabled peers. According to this principle, the first consideration of a child's educational placement is how and where he or she would be educated if not disabled, and can the child learn in that environment with appropriate aids and services.

THE ISSUE OF INCLUSION

While initially the LRE principle of appropriate education was interpreted to mean adequate equal access, more recent cases have set a standard that a child should be educated in a place where "significant learning" takes place and "meaningful educational benefit" occurs. Courts have left the enactment of higher standards to the discretion of individual states. Current advocates in the field fall on a continuum of their own, from full inclusion to inclusion and separation of the severely disabled. Federal courts have differed in determining what is an appropriate LRE and have set differing standards across states. With the reauthorization of Individuals With Disabilities Education Act (IDEA), Farley (2002) suggests that the Supreme Court evaluate these separate standards currently used to determine LRE and devise a single national test to guide school districts.

THE ROLE OF THE SCHOOL PSYCHOLOGIST IN LRE

Debate continues in this area as to how to implement LRE. It is the IEP team's responsibility to tailor the options to the individual. The school psychologist, as an integral part of the IEP team, is important in helping to determine the appropriate setting as well as interpreting assessment (both formal and informal) results.

Generally, discussion about LRE includes the physical context; that is, whether the child should be in a regular classroom setting. It may be more important to evaluate the social organization of the setting rather than just the physical aspects. In this manner, the specific activities are evaluated to determine the appropriateness for the particular child. Evaluating the child within the interaction present during a specific activity provides a more appropriate context in which to determine placement. School psychologists are in a prime position to assist with such determination because they are trained to conduct functional behavioral analyses, have a well-developed understanding of social development and context, and are able translate these aspects for school professionals and parents to provide additional insight into the child's needs. These abilities are also most in tune with the reauthorization standards of IDEA.

Kavale and Forness (2000) rightly point out that ignoring research evidence on the appropriateness of placement based on functional analysis has led to the practice of inclusion even in situations that are not in the best interest of the child. Evaluating the social ecology of the classroom as well as the academic requirements is an important step that school psychologists can provide. Consideration of all the information is necessary to provide the best possible education for each child. In line with these concerns is the emerging concern of the effect of the mainstreamed child on the other students in the class (Yell, 1995). Looking at the sociocultural aspects of the classroom has become even more important for the appropriate planning for the child.

IMPORTANT LEAST RESTRICTIVE ENVIRONMENT COURT CASES

Mattie T. v. Holladay (1979): This class action suit sought to right the exclusion, neglect, discriminatory evaluation, and inappropriateness of placement of 26 disabled students in Mississippi. The benchmark order from this case launched both the idea of LRE and the concept and application of Child Find, requiring schools to actively identify disabled students and evaluate and serve them accordingly.

Roncker v. Walters (1983): Against the family's wishes for greater inclusion for their child, a district wanted to move this educable mentally retarded (EMR) student, who was not progressing in a regular education program, to a segregated placement. This case clarified the importance of education in the general education classroom and reemphasized the importance of the student being integrated to the maximum extent appropriate.

Greer v. Rome (1991): This case set the standard for considering a "continuum of options" before deciding on a more restrictive setting. An IEP committee must consider what the appropriate LRE is.

Oberti v. Board of Education of the Borough of Clementon School District (1993): This landmark case established the idea of *inclusion* as a right not a privilege. The burden of proving compliance with LRE falls on the school, and the court voiced the opinion that inclusion promotes successful societal integration and functioning.

—*Margaret Semrud-Clikeman*
and Allison Cloth

See also Due Process; Functional Behavioral Assessment; Individuals With Disabilities Education Act; Mainstreaming; Resource Rooms; Special Education

REFERENCES AND FURTHER READING

Farley, S. E. (2002). Least restrictive environments: Assessing classroom placement of students with disabilities under IDEA. *Washington Law Review, 77,* 809–842.

Kavale, K., & Forness, S. R. (2000). History, rhetoric, and reality—Analysis of the inclusion debate. *Remedial and Special Education, 21,* 279–296.

Prasse, D. (1995). School psychology and law. In A. Thomas & J. Grimes (Eds.), *Best practices in school psychology* (Vol. 3, pp. 41–50). Washington, DC: National Association of School Psychologists.

Yell, M. L. (1995). Least restrictive environment, inclusion, and students with disabilities—A legal analysis. *Journal of Special Education, 28,* 389–404.

LICENSING AND CERTIFICATION IN SCHOOL PSYCHOLOGY

Historically, there has been a distinction between licensure and certification. Licensure limits the practice of a profession to those individuals who hold a license in a specific field. Certification permits use of a particular title or "certifies" that the person has completed a specific training program. Some states may use either term, but conform most closely to the concept of licensing by giving legal authority to individuals to provide services. In all cases, it is implicit or explicit in the applicable laws that the professional subscribes to codes of conduct and ethical principles adopted by the profession. For this entry, licensure is equivalent to certification, unless otherwise noted.

In most states, departments of education are given the responsibility and authority to establish requirements for licensing of school psychologists, evaluating applicants' credentials, issuing licenses, and assuming disciplinary authority over those who are credentialed. Training is at the graduate level only. To work in the public schools, most states require that school psychologists complete a state-approved graduate program of at least 60 semester hours, which may or may not require a formal, professionally supervised internship. Licensing may be at the doctoral and nondoctoral levels, and some states have separate procedures for each level. Some activities may be restricted to doctoral level school psychologists such as working with students who have emotional and behavioral problems.

NATIONAL SCHOOL PSYCHOLOGY CERTIFICATION SYSTEM

In 1988, the National Association of School Psychologists (NASP) approved the National School Psychology Certification System (NSPCS), which established standards by which school psychologists should be trained. School psychology programs may apply to NASP to offer approved programs, which will culminate in a graduate being eligible to be endorsed as a Nationally Certified School Psychologist (NCSP). Students must complete a course of study of at least 60 semester hours, which includes a 1,200-hour internship, as well as passing the national examination in school psychology. NASP approves both nondoctoral and doctoral programs. Graduate programs may, at their discretion, require that students take and pass this examination as a graduation requirement. As of 2004, 21 state departments of education accept the NCSP credential as making the applicant automatically eligible for licensure as a school psychologist. The NCSP is a certificate and does not permit a school psychologist to provide services unless licensed by a state. Holding the NCSP only verifies that the school psychologist has completed a NASP-approved program. Conversely, a school psychologist may not have the NCSP, yet be licensed by a state. Holders of the NCSP must complete at least 75 clock hours of continuing education every three years to retain it.

INDEPENDENT PRACTICE FOR SCHOOL PSYCHOLOGISTS

Every state has a separate mechanism for licensing of psychologists who work in nonschool settings or independent practice as a psychologist. In general, independent practice is limited to persons who hold a doctoral degree (PhD, PsyD, or EdD) in school, clinical, or counseling psychology. (Some states, such as Indiana, have limited independent practice options for nondoctoral or unlicensed doctoral school psychologists.) Most state licenses for independent practice are generic (i.e., they do not license by specialization area, but it is assumed that the person practices within one's scope of training and experience). Failure to practice within one's area of competence is considered unethical and illegal, and could result in disciplinary action. Students in doctoral programs in school psychology may choose to complete programs of studies which include a 1,500-hour internship and lead to licensure as an independent practitioner. Doctoral programs accredited by the American Psychological Association meet this requirement. Following receipt of the doctoral degree, a candidate for licensure as a psychologist is required to complete postdoctoral supervised experience of at least 1,500 hours and successfully pass the Examination for the Professional Practice of Psychology (EPPP). Most states also require an examination covering state laws and ethics, which may be written and/or oral. Each state sets its own postdoctoral experience requirements and passing score on the EPPP. Following approval for independent practice, the licensed psychologist often must complete continuing education hours annually or over several years (depending on the state) to retain the license. Doctoral level school psychologists who have a license for independent practice also are eligible to be licensed separately by state departments of education. There may be some minor differences in requirements for either license across states.

—*Thomas J. Huberty*

See also American Psychological Association; Careers in School Psychology; National Association of School Psychologists; School Psychologist

M

MAINSTREAMING

Hallahan and Kauffman (2000) defined mainstreaming as "the placement of students with disabilities in general education classes for all or part of the day and for all or only a few classes" (p. 66). Students with disabilities may be assigned to a continuum of educational placements from general education classroom, on one end of a continuum, to institutionalization on the other. A student's placement within this continuum is determined by his or her Individualized Education Plan (IEP) committee. Several factors contributed to the mainstreaming movement such as normalization, deinstitutionalization, early intervention and early childhood programs, technology advances, and legislative actions such as the 1990 Individuals With Disabilities Education Act (IDEA) (previously known as the Education for All Handicapped Children Act [1975]). Developments in the past decade have moved the discussion of mainstreaming toward inclusive education, whose advocates propose that all students' educational needs can be met in general education classrooms.

—*Wade R. Arnold*

See also Special Education

REFERENCES AND FURTHER READING

Hallahan, D. P., & Kauffman, J. M. (2000). *Exceptional learners: Introduction to special education* (8th ed.). Needham Heights, MA: Allyn & Bacon.

MANIFESTATION DETERMINATION

When a student with a special education disability violates school discipline policy that ordinarily would result in suspension or expulsion, manifestation determination is completed to ascertain whether the behavior that violated school discipline policy was a result of the student's disability. Manifestation determination also assesses the educational placement and program (called the Individualized Education Plan [IEP]) of the student to determine whether the program was adequately meeting his or her educational needs. If the misbehavior is deemed to be a result of the student's disability or if the district does not have positive behavior support interventions in place for the student, then the school's discipline policy may not be applied to the special education student.

Manifestation determination was mandated under the Individuals With Disabilities Act 1997 (IDEA 1997) to clarify procedures under which school personnel could suspend a special education student from school or apply the existing school discipline policy to the student's problem behavior. Schools are charged with developing prevention programs to reduce or eliminate future occurrences of behavior problems. In this vein, schools should develop clear expectations or rules for students' behavior, and the consequences for misbehavior, and inform parents and students of these expectations and potential consequences.

GENERAL PROCEDURES

Disciplinary actions taken by schools for any behavior problem may result in in-school disciplinary actions or out-of-school disciplinary actions. For students with disabilities, any in-school disciplinary action may be used as long as it does not violate the student's IEP. IDEA 1997 requires schools to treat special education students that are suspended or expelled from school differently than the rest of the student body. The removal of a student with a disability from school for disciplinary reasons constitutes a "change of placement" if the absence from school is more than 10 cumulative or consecutive days (during a school year), and the suspension(s) constitute a "pattern of removal." *Pattern of removal* is vaguely defined but generally refers to the length of time a student is removed, the proximity of the removals to one another, or the length of each removal. The student's special education teacher is charged with determining if a *change of placement* has occurred by examining the pattern of removal. If a pattern of removal has occurred and after the 10th day of suspension, the parents must be notified that a placement change has occurred. If the parents or guardians disagree with the assessment results, findings, recommendations, or placements resulting from the manifestation determination process, they may invoke their right to a due-process hearing with an impartial hearing examiner.

DATA COLLECTION PROCEDURES

After the parents have been notified, the IEP team has 10 business days to collect data for the manifestation determination. The IEP team decides on the types of information needed to determine if the behavior(s) in question is a manifestation of the student's disability. The types of information collected must include a current functional behavior assessment (FBA), a review of school records, any previous psychoeducational evaluation or diagnostic reports, the child's current IEP and placement, and, when possible, an observation of the child. Interviews will frequently be conducted with the child, the child's teacher, and the parents. Using the above-mentioned information, the IEP team must determine whether:

- The IEP and placement were appropriate.
- Positive behavior intervention strategies were employed.

- The child's disability did not impair his or her understanding of the consequences of the misbehavior.
- The child's disability did not impair his or her ability to control the behavior subject to disciplinary action.

If the child's IEP or educational placement was not considered to adequately meet the student's needs, then the team must conclude that the behavior was a manifestation of the student's disability. In this scenario, the child cannot be subject to long-term removal from school, and the district must take immediate action to remedy the deficiencies in the placement or IEP. Based on the available data, the IEP team may recommend a change of placement; however, parental consent is required. A 45-day interim placement may be used if the misbehavior involved weapons or drugs. If the child's behavior was not considered to be a manifestation of his or her disability, then the district may proceed with the existing suspension or expulsion policies.

PERSPECTIVES ON MANIFESTATION DETERMINATION

The manifestation process is similar to the well-known legal precedent of determining if a person should be held responsible for his or her criminal behavior because of a preexisting mental condition. The criminal behavior of persons with mental conditions that preclude their ability to judge right from wrong frequently lead to mental health treatment rather than harsher prison sentences. This view features a medical model orientation that states that the problem or disorder is within the person and is not influenced by the environment and is therefore "context independent." This view is not currently accepted by contemporary psychologists as nearly all mental disorders are viewed as *context dependent*, or are significantly influenced by environmental conditions.

Katsiyannis and Maag (2001) argue that disability categories are socially constructed rather than medically validated. Socially constructed disability categories are subject to social and political pressures within the school and in society. As a result, it is extremely difficult to develop scientifically validated assessment and treatment approaches for students with similar educational disabilities. These problems magnify the dilemma of stating with certainty that the student's behavior was caused by the disability.

Katsiyannis and Maag (2001) proposed an alternative skills assessment model to improve the manifestation determination process. In this approach, the goals of assessment are to ascertain whether the student possesses the skills required to engage in appropriate behavior, analyze problem situations and interpret them, and enable the student to self-monitor his or her own behavior. Student and teacher interviews, self-report scales, and social role-plays would be employed to gather information on the above-mentioned questions. With a greater use of instruments and approaches for directly observing the behavior of the student in question, this approach has greater scientific credibility and holds promise for improving the manifestation determination process.

—*Steven W. Lee*

See also Diagnosis and Labeling; Discipline; Expulsion; Functional Behavioral Assessment; Individuals With Disabilities Education Act; Special Education; Suspension; Violence in Schools

REFERENCES AND FURTHER READING

Katsiyannis, A., & Maag, J. W. (2001). Manifestation determination as a golden fleece. *Exceptional Children, 68,* 85–96.

MASTERY LEARNING

Mastery learning is "both a philosophy of instruction and a set of methods for teaching and assessing" (Gentile & Lalley, 2003, p. 172). As a philosophy, it endorses the belief that, except for the most severely cognitively impaired, all children can learn what the schools are accountable for teaching. As a set of teaching and testing methods, it requires that each student be assessed in a criterion-referenced manner—that is, without reference to the performance of others—on how well he or she is achieving the required instructional objectives.

The belief that all children can learn was a central tenet of Benjamin Bloom's initial formulation of mastery learning in 1968. He deduced this from John Carroll's 1963 model of school learning, in which Carroll rejected the traditional norm-referenced view of aptitude as an intellectual trait of cognitive complexity or capacity in favor of a criterion-referenced measure of time needed to learn a preestablished standard. Individual differences still existed, but they would be measured by rate of achieving mastery for a given domain of instructional objectives (e.g., in math vs. history vs. music).

Bloom championed this notion, suggesting that by using criterion-referenced techniques to hold students accountable for achieving important instructional objectives, and by requiring that students remediate and retest, they would all eventually attain mastery. Bloom's methods, called Learning for Mastery, allowed traditional group-based instruction, with individualization occurring as needed depending upon the results of mastery testing. Another system, derived independently from a behavioral contingency management approach by Fred S. Keller (1968), required a totally individualized approach to instruction. Keller's Personalized System of Instruction was more popular in higher education settings than in public schools.

Both systems have the following common features, which serve to define mastery learning (e.g., Block & colleagues, 1989; Gentile & Lalley, 2003):

1. Clearly stated mastery objectives, published for all and sequenced to facilitate transfer of previous knowledge and skills to current and future lessons

2. A preestablished passing standard that is sufficient to guarantee adequate original learning (e.g., 75% correct or more)

3. Criterion-referenced grading, with correctives and retesting required to demonstrate attainment of those objectives

4. Grading incentives to encourage students to go beyond initial mastery and strive for fluency in the material, to better organize, apply, and even teach it

The most common failings in implementing mastery learning occur when mastery is conceived as the endpoint of learning. Mastery, rather, implies only that initial learning of knowledge or skills is sufficient so that when it is forgotten, as it inevitably will be, it can be relearned quickly. With sufficient practice beyond original learning, called overlearning, the material or skill can become automatized, relatively permanent in memory, and sufficiently fluent to be available for transfer. Thus, a mastery learning scheme must award the lowest passing grade for initial acquisition of the required objectives (even if the score on the test is 100% correct) and reserve higher grades for students who complete projects or otherwise demonstrate applications or higher-level analyses of the course content or skills.

—J. Ronald Gentile

See also Classroom Climate; Criterion-Referenced Assessment; Learning; Norm-Referenced Assessment

REFERENCES AND FURTHER READING

Block, J. H., Efthim, H. E., & Burns, R. G. (1989). *Building effective mastery learning schools.* New York: Longman.

Bloom, B. S. (1968). *Mastery learning. UCLA-CSEIP evaluation comment. 1*(2). Los Angeles: University of California at Los Angeles. Reprinted in J. H. Block (Ed.). (1971). *Loves through time.* Berkeley, CA: Bancroft Books.

Block, J. H. (1971). *Mastery learning: Theory and practice* (pp. 47–63). New York: Holt, Rinehart & Winston.

Carroll, J. B. (1963). A model of school learning. *Teachers College Record, 64*, 723–733.

Gentile, J. R., & Lalley, J. P. (2003). *Standards and mastery learning: Aligning teaching and assessment so all children can learn.* Thousand Oaks, CA: Corwin.

Keller, F. S. (1968). Goodbye teacher. *Journal of Applied Behavior Analysis, 1*, 79–89.

MATHEMATICS CURRICULUM AND INSTRUCTION

The mathematics curriculum in K–12 schools is organized across four major areas, number systems, algebra, geometry and measurement, and statistics and probability. While emphasis varies, each grade level's curriculum will likely include experiences with topics in each area. During their study of mathematics, students are expected to learn concepts and procedures, and both are required for mathematical expertise.

The study of numbers begins early with whole numbers and the process of counting. As students age, the number systems they study increase to include integers, rational numbers, and real numbers. Students learn to represent numbers in a variety of ways. For example, the number 5 may be represented by 5 beans, as the difference between 12 and 7, as a product of 20 and ¼, and as the square root of 25. Students learn to write numbers as fractions, decimals, and percents and to complete computation problems with numbers written in various forms. Understanding that numbers can be represented in many different ways is key to developing common sense about numbers and being able to use them in various real-world settings.

The study of algebra begins with a study of patterns by young children. Some patterns involve counting; others involve computational relationships. Older students begin to write patterns using variables and then use variables as unknowns in equations and inequalities and when solving problems. Students learn to represent functions using a table of values, an equation, and a graph. The ability to describe patterns in different ways and to use a variety of different representations is key to developing algebraic thinking.

The study of geometry and measurement includes shapes, their properties and relationships. Students begin exploring common two- and three-dimensional shapes. As they study more complex shapes, they also analyze shapes for their properties, noting such characteristics as number of sides, sum of angle measures, and sides or angles of equal measure. Students learn that some shapes are congruent and some are similar. They also learn how sets of shapes are related, such as all squares are parallelograms. Students study perimeter, area, and volume and their use in the real world.

The study of statistics and probability centers on ways to display and analyze data. Young students create bar graphs of information about themselves and their surroundings. Older students learn other ways to display data and how to select the best representation for a particular set of data. Measures of central tendency (mean, median, and mode) are studied as well as measures of variability, such as the range and standard deviation. Concepts of chance and likelihood provide an introduction to probability; students then learn to calculate the probability of an event occurring and use concepts of probability to analyze information in the real world.

During the study of mathematics, students in all grades develop their problem-solving and reasoning processes. A primary purpose of studying mathematics is developing abilities useful in solving problems that arise in both real-world and mathematical settings. Systematic reasoning is a critical part of mathematics, so students need to engage in the process of making conjectures and developing sound deductive arguments. Problem solving and reasoning should be an integral part of the study of all content areas in mathematics.

Two different views of learning influence mathematics teachers' instruction. First, the *constructivist view* describes how learning occurs as students construct, enhance, and restructure their own knowledge as a result of their thought processes, direct interaction with their environment, and social interaction with other people. In the constructivist approach, students are encouraged to construct meaning in their own way from their own experiences (Karp & Voltz, 2000). The second approach is based on *behavioral theories*, in which researchers view learning as the direct transfer of knowledge from the teacher to the learner. In direct instruction, the teacher explains and demonstrates, asks questions, and provides practice on the topic to be learned. Students derive knowledge from the information presented by the teacher. While constructivism has shaped the current reform in mathematics education, aspects of many theories may help students learn.

The focus of mathematics instruction is not just rote memorization but learning mathematical concepts and procedures with understanding. Researchers have investigated ways to help all students gain mathematical understanding that include using manipulatives, helping students solve problems, using technology, and writing and reflecting.

USING MANIPULATIVES

Concrete materials, or manipulatives, can be used to represent mathematical concepts. To develop a deep understanding of mathematical ideas, all students need to see and experience an idea in different ways. For example, students beginning to understand the idea of *one-half* need experiences with that concept using different materials, such as one-half of a candy bar, one-half of a group of oranges, and one-half located on a number line. While concrete materials are more common in elementary school, middle and high school algebra and geometry students benefit from using algebra tiles to model factoring and multiplying polynomials, and using models of two- and three-dimensional geometric figures to investigate measures, properties, and relationships.

Some researchers (Fleischner & Manheimer, 1997) recommend a sequence of activities for any topic that begins with the use of concrete materials followed by work with semiconcrete (pictorial) and abstract

representations. For example, students need to see connections among the two-digit number, 11, represented concretely as one set of ten blocks and one more block, a picture of those blocks, and the numeral 11. Individual students will need more or less work with concrete and pictorial representations, but research shows that students with learning difficulties benefit from extended practice with manipulative materials.

SOLVING PROBLEMS

Learning to solve problems is an important part of learning mathematics. In addition to some traditional word problems, students are expected to solve more complex, often real-world–based, problems. However, students find problem solving to be difficult, and students with learning disabilities are even less successful than students without disabilities.

Many teachers and written materials present a version of Polya's (1957) suggestions for solving problems. His four steps are:

1. Understand the problem.

2. Devise a plan.

3. Carry out the plan.

4. Look back.

Research shows that students have particular difficulty making sense of some problems and representing them in mathematical form. Addressing this difficulty, teachers and researchers have enhanced the four steps with specific strategies or extra steps. Frequent suggestions include paraphrasing the problem and identifying important words as specific aspects of understanding the problem and drawing a picture or diagram as a part of devising a plan.

USING TECHNOLOGY

Both calculator and computer technology have changed aspects of teaching and learning mathematics. Calculators can be used to explore, develop, and reinforce numerical concepts of estimation and computation, but teachers must help students learn how and when to use the calculator with recognition of its constraints. Students need to be aware that calculators approximate values that have more digits than the display can accommodate. For example, a calculator that can display 10 digits would show 0.6666666667 as a value for two-thirds rather than the repeating decimal. Some calculators have built-in capability to simplify numerical expressions using order of operations, while other calculators do not. For example, a calculator with the capability to implement order of operations will correctly determine that $3 + (5) \times 4$ equals 23, but a calculator without order of operations will indicate that $3 + 5 \times 4$ is 8×4 or 32. When students use the calculator for computation, teachers need to ensure that they understand the algorithms upon which the calculations are based.

Middle and high school students use graphing and dynamic geometry tools. Using graphing technology, many students discover mathematical ideas on their own. In particular, students can generate a large set of examples, then make conjectures based on observed similarities or differences. For instance, as students graph several linear functions that pass through the origin but have different values for the slope, students can see the relationship between the size of the slope and the steepness of the line. Dynamic geometry tools on either calculators or computers can be used to make and test conjectures and explore theorems about geometric shapes. Such activities provide students opportunities to explore why rules, properties, and relationships are true.

WRITING AND REFLECTING

Mathematics teachers are using writing to encourage students to reflect on their experiences and to think about their learning. Young students frequently combine their writing with pictures or diagrams to illustrate their ideas. As students age, they should increase their use of correct mathematical language to express their ideas and provide more detailed explanations and reflections. When students communicate their ideas in writing, they learn to clarify, refine, and consolidate their thinking. In the process, students can also discover new ideas and make new connections. One child said, "when you write about math, you get more ideas" (Whitin & Whitin, 2000, p. 4).

Writing has come to be an important part of problem-solving instruction in many mathematics classrooms. Students are writing to communicate their solutions to problems; that is, they are writing a description of the entire problem-solving process that led to an answer. In this type of writing, students are encouraged to describe the strategies they used and explain why their solution makes sense. Such justification is expected because many problems have various methods of solution and sometimes more than one correct answer.

CONCLUSION

Because all students need to learn mathematics, education professionals are working to provide high-quality materials and methods in all K–12 classrooms. Both curriculum and instruction must play roles in meeting the goal of "high expectations and strong support for all students" (National Council of Teachers of Mathematics, 2000, p. 12).

—*A. Susan Gay*

See also Mathematics Interventions and Strategies

REFERENCES AND FURTHER READING

Fleischner, J. E., & Manheimer, M. A. (1997). Math interventions for students with learning disabilities: Myths and realities. *School Psychology Review, 26*, 397–413.

Karp, K. S., & Voltz, D. L. (2000). Weaving mathematical instructional strategies into inclusive settings. *Intervention in School and Clinic, 35*, 206–215.

National Council of Teachers of Mathematics. (2000). *Principles and standards for school mathematics.* Reston, VA: National Council of Teachers of Mathematics.

Polya, G. (1957). *How to solve it* (2nd ed.). Princeton, NJ: Princeton University Press.

Whitin, P., & Whitin, D. J. (2000). *Math is language too: Talking and writing in the mathematics classroom.* Urbana, IL: National Council of Teachers of English.

MATHEMATICS INTERVENTIONS AND STRATEGIES

Since the National Council of Teachers of Mathematics released its *Standards* in 1989, reform of mathematics curriculum to increase students' understanding of mathematical concepts has been a major issue of discussion. Most agree on the goal; however, fierce debates have arisen about the best instructional methods to reach those goals. Some have stressed discussion of problem-solving strategies and the emergence of mathematical discussion between students as the most critical elements in mathematics reform.

Others have feared that by minimizing the teaching of arithmetic computation and simple word problems, many students—especially those with learning disabilities, individuals with psychological processing or learning difficulties, and other learning problems—would never develop conceptual understanding.

In 2001, the National Research Council issued a report on lessons learned from experimental, development, and case-study research on teaching and the learning of mathematics. This document, *Adding It Up,* concluded that mathematical proficiency includes:

- Understanding mathematical concepts
- Fluent and accurate computational ability
- Strategic competence
- Adaptive reasoning

The latter two reflect insights gained from cognitive science and developmental psychology. Strategic competence is the ability to use either words or pictures to represent a problem and potential solutions, and the ability to develop multiple strategies for solving mathematical problems. Adaptive reasoning is the ability to justify strategies, and to analyze strengths and weaknesses of solutions proposed by others. These are ambitious goals, but they should be the objectives of a mathematics intervention.

Between 1996 and 2002, several researchers synthesized the experimental research on effective mathematics interventions for students who struggled with mathematics. Although the body of research is small, and many of the measures only tap one or two of the elements of mathematics proficiency noted previously, the syntheses suggest several features of instructional interventions that are likely to enhance achievement for these students. Some of the more promising interventions feature mediated verbal rehearsal, the use of visual representations, peer-assisted learning, and strategies for the efficient retrieval of basic arithmetic facts. These would seem to be indicators of teaching situations or interventions that are likely to be successful for this group of struggling students.

One technique, sometimes called mediated verbal rehearsal, that seems to be effective is taught in the following sequence:

- Providing examples
- Demonstrating proficient math solutions to students

- Requiring students to solve similar types of problems
- Requiring students to verbalize their justifications for their solutions

This technique appears to work when the teacher gives students feedback about the solution and justification. This approach attempts to build what the National Research Council calls strategic competence and adaptive reasoning in students.

The intervention research also supports the use of visual representations (e.g., figures, drawings, diagrams) of mathematical problems. This would seem to support the idea that students with learning problems are helped when they are required to represent mathematical relationships and problems in multiple ways.

Students with learning problems benefit from peer-assisted instruction. Typically a student who is struggling is paired with a more proficient student. However, both play the role of tutor and tutee. This enables the less proficient student to carefully watch, monitor, and question what and why the peer is solving a problem in a particular fashion. It also allows the more proficient peer to ask the student with a learning problem to articulate why the decision was made, to suggest that the student draw out a picture of the problem or put his or her reasons for a strategy choice into words. Tutors and tutees can be trained in a variety of techniques that promote this type of dialogue about mathematics. There is some evidence that more expert tutors or interventionists can use a similar methodology, especially when students are working on more complex mathematical material.

Some important findings have emerged from the research on the nature of mathematics difficulties and disabilities. A key finding is that students with mathematics difficulties tend to be unable to rapidly retrieve basic arithmetic facts (also known as arithmetic combinations). Proficient students often easily and quickly retrieve these combinations, such as $9 + 8$, or 7×6. Students with mathematics difficulties often resort to inefficient procedures such as counting on their fingers. When students cannot quickly recall that $9 + 8$ is 17, or 7×6 is 42, they are likely to get lost in more mathematically advanced discussions. We know that efficient retrieval of basic arithmetic combinations/facts is a goal of mathematics interventions. However, we are less certain about what are the best teaching strategies beyond extensive drill on memorization of these combinations. Increasingly, researchers are arguing for approaches that immerse students in learning these combinations, but also using them as a means to build understanding of mathematical relations and concepts. To date, little research has compared the relative effectiveness of pure drill (often through computer exercises) as an intervention with intensive teaching of the strategies underlying the arithmetic facts. This is a critical area in mathematics intervention research. It is possible that a mixture of both approaches is optimal.

Currently, the findings from the intervention research provide only broad guidelines on how to teach or how to effectively intervene when students experience difficulties in learning mathematics. Research should be useful to school psychologists, however, as a guide to what seems to be effective practice. Assisting with setting up peer tutoring programs or cross-age tutoring programs is likely to be helpful. In addition to implementing or helping teachers to implement interventions that boost the math achievement of students, school psychologists should keep abreast of advances in measures for screening students who require early intervention and work with teachers to set up progress monitoring systems for students who do poorly in mathematics based on state assessments.

—*Russell Gersten and Jonathan R. Flojo*

See also Academic Achievement; Cooperative Learning; Grades; Homework; Learning; Learning Styles

REFERENCES AND FURTHER READING

Baker, S., Gersten, R., & Lee, D. (2002). A synthesis of empirical research on teaching mathematics to low-achieving students. *The Elementary School Journal, 103*(1), 51–73.

Fuchs, D., & Fuchs, L. S. (2001). Principles for the prevention and intervention of mathematics difficulties. *Learning Disabilities Research & Practice, 16*(2), 85–95.

Geary, D. C. (1993). Mathematical disabilities: Cognitive, neuropsychological, and genetic components. *Psychological Bulletin, 114*, 345–362.

Hanich, L., Jordan, N., Kaplan, D., & Dick, J. (2001). Performance across different areas of mathematical cognition in children with learning disabilities. *Journal of Educational Psychology, 93*(3), 615–626.

Kirkpatrick, J., Swafford, J., & Findell, B. (Eds.). (2001). *Adding it up: Helping children learn mathematics.* Washington, DC: National Academy Press.

MEDIA AND CHILDREN

Every day children are exposed to the best and worst of our society thorough media. The media include television, radio, Internet, video games, and other forms of electronic devices. For better or worse, media impacts children's achievement, behavior, and health. Significant mediating factors include parental supervision, amount and type of media, and child characteristics.

The results of a nationwide survey of 3,155 youngsters found that the average American child has access to an impressive array of electronic media—three televisions, three tape players, three radios, two CD players, one video game player, and one computer. They found that children 8 to 18 years of age average nearly 6.75 hours with media every day. Sixty-five percent of these children and adolescents watch TV with their meals and have a TV in their bedrooms, while 61% stated they had no rules about TV in their homes. Only 5% of these youngsters watched TV with their parents. Although 21% have computers, respondents averaged only 21 minutes per day playing computer games. In addition, older teens spend, on average, 87 minutes per day listening to music. Children 2 to 7 years of age average 3.5 hours per day with media and 32% of this group have a TV in their bedrooms.

MEDIA'S IMPACT ON ACHIEVEMENT
Preschool Level

Before kindergarten, parents who select educational TV programs like *Sesame Street* provide their child with a solid advantage. Longitudinal research has found positive outcomes for students watching *Sesame Street*. Using Center for Research on the Influences of Television on Children (CRITC) data, Wright and colleagues (2001) found positive correlations between *Sesame Street* and scores in reading, math, vocabulary, and readiness even when factors like socioeconomic status were statistically controlled. Huston and colleagues (2001) found that when compared to nonviewers, high school students who had watched *Sesame Street* as preschoolers read more books; academically outperformed nonviewers in English, science, and math; and were more highly motivated to achieve. They also found that males who watched *Sesame Street* as five-year-olds were less aggressive as teens than those who did not watch.

Committed to children's best interests, the producers of *Sesame Street* use child development principles to teach concepts. Fisch (2002) reviewed educational TV and noted improvements in students' language skills from shows including *Barney & Friends*, *Between the Lines*, *Blue's Clues*, and *Electric Company*. Reading comprehension skills were improved in students watching *Reading Rainbow* with increases in library usage noted.

In Huston's early learning model, TV's educational programs promote language skills, motivation, and behaviors needed to sustain attention and concentration. As a result, students experience early academic success, which firmly sets the foundation for future success.

Elementary Level

While educational programs are excellent examples of TV's promise, the reality is that TV incessantly promotes itself as entertainment. Cunningham and Stanovich (1998) reported that individuals reading popular magazines had three times more opportunities to learn new vocabulary words than those watching prime-time TV. A three-year Dutch study of second and fourth graders found that TV negatively influenced reading comprehension skills by reducing recreational reading and depreciating reading's value. They also found that reading subtitles on televised programs improved reading.

Studies have shown significant math gains and a better attitude toward math in students who viewed *Infinity Factory* and *Square One TV*. In science, *3–2–1 Contact* and *Bill Nye the Science Guy* enhanced students' scientific knowledge while promoting problem-solving skills and a positive attitude toward science.

Secondary Level

Keith and colleagues (1986) studied the cumulative effect of TV viewing on high school seniors. When high-ability students spent more than one hour per school day watching TV, their academic achievement declined. Students from low socioeconomic status families and low-ability students watched more TV than more economically advantaged and more capable students. Gentile and Walsh (2002) investigated

family media habits and found that a TV in a child's bedroom correlated with lower school performance even when statistically controlling for income and race. Thirty-eight percent of American children have a TV in their bedrooms. African American and Hispanic children are more likely than whites to have a TV in their bedrooms, and children from low-income families are more likely to have a bedroom TV than those from higher-income families.

Gentile and Walsh (2002) also found that:

- Children whose families leave the TV on when no one is watching it perform poorly academically.
- Children with a TV in their bedrooms watch 5.5 hours more TV each week than those who do not.
- Children who participate in alternate activities do better in school than those who do not.

In general, children who watch less TV are monitored more by parents; their families have more knowledge about media and media effects, use electronic and print media more carefully, and participate in alternate activities rather than using media.

Intellectually bright students watch beneficial TV shows, while low achievers prefer violent programs. Students with disabilities watch more TV than their peers. The emotionally disturbed students watch more crime stories and cartoons and frequently identify with their favorite TV character. Students with learning disabilities may believe that TV reflects reality and have difficulty understanding special effects and TV ads.

MEDIA'S IMPACT ON BEHAVIOR

Historically, the impact of media on aggressive behavior has been a concern since the 1930s. Major investigations have all conclusively determined that televised violence is a contributing factor to aggression in children. Studies have found that TV violence poses a serious risk of harm to children. Parke and Slaby (1983) documented four effects of violent media:

1. The *aggressor effect* increases aggressiveness toward others.

2. The *victim effect* makes the viewer see the world as a mean place, which requires one to protect oneself.

3. The *bystander effect* makes viewers become apathetic and desensitized to the needs of others.

4. The *appetite effect* makes viewers want to seek out more violent material.

In a 15-year longitudinal study, Huesmann and colleagues (2003) investigated the effects of violent media on children 6 to 10 years of age. Statistically controlling for socioeconomic status, intellectual ability, and parenting factors, media violence predicted adult aggressiveness. Men who were high TV-violence viewers as boys were three times more likely to be convicted of crimes than other men in the study. Further, these men were significantly more likely to be aggressive toward their spouses, react to an insult by shoving another person, and to have a moving traffic violation. Women who were high TV-violence viewers as girls were four times more likely to assault another adult than other women. Further, they were more likely to throw something at their spouses, commit a criminal act, and to have a moving traffic violation.

Consuming two to four hours of TV daily, a typical child will see 8,000 murders and more than 100,000 acts of violence by the time he or she leaves elementary school. Researchers conclude that video games prime aggressive ideas, reinforce overlearning of aggressive scripts, and increase perceptions of others as being hostile. Increased time with TV and computerized games along with decreased outdoor play have contributed to the growing problem of childhood obesity. Studies show that when elementary children restrict their TV viewing, significant decreases in body mass index are measured. Not just physical health is affected by media access. Although parents reported positive academic benefits with declines in face-to-face social interactions, lower scores on self-ratings of psychological well-being were observed.

PARENTAL CONTROLS

It is obvious that parents have tremendous responsibility in raising their children. Parents should ask the following questions about a TV program, "Is it developmentally appropriate for their child? Does the program promote their child's emotional development such as trust, the foundation of relationships?" Other questions focus on children's needs to be connected in meaningful relationships, to be empowered with the belief of making a positive difference in nonviolent ways, to respect diversity, and to act responsibly and morally. In 1998, Cantor reminded parents of the extraordinary precautions most take to safety proof their home for their baby. Over time, television poses just as great a risk to a child's well-being in a myriad of ways, from usurping family rituals like dinnertime to undermining social values. In her research, Cantor documented that media programs can frighten children, create anxiety, and interfere with their sleep.

Practical Solutions

DeGaetano and Bander (1996) provided the following practical tips for parents on supervising the TV habits of their children:

- Establish the contingency of doing some developmentally appropriate physical activity before TV is watched.
- Establish homework as priority over TV.
- Start each school day without TV.
- Set 10 minutes aside for family discussions for each hour of TV watched.
- Use a timer to log time children spend on playing, reading, homework, household chores, and media.
- Hold nightly family reading time.
- Encourage writing.
- Provide developmental activities as alternatives to TV.
- During coviewing, ask questions about the TV shows such as the children's likes and dislikes.
- Treat violent TV and movies as a "hot stove" for children.

Jason and Hanaway (1997) recommend three ways to reduce TV watching by youngsters. They defined them as low-tech, middle road, and high-tech solutions. *Low-tech solutions* de-emphasize the omnipresence of television by:

- Keeping only one TV for family viewing and getting rid of extra TVs
- Keeping TV sets out of the kitchen and bedrooms
- Discussing ways to reduce TV watching
- Setting limits on amount of TV time
- Closing the doors of the entertainment center or simply covering the TV when it is not in use

The *middle road strategy* uses behavior management principles. First, parents and children keep a log of activities and sign a contract for TV rules. Next, children earn tickets to watch TV by first engaging in developmentally appropriate activities. Finally, the *high-tech strategy* uses electronic tools such as Addi Jurs' The Switch, CinTel's Super Vision, and Randal Levenson's TV Allowance. Also, newer TVs are equipped with the V-chip. Kaiser Family Foundation's (2001) report indicated that only 17% of parents with V-chip TVs used it to block programs with sex and violence. Instead, they relied on the seven TV parental guideline ratings as guides for their children's time with TV.

SUMMARY

Parents need to defend their children's right to develop their potential as responsible citizens by limiting TV, coviewing and discussing TV programs, keeping TV out of their children's bedroom, turning off the TV during dinner time, and turning off violent TV programs. Also, parents should use the V-chip to keep unwanted programs out of the home. Parents should encourage their children to develop physical and mental skills by engaging in developmentally appropriate activities and extracurricular school activities. Finally, parents should use TV as a communication tool to enhance their children's potential, not an electronic babysitter.

Point Versus Counterpoint: Media and Children

Media ranging from television, radio, Internet, e-mail, and video games are universally available. They function as important communication, education, and entertainment tools. However, the question is how would you like your children to spend the 1,000 hours the average child spends each year engaged with media? Balancing the advantages and disadvantages of media requires active parent oversight.

At best, TV, the "great equalizer," offers a wide variety of programming: up-to-date news, weather, and sports; quality programs like *Sesame Street*; entertainment; and opportunities to expand one's knowledge about a topic. At its worst, TV exposes children to violence, bigotry, and profanity as well as distracting children from more meaningful activities. What's bad about TV? At the least, time devoted to consuming media can usurp family time as well as study time, and exercise time. Critics claim the "great antisocializer" is a contributing factor to the violence in our society. The American Psychological Association takes the positions that viewing violence begets violence and that viewing violence is one of four factors contributing to violence in the schools.

Oliver (2002) reviewed studies showing that individuals select different forms of media based on their individual traits such as need for cognition, sensation seeking, empathy, and aggressiveness. For example, people who score high on authoritarianism enjoy reality-based police programs. Oliver found that people select, interpret, and recall events that support their views. Huesmann and colleagues (1984) concluded that televised violence may affect any child regardless of his or her level of aggression. They also indicated that elementary children became more aggressive when they consistently watched TV violence, identified with aggressive TV characters, believed TV violence was real life, and struggled academically.

Ferguson (2002) defends the media, pointing out that the American culture itself is a violent one. He argued that the research effect sizes are small and account for only 1.2% to 9.6% of the variance in violent behavior.

While people might debate the advantages and disadvantages of television, parents as first teachers must decide in favor of their children's best interests. Parents must actively discuss with their children the advantages and disadvantages of television and other media. Kurz (2001) stated that educators should support National TV-Turnoff week because of the television's adverse effects.

—Albert F. Hodapp and Joan B. Hodapp

See also Aggression in Schools; Computer Technology; Homework; Latchkey Children; Parenting; Violence in Schools

REFERENCES AND FURTHER READING

Cantor, J. (1998). *"Mommy, I'm scared": How TV and movies frighten children and what we can do to protect them.* San Diego, CA: Harcourt Brace.

Cunningham, A. E., & Stanovich, K. E. (1998, Spring/Summer). What reading does for the mind. *American Educator*, 8–15.

DeGaetano, G., & Bander, K. (1996). *Screen smarts: A family guide to media literacy*. Boston: Houghton Mifflin.

Ferguson, C. J. (2002). Media violence: Miscast causality. *American Psychologist, 57*, 446–447.

Fisch, S. M. (2002). Vast wasteland or vast opportunity? Effects of educational television on children's academic knowledge, skills, and attitudes. In J. Bryant & D. Zillman (Eds.), *Media effect: Advances in theory and research* (2nd ed., pp. 397–426). Mahwah, NJ: Erlbaum.

Gentile, D. A., & Walsh, D. A. (2002). A normative study of family media habits. *Applied Developmental Psychology, 23*, 157–178.

Huesmann, L. R., Lagerspetz, K., & Eron, L. C. (1984). Intervening variables in the TV-violence-aggression relation: Evidence from two counties. *Developmental Psychology, 20*, 746–775.

Huesmann, L. R., Moise-Titus, J., Podolski, C. L., & Eron, L. D. (2003). Longitudinal relations between children's exposure to TV violence and their aggressive and violent behavior in young adulthood: 1977–1992. *Developmental Psychology, 39*, 201–221.

Huston, A. C., Anderson, D. R., Wright, J. C., Linebarger, D. L., & Schmitt, K. L. (2001). Sesame Street viewers as adolescents: The recontact study. In S. M. Fisch & R. T. Truglio (Eds.), *"G" is for growing: Thirty years of research on children and Sesame Street*. Mahwah, NJ: Erlbaum.

Jason, L. A., & Hanaway, L. K. (1997). *Remote control: A sensible approach to kids, TV, and the new electronic media*. Sarasota, FL: Professional Resource Press.

Kaiser Family Foundation. (2001, July). *Parents and the V-chip 2001: A Kaiser Family Foundation survey*. Menlo Park, CA: Author. Available online at http://www.kff.org

Keith, T. Z., Reimers, T. M., Fehrmann, P. G., Pottebaum, S. M., & Aubey, L. W. (1986). *Journal of Educational Psychology, 78*, 373–380.

Kurz, J. (2001, March). Turn off TV-turn on life. *Communique*, 32.

Oliver, M. B. (2002). Individual differences in media effects. In J. Bryant & D. Zimmerman (Eds.), *Media effects: Advances in theory and research*. (2nd ed., pp. 507–523). Mahwah, NJ: Erlbaum.

Parke, R. D., & Slaby, R. G. (1983). The development of aggression. In P. H. Mussen (Series ed.), *Handbook of child psychology* (Vol. 4). New York: Wiley.

Wright, J., Huston, A. C., Scantlin, R., & Kotler, J. (2001). The early window project: *Sesame Street* prepares children for school. In S. M. Fisch & R. T. Truglio (Eds.), *"G" is for growing: Thirty years of research on children and Sesame Street*. Mahwah, NJ: Erlbaum.

MEMORY

Memory is the ability to encode, process, and retrieve information. As a skill, it is inseparable from intellectual functioning and learning. Individuals deficient in memory skills would be expected to have difficulty on a number of academic and cognitive tasks. Although memory is linked to performance in several academic (e.g., reading) and cognitive (e.g., problem solving) areas, it is critical for learning for three reasons (Swanson & colleagues, 1998). First, it reflects applied cognition; that is, memory functioning reflects all aspects of learning. Second, several studies suggest that the memory skills used by students do not exhaust, or even tap, their ability; therefore, we need to discover instructional procedures that capitalize on that untapped potential. Finally, several cognitive intervention programs that attempt to enhance the overall cognition of children and adults rely on principles derived from memory research.

MODELS OF MEMORY

Most research on memory, whether of developmental or instructional interest, draws from information processing literature because it contains the most influential model in cognitive psychology to date. The information processing model focuses on how input is transformed, reduced, elaborated, stored, retrieved, and used. The central assumptions of the model are:

- A number of operations and processing stages occur between a stimulus and a response.
- The stimulus presentation initiates a sequence of stages.
- Each stage operates on the information available to it.
- These operations transform the information in some manner.
- This new information is the input to the succeeding stage.

One popular means of explaining cognitive performance is by drawing upon fundamental components that are inherent in most models of information processing. Three components are fundamental:

1. *Constraint or structural component*—This is akin to the hardware of a computer, which defines the parameters within which information can be processed at a particular stage (e.g., sensory storage, short-term memory, working memory, long-term memory).

2. *Strategy component*—This is akin to the software of a computer system, which describes the operations of the various stages.

3. *Executive component*—This is overseeing and monitoring learners' activities (e.g., strategies).

This model views information as flowing through component stores in a well-regulated fashion, progressing from the sensory register, to short-term memory, and finally to long-term memory. These stores can be differentiated in children's functioning by realizing that:

- Short-term memory has a limited capacity, and thus makes use of rehearsal and organizing mechanisms.
- Storage in long-term memory is mostly semantic (e.g., by using categorical taxonomies or associations).
- Two critical determinants of forgetting in long-term memory are item displacement (new incoming items replace old items) and interference (relevant items cannot be discriminated from irrelevant items), possibly as a result of a lack of retrieval strategy.

Some researchers argue for a connectionist model of information processing, whereby learning and memory occur over repeated associations (i.e., strength of activations) rather than stages or storage compartments. Such an activation model suggests that the focus on short-term memory or on long-term memory storage is not as important as a memory system based on the strength of associations, whereby associations are built on phonetic, semantic, and/or visual–spatial information. For example, frequent or common words are easier to remember than infrequent or uncommon words because of their repeated occurrence, familiarity, and association with other items.

Others' perspectives focus on working memory. Working memory is viewed as a more dynamic and active system because it simultaneously focuses on processing and storage demands, whereas short-term memory focuses primarily on the storage of information and is considered a more passive system. Baddeley (1986) describes working memory as a limited-capacity central executive that interacts with a set of two passive storage systems used for temporary storage of different classes of information: the speech-based phonological loop and the visual sketch pad. The phonological loop is responsible for the temporary storage of verbal information; items are held within a phonological store of limited duration, and the items are maintained within the store via the process of articulation. The sketch pad is responsible for the storage of visual–spatial information over brief periods and also plays a key role in the generation and manipulation of mental images. The central executive is primarily responsible for coordinating activity within the cognitive system, but it can also devote some of its limited capacity to increasing the amount of information that can be held in the two subsystems. For example, to read words one must monitor (executive system) the accessing of phonological representations (phonological loop) as well as orthographic features (sketch pad).

RESEARCH ON MEMORY, LEARNING DIFFICULTIES, AND INTERVENTION

The study of memory in students with learning difficulties has been strongly influenced by the hypothesis that variations in memory performance are rooted in the children's acquisition of mnemonic strategies (Swanson & colleagues, 1998). An example of a mnemonic strategy is the recall of number sequences (1, 2, 3, 4) using a rhyme (e.g., 1–2 buckle my shoe, 3–4 shut the door). Strategies are deliberate, consciously applied procedures that aid in the storage and subsequent retrieval of information. Most strategy training studies that include children can trace their research framework back to earlier research on metacognition and/or research on production deficiencies by Flavell (1970). Metacognition refers to knowledge of general cognitive strategies (e.g., rehearsal); awareness of one's own cognitive processes; the monitoring, evaluating, and regulating of those processes; and beliefs about factors that affect cognitive activities. In this research, a distinction is made between the concepts of mediational and production deficiencies.

Mediational deficiencies mean the inability to use strategies efficiently. For example, young children may not spontaneously produce a potential mediator to process task requirements, but even if they did, they would fail to use it efficiently to direct their performance.

Production deficiencies suggest that children can be taught efficient strategies that they fail to produce spontaneously and that these taught strategies direct and improve their performance. An example of a production deficiency is when a child is taught a strategy to remember information from a passage, but fails to use that strategy. However, when prompted by the teacher to use the strategy the child's remembrance of information improves. In contrast, a mediation deficiency occurs when the child uses a powerful strategy to remember information, but the strategy fails to improve their performance.

A large body of research suggests that remembering becomes easier with age because control processes become more automatic through repeated use. Control processes in memory reflect choices as to which information to scan as well as choices of what and how to rehearse and/or organize information. Rehearsal refers to the conscious repetition of information, either vocally or subvocally, to enhance recall at a later time. Learning a telephone number or a street address illustrates the primary purpose of rehearsal. Other control processes include organization (such as ordering, classifying, or tagging information to facilitate retrieval) and mediation (such as comparing new items with information already in memory). Various organizational strategies studied that have been linked to helping children with learning difficulties include:

- *Chunking*—Grouping items so that each one brings to mind a complete series of items (e.g., grouping words into a sentence)
- *Clustering*—Organizing items into categories (e.g., animals, furniture)
- *Mnemonics*—Idiosyncratic methods for organizing information (e.g., associating items to be remembered with people known to the person)
- *Coding*—Varying the qualitative form of information (e.g., substituting pictures for words)

Studies have also been directed to procedures to help children with learning difficulties mediate information, such as:

- Using preexisting associations, thereby eliminating the need for new ones
- Using instructions, asking the student to mediate information verbally or through imagery, to aid in organization and retrieval
- Employing cuing, using verbal and imaginary cues to facilitate recall

An example of a study to enhance mediation of information was provided by Mastropieri and colleagues (1985). They conducted two experiments in which adolescents with learning disabilities recalled the definitions of vocabulary words according to either a pictorial mnemonic strategy (the keyword method) or a traditional instructional approach. The keyword method involved constructing an interactive visual image of the to-be-associated items. For example, to remember that the English word *carlin* means old woman via the keyword method, the learner is directed to notice that the first part of *carlin* is the familiar word "car." Then the learner constructs an interactive image that relates a car and an old woman, such as an elderly woman driving an old car. The results indicated that the keyword strategy was substantially more effective than the traditional approach.

Pressley (1994) states that good memory performance is a product of strategies, knowledge, metacognition, motivation, and capacity. None of these factors operates in isolation, but rather effective cognition is a product of all these components and interactions. Sometimes strategic processing will be more prominent in cognition than other factors, sometimes relating content to prior knowledge will be the most salient mechanism, and still on other occasions there will be obvious reflections by a child on the task demands (on what he or she knows how to do in this particular situation or situations similar to it that have been encountered in the past). Sometimes metacognition is the more salient component used by the child when performing a task. Sometimes the child's motivation will be especially apparent, and if observed at that time, the observer would report that the individual succeeded simply by trying hard.

Based on extensive literature (Swanson & colleagues, 1998), some very practical concepts and principles from memory research can serve as guidelines for the instruction of students with learning difficulties. Effective instruction must entail information about a number of strategies, about how to control and implement those procedures, and about how to gain recognition of the importance of effort in producing successful performance. Furthermore, any of these components taught in isolation is likely to have a rather diminished value in the classroom context.

—*H. Lee Swanson*

See also Learning; Learning Disabilities; Mastery Learning; Mathematics Interventions and Strategies; Neuropsychological Assessment; Reading Interventions and Strategies; Spelling Interventions and Strategies; Writing Interventions and Strategies

REFERENCES AND FURTHER READING

Baddeley, A. D. (1986). *Working memory*. London: Oxford University Press.

Flavell, J. H. (1970). Developmental studies of mediated memory. In H. W. Reese & L. P. Lipsitt (Eds.), *Advances in child development and child behavior* (Vol. 5, pp. 181–211). New York: Academic.

Mastropieri, M. A., Scruggs, T. E., Levin, J. R. Gaffney, J., & McLoone, B. (1985). Mnemonic vocabulary instruction for learning disabled students. *Learning Disability Quarterly, 8,* 57–63.

Pressley, M. (1994). Embracing the complexity of individual differences in cognition: Studying good information processing and how it might develop. *Learning & Individual Differences, 6,* 259–284.

Swanson, H. L., Cooney, J., & O'Shaughnessy, T. (1998). Memory. In B.Y. L. Wong (Ed.), *Understanding learning disabilities* (2nd ed., pp. 107–162). San Diego, CA: Academic.

MENTAL AGE

Mental age (MA) is also known as an age norm, age equivalent score, or test age. It is defined as the age at which an individual performs on an intelligence test (Sax, 1997). For instance, a person who obtains the same number of points on an intelligence test as the average 8-year-old child is said to have a mental age of 8 years. A person's mental age does not necessarily correspond to his or her chronological age. Thus, a 7-year-old who obtains the same number of points as the average 11-year-old is said to have a mental age of 11 years.

The concept of mental age was introduced by Alfred Binet and Theodore Simon in 1908. Binet and Simon measured mental age by developing questions that would predict academic achievement. Earlier intelligence tests divided the mental age by the chronological age and multiplied this number by 100 in order to determine the intelligence quotient (IQ). Using this formula, a person's IQ was a person's mental age relative to his or her chronological age. Today, this formula is generally not used to obtain an IQ score because it does not take into account the "age of arrest," which means that intelligence levels off in adulthood.

When performance on intelligence tests is examined throughout a person's lifetime, it is found that there is an increase in a person's scores throughout childhood and adolescence, a flattening effect when a person is in his or her teens or early twenties, and a decrease in performance after this time. Therefore, IQ tests today produce a mental ability score based on a person's performance relative to the performance of similar-age peers.

An additional problem with MA is that mental age units are not equal throughout the developmental period because mental growth does not occur at an equal rate across ages. For example, a child develops at a much higher rate between the ages of 2 and 3 years than between the ages of 11 and 12 years. For this reason, test scores vary more at different ages, thus making accurate interpretation of mental age scores difficult if not impossible. Another limitation of using mental age is that a global mental age does not accurately reflect the differences in a person's skills and abilities. It cannot tell you, for instance, that a person scored significantly better on tasks of a verbal nature, but performed poorly on nonverbal tasks. Despite the limitations of using mental age in interpreting test scores, mental age continues to be used because it is an interpretation that is widely understood by the general public.

—*Rebecca Miller*

See also Mental Retardation; Social Skills; Theories of Human Development

REFERENCE AND FURTHER READING

Sax, G. (1997). *Principles of educational and psychological measurement and evaluation* (4th ed.). Belmont, CA: Wadsworth.

MENTAL RETARDATION

The most widely used definition of mental retardation (MR) in the United States is:

Mental retardation is a disability characterized by significant limitations both in intellectual functioning and in adaptive behavior as expressed in conceptual, social, and practical adaptive skills. This disability originates before age 18.

This definition is from the American Association of Mental Retardation (AAMR), which has had responsibility for defining mental retardation since 1921 (Luckasson & colleagues, 2002).

Intellectual functioning is generally assessed by means of a standardized intelligence test, resulting in an intelligence quotient (IQ). The IQ must be below 70 or 75 for a person to be considered mentally retarded. Adaptive behavior or skills include conceptual (e.g., receptive and expressive language), social (e.g., interpersonal skills), and practical (e.g., personal self-help skills). Adaptive skills can be assessed by adaptive behavior scales, observations, and anecdotal records. When applying this definition, AAMR states that professionals must consider the following five assumptions:

1. Limitations in present functioning must be considered within the context of community environments typical of the individual's age, peers, and culture.

2. Valid assessments must consider cultural and linguistic diversity as well as differences in communication, sensory, motor, and behavioral factors.

3. Limitations often coexist with strengths within an individual.

4. Descriptions of limitations help develop a profile of needed supports.

5. Life functioning of a person with mental retardation will generally improve with appropriate personalized supports over a sustained period.

Once a person has been identified as an individual with MR, AAMR advocates determining the level of supports (intermittent, limited, extensive, pervasive) needed to provide the person with the ability to function as independently as possible within the community. Intermittent supports are episodic or short-term (*as needed*), and may be either low or high intensity. The key factor to limited support is consistency despite less time, fewer staff, and/or lower costs. Extensive supports occur regularly and are not time-limited. Pervasive supports are both constant and high intensity, involve more staff, are the most intrusive, and occur in the most environments. Thompson and colleagues (2004) developed the *Supports Intensity Scale* to assist professionals in determining the level of support needs for an individual in seven areas of competence: home living, community living, lifelong learning, employment, health and safety, social interaction, and protection and advocacy (e.g., protecting self from exploitation, exercising legal responsibilities). Additional information is also gathered on exceptional medical (e.g., respiratory care, skin care) and behavioral needs (e.g., self-directed destructiveness, sexual). The composite score from the scale is used to determine the need for supports and the level of intensity.

Another frequently used definition for MR is provided by the American Psychiatric Association's *Diagnostic and Statistical Manual of Mental Disorders, Fourth Edition* (*DSM-IV*) (1994), which provides thorough diagnostic criteria for medical and health care professionals in the United States. The *DSM-IV* version is based on the 1992 AAMR definition, but it retains the levels of severity (mild, moderate, severe, and profound) used in the 1972 AAMR definition. Approximately 85% of individuals classified as mentally retarded fall within the mild range (IQ from 50–55 to approximately 70), 10% fall within the moderate range (IQ 35–40 to 50–55), 3% to 4% fall within the severe range (IQ 20–25 to 35–40), and 1% to 2% fall within the profound range (IQ below 20–25). Deficits must also occur in at least two of the following adaptive functioning areas: communication, health, leisure time, safety, school, self-care, social, taking care of a home, and work. Again, age of onset must occur before age 18 years.

MR is also defined by programs mandated and funded by the U.S. government. The AAMR definition is closely linked to the federal definition found in the Individual With Disabilities Education Act (IDEA) (1997), which is the major special education law in the United States. Students determined eligible under the category of MR qualify for special education and related services.

While various definitions emerged and changed in the 1990s, a hot debate has ensued over whether the term *mental retardation* itself is appropriate. Self-advocates, along with family members and professionals, have argued passionately for a change in language to something less degrading and stereotyping. Other terms currently used include intellectual disability and cognitive disability/delay. The President's Committee on Mental Retardation is now The President's Committee for People with Intellectual Disabilities. This name change reflects a tremendous shift from looking at the disability to focusing on people. Members of AAMR voted to maintain the

Table 1   Selected Causes of Mental Retardation

Chromosomal	Prenatal	Metabolic	Perinatal & Postnatal	Genetic
• Angelman syndrome • Down syndrome • Fragile X syndrome • Klinefelter syndrome • Prader-Willi syndrome • Rett syndrome • Williams syndrome	• Maternal malnutrition • Folic acid deficiency • Maternal infections • Congenital rubella • HIV • Toxoplasmosis • Maternal substance abuse • Fetal alcohol syndrome (FAS)	• Phenylketonuria (PKU)	• Encephalitis • Trauma • Difficult or complicated birth • Prematurity • Severe head injury • Malnutrition • Severe emotional neglect or abuse • Exposure to lead • Exposure to mercury	• Tay-Sachs disease • Microcephaly • Hydrocephalus

term mental retardation in their association name and journal title (*The American Journal on Mental Retardation* and *Mental Retardation*, respectively), while members of the Council for Exceptional Children (CEC) in 2002 renamed the Division on Mental Retardation and Developmental Disabilities to the Division on Developmental Disabilities (DDD). As a result, the division's journal became *Education and Treatment in Developmental Disabilities*, replacing *Education and Treatment in Mental Retardation and Development Disabilities*. Smith (2003) felt this was a critical, first step in "abandoning the myth of mental retardation" (p. 361). CEC-DDD continues to affirm its commitment to all individuals who experience a need for mild to extensive supports.

ETIOLOGY OF MENTAL RETARDATION

MR occurs for a number of reasons, some genetic or hereditary, others the result of poor maternal nutrition or prenatal toxicity, and still others for no known identifiable cause. Some argue that knowing the etiology of MR does not enhance the ability to provide educational services or other forms of support and simply provides an unnecessary label. Research, however, suggests that even subtle differences among various syndromes can lead to a better understanding and thus better services. Table 1 lists some of the most common known reasons for MR. Yet, even within a particular syndrome, the severity of MR can vary greatly. Generally, the more severe the MR the earlier it is detected. Often children are not classified as having mild MR until they fall behind in school. MR can also occur in combination with another type of

disability. Often there are medical, physical, and/or mental health problems as well. As noted earlier, in order to be classified as having MR, there must be deficits in adaptive behavior. Therefore, persons with MR will experience problems with communication, social, motor, and/or self-help skills.

EDUCATIONAL SERVICES FOR STUDENTS WITH MENTAL RETARDATION

According to the Twenty-fourth Annual Report to Congress on the Implementation of the Individuals With Disabilities Education Act (U.S. Department of Education) (2002), slightly less than 1% of children, ages 6 to 21 years are mentally retarded. When compared to other students with disabilities served under the Individuals With Disabilities Education Act (IDEA), 10.6% of the students were labeled mentally retarded—the third largest category. The percentage of students with specific learning disabilities and speech or language impairments was higher.

Despite gains in the use of tests that are culturally and linguistically nonbiased, African American children are still overrepresented in special education under the category of MR, whereas students of Hispanic origin have lower rates of identification. Similarly, advocates of inclusion or integration of students with disabilities into general education settings have not achieved as much as has been anticipated for children who are mentally retarded, especially older students. Most students (ages 6–21 years) are educated in public schools with very few served in separate public or private facilities, residential facilities, and home/hospital environments. Within a school setting, half of these 6- to 21-year-old students with MR are served outside the regular classroom 60% or more of the time.

HISTORICAL PERSPECTIVE

Services and education for individuals with MR began in Europe and were brought to the United States by Edouard Seguin, a French physician who had studied under Jean-Marc Gaspard Itard (famous for his ground-breaking study of Victor, Wild Boy of Aveyron) and Jean-Etienne Dominique Esquirol. Esquirol categorized "intellectual deficiency" into idiots and imbeciles. Imbeciles could develop to a certain extent, while someone classified as an idiot demonstrated little skill, thought, or use of their senses. Later the terms moron, feeble-minded, and borderline would be added to explanations and classification structures used to describe individuals with cognitive delays. Seguin collaborated with Samuel Howe, who opened the Massachusetts School for Idiotic and Feeble-Minded Youth in 1848 as an experimental boarding school. The success of this school and others to provide an education offered hope to parents and led many to advocate for the establishment of state training schools. Unfortunately, these early schools led to large, impersonal institutions where children and adults received less than adequate care, education, and training. However, Sequin's educational approach is still felt today.

The widespread development of institutions coincided with the worldwide eugenics movement and the development of standardized intelligence testing. It would take more than 100 years for society to recognize the injustice perpetuated by institutionalization and subsequent forced sterilization. In 2002, Governor Mark Warner of Virginia became the first to offer an official apology for the gross abuse of human rights of those who were poor, mentally ill, or mentally retarded in the name of eugenics, as well as the faulty reasoning behind the intent to wipe out hereditary disorders and human shortcomings. Four other governors (Oregon, California, North Carolina, and South Carolina) followed suit. Physicians in a total of 33 states conducted more than 65,000 sterilizations of men, women, boys, and girls. State laws permitting forced sterilization were modeled after Virginia's. Although some states have repealed their eugenics laws, the Supreme Court ruling in *Buck v. Bell* (1927) still stands.

Much shame and misguided advice by medical practitioners led many parents to place their children in institutions or to hide their children away at home. The trend began to change when Pearl S. Buck, a renowned author, wrote a book about her daughter, Carol, born in 1920, who was mentally retarded. *The Child Who Never Grew* first appeared in 1950 and provided parents with hope and affirmation of all they had felt and been through. Dale Evans Rogers, wife of Roy Rogers, also wrote a moving story entitled *Angel Unaware* (1953, 1984) about their daughter, Robin, who was born with Down syndrome and only lived for two years. Both women were well known and respected. Their heartfelt stories of their daughters touched many lives. For the first time, many felt they could openly discuss their children with MR. The closet door was opening. Public awareness and acceptance became even greater when President John F. Kennedy and his family, particularly his sister, Eunice Shriver, championed the rights of individuals with MR. Their sister Rosemary, an individual with mental retardation, served as the impetus. President Kennedy initiated the President's Panel on Mental Retardation in 1961, and Eunice Shriver redefined athletic competition with the founding of the Special Olympics in 1968. Society would never again view individuals with MR as totally incapable. Spurred by U.S. Senator Robert Kennedy's tour of several institutions in Massachusetts and the ensuing reports in the news media, Blatt and Kaplan (1966; reprinted in 1974) published *Christmas in Purgatory: A Photographic Essay on Mental Retardation*. This book provided the general public with a stark view of the reality of life in the institution. It was not a pretty picture.

Several states have enacted laws allowing for the death penalty in cases where the defendant is an individual with MR. The State of Virginia again played a role in another landmark decision by the U.S. Supreme Court when the court ruled on June 20, 2002, in the case of *Atkins v. Virginia*, that it was unconstitutional to execute individuals with MR. James W. Ellis, a law professor at the University of New Mexico Law School and past president of AAMR, represented Atkins and has written a guide for state legislatures to assist in implementing the *Atkins* decision. Unfortunately, a number of people with MR remain in the criminal justice system. Their disability often works against them when arrested or confronted by law enforcement officers (Davis, 2000). Also, persons with MR are twice as likely to be a victim of criminal activity. Law enforcement officers, members of the criminal justice system, and advocates need to work together to understand the nuances of working with offenders and victims who have MR.

TRENDS IN EDUCATION AND SERVICE

The civil rights movement in the United States spawned a "disability rights" movement. *Brown v. the Board of Education* (1954) became a legal landmark in the desegregation of schools. Schools could no longer deny admittance or segregate children based on race or ethnicity. Seventeen years later in the *Pennsylvania Association for Retarded Citizens (PARC) v. Commonwealth of Pennsylvania* (1971) case, it was successfully argued that all children, regardless of mental age, were entitled to a free and appropriate public education in the least restrictive environment. A free and appropriate public education (FAPE) would become the hallmark of educational services for individuals with disabilities. Access to education was the key to opening the future for individuals with MR. Deinstitutionalization and the passage of the Education for All Handicapped Children Act in 1975, now known as IDEA, helped to solidify the process of integrating persons with MR into their communities and to provide families with necessary supports to keep their children at home, to receive a free and appropriate public education, and to prepare them for adult life as contributing members of society.

The need to speak for themselves, have choices, and participate in decision making has been a critical component of the disability rights movement, especially for individuals with MR. Acquiring self-determination skills supports the notion that individuals with MR can and should make choices about a number of aspects resulting in autonomy (Drew & Hardman, 2004). Learning self-determination skills should start at a young age and continue throughout life. Additionally, parents and professionals should assist students and adults in recognizing options from an array of choices, understanding potential consequences of their choices, following through, analyzing results, and making any necessary adjustments in the future.

As people with MR achieve stable and longer lives, there is a growing demand for services coupled with issues related to aging caregivers, nutrition, and access to health care services (Rizzolo & colleagues, 2004). The closing of large institutions created a need for smaller, community-based options. Long waiting lists and a lack of suitable options created serious problems in finding places for individuals with MR to

Photo 1   Gail Boger, a child with Down syndrome, circa 1910.

reside once their families could no longer care for them. It appears that individuals with MR will live into retirement and outlive their parents. Unfortunately, when deinstititutionalization occurred, planning for adequate health care within the community did not take place. Children with MR live with chronic emotional, behavioral, developmental, or physical problems and thus use more health care and related services (Krauss & colleagues, 2003). More than 20% of children with MR, whose parents completed a national survey, had problems accessing health care, especially in getting referrals and finding well-trained providers. If the parent was also in poor health, the child was at greater risk. However, those who had Medicaid coverage and other public health coverage encountered few problems. Medical providers (e.g., dentists, nurses, opthamologists, physicians, psychologists) need more training to work with patients with

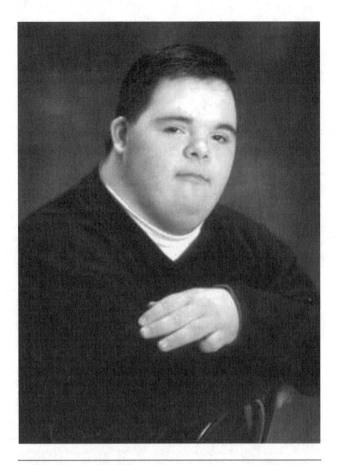

Photo 2   Mike Duarte, born with Down syndrome in 1980.

MR, and individuals with MR need to acquire skills to communicate with their health care providers and have the opportunity to express their opinions about the health care system and how it might be improved.

Individuals with MR struggle against negative perceptions, prejudice, and lack of options. Strong advocates, legislation, and litigation have helped people with the label of mental retardation fight for dignity and respect, gain access to education and community services, and pursue options to assure a full and satisfying life. Professionals, parents, and self-advocates have learned that despite limits in cognitive ability and adaptive skills, individuals with MR do learn, and they can lead satisfying lives as contributing members of society.

In the early 1900s a child with Down syndrome, Gail Boger, was born into a family in Missouri. He was the youngest of three children and the author's great uncle. This child remained at home until his death at the age of 12 years (Photo 1). Although this sounds young, the average life expectancy of a person with Down syndrome at that time was only nine years

(Rizzolo & colleagues, 2004). He did not go to school, but instead he learned skills at home. While his life coincided with an increase in the institutionalization of children and adults considered "feeble-minded" and the eugenics movement, his parents chose instead to keep him at home and honor his place in the family with a pictorial record.

The 1970s saw a shift in attitudes as the deinstitutionalization movement began in full force. By the 1980s, when Mike Duarte was born (Photo 2), possibilities and educational opportunities had dramatically shifted. Mike grew up alongside his two sisters in his family home, where he still lives. He attended an early intervention program, began kindergarten at age 5 years, and was included in general education classrooms (where he worked on functional life skills) until he exited the school system at age 21 years. During the course of his education, he learned to interact with his same-age nondisabled peers, in other words he made friends; acquired independent self-help skills; became responsible enough to stay at home unsupervised for moderate lengths of time; learned to ride public transportation; acquired numerous leisure skills; and began to explore vocational options. Currently, Mike and his parents are working with Vocational Rehabilitation and local community providers to determine an appropriate vocational path and provide him with ongoing support and services. While Mike will most likely not experience the level of independence seen in his sisters, he will continue to have a meaningful life. Those closest to him continue to offer support and strive to help him achieve his dreams and reach his potential.

As Gold (1980) so eloquently stated, mental retardation has never really been something that resides within a person. Rather, mental retardation and its perceived level of severity correlate solely to society's ability and willingness to provide education, training, and supports. With adequate levels of support, any individual can learn and become a valuable, contributing member of society.

—*Christine Macfarlane*

See also Academic Achievement; Intelligence; Learning; Retention and Promotion

REFERENCES AND FURTHER READING

American Psychiatric Association. (1994). *Diagnostic and statistical manual of mental disorders* (4th ed.). Washington, DC: Author.

Atkins v. Virginia, 536 U.S. 304 (2002).

Blatt, B., & Kaplan, F. (1974). *Christmas in purgatory. A photographic essay on mental retardation.* Syracuse, NY: Center on Human Policy Press. (Original work published 1966)

Brown v. Board of Education, 347 U.S.483 (1954).

Buck, P. S. (1992). *The child who never grew.* Bethesda, MD: Woodbine House. (Original work published 1950)

Buck v. Bell, 274 U.S. 200 (1927).

Davis, L. A. (2000). *People with mental retardation in the criminal justice system.* Silver Springs, MD: The Association for Retarded Citizens (ARC).

Drew, C. J., & Hardman, M. L. (2004). *Mental retardation: A lifespan approach to people with intellectual disabilities* (8th ed.). Upper Saddle River, NJ: Pearson/Merrill Prentice Hall.

Education for All Handicapped Children Act, Public Law 94–142, Title 34 C.F.R. 301.1 (1975).

Ellis, J. W. (n.d.). *Mental retardation and the death penalty: A guide to state legislative issues.* Retrieved June 26, 2004, from http://www.deathpenaltyinfo.org/MREllisLeg.pdf

Gold, M. W. (1980). *Try another way manual.* Champaign, IL: Research Press.

Individuals With Disabilities Education Act (IDEA), Public Law 105–17, Title 34 C.F.R. 300 (1997).

Krauss, M. W., Gulley, S., Sciegaj, M., & Wells, N. (2003). Access to specialty medical care for children with mental retardation, autism, and other special health care needs. *Mental Retardation, 41,* 329–339.

Luckasson, R., Borthwick-Duffy, S., Buntinx, W. H. E., Coulter, D. L., Craig, E. M., Reeve, A., et al. (2002). *Mental retardation: Definition, classification, and system of supports* (10th ed.). Washington, DC: American Association on Mental Retardation.

Pennsylvania Association for Retarded Citizens v. Commonwealth of Pennsylvania, 334 F. Supp. 1257 (E.D.PA, 1971).

Rizzolo, M. C., Hemp, R., Braddock, D., & Pomeranz-Essley, A. (2004). *The state of the states in developmental disabilities.* Washington, DC: American Association on Mental Retardation.

Rogers, D. E. (1984). *Angel unaware.* Grand Rapids, MI: Fleming H. Revell. (Original work published 1953)

Smith, J. D. (2003). Abandoning the myth of mental retardation. *Education and Training in Developmental Disabilities, 38,* 358–361.

Thompson, J. R., Bryant, B. R., Campbell, E. M., Craig, E. M., Hughes, C. M., Rotholz, D. A., et al. (2004). *Supports Intensity Scale (SIS).* Washington, DC: American Association on Mental Retardation.

MENTORING

Mentoring is a relationship in which an older person provides ongoing guidance, instruction, and encouragement to another, younger individual, usually a youth, with the goal of further developing that individual's competence and character (Rhodes, 2002a). Typically viewed as older and wiser, *mentors* develop supportive relationships with younger youth, who are referred to as *mentees* or *protégés.*

NATURAL VERSUS PROGRAM-BASED MENTORING

A major distinction in the definition of mentors and mentoring relationships is between natural mentors and program-based mentors. Natural mentoring, as the name suggests, emerges naturally. Youth often develop natural mentoring relationships with adults who pay special attention to them, and who provide guidance, encouragement, and a sympathetic ear. In the context of school, natural mentors may include teachers, coaches, counselors, psychologists, administrators as well as many other "older and wiser" individuals. Outside of schools, youth may develop natural mentoring relationships with adults in their extended family, neighborhood, religious organizations, and in recreational settings.

Program-based mentoring refers to a formalized process by which an organization recruits an individual to serve as mentor to a youth. The adult and youth usually have had no prior contact or relationship, and their interaction results from being matched together in a mentoring relationship. Big Brothers Big Sisters (BBBS) of America is the largest formal mentoring program in the United States and has been actively recruiting adults to work as mentors with youth for 100 years. Initially, BBBS recruited men to work with boys from fatherless homes, but today this organization serves both boys and girls and reaches beyond those from single-parent homes to support the development of competence and character of youth from a variety of settings.

COMMUNITY-BASED VERSUS SCHOOL-BASED MENTORING PROGRAMS

The context of mentoring plays a significant role in shaping the nature of program-based mentoring relationships. The majority of mentoring programs are based on or originate in the community through BBBS and other organizations such as Boys and Girls Clubs of America and the Young Men's and Young Women's Christian Associations (YMCA and

YWCA). However, schools also have emerged as a viable context for mentoring. Some advantages of school-based mentoring programs include significantly lower operational costs. Herrera and colleagues (2000) estimate school-based programs cost approximately half as much as community-based programs. School-based programs also provide increased access to youth, and greater opportunities for school staff and program coordinators to supervise mentors and provide mentors with immediate support, instruction, and feedback. Mentors often prefer school-based mentoring because it is less time-consuming. Typically, school-based mentors meet with their mentees once per week for an hour, whereas community-based programs often encourage weekly meetings of three to four hours.

HISTORY OF MENTORING

The term *mentor* has held the same meaning for more than 1,000 years. The word originated from the character Mentor in Homer's *The Odyssey* (see Baker & Maguire, in press). Mentor was a trusted friend of Odysseus, the king of Ithaca. When Odysseus went to fight in the Trojan War, Mentor was asked to watch over, befriend, and provide council and support to Odysseus's son, Telemachus. For hundreds of years, adults have served as mentors to youth in work apprenticeships. However, formal mentoring programs did not emerge until the early 20th century with the help of Jane Addams and Ernest Coulter, who encouraged the juvenile courts system to address delinquency. Adults working with needy or problem youth became known as Big Brothers, long before BBBS was founded. (Big Brothers was founded in 1904, and Big Brothers and Big Sisters maintained separate identities until 1978 when they merged to become Big Brothers Big Sisters of America.) Perhaps the most public statement in support of formal mentoring programs was President George W. Bush's pledge to commit 150 million dollars to mentoring programs. Although intuitively appealing and a popular approach to intervention, there has been limited research on the effectiveness of mentoring programs to date.

MENTORING RESEARCH AND LITERATURE

In 1936, Richard C. Cabot, a Harvard-trained physician, initiated the first systematic study on the effects of mentoring in his Cambridge–Somerville Youth Study (CSYS), which examined various intervention programs for delinquent youth (Baker & Maguire, in press). The 30-year follow-up study revealed the potentially negative effects of poorly run intervention programs that do not sufficiently counter delinquent youth's tendency to undermine authority (Dishion & colleagues, 2003). They found that youth who participated in a comprehensive intervention program that included mentoring fared worse 30 years later than youth who had not participated. These negative results, they argued, resulted from aggregating delinquent youth together in the intervention. Based on these findings and more recent studies consistent with this view, it can be argued that psychologists coordinating mentoring programs in schools should avoid including solely children viewed as at risk for underachievement or delinquency.

Until recently, the enthusiasm for mentoring has eclipsed the few systematic efforts conducted to assess whether mentoring works. The intuitively appealing nature of mentoring and concomitant enthusiasm for mentoring has been tempered by research illustrating that successful mentoring programs take a lot of work, planning, dedication, and resources (e.g., time, funding, and staff energy) to be effective. Nearly 20 years before *The Kindness of Strangers* (Freedman, 1993) heralded a wave of enthusiasm for mentoring, which crested at the end of the 20th century, Goodman (1972) conducted the first systematic study of college-age mentors to youth. This was the first study of youth mentoring to reveal its positive effects on youth's social skills, self-esteem, and relationships with other adults. Goodman's study also foreshadowed more recent research findings by revealing the importance of ongoing training and the duration of the mentoring relationship, the differential effectiveness of shy and extroverted mentors, and the impact of mentoring on the college mentors themselves. The more recent and frequently cited study of the BBBS program reveals that youth who receive mentors are less likely than those without a mentor to engage in substance use, fighting, or skipping school, and are more likely to report improved relationships with their parents (Grossman & Tierney, 1998). However, there are limitations to this study, the most significant of which is that all outcomes were self-reported by the youth. No teacher, parent, or significant adults' reports of the effectiveness of the mentoring program were collected.

The sophistication of research on mentoring's effectiveness has been increasing in recent years (Rhodes, 2002b), and now there are a number of research-based publications on mentoring (Rhodes 2002a) that balance the naïve enthusiasm of much of the earlier mentoring literature. DuBois and colleagues (2002) conducted one of the most important studies of youth mentoring. In 1999, they undertook a meta-analysis of all the available research in the field of mentoring. Among the hundreds of articles touting the potential of youth mentoring, DuBois and colleagues found that only 55 studies had comparison groups and measured outcomes before and after mentoring. The authors' study was the first systematic effort to examine the effectiveness of mentoring practices that had previously been proposed by those in the field. They tested several theoretically based "best practices," as well as other commonly used components of mentoring programs, and found that the most effective mentoring programs employed a larger number of identified mentoring best practices than did the less effective programs. Consistent with Goodman's findings, some of DuBois and colleagues' best practices include the systematic matching of mentors and mentees and the provision of ongoing training and supervision to mentors. Table 1 provides a set of best practices for the mentoring field (MENTOR/National Mentoring Partnership, 2003). These best practices provide guidelines for school psychologists, counselors, teachers, and administrators who intend to develop and implement school-based mentoring programs.

Other findings revealed by DuBois and colleagues' (2002) meta-analysis and more recent research (e.g., Rhodes, 2002a, 2002b) are worth noting. For example, although providing structured activities emerged as a best practice, more recent research has revealed that recreational and sport activities as well as casual discussions about family, friends, and personal issues were strong predictors of whether the mentees came to see their mentors as significant persons in their lives (DuBois & colleagues, 2002). Therefore, even in school settings, activities that promote connectedness between the mentor and mentee may be more effective at unleashing the potential effects of mentoring than academic or goal-focused activities.

School psychologists are likely to perform several roles in the development and maintenance of school-based mentoring programs. They may be responsible for identifying students who might benefit from a mentor; when they do, they should avoid selecting only students who are at risk for problem behaviors and underachievement. Such students do not appear to be the best candidates for mentoring, and their problem behaviors may worsen as a result if gathered into a group-based intervention. School psychologists may be responsible for training and supervising the adults who work as mentors; during the training, they should attempt to incorporate as many of the best practices of youth mentoring as possible. Finally, school psychologists may be responsible for collecting data for evaluation purposes; they should begin this work by turning to the burgeoning literature on youth mentoring or the *Handbook of Youth Mentoring* (DuBois & Karcher, in press) to identify instruments and procedures specific to this important task. In program coordination and evaluation, school psychologists should include parents by facilitating contact between mentors and parents and by including parents' perspectives when assessing important outcomes. As planners, coordinators, and evaluators, school psychologists can play a central role in the development of successful youth mentoring programs.

—Michael J. Karcher, Laura Roy-Carlson,
Chiharu Allen, and Debby Gil-Hernandez

See also Intervention

REFERENCES AND FURTHER READING

Baker, D. B., & Maguire, C. (in press). Mentoring in historical perspective. In D. L. DuBois & M. J. Karcher (Eds.), *Handbook of youth mentoring*. Thousand Oaks, CA: Sage.

Dishion, T. J., McCord, J., & Poulin, F. (2003). When interventions harm: Peer groups and problem behaviors. *American Psychologist, 54,* 755–764.

DuBois, D. L., Holloway, B. E., Valentine, J. C., & Cooper, H. (2002). Effectiveness of mentoring programs for youth: A meta-analytical review. *American Journal of Community Psychology, 30,* 157–197.

DuBois, D. L., & Karcher, M. J. (in press). *Handbook of youth mentoring*. Thousand Oaks, CA: Sage.

DuBois, D. L., Neville, H. A., Parra, G. R., & Pugh-Lilly, A. O. (2002). Testing a new model of mentoring. *New Directions for Youth Development, 93*(Spring), 21–57.

Freedman, M. (1993). *The kindness of strangers: Adult mentors, urban youth, and the new voluntarism.* San Francisco: Jossey-Bass.

Goodman, G. (1972). *Companionship therapy: Studies in structured intimacy.* San Francisco: Jossey-Bass.

Grossman, J. B., & Tierney, J. P. (1998). Does mentoring work? An impact study of the Big Brothers Big Sisters Program. *Evaluation Review, 22*(3), 403–426.

Herrera, C., Sipe, C. L., & McClanahan, W. S. (2000). *Mentoring school age children: Relationship development*

Table 1   Effective Practices in Youth Mentoring

Designing a Program

- Design specific program goals and procedures.
- Establish an evaluation component to the mentoring program.

Initial Procedures

- Define clear roles for staff and advisors of the mentoring program.
- Establish criteria for matching youth with mentors (e.g., gender, race, interests).*
- Establish a public relations component.
- Establish a system to maintain regular contact with mentors/mentees.
- Design a plan for staff support.

Funding

- Design a financial plan (budget management, timeline, system for managing finances).
- Plan for future funding.
- Document staff information and mentor/mentee matches.

Mentor/Mentee Relationships and Participation

- Conduct mentor/mentee orientation.†
- Recruit mentors in helping roles/professions (e.g., teachers, counselors, psychologists).†
- Use screening procedures (e.g., background checks, interviews, etc.).*
- Communicate clear guidelines of where and when mentors/mentees will meet.
- Clarify expectations regarding frequency of mentor/mentee contact.*
- Clarify expectations regarding duration of relationships.*

Parental Involvement

- Conduct parent orientation.
- Encourage parent support and involvement.†
- Encourage parental feedback.

Program Implementation and Maintenance

- Supervise mentors (provide guidance from staff).*
- Monitor mentors (mentor activity logs).*
- Provide ongoing mentor support (mentors discuss feelings/experiences with staff).*
- Provide structured activities for mentors and youth (e.g., events planned by host organization).†
- Provide ongoing training of mentors.†
- Monitor implementation.†
- Help mentors/mentees reach relationship closure.
- Reflect on and disseminate findings from the evaluation.
- Recognize contributions of program participants.

*Theory-driven best practices lacking empirical support (DuBois & colleagues, 2002).

†Empirically supported (evidence-based) best practices (DuBois & colleagues, 2002).

Adapted from MENTOR/National Mentoring Partnership. (2003). *The elements of effective practices.* Alexandria, VA: Author. (Used with permission).

in community-based and school-based programs. Philadelphia: Public Private Ventures.

MENTOR/National Mentoring Partnership (2003, September). *Elements of effective practice* (2nd ed.). Retrieved May 12, 2004, from http://www.mentoring.org/common/effective_mentoring_practices/pdf/effectiveprac.pdf

Rhodes, J. E. (2002a). *Stand by me: The risks and rewards of mentoring today's youth.* Cambridge, MA: Harvard University Press.

Rhodes, J. E. (Ed.).(2002b). A critical view of youth mentoring [special issue]. *New Directions for Youth Development, 93*(Spring), 21–57.

MIDDLE SCHOOL

The U.S. Department of Education defines middle-level schools as involving no grade lower than fifth and no grade higher than eighth. Two generic labels are commonly used to describe middle-level schools. The label "middle school" typically refers to schools comprising grades sixth through eighth; the term "junior high school" usually refers to schools having grades seventh through ninth. These differing definitions contribute to some difficulties in identifying and communicating trends in school composition.

According to the National Middle School Association (NMSA) (2003), the percentage of middle schools and the percentage of children attending them have increased dramatically since the 1970s; the reverse has occurred for junior high schools. In 1971 there were 10,445 total middle-level schools, of which 1,662 (16%) had sixth through eighth grades. In 2000 there were 14,107 middle-level schools, of which 8,371 (59%) had sixth through eighth grades. This represents an increase of 404%. In contrast, the number of grades seventh through ninth (junior high) schools decreased from 45% of the total to 5% of the total during that same time span (NMSA, 2003).

THE EVOLUTION, DEFINITION, AND PURPOSE OF MIDDLE SCHOOLS

During the 1800s, the eight-four (elementary school-high school) pattern dominated education. It provided basic skills and vocational training to large numbers of students, and college preparation for some. During the late 1800s psychologists, such as G. Stanley Hall, began to identify the unique biological, social, and cognitive changes underlying early adolescent development, which then were seen as requiring educational curricula and methods different from the existing elementary and secondary forms. For example, in contrast to the high school emphasis on subject mastery, early adolescents were viewed as needing a more exploratory curriculum presented in a more nurturing atmosphere that fostered personal growth.

At the same time, many educators felt that starting secondary education sooner might help stem the very high dropout rate following sixth grade. In response to these emphases, the National Education Association (NEA) recommended restructuring education programs to better prepare students for high school and to better meet the developmental needs of early adolescents. The first junior high schools, established in Columbus, Ohio, in 1909, incorporated grades seven through nine. Although purportedly focused specifically on the needs of middle-level students, the early junior high schools provided little by way of a unique curriculum focused on the needs of developing adolescents. Nor were teachers specifically trained to deal with the issues and concerns of those leaving childhood and entering the adolescent years. A major criticism of junior high schools, then and now, is that they largely represent administrative reorganizations dividing the secondary school into different units but lacking a unique curricular approach tuned to emerging adolescents. Of note, criticisms of current middle schools are very similar.

By the late 1950s, these criticisms—along with increases in school enrollment and pressures on school enrollments because of school desegregation—fostered the development of middle schools. In 1982 and again in 1995 the NMSA published *This We Believe*, a statement of practice and philosophy of middle school education that attempted to distinguish it from junior high education. In 1989 the Carnegie Council on Adolescent Development published *Turning Points*, urging reform in middle-level education. The confluence of these events resulted in the growth of middle schools presumably based on a philosophy of education distinguishing it from junior high schools (Table 1).

THE EFFECTIVENESS OF MIDDLE SCHOOLS

One set of problems in determining if middle schools meet their goals entails research design issues, such as:

- Neither students nor teachers are randomly assigned to schools.
- There are multiple choices for the unit of analysis (e.g., the individual school versus a collection of schools).
- An appropriate comparison group (e.g., junior high schools or national norms) must be determined.

Another set of concerns centers on determining the degree to which middle schools provide the suggested curricular components, generalization to other districts, and related issues.

Table 1   Some Differences Between Middle School and Junior High School Foci and Goals

Middle School	Junior High School
Student-centered instruction	Subject-centered instruction
Creative exploring and experimenting with subject matter	Mastery of concepts and skills in separate subject matter
Intramural athletic programs	Interscholastic athletic programs
Interdisciplinary teams for instruction	Department organizational structure for instruction
Usually grades 6, 7, and 8	Usually grades 7, 8, and 9
Exploratory curriculum	Fixed curriculum
Preparation of student for continuous learning	Preparation of student for high school curriculum
Focus on student needs by teams of teachers	Focus on subject matter by individual teachers
Fostering cooperation	Fostering competition

Compiled from: Carnegie Council on Adolescent Development. (1989). *Turning points: Preparing American youth for the 21st century.* New York: The Carnegie Corporation of New York; National Middle School Association (NMSA). (1982, 1995). *This we believe: Developmentally responsive middle level schools.* Columbus, OH: Author.

In their Research Summary #12, the NMSA (1995) reported that there are some enhanced achievements and engagement in academics in middle-level students taught via team teaching methods, a hallmark of middle schools. Recent research demonstrates a critical reason teaming is related to enhanced student achievement is the emphasis on team common planning time (Vars, 1993). The greater the amount of common planning time, the better the student achievement.

Research also shows that academic success often decreases during any transition. Students who attend a K–8 school will only make a single transition, that is, to high school (Johnston & Markle, 1986). Other students may transition from elementary school to middle school, and then from middle school to high school. Educators have addressed the transition issue with the creation of transition teams and/or programs to assist students in their move from middle school to high school (Alstaugh, 1998). Research shows that SES, school size, and differences in the makeup of the student body can all play a role in determining success of transition programs (Clark & Clark, 1994). Transition teams can help make students and parents more aware of the upcoming changes. Support can be offered through a transition team comprised of eighth and ninth grade students, parents, and teachers to provide transitioning students with the information and assistance preceding the year of a school change and during the transition year itself.

Other research on the claimed value of middle schools, such as enhancing personal growth, allowing exploration, and achievement in specific subject areas, is sorely needed (Carnegie Council on Adolescent Development, 1989).

THE SCHOOL PSYCHOLOGIST IN MIDDLE SCHOOL

All psychologists who want to work in the schools receive special training and education in an effort to properly prepare them for the responsibilities of a school setting. Coursework and fieldwork in testing students, counseling students, providing teachers and parents with necessary workshops, consulting with faculty and parents, and assessing students' emotional and academic concerns are all parts of a school psychologist's training (Gutkin & Reynolds, 1999).

A school psychologist's responsibilities, at any grade level, vary depending on the type of students, the school district's needs, expectations of administrators, and local and federal standards. Standards can dictate how many student cases a psychologist is managing or standards may dictate the amount of time between which cases must be revisited (Hartshorne & Jacob-Timm, 1998).

A psychologist working in a middle school may be expected to understand the developmental, social, emotional, physiological, academic, and behavioral needs of young adolescents. Consistent with the philosophy of middle schools, a middle school psychologist may regularly meet with a team of teachers when discussing the concerns of one student, because middle schools are most often designed to assign a team of teachers to each group of students. This allows for all of the adults working in the school who interact with the student to communicate and collaborate on assisting the student. Additionally, a middle school psychologist may lead groups for students on anger management, social skills, parental divorce, and other similar topics, because young adolescents are facing these issues.

Although administrators may seek out psychologists who are uniquely prepared to work in a middle school, they likely will have difficulty hiring psychologists who have specific middle school training or experience. Many school psychologists lack this expertise because training programs are not required, or designed, to prepare psychologists to work in specific school settings. A psychologist applying for a job in a middle school may have little to no training or experience working in a middle school.

Because teacher-training programs are divided among specialties in early education (K–5) and secondary education (subject specific), it is equally difficult to hire teachers with training specifically focused on teaching middle school students. Despite the educational system's movement to create middle schools and design an educational philosophy salient to young adolescents in the middle schools, training programs for both teachers and school psychologists are not addressing the training needs for these professions. If our country's desire to create middle school facilities that adhere to middle school educational philosophy sincerely exists, our country's training programs need to create curricula to prepare teachers, psychologists, and other staff to work in a middle school. This means training school staff in the middle school philosophy.

CONCLUSION

The middle school movement grew during the 1950s and 1960s because of dissatisfaction with the effectiveness of junior high schools. By the 1970s the number of middle schools increased dramatically because it was felt that middle-level education needed to focus more on being exploratory, on helping young adolescents with specific developmental needs (which are different from those of children or older adolescents),

and on easing the transition to high school. Although middle schools far outnumber junior high schools, research evidence demonstrating their advantage in terms of academic achievement, personal growth, and ease of transition to high school is severely lacking. Moreover, criticisms originally raised about junior high schools, such as their being little more than miniature high schools in their curriculum and orientation toward instruction, frequently are raised about middle schools. Many would argue that the promise of middle schools has yet to be realized.

—*Jerome B. Dusek and Lauren A. Arbolino*

See also Theories of Human Behavior and Development

REFERENCES AND FURTHER READING

Alstaugh, J. L. (1998). Achievement loss associated with transition to middle school and high school. *Journal of Educational Research, 92,* 20–25.

Carnegie Council on Adolescent Development. (1989). *Turning points: Preparing American youth for the 21st century.* New York: The Carnegie Corporation of New York.

Clark, S., & Clark, D. (1994). Restructuring the middle level school: Implications for school leaders. Albany, NY: State University of New York Press.

Gutkin, T. B., & Reynolds, C. L. (1999). *Handbook of school psychology.* New York: John Wiley.

Hartshorne, T. S., & Jacob-Timm, S. (1998). *Ethics and law for school psychologists.* New York: John Wiley.

Johnston, J. H., & Markle, G. C. (1986). *What research says to the middle level practitioner.* Columbus, OH: National Middle School Association.

National Middle School Association (NMSA). (1982, 1995, 2003). *This we believe: Developmentally responsive middle level schools.* Columbus, OH: Author.

Vars, G. F. (1993). *Interdisciplinary teaching: Why and how.* Columbus, OH: National Middle School Association.

MONTESSORI SCHOOLS

Maria Montessori, born in Italy in 1870, developed her own theories of child development and learning, which serve as the foundation for Montessori schools. Montessori believed that schools should be designed to facilitate the natural development and independence of children. Given the freedom to choose their activities and work at their own pace, children take responsibility for their own learning. Opportunities for learning are facilitated through a prepared environment that introduces specific learning materials to children based on their developmental level and interests. Once the materials are introduced to children, they are able to work with them independently thereby satisfying their inner desire to learn. Such an approach is intended to allow children to enhance their self-discipline as they mature from childhood to adulthood.

Beginning with the inception of the first Montessori school in 1907, *Casa dei Bambini*, Montessori's educational philosophy and methods have expanded to locations worldwide. In 1909, teacher training programs began in Italy and were extended to international locations several years later. Montessori developed the Association Montessori Internationale (AMI) in 1929 to ensure that her work would continue after her death in a manner consistent with her philosophy and teachings. The AMI has developed its operations to include 50 accredited training programs in 18 countries worldwide (Association Montessori Internationale, 2001). It is estimated that as many as 5,000 Montessori schools are operating in the United States alone (Ruenzel, 1997).

Children of different ages share the same Montessori classroom. Groupings often include children ages 2 months to 3 years, 3 to 6 years, and 6 to 12 years; and activities within the classroom are prepared according to the developmental level of the group. Although Montessori programs can be designed for children of all ages, much attention has been given to programs designed for children ages 3 to 6 years. Indeed, Montessori considered children in this age range to have an *absorbent mind,* which allows them to naturally and effortlessly absorb skills and abilities from their environment. To facilitate their growth, the classroom contains activities to engage children in developing their skills in five major areas:

1. Practical life skills for daily living such as sweeping, pouring, or polishing

2. Sensory development

3. Language

4. Mathematics

5. Culture, or areas such as history, anthropology, and biology

The role of teachers in Montessori classrooms is to maintain an organized environment, arrange materials so they are attractive to the children, present activities to the children based on individual needs, and observe the children's work and development.

Research on outcomes for children participating in Montessori schools has yielded mixed results. Some studies indicate that children in Montessori schools perform better than children in traditional preschool programs on tasks requiring creativity and school readiness. Montessori students' performance on tests related to general intelligence, academic achievement, and attention have generally not been significantly different from traditional preschool programs (Chattin-McNichols, 1981). However, conclusions from research comparisons should be viewed with caution. Differences may result from limitations in research designs rather than true differences between the programs.

—*Tracey R. Bainter*

See also Class Size; Learning; Motivation; Preschoolers

REFERENCES AND FURTHER READING

Association Montessori Internationale. (2001, November). *Association Montessori Internationale training centres.* Available online at http://www.montessori-ami.org/6training/6atraining.htm

Chattin-McNichols, J. P. (1981). The effects of Montessori school experience. *Young Children, 36*(5), 49–66.

Ruenzel, D. (1997). The Montessori method. *Education Week on the Web.* Available online at http://www.amshq.org/links.html

MOTIVATION

Motivation is the force behind behavior and provides an explanation for why people do things. Motivation influences what people do—meaning their choice of actions, as well as how they act; the intensity, persistence, and quality of their actions. Motivational theories help to explain people's achievements as well as their failure to achieve. They provide a way of understanding accomplishments and success, especially in the face of challenge and adversity. They also help to explain unexpected outcomes such as the lackluster performance of talented individuals or the triumph of an underdog who exceeds all expectations.

Motivation is especially prized in learning situations, whether the instruction takes place in a fourth grade classroom or on a soccer field. Without putting forth effort and actively engaging in the activity, even the most capable individuals will not benefit from the opportunity to learn. Motivation for learning is a particular kind of motivation that is concerned with the goals, activities, and behaviors involved in acquiring skills, knowledge, or competence (Brophy, 2004; Stipek, 2002). When students are motivated to learn, they put forth effort, they are engaged, they show greater persistence in the face of failure, and they take risks (attempting challenging tasks). As a result, they learn more, have deeper understandings of ideas, perform at higher levels of achievement, and are more likely to stay in school. Students who are motivated to learn also report greater satisfaction and enjoyment of learning, higher self-worth, and a greater sense of well-being.

An individual's motivation can vary depending on a number of factors including personal characteristics—age, ability, experience, values, and beliefs—and contextual characteristics—subject matter (gym versus math), task difficulty, task features (worksheet versus science project), task structure (individual, competitive, cooperative), teacher expectations, and the quality of the student–teacher relationship. Thus, a student may not have any interest in learning about history or physics, but may show initiative, effort, and persistence in studying art or literature. Rather than viewing people as being either motivated or not, most models of motivation view people as being differentially motivated to pursue some actions and not others. Individuals possess multiple motivations that at times compete for action (desire to watch that favorite television show and the desire to study for a science test). The key question for learning is how and why are students motivated to learn and achieve?

THEORETICAL APPROACHES TO MOTIVATION

Motivation is generally viewed as a multifaceted construct that has behavioral, cognitive, and affective dimensions. Different theoretical perspectives have variously focused on:

- Behaviors such as effort, engagement, persistence, and performance
- Thoughts such as expectations, self-perceptions, and goals
- Emotions such as pride, shame, and guilt

Motivation for learning is evidenced by the academic goals that students set, the quality of their engagement in tasks, their choices in courses (e.g., calculus or tennis), their persistence in the face of failure or challenges, their performance on learning activities, and the pride with which they experience their accomplishments. Thus, motivation for learning is not viewed simply as a unitary characteristic, of which people have more or less, but as a multidimensional construct. Most approaches fall under one of the following theoretical perspectives: behavioral, intrinsic motivation, or cognitive.

Behavioral

The dominant approach to motivating learning, especially in schools, has been the behavioral model, which involves the use of rewards and incentives to elicit desired behaviors. The use of external reinforcement is commonplace in schools and may take the form of tickets doled out for good citizenship, candy dispensed for turning in homework, or extended recess awarded for paying attention during an assembly. According to this model, behavior is controlled by its consequences. Thus, students are more likely to engage in learning behaviors that result in rewards and avoid behaviors that lead to punishment or undesirable outcomes. When students engage in learning activities to obtain rewards outside of the task, this type of motivation is referred to as extrinsic motivation. For example, when students study state capitals to obtain a sweet or learn multiplication tables to earn the chance to watch a video, the motivation is viewed as being extrinsic, or external, to the activity. The use of material or social incentives can be powerful in producing the motivation to engage in learning activities. The use of rewards for engaging in learning behaviors is popular because it is relatively easy to implement, targets specific behaviors, and its effectiveness can be easily monitored. There is disagreement in the field, however, over whether and under what conditions the use of rewards may undermine students' intrinsic motivation (Cameron & Pierce, 1994; Deci & colleagues, 2001). Critics of the use of rewards for learning are concerned that students' interest in a topic becomes replaced solely by an interest in the reward.

Intrinsic Motivation

There are many occasions, however, when students engage in learning activities without the promise of rewards or the threat of punishment. They eagerly pursue interests in dinosaurs, pyramids, or tornadoes, for example. When people engage in activities for their sheer enjoyment, the motivation is considered to be intrinsic. Intrinsic motivation can be a powerful motivator because engaging in an activity doesn't depend on the existence of external reinforcers to make it worthwhile; simply doing the activity is inherently valuable and satisfying.

An intrinsic motivation approach assumes that people have a natural tendency to seek experiences that increase their competence, elicit curiosity, and promote autonomy. Learning activities that are optimally challenging (not trivially easy or too difficult), are novel and interesting, and offer choice and self-direction, tap into intrinsic motivation, and provide the opportunity for individuals to increase mastery, satisfy their curiosity, and enhance their sense of personal control.

One way of portraying the subjective experience of being intrinsically motivated is with the concept of flow (Csikszentmihalyi, 1997). The flow state is characterized by being so fully immersed in an activity that people lose track of time and become unaware of what is going on around them. Their attention is riveted and sharply focused, and there is a striking lack of self-consciousness. While observed in recreational activities such as chess, basketball, and painting, flow has also characterized the work of writers, inventors, and musicians. Among children, flow is most commonly seen at play, particularly with videogames, but may also be seen in learning activities such as reading, solving mathematical problems, or writing in a journal. Flow is not easily achieved in situations where there is little control over one's learning and the actions needed to perform the task such as those commonly found in schools.

Cognitive

Cognitive approaches view people's thoughts and beliefs as playing a central role in motivation and learning. According to this view, people's perceptions indirectly affect achievement by influencing how they think, feel, and act in learning situations. How people interpret and understand events is considered more important than what actually happens. People are viewed as acting on their understandings, however accurate or inaccurate, and these serve as powerful determinants of learning behaviors. For example,

students who selectively focus on the difficulty of tasks and their low performances in school may begin to see studying as futile and give up trying when presented with tasks that are within their ability to achieve. A variety of people's beliefs and thoughts play a critical role in how they interpret, engage, and perform in learning situations. These beliefs change with age, becoming more accurate, complex, and stable.

Specific types of thoughts and beliefs that are related to motivation and learning include an individual's self-perceptions of competence, self-efficacy beliefs, causal attributions, and achievement goals. Self-perceptions of competence refer to people's estimates of their ability. These perceptions influence a student's choice of tasks, effort, persistence, causal attributions, and achievement. Young children tend to overestimate their abilities and, accordingly, often maintain high expectations for future success even in the face of failure. As children develop, their perceptions of competence decline, but become more accurate. Self-efficacy is the belief that one is capable of performing in specific areas such as language arts, biology, or gym. Self-efficacy beliefs are task- or situation-specific and include the belief that one's actions can lead to desired outcomes (Bandura, 1997).

Causal attributions are beliefs about why things happen. When people succeed or fail in learning situations, they are assumed to naturally search for reasons for these outcomes (Weiner, 1992). For example, when students who diligently studied for an exam do poorly, they may attribute this result to external reasons, such as a difficult test, or to internal reasons, such as lack of ability. Depending on whether the explanation is internal or external to the individual (e.g., ability versus ineffective teacher), stable or unstable (e.g., ability versus effort), and controllable or uncontrollable (e.g., study strategies or difficulty of the exam), this increases or decreases their expectation for future success. Causal beliefs for success that are stable and internal lead to stronger expectations for future success. Failure attributions that are stable and internal lead to weaker expectations for future success. Thus, believing that one excelled in a biology class because of one's ability would result in a stronger expectation to succeed in the future than attributing it to an easy topic. In the case of failure, believing that it was caused by ability would decrease the expectation for future success more than attributing it to lack of studying. When causal attributions are made to unstable causes, future expectations are not strengthened. Thus, attributing success to a good teacher or an easy exam is not likely to lead to greater expectations for future success.

Achievement goals refer to people's reasons for engaging in achievement-related behaviors (Ames, 1992; Dweck, 1999). Two main types of goals that have been identified are learning (or mastery) goals and performance goals. Students with mastery goals are concerned with developing new skills and increasing their competence. Students with performance goals are concerned with obtaining recognition of their competence. Two subtypes of performance goals have been further distinguished. First, performance-approach goals are focused on demonstrating competence. For students with this self-enhancement goal, the primary purpose of achievement activities is to obtain positive evaluations of their ability. Students with this goal are also likely to put forth effort on learning tasks, but choose tasks that are less challenging. They take few risks, such as answering questions only when they are certain that they are correct. Second, performance-avoidance goals are focused on avoiding negative judgments of ability. Individuals with these self-defeating goals are likely to engage in failure-avoiding tactics such as choosing trivially easy tasks, putting forth minimal effort, or procrastinating.

CONTEXTS OF MOTIVATION

It is important to put each of these approaches in context and to recognize that motivation to learn doesn't develop independently of particular learning situations. Whether one uses a behavioral, intrinsic, or cognitive theoretical perspective to explain motivation, the nature of learning contexts also influences students' motivation. Contextual characteristics such as teacher instructional practices, beliefs, and relationships can cultivate or undermine students' motivation. For example, teachers who support the autonomy of students by providing choices in the classroom rather than being unilaterally directive and controlling have students who have higher levels of intrinsic motivation.

The social features of the context also play a crucial role in fostering motivation. Students who experience a sense of belongingness, who feel connected and a part of a community, are more likely to be motivated in school (Osterman, 2000). When students experience a sense of relatedness with peers and/or teachers, they are more likely to be engaged and invested in learning at school. Instructional practices, teacher control

orientations, school and class size, grouping structures, scheduling practices, and school norms and policies can foster belongingness or fuel alienation.

SCHOOL PSYCHOLOGISTS' ROLES

One of the primary roles of school psychologists is to help determine whether a disability that affects learning is present among students having difficulty in school. The identification of a disability may explain why a student is struggling in school, and appropriate interventions may be provided to accommodate or remediate the impairment. Students, however, often fail to perform in school even in the absence of a disability. School psychologists can help to differentiate between students who have a genuine disability that interferes with learning and students who are capable of achieving but are not performing at expected levels. To reliably ascertain whether a student has a learning disability, for instance, it is essential to determine: Is the lowered performance primarily caused by an inability to fully process sensory input, or it is caused by a lack of interest, lack of effort, or, in other words, diminished motivation? It is not unusual for students with disabilities that affect learning to also exhibit reduced motivation given their history of academic difficulties. Thus, it is important to assess students' motivational characteristics in addition to their academic and cognitive functioning. Students who display motivation to learn are more likely to have higher levels of engagement, experience flow, have higher expectations, be more optimistic about their future performance, persist in the face of failure, take risks, and achieve at higher levels. School psychologists can assess the motivational characteristics of students and develop interventions involving teachers, parents, peers, and individual students to promote the development of optimal motivation.

Assessment of Motivation

Recognizing that motivation is multifaceted and that people can be motivated in a variety of ways implies that motivation should be assessed in multiple ways and in specific learning situations. Accurate descriptions of motivation are obtained by assessing motivation:

- In specific subject matter areas
- In relation to the instructional context

- In specific contexts (e.g. home versus school, formal versus informal)
- With multiple data sources (e.g., self-reports, teacher reports, parent reports)

School psychologists assess motivation with multiple measures including observations, interviews, review of work samples, self-report measures, and rating scales. They can obtain valuable information by simply observing a student's behavior in a classroom. A common focus of observation is a student's engagement in learning activities. This may be measured by observing and recording the participation rates of students, time on task, work completion, persistence, and the quality of work samples. Interviews with students can provide valuable information about their learning behaviors, enjoyment of learning activities, and their motivational beliefs. These conversations can also inform the development of interventions by identifying potential reinforcers, areas of personal interest, and interpretations of their achievement outcomes.

Individuals involved in students' learning may be asked to complete rating scales that assess behaviors and attitudes related to motivation. Examples of published and research tools that assess motivational processes include the Academic Competence Evaluation Scales (DiPerna & Elliott, 2000), Children's Academic Intrinsic Motivation Inventory (Gottfried, 1986), and the Patterns of Adaptive Learning Scales (Midgley & colleagues, 1998).

Motivational Interventions

School psychologists use the results of assessments to design interventions that promote motivation for learning. The most commonly used method to increase motivation in schools is providing incentives for desired learning behaviors. From preschool onward, parents as well as teachers bestow rewards on students who are good citizens, name the capitols of the 50 states, sit quietly, and read every day. Students receive material reinforcers such as candy, erasers, pencils, or stickers, as well as rewards that include extended recess, time on the computer, an opportunity to watch a video, school- or classwide recognition, or special privileges (e.g., line leader). The provision of rewards works best when the desired behavior is specifically defined and substantively related to the reward (e.g., a book rather than a candy bar for reading). It also is more effective when the reward is tied to a specific standard of performance and not merely to the presence or absence of the behavior. For example, tying rewards to completing 20 math problems with 90% accuracy is more effective than setting goals of simply completing the math problems. Designing the reinforcement to be contingent on the quality of the performance is essential for keeping the focus on learning.

Rewards are especially effective in the short run to change behavior, but less effective in changing behavior over the long term. Eventually, rewards need to be phased out and replaced by an internal sense of motivation that doesn't rely on the continued receipt of external rewards. Intrinsic motivation approaches have the goal of increasing the satisfaction and enjoyment that individuals derive from an activity. Students read a book, invent a new form of transportation, or write a short story, not to receive a concrete reward or to avoid punishment, but because of the satisfaction they derive from the activity. Strategies that increase intrinsic motivation include selecting tasks that have intermediate levels of challenge or difficulty, designing activities that are interesting and novel, and providing choices in learning that increase students' sense of personal agency. For example, designing instructional activities that enhance the learning experience by creating situational interest, can lead to the development of personal interest in a topic. Teachers who communicate feedback in an informational rather than a controlling manner facilitate autonomy and self-regulation in students.

Cognitive interventions focus on changing the beliefs of individuals to promote adaptive responses to achievement situations. Interventions that foster perceptions of competence, self-efficacy, mastery and learning goals, and adaptive causal attributions can increase students' efforts and engagement in learning activities. Classroom learning structures can also affect motivational beliefs and learning. Competition can promote social comparisons and heighten awareness about performance evaluations, turning attention away from learning and the task at hand. Cooperative and individual learning structures are more effective in fostering learning and mastery goals. The development of learning communities that enhance a sense of belonging can promote students' motivation by creating supportive environments that enable students to take risks, to put forth effort, and to engage in learning.

School psychologists also deal with motivational problems that most children commonly experience throughout the course of schooling. These may take the form of test anxiety, perfectionism, or boredom with school activities. These problems often involve performance goals, unrealistically high expectations, and low task value, respectively. School psychologists can help with these ordinary motivational problems by developing interventions that reduce anxiety, focus attention on the task instead of on performance evaluations, foster realistic expectations, and increase task value by highlighting the instrumental value of school activities.

—Evelyn R. Oka

See also Ability Grouping; Behavior Intervention; Cooperative Learning; Dropouts; Homework; Learning; Self-Management

REFERENCES AND FURTHER READING

Ames, C. A. (1992). Classrooms: Goals, structures, and student motivation. *Journal of Educational Psychology, 84,* 261–271.

Bandura, A. (1997). *Self-efficacy: The exercise of control.* New York: Freeman.

Brophy, J. (2004). *Motivating students to learn* (2nd ed.). Mahwah, NJ: Erlbaum.

Cameron, J., & Pierce, W. D. (1994). Reinforcement, reward, and intrinsic motivation: A meta-analysis. *Review of Educational Research, 64,* 363–423.

Csikszentmihalyi, M. (1997). *Finding flow: The psychology of engagement with everyday life.* New York: Harper & Row.

Deci, E. L., Koestner, R., & Ryan, R. M. (2001). Extrinsic rewards and intrinsic motivation in education: Reconsidered once again. *Review of Educational Research, 71,* 1–28.

DiPerna, J. C., & Elliott, S. N. (2000). *Academic Competence Evaluation Scales.* San Antonio, TX: The Psychological Corporation.

Dweck, C. S. (1999). *Self-theories: Their role in motivation, personality, and development.* Philadelphia: Psychology Press.

Eccles, J. S., & Wigfield, A. (2002). Motivational beliefs, values, and goals. *Annual Review of Psychology, 53,* 109–132.

Gottfried, A. E. (1986). *Children's academic intrinsic motivation inventory.* Odessa, FL: Psychological Assessment Resources.

Midgley, C., Maehr, M. L., Hruda, L. Z., Anderman, E., Anderman, L., Freeman, K. E., et al. (1998). *Manual for the patterns of adaptive learning scales (PALS).* Ann Arbor: University of Michigan.

Osterman, K. F. (2000). Students' need for belonging in the school community. *Review of Educational Research, 70*(3), 323–367.

Stipek, D. (2002). *Motivation to learn* (4th ed.). Boston: Allyn & Bacon.

Weiner, B. (1992). *Human motivation: Metaphors, theories, and research.* Newbury Park, CA: Sage.

MOTOR ASSESSMENT

Motor skills are generally evaluated during an assessment in the schools by an occupational and/or physical therapist. Motor performance is also considered an important part of a neuropsychological evaluation. A neuropsychological evaluation assesses the relationship between brain activity and behavior (Teeter & Semrud-Clikeman, 1997). There are occasions when a school psychologist may need to provide additional measures of motor skills to provide support for a child or adolescent in the area of handwriting and copying.

Motor skills can be divided into several areas. The most obvious division is between fine and gross motor skills. Gross motor skills are the bigger movements (e.g., running and jumping) that use the large muscles in the arms, legs, torso, and feet; whereas fine motor skills are small movements (e.g., grabbing something with the thumb and forefinger) that use the small muscles of the fingers, toes, wrists, lips, and tongue. In order to more fully understand these measures, it is important to first review the structures that contribute to motor functioning.

NEUROANATOMY

The motor system is contained within the front part of the brain. This motor strip controls the execution and maintenance of simple motor functions. It is a crossed system so that the right hemisphere motor strip located on the right side of the brain controls the left side of the body, and vice versa. The premotor cortex lies in front of the motor strip and directs the primary motor cortex.

In addition to the frontal lobes, the parietal lobe is also involved with the motor system. The parietal lobe lies in the superior portion of the back of the brain. This section allows for not only the perception of touch and temperature, but also an awareness of the position and movement of body parts (kinesthetic sense). Similar to the motor system, the sensory system is also a crossed system. It is particularly important for motor skills in that the primary parietal region allows for a rapid cross-communication with the motor system, which is necessary for the execution of motor behavior (Teeter & Semrud-Clikeman, 1997).

In addition to the sensory and motor cortices, the ability to integrate motor skills and visual information is an important part of motor control. The juncture of the occipital, parietal, and temporal lobes has been implicated in visual–motor integration. This juncture lies in the posterior portion of the brain where the three lobes connect. For some children, fine motor skills may be intact but they experience difficulty integrating what they see with what their hands/fingers are reproducing. These children may have difficulties in visual–motor integration, but have adequate fine motor skills. Similarly, a child with fine motor skill deficits may experience difficulties with visual–motor tasks that are not caused by perceptual deficits. Fine motor skills are those that allow a person to complete a task with his or her hand, while perceptual skills are those that allow understanding of what the person sees.

The school psychologist needs to tease apart the difficulties a child may have through the use of fine motor tests as well as perceptual tasks that are not heavily involved motorically. For example, child with cerebral palsy may perform poorly on a visual–motor task because of obvious motor problems and should be tested for perceptual accuracy on tasks that do not have a motor component. Similarly children with tremors, arthritis, or motor slowing may do poorly on measures of visual–motor integration for these reasons and not because of perceptual difficulties. In addition, children with motor difficulties may do poorly because of their positioning. It is very helpful to have a physical therapist or occupational therapist assist the psychologist in positioning the child for optimum performance.

EVALUATION OF GROSS MOTOR SKILLS

The evaluation of gross motor skills is completed generally by a physical therapist and/or adaptive physical education teacher. Most school psychologists do not evaluate gross motor ability. However, it is important to be aware of qualitative differences in the child's ability to walk, his or her gait, and the fluidity of movement. A child who runs awkwardly, falls frequently, or walks on his or her tiptoes needs to be referred for an evaluation by a specialist in this area.

For younger children, evaluation of motor skills is an important aspect of the evaluation. The Bayley Scales of Infant Development, Mullen Scales of Early Learning, and the Denver Developmental Screening Test include measures of gross motor skills. In addition, the Vineland Adaptive Behavior Scales provides an evaluation of the child's fine and gross motor skills.

Treatment for gross motor skills deficits is generally completed by a physical therapist for children with severe deficits and may be accommodated by an adaptive physical education class for those with moderate to severe difficulty. For children with significant motor impairment, it is often a good idea for a neurologist to evaluate the child to determine whether a more significant problem is contributing to the child's difficulty. Often the first sign of a brain tumor or other neurological deficit is a decline in motor performance. For children who are developmentally delayed, the motor system is a good marker for the integrity of their neurological development. Thus, young children whose development is questionable should have an evaluation of their motor skills.

EVALUATION OF FINE MOTOR SKILLS

Tests of motor performance are a vital part of most neuropsychological assessments because of the observed connection of motor impairment to functional outcomes. Children who have difficulty completing tasks that involve buttoning, drawing, or tracing often have brain functions that are compromised. This difficulty often translates into difficulty adapting to one's environment and functioning independently.

Tests of fine motor skills are not often used by school psychologists but with training can be helpful in determining the extent of a child's motor deficits. Specific measures used for assessing the various aspects of fine and gross motor ability include handedness preference, strength, speed, and dexterity. Although performance with the preferred hand is usually slightly superior to that with the nonpreferred hand on tasks of fine motor ability, equal performance or better performance with the nonpreferred hand occurs frequently in the normal population. Therefore, neurological impairment cannot be surmised from a lack of laterality unless this pattern is observed across several tasks. Laterality refers to the preference most of us have for one side of the body or the other. For example, most people are right-handed, right-eyed, and right-legged—that is, they prefer to do activities with their right side. Impaired motor performance or lateralized deficits on a variety of motor tasks is quite rare in the normal population and may be more suggestive of a neurological disturbance in the contralateral hemisphere, because motor skills are controlled by the opposite side of the brain. Poor attention, lack of effort, and lower cognitive functioning are also typical explanations for poor performance on motor measures.

Finger dexterity is an area of fine motor evaluation that should be included in many neuropsychological and school psychological evaluations. Measures include the Purdue Pegboard and the Grooved Pegboard. These measures are easily used by a school psychologist and norms are available. The Purdue Pegboard is a timed measure of motor speed and finger and hand dexterity. It involves the child placing pins in one of two rows of holes, using each hand separately and then together. Scores are obtained for each hand and for both hands. It is expected that the dominant hand will perform better than the nondominant and that both hands together will perform the best.

The Grooved Pegboard is a timed measure of motor speed where a child is asked to place keyhole-shaped pegs into holes in a four-inch square pegboard, using only one hand at a time. For the dominant hand, the time is expected to be faster than for the nondominant hand. One can also qualitatively evaluate the method that the child uses to complete the pegboard.

In addition to these measures, there are sensorimotor and visual–spatial scales on the NEPSY. These scales evaluate a child's ability to touch each finger sequentially with his or her thumb, imitate hand positions, and complete a maze as quickly as possible. In addition, the child is asked to copy figures that become increasingly more difficult and to judge where an arrow will hit a target.

Measures of visual–motor integration include the Bender-Gestalt Test and the Test of Visual–Motor Integration (VMI). These tests require a participant to copy geometric designs in clearly delineated squares of space equal to the original. The 24 designs increase in complexity, starting with a vertical line and progressing to three-dimensional figures. In addition to the VMI and Bender, the Developmental Test of Visual Perception-2 can be very helpful in evaluating eye–hand coordination, copying, spatial relations, visual closure, and visual–motor speed (how fast the child is able to complete a task). This measure also allows a comparison of subtests that are not as involved motorically from those that are motor driven. This difference is important for determining whether poor performance is caused by a motor difficulty alone or whether there are perceptual problems that are interfering with performance. If there are both perceptual and motor difficulties, intervention is more difficult and the prognosis would be more guarded than for motor problems alone.

Treatment for fine motor skill deficits for those children with severe difficulty often involves an occupational therapist. An occupational therapist assists the child in learning activities of daily living such as buttoning, zipping, and tying shoes. In addition, support is frequently given for copying figures through the use of tracing as well as dot-to-dot figures. Moreover, an occupational therapist also provides support to the classroom teacher and parent with a program to continue the work past the therapy hour (in the classroom or at home). The occupational therapist may see the child 15 to 45 minutes per week, and a supportive program can only assist the child in making good progress. The treatment is generally age-based with more hands-on activities planned for younger children and more handwriting and copying activities for older children.

In summary, fine and gross motor skills can affect a child's learning ability as well as his or her ability to socialize. Children with significant gross motor skills have difficulty participating in group activities such as soccer or Little League, mainstays of many young children's social experiences. These difficulties can cause these children not to feel part of their peer group and to become less socially adept. In addition, children with significant fine motor delays may have difficulty with dressing and caring for their own needs. Adaptation needs to be encouraged. The use of Velcro fasteners are very helpful for many of these children.

The school psychologist may supplement his or her testing with testing by an occupational or physical therapist to complete an Individualized Education Plan (IEP) appropriately. The IEP is an individualized plan to assist the child with special education needs. Related services such as occupational and physical therapy are included in the IEP. In some cases the school psychologist will be called upon to interpret neuropsychological and neurological reports and needs to be conversant in what the tests measure and what the results mean. In other instances, the school psychologist may provide the only measures of visual–motor and/or fine motor skills, and these findings can be incorporated into an appropriate intervention program.

—*Margaret Semrud-Clikeman and Jenifer Walkowiak*

See also Sensorimotor Stage of Development

REFERENCES AND FURTHER READING

Teeter, P. A., & Semrud-Clikeman, M. (1997). *Child neuropsychology*. Boston: Allyn & Bacon.

MOVIES. *See* MEDIA AND CHILDREN

MULTICULTURAL EDUCATION

Much has changed since multicultural education first became a "hot topic" for researchers, educators, and parents. What we know today about multicultural education is very different from what we knew in the past. The United States, as well as many other countries, has evolved into a country rich with diversity among its people, their cultures, and their backgrounds. Students in today's schools come from homes of different economic, linguistic, religious, and ethnic traditions. The National Center for Educational Statistics reported that in 2000 39% of the students in U.S. schools were considered part of a minority group, and in many parts of the country the percentages were much higher. Conditions of poverty, community violence and crime, societal and individual prejudice, and racism continue to create additional challenges for students trying to learn. While the diversity of the U.S. school population is growing, many students from these backgrounds are being left behind academically. In addition, the reliance on high-stakes tests, such as state standards tests, widens the gaps in academic achievement for diverse groups. This is one of the key reasons that applying multicultural education in schools is so important.

Multicultural educators and researchers have long debated the definitions, meanings, goals and approaches of multicultural education. Banks and Banks (2001) and Sleeter and Grant (1999) have written much about multicultural education. The works of these authors are described here because they offer useful definitions, descriptions of different understandings and approaches, and discussion of their relative strengths and shortcomings as the approaches are used in schools.

Banks and Banks (2001), two of the leading figures in the field of multicultural education, propose that multicultural education is at least three things: an idea or concept, an educational reform movement, and a process. They say that multicultural education incorporates the belief that all students, regardless of gender, social class, ethnicity, or culture, should have an equal opportunity to learn. Korn and Bursztyn (2002) add that multicultural education is a way to fill the gap between the cultures of home and school with multicultural curricula. Sleeter and Grant (1999) use the term *multicultural education* to encompass educational practices directed toward issues of race, culture, language, social class, gender, disability, racism, classism, and sexism.

Much like the definition of multicultural education, there is a debate about its goal(s). The consensus among most scholars and researchers appears to be that the major goal of multicultural education is to address the inequality in education by promoting an understanding and appreciation of cultural diversity (Davidman & Davidman, 1994).

CONTRIBUTIONS OF BANKS AND BANKS

Banks (1994) states that there is general agreement among most multicultural education scholars and researchers that institutional changes must be made for multicultural education to be implemented successfully (e.g., changes in curricula, teaching materials, learning styles, attitudes, and school culture). He articulates five dimensions of multicultural education (see Table 1) that describe the different ways to accomplish the goal of multicultural education.

Of Banks's five dimensions of multicultural education, *content integration* is the most common approach used in schools today. Table 2 shows examples of each approach of content integration, along with the advantages and disadvantages of each approach. The *contributions approach,* the most widely used in schools, is easy to integrate without changing the structure and goals of the mainstream curriculum, and knowledge can be spread quickly (Banks & Banks, 2001). However, numerous disadvantages outweigh the advantages of this approach. A major disadvantage is that curriculum remains unchanged or unaltered, thus it leads to only telling "half of the story." Content is limited to special months and holidays without regard for important concepts and issues related to oppression and struggles of diverse groups. Students may end up studying the strange and exotic characteristics of diverse cultures, which may reinforce stereotypes and misconceptions (Banks & Banks, 2001). For example, heroes and heroines who are more radical and less conforming, such as Malcolm

Table 1 Five Dimensions and Definitions of Multicultural Education

Dimension	Definition
Content integration	The extent to which teachers use examples as content from a variety of cultures in their teaching
Knowledge construction	The extent to which teachers help students process, understand, investigate, and determine how biases within a discipline influence the ways in which knowledge is constructed
Prejudice reduction	Focus on the characteristics of students' racial attitudes and how to modify these attributes by teaching methods and materials
Equity pedagogy	The modification in teaching that facilitates academic achievement of students from diverse racial, cultural, gender, and social-class groups
Empowering school culture and social structure	The examination of grouping and labeling practices, sports participation, unequal achievement, and the interaction of staff and students across ethnic and racial lines to create school culture that empowers students from diverse racial, ethnic, and gender groups

X and The Black Panthers, are often overlooked and therefore "invisible" in this stage of integration.

Teachers may find the *additive approach* attractive. It allows them to "add" ethnic content without putting a considerable amount of time and effort into restructuring the curriculum, which Banks and Banks (2001) suggest would take substantial training and rethinking of the curriculum and its purpose, nature, and goals. However, adding a book or unit that lacks genuine ethnic content, concepts, and experiences is problematic; it continues to perpetuate only a mainstream viewpoint rather than the perspectives of the ethnic cultures that participate and are affected by these events and issues.

The change in curriculum and pedagogy in the *transformation approach* distinguishes it from the aforementioned approaches. Korn and Bursztyn (2002) describe this approach as more comprehensive and radical because it changes the curriculum to encourage student empowerment and social action. They note that transformation goes beyond the study of heroes, holidays, and people. It considers the practices that are part of understanding the children's experiences. This approach has three strengths:

1. It builds students' knowledge and awareness of the ways in which culturally and linguistically diverse groups have contributed to and participated in the formation of U.S. society and culture.

2. It assists in the reduction of stereotypical views, stigmas, and misconceptions.

3. Students from diverse cultural groups can identify with the school curriculum when they are able to see their cultures being represented in the curriculum.

This involves a significant amount of time and effort to train teachers. Both the curriculum and the teacher are transformed. Teachers engage in a continual and ongoing process of self-awareness and curriculum change.

The *social action approach* is comprised of all the components of the transformation approach, plus components that call for students to take action and make decisions that are related to the issues, concepts, or problems that they study. The social action approach enables students to improve skills in decision making, social action, data gathering, and group interaction (Banks & Banks, 2001). It also develops their ability to analyze their values and the values of others. The social action approach takes a considerable amount of time to plan and teach (Banks & Banks, 2001). Educators using this approach are encouraged to help students focus on considering and taking action, rather than being preoccupied with problems.

CONTRIBUTIONS OF SLEETER AND GRANT

Sleeter and Grant (1987, 1999) argue that much of the existing literature addresses only limited aspects of multicultural education. Recognizing that

Table 2　　Four Approaches to Content Integration

Approach Name	Description	Examples
Contributions	Primary focus on ethnic heroes, holidays, cultural elements (e.g., food, dances, and music) and artifacts with little attention to other aspects of ethnic content.	(a) Celebrations of the accomplishments and contributions of African Americans and Black History in February. (b) The study of Native American culture during the Thanksgiving holiday.
Additive	The addition of content, concepts, themes, and perspectives to the curriculum without change in the basic structure, purpose, and characteristics of the curriculum.	(a) A teacher requires students to read The *Joy Luck Club* (1994), a best selling novel that depicts the complexities of the relationship between Chinese immigrant mothers and their American-raised daughters. (b) The addition of a unit on African Americans in education during the study of U.S. history and segregation.
Transformation	Transforms the curriculum and enables students to view concepts, issues, themes, and problems from several perspectives and points of view. Often a major shift in the way teachers teach, understand, and connect with students (Korn & Bursztyn, 2002).	A teacher redesigns her literacy curriculum and methods of instruction to include more group projects based on the students' home cultures, resulting in a very different way of teaching.
Social Action	All components of the transformation approach, plus it calls for students to take action and make decisions related to the issues, concepts, or problems they study. Students gather data, analyze their values and beliefs, expand their knowledge, identify alternative courses of action, and decide what, if any, actions they will take.	(a) A class studies prejudice and discrimination in their school and decides to take action to improve race relations in the school (Banks & Banks, 2001). (b) A teacher designs an English unit and requires students to complete a social action project on the under-representation of individuals with disabilities in television and film. The students gather data on the number of individuals with versus the number without disabilities in television and film, analyze the differences, and write a letter to filmmakers and producers of television programs suggesting ways to improve the visibility of individuals with disabilities in film and TV.

From Banks, J. A., & Banks, C. A. M. (Eds.). (2001). *Multicultural education: Issues and perspectives* (4th ed.). New York: Wiley.

"multicultural education means different things to different people" (Sleeter & Grant, 1987, pp. 31–32), they reviewed and examined a wide variety of literature from various educators and researchers on this topic. They developed a taxonomy or classification system to help define multicultural education, examine its use, and identify shortcomings of the approaches. Five categories of multicultural education emerged as a result of their examination:

1. Teaching the culturally different

2. Single group studies

3. Human relations

4. Multicultural education

5. Education that is multicultural and social reconstructionist

Table 3   Five Approaches to Multicultural Education

Description of Approach	Critique
Teaching the Culturally Different: Views multicultural education as something one does mainly with students who are of color. Main goals are: (a) helping educators teach students from diverse backgrounds, and (b) making a commitment to educational achievement of children of color and development of positive group identity.	Materials discuss race and ethnicity; limited attention is given to other forms of diversity such as language, sexual orientation, religion, and gender. Limited progress has been reported in recommendations for practice, goals, and suggestions for instruction. This approach puts too much responsibility for eliminating racism on people of color and their teachers rather than on the general mainstream population.
Human Relations: Views multicultural education as a means to help students of different backgrounds communicate, get along better, and feel good about themselves.	The approach lacks long-term goals; it ignores the impact that institutional discrimination, powerlessness, poverty, and privilege can have on communication and appreciation for one another.
Single Group Studies: Uses lessons or units that focus on the experiences and cultures of specific groups such as a particular ethnic group (e.g., African American, Native American, Asian, or Filipino). Can focus on developing acceptance, appreciation, and empathy for America's rich cultural and linguistic diversity (King, 1980), or on reflective decision making used for resolving personal problems (Banks, 1973).	The goals of this approach are sometimes unclear and authors of single group studies admit to having different goals. This approach emphasizes teaching about the contributions of ethnic groups without raising awareness of racial oppression or activating social action. Also, this approach lacks attention to other forms of human diversity; the case of "single" versus "multiple."
Multicultural Education: Designed to promote: (a) strength and value of cultural diversity, (b) human rights and respect for cultural diversity, (c) alternative life choices for people, (d) social justice and equal opportunity for all people, and (e) equity in distribution of power among members of all ethnic groups (Gollnick, 1980; Gollnick & Chinn, 1998).	This approach has well-developed goals and includes promising models of curriculum, instruction, and teaching guides. Although this approach is the most popular of the five approaches, it needs improvement in at least two areas. Authors should: (a) give equal weight to both curriculum and instruction, and have more discussion on policy, language, and bilingualism from a multicultural perspective; and (b) consider the intersection of race, class, and gender factors when examining oppression.
Education That is Multicultural and Social Recontructionist: Designed to promote cultural pluralism and to prepare people to take social action against social structural inequality. Goals expand beyond the multicultural education approach, with more emphasis on helping students gain a better understanding of the causes of oppression, inequality, and ways to resolve social problems. Understanding of concepts and issues and skills in social action are developed through it. Students engage in democratic decision making about substantive schoolwide concerns.	This approach gained popularity in the schools during the 1990s. Unlike other approaches, this approach promotes learning to form coalitions across race, class, and gender lines. Forming coalitions is a complex skill important in a multicultural democratic society. A shortcoming of this approach is that it is relatively new, with few studies or examples available to guide people who want to implement experiences with a wide range of people, perspectives, and activities. Some think this approach is good but not feasible. Some criticize it because when students think for themselves and are empowered with skills in social action, they may challenge their teachers or school systems.

Sleeter, C. E., & Grant, C. A. (1999). *Making choices for multicultural education: Five approaches to race, class, and gender.* Upper Saddle River, NJ: Prentice Hall.

Table 3 summarizes the five categories and Sleeter and Grant's critique of each one. They believe that the fifth category offers the most promise for addressing today's multicultural education needs. This approach involves teaching skills in social action and promoting the development of understandings that are constructed out of one's experience with diverse perspectives and considerations. Students move from being thinkers to actors who can "work collaboratively to speak out, be heard, and effect change" (Sleeter & Grant, 1999, p. 221), thereby taking charge of their lives.

Whichever approach to multicultural education is used, it should include more than awareness of culture. "Multicultural education embodies a perspective rather than a curriculum" (Carr, 2002). Carr, Manager of the California Department of Education, Special Education Division, advocates that teachers need to use a multicultural education approach that supports and encourages greater appreciation, tolerance, and understanding of diverse cultural groups, learning styles, and curriculum. Students need to learn who they are in relation to the world and to their own environment. Multicultural education includes infusing a child's language and cultural knowledge throughout classroom routines and curriculum. It also includes culturally responsive teaching, which Gay (2002) defines as using characteristics, experiences, and perspectives of culturally diverse students as tools for effective teaching. As a result, teaching is consistent with students' experiences and holds personal meaning; each child is engaged and encouraged to learn and succeed. More importantly, multicultural education offers students of all backgrounds knowledge and skills in working with people representing a variety of backgrounds. Multicultural education offers the depth and tools to prepare students for productive actions and contributions in today's world.

—*Tonika Duren Green and Colette L. Ingraham*

See also Cross-Cultural Assessment; Race, Ethnicity, Class, and Gender; School Reform

REFERENCES AND FURTHER READING

Banks, J. A. (1973). Teaching black studies for social change. In J. A. Banks (Ed.), *Teaching ethnic studies* (pp. 149–179). Washington, DC: National Council for the Social Studies.

Banks, J. A. (1994). *Multicultural education: Theory and practice* (3rd ed.). Needham Heights, MA: Allyn & Bacon.

Banks, J. A., & Banks, C. A. M. (Eds.). (2001). *Multicultural education: Issues and perspectives* (4th ed.). New York: Wiley.

Carr, B. (2002). Accepting the challenge. *The Special Edge, 15*(2), 1.

Davidman, L., & Davidman, P. T. (1994*). Teaching with a multicultural perspective: A practical guide.* White Plains, NY: Longman.

Gay, G. (2002). Preparing for culturally responsive teaching. *Journal of Teacher Education, 53*(2), 106–116.

Gollnick, D. M. (1980). Multicultural education. *Viewpoints in Teaching and Learning, 56,* 1–17.

Gollnick, D. M., & Chinn, P. C. (1998). *Multicultural education in a pluralistic society* (5th ed.). Upper Saddle River, NJ: Prentice Hall

King, E. W. (1980). *Teaching ethnic awareness.* Santa Monica, CA: Goodyear.

Korn, C., & Bursztyn, A. (Eds.). (2002). *Rethinking multicultural education: Case studies in cultural transition.* Westport, CT: Bergin & Garvey.

Mayer, D. P., Mullens, J. E., & Moore M. T. (2000). *Monitoring school quality: An indicators report* (NCES 2001–030). Washington, DC: U.S. Department of Education, National Center for Education Statistics. Available online at http://nces.ed.gov/pubs2001/ 2001030.pdf

Sleeter, C. E., & Grant, C. A. (1987). An analysis of multicultural education in the United States. *Harvard Educational Review, 57,* 421–444.

Sleeter, C. E., & Grant, C. A. (1999). *Making choices for multicultural education: Five approaches to race, class, and gender.* Upper Saddle River, NJ: Prentice Hall.

Tan, A. (1994). *The joy luck club.* New York: Prentice Hall.

Wirt, J., Choy, S., Gerald, D., Provasnik, S., Rooney, P., Watanabe, S., et al. (2002). *The condition of education 2002* (NCES 2002–025). Washington, DC: U.S. Government Printing Office. Available online at http://nces.ed.gov/ pubsearch/pubsinfo.asp?pubid=2002025.

MULTIDISCIPLINARY TEAMS

Multidisciplinary teams (MDTs) are decision-making groups composed of individuals with expertise in differing knowledge and skill areas. MDTs are used in a variety of settings in the helping professions. In education, MDTs make decisions about whether a student will receive special education services and develop the student's Individualized Education Plan (IEP). Their use in the provision of special education services was first required in 1975 by the Education for All Handicapped Children Act (Public Law 94–142). The rationale for why these teams are multidisciplinary is that decisions in complex situations are best made with input from individuals with diverse perspectives. MDTs offer the school psychologist and others the opportunity for increased communication with those who have different professional specializations.

The term *multidisciplinary* means that the team is composed of individuals from different professions.

Other names used for MDTs include child study teams, IEP teams, appraisal teams, and placement committees. Knowing that a school team is multidisciplinary does not explain how the team members interact with one another. Collaboration, rather than a series of individual reports, is strongly recommended. Some models of team functioning involve minimizing the distinctions between professional roles, even to the extent that team members train other team members from different professions to perform some of their traditional job functions.

The Individuals With Disabilities Education Act 1997 (IDEA 1997) specifies the individuals who are to be involved in making special education decisions concerning eligibility, the IEP, and placement. Parents are to be participants in each of these decisions. After evaluation data have been collected from interviews, tests, observations, and school records, the law requires that a group of qualified professionals and the parents use the data to determine whether the student meets the legal definition of a child with a disability. The team that develops the child's IEP is to include the parents, regular education teacher, special education teacher, an individual who can interpret the implications of the evaluation data for the student's instruction (e.g., a school psychologist), and a school representative who knows about the general curriculum, specialized instruction, and available school resources. Some teams also include the student, counselor, social worker, nurse, speech-language pathologist, physical therapist, occupational therapist, and/or persons from outside agencies. Others, including the student, may participate on the IEP team under certain circumstances. Determination of the educational placement of a child with a disability is made by a group composed of the parents and others who are knowledgeable about the child. They consider the data from the comprehensive evaluation and placement options in making decisions on behalf of the child. The three decisions—eligibility, IEP, and placement—can be made by the same MDT, or a different one; the MDT can be any of the groups defined in IDEA as responsible for these decisions. It is the responsibility of the school district to make sure the correct individuals participate in each decision.

The student's regular education teacher knows which learning and behavior strategies have helped the student and what modifications and supplements to the general education program are needed. The special education teacher has expertise in the special education methods that the student needs to succeed in school. Most students with disabilities receive their educational instruction from both regular and special education teachers. It is important that these key people in the implementation of the IEP be involved in its development.

The school psychologist likely gathered much of the evaluation data that the MDT used to determine whether the child met the legal requirements for eligibility for special education services, and can interpret the data as needed by other team members. At the IEP meeting, the school psychologist should explain the instructional implications of the evaluation data.

The principal acts as the representative of the school district to make sure that the instructional plans in the IEP can be implemented. This requires knowledge of the general education curriculum and the school district's resources, qualifications to supervise the provision of special education services, and authority to commit resources of the district to implement the IEP.

Parents are the experts on their own children and as such have valuable contributions to make in special education decisions. They have been with the child in many environments, not just the school; know the child's medical, educational, and social–emotional histories; and can explain the home environment. Of all the MDT members, it is the parents who will have the longest involvement in the student's life.

Students must be invited to participate on the MDT when transition needs and services are to be considered. Because transition service needs must be included in the IEP by the time the student is 14 years of age, adolescents with disabilities often participate on their own IEP teams. Parents may decide that it is appropriate for younger students to participate, but their inclusion on MDTs is much less frequent. Adolescents on MDTs have the opportunity to share their perspectives, needs, and goals with the adults who are providing their support and guidance. Their presence on the MDT enhances the team experience for parents and regular education teachers, and results in administrators focusing more on the student's strengths, interests, and needs (Martin & colleagues, 2004).

Other persons, like the school nurse or social worker, may participate on MDTs, particularly when their services are to be provided as part of the student's IEP. Someone representing the agency that is likely to provide the student's future transition services needs to be on the IEP team when the services

A multidisciplinary team helps to ensure that decisions in complex situations are made with input from individuals with diverse perspectives.

are discussed. In any individual situation, the parents or the school district might want to invite other persons to the meeting. For example, the physician who is managing a student's medications could explain their effects on the child's behavior and could learn from other MDT members how the medications may be affecting the child's school performance.

MDT members may contribute more in the meeting if the number of participants doesn't get too large. Parents are particularly likely to be intimidated in a situation in which a sensitive subject like their child's education is being discussed by individuals who may know each other but who are newly acquainted with the parents. In general, who is on the team affects the experience of other team members in terms of who talks more and what is talked about (Martin & colleagues, 2004).

Ideally, all MDT members participate as equal partners in decision making. Unfortunately, broad participation by diverse team members does not necessarily improve problem solving or outcomes for students (Fuchs & colleagues, 1996).

School psychologists are typically trained to facilitate groups in the problem-solving process. The use of effective communication skills and conflict-resolution strategies will move the group beyond the sharing of a series of reports to meaningful communication.

—*Nancy. A. McKellar*

See also Diagnosis and Labeling; Individuals With Disabilities Education Act; Individualized Education Plan; Least Restrictive Environment; Special Education; Student Improvement Teams

REFERENCES AND FURTHER READING

Fuchs, D., Fuchs, L. S., Harris, A. H., & Roberts, P. H. (1996). Bridging the research-to-practice gap with mainstream assistance teams: A cautionary tale. *School Psychology Quarterly, 11*, 244–266.

Individuals With Disabilities Education Act Amendments of 1997, Public Law 105-17, 20 U.S.C. 1401, et seq.

Martin, J. E., Marshall, L. H., & Sale, P. (2004). A 3-year study of middle, junior high, and high school IEP meetings. *Exceptional Children, 70*, 285–297.

N

NATIONAL ASSOCIATION OF SCHOOL PSYCHOLOGISTS

The National Association of School Psychologists (NASP) was founded in St. Louis, Missouri, in March of 1969 in order to better represent the interests of school psychologists, particularly those trained at the nondoctoral degree level. The NASP was, in part, a response to the need for national representation in legislation affecting education, as well as a need to organize the efforts and build communications among the existing school psychology associations across the country. The St. Louis meeting followed an earlier meeting in Columbus, Ohio, called by the Ohio School Psychologists Association to consider founding a national group.

1969–1979

The NASP grew rapidly in size and representation from 1970 to the present (see the timeline). In its first decade, it successfully established its governance structure; a code of ethics; standards documents for training, credentialing, and practice; a continuing professional development program; and a national newsletter and journal. It also attained constituent membership with the National Council for Accreditation of Teacher Education (NCATE), which led to its formal involvement in NCATE's accreditation process; and in the late 1980s NCATE granted permission for NASP to approve school psychology programs. Annual conventions were organized and have been held every year since 1969. Relationships with the Division of School Psychology of the American Psychological Association (APA) were often difficult, but led to joint efforts to establish a committee on international school psychology, and to influence major federal legislation (Public Laws 94–142 & 93–380). Differences between NASP and the APA regarding training and credentialing, and related program accreditation, led to the formation of the APA/NASP Task Force in 1978 (later renamed the APA/NASP Interorganizational Committee, until it was disbanded in 2002). Although the issue of entry-level training (doctoral versus nondoctoral) has plagued school psychology since its inception, no resolution of the issue was achieved by the APA/NASP joint effort.

1980–1989

During the 1980s NASP successfully promoted its training and credentialing guidelines, established its National Certification in School Psychology (NCSP) program, and initiated a process for approving training programs. It formalized efforts to better represent school psychology through the creation of the Governmental and Professional Relations Committee (GPRC) in Washington, DC, especially reauthorizations of special education legislation. The accomplishments of the GPRC set the stage for even stronger and more successful efforts in the next decade. The NASP's Assistance to States Committee fostered growth in the number and strength of state associations and their relationships with NASP. The 1980s was also a period when the NASP ventured beyond its professional resource publications (e.g., standards and training directories) to revenue-producing publications, among the most successful being *Best Practices in School Psychology*. Also established was the Children's Fund Auction held annually at the national convention.

1990–1999

In the 1990s, the association established an independent office in the Washington, DC, area to centralize operations and maximize its influence on national legislation affecting education and psychology. The office was the culmination of a series of earlier management efforts including part-time executive directors, a four-manager system from 1976 to 1987, and a contract with a multiassociation management firm in Washington, DC. The stability, visibility, and success of NASP's central office under the leadership of Executive Director, Susan Gorin cannot be overstated. The area of GPR continued to flourish, concentrating on federal legislation (e.g., Individuals With Disabilities Education Act [IDEA], Medicaid funding), and achieving nationwide recognition for its efforts in the area of school violence. Publications expanded in the 1990s as did membership and revenues. Also in this decade, NASP established its Minority Fellowship Program, a visible outcome of efforts to improve minority representation in school psychology since the 1970s.

NASP TODAY

With more than 22,000 members, the NASP is the largest organization whose efforts are directed solely to school psychology. The mission of NASP is to promote educationally and psychologically healthy environments for all children through research-based, effective programs that prevent problems, enhance independence, and promote optimal learning. This is accomplished through current research and training, advocacy, program evaluation, and professional service. Its policies represent the interests of all school psychologists irrespective of level of training and locus of practice. The NASP is not a union and does not engage in collective bargaining on behalf of its members.

Regular membership is available to persons directly involved in the field of school psychology. Student membership is available for those in training, and there is an associate membership available

for nonschool psychologists. Members receive the newsletter and journal, and may obtain other services, including professional liability insurance. The association offers a program of national certification, the requirements for which are consistent with its standards for training, credentialing, service provision, and ethics. More information and text of the Professional Conduct Manual of NASP (ethics code) are available at http://www.nasponline.org/pdf/ProfessionalCond.pdf.

The NASP convention, held either in the United States or Canada, is attended by more than 4,000 people annually. Workshops, special events, and other presentations are included that serve as continuing education activities for practitioners required to maintain state and/or NCSP credentials.

Policies of the NASP are enacted by a governance structure of nationally elected officers and state-elected delegates. Since its founding, representation has been based on geography and not on special interest groups within the field of school psychology. However, several interest groups organized around specific topics (e.g., neuropsychology) are sponsored by the NASP and often have their own listserv, newsletter, and convention programs. A comprehensive set of committees and boards interact with the governance structure and the Bethesda, Maryland, office staff to facilitate policy and program implementation. A nationwide network of state associations of school psychologists affiliates with the NASP and participates in the granting of annual awards, including the NASP School Psychologist of the Year.

Among its many publications are its newsletter, *Communiqué,* and its quarterly journal, *School Psychology Review.* Other publications include directories of training programs and credentialing requirements, code of ethics, standards documents, guides on special topics such as school violence, and books used in training and practice. Its Web site and listservs offer additional sources of information.

Governmental and professional relations continue to be a major activity area. Therein, the association collaborates with numerous related professional groups (e.g., American Psychological Association and the Council for Exceptional Children) to promulgate federal and state legislation and regulations that will enhance the practice of school psychology and improve the lives of children and youths, families, and educators. In the area of accreditation, the NASP collaborates with the National Council for

Timeline of the National Association of School Psychologists (NASP)

1969: NASP founded in St. Louis, Missouri; Pauline Alexander chosen as first President.

1972: First editions of both the NASP *Communiqué* and the *School Psychology Digest* (changed in 1980 to *School Psychology Review*) published. Training guidelines for school psychology programs and a *Survey Listing of Institutions Offering Graduate Training in School Psychology* published.

1977: First edition of NASP's *Directory of School Psychology* Training Programs in the United States and Canada published; edited by Doug Brown and John Lindstrom.

1978: Guidelines for credentialing, training, and provision of services approved. American Psychological Association (APA)/NASP Task Force established (later called Interorganizational Committee; disbanded in 2002).

1979: Membership roster is 5,141.

1980: Spring Hill Symposium held in Wayzata, Minnesota.

1981: Olympia Conference on the Future of School Psychology held in Oconomowoc, Wisconsin.

1982: Memphis City Schools Mental Health Center receives first NASP and Division of School Psychology-APA Joint Award for Excellence.

1985: First edition of *Best Practices in School Psychology* published by NASP, edited by Alex Thomas and Jeff Grimes.

1988: Training program approval process approved by National Council for Accreditation of Teacher Education. Revenue exceeds $1,000,000.

1989: Membership roster is 15,156.

1989: National Certification in School Psychology founded.

1990: NASP opens first independent office in Silver Spring, Maryland.

1992: Revenue exceeds $2,000,000.

1997: Governance structure and regions reorganized.

1999: Membership roster is 21,488.

2002: Chicago Convention sets record attendance of 4,397. Conference on the Future of School Psychology held at Indiana University-Bloomington.

---

the Accreditation of Teacher Education to approve those programs that meet NASP training standards.

The NASP collaborates with the Division of School Psychology of the American Psychological Association, although the two groups have sharp differences on matters of training and credentialing. The APA advocates for doctoral-level training and credentialing as school psychologists, with nondoctoral practitioners holding different titles and being under supervision. In contrast, the NASP represents both doctoral and nondoctoral school psychologists and advocates for their independent practice in any setting so long as their preparation is consistent with NASP standards. The APA and NASP relationship has been generally positive and has involved several joint efforts including the APA/NASP Task Force (1978–2002), the Spring Hill (1980) and Olympia (1981) Conferences, a Joint Award for District Program Excellence, and the 2002 Futures Conference.

Historical and contemporary information about the NASP is available in Fagan (1993), Fagan and Bose (2000), Fagan and colleagues (2000), Fagan and Wise (2000), as well as special issues of the *School Psychology Digest* (Vol. 8, No. 2) and *School Psychology Review* (Vol. 18, No. 2). Perspectives on the future of school psychology appear in special issues of *Psychology in the Schools* (2000, Vol. 37, No. 1), and *School Psychology Review* (2000, Vol. 29, No. 4).

—*Thomas K. Fagan*

See also American Psychological Association; Licensing and Certification in School Psychology; School Psychologist

REFERENCES AND FURTHER READING

Fagan, T. K. (1993). Separate but equal: School psychology's search for organizational identity. *Journal of School Psychology, 31,* 3–90.

Fagan, T., & Bose J. (2000). NASP: A profile of the 1990s. *Communiqué, 29*(2), 10–11.

Fagan, T. K., Gorin, S., & Tharinger, D. (2000). The National Association of School Psychologists and the Division of School Psychology-APA: Now and beyond. *School Psychology Review, 29*(4), 525–535.

Fagan, T. K., & Wise, P. S. (2000). *School psychology: Past, present, and future*. Bethesda, MD: National Association of School Psychologists.

NATIVE AMERICANS. *See* Race, Ethnicity, Class, and Gender; Consultation: Cross-Cultural; Cross-cultural Testing; Multicultural Education

NEUROPSYCHOLOGICAL ASSESSMENT

Neuropsychology is the study of brain–behavior relationships that use both neuropsychological and psychological theories and methodologies; it is the clinical application of brain–behavior relations. Neuropsychological assessment is the assessment of those individuals with congenital or acquired neurological disorders and/or diseases that result in impaired functions, as well as psychiatric illnesses.

Other related definitions state that neuropsychological assessment focuses on the study of various behavioral domains related to neurological structures, or *functional systems*, in the brain and the relationship between these behaviors and the integrity of the central nervous system (CNS) (Hynd & Hooper, 1992). Behavioral domains often included in these definitions are:

- Cognitive ability
- Sensory-motor ability
- Memory
- Attention
- Achievement
- Emotional functioning
- Executive functioning (e.g., the ability to control and maintain attention)

Neuropsychological assessment is not simply the inclusion of specific components in the assessment battery; it is the conceptualization and interpretation of the findings in conjunction with current knowledge of development and brain–behavior relations.

WHO CAN ETHICALLY CONDUCT NEUROPSYCHOLOGICAL ASSESSMENTS?

As with all psychological assessment, competency, as defined by training and experience, is needed to ethically conduct neuropsychological assessments. As with any specific measure, individuals may attain specialized training and supervised practice in administering any number of neuropsychological measures; the broader issue of competency relates to the practitioner's ability to then interpret these measures within the context of brain–behavior relations as opposed to a surface examination of obtained scores.

The level of competency and experience required before one can call oneself a "neuropsychologist" is defined by multiple professional boards. As recently as 2003, the specialty definition for clinical neuropsychology was approved by the APA Commission for the Recognition of Specialties and Proficiencies in Professional Psychology (CRSPPP). Multiple professional organizations (e.g., APA Division 40, International Neuropsychological Society) have concurred with these somewhat general requirements for competency. From the CRSPPP definition, competence includes specific knowledge and skills related to:

- Functional neuroanatomy and neuropathology
- Neurological and related disorders
- Child development
- Behavioral pathology
- Psychopharmacology
- Ontology of neuropsychological processes, as well as decrements in those same neuropsychological processes as a function of normal aging
- Psychophysiology and pathophysiology as related to various disorders

These competencies are in addition to the basic skills and knowledge incumbent of all practitioners including test administration and interpretation, sociocultural factors and their influence on behavior, and linkage between assessment and intervention strategies.

Although licensure is not specific to clinical neuropsychology, specialty status can be obtained from the American Board of Professional Psychology (ABPP). Eligibility requirements for a specialty in clinical neuropsychology include:

- A doctoral degree from a professional psychology program that is accredited by the APA or the Canadian Psychological Association (CPA), or that is listed in the publication *Doctoral Psychology Programs Meeting Designation Criteria*
- Licensure or certification as a psychologist in the state, province, or territory in which the psychologist practices
- A general internship that includes a special focus in neuropsychology *and* two years of postdoctoral training experience in clinical neuropsychology **or** successful completion of an approved clinical neuropsychology residency *and* (licensed) practice at the independent level *and* a variety of training and experiences that prepares the specialist in neuropsychology (e.g., basic neurosciences, psychopathology, assessment, intervention)

Beyond minimal competency, to be granted board certification in the specialty area by the ABPP, a psychologist must demonstrate advanced competencies required by the specialty.

CONTRIBUTIONS OF NEUROPSYCHOLOGICAL ASSESSMENT FOR YOUTHS IN EDUCATIONAL SETTINGS

Neuropsychological testing has become a popular topic when studying disabilities that affect children and their education. Historically, the assessment and identification of children for special education services in schools has consisted of cognitive ability and achievement tests as the primary assessment tools. One of the most common issues concerning neuropsychological testing in schools is the appropriateness and usefulness of neuropsychological tests in contributing additional information beyond that of traditional psychoeducational testing, as well as the validity and reliability of such measures, information gained, and the relevancy in creating intervention plans. Hynd and Hooper (1992, p. 3) asserted that from a biological and psychological perspective "better characterization of a disease or disorder will lead to a better understanding of etiology and the most effective means of differential treatment"; therefore, the most thorough assessment of a child's functioning would be the most beneficial.

Many authors have supported the need for neuropsychological testing in schools because of its

Table 1 Domains of Neuropsychological Assessment *(NEPSY)*

Domain	NEPSY Subtests
Auditory/ linguistic functioning	Auditory Attention and Response Set
	Phonological Processing
	Comprehension of Instructions
	Oromotor Sequences
Motor functioning	Finger Tapping
	Imitating Hand Positions
	Visuomotor Precision
	Manual Motor Sequences
	Design Copy
	Oromotor Sequences
Visual–spatial functioning	Design Copy
	Arrows
	Block Construction
	Route Finding
Sensory perception	Finger Discrimination
	Design Copy
Attention/ concentration	Auditory Attention and Response Set
	Visual Attention
	Statue
Learning/ memory	Memory for Faces
	Memory for Names
	Narrative Memory
	Sentence Repetition
	List Learning
Executive functions	Tower
	Statue
	Design Fluency
	Knock and Tap

usefulness in identifying individual strengths and weaknesses that lead to better intervention options and the creation of a more holistic view of a student's functioning. Hartlage and Williams (1990) further emphasized the importance and relevance of creating interventions based on neuropsychological assessment because of the critical changes in the central nervous system and frontal lobes (i.e., front portion of the brain) during childhood.

THE STRENGTHS AND WEAKNESSES OF MEASURES USED IN NEUROPSYCHOLOGICAL ASSESSMENT

As with any assessment, neuropsychological assessment should incorporate measures that are psychometrically sound, valid, and fair. Historically, measures used with children and youths have been based on neuropsychological measures of adults (Riccio & Wolfe, 2003). Further, child neuropsychology has been criticized for its failure to incorporate and understand measurement issues in test use and construction. Specific concerns have been raised on the availability of adequate normative data across the life span. A second concern is related to the need to establish reliability and validity of scores as well as their subsequent interpretation (Riccio & Reynolds, 1998). With developmental issues, a prominent focus of child assessment, the sensitivity of neuropsychological measures to neurobehavioral and neurodevelopmental differences in children is important. In recent years, there has been an increase in the number of studies to establish normative data and to investigate the validity and reliability of obtained scores. At the same time, at least one comprehensive battery was developed for children to obtain a developmental neuropsychological assessment (the NEPSY; Korkman & colleagues, 1998). Table 1 gives the tasks and domains covered by the *NEPSY* for children ages 3 to 12 years.

—*Cynthia A. Riccio and Kelly Pizzitola Jarratt*

See also Behavioral Assessment; Bias (Testing); Communication Disorders; Intelligence; Learning; Reliability; Social–Emotional Assessment

REFERENCES AND FURTHER READING

Hartlage, L. C., & Williams, B. L. (1990). Neuropsychological assessment in the childhood and adolescent years. In A. M. Horton Jr. (Ed.), *Neuropsychology across the life-span* (pp. 43–64). New York: Springer.

Hynd, G. W., & Hooper, S. R. (1992). *Neurological basis of childhood psychopathology.* Newbury Park, CA: Sage.

Korkman, M., Kirk, U., & Kemp, S. (1998) *NEPSY: A developmental neuropsychological assessment.* San Antonio, TX: Psychological Corporation.

Riccio, C. A., & Reynolds, C. R. (1998). Neuropsychological assessment of children. In M. Hersen & A. Bellack (Series Eds.) & C. R. Reynolds (Vol. Ed.), *Comprehensive clinical psychology* (Vol. 4, Assessment) (pp. 267–301). New York: Elsevier.

Riccio, C. A., & Wolfe, M. E. (2003). Neuropsychological perspectives on the assessment of children. In C. R. Reynolds & R. W. Kamphaus (Eds.), *Handbook of psychological and educational assessment of children: Intelligence, aptitude, and achievement* (2nd ed., pp. 305–324). New York: Guilford.

NO CHILD LEFT BEHIND ACT OF 2001, THE

The No Child Left Behind Act of 2001 (NCLB) was passed by the U.S. Congress with broad bipartisan support and signed by President George W. Bush on January 8, 2002. The most comprehensive education legislation in a generation, it is founded on the major themes of school choice, accountability through the implementation of high standards, public reporting of test results, research-based reforms for ineffective schools, and a guarantee of yearly progress. The law necessitates substantial changes in state assessment and accountability systems to ensure alignment with federal guidelines.

NCLB mandates that schools:

- Design curriculum and instruction to ensure that all students meet clear and challenging academic standards.
- Develop teacher preparation and professional development programs that ensure teachers are prepared to teach the standards.
- Conduct assessments that measure how well students are meeting the standards.
- Implement an accountability system determining whether students make adequate yearly progress toward meeting the standards.

A school demonstrates adequate yearly progress when at least 95% of the students (and 95% of each major subgroup of students) take the assessment and the proportion of students (in total and in each major subgroup) who demonstrate proficiency on state assessments of reading and mathematics meets or exceeds a state-established minimum.

NCLB holds each state, school district, and school accountable for the academic achievement of its students, with a particular emphasis on closing the achievement gap between minority and nonminority students and those living in low-wealth and high-wealth districts. This is partly accomplished by insisting that schools measure the performance of advantaged and disadvantaged subgroups of students, including those with limited English proficiency (flexibility in defining this group of students is given to the states), diverse racial/ethnic backgrounds, disabilities, and low income. NCLB also targets students who need reading assistance and those who are homeless, migrants, neglected, and/or delinquents. NCLB requires that schools develop plans to have highly qualified teachers teaching core academic subjects. Each school must take steps to ensure that in the 2006–2007 school year "poor and minority children are not taught at higher rates than other children by inexperienced, unqualified, or out-of-field teachers" (20 U.S.C. § 6301).

NCLB requires schools to develop challenging academic content standards and assessments. A central principle of the Act is that all students, including those with disabilities, learn more when they are challenged to meet high expectations for their performance. Schools are classified as in need of improvement when they have not made adequate yearly progress for at least two consecutive years in getting all students to achieve proficiency at the state's established standards. Each major subgroup of students must meet these criteria. Schools may also be allowed to meet another indicator of academic success established by the state as an alternative to the adequate yearly progress guideline. NCLB mandates that minimum percentages of all students in grades three through eight demonstrate proficiency in reading and math each year, increasing incrementally over a 12-year period until 100% of students are proficient by 2014. The U.S. Department of Education has considered allowing states to permit some students with significant disabilities to meet alternative standards for achievement, but it recommends that this group should not exceed 0.5% of the total student population.

There are significant consequences for schools that fail to make adequate yearly progress. Schools that fail to meet achievement goals for two consecutive years must:

- Develop a two-year school improvement plan with input from parents, staff, the school district, and outside experts.
- Notify parents of public school choice and provide transportation to an available school of choice.

- Obtain technical assistance geared at achieving school reform and provide professional development for teachers.

When schools in improvement status fail to make adequate yearly progress for a third consecutive year, they must also provide tutoring or other supplemental services to improve their students' academic achievement. Four years of failing to make adequate yearly progress demands that schools select at least one of the following options:

- Replace key staff.
- Adopt new, scientifically research-based curriculum and provide professional development.
- Decrease school management authority.
- Employ an outside consultant to advise school management.
- Extend the school day or school year.
- Restructure the internal school organization.

Schools are released from their improvement category status only when they meet adequate yearly progress for two of the next three years.

NCLB encourages substantial participation in schools by parents and families. Annual report cards measuring school performance and teacher quality are disseminated and include:

- Annual data about a school's level of student achievement compared to state standards
- Two-year trend data matched against state standards
- The percentage of students not tested and, therefore, not represented in the results
- Graduation and attendance rates
- The names of schools classified as being in need of improvement
- Teacher credentials and qualifications
- A comparison of academic achievement for all subgroups with the larger student body

Additionally, if a school has been determined to be in need of improvement, information must be made available about academic improvement plans developed to meet the standards of NCLB. School districts must also implement policies to allow students who attend persistently dangerous schools or become victims of violent crimes while at school, to attend a safe school within the district. Parents may opt to transfer their children out of a school designated as in need of improvement.

Like nearly all far-reaching education legislation at the federal level, NCLB has not been without its share of controversy. Advocates maintain that the Act will raise the academic performance of students via higher expectations, teachers with better training, and accountability for outcomes. Detractors describe the accountability provisions as penalties imposed on struggling schools and note that possible funding shortfalls in NCLB render the Act an unfunded mandate on states and their schools.

—Robert J. Kubick Jr. and Caven S. Mcloughlin

See also Academic Achievement; Individuals With Disabilities Education Act; School Reform

REFERENCES AND FURTHER READING

Mcloughlin, C. (2003, September). No child left behind primer for parents and educators: The federal 'No Child Left Behind Act of 2001.' *Communiqué, 32*(1), insert.

U.S. Department of Education. (2003). *No child left behind: A parents' guide.* Jessup, MD: Educational Publications Center.

U.S. Department of Education, Office of Elementary and Secondary Education. (2002). *No child left behind: A desktop reference.* Washington, DC: Author.

NORM-REFERENCED TESTS

Norm-referenced tests compare an individual's score to a representative sample of scores obtained from the same measure. The norm group is typically drawn from the general population. Tests are normed by selecting a group that is drawn from the general population and may be matched on variables such as gender, age, race/ethnicity, socioeconomic status, type of school, grade level, and others. An individual's score is then directly compared to the individual's norm group. The standardization of a norm-referenced test creates a scale in which an individual's score results in a ranking within the scores obtained from the norm group (Sattler, 2001). The score is determined to be high or low based on the scores obtained from the norm group.

In educational and school psychology, norm-referenced tests are an important tool that serves many functions. Norm-referenced tests may provide information that may not be obtained from other sources. Norm-referenced tests have been used to obtain information on intelligence, achievement, and behavior (Sattler, 2001). They may also be used to gather information on students' rankings on broad educational outcomes such as math calculation or reading comprehension. Additionally, information gathered from norm-referenced tests can be used to identify children with special needs. Thus, the scores derived from these tests may lead educators to place students with special services.

Witt and colleagues (1998) describe several advantages and disadvantages of using norm-referenced tests in educational settings. One advantage of norm-referenced tests is to help determine whether students require special services. Students may receive special services based on how their scores fall within their normative group. Another advantage of norm-referenced tests is that they do not usually require an extensive amount of time to administer. A third advantage is that scores derived from norm-referenced tests are typically easy to explain to parents. For example, most parents understand what it means for their child to perform at the 99th percentile. Of all individuals taking the test, their child performed better than 99% of the test takers. Finally, another advantage of norm-referenced tests is that there is an abundance of technical data supporting the tests' standardization, reliability, and validity.

There are some disadvantages of using norm-referenced tests in educational settings. One disadvantage is that the information gathered from a norm-referenced test is often too broad in scope and does not inform educators of students' specific weaknesses that may be in need of remediation. By the same token, information from norm-referenced tests does not inform students' educators of academic strengths. Another disadvantage of using norm-referenced tests is that the items on the tests are not typically derived from students' current curriculum. Therefore, the norm-referenced test is assessing broad educational knowledge, but not classroom content.

There are many examples of norm-referenced tests in current use in educational settings. One is the California Achievement Test (CAT), which is a group-administered achievement test frequently used by public school systems. The CAT's standardization sample consists of thousands of students drawn from across the nation. The CAT's standardization sample is stratified by grade level, type of school, geographic region, and community type.

—Jennifer T. Freeland

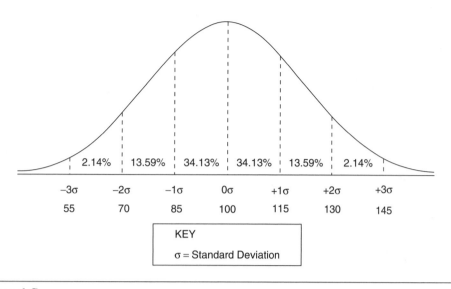

Figure 1   Normal Curve

See also Bias (Testing); Criterion-Referenced Assessment; Grade Equivalent Scores; Normal Distribution; Percentile Ranks; Reliability; Statewide Tests

REFERENCES AND FURTHER READING

Sattler, J. M. (2001*). Assessment of children: Cognitive applications* (4th ed.). La Mesa, CA: Jerome M. Sattler.

Witt, J. C., Elliott, S. N., Daly, E. J., Gresham, F. M., & Kramer, J. J. (1998). *Assessment of at-risk and special needs children* (2nd ed.). Boston: McGraw-Hill.

NORMAL DISTRIBUTION

The normal distribution is a hypothetical distribution of individual scores on any test. The normal distribution is a symmetrically shaped bell curve with the largest number of scores in the middle of the distribution and the smallest number of scores in the tails of the distribution (Figure 1). Because the normal curve is symmetrical, the measures of central tendency (i.e., the mean, median, and mode) will be the same. The mode is the most frequent score in the distribution, the mean is the average score in the distribution, and the median is the middlemost score or the midpoint of the distribution (Cohen & Swerdlik, 1999).

The normal distribution can be "divided into areas defined in standard deviation units" (Cohen & Swerdlik, 1999, p. 107). Figure 1 shows a hypothetical distribution of mathematics achievement test scores with a mean of 100 and a standard deviation of 15. In this example, 34.13% of all scores will fall between the mean and 1 standard deviation above or below the mean. Stated another way, approximately 34% of all mathematics achievement test scores will lie between the scores of 85 and 100, or 100 and 115. Continuing with this example, 13.59% and 2.14% of all scores will lie between 1 and 2, and 2 and 3 standard deviations above or below the mean, respectively. In other words, approximately 14% of all scores will fall between 70 and 85, or 115 and 130, and approximately 2% of all scores will lie between 55 and 70, or 130 and 145. These relationships between the percentages of test scores and standard deviation units are important when discussing test score interpretations.

—*Patricia A. Lowe*

See also Percentile Ranks; Standard Deviation

REFERENCES AND FURTHER READING

Cohen, R. J., & Swerdlik, M. E. (1999). *Psychological testing and assessment: An introduction to tests and measurement* (4th ed.). Mountain View, CA: Mayfield.

O

OBESITY IN CHILDREN

Childhood obesity is a serious problem in the United States because of its association with detrimental social and physical outcomes and its rising prevalence in recent years. Although several proposed methods for determining childhood obesity exist, the most widely used is to define childhood obesity as equal to or above the 95th percentile on the body mass index (BMI). Epidemiological studies employing the BMI method suggest that approximately 11% to 15% of children in the United States are obese. Estimates suggest that the prevalence of childhood obesity has risen by 4% over the previous decade (Centers for Disease Control and Prevention, 2004). Although obesity rates have increased for both sexes and all racial–ethnic groups studied, it appears that rates of obesity may be higher among minority groups, including African Americans and Mexican Americans, when compared to whites.

Childhood obesity has multiple possible causes, which can be best understood by considering the combined effect of societal, genetic, and behavioral factors. Two important trends in society may increase the risk for childhood obesity. The first issue deals with consumption. The Food Guide Pyramid, created by the U.S. Department of Agriculture (USDA) and supported by the Department of Health and Human Services (HHS), outlines the recommended intakes for five food groups, with foods listed from bottom to top in order of portion size. According to the pyramid, carbohydrates from grains should be eaten in the greatest quantity, followed by fruits and vegetables,

protein and dairy, and fats. Only 1% of children are meeting the nutritional intake recommendations from the Food Guide Pyramid, suggesting deficits in proper nutrition. This may be related to the availability and ingestion of convenient, inexpensive, flavorful, and high-fat foods.

The second societal trend is that children lead a more sedentary lifestyle, partly because of monetary cutbacks in America's physical education programs. Research supports the idea that childhood obesity is related to increased time engaged in sedentary activities such as television watching, video game playing, and working on computers. The research demonstrates that child obesity is linked to video games and the level of body fat is related to television watching. In addition, research indicates that the more time a child spends engaging in such sedentary activities the greater the likelihood that the child will be obese; and that the relation between lack of physical exercise and being overweight begins early, during the preschool years. Within this environment, certain children may be at particular risk for obesity. Genetic variables play a role in childhood obesity as these variables may influence metabolism, muscle characteristics, and taste preferences. For example, infants are born with a preference for salty and sweet tastes, and excess consumption of these preferred foods would likely lead to obesity (Birch & Fisher, 1998). Further, parental feeding behaviors affect children's eating habits. Once parents put their children on a solid food diet, they have the ability to create food preferences in their children. For example, children whose diet is greatly restricted are more likely to eat large portions of those forbidden foods when given the freedom of choice, creating a possible future pattern of overeating (Birch & Fisher, 1998).

Childhood obesity is associated with significant risk for health and psychological problems. A review of relevant literature reveals that obese children are more likely to develop hypertension, diabetes, and sleep apnea (Dietz, 1998). Twenty percent of overweight children have two or more of these problems. Further, being obese as a child greatly increases one's likelihood of being obese as an adult; the probability increases with the severity of the childhood overweight condition, and leads to future health threats including possible increased risk for coronary heart disease, colon caner, and diabetes, as well as an associated increased risk of mortality (Dietz, 2002). Obesity in children can also carry a significant risk of social discrimination and psychological problems. Children tend to equate obesity with laziness and sloppiness and view obese children as less attractive, less intelligent, and less popular (Birch & Fisher, 1998). Further, obese children tend to suffer from weight-related teasing by peers. Perhaps in part because of social discrimination, obese children may experience low self-esteem and body dissatisfaction, and they are more likely to develop body image distortion and eating disorders. Overall, severely obese children have a lower quality of life than their normal-weight peers, comparable to children diagnosed with cancer.

There are many different approaches to treating childhood obesity, including modification of eating and exercise behavior. The goal of any nutrition program is to have the child ingest fewer calories than he/she expends each day while following current U.S. dietary guidelines. In contrast to adults, children's eating patterns may be more amenable to change. Most studies have focused on decreasing caloric intake and increasing healthy food consumption. Although exercise programs alone are ineffective, they may increase weight loss when combined with decreased caloric intake. While there is no clear answer to the best exercise approach, lifestyle exercise seems to be superior to structured aerobic activity. Incorporating exercise into children's daily routine, such as taking the stairs instead of the elevator, or engaging in hobbies that require physical activity, may be more effective at producing long-term results. In addition, research indicates that incorporating behavior therapy techniques such as self-monitoring (e.g. keeping a daily food diary) and parental positive reinforcement (e.g.,

praising healthy food choices) increases weight loss. Based on literature reviews demonstrating that weight loss programs for children are most effective when parents are highly involved, it has been recommended that parents take a leading role in childhood obesity treatment and prevention (Zametkin & colleagues, 2003). A number of specific parental skills have been proposed as part of a family-based intervention for child obesity including both the parents and child taking responsibility for child's food choices, preparing healthy meals, engaging in problem solving when faced with setbacks, and engaging in physical activities as a family (Golan & Weizman, 2001).

Because obese children can be greatly affected by their social environment, it is also important to incorporate schools into children's weight-loss programs— recent research shows the added efficacy of adult involvement (Goldfield & Epstein, 2002). Trained individuals in the schools can implement enjoyable exercise programs that children will want to continue after treatment has ended. In addition, schools can incorporate nutrition programs teaching children proper eating habits.

The school psychologist can also take an active role in the assessment and treatment of childhood obesity. The school psychologist should identify the cultural and societal influences, such as the media and the child's family, that affect the child's eating patterns and beliefs about food; begin to educate the child on proper nutrition, exercise, and self-acceptance; and then help the child set reasonable goals for weight loss. By networking with other school psychologists, nutritionists, and health educators, a school psychologist can gain comprehensive knowledge on weight loss and maintenance practices. She or he should also address the issues that arise from weight-related teasing by peers, and possibly engage in role playing to educate the child on how to cope with such situations. Thus, the most effective treatment of obesity in children may be a combination of parental and school-guided behavioral programs focused on decreasing caloric intake and establishing a healthy diet, while incorporating physical activity into the child's life. With proper intervention, it may be possible to decrease the growing childhood obesity trend.

—*Jessica S. Benas, Elizabeth C. Scafidi, and Michael A. Friedman*

See also Eating Disorders; Pica; Prevention; Self-Management

REFERENCES AND FURTHER READING

Birch, L. L., & Fisher, J. O. (1998). Development of eating behaviors among children and adolescents. *Pediatrics, 101,* 539–549.

Centers for Disease Control and Prevention. (2004). *Defining overweight and obesity.* Retrieved May 10, 2004, from http://www.cdc.gov/nccdphp/dnpa/obesity/defining.htm

Dietz, W. H. (1998). Health consequences of obesity in children and adolescents. In C. Fairburn & K. Brownell (Eds.), *Eating disorders and obesity* (2nd ed., pp. 473–476). New York: Guilford.

Dietz, W. H. (2002). Medical consequences of obesity in children and adolescents. In C. Fairburn & K. Brownell (Eds.), *Eating disorders and obesity* (2nd ed. pp. 473–476). New York: Guilford.

Golan, M., & Weizman, A. (2001). Familial approach to the treatment of childhood obesity: Conceptual model. *Journal of Nutrition Education, 33,* 102–107.

Goldfield, G. S., & Epstein, L. H. (2002). Management of obesity in children. In C. Fairburn & K. Brownell (Eds.), *Eating disorders and obesity* (2nd ed. pp. 573–577). New York: Guilford.

Zametkin, A. J., Zoon, C. K., Klein, H. W., & Munson, S. (2004). Psychiatric aspects of child and adolescent obesity: A review of the past 10 years. *Journal of the American Academy of Child and Adolescent Psychiatry, 43,* 134–150.

OBSESSIVE–COMPULSIVE DISORDER

Obsessive–compulsive disorder (OCD) is a debilitating disorder characterized by recurrent obsessions and/or compulsions that cause significant impairment in an individual's daily functioning (American Psychiatric Association [APA], 2000). Adults diagnosed with OCD often realize that their obsessions or compulsions are excessive or unreasonable; however, children with OCD may not be able make this determination. The individual's obsessions and/or compulsions cause significant distress and can significantly interfere with social, school, and occupational activities, and relationships. Given the intrusive nature of OCD's symptomatology and the distress that the disorder causes, it is imperative that school psychologists are aware of the nature of the disorder and how to accurately diagnose and treat children with OCD.

OCD can occur in children as young as 4 years old (Chansky, 2000), with a mean age of onset occurring between 6 and 11 years of age and bimodal peaks in early childhood and early adolescence (Piacentini & Bergman, 2000). More than a million children in the United States suffer from OCD (Chansky, 2000),

and OCD has a lifelong prevalence estimated at 1% (Flament & colleagues, 1988). Pauls & colleagues (1995) found that 80% of adults with OCD identify the onset of symptoms before the age of 18 years. Rates of OCD in individuals vary from study to study; however, it is generally accepted in the literature (Snider & Swedo, 2000) that OCD affects 2% to 3% of the total population. It is estimated that 1 in 200 youngsters experience diagnosable OCD (March & colleagues, 1995). However, many researchers conclude that OCD is underreported in children and youth because of an inability to properly recognize and diagnose the disorder. OCD is more common in boys than girls; however, by adulthood, OCD occurs equally across the sexes. Developmentally, most children experience minor obsessive–compulsive symptoms as part of the normal process of achieving mastery and control over their environment. However, the difference between normative obsessions or compulsions and pathological symptoms is that OCD symptoms produce "dysfunction rather than mastery" (March, 1995).

OCD is best conceptualized as a neurobehavioral disorder (March & Mulle, 1998). The etiology of OCD is complex, with evidence supporting a genetic component (Pauls & colleagues, 1995), faulty circuitry between the basal ganglia to the cortex (Rauch & colleagues, 1994), and neurotransmitter and neuroendocrine abnormalities (Swedo & Rapoport, 1990). Additionally, in a subgroup of children with OCD, symptoms may develop or be exacerbated by the presence of group A β-hemolytic streptococcus (GABHS) infection. This onset is known as "pediatric autoimmune neuropsychiatric disorder associated with streptococcus" (PANDAS) (March & Mulle, 1998). Research supports both biological and neurobehavioral conceptualizations of the disorder.

Children suffering from OCD often experience difficulties in familial, social, academic, and normal-life functioning. Students may exhibit academic difficulties resulting from perfectionism and slowness in completing scholastic assignments, or tests (March & Mulle, 1998). Children may also find it difficult to function effectively in socially complex environments where they might be ridiculed for being seen performing embarrassing compulsions. Youths with OCD often feel that they need to hide their compulsions, creating both physical and emotional isolation from their peers and family.

Several researchers have documented the most common obsessions and compulsions in youths with

OCD. The most common obsessions in children and adolescents are related to:

- Germs and/or contamination
- Fears of harm to self and/or others
- Symmetry urges (i.e., needing to line up objects so they are even or needing body movements to be even on both right and left sides)
- Religiosity/scrupulosity

The most common compulsions in children and adolescents are (Chansky, 2000; Snider & Swedo, 2000; Swedo & colleagues, 1989):

- Washing and/or cleaning
- Checking and/or repeating
- Counting
- Touching
- Ordering

Another complicating factor for youths with OCD is the presence of other comorbid conditions. Additional mood, tic, disruptive behavior, and learning disorders are commonly found in both clinical and epidemiological samples of youths with OCD (Flament & colleagues, 1988; Riddle & colleagues, 1990). In fact, comorbidity may occur in up to 80% of childhood cases (Piacentini & Bergman, 2000). The presence of comorbidity often complicates accurate diagnosis and treatment. For example, symptoms of distractibility might be caused by inattention related to obsessions and/or mental rituals instead of inattention associated with attention deficit hyperactivity disorder. Accurate diagnosis is critical so that youths with OCD can receive appropriate and prompt treatment.

School psychologists and teachers can play a major role in the identification, assessment, and treatment of obsessive–compulsive disorder (Adams & colleagues, 1994). Students with OCD may experience problems navigating demands at schools. OCD symptoms may include:

- Rewriting and/or rereading
- Erasing and/or redoing assignments
- Excessive hand washing
- Excessive worries about schoolwork

These symptoms detract from successful academic and social tasks that the school environment requires. Effective diagnosis includes the use of diagnostic interviews—such as the Anxiety Disorders Interview for the *DSM-IV* (Silverman & Albano, 1997) or the Children's Yale-Brown Obsessive Compulsive Scale (Goodman & colleagues, 1989)—and systematic behavioral observations.

Depending upon the severity of the OCD symptoms, cognitive–behavior therapy (CBT) with or without medication management is the best course of treatment for youths with OCD (Snider & Swedo, 2000). CBT is a treatment approach that uses performance-based procedures and cognitive intervention strategies to create changes in thinking, feeling, and behavior (Kendall, 2000). One component of CBT, called "exposure and ritual prevention," gradually exposes the youth with OCD to his or her feared stimuli, while systematically helping the youth refrain from engaging in the OCD rituals. Whether CBT alone or in combination with medication is used to treat OCD, it is critical that the school psychologist, teachers, parents, and the student are all involved with the treatment plan. A comprehensive, ecological treatment plan including school-based consultation that augments traditional cognitive behavioral therapy for OCD may increase family and academic functioning, reduce stress, and expedite the effects of cognitive–behavioral therapy.

OCD is a disorder of childhood and adolescence that causes a great deal of distress for the youth and his or her family. Additionally, given that OCD's symptomatology often manifests in the school setting, it is crucial that school psychologists and school personnel are aware of the nature and course of the disorder. School psychologists are in a unique position to aid in accurate diagnosis and treatment of youths with OCD.

—*Susan M. Swearer and Kisha M. Haye*

See also Comorbidity; Counseling; *DSM-IV*; Interviewing; Psychopathology in Children

REFERENCES AND FURTHER READING

Adams, G. B., Waas, G. A., March, J. S., & Smith, M. C. (1994). Obsessive compulsive disorder in children and adolescents: The role of the school psychologist in identification, assessment, and treatment. *School Psychology Quarterly, 9*(4), 274–294.

American Psychiatric Association. (2000). *Diagnostic and statistical manual of mental disorders* (4th ed., text rev.). Washington, DC: Author.

Chansky, T. E. (2000). *Freeing your child from obsessive compulsive disorder.* New York: Crown.

Flament, M. F., Whitaker, A., Rapoport, J. L., Davies, M., Berg, C. Z., Kalikow, K., et al. (1988). Obsessive compulsive disorder in adolescence: An epidemiological study. *Journal of the American Academy of Child and Adolescent Psychiatry, 27*(6), 764–771.

Goodman, W. K., Price, L. H., Rasmussen, S. A., Mazure, C., Fleischmann, R. L., Hill, C. L., et al. (1989). The Yale-Brown Obsessive Compulsive Scale: I. Development, use, and reliability. *Archives of General Psychiatry, 46*(11), 1006–1011.

Kendall, P. C. (Ed.). (2000). *Child and adolescent therapy: Cognitive-behavioral procedures.* New York: Guilford.

March, J. S. (1995). Cognitive-behavioral psychotherapy for children and adolescents with OCD: A review and recommendations for treatment. *Journal of the American Academy of Child and Adolescent Psychiatry, 34*(1), 7–18.

March, J. S., Leonard, H. L., & Swedo, S. E. (1995). Pharmacotherapy of obsessive-compulsive disorder. In M. Riddle (Ed.), *Child and adolescent psychiatric clinics of North America* (pp. 217–236). Philadelphia: WB Saunders.

March, J. S., & Mulle, K. (1998). *OCD in children and adolescents: A cognitive behavioral treatment manual.* New York: Guilford.

Pauls, D. L., Alsobrook, J. P., Goodman, W., Rasmussen, S., & Leckman, J. F. (1995). A family study of obsessive-compulsive disorder. *American Journal of Psychiatry, 152,* 76–84.

Piacentini, J., & Bergman, R. L., (2000). Obsessive-compulsive disorder in children. *The Psychiatric Clinics of North America, 23,* 519–533.

Rauch, S. L., Jenike, M. A., Alpert, N. M., Baer, L., Breiter, H. C., Savage, C. R., et al. (1994). Regional cerebral blood flow measured during symptom provocation in obsessive-compulsive disorder using oxygen 15-labeled carbon dioxide and positron emission tomography. *Archives of General Psychiatry, 51*(1), 62–70.

Riddle, M. A., Scahill, L., King, R., Hardin, M. T., Towbin, K. E., Ort, S. I., et al. (1990). Obsessive-compulsive disorder in children and adolescents: Phenomenology and family history. *Journal of the American Academy of Child and Adolescent Psychiatry, 29*(5), 766–772.

Silverman, W., & Albano, A. (1997). *Anxiety disorders interview schedule for DSM-IV: Parent & child versions (ADIS-P & C).* Albany, NY: Graywind.

Snider, L. A., & Swedo, S. E. (2000). Pediatric obsessive-compulsive disorder. *Journal of the American Medical Association, 284,* 3104–3106.

Swedo, S., & Rapoport, J. (1990). Neurochemical and neuroendocrine considerations of obsessive-compulsive disorder in childhood. In W. Deutsch, A. Weizman, & R. Weizman (Eds.), *Application of basic neuroscience to child psychiatry* (pp. 275–284). New York: Plenum.

Swedo, S. E., Rapoport, J. L., Leonard, H., Lenane, M., & Cheslow, D. (1989). Obsessive-compulsive disorder in children and adolescents: Clinical phenomenology of 70 consecutive cases. *Archives of General Psychiatry, 46*(4), 335–341.

OPERANT CONDITIONING. *See*
BEHAVIOR; CONDITIONING: CLASSICAL AND OPERANT

OPPOSITIONAL DEFIANT DISORDER

Oppositional defiant disorder (ODD) is a childhood disorder that is characterized by undercontrolled, noncompliant, defiant, and socially disruptive behavior. ODD is classified as a disruptive behavior disorder along with attention deficit hyperactivity disorder (ADHD) and conduct disorder (CD). The *Diagnostic and Statistical Manual of Mental Disorders, Fourth Edition-Text Revision* (*DSM-IV-TR*) specifies that youth must exhibit four of the following behaviors for at least six months for a diagnosis of ODD to be made (American Psychiatric Association, 2000):

- Loses temper
- Argues with adults
- Defies or refuses to comply with rules or adult's requests
- Annoys others deliberately
- Blames others for mistakes
- Is easily annoyed by others
- Is often angry and resentful
- Is often spiteful and vindictive

The *DSM-IV-TR* also specifies that a diagnosis should only be made if oppositional and defiant behavior significantly impairs an individual's academic, social, and adaptive functioning.

According to the *DSM-IV-TR*, ODD typically manifests itself before the age of 8 and affects anywhere from 2% to 16% of youth, depending on the diagnostic tools used (American Psychiatric Association, 2000). Before puberty, the *DSM-IV-TR* reports higher prevalence rates of ODD in boys than girls; however, it is presumed that gender rates are equal after puberty (American Psychiatric Association, 2000). Research has not uncovered a direct link between any one risk factor and ODD, rather the interaction between multiple factors most likely influences the development of this disorder (Burke & colleagues, 2002). The search for causes of ODD is further complicated by the fact that most research has focused on aggression, delinquency, and CD rather than on ODD. Social and biological influences that continue to be explored as possible links to ODD include temperament of children and parents (Barkley, 1997; Burke & colleagues, 2002), inconsistent and harsh discipline (Frick & colleagues, 1992), response to chronic illness (Beratis, 1993), neuroanatomy, and the under-arousal of the autonomic nervous system (Burke & colleagues, 2002).

Research shows that ODD is frequently accompanied by other disruptive behavior disorders (e.g., ADHD, CD), developmental disorders (e.g., mental retardation), and affective disorders (e.g., depression). Wenning and colleagues (1993) found that 79% of their subjects originally diagnosed with ODD also had a diagnosis of depression or developmental disorder, leaving only 21% of their sample with a sole diagnosis of ODD. Some comorbid conditions that frequently occur with ODD include: ADHD; reading, writing, and math disorders; expressive and receptive language disorders; and depression. The comorbidity of ODD with other disorders increasingly complicates the accurate assessment and delivery of treatment to children with ODD because practitioners and teachers may unintentionally overlook affective or developmental disorders because they are focused on the overt, disruptive symptoms of ODD. Because hostile, defiant, and negative behaviors are challenging and frustrating to parents and teachers, there is a tendency to focus on these behaviors to the exclusion of social, academic, and language deficits. Teachers may attribute failure to comply with commands to the student's oppositional nature, rather than considering the possibility that a student may have difficulty in receptive language.

A thorough understanding of ODD by parents and professionals is critical because accurate diagnosis that leads to effective early intervention can diminish the negative impact this disorder has on a student's academic, adaptive, and social skills.

Another salient reason for early intervention is that approximately 25% of youths diagnosed with ODD will later develop CD (Lahey & colleagues, 1992), another disruptive behavior disorder characterized by increased physical aggression and more serious rule violations that infringe upon the basic rights of others.

DIAGNOSIS OF OPPOSITIONAL DEFIANT DISORDER AND THE ROLE OF THE SCHOOL PSYCHOLOGIST

An accurate diagnosis of ODD can be complicated by a variety of issues. First, ODD often occurs with other disorders and conditions. Consequently, school psychologists should always conduct a comprehensive evaluation by using multiple methods and informants to account for the possibility of comorbid conditions. Evaluators should not only explore the behavioral excesses characteristic of ODD, but they should also assess the student's academic, language, and social skills with appropriate measures. Students, parents, and teachers should also be interviewed in order to obtain factual information as well as to assess each informant's preferences for intervention and their motivation to participate in a treatment program. Although the vast majority of research has been conducted on males, it is important for practitioners to remember not to overlook females because they may also present with ODD.

A second issue that arises when diagnosing ODD is that some defiance and noncompliance are developmentally appropriate for preschoolers and adolescents as they seek to establish autonomy from their caregivers. As a result, it is important for school psychologists to have a thorough understanding of child and adolescent development so that developmentally appropriate defiance is not misconstrued as aberrant behavior. Determining whether the student's behavior exceeds age-appropriate norms may be accomplished by using comprehensive child behavior rating scales. By conducting classroom observations, school psychologists may directly compare the student to his or her classmates in terms of on-task behavior and the length of time it takes to respond to requests.

An assessment should not only determine whether a student meets the criteria for ODD, it should also provide information that will guide the school psychologist, teachers, and parents in developing an effective treatment plan. Conducting a functional assessment and analysis of the student's disruptive behavior allows school psychologists to confirm specific hypotheses about the student's behavior and, in turn, develop a treatment plan that specifically addresses the individual's problematic behavior. Possible reasons for a student's oppositional behavior may be to avoid an unpleasant task or to obtain attention from peers, parents, and/or teachers. An assessment of ODD should always involve gathering information about a student's strengths because the strengths can be used to develop effective interventions.

TREATMENT FOR OPPOSITIONAL DEFIANT DISORDER

A variety of treatments for disruptive behavior disorders have been described in the literature. Parent training programs have demonstrated improvements in

ODD symptoms by focusing on teaching parents effective methods for managing their children's behavior (Barkley, 1997; Forehand & McMahon, 1981; Patterson, 1974; Webster-Stratton, 1984). Other school-based interventions that have demonstrated success with ODD include social skills training, problem-solving training, effective classroom management, self-management training (managing one's own behavior), and home–school communication. Youths with ODD may also be deemed eligible for special education services under the category of a behavioral disorder (BD) in states that have this eligibility category, or other health impaired (OHI), learning disabilities (LD), or emotional disturbance (ED) if the youth has a comorbid condition. While all of the interventions described have some merit, Burke and colleagues (2002) emphasized that the most successful interventions for youths with disruptive behavior disorder are multifaceted and address multiple risk factors. School psychologists may better serve youths with ODD and their families by consulting with the families and teachers about treatment strategies, facilitating home–school communication, and providing training for parents and students.

—*Melinda Russell Stamp*

See also Aggression in Schools; Attention Deficit Hyperactivity Disorder; Counseling; Depression; *DSM-IV*; Parenting; Psychopathology in Children

REFERENCES AND FURTHER READING

American Psychiatric Association. (2000). *Diagnostic and statistical manual of mental disorders.* (4th ed., text rev.). Washington, DC: Author.

Barkley, R. A. (1997). *Defiant children: A clinician's manual for assessment and parent training.* New York: Guilford.

Beratis, S. (1993). Psychosocial status in pre-adolescent children with β-thalassaemia. *Journal of Psychosomatic Research, 37*(3), 271–279.

Burke, J. D., Loeber, R., & Birmaher, B. (2002). Oppositional defiant disorder and conduct disorder: A review of the past 10 years, part II. *Journal of the American Academy of Child and Adolescent Psychiatry, 41*(11), 1275–1293.

Forehand, R. L., & McMahon, R. J. (1981). *Helping the noncompliant child: A clinician's guide to parent training.* New York: Guilford.

Frick, P. J., Lahey, B. B., Loeber, R., Stouthamer-Loeber, M. G., & Hanson, K. (1992). Familial risk factors to oppositional defiant disorder and conduct disorder: Parental psychopathology and maternal parenting. *Journal of Consulting and Clinical Psychology, 60*(1), 49–55.

Lahey, B. B., Loeber, R., Quay, H. C., Frick, P. J., & Grimm, J. (1992). Oppositional defiant and conduct disorders: Issues to be resolved for *DSM-IV. Journal of the American Academy of Child and Adolescent Psychiatry, 31*(3), 539–546.

Patterson, G. R. (1974). Interventions for boys with conduct problems: Multiple settings, treatments, and criteria. *Journal of Consulting and Clinical Psychology, 42,* 471–481.

Webster-Stratton, C. (1984). Randomized trial of two parent-training programs for families with conduct-disordered children. *Journal of Consulting and Clinical Psychology, 52,* 666–678.

Wenning, K., Nathan, P., & King, S. (1993). Mood disorders in children with oppositional defiant disorder: A pilot study. *American Journal of Orthopsychiatry, 63*(2), 295–299.

ORGANIZATIONAL CONSULTATION AND DEVELOPMENT

Organization development (OD) is a term that refers to a planned and sustained long-term effort to improve the ability of an organization to achieve its self-identified goals within an atmosphere that promotes the growth and well-being of its individual members. Organizations that are successful in attaining both of these elements are thought of as "healthy organizations." Organizational consultation is the process through which one or more professionals facilitates the efforts of an organization to achieve a healthy state.

Organization development is relevant to organizations of many different kinds, including companies, schools, professional associations, and community agencies. Although OD frequently focuses on an entire organization, it also could be used to address the effectiveness of major units within an organization (e.g., a company's personnel department or the staff development office for a school district).

OD is a relatively young field, with some of the earliest efforts not emerging until after World War II. In his seminal article, "Toward a General Theory for the Behavioral Sciences," Miller (1955) proposed a systems theory as a way to understand the interconnectedness of all living things. In the years since Miller first advanced the idea, systems theory has come to serve as a cornerstone for the field of organization development. From this perspective, an organization is viewed as being composed of parts that are organized in a purposeful way in order to achieve its goals. There is thought to be reciprocal influence among the parts on each other, as well as on the organization as a whole, and vice versa (i.e., the organization also influences each of its individual parts). Further, even the organization is thought to be one part of a larger system that it influences and by which it, in turn, is also influenced. The systems theory perspective provides a helpful framework for understanding an organization, how it functions, and how changes in any element of the organization impact other elements and the organization as a whole.

The earliest applications of organization development were found in military and industrial settings, but did not appear in schools until the early 1960s. However, the use of OD to improve the effectiveness of schools has increased dramatically since the publication of *A Nation at Risk* (National Commission on Excellence in Education, 1983), which was largely responsible for launching the current "school reform" movement. Moreover, state and federal legislation that both mandate accountability for student academic achievement (as demonstrated through high-stakes testing) and emphasize the use of evidence-based practices, meaningful parental involvement in educational decision making, the use of problem solving as a conceptual framework for the organization, and delivery of student services and other major changes in education. This zeitgeist has intensified the need for individuals who are skilled in organization change methods.

Historically, OD has not been a professional service emphasized by school psychologists and has not been emphasized during their graduate-level training. However, preparation in this area is now required in many programs and by national training standards. In addition, school psychologists have become involved in school change initiatives in part because of their strong foundation in the behavioral sciences and their understanding of the ecology of schools from a systems perspective. School psychologists typically engage in organization development through one of two avenues. They are sometimes hired by schools or other organizations as consultants for the specific purpose of engaging in organization development. More likely, they are hired as school psychologists—more than 80% of schools employ school psychologists (Curtis & colleagues, 2002)—and organization development is one of many professional services they provide.

In many cases, the initiation of OD results from the perceived need and desire of the organization to address a specific problem that it is confronting. However, while the short-term goal of OD may be the reduction or elimination of a specific problem, the primary purpose of intervention is to increase the problem-solving capacity of the organization. The goal of the organizational consultant is to enhance the ability of the organization to analyze and effectively address whatever problems it faces. However, while increased overall problem-solving capacity is the primary goal, "it typically is the precipitating problem that provides an opportunity to engage in a longer, sustained effort for system-level change" (Curtis & Stollar, 2002, p. 227).

Curtis and Stollar (2002) identify a number of skills that they contend are essential for the organizational consultant, beginning with effective communication skills. "The ability to listen, ask open-ended questions, paraphrase, and summarize and synthesize information, all within a nonjudgmental climate, are especially important" (p. 226). They suggest that these skills become even more critical for school psychologists who are engaging in change efforts from within the organization because other members of the group may resist or resent colleagues whose behaviors alter their collegial relationship. In other words, some behaviors (e.g., giving the group feedback about being off task or not following procedures) could result in perception of the individual as acting like she or he is an expert. Curtis and Stollar also identify collaborative planning and problem-solving skills and group process skills as essential for school psychologists who wish to engage in organizational change efforts. In addition to these skills, external consultants also need skills that would enable them to enter and to terminate the consultative relationship effectively.

Most researchers and authors in OD emphasize that the primary responsibility for meaningful and lasting change lies with members of the organization rather than with the organizational consultant. Therefore, the role of an external consultant is primarily that of facilitator of the efforts of organizational members. "The role of the system consultant is to facilitate the efforts of the group to achieve the goals that the group has decided upon, in a manner that the group chooses" (Curtis & Stollar, 2002, p. 226). "The OD consultant's role is to help employees create their own solutions, systems, and concepts" (Harvey & Brown, 2001, p. 106). However, the facilitative role of the external consultant may be changing somewhat. Harvey and Brown (2001) suggest, "The OD practitioners of today are no longer just process facilitators, but are expected to know something about strategy, structure, reward systems, corporate culture, leadership, human resource development, and the nature of the business of the client organization" (p. 105).

The rapidly changing nature of today's world and the demands and stresses that such changes place on organizations such as schools increase the importance of organizational consultation and development. Professionals with the knowledge and skills needed to engage in organization development will very likely be increasing in demand as resources to assist organizations in facing new challenges.

—Michael J. Curtis

See also Careers in School Psychology; Consultation: Behavioral; Consultation: Conjoint Behavioral; Consultation: Ecobehavioral; Consultation: Mental Health; Ethical Issues in School Psychology; Evidence-Based Interventions; Program Evaluation; School Psychologist; School Reform

REFERENCES AND FURTHER READING

Curtis, M. J., Grier, J. E. C., Abshier, D. W., Sutton, N. T., & Hunley, S. A. (2002). School psychology: Turning the corner into the twenty-first century. *Communiqué, 30*(8), 1–5.

Curtis, M. J., & Stollar, S. A. (2002). Best practices in system-level change. In A. Thomas & J. Grimes (Eds.), *Best practices in school psychology: IV* (pp. 223–234). Bethesda, MD: National Association of School Psychologists.

Harvey, D., & Brown, D. R. (2001). An experiential approach to organization development (6th ed.). Upper Saddle River, NJ: Prentice-Hall.

Miller, J. G. (1955). Toward a general theory for the behavioral sciences. *American Psychologist, 10*(9), 513–531.

National Commission on Excellence in Education. (1983). *A nation at risk*. Washington, DC: U.S. Department of Education.

OTITIS MEDIA

Otitis media (OM) is an inflammation of the middle ear that can occur in one or both ears. It is the most common disease of childhood, after respiratory tract infections. OM is often caused by a buildup of infectious fluid within the eustachian tube, a slender canal in the inner ear. Symptoms of acute OM can include complaints of pain or tugging at the ear (in nonverbal children), a pus-like ear discharge, irritability, fever, poor appetite, and short-term hearing loss. OM with effusion indicates the presence of a watery or mucus-like fluid in the ear without symptoms of infection (i.e., complaints of pain, irritability, etc.). Instead, it is characterized by mild to moderate hearing loss and possible reports of an itchy feeling deep within the ear; OM with effusion is common in children recovering from acute OM.

INCIDENCE

Almost all children have acute OM at some time, but between 5% and 20% of children have chronic and recurrent OM with effusion. OM is most prevalent between the ages of 3 months and 3 years and is the most frequent reason for clinic visits in children younger than 15 years of age. Approximately 66% of children have at least one OM episode by the age of 3; 50% have two or more episodes of OM. The younger a child is when the first incidence of OM occurs, the more likely the child is to experience recurrent episodes. OM is fairly common during winter months because of the increased number of people suffering from colds and upper respiratory illnesses. Children with Down syndrome, cleft palate, or other craniofacial anomalies are particularly at risk for OM because of the structure of their eustachian tubes. Approximately 50% of all children with a cleft palate experience recurrent OM. Additional risk factors include family history, bottle-fed as an infant, exposure to second-hand cigarette smoke, pollution, high allergen levels, and day-care settings.

DIAGNOSIS AND TREATMENT

Diagnosis of OM can only be made by visual inspection of the ear by a medical professional. Treatment consists of a course of antibiotics, which generally relieves symptoms within 48 to 72 hours; approximately 50% cases clear up within 3 weeks. Persistent cases may require additional, extended medical treatments. A follow-up examination of the ear by a physician is necessary to confirm complete resolution of the condition and reduce OM recurrence. When OM is recurrent (i.e., three or more acute infections within 6 months), tubes may be surgically inserted into the ear to facilitate fluid drainage and avoid accumulation. The tubes typically remain in place for 6 to 12 months. It is important to monitor treatment adherence to ensure the child's complete recovery. It is also recommended that any child having recurrent OM with effusion be assessed by an audiologist and a speech pathologist. Additional suggestions for intervention include minimizing exposure to harmful environmental factors such as cigarette smoke, pollution, allergens, and situations in which there is an increased risk for illness or infection (e.g., day-care settings). Parents also should be instructed against bottle-feeding while the child is lying down. Medical personnel may also wish to disseminate preventative care information such as advocating the use of ear plugs while swimming.

OUTCOMES

Complications from recurrent or long-term OM may lead to damage of the middle ear structures; irreversible hearing loss; and, in rare instances, meningitis, encephalitis, and hydrocephalus. Children who sustain intermittent hearing loss as a result of OM may develop difficulty discriminating sounds, which can lead to auditory processing and learning deficits. Children who develop permanent hearing loss can be at further risk for developing speech and language impairments, attention difficulties, and learning difficulties. The school psychologist can be instrumental in identifying children with OM who are at risk for developing auditory processing and/or learning problems, and facilitating their assessment. Specific classroom management strategies to use include minimizing background noise, preferential seating (e.g., not by the pencil sharpener), and making speech louder and clearer. Specific instructional management strategies to use include increasing children's attention to language by using both written and verbal communication and promoting language learning with techniques such as learning vocabulary for new material or teaching the roots of words.

—*Becky M. Siekierski and William A. Rae*

OUTCOMES-BASED ASSESSMENT

Assessment and evaluation are two important components of a school psychologist's role. Outcomes-based assessment is a traditional, well-established form of measuring student achievement. It evolved from the testing movement of the early 1900s, the accountability movement of the 1920s, and the evaluation of educational programs of the 1930s. Outcomes-based assessment is defined as the measurement of student achievement in regard to critical, prioritized goals and objectives. While outcomes can be measured in a variety of ways, such as authentic and alternative assessment, outcomes-based assessment is typically associated with statewide and district testing programs in the United States and in entities such as the National Assessment of Educational Progress (NAEP) and the National Assessment of Vocational Education (NAVE). Outcomes-based assessment also has an international emphasis, which is widespread.

It is important to distinguish between outputs and outcomes. The Government Performance and Results Act of 1993 (GPRA) views outputs as the number of students graduating from a school system, the types of curricula taken, academic and vocational credits earned, and so forth; whereas outcomes focus on what students have learned, what they can do now, and what they can do in the future. The evaluation of federally funded programs is increasingly stressing the need for outcomes-oriented data.

As noted, outcomes-based assessment is prominent in school proficiency tests, with results being reported publicly and distributed widely to varied audiences, including parents. Publicizing results (to describe the performance of districts, schools within districts, and individual students usually against established standards and criteria) is referred to as "high-stakes testing." Complicating the picture is the fact that standards are partially dependent on the reasoned judgments of individuals, such as teachers and subject-matter experts.

There are advantages and disadvantages associated with high-stakes testing and the use of results obtained from it (Cizek, 2001). On the positive side, the testing and the subsequent results:

- Provide a benchmark for how well the schools are doing
- Illuminate areas in need of improvement
- Help restructure and improve the curricula
- Are accepted as meaningful by many educators and groups in society

If the testing and subsequent results at the district, school, or individual level are below standard, negative consequences may follow. Schools may be viewed as deficient; teachers may be pressed to teach to the test; and some students may be labeled as nonachievers and may not graduate, or may receive a *tagged* or differentiated high school diploma indicating their inability to reach the (e.g., district, state) standard. This outcome may be especially relevant for students who are adolescents with special needs.

School psychologists, particularly those working in smaller school systems, would usually be the professionals most knowledgeable about proficiency testing and test results because of their training and experience. By default, school psychologists may see a shift in their role from administering specialized assessment instruments to individuals for diagnostic purposes to that of interpreting proficiency test results, conducting training sessions on the nature of those results, and working with teachers and administrators to develop plans and strategies for enhancing district, school, and individual achievement. In the near future, this shift may expand their general duties in the areas of program evaluation, curriculum refinement, and improved development of instructional strategies; such changes in their role will affect how students in graduate programs of school psychology are trained.

—*James W. Altschuld and James T. Austin*

See also Academic Achievement; Authentic Assessment; Performance-Based Assessment; School Reform

REFERENCES AND FURTHER READING

Cizek, G. J. (2001). More unintended consequences of high-stakes testing. *Educational Measurement: Issues & Practice, 23,* 19–27.

Government Performance and Results Act, Public Law 103–62 §20 (1993).

Paris, S. G. (2000). Trojan horse in the schoolyard: The hidden threats in high-stakes testing. *Issues in Education 6*(1,2), 1–16.

Rosenfield, S., & Nelson, D. (1995). *The school psychologist's role in school assessment.* Greensboro, NC: ERIC Clearinghouse on Counseling and Student Services.

OVERCORRECTION.

See BEHAVIOR INTERVENTION; CONDITIONING: CLASSICAL AND OPERANT

P

PARENT EDUCATION AND PARENT TRAINING

Parent education (PE) refers to programs designed to enhance general parenting skills, usually independent of specific child behavior problems. Parent training (PT) is a general term that refers to several related interventions designed to help parents address child noncompliance and/or disruptive behaviors.

Both PE and PT programs promote parenting skills that are consistent with Baumrind's (1971) conceptualization of authoritative parenting (i.e., parenting that is responsive to the child's emotional needs, and yet requires child compliance with parents' instructions and directions). An impressive body of research suggests that authoritative parenting is associated with better child compliance, child psychosocial adjustment, and social competence. Longitudinal studies also indicate better long-term outcomes among children raised by authoritative parents, as compared to children of parents that use other child-rearing styles (e.g., authoritarian, in which parents demonstrate high levels of control but low levels of responsiveness; and permissive, in which parents demonstrate high levels of responsiveness but low levels of control).

While both PE and PT programs tend to promote authoritative parenting, as noted above, PT programs tend to be prescribed for parents of children with identified behavior problems, while PE programs are often seen as more preventative in nature, and are designed to enhance general parenting skills. This distinction has implications for the specific components of each type of program.

PARENT EDUCATION

As the name implies, PE programs are didactic in nature, and may impart knowledge about children's physical, emotional, and social development; parenting skills; parenting stress management; and children's home and school environment. Programs vary in their emphasis, but may include specific instruction about discipline strategies, child education and school readiness, nutrition, appropriate expectations for child social and physical development, and family role expectations. Specialized PE programs have also been described for parents of children in higher-risk situations (e.g., children at risk for abuse, children with developmental delays, families undergoing divorce).

PE programs occur in both individual and group formats. Group PE programs may be advantageous for at least two reasons: They may be more cost-effective than individual sessions, and parents may find additional sources of social support via group membership. However, individual PE programs may offer some advantages as well. They may be more easily tailored to individual parent's needs, and be more flexibly scheduled than group sessions.

Regardless of format (i.e., group vs. individual) PE programs are generally led or facilitated by a mental health professional, developmental specialist, or health care provider (e.g., a nurse), although in some programs, trained parent educators may facilitate or cofacilitate PE groups. The group leader or facilitator provides information and solicits comments, usually with the goal of helping the learners make applications and generalize the material. This didactic orientation has been criticized, along with the term "Parent Education," for perpetuating a power differential between the teacher and the learner (i.e., that the teacher is seen as the expert, and the parent/learner is seen as having little expertise). This view of parents is believed by some to undermine the parent's sense of authority and competence. Obviously, programs vary in the degree to which a power differential exists.

Corresponding to the wide variety in the content and scope of PE programs, there is considerable variety in the resulting outcomes. Several program evaluations have found positive changes in parenting-related distress, improved parental attitudes, and use of authoritative parenting practices. Other studies have found improved nurturance among parents who completed PE programs, as well as enhanced self-reported parental competence, and more positive parent-child interactions. Despite these positive reports, some evidence suggests that the gains may be short lived and that they are dependent on social context. That is, changes in parenting practices may be, to some degree, dependent upon the values of the cultures and subcultures in which the families live. Few studies have examined child variables (e.g., language development, adjustment) as outcomes of PE programs.

PARENT TRAINING

While PE programs are designed to improve general parenting skills, PT programs are designed to teach parents to address their children's disruptive behaviors. So, unlike many forms of child therapy, in which the child works directly with a therapist, PT programs teaches parents to serve as the primary therapist for their child, while the clinician serves as a consultant or trainer for the parent. In most PT programs, parents learn methods of positively reinforcing appropriate behaviors, methods of decreasing reinforcement of inappropriate child behaviors, techniques to increase the stimulus value of their instructions (i.e., increase the likelihood that children will attend to the parents' instructions), and, in some PT programs, methods of helping their children to appropriately communicate their feelings. Specific skills may include attending, rewarding, ignoring, giving directions, and time-out procedures.

Several theoretical traditions have significantly contributed to the development of modern PT programs. Constance Hanf is often considered the grandparent of current behavioral PT programs, applying operant behavioral principles to parent-child interactions in the 1960s. Various humanistic theorists have also contributed to some modern PT programs, particularly those that emphasize children's communication of their emotional states. Four PT programs are described in the following sections to highlight program components.

Helping the Noncompliant Child (McMahon & Forehand, 1984, 2003). This intervention teaches parents to manage noncompliance in three- to eight-year-old children by helping parents communicate expectations clearly and providing appropriate consequences for child behavior. This program emphasizes implementation of operant behavioral principles and makes use of a child-directed play component (i.e., a time in the therapy session in which the child sets the direction and tone of the activity) to help parents implement attending and rewarding skills in the therapy sessions. McMahon and Forehand emphasize the necessity of scheduled practice time during the week so parents can further develop their attending and rewarding skills in the home environment. This program helps parents decrease environmental reinforcement of inappropriate behaviors by teaching ignoring strategies and time-out. These components are based on the assumption that behavior that is deprived of reinforcement is less likely to reoccur.

Helping the noncompliant child has been the focus of much empirical research and has been nationally recognized as a best practice for family-based treatment. In longitudinal investigations, treated families were functioning similar to the (nonclinical) comparison sample 4½ and 10 years after the intervention.

Parent-Child Interaction Therapy (PCIT) (Foote & colleagues, 1998). PCIT is a short-term, evidence-based intervention designed for families with children between the ages of two and six experiencing a range of behavioral, emotional, and family problems. Two main phases define PCIT with child-directed interaction as the initial focus and parent-directed interaction implemented once the primary phase has been mastered. This parent training program combines basic behavioral principles with more traditional play therapy techniques and problem-solving skills. PCIT places a strong emphasis on changing the way parents and children interact, thus incorporating elements of developmental psychology, attachment theory, and social learning theory.

Research indicates that PCIT results in clinically significant improvements in the interactional style of parents and children and in the behavior problems of children at home and at school. Longitudinal studies have found that parents who completed PCIT continued to report significant changes in their children's behavior three to six years after completing treatment. Parents also report high levels of satisfaction with the content and process of PCIT and more confidence in their abilities to manage their children's behavior.

Incredible Years Parents Training Series (Webster-Stratton & Reid, 2003). This program is based on the theory that ineffective parenting, family-, school-, peer-, and community-risk factors influence the development of child conduct problems. The *Incredible Years Training Series* targets adults (parents and teachers) who work with children between the ages of two and eight years. The parent program focuses on promoting authoritative parenting skills and parents' self-confidence by replacing critical and violent discipline with more positive strategies such as ignoring, imposing logical and natural consequences, and problem solving.

Empirical research on this program shows significant improvement in parental attitudes and parent-child interactions, while significantly reducing parents' reliance on violent and critical discipline, and child conduct problems. Research also demonstrates a significant improvement in parental communication, problem solving, and collaboration skills when compared to parents who did not complete the program.

Parent Management Training for Conduct Disorder (Kazdin, 2003). The Parent Management Training (PMT) program combines cognitive problem-solving skills training with parent management training. Parents learn specific procedures to alter interactions with their children, to promote prosocial behavior, and to decrease inappropriate behavior. As with other parent training programs, PMT relies on operant behavioral principles to increase the frequency of positive behaviors. Parents are also trained to identify, observe, and define problem behaviors in new ways, while developing and using a token economy system. Empirical studies indicate that PMT produces reliable and significant reductions in antisocial behavior, while increasing prosocial behavior.

CULTURAL DIVERSITY IN PARENT TRAINING AND PARENT EDUCATION

While extensive empirical research has found success for PT programs, recent explorations of the literature have revealed only a handful of studies examining cultural diversity and parent training (Forehand & Kotchick, 1996). Most programs do not address cultural or contextual variables that affect parents' and children's views of appropriate behavior and discipline, and very few investigations have been conducted examining differences in PE and PT outcomes across demographic groups. The few studies that have been conducted suggest that social and cultural contexts have a significant impact on parents' perceptions of the acceptability of material presented in PE programs. This remains an issue for further scientific inquiry.

—*Ric G. Steele and Margaret M. Richards*

See also Conditioning: Classical and Operant; Parenting; Theories of Human Development

REFERENCES AND FURTHER READING

Baumrind, D. (1971). Current patterns of parental authority. *Developmental Psychology Monograph, 4*(1, Pt. 2).

Forehand, R., & Kotchick, B. A. (1996). Cultural diversity: A wake-up call for parent training. *Behavior Therapy, 27,* 187–206.

Foote, R. C., Schuhmann, E. M., Jones, M. L., & Eyberg, S. M. (1998). Parent-child interaction therapy: A guide for clinicians. *Clinical Child Psychology and Psychiatry, 3,* 361–373.

Kazdin, A. E. (2003). Problem-solving skills training and parent management training for conduct disorder. In A. E. Kazdin & J. R. Weisz (Eds.), *Evidence-based psychotherapies for children and adolescents* (pp. 241–262). New York: Guilford.

McMahon, R. J., & Forehand, R. (1984). Parent training for the noncompliant child: Treatment outcome, generalization and adjunctive therapy procedures. In R. F. Dangel & R. A. Polster (Eds.), *Behavioral parent training: Issues in research and practice* (pp. 298–328). New York: Guilford.

McMahon, R. J., & Forehand, R. L. (2003). *Helping the noncompliant child: Family based treatment for oppositional behavior* (2nd ed.). New York: Guilford.

Webster-Stratton, C., & Reid, M. J. (2003). The incredible years parents, teachers, and children training series: A multifaceted treatment approach for young children with conduct problems. In A. E. Kazdin & J. R. Weisz (Eds.), *Evidence-based psychotherapies for children and adolescents* (pp. 224–240). New York: Guilford.

PARENT-TEACHER CONFERENCES

A parent-teacher conference is an interactive meeting between a parent and a teacher where the primary focus is on the child's academic, behavioral, emotional, psychological, or social functioning. Parents and teachers need to collaborate and keep the interest of the child as their main focus (Comer, 2003; Comer & colleagues, 1996; Dettmer & colleagues, 2002; Epstein, 1995). A parent-teacher conference can occur at any time of the school year to address the needs of the child or the concerns of a parent or a teacher. Conferences can also provide an opportunity for parents to talk with teachers about the progress their child is making in the classroom. Conferences, which are scheduled and conducted regularly with school personnel, provide a means for parents and teachers to discuss educational issues impacting the student (Bauer & Shea, 2003).

Parent-teacher conferences can be scheduled in a variety of ways. Two of the times when one can expect a parent-teacher conference are in the fall and the spring of the school year. In the fall, a parent-teacher conference provides parents with an opportunity to meet the teacher, tour the school, and understand the curriculum and expectations set forth for the specific grade or course. In the winter or early spring, a parent-teacher conference provides the opportunity for parents and teachers to discuss the progress made by the student. This would also be a reasonable time to consider and begin to discuss any specific educational considerations for the next academic year.

TYPICAL REASONS FOR THE PARENT-TEACHER MEETINGS

There are many reasons why a parent-teacher conference might be scheduled. Students who do not make adequate academic progress or students who are experiencing academic, behavioral, emotional, psychological, or social concerns in the class or in the school are reasons why a parent-teacher conference might be scheduled. These conferences might be scheduled by the teacher to help a parent understand what is occurring in the classroom. The conferences might also be requested by the parent to express a concern or inquire about the progress made by the student. In some instances, a principal or other school administrator might call a conference with the parent or with the parent and the teacher to discuss academic, behavioral, emotional, psychological, or social issues the student is encountering.

CONFERENCE EXPECTATIONS

For regularly scheduled parent-teacher conferences at the beginning of the school year or at the beginning of the semester, parents can expect to have an opportunity to meet individually with their child's teacher. This meeting can occur in the teacher's classroom, school conference room, or other available room within the school building. The teacher meets with the parent for the scheduled amount of time, which may range from 10 to 30 minutes. This time range will depend upon the issues that need to be discussed during the meeting. During this time, the parent and teacher can discuss the student's academic progress, address class or school issues, and examine behavior or social issues of interest or concern to the parent. Specific suggestions for the parents and the teachers are listed below for consideration.

SUGGESTIONS FOR PARENTS

For a variety of reasons, parents may feel uneasy about attending a conference at their child's school. Their conference experience can be enhanced with preparation, as described in the following sections.

Prior to the Conference Meeting

- Write down a few questions to ask the teacher or principal.
- Ask someone to plan to go with you to the meeting if this would be helpful to you.
- Be sure you know the place and time of the meeting.

During the Conference Meeting

- Ask the teacher or principal the questions you have prepared.
- Take notes or have your spouse or friend take notes for you.
- Listen carefully to what the teacher or principal has to say.
- Ask questions of the teacher or principal to help clarify points discussed.
- Bring an interpreter if you have difficulty with the language that is spoken at the meeting.

- Ask the teacher for examples of your child's work if you have not seen any of the work at home.
- Ask what suggestions the teacher or principal can give you to help you assist your child.
- Ask how you can work together with the school to assure that your child is making adequate progress.

After the Conference Meeting

- Look at the notes taken during the meeting.
- Jot down any additional questions thought of after you returned home.
- Call or e-mail the teacher and ask those questions.
- Follow up with any suggestions that were made during the conference.
- Share the conference information with others in the family, when appropriate.
- Contact the teacher or principal to thank him or her for the information or assistance you received during the conference.
- Schedule a follow-up conference, when appropriate.

SUGGESTIONS FOR TEACHERS

Teachers may feel anxious about conducting a conference. Here are a few suggestions that may assist a teacher in thinking about, preparing for, and conducting a smooth parent-teacher conference.

Prior to the Conference Meeting

Contacting the Parents (Through One or More Methods)

- Send home information with the student to help the parents know what to expect from the conference.
- Send home an informational note with an agenda attached.
- Write and send a personal letter to the parents.
- Call the parents on the phone to invite them to the meeting.
- Send an e-mail to the parents to encourage their attendance.
- Post a personal greeting to all parents on the school's Web site.

- Send home a regular newsletter and include a personal greeting to the parents that encourages them to come to the meeting.

Creating a Conversation-Friendly Environment

- Set up a comfortable environment to help facilitate the meeting.
- Eliminate any physical "barrier" between the parents and the teacher.
- Have a round table with chairs around it and sit facing one another.

During the Conference Meeting

Beginning With Welcome and Introductions

- Greet the parents as they walk into the meeting.
- Introduce yourself and help the parents feel comfortable.
- Offer them refreshments if available.
- Establish a rapport with the parents.

Sharing Information

- Introduce your subject area to the parents; help them understand what you teach and how your class is conducted.
- Have child's work available for the parents to review.
- Have policies ready to review or visibly post them.
- Have a handout for the parents on curriculum, policies, and upcoming events.

Focusing on Strengths

- Note the positive attributes of the student.
- Indicate how the student contributes to the class.

Focusing on Growth Areas

- Address the specific areas that need improvement.
- Suggest strategies or activities that parents could try at home to address areas that need improvement.

Building Rapport

- Remind the parents that you wish to work with them to help their child.
- Remind them that you want their child to achieve.
- Listen to the parents' requests or concerns.
- Be sure you understand specific concerns and ask for clarification when needed.
- Proceed with caution when asking questions, be sure they are appropriate.
- Build consensus and resist the urge to blame (Comer & colleagues, 1996).
- Address requests or concerns as directly as possible.
- Use a problem-solving approach where you identify the problem, discuss the options, explore the consequences, and target a possible solution. (Dettmer & colleagues, 2002).

Using Appropriate Communication Skills

- Provide descriptive behaviors from a positive perspective.
- Be objective and descriptive in your choice of words.
- Reflect back what you hear the parents saying.
- Encourage the parents to converse about their child.
- Make eye contact with the parents.
- Smile, give head nods, and other appropriate affirmations.
- Be careful not to overdo with the affirmations.
- Lean towards the parents and show interest in their conversation.
- Focus on the parents as you converse with them.
- Resist the temptation to multitask during the conference.
- Be cautious that you don't inadvertently use barriers during the conference.

After the Conference Meeting

- Thank parents for attending.
- Invite parents to stay in touch; give them a way to contact you.
- Send a note to the parents to thank them for their ideas.
- Send an e-mail to parents to let them know you appreciated their suggestions.

- Schedule a follow-up meeting when necessary.
- Make notations of ideas or suggestions that occurred during the meeting.
- Follow up on any of the specific suggestions or ideas recommended at the meeting.

Parent-teacher conferences can be very productive opportunities to share information about the progress a student is making or to discuss specific issues or concerns facing a particular student (Bauer & Shea, 2003). When the true focus of the parent-teacher conference is the child's best interest, the conference can move along smoothly. School experiences can evoke the strengths of children, their parents, and their teachers if the collaboration of administrators, teachers, and parents is fostered and enhanced (Comer & colleagues, 1996).

—Gloria A. Dye

See also Grades; Homework; Individualized Education Plan Meeting; School–Home Notes; Student Improvement Teams

REFERENCES AND FURTHER READING

Bauer, A. M., & Shea, T. M. (2003). *Parents and schools: Creating a successful partnership for students with special needs.* Upper Saddle River, NJ: Merrill/Prentice Hall.

Comer, J. P. (2003, November/December). Fundamental success. *The Crisis*, 30–33.

Comer, J. P., Haynes, N. M., Joyner, E. T., & Ben-Avie, M. (Eds.). (1996). *Rallying the whole village: The Comer process for reforming education.* New York: Teachers College Press.

Dettmer, P., Thurston, L. P., & Dyck, N. (2002). Consultation, collaboration and teamwork for students with special needs. (4th ed.). Boston: Allyn & Bacon.

Epstein, J. L. (1995). School/family/community partnerships: Caring for the children we share. *Phi Delta Kappan*, 76(9), 701–712.

PARENTING

Parenting refers to a number of complex and interrelated ideas and practices. Bradley and Corwyn (1999) have constructed a framework in which parenting is conceptualized as a set of five functions performed by parents. Parents provide their children with:

1. Basic physical and psychological sustenance

2. Adequate cognitive and social stimulation

3. Emotional support

4. Appropriate structure

5. Surveillance (keeping track of the child and his or her environment in order to protect the child)

Quality of parenting can be assessed by taking into account the extent to which each of these tasks is fulfilled.

There are various and simultaneous contexts that must be included in any serious consideration of parenthood. A parent is nested in an immediate family, a neighborhood, a cultural norm, racial and ethnic currents, immigrant status, social and economic factors, a political climate, and a historical period. An even more finely grained rendering of the topic of parenting might concern itself with distinctions between mothering and fathering. Additionally, there are many potentially interesting questions such as the impact of single-parenting, dual-career parenting, gay and lesbian parenting, and so forth. Thus, there are numerous factors that come into play when one contemplates the meaning of parenthood. Clearly, parenting is a multilayered dynamic system of values, behaviors, and roles.

CULTURAL VARIATIONS

Parenting beliefs and practices are shaped by culture. One culture might promote independence and autonomy, while another might encourage less exploration and greater social courtesy. When discussing the impact of cultural variations in parenting practices, it is difficult to determine where stereotypes leave off and real distinctions among groups exist. Often, a distinct group subsumes many different subgroups that espouse different traditions. For example, the group considered to be Latino is quite varied. It includes Mexican, Puerto Rican, Cuban, and Central and South American, as well as people of other Hispanic origin. Some groups do not share a common language. Among Asians, there are Taiwanese, Japanese, Vietnamese, and Korean to mention a few. Asian parenting practices vary according to the ethnicity, culture, and language. Moreover, parenting practices change with increased assimilation into the dominant culture.

Although it can be helpful to pay attention to cultural origins and beliefs of any particular group, it is vital to avoid the imposition of evaluative comparisons with other cultural groups. In addition, the role of grandparents and other members of the extended family as parenting agents must factor into an understanding of different child-rearing practices. Likewise, a discussion of cultural influences on parenting must take into account immigration patterns and acculturation trends. Finally, cultural differences are often confounded by social and political contexts. Poverty, prejudice, and the various stressors that accompany these conditions are decisive in determining parenting practices.

ACADEMIC ACHIEVEMENT AND SOCIAL–EMOTIONAL DEVELOPMENT

Parental involvement in academic activities fosters good school performance. There are many styles of parenting that foster different degrees of parental involvement. Baumrind (1967) identified a parenting classification system that has generated a great deal of research and has exerted much influence on generations of parenting researchers. Baumrind put forward four parenting styles:

1. Authoritative

2. Authoritarian

3. Rejecting–Neglecting

4. Permissive

According to this schematization, an authoritative parenting style is characterized by high parental warmth, high behavioral expectations, and high use of democratic parenting strategies; whereas an authoritarian style also espouses high behavioral expectations, but exhibits low parental warmth and low use of democratic strategies. Although each of these styles predicts children's academic achievement, the relationship is complex. For example, authoritative parenting is more successful than authoritarian methods in promoting academic achievement in middle-class children. However, it has been found that parenting style interacts with other variables such as a child's ethnicity and socioeconomic status, and the interactions among these different variables predict different academic achievement outcomes.

As children grow and develop, their thinking patterns change while their emotional and social needs broaden. Children move from concrete thinking to abstract thinking. Parents must be in sync with these changes and encourage their children to participate more in decision-making and problem-solving activities in all areas of their lives, including extracurricular events such as sports, performing arts and music, academic elective subjects, social issues, and discretionary purchases. As children grow up, peers play an increasingly important role in their lives. Social spheres widen and parents must balance the child's needs for autonomy with their desire for parental control. This is not always harmonious. However, children need practice to improve their skills in navigating uncharted waters. Although most children manage quite well, some children will falter during these transitions. The parent-child tie is enormously important during these occasions. If a prudent, incremental, and sound increase in autonomy is permitted to occur, parents and children can maintain strong ties and communication patterns during these vital developmental phases.

THE SCHOOL PSYCHOLOGIST'S ROLE

The school psychologist plays an important role in facilitating parenting practices that support children and youths. School psychologists serve several clients simultaneously: school personnel, pupils, and parents. Promoting parental participation in schools and working together with parents, pupils, and school personnel is one of the functions and responsibilities of school psychologists. The more involved parents are in their child's school, the greater the child's academic success, attitudes toward school, academic engagement, and the higher the child's self-concept. School psychologists can promote parental activities such as fund raising, serving as advocates for teachers and the school, and working collaboratively with school board members. Parents benefit from a partnership with the school by acquiring added knowledge about their child's development, learning about the school's goals, and developing means to advocate for their children.

School psychologists can direct parents toward appropriate involvement with their children's homework, school projects, and participation in educational trips. School psychologists can teach parents about children's cognitive, emotional, and social development. They can impart scientifically sound information about child-rearing techniques through the introduction of formal workshops, classes, and other types of educational programs for parents. Various types of parent training programs can be provided to parents and give parents the opportunity to discuss parenting, role play, read relevant material, view videotaped instruction, and achieve personal growth. Parent education programs' goals include improving communications skills, school achievement, discipline practices, and literacy promotion. It is vital to design or select parent education programs that are culturally sensitive, because a one-size-fits-all type of program can miss the mark when working with diverse populations.

Through scientific investigations school psychologists can help parents support healthy child development. By carrying out empirically based research on parent-child relations, parenting practices, and a host of related matters, school psychologists can contribute to the formulation of policies and practices that address the needs of children and youths.

In addition, school psychologists can influence parenting practices that support children by offering special forums that address concerns about:

- Substance use
- Sex education
- Child abuse and neglect
- Depression
- Self-harming activities
- Eating disorders
- Other relevant health matters

Also, school psychologists can work with parents on developing public awareness campaigns designed to increase community initiatives in these areas of child health and development.

Furthermore, school psychologists can provide resources to parents that will facilitate their development and maintenance of self-confidence in their child-rearing abilities. For example, school psychologists are in a position to offer knowledge about developmental trends in children, to teach techniques for stress reduction, and to provide knowledge that leads to realistic expectations of child behavior. Efforts should be made to inculcate a sense of parental competency. Parents who feel proficient in their child rearing, tend to be warm and responsive toward their children, which, in turn, leads to healthier parent-child interactions.

—Lawrence Balter

See also Abuse and Neglect; Divorce Adjustment; Homelessness; Latchkey Children; Media and Children; Parents As Teachers; Race, Ethnicity, Class, and Gender; Resilience and Protective Factors; School Refusal; Single-Parent Families

REFERENCES AND FURTHER READING

Baumrind, D. (1967). Child care practices anteceding three patterns of preschool behavior. *Genetic Psychology Monographs, 75,* 43–88.

Bornstein, M. H. (Ed.). (1991). *Cultural approaches to parenting.* Hillsdale, NJ: Erlbaum.

Bradley, R. H., & Corwyn, R. F. (1999). Parenting. In L. Balter & C. Tamis-LeMonda (Eds.), *Child psychology: A handbook of contemporary issues.* Philadelphia: Psychology Press.

Briggs, R., & Balter, L. (2002). Parental involvement in educational settings: The school psychologist's role in creating successful partnerships. *Psychoeducational Center Reports,* New York University School Psychology Programs.

Cheng Gorman, J., & Balter, L. (1997). Culturally sensitive parent education: A critical review of quantitative research. *Review of Educational Research, 67*(3), 339–369.

Gutman, L. M. (2000). Academic achievement. In L. Balter (Ed.), *Parenthood in America: An encyclopedia.* Santa Barbara, CA: ABC-CLIO.

Huston, A. C. (1999). Effects of poverty on children. In L. Balter & C. Tamis-LeMonda (Eds.), *Child psychology: A handbook of contemporary issues.* Philadelphia: Psychology Press.

PARENTS AS TEACHERS

The Missouri Department of Elementary and Secondary Education founded Parents As Teachers (PAT) in 1981. In 1986, Ohio, Texas, and Connecticut became the first three states outside of Missouri to implement PAT programs. In 1991, PAT attained international status when Australia began providing services. In 1994, the organization received public commendation from the United States Secretary of Education, as evaluations of PAT programs showed significant gains for high-needs children and their parents. By 1998, the number of PAT programs reached more than 2,000 sites including 49 states in the United States, Australia, Canada, England, and New Zealand. With certification of the first PAT program in Hawaii on July 12, 2001, PAT officially reached all 50 states. New developments in PAT include the *Born to Learn Curriculum: Prenatal to 3 Years,* which was translated into Spanish, and the development of standards for assessing the overall quality of PAT programs.

The philosophy of PAT is that babies are born to learn. The vision is that parents will be their child's best first teachers. Therefore, PAT services are driven by the idea that parents are the critical players in establishing the best possible foundation for learning and development for their children.

PAT provides several services for families with children younger than the age of three years. There are four key components common to all of the PAT programs:

1. Families receive personal visits in their home from a parent educator who educates the family regarding age-appropriate expectations for their child.

2. Parent meetings allow parents to share their concerns with other parents and to increase their parenting knowledge.

3. Screenings of the child's health, hearing, vision, and overall development are conducted periodically. Screenings provide an avenue for early detection of potential learning problems.

4. The founders of PAT were cognizant of the fact that families may have needs extending beyond the scope of PAT services. This provides the parents with links to resources within their community.

Numerous research studies on PAT programs throughout the country have confirmed positive effects in terms of child, parent, and family outcomes (Pfannenstiel, 1999). For example, *The School Entry Assessment Project* included more than 3,000 PAT participants. Findings indicate that children who participate in PAT combined with other prekindergarten experiences such as Head Start are the highest performing group upon school entry. Outcome measures included:

- Communication
- Mathematical knowledge
- Working with others
- Conventional knowledge

Other results indicate that children who receive PAT and early childhood special education (ECSE) services are rated by their teachers as similar in preparation to their average peers upon entering school. This finding suggests the possible contribution of PAT in ameliorating early developmental delays.

In an effort to reach a large number of children and their families, some school districts choose to pool their resources into consortia. By doing so, they are able to serve a larger number of children and their families than they would if they provided services as independent districts.

—*Kari L. Manier*

See also Head Start; Parenting; Preschoolers; Single-Parent Families

REFERENCES AND FURTHER READING

Pfannenstiel, J. (1999). *School entry assessment project: Report of findings.* Overland Park, KA: Research and Training Associates.

PEDOPHILIA

Pedophilia is a disorder in which an adult shows a strong and consistent preference to engage in sexual relationships with a prepubescent child younger than 13 years of age. The person with pedophilia must be at least 16 years of age and at least five years older than the child (*Diagnostic and Statistical Manual of Mental Disorders, Fourth Edition* [*DSM-IV*], 1994). Persons with pedophilia may be exclusive, that is only sexually attracted to children, or nonexclusive, where they are sometimes attracted to adults. Some restrict their interactions to children of their own gender, while others are attracted to children of both genders. Incidence reports about the disorder vary widely across studies and reflect a number of differences in its operational definition. Approximately 0.1% of men are believed to be pedophiles; data on the prevalence rate among females are not available. The statistic for male perpetrators is probably underestimated because so many cases go unreported. Approximately 35% of pedophiles are homosexual. Male-on-male pedophiles are far more numerous than heterosexual pedophiles. It is estimated that approximately 80% of pedophilic victims are boys molested by adult males. The most preferred age of female victims is 8 to 10 years, while male victims tend

to be slightly older. The range of sexual behaviors in pedophilia extend from gentle fondling, self-masturbation, or actual genital and/or oral penetration of the child involving either the penis, fingers, or objects with varying degrees of force. It is not unusual for the adult to develop some kind of emotional bond with the child and try to meet the child's physical and material needs to encourage the child's loyalty and commitment.

Although it is difficult to develop a precise profile of a pedophile, some generalizations exist. Most pedophiles are adult males who rationalize these behaviors, devote a good deal of time to sexually fantasizing about children, often view various forms of child pornography, and typically engage in other kinds of socially approved behaviors to compensate for this behavior. Many pedophiles have childhood histories of being sexually abused.

A number of treatment approaches have been used with pedophiles, although this disorder is generally highly resistant to psychological intervention. Therapeutic strategies include treating the pedophilia as symptomatic of the person's own posttraumatic stress disorder or viewing the behavior as an addiction and using 12-step support groups to deliver treatment. Some promising approaches are behavior therapy using aversion techniques, where the pedophilic actions become associated mentally with unpleasant thoughts developed during visual imagery, desensitization, covert sensitization, and/or cognitive restructuring. Victim empathy and relapse prevention training programs often are used as adjuncts to the behavior therapy. Several antiandrogen medications have also been found to be effective in controlling this disorder but remain controversial control mechanisms (Crawford, 1981).

—*Raymond E. Webster*

REFERENCES AND FURTHER READING

American Psychiatric Association. (1994). *The diagnostic and statistical manual of mental disorders* (4th ed.). Washington, DC: Author.

Crawford, D. (1981). Treatment approaches with pedophiles. In M. Cook & K. Howells (Eds.), *Adult sexual interest in children* (pp. 181–217). London: Academic.

PEER MEDIATION

As acts of aggression and disruptive behavior occur more frequently in schools, the need for programs to help students resolve conflict increases. There are many types of conflict resolution programs. A common type is the peer mediation program. Peer mediation programs empower students to manage their own conflict through training in problem solving and negotiation.

Although conflict occurs regularly in schools, many children don't possess the skills necessary to manage conflict constructively. In fact, research suggests that untrained students primarily resolve conflict with destructive strategies such as verbal threats or force (Johnson & colleagues, 1992). The purpose of peer mediation is to help students manage conflict by understanding others' perspectives and working cooperatively. Peer mediators are neutral third parties who facilitate negotiation by listening to peers' problems, clarifying concerns, and assisting in the problem-solving process. In this way, peer mediation provides a structured opportunity for students to discuss their feelings and develop a solution that benefits both parties.

Peer mediation programs are classified as either cadre or total student body approaches (Johnson & Johnson, 1996). While only a small number of students serve as peer mediators with a cadre approach, the total student body approach focuses on training every student in conflict resolution and peer mediation. Peer mediators are selected through a self-, peer-, or teacher-nomination process. Selected peer mediators should be assertive, effective communicators and representative of the entire student population (Burrell & Vogl, 1990). Training should include discussions, role play, and other skill-building activities to allow students to practice what they learn. Ongoing support and training is also important for peer mediators to improve upon their skills.

There are many potential advantages of peer mediation. When schools implement peer mediation programs, they foster an environment that empowers students to control their own behavior (Johnson & Johnson, 1994). Furthermore, research suggests that peer mediation and conflict resolution training has positive effects on self-esteem, school climate, students' attitude toward conflict, and academic achievement (Johnson & Johnson, 1996). Moreover, peer mediation has led to a decrease in discipline referrals and suspensions (Johnson & Johnson, 1996). Nevertheless, there are several challenges that affect successful mediation. For example, some students have difficulty remaining neutral (Hale & Nix, 1997), expressing feelings, and reversing perspectives

(Johnson & colleagues, 1992). Likewise, mediators have reported loss of friendships and a negative popularity status (Humphries, 1999). Empirical research on peer mediation is limited. Most studies involve self-reports or testimonials made by individuals who are dedicated to the success of peer mediation programs (Johnson & Johnson, 1996). Therefore, more research is necessary to determine the effectiveness of these widely implemented programs.

—*Amy Kiekhaefer*

See also Bullying and Victimization; Discipline; Friendships; Gangs; Mentoring; Peer Pressure; Peer Tutoring; Prevention; Problem Solving; Violence in Schools

REFERENCES AND FURTHER READING

Burrell, N., & Vogl, S. (1990). Turf side conflict mediation for students. *Mediation Quarterly, 7*(3), 237–250.

Hale, C., & Nix, C. (1997). Achieving neutrality and impartiality: The ultimate communication challenge for peer mediators. *Mediation Quarterly, 14*(4), 337–352.

Humphries, T. (1999). Improving peer mediation programs: Student experiences and suggestions. *Professional School Counseling, 3*(1), 13–19.

Johnson, D., & Johnson, R. (1994). Constructive conflict in the schools. *Journal of Social Issues, 50*(1), 117–137.

Johnson, D., & Johnson, R. (1996). Conflict resolution and peer mediation programs in elementary and secondary schools: A review of the research. *Review of Educational Research, 66*(4), 459–506.

Johnson, D., Johnson, R., & Dudley, B. (1992). Effects of peer mediation training on elementary school students. *Mediation Quarterly, 10*(2), 89–98.

PEER PRESSURE

According to Robyn Feller's *Everything You Need to Know About Peer Pressure* (1993), peer pressure is what causes people to do things that are popular in order to fit in with others. Accordingly, it can be a very powerful driving force in the lives of adolescents. Peer pressure is a common experience of life for most teenagers. Peers are usually regarded as the people who are of similar age to a person, such as the other members of class in school, or the other boys in a troop of Boy Scouts. Because peer status is especially important during middle school and high school, pressures from other teens can be a driving force that influences the behavior of teenagers positively or negatively. Adolescents spend so much of their time with their peers, so it makes sense that these peers can influence them both positively and negatively.

As Feller (1993) points out, young people can often influence each other in very positive ways, such as pressuring friends to stay in school, getting good grades, or joining a sports team. Friends may encourage each other to participate in peer tutoring in the school's resource room, or work out conflicts appropriately with other students in peer mediation. Not only is this type of positive pressure enriching for young people, it also develops social skills and can aid in a sense of self-worth and self-exploration for students.

Peer pressure is more commonly thought of negatively, such as when it is used to exclude students socially from a certain group or to coerce students into performing negative behaviors (e.g., using illicit drugs, drinking, cheating on a test). Peer pressure strongly influences behavior in children and adolescents, influencing them to say the "right" thing, wear the "right" clothes, or act a certain way. Peer pressure may be used to coerce children and adolescents to join gangs. Gang behavior uses peer pressure to promote negative behaviors, such as theft, destruction of property, or the injury of another student.

Currently, research studies (Simons-Morton & colleagues, 2001) show that middle school students are much more likely to drink or smoke if they have friends that do so. This is just one of many studies that gives credence to the idea that students can be influenced by the peers around them.

Parents, teachers, and psychologists use positive peer pressure as a method to change a child's behavior in school. Teachers may orchestrate peer pressure to get students to exhibit appropriate behaviors or to follow class rules. Psychologists use peer pressure in group counseling to promote support and encouragement among group members.

—*Jill S. Lange*

See also Cheating; DARE Program; Peer Mediation; Peer Tutoring; Smoking (Teenage); Social Skills; Substance Abuse

REFERENCES AND FURTHER READING

Feller, R. M. (1993). *Everything you need to know about peer pressure.* New York: Rosen.

Simons-Morton, B., Haynie, D. L., Crump, A. D., Eitel, P., & Saylor, K. E. (2001). Peer and parent influences on smoking and drinking among early adolescents. *Health Education & Behavior, 28*(1), 95–107.

PEER TUTORING

Peer tutoring is an instructional strategy that uses pairs of students to teach one another academic skills. Peer tutoring has been used successfully across a wide range of students, subject areas, educational settings, and grade levels. It is a promising strategy for diverse students including low income, ethnic minority, and language minority students. This strategy has been implemented to enhance student learning in the areas of mathematics, reading, spelling, social studies, science, and history. Peer tutoring has been used in regular and special education settings with students of all abilities and grade levels. As opposed to more traditional teacher-led models of instruction, peer tutoring has the advantage of engaging students in active rather than passive learning. It enables the classroom teacher to serve as a facilitator, moving around the classroom as students are engaged in learning with their peers.

The documented effects of peer tutoring include increases in academic skills, on-task behavior, social skills, self-concept, and academic motivation. The components of peer tutoring include providing structure so that students have well-defined roles, interdependent reward contingencies in which both students' contributions enable them to earn team rewards, evaluation on the basis of individual student progress, and opportunities for self-management.

Two well-researched models of peer tutoring applied to whole classrooms include Reciprocal Peer Tutoring (RPT) and Classwide Peer Tutoring (CWPT). RPT was originally developed by Fantuzzo and colleagues for pairs of low-achieving urban elementary school students. RPT uses a structured format and a student-managed group reward contingency, and provides opportunities for students to alternate between tutor and tutee roles. RPT has been effectively used in the context of elementary school mathematics education with students in grades three through five, although it may be modified for other purposes. CWPT was developed by Greenwood and other researchers from the Juniper Gardens Children's Project at the University of Kansas, and can be applied to classrooms of students within the same grade level. The core features of CWPT include reciprocal teaching, curriculum, tutor training, and motivational strategies that include team competition (Greenwood & colleagues, 2002). CWPT has been used in both elementary and secondary school settings and has been applied to reading, spelling, and mathematics education with positive results.

Two additional evidence-based models of peer tutoring developed on the basis of CWPT are Peer-Assisted Learning Strategies (PALS) (Fuchs & colleagues, 1996) and Classwide Student Tutoring Teams (CSTT) (Maheady & colleagues, 1991). PALS includes some additional peer teaching strategies and can be linked to computerized curriculum-based measurement evaluation programs. PALS has been used quite successfully to enhance elementary school reading and mathematics instruction. CSTT was developed to support secondary level instruction in mathematics, social studies, science, and history. CSTT combines the peer teaching procedures of CWPT with aspects of the Teams-Games-Tournaments model (TGT) (Devries & Slavin, 1978), which uses mixed ability teams of four to five students in team competition.

Overall, peer tutoring is a promising evidence-based strategy for enhancing student learning in diverse classrooms.

—*Marika Ginsburg-Block*

See also Classroom Climate; Classwide Peer Tutoring; Study Skills

REFERENCES AND FURTHER READING

Devries, D., & Slavin, R. (1978). Teams-games-tournaments (TGT). Review of ten classroom experiments. *Journal of Research and Development in Education, 12*, 28–38.

Fuchs, D., Fuchs, L. S., Mathes, P. G., & Simmons, D. C. (1996). *Peer-assisted learning strategies in reading (PALS): A manual.* (Available from Box 328, Peabody College, Vanderbilt University, Nashville, TN, 37203.)

Greenwood, C. R., Maheady, L., & Delquadri, J. (2002). Classwide Peer Tutoring programs. In M. R. Shinn, H. M. Walker, & G. Stoner (Eds.), *Interventions for academic and behavior problems II: Preventive and remedial approaches* (pp. 611–649). Bethesda, MD: National Association of School Psychologists.

Maheady, L., Harper, G. F., Sacca, M. K., & Mallette, B. (1991). Classwide student tutoring teams (CSTT): *Instructor's manual and video package.* Fredonia, NY: SUNY College at Fredonia, School of Education.

PERCENTILE RANKS

Percentile ranks are a commonly used form of norm-referenced score transformation. They are reported for most ability, aptitude, and achievement tests as well as for attitude, personality, and interest inventories.

Percentile ranks are expressed as whole-number values that range between 1 and 99 to indicate the position or rank of the respondent's score in a reference group of test takers. For example, if 100 individuals completed a test, a percentile rank of 40 would indicate that the respondent's score was equal to or higher than 40 of the 100 individuals in the norm group. In the case of nationally standardized tests with larger norm groups, a percentile rank of 40 would indicate that the respondent had earned a score equal to or higher than 40% of the people in the norm group.

Percentile ranks have one very serious disadvantage—they are not equal units of measurement. Because they are not equal units, score differences in the middle of the distribution appear larger than score differences in the tails of the distribution. For this reason, one must be very careful when interpreting percentile ranks.

In general, approximately 68% of people earn percentile ranks between 16 and 84. Percentile ranks in this range are considered average or typical. In a normal distribution, these percentile ranks include the area between one standard deviation above and one standard deviation below the mean of the distribution. Percentile ranks in the tails of the distribution represent large differences in scores. For instance, the difference between percentile ranks of 95 and 99 or between 10 and 15 represent much larger differences than do the differences between, for example, 40 and 45 or 70 and 75.

Test profiles attempt to show visually that the differences in the middle of the distribution are closer together by compacting the distribution in the middle range and expanding the range in the tails of the distribution. Particular attention should be given to the graphic on the profile for achievement tests when interpreting percentile ranks to students and their parents.

Understanding this characteristic of percentile ranks is very important in comparing scores on a standardized achievement test. Students who earn percentile ranks of 40 in reading and 60 in mathematics are scoring in the average or typical range for both subject areas. The student and his or her parents should not be led to believe that the student's achievement in mathematics is higher or better than the achievement in reading. Conversely, students who earn percentile ranks of 5 in reading and 15 in mathematics have performed much better in mathematics than in reading, although their overall achievement is lower than most students of their age or grade in school. The same differences apply for the upper end of the distribution. Students who earn percentile ranks of 97 in mathematics and 90 in reading have higher levels of achievement in mathematics than they do in reading.

—*Nona Tollefson*

See also Academic Achievement; Grade Equivalent Scores; Intelligence; Stanines

PERFORMANCE-BASED ASSESSMENT

Since the late 1980s, many states, districts, and schools have developed performance assessments (PAs) to measure students' achievement of educational standards. PA comprises assessment techniques in which students must, independently or in small groups, construct responses to complex tasks that emulate realistic problems faced within an academic domain. For example, PA in mathematics might require students to estimate the amount of paint needed to cover a house by applying concepts of geometry, algebra, proportions, and other mathematical principles.

Although PA, authentic assessment, and portfolio assessment share the use of constructed responses and realistic problems, standards-based PA is unique because its content and outcomes are judged relative to specific academic standards. Educators develop and select PA tasks to assess students' mastery of specific academic standards, and judge students' performances with respect to their achievement of standards (e.g., progressing, partially proficient, proficient, advanced). Judges typically use rubrics that describe the proficiency categories and the criteria for rating student performance within each category. Also, standards-based PA typically restricts itself to on-demand assessment tasks (i.e., those that the student receives and completes in one setting), in part to ensure fairness (i.e., so that all students complete the task under the same conditions).

Because standards-based PA tasks are aligned with academic standards, PA intends to encourage teachers to improve instructional practices, educational equity, and otherwise increase their efforts toward educational reform (Khattri & colleagues, 1995). PA is also intended to challenge students to engage in higher-order thinking, to integrate and synthesize ideas, and to motivate students in ways multiple-choice tests cannot. Although some agencies use PA primarily to inform educators of a school's or system's effectiveness (e.g., reporting only group results), other agencies may use PA (usually in combination with other assessment methods) to describe individual student proficiency, make retention and promotion decisions, or even make graduation decisions.

Although PA may be popular among educators, research is equivocal in supporting its benefits. Psychometrically, PA often suffers from inadequate reliability (e.g., poor agreement among judges) and from task specificity (Shavelson & colleagues, 1999). These problems caution educators to be wary of rating students' proficiency unless judges are rigorously trained and students are assessed on a wide variety of PA tasks. PA is also expensive to develop, administer, and score, and may maintain or even exacerbate equity concerns for ethnically, culturally, and linguistically different students (Braden, 1999). Although some argue group-based PA (which requires students to work together in small groups to complete a task) is more equitable than individual PA (Neuberger, 1993), research suggests that student grouping influences individual outcomes (Webb & colleagues, 1998). Standards-based PA is most likely to benefit students and educators when it is used in conjunction with other methods of assessment (e.g., multiple-choice tests, grades, portfolios) to inform students, educators, and other stakeholders about students' mastery of educational standards.

—*Jeffrey P. Braden*

REFERENCES AND FURTHER READING

Braden, J. P. (1999). Performance assessment and diversity. *School Psychology Quarterly, 14*(3), 304–326.

Khattri, N., Reeve, A. L., Kane, M. B., & Adamson, R. J. (1995). *Studies of educational reform: Assessment of student performance (Vol. 1: Findings and conclusions)*. Washington, DC: Office of Educational Research and Improvement (ERIC Document No. ED 397 352).

Neuberger, W. (1993, September). *Making group assessments fair measures of students' abilities*. Paper presented at the

CRESST Conference on "Assessment Questions: Equity Answers," Los Angeles, CA.

Shavelson, R. J., Ruiz-Primo, M. A., & Wiley, E. W. (1999). Note on sources of sampling variability in science performance assessments. *Journal of Educational Measurement, 36*(1), 61–71.

Webb, N. M., Nemer, K. M., Chizhik, A. W., & Sugrue, B. (1998). Equity issues in collaborative group assessment: Group composition and performance. *American Educational Research Journal, 35*(4), 607–661.

PERSEVERATION

Perseveration is the repetition of a behavior to a marked degree that interferes with other activities. It manifests itself in either a verbal or nonverbal manner, or both. Furthermore, to the outside observer, this repetition may appear purposeless in nature because children will persist despite discouragement and an apparent lack of incentives. It should be noted, however, that perseveration can offer sensory stimulation for some children. In children, perseveration can be characteristic of a variety of mental disorders or syndromes such as mental retardation, communication disorders, pervasive developmental disorders, attention deficit hyperactivity disorder, tic disorders, stereotypic movement disorder, schizophrenia and other psychotic disorders, and obsessive–compulsive disorder. Additionally, perseveration can result from brain injury and substance abuse. In terms of educational implications of perseveration, children who perseverate are likely to experience difficulty focusing on and transitioning between school activities. As such, children may benefit from structured environments, prompting, schedules, and positive reinforcement.

—*Gina Coffee Herrera*

PERSONALITY ASSESSMENT

As it currently stands, the assessment of child and adolescent personality involves two predominant activities for school psychologists:

1. To identify and provide services to emotionally disturbed students as part of the Individuals With Disabilities Education Act (IDEA)

2. To better understand the significant number of social–emotional and behavioral problems that nonspecial education students manifest in today's schools and communities

But, more functionally, personality assessment should provide pragmatic recommendations and action plans that decrease or resolve current child and adolescent problems such that they can be prevented in the future. Moreover, from a health and mental health perspective, personality assessment should also provide parents and educators with insight and direction into such problems as truancy; drug abuse; dropping out; teenage pregnancy; suicide; and the emotional impacts of divorce, poverty, rejection, and academic failure. In totality, then, personality assessment is a process of collecting valid data to explain the causes for or contingencies relevant to a student's social–emotional, behavioral, or affective difficulties. This assessment is only meaningful when linked with viable, acceptable, and socially valid interventions that are successfully implemented with ongoing attention to treatment integrity and evaluation.

FOUR CONTEXTS FOR PERSONALITY ASSESSMENT

Personality assessment should be conducted within four contexts. First, it is essential that school psychologists understand normal and abnormal personality development and apply this information to empirical models that attempt to explain students' social–emotional, behavioral, and affective development. Second, personality assessment must be conducted within an ecological context, recognizing that social, emotional, and affective behavior occurs within a child's or adolescent's interdependent domains of self, home, peers, school, and community. Third, personality assessment in the schools should occur within a context that recognizes that students often are referred for school-based assessment as a function of their (usually, inappropriate) behavior or affect at school, and that the (equally inappropriate) goal of the referral is to identify the student's "psychological deficit" and "fix" him or her. Instead of adopting and reinforcing this perspective, the assessment should evaluate the student within the context of an instructional environment that includes the student, the teacher, the instructional process, and the curricula being delivered.

More specifically, along with a functional assessment of the student's inappropriate behaviors, the assessment also should focus on students' skills and assets, the ways that they develop resilient responses to challenging events and environments, and the enabling conditions that facilitate their growth and development (Gable & colleagues, 1998; Tilly & colleagues, 1998). The assessment, then, provides information that can help psychologists and educators differentiate where the student is making good social, emotional, or behavioral growth, and where he or she is exhibiting inappropriate behavior and/or affect. This approach also must be sensitive to situation- and setting-specific behavior, and it should guide the school psychologist's thinking so that personality assessment becomes (a) an empirically-based problem-solving process, that (b) links assessment directly to intervention, and that (c) integrates referred problems and their needed solutions into a realistic and holistic context.

As a last context, when personality assessment is conducted solely under IDEA, it is usually done to determine either whether the student is eligible for services for emotional disturbances or whether a specific inappropriate act was a manifestation of a behavioral or emotional disability. Relative to eligibility, the best reason to initiate an assessment is the lack of sufficient progress in resolving a student's specific social, emotional, or behavioral concerns that have already been functionally analyzed and addressed (albeit, unsuccessfully) through systematic, classroom-based intervention. Given this, the personality assessment process would build from the functional assessment and intervention data, and move into more intensive analyses including the ecological contexts involving the student. Once again, the primary goal of the assessment is to determine functionally "why" the referred situation is occurring, not "whether" the student qualifies as eligible for services.

CLASSIFICATION SYSTEMS OR APPROACHES RELATED TO PERSONALITY ASSESSMENT

Framing the personality assessment process are three influential classification systems or approaches. While the functional assessment of a student's behavior and affect is more relevant to planning viable and effective intervention programs, the presence of these classification systems cannot be ignored given their widespread use and their determination of much of our diagnostic nomenclature.

The *Diagnostic and Statistical Manual of Mental Disorders, Fourth Edition* (*DSM-IV*) (American Psychiatric Association, 1994) attempts to describe specific disorders of infancy, childhood, and adolescence as behaviorally as possible. Among the strengths of the *DSM-IV* are the research reviews and clinical trials that preceded its publication, as well as the "common" diagnostic language and assessment goals that result when practitioners evaluate students using its criteria. Among the *DSM-IV*'s weaknesses are its:

- Dependence on a medical model perspective of behavior and pathology
- Focus on criteria that more describe a referred student's problem than help to functionally assess why it is occurring
- Excessive differentiation of the cited mental disorders with more than 350 different diagnoses or labels
- Relative lack of diagnostic agreement among clinicians
- Lack of clear applicability, for some diagnoses, in school-versus-home or community treatment settings

The empirically based classification approach results from many researchers' factor analyses of characteristics exhibited by emotionally disturbed and behaviorally disordered children and adolescents. At a broadband level, two factors—internalizing or overcontrolled and externalizing or undercontrolled—have consistently been identified. These factors broadly describe students who demonstrate depressed, withdrawing, or uncommunicative behavioral styles versus hyperactive, aggressive, or delinquent behavioral styles, respectively. At a narrowband level, many different behavioral clusters have been identified, some of which vary developmentally across age, gender, and sample. To date, the following narrowband factors have been most consistently identified, largely through behavior rating scale research:

- Aggressive, delinquent, or conduct disordered behavior
- Attention problems/motor excess
- Thought problems/psychotic behavior
- Social problems/immaturity
- Anxious, withdrawn, depressed behavior
- Somatic complaints

From a psychometric perspective, the factor analytic approach, along with the resulting broadband and narrowband factors, represents a very sophisticated approach to classifying and comparing behavior. However, this classification approach does not facilitate an accurate identification of all problems or the development of appropriate interventions in every case. In fact, it must be emphasized that the factors derived from this approach are statistical clusters of correlated behaviors or characteristics, and that there were numerous theoretically and empirically based decisions made by the researchers that influenced which items appear on which factors. Thus, although behavior rating and objective personality assessment often are used as part of a personality assessment, it should be noted that:

- Some of their factors may be multidimensional despite the fact that their names suggest single clinical entities.
- The specific items clinically endorsed during an assessment may relate correlationally, as opposed to causally, to the named factor where it appears.
- The named factor may or may not directly relate to a clinical diagnosis, for example, as defined in the *DSM-IV*.

(Note: some of the assessment scales used are the Child Behavior Checklist, Personality Inventory for Children and for Youth, Children's Personality Questionnaire, Early School and High School Personality Questionnaires, Minnesota Multiphasic Personality Inventory-Adolescents, and Millon Adolescent Personality Inventory.)

The classification approach used by IDEA involves a definition of emotional disturbance (ED) that:

- Is primarily educational and that does not lend itself to psychological differentiation or analysis
- Requires a state or district to behaviorally operationalize in order to be used in any consistent manner
- Necessitates only a yes or no "diagnostic" decision
- Encourages a "medical-model" perspective of disturbed behavior
- Excludes (without definition) "socially maladjusted" students
- Ignores the fact that many students exhibit two or more co-occurring behavioral or affective disorders

Expanding briefly, the IDEA definition focuses on conditions that "adversely affect educational performance," desensitizing our schools to students who progress educationally but still need socialization or mental health services. The definition leaves such characteristics as "inappropriate types of behaviors or feelings," "under normal circumstances," "over a long period of time," and "to a marked degree" to state, school district, or individual multidisciplinary teams to operationalize. Finally, the definition permits a simplistic "yes, the child qualifies as an ED child," or "no, the child does not qualify" mentality, which suggests that the student owns or does not own the causal pathology. Thus, as a guide for personality assessment, the ED definition and criteria provide little guidance and, indeed, may result in a number of "false-negative" decisions relative to students with psychological needs who, nonetheless, are not exhibiting educational problems. Moreover, this approach potentially discourages an ecological perspective that focuses on functional assessment, intervention, and problem resolution.

THE PERSONALITY ASSESSMENT PROCESS

As an ecological problem-solving process to explain a student's social–emotional, behavioral, or affective difficulties, personality assessment is conducted to validate specific hypotheses that explain why a student is exhibiting those difficulties so interventions, linked to the data, can be developed and implemented. Six broad hypothesis domains are generally used to help explain a student's difficulties:

1. Family, neighborhood, and community

2. School district and school

3. Classroom and peer

4. Teacher and instructional

5. Curricular

6. Student conditions

In completing their assessments, school psychologists use four primary data collection approaches:

1. Review and analysis of records and previous assessment and intervention data

2. Interviews with individuals who have significant knowledge and experience with the student (including the student)

3. Behavioral observations and functional analyses of the student and others related to the concerns

4. Assessments with formal personality tools and techniques

Using these data, school psychologists also recognize and differentiate between causal and correlational explanations of referred problems. Causal pathways involve conditions and characteristics that directly cause specific student outcomes. Critically, many of the student, teacher, and curricular conditions noted previously tend to be causal to student outcomes. Correlational pathways involve conditions that influence student outcomes, increasing or decreasing the probability that they occur, but not assuring their occurrence. Thus, many of the peer, classroom, school, district, family, and community characteristics tend to be more correlational.

Personality assessment, then, is a process and not a product. It is not simply the administration of a battery of broadband or narrowband scales that globally describe or label a student's "pathology." Indeed, it is an integrated process that strategically uses its assessment outcomes to formulate functional interventions. Personality assessment uses a multimethod, multisource, multisetting approach. And, it focuses on direct assessment wherever possible, avoiding or minimizing approaches that require interpolations or subjective interpretations from the data collected. Finally, appropriate personality assessment is culturally sensitive and free from bias. In the end, the success of the personality assessment process should be based on the behavioral and treatment changes that occur from the resulting treatment program.

—*Howard M. Knoff*

See also Applied Behavior Analysis; Behavioral Assessment; Buros Mental Measurements Yearbook; Projective Testing; Psychopathology in Children; Social–Emotional Assessment; Theories of Human Development

REFERENCES AND FURTHER READING

American Psychiatric Association. (1994). *Diagnostic and statistical manual of mental disorders* (4th ed.). Washington, DC: Author.

Gable, R. A., Quinn, M. M., Rutherford, R. B., & Howell, K. W. (1998). *Assessing student problem behavior-Part II: Conducting the functional behavioral assessment.* Washington, DC: American Institutes for Research, Center for Effective Collaboration and Practice.

Reschly, D. J., Tilly, W. D., & Grimes, J. P. (Eds.). (1998). *Functional and noncategorical identification and intervention in special education.* Des Moines: Iowa Department of Education.

Tilly, W. D., Kovaleski, J., Dunlap, G., Knoster, T. P., Bambara, L., & Kincaid, D. (1998). *Functional behavioral assessment: Policy development in light of emerging research and practice.* Alexandria, VA: National Association of State Directors of Special Education.

PHENYLKETONURIA

Phenylketonuria (PKU) is a rare, inborn metabolism error resulting from a deficiency of phenylalanine hydroxylase (an enzyme) transmitted by an autosomal (i.e., nonsex chromosome) recessive gene. The incidence of PKU in the United States is approximately 1:15,000, and 1 in 60 persons (generally mothers) is a carrier of the gene.

The most serious outcomes of PKU are moderate to severe mental retardation and behaviors such as hyperactivity, inattention, perceptual–motor problems, aggressiveness, negative mood, and motor difficulties. Children untreated for PKU are normal at birth, but begin to show slowed brain development by four months.

Well-established screening procedures (via blood analysis) are used to test every child for PKU at birth. Managing the disorder via dietary supplements from the first month of life can result in normal development. PKU diets use synthetic foods that provide amino acids with minimal or no phenylalanine. A diet free of phenylalanine must be supplemented with low-protein dietary supplements and measured amounts of fruits, vegetables, and synthetic foods to maintain essential phenylalanine levels. Dietary compliance for both parents and children may be a significant problem. Misunderstanding, mismanagement, or lax attention to the diet may delay development of the child. Instruction in nutrition education is useful for parents of children with PKU. Specific dietary instructions should be shared with educators, babysitters, friends, and family members. As children reach adolescence, more difficulties may develop with peer pressure.

School personnel can assist parents and children with PKU in maintaining and monitoring the diet.

—Karen T. Carey

PHONEMIC AWARENESS

Phonemic awareness can be described as a bridge between spoken and written language. Specifically, phonemic awareness refers to the consciousness of sounds within spoken words. It is an auditory understanding and not directly tied to letter–sound correspondences, yet it is fundamental to reading.

HISTORY

Historically, educators believed there were two main components in learning to read—visual and auditory elements. Therefore, it was believed that if students were taught the letters (visual) and the sounds (auditory), which is essentially phonics, then students would learn how to decode words. Even though many children learned to read this way, there were some children who struggled to read. During the 1960s, two Russian psychologists, Zhurova and Elkonin, began to realize that there was a relationship between phoneme segmentation (clearly saying each sound within a word) abilities and reading achievement. Research by Liberman, as cited by Blachman (2000), in America confirmed that children who could read well were able to segment phonemes within words; however, the poor readers were unable to analyze and complete these tasks. Therefore, beginning readers need to recognize that speech is composed of segmented units called phonemes. Phonemes are abstract, and they are the smallest units of sound within spoken words.

THEORY AND RESEARCH

Extensive research has been completed since these early studies. As cited by Blachman (2000), the results continue to provide evidence that phoneme awareness remains a strong predictor of reading ability and children lacking in this ability stay behind as poor readers.

Numerous researchers, such as Ehri (1979) and Perfetti (1985), have identified a reciprocal relationship between early phonological awareness and early literacy acquisition. The hypothesis of this relationship means that phonological awareness, such as rhyme and alliteration (the repetition of the same sounds or the same kinds of sounds at the beginning of words), may facilitate literacy development, and that reading instruction may, in turn, influence more reflective phonemic awareness, which contributes to an increase in overall reading scores. Therefore, one can say that phonemic awareness is both a cause and a consequence of learning to read.

Yopp's (1995) work enables educators to understand the difference between phonological and phonemic awareness. Phonological awareness refers to a global understanding of language, such as having an ear for rhyme, alliteration, and identifying syllables. Phonemic awareness is the manipulation of sounds within words, such as matching sounds; counting phonemes; identifying beginning, middle, and ending sounds; and segmenting and blending, which are simple tasks. Phonemic awareness also includes compound tasks such as deleting and substituting phonemes, which require children to handle complex tasks in memory.

INTERVENTION PROCESSES

Early family and preschool literacy experiences such as being read to and language play appear to assist children with a positive advantage in literacy. Many children will naturally acquire some phonemic awareness from hearing stories, participating in language play, and learning to read and spell even if phonemic awareness is not explicitly taught to them. However, the review of research by the National Reading Panel (2000) shows that direct instruction does improve phonemic awareness, which positively impacts reading scores.

The daily time that is recommended for phonemic awareness training should be based on the reason for the instruction as well as situational factors. Overall, phonemic awareness training should be used in moderation because it is a means rather than an end. The maximum allotted instructional time period should be 30 minutes, as concluded by the National Reading Panel (2000).

Phonemic awareness training may differ based on the children's developmental level rather than specific grade level. However, general guidelines for the grades can be provided. For example, at a preschool and kindergarten level in which students have little phonological awareness, the students will learn from listening exercises such as rhyme (e.g., *cat* and *hat*) and alliteration (e.g., the *big black beagle barked ballistically*). They will also be asked to count the number of sounds in words, and to identify the beginning, middle, or final sound. First graders will continue to experience these simple tasks, but a much greater emphasis is placed on segmenting sounds (e.g., *cat* becomes *c-a-t*) and blending sounds (e.g., *c-a-t* becomes *cat*). As first-grade students learn to read, they also study how to substitute phonemes (e.g., take the /b/ off *bat* and replace it with /c/ to make *cat*) and delete phonemes (say *plate* without the /p/). Many times, phonemic awareness instruction begins to taper off after first grade, so greater time may be devoted to additional reading and writing components. However, for students who need the assistance, second-grade instruction may continue to focus on substituting and deleting phonemes. Substituting and deleting phonemes are complex tasks that are strengthened as a result of basic reading knowledge and are a consequence of reading.

Furthermore, the application of writing and spelling also contributes to the development of phonemic awareness. For example, when children write the word *snake*, they must use their phoneme discrimination to print the sounds they hear. Adults may gain insight into how children perceive the alphabetic system and monitor children's phoneme awareness by permitting children to use invented spellings.

One instructional tool that helps students analyze sounds is the Elkonin box. This tool requires students to say a word slowly and move a chip into the box for each sound they pronounce. Ball and Blachman, cited by Blachman (2000), expanded on Elkonin's work by using a "say-it-and-move-it" procedure. First, kindergarten students take blank tiles and move them as they pronounce each phoneme. Next, letter–sound correspondences are introduced and students participate in activities that emphasize sound–symbol relationships. Results show that students can begin segmenting by using blank tiles. Then as students are developmentally ready, letters should be added to the instruction because the letters seem to facilitate the transfer to reading and spelling.

Some children experience problems with phonological processing when their sound representations in memory are less stable than those of proficient readers. For these students who struggle or who may have a disability, it is recommended that their phonemic awareness interventions be longer, more intense, and more explicit. One method that has been used to help these children is the Lindamood Phonemic Sequencing program (formally called the Auditory Discrimination in Depth [ADD] program), developed by Lindamood

and Lindamood in 1975. This approach helps children identify and monitor their articulations and mouth movements so the students discover when one phoneme ends and another begins. Sounds are given labels such as *lip poppers* or *tip tappers*, which help children to master sounds. The instruction is then connected to letters to assist reading development.

ASSESSMENT APPROACHES

The simple and compound tasks that have been described in the previous section are also used to assess students' phonemic awareness ability. The National Reading Panel (2000) informed educators that phonemic awareness assessment is more effective when specific phonological analysis tests are used rather than standardized reading and spelling tests. Several tests that have been used include:

- The Lindamood Auditory Conceptualization Test (1975). This test assesses how well children can discriminate one speech sound from another within a given word, and the children's ability to perceive and compare the number of sounds and the order of sounds within words.
- Dynamic Indicators of Basic Early Literacy Skills (DIBELS) (1996), developed by the University of Oregon. This test has two subtests that measure phonological awareness; one that asks children to identify and produce initial sounds of a word and the second that assesses children's ability to produce sounds within a word.
- The Yopp-Singer Test of Phoneme Segmentation (1975). This test is a simple, quick assessment that teachers may use to learn more about their students' phonemic abilities and to effectively plan instruction.

ROLE OF SCHOOL PSYCHOLOGIST

School psychologists have been trained to conduct assessments and observations of students and to assist in the planning of intervention. School psychologists often begin by analyzing a child's cognition and achievement. If the formal tests for cognition and achievement indicate that the area of reading is a challenge to a student, then the school psychologist usually administers one of the phonemic awareness assessments to gain a better and more in-depth understanding of the child's phonological abilities.

The school psychologist plays an instrumental role on a multidisciplinary team that plans a child's intervention. Even though the teacher or reading specialist may be the person providing the intervention, the school psychologist continues to maintain a role by monitoring progress and conducting follow-up testing.

CONCLUSION

Phonemic awareness, an auditory understanding of sounds, plays an instrumental role in learning to read. Several different tasks such as blending, segmenting, and deleting and substituting may be categorized into simple and compound phonemic awareness. Simple tasks facilitate reading development, and compound tasks appear to be strengthened as a result of the reading process. Supplemental phonemic awareness instruction with letters may aid in the transition of prereaders to reading and spelling. Assessments may be used to gain further understanding and analysis of a child's phonemic awareness, and the school psychologist will be able to provide guidance in the assessment and intervention process.

—*Donita Massengill*

See also Academic Achievement; Curriculum-Based Assessment; Early Intervention; Learning; Reading Interventions and Strategies

REFERENCES AND FURTHER READING

Blachman, B. A. (2000). Phonological awareness. In M. L. Kamil, P. B. Mosenthal, P. D. Pearson, & R. Barr (Eds.), *Handbook of reading research* (Vol. 3, pp. 483–502). Mahwah, NJ: Erlbaum.

Ehri, L. C. (1979). Linguistic insight: Threshold of reading acquisition. In T. G. Waller & G. E. MacKinnon (Eds.), *Reading research: Advances in theory and practice* (Vol. 1, pp. 63–144). New York: Academic.

Good, R. H. (2001). *Using dynamic indicators of basic early literacy skills (DIBELS) in an outcomes-driven model: Steps to reading outcomes.* Washington, DC: U.S. Dept. of Education, Office of Educational Research and Improvement, Educational Resources Information Center.

Kaminski, R., & Good, R. H., III. (1996). Toward a technology for assessing basic early literacy skills. *School Psychology Review, 25*(2), 215–227.

Lindamood, C., & Lindamood, P. (1975). *The ADD program: Auditory discrimination in depth.* Austin, TX: DLM Teaching Resources.

National Reading Panel. (2000). *Teaching children to read: An evidenced-based assessment of the scientific research literature on reading and its implications for reading instruction.* Washington, DC: National Institute of Child Health and Human Development, Report of NIH Pub. No. 00–4769. Retrieved April 12, 2004, from http://www.nationalreading panel.org

Perfetti, C. A. (1985). *Reading ability.* New York: Oxford University Press.

Yopp, H. (1995). A test for assessing phonemic awareness in young children. *The Reading Teacher, 49*(1), 20–29.

PICA

Pica is an eating disorder typically defined as the persistent eating of nonnutritive substances for a period of at least one month at an age in which the behavior is developmentally inappropriate. Individuals suffering from pica mouth and/or ingest a variety of substances, including, but not limited to, clay, dirt, stones, hair, feces, lead, plastic, paper, paint chips, chalk, and wood. Pica's etiology is unknown; however, hypotheses ranging from psychosocial causes to biochemical factors have been implicated. The prevalence of pica is also unknown because the disorder is often unrecognized or underreported. However, it is most commonly reported in children and individuals with mental retardation. Complications associated with pica range from mild to life-threatening, depending on the materials ingested and the subsequent medical consequences. Individuals diagnosed with pica undergo therapy, dietary modifications, and pharmacotherapy if needed. Pica usually remits spontaneously and, therefore, should not cause any serious complications or educational deficits if treated early in its onset.

—*Tonishea Coleman*

See also DSM-IV

PLAY-BASED ASSESSMENT. *See*
Authentic Assessment; Classroom Observation; Developmental Milestones; Infant Assessment; Preschool Assessment

PORTFOLIO ASSESSMENT

Portfolios are systematic collections of students' work samples over time and may contain materials that focus on particular content areas (i.e., math *or* language arts), or they may take in materials from across students' school experience (i.e., math *and* language arts). They serve multiple purposes and are used to highlight students' best work, document their achievements, and evaluate their level of performance. Additionally, they are programmatically implemented at varying levels of educational organization from large-scale programs across states and districts (Kentucky and Vermont), to smaller units such as schools, classrooms, or even particular students.

The use of portfolios in schools provides information that cannot be obtained in norm-referenced, standardized assessments (e.g., standardized achievement tests). In recent years, there has been a trend to use "authentic" assessment approaches that describe and evaluate students' performance within the actual context of their specific classrooms. Portfolio assessment falls under the domain of the authentic approach. Where standardized assessments may be characterized as being objective, standardized, and reliable (similar results in equivalent circumstances), authentic assessments are described as being subjective, individualized, and ecologically valid (i.e., they are sensitive to the unique people and processes in a given location) (Wiggins, 1998). Portfolios are "authentic" in that they are based upon an individual student's actual curriculum and instruction within the context of his or her classroom. The norm-referenced group for a standardized achievement assessment may be national (e.g., Woodcock-Johnson Test), although its content may be only generally related to a student's curriculum experience.

ESSENTIAL CHARACTERISTICS

Because portfolios are used across a wide range of settings and for disparate purposes, the term itself has become generic. A portfolio may refer to a year-end collection of reflective writing assignments for a high school student or to a competency-based portfolio used for special education documentation for a second grader receiving educably mentally handicapped (EMH) services (i.e., services specifically for a student with mental retardation). Even though the content and use of portfolios is quite varied, some general features are usually associated with them (McMillan, 2004).

The content is not random and collected haphazardly, but rather purposefully, in that work samples and documents are chosen in a systematic manner. Selection and inclusion of portfolio materials are guided by the preestablished purpose of the portfolio. If the goal is to demonstrate competency in three different forms of writing, then works reflecting this outcome would be collected. Examples come directly from the students and are samples of "performance in context" (Woolfolk, 2004).

Another major benefit of this approach is the collection of authentic works, for example, book reports, writing logs, and paper drafts that come directly from students' instructional experiences. In some cases, portfolios are designed to foster a reflective process wherein students write about and evaluate their sample. A language arts portfolio may contain successive drafts of a paper that a student has evaluated and edited. A teacher may use these writings to link assessment and instruction. For example, the writings may highlight a need to spend more instructional time on word choice and organization. Ultimately, portfolios need clear guidelines for scoring. Evaluation should follow a rubric that is reliable and uses sound criteria.

THREE TYPES OF PORTFOLIOS

Portfolios come in three basic forms: showcase, documentation, and evaluation. Showcase portfolios consist of samples of a student's best work in either one or several work areas. A third grader's showcase might consist of five each of her best stories, math problem worksheets, and letters to friends. The items are collected and reflected upon throughout the year and then sent home on the last day of school. Documentation portfolios show development over the course of a circumscribed period of time, such as through a unit or subject area. Evaluation portfolios may be used to assess multiple students' level of attainment of some particular skill or competency. To accomplish this goal, the documents are more uniform across students with a necessary focus on standardization of content and scoring. For example, content of all of the portfolios in a particular classroom would be drawn from the same proscribed assignments and evaluated through the same scoring rubric.

LIMITATIONS

Portfolios are not without limitations, especially when used for evaluation. Main characteristics, such as the systematic collection of authentic materials, also contribute to limitations on their use and generalizability. When a teacher commits her entire class to the portfolio process, she or he will need to start with a well-defined instructional purpose and create valid rubrics to reliably score the many assignments that will be collected in each student's portfolio. Salvia and Ysseldyke (2004) point out that teachers have to adequately address issues ranging from scoring to bias to time and money. They specifically mention problems with score interpretation, aggregation, and reliability, subjectivity in evaluation, and the time investment necessary to effectively implement a portfolio process across each of an individual teacher's classes.

THE USE OF PORTFOLIOS IN ASSESSMENT

Generically portfolios have applications to the work of school psychologists through their virtue of being potentially data-rich collections of students' specified work samples over a period to time. However, their usefulness in assessment and decision making depends upon, first, the portfolio's relevance to the issue under consideration (e.g., an art portfolio may not be of much use to a school psychologist considering a student's reading fluency) and, second, issues such as the scoring rubric's validity and reliability. The rubric must have the properties of measuring what it claims to evaluating (e.g., descriptive vs. figurative language in an essay) and of doing so in the same manner for each student (knowing which student wrote the essay should not affect the results). Portfolios that meet these criteria can be used for assessment in a number of cases.

Augmentation

Portfolios can bolster traditional assessment practices by augmenting assessments that were standardized on a national sample to a hypothetical national curriculum. By providing an ecologically valid comparison to other students who are receiving the same curriculum and instruction, a student's achievement can be considered from a local context. The strength of portfolios comes from being able to ascertain how a student compares to peers who have had the same instruction and curriculum in the same classroom environment.

Documentation

Students who are involved in the child study or prereferral process, in which a team discusses the student and tries new strategies, are mandated to receive alternative interventions before being referred for special education assessment. Portfolio assessment offers a means to document a student's response to intervention.

Regular Education

Portfolio assessment can be used as a component of a regular education problem-solving model to help school psychologists and regular education teachers screen for students at risk for academic failure. Especially in districts that have local norms, portfolios can be used to screen students for early indications of academic difficulties.

Linkage

Portfolios may be very useful in linking assessment to instruction in regular education. School psychologists may use portfolios as a part of curriculum-based assessment in which students' progress is monitored and instruction planned by assessing their accuracy in bona fide classroom assignments and then planning interventions based upon the student's level of performance. For example, if a teacher requests help with a student who is "illiterate," a portfolio may be an essential element for establishing and documenting the initial baseline of the student's word recognition (words they can identify and know the meaning of), fluency (the speed and accuracy of reading), and comprehension (understanding what is read). Portfolio samples of the student's actual work will both support the assessment of the instructional match and the evaluation of the effectiveness of the intervention(s).

Instructional match, that is, the fit between the curriculum materials being used, the instructional methods employed, and their correspondence with students' specific levels of ability, can be ascertained and used to meet a student at his or her current level of skill. For example, a portfolio assessment of a student presumed to be struggling with composing stories based upon class readings may actually highlight the need for the student to first develop better reading fluency to be able to understand what he or she is to write about. Once interventions are decided upon and put into practice, their effectiveness can be documented through the targeted collection of school work in a portfolio.

Professional Training

Recent changes to accreditation standards (e.g., National Council for Accreditation of Teacher Education, National Association of School Psychologists) have required that professional training programs collect data on "outcome" measures for the efficacy of a program. Many universities are using electronic portfolios to meet this demand. Some school psychology programs (e.g., University of North Carolina) require each preservice student to create and maintain an electronic portfolio that demonstrates their acquisition of skill and content related to these outcome measures. Each student in the University of North Carolina program is required to keep an electronic portfolio in which he or she collects work samples related to the National Association of School Psychologists' core competencies. The students write about how their portfolio materials demonstrate mastery of standards and present the portfolios to their advisor at the end of each academic year. These types of portfolios are likely to become ubiquitous in training programs.

—*Steve Knotek*

See also Authentic Assessment

REFERENCES AND FURTHER READING

McMillan, J. H. (2004). *Classroom assessment: Principles and practice for effective instruction* (3rd ed.). Boston: Allyn & Bacon.

Salvia, J., & Ysseldyke, J. E. (2004). *Assessment in special and inclusive education* (9th ed.). Boston: Houghton Mifflin.

Wiggins, G. P. (1998). *Educative assessment: Designing assessment to inform and improve student performance.* San Francisco: Jossey-Bass.

Wolf, D. (1989). Portfolio assessment: Sampling student work. *Educational Leadership, 46*(7), 35–39.

Woolfolk, A. (2004). *Educational Psychology* (9th ed.). Boston: Allyn & Bacon.

POSITIVE BEHAVIOR SUPPORT

A relative newcomer to the literature on management of difficult behavior, and even more recently school reform, positive behavior support (PBS) traces its origins to the science of applied behavior analysis. As such, it is an extension of operant conditioning learning theory into a broader context of "discipline," or the management of problem behavior in family, school, and community settings. Operant conditioning originated in the early 20th century from animal learning experiments conducted by Skinner and students at Harvard University. These experiments led to a breakthrough in conceptions of how organisms learn by showing that particular forms of behavior are learned in response to what follows them (i.e., reinforcement or punishment) in a contingent relationship, hence the term *operant conditioning*. Its extension to child-learning and applications to the modification of human behavior can be traced to the mid-1960s and the appearance of the *Journal of Applied Behavior Analysis*.

The term *positive behavior support* first appeared in the late 1980s and early 1990s and was largely identified with research in special education as distinguished from applied behavior analysis, which has been from its outset more closely identified with clinical and child psychology. With its focus on problem behavior, often associated with disabilities in the broader context of schools, PBS distanced itself from the use of punishers, or aversive consequences for management of problem behavior. The "positive" in PBS reflects the emerging theoretical perspective that even the most challenging behavior can be managed without resorting to all but the mildest forms of punishment. This position has engendered controversy that continues in various forms to the present day. Many researchers and practitioners associated with applied behavior analysis argue that punishment has always been a small and decreasing part of that applied science, and that PBS, with its broader context of application and its close ties to the normalization-inclusion movement within special education, lacks some of the scientific rigor that has historically been a hallmark of applied behavior analysis.

Positive behavior support is addressed to broad outcomes framed as comprehensive lifestyle changes and enhancements in quality of life. The conceptual "heart" of PBS is functional behavioral assessment (FBA), a comprehensive approach to assessment that is addressed to the question of why a problem behavior is occurring. It asks, what function is this behavior serving for the individual, and what alternatives might be identified that can be taught to the individual that are socially acceptable and that can replace the problem behavior in the individual's repertoire? This emphasis on the functions of challenging behavior positions PBS as a pedagogy and thus enables its practitioners and researchers to fully identify with and contribute to the teaching-learning mission of schools.

Positive behavior support has emerged as a highly contextualized applied science that focuses on conducting rigorous research with carefully controlled applications in complex "naturalistic" school and community environments. The "support" part of PBS reflects its emphasis on prevention, first of the emergence of even more antisocial behavior if not addressed early on; and secondly, of the possibility of removal of the individual from mainstream participation in school and community life because of unchecked antisocial behavior.

Research on PBS has led to the formation of an applied pedagogy at three distinct levels of application. Level 1, individual support reflects the following logic. An individual is identified who is at risk of being removed from a mainstream social context, say a classroom, for reasons of challenging behavior. The problem behavior is carefully defined so that it can be clearly measured. A functional behavioral assessment is conducted, which may include documentation reviews, standardized tests, medical and physical reviews, contextual observations, interviews, and so forth. From this information, a hypothesis is formed as to the function of the problem behavior and possible prosocial replacement behaviors that might be successfully taught to the individual. For example, a child in a second grade classroom displays an annoying behavior of vocalizing during a period of quiet workbook time. Efforts by the teacher only exacerbate the problem, leading to the child's removal from the classroom. An FBA results in a hypothesis that the annoying behavior is serving the function of escape from the workbook task. A decision is made to teach the child to raise his or her hand (prosocial behavior) to which the teacher responds by allowing him or her to engage in another less demanding task. The student is allowed to return to the more difficult task on his or her own time. Measures of "inappropriate vocalization" (problem behavior) are noted in this example to reflect decreases over time inversely proportionate to increases in "raising hand to request activity change."

Much research into individual support has tended to be concentrated on problems that:

- Serve the function of enhancing or reducing sensory stimulation (i.e., problems of autism and disturbances of sensory integration)
- Focus on seeking attention
- Seek to escape from or avoid difficult tasks

From the FBA process and its resultant hypothesis, a behavior support plan is developed, ideally by an interdisciplinary team of individuals who can "network" the various stakeholders in the process such as teachers, students, and family members, so that the entire social life space of the individual is engaged in the replacement process. Careful data are collected to evaluate progress, and adjustments to the plan are made if needed, to maximize the probability of a successful outcome. The individual support process is discontinued when the presenting problem is solved.

Level 2 and level 3 applications of PBS refer, respectively, to group and universal applications of the pedagogy. Examples of level 2, or group applications, that have appeared in the research literature have dealt with unruly hallway behavior in urban schools during transition periods; problems of classroom management; problems of noisy and unruly behavior during lunchtimes in a school cafeteria; and problems occurring in school yards during recess. In level 3 applications, the term "universal" refers to an extension of PBS interventions to the broader contexts of entire social systems such as schools, community settings, and combinations of these.

The bulk of PBS level 3 research has emerged as "schoolwide" applications. This process typically takes two to three years to fully instantiate in a single school, and requires extensive technical assistance as well as professional and staff development activities. These usually take the form of ongoing, longitudinal training sessions conducted by district-level or external providers with requisite expertise, and have been shown to produce significant positive outcomes in academic as well as social indicators for students, particularly in urban, "inner city" schools. One "target" of schoolwide PBS, for example, is a significant reduction in reliance by teaching staff on exclusionary discipline tactics such as office referrals, suspensions, detentions, and expulsions. When teachers learn to manage problem behavior in the context of the general education curriculum and classroom teaching, fewer referrals out of class occur and the resultant increase in instructional time becomes associated with higher state assessment scores and other measures of academic performance.

Schoolwide PBS teaches the social expectations of the school to all students, not just those identified for specialized supports. Often these applications will include some form of "tickets" or other tangible rewards for appropriate behavior on the part of all students. As with a token economy, these tickets may be exchangeable for some desirable items such as coupons for fast food restaurants, pictures posted on the "wall of fame," and so forth. These "catch-em-being-good" (or acknowledgment) awards have been shown through research to be identified with positive changes in "school climate," a broad indicator of potential positive trends in academic performance, particularly on the part of inner city and other low-achieving schools.

In summary, positive behavior support (PBS) is an applied pedagogical science. An outgrowth of applied behavior analysis, it extends basic principles of reinforcement and stimulus control (i.e., features of the environment that come, through conditioning, to signal to the person that a particular response will be met with reinforcement or punishment) to a broader context of schools, family settings, and the community. It is of interest to school psychologists because of its focus on prevention and schoolwide problem-solving opportunities. Of the variety of school-based professionals, school psychologists are perhaps best trained and equipped to provide the requisite training and technical assistance needed within schools to successfully undertake or guide the functions of behavioral assessment; team problem solving; systematic data collection and analysis; and the provision of new information to school personnel growing out of the expanding base of positive behavior support. That PBS is growing in scope and application is reflected in its status as mandated school praxis in the Individual With Disabilities Education Act (IDEA); in its National Technical Assistance Center Web site; emergence of an international scholarly journal dedicated to the dissemination of research on its applications, *The Journal of Positive Behavior Interventions;* and the existence of an international guild, the Association for Positive Behavior Support.

—Wayne Sailor

See also Applied Behavior Analysis; Classroom Climate; Conditioning: Classical and Operant; Functional Behavioral Assessment

REFERENCES AND FURTHER READING

Crone, D. A., & Horner, R. H. (Eds.). (2003). *Building positive behavior support systems in schools.* New York: Guilford.

Koegel, L. K., Koegel, R. L., & Dunlap, G. (Eds.). (1996). *Positive behavioral support: Including people with difficult behavior in the community.* Baltimore: Paul H. Brookes.

Lucyshyn, J. M., Dunlap, G., & Albin, R. W. (Eds.). (2002). *Families & positive behavior support: Addressing problem behavior in family contexts.* Baltimore: Paul H. Brookes.

Turnbull, A., Edmonson, H., Griggs, P., Wickham, D., Sailor, W., Freeman, R., et al. (2002). A blueprint for schoolwide positive behavior support: Implementation of three components. *Exceptional Children* 68(3), 377–358.

POSITIVE REINFORCEMENT. *See*

Applied Behavior Analysis; Behavior; Behavior Intervention; Functional Behavior Assessment; Premack Principle; School Discipline; Verbal Praise

POSTTRAUMATIC STRESS DISORDER

Posttraumatic stress disorder (PTSD) is a condition that may occur as a result of experiencing a traumatic event. People who have PTSD suffer from difficult memories and painful feelings that do not seem to improve over time. PTSD is defined in the *Diagnostic and Statistical Manual of Mental Disorders, Fourth Edition-Text Revision* (*DSM-IV-TR*) (American Psychiatric Association, 2000). This is the reference book that physicians, psychiatrists, and psychologists use to diagnose mental disorders. Approximately 8% of the adult population of the United States will suffer from PTSD at some point during their lives, according to the *DSM-IV-TR*. Overall prevalence for children and adolescents is not known, but the incidence of PTSD in children exposed to traumatic events ranges from 8% to 75% for war, 19% to 100% for criminal victimization, and 0% to 91% for natural disasters (Saigh & colleagues, 1996).

Sometimes the diagnosis of PTSD has already been made and treatment is underway when a child comes to school. However, some children have undiagnosed or untreated PTSD. They may be referred to school psychologists for their behavior or learning problems. School psychologists can help teachers work with these children in the classroom. School psychologists can provide information that will help in the diagnosis of PTSD and assist in locating appropriate treatment.

HOW IS POSTTRAUMATIC STRESS DISORDER DIAGNOSED?

PTSD is a serious mental disorder that requires professional diagnosis and treatment. A psychiatrist or psychologist can diagnose PTSD by observing the conditions discussed in the following sections.

Exposure to Trauma

PTSD can only occur if an individual has experienced or witnessed a traumatic event that overwhelms the person's defenses and coping skills. Traumatic events have two characteristics:

1. The person experiencing or witnessing the event is afraid that someone will be hurt or killed. Actual death or serious injury may occur.

2. The person feels intense fear, helplessness, and horror. Children may show agitation and disorganized behavior.

The fear of death or injury and feeling powerless to stop what is happening combine to make the event traumatic.

PTSD occurs as a result of trauma, but experiencing trauma does not necessarily lead to PTSD. Approximately 70% of people experience potentially traumatic events during their lives, but most do not develop PTSD (Saigh & colleagues, 1996). Different people react differently to traumatic events. Some people recover quickly, while others struggle with their reactions and feelings long after the event.

Some types of traumatic events are more difficult to cope with than others. People are more likely to have long-lasting problems as a result of trauma if it is repeated or if another person, especially a friend or family member, caused the trauma (Allen, 1995). Greater amounts of trauma lead to a greater likelihood of PTSD symptoms (Allen, 1995).

Reexperiencing the Trauma

Reexperiencing trauma happens when memories of the traumatic event keep coming back even though they are unwanted. These memories might be recollections that keep coming to mind or they might be flashbacks, when it seems as though the traumatic event is actually happening all over again. Children who have experienced trauma sometimes play out the event over and over again with toys or dolls, but their play is not satisfying or fun. People frequently have nightmares about traumatic events they have experienced.

Avoidance of Reminders of the Trauma

A desire to avoid unwanted memories by trying to avoid reminders of the event is another characteristic of PTSD. People who experience trauma stay away from places or people that remind them of the event and do not want to talk about what happened. Details of the trauma may be hard to remember. An individual may also become withdrawn and distant from other people or show little emotion.

Increased Arousal

People who have experienced a traumatic event become overly sensitive and alert to what is going on around them. They may be easily startled by noises or have trouble sleeping. They may be irritable or find it hard to pay attention to other people, to family members, or to school, and work. Often the quality of school assignments or job performance decreases as the person is unable to concentrate on important daily tasks.

Duration of Symptoms

The symptoms of repeated memories, avoidance of reminders of the event, and increased arousal occur more than one month after the traumatic event. Many people who experience trauma start to recover within a few weeks as their lives begin to return to normal. However, for some people the disturbing thoughts and memories do not seem to go away. They continue to struggle with persistent painful feelings and symptoms. When this continues without improvement for more than one month, acute PTSD may be present. Chronic PTSD occurs when symptoms continue longer than three months.

Significant Impairment in Functioning

The changes that have occurred as a result of trauma significantly impair the person's everyday functioning. Life does not return to normal. Children's behavior may regress and be more like that of younger children. Children may develop fears related to the trauma or other fears such as fear of the dark or fear of being alone. Schoolwork suffers and grades may fall. Adolescents may drop out of school. Children and adolescents may behave badly, get in fights, or complain of physical symptoms such as headaches or stomachaches. Adults may be unable to return to work or to perform their jobs as before. Personal relationships may also suffer when people argue, blame one another, or find it difficult to trust others. The quality of life for the person who has suffered the trauma is worse than before.

Other disorders may occur along with PTSD. These include attention problems, depression, anxiety, substance abuse, and defiant or antisocial behavior. School failure and high-risk behaviors such as drug use, sexual activity, and reckless driving may occur with PTSD. Severe trauma resulting in PTSD can even contribute to long-term personality changes.

POSTTRAUMATIC STRESS DISORDER TREATMENT

Treatment for PTSD depends on the age and symptoms of the person. The first step in treatment is to help the individual return to daily activities such as work or school. Medication can help to keep symptoms under control. Hospitalization may be needed for safety. A stable and predictable routine in a safe environment can reduce anxiety and increase trust in other people.

Therapy provides individual support and may also assist in repairing family relationships. Learning about trauma and PTSD helps in understanding difficult symptoms and reactions. Participating in a group made up of people who have experienced similar events can be beneficial. Family counseling helps family members learn new ways of communicating and working with each other after a traumatic loss.

After the individual has become stronger and normal functioning has been restored, the therapist may begin to examine the details of the trauma itself. This type of therapeutic work occurs toward the end of treatment. It should only be done by a trained, experienced, and trusted professional therapist. Trauma therapy can help people understand and redefine the trauma as a manageable memory of an event rather than an as a catastrophe that continues to overwhelm their lives.

School psychologists serve three important functions with respect to PTSD (McNally, 1996):

1. They assist in making schools safe places for children and adults.

2. They help teachers and parents understand that learning and behavior problems can be a direct result of PTSD, and are not caused by laziness or lack of motivation.

3. They assist with a comprehensive evaluation to determine the risk and protective factors involved for an individual child who may have PTSD, such as intellectual ability and family support.

—*Julia Shaftel*

See also Abuse and Neglect; Counseling; *DSM-IV*; Fears; Psychopathology in Children; Violence in Schools

REFERENCES AND FURTHER READING

Allen, J. G. (1995). *Coping with trauma: A guide to self-understanding.* Washington, DC: American Psychiatric Press.

American Psychiatric Association. (2000). *Diagnostic and statistical manual of mental disorders* (4th ed., text rev.). Washington, DC: Author.

McNally, R. J. (1996). Assessment of posttraumatic stress disorder in children and adolescents. *Journal of School Psychology, 34,* 147–161.

Saigh, P. A., Green, B. L., & Korol, M. (1996). The history and prevalence of posttraumatic stress disorder with special reference to children and adolescents. *Journal of School Psychology, 34,* 107–131.

PRACTICE EFFECTS. *See* Behavior; Learning; Mastery Learning

PRADER-WILLI SYNDROME

Prader-Willi syndrome (PWS) is a rare neurobehavioral genetic disorder that affects numerous organ systems. It occurs in approximately 1 in 10,000 to 30,000 births and affects all races and genders. PWS impacts the functioning of the hypothalamus, a regulation center located in the brain, resulting in decreased growth hormone, altered reproductive hormones (e.g., hypogonadism), disruption in appetite control, and altered regulation of the autonomic nervous system (the nervous system associated with involuntary reactions). In infancy, PWS is associated with a poor sucking reflex and weak muscle tone. In later childhood, it is associated with:

- Excessive food seeking (with subsequent morbid obesity)
- Delayed development
- Mental retardation or learning disability (Intelligence test scores can range from 20 to 115; an average intelligence score for an individual with no disabilities is 100.)
- Characteristic physical features (e.g., short stature, small hands, small feet, almond-shaped eyes, small mouth with thin upper lip and down-turned corners, fair skin and hair)

Children and adolescents with PWS often have rigid thought processes, perseverative or obsessive thinking, and tenuous emotional control. A regular education classroom setting is preferred, although the child's developmental or emotional status may require a more restricted classroom environment. Teachers should use positive reinforcement for appropriate behavior and avoid emotional overstimulation. The classroom environment should be structured with clear, consistent rules provided. Holistic and spatial teaching approaches, such as showing the end product then breaking down the steps or using manipulatives, can be effective. A multimodal treatment approach is recommended with a combination of behavioral, emotional, linguistic, physical, and pharmacological interventions.

—*Katherine Newton and William A. Rae*

PREMACK PRINCIPLE

The Premack Principle is an operant conditioning principle that originated in David Premack's research with animals. According to Premack's (1965) principle, a behavior that has a higher probability of occurring may be used as a reinforcer for a behavior that has a lower probability of occurring. To increase the occurrence of a less preferred activity, a more preferred behavior should be made contingent upon the occurrence of the less-preferred, low-frequency behavior.

Several researchers replicating Premack's findings have conducted studies with both animals and humans to provide evidence supporting the Premack Principle. For example, Allen and Iwata (1980) were able to increase exercising behavior among a group of individuals with developmental disabilities by making time for playing games (high-probability behavior) contingent upon engaging in exercise (low-probability behavior). In another study, Geiger (1996), demonstrated the effectiveness of the Premack principle in middle school classrooms. By making recess, a high-probability behavior that children willingly engage in, dependent upon the demonstration of appropriate classroom behavior and completion of work in the classroom (low-probability behaviors), appropriate behavior and work completion increased.

—*Mary Lea Johanning*

See also Behavior Intervention; Conditioning: Classical and Operant

REFERENCES AND FURTHER READING

Allen, L. D., & Iwata, B. A. (1980). Reinforcing exercise maintenance: Using existing high-rate activities. *Behavior Modification, 4,* 337–354.

Geiger, B. (1996). A time to learn, a time to play: Premack's principle applied in the classroom. *American Secondary Education, 25,* 2–6.

Premack, D. (1965). Reinforcement theory. In D. Levine (Ed.), *Nebraska symposium on motivation,* (Vol. 13, pp. 123–188). Lincoln, NE: University of Nebraska Press.

PRESCHOOL ASSESSMENT

Preschool assessment is defined as the systematic observation and evaluation of children younger than school age typically children ages three to five years who have not yet entered kindergarten. The process may include the assessment of preacademic skills, language development, cognitive ability, social and emotional status, hearing and vision screening, and motor skills. The assessment of children in this age range presents unique challenges and a thorough understanding of the normal developmental patterns of young children is essential for accurate interpretation of assessment information. The results of preschool assessments do not have the reliability, or stability over time, seen in the evaluation of older children. Even so, when done with this caution in mind, assessment tools designed for young children can provide a broad range of information that leads to effective treatment through in-home services, preschools, or referral to other appropriate agencies or therapists with the goal of implementing effective interventions plans.

The importance of early intervention for young children with special needs has been well established. Federal law requires early identification and makes provision for services for preschool children. An assessment process is necessary to access these services and helpful in determining the nature and extent of the services needed. In addition to making a determination regarding the need or eligibility for services, the goal of preschool assessment is to determine a child's strengths and weaknesses, assess the degree and type of deviation from normal development, and design appropriate interventions. The process is not designed to make a definitive determination regarding functioning or make firm predictions about future development; rather, the focus is on current levels of functioning and the identification of strategies that will facilitate ongoing development.

Assessment of the functioning of preschool children has been fraught with controversy, just as the assessment of older children and adults. Questions arose regarding the very nature of intelligence, the role of the environment, and reliability of tests developed. By the 1960s, however, evaluation of young children increased significantly because of the involvement of the government in providing educational opportunities for special populations. With the establishment of Head Start and Follow Through, federally funded preschool programs that required documentation of their effectiveness through assessment, the need for evaluation instruments became apparent. These instruments represented a shift in the conceptualization of cognitive functioning. The emphasis moved from assessment of intelligence as a fixed entity to looking at the whole child, comprised of many different skills and abilities.

With the passage of Public Law 94–142, the first comprehensive legislation regarding special education, a free and appropriate public education was mandated for all children regardless of handicapping conditions. Public Law 99–457 extended the guaranteed rights to preschoolers (three to five years), with the option to extend these services to toddlers and infants. The reauthorization of Public Law 94–142 in 1990 renamed this legislation the Individuals With Disabilities Education Act (IDEA). This legislative act guaranteed special education services to young children and identified the same categories as provided for older children. Concerns developed regarding the specific identification of children in this group, given the nature of the development of young children and the assessment instruments available. Public Law 102–119 gave states the ability to use another category for preschool children, which is broader in nature. This category of developmental delay still required the use of appropriate diagnostic instruments and procedures. The most recent reauthorization occurred in 1997 by Public Law 105–17, which directly dealt with provision of services to all children with disabilities from birth to 21 years.

Embedded in these legislative requirements are guidelines for the assessment of young children. The tests used must be valid, administered by trained individuals, and capable of addressing the needs of the child within the educational setting. Multiple measures must be used and they must be free of bias. To this end, a child's native culture and language must be considered and the tests must be administered in the child's native language if appropriate. All areas of functioning must be addressed and input from a variety of sources including parents must be considered. A multidisciplinary group, including teachers, parents, school administrators, and those involved in the assessment process, is required to translate this information into appropriate educational programming.

Since the inception of laws requiring the provision of services for preschool children, there has been an increasing interest in the development of assessment instruments for this age range. Use of the appropriate instruments is only a part of the process of successful evaluation. Although specific criteria have been established to earn the credentials necessary to work with these children, universities offer classes in preschool assessment, and students are able to access practicum and internship sites where there are opportunities to gain these skills; many psychologists in practice are not specifically trained and therefore not qualified to carry out this specialized form of assessment.

As new tests are being developed and marketed, older tests continue to be refined and renormed. The type and variety of assessment instruments available reflects the idea that many aspects of development must be addressed when assessing a young child and that there are many sources of relevant information that must be considered. A better understanding of the development of reading skills, reinforced by the findings of the research conducted by the National Institutes of Mental Health—which examines the causes and treatments for reading difficulties—has encouraged the development of new tests that assess phonological awareness and processing, defined as understanding, manipulating, and learning the speech sounds corresponding to letters of the language. Clinicians are identifying and treating developmental, behavioral, and mood disorders such as depression, attention deficit hyperactivity disorder, and anxiety, in part because of an increased willingness and ability to assess these conditions in young children.

Although the process of assessing young children steadily improves, controversy continues regarding the application of assessment results in making program decisions. School programs that adopt the philosophy of the Gesell Institute and like-minded researchers and educators may recommend grade retention or late entry into kindergarten, believing that there is a predetermined pattern of growth and development for each child and that with time the child will develop skills in the deficit areas without the benefit of special education services. The current position of the National Association of School Psychologists states that retention is not a suitable practice except in rare situations, such as an illness that causes a child to miss a significant part of the school year. Repetition of a grade has not proved to be an effective strategy for improving academic functioning in children with delays. Assessment and subsequent reassessment of young children provide information necessary to develop the practices that offer the most benefit and eliminate those practices that are not helpful.

GOALS OF ASSESSMENT

Controversy has surrounded the entire process of preschool assessment, and some even question whether preschoolers should be assessed at all. Concerns are expressed about the effects of labeling children, the difficulty in predicting future problems, and the validity of the evaluation results with respect to preschoolers. But federal laws mandate that children meet eligibility requirements before they can be assigned to intervention programs and preschool assessment processes have flourished as a result. While evaluation methods provide a description of a preschooler's skills

and development, the assessment process has also been charged with providing information that can be used to make eligibility decisions. The goal of assessment is to provide a description of the child's current levels of functioning, information relevant to placement decision, and the means to develop an appropriate intervention plan.

The Position Statement on Early Childhood Assessment prepared by the National Association of School Psychologists (1999) promotes assessment practices for young children that are:

- Developmentally appropriate, ecological, comprehensive, skills-based, and family focused
- Conducted by a multidisciplinary team
- Based on comprehensive, educational, and/or behavioral concerns, rather than isolated deficits identified by individual assessments
- Nondiscriminatory in terms of gender, ethnicity, native language, family composition, and/or socioeconomic status
- Technically adequate and validated for the purpose for which they are used, including the provision of norms, which compare children with their peers, for minority children and children with physical disabilities

Richard Nagle (2000) identifies four goals for assessment of preschoolers: screening, diagnosis, individual program planning and monitoring, and program evaluation.

Screening

The purpose of screening is to identify children who are at risk and would benefit from early intervention programs. Typically the procedures are general in nature and involve brief assessments of multiple areas of functioning. More comprehensive assessment is recommended if a child is identified with a potential difficulty. One of the difficulties with screening procedures, particularly with young children, is the possibility of inaccurately identifying children with normal development as those in need of services. Preschool screening processes are often overwhelming for children who are shy or cautious or have difficulty with rapid transitions. When evaluated under different circumstances, these children do not evidence any delays. A high rate of false-positive identifications, results which indicate a problem when none exists, can use staff time inefficiently and cause undue concern on the part of the parent. The screening process, can, however, identify many children who may not otherwise come to the attention of the school staff. Parents with concerns may be more likely to come to a community-based screening process than seek out an individualized evaluation. Screening can lead to earlier implementation of interventions for many children.

Diagnoses

There are typically three main goals of a diagnostic process:

1. Specification of the child's individual needs

2. Identification of specific services to meet individual needs

3. Determination of eligibility for services

The diagnostic process must be comprehensive and include multiple sources and assessment procedures, following the guidelines established by law. Because of the assessment challenges presented by this population, the evaluation process may require adaptation and additional time. More frequent assessment and observations are necessary to gain a clear picture of a child's functioning to keep up with the rapid changes that occur in development. The results of a diagnostic process must always be viewed with caution.

Individual Program Planning and Monitoring

Once the child's needs are determined, this information must be linked to intervention to address those needs. The evaluation results should flow directly into the planning of an appropriate educational plan. If an evaluation focuses solely on determination of eligibility and results in placement in an early intervention program that identifies general developmental goals for all children involved, then the process has not fulfilled the requirements of the law and does not provide appropriate individualized services. The information obtained must be interpreted and applied to individual goal development and instructional planning. The child's performance in the program must be monitored to determine progress made, need for change of goals and objectives, or change of intervention strategies.

To be effective, the process of monitoring and making needed changes must be undertaken at more frequent intervals for younger children than for older children.

Program Evaluation

The evaluation of the effectiveness of a program can be undertaken in a variety of ways. In general, it is important to determine if the program is meeting the identified outcome objectives. These objectives can relate to immediate as well as long-term outcomes. As school districts are facing increasing financial deficits because of funding cuts, program evaluation can be an important factor in determining whether a program will be eliminated or continued.

CHALLENGES OF ASSESSMENT

Young children present challenges that are not typically present when assessing older children, adolescents, or adults. Any assessment process must take into account the state of the child, the environment, the relationship between examiner and the child, and the validity and reliability of the assessment techniques, defined as the extent to which the test measures what it purports to measure and stability over time. Each of these factors presents unique challenges for the preschool child and is significantly important in determining the accuracy of the assessment process. Modifications are often required for young children in order to allow the process to be completed. In addition, there are challenges intrinsic to the developmental process itself.

As a child grows, the developmental course becomes more even and predictable; however, young children have developmental patterns that are characterized by periods of rapid and slower development. Many parents report that as one skill develops, another may remain at the same level. These patterns can make test interpretation difficult. A child may not be able to display a skill during the evaluation process, but it may be fully present only days or weeks later. A child may appear delayed in terms of test scores, then display scores within normal limits or even advanced in a very short period of time, without any specific intervention. This factor has led many pediatricians to counsel parents against early assessment, telling the family that the child "will grow out of" the difficulties presented. Although this may at times be true, too many children do not fulfill this prophecy and do not receive the intervention they need. One of the challenges to accurate assessment is to determine what constitutes a "real" delay as opposed to as skill that is developing but not yet fully expressed during the assessment process. All assessment results must be interpreted with this caution regarding accuracy.

Direct assessment of young children can also present difficulties that challenge the validity of test results. Failure to demonstrate a skill may indicate a delay; however, it may also indicate that the child does not understand the language of the instruction given, that the child's shyness interferes with responding, or that the child lacks necessary test-taking skills. For example, a child may have an understanding of a vocabulary word presented by the examiner and may be able to associate the given word with a picture, but the child does not understand the direction "point to . . . ." In this case, it may be assumed that the child is not familiar with a word when in fact the child is just not able to respond correctly to the response format. It is often necessary to train a pointing response before an assessment process.

Young children demonstrate a wide range of language skills, all within normal limits. A child with language skills that are slower to develop may not be able to respond to tasks requiring verbalization, even though the child knows the information. Even children with advanced language development may be difficult to assess because of problems with intelligibility.

Another challenge involves the assessment process itself. If standardized tests are used, the examiner must understand how to administer them in the standardized format; however, it is just as important for the examiner to have the ability to alter the standardized procedures to achieve an accurate assessment. The examiner must be able to go beyond the standard procedure, offering alternate probes and response requirements. This testing the limits process can involve rephrasing a question or giving additional time. The examiner must know what specific skill is being assessed and how to change the process in order to determine if the skill is present. The examiner must also be able to modify the response format. For example, a child may not be able to point to a picture response but can indicate yes or no by gesture when the examiner points to the choices. It is important that every alteration of standardized procedure be documented and that test results be interpreted within the context of the altered administration. At times it is necessary to first teach specific behaviors, such as pointing, if an accurate assessment is to

be made. The examiner must have an array of strategies available that will serve to engage the child and maintain attention. Test sessions with young children are typically brief and the examiner must be able to assess the level of investment.

Many young children have temperamental or behavioral difficulties that interfere with the assessment process. These are not deviant behaviors; rather they are part of normal development. Young children may have more difficulty than older children in adapting to the unfamiliar setting, separating from a parent, or relating to the examiner. It is important for the examiner to make changes in the setting as well as personal demeanor to make the child more comfortable. It is important to offer appropriately sized furniture and remain at the child's eye level. Some children will not respond directly to the examiner even with appropriate modifications. They may, however, be able to make use of a prop such as a stuffed animal to point to pictures or relay information. When presented with a page of pictures, a child may not be able to indicate a choice independently but may be able to respond with yes or no when the examiner points to each picture. Many of the adaptive techniques that are necessary when assessing young children are not standardized procedures; however, they allow the examiner to obtain important information about skill development, the conditions under which the child can display the skill, and whether the child can learn with modeling or instruction. It is imperative that the examiners discuss these procedural deviations and incorporate them into an understanding of the child.

Preschool assessment processes rely heavily on observation in addition to testing. It is important to obtain observation data from several settings. If a child is not in a preschool setting where observations by teachers can be obtained, the examiner must rely solely on parental information. A single source of information can be biased because of the caregiver's familiarity with the child. This familiarity may have a positive as well as negative impact. For example, a parent may be able to interpret responses from a speech-impaired child that the examiner could not; however, the caregiver may also "fill in" for the child and assume the child is capable of a skill, not recognizing the level of support and facilitation provided.

Another challenge in preschool assessment involves the ability of a young child to make transitions. These difficulties can be noted as the child is moved out of the classroom and into the testing setting, as well as in the testing process as the examiner moves to new items and tasks. Transitional objects can be helpful, or a teacher or aide escort to the new location may ease the transition. Young children are also less skilled in managing the frustration that can result as the child repeatedly reaches the ceiling of a test, or the place at which a task becomes too difficult to complete. The examiner must develop and employ methods other than verbal explanation to manage this frustration.

Alterations in the physical setting must be made for young children. Many children are not accustomed to sitting at a table, particularly one that is too large. The examiner may need to invest in the appropriate size furnishings or may prefer to work on the floor with a child. Some assessment approaches, such as play-based assessment (a technique developed by Toni Linder), make use of a more natural setting and involve observational techniques and guided play to assess levels of functioning. This process must take place in a room equipped with specific materials, additional staff, and videotaping equipment.

In contrast to older children, preschoolers do not have the same sense of what is required of them and the ability to comply despite their apprehension. Older students can understand the explanations of the purpose of the process and can delay gratification. Young children will not comply if they are unwilling, anxious, frightened, or shy, unless modifications and immediate gratification can be incorporated into the process.

The tests themselves also present challenges to accurate assessment. Reliability issues surface from many of the behavioral issues identified. In addition, the instruments may not be sensitive enough to individual differences. The items are often general and each correct response can result in a substantial increase in the score, while a failed response will yield a much lower score. The tests are not sensitive to the incremental steps in the development of a skill; therefore, a score may underestimate a child's ability. Because preschoolers' skill development is limited, the instruments may not have an adequate lower, or floor, level necessary to determine if a discrepancy exists between actual and expected levels of functioning. There are not enough items at the lower end of a test to determine if a child's performance is significantly lower than the norm.

METHODS OF ASSESSMENT

There continues to be debate regarding the methods and instruments to be used in the assessment of a preschool child. While there is agreement that the process must include multiple sources and methods, there is not widespread agreement of the specific procedures to use. Currently there is a move toward alternative methods of assessment, such as criterion-referenced or curriculum-based assessment, which seek to determine whether a child has mastered specific content rather comparing the child's performance to a representative sample of children at the same age or grade level. Even so, standardized norm-referenced instruments continue to be widely used.

Testing methods can be thought of as standardized or traditional methods as opposed to alternative methods. Those in favor of alternative testing methods point out that traditional methods are limited in their usefulness because of their technical inadequacies as well as the artificial, standardized manner in which they must be administered. They argue for a more natural observational assessment. Users of standardized tests counter that norm-based assessment instruments allow meaningful comparisons between children, which provides a more accurate view of the nature and extent of the delays. An effective evaluation process most likely involves a combination of these philosophies. The selection of tests or procedures depends, in part, on what type of process the child will allow. Use of nontraditional observational methods will be critical for a child who will not leave the classroom, refuses to respond verbally, or has difficulty with transition. Other children may respond well to the standardized testing process and thrive on the individual attention, while appearing shy and withdrawn in the classroom.

Traditional methods include tests such as the Weschler Preschool and Primary Scale of Intelligence-Revised, the Stanford-Binet V, the Bayley Scales of Infant Development, Second Edition; the Cognitive Abilities Scale, Second Edition; the Differential Ability Scales; and the Woodcock-Johnson III Tests of Achievement and Woodcock-Johnson III Tests of Cognitive Ability. Alternative methods may include play-based assessment, curriculum-based assessment, in which a child's mastery of content is measured, and observational approaches.

In either approach, extensive contact with the parent is a necessary component. An extensive history as well as an assessment of family functioning should be obtained. Various checklists are available that can help structure this process. This portion of the assessment is particularly critical if the child is not involved in a preschool program. The parents can provide valuable information as well as corroborate or invalidate test findings. A delay or deficit as determined on a performance test must always be checked by those familiar with the child's normal behavior; therefore, a child may not have demonstrated mastery of a task in the testing setting, but a parent or teacher may provide information attesting to the child's mastery of the skill. Interpreting test results without confirmation or allowance for skills mastered but not demonstrated, will not yield a true view of a child's abilities; rather, it will provide a picture of the child's functioning within a circumscribed setting. Often this is valuable information; however, it should not be interpreted as an accurate estimate of skill development.

The difficulty surrounding the selection of assessment instruments again highlights the unpredictable nature of preschool evaluation. The key to accurate assessment is a solid understanding of the development and behavior of young children and the flexibility to adapt testing procedures to the individual child.

DOMAINS OF ASSESSMENT

Regardless of the method of assessment, the areas to be addressed remain similar. The overriding goal is to determine if a child is developing normally and if that development is occurring at the appropriate rate. The acquisition of information from an assessment process provides the specificity needed to develop a plan to address the areas of delay or deficiency.

Some of the areas to be assessed and the tests used for the assessment are discussed in the following sections.

Fine and Gross Motor Skill Development

A comprehensive evaluation of motor skills is not within the scope of most school or clinical psychologists; however, these skills can be screened and further assessment by an occupational therapist recommended if needed.

Tests: The Berry-Buktenica Developmental Test of Visual-Motor Integration, fifth edition (Beery & colleagues, 2004), play-based assessment.

Cognitive and Learning Ability

There is controversy regarding the administration of intelligence tests to young children. Caution is

certainly in order in relation to the actual scores obtained; however, tests of intellectual functioning can be used as a process instrument and provide useful information regarding a child's learning.

Tests: The Weschler Preschool and Primary Scale of Intelligence-Revised (WPPSI-R) (Weschler, 2002), the Stanford-Binet V (Roid, 2003), Woodcock-Johnson III Complete Battery (Woodcock & colleagues, 2001), curriculum-based measures, play-based assessment.

Language and Speech Development

The administration of tests that assess language development should be an integral part of a preschool evaluation. The ability to understand language, or receptive language, as well as the ability to express verbal information (referred to as expressive language skills) can be assessed. Observation is critical in this area because many children hesitate to speak extensively to an unfamiliar person. If a language delay is suspected, a speech-language pathologist should be involved to assess functioning.

Tests: Peabody Picture Vocabulary Test-Revised (Dunn & Dunn, 1997), Expressive Vocabulary Test (Williams, 1997), Bracken Test of Basic Concepts (Bracken, 1998).

Basic Skills

A preschool evaluation should also include assessment of basic skills, particularly as a child nears the age for entry into kindergarten. This involves knowledge of general information; color naming; shape, letter, and number identification; and the application of fine motor skills to academic tasks such as writing. Assessment of basic skills also includes evaluation of phonological awareness and processing, which are the skills underlying reading, as well as beginning math and writing skills.

Tests: Woodcock-Johnson III Tests of Achievement, Woodcock-Johnson III Tests of Cognitive Abilities (Woodcock & colleagues, 2001), and the Phelps Kindergarten Readiness Scale-Second Edition (Phelps, 2003).

Behavior and Attention

Although school psychologists typically do not diagnose attention or behavior problems, it is certainly possible to determine if difficulties in these areas exist and affect performance. If problems are suspected, referral to the appropriate treatment source can be initiated. Observation of behavior both in the testing setting as well as in the home and classroom is essential. Issues such as impulsivity, distractibility, tolerance for frustration, withdrawal, communication difficulties, and anxiety can be addressed. A child's learning style and approach to problem solving can be observed as test items are administered. This information can be as useful as the actual test scores.

Tests: Behavior rating scales: attention deficit hyperactivity disorder (ADHD) rating scales.

The proficiencies necessary to assess the skills and abilities of preschool children are not simply a downward extension of the techniques and tests necessary to evaluate older children and adults. The process is unique to the population and presents many challenges, but it is necessary to ensure that young children and their families are provided with the services they need.

—*Carleen Franz*

See also Intelligence; Special Education; Theories of Human Development

REFERENCES AND FURTHER READING

Beery, K. E., & Beery, N. A. (2004). *The Beery-Buktenica developmental test of visual-motor integration* (5th ed.). Minneapolis, MN: NCS Pearson.

Bracken, B. A. (1998). *Bracken basic concept scale-revised.* San Antonio, TX: Psychological Corporation.

Bracken, B. A. (1999). *The Psychoeducational Assessment of Preschool Children* (3rd ed.). Boston: Allyn & Bacon.

Dunn, L. M., & Dunn, L. M. (1997). *Peabody picture vocabulary test* (3rd ed.). Circle Pines, MN: American Guidance Services.

Hall, S. L. (1999). *Straight talk about reading: How parents can make a difference during the early years.* Chicago: Contemporary Books.

Lichtenberger, E. O., & Kaufman, A. S. (2004). *Essentials of WPPSI-III assessment.* Hoboken, NJ: Wiley.

Lidz, C. S. (2003). *Early childhood assessment.* Hoboken, NJ: Wiley.

Nagle, R. J. (2000). Issues in preschool assessment. In B. A. Bracken (Ed.), *The psychoeducational assessment of preschool children* (3rd ed., pp. 19–32). Boston: Allyn & Bacon.

National Association of School Psychologists. (1999). *Position statement on early childhood assessment.* Bethesda, MD: Author.

Nuttall, E. V., Romero, I., & Kalesnik, J. (1999). *Assessing and screening preschoolers: Psychological and educational dimensions* (2nd ed.). Boston: Allyn & Bacon.

Phelps, L. (2003). *Phelps Kindergarten Readiness scale (2nd ed.).* Brandon, VT: Psychology Press.

Roid, G. H. (2003). *Stanford-Binet intelligence scales* (5th ed.). Itasca, IL: Riverside.

Wechsler, D. (2002). *Wechsler Preschool and Primary scale of Intelligence – Revised.* San Antonio, TX: The Psychological Corporation.

Williams, K. T. (1997). *Expressive vocabulary test.* Circle Pines, MN: American Guidance Service.

Woodcock, R. W., McGrew, K. S., & Mather, N. (2001). *Woodcock-Johnson III Tests of Achievement.* Itasca, IL: Riverside.

PRESCHOOLERS

The preschool years are increasingly being recognized as the ideal time to identify potential developmental problems and provide remediation. This period, which includes ages three to five years, is notable for remarkable growth. Preschoolers are particularly well primed to incorporate new information into their existing cognitive and behavioral repertoires, or create new behaviors to adjust to novel information. This form of adaptation is highly flexible and active during the preschool years, making this age well suited to instruction and intervention.

Preschoolers are maturing across several domains of development, including:

- Fine and gross motor skills
- Speech and language development
- Cognitive development
- Social skills and competence
- Self-help and adaptive skills

Maturational changes in biological structures precede the emergence of developmental milestones. Critical and precise physical changes in muscle mass, bone growth, neuronal connectivity, sensory–motor integration, and other physiological transformations support the newly acquired skills of the preschooler.

Although preschoolers are biologically primed for growth in these developmental areas, growth is maximized through interaction and practice with their environment. Play is used as the primary means through which preschoolers practice their burgeoning skills and enhance development across the five domains indicated previously. For instance, a young child who engages in a fantasy play scenario with a same-age peer in the kitchen play set learns valuable skills, including:

- Interactive social skills (e.g., negotiation, fairness, and social problem solving)
- Cognitive skills (e.g., classification of foods, sequencing of cooking steps, and consequential thinking)
- Fine motor skills (e.g., stirring, mixing, and holding utensils)
- Self-help skills (e.g., feeding, basic food preparation, and clean-up)
- Communication skills (verbal *scripts* that are enacted by the two children depicting a variety of real-life scenarios or themes)

Preschool and child care centers provide the ideal environment to meet the enrichment needs of a developing preschooler. Typically, the preschool years mark the initial entry into early childhood care and/or education. Parents often wait until their child is at least three years old to enroll him or her in a child care or preschool setting, because at that age the child exhibits increased independence and an ability to separate from caregivers, and is toilet-trained (a requirement of many child care sites).

This early school experience is instrumental in preparing for school readiness and fostering growth. A high-quality day care or preschool experience, characterized by low adult-to-child ratios, safe and stimulating environments, and hands-on instruction is associated with the greatest gains in development (Frede, 1995). These gains include enhanced social and cognitive development (particularly social competence), self-regulation, and communication skills, which also serve as resiliency variables against future school failure, referral to special education, and dropouts (National Association of School Psychologists [NASP], 1998). Unfortunately, many child care programs are considered poor or mediocre by experts, and as many as 33% are rated as inadequate and potentially harmful to a child's development and safety (Children's Defense Fund, 2001). Full-time child care costs can easily reach $5,000 to $10,000 a year, far beyond the affordability of many single-parent families and families living at or near the poverty level (Children's Defense Fund, 2001).

Recognizing the importance and need for a quality early childhood education, the federal government established Head Start in 1965 to provide low-income children and their families with a comprehensive range of services, including early childhood education; medical, dental, and mental health; nutrition; and parent involvement (About Head Start, 2002). In 1994, through the reauthorization of Head Start program, Congress established Early Head Start, which extends services from birth to three years, and includes assistance for pregnant women (About Head Start, 2002).

In addition, federal resources are made available to states to finance programs encouraging universal preschool, affordable child care options, and early intervention, such as through the federal Child Care and Development Fund and the Title XX Social Services Block grant. Despite the availability of these federal financial incentives, the existing programs vary greatly from state to state, and perilously rely on state budget cycles that are often late and politically driven. Consequently, the responsibility of financing early childhood education and child care remains the responsibility and burden of parents.

For parents with the means to afford a private preschool program, there are many available with excellent facilities, teachers, and curricula. For instance, Montessori preschool programs use a specific teaching style and curriculum developed by their founder, Dr. Maria Montessori, in the early 20th century. The hallmark of a Montessori education is active, innovative learning through discovery experiences with materials designed to foster growth in physical, social, emotional, and cognitive areas (American Montessori Society, n.d.).

State licensing and certification boards are responsible for overseeing the quality of care at child care and preschool centers. These boards dictate the minimal acceptable standards for staffing, facilities, and educational activities, and these standards vary greatly from state to state. Unfortunately for parents, licensing boards can only inform them whether a program has met minimal criteria and has had a violation of standards. Instead, parents are encouraged to contact state and national accreditation boards, funded by independent nonprofit agencies, which provide standards of education and care that exceed minimal expectations, and, in fact, reflect best practices in early childhood education. For instance, the National Association for the Education of Young Children (NAEYC) (2002) demands more rigorous standards in their accreditation process. Programs that hold the NAEYC accreditation meet or exceed a number of important criteria associated with an enriching and safe educational experience, including warm, responsive teacher-child interactions, an appropriate curriculum, qualified staff with professional development opportunities, and a stimulating and protective physical environment.

School psychologists' role in serving preschoolers has increased significantly within the past two decades, preceded by federal legislation in 1975 extending psychological services to handicapped children ages three years and older through Public Law (P.L.) 94–142, the Education for All Handicapped Children Act, and augmented by P.L. 99–457 in 1986, which extended services to birth and mandated a free and appropriate public education to children with disabilities who are three to five years of age (Fagan & Wise, 2000; Nagle, 2000). As special education services became available to preschoolers, eligibility and disability classifications were required to determine the appropriate education plan. School psychologists were sought to fulfill this requirement, in part because of their knowledge of psychometric measures in early childhood, familiarity with special education laws and education systems, and training in collaborative consultation.

School psychologists typically work on a multidisciplinary assessment team, which may include a speech-language pathologist (SLP), an occupational therapist (OT), and/or a physical therapist (PT), as well as regular and special education preschool teachers. A child referred to this team will be evaluated across the five domains previously mentioned (cognitive, communication, fine and gross motor skills, adaptive and self-help skills, and social skills).

Although the school psychologist can administer assessments across all five domains, typically he or she assesses cognitive, adaptive, and social skills functioning, while the SLP assesses communication skills, and the OT and PT assess fine and gross motor functioning, respectively. Teams work closely with the child's preschool teachers and family to ascertain the nature of the problem, collect data from multiple settings, and encourage a robust school–home network.

In addition to assessment, many school psychologists work with behaviorally disordered and/or maltreated youngsters as a play therapist, to ameliorate behavioral problems and train them in social problem solving to prevent future conflicts. The psychologist very often includes a family counseling component into the therapeutic intervention, as early childhood problems result from, and are exacerbated by, situational problems in the home (e.g., marital conflict, disagreement over discipline, sibling rivalry, and poor parenting style).

The psychologist also works as a consultant to preschool teachers, by developing individual and class-wide behavioral management plans, advising teachers on a child's disability, providing validated intervention strategies, and informing teachers of legal and ethical issues, including the utility and applicability of assessment results (NASP, 1991). Finally, psychologists serve as consultants to teachers and school administrators on ecological-behavioral management (i.e., arranging the environment to maximize visual appeal, attention, and safety while minimizing distractions and disruptions).

School psychologists' role in working with preschoolers has been well established, and recent federal legislation predicts an increasingly important role in the future (Gredler, 2000). For instance, Individuals with Disabilities Education Act (IDEA) regulations in 1999 mandated positive behavior supports and functional behavioral assessment for children, including preschoolers, whose behavior impedes their learning or that of others (Reschly, 2000). Furthermore, a primary concern of legislators and elected officials has been school readiness, as professionals, parents, and policy makers attempt to thwart the continuing crisis of poor achievement, grade failure, and dropouts (Fagan & Wise, 2000). This underscores the need for quality early childhood education programs, and school psychologists serve a vital role in assuring program quality, preventing difficulties for at-risk children, and identifying appropriate services for children already experiencing difficulties.

—*Paul C. McCabe*

See also Early Intervention; Preschool Assessment

REFERENCES AND FURTHER READING

About Head Start. (n.d.). Available online at http://www .2.acf.dhhs.gov/programs/hsb/about/index.htm

American Montessori Society. (n.d.). *The American Montessori society profile.* Available online at http://www .amshq.org

Children's Defense Fund. (2001, April). *Child care basics.* Available online at http://www.childrensdefense.org/cc_ facts.htm

Fagan, T. K., & Wise, P. S. (2000). *School psychology: Past, present, and future.* (2nd ed.). Bethesda, MD: National Association of School Psychologists.

Frede, E. C. (1995). The role of program quality in producing early childhood program benefits. *The Future of Children, 5*(3), 115–132.

Gredler, G. R. (2000). Early childhood assessment and intervention: What the future holds. *Psychology in the Schools, 37,* 73–79.

National Association for the Education of Young Children. *NAEYC accreditation.* (n.d.). Available online at http://www.naeyc.org/accreditation

National Association of School Psychologists. (1991). *Position statement on early childhood assessment.* Available online at http://www.nasponline.org/information/pospaper_eca.html

National Association of School Psychologists. (1998). *Position statement on early childhood care and education.* Available online at http://www.nasponline.org/information/pospaper_earlychild.html

Nagle, R. J. (2000). Issues in preschool assessment. In B.A. Bracken (Ed.), *The psychoeducational assessment of preschool children* (3rd ed). Needham Heights, MA: Allyn & Bacon.

Reschly, D. J. (2000). The present and future status of school psychology in the United States. *School Psychology Review, 29,* 507–522.

PREVENTION

School psychology interventions intended to improve the academic or social success of children involve shaping developmental processes in classrooms, in individual interactions with children, and at the level of the school organization. Increasingly, school psychology recognizes the value of taking action prior to the emergence of problems. This perspective can be characterized as a prevention-oriented focus to service delivery (Roberts, 1996).

RISK AND PREVENTION

Risk refers to a probability linking a "risk factor" such as poor academic skills with an outcome such as dropping out of school. Risk does not describe a causal relation, although a risk factor may be part of an etiological process. If in a given school 85% of 3rd graders with test scores below the 25th percentile drop out before 12th grade, the 25th percentile could be used as a cut score for distinguishing a group of 3rd graders with a high probability (high risk) of dropping out. Risk status is ideally linked with delivery of interventions. In a preventive-oriented service delivery system, resources are deployed at various stages prior to the time at which problem outcomes are expected to appear. Implementation of interventions—for example, smaller class size and intensive instruction in reading,

mathematics, and content knowledge for children whose grades on standardized test scores fall below the 25th percentile—might lead to only 15% of children who score below the 25th percentile dropping out.

Primary prevention is aimed at the entire population, without regard to risk status, and is delivered before the causal process thought to underlie the problem outcome begins, for example, inoculating all children for certain diseases. The aim of primary prevention is to eliminate the problem outcome in the population. Secondary prevention actions are delivered to a particular group—a high-risk group—whose probability of attaining the problem outcome is elevated. The link between high-risk status and secondary prevention enables the action to be targeted more narrowly than for primary prevention efforts. Prekindergarten programs for poor four-year-old children are examples of secondary prevention. Secondary prevention actions are delivered *before* the problem outcome is incurred by the group members and are evaluated in terms of how they lower the risk coefficient for the target group. Tertiary prevention actions are delivered after a problem outcome has occurred. These actions basically involve remediation of the effects of a problem outcome and are offered only to individuals who have incurred problem outcome status. Special education or programs for children with certain disorders or disabilities are examples of tertiary prevention efforts. In actuality, the distinctions between these services are blurred; however, services are more preventively oriented when they are delivered early, on a widespread basis and in the absence of having clearly attained problem outcome status.

Cowen (1999) points out a fourth form of intervention, competence enhancement. Prevention approaches have as their goal the elimination of pathology, such as reducing reading failure, whereas competence enhancement focuses on improving positive outcomes for all children. Traditional prevention approaches are biased by a focus on negative outcomes. In Cowen's view, this focus could reduce efforts to promote health in the population. For example, in dental health, a focus on eliminating cavities and tooth decay led to the widespread use of fluoride. But tooth decay still increased in children who did not brush their teeth or receive regular teeth cleaning. The focus on preventing negative outcomes neglected the larger needs to promote dental health. Clearly, prevention and health promotion are not the same.

Wellness or competence enhancement approaches promote healthy human development and focus efforts on deploying resources to all individuals. The emphasis on providing high-quality literacy instruction to all children in contrast to identifying disabilities in some children who fail to learn to read is an example of this distinction. Wellness enhancement is complementary to risk reduction and contributes to a multilevel, proactive approach that includes competence enhancement and programs for children who need additional support (Cowen, 1999).

PREVENTION IN THE SCHOOLS

Prevention science has grown substantially in the past decade, contributing to an emerging empirical literature on program evaluation, design, and implementation, as described briefly in the following sections.

Primary Prevention

Durlak & Wells's (1997) meta-analysis of primary prevention efforts supports the effectiveness of programs that modify the school environment and help children negotiate transitions. One example is the School Transitional Environment Project (STEP), which focuses on promoting health in the transition from elementary school to junior high or from junior to senior high school; this focus on transition is warranted because of evidence suggesting that these transitions may heighten risk for some and create opportunities for others (Felner & colleagues, 2001). STEP increases the ability of the school to respond to children's needs by creating schools within schools. "Teams" of 60 to 100 students have classes together and have consistent homeroom advisors and/or counselors. Time is allotted for all teachers to meet and discuss students, to integrate curriculum, and to increase coherence and support available to students. These efforts reduce complexity for students and build a sense of continuity and community. Felner and colleagues (2001) reported a 40% to 50% decline in school dropouts, maintenance of achievement levels, and fewer child- and teacher-reported behavioral and emotional problems. Not surprisingly, teachers also reported higher job satisfaction and less burnout (Felner & colleagues, 2001).

Common dimensions of successful schools, according to Felner and colleagues (2001), include promoting a sense of belongingness and agency; engaging families; an integrated, quality curriculum; ongoing professional development; high expectations for students; and opportunities for success. These attributes are also exemplified in the well-known school-reform program called Success for All (SFA) (Slavin & colleagues, 1996). SFA emphasizes the management of instructional time and resources; a focused curriculum in reading, math, and language arts; assessment linked to intervention and instruction; and the early delivery of intensive instruction and tutoring to children having difficulty learning. This whole-school reform effort has proved successful in raising academic achievement, reducing negative behavioral outcomes, and reducing rates of special education placements (Slavin & colleagues, 1996). An extension of SFA called Roots and Wings has many of the same attributes of SFA but has a more comprehensive curriculum, and has also shown positive results when implemented in a number of elementary schools.

The Child Development Project (CDP) (Battistich & colleagues, 1997) promotes social and moral development, community, and active caring for children within the school to improve mental health and academic success. The need for schools to become "caring communities" is most commonly identified at the middle and high school levels where preadolescent and adolescent disengagement and lack of connection to school goals are most marked. CDP involves extensive analysis and reshaping of the school environment as a prerequisite for changes sought at the classroom level. CDP interventions address concerns such as caring, relationships, student autonomy, and values needed at the classroom and the school levels.

In the San Ramon Project, CDP focused on changing discipline practices and teaching styles (i.e., emphasizing cooperative learning and making curriculum meaningful); and broadening the focus of schools' social and ethical dispositions, attitudes and motivations, and metacognitive skills in addition to facilitating academic development. Battistich and colleagues (1997) summarized the evaluation of two years of implementation data in 24 (12 were comparison or no-treatment control schools) highly diverse schools. Findings indicated positive changes for the 12 CDP schools. CDP produced changes in teachers' observed warmth and supportiveness to students and low use of extrinsic control measures—both of which were partially responsible for children's increased engagement and achievement—and positive behavior toward peers and adults. Students reported an increase in the enjoyment of the classroom and motivation to learn.

Secondary Prevention

Secondary prevention approaches focus on delivering resources to children identified through systematic screening processes as highly likely to demonstrate academic and social problems at a later time.

Project Fast Track has a focus on enhancing social and emotional competencies and reducing negative, aggressive behavior for children performing low on both behavioral and academic indicators. The approach is multifaceted, involving academic tutoring and social skills groups, and the classroom teachers' use of the Promoting Alternative THinking Strategies (PATHS) curriculum (Greenberg & colleagues, 1995). PATHS is designed to help children identify and label feelings and social interactions, reflect on those feelings and interactions, generate alternative behavior, and test such alternatives. Teachers are trained to add lessons to their first-grade curriculum that teach children emotional understanding, communication skills, self-control, and social participation. In the context of this multifaceted intervention, teachers who had a better understanding of the importance of teaching PATHS skills generalized the lessons taught in the PATHS curriculum to their interactions with students throughout the day. These teachers, who also had effective management skills, reported more decreases in aggressive behavior in their classrooms. In one study, teachers implemented PATHS with regular and special education children in the second and third grades (Greenberg & colleagues, 1995). Teachers were trained to teach sixty 30-minute lessons on self-control, emotions, and problem solving to their classes. Children who received the intervention had a larger emotional vocabulary, a more advanced ability to connect basic emotions to personal experiences, a more advanced understanding of recognizing emotional cues in others, and the belief that they could manage their feelings more than the children who did not receive the intervention (Greenberg & colleagues, 1995).

In sum, the emerging empirical literature of preventive interventions and whole-school reform efforts very clearly supports the value of these efforts for improving student social and academic performance. This empirical literature clearly provides the evidentiary basis to inform school psychologists' practice in moving toward a prevention focus. It is expected that the next decade will see an expansion of research on prevention and a re-organization of services provided to children, with an emphasis on school-based prevention and competence enhancement strategies.

—Robert C. Pianta

See also Bullying and Victimization; Cheating; DARE Program; Discipline; Early Intervention; Gangs; Parents As Teachers; Peer Mediation; Resilience and Protective Factors; Substance Abuse; Violence in Schools

REFERENCES AND FURTHER READING

Battistich, V., Solomon, D., Watson, M., & Schaps, E. (1997). Caring school communities. *Educational Psychologist, 32*(3), 137–151.

Cowen, E. (1999). In sickness and in health: Primary prevention's vows revisited. In D. Cicchetti & S. L. Toth (Eds.), *Rochester symposium on developmental psychopathology: Developmental approaches to prevention and intervention* (Vol. 9, pp. 1–24). Rochester, NY: University of Rochester.

Durlak, J., & Wells, A. (1997). Primary prevention mental health programs for children and adolescents: A meta-analytic review. *American Journal of Community Psychology, 25*(2), 115–152.

Felner, R., Favazza, A., Shim, M., Brand, S., Gu, K., & Noonan, N. (2001). Whole school improvement and restructuring as prevention and promotion: Lessons from project STEP and the project on high performance learning communities. *Journal of School Psychology, 39,* 177–202.

Greenberg, M., Kusche, C., Cook, E., & Quamma, J. (1995). Promoting emotional competence in school-aged children: The effects of the PATHS curriculum. *Development and Psychopathology, 7,* 117–136.

Roberts, M. C. (1996). *Model programs in child and family mental health.* Mahwah, NJ: Erlbaum.

Slavin, R. E., Madden, N. A., Dolan, L. J., & Wasik, B. A. (1996). *Every child, every school: Success for all.* Thousand Oaks, CA: Corwin.

PROBLEM SOLVING

Much of life involves solving problems. From major decision making (e.g., purchasing a new car, choosing an academic major), to responding to daily hassles (e.g., having a flat tire) and stressful life events (e.g., unemployment, divorce, or death of significant others), how people solve various life problems has been an important subject of research and practice for mental health professionals. Formally defined, problem solving is a goal-directed process that includes identifying the problem, generating solutions, selecting the best solution(s) and implementing it (them), and evaluating the outcome(s).

Historically, the scholarly effort to define the problem-solving process with life problems finds its roots in the work of D'Zurilla and Goldfried (1971). They proposed a five-stage model of the problem-solving process:

1. General Orientation Stage: Individuals recognize and approach a problem with a certain cognitive and motivational frame of mind.

2. Problem Definition and Formulation Stage: Individuals define the problem in specific terms and identify specific goals to solve the problem.

3. Generation of Alternatives Stage: Individuals produce a list of appropriate and possible solutions.

4. Decision-Making Stage: Individuals evaluate a variety of possible solutions based on expected consequences.

5. Selection of the Best Solutions, Solution Implementation, and Verification Stage: Individuals select the best solution, implement it, and evaluate the actual outcomes of the selected solution.

Even though these five components were identified more than 30 years ago, scholars still hold to their validity for describing the problem-solving process, with only a few minor modifications.

Current research and practice pertaining to problem solving owe a great debt to D'Zurilla and Goldfried's (1971) problem-solving process model. For example, a great deal of research has centered on the construct of *problem-solving appraisal* (i.e., an individual's perceived ability, style, behavior, and attitude in solving the problem) as measured by the Problem Solving Inventory (PSI) (Heppner, 1988). More than 120 studies over a 20-year period between 1982 and 2002 have investigated the link between the level of effectiveness in problem-solving appraisal and various outcome variables, including psychological distress. The research has consistently suggested that effective problem solvers show better psychological, physical, and educational adjustment.

The problem-solving process model has had a direct influence on professional practice in psychology through the development of problem-solving training and problem-solving consultation. Problem-solving consultation (PSC) is an indirect form of service delivery where school psychologists work with teachers or parents who have students with academic, behavioral, social, and/or emotional problems. Although PSC does not involve direct problem-solving training with individual consultees (i.e., teachers and parents), the consultation components and process make direct use of the problem-solving framework, such as problem identification, problem analysis, treatment design and implementation, and treatment evaluation. Behavioral consultation, one of the more popular subtypes of PSC, underscores the importance of:

- Conducting collaborative consultations between a school psychologist and consultee(s)
- Setting the primary goal to be behavioral change of the client (usually the child)
- Conducting multiple interviews corresponding to the problem-solving process

The effectiveness of PSC across a variety of academic and behavioral problems is well documented. For example, Galloway and Sheridan (1994) found that PSC was effective in helping teachers and parents with underachieving students and with children diagnosed as attention deficit hyperactivity disorder. Knoff and colleagues (1995) through investigating teachers' perception of effective school psychology consultation, suggest that PSC, particularly behavioral consultation, is a preferred and important service in school psychology; and PSC tends to improve teachers' self-efficacy regarding their skills and ability to define problems and instruct the problematic child.

There appears to be substantial evidence of a strong association between problem-solving appraisal, Problem-Solving Training (PST) and Problem-Solving Consultation (PSC), and psychological, physical, and educational adjustment. Nonetheless, there are two major issues that need further consideration. First, with regard to problem-solving appraisal, the readers should use caution by differentiating the perceived effectiveness of problem solving and the actual problem-solving ability or skills—although in many instances these two constructs may overlap. For example, if a person does not have a realistic sense of his or her actual problem-solving skills, there would be a discrepancy between his or her perception, and actual behavior. Second, directly concerning the role and function of school psychologists, PSC appears to fit very well in a mental health model of practice, as it gives teachers and parents the tool to prevent, or at least effectively handle, a myriad of different problems.

The problem-solving approach (i.e., problem identification, problem analysis, treatment design and implementation, and treatment evaluation) can be a very effective tool in applied psychology. Given that the way people deal with their ever-changing life-situations and problems substantially affects their psychological, physical, and educational adjustment, it appears as it would behoove mental health professionals to promote problem-solving skills in their clientele.

—*Dong-gwi Lee*

See also Consultation: Behavioral; Consultation: Conjoint Behavioral; Consultation: Ecobehavioral; Early Intervention; Interviewing; Multidisciplinary Teams; School Psychologist; Special Education

REFERENCES AND FURTHER READING

D'Zurilla, T. J., & Goldfried, M. R. (1971). Problem solving and behavior modification. *Journal of Abnormal Psychology, 78,* 107–126.

Galloway, J., & Sheridan, S. M. (1994). Implementing scientific practices through case studies: Examples using home-school interventions and consultation. *Journal of School Psychology, 32,* 385–413.

Heppner, P. P. (1988). *The Problem Solving Inventory (PSI): Manual.* Palo Alto, CA: Consulting Psychologists.

Knoff, H. M., Sullivan, P., & Liu, D. (1995). Teachers' ratings of effective school psychology consultations: An exploratory factor analysis study. *Journal of School Psychology, 33,* 39–57.

PROGRAM EVALUATION

Program evaluation is the systematic investigation of the worth or merit of a program. Program evaluation can provide evidence of achievement of program goals and purposes, identify effective program components, determine the reasons why some program components are successful and others are not, identify potential program improvements, and examine a program's cost-effectiveness. Evaluators gather information that describes how a program was conceptualized, designed, and implemented and they examine the success of the program in meeting its expected outcomes. Evaluation can be conducted by the program's staff, by an outside evaluator, or by a combination of both.

THE EVALUATION PROCESS

Each program consists of a set of planned activities and anticipated outcomes. The activities are the processes that are hypothesized to lead to program outcomes, which are the specific changes in program participants' behavior, knowledge, skills, status, and level of functioning. Outcome indicators are the specific measurable aspects of the outcomes (W. K. Kellogg Foundation, 2001). Using a tutoring program as an example, the activities include the frequency of tutoring, the structure of the lessons, and the materials used in the sessions. The expected outcome is improved academic performance for participants. Program staff can identify several different outcome indicators, for example improved performance on tests.

Program evaluation has two broad purposes: formative, which examines the program as it is being implemented, and summative, which describes the program's worth or impact after the program is completed. Formative evaluation occurs during the planning and implementation of the program. It attempts to determine the probability of program success and provides information about modifications or changes that might increase the program's ability to achieve the intended results. Summative evaluation occurs after the program has been completed and presents conclusions about overall program success as measured by the outcome indicators. Referring back to the example of the tutoring program, formative evaluation could examine patterns of student attendance and the extent to which staff is providing appropriate tutoring. Summative evaluation could examine participants' test performance as related to their attendance in the tutoring intervention.

The first step in an evaluation study is to focus the evaluation. The evaluator, in collaboration with program stakeholders (e.g., those with direct interest, involvement, or investment in the program such as program staff, program participants, funders, etc.), identify the purpose of the evaluation and develop evaluation questions based on program inputs and expected outcomes.

Once evaluation questions are generated, the evaluator develops an evaluation design and methodology to guide data collection and analysis. This step requires that the evaluator identifies data necessary to answer the evaluation questions, methods of data collection, sampling strategy, and data collection instruments.

Evaluators use qualitative and quantitative data, collected through methods such as surveys, observations, focus groups (a group interview of 6–10 people), analysis of existing data, and results of standardized tests. Finally, the evaluator analyzes the data, interprets findings, and communicates the results to key stakeholders.

DIFFERENCES BETWEEN EVALUATION AND RESEARCH

Evaluation studies use the same techniques and processes as other social science research, yet they are different in terms of the goals of the study, the types of questions that are asked, and the way that the results are presented and used. The goal of program evaluation is to provide program stakeholders with information about the value of a program or about the ability of the program to meet an expected outcome. The goal of research, to contribute new knowledge to a field, is broader. Evaluation can contribute to the field by adding information about a specific program or type of program, but typically evaluations focus on gathering program-specific information rather than studying a problem or issue more broadly.

Evaluation questions are directly related to the program and come from the stakeholders who will use the evaluation results for program implementation or improvement. Evaluators help to develop the evaluation questions but ultimately, the questions need to be of value to the stakeholders. In contrast, research questions are often based on the researcher's inherent interest in a topic area of study.

A third difference between the two is in the way that results are presented. Stakeholders of evaluation studies typically want to know specific information about the outcomes associated with the program, while the users of research typically have more general interests. Evaluation results are often presented in oral and written form to program stakeholders, directors, funders, and staff. They may or may not be available to a wider audience. In contrast, the results of research studies are widely disseminated in academic presentations and publications.

PRINCIPLES OF PRACTICE

Program evaluators follow a set of five guiding principles for evaluators, as developed by the American Evaluation Association:

1. Systemic inquiry

2. Competence

3. Integrity/honesty

4. Respect for people

5. Responsibility for general and public welfare

The principles require that evaluators apply systemic inquiry, that is, use the highest technical standards of data-based investigation to increase the accuracy and credibility of the findings. Second, evaluators must have the competence to conduct the proposed evaluation. They must practice with integrity and honesty, demonstrate respect for those affected by the evaluation, and accept responsibility for general and public welfare as related to the evaluation and its findings.

In addition to these principles, the Joint Committee on Standards for Educational Evaluation (1994) has developed a set of standards for evaluating educational programs. The principles focus on four attributes of evaluation: utility, feasibility, propriety, and accuracy. The standards require that evaluators provide clients with useful information (utility); conduct evaluation that is realistic, practical, and efficient (feasibility); follow legal and ethical guidelines and show due regard for the welfare of participants and those affected by its results (propriety); and use a technically sound and appropriate design (accuracy).

PROGRAM EVALUATION MODELS

Models of program evaluation provide a framework for conceptualizing and conducting evaluation. The models differentiate themselves by emphasizing different aspects of the evaluation process and by helping practitioners plan and implement evaluations that are responsive to different stakeholder needs. The evaluation literature includes reference to more than 20 different evaluation models. Five commonly used models are described in the following paragraphs.

Experimental or field trials involve random assignment of individuals to a treatment group and identification of differences in relevant outcomes between the two groups. Random assignment of an appropriate number of participants minimizes preexisting differences between the groups that may affect the outcomes. This model of evaluation is useful because it can show causality (i.e., it can provide evidence as to whether the intervention caused the observable outcomes).

In contrast to evaluation using experimental design, which focuses primarily on outcomes, theory-driven evaluation (Donaldson, 2003) examines not only the outcomes but the mechanisms that are hypothesized to have led to the outcomes. This type of evaluation considers the program's conceptual framework or program theory and identifies connections between program theory and outcomes. Program theories describe the ways in which program components are hypothesized to affect outcomes. Program theories are based on prior research, previous evaluation findings, and stakeholders' experiences with the way in which the program is working or has previously worked. The evaluation examines whether and how the program components led to the expected outcomes, how the program works and when it works. The evaluator must be familiar with the content area of the program in order to help analyze program theory and assist key stakeholders in identifying and prioritizing evaluation questions.

The third model, Stufflebeam's (2000) Context, Inputs, Process, Product (CIPP) model of evaluation does not describe or analyze the program theory but focuses on the program context, input, processes, and products. These four components provide a range of information for program staff during implementation and provide summative judgments about the program at its conclusion. An evaluation can include all or some of the components to meet stakeholder needs. The model emphasizes stakeholder involvement and has the goal of helping stakeholders to improve programs rather than simply evaluating the end outcomes.

Another model of evaluation that focuses on providing program staff and stakeholders with meaningful information is Patton's (1997) utilization-focused evaluation. Stakeholders are actively involved in the entire process, which answers evaluation questions and helps clients see the utility of the evaluation results. Evaluators collaborate with a set of key program stakeholders to identify evaluation questions, which may change as the evaluation progresses to ensure that the evaluation examines the aspects most relevant to the stakeholders. Utilization-focused evaluation contends that the critical feature of evaluation is the way in which the results are used. An evaluation is viewed as successful if the results lead to program improvement.

The final model of evaluation, empowerment evaluation (Fetterman, 2003), is also client-centered in that the evaluator helps clients to conduct their own evaluation by serving as a coach or facilitator. The evaluator helps organizations to define their mission, take stock of organizational strengths and weaknesses, determine strategies to accomplish program goals, and identify ways to measure progress towards meeting those goals. The model emphasizes training program staff to learn how to conduct evaluation, reflect on their own practice, and improve programs.

PROGRAM EVALUATION IN THE SCHOOLS

Educators are under increasing scrutiny to demonstrate results, show accountability, and ensure that students are meeting learning standards. The attempts to increase student achievement have resulted in increased educational reform efforts at the national, state, and local levels. Reform efforts include changes to traditional educational programs such as teaching methods, schedules, and curriculum to improve student outcomes.

The application of program evaluation to monitor the effectiveness of reform efforts and to monitor educators' success at increasing student achievement is becoming more common. Funders, including the federal government and private foundations, review program results to determine future funding. The federal government has a center for educational evaluation and many state departments of education and school districts have evaluation offices to monitor and evaluate programs. While evidence regarding the effectiveness of programs and reform efforts can be gathered by researchers, evaluators can provide additional information to school personnel by measuring and supporting program implementation as well as outcomes.

ROLE OF THE SCHOOL PSYCHOLOGIST IN PROGRAM EVALUATION

Few school psychology practitioners conduct and publish research, with the exception of action research in the schools. However, school psychologists who evaluate the effectiveness of interventions for individuals or groups of students engage in a type of program intervention. By learning about more formal program evaluation practices and techniques, school psychologists can examine program components that affect outcomes, including the program theory, inputs, context, extent of implementation, and examine the connection between the intervention and student-level outcomes. Becoming more proficient in the methods of program evaluation would allow school psychologists to efficiently monitor and evaluate outcomes associated with interventions.

Typically school psychology programs include coursework in research methods and statistics. Fewer programs offer coursework specific to program evaluation. Even among programs that offer program evaluation courses, they are typically not a requirement. However, school psychologists who engage in program evaluation and applied research to examine school reform efforts are encouraged to increase their knowledge and skills in conducting program evaluation.

—*Tania Jarosewich*

See also Formative Evaluation; Special Education; Summative Evaluation

REFERENCES AND FURTHER READING

Donaldson, S. I. (2003). Theory-driven program evaluation in the new millennium. In S. Donaldson & M. Scriven (Eds.), *Evaluating social programs and problems: Visions for the new millennium* (2nd ed., pp. 109–144). Mahwah, NJ: Erlbaum.

Fetterman, D. (2003). Empowerment evaluation strikes a responsive cord. In S. I. Donaldson & M. Scriven (Eds.), *Evaluating social programs and problems: Visions for the new millennium* (2nd ed., pp. 63–76). Mahwah, NJ: Erlbaum.

Joint Committee on Standards for Educational Evaluation. (1994). *The program evaluation standards: How to assess evaluations of educational programs.* Thousand Oaks, CA: Sage.

Patton, M. Q. (1997). *Utilization-focused evaluation: The new century text* (3rd ed.). Thousand Oaks, CA: Sage.

Stufflebeam, D. L. (2000). The CIPP model for evaluation. In D. L. Stufflebeam, G. F. Madaus, & T. Kelleghan (Eds.), *Evaluation models: Viewpoints on educational and human services evaluation.* Boston: Kluwer Academic.

W. K. Kellogg Foundation Logic Model Guide. (2001, December). Retrieved July 12, 2004, from http://www.wkkf.org/Pubs/Tools/Evaluation/Pub3669.pdf

PROJECTIVE TESTING

Projective techniques are tests that involve the use of open-ended stimuli such as inkblots as well as pictures, drawings, and words. In projective testing, an examinee is asked to respond to the stimulus and supply structure to the unstructured test material and this structure reflects fundamental aspects of the examinee's personality. In supplying structure to unstructured test material, the individual reveals his or her desires, conscious and unconscious needs, fears, perceptions, and inner conflicts. This is known as the projective hypothesis. Thus, projective tests are indirect methods of assessing an examinee's personality (Cohen & Swerdlik, 1999).

Projective tests are used in the schools to assess behavioral, emotional, and social functioning of students. Students typically evaluated with projective tests are individuals who are experiencing behavioral, emotional, and/or social difficulties such as students who are unable to establish and maintain relationships with teachers or friendships with peers; students who are depressed or anxious; or students who have a thought disorder. When students' behavioral, emotional, and/or social problems have an adverse impact on their educational performance, these students may meet the eligibility requirements for special education and related services under the emotional disturbance (ED) category of the Individuals With Disabilities Education Act (IDEA).

Projective tests that are commonly used in the schools include picture drawings (e.g., drawings of a person, family, school setting, house, or tree), thematic storytelling techniques (e.g., telling stories about pictures), and sentence completion tests (e.g., completing sentences given sentence stems). Inkblot tests are used less frequently in the schools because of the amount of time and advanced training needed to administer, score, and interpret these tests.

Controversy exists surrounding the psychometric soundness of projective tests. Many have argued that projective tests are not sound instruments from a measurement perspective. Standardized administration and scoring procedures are two standards used to evaluate the quality of a measure. Many projective tests do not have standardized administration and scoring procedures. The lack of objectivity in scoring examinees' responses may produce spurious evidence of validity where none exists and subtle differences in verbal instructions given by examiners to examinees may alter the examinees' test performance. Another criterion for assessing the quality of a measure is the norms of the test. Many projective tests do not have norms (i.e., a large, current and diverse sample of people that have taken the test), have inadequate norms, or do not describe their norming sample in sufficient detail. When norms are lacking, inadequate, or not described in sufficient detail, faulty interpretations of examinees' responses may result. Problems assessing interscorer reliability (i.e., consistency of raters' scoring), internal consistency reliability (i.e., uniformity of the item content), and test-retest reliability (i.e., consistency of examinees' responses over time) have been reported, resulting in spuriously low or high reliability estimates. Validity, another standard for evaluating the quality of a measure, refers to the instrument measuring what it is purported to measure. Most validation studies conducted with projective tests have reported inconclusive results because of methodological problems (i.e., experimental control) and/or problems analyzing the data (i.e., statistical analysis) (Anastasi, 1988). Thus, when evaluating the validity and other psychometric properties of projective techniques, school psychologists should be aware that the psychometric soundness of the majority of these measures has not been demonstrated (Cohen & Swerdlik, 1999).

In contrast, some individuals have found projective tests to be quite useful in practice. Projective tests may provide helpful information to practitioners on how individuals organize their experiences, which are unique to each individual's personality (Cohen & Swerdlik, 1999). Others have suggested that projectives are not truly tests but are clinical tools and these clinical tools should not be evaluated in terms of the usual psychometric procedures. The real value of projective techniques is more likely to emerge when trained clinicians interpret these clinical tools qualitatively rather than score these instruments quantitatively and interpret these measures as psychometric instruments (Anastasi, 1988). As for now, the controversy continues about the true value of projective techniques and in their use, including their use with students in the schools.

—*Patricia A. Lowe*

See also Diagnosis and Labeling; Personality Assessment; Reliability; Social–Emotional Assessment; Validity

REFERENCES AND FURTHER READING

Anastasi, A. (1988). *Psychological testing* (6th ed.). New York: Macmillan.

Cohen, R. J., & Swerdlik, M. E. (1999). *Psychological testing and assessment: An introduction to tests and measurement* (4th ed.). Mountain View, CA: Mayfield.

Prevatt, F. F. (1999). Personality assessment in the schools. In C. R. Reynolds & T. B. Gutkin (Eds.), *The handbook of school psychology* (3rd ed., pp. 434–451). New York: Wiley.

PSYCHOMETRIC *g*

Psychometric *g* is the general factor that underlies individual differences on cognitive ability tests. All cognitive tests measure *g* to some extent, but intelligence quotient (IQ) tests tend to measure it particularly well. Psychometric *g* is not a cognitive ability per se, but a property of the brain that causes cognitive tests and performances to correlate with one another. Psychometric *g* is related to the complexity of cognitive processing, not to the surface characteristics of tests (i.e., content). Individual differences in *g* also appear to be related to both genes and the environment. Psychometric *g* explains 80% to 90% of the differences in scholastic and occupational outcomes that can be predicted from tests. Personality traits such as conscientiousness and ambition are thought to interact with *g* to produce individual differences in many real-world outcomes. Intervention studies suggest that *g* is susceptible to environmental intervention, but that there are limits to its malleability.

—*John H. Kranzler*

See also Intelligence

PSYCHOPATHOLOGY IN CHILDREN

Psychopathology in children can be defined as behaviors, emotions, and thoughts that are maladaptively deviant. Maladaptive deviance includes aspects of functioning that deviate markedly from norms for a child's developmental level, that may impair developmental advances and acquisition of adaptive skills, and/or that may be harmful to the child or others.

THE *DSM-IV* APPROACH

Child psychopathology is currently viewed from a variety of perspectives. One important perspective is embodied in the American Psychiatric Association's (1994) *Diagnostic and Statistical Manual of Mental Disorders, Fourth Edition* (*DSM-IV*), which defines child psychopathology in terms of categories of disorders. For example, the *DSM-IV* defines attention deficit hyperactivity disorder (ADHD), predominantly inattentive type, by nine symptom criteria such as "often has difficulty organizing tasks and activities" and "is often forgetful in daily activities." A child who is deemed to display at least six of the nine symptoms and who also meets criteria for age of onset, duration of the symptoms, and impairment is diagnosed as having ADHD, predominantly inattentive type. The criteria are the same for both genders, all ages, and all sources of information.

The most common *DSM-IV* diagnoses for children include ADHD, conduct disorder, oppositional defiant disorder, separation anxiety disorder, generalized anxiety disorder, dysthymia, major depressive disorder, and adjustment disorder. The *DSM-IV* approach implies that there are categorical differences between mental health and each type of disorder. If a child meets criteria for a disorder and is judged to be impaired by the disorder, then the child is not mentally healthy.

THE EMPIRICALLY BASED APPROACH

A second important perspective is embodied in the empirically based approach. Rather than defining disorders by the same criteria for both genders, all ages, and all sources of data, the empirically based approach uses statistical methods to identify patterns of problems that are actually reported for children of each gender at different ages according to multiple sources of data. The sources of data can include parents, teachers, interviewers, observers, and the children themselves. The empirically identified patterns of problems are designated as syndromes, in the sense of "problems that tend to occur together."

To reflect variations in the frequency and intensity of children's problems, the problems are assessed quantitatively by having parents, teachers, and others rate each problem using scales such as *0 = not true, 1 = somewhat or sometimes true,* and *2 = very true or often true* of the child. A child's score on a syndrome is the sum of the child's scores on all items comprising the syndrome.

To help users judge the degree of deviance indicated by each syndrome score, the syndromes are displayed on profiles that compare syndrome scores with norms for the child's age and gender. Thus, for example, if a teacher rates 13-year-old Jason, the teacher's ratings of problems comprising the attention problems syndrome are summed to obtain Jason's score for attention problems. Figure 1 illustrates how scores for each syndrome are compared with scores for a national sample of boys who were rated by their teachers. Another page of the profile (not shown in Figure 1) displays Jason's scores on subscales of the attention problems syndrome designated as inattention and hyperactivity-impulsivity.

Figure 1 shows two broken lines printed across Jason's profile. To help users judge the degree of deviance indicated by a syndrome score, the broken lines demarcate a borderline clinical range. The borderline clinical range is between scores in the normal range (below the bottom broken line, which is at the 93rd percentile) and scores in the clinical range (above the top broken line, which is at the 97th percentile). Scores in the borderline range are high enough to be of concern, while scores in the clinical range indicate a likely need for professional help.

Because Jason's score on the attention problems syndrome was higher than scores obtained by 97% of normal boys, his teacher's ratings indicate a need for professional help. However, because children's problems often vary from one context to another, ratings of Jason by all his teachers, his parents, and by Jason himself should be compared. Even if Jason scores high on attention problems according to multiple informants, his profile may also reveal high scores on other syndromes, as shown in Figure 1. This would argue for treatment that is not limited to attention problems.

Data from teachers, parents, youths, and others can be compared to distinguish between problems that are reported only for particular situations or only by a particular informant, such as a teacher, versus those that are consistent across situations and informants (Achenbach & Rescorla, 2001).

Empirically identified syndromes include:

- Aggressive behavior
- Anxious or depressed
- Attention problems
- Rule-breaking behavior
- Social problems
- Somatic complaints
- Thought problems
- Withdrawn or depressed

The same forms that are scored according to empirically based syndromes can also be scored according to *DSM*-oriented scales (Achenbach & Rescorla, 2001).

The empirically based approach avoids implying that all mental disorders are categorically different

TRF/6-18 - Syndrome Scale Scores for Boys 12-18

ID:0001
Name: Jason

Gender: Male
Age: 13

Date Filled: 06/06/2002
Birth Date: 05/05/1989

Clinician: Ortiz
Agency: Student Services
Verified: Yes

Informant: L. Smith
Relationship: Classroom Teacher {F}

	Internalizing					Externalizing	
	Anxious/ Depressed	Withdrawn/ Depressed	Somatic Complaints	Social Problems	Thought Problems	Attention Problems	Rule-Breaking Behavior	Aggressive Behavior
Total Score	12	6	1	12	3	40	7	16
T Score	73-C	63	58	77-C	64	72-C	65-B	67-B
Percentile	>97	90	79	>97	92	>97	93	96

Anxious/Depressed
2 14. Cries
0 29. Fears
0 30. FearSchool
0 31. FearDoBad
0 32. Perfect
2 33. Unloved
2 35. Worthless
2 45. Nervous
0 50. Fearful
0 52. Guilty
1 71. SelfConsc
2 81. NoCriticism
1 91. TalkSuicide
0 106. AnxPleas
0 108. FearMistk
0 112. Worries

Withdrawn/Depressed
1 5. EnjoysLittle
0 42. PreferAlone
2 65. Won'tTalk
0 69. Secretive
0 75. Shy
1 102. LacksEnergy
2 103. Sad
0 111. Withdrawn

Somatic Complaints
0 51. Dizzy
1 54. Tired
0 56a. Aches
0 56b. Headaches
0 56c. Nausea
0 56d. EyeProb
0 56e. SkinProb
0 56f. Stomach
0 56g. Vomit

Social Problems
0 11. Dependent
1 12. Lonely
2 25. NotGetAlong
2 27. Jealous
2 34. OutToGet
0 36. Accidents
0 38. Teased
2 48. Not Liked
2 62. Clumsy
0 64. PreferYoung
0 79. SpeechProb

Thought Problems
1 9. MindOff
0 18. HarmSelf
0 40. HearsThings
0 46. Twitch
0 58. PicksSkin
0 66. RepeatsActs
0 70. SeesThings
0 83. StoresUp
0 84. StrangeBehav
0 85. StrangeIdeas

Attention Problems
2 1. Acts Young
0 2. Noisy
2 4. FailsToFinish
2 7. Brages
2 8. Concentrate
2 10. SitStill
1 13. Confuse
1 15. Fidgets
1 17. Daydream
1 22. Directions
1 24. Disturbs
2 41. Impulsive
2 49. DiffLearn
2 53. TalksOut
1 60. Apathetic
2 61. PoorSchool
2 67. DisruptDisc
2 72. Messy
2 73. Irresponsible
1 74. ShowOff
1 78. Inattentive
1 80. Stares
2 92. Underachiev
1 93. TalkMuch
1 100. FailsToDo
0 109. Whining

Rule-Breaking Behavior
0 26. NoGuilt
2 28. BreaksRules
0 39. BadFriends
0 43. LieCheat
0 63. PreferOlder
0 82. Steals
1 90. Swears
0 96. ThinksSex
2 98. Tardy
2 99. Tobacco
0 101. Truant
0 105. AlcDrugs

Aggressive Behavior
2 3. Argues
2 6. Defiant
0 16. Mean
1 19. DemAtten
1 20. DestroyOwn
0 21. DestroyOther
1 23. DisbSchool
1 37. Fights
0 57. Attacks
0 68. Screams
0 76. Explosive
2 77. Frustrated
2 86. Stubborn
2 87. MoodChang
0 88. Sulks
0 89. Suspicious
0 94. Teases
0 95. Temper
0 97. Threaten
1 104. Loud

Copyright 2001 T.M. Achenbach   B = Borderline clinical range; C = Clinical range   Broken lines = Borderline clinical range

Figure 1 Profile of Empirically Based Syndromes Scored From a Teacher's Report Form Completed for 13-year-old Jason (original work based on Achenbach & Rescorla, 2001).

from mental health. Instead, it assesses problems quantitatively and compares children with normative samples of peers to guide judgments about whether children need help, in what situations they need help (e.g., home, school, or both), and what kind of help they most need. The empirically based approach also assesses competencies, strengths, and adaptive functioning, which are essential for deciding how to help children.

TREATMENT

Treatments for children's problems include medications, behavioral and cognitive-behavioral therapies, psychotherapy, family therapy, group therapy, and educational interventions. Parents and teachers are often involved in treatment, and multiple treatments are often applied to the same child. Because no single treatment is likely to resolve all problems, different treatments must be coordinated to deal with particular aspects of problems, as well as to strengthen competencies.

Numerous studies have demonstrated the efficacy of several kinds of treatment (Weisz & Jensen, 1999). However, there is less evidence that typical mental health services are efficacious. Although typical mental health services may face practical challenges not faced by controlled studies, more systematic application of efficacious treatments could improve the outcomes of mental health services (Weisz & colleagues, 1995).

CONCLUSION

The *DSM-IV* approach and the empirically based approach provide categorical versus quantitative perspectives on psychopathology and mental health. Some of the *DSM-IV*'s diagnostic categories are defined by symptoms like those that comprise empirically based syndromes, and *DSM-IV*-oriented scales can be scored from the same assessment forms as empirically based syndromes. Various treatments for child psychopathology are efficacious, but these treatments need to be used more systematically in typical mental health services.

—*Thomas M. Achenbach*

See also Aggression in Schools; Autism Spectrum Disorders; Depression; *DSM-IV*; Obsessive–Compulsive Disorder; Oppositional Defiant Disorder; Posttraumatic Stress Disorder

REFERENCES AND FURTHER READING

American Psychiatric Association. (1994). *Diagnostic and statistical manual of mental disorders* (4th ed.). Washington, DC: Author.

Achenbach, T. M., & Rescorla, L. A. (2001). *Manual for the ASEBA school-age forms and profiles.* Burlington, VT: University of Vermont Research Center for Children, Youths, and Families.

Weisz, J. R., & Jensen, P. S. (1999). Efficacy and effectiveness of child and adolescent psychotherapy and pharmacotherapy. *Mental Health Services Research, 1,* 125–157.

Weisz, J. R., Donenberg, G. R., Han, S. S., & Weiss, B. (1995). Bridging the gap between laboratory and clinic in child and adolescent psychotherapy. *Journal of Consulting and Clinical Psychology, 63,* 688–701.

PSYCHOTHERAPY

Psychotherapy has been described as including four major factors:

1. A relationship in which the client has confidence that the therapist is competent and cares about his or her welfare

2. The expectancy or hope shared by the therapist and the client that benefits will result from the process

3. An underlying conceptual framework that provides a rationale for understanding and a set of procedures designed to alleviate the client's distress and functional impairment that require the active participation of both client and therapist

4. A practice setting that is socially defined and accepted as a place of healing

Additional factors that influence the process and outcome include aspects of the client (e.g., nature of the problem, ability to understand and engage in the process, motivation for change, and resources outside of the psychotherapeutic relationship such as parental involvement and support) and characteristics of the therapist (e.g., competence and personality features). Psychotherapy is intended to enhance the client's mental health, flexibility, quality of relationships, and well-being. This occurs through a process of development and change in cognition, perceptions, self-understanding, relational capacities, and overt behavior in the client that promotes a decrease in distress and an increase in adaptive functioning. For children and adolescents, collaborative work with families and schools are designed to promote and maintain complementary change as well.

WHY SEEK PSYCHOTHERAPY AND WHO SEEKS IT?

Psychotherapy is usually sought when an individual is experiencing significant subjective emotional and cognitive distress and impairment in their relational or achievement-, school-, and/or work-related functioning. Psychotherapy may also be sought by others in the individual's life who are concerned for the individual or are affected significantly by the client's distress or behavior. This latter motivation is often the case for children and adolescents who are referred for psychotherapy. At younger ages, psychotherapy typically is initiated by a parent, teacher, or health provider and involves extensive collaborative work with parents and often schools. Adolescents will sometimes self-initiate a request for psychotherapy when they understand it as a potential resource.

A child or adolescent may begin psychotherapy for a variety of reasons, including:

- Experiencing or witnessing abuse, assault, or trauma
- Adjusting to a loss (illness or death in the family, family divorce or restructuring, ending of a significant relationship)
- Adjusting to a chronic medical condition
- Experiencing relational difficulties
- Expressing suicidal ideation or following up after a suicidal attempt

Also, the effects of unrealistic or unhealthy parental or school expectations; living with parental psychopathology or drug and alcohol abuse; social and emotional adjustment to a neurodevelopmental disorder (language and learning disabilities); and prejudice or harassment related to racism, homophobia, or sexism may be reasons treatment is sought. Lastly, psychotherapy is often initiated when a single or coexisting mental disorders (mood, anxiety, conduct, or control disorders) are diagnosed.

PSYCHOTHERAPY VERSUS COUNSELING: IS THERE A MEANINGFUL DIFFERENCE?

A debate exists on whether psychotherapy and counseling differ in terms of process and outcome.

Rather than enter into a controversy, some professionals simply choose not to make a distinction, while others contend that it is impossible to differentiate the two. Still others maintain that there are significant differences, typically based on theoretical orientation and depth of treatment. The "difference" group views counseling as a learning-oriented process with the goal of helping clients to learn or acquire new skills that will enable them to cope and adjust to life situations. In contrast, psychotherapy is viewed as a process in which the therapist assists the client in altering his or her thoughts, perceptions, emotions, relationships, and behavior, and possibly reorganizing or affecting the development of personality. The terms are often interchangeable in contemporary practice, possibly leaving the consumer perplexed. For clarification, it is suggested that the client or parents of the client clarify with the practitioner the nature of the services to be provided, including theoretical orientation, process, and expected outcome of treatment, and which "term" might be more accurate or comfortable. In general, schools seem most comfortable with the term counseling; schools typically offer guidance counseling, crisis counseling, developmental guidance, and career guidance.

HOW HAVE HISTORICAL AND THEORETICAL PERSPECTIVES AFFECTED THE DEVELOPMENT OF PSYCHOTHERAPY?

All schools of psychotherapy are bound together by rationales that include theoretical formulations related to personality and psychopathology, and a set of principles and techniques to apply in practice. The most influential schools have been based on four major theories of personality development and psychopathology:

1. Psychoanalytic theory (and its derivatives)
2. Behavioral theory (including behavior modification, social learning, and cognitive–behavioral)
3. Humanistic theory
4. Family systems theory (not addressed in this article)

Psychoanalytic psychotherapy was the exclusive form of psychotherapy during the early part of the 20th century. Early psychoanalytic theories of treatment sought to enable the client to become aware of suppressed memories as well as the consequences that past experiences asserted upon the client's present psyche. In so doing, it would then be possible to work toward the client's realization of the connection between his or her unconscious past and the conscious reality he or she was presently experiencing. Eventually, psychoanalytic psychotherapy evolved to place greater importance upon interpersonal and social determinants of personality and psychopathology. This shift was paralleled by an increased focus on the importance of the therapeutic relationship as an effective therapeutic agent. In the course of this shift, certain key concepts, such as transference and countertransference, were reconceptualized to reflect the impact of early relationships on current relational functioning. Transference refers to the thoughts and/or feelings directed toward the therapist (e.g., child feels love toward the therapist). In countertransference the therapist projects his or her feelings upon this client (e.g., caring for the patient). Within this approach, which is often referred to as psychodynamic or interpersonal psychotherapy, the therapist seeks to understand the impact of early relationships on current relational functioning. The therapist then uses the current therapeutic relationship to "correct" earlier relational disappointments and harm by providing a corrective emotional experience; that is, the therapist responds to the client in ways that do not confirm the client's expectations based on earlier nonsupportive or hurtful relationships. The client internalizes the qualities of the therapeutic relationship to further develop his or her relational schemes in ways that provide the client with more adaptive choices and counteract earlier established maladaptive patterns of relating and reacting.

Behavioral therapy became recognized in the 1950s as an alternative to traditional psychotherapy. The behavioral perspective focuses on the present rather than past conditions to find factors that are maintaining current problematic behavioral patterns. Behavioral therapy targets the child's overt behavior and emphasizes treatment in the context of family and school. In the 1970s, many with a behavioral perspective began to move away from a strictly stimulus–response model (e.g., stimulus or environmental conditions give rise to behavior) to one that gave weight to the cognitive processes as well. Cognitive–behavioral therapy is based on a problem-solving approach that emphasizes changing an individual's dysfunctional thoughts, emotions, and behavior. This approach places an emphasis on analyzing current problems, defining concrete goals, and developing strategies so that the client can achieve specific, measurable changes. When working with children and adolescents from a cognitive–behavioral perspective, it important to support them through their thought processes, guide them in identifying alternate solutions, encourage and reward them for effort, and aid them in implementing and practicing the skills needed to manage problems and interactions with others.

Humanistic psychotherapy moved into the forefront in the 1960s as a reaction to the clash between those who adhered to psychoanalytic theories and those who followed a behavioral orientation. The concept that most characterizes this approach is dedication to a phenomenological approach. This approach subscribes to humanity's unique ability to possess an awareness of one's own thoughts and to use this ability to interpret one's own world, and use this analysis toward achieving the realization of one's own independent self. Moreover, it focuses on the individual's perception of reality in order to understand behavior. All the theories under this orientation emphasize the process of actualization and growth. There have been several subsets of the humanistic approach, among the most common being Gestalt psychotherapy and experiential psychotherapy.

An integrative approach to psychotherapy has been embraced in the past 20 years. Such an approach advocates not being confined by a single paradigm; rather it promotes constructing a theoretical orientation that draws from multiple theoretical traditions. The integrative movement has been validated by research findings indicating that psychotherapy from different major theoretical perspectives is equally effective, as well as meaningfully more effective than no treatment or placebo conditions. Some attribute the effects to factors shared across the schools of psychotherapy discussed in the description of psychotherapy presented earlier.

WHAT ARE THE UNIQUE ASPECTS OF PROVIDING PSYCHOTHERAPY TO CHILDREN AND ADOLESCENTS?

There are unique and challenging aspects to how children and adolescents, their family systems, their school environments, and the collaborative framework involved in their counseling experiences affect the psychotherapy process. It is important to examine these influencing factors, as extensive work with significant others in these systems is highly recommended. In addition, parental consent is needed for child and adolescent psychotherapy, as well as consulting with others involved. Thus, in addition to psychotherapy sessions with the child, consultation with parents, teachers, whole families, as well as family–school meetings may be set up. Because of the complexities of multiple relationships, boundaries and confidentiality between the psychotherapist and the child client and others involved need to be explicitly negotiated and clarified throughout the process.

Furthermore, children's verbal and cognitive abilities, as well as the organization of their personalities are in development, and most children lack an explicit understanding of psychotherapy and the purposes and goals of treatment. These unique aspects provide opportunities for psychotherapists to educate children and the adults in their lives about the potential benefits of psychotherapy, to work with children early in their personality development, and to influence significant others in children's lives. In addition, in psychotherapeutic work with children, along with the verbal mode that is common with adults, the modalities of play, art, and games are common. For adolescents, although the verbal mode is dominant, games and even physical activities may comprise part of the process.

WHAT ARE THE ADVANTAGES AND DISADVANTAGES TO PROVIDING PSYCHOTHERAPY IN SCHOOL SETTINGS?

Schools are a natural setting where children come to learn and develop socially and emotionally. Although schools are united in their commitment to promoting academic achievement, schools and their administrations vary in their attitudes, acceptance, and resources to provide site-based mental health and health services, including counseling and psychotherapy. Within a supportive school atmosphere, mental health services can enhance learning and development, as well as overall school climate. In addition to flexible access to children, access to and collaboration with teachers and other involved school staff is readily obtained. In addition, the practitioner has the opportunity to experience a complete cohort of children in a particular school, to get a sense of fit between the child and his or her norm group, and to implement indicated system interventions. There also may be the opportunity, depending on the continuum

of services available in the school, to help coordinate a combination of individual-, group-, and family-related services to address a child's needs. There also is an opportunity for long-term follow-up, even over several years, to track the development of an individual child and his or her family. In contrast, access to parents may be more challenging with the provision of school-based psychotherapy, and confidentiality and boundaries may be challenging to maintain. In addition, some children, adolescents, and their parents may choose to seek psychotherapy services outside of the school, to ensure privacy and confidentiality more fully. The decision on which setting may be most appropriate for a child obtaining psychotherapy services should be thoughtfully made.

WHAT IS THE ROLE OF SCHOOL PSYCHOLOGISTS IN PROVIDING OR REFERRING A CHILD FOR PSYCHOTHERAPY?

Many school-based school psychologists, at the specialist and doctoral levels, have voiced a desire to provide or expand school-based counseling and psychotherapy for children and adolescents. The opportunity to do so will be impacted by many attitudinal, systemic, and resource issues, alluded to previously. An additional factor to consider is the education, training, and competence of the individual school psychologist. School psychologists vary greatly in their preparation to provide psychotherapy, based on their graduate school education and training, supervised internship, postdoctoral experiences, and continued education and training. As a general rule, school psychologists are more prepared to offer behavior and cognitive–behavioral therapy than family therapy and psychotherapy from a psychodynamic perspective, although some will be very well prepared in these areas and also be able to offer psychotherapy from an integrated perspective.

School-based school psychologists, through their assessment and consultation functions, also have a key role in referring children and families to public and private facilities within the community for mental health services, including psychotherapy. It is extremely important for referring school psychologists to be well informed about community services and to assist referred individuals with the process, which can be complex and confusing at times. Lastly, school psychologists that are licensed for independent practice (which in most states requires meeting the doctoral licensing requirements) provide psychotherapy in other settings, including clinics and independent practices. Their thorough training in integrating the child, family, school, and community impact on development prepares these professional psychologists to offer psychotherapy to children and adolescents whose mental health needs include a school component.

—*Deborah Tharinger and Michelle Perfect*

See also Abuse and Neglect; Confidentiality; Counseling; Crisis Intervention; Informed Consent; Interviewing; Psychopathology in Children

PSYCHOTROPIC MEDICATIONS

Important advances in psychotropic medications and significant developments in neuroscience have complemented our growing knowledge about the structural and functional differences of the central nervous system (CNS) in children diagnosed with learning disorders and emotional problems (Brown & Sammons, 2002). However, in spite of these recent advances, researchers and clinicians note that clinical use of psychotropic medications in children exceeds our knowledge about the efficacy and safety of these drugs. Unfortunately, no statistical database exists on how many children and adolescents are receiving psychotropic medications for specific disorders. However, some surveys with specific psychotropic drugs (i.e., stimulants) suggest increased use of these drugs (Safer & colleagues, 1999). The psychiatric disorders for which psychotropic medications have been most used include attention deficit hyperactivity disorder (ADHD), autism, enuresis, mental retardation, and Tourette's syndrome.

The rationale for distinguishing between adult and pediatric psychopharmacology includes the differences in medical and psychological practice between the two populations. These include physiological factors (e.g., differences in body weight, drug absorption, and drug interactions) and psychological factors (children and adolescents usually have a different cognitive framework from adults to describe positive and adverse effects of drugs) (Werry & Aman, 1998). Furthermore, children almost always rely on caregivers to administer medication and to report on the positive and negative effects of various medications. In addition,

psychotropic medication is only one of many treatments children may receive.

Assessment of psychotropic drug effects in the pediatric population is monitored in the areas of learning, physical functioning, and psychosocial functioning. Therefore, assessment must be conducted from different informants (caregivers, teachers, clinicians) and in various settings (home, school) (Brown & Sawyer, 1998). Assessments usually include behavioral rating scales, direct observations of behavior, physical effects, structured interviews, and, sometimes, specific laboratory measures of psychological performance (e.g., continuous performance tasks of concentration and attention). While the search continues for ideal measurements to predict response to psychotropic drugs, so far no such instrument has been developed (Brown & Sammons, 2002).

DISORDERS FOR WHICH PSYCHOTROPIC MEDICATIONS ARE EFFECTIVE

Although information about the incidence of children being treated with psychotropic drugs is not available, the disorders that are most often treated by psychotropic drugs include attention deficit hyperactivity disorder (ADHD), autism spectrum disorders, mental retardation, developmental disabilities, seizure disorders, mood disorders, enuresis, and Tourette's syndrome (Werry & Aman, 1998).

Attention Deficit Hyperactivity Disorder

ADHD is the most common behavioral disorder pediatricians see. In general, ADHD has been responsive to stimulant agents. Recently, concern has mounted about the increase in stimulant use and possible "overuse" (Safer & colleagues, 1999). Increased use is related to children being managed on stimulants for a long time, better identification of children with ADHD-inattentive type, more girls receiving treatment, and more children taking medication during the summer. Notwithstanding their increased use, the stimulants have been the most carefully documented treatment in child psychiatry (Kutcher, 1997).

Autism Spectrum Disorders

Little is known about the cause and cure of autism. However, some psychotropic medications have been successfully used to reduce behaviors such as aggression, obsessions, overactivity, and stereotypies. A recent survey suggests that nearly 33% of one state's population of children with autism were receiving psychotropic medications, the most common being the stimulants and the antipsychotics (Werry & Aman, 1998). The selective serotonin reuptake inhibitors (SSRIs) have been recommended to manage obsessive and ritualistic behaviors in this population.

Tourette's Syndrome

Tourette's syndrome is characterized by involuntary, repetitive, and stereotyped motor or vocal behavior. It is associated with several developmental and psychiatric disorders (e.g., ADHD, learning disabilities, obsessive–compulsive disorder). In previous years, antipsychotic medications such as haloperidol were often used to manage Tourette's syndrome (Kutcher, 1997). However, because of concerns about adverse side effects, drugs with a more favorable side effect profile ("atypical" antipsychotics) have been used increasingly (olanzapine, risperidone, or ziprasodone). While information on their safety and efficacy is encouraging, more controlled trials clearly are needed to establish further safety and efficacy.

Enuresis

Although children with enuresis are usually treated with behavioral methods, there is some interest in using medications for this disorder. Medications for managing enuresis include the tricyclic antidepressants (a classification of antidepressant medications that are hypothesized to potentiate the adrenergic synapses by blocking the reuptake of norepinephrine at the nerve endings) and the antidiuretic hormone desmopressin (a synthetic version of the naturally occurring hormone vasopressin, a hormone affecting renal functioning or water retention) (Phelps & colleagues, 2002). However, these drugs have high relapse rates, and potentially fatal cardiac effects have often been an adverse effect of the tricyclic antidepressant (Werry & Aman, 1998).

Affective and Mood Disorders

Compared to some of the disorders mentioned above, little clinical research has looked at how to use psychotropic drugs to manage affective and mood disorders. Some experts believe that the prevalence of use of antidepressants (including tricyclic antidepressants and SSRIs) and anxiolytics (psychotropic medications used to manage anxiety disorders) is greater than the information available about their safety and efficacy for children and adolescents. Nevertheless, encouraging recent studies support the safety and efficacy of the SSRIs in managing affective and mood disorders in pediatric populations (Brown & Sammons, 2002).

Mental Retardation and Developmental Disabilities

Psychotropic drug use, including the antipsychotic and stimulant agents, continues to increase for people with mental retardation and developmental disabilities. However, professionals are concerned about the limited ability of these individuals to report adverse effects.

CLASSES OF PSYCHOTROPIC MEDICATIONS

Psychotropic medications are categorized by a classification system that includes the stimulants, antidepressants, antipsychotics, anxiolytics, mood stabilizers, and anticonvulsants.

Stimulants

Stimulants are the first-line pharmacological treatment for ADHD (Brown & Sawyer, 1998; Phelps & colleagues, 2002). They do not affect the natural course of the disorder but help manage its specific symptoms. Many types of stimulants are available to clinicians, including dextroamphetamine (i.e., Adderall and Dexedrine), magnesium pemoline (Cylert), and methylphenidate (i.e., Ritalin, Concerta, Metadate CD, and Focalin). It is thought that these drugs take effect by increasing the reuptake of dopamine or norepinephrine at the synapse. Because of its severe side effect of liver toxicity, magnesium pemoline is no longer recommended to manage ADHD.

Methylphenidate and dextroamphetamine compounds have short- and long-acting forms. Ritalin and Focalin are the short-acting forms of methylphenidate, and Dexedrine and Adderall are the short-acting forms of dextroamphetamine. An advantage of the long-acting preparations is that doses may be given less often. Therefore, these stimulants (e.g., Concerta, Metadate CD, Adderall XR) are increasing in popularity because of the convenience of once-a-day dosing.

The adverse side effects most commonly noted of the stimulants include abdominal pains, appetite suppression, headaches, insomnia, irritability, rebound phenomena (observed when children discontinue stimulant drug therapy; often their inattentiveness and overactivity appear to worsen in response to cessation of the stimulant medication) and tics (Werry & Aman, 1998).

Antidepressants

Antidepressant agents are usually used to treat symptoms of depression in the pediatric population. These agents have also been shown to improve symptoms of ADHD, obsessive–compulsive disorder, (OCD) and enuresis. The SSRIs are the first line treatment for depression (Werry & Aman, 1998). These exert their effects by selectively blocking serotonin reuptake. The SSRIs currently available are fluoxetine HCl (Prozac), sertraline HCl (Zoloft), paroxetine HCl (Paxil), fluvoxamine (Luvox), and citalopram (Celexa). The only SSRI that has received Food and Drug Administration (FDA) approval for use with children and adolescents is sertraline HCl (Werry & Aman, 1998). Fluvoxamine also is approved for children and adults to manage OCD. Some common adverse side effects for the SSRIs include dry mouth, nausea, restlessness, and weight gain. However, these effects are usually mild and fleeting. Less common adverse side effects include blurred vision, dermatitis, and sexual dysfunction (Werry & Aman, 1998). Another complication of SSRI treatment is serotonin syndrome, caused by excess serotonin in the CNS. The symptoms of serotonin syndrome include CNS irritability, coma, hypothermia, seizures, and death. Research on the safety and efficacy of the SSRIs is still in its infancy.

Buproprion (Wellbutrin), an atypical antidepressant that has been effective in treating ADHD, has its main effects on dopamine and norepinephrine reuptake (Werry & Aman, 1998). It is also approved for use in quitting smoking (Zyban). Buproprion may be a viable alternative to stimulant medication if there is a family history of tics, for which stimulants might not be recommended, or if a family member is at risk for selling or abusing stimulants. The side effects of buproprion include agitation, confusion, insomnia, irritability, and possible hypertension (Werry & Aman, 1998). Buproprion is not recommended for patients with a history of an eating or a seizure disorder.

When compared to placebos, tricyclic antidepressants (a classification of antidepressant medications

that are posited to potentiate the adrenergic synapses by blocking the reuptake of norepinephrine at the nerve endings—e.g., Elavil, Norpramin, Pamelor, and Tofranil) have not been shown to be effective in managing depression or enuresis in children and adolescents (Brown & Sawyer, 1998). In addition, the side effects can be severe with the possibility of cardiac complications including sudden death. Therefore, these agents are not recommended for treating depression in pediatric populations (Werry & Aman, 1998).

Antipsychotics

In the past, haloperidol (Haldol) was the treatment of choice for childhood psychosis. Its efficacy is well established, although it has a high incidence of extrapyramidal side effects (a constellation of medication side effects causing odd muscular reactions caused by the antipsychoptic's action on dopamine receptors; includes acute dystonia, akasthisia, akinesia, and Parkinsonian side effects). Therefore, the atypical antipsychotics including olanzapine (Zyprexa), risperidone (Risperdal), ziprasidone (Geodon), quetiapine fumarate (Seroquel), and clozapine (Clozaril) are prescribed more often because their side effect profile is better than other antipsychotic agents (Brown & Sammons, 2002). Adverse side effects include sedation, weight gain, and anticholinergic effects (e.g., dry eyes, mouth, and/or throat; constipation). Clozapine is associated with severe and possibly fatal side effects including potentially fatal cardiac complications (Brown & Sammons, 1998).

Anxiolytics

Most scientific research supports using behavioral therapy to treat childhood anxiety disorders (Phelps & colleagues, 2002). Few studies exist on the efficacy of anxiolytic medications in children. Buspirone (BuSpar) has been effective in treating generalized anxiety disorder in children. It has a mild side effect profile, but drug-to-drug interactions may occur. While there is no evidence that buspirone causes tardive dyskinesia (appears after long-term—three months or more—treatment with antipsychotics and generally appears as abnormal involuntary movements of the mouth, face, tongue, and neck), occasional extrapyramidal side effects have been noted. Although clomipramine (Anafranil) has been effective in managing OCD, its side-effect profile may be severe because it is structurally similar to the tricyclics. Clonazepam (Klonipin) also is effective for anxiety and panic attacks. As with any benzodiazepine (a classification of antianxiety medications hypothesized to enhance GABA [gamma-aminobutyric acid], the main inhibitory neurotransmitter in the CNS [e.g., Ativan, Klonopin, Xanax]), however, the risk of long-term dependence is possible. Therefore, these medications are recommended only when other treatments have failed (Brown & Sammons, 2002).

Anticonvulsants and Mood Stabilizers

Lithium may be effective in managing bipolar disorder in adolescents, but so far no studies have evaluated lithium use with younger children.

In addition to managing seizure disorders, anticonvulsant medications such as phenobarbital, phenytoin (Dilantin), carbamazepine (Tegretol), and valproate (Depakote, Depakene) can also be effective in treating behavioral disorders such as aggressive behaviors and manic episodes (Brown & Sawyer, 1998). More studies are needed on the newer anticonvulsants, including gabapentin (Neurontin), tiagabine HCl (Gabitril), and lamotrigine (Lamictal), before they can be endorsed for treating cyclical mood disorders in children and adolescents.

Alpha-Adrenergic Medications

Clonidine HCl (Catapres), an alpha-adrenergic agent used to treat hypertension, is also effective in treating ADHD, specifically impulsivity and overactivity (Brown & Sammons, 2002). Guanfacine HCl (Tenex) is an agent that acts longer than clonidine and has fewer adverse effects. Adverse side effects of alpha-adrenergic agents include sedation and hypotension.

ATTITUDES, CONSUMER SATISFACTION, AND LEGAL ISSUES

Caregivers and teachers may view behavioral therapies or other forms of psychotherapy as better treatment options than psychotropic agents (Brown & Sawyer, 1998). Generally, research indicates that caregivers are more accepting of psychotropic agents when they are combined with psychotherapy and when their efficacy is assessed by controlled clinical trials (Brown & Sawyer, 1998). Children and adolescents' attitudes toward psychotropic medication are also important and predict compliance with treatment.

In spite of these issues, the well-informed practitioner must also consider critical issues including informed consent, children and adolescents' right to refuse treatment, custody issues, confidentiality, and the best interest of the child or adolescent.

CONCLUSION

There are numerous psychotropic medications available for children and adolescents. However, controlled clinical trials with these agents have not kept pace with their widespread use. It is anticipated that in future years, research will identify further the efficacy of these medications on learning and behavior, as well as the short-term and long-term safety of these agents for children and adolescents.

—Angela La Rosa, Ronald T. Brown, and Lilless McPherson Shilling

See also Aggression in Schools; Attention Deficit Hyperactivity Disorder; Autism Spectrum Disorders; Depression; Enuresis; Mental Retardation; Personality Assessment; Social–Emotional Assessment; Substance Abuse; Tourette's Syndrome

REFERENCES AND FURTHER READING

Brown, R., & Sammons, M. (2002). Pediatric psychopharmacology: A review of new developments and recent research. Professional Psychology Research and Practice, 33, 135–147.

Brown, R., & Sawyer, M. (1998). Medication in school-age children: Effects on learning and behavior. New York: Guilford.

Kutcher, R. (1997). Child and adolescent psychopharmacology. Philadelphia: W. B. Saunders.

Phelps, L., Brown, R., & Power, T. (2002). Pediatric psychopharmacology: A collaborative approach. Washington, DC: American Psychological Association.

Safer, D., Zito, J. M., & Fine, E. M. (1999). Increased methylphenidate usage for attention deficit disorder in the 1990s. Pediatrics, 98, 1084–1088.

Werry, J., & Aman, M. (1998). Practitioner's guide to psychoactive drugs for children and adolescents (2nd ed.). New York: Kluwer.

PUBERTY

Puberty represents the process of moving from reproductive immaturity to maturity (Alsaker, 1996). Changes occur with respect to overall body stature and composition, hormone levels, and the development of primary and secondary sex characteristics. This process can take two to six years to complete; four years is considered average. Whereas puberty is considered one of the true universals of human development, one of its hallmarks is the tremendous variability that exists between and within individual adolescents. Furthermore, although puberty is seen as a predominantly biological event, the changes it brings interact in a variety of ways with aspects of the adolescent's environment, and can significantly impact other aspects of development and functioning (Alsaker, 1996; Dubas & colleagues, 1991).

Slap (1986) provides a comprehensive accounting of the physical and physiological changes females and males experience during puberty. In females, the onset of puberty is typically marked by the appearance of breast buds and the beginning of the height spurt. The average age for these events is 10 years, with a typical age range of 8 to 13 years for both. Breast development is typically completed by 14 years and adult stature is achieved by an average age of 13 years, with a normal range for both of 10 to 16 years. Pubic hair begins to appear around 10.5 years on average, with a range of 8 to 14 years, and is typically completed by 14.5 years, with a range of 14 to 15 years. The average age of menarche is 12.5 years, with a range of 10.5 to 15.5 years.

In males, the testes begin to enlarge at an average age of 11.5 years, with a range of 9.5 to 13.5 years. Enlargement of the penis and the appearance of pubic hair begin at an average age of 12 years, with a range of 10 to 15 years; penile growth is completed at an average age of 14.5 years, with a range of 12.5 to 16 years, and pubic hair growth is completed at 15.5 years, with a range of 14 to 17 years. First ejaculation (semenarche or spermarche), usually in the context of a nocturnal emission ("wet dream"), occurs at an average age of 13 years, with a range of 12 to 16 years. The average age for the beginning of the height spurt is 12.5 years, with a range of 10.5 to 16 years; adult stature is reached at an average age of 15.5 years, with a range of 13.5 to 17.5 years. The appearance of facial hair and deepening of the voice begin at an average age of 14 years, with a range of 12.5 to 15.5 years.

Multiple factors must be appreciated when trying to understand adolescents' reactions to puberty. Boys generally feel more positive about their changes than girls do; girls tend to be more ambivalent, experiencing a mix of anxiety, excitement, and pride. The amount of information about and preparation for the respective changes is an important predictor of positive adjustment. Girls who are not prepared for menarche and boys who are not prepared for semenarche often experience undue anxiety and shame. Cultural standards of physical attractiveness for males versus females and the fact that adolescents' pubertal body changes are said to have "social stimulus value" (meaning that others notice the changes and react to them) also come into play. For example, puberty brings an increase in lean body mass (i.e., muscle) for males, but a decrease in lean body mass (and an increase in body fat) for females. Depending on the degree to which these normal changes in body shape and composition occur for boys versus girls, the adolescent's body image and overall self-esteem may be enhanced or diminished.

It is important to distinguish between pubertal status versus timing. Pubertal status is an objective measure; it refers to how far along an adolescent is with respect to the physical and/or biological changes. Pubertal timing is a normative measure, characterizing the adolescent's development as either early, on time, or late as compared to a specific peer cohort. Adolescents who are early (or late) would be the first (or last) 20% of their cohort. Research has shown that adolescents' perceptions of their pubertal timing are powerful predictors of their adjustment to the changes (Dubas & colleagues, 1991). However, their perceptions are not always accurate, especially in early adolescence. Generally speaking, adolescents who believe they are developing at about the same time and rate as the majority of their peers are most positive about their experiences.

Developing early has been associated with certain risk factors for girls; because their changes may begin as early as seven years of age, these girls are typically ill-prepared for them. Early maturing girls are often subjected to teasing, and they tend to associate with older peers and begin dating earlier. Late-maturing girls often report dissatisfaction with what they feel is a lack of attention from boys. However, being a late-developing female is a welcomed set of circumstances in competitive sports that favor a prepubescent body shape (e.g., gymnastics, ice-skating). Early maturing boys seem to enjoy some advantages over their on-time or late-developing peers, as they tend to be taller and stronger; they often excel in athletics and are treated by others (including adults) as more mature. This often serves to increase self-esteem, but can also increase stress, as others (including adults, peers, and parents) may have very high expectations for the early developing male and his behavior based only on his physical appearance. Late-maturing males are often unhappy with their physical development; their smaller stature tends to be a disadvantage socially and athletically, and looking more "childlike," they may be treated as such by others. Some cope by developing very strong interpersonal skills; as a result, by late adolescence and early adulthood, these young men may fare better than their peers who developed early (Peskin, 1972).

What triggers puberty? Heredity and genetics certainly play a role, but so do environmental factors like nutrition and stress. Essentially, puberty results from a reactivation of the intense hormonal activity that was begun during the prenatal period. The major influences in this reactivation are the hypothalamus, the pituitary and adrenal glands, and the gonads (i.e., ovaries, testes), which produce sex hormones in abundance, at least in contrast to childhood when their concentration was minimal. The characterization of puberty as a time of "raging hormones" is not wholly inappropriate, but the status of hormones as a direct cause of behavioral and/or mood disruptions is not a given. For example, extreme (high or low) concentrations of testosterone and estrogen are associated with unstable mood, but moderate concentrations are associated with more positive moods. Estrogen increases as a result of stress; early adolescence brings with it many stressors other than adjusting to a changing body, like school transitions and changes in relationships with parents.

—Lesa Rae Vartanian

See also Friendships; Gangs; Social Skills

REFERENCES AND FURTHER READING

Alsaker, F. D. (1996). Annotation: The impact of puberty. *Journal of Child Psychology and Psychiatry, 37,* 249–258.

Dubas, J. S., Graber, J. A., & Petersen, A. C. (1991). A longitudinal investigation of adolescents' changing perceptions of pubertal timing. *Developmental Psychology, 27,* 580–586.

Peskin, H. (1972). Pubertal onset and ego functioning. In J. Kestenberg (Ed.), *The adolescent: Physical development, sexuality and pregnancy.* New York: MSS Information.

Slap, G. B. (1986). Normal physiological and psychosocial growth in the adolescent. *Journal of Adolescent Health Care, 7,* 13S–23S.

PUNISHMENT. *See* APPLIED BEHAVIOR ANALYSIS; BEHAVIOR; BEHAVIOR INTERVENTION; FUNCTIONAL BEHAVIOR ASSESSMENT

QUALITATIVE RESEARCH

The term *qualitative research* refers to the study of phenomena in their natural environments and to ascribing meaning to these phenomena through authentic interaction and interpretation. In qualitative research, the researcher becomes a participant in the data-gathering process. This is in sharp contrast to quantitative research methods, which strive to systematically manipulate the environment in which observations are being conducted, for the purpose of eliminating any extraneous sources of influence which may impact the behavior of subjects.

Qualitative researchers generally deal with relatively small samples of individuals and collect data that are more exhaustive with respect to describing the complexity of those individuals and their environments. Qualitative researchers concern themselves with the description and interpretation of phenomena that may not be so easily assessed, for the purpose of garnering a deeper understanding of the processes that underlie them. For this reason, qualitative research methods provide a very important counterpoint to the studies conducted by quantitative researchers, and, consequently, they are valued by many social scientists.

MODELS AND METHODOLOGIES USED BY QUALITATIVE RESEARCHERS

Among the most common strategies employed in qualitative research are case studies, the life history method, ethnography, grounded theory, participatory action research, and clinical models. The case study is

perhaps the most popular model for qualitative research. It involves an in-depth description and interpretation of a single case (*case* may be defined as any entity of interest, usually an individual, but sometimes a larger group, such as a classroom of children). Multiple methods are typically employed to collect data for case studies, including field notes, structured interviews, observations, conversations, document analysis, and many other sources. The life history method is a kind of case study that relies almost solely on the interpretation of historical documents such as biographies, autobiographies, and narrated accounts of history, to create a modern representation of another time and place.

Ethnography is the branch of social science dedicated to descriptions of peoples and their cultures. The purpose is to create representations of human group behavior through interactions with the group studied. Grounded theory refers to an approach to data gathering that is similar to ethnography, in that it consists of collecting detailed materials through field study. In grounded theory, data gathered using interviews, observations, and other methods are studied to discover phenomena and develop a theory that underlies the actions of the people being studied.

Participatory action research and clinical models are two related disciplines in qualitative research, differentiated from other strategies by their focus on not only interacting with the environment, but also actively influencing the settings in which data are being collected. That is, practitioners of both participatory action research and clinical models are purposeful, directed agents of change. The two approaches differ—participatory action researchers are dedicated to large-scale social change, often reacting to perceived injustices in the community, while clinical researchers are concerned with the diagnosis and treatment of the individuals being studied.

There are many examples of qualitative research to be found in the schools. Many of these involve case studies of students and their reactions to changes implemented in their schools (e.g., Herr & Brooks, 2003). Others employ clinical approaches to children with behavioral problems, documenting the study and remediation of problematic behaviors (e.g., Robertson, 1998).

—*William P. Skorupski*

See also Research

REFERENCES AND FURTHER READING

Denzin, N. K., & Lincoln, Y. S. (2000). *Handbook of qualitative research.* London: Sage.

Herr, L. M., & Brooks, D. W. (2003). Developing and sustaining K-12 school technology innovation through lottery grant awards: A multiple case study. *Journal of Science Education and Technology, 12,* 153–182.

Robertson, D. F. (1998). Homeless students: A search for understanding. *International Journal of Leadership in Education, 1,* 155–168.

R

RACE, ETHNICITY, CLASS, AND GENDER

Race has been recognized as being scientifically nonexistent, yet socially real. Some have argued that genetic evidence (e.g., DNA) indicates that most physical variation occurs within so-called *groups*. Hence, there is more recognized *within* racial group variation than *between* racial group variation. Contemporary scholars argue the term *race* was invented in the 18th century to refer to the populations brought together in colonial America. The term was originally tied to the theorem of the Great Chain of Being (Armelagos & Goodman, 1998). The "scientific" research and the popular culture of the time supported, justified, and expanded fictitious beliefs about the various populations. These ideas became deeply embedded in American thought and eventually spread to other areas of the world. The early emphasis placed on race and the supposed related meanings gave way to racism. It has been said that if race is not a sufficient cause of racism, it is a necessary cause. Consequently, it has also been argued that the concept of *race* is a prime example of how politics can be embedded in science (Armelagos & Goodman, 1998).

Race enters into psychotherapy in ways that parallel its operation in society. Therefore, biases held by either the client or therapist can affect the assessment and treatment of those seeking psychological counseling. Many concepts of psychological assessment work from a European (or Western)-based system of understanding and treatment of problems. A major departure from what can be called European psychology is Black psychology, which focuses on understanding and treating clients from an African perspective that may also be more helpful to those who commonly employ an African/African American worldview (Wilson, 1993). An ability to relate to individuals who may process information differently can lead to better intervention and counseling by preventing misattribution caused by unfamiliarity with a person's worldview.

In many situations, the term *race* has been synonymous with *ethnicity*. Ethnicity can be seen as a subset of race in some instances. For example, throughout the African continent there are numerous ethnic groups (sometimes called tribes) such as the Ashanti, the Igbo (or Ibo), the Zulu, and the Yoruba, just to name a few. All of the ethnic groups would be in the same racial category—Black—but have more or less differing worldviews, customs, rituals, and practices. Thus, ethnicity can be contained within the race categorization and also be synonymous with race as a descriptor (e.g., African American).

One common theme in the ethnic discourse is the notion of culture, or shared history of a given people. It is this shared history, with common rituals, worldviews, philosophies, speech/language, mode of dress, and/or music, that bind individuals to a particular group. It can be said that the more one has in common and identifies in these various areas, the more one is part of this group.

Issues of race and ethnicity have been addressed in the field of education. The growth in multicultural initiatives is evidence of the push for including historical representation of ethnic minorities in the curriculum. Some have argued that academic success among ethnic minority students in the United States has been under-realized because in some instances students have resisted a school culture that attempts to make everyone fit mainstream American values (Fordham, 1988). Others have argued that many of the problems associated with ethnic minorities have come as a result of being inadequately educated, or educated away from one's own self-interest for the benefit of the status quo. As a result of the inadequate education, many problem behaviors have developed in these communities and they persist (Akbar, 1998).

It is not the race of the client, therapist, student, or teacher that should be of most concern. It should, however, be acknowledged, addressed, and resolved that race and ethnicity, as real and unreal as they may be, often have definite implications and outcomes. In addition, one's culture should be taken into account to adequately teach and treat those in need (Wilson, 1993).

Class structure in a capitalist society such as the United States refers to the social ranking of individuals, families, and other groups according to their economic status. For example, the terms underclass, working class, middle class, and upper class denote a stratification of society that is based on income and social standing in a particular community (Bottomore, 1991). During the latter half of the 20th century, critics of class structure pointed to a number of radical social movements that resisted the notion of limits being placed on a person's mobility because of class or any number of other identity markers (e.g., gender, race, ethnicity, sexual orientation). However, with the rise of newer communication technologies and global capitalism has come a new class divide—one that separates people into two groups: a group that has access to these newer technologies and the jobs they create, and a group that has little or no such access.

An examination of some of the assumptions underlying class structure reveals a society's influence on young people's self-perceptions and identity formations. For example, individuals who perceive themselves (and are perceived by others) as being low-achieving students often end up the recipients of what Finn (1999) calls a "domesticating" education—that is, an education that stresses "functional literacy, literacy that makes a person productive and dependable, but not troublesome" (pp. ix-x). It is a second-rate kind of educational arrangement that typically leads to lower expectations and to social and economic inequalities. This cycle of inequalities continues as part of a pattern in which young people learn to identify with others in their culture who may be working class or poor like themselves. Because these identities

form early in life, it is important for educators to attempt to understand young people's history and background and avoid generalizing about "what works" for one class of people as opposed to another. Interventions that challenge traditional notions of learning within developmental psychology must also look for richer and more diverse assessments of young people's learning than are available in the current climate of high-stakes testing, with its emphasis on factual rather than higher-order thinking.

Gender denotes the attributes that are culturally ascribed to men and women. It is not a synonym for one's biological sex status (male or female). Scholars of late argue that gender is culturally and socially constructed through language (Payne, 1996). That is, the very things that seem to draw attention to one's maleness or femaleness are, in effect, not innate, but rather acquired through the cultural and social contexts in which we learn to speak, read, write, act, dress, and so on. The point of arguing for a culturally constructed notion of gender is that it is thought to facilitate a disruption of the traditional view of men and women in which the male is dominant and the female is subordinate—a condition that historically has led to social injustices and economic inequities. By disrupting the traditional view, feminists seek to make people more aware of how language has played a role in constituting male privilege throughout the centuries.

Issues of gender bias and prejudice in schools affect group dynamics within instructional contexts. For example, the research literature on student-led discussion groups in grades 6 through 12 demonstrates that peers, acting as "more knowledgeable others" (e.g., more academically capable students tutoring peers who are struggling to read), can facilitate meaningful interpretation of texts. However, what is less well understood is how the potential for stereotyping on the basis of gender can create situations in which some students' voices are valued over others. For example, studies conducted on girls' loss of voice, resiliency, and self-esteem as they approach adolescence suggest that many young women go through a process in which they begin to see themselves as the stereotypical female that society seemingly defines for them. In some instances, preadolescent females may begin to voice their opinions less in class discussions because a strong female voice is deemed unfeminine. Interventions aimed at changing this process point to the need for instructional strategies that better position young women to join in peer-led discussion groups with confidence and ease.

In summary, race, ethnicity, class, and gender are anything but "neutral" concepts. Each is socially, historically, and culturally embedded in a wide array of patterned behaviors, beliefs, and attitudes that give these concepts their meanings. More than simply theoretical constructs, race, ethnicity, class, and gender are capable of producing material effects that can have real consequences on people's everyday lives, whether in school or in clinical settings.

—*Donna E. Alvermann and Preston Hughes, IV*

See also Ability Grouping; Americans with Disabilities Act; Bias (Testing); Friendships; Intelligence; Multicultural Education; Resilience and Protective Factors

REFERENCES AND FURTHER READING

Akbar, N. (1998). *Know thy self.* Tallahassee, FL: Mind Productions.

Armelagos, G. J., & Goodman, A. H. (1998). Race, racism, and anthropology. In A. H. Goodman & T. L. Leatherman (Eds.), *Building a new biocultural synthesis: Political-economic perspectives on human biology.* Ann Arbor: University of Michigan Press.

Bottomore, T. (Ed.). (1991). *A dictionary of Marxist thought* (2nd ed.). Cambridge, MA: Blackwell.

Davies, B. (1994). *Poststructuralist theory and classroom practice.* Geelong, Australia: Deakin University Press.

Finn, P. J. (1999). *Literacy with an attitude: Educating working-class children in their own self-interest.* Albany, NY: State University of New York Press.

Fordham, S. (1988). Racelessness as a factor in black student's school success: Pragmatic strategy or pyrrhic victory? *Harvard Educational Review, 58*(1), 54–84.

Payne, M. (Ed.). (1996). *A dictionary of cultural and critical theory.* Malden, MA: Blackwell.

Wilson, A. (1993). *The falsification of African consciousness: Eurocentric history, psychiatry, and the politics of white supremacy.* New York: African World Infosystems.

RADIO/MUSIC. *See* COMPUTER TECHNOLOGY; MEDIA AND CHILDREN

REACTIVE ATTACHMENT DISORDER OF INFANCY AND EARLY CHILDHOOD

The essential feature of a reactive attachment disorder (RAD) is a marked disturbance in social relatedness that begins before age five years (in most contexts) and is associated with gross pathological care, which is presumed to be the cause of the disturbed social relatedness (*Diagnostic and Statistical Manual of Mental Disorders, Fourth Edition* [*DSM-IV*], American Psychiatric Association, 1994). Gross pathological care includes a persistent disregard for the child's basic emotional and/or physical needs—a condition associated with child maltreatment. It can also include a lack of opportunity for the child to form a stable attachment with a primary caregiver, a circumstance that is associated with orphanages and multiple moves in the foster care system. However, gross pathological care does not always result in the development of RAD.

The *DSM-IV* delineates two subtypes of RAD: an *inhibited type* in which the child "shows a pattern of excessively inhibited, hypervigilant, or highly ambivalent responses" to the caregiver; and a *disinhibited type* in which the child "exhibits indiscriminate sociability or a lack of selectivity in the choice of attachment figures" (p. 116). Children with the inhibited type tend to be withdrawn and constricted in their behavior, whereas children with the disinhibited type show no fear of strangers and will often treat new acquaintances in an inappropriately friendly and intimate manner. RAD is distinct from mental retardation or autism in that children with mental retardation develop appropriate attachments, and in autism, there is typically no gross pathological care. Autism and other pervasive developmental disorders also involve a qualitative impairment in communication and stereotyped patterns of behavior. Contemporary studies of attachment disorders in Romanian orphans (O'Connor & Rutter, 2000; Zeanah, 2000) provide some prevalence data. In a Canadian study (Zeanah, 2000) of 56 children ages three to five years who were adopted from Romania, secure attachment was initially found in only 30% of the children, while insecure, controlling attachment was observed in 42% of the children. Parent-reported attachment security increased significantly as the children became older (11 to 39 months), but there was no change in the level of indiscriminant friendliness toward nonfamily members. In a British study (O'Connor & Rutter, 2000) of 165 children ages four to six years adopted from Romania (144 were from institutions), the investigators found that only seven of the children exhibited marked/pervasive signs of attachment disorder. Duration of deprivation was linearly related to the number of signs of attachment disorder; however, more than 80% of the children adopted from Romanian institutions exhibited no marked/severe signs of attachment disorder at either age four or six years. The fundamental assumption underlying the development of RAD is that a child's attachment to a primary caregiver is biologically based and that only in extreme circumstances will the child not develop an attachment to his or her primary caregiver (Bowlby, 1969, 1982). The developmental course of RAD varies depending upon the age of the infant when he or she experienced gross pathological care, the amount and frequency of disruptions in the attachment relationship, the duration and severity of deprivation, the quality of the parent-infant relationship before and after the deprivation, and the implementation of any interventions. Many children who receive consistent, sensitive, and responsive caregiving following a period of gross pathological care will attain normal development, whereas those who do not will continue to exhibit symptoms of RAD (Howe, 1998).

The majority of treatment approaches have focused on early infancy, with interventions designed to improve the infant-parent relationship. The interventions center on addressing the child's emotional and behavioral difficulties and improving the parents' ability to understand and respond appropriately to their child's underlying needs for security and safety. Some interventions have included parent education on developmental issues relevant to the child's problems and direct "coaching" of the parent while the parent is interacting with the child in contrived situations. These interventions have been implemented in order to directly modify both the parents' and child's behavior and to improve parent-child communication, negotiation, and interaction (Greenberg & colleagues, 1997). This approach has also been modified and used with school-age children in the school setting.

Educational outcomes for children with RAD vary depending upon the nature and severity of the neglect that the child has experienced. These children may have physical problems associated with neglect such as poor dental hygiene, poor nutrition, and retarded growth. They may experience academic difficulties because of understimulation and/or nonattendance in school, and impaired peer relationships because of withdrawn behavior or indiscriminate friendliness (Crosson-Tower, 2002).

—*Linda Webster*

See also Autism Spectrum Disorders; *DSM-IV;* Infant Assessment; Mental Retardation; Preschoolers

REFERENCES AND FURTHER READING

American Psychiatric Association. (1994). *Diagnostic and statistical manual for mental disorders* (4th ed.). Washington, DC: Author.

Bowlby, J. (1969, 1982). *Attachment and loss* (Vol. 1). New York: Basic Books.

Crosson-Tower, C. (2002). *Child abuse and neglect.* Boston, MA: Allyn & Bacon.

Greenberg, M. T., DeKlyen, M., Speltz, M., & Endriga, M. C. (1997). The role of attachment processes in externalizing psychopathology in young children. In L. Atkinson & K. J. Zucker (Eds.), *Attachment and psychopathology* (pp. 196–222). New York: Guilford.

Howe, D. (1998). *Patterns of adoption.* Oxford, UK: Blackwell Science.

O'Connor, T. G., & Rutter, M. (2000). Attachment disorder behavior following early severe deprivation: Extension and longitudinal follow-up. *Journal of American Academy of Child & Adolescent Psychiatry, 39,* 703–712.

Zeanah, C. H. (2000). Disturbances of attachment in young children adopted from institutions. *Developmental and Behavioral Pediatrics, 21,* 230–236.

READING INTERVENTIONS AND STRATEGIES

Children experience difficulties in learning to read for a variety of reasons, including cognitive factors such as decoding (ability to pronounce written words) problems, psychological reasons such as lack of interest and motivation, and environmental differences such as inadequate facilities at home as well as in the classroom. The school psychologist must consider all these potential sources of impediment to acquiring reading skills and then develop a plan to address the cause(s). The existing policy—diagnosing poor readers who have a learning disability (LD) and poor readers who do not have a learning disability by administering an intelligence test and a reading achievement test—is not helpful in identifying the source of the reading problem, nor does it help in devising appropriate remedial procedures (Aaron, 1997). A more serious problem is that, so far, there is no convincing evidence that labeling children as LD and placing them in special education resource rooms produces any improvement in their reading achievement (Bentum & Aaron, 2003).

An uncomplicated way to understand the nature of the reading deficit is to organize the potential sources of reading difficulties into a coherent model and then proceed with the diagnosis by following the model. On the basis of the theories of reading and research of experts as well as our own, we (Aaron & Kotva, 1999; Joshi & Aaron, 2000) have developed a model of reading acquisition called the Component Model.

THE COMPONENT MODEL OF READING

A component, as applied to psychological phenomena, is a mental process that is independent of other psychological processes. The failure of any one of the processes in the Component Model of reading can result in reading difficulties. For example, decoding (the ability to pronounce the written word) is one such operation; linguistic comprehension is an example of another operation. A child may not be able to decode written text but can listen and comprehend spoken language much better. He or she will, nevertheless, be a poor reader because the weak decoding process can affect reading independent of the comprehension process. Conversely, an individual who can decode written words fairly well but has weak linguistic comprehension skills will also be a poor reader. These two operations, decoding and comprehension, are part of the Cognitive Module of the reading Component Model. The Component Model of reading contains three modules that are relatively independent of each other. Each module, in turn, contains several operations. Table 1 gives the three modules and their operations.

THE COGNITIVE MODULE: ITS CONSTITUENTS

The Cognitive Module of the reading Component Model has five operations, which are classified under two major constituents: word recognition and comprehension.

Word Recognition

The ability to recognize the written word is a prerequisite for reading. Word recognition subsumes two related skills, decoding and sight-word reading.

Decoding. The basic speech sound, which can alter the meaning of a word, is a phoneme. A letter of the alphabet or a group of letters that represent a single phoneme is called a grapheme. Initial stages in reading involve transforming graphemes into phonemes and is also referred to as decoding.

Table 1   The Constituents of the Component Model of Reading

Cognitive module:	Word Recognition:	Decoding, Sight-word reading
	Comprehension:	Vocabulary, Sentence comprehension, Passage comprehension
Psychological module:	Motivation & interest Locus of control Learned helplessness Learning styles Teacher expectation Gender differences	
Ecological module:	Home environment, culture, & parental involvement Classroom environment Peer influence Dialect English as second language	

What is the advantage of grapheme–phoneme conversion and decoding the print? The sound format of words is the best way to keep words in short-term memory. Thus, decoding is an essential skill for sentence comprehension. After the reading experience of two or three years, children become proficient decoders and subsequently become sight-word readers.

Sight-Word Reading. Contrary to what one may think, sight-word reading does not involve processing the word as a single unit, or a single picture. During sight-word reading, individual letters in the written word are processed, but they are processed all at once, in parallel. Eye movement studies provide the best support for the view that when we read, we process all the letters in a word (Just & Carpenter, 1987). Recognizing a written word by sight is very much like facial recognition. It is quick, simultaneous, and automatic; it is also not attention demanding.

Since sight-word reading involves processing the letters in the words, it is essential that the beginning reader possess letter knowledge. Without such knowledge, the child cannot decode the words smoothly. It follows then, that decoding skills are a prerequisite for sight-word reading.

Comprehension

Because language is expressed mainly in two forms, spoken and written, the term *comprehension* refers to an understanding of both spoken and written language. Beyond the modality difference, the same brain mechanisms are involved in comprehending spoken and written language. This is supported by research studies, which show that the correlation between listening comprehension and reading comprehension can be as high as .80. Comprehension of written text requires three elements:

1. Knowledge of words (vocabulary)

2. Understanding sentences

3. Understanding passages

Knowledge of Words. Vocabulary knowledge and reading comprehension are highly related to each other, the correlation being as high as .80. In general, people who read more have a high level of vocabulary. Children who have a rich vocabulary tend to read more because they enjoy reading; this leads to greater vocabulary knowledge. Children who have limited vocabulary avoid reading as much as they can, and their vocabulary knowledge stagnates. This results in an ever-widening gap between good readers and poor readers. Eventually, this results in the so-called *Matthew Effect*, taken from the Bible and applied to the reading–vocabulary symbiosis: "For everyone who has, more will be given; he will have abundance; but from him who does not have, even what he has will be taken away" (The Gospel according to St. Matthew, Chapter 25, verse 29).

Understanding Sentences. Having a large vocabulary itself does not guarantee the comprehension of sentences and connected texts. To understand sentences, the reader should, first of all, be able to interpret the sentence correctly. Some of the sentences children encounter in upper grades do not state the meaning explicitly. The child has to infer the information that is not given. A knowledge of syntax (grammar) is also essential for understanding sentences, because written sentences are complex in the sense they have many embedded clauses in them.

Understanding Passages. Just as sentences are more than a collection of words, text is not a mere aggregation of sentences. Linguists describe connected texts as having their own grammar. That is, they have a

beginning, a message, and an end. This is referred to as the grammar of the story. Understanding the grammar of the story facilitates comprehension.

THE PSYCHOLOGICAL MODULE: ITS CONSTITUENTS

Psychological aspects related to learning are also important for the acquisition of reading skills. If a child is not interested in learning to read, no amount of instruction can make him or her a good reader.

Motivation and Interest

Motivation is defined as the process of initiating, sustaining, and directing one's own activity. Motivation leads children to read. Reading becomes an alluring activity when children find it interesting. Psychologists classify motivation broadly as extrinsic and intrinsic. External factors that motivate children to read are simple rewards such as gold stars, candy, and verbal praise by the teacher. Intrinsic motivation is a desire to read that comes from within the child.

Locus of Control

Julian Rotter, who introduced the concept of *locus of control* into the psychological literature, classified it into two discrete categories, external and internal. When a person feels that life's events are the result of chance, luck, fate, or control by others, he or she feels the location of control is external; when a person feels that the outcomes of events are the consequences of his or her own actions, the locus is said to be internal. This variable is said to have significant influence on children's learning.

Learned Helplessness

After repeated failure, a child will not try to learn; he or she will just give up. In other words, the child has learned to be helpless. Behaviorally, this can lead to a lack of interest and effort on the part of the child. In the long term, the child expects to fail and fulfills this prophecy by failing.

Learning Styles

Learning styles are described as reasonably stable patterns of behavior that indicate learning preferences. According to Marie Carbo (1983), who is the leading proponent of learning styles, the concept of learning styles has four dimensions:

1. Cognitive: Includes factors such as modality preferences (auditory vs. visual)

2. Affective: Includes personality characteristics such as anxiety level, expectancy, and level of motivation

3. Physiological: Includes gender differences, daily rhythms (morning vs. afternoon person), and "left-brain" or "right-brain" proclivity

4. Psychological: Includes factors such as self-concept, locus of control, and sociability (loner vs. group person)

The instructional implication is that matching the method of instruction with the learning style of the child should reduce learning difficulties.

There are several problems associated with the concept of learning styles. For one thing, we have no reliable instruments to assess the learning styles of children. For instance, it is not an easy matter to decide who is left-brained and who is right-brained. Nor is it easy to determine if a child is an auditory learner or a visual learner. It is also well-known that optimal learning occurs when the child can see, hear, and touch what he or she has to learn. In spite of the many claims, the findings of research on the effectiveness of matching teaching with learning styles is equivocal.

Teacher Expectation

The concept of teacher (or parent) expectation refers to inferences that teachers make about the future behavior and achievement of a child, based on what the teacher knows about the child now. These expectations affect learning outcomes because teachers, either consciously or unconsciously, tend to behave in conformity with their expectations and children respond accordingly and fulfill these expectations. Teachers themselves may not be conscious of their expectations and actions and, for the most part, are unaware of their own behavior. The school psychologist can be of much help here.

Gender Differences

As early as 1919, Hinshelwood, a British physician, reported that more boys than girls have reading difficulties. Since then, a gender difference has been observed by many other investigators. Although the higher incidence of reading disability in boys is frequently encountered, the reason for the observed gender difference is disputed. Two explanations theorized are constitutional and environmental. The constitutional explanation of a gender difference in reading ability is linked to cerebral hemispheric differences in the brains of the two sexes.

The environmental explanation is equally viable. The explanation goes something like this: in American culture, there seems to be an ethos that reading, writing, and other literacy pursuits are "girlish" things; math and athletics are "boyish" things. It is also pointed out that boys, being aggressive and restless, are likely to attract the attention of teachers more often than girls. The net result is that more boys than girls are referred for diagnostic evaluation.

THE ECOLOGICAL MODULE: ITS CONSTITUENTS

The importance of home in the acquisition of literacy skills by children is succinctly expressed by statements such as "home is the first school" and "family is the nation's smallest school." Needless to say, several environmental factors associated with home, school, and culture affect the acquisition of reading and writing skills.

Home Environment, Culture, and Parental Involvement

Describing the family as the nation's smallest school, it has been estimated that 90% of the differences in academic achievement seen among students and their schools could be explained by five factors:

1. The presence of two parents in the home

2. Quantity and quality of reading materials in the home

3. Number of hours spent watching TV

4. Number of days absent from school

5. Number of pages read for homework

Activities such as joint storybook reading, playing word games, and visiting libraries promote reading skills. Children tend to do what they see, particularly what they see their parents do. Another factor is a potential difference between the school culture and the home culture. For example, the teacher expects the child to do well at school, but doing well in school is not at the top of the list of parental expectations for the child. Remedial strategies and interventions cannot be planned without taking the home environment into account. The school psychologist can play an important role in bridging the gap between home and school.

Classroom Environment

Young children are quite active; they become restless and lose concentration if they are required to sit in one place for more than a few minutes. For this reason, the classroom has to be arranged in such a way that it provides plenty of opportunities for movement, action, and interaction with peers and the teacher.

A classroom environment that is rich in literacy materials is an important factor in promoting literacy learning among children. Researchers report that space allocation and arrangement, and accessibility of materials and learning tools have a positive influence on children's literacy learning.

For optimal learning–teaching outcomes, seating of the children can be arranged in a semicircle so that the distance between the teacher and the child is the same for all children. The result is that no child sits always in the front part of the classroom and no child is cast away to the rear of the classroom. Wild departures from these ideal environmental conditions can result in reading difficulties.

Peer Influence

The influence of peers on children's behavior is well recognized in psychological literature. It is a powerful factor. Peer influence can operate both positively and negatively on a child. Positive peer influences can be exploited by setting up many learning experiences for the children through organizing them into small groups in which learning occurs.

Dialect

Dialect is a regionally or socially distinctive variation of language characterized by a particular accent, set of words, and even grammar. Even though it is relatively easy to distinguish between a dialect and a language, the difference is largely a matter of degree. People are said to speak different languages when they do not understand each other; they are said to speak dialects if they can understand each other, even though not perfectly. A single dialect, usually spoken by a majority of people, comes to predominate as the official or standard form of the language. Thus, the English spoken by a majority of people (and not because it possesses some singular linguistic feature that sets it apart from other dialects) becomes Standard English (SE).

In the United States, many dialects are spoken, including Black English (BE), which is also known as Vernacular Black English or Ebonics. Many African American children and students can speak both BE and SE and can switch the two as the situation demands. BE can vary from SE in phonology and grammar.

English as a Second Language

Bilingualism exists in degrees. A child may come from a home where only a language other than English is spoken or from a home where both English and another language are used. It is understandable that reading and writing pose special difficulties for a child from a home where English is used as a second language (ESL). Learning to read and write in a second language is especially difficult for an ESL child with reading difficulties.

ASSESSMENT OF THE COGNITIVE, PSYCHOLOGICAL, AND ECOLOGICAL ELEMENTS OF READING

Assessment of Decoding Skills

Almost all standardized tests of reading achievement have a subtest for assessing decoding skills. Also known as "word attack" tests, these tests contain a list of nonwords (such as *daik* and *birk*). Because the child has not encountered such nonwords before, word familiarity is controlled.

It has to be pointed out that not all nonwords are alike. A nonword such as *dake* is said to be "friendly" because it has many neighbors (e.g., make, bake, rake, etc.). A child can successfully read *dake* simply by substituting the first letter in the word and reading it by analogy. In contrast, words such as *daik*, do not have many neighbors and, therefore, cannot be read by analogy. A list of such "unfriendly" nonwords, is, therefore, a better test than the ones used by many standardized tests.

Another problem with standardized word attack tests is that many of them are not timed. Experience shows that some poor decoders, given sufficient time, can decode many nonwords. The results obtained from such untimed tests can be misleading. In the classroom, the teacher (or the school psychologist) can construct his or her own list of nonwords. If care is taken to include only "unfriendly" nonwords and administration of the list as a timed test, an objective measure of decoding skills can be obtained.

Assessment of Sight-Word Reading Skills

Sight-word reading is an automatic process resulting in the very fast naming of a word. We've known for more than 100 years that skilled readers can name a written word as fast as they can name a written letter. This is possible because all the letters in a word are processed simultaneously and in parallel. Therefore, when a child names a written word as fast as he or she can name a written letter, we know the child has read that word by sight. To assess sight-word reading skills, the teacher can make a list of 20 common words already taught in the classroom and ask the child to name them and note the time. Subsequently, the teacher can also record how much time it takes the child to name a list of 20 letters of the alphabet. When letter-naming time and word-naming time are close to each other, the child can be considered to have read those words by sight.

Assessment of Vocabulary Knowledge

There are two ways of assessing vocabulary knowledge. One is informal and the other is formal. It should be understood that children know more words than they use in their day-to-day conversation. Therefore, mere sampling of speech will not provide a reliable measure of a child's vocabulary knowledge. The informal way of assessing vocabulary is to construct a vocabulary inventory by selecting words from the textbook the child uses in the classroom. Curriculum-based assessment uses this approach. The child can then be asked "what does that word mean?" or to embed the word in a sentence to make it meaningful.

Formal assessment of vocabulary relies on standardized tests. The most frequently used test is the Peabody Picture Vocabulary Test. In this test, four pictures of objects, animals, or actions are presented. The child is given one word and is asked to point to the one picture that matches the target word. An advantage of this test is that no verbal response is required; it also can be administered to very young children as well as to adults.

Assessment of Comprehension of Sentences and Written Passages

As it is in the case of vocabulary, assessment of comprehension can be carried out in two ways: informal and formal. Informally, the child can be asked to read a passage from his or her textbook and then answer some questions. In addition to the number of questions answered correctly, the behavior of the child during oral reading can also provide important clues about the child's reading skills. When the child makes an oral error and goes back and corrects the mistake, it shows that the child is monitoring his or her own comprehension and takes corrective action. Children whose comprehension is not up to par are likely to rush through the text without correcting their own reading mistakes.

All standardized tests of achievement have a subtest of reading comprehension. However, these tests have adopted different strategies to assess comprehension. The Woodcock Language Proficiency Battery-Revised subtests are in the cloze format in which a word is deleted from the sentence and the reader has to supply the word. The Stanford Diagnostic Reading Test (SDRT) and the Gates-McGinitie tests require the child to read a paragraph and answer multiple-choice questions. The Peabody Picture Vocabulary Test presents a choice of four pictures from which the reader chooses the one that fits the written sentence.

It is apparent that tests differ in the ways they assess comprehension and are, therefore, not likely to yield identical results. The Woodcock Language Proficiency Battery, made up mostly of sentences, does not put much stress on memory. The Stanford Diagnostic Reading Test, which uses a paragraph format, is closer to real-life reading, and, therefore, ecologically more valid. The Peabody Individual Achievement Test involves much reasoning and has many features of a test of reasoning and intelligence. It is important that the school psychologist pay attention to which test was used for assessing reading comprehension.

Assessment of Spelling Skills

It is a widely held belief that spelling is a visual memorization task. However, developmental studies of spelling indicate that it is more closely related to phonological skills than to rote visual memory (Treiman, 1993). As a result, spelling errors committed by children often reflect their efforts to "phoneticize" English words (e.g., "girl" spelled as *gal* and "light" spelled as *lite*).

Standardized tests of spelling ability (e.g., the Wide Range Achievement Test) use a list of words to assess spelling skills. It is possible that the list contains words with which the child is not familiar. The child will phonetically spell many of these unfamiliar words, which will lead to errors. Under such circumstances, should we conclude that the child has a spelling weakness or that his or her vocabulary knowledge is limited? The best way to assess spelling performance is by using words with which the child is familiar.

There is another point to be made here. Consider two third graders who were given a spelling test that consisted of words such as "horse," "school," "book," and "leaf." Child *A* spelled them as "house," "scool," "bok," and "leef" whereas child *B* spelled these words as "ose," "oolcs," "koo," and "lf." Both children receive a zero on the test. Such a quantitative evaluation places both children on the same level and is of little instructional value. Instead, qualitative analysis of spelling provides a more accurate view of the child's spelling skills in addition to giving hints for spelling instruction.

IDENTIFYING THE SOURCE OF A READING PROBLEM (DIFFERENTIAL DIAGNOSIS)

The main purpose of the diagnostic procedure is to identify the source of reading difficulty. With reference to the Cognitive Module, this can be accomplished by administering a standardized test of reading comprehension and a test of listening comprehension.

Decoding Problems

If listening comprehension is within average range but reading comprehension is below average, then weak word recognition skills are the source of reading difficulty. This diagnosis can be further confirmed by a low word-attack score, poor spelling performance, and slow naming of written words. Remedial instruction would then focus on improving word recognition skills.

Comprehension Problems

In contrast, if the child performs at a below-average level on both reading and listening comprehension, the remedial instruction will focus on improving comprehension skills. Word recognition skills of these children should also be assessed. Standardized batteries such as Woodcock Language Proficiency Battery and Wechsler Individual Achievement Test have subtests of reading and listening comprehension.

The combination of a higher listening comprehension score and a lower reading comprehension score is the most frequently encountered pattern seen in children with reading disability. Occasionally, the opposite pattern—higher reading comprehension score and lower listening comprehension score—is seen. This is often indicative of attentional problems (Aaron & colleagues, 2002; Aaron & colleagues, 2004).

Assessment of the constituents of the Psychological Module and the Ecological Module are carried out through observation and interview procedures.

INSTRUCTIONAL PROCEDURES

Remedial Approaches: The Cognitive Module

Instructional Procedures for Improving Word Recognition Skills: Decoding

In general, remedial methods attempt to deal with two main problem areas in reading, word recognition skills and comprehension skills. Other areas of concern to teachers are vocabulary development, fluency development, and spelling development.

Awareness of units in spoken language develops as early as nursery school. First, children are able to recognize and repeat rhyming words. Subsequently, by age three or four years, they can identify syllables in multisyllabic words. Finally, some (but not all) children can identify phonemes. Phonemes are not as easily recognizable as rhymes or syllables because in speech, phonemes overlap each other much like the shingles on a roof. In recent times, sensitivity to phonemes has come to be described under the label of phoneme awareness. The ability to recognize rhymes and syllables, along with phoneme awareness, is collectively referred to as phonological awareness. A good deal of research shows that sensitivity to phonemes and word recognition skills are closely related. Although it is uncertain whether phoneme awareness results in better word recognition skills or reading experience results in better phoneme awareness, it is well established that phoneme awareness training improves reading skills, particularly those of poor readers. This phenomenon is true not only in English but also in languages such as Dutch, Italian, and Norwegian. Phoneme awareness training can be the starting point for children with word recognition difficulties.

A simple but interesting task that can be useful for creating an awareness of sounds in the language is picture sorting. In this task, children are asked to sort pictures with similar initial or final sounds in their names on the basis of some criterion set by the teacher. The same task can be presented orally.

In their book *Phonemic Awareness in Young Children*, Adams and colleagues (1998) provide step-by-step instructions for creating phonological awareness in children, starting with rhyming activities and culminating in word identification.

In making a transition from oral language to written language, from phoneme awareness to word recognition, the following steps are used:

- Associating sounds with colored blocks or tiles
- Replacing colored blocks or tiles with letters of the alphabet
- Blending constitutional sounds in simple words and pronouncing the words
- Copying words on to sheets of paper
- Spelling the words from memory introduced in the previous step

A knowledge of the structure of words and how they are formed can be of much help in acquiring word recognition skills and in vocabulary development. Known as morphological awareness, this includes not only knowing words, but knowing about words (i.e., the origin of words such as Latin, French, etc.) and roots of words (free morphemes).

Instructional Procedures for Improving Word Recognition Skills: Fluency and Sight-Word Reading

Sight-word reading skills develop slowly; but by the time children are in the third grade, most of them are able to read many common words by sight. It should be remembered that even skilled adults have to decode the word in order to pronounce it. The first step, therefore, would be to improve the decoding

skills of a child who does not have well-developed sight-word reading skills. Beyond this step, familiarity with the printed word is an important factor that promotes sight-word reading skills. This can be accomplished by reading, reading, and more reading. Such reading experience should involve meaningful sentences, not isolated words. Repeated exposure to words brings these words into the child's sight-word repertoire. Simply printing words on cards and exposing them to the child again and again will not make a child a good sight-word reader. The child may be able to read a handful of words by sight, but, beyond that, memory limits further progress.

Not all educators favor a phonics instructional approach. Their argument is that the skill and drill approach to reading instruction is meaningless and uninspiring for children who may lose interest in the entire enterprise of reading. On the other hand, if meaningful materials are used, they are likely to become avid readers. This philosophy of reading instruction is often referred to as the whole language approach (Goodman, 1986). The disagreement between the skills approach and the meaning approach to reading instruction has a history of more than 100 years behind it and is known as the *reading war*.

Instructional Strategies for Promoting Spelling Skills

Spelling has to be explicitly taught. In teaching spelling to children, the following principles are recommended (Moats, 1995):

- Provide spelling exercises and tasks according to the child's vocabulary level, not on the basis of the child's chronological age.
- Provide phoneme awareness to the child, if necessary. There is evidence that this type of training improves children's spelling (Arra & Aaron, 2001).
- Use as many modalities as possible for spelling instruction.
- Embed spelling words in sentences. This makes the words meaningful and, simultaneously builds up vocabulary knowledge.
- Focus on letter patterns. Use a family of words based on their onsets and rimes for instruction.
- Keep in mind the student's spelling skills level when preparing lists of spelling words. The list size will have to be individualized.

- Give four or five spelling words per day to children in primary grades and to children who have difficulty with spelling.
- Have the students take a test on these words the following day. Missed words are included in the next day's spelling list.
- Analyze spelling errors and direct the student to compare the misspelled word(s) with the correct spelling. When possible, explain to the student why he or she might have committed the spelling error(s) by using a phonological analysis of the errors.

It also has to be kept in mind that spelling is more resistant to instructional efforts than decoding or reading.

Instructional Procedures for Improving Vocabulary Knowledge

Vocabulary instruction is not mere teaching of dictionary definitions of words. The most critical element in vocabulary learning is meaning within a context. This is so because meaningful information is remembered well, whereas meaningless rote memorization does not last long. Words can be made meaningful by encountering them in a situation while reading or constructing sentences using new words. Teachers can introduce new words, embed them in sentences, and make them meaningful.

Visualizing word families by constructing semantic maps is another way of improving vocabulary knowledge.

Reading to children or reading with children is a simple way of introducing new words. Reading to children should be made an interactive process. The parent or the teacher stops, asks questions, and asks the child to repeat what he or she has heard.

Games such as Scrabble are also a means of making children think about words. Children should know not only the words, but they should also know about the words.

Instructional Strategies for Promoting Reading Comprehension

The ultimate goal of reading is to comprehend the written material. It was noted earlier that both listening comprehension and reading comprehension are mediated by the same cognitive mechanisms. For this reason, training in listening comprehension is the starting point with very young children or children

who have decoding deficits. The listening comprehension training focuses mainly on teaching the child to pay attention while listening to a story, to be able to identify the main points, and to summarize the story at the end.

After listening comprehension training, reading is introduced. The children are asked to memorize and use the following seven strategies as they read:

1. Determining the purpose of reading: The child should ask, "What is the purpose of my reading this?" Many children mistakenly think that reading aloud without making mistakes and reading fast are the goals of reading.

2. Activating background information: The child should pause after reading the title of the text and think aloud what the passage is about.

3. Stopping and reflecting: After reading a paragraph, the child should pause and reflect what he or she has read so far.

4. Seeking help: If questions arise, the child should ask the teacher or refer to the dictionary.

5. Using pictures and maps: The child should often look at pictures and maps in the text and use them as visual aids.

6. Questioning self: The child should self-monitor his or her own comprehension.

7. Summarizing: When the end of the story is reached, the child should be able to summarize the contents in one or two sentences, without looking at the text.

For children with word recognition problems, decodable books can be used. Stories in decodable texts are constructed out of simple words, which are often repeated.

Remedial Approaches: The Psychological Module

Motivation

There are some simple principles that can be implemented by parents and teachers for promoting intrinsic motivation in children. First, children should be made to know that behind the scribbles in the book are hidden interesting stories that are to be discovered. This is accomplished by reading aloud interesting stories to children according to age level and ability.

Educators recommend that reading-aloud time should meet three conditions:

1. Children must see value in reading.

2. Children should see that reading brings enjoyment and satisfaction.

3. The book chosen should be such that the child would feel confident and would want to read it for himself or herself. It is important to set a fixed time of around 20 minutes per day so that children look with anticipation for the read-aloud moments.

An activity will be motivating if it is challenging but not beyond the skill of the reader. Children should be given some degree of autonomy in choosing the book to be read. Another important fact to keep in mind is that reading to children should not be a one-way activity. The teacher/parent should actively involve the child during reading by stopping, pondering, and asking the child questions. Additionally, if the child sees his parents in the act of reading and enjoying it, he or she is likely to emulate their behavior.

Locus of Control

Reliance on factors such as chance, luck, and fate bring forth inconsistent outcome and often failure. Creating opportunities in which the child can succeed can build confidence.

Learned Helplessness

The best thing parents can do is to create opportunities for their children to be successful as much as possible. Success could be realized by adjusting tasks in which the child can succeed. This can be accomplished by assigning reading material according to ability level, cutting down on the number of pages to be read, reducing the number of spelling words, and providing additional time to complete reading and writing exercises. Feedback should be constructive; judgmental statements are to be avoided.

Learning Styles

It has to be noted that learning style is not to be confused with individual differences among children. Children do differ in their family background, in the first language and dialects they use, in their interests, and in their ability level. Children also differ in their anxiety level. Helping the anxious child to relax and making such a child feel comfortable are part of a teacher's social skills. Young children also need lots of hands-on activities and learn best when they can move around freely. It is also known that some children benefit from group work and peer instruction. These educational practices, however, are not derived from the concept of learning style.

Teacher/Parent Expectations

- We all form expectations of others, often unconsciously, and this does influence our behavior.
- Teachers should keep expectations for the individual child current by paying close attention to his or her progress.
- Teachers should be flexible enough to alter expectations.
- Teachers should give more importance to current performance than to past performance.
- Teachers should set flexible goals for the child.
- Teachers should stress the continuous progress of the child and not how he or she compares to other children or to standardized norms.
- Teachers should emphasize constructive feedback rather than judgments such as "good" and "poor" or "right" and "wrong."
- Teachers should recognize and reward the child for his or her real progress and not for trivial attainments.

Gender Differences

Notions about gender differences can influence parents' expectations ("Boys will be boys") and thus create a mindset which, in turn, can affect instructional practice. The best way to avoid such gender-based expectations is to be aware that these studies deal with averages and not individuals. That is, in any given area, there are boys who perform better than girls and there are girls who perform better than boys.

Remedial Approaches: The Ecological Module

Home Environment

Parents are the primary models children tend to emulate. It is, therefore, important that parents present themselves as avid readers. During case conferences, this fact should be stressed and parents should be made to realize the importance of their role in their children's education.

The school psychologist should realize that if the gap between the home culture and school culture is wide, children may perceive reading-related tasks as irrelevant. Parent-teacher-child conferences provide an opportunity for reducing cultural differences between school and home.

Classroom Environment

Dividing children into small groups can introduce variety in classroom instruction. Such a grouping need not be based on ability, but rather it is better to have children of different ability levels in each group.

The seating arrangement of children and sufficient room for children to move around are features that are essential elements of the classroom environment.

Dialect

Emphasizing the functional value of learning and using the standard dialect may not be effective with most minority children. For example, statements such as "You will get a good job only if you speak like most people do" and "You have to learn to speak and write the way you are taught in the school" may sound very unrealistic to minority children. Instead, enticing the child to use SE because the majority of the people in this country use SE is likely to be an agreeable proposition for many minority children.

It will be helpful for the teacher or the parent to draw the attention of the child to phonological and grammatical differences between Standard English and Black English. In addition, special attention to spelling can make children sensitive to phonemes they tend to omit or substitute. Drawing the attention of the student to the influence of dialect on written language can be helpful in avoiding some grammar mistakes. This is so because many students tend to write the way they speak.

English as a Second Language

While admittedly the acquisition of reading and writing skills will be far more difficult for an ESL child than it is for the child whose mother tongue is English, written language can actually be of help in learning SE because written language is formal, whereas spoken language is colloquial. Phonology and vocabulary can be introduced with much less difficulty than grammar and morphology (word inflections). Peers of the ESL child can be a good source for acquiring SE skills.

Instructional Strategies Designed for Teaching Children at Risk

It is said that for no apparent reason, 10% to 20% of school children experience difficulty in learning to read. This condition is recognized by different labels such as learning disability, specific reading disability, and dyslexia. Since it was first recognized that some children with normal mental ability experience an inordinate amount of difficulty in learning to read, specialized methods for teaching these children have been developed and promoted. Fernald and Keller in 1921, Monroe in 1932, and Orton in the 1930s were the pioneers who developed such methods. These methods focused primarily on developing word recognition skills through phonics-based instruction.

The Orton-Gillingham Approach

The Orton-Gillingham approach was first presented in 1960 by Anna Gillingham, a close associate of Samuel Orton, a physician who practiced medicine in Iowa in the 1920s and 1930s. During his practice, Orton gained extensive experience in dealing with children who had educational problems. Later, he and Gillingham operated a clinic together in New York, and there they developed their instructional method.

The original publication was revised several times, with the seventh edition appearing in 1979 under the title, *Remedial Training for Children With Specific Disability in Reading, Spelling, and Penmanship* (Gillingham & Stillman, 1979). Several phonics-based versions of the Orton-Gillingham approach have been developed in recent years by other authors.

The three important features of the Orton-Gillingham approach are:

1. It teaches phonics directly by introducing letter names and their sounds first, and blending skills soon after.

2. It uses a multisensory approach by teaching letter-sound associations through auditory, visual, and kinesthetic modalities.

3. It follows a systematic step-by-step approach proceeding from the simple to the complex.

Even though this method has been practiced extensively with dyslexic children and adolescents, very few research studies had been conducted and reported to validate the effectiveness of the Orton-Gillingham approach. The primary reason for the paucity of research is that this method is used primarily in clinical settings on a one-to-one basis, which does not generate extensive data that can be statistically analyzed. Two studies, one by Kline and Kline (1978) and another by Joshi and colleagues (2002), reported successful outcomes.

Beth Slingerland (1977) developed a closely related guide for teaching children with specific reading disabilities that uses a multisensory approach. In many respects, the Slingerland procedures are very similar to the Orton-Gillingham approach. In fact, Slingerland spent some time with Anna Gillingham and Bessie Stillman, authors of the Orton-Gillingham method.

Spalding's Writing Road to Reading

The Writing Road to Reading by Romalda Spalding was first published in 1957. Spalding acknowledges her indebtedness to Samuel Orton, under whom she practiced her remedial methods for three years. During the span of nearly four decades, it has been widely tested with good results. A fifth revised edition of the program was published in 2003. It is a structured method of teaching phonics and is available in the form of a single book, which makes the implementation of the procedures relatively easy. Even though this method is intended for use in the regular classroom, it is equally valuable to remedial teachers. The Spalding program is also called the Unified Phonics Method because it incorporates hearing, speaking, and writing, as well as reading comprehension.

Although much of the material in *The Writing Road to Reading* is borrowed from the Orton-Gillingham approach, the Spalding method differs from it in two important respects: emphasis on letter sounds rather than letter names, and the emphasis on spelling through writing.

Reading Recovery Program

Reading Recovery (RR) is another widely known program that does not follow a rigid sequential format but has a meaning orientation. RR was developed by Marie Clay and became a nationwide program in New Zealand in 1979 and was later introduced in the United States and Australia in 1984. Developed as a program designed to be preventive in nature, RR is implemented soon after reading problems are recognized during the first year at school. Some of the salient features of the RR program are:

- It is designed for at-risk readers in the first grade.
- Each program is individually designed, and there is no standardized or scripted procedure for instruction. The RR program uses storybooks and does not use highly structured books and worksheets. The RR teacher a spends considerable amount of time in identifying the child's weaknesses and strengths. Children are tutored individually. However, some school systems tutor children in small groups of two or three. The instructional program is approximately 30 minutes per day and is supplementary to the regular classroom teaching. Classroom teachers and RR teachers work as a team.
- RR is temporary and lasts until the child has reached a level of reading skill expected at his or her grade level. Under normal circumstances, this period is expected to be approximately 12 weeks.
- Writing is given as much importance as reading. Every day, the child writes as much as he or she can alone. The child is also asked to read what he or she has written.
- RR teachers are required to undergo special training, which may be a year in duration. They also continue to participate in in-service programs.

According to one report, at the end of first grade, more than 66% of the students who had completed the program were reading at or above the first grade level.

Some of the concerns about RR are that progress is measured by informal tests and not by standardized tests. There is also a possibility that the effects may wear off after students reenter the regular classroom. Success rates reported may be based on children who have improved and were discontinued from the program and not on the entire population of children participating in the RR program. Yet another concern is the extensive training teachers have to undergo and the nature of the one-to-one teaching format, both of which may not be cost-effective.

—P. G. Aaron

See also Academic Achievement; Cooperative Learning; Grades; Homework; Learning; Learning Styles

REFERENCES AND FURTHER READING

Aaron, P. G. (1997). The impending demise of the discrepancy formula. *Review of Educational Research, 67*(4), 461–502.

Aaron, P. G., Joshi, R. M., Hyyon, P., Smith, N., & Kirby, E. (2002). Separating genuine cases of reading disabilities from reading difficulties caused by attention deficits. *Journal of Learning Disabilities, 35*(5), 425–435.

Aaron, P. G., Joshi, R. M., & Phipps, J. (2004). A cognitive tool to diagnose predominantly inattentive ADHD behavior. *Journal of Attention Disorders, 7,* 125–135.

Aaron, P. G., & Kotva, H. (1999). Component Model-based remedial treatment of reading disabilities. In I. Lundberg, F. Tonnessen, & I. Austad (Eds.), *Dyslexia: Advances in theory and practice.* Boston: Kluwer Academic.

Adams, M. J., Foorman, B., Lundberg, I., & Beeler, T. (1998). *Phonemic awareness in young children.* Baltimore, MD: Paul H. Brookes.

Arra, C., & Aaron, P. G. (2001). Effects of psycholinguistic instruction on spelling performance. *Psychology in the Schools, 38,* 357–363.

Bentum, K., & Aaron, P. G. (2003). Does reading instruction in learning disability resource rooms really work? A longitudinal study. *Reading Psychology, 24,* 361–381.

Carbo, M. (1983). Research in reading and learning style: Implications for exceptional children. *Exceptional Children, 49,* 486–493.

Clay, M. (1985). *The early detection of reading difficulties* (3rd ed.). Portsmouth, NH: Heinemann.

Clay, M. (1993). *Reading recovery: A guidebook for teachers in training.* Portsmouth, NH: Heinemann.

Gillingham, A., & Orton, S. (1979). *Remedial training for children with specific disability in reading, spelling, and penmanship* (7th ed.). Cambridge, MA: Educators Publishing Service.

Goodman, K. (1986). *What's whole in whole language?* Portsmouth, NH: Heinemann.

Joshi, R. M., & Aaron, P. G. (2000). The Component model of reading: Simple view of reading made a little more complex. *Reading Psychology, 21,* 85–97.

Joshi, R. M., Dahlgren, M., & Boulware-Gooden, R. (2002). Teaching reading through multisensory approach in an inner city school. *Annals of Dyslexia, 53,* 235–251.

Just, M. A., & Carpenter, P. A. (1987). *The psychology of reading and language comprehension.* Boston, MA: Allyn & Bacon.

Kline, C., & Kline, C. (1978). Follow-up study of 216 dyslexic children. *Bulletin of the Orton Society, 25,* 127–144.

Moats, L. C. (1995). *Spelling development, disabilities, and instruction.* Baltimore, MD: York.

Slingerland, B. (1977). *A multi-sensory approach to language arts for specific language disability in children.* Cambridge, MA: Educators Publishing Service.

Spalding, R. B. (2003). *The writing road to reading.* New York: Harper Collins.

Treiman, R. (1993). *Beginning to spell: A study of first grade children.* New York: Oxford.

Woodcock, R. W. (1991). *Woodcock Language Proficiency Battery-Revised.* Itasca, IL: Riverside.

RECIPROCAL DETERMINISM

Reciprocal determinism is a construct proposed by Albert Bandura within his social learning theory. Social learning theory focuses on behavior and learning within social contexts, and it posits that an individual's behavior changes after direct experience or after observing a model's behavior (otherwise known as vicarious learning). The four processes involved in vicarious learning are paying attention, retaining, reproducing, and having the motivation to emit a model's behavior.

Reciprocal determinism suggests that individuals function as a result of a dynamic and reciprocal interaction among their behavior, environment, and personal characteristics (Bandura, 1997). Personal characteristics include one's thoughts, emotions, expectations, beliefs, goals, and so forth. Behavior is conceptualized as a person's skills and actions. Lastly, environment is considered to be a person's social and physical surroundings. All three systems interact with each other; therefore, a change in one will influence the others as well. Reciprocal determinism indicates that people do have a say in their future, because of reciprocal interactions.

Reciprocal determinism is relevant to school learning. A child's behaviors may be the result of an interaction between the environment and his or her personal characteristics. For instance, a child may be frustrated by a mismatch between his or her academic abilities and the instruction or curriculum. This frustration may lead to disruptive behaviors, which result in the teacher becoming upset as well. Therefore, understanding reciprocal determinism may be very helpful in reducing disruptive or aggressive behaviors and in altering negative and defeating cycles. Likewise, from an academic perspective, if a child is experiencing difficulties in a class, it is important to consider environmental issues (i.e., instruction, curriculum, home and social environment, etc.) that could be affecting the child's academic performance. Very importantly, when a school psychologist recognizes that a change in one system will influence the others, his or her following decisions should be made in favor of interventions that will have the most positive impact on that system.

—*Jennifer Lang*

RELIABILITY

Reliability, which is the consistency of test scores or ratings, is one of several ways to assess the quality of a measure. Three major types of reliability, including brief descriptions, are:

1. *Interrater reliability* refers to the consistency of the ratings made by two or more observers on the behavior (e.g., classroom behavior) of one or more students.

2. *Internal consistency reliability* (e.g., split-half reliability, parallel forms reliability, and coefficient alpha) refers to the degree of uniformity of the item content of a measure. In other words, the degree to which the items on a measure are similar in content to each other. To evaluate the internal consistency reliability, a single administration of the measure is given and then the degree of homogeneity of the item content of the measure is examined.

3. *Test-retest reliability* involves repeated administrations of the same measure, such as a reading achievement test, to the same individuals on two or more occasions to determine whether the test scores obtained on the measure are similar or consistent over time.

The reliability of test scores or ratings is important to school psychologists and other professionals who administer tests or conduct classroom observations in educational settings. Test scores or ratings must be reliable in order to have confidence in the results obtained from these measures or classroom observation forms. Test scores and observer ratings help educators and parents make decisions about educational

programs for students and to monitor student progress in these programs. Thus, test scores or ratings need to be reliable.

—*Patricia A. Lowe*

See also Bias (Testing); Cross-Cultural Assessment; Ethical Issues in School Psychology; Norm-Referenced Tests; Statewide Tests

REFLEX. *See* DEVELOPMENTAL MILESTONES; NEUROPSYCHOLOGICAL ASSESSMENT

REPORTS (PSYCHOLOGICAL)

Psychological reports are summary documents written by mental health professionals to help others understand a person and the context in which the person lives (Tallent, 1993). Reports often describe a specific referral question and review the assessment process used to derive the included interpretations and intervention recommendations. In school settings, it is most commonly the school psychologist who creates a case study report aimed at helping both family members and school personnel gain a clear understanding of the academic and/or social–emotional needs of a child and the rationale for any suggested categorizations (e.g., special education placement) or interventions. Sometimes the school psychologist is one member of a larger multidisciplinary team that works conjointly to assess all aspects of a student's individual functioning and environment, and produces one comprehensive assessment report. Diagnostic and intervention decisions reflect the collective agreement of the team members (e.g., speech pathologists, occupational therapists, school social workers, school psychologists, and teachers).

Psychological reports serve as a means of communication between school personnel (e.g., teachers, social workers, psychologists, and administrators), family members, and outside professionals (e.g., medical doctors and clinicians). Thus, the author of such documents must recognize the need for "user friendly" reports that are jargon-free and contain interpretations easily understood by all readers. Recommendations should be specific, realistic, and practical, and be written with the intent of creating positive change for the student.

Although psychological reports may vary in style and format based on the author's professional role and personal style, a typical psychological report includes the following subsections (Sattler, 2001; Wolber & Carne, 1993):

- Identifying information about the examiner and examinee
- Reason for referral
- Assessment instruments and evaluative procedures
- Background information
- Behavioral observations during the assessment
- Assessment results (often divided into two sections called intellectual/cognitive functioning and personality functioning)
- Clinical impressions and recommendations
- Summary

A useful psychological report includes only information relevant to the purpose of the report and integrates testing results, behavioral observations, and background information gathered from all necessary sources (i.e., parents, school records and personnel, medical charts, and previous psychological treatment records). Psychologists should base interpretations on assessment findings rather than on speculation. It is critical that school psychologists gather data from a variety of sources and settings in order to corroborate and/or elaborate on formal test results. All information should be reported in a clear, concise manner. Readers are more appreciative of a report that is well organized, not too complex, has practical recommendations, and has a more tentative tone than one that is lengthy, contains too much theory or jargon, comes across as authoritative, and suggests unrealistic interventions (Tallent, 1993).

Once the school psychologist's report is written, it becomes part of the student's official academic file and is subject to the legal and ethical principals and standards governing the profession. Specific ethical principles and standards regarding confidentiality, the assessment process, and the maintenance of records serve as guidelines for how psychologists should prepare and disseminate such information. Separate ethical principles and standards also address the use of word processing or computerized report writing programs. Parents and eligible students have a right to inspect and review a student's academic record under a federal law commonly known as the Family Educational Rights and Privacy Act (FERPA).

The following is a psychological report for a student named Sam. The report begins by describing the referral problems or questions to be answered through the psychological evaluation. It then describes the background or context of the problems Sam is experiencing in reading and math. This background information provides the backdrop against which the assessment tools (tests or procedures) are selected to be administered to Sam and other important adults in his environment. The results from the tests or procedures administered are described and interpreted, and conclusions are drawn regarding the factors (uncovered through the assessment process) that are contributing to Sam's educational problems. Recommendations for interventions that might help Sam improve in reading and math, which have been linked to findings, are provided at the end.

Psychological Report

Name: Sam	DOB: 11/20/92
Address: Kansas	Parents: Will & Cindy
School: Blue Bird	Date of Evaluation:
Elementary (BBE)	10/6/00
Phone: (xxx) xxx-xxxx	Grade: 2nd

Reason for Referral:

Sam was referred to the CARE team in September, 1999, by his first grade teacher, K. J. The CARE team is a group of general education teachers, special education teachers, and other professionals who meet to problem solve strategies to help students experience success within the general education classroom. Miss J was concerned about Sam's low achievement in the areas of math and reading. She reported that Sam was far below his peers in these areas. Despite numerous modifications, Sam remained behind peers and the team felt a comprehensive evaluation was necessary. This is an initial evaluation to determine whether Sam is eligible to receive special education services.

Background Information:

School History

According to Sam's educational file, Sam has attended Blue Bird Elementary (BBE) since his school career started. He has never been held back; however, his kindergarten teacher did rate him as a fair candidate for retention. He has no history of receiving special education services, but has had a modified curriculum. In first grade, CARE team problem-solving helped provide interventions and modifications to assist Sam, but little progress was reported.

Information obtained from Sam's educational file revealed that Sam's grades throughout his school history have been mostly S's (Satisfactory). In kindergarten, Sam received all S's; however, his grade card showed that there were skills he did not master by the end of the year. These skills included recognizing the alphabet out of order, recognizing initial consonant sounds, beginning to recognize words, and knowing number words. He also couldn't recite the alphabet in order until the last quarter of the year.

Sam again received mostly S's in first grade (on a modified curriculum), with S's in math, spelling, and language. The area in which he struggled the most was work habits, in which he received a U (Unsatisfactory). The teacher commented that he needed to work on listening attentively and following directions. The area in which Sam was strongest was social development. In this area he received S+'s and E's (Excellent), with his teacher commenting that he worked with others and was courteous. Up to this point in second grade, Sam has not received any official grades, but his teacher reports that he is performing significantly below peers in all areas. Due to Sam's age, he has not yet taken any standardized group achievement tests.

According to Sam's educational file, he missed 2 days during the first semester of kindergarten and 7½ days during the second semester. In first grade Sam missed 3½ days during the first semester and 12 days during the second. Sam was absent approximately 1 of every 6 days during the second half of his first grade year. There is no reported history of disciplinary problems in Sam's file.

According to Sam's psychological file, modifications used in the first grade included small group instruction for reading in the Discovery Room. Sam was allowed to retake spelling lists as often as needed, and his list was reduced to 6 words instead of 10. Praise for work well done was used frequently. Rewards, consisting of prizes from the treasure box, were earned when the teacher found him working independently. A behavior system to increase on-task behavior was utilized. Sam's workload was reduced by approximately half. The length of his reading assignment was modified, assigning him short phrases and sentences when reading class books. Sam was allowed to bring in a book from home to read to the class. Individual directions were given to him after group instructions. In spite of some growth academically, Sam is still far below peers.

Sam was described by his first grade teacher as "an extremely active and usually a happy child. He also likes to socialize with others in class." Miss J reported that Sam often had difficulty working with children in small groups in the classroom; however, Sam's current teacher reports that he displays good social skills and is able to maintain friendships with same-age peers. She states that he is not a problem behaviorally, but that there is a noticeable difference in his behavior when he hasn't taken his Ritalin. At these times he will become preoccupied with something, such as a hangnail on his finger, and lose focus. According to Sam's mother, he enjoys playing soccer and flying kites. He is also involved in farm activities.

Medical History

According to Sam's mother, there were no pre-, peri-, or postnatal complications. Sam was a full-term baby born by vaginal delivery. He weighed 7 pounds. Developmental milestones were reported as acquired within normal limits. In August of 1996, when Sam was 2 years, 9-months-old, he had an incident in which he nearly drowned in a motel swimming pool. Sam's mother suspects that he was under water for one to two minutes. When his cousin pulled him up, he had a faint heartbeat but was not breathing. After Mrs. H began CPR, Sam vomited water and resumed breathing.

In the Fall of 1999, he was diagnosed with Attention Deficit Disorder and is on Ritalin (20 mg slow-release in the morning and 7½ mg at noon). His mother believes that this dosage is working well for Sam. His parents do not have any behavior concerns. According to school records, Sam passed both vision and hearing screenings in the Fall of 1998.

Sam's mother reported that asthma has weakened his vocal cords, leading to scar tissue and nodules. According to the speech pathologist, he had a speech/language evaluation for voice concerns at the hospital approximately a year before kindergarten, but no services were deemed needed. Sam was evaluated by the speech pathologist at BBE in the Spring of 2000. His language skills were screened with the Clinical Evaluation of Language Fundamentals-Third Edition Screening Test. Sam did not meet criteria to pass this screening instrument. It was also noted during this screening that Sam's voice quality is hoarse and scratchy. He also had some aphonic (loss of voice) episodes while engaging in conversation. The teacher and special education teacher have mentioned Sam's voice quality as a concern. Sam's parents may want to consider consulting their pediatrician about this problem.

Social

According to multiple sources, Sam has fair to good social skills. His mother reports that Sam has friends and gets along well with them. His current teacher also reports that he has same-age friends and is able to maintain these friendships. His previous teacher reported that he had some problems working in small groups; however, according to his current teacher, he works better in small groups.

Family

According to a parent questionnaire, Sam lives with his father, Will, his mother, Cindy, and his 10-year-old brother Nick. Nick is a fourth grader at Blue Bird Elementary. According to the questionnaire, there is no history of educational, medical, or psychological problems among these family members. Mrs. H describes the family as fairly close, with occasional disputes, but nothing she would characterize as major problems.

Background of Referral Problem

Sam's academic functioning appears to have been a consistent concern since the beginning of his school career at BBE. He was referred to the CARE team by both his kindergarten and first grade teachers for being behind his same-age peers in the curriculum. In first grade, he received various interventions and modifications both in and outside of the classroom. Miss J reported some progress, but still identified him as being substantially lower than peers.

Currently, Sam's second grade teacher, Mrs. G, describes him as being significantly behind his peers academically. She describes him as being a hard worker, but not able to produce the same quality of work as his peers. She states that he often does not participate in group activities. His problems are the worst when he hasn't taken his medication and is unable to focus. During these times, he becomes preoccupied and doesn't get anything accomplished. He

also struggles when Mrs. G is presenting lessons to the entire class. She feels that he becomes lost easily during these times. He is at his best when working in small groups and receiving individual attention and instructions. According to a parent interview, Sam's mother views Sam's academic progress as being inconsistent. Some weeks he does well, then other weeks he will really struggle. For example, he may do well in math for one month then say he's not interested and do poorly.

Previous Evaluations:

None.

Assessment Tools:

Classroom Observation

Wechsler Intelligence Scale for Children–Third Edition (WISC-III)

Test of Visual-Motor Integration (VMI)

Wechsler Individual Achievement Test (WIAT)

Phonemic Awareness Inventory

Developmental Reading Assessment (DRA)

Informal Oral Reading Inventory

Listening Comprehension Probe

Reading Probe

Spelling Probe

Untimed Writing Sample

Dictation Analysis

Written Language Probe

First Grade Cumulative Math Test

Math Probe

Results:

Classroom Observations

An observation was conducted in Sam's second grade classroom during a group reading activity. Sam was on task 82.5% of the time and a typical peer was on task 92.5% of the time. When Sam was off task, he was typically looking off into space, but was never

observed to be disruptive. As the group was instructed to read aloud, Sam would watch the teacher or look at his book, but did not participate with the group.

Testing Observations

During testing, rapport was easily established. Sam appeared to be hesitant to be taken from the classroom, but quickly became comfortable in his new environment. He was excited when asked about events that had happened over the weekend and appeared to enjoy telling stories about his life. He was calm and able to sit in his chair for more than an hour at a time. Sam was both attentive and cooperative throughout the testing; however, he did ask to have several of the math questions repeated. He was persistent at tasks, such as putting together puzzles, even as they became more difficult. Due to Sam's persistence and cooperation, it is this examiner's opinion that the results are a fair representation of his abilities.

Cognitive Assessment

Sam is operating in the average range of intellectual functioning (FSIQ–95 +/– 5; 37%). No significant discrepancy is noted between Sam's average verbal comprehension/conceptualization skills (VIQ–95 +/– 5; 37%) and his average perceptual organizational abilities (PIQ–95 +/– 5; 37%). His relative strengths are in the areas of simultaneous processing and visual closure. He was able to look at a picture with an important piece missing and identify the piece.

Visual–Motor and Achievement Assessment

Sam had no difficulty copying simple shapes (circle, square, rectangle, diamond, or triangle) or simple lines (horizontal, diagonal, or vertical). He started to display difficulties when the designs became more complex (lines within shapes), but he scored in the 82nd percentile for visual-motor skills and at an age equivalence of 10 years, 6 mos. He also used the correct tripod grasp of the pencil with minimal prompting.

Compared to Sam's overall ability, his math and reading scores are lower and fall in the low average range. Sam's reading comprehension skills fell in the 7th percentile. He was able to answer questions about very simple stories that he had read, but had a hard

time when the stories became longer. He would substitute words in the story when he couldn't read them based on the accompanying picture. In contrast, Sam demonstrated above average skills in the area of listening comprehension. He was able to listen to a story and then answer very specific questions about the story.

In the math areas, Sam again scored in the low average range. His Mathematics Composite score of 82 places him in the 12th percentile. His strategy on most of the problems was to count with his fingers. This strategy was often used inaccurately, particularly with story problems. Sam had problems counting with his fingers when the numbers presented were larger than 10. On some problems, he appeared to use no strategy at all; quickly stating a random answer.

Formal and informal measures and curriculum-based measurements (CBMs) were administered in the Spring of 2000 by the resource teacher to gain a more complete picture of Sam's functioning. The following measures are grouped by achievement area.

Reading

The Phonemic Awareness Inventory was administered to assess Sam's understanding of spoken language and how language fits together. Sam was able to identify words that were the same and different (fat-bat, nut-nut), and create a rhyming word to match a word given to him. He was able to name the sound he heard at the beginning, middle, and end of words. Sam was also successful at counting the number of syllables in a word and blending speech sounds. Syllable segmentation, breaking a word into its individual sounds, leaving off beginning and ending sounds, and replacing sounds was difficult for Sam.

A Developmental Reading Assessment (DRA) was administered to assess and observe Sam's development as a reader.

Oral Reading –

Level 3	Independent	100% accuracy	Grade 1.0
Level 4	Instructional	96% accuracy	Grade 1.1
Level 6	Frustrational	85% accuracy	Grade 1.2

There were several strategies that Sam was observed to use during the assessment. Sam had left-to-right and top-to-bottom directionality for reading. He was able to differentiate words and letters and had one-to-one matching when reading early predictable books. He used his finger to track each word as he read with prompting. Sam was also able to look through the pictures in a book before actually reading them and draw pertinent information from the pictures. He commented on each picture as a separate event.

Sam read very slowly, methodically, and word-for-word, especially as the text became more difficult. When Sam came to a word in the text that he did not know, he would pause and try to sound the word out. He did not appear to be looking at the pictures for clues and he did not reread to check if the word made sense.

An analysis of Sam's reading errors show that his most frequent reading error was substitution. In other words, he read an incorrect word for the word written in the text (there/here, where/why, etc.). When Sam substituted an incorrect word, the word he read was frequently graphically similar at the beginning 73% of the time. The substituted word was graphically similar in the middle 36% of the time and similar at the end 18% of the time. Sam's errors did not change the meaning of the sentence 27% of the time, while he substituted a word of the correct class (noun for a noun, adverb for an adverb) 45% of the time. Sam self-corrected 27% of the errors that he read.

An informal oral reading inventory was administered to determine an instructional reading level.

Independent level	Level	Preprimer
Instructional level	Level	Primer
Frustrational level	Level	1st grade

A listening comprehension probe was administered to assess Sam's ability to understand and interpret oral language when a story or information was read to him. Passages from the QRI (Qualitative Reading Inventory) were read aloud to Sam. He was then asked to recall as much information as he could from the passage, and also answer explicit questions about the passage.

| Instructional level | level 1 (first grade) 100% explicit, 63% implicit |

When asked to recall information on his own about the passages read to him, Sam was able to recall events from the story. He was able to discuss background information, events from the story, and how the story was resolved. When asked direct questions about the passages that were read, Sam was capable of discussing what he remembered from the passage. It was easier for Sam to remember direct information from the text rather than information he had to infer.

On the CBM reading probe administered to Sam in January of his first grade year, he was able to read 11 words per minute. The typical range of scores for other first graders in the district was 0–110. In April of the same year, he was able to read 14 words per minute, with the typical range of scores being 10–168.

Spelling

Sam was administered a spelling probe (Grades 1–2) to show his knowledge of basic spelling skills. On this probe, he correctly spelled 9 out of 20 words, or 45%. According to the assessment, Sam's spelling skills fall slightly above the first grade level of 8/20 or 40%. In looking at the results of the assessment, it is apparent that Sam is beginning to understand spelling rules. However, when asked about spelling in tests and daily work, his teacher reports that he is on a modified list and that his spelling is very inconsistent.

Written Language

On an untimed writing sample, Sam was asked to choose one of several photographs to write about. He was then provided with unlimited time to write as much as he wanted about the picture. Sam chose a picture of a boy with a falcon over his head. He created a 10-word story that described what was happening in the picture and what the bird was doing. There were 4 spelling errors (60% spelled correctly) in the passage, and Sam did not include any punctuation in the story. Sam also used capital letters in the middle of the sentence and at times put capital letters in the middle of words.

On a dictation analysis task, Sam was asked to dictate a story to the administrator after making a story map with administrator assistance. Again, he was given some pictures to look at, and he chose to write about a cat lifting weights. Sam needed some assistance in order to come up with ideas to put on the story map. He dictated four sentences. When read back to Sam, he did notice two mistakes and made appropriate changes to make the story more fluent.

On the CBM written language probe administered in April of 2000, Sam scored 13 in the area of Total Words Written, with scores of typical peers in the district falling in the range of 8 to 37. He scored 10 in the area of Words Spelled Correctly (range = 3–31), 5 in the area of Correct Word Sequence (range = 0–28), and 10 in the area of Incorrect Word Sequence (range = 0–17).

Math

On a first grade cumulative math test, Sam completed 61% correctly. He was able to count objects and order numbers to 99, but had difficulty completing addition and subtraction facts, determining fractional parts of a set, determining appropriate measurements, and solving word problems.

Sam scored 88% on the computation probe, which included problems such as single-digit and double/single addition and subtraction. Sam used finger counting in order to solve most of the problems, although he did know some facts by memory. In the problem 10 + 5, he made a reversal in his numbers by answering 51.

On questions about money, Sam identified the names and knew the value of all the coins (quarter, dime, nickel, penny). He was able to identify time to the hour and half hour, and was able to create those times. He was unable to identify or create times for 15 minutes after the hour, and he often reversed where the hour hand should be for the 15-minute times. He was able to count by 2's, 5's, and 10's without assistance. He could also count backwards from 10–0 and from 20–0.

On the CBM math probe administered in January of 2000, Sam received a score of 10 for addition, with the typical range of peers in the district being 0 to 45. He scored 9 in the area of subtraction, with the range being 0 to 29, and 9 in mixed math, with the range being 0 to 32. On the April math probe, Sam received a score of 6 for addition, with a range of 11 to 66, 10 for subtraction, with a range of 1 to 36, and 9 for mixed math, with a range of 0 to 46.

Personality and Behavioral Assessment

According to interviews with Sam's mother and current teacher, he is not a problem behaviorally, although he does have problems focusing (particularly when not on medication). On a parent questionnaire used to gain more information about how Sam acts at home, Sam's mother reported that she sees Sam's personality as "quiet, sensitive . . ." a child who likes to "play alone as well as with others." She also reported that he is "fun-loving, humorous, and kind and thoughtful of others." Sam's mother checked the following characteristics on the parent questionnaire regarding Sam: "he has difficulty handling criticism, he is shy but truthful and creative, with a respect for authority." She feels he is easily upset and has difficulty following directions as well as a short attention span. She finds the short attention span

and difficulty completing tasks the most difficult things about raising Sam.

Summary and Conclusions:

Sam demonstrates a significant gap in achievement in the curriculum when compared to same-age peers. This gap has not narrowed in spite of small group instruction all year and extreme teacher modifications to his instruction and curriculum.

Although Sam's overall intellectual functioning falls in the average range, his academic functioning is significantly lower in most areas as measured by a standardized achievement test, curriculum-based measurements, cumulative tests, and informal measures.

The area of greatest concern for Sam appears to be reading. In looking at both the CBM and DRA results, it can be determined that Sam was reading at an emergent level when evaluated in the spring of 2000. At this time, he was at least one grade level lower than his first grade peers. Sam struggles with reading, and he is unable to apply different decoding strategies when reading, such as looking at the picture, "chunking" words, or rereading to decode. In examining his reading errors, it appears that Sam often relies on the initial letter/s of a word in order to decode it. Some of his reading errors might occur because he may focus only on the initial sound, and misread the remainder of the word. When substituting words in a reading passage, the substitutions changed the meaning of the sentence 73% of the time. This makes it difficult for Sam to understand what he is reading.

Other areas of concern for Sam are math, spelling, and written language. In these areas, Sam performs lower than his overall ability would suggest and is below average when compared to peers based on both standardized and curriculum-based measures.

Reports from Sam's mother and past and present teachers indicate that Sam may still experience some difficulty attending to tasks and staying focused, particularly when not taking his medication. A classroom observation and testing situations showed that Sam can be attentive and persistent under certain circumstances.

Sam's present levels of performance qualify him under law to be eligible to receive special education services for a child with a specific learning disability in the area of reading comprehension. Despite numerous modifications, Sam continues to demonstrate a severe discrepancy between achievement and intellectual ability in the area of reading comprehension. This discrepancy is not determined to be caused by a visual,

Psychometric Summary Sheet

Wechsler Intelligence Scale for Children-Third Edition
(WISC-III)   9/11/00

Index Scores	Standard Score	Percentile Rank
Verbal	95	37
Performance	95	37
Full Scale	95	37

Verbal Subtests	Scaled Score	Percentile Rank
Information	10	50
Similarities	9	37
Arithmetic	7	16
Vocabulary	11	63
Comprehension	9	37
Digit Span	9	37

Performance Subtests	Scaled Score	Percentile Rank
Picture Completion	14	91
Coding	7	16
Picture Arrangement	7	16
Block Design	9	37
Object Assembly	9	37
Symbol Search	7	16

Wechsler Individual Achievement Test (WIAT)   9/18/2000

Composite Scores	Standard Score	Percentile Rank
Reading	81	10
Mathematics	82	12

Subtest Scores	Standard Score	Percentile Rank
Basic Reading	86	18
Math Reasoning	86	18
Spelling	86	18
Reading Comprehension	78	7
Numerical Operations	83	26
Listening Comprehension	112	67

Phonemic-Awareness Inventory

Level 1

Whole Word Discrimination	9/9	100%
Rhyming Word Recognition	6/6	100%
Rhyming Word Application	8/9	89%
Syllable Counting	5/6	83%

Level 2

Syllable Segmentation	5/9	55%
Oral Synthesis-Blending Sounds	14/14	100%

Level 3

Approximation	6/6	100%
Phoneme Isolation	12/12	100%
Beginning	4/4	100%
Middle	4/4	100%
End	3/4	75%

Level 4

Segmentation	5/9	55%

Level 5

Phoneme Deletion	16/20	80%
Phoneme Substitution	4/9	44%

Curriculum-Based Measurements

() = 1st grade norm

January Reading Probe

11 WPM (0-110)

April Reading Probe

14 WPM (10-168)   Z-score = −1.28

Spelling-Test A (Grade 1-2)   9/20   45%

Test A Analysis

Long Vowels	4/5	(lowe/low)
Short Vowels	6/7	(letr/letter)
Consonant Blends	1/3	(thriye/try, fllat/flat)
Consonant Digraphs	1/3	(bak/back, wite/white)
Vowel Digraphs	5/5	
Vowel/Consonant/e	1/1	
Bossy 'r'	0/2	(torde/tardy, yuer, year)
Long 'A' Sound With 'ay'	1/1	
Long 'Y' Sound	0/1	(thriye/try)
Short 'y' Sound	0/1	(torde/tardy)
Diphthongs	0/1	(tooy/toy)
Schwa	0/2	(letr/letter, uther/other)
Nonphonic Spellings	0/2	(mene/many, uther/other)
Reversals- none		

Written Language

Curriculum-Based Measurement (CBM) Scores
April Writing Probes

		Median	Z score
Total Words Written:	13 (8-37)	18	−0.50
Words Spelled Correctly:	10 (3-31)	13	−0.33
Correct Word Sequence	5 (0-28)	9	−0.44
Incorrect Word Sequence	10 (0-17)	9	

Math-skills analysis (1st grade cumulative test)

Count how many objects in a collection have a given attribute	2/2	satisfactory
Compare two numbers, 0 through 99	1/1	satisfactory
Order numbers to 99	1/1	satisfactory
Find how many in all given several sets	1/1	satisfactory
Subtract to compare groups	1/1	satisfactory
Write addition and subtraction sentences	1/2	unsatisfactory
Complete addition and subtraction fact families	0/1	unsatisfactory
Identify 1/2, 1/3, or 1/4	2/2	satisfactory

Determine fractional parts or a set	0/2	unsatisfactory
Identify sides and corners of a figure, symmetry	2/3	satisfactory
Time to half hour, inches, centimeters, heavier	2/3	satisfactory
Determine appropriate measurement	0/1	unsatisfactory
Choosing correct number sentence for word problem	2/2	satisfactory
Solving word problems	2/6	unsatisfactory

CBM Scores

January Math Probes
   Addition: 10 (0-45)
   Subtraction: 9 (0-29)
   Mixed Math: 9 (0-32)
April Math Probes

	Median	Z-score
Addition: 6 (11-66)	32	−1.73
Subtraction: 10 (1-36)	20	−0.91
Mixed Math: 9 (0-46)	19	−0.77

motor, or hearing impairment; mental retardation; emotional disturbance; or environmental, cultural, or economic disadvantage.

Recommendations:

As much extra time as possible in working with Sam by the teacher, student teacher, or paraprofessional in the regular education classroom would be helpful to increase his success. Many repetitions, as well as intensity of interaction may help him to grasp new concepts faster and easier.

Small-group instruction, with individual reinforcement for him, is the best model for keeping Sam's attention and giving him more chances for interaction and teacher monitoring of skills. A minimum of whole group instruction might be best for Sam unless he can be individually reinforced during this time.

Sam may work best in a structured classroom in which he can receive some preferential attention for task completion. A behavior system, such as the one that was implemented in first grade, may be helpful if Sam continues to have problems focusing.

Continuous monitoring of Sam's medication taking would be helpful. This might help to decrease the amount of time Sam loses focus.

Sam would benefit from further emphasis and encouragement of phonics skills, including sound and letter manipulation, which may help him sound out more quickly and accurately.

Encouraging Sam to use strategies other than sounding out, such as skipping a word and going back, may help increase his reading accuracy and fluency. Continued participation in a small-group, guided reading setting in the Discovery Room may be important to help foster the use of those other strategies. Frequent practice of sight words and repeated readings of material that Sam has already read may also help increase his reading accuracy.

Small-group instruction focusing on guided writing may help Sam increase his writing skills. This small-group focus could include practice of frequently written words, spelling, punctuation, grammar prompting, and assistance with prewriting and story development skills.

Because Sam relies heavily on finger counting in order to complete computation problems, teaching him the touch math method may help increase his computation speed and accuracy. This method will supply him with the tactile impact that he needs in order to count up or down to solve computation problems without taking as much time as counting on fingers.

Current second grade curriculum for fine-motor and visual-motor tasks is appropriate. Sam will participate in a special program sponsored by the occupational therapist called "Handwriting Day" (which has already been arranged with his teacher to take place 2nd quarter).

—*Tracy K. Cruise*

See also Confidentiality; Ethical Issues in School Psychology; Multidisciplinary Teams

REFERENCES AND FURTHER READING

Sattler, J. M. (2001). *Assessment of children: Cognitive applications*. San Diego, CA: Author.

Tallent, N. (1993). *Psychological report writing* (4th ed.). Englewood Cliffs, NJ: Prentice Hall.

Wolber, G. J., & Carne, W. F. (1993). *Writing psychological reports: A guide for clinicians*. Sarasota, FL: Professional Resource Press.

RESEARCH

Research in school psychology is defined broadly as any data collected systematically that may be applied to benefit individuals primarily from birth through age 18 years. Recently, however, there has been an impetus for school psychologists to study and conduct research on issues pertaining to individuals across the life span, because learning is believed to continue indefinitely. Although research in school psychology is usually conducted in schools or other educational settings (e.g., residential facilities for individuals with disabilities, therapeutic nurseries), there is no particular limitation imposed on where data may be collected. Similarly, there is no limitation placed on who may collect the data (e.g., academicians, practitioners, graduate students, or paraprofessionals). The participants in research studies may include young children, college students, individuals with specific disorders (e.g., learning disabilities, autism, attention deficit disorder), or other individuals.

HISTORY OF RESEARCH IN SCHOOL PSYCHOLOGY

In 1879, the first psychological laboratory was founded by Wilhelm Wundt in Germany, and in 1896 Lightner Witmer established the first psychological clinic at the University of Pennsylvania. Witmer is often cited as the founder of school psychology in the United States, and each year the Lightner Witmer award is given to a new scholar-researcher who has made significant contributions to research in school psychology. Although it has been generally recognized since the dawn of time that individuals differ with respect to intelligence, personality, achievement, and other characteristics, it was not until the 19th century that the scientific research on individual differences emerged. During this period, research focused on inheritance of intelligence with variables that included sensorimotor abilities (e.g., reaction time, sensory discrimination).

In 1905, the first intelligence test (the Binet-Simon Intelligence Scale) was published. Following early research endeavors, there was a period of rapid growth and development in psychological research including the measurement of intelligence; individual differences in achievement, personality, vocational interests; and numerous other domains (e.g., suitability for military duty). Research over the past 100 years has evolved in many ways—the breadth of topics investigated, the sophistication of the data collection techniques used (e.g., computers and other specialized equipment such as polygraph machines), and the

knowledge base and understanding of how to interpret research findings have grown by leaps and bounds. Additionally, ethical guidelines have emerged, and they strictly govern research practices to protect the rights of participants in all research-related activities.

TYPES OF RESEARCH AND DATA COLLECTION METHODS

In general, there are two types of research (basic and applied), and they differ in their primary goals. The goals of basic research usually involve formulating theories, establishing relationships among different psychological constructs or variables, and providing knowledge for the sake of gaining knowledge. Applied research uses the results of basic research and applies them to solve everyday problems that children and adolescents encounter or to assist school personnel in serving their constituents. Although one may think that these two types of research are mutually exclusive, nothing could be farther from the truth. In fact, they are probably inextricably bound and inform each other in a reciprocal and evolving manner.

In addition to the two broad types of research in school psychology, there are two major methods of collecting and presenting research findings: quantitative and qualitative methodologies. There are several subtypes of each method, and they tend to involve different means for collecting the data and analyzing and reporting the results. As the name suggests, quantitative methods involve quantifying something (e.g., how many words are read by two groups of second graders) and perhaps comparing groups on the variable in question. Qualitative methods usually involve describing a phenomenon (e.g., how a third grader solves a math problem) so that the process can be understood and studied via a quantitative method. However, in most research a variety of methods are used because school psychologists believe and accept that there is more than one way to examine variables. They also believe that it is important to explore any and all ways to answer questions that can be applied to help children and adolescents. In fact, school psychologists have found that flexibility in the type(s) of selected research methodologies leads to richer and more valuable outcomes. Thus, school psychology researchers often combine quantitative and qualitative research methodologies to maximize the generalizability of their findings.

DOMAINS OF RESEARCH IN SCHOOL PSYCHOLOGY

The domains of research in school psychology include:

- Assessment
- Interventions
- Psychopathology or disorders
- Consultation
- Research methodologies

Each of these domains contributes valuable information about how children and adolescents learn, grow, and cope in today's society. Assessment research in school psychology usually involves evaluating a child's functioning in areas such as cognition (e.g., intelligence quotient [IQ]), achievement (e.g., reading), behavior (e.g., study habits), and personality (e.g., extroversion vs. introversion). For example, assessment research may investigate the impact of study habits and intelligence on reading comprehension. It also may involve determining what assessment methods may be the most useful under myriad conditions. Although many individuals in and outside of the field have equated assessment with testing, testing is only one method of assessment. Other methods of assessment include informal and formal observations; interviews; and curriculum-based, performance-based, and authentic assessments.

Research in interventions in school psychology involves determining the nature and extent of what specific strategies or treatments may be useful for a certain gender, age group, ethnic group, or ability level under certain conditions. A wide range of interventions exist today including behavior modification, individual and group counseling, parent training, psychopharmacology, and crisis intervention. Recently, many professionals in school psychology have been active in compiling a database on the most effective interventions for learning (e.g., early literacy) and behavior problems (e.g., attention deficit disorders). Additionally, psychopharmacological interventions with young children have been widely debated topics.

Another major area or domain of research in school psychology is the development of psychopathology or psychological disorders, especially those that have a negative impact on children's and adolescents' learning. Examples of developmental disorders (those disorders that begin early in life for a variety of reasons) include mental retardation, autism, learning disabilities, and attention deficit hyperactivity disorder. Research is devoted to determining the nature and causes of these disorders as well as what treatments may be most effective in alleviating or managing them. Additional psychological disorders that may be researched by school psychologists include substance abuse (e.g., alcohol and tobacco use), eating disorders (e.g., anorexia, bulimia), and severe behavior problems (e.g., conduct disorder).

Consultation is a unique intervention process that involves indirect service delivery. It is being used more and more in educational settings and includes working with other professionals, parents, and other individuals who play a part in the learning process. Research in consultation involves uncovering the best ways to effect change in an educational system as well as the best ways to engage others as helping agents in children's and adolescents' lives. Research may, for example, focus on the efficacy of consulting with classroom teachers to reduce disruptive behavior as compared to school psychological services rendered to the children exhibiting these behavioral difficulties. Several types of consultation are described in the literature including behavioral, instructional, mental health, and organizational systems.

Finally, although it may sound strange, research in school psychology also involves determining the best research methods to use to answer questions or solve problems. Researchers are always trying to devise new and innovative methods of collecting, analyzing, and reporting data. Thus, a small but fair amount of research is devoted to increasing the utility or applicability of research methods and techniques.

COMMON TOPICS OF RESEARCH

There are many topics of research in school psychology. Most of the topics listed here fall under one of the broad domains discussed previously. This list is provided to give a sense of the breadth and depth of research topics in school psychology. Some of these topics are defined further in this volume. The most frequently researched topics in school psychology are, but are not limited to, reading and other academic domains, intelligence, instruction, special education, counseling, parenting, legal issues, ethics, professional training, violence prevention, social skills, pharmacology, and psychopathology. Trends in school psychological research are consistent with concerns of the times and research attempts to solve problems confronting children and adolescents in our society.

LOCATING RESEARCH IN SCHOOL PSYCHOLOGY

The primary source for reading about research conducted in school psychology is professional journals. The major school psychology journals are:

- *Journal of School Psychology*
- *Psychology in the Schools*
- *School Psychology International*
- *School Psychology Quarterly*
- *School Psychology Review*

These journals publish some of the finest research articles in the field and are highly respected by school psychologists and other professionals. They contain articles on many of the research topics identified previously and examples of basic and applied research as well as quantitative and qualitative research methodologies. Most school psychologists subscribe to and regularly receive one or more of these journals. The *School Psychology Quarterly* is the official Division 16 (School of Psychology) journal of the American Psychological Association (APA), and *School Psychology Review* is the official journal of the National Association of School Psychologists (NASP). Division 16 of the APA and NASP are the two largest national school psychology associations.

There are 16 secondary and 26 tertiary journals that publish research and provide information on research topics. In addition, there are two other major publications produced by school psychology national organizations. *The School Psychologist* (published four times annually) is the official newsletter of Division 16 of the APA, and *Communiqué* (published eight times annually) is the official newsletter of NASP. These newsletters print research articles, book and test reviews, commentaries, current information on federal mandates, position statements, and many more interesting and important topics and features in a reader-friendly manner. APA and NASP also sponsor annual conferences in which school psychologists and other psychologists share the results of their research.

Another source of research in school psychology is the Internet and the World Wide Web. Most individuals are aware of the information explosion that has occurred because of access to the Internet and the millions of Web sites available on-line. The Internet has become a valuable source of information regarding research on children and adolescents. However, at the same time, readers are cautioned about believing everything they read on the Internet. There are many Web sites that provide inaccurate and potentially harmful information ranging from what to expect from children and adolescents to how to treat them.

In addition, there are literally thousands of texts that publish the results of quantitative and qualitative research, theoretical articles, and professional opinions. Space limitations preclude the listing of many of these texts. However, there are several excellent texts devoted to school psychology research, practice, and ethics. Although these texts are written for professionals in the field, they also may be helpful to parents, teachers, and others who have an interest in the well-being of children and adolescents. These texts include *Best Practices in School Psychology-IV; Children's Needs II: Development, Problems and Alternatives; Helping Children at Home and School: Handouts From Your School Psychologist* (all published by the NASP) and *The Handbook of School Psychology-Third Edition* (published by John Wiley).

TRENDS AND FUTURE DIRECTIONS IN SCHOOL PSYCHOLOGY RESEARCH

It is difficult to state exactly what the trends and future directions in school psychology research are, because there are many and they constantly change with the times and sociopolitical agendas. However, the following three areas have been the focus of attention in recent years and will probably continue to be researched in the years to come. The first area is violence and violence prevention. Almost everyone is aware of the amount of violence in American society as well as in other societies around the world. Unfortunately, a high percentage of violence occurs in schools, ranging from bullying to the use of deadly weapons. School psychologists are especially adept at conducting, disseminating, and consuming research in violence prevention and related areas. Funding for violence prevention has been very high for many years and probably will not be decreased any time soon.

A second trend of school psychology research is early intervention. There is little doubt that prevention of and early intervention for learning and behavior problems benefit many children. In addition, from an economic perspective, early intervention may save millions of dollars in health care, special education costs, and so forth. Although it is known that prevention and early intervention are viable "treatments" and that they work in general, the focus of research efforts should be directed toward determining what works for whom under what conditions. When assessment and interventions for young children are streamlined, positive effects on society as a whole may occur.

The third trend of research in school psychology may be called *disorder-specific* interventions. This research involves uncovering what constitutes the most effective treatments or interventions for specific learning and behavior problems. For example, it is now known that increasing young children's phonological awareness (including awareness of sound–symbol correspondences) assists them greatly in learning how to read. Also, it can be helpful for young children who already demonstrate difficulties in learning how to read. Another example is behavior modification, which is used to treat children and adolescents who exhibit a wide range of behavior problems. Although neither of these "interventions" has been the only one to be successful for these difficulties, the research literature clearly shows their superiority to other forms of treatment.

It seems that an additional area that needs to be explored continuously is how school psychologists can apply what is learned from research to educational settings as well as how practice or work that takes place in applied settings can inform research. As Phillips (1999) indicates in *The Handbook of School Psychology-Third Edition,* "But science and practice are still not joined in the most meaningful and significant sense, and if future efforts are to be more successful, both the science and the practice of school psychology must be changed, even transformed, in important ways" (p. 56). Thus, constant efforts must be directed at the science–practice link if there is to be a significant benefit to our children and adolescents in educational settings.

In conclusion, research in school psychology includes a range of methodologies, is conducted by individuals who work in various settings, and may be basic or applied in nature. Research in school psychology, together with research from other branches of psychology, has provided practitioners, parents, educators, and others with essential information that has promoted the well-being of children and society as a whole. Research is exciting in that countless problems that have confronted our society, once deemed too insurmountable, have become more manageable through ongoing research efforts. Research has improved our knowledge of and ability to intervene with certain disorders, reduce the prevalence of other disorders, assist children to learn more effectively, facilitate parenting skills, enhance self-esteem, reduce violence, and so forth. There will always be a great need for more research because there will always be new questions to answer—research will, over time, provide those answers. What needs to be done and how it can be done remain unanswered, yet all questions may be answered via research in school psychology.

—*Vincent C. Alfonso and Melissa B. Tarnofsky*

See also Careers in School Psychology; Diagnosis and Labeling; Division of School Psychology (Division 16)

REFERENCES AND FURTHER READING

Aiken, L. R. (2003). *Psychological testing and assessment.* Boston: Allyn & Bacon.

Phillips, B. N. (1999). Strengthening the links between science and practice: Reading, evaluating, and applying research in school psychology. In C. R. Reynolds & T. B. Gutkin (Eds.), *The handbook of school psychology* (3rd ed.). New York: John Wiley.

Reynolds, C. R., & Fletcher-Janzen, E. (Eds.). (2002). *Concise encyclopedia of special education* (2nd ed.). New York: John Wiley.

RESILIENCE AND PROTECTIVE FACTORS

RISK AND RESILIENCE

Risk and resilience have been conceptualized as opposite poles "of individual differences in people's response to stress and adversity" (Rutter, 1987, p. 316), with risk representing the negative pole (e.g., succumbing to adversity) and resilience the positive (e.g., overcoming adversity). Over the past five decades, a large and consistent body of research has shown that children's futures are made considerably dimmer by exposure to multiple, chronically adverse living conditions such as poverty, family dysfunction, parental illness or incompetence, abuse, and poor physical health. Negative outcomes of these conditions include (Doll & Lyon, 1998):

- Increased delinquent activity/criminality
- Lower measured intelligence
- Increased educational and learning problems
- Increased likelihood of physical and mental health problems
- Increased likelihood of teenage parenthood
- Increased likelihood of unemployment
- Decreased likelihood of social competence

However, most of these same studies describe complex transactional relationships by which vulnerable children are protected against adult dysfunction through an interplay among characteristics of:

- The child (e.g., easy temperament, achievement oriented)
- The caregiver (e.g., a desire to protect the child from burdensome family hardships)
- The environment (e.g., a high level of support from extended family, friends, and other adults, including those in schools)

Taken together, the results of these studies suggest that understanding the dynamic ways in which individuals successfully negotiate risk situations holds more promise for understanding resilience than amassing lists of discrete attributes of presumably resilient individuals (Doll & Lyon, 1998).

Resilience research, therefore, is no longer preoccupied with describing static or isolated patterns of risk and resilience. Instead, attention has shifted toward: (a) explaining the specific mechanisms by which constellations of risk propel a child toward poorer adult outcomes, and the ways in which these mechanisms are interrupted by protective factors (Rutter, 1987); and (b) understanding how these mechanisms organize into developmental trajectories that facilitate or hinder adult competence. This understanding is dependent on sources of risk and resilience at different points in children's lives, variables that change the magnitude and direction of their lives, and the points in time when these influential variables are introduced, as well as how they are maintained. Addressing both aspects of negotiating risk (e.g., specifying mechanisms and investigating their influence on developmental trajectories) is essential if

social and educational programs are to be successful in helping protect vulnerable children.

PROTECTIVE FACTORS

Although the precise mechanisms underlying resilience are just beginning to be understood, several decades of longitudinal research provide at least working knowledge about protective factors that are key to ameliorating conditions of risk. These protective factors may be organized into two groups, those pertaining to characteristics of the individual and those related to the context or environment (Doll & Lyon, 1998).

Individual Characteristic Protective Factors

- Intellectual ability
- Positive temperament or easygoing disposition
- Positive social orientation, including close peer friendships
- High self-efficacy, self-confidence, and self-esteem
- An achievement orientation with realistically high expectations
- A resilient belief system, or faith
- A higher rate of engagement in productive activities

Contextual Protective Factors

- A close, affectionate relationship with at least one parent or caregiver
- Effective parenting (characterized by warmth, structure, and realistically high expectations)
- Access to warm relationships and guidance from other extended family members
- Access to and relationships with positive adult models in a variety of extrafamilial contexts
- Connections with at least one or a variety of prosocial organizations
- Access to responsive, high-quality schools

While these protective factors may appear simple at first glance, it must be remembered that they unfold within the complex and continuous process of human development. As Pianta and Walsh (1998) have noted, "vulnerability and protective mechanisms operate within a window of opportunity—a period of relative plasticity—when responses to risk are being formulated"

(p. 414). Hence, protective factors may be best understood as a complex transaction between the individual and his or her contexts, with issues of timing and quality of relationships being critical in ameliorating risk and facilitating development of competence.

THE FUTURE OF RESILIENCE RESEARCH AND PROGRAMS

Most researchers agree that the most powerful means of uncovering resilience mechanisms will be found in prospective, longitudinal prevention studies, where processes thought to promote resilience and reduce risk are deliberately implemented and their impact tracked over time in relation to important adult outcomes. Such studies have the potential to reveal the intricate relationships between early precursors and later outcomes that stretch across childhood and adolescence into adulthood. These studies must begin in early childhood in order to examine mechanisms and processes operating during critical early developmental periods. The investigations must be prospective and manipulate variables systematically to clarify links between mechanisms and later outcomes, elucidating trajectories that Robins and Rutter (1990) have termed the "straight and devious pathways from childhood to adulthood."

These types of studies will require different research designs, data collection methods, and data analysis techniques that have been used in most previous research on risk and resilience. Additionally, because protective factors are typically maintained within caregiving relationships that are authentic and persist over time, newer studies will need to occur in natural environments rather than laboratory settings.

This kind of research stretches across decades and requires that we rethink the systemic supports for psychosocial intervention/prevention programs that now exist. Longitudinal prevention studies will require funding that extends beyond the three- to five-year periods of most current social science grants. These studies will demand dependable collaboration between youth service providers with access to families and researchers with the methodological sophistication to examine risk and resilience relationships.

Schools can play a vital role in the advancement of resilience research by virtue of the fact that they deal daily with the problems of students who are seriously at risk for a wide variety of poor educational and psychosocial outcomes. Schools contain a large and captive audience of at-risk students who would be difficult to aggregate under other circumstances for purposes of long-range prevention and intervention efforts. However, schools need to be mindful of the fact that resilience programs represent yet another area where it may be easy to place "the cart before the horse." The research base on resilience is still developing, and as yet only a partial understanding of the mechanisms involved in successfully negotiating risk situations has been achieved. Children who live in conditions of chronic risk are unlikely to profit from programs that are short-lived, poorly organized, or do not plan for follow-through from grade to grade and from school building to school building. Such programs often represent popularized notions of resilience that are based loosely on resilience research, if at all. Regrettably, a number of the current resilience efforts in schools seem to be of this ilk. Such programs seem destined to go the way of the numerous educational fads that have preceded them, but in the process may also damage the prospects of those programs that are supportable. Pianta and Walsh (1998) have provided a set of generalizations for school-based programs aimed at fostering resilience. These include:

- Mobilize resources early in the interest of interrupting cycles of risk.
- Pay close attention to adult-child and peer relationships in the service of building educational and social competence.
- Provide only comprehensive, integrated programs to children and youth rather than discrete skills-based or isolated pull-out programs, which offer little hope of long-term impact.

Programs based on these broad principles may well succeed in interrupting chronic cycles of risk and promoting resilience in many school-age children and youth.

—*Mark Lyon*

See also Abuse and Neglect; Attention Deficit Hyperactivity Disorder; Divorce Adjustment; Dropouts; Learned Helplessness; Self-Concept and Efficacy; Self-Injurious Behavior; Violence in Schools

REFERENCES AND FURTHER READING

Doll, B., & Lyon, M. A. (1998). Risk and resilience: Implications for the delivery of educational and mental health services in schools. *School Psychology Review, 27,* 348–363.

Pianta, R. C., & Walsh, D. J. (1998). Applying the construct of resilience in schools: Cautions from a developmental systems perspective. *School Psychology Review, 27,* 407–417.

Robins, L. N., & Rutter, M. (Eds.). (1990). *Straight and devious pathways from childhood to adulthood.* New York: Cambridge University Press.

Rutter, M. (1987). Psychosocial resilience and protective mechanisms. *American Journal of Orthopsychiatry, 37,* 317–331.

RESOURCE ROOMS

Since 1975, the Resource Room has been an alternative instructional placement for students who are eligible to receive special education services. A less restrictive alternative to self-contained classrooms, the Resource Room option allows the student to spend the majority of the day with grade-level peers. The student comes to the Resource Room for no more than a few hours each week. In the Resource Room, teaching methods geared to students with learning differences are employed. It is not a study hall or a place for review. Rather, Resource Room instruction provides an alternative to the general curriculum in specific academic areas (such as reading or arithmetic), taught by trained special education teachers, to meet the needs of the individual student. Resource Room placement is appropriate for the student who needs more intervention than can be provided in a regular classroom.

—*Cheryl H. Silver*

See also Least Restrictive Environment; Special Education

RESPONSE COST. *See* APPLIED BEHAVIOR ANALYSIS; BEHAVIOR INTERVENTION; BEHAVIORAL ASSESSMENT; BEHAVIORAL CONCEPTS AND APPLICATIONS BEHAVIOR

RESPONSIVENESS TO INTERVENTION MODEL

The term *learning disabilities* is a disability category that includes persons with severe underachievement in academic areas that is caused by a neurological delay or dysfunction. This underachievement is not related to mental retardation, sensory impairments, or environmental influences such as lack of educational opportunity or poor instruction. The history of learning disabilities (LD) has included much controversy about the procedures and criteria for identifying students with LD. Responsiveness to intervention (RTI) has gained momentum as a means of determining whether a student has a learning disability. RTI is an assessment method that incorporates intense instruction focusing on improving the LD student's skill deficits (e.g., word recognition deficits) with careful monitoring of the student's progress. RTI intends to rule out that poor instruction is responsible for the student's skill deficits. Thus, RTI can be very helpful for assessing the quality of instruction for all students in a school.

RTI is proposed as a valuable model for schools because of its potential utility in identifying students with LD and preventing academic failure among all students. Students need and benefit from a close match of their current skills and abilities with the instructional and curricular choices provided within the classroom. When a mismatch occurs, student learning and outcomes are lowered. For some students, typical classroom instruction is appropriate and meets their needs, but for others, success is not easy. The hypothesis is the earlier that these floundering students can be identified and provided appropriate instruction, the higher the likelihood that they can be successful and maintain their class placement. Thus, their underachievement is reduced or eliminated.

Some advocates propose that RTI can have an important role in LD determination because of its emphasis on careful monitoring of student learning and providing high-quality instruction. One commonly accepted characteristic of LD is that students with LD do not learn at the same speed or level as other students with similar age, educational opportunities, and assessed ability level. They are regarded as underachievers. This intrinsic difference means that the difficulties are attributable to the youngster, presumably because of an undetected neurological problem, and not the classroom instruction.

The use of aptitude-achievement discrepancy formulas was one way of quantifying a student's level of underachievement. The underachievement was computed by calculating the difference between a student's ability score (from an ability test) and achievement score (from an achievement test). If the difference or discrepancy between these two scores was of sufficient magnitude, the student was considered as having significant underachievement. RTI provides another method of assessing underachievement. Students who are underachieving even when they are provided high-quality instruction might have a learning disability.

RESPONSIVENESS TO INTERVENTION CRITICAL FEATURES

RTI as an assessment method is designed to match students with appropriate instruction, thereby helping learners who are experiencing difficulty. Therefore, RTI may be one of the best new approaches for linking assessment with instruction. The core features of RTI include:

1. *High-quality classroom instruction.* Students receive high-quality instruction in their general education setting. Before students are singled out for specific assistance, one has to have assurance that the typical classroom instruction is of high quality. The quality of instruction is based on numerous considerations including that the instructor is adequately prepared with appropriate background education, delivers the curriculum as intended, uses appropriate instructional and assessment methods, and is consistent in instruction. Comparing students' learning rates and achievement in different classrooms at the same grade level is one means of assessing the quality of instruction.

2. *Research-based instruction.* General education's classroom practices and the curriculum vary in their efficacy. Thus, ensuring that the practices and curriculum have demonstrated validity is important. Research-based instruction means that appropriate experiments have been completed that demonstrate the efficacy of the particular instructional methods and curriculum. If not, one cannot be confident that a student's limited gains are independent of classroom experiences.

3. *Universal screening.* School staff conducts universal screening of all students' academics and behavior three times per year (e.g., fall, winter, and spring). This feature focuses on specific criteria for judging the learning and achievement of all students, not only in academics but also in related behaviors (e.g., class attendance, tardiness, truancy, suspensions, and disciplinary actions). The screening results are useful in two ways. First, the results can indicate the quality of classroom instruction and possible changes in teaching, curricula, or instructional methods. Second, those screening results are applied in determining which students need closer monitoring or an intervention.

4. *Continuous progress monitoring.* Students' classroom progress is monitored continuously. Thus, staff can readily identify the learners who are not meeting the classroom-level benchmarks or other expected standards. Progress-monitoring data are collected weekly or during alternate weeks. Various curriculum-based assessment models are used in this role (e.g., number of words read correctly from the reading curriculum or arithmetic problems correctly solved within a fixed time interval, such as one or two minutes).

5. *Research-based interventions.* When a student's screening results or progress-monitoring results indicate a deficit, an appropriate instructional intervention is implemented, perhaps an individually designed instructional package or a standardized treatment. The decision whether to use an individually designed instructional package or a standardized treatment is made when the school or school district is setting up their procedures. In some school districts, both approaches are used in a fixed sequence. If the student doesn't respond to the standard treatment protocol, an individually designed intervention is determined and implemented.

The standardized treatment protocols are the interventions that researchers have validated as effective, meaning that the experimental applications were completed with the proper experimental controls to demonstrate that the intervention works. School staff is expected to implement specific, research-based interventions to address the student's difficulties. These interventions might include a "double dose" of classroom instruction and/or different instructional method. These interventions are not adaptations of the current curriculum or accommodations, because one would expect those procedures to be implemented already. Research-based interventions are 8 to 12 weeks in length and are designed to increase the intensity of the learner's instructional experience. These protocols include specific information about the number of minutes per day, the number of days per week, the number of weeks that an intervention will be implemented, as well as the specific skills addressed, where the instruction will be provided, who will provide the instruction, and the materials used for instruction and assessing progress. Furthermore, the following two procedures should be implemented to ensure that a robust outcome is obtained and that it is directly related to the intervention(s):

1. *Progress monitoring during interventions.* School staff uses progress-monitoring data to determine interventions' effectiveness and to make any needed modifications. Carefully defined data are collected, perhaps as often as daily, to provide a cumulative record of the learner's response to the intervention. This progress monitoring is very specific in that the tasks and responses are very closely tied to the specific intervention the learner receives. These assessment data often do not have the normative information that permits comparison with other classmates or peers.

2. *Fidelity measures.* While the classroom instruction and interventions are designed, implemented, and assessed for learner effectiveness, fidelity measures are completed on individuals providing instruction. A fidelity measure indicates the degree to which the intervention was implemented as intended and with consistency. Staff members other than the classroom teacher have an important role in completing fidelity measures, which can be an observational checklist of critical teaching behaviors.

RESPONSIVENESS TO INTERVENTION ATTRIBUTES

RTI has been implemented in a number of different ways. Some attributes common to the many different RTI versions include:

- Multiple tiers of increasingly intense student interventions. That is, if student progress is unsatisfactory, then a more intense dosage of instruction is considered (e.g., Fuchs & colleagues

2003). Thus, these tiers of interventions are often described with the public health framework of primary, secondary, and tertiary. The primary intervention is for the population of students in a school (e.g., students in a classroom). Students who need a stronger intervention are provided a secondary level intervention. The tertiary tier is for those students needing the most intense of all available interventions. Interventions continue for 6 to 12 weeks, and intervention cycles may be repeated.

- Implementation of a differentiated curriculum. The differentiated curriculum means that students have the option to receive a different curriculum for their secondary or tertiary intervention. The assumption is that a different curriculum and its instructional methods might better address the students' learning difficulties. Students in a secondary or tertiary RTI tier are provided a curriculum that addresses the specific deficit indicated by the screening results or classroom progress monitoring. An area of concern is that schools do not have clear guidelines about how the intensity of instruction needs to be increased (e.g., size of grouping, amount of time, and choice of intervention).

- Instruction delivered by staff other than the classroom teacher. Classroom teachers have a significant responsibility for all learners in the primary level of intervention and integrating the higher tiers of instruction and curriculum provided to students. Resource staff (e.g., a reading teacher or a title I teacher) deliver instruction to learners at the higher tier levels.

- Varied duration, frequency, and time of interventions. The different intervention tiers can vary in several features (e.g., duration, frequency, staff roles, and time). A characteristic of RTI models is that those features are specified for the learners so that teachers, parents, and other staff involved have a clear blueprint for understanding the student's intervention.

- Categorical or noncategorical placement decisions. School district staff implement RTI using categorical and noncategorical service delivery models. In a categorical model, the students' disability is considered in the grouping of students (e.g., students with learning disabilities received instruction with other students with learning disabilities). In noncategorical models, the students' disability areas are not of primary consideration in providing instruction. This noncategorical feature is attractive to many educators who believe RTI can fit with their broader framework for serving students with varied disabilities.

- Prevention and LD identification. RTI has application for preventing academic difficulties and for LD identification. As a preventive, early intervention framework, RTI can inform parents and staff about youngsters who are not progressing as well as their peers and help inform parents and staff about the appropriateness of selected interventions. For LD determination, RTI provides a framework for ensuring that students have received appropriate learning experiences as required in LD identification. One attribute of LD is that the students have not achieved commensurate with their peers when given appropriate learning experiences. Other parts of LD identification require that the students demonstrate a significant discrepancy between ability and achievement and that the discrepancy is not related to other factors such as other disabilities or educational, economic, or cultural differences.

RESPONSIVENESS TO INTERVENTION ISSUES

With the increasing emphasis on having a scientific basis for practices, RTI is noticeably lacking in supportive scientific evidence. The concept has broad appeal as a prevention model for reading and behavior problems and some experimental evidence supporting that application. To date, however, broad scale, rigorous experimental or evaluative evidence is lacking for RTI's application for LD determination. School district applications, commonly considered as important testaments to RTI's value, do not specifically identify students with LD but rather identify students for a noncategorical special education model. RTI has much to offer for improving services to students in the whole school; how RTI increases the validity of LD determination is unknown.

A second issue is in the category of "necessary, but not sufficient" information. Underachievement is considered one distinguishing characteristic of students with LD, but students can have underachievement and not have a learning disability. Aptitude–achievement

discrepancy and RTI are two distinct ways of assessing a student's underachievement. By themselves, they are not sufficient information for making an LD determination. A difficulty for the LD field remains that other features considered important to LD (e.g., average or above-average ability level, processing deficits, and uneven profile of skills and abilities) have limited empirical support. Processing deficits include a variety of specific aptitudes or abilities (such as attention, perception, recognition, short-term memory, recall, organization, and expression) that influence one's ability to understand and interact effectively and efficiently with everyday situations. The challenge is to determine the appropriateness of such processing constructs and corresponding assessments that can further differentiate students with LD from other students experiencing difficulty in the curriculum.

A critical issue for implementation is that RTI activities take place within the general education framework, and such activities as universal screening, progress monitoring, and multiple tiers of interventions rely on the close cooperation of general education staffs. RTI involves a significant shift in roles and responsibilities and the interaction patterns among staff. The working relationship among staff will be very important to successful RTI implementation and assessing that classroom-level instruction is research-based, of high quality, and implemented with fidelity. A related concern is that when a student does respond positively to an intense intervention in terms of improved learning rate and at a higher achievement level, the conditions that lead to that improvement may be very burdensome to classroom staff. Maintaining that level of intervention may be difficult, and staff might consider that a special education placement is a better option for the youngster. On the other hand, because the student was responsive to the intervention, is the appropriate conclusion that the student does not have a disability?

For some school staff, who are concerned about practicality and feasibility issues, the RTI component may look like a more complicated, intensive model of prereferral intervention. Prereferral intervention involved a set of procedures intended to reduce the number of referrals to special education. The assumption was that if classroom teachers implemented specific interventions within the classroom, the students would benefit and the costs of a comprehensive evaluation and time requirements would be reduced. While this approach was desirable, implementation was difficult to achieve. RTI likely faces similar implementation difficulties.

An additional point to consider is that no one model of RTI exists. Current implementations differ on a number of features that influence the validity of the results:

- Number of tiers in the model
- Normative framework for cutoff scores on screening measures
- Agreement on what constitutes high-quality general education instruction
- Agreement on what constitutes appropriate interventions for each tier
- How long an intervention should be conducted
- Delineation of student responses that indicate adequate or inadequate progress to an intervention
- Specification of other necessary information as a basis for LD determination

Some other practical points include which budget will support the tiers of intervention (e.g., are screening and interventions a general education or special education activity?) and at what point do parents need to be involved and due-process protections applied? Due-process protections are the legal safeguards that are afforded to parents in relation to schools' assessment and intervention activities with children. An example of those protections is that a parent or guardian must provide informed consent before an evaluation or change of class placement can be completed with a youngster. The due-process protections ensure that parents have a right to formal hearing if they are challenging the school's plans regarding their child.

SCHOOL PSYCHOLOGIST'S ROLE

School psychologists potentially have a number of important roles in RTI models. As in their current role, they will continue to be the staff member who interprets students' learning and behavior within a developmental and psychological framework. Parents and teachers can provide excellent descriptions of students' behavior (e.g., the student has difficulty paying attention for long periods of time, can't stay in his or her seat, is aggressive toward other students, doesn't interact with peers, seems sad or depressed, has trouble sounding out words, doesn't read fluently, can't remember multiplication facts, and has trouble copying from the chalkboard to paper). Parents and teachers look to

psychologists to interpret those behaviors, provide meaning, and increase understanding. Thus, an important role is for the psychologist to interpret such behaviors within a social competency perspective (e.g., teacher-student, child-peer, or parent-child interactions) or an information processing or psychological processing framework (e.g., describing the role that attending, memory, recall, self-monitoring, and motor skill integration can have in a student's learning and achievement). The school psychologist is frequently the best and often the only resource person within a school to offer these perspectives. These perspectives will be very important in the analysis, design, and implementation of any student's RTI intervention.

Further, school psychologists' experiences in assessment and instructional and behavioral interventions will assist in RTI implementation through strategic planning, staff development, and technical assistance to school staff and parents. In a technical role, they can help in the development and implementation of behavioral observation and curriculum-based assessment measures important to student screening and progress monitoring. School psychologists can help schools address the needs of all students through accurate monitoring of students' learning rates, achievements, and behaviors, as well as the development and outcomes of interventions.

Fidelity checks are an important part of RTI. School psychologists can have an important role in helping schools establish the procedures for fidelity checks. If instruction is not of high quality and delivered with fidelity, students are perceived as having problems and efforts are directed toward those students rather than the larger issue of poor or inconsistent instruction affecting all students.

—Daryl F. Mellard

See also Learning Disabilities

REFERENCES AND FURTHER READING

Case, L., Molloy, D., & Speece, D. (2003). Responsiveness to general education instruction as the first gate to learning disabilities identification. *Learning Disabilities Research and Practice, 18,* 147–156.

Fuchs, L. S. (2003). Assessing intervention responsiveness: Conceptual and technical issues. *Learning Disabilities Research and Practice, 18,* 172–186.

Fuchs, D., Mock, D., Morgan, P., & Young, C. (2003). Responsiveness to intervention: Definitions, evidence, and implications for the learning disabilities construct. *Learning Disabilities Research and Practice, 18,* 157–171.

Hickman, P., Linan-Thompson, S., & Vaughn, S. (2003). Response to instruction as a means of identifying students with reading/learning disabilities. *Exceptional Children, 69*, 391–410.

RETENTION AND PROMOTION

Grade retention is defined as the practice of requiring a student who has attended a given grade level for a full school year to remain at that same grade level for the following school year. Other commonly used terms to describe grade retention are "being retained," "being held back," "nonpromotion," and "flunking." Recent estimates suggest that 5% to 10% of students are retained annually in the United States, which translates to more than 2.5 million children every year who are required to complete an extra year of school. The use of grade retention as an academic intervention has increased over the past 30 years. Grade retention is increasingly popular within the current sociopolitical climate, which emphasizes high standards and accountability.

Considering its popularity as an academic intervention, one might assume that grade retention is highly effective and beneficial for students who are struggling—academically, behaviorally, and/or socially—within the school context. However, the convergence of research suggests that grade retention is quite the opposite—in other words, it is an ineffective and discriminatory policy. Considering the abundance of information research has provided regarding the effectiveness (lack thereof) of grade retention as an intervention to address academic, social–emotional, and behavioral problems, the increasing use and expense in the United States has led to numerous debates. The relevant research provides essential information regarding:

- Individual, family, and demographic characteristics of retained students
- The effectiveness of grade retention in addressing academic, social–emotional, and behavioral problems
- Long-term outcomes associated with grade retention
- The perceived stressfulness of grade retention from students' perspectives

CHARACTERISTICS OF RETAINED STUDENTS

Numerous studies have examined the gender and ethnic characteristics of retained students. Boys are twice as likely to repeat a grade as girls, and retention rates are higher for minority students, particularly African American and Latino children. In general, retained students have lower achievement scores relative to the average student in a classroom. Yet, it is essential to consider additional characteristics of this population because low achievement is not a distinguishing characteristic among retained and promoted students when studied in isolation. Compared to equally low-achieving but promoted peers, research reveals that retained students do not consistently have lower intelligence quotient (IQ) scores. However, children who are retained are more likely to have mothers with lower IQ scores than their peers who are promoted despite low academic achievement. Another significant factor in determining whether a student will be retained is the level of parents' involvement in school and their attitude toward their child's education. Low parent involvement and a less-than-positive attitude toward their child's education are associated with a child who is more likely to be retained.

Students who are retained are often reported as experiencing difficulties in both intrapersonal and interpersonal areas. Within these realms, factors contributing to the decision to retain include significantly less confidence, less self-assuredness, less engagement, greater levels of immaturity, and evidence of more behavior problems compared to their similarly low-achieving, but promoted peers. Teachers have also reported that retained students are less popular and less socially competent than their peers. Thus, it is evident that social behavior plays a significant role in the decision of whether to use retention as an intervention. Available research indicates that retained students are a diverse group of children with an assortment of challenges influencing their low achievement, behavior problems, and poor classroom adjustment.

EFFECTIVENESS OF GRADE RETENTION

Statistical meta-analyses provide a synthesis of studies of grade retention research published between 1925 and 1999. Meta-analysis methodology incorporates a statistical procedure that yields an "effect size." The use of effect sizes is a means for researchers to systematically pool results across studies. Analyses resulting in a negative effect size indicate that an intervention (i.e., grade retention) had a negative or harmful effect relative to the comparison groups of promoted students. Meta-analyses examining the effectiveness of grade retention have included academic achievement, behavior problems, and social adjustment.

Effects on Academic Achievement

Overall, academic advantages for retained students relative to comparison groups of low-achieving promoted peers have not been demonstrated in the research. A meta-analysis of research examining the effectiveness of grade retention (Holmes, 1989) reported that among 63 published studies, 54 yielded negative achievement effects for retained students. Only nine studies revealed positive short-term achievement effects (during the repeated grade the following year), and these short-term benefits were found to diminish over time, disappearing entirely in later grades. The overall effect sizes for academic achievement outcomes in the Holmes and Matthews (1984) and Holmes (1989) meta-analyses were −.44 and −.19, respectively.

The most recent meta-analysis examining 20 studies published between 1990 and 1999 (Jimerson, 2001) revealed that 5% of 169 analyses of academic achievement outcomes resulted in significant statistical differences favoring the retained students, whereas 47% resulted in significant statistical differences favoring the comparison groups of low-achieving peers. Of the analyses that did favor the retained students, 33% of them reflected differences during the repeated year (e.g., second year in kindergarten). Moreover, these initial gains were not maintained over time. Analyses examining the effects of retention on language arts, reading, and math yielded moderate to strong negative effects (ES = −.36, −.54, −.49, respectively). Notably, decisions regarding grade retention are often based on reading skills; however, research reveals that grade retention appears to be an ineffective intervention to improve reading skills. Thus, grade retention appears to be contraindicated for children with reading problems. These findings indicate that across published studies, low-achieving, but promoted students outperformed retained students in language arts, reading, and math. The overall average effect size across academic achievement outcomes

was −.39. Altogether, the results of meta-analyses examining more than 80 studies during the past 75 years, including nearly 700 analyses of achievement, do not support the use of grade retention as an early intervention to enhance academic achievement.

Effects on Social Adjustment and Behavior

Relatively fewer studies have addressed the social adjustment and behavioral outcomes of retained students. The results of these studies indicate that grade retention fails to improve problem behaviors and can have harmful effects on social–emotional and behavioral adjustment as well. The Holmes (1989) meta-analysis examined more than 40 studies including 234 analyses of social–emotional outcomes. It concluded that, on average, the retained students displayed poorer social adjustment, more negative attitudes toward school, less frequent attendance, and more problem behaviors in comparison to groups of matched controls. Jimerson's (2001) meta-analysis examined 16 studies that yielded 148 analyses of social–emotional adjustment outcomes of retained students relative to a matched comparison group of students. The overall average effect size regarding social adjustment and behavior outcomes across studies published between 1990 and 1999 was −.22. Related research reveals that retained students may be teased or have difficulties with their peers. Overall, results of the meta-analyses of more than 300 analyses of social–emotional and behavioral adjustment (from more than 50 studies during the past 75 years) do not support the use of grade retention as an early intervention to enhance social–emotional and behavioral adjustment.

High School Dropout and Grade Retention

There is considerable literature examining high school dropout rates that identifies grade retention as an early predictor variable. Grade retention has been identified as the single most powerful predictor of dropping out, even when controlling for other characteristics associated with dropping out. A review (Jimerson & colleagues, 2002) of 17 studies examining factors associated with dropping out of high school prior to graduation supports the findings that grade retention is one of the most robust predictors of

---

Point Versus Counterpoint: Grade Retention

The case for:

The most common reasons provided in support of grade retention include: immaturity, not meeting educational standards, traumatic injuries, and personal experiences with retention (i.e., anecdotal evidence). Immaturity—physically, socially, and/or behaviorally—is a common reason given when retention is recommended for a child in the elementary grades, the position is often advocated that this will "give the child a year to grow." In some instances, late birthdays are offered as a supporting reason provided for the recommendation of retention for many "immature" students. A phrase that is often mentioned by proponents of retention is, "It was successful for ___ when retained." Many education professionals cite examples of positive outcomes in students for whom they recommended retention. Particularly in the elementary grades, educational professionals are less hesitant to retain, believing that retention would be less deleterious for a student in kindergarten or first grade, relative to middle school or high school. The high academic and behavioral standards expected of students beginning in the elementary years impact decisions regarding retention for students now more than ever. In some cases, if a child is unable to meet district or state standards, it is required that he or she be retained. Even if not required, anticipating that a child will experience great difficulty if promoted to the next grade level, teachers are faced with a difficult decision whether to promote or retain. Lastly, students who have experienced a traumatic injury (e.g., brain injury) are sometimes recommended for retention. The rationale is that the student missed an excessive amount of school days because of the injury and may need time to recover and catch up with his or her peers.

The case against:

Extensive and long-term research focusing on the effectiveness of grade retention reveals that it is associated with deleterious outcomes. While short-term improvements among retained students may be noted in a few studies, the long-term negative effects of retention are consistently documented. Students who have been retained are at a much greater risk of dropping out of high school, engaging in antisocial behaviors, and experiencing poorer educational and employment opportunities. Furthermore, students at various grade levels have rated the prospect of being retained as one of the most stressful life events. Considering the cumulative evidence, students who have been retained do not excel in any areas above and beyond their lower-achieving, yet promoted peers. Thus, given the convergence of research, the use of grade retention as an academic intervention is discouraged. Instead, those interventions that have been demonstrated to be effective in facilitating academic and developmental outcomes should be implemented. The primary objective should be to promote the social and cognitive competence of students and enhance their academic success.

school dropout. All studies of school dropout that included grade retention found that it was associated with subsequent school withdrawal. Several of these studies included statistical analyses controlling for many individual and family variables commonly associated with dropping out (i.e., social–emotional adjustment, socioeconomic status, ethnicity, achievement, gender, parental level of education, and parental involvement). Research indicates that retained students are between 2 and 11 times more likely to drop out during high school than nonretained students, and that grade retention increases the risk of dropping out between 20% and 50%.

Long-Term Outcomes Associated with Grade Retention

In addition to increasing the likelihood of dropping out of high school, grade retention is associated with other long-term negative outcomes. The results of longitudinal research provide evidence that retained students have a greater probability of poorer educational and employment outcomes during late adolescence relative to a comparison group of low-achieving, but promoted students. Specifically, retained students are reported to have lower levels of academic adjustment at the end of 11th grade, more likely to drop out of high school by age 19 years, and less likely to receive a diploma by age 20. They were also less likely to be enrolled in a postsecondary education program, received lower education/employment status ratings, and were paid less per hour.

STUDENTS' PERSPECTIVES ON GRADE RETENTION

It is also important to consider children's perspectives regarding grade retention. In a study published in 1987, students in first, third, and sixth grade were asked to rate 20 stressful life events that included such occurrences as losing a parent, going to the dentist, and getting a bad report card. The results indicated that sixth-grade students reported only the loss of a parent and going blind as more stressful than grade retention. This study was replicated in 2001, and it was found that sixth-grade students rated grade retention as the single most stressful life event, higher than both the loss of a parent and going blind. A developmental trend was noted in both studies, with the reported stress of grade retention increasing from first, to third, to sixth grade. Thus, research indicates that children perceive grade retention as extremely stressful.

While retention may seem appealing in the short term as a solution for children who are experiencing academic, behavioral, and/or social difficulties in school, there is substantial empirical evidence contraindicating

its use. Research during the past century examining the effectiveness of grade retention consistently indicates the potential for negative outcomes. In light of this cumulative research evidence, it is imperative that educational professionals and parents alike consider evidence-based alternatives (i.e., empirically supported alternative strategies) to promote the social and cognitive competence of children at risk for academic failure.

—*Shane R. Jimerson and Sarah M. Woehr*

See also Academic Achievement; Friendships; Grades; Race, Ethnicity, Class, and Gender; Special Education

REFERENCES AND FURTHER READING

Holmes, C. T. (1989). Grade-level retention effects: A meta-analysis of research studies. In L. A. Shepard & M. L. Smith (Eds.), *Flunking grades: Research and policies on retention* (pp. 16–33). London: Falmer.

Holmes, C. T., & Matthews, K. M. (1984). The effects of non-promotion on elementary and junior high school pupils: A meta-analysis. *Reviews of Educational Research, 54,* 225–236.

Jimerson, S. R. (2001). Meta-analysis of grade retention research: Implications for practice in the 21st century. *School Psychology Review, 30,* 420–437.

Jimerson, S. R., Anderson, G. E., & Whipple, A. D. (2002). Winning the battle and losing the war: Examining the relation between grade retention and dropping out of high school. *Psychology in the Schools, 39*(4), 441–457.

RETT'S DISORDER. *See* AUTISM SPECTRUM DISORDERS

S

SATIATION. *See* BEHAVIORAL
CONCEPTS AND APPLICATIONS

SCHEDULES OF REINFORCEMENT

The term *schedule of reinforcement* refers to the timing with which reinforcement is delivered for a certain behavior. This scheduling is important because different schedules produce different effects on behavior. The most basic type of schedule is one in which reinforcement follows every occurrence of the behavior. This type of schedule is referred to as continuous reinforcement (CRF) and should be used when teaching new behaviors; it is characterized by high rates of responding. For example, if Bob is shy but responds well to teacher praise, the teacher may institute a CRF schedule in which every time Bob offers an answer in class, teacher praise immediately follows. For this type of schedule to be truly continuous, each and every instance of the behavior must be followed by reinforcement.

A classroom teacher with many students and responsibilities may find it difficult and cumbersome to try to reinforce each and every occurrence of a particular behavior. Fortunately, the principles of learning and what we know about the effects of different schedules of reinforcement suggest that the teacher doesn't have to, and actually shouldn't, reinforce on a continuous schedule for very long. In fact, once the teacher gets the behavior going in the desired direction (e.g., it starts to increase and shows signs of acquisition), it is actually better to start to gradually taper the frequency of reinforcement. Teachers must be careful, however, not to terminate or fade the schedule too quickly once the student begins to respond under the CRF schedule.

In contrast to CRF, the term *intermittent reinforcement* is used to describe schedules in which reinforcement occurs every so often, but not after each response. In classrooms, intermittent schedules are very useful because they are not as prone to satiation effects (behaviors stop because too many reinforcers have been delivered) as are CRF schedules, are not as cumbersome to implement and administer, and produce behaviors that are more resistant to extinction, meaning that these behaviors won't extinguish easily if the teacher forgets to reinforce occasionally. Intermittent schedules also produce behavior that occurs at a high, steady rate. In general, intermittent schedules can be categorized into ratio and interval schedules, and each of these can be further classified as fixed or variable; thus, we can have fixed ratio, variable ratio, fixed interval, and variable interval schedules.

RATIO SCHEDULES

As the name implies, a ratio schedule focuses on the number of occurrences of a behavior. This predetermined number of occurrences determines when a reinforcer is delivered. The first type of ratio schedule is a fixed-ratio schedule of reinforcement (FR). The CRF schedule mentioned earlier is actually a special type of fixed-ratio schedule called an FR1 schedule, because every occurrence of the behavior produces reinforcement.

The number following the symbol FR designates how many times the behavior must occur before reinforcement is delivered. For example, in an FR4 schedule, reinforcement would follow the fourth occurrence of the behavior. Say that a student is working on a math worksheet and the teacher wanted to reinforce problem completion. Under an FR4 schedule, no reinforcement would follow completion of the first three problems, but once the student completed the fourth problem, the teacher would deliver reinforcement.

Sometimes, teachers may inadvertently move to higher ratios too quickly. When first introducing reinforcement, especially with new behaviors, it is most effective to start with CRF (i.e., FR1) schedules, and then gradually move to higher ratios. Reinforcement that follows fewer responses (e.g., CFR, FR2), is a very rich schedule of reinforcement. Moving to higher-ratio requirements is called thinning the reinforcement schedule. Eventually, it is appropriate in classrooms to move to thinner schedules of reinforcement, but thinning these schedules out too quickly can inadvertently produce extinction effects. The term *ratio strain* is used to describe instances in which a rich ratio schedule is thinned out too quickly. For example, if a teacher initially reinforces a student for correct letter recognition on an FR1 (or CRF) schedule and then immediately moves to an FR10 schedule, student responding may quickly extinguish.

Fixed-ratio schedules lead to very predictable patterns of student response when used in classrooms. Ratio schedules often lead to moderate and consistent rates of responding. Additionally, as the ratio increases in size, students may demonstrate a pause in responding immediately after the reinforcer is delivered. This is known as a postreinforcement pause. With larger ratios, the student will demonstrate larger pauses. With very small FR schedules, the postreinforcement pause may not be noticeable.

In most classroom settings fixed-ratio schedules (except for FR1 or CRF for new behaviors) are less commonly used for extended periods of time. A variable-ratio schedule (VR) is more common and is one in which reinforcement occurs after some average number of responses rather than a fixed number. For example, under a VR4 schedule, the teacher would reinforce after an average of four responses. Under such a schedule, the teacher could deliver reinforcement after two, four, eight, or more responses, as long as the average delivery of reinforcement equals four. In a classroom, a teacher may give a student stickers under a VR schedule for proper hand-raising behavior. Under a VR2 schedule, the teacher would deliver a sticker, on average, after every two hand raises. The teacher would benefit from planning out the averages before instituting the schedule to keep up with the requirements of the VR schedule.

Because of the unpredictable nature of reinforcement delivery, VR schedules typically produce higher and steadier rates of behavior than FR schedules. Additionally, VR schedules produce behavior that is more resistant to extinction than FR schedules. Lastly, VR schedules do not typically result in postreinforcement pauses as is seen with FR schedules.

INTERVAL SCHEDULES

Interval schedules deliver reinforcement based on time and the occurrence of a target behavior. Under a fixed-interval schedule (FI), reinforcement is delivered for the first response following a fixed period (i.e., interval) of time. For example, in an FI3-minute schedule, the teacher would reinforce a student (perhaps with stickers) the first time the behavior of interest (e.g., on task) occurs after a three-minute period. Under FI schedules, responding is slower near the beginning of the interval and continues to increase, becoming more frequent at or near the end of the interval. This is known as fixed-interval scalloping. Fixed interval schedules are typically easier for teachers to manage because timers can be used to signal the delivery of reinforcement, and unlike with ratio schedules, teachers need not monitor and keep up with each occurrence of student behavior.

In a variable-interval schedule (VI), reinforcement is delivered after some average period of time. This period of time is not fixed and averages some predetermined amount of time. Altering the above example, the teacher may decide to give smiley stickers for the first occurrence of on-task behavior by each student after three minutes, then after eight minutes. This type of schedule would be referred to as a VI5-minute schedule of reinforcement in that reinforcement is delivered every five minutes on average. Similar to VR schedules, the delivery of reinforcement at variable times leads to higher and more consistent levels of student responding than either of the fixed schedules, and variable-interval schedules are not associated with the scalloped responding seen with FI schedules. Using a VI schedule also typically produces behaviors that are highly resistant to extinction.

CONCLUSION

When teachers understand and monitor the delivery of reinforcement, they increase their chances of success in their classrooms. Continuous reinforcement is preferred when teaching new behaviors, but teachers should strive to eventually transition to intermittent schedules. Reinforcement can be delivered based on the number of times a behavior occurs (ratio schedules) or on the passage of time (interval schedules). Additionally, the delivery of reinforcement can be fixed (by occurrences or time) or variable. With any FR or FI schedule, teachers can expect some pauses in behavior following the delivery of reinforcement as a function of the schedule. In an FR schedule, there will be pauses immediately following the delivery of reinforcement (postreinforcement pause). With FI schedules, responding will be less frequent at the beginning of the interval and more frequent near the end (fixed-interval scallop). Variable schedules (VR and VI) are associated with steadier rates of responding without pauses or scallops. Intermittent schedules are typically more resistant to extinction than continuous reinforcement. Effective use of these schedules of reinforcement can enhance the teaching and ultimate acquisition of new behaviors and assist in the management of problematic behaviors in the classroom.

—Daniel H. Tingstrom
and James W. Moore

See also Behavior; Behavior Intervention; Generalization; Self-Management

REFERENCES AND FURTHER READING

Alberto, P. A., & Troutman, A. C. (2003). *Applied behavior analysis for teachers* (6th ed.). Upper Saddle River, NJ: Prentice Hall.

Cooper, J. O., Heron, T. E., & Heward, W. L. (1987). *Applied behavior analysis.* Upper Saddle River, NJ: Prentice Hall.

Malott, R. W., Malott, M. E., & Trojan, E. A. (2000). *Elementary principles of behavior* (4th ed.). Upper Saddle River, NJ: Prentice Hall.

SCHOOL CLIMATE

School climate is a complex construct consisting of multiple components (Freiberg, 1999). Various aspects include the:

- Quality of interpersonal relations between students and teachers
- Extent to which the school is perceived as a safe and caring place
- Degree to which students, parents, and staff are involved in collaborative decision making
- Degree to which there are high expectations for student learning

A school that has a positive school climate is perceived as welcoming (to students, parents, and staff) and is characterized by respectful interactions between individuals. Students are motivated to achieve, and staff convey the importance of school and learning. The school is clean, well maintained, and inviting. The combination of these characteristics results in the school being perceived as a good place.

Over the years research has documented a variety of outcomes that are associated with school climate (Lehr & Christenson, 2002). It is consistently identified as a variable that is a key ingredient of effective schools and is positively associated with academic effectiveness. Studies demonstrate a link between positive school climate and higher levels of achievement in reading, math, and writing. In addition, students who attend schools with positive school climates are more likely to have favorable attitudes toward school (motivation for schooling, academic self-concept) and satisfaction with schooling. Fewer behavior problems and higher levels of attendance are also associated with a positive school climate.

A variety of school characteristics related to school climate are also associated with negative school outcomes. For example, schools with weak adult authority, punitive discipline, a climate of low expectations, and absence of caring relationships between staff and students have higher absentee levels and higher dropout rates. Schools that have large enrollments also risk higher proportions of students who feel alienated and become disengaged from school and learning.

These findings have implications for school policies and practices that educators can influence. School policies that foster positive climates include a strong academic press and relevant curriculum, purposeful inclusion of all students in academic activities and learning, and high-quality instruction. In addition, schools with discipline policies that are clear, fair, and effective, tend to engage students in school and yield more positive outcomes (e.g., fewer disciplinary problems, higher rates of attendance). Schools that are organized into smaller learning communities allow more opportunities to create positive climates that can engage students, in part, by providing more individual attention and through relationship building.

Many programs and strategies have been developed to foster positive school climates (Scherer, 1998). It is clear that there is not one best program or strategy to use. Efforts range from single strategies that are designed to address an aspect of a school climate to large-scale programs within the context of school reform. For example, to create a more welcoming learning community, students and staff may decide to implement a strategy in the morning where students are greeted by name and with a smile as they enter the school. In other cases, a school climate committee may be formed that works collaboratively to assess the school's climate, determine areas of strength and need, set goals, and design interventions that address the identified issues. More recently, efforts to create more positive learning environments have occurred within the context of implementing universal interventions that are delivered to all students within a school (e.g., positive behavioral supports). Other programs that promote peaceful conflict resolution, prevent bullying, or increase school safety are also examples of programs that can be used to improve school climate. Building positive learning environments is a continuous process that must be revisited and modified regularly. Efforts to improve school climate that adhere to best practices include initial measures of key stakeholders' perceptions of school climate (e.g., students, parents, staff, community members), and ongoing measures that provide feedback about the impact of the intervention as it is being implemented.

School psychologists are in key positions to effect positive changes in school climate. School psychologists can work in collaboration with other key players to create positive learning environments that engage students, parents, and staff. Disseminating information about the impact that school climate can have on student outcomes is an important contribution. Additionally, school psychologists can offer knowledge about associated research, ways of measuring school climate, and examples of effective strategies. Addressing issues associated with school climate is a powerful, preventive approach that can be used to facilitate student engagement with school and learning resulting in positive student outcomes.

—*Camilla A. Lehr*

See also Discipline; Dropouts; High School; Middle School; Multicultural Education; School Reform; Violence in Schools

REFERENCES AND FURTHER READING

Freiberg, J. H. (1999). *School climate: Measuring, improving and sustaining healthy learning environments.* London: Falmer.

Lehr, C. A., & Christenson, S. L. (2002). Promoting positive school climate. In A. Thomas & J. Grimes (Eds.), *Best practices in school psychology IV* (pp. 929–947). Bethesda, MD: National Association of School Psychologists.

Scherer, M. M. (Ed.). (1998). Realizing a positive school climate. *Educational Leadership, 56*(1), 8–71.

SCHOOL COUNSELORS

A school counselor is a licensed professional educator trained to address the needs of students by implementing a standards-based school counseling program. School counselors are employed in elementary, middle/junior high, and senior high schools, and in postsecondary settings. Their work requires attention to developmental stages of student growth, as well as to the needs, tasks, and student interests related to those stages. School counselors work with all students, including those who are considered at risk and those who have special needs. Although best known for their role in counseling students with mental health concerns, school counselors also are responsible for prevention and health promotion programs. They are specialists in human behavior and education, and they provide assistance to students through four primary interventions:

1. Counseling (individual and group)

2. Large-group guidance

3. Consultation

4. Coordination

Their school psychologist colleagues also work to optimize students' health and learning, but they typically provide assistance through consultation and assessment.

—*Shane J. Lopez and*
Heather N. Rasmussen

See also Counseling

SCHOOL–HOME NOTES

A school–home note, otherwise referred to as a daily report card, is a means of sharing information from classroom to home and back to classroom regarding a student's behavior and/or academic performance. This procedure requires that parents and teachers communicate to alleviate the student's difficulties in the classroom. Parents may provide consequences at home that may increase the likelihood of success. A school–home note allows for parents to become directly involved with the progress of their student. It also involves minimal time on the part of the teacher.

According to Kelly (1990), a quality school–home note program involves a parent-teacher conference in which acceptable or desirable behavior for the student is discussed. Next the parents and teacher should define specific, observable behaviors and form clearly defined goals for improvement. After the target behavior and goals have been identified, the parents and the teacher include the student and develop the school–home note with clear expectations for each member. Then, with the help of the child, a set of daily and weekly rewards should be provided for satisfactory performance. Finally the school–home note should be implemented with frequent verbal feedback and praise along with the promised consequences.

The behaviors that can be addressed by a school–home note include classroom behavior and academic problems. Kelly (1990) identified recommended behaviors to be targeted by a school–home note program:

- School work completion
- Using class time well
- Talking only with permission
- Being prepared for class
- Handing in homework
- Playing nicely with other children

Elliot and colleagues (1999) state that school–home notes may not be appropriate for students with severe behavior problems and academic deficiencies, or for students who come from a dysfunctional family. They also state that a school–home note has a variety of advantages. It requires collaboration between parents and teachers in problem solving and provides frequent feedback emphasizing positive rather than negative behavior. The focus on positive behavior may increase a student's self-esteem and motivation. The small time commitment required for implementation increases the likelihood of acceptability and follow-through of the program. The increased parental involvement may also enhance the support of the intervention and its ability to be maintained in different environments.

A school psychologist may assist the parent or teacher in the development of the school–home note. This may be done through "conjoint behavioral consultation" when both the parent and the teacher are included.

—*Amy Conklin*

See also Consultation: Conjoint Behavioral; Intervention; Motivation; Parenting

REFERENCES AND FURTHER READING

Elliot, S. N., Busse, R. T., & Shapiro, E. S. (1999). Intervention techniques for academic performance problems. In C. R. Reynolds & T. B. Gutkin (Eds.), *The handbook of school psychology* (pp. 664–685). New York: John Wiley.

Kelly, M. L. (1990). *School-home notes promoting children's classroom success.* New York: Guilford.

SCHOOL PSYCHOLOGIST

The history of school psychology may be appropriately described as one of continuous evolution and expansion. Yet the foundations of many, if not most, current practices and professional issues are found in the earliest years of the profession. For example, the roles of the school psychologist (testing and placement, assessment and treatment, consultant and health care provider), the inextricable relationship between school psychology and special education, and the influence of social reforms and state and federal legislation on the profession were all anticipated in the earliest years of the profession's development.

THE EARLIEST YEARS

The beginning of school psychology is commonly associated with Lightner Witmer and the opening of the first "psychological clinic" at the University of Pennsylvania in 1896. As a result of requests he received to help children with school-related problems, Witmer turned part of his scientific laboratory into a clinic to diagnose and treat children with such problems. Witmer suggested the term "clinical" psychology to describe his research and services for children. As a result he is considered the founder of both clinical and school psychology. Witmer's primary interest was the application of the young science of psychology to solve problems for individual children, especially problems related to school.

At roughly the same time, work by Francis Galton, James Cattell, and Alfred Binet on the development of mental tests was to have a powerful influence on the field of school psychology. Both Galton and Cattell conducted experimental attempts to develop individual intelligence tests. However, modern intelligence testing and its application to education are most directly linked to the work of Binet. In 1904, Binet was appointed to a commission by the French government to develop a test to identify children most likely to benefit from placement in special classes. Working with a colleague, Theodore Simon, Binet developed a series of tests published in 1908, the Binet-Simon Scales of Intelligence. Binet introduced the notion of a mental "level" and proposed the first classification of intelligence based on the test results. A mental level was determined by how far the score of a particular child was in years from the average score of normal children of the same age. Binet then proposed that a child with a mental level that was two years below the average score of normal children of the same age should be classified as below normal and placed in special classes. The Binet-Simon test was revised in 1916 by Lewis Terman at Stanford University and later became known as the Stanford-Binet Intelligence Scales. With this revision, the concept of a mental level or mental age was replaced with the intelligence quotient (IQ), defined as the mental age divided by the chronological age. The Stanford-Binet became widely used in the United States, and intelligence testing and the identification of children with special needs became a foundation of early school psychology.

The period between 1890 and 1920 is generally considered a progressive era of social reform, and many of these reforms either directly or indirectly promoted interest in the emerging profession of school psychology. Important events during this time included the enactment of child labor laws (which recognized childhood as a unique period of life), the development of juvenile courts and associated child guidance clinics, and, perhaps most important to school psychology, the enactment of compulsory education laws.

Compulsory education laws brought many children from widely diverse backgrounds into school for the first time. The combination of a dramatic increase in enrollment and the wide variation of students' ability and achievement levels created a need for professionals who could assist in "sorting" children into appropriate educational levels and placements, including classes for children who were truant, delinquent, or labeled as "backward." Compulsory education simultaneously highlighted the need for special education services that would help children who were struggling in the classroom. If all children were compelled to attend school, then schools might logically be required to provide services for all children. Thus, two of school psychology's most enduring roles—the school psychologist as a "sorter" of children into educational placements and as a "gatekeeper" regulating the flow of children into special education—were facilitated by compulsory education.

The term *school psychologist* was first used in a 1911 publication. However, the term did not enter general usage until many years later. Rather, the term *clinical* was used generically in the early 20th century to refer to all applied psychologists—engaged in solving practical problems of the school or workplace. The first clinic facilities associated with a school were established in the Chicago Public Schools in 1899 as a research facility associated with the larger Child Study Movement founded by G. Stanley Hall and devoted to the depiction of children's behavior. However, the clinic later provided services that included group testing and individual treatments. Child guidance clinics, previously associated with delinquency and the early juvenile courts, also began to provide therapy services in the schools in the 1920s. However, these early clinical services in the schools were short-lived as educators questioned their usefulness for school-related problems.

The first person with the official title of a School Psychologist is generally considered to be Arnold Gesell, who was hired by the state of Connecticut in 1915. His primary function was to test children for possible special class placement.

PROFESSIONAL DEVELOPMENT

The creation and growth of the profession of school psychology gained momentum between the 1920s and

1960s. The development of a professional identity and organizations and descriptions of roles and functions, as well as the formation of training and certification programs were preeminent concerns during this time.

An important milestone was the publication in 1930 of the first text with an exclusive focus on school psychology entitled, *Psychological Service for School Problems* by Gertrude Hildreth. The text described the activities of the school psychologist and suggested possibilities for the further development and expansion of the field. It might be noted that Hildreth's account of a typical day for a school psychologist is remarkably similar to current practice in many areas of the United States.

Professional organizations play an essential role in the development, growth, and continued strength of every profession. School psychologists are represented by two prominent professional organizations. The first professional organization founded exclusively for school psychologists was the Division of School Psychology (Division 16) within the American Psychological Association (APA). Division 16 was founded in 1945 to represent the interests of psychologists practicing in school settings. Full membership in APA (and thus Division 16) requires a PhD. As the number of practicing school psychologists grew (from roughly 200 in 1920 to 5,000 in 1970 [Fagan, 1992]), many began to believe that Division 16 and the APA were not adequately representing the unique interests of nondoctoral school psychology practitioners. In 1969, the National Association of School Psychologists (NASP) was formed to actively promote the interests of practicing school psychologists.

The first training program specifically for school psychologists was developed at New York University in the 1920s, followed by Pennsylvania State University in the 1930s. Similarly, the first state credentials for school psychologists were established by New York and Pennsylvania in the 1930s. School psychology training programs increased in number throughout the mid-20th century (there are currently more than 200 programs in the United States). State credentialing of school psychologists followed a parallel course of development with all states providing certification by 1977.

FEDERAL LEGISLATION AND DRAMATIC EXPANSION

If the period between the 1920s and 1960s was one of gradual growth in the number of school psychologists,

the 1970s and 1980s were a time of dramatic expansion. The roughly 5,000 school psychologists in 1970 grew to an estimated 22,000 just 20 years later (Fagan, 1992). This rapid expansion of the field is considered a direct result of federal legislation. In 1975, the Education for All Handicapped Children Act was signed into law (commonly known as Public Law 94–142). This law mandated a "free and appropriate" public education for all handicapped children, many of whom had been excluded from public schools up until this time. The law placed an emphasis on special education but also mandated "related" services that included psychological services. The law further defined specific categories of handicaps that entitled children to special education. The school psychologist subsequently became essential to determining the existence of these specific handicaps, and consequently a child's eligibility for now-mandated special education. As a result, the demand for school psychologists dramatically increased across the United States. The Education for All Handicapped Children Act was revised and reauthorized in 1990 and retitled the Individuals With Disabilities Education Act (IDEA).

The Education for All Handicapped Children Act has been described by some as a mixed blessing for school psychology. While the law expanded the prominence and number of job opportunities, it also solidified the role of the school psychologist as the "gatekeeper" to special education. As a result, some have suggested that the legal mandate for assessment and classification came at the expense of limiting school psychologists' opportunities to conduct treatment and consultation. School psychologists currently continue to spend a majority of their time conducting assessment-related activities. However, Witmer's early emphasis on the treatment of school-related problems for individual children continues to thrive and expand, while many of Hildreth's suggestions for the expansion of school psychological services, such as direct assessment and intervention for academic problems, have become more common.

CURRENT IDENTITY OF SCHOOL PSYCHOLOGY

School psychology in the 21st century has evolved beyond its origins to address the needs of children and their families in all settings. In the United States, school psychologists work in schools, mental health agencies, hospitals, private practice, and other locations that provide services to families. The two largest professional associations, NASP and the American Psychological Association's Division 16, offer complementary perspectives on training and practice, the first serving as the main voice of psychologists employed in schools, the latter providing a link to all other domains and practice settings of psychology.

For school-based practitioners, changes in federal priorities for education have influenced expectations for service. Beginning in the late 1990s, leaders in the profession have urged both psychologists and educators to shift service priorities away from assessment, focusing more on interventions that address the academic needs of children. A related movement in the mental health fields that recognized the influence of the environment on behavior produced two additional shifts in service priorities: inclusion of all children in general education settings, and involvement of the family in every phase of service planning and delivery.

The NASP has continued to update training and practice guidelines, distributing the following publications to training programs and practitioners:

- *Standards for Training and Field Placement Programs in School Psychology*
- *Standards for the Credentialing of School Psychologists*
- *Professional Conduct Manual*
- *Principles for Professional Ethics and Guidelines for the Provision of School Psychological Services*

As part of a strategy to improve the delivery of school psychological services, NASP has instituted a national certification system. A Nationally Certified School Psychologist (NCSP) meets specific training and practice standards and is responsible for ongoing professional development. The NCSP system allows a uniform standard of preparation and practice to be implemented nationwide.

Training programs in school psychology usually offer a degree based on 60 semester-hours of graduate preparation (the NASP standard) or an advanced program of studies leading to the PhD. NASP, through its program-approval process and affiliation with the National Council for Accreditation of Teacher Education (NCATE), and APA, via its program-accreditation process with doctoral-level programs in professional psychology, provide two avenues and structures for program development. Because APA does not accredit nondoctoral programs, the majority of school psychology programs, which are nondoctoral, strive to address NASP standards.

JOB DESCRIPTION AND EMPLOYMENT SETTINGS

Given the ways in which kindergarten through 12th grade (K–12) education is funded and administered, there is wide variation in the duties of school-based psychologists. School psychologists tend to:

- Provide assessment
- Plan and deliver interventions with children and families (school and nonschool setting)
- Counsel students in individual and group settings
- Provide consultation to teachers, administrators, community agencies, and other agencies

Many psychologists engage in duties beyond the classroom, providing supervision to other professionals, participating in grant writing and programs funded by private and governmental agencies, engaging in training activities, conducting research and evaluation, and other duties required by the employer. Depending on the state, school psychological services can be based in a school district, other education or mental health agencies that support schools, or other professional groups that contract to the schools.

School psychologists employed in settings outside of K–12 education might work at a university (as a trainer or psychologist in a health clinic), a hospital or other health care provider setting, private practice, and additional private and public sector locations that require the skills of a psychologist.

SUPPLY AND DEMAND IN THE JOB MARKET

The current outlook for employment is stable or improving. The American Association for Employment in Education, which monitors employment trends across the United States, has noted overall shortages in recent years that tend to be concentrated in the Midwest, Northeast, and South Central regions of the United States. Training programs report stable or growing numbers of applicants, promising a steady supply of new professionals. Some concern has been expressed (Curtis & colleagues, 2003) regarding

Typical Workday of a School Psychologist

School psychologists tailor their services to the particular needs of each child and situation. School psychologists use many different approaches, but most provide these core services:

Consultation	* Engaging in problem-solving activities with teachers, parents, and administrators about problems in learning and behavior * Helping others understand child development and how it affects learning and behavior * Strengthening working relationships between educators, parents, and community services
Assessment	Using tests and other materials to assess: * Academic skills * Classroom behavior * Personality and emotional development * Social skills * Eligibility for special education
Intervention and Prevention	* Working directly with children and families * Solving conflicts and problems in the classroom * Providing counseling services to children and families * Supporting teachers by offering social skills training, behavior management, and other strategies * Offering crisis intervention * Developing schoolwide programs that enhance mental health
Education	Delivering in-service workshops and other group presentations on topics such as: * Teaching and learning strategies * Classroom management techniques * Working with students who have disabilities or unusual talents * Substance abuse * Crisis management
Research and Planning	* Evaluating school services and grant-funded activities * Serving as resident experts on research methodology * Conducting research to expand the professional literature on practice
Health Care Provision	* Collaborating with other professionals to provide mental health services * Working with children and families as a case manager or advocating to ensure the integration of services * Promoting healthy school environments

NOTE: The typical workday will vary widely in every state. Each practitioner will be involved during the school year in a unique mixture of roles and services. We suggest contacting a local school psychologist to discover how practitioners in your area are involved with children, families, and schools.

the future supply of trainers for school psychology programs.

COMPETITIVENESS IN SALARY AND FRINGE BENEFITS WITH OTHER PROVIDERS OF PSYCHOLOGICAL SERVICES

Salaries for school psychologists are influenced by employment setting, years of experience, and educational degree. NASP monitors salaries in the United States. Some data are available online, although current information may not be available. As might be expected, salaries tend to be higher than those for teachers (in many cases, significantly higher). The APA, representing all areas of psychology, has published salary data on employment in nonschool settings. Once again, the setting and the professional's degree and experience influence compensation. In general, school psychologists at the doctoral level earn salaries similar to other psychologists in academic settings, but tend to earn less in nonacademic settings. Benefit packages generally are no different for school psychologists in comparison to other psychologist professions.

LICENSURE REQUIREMENTS

The ability to practice as a school psychologist is regulated across the United States. School-based professionals are required to follow credentialing requirements for the state in which they practice. The NASP offers information on such requirements, which apply at doctoral and nondoctoral levels.

School psychologists in other settings, most importantly at the doctoral degree level, tend to seek licensure as psychologists within the state in which they are employed. Licensure requirements vary in terms of training expectations, postdoctoral supervision, and scores on licensure examinations. The Association of State and Provincial Psychology Boards (ASPPB) provides information on each state's requirements for practice as a psychologist.

FUTURE DIRECTIONS

A 2002 conference considered the future of the profession. Ehrhardt-Padgett, and colleagues (2003) promoted the following agenda for preparing to meet future service needs:

- Acknowledging educational change
- Considering mental health needs
- Using assessment data to plan for intervention
- Engaging in group-focused service delivery
- Promoting collaboration and partnership practices
- Affirming cultural uniqueness of students

Other directions that have been suggested include a shift to a more community-based orientation that acknowledges the importance of home, school, and community influences on children's development. The profession approaches the future with a strong commitment to children, families, and schools.

—Stewart W. Ehly and John A. Northup

See also American Psychological Association; Careers in School Psychology; Division of School Psychology (Division 16); Licensing and Certification in School Psychology; National Association of School Psychologists; Social Workers (School); Special Education

REFERENCES AND FURTHER READING

Curtis, M. J., Grier, J. E. C., & Hunley, S. A. (2003). The changing face of school psychology: Trends in data and projections for the future. *School Psychology Quarterly, 18,* 409–430.

Ehrhardt-Padgett, G. N., Hatzishristou, C., Kitson, J., & Meyers, J. (2003). Awakening to a new dawn: Perspectives on the future of school psychology. *School Psychology Quarterly, 18,* 483–496.

Fagan, T. K. (1992). Compulsory schooling, child study, clinical psychology, and special education: Origins of school psychology. *American Psychologist, 47,* 236–243.

SCHOOL REFORM

Comprehensive school reform (CSR) is a school-improvement approach, especially for low-performing, high-poverty schools, which involves changes in key aspects of a school, from classroom instruction and management to school governance. Rather than adopt strategies to bring about change in individual components (e.g., implementing an innovative reading program, providing a professional development seminar to teachers, adding a computer lab), CSR is an attempt to move toward an overarching framework that guides curriculum, instruction, assessment, professional development, discipline, and other school elements in an integrated fashion (Traub, 1999). The U.S. Department of Education defines CSR on the basis of 11 components (Table 1). A critical feature of CSR (component 11) is the implementation of practices that have been proved to be effective through scientifically based research; that is, the academic performance of students in schools who participate in CSR programs is significantly higher than that of students in nonparticipating schools. The six components of scientifically based research are:

1. Empirical methods
2. Rigorous and adequate data analysis
3. Measurements or observations that provide valid and reliable data
4. Experimental or quasiexperimental evaluation design, in which schools are assigned randomly to experimental or control conditions and the researcher systematically varies procedures implemented in each school
5. Replicability
6. Evaluation by independent expert reviewers

Table 1   Eleven Components of Comprehensive School Reform

1. Employs scientifically based and replicable methods for student learning, teaching, and school management

2. Integrates instruction, assessment, classroom management, professional development, parental involvement, and school management

3. Provides high-quality and continuous teacher and staff professional development

4. Includes measurable goals and benchmarks for student achievement

5. Is supported schoolwide by teachers, principals, administrators, and other staff

6. Provides support for teachers, principals, administrators, and staff through shared leadership and responsibility

7. Provides for involvement of parents and community members

8. Uses high-quality external technical support and assistance from entities with expertise in school reform program development and implementation

9. Includes a plan for annual evaluation of implementation and student outcomes

10. Identifies federal, state, local, and private resources to support and sustain school reform initiatives

11. Has scientifically based evidence documenting improvement (or the potential for improvement) of academic achievement

HISTORY OF SCHOOL REFORM

The problems of society as a whole are reflected in the history of school reform. Throughout history, society has attempted to solve nationwide issues in education through school reform efforts. As a result of the Cold War between the United States and Soviet Union in the 1950s and 1960s and Sputnik's launch in 1957, Americans believed our country's schools had failed and were behind those in the Soviet Union. This led to a focus on improving the teaching of math, science, and foreign languages, and shifted attention to promoting education and achievement among high-achieving students.

In 1958, the National Defense Education Act (NDEA) expanded testing in schools and called for new programs in science, math, and foreign languages. As we entered the 1960s, a booming economy led to optimism that government could solve many of society's problems. President Lyndon Johnson's "Great Society" grew out of this optimism and was an attempt to solve societal problems such as poverty and racial discrimination. In 1965, the Elementary and Secondary Education Act (ESEA) was signed by President Johnson. ESEA was an education reform movement that focused on helping disadvantaged

students succeed at school through additional resources and services such as Title I.

The Civil Rights Movement of 1970 drew attention to the inequality of education. Rather than emphasizing teaching of high-achieving students, the focus shifted to providing equal access to education. The 1974 Equal Educational Opportunities Act (EEOA) was a result of this movement. This act specified that no state can deny equal educational opportunity on the basis of race, color, sex, or national origin.

The booming economy of the 1960s gave way to economic instability in the 1980s. The lack of a stable economy and a revived Cold War, again, contributed to beliefs that improvements in education were needed to compete globally in the work force. Concern shifted from providing equal opportunities back to producing top students. *A Nation at Risk* (National Commission on Excellence in Education [NCEE], 1983) contributed to society's concerns with education. This report claimed that our educational system was not preparing students to be competitive in the global market; it cited the decline of educational achievement among high school graduates as evidence of problems in our educational system.

At the start of the 1990s, educators determined the best answer to school reform was to balance the goal of equality from the 1960s with the goal of excellence from the 1980s. To achieve this, President George H. W. Bush invited all 50 governors for an education summit. This meeting led to the Goals 2000: Educate America Act (1994), which articulated educational goals and provided financial support for schools to achieve these goals. It also mandated accountability in grades 4, 8, and 12, in hopes of providing equal access to education and high academic standards for all students, regardless of socioeconomic, racial, and linguistic background.

In 1998, the Comprehensive School Reform Demonstration (CSRD), which arose from ESEA, gave funds to support the initial implementation of a school's reform initiative. These funds targeted schools that were in need of raising student achievement, especially for low-income and minority students, and used a research-based reform model in which the school-based practices funded through CSRD were derived from scientific research. In 2001, the No Child Left Behind (NCLB) Act, signed by George W. Bush, promised to provide all children access to high-quality education. This promise was to be upheld through accountability for test scores, scientifically based instruction methods, parental choices, and the ability to consolidate and reallocate funds received under various grants and programs. The CSRD program was incorporated into NCLB and renamed the Comprehensive School Reform Program (CSRP). The CSRP provides grants (minimum $50,000 per year) to schools to design and implement scientifically based strategies for school reform, with the assistance of external developers and entities. Since the authorization of CSRP, Congress has steadily increased its support for school reform. In 2003, the allocation for CSRP was $310 million; schools receiving funds through CSRP had an average poverty rate of 70%.

DESCRIPTION OF MAJOR SCHOOL REFORM MODELS

Consistent with CSRP (component 8), many schools are turning to external groups such as university-based research and development centers for assistance in designing school reform programs. Despite differences in specific processes for improving student outcomes and diverse opinions about the benefits of school reform (see Point-Counterpoint box), CSR models provide a design for whole-school change and help

schools address multiple components (see Table 1). Many CSR models incorporate additional variables that influence student success, including:

- Adoption of achievement standards and accountability to the community
- Inclusion of all students, regardless of disability status, in the total school experience
- Use of discipline procedures to promote positive behavior and social–emotional competence

Several reviews of models have been published in the last five to eight years to help schools select and implement CSR programs. The most recent report was published by the Center for Research on the Education of Students Placed At Risk (CRESPAR). Through CRESPAR, Borman and colleagues (2002) conducted a meta-analysis of research on achievement effects of 29 widely implemented school reform models. The following is a description of six models that have strong or promising evidence of positive effects on student achievement.

Success for All

Success for All (SFA), developed by Robert Slavin and Nancy Maddan, is a comprehensive approach to ensure success in reading, minimize special education referrals, increase attendance, and address family needs. The key component of SFA is a highly structured reading and language arts curriculum, in which students receive 90 minutes of daily instruction in multiage, homogeneous ability groups; 20 minutes of tutoring is also provided for early readers who have significant difficulty learning to read. Continuous assessment of progress is critical in that reading group assignments are revised every eight weeks based on students' reading skills. Parent involvement is also an integral feature of SFA; each school has a Family Support Team to encourage parent involvement (e.g., reading to students) and help parents address problems at home that may affect students' ability to learn and succeed in school. Two keys to effectiveness of SFA are the program facilitator, who provides mentoring and support to the school as needed, and the staff support teams that assist teachers with implementation of the program and curriculum. The scientific base for SFA is strong. More than 16 empirical studies have documented significantly higher performance on standardized reading tests for students in

SFA schools, compared to similar students (age, ability) in matched control schools (i.e., schools that did not implement a school reform model), including schools that provide one-on-one tutoring.

Direct Instruction

The goal of Direct Instruction (DI) is to increase student achievement through carefully focused and structured instruction. The DI model aims to provide intense, efficient lessons that allow learners to master basic academic skills. A central tenet of the DI model is that explicit instruction minimizes errors and accelerates learning. The curriculum and instructional methods, evolving from work on teacher-directed instruction by Siegfried Engelmann in the 1960s, are the most important aspects of a DI model. DI provides highly scripted, interactive lessons geared toward small, homogeneous ability-grouped students. Programs are designed around a system of teaching that includes:

- Scripted lesson plans
- Rapid-paced interactions
- Immediate corrective feedback
- Achievement-based grouping
- Frequent assessment

To implement DI, schools must purchase required curriculum materials. Inherent in a DI approach is setting the instructional pace according to the performance level of each instructional group. Because DI relies on grouping students by achievement levels, frequent assessment of progress is essential. Teachers monitor student progress every 5 to 10 days using brief academic probes. DI has a strong evidence base, documenting benefits in both academic skills and social–emotional outcomes, such as improvements in self-esteem, attitudes toward school, and success attributions. The model makes limited organizational demands on schools, other than requiring all literacy teachers to teach their content at the same time to allow for cross-class grouping (i.e., grouping students for instruction on the basis of achievement level instead of grade level).

School Development Program

The School Development Program (SDP) is based on the work of James Comer, who believes that healthy child development is the keystone to academic achievement. The goal of SDP is to promote the development of students' personal strengths, which enables them to succeed in school. Implementing SDP requires significant schoolwide organizational change. Three core mechanisms comprise the basic operational structure for SDP:

1. The School Planning and Management Team (teachers, classroom aides, parents, support service staff, and principal) develops, implements, and evaluates a school plan, and coordinates all school activities, including professional development programs.

2. The Student and Staff Support Team (teachers and support service staff) meets weekly to support individual teachers with challenging students and promote the development of positive schoolwide learning environments.

3. The Parent Team supports activities to involve parents.

Central to the work of these teams are three operations, including a Comprehensive School Plan (detailing specific goals), a Staff Development Plan (specifying teacher training to meet goals), and a Monitoring and Assessment System to evaluate progress toward the goals. Finally, SDP schools and staff are guided by three core principles of the Comer process. The first, termed "no fault," focuses on solution-oriented problem solving (rather than blaming). The second principle is consensus decision making, achieved through dialogue and understanding of different points of view. The final principle is collaboration; principals and teams share responsibility in implementing program components. Research indicates that in SDP schools (compared to non-SDP schools), students exhibit higher achievement and self-concept, and have significantly lower rates of absenteeism and suspension.

Community for Learning

The goals of Community for Learning (CFL), developed by Margaret Wang, are to improve academic performance and to promote independent learning among students through coordination of classroom instruction and community services. The CFL program is based on the principle that learning is affected by a variety of environments outside of school. A central component is a system of shared decision making involving school staff, parents, and community. CFL relies on an evidence-based instructional model called the Adaptive Learning Environments Model (ALEM), which incorporates five instructional features:

1. Individualized learning plans

2. Flexible grouping strategies

3. Alignment of school curriculum with district/ state standards

4. Student-centered learning materials matched to students' interests and learning styles

5. Criterion-referenced assessment and daily progress monitoring (i.e., assessment of student performance in relation to skill objectives rather than norms)

The research base for CFL, in terms of positive effects on student achievement, is promising. Empirical studies have documented higher reading and mathematics achievement test scores for students participating in the program, compared to nonparticipating students. Research has also found that mainstreamed special education students in CFL schools perform better on achievement tests than similar students not using the approach.

High Schools That Work

High Schools That Work (HSTW), developed by the Southern Regional Education Board, combines the content of college preparatory courses with vocational studies to improve the academic achievement of students who are not planning to attend college. Within HSTW, a challenging high school experience is provided for vocational students by setting high standards and requiring "college-bound" academic courses. The centerpiece of HSTW is a curriculum that blends essential content of college-preparatory mathematics, science, language arts, and social studies courses with career and technical studies in grades 9 through 12. In addition to strengthening the academic focus, HSTW schools provide rigorous vocational courses and structured learning experiences in work environments. The stronger integration of college-preparatory courses and vocational training requires collaboration among academic and vocational teachers, as well as individualized advising for students. Teachers

receive training to merge academics into vocational studies, including:

- Using student-centered assignments (e.g., designing a blueprint for a house in lieu of taking a math exam on measurement)
- Providing tutoring outside of school
- Using assessment information to identify strengths and weaknesses to improve instruction

A final component of HSTW is a school advisory council composed of students, parents, teachers, community members, and business leaders to coordinate the implementation of the program. The evidence base for HSTW is promising, with 10 studies documenting positive effects on student achievement (improved performance on the National Assessment of Educational Progress). The positive results are stable across a variety of schools, and consistent between urban and rural school environments.

Accelerated Schools

The Accelerated Schools (AS) approach, developed by Henry Levin, is predicated on the belief that at-risk students should have the same curriculum and instruction as typical or gifted students. Through AS, at-risk students learn at an accelerated pace to catch up (by grade six) with more advantaged students. The AS approach is grounded in three principles. The first is unity of purpose, which means that parents, teachers, students, and administrators work toward a common set of goals. The second is site-based decision making and responsibility, in which all members of the school community share in and are accountable for decision making. The third principle is building on strengths, which means that schools draw on the expertise and experience of everyone in the school community. To implement this model, schools have two individuals (one within the school staff and one from within or outside the district administration) who provide training and technical assistance to implement the model. The instructional emphasis is on collaborative inquiry; incorporating hands-on learning; and shared, collaborative problem solving.

Studies of school reform and the process of school change have identified several common factors that have an effect on the success or failure of CSR efforts, irrespective of the specific model. First, the quality

---

Point Versus Counterpoint: School Reform

The case for:

- Providing good education to all children is a central concern; reform efforts that emphasize academic achievement and goals for improvement will help all students perform better.
- Standards allow all students to attain high levels of achievement and promote accountability for improved teaching and learning.
- Students with disabilities and minority students have low expectations and weak instruction; they will benefit from reform efforts that provide high-quality instruction.
- No school can produce successful students without resources to provide an adequate education; resources (e.g., space, computer labs) linked to reform will help students succeed.
- It costs more to educate a child in special education than general education. Reform programs allow children to remain in general education.

The case against:

- Changing standards will not accomplish goals if schools lack resources.
- Implementing reform initiatives is not an efficient way to solve education problems. Teachers and administrators need to do a better job of implementing strategies already in place.
- There is limited knowledge about which reform programs have the greatest impact.
- Most reform models were not designed for students with disabilities.
- Standards-based reform efforts may work against some students. Minorities and students with disabilities are at risk of failing high-stakes tests and, in turn, will suffer consequences such as being retained or denied a high school diploma.
- High-stakes testing pressures schools to achieve high pass rates; administrators may refer low-achieving students to special education to achieve these high pass rates.

---

and level of implementation of the CSR model is highly related to positive outcomes. Second, clearly defined CSR programs are implemented with greater integrity and, in turn, have stronger effects on student outcomes than programs that are less clearly defined. Third, professional development and training components are critical for successful implementation. And, fourth, the greatest impact is achieved when all teachers, staff, and administrators embrace the principles and policies associated with the reform design (Slavin & Fashola, 1998). Overall, the potential and current success of CSR programs demonstrates that research-based models of educational improvement can be implemented on a schoolwide basis successfully. With the recent proliferation of CSR models and simultaneous growth in research, combined with significant funding available through CSRP, the potential for research-based school reform in this country has never been greater.

—Maribeth Gettinger and Kristen Kalymon

See also Academic Achievement; Charter Schools; Discipline; Outcomes-Based Assessment; Performance-Based Assessment; Special Education; Statewide Tests

REFERENCES AND FURTHER READING

Borman, G. D., Hewes, G. M., Overman, L. T., & Brown, S. (2002). *Comprehensive school reform and student achievement: A meta-analysis* (Report No. 59). Baltimore, MD: CRESPAR, Johns Hopkins University.

National Commission on Excellence in Education (NCEE). (1983). *A nation at risk: A report to the nation.* Washington, DC: Author.

Slavin, R. E., & Fashola, O. S. (1998). *Show me the evidence! Proven and promising programs for America's schools.* Thousands Oaks, CA: Corwin.

Traub, J. (1999). *Better by design? A consumer's guide to schoolwide reform.* Washington, DC: Thomas B. Fordham Foundation.

Wang, M. C., Haertal, G. D., & Walberg, H. J. (1998). *What do we know: Widely implemented school improvement programs.* Philadelphia: Center for Research in Human Development and Education.

SCHOOL REFUSAL

School refusal is used to describe behaviors associated with children who refuse to attend school for many reasons. Estimates of prevalence generally range from 2% to 5%. School refusal may happen at any age, although it is most commonly associated with school transitions (such as preschool to elementary school, elementary to middle school, etc.) or following stressful events (divorce, death, move) or holiday recesses. Children with poor academic or social skills may also be at a higher risk.

The severity of school refusal behavior varies, ranging from frequent complaints and reluctance to attend school, to frequent absences for entire or partial days, to more severe instances of absences for weeks, months, or even longer. Many school refusers complain of somatic ailments such as headaches or stomachaches.

Although both truants and school refusers avoid school, a distinguishing characteristic is that parents of school refusers know where their child is when he or she is not at school (typically at home or at the parent's place of work). The parents of truant children typically are unaware of their child's whereabouts. The school refuser is typically avoiding or escaping negative situations or seeking adult attention, whereas the truant frequently avoids school in order to engage in delinquent behavior.

Children with school refusal behavior are a heterogeneous group, which makes diagnosis and treatment difficult. Behaviors associated with school refusal may include severe anxiety, crying, panic, depression, social anxiety, separation anxiety, sever acting out (kicking, biting, screaming, clinging, etc.).

OUTCOMES

Untreated, school refusal behavior may result in negative outcomes for the child and the family. Academic difficulties frequently result when the child misses significant amounts of school because he or she has fallen behind academically. The academic problems make it even more difficult for the child to return to school. Frequent absences may result in impaired peer and social functioning, which makes returning to school more complicated. Some children with unresolved school refusal behavior become adults with significant fears of social situations, difficulty leaving the house (agoraphobia), and difficultly maintaining employment. School refusal behavior can also create significant stress within the family because of parents' absences from work to take care of their child or having to go to meetings with school personnel to discuss their child's problematic behavior, as well as daily conflict and emotional stress associated with their child's extreme or manipulative school avoidance behaviors. The problems are exacerbated if there are additional difficulties within the family such as parental conflict, poor parenting, financial, or emotional issues.

CAUSES

In the past, these behaviors were thought to be caused by school phobia, an unreasonable and extreme fear of attending school. Other researchers believed that school refusal was a separation anxiety disorder. Separation anxiety, which consists of the child becoming upset when separated from primary caregivers, is a normal developmental stage for very young children. Developmentally inappropriate and excessive anxiety concerning separation from home or from caregivers that impacts a child's ability to function is typically considered to be separation anxiety disorder. Frequent absences from school may be one of the behaviors exhibited by children with separation anxiety disorder.

Parenting and family factors have also been blamed for school refusal behavior. In some cases, the parents may be unable to separate from their child, or are unable to understand their role in maintaining the behavior. Sometimes the child who refuses to attend school has been considered to be a "barometer" for the family's financial, emotional, or parenting difficulties. Families that are experiencing a crisis may have great difficulty coping with a child who refuses to attend school.

Current research indicates that school refusal has multiple causes and different levels of severity. There is rarely a single cause for this behavior, which makes diagnosis and treatment particularly challenging. This is important because treatment must address the multiple causes of this distressing and complex set of behaviors.

Children may refuse to attend school for any or a combination of the following reasons:

- Avoid anxiety-provoking situations related to feelings of depression, anxiety, unspecified fear, specific fear (tornadoes, house fire), separation from parent (separation anxiety, depression, generalized anxiety)

- Escape social situations that cause anxiety (social anxiety, bullying)
- Avoid performance or evaluation activities (performance anxiety)
- Seek attention from family or others in a manipulative manner; may follow a true health-related absence
- Seek rewards of staying at home (sleeping in, watching television, playing video games, eating snacks)
- Avoid adult supervision in order to engage in antisocial behavior, typically considered to be "truant"

DIAGNOSIS AND TREATMENT

School personnel are usually the first to notice excessive absences. Diagnosis and treatment requires collaboration between the school, family, primary medical care provider, and mental health providers. Because of frequent complaints of physical symptoms (headache, sore throat, stomachache), it is important for the physician to determine if underlying medical causes are present. It is also important that medical excuses for the child's absences not be written unless there is a documented medical condition present.

Other indications of possible school refusal behavior include:

- Patterns of absences (following weekends, holidays, vacations, test days, oral presentations)
- Excessive visits to the school nurse, requests to call parents
- Frequent tardiness and arrivals at school upset with a frustrated or angry parent
- Expressions of anxiety about parent or other family member; fears that something "bad" will happen because the child is not at home
- Complaints about being at school (crying, trying to leave, clinging to parent)

The child's teacher or parent should consult with the school psychologist or other school support staff as soon as these behaviors become apparent. The best outcomes occur with rapid treatment, before the behaviors become a pattern.

Because school refusal requires a multisourced assessment, it should involve a variety of methods such as observations; interviews; checking past attendance,

academic, and health records; and questionnaires. Information regarding the child's development, emotional functioning, social skills, and family factors is important. Information should be obtained from the child, family, and teachers. Academic achievement testing may be necessary. It is important to understand if the child is escaping situations that cause anxiety or is seeking attention.

Assessment should also include investigating what happened before the behavior (antecedents) and what happens after the child refuses to go to school (consequences). The antecedents may help the school psychologist and teaching staff to understand the initial cause of the behavior, whereas the consequences may help them to understand what may be maintaining the behavior. An example of an antecedent could be the child refusing to go to school initially because of fears of poor academic performance. The child cries and refuses to go to school. At home the child watches TV, plays with toys, and receives adult attention as a consequence. The rewards of staying at home are far greater than going to school, which is perceived as being aversive. Treatment would then consist of managing the negative aspects of school, while reducing the positive rewards for staying home. Treatment that only focuses on one aspect (anxiety of school) may not be as effective as strategies that address both the antecedents and the consequences (being rewarded at home).

Treatment strategies need to be guided by this information. The home and school, at a minimum, need to collaborate; community medical and mental health providers may need to be included. Factors to consider for treatment include duration of the behavior, age of the child, and the parenting and coping skills of the family.

Treatment planning should emphasize a rapid return to school. Academic and social support strategies may help to decrease problems associated with school and ease reentry. Some academic requirements may need to be adjusted or tutoring provided. Some required activities that make the child anxious (such as oral reading, test taking, or class presentations) may need to have other activities substituted (such as presenting the information to the teacher instead of the class). Teaching the child specific social or coping skills may be needed. Behaviors associated with school attendance (getting up, getting dressed, being ready on time, not crying, etc.) should be reinforced. Reward systems and other behavior reinforcement strategies are frequently used to increase school attendance. Anxious students may need to be welcomed by staff when they enter the school, and a "safe" or "quiet" room provided if the child becomes distressed. Negative school climate issues such as bullying should be addressed.

If the child or family experiences significant difficulties with depression or anxiety, mental health treatment from a school psychologist or other mental health provider may be necessary. Sometimes medications may be prescribed to help alleviate symptoms. Mental health support for the child and family may assist with family issues that may be exacerbating the behaviors. Parents will frequently need help in managing the refusal behaviors and in not unintentionally rewarding school absences. Treatment is most successful if it is a team effort. Rapid response is critical.

—Leslie Z. Paige

See also Cognitive–Behavioral Modification; Dropouts; Fears; Separation Anxiety Disorder

REFERENCES AND FURTHER READING

Kearney, C. A. (2001). *School refusal behavior in youth: A functional approach to assessment and treatment.* Washington, DC: American Psychological Association.

King, N. J., Ollendick, T. H., & Tonge, B. J. (1995). *School refusal: Assessment and treatment.* Boston: Allyn & Bacon.

Paige, L. Z. (1997). School phobia, school refusal, and school avoidance. In G. G. Bear, K. M. Minke, & A. Thomas (Eds.), *Children's needs II: Development, problems, and alternatives* (pp. 339–347). Bethesda, MD: National Association of School Psychologists.

Wimmer, M. B. (2003). *School refusal: Assessment and intervention within school settings.* Bethesda, MD: National Association of School Psychologists.

SECTION 504

Section 504 of the Rehabilitation Act of 1973 is a major piece of federal antidiscrimination legislation designed to protect the civil rights of individuals with disabilities. For years, section 504 was concerned with employment practices. Recently, the Office for Civil Rights (OCR) of the U.S. Department of Health and Human Services has become more concerned with enforcing section 504 in education.

No state or local school district that receives federal funds can discriminate against students, parents, or staff members with disabilities. While section 504 is frequently considered with reference to making academic accommodations for students with disabilities, it also applies to providing accommodations such as ramps to get into schools, adequacy of restrooms for wheelchairs, and other accommodations for students, parents, and staff with disabilities.

The Office for Civil Rights (OCR) of the U.S. Department of Health and Human Services, which is the federal agency that monitors section 504, describes a qualified student with a disability as one who is:

- Of an age during which persons without disabilities are provided such services
- Of any age during which it is mandatory under state law to provide such services to students with disabilities
- A student for whom a state is required to provide a free appropriate public education under the Individuals With Disabilities Education Act (IDEA)

For an individual to be covered under section 504, the individual must have a disability, as defined in the Act, and be otherwise qualified. This means that a person with a disability must be qualified to do something (i.e., work, attend school) before the presence of a disability can be a factor in discrimination. Under section 504, a person is considered to have a disability if that person (29 U.S.C. Sec.706[8]):

- Has a physical or mental impairment that substantially limits one or more of the individual's major life activities
- Has a record of such an impairment
- Is regarded as having such an impairment

The Act defines a physical or mental impairment as:

(a) any physiological disorder or condition, cosmetic disfigurement, or anatomical loss affecting one or more of the following body systems: neurological; musculoskeletal; special sense organs; respiratory, including speech organs; cardiovascular; reproductive; digestive; genitourinary; hemic and lymphatic; skin; and endocrine; or (b) any mental or psychological disorder such as mental retardation, organic brain syndrome, emotional or mental illness, and specific learning disabilities.

Section 504 requires that the person have a physical or mental impairment that substantially limits one or more of the person's major life activities. The second part of the definition relates to the impact of the physical or mental impairment on a major life activity. The Act defines a *major life activity* as (34 Code of Federal Regulations Part 104.3):

- Caring for one's self
- Performing manual tasks
- Walking
- Seeing
- Hearing
- Speaking
- Breathing
- Learning
- Working

For many school-age children, the major life activity affected is learning. Some children not covered under IDEA are covered under section 504, and are, therefore, eligible for certain protections and services.

For a child to be eligible under section 504, the school must determine that the child has a disability, as defined in section 504, and that the disability results in a substantial limitation of a major life activity. School personnel must collectively use their professional judgment to make this determination. While the school determines eligibility, information from physicians, psychologists, or other professionals plays a critical role in the determination.

Because the definition of disability (see entry on Individuals With Disabilities Education Act) and the requirements for eligibility under IDEA are more restrictive than those used in section 504, all children eligible for services under IDEA are eligible for protections or accommodations under section 504.

Section 504 also requires that related services be provided for students with disabilities if these services are required to meet the students' educational needs and are available to other students. Unlike IDEA— which defines related services as those that are necessary to enable a student to benefit from special education—related services can be provided under section 504 to children who do not receive any other special education services or interventions.

—*Tom E. C. Smith*

See also Due Process; Individualized Education Plan; Individuals With Disabilities Education Act; Special Education

SEIZURE DISORDERS

Seizure disorders, or convulsions, are the most common neurological condition of childhood. Seizures are the outwardly visible sign of an abnormal electrical discharge in the brain, which, depending on the type, are associated with various degrees of loss of consciousness and/or involuntary motor activity. Seizure disorders are usually placed in one of three broad classifications (partial, generalized, or unclassified), with more specific categories described within each classification.

Partial seizures typically involve a more limited number of nerve cells in the brain than generalized seizures and account for up to 40% of the seizures diagnosed. Partial seizure disorders are classified into three types, which refer to the degree of consciousness involved:

1. Simple partial

2. Complex partial

3. Partial with secondary generalization

Simple partial seizures typically do not impair consciousness, but they do manifest asynchronous movements that usually involve the neck, face, and/or extremities that last for 10 to 20 seconds. In contrast, complex partial seizures (with or without an aura) do involve an impairment of consciousness. Approximately 33% of children with seizures report an aura consisting of a vague, unpleasant feeling and/or undifferentiated fear. Presence of an aura usually indicates a focal onset of a seizure. Children undergoing this type of seizure often engage in automatic, uncoordinated, purposeless behaviors such as walking or running in a repetitive, nondirective fashion; rubbing objects; picking at clothing; and blank stares. Partial seizures with secondary generalization refer to seizures that spread to other parts of the brain and show a convulsion.

Generalized seizures involve larger areas of the brain than partial seizures and typically involve a loss of consciousness. They are categorized—depending on the type of body involvement exhibited during the seizure—as absence, tonic-clonic, myoclonic, or atonic. Absence seizures (previously called petit mal seizures) are seen most commonly in children. This type of seizure involves abrupt changes in consciousness characterized by a rapid cessation of motor activity and a blank, staring appearance with eyelid flickering.

These seizures are never associated with an aura and rarely last more than 30 seconds. Historically, absence seizures have been misdiagnosed as a form of attention deficit because the children were observed to not be paying attention. In contrast, tonic-clonic seizures (previously called grand mal seizures) involve sudden loss of consciousness with convulsions that involve stiffening then jerking of the limbs. These may follow a partial seizure. Tonic seizures involve stiffening of extremities without jerking, while clonic seizures involve the jerking without the stiffening of the extremities. The rest of the specific generalized seizure disorders involve minor motor seizures. Myoclonic seizures involve brief, involuntary, rapid muscle contractions. Atonic or astatic seizures are sometimes called drop attacks because they involve abrupt loss of posture tone, which may result in falling forward. Atypical generalized seizures are those that don't fit into the typical categories. Unclassified seizures are typically initial seizures where more information is needed before a classification can be made.

PREVALENCE AND ETIOLOGY

The etiology of seizure disorders is complex, and may not be known in more than 50% of children who experience them. Known etiologies include:

- Head trauma
- Toxic or metabolic conditions such as birth asphyxia, poisoning, drug withdrawal, or blood sugar imbalances
- Vascular conditions such as high blood pressure, problems with blood vessels, or vascular diseases such as lupus
- Infections such as meningitis, encephalitis, or systemic infections
- Brain tumors
- Malformations of the brain
- Degenerative disorders of the brain such as Rett syndrome
- Genetic disorders with chromosomal abnormalities such as Down or fragile X syndrome
- Genetic epilepsies such as absence or photosensitive epilepsies
- Febrile (from high fever) seizures

PREVALENCE AND SYMPTOMS

The lifetime risk of having at least one seizure is 8% to 11%, with the most common initial onset times in the first two years of life and at puberty. The symptoms of a seizure depend on the type of seizure and the individual. Changes in consciousness and motor activity are the most common symptoms. Sometimes individuals will be able to detect the onset of a seizure with changes in sensory perception such as light auras or sounds. For other individuals, there may be no noticeable indications prior to the seizure.

TREATMENT

Treatment of seizure disorders falls into three categories: prevention of known causal agents, pharmacological, and surgical. Prevention of, or limited exposure to, possible causal agents—such as sensory stimuli like flashing lights or certain drugs—can be used for certain individuals if the cause is known. Pharmacological treatments are the most common treatment and include a range of medications. Typical medications include—indicated by generic name then brand name—carbamazepine (Tegretol), ethosuximide (Zarontin), phenobarbital, phenytoin (Dilantin), primidone (Mysoline), and valproate (Depakene or Depakote). Each medication has its own schedule of administration and potential side effects. One typical goal of pharmacological treatment is to reduce the types and amount of medication needed; however, given the complexity of some seizures, this may not be possible. For some with seizures, there is limited or no response to medication. These types of seizures are called intractable epilepsy. Surgical interventions are dependent on the type and location of the seizure, and are typically used sparingly.

EDUCATIONAL IMPLICATIONS AND INTERVENTION

Educational implications for children who have seizures are somewhat dependent on the type of seizures. With impairment of consciousness, there may be a need to reteach material that was presented just before the seizure occurred. Ongoing assessment of instructional knowledge is essential for the student who may be having seizures. Teaching to fill in gaps of knowledge, teaching all the steps in sequence, or providing additional instruction may be needed to ensure mastery of material. With some seizure disorders, decreases in cognitive functioning may occur over time. This requires careful monitoring, frequent assessment, and possibly the need to reteach material that was mastered earlier. Children whose learning is affected by seizures are eligible for special education services through the Individuals With Disabilities Education Act (IDEA), usually under the category of other health impaired (OHI). This will allow the education program to be tailored to the needs of the individual.

For the child who has an identified seizure disorder, education of the staff is essential. In particular, education about immediate intervention and postvention will make the occurrence of a seizure more matter of fact and less traumatic, and may prevent serious injury. Most important is having an action plan.

Prevention activities include educating staff and students about seizures and what may happen, first aid training of personnel most likely to be responding to a seizure, and adhering to medical treatment schedules. In the education plan, first aid training is important for all teachers who have contact with a student who has seizures as well as other staff such as cafeteria workers and bus drivers. Information about seizures for classmates should be tailored to the age of the students, and the type of seizure activity they may be observing. For example, younger students may need to hear that seizures are not contagious, while older students may notice absence seizures and report them to the teacher. Students are also part of the immediate action plan by helping to summon team members and by clearing space for safety if needed. All faculty must adhere to the medical regimen, and must know what to do in atypical situations such as field trips or other changes in the typical school day.

Immediate intervention in the case of a seizure should include summoning of the team, securing the safety of the student experiencing the seizure as well as the rest of the students, and some degree of privacy such as a partition or a light blanket on the student in case of incontinence. Other interventions are dependent on the situation, but may involve outside resources such as community emergency response personnel.

Postvention includes allowing the student with the seizure time to recover, and depends on the individual and the type of seizure. The student may stay in the classroom or may need to go to the nurse's office or other designated area. The rest of the students in the classroom should be debriefed about the incident. If the students are well prepared ahead of time, or if this is reoccurring, the debriefing may be very limited in scope. If this is a first time, or if students have not been prepared, more debriefing and education is needed. Once debriefing has occurred, it is important to return to the typical schedule as soon as possible. For the student who has had the seizure, it is important

to debrief what happened just before and during the seizure, and then allow the student to return to the normal schedule as soon as possible. It is likely that reteaching will be needed, as some impairment may have been occurring before the actual seizure. It will also be necessary to debrief with the response team as soon as possible to ensure smooth functioning.

—*Constance J. Fournier and William A. Rae*

SELECTIVE MUTISM

Selective mutism (SM) is a disorder of childhood of unknown cause. It is characterized by a lack of speech in many social settings and is often first noticed when a child begins school. Adolf Kussmaul first identified SM in publication in 1877, as aphasia voluntaria. In 1934, Moritz Tramer renamed it Elective Mutism. The *Diagnostic and Statistical Manual of Mental Disorders, Fourth Edition-Text Revision (DSM-IV-TR)* (2000) identifies six major characteristics that must be satisfied for a diagnosis:

1. There is a persistent lack of speech in many social settings such as school.

2. The individual is able to produce clear and spontaneous speech in some settings and with some individuals, most often at home.

3. The lack of speech interferes with education or social communication.

4. The lack of speech must last beyond the first month of school.

5. The lack of speech is not caused by lack of knowledge of the language.

6. The lack of speech is not caused by the effects of another disorder (e.g., pervasive developmental disorder, autism, communicative disorder, schizophrenia, or psychosis).

SM is a rare disorder. Prevalence studies provide widely ranging estimates from 0.06% to 0.89%. The frequency of SM is higher for girls than boys, with a ratio of 1.6:1.

SM was originally thought to be primarily related to oppositional defiant behavior in a child, leading to a refusal to speak in an effort to control other individuals in his or her environment. Another initial theory was that the onset of SM was induced by a trauma such as physical or sexual abuse. These theories have not received support. Research into the etiological factors and familial characteristics since 1995 has supported the theory that SM behaviors are anxiety related and stimulated when the individual is in a social situation requiring speech. In this model, the child is unable to speak initially because of anxiety. Later, the individual continues not speaking in an attempt to control his or her anxiety level. Over time, the individual makes fewer efforts to speak; thus, the pattern of SM behavior develops. Research also supports the association between SM in children and familial factors of anxiety disorders, social phobias, and parents who themselves were reluctant speakers.

The interpretation of children with SM behaviors as being oppositional is still prevalent. Demanding speech from a child can exacerbate the disorder. Long-term negative effects on educational performance and occupational outcomes are assumed but as yet unsubstantiated. Other associated features may include shyness, behavioral inhibition, and enuresis.

Interventions from different theoretical models have been developed and include psychodynamic therapy, family systems therapy, cognitive–behavioral interventions, applied behavioral analysis, and biological approaches. Investigation into the effectiveness of these treatment methods supports the conclusion that behavioral and cognitive–behavioral interventions (e.g., fading, shaping, extinction, and positive reinforcement) are more effective than no treatment. Evidence of the effectiveness of the other treatment methods (e.g., psychodynamic therapy and family systems therapy) has not been substantiated. Medication such as selective serotonin reuptake inhibitors (SSRIs) has demonstrated some success in reducing anxiety sufficiently to establish speaking behaviors in children and is best used in conjunction with other therapeutic methods such as behavioral and cognitive–behavioral therapy.

—*Frances Haerberli*
and Thomas R. Kratochwill

See also Applied Behavior Analysis; Behavior Intervention; Behavioral Assessment; *DSM-IV*

REFERENCES AND FURTHER READING

American Psychiatric Association. (2000). *Diagnostic and statistical manual of mental disorders* (4th ed., text rev.). Washington, DC: Author.

SELF-CONCEPT AND EFFICACY

According to Bandura (1997), self-efficacy is defined as "people's beliefs in their capabilities to produce desired effects by their own actions" (p. vii). In more general terms, self-efficacy is defined as an individual's own beliefs about what he or she is capable of doing. An individual's ability to actually achieve a goal is related to whether or not he or she believes that the goal can be successfully achieved (Bandura, 1986). Self-efficacy is usually specific to certain areas, meaning that an individual believes that he or she is more capable in some areas than in others (e.g., first grade student may have high self-efficacy for correctly completing addition problems but low self-efficacy for correctly solving multiplication problems). Individuals develop their sense of self-efficacy through direct experiences, observing other people's experiences, and listening to other people's comments about what they think he or she is capable of doing.

The development of self-efficacy is related to aspects of social–cognitive theory. According to this theory, self-efficacy beliefs are influenced by the development of symbolic thought (i.e., language), an understanding of cause-and-effect relationships, and the ability to engage in self-observation and self-reflection. In addition to these cognitive or internal aspects, a child's development of self-efficacy is also influenced by the responses of the social environment (namely the child's parents) to his or her actions. A child develops a sense of self-efficacy by trying to manipulate the people around him or her. After the child's attempt at manipulation, the people in the environment may respond to the child's actions and thus help the development of self-efficacy, or they may not respond and thus slow the development of self-efficacy (Bandura, 1997).

Self-concept refers to an individual's own perceptions, both positive and negative, of his or her attributes, traits, and abilities. Components of one's self-concept include self-esteem (i.e., one's feeling of self-worth), self-efficacy, and how stable and structured one's beliefs are.

Individuals develop a sense of self-concept through their own experiences and through observing other people's experiences. Comparing one's abilities to other people's abilities is also an important aspect in the development of self-concept. In addition, one's self-concept becomes more sophisticated as a result of development. In young children, their self-concept is more concrete, meaning they define themselves in terms of their physical characteristics, name, or behaviors, but as children enter school, their self-concepts become more abstract as a result of a better understanding of their abilities (Schunk, 2004). An individual's self-concept is also thought to become more differentiated over time, meaning that there is a general or global self-concept and then numerous sub-areas of self-concept for specific areas such as math self-concept and science self-concept (Schunk, 2004).

Self-concept can be assessed through several techniques, but the assessment is usually based on self-report measures. One of the most frequently used techniques for assessing an individual's self-concept is through rating scales. With rating scales, an individual is presented a series of statements (e.g., "I am good at science," or "Overall, I am satisfied with myself") and then asked to indicate his or her level of agreement or disagreement with each statement. The responses are then tabulated to determine either specific-area self-concept scores or general self-concept scores. Another assessment technique is a checklist in which the individual is presented with a list of adjectives and then asked to check all the adjectives that apply to him or her. The adjectives are all preassigned to specific categories so the examiner can review the individual's responses and develop a self-concept score based on the categories. In a third assessment technique, called a Q Sort, the individual sorts cards that have self-descriptors written on them into a specific number of piles that range from the descriptions that are "most like me" to the ones that are "least like me." A final assessment technique is free responses, which require the individual to complete partial statements such as, "I feel happiest when . . ." (Strein, 1995).

After completing an assessment of an individual's self-concept, an examiner may determine that interventions are necessary to increase the individual's self-concept. There are several general techniques that may be used to increase a student's self-concept including:

- Demonstrating to the student that he or she has the ability to learn and that he or she has made progress
- Providing positive feedback
- Using models appropriately
- Decreasing the occurrence of negative social comparisons

In addition, interventions to address the general self-concept are typically ineffective, so interventions should be designed to address specific areas, and the success of these interventions may ultimately lead to an overall improved general self-concept (Schunk, 2004).

—*Megan E. Luhr*

See also Dropouts; Learning Styles; Motivation; Personality Assessment

REFERENCES AND FURTHER READING

Bandura, A. (1986). *Social foundations of thought and action.* New York: Prentice Hall.

Bandura, A. (1997). *Self-efficacy: The exercise of control.* New York: Freeman.

Schunk, D. H. (2004). *Learning theories: An educational perspective* (4th ed.). Upper Saddle River, NJ: Pearson Prentice Hall.

Strein, W. (1995). Assessment of self-concept. In W. Schafer (Ed.), *Assessment in counseling and therapy.* ERIC/CASS Digest (ERIC Document No. ED389962). [Reprinted in Garry Walz and Jeanne Bleuer (Eds.). (2001). *Assessment: Issues and challenges for the new millennium.* Greensboro, NC: ERIC Clearinghouse on Counseling and Student Services.]

SELF-FULFILLING PROPHECY

The principle of self-fulfilling prophecy states that a person will live up (or down) to others' expectations, predictions, or preconceived notions regarding his or her behavior. Positive expectations or predictions about behavior tend to lead to positive outcomes, whereas negative expectations or predictions tend to lead to negative outcomes. Simply put, expectations for behavior are likely to come true. As cited in Papalia and colleagues (2002), Rosenthal and Jacobson conducted a study on the self-fulfilling prophecy in a school setting. In this study, teachers were informed that certain students showed potential for extraordinary cognitive gains as measured by an intelligence test. Over the course of the year many of these children actually showed unusual gains. These students' behavior was related to the expectations set by their teachers. Teachers, parents, and other adults' beliefs about a student's behavior may have a significant impact on the actual behavior demonstrated by the individual student. Based on the principle of self-fulfilling prophecy, setting high expectations for all students may increase positive behaviors and outcomes for all students in schools today.

—*Martha Boehlert*

See also Dropouts

REFERENCES AND FURTHER READING

Papalia, D. E., Wendkos Olds, S., & Duskin Feldman, R. (2002). *A child's world: Infancy through adolescence* (9th ed.). New York: McGraw-Hill.

SELF-INJURIOUS BEHAVIOR

Self-injurious behavior is among the most perplexing and serious forms of psychopathology in children with developmental disabilities. It is defined as the repetitive and deliberate infliction of harm to one's own body (American Psychiatric Association, 1994). Common forms of self-injury include self-biting; self-punching; and repetitive banging of the head and limbs against solid, unforgiving surfaces such as walls, tables and floors. Less common forms of self-injury include repeatedly dislocating and relocating joints; eye gouging; pulling out one's own hair, teeth, or fingernails; pica, and self-mutilation of the genitals and rectum. Self-injurious behavior affects 8% to 14% of the child population with autism and/or mental retardation. The vast majority of these children are nonverbal with IQs below 50. Fortunately, most children with self-injurious behavior respond favorably to treatment. Behavior therapy using positive reinforcement, medication, and various combinations of behavior therapy and medication are frequently reported as successful in virtually eliminating the problem. However, there remains a significant minority of children with special needs who are unresponsive to treatment. Self-injury in this refractory group is at high risk of escalating to life-threatening proportions and results in the affected children being consigned to the use of highly restrictive protective equipment such as helmets, padded mitts, arm and leg restraints, and other individually tailored articles of protective clothing.

MOTIVATIONAL AND BIOLOGICAL HYPOTHESES OF SELF-INJURY

The mechanisms by which self-injurious behavior is developed and maintained are not well understood. For the most part, children who engage in self-injury are a heterogeneous and ill-defined group. That is to say, the reasons underlying why one child engages in self-injury may be entirely different from why another child engages in self-injury, even if the self-injurious behavior of the two children in question takes the same form. In this regard, researchers (Baumeister & Rollings, 1976; Winchel & Stanley, 1991) have delineated a number of motivational and biological hypotheses fundamental to children with special needs who engage in self-injurious behavior. Importantly, none of the proposed hypotheses discussed below are viewed as excluding each other. The likelihood of one hypothesis overlapping with one or more of the other hypotheses is highly probable and, in fact, is to be expected.

Positive Reinforcement

Self-injurious behavior is learned and maintained through operant conditioning using a positive reinforcement paradigm. Children may engage in self-injury because it gains them access to something that they prefer such as social attention (usually in the form of a comforting behavior), which is delivered to them contingent upon performance of the self-injurious act. Self-injury is a dramatic event that often leads to the use of physical management techniques by parents and teachers as a means of protecting the child from harm. Favell and colleagues (1978) caution that some children with special needs may find physical management to be rewarding (i.e., the equivalent of social attention), which may result in a paradoxical effect of increasing the frequency of the self-injurious behavior that it was designed to stop.

Negative Reinforcement

Self-injurious behavior is learned and maintained through operant conditioning using a negative reinforcement paradigm. Children may engage in self-injury because it allows them to terminate or escape from a condition that they find to be aversive, such as a physical exercise routine, contingent upon performance of the self-injurious behavior. Self-injury is an event that draws immediate attention and concern from adults. Parents, teachers, and other caretakers, acting in good faith, may modify or suspend limits or demands on a child because it has the effect of stopping the self-injury, at least for the time being. Unfortunately, it also teaches the child that self-injury is an effective way to communicate protest and to escape from nonpreferred tasks. In the long run, it has the effect of worsening the child's self-injury problem.

Self-Stimulation

Self-injurious behavior occurs in response to either insufficient or overabundant levels of environmental stimulation. Children with special needs may possess perceptual hypersensitivities as well as hyposensitivities. For example, some children show tactile defensiveness when touched, even lightly, while other children show a high threshold for tolerating pain. Homeostasis is a condition wherein all forms of stimulation are balanced for the child. When the child's homeostasis or balance of stimulation is disrupted and he or she becomes either overaroused because of an abundance of environmental stimulation or underaroused because of a lack of environmental stimulation, self-injurious behavior may serve a compensatory function and act to restore homeostatic balance.

Developmental

Self-injurious behavior occurs to "fix" an otherwise normal and transient stage of development. Self-injury has been observed in 11% to 17% of normally developing babies before the age of 30 months, usually in the form of head banging in the crib and usually with clear communicative intent (e.g., Pick me up; Feed me; Burp me; Change my diaper; I'm sick, etc.). The advent of language in the normally developing child results in no further observations of self-injury. For children with special needs who fail to acquire language, self-injury may become "fixed" because it has proved to be an efficacious means of communicating protest and/or discomfort. Finger sucking and toe walking are additional examples of possible "fixing" of normal and transient stages of development that may result in self-injury.

Organic

Self-injurious behavior is the product of a genetic disorder where severe self-injury is characteristic of the disorder. A complex motor tic, such as the self-slapping or skin picking associated with Tourette's syndrome, is another example of a genetic disorder that may involve self-injury. Self-injurious behavior may also be the product of a nongenetic physical disorder such as epilepsy (Gedye, 1989), otitis media,

migraine headache, or toothache. Children with autism and/or mental retardation who are nonverbal and lack an effective means for communicating illness may resort to self-injury in the form of repeatedly pressing or hitting an affected area, possibly to achieve an anesthetic effect, or they may merely attack the affected area out of frustration over the discomfort it creates.

Biologic

The imbalance of two brain chemicals, dopamine and serotonin, are hypothesized as playing a major role in the advent and maintenance of self-injurious behavior in children with special needs (Schroeder & colleagues, 2001). However, there is increasing attention to the possible role of endorphins in the syndrome of self-injurious behavior. Endorphin is a morphine-like chemical produced by the body in response to injury. The most widely postulated theory involving endorphins and self-injury suggests that some children engage in self-injurious behavior in order to gain access to endorphins and, more specifically, their narcotic effect. It is further speculated that these same children continue to hurt themselves day after day because they become addicted to the rewarding sensory consequence of the endorphins.

ASSESSMENT OF SELF-INJURY

Self-injurious behavior does not occur without a reason. The assessment of self-injury, therefore, must go beyond identifying the characteristics or type of self-injury and its magnitude or severity (Iwata & colleagues, 1990). The assessment of self-injury should be designed to identify the reason why the child engages in the behavior as well as self-injury's role in the child's behavioral repertoire (Bosch, 2001). This approach is known as the functional assessment of behavior. Conducting a functional assessment of self-injurious behavior is critical in determining which of the previously mentioned motivational and biological hypotheses is operational for any specific child. The functional assessment of self-injury includes analyzing both the antecedent and consequent conditions that surround the self-injurious behavior. That is, assessing the conditions that immediately preceded the self-injury as well as what resulted for the child after he or she engaged in the self-injurious behavior. The goal of the functional assessment is to delineate the circumstances that prompted or cued the child to engage in self-injury and identify the function or role served by the self-injurious behavior, such as:

- Did it result in social attention?
- Did it allow the child to escape a nonpreferred or unpleasant situation?
- Was it a response to isolation or boredom?
- Did it appear to have a communicative intent such as protest?
- Does the child have a genetic disorder or a medical disorder that could explain its presence?
- Did it appear (ironically) to provide relief from discomfort?

These and similar questions must be addressed through a careful analysis of conditions surrounding the self-injurious event in order to determine the function or role played by self-injury and, consequently, how best it may be treated (Iwata & colleagues, 1992).

TREATMENT OF SELF-INJURY

More than $20 billion has been spent in the care and treatment of children with autism and/or mental retardation who have engaged in self-injurious behavior during the past five years. Approximately 65% of children with self-injury respond favorably to behavior therapy using positive reinforcement strategies (Repp & Singh, 1990). An additional 30% respond favorably to behavior therapy in combination with various medications. However, successful treatment of the remaining 5% is elusive and very expensive. Controversy abounds in the treatment of self-injury when a child has been unresponsive to conventional therapy and the behavior has worsened to levels where the child's life is at stake. Highly restrictive protective equipment is invariably applied in these cases and, in some instances, mechanical restraint may be necessary to ensure the child's safety. In such cases, there is considerable debate as to whether an experimental method such as faradic electric shock should be employed.

—*Rowland P. Barrett*

See also Abuse and Neglect; Aggression in Schools; Behavior Intervention; Mental Retardation; Traumatic Brain Injury

REFERENCES AND FURTHER READING

American Psychiatric Association. (1994). *Diagnostic and statistical manual of mental disorders* (4th ed.). Washington, DC: Author.

Baumeister, A. A., & Rollings, J. P. (1976). Self-injurious behavior. In N. R. Ellis (Ed.), *International review of research in mental retardation.* (Vol. 8, pp. 1–34). New York: Academic.

Bosch, J. J. (2001). An interdisciplinary approach to self-injurious and aggressive behavior. *Journal of Developmental and Physical Disabilities, 13,* 169–178.

Favell, J. E., McGimsey, J. F., & Jones, M. L. (1978). The use of physical restraint in the treatment of self-injury and as positive reinforcement. *Journal of Applied Behavior Analysis, 11,* 225–241.

Gedye, A. (1989). Extreme self-injury attributed to frontal lobe seizures. *American Journal on Mental Retardation, 94,* 20–26.

Iwata, B. A., Dorsey, M. F., Slifer, K. J., Bauman, K. E., & Richman, G. S. (1992). Toward a functional assessment of self-injury. *Journal of Applied Behavior Analysis, 27,* 197–209.

Iwata, B. A., Pace, G. M., Kissel, R. C., Nau, P. A., & Farber, J. M. (1990). The self-injury trauma (SIT) scale: A method for quantifying surface tissue damage caused by self-injurious behavior. *Journal of Applied Behavior Analysis, 23,* 99–110.

Repp, A. C., & Singh, N. N. (1990). *Perspectives on the use of nonaversive and aversive interventions for persons with developmental disabilities.* Sycamore, IL: Sycamore Publishing.

Schroeder, S. R., Oster-Granite, M. L., Berkson, G., Bodfish, J. W., Breese, G. R., Cataldo, M. F., et al. (2001). Self-injurious behavior: Gene-brain behavior relationships. *Mental Retardation and Developmental Disabilities Research Reviews, 7,* 3–13.

Winchel, R. M., & Stanley, M. (1991). Self-injurious behavior: A review of the behavior and biology of self-mutilation. *American Journal of Psychiatry, 148,* 306–317.

SELF-MANAGEMENT

Self-management refers to actions individuals take to independently change or maintain their own behavior. This is in contrast to strategies and interventions directed by others, such as teachers and parents, to change an individual's behavior. Terms regularly seen in the literature related to self-management include self-regulation, self-control, and self-determination. Theoretically, self-management strategies have been described from both behavioral and cognitive viewpoints. The differences lie primarily in the focus of the intervention with a large amount of overlap in actual procedures. Specifically, behavioral self-management strategies emphasize what the individual does after the target behavior occurs (e.g., recording whether or not a task was completed); whereas cognitive self-management strategies emphasize what the individual says, thinks, or does before engaging in the target behavior (e.g., saying the steps needed to solve a problem out loud before attempting the problem). Although there are differences in terminology and explanation for efficacy, cognitive and behavioral approaches to self-management share relatively the same objectives. Students are taught to monitor and evaluate their own behavior and make adjustments when needed. The ultimate goal is for students to perform the necessary steps of a desired behavior without the need for supervision from others.

Although there are many different types of self-management procedures, those described most frequently in the school psychology self-management literature are self-monitoring, self-evaluation, self-reinforcement, self-instruction, and social problem solving. Self-management programs typically are comprised of one or some combination of these strategies (Shapiro & Cole, 1994).

SELF-MONITORING

Self-monitoring requires individuals to pay attention to a specific aspect of their behavior, and then indicate whether or not the behavior being monitored has occurred (i.e., "Did I do it?"). For example, a student who frequently talks out in the classroom during independent seat work might be asked to self-monitor hand-raising behavior, and record when this occurs. Checklists are commonly used when self-monitoring. On a homework checklist, a student may check off the following steps when completing an assignment:

- Do I have the necessary supplies?
- Did I read the directions?
- Did I complete the assignment?
- Did I turn it in on time?

Both audio and visual cues can be used to prompt students to self-monitor. For example, picture prompts may be provided depicting targeted behaviors, or a tone may be emitted from a tape recorder. These signal students to record whether they were engaging in the specified behavior at predetermined intervals.

Self-monitoring has resulted in behavior change in the absence of other interventions. Thus, simply paying attention and recording specified behaviors may result in desired behavior change.

SELF-EVALUATION

Self-evaluation requires individuals to evaluate the quality of their own behavior against a predetermined criterion for a given behavior (i.e., "How well did I do?"). Self-evaluation typically is used in conjunction with self-monitoring as part of a self-management program. Students may evaluate their behavioral or academic performance using a rating scale (e.g., 5 being excellent and 1 being unacceptable). Students often need training on how to accurately and consistently evaluate their own behavior. This can be done using a matching system wherein a teacher, peer, or parent rates the behavior and the target student attempts to match their rating. Matching may be faded as the student learns to rate his or her own behaviors accurately and consistently. Backup reinforcers have been used in some interventions when student ratings match teacher ratings.

In addition to using ratings for behavioral evaluations, academic behaviors (e.g., mathematics and spelling) can be objectively assessed by evaluating the accuracy of individual items. One example of using self-evaluation for academic behaviors is the "Cover, Copy, and Compare" technique (Skinner & colleagues, 1989). In the Cover, Copy, and Compare intervention, students are given a worksheet containing unsolved academic problems on the right side of the page (e.g., mathematics computation, vocabulary definition, or spelling words), with corresponding answers to these problems appearing on the left side of the page. Students are first instructed to look at the initial problem and its corresponding answer. Next, students are told to cover the correct answer on the left side of the page (with paper, an index card, or the like), and then solve/write down the answer on the right side of the page. Finally, the students are asked to uncover the correct answer to the problem on the left and evaluate if their answer was correct.

SELF-REINFORCEMENT

Self-reinforcement components require students to determine whether the criteria were met and to select and self-administer reinforcement contingent upon meeting the criteria (i.e., "Did I meet my goal?"). Self-reinforcement has been effective as part of multi-component self-management programs.

SELF-INSTRUCTION

Self-instruction is a cognitive-based self-management procedure in which students are taught to use self-statements to guide academic and social behaviors. Meichenbaum (1977) outlined a step-by-step training procedure that requires students to move gradually from assisted overt verbalizations to unassisted covert verbalizations (i.e., self-talk). Similarly, social problem-solving training is a cognitive-based intervention that focuses on teaching students to recognize interpersonal problems, generate solutions, evaluate consequences of solutions, select a solution, and follow through on the solution.

ADVANTAGES AND DISADVANTAGES OF SELF-MANAGEMENT INTERVENTIONS

Few disadvantages have been documented in the use of self-management strategies. This is at least partially related to the types of problems addressed using self-management (i.e., simple, discrete behaviors). External control techniques (e.g., teacher-managed interventions) raise concerns regarding generalization of the intervention (i.e., transfer of the skills beyond the immediate intervention setting), and passivity and motivation of the student. Self-management procedures theoretically are designed to increase generalizability, as students are not dependent on another for monitoring and evaluating behaviors. However, not all self-management procedures result in generalization in other settings, indicating a need for more research to identify the variables that promote generalization. Interventions that target general academic behaviors (e.g., checking work) rather than specific behaviors (e.g., checking spelling accuracy) are inherently more generalizable.

Another advantage cited for self-management procedures is the efficacy of self-management interventions across a wide variety of behaviors, settings, and populations. In some cases, self-management interventions are as effective or more effective than teacher-managed interventions. Additionally, self-management interventions are less intrusive, and teachers report preferring self-management over some teacher-managed interventions (e.g., token economies). However, many of the self-management interventions include some type of external reinforcement (e.g., token systems) and involvement from teachers (e.g., matching). While these components are often reduced or eliminated over time, significant up-front time from teachers and parents is often needed for teaching and maintaining behaviors, and there are few examples of students using self-management interventions with only natural consequences in place.

SELF-MANAGEMENT POPULATIONS AND BEHAVIORS

Substantial research has supported the use of self-management interventions, documenting positive gains for a wide variety of students (Shapiro & Cole, 1994). Self-management interventions have produced positive changes for students with various school difficulties and disabilities, including students with autism, learning disabilities, emotional and behavioral disorders, health-related concerns, and mild to severe cognitive impairments. Additionally, self-management has been used in special education and general education classrooms, and on an individual or a classwide basis. Generally, self-management strategies can be effective for all ages or disability groups; however, adapted procedures may be needed depending on the population and the goal. For example, students with attention deficit hyperactivity disorder (ADHD) may need more specific feedback for both their desirable and undesirable behaviors.

Self-management is an effective intervention strategy for behaviors ranging from academic to behavior problems. Specifically, self-management has been used effectively for:

- Improving academic performance behaviors, homework completion, academic productivity, academic accuracy, and specific academic skills
- Decreasing disruptive and off-task behaviors
- Teaching social skills, such as appropriate and inappropriate social responding and conversational interactions
- Teaching vocational/domestic skills
- Teaching self-control strategies, such as problem orientation ("What do I have to do first?"), self-questioning, self-instructional training, and problem-solving skills

SELF-MANAGEMENT EXAMPLE

Interventions typically include a variety of self-management components (self-monitoring, goal-setting, evaluation, reinforcement). Rhode and colleagues (1983) provide one example of a self-management intervention used in a classroom setting. This procedure has been adapted successfully for use with various behaviors, populations, and settings.

Baseline Phase

Before implementing the self-management intervention, the target behaviors for intervention and the objective criterion for rating student behaviors and/or quality of student performance (e.g., a rating scale from 1 for poor to 5 for excellent) are established. The setting for implementing the intervention is also determined, as well as the specific length of rating intervals that will be used for evaluation. For example, ratings initially may occur every 15 minutes during math class, then be extended based on student performance. After establishing the intervention procedures, the teacher rates the student's performance on the target behaviors at the end of the predetermined rating interval(s); this is the baseline performance. The teacher does not tell the student the rating he or she received, as the ratings at this point are intended for practice in rating consistently, using the full range of the rating scale, and to establish a reward criterion. The baseline phase lasts for approximately one week, depending upon stability of student performance.

Teacher-Directed Phase

The objective of the teacher-directed phase is to teach students to accurately use the rating scale, provide frequent and meaningful teacher feedback, and to achieve a desired level of performance. At the end of the evaluation interval, the teacher informs the student of the rating he or she received, and provides feedback about why the particular rating was given. The teacher ratings correspond to points that are accumulated and exchanged for backup rewards. A general rule of thumb for this phase is to continue until the student reaches the teacher's predetermined criterion for the target behavior for at least three consecutive days.

Matching Phase

The matching phase teaches students to accurately evaluate their own behavior, while matching the accuracy of their ratings to those evaluations given by the teacher. After the evaluation interval, both the student and teacher independently rate the student's behavior, and then compare the evaluations. If the student and teacher ratings match exactly, the student earns the designated number of points he or she determined should be awarded, plus one bonus point for matching with the teacher. If the total of the student and teacher ratings are within one point of each other, the student keeps the evaluation points he or she assigned but with no bonus. If there is a two-point or more discrepancy between the student's and teacher's ratings in either direction, no points are earned for the entire interval. Similar to the

teacher-directed phase, student ratings correspond to points that are accumulated and exchanged for backup rewards. Also, students receive teacher feedback about their performance, especially when point discrepancies occur. This phase continues until the student achieves a desired level of performance and accurately rates his or her behavior for at least three consecutive days. This phase may last for two to three weeks, depending upon student performance and the behaviors targeted.

Fading and Self-Management Phase

Once the student consistently provides accurate judgments of his or her behavior and the behavior has achieved the desired level, intervention components are faded (i.e., reduced or eliminated) toward complete self-management. First, one can gradually fade the teacher-directed component by decreasing the frequency of student and teacher matches. Additionally, the length of the self-evaluation interval can be extended so students rate their behavior less frequently, such as at the end of the class period rather than several times throughout the period. The reinforcement schedule also could be extended by increasing the number of points needed for backup rewards, or by exchanging points at less frequent intervals. The rate of fading procedures is determined by student responsiveness and the degree to which the student continues to accurately assess his or her behavior. Fading of intervention procedures continues until the rating system and rewards are completely removed, and students are managing their own behavior with natural consequences or self-management.

—Sheri L. Robinson and Kathryn E. Hoff

See also Applied Behavior Analysis; Behavior Intervention; Social Skills; Study Skills

REFERENCES AND FURTHER READING

Meichenbaum, D. (1977). *Cognitive-behavior modification.* New York: Plenum.

Rhode, G., Morgan, D., & Young, R. (1983). Generalization and maintenance of treatment gains of behaviorally handicapped students from resource rooms to regular classrooms using self-evaluation procedures. *Journal of Applied Behavior Analysis, 16,* 171–188.

Shapiro, E., & Cole, C. (1994). *Behavior change in the classroom: Self-management interventions.* New York: Guilford.

Skinner, C., Turco, T., Beatty, K., & Rasavage, C. (1989). Cover, copy, and compare: A method for increasing multiplication performance. *School Psychology Review, 18,* 412–420.

SENSORIMOTOR STAGE OF DEVELOPMENT

The sensorimotor stage of development begins at birth with the simple reflexes of the neonate and terminates at around two years of age with the onset of symbolic thought representing early childlike language. Within this stage of development, Piaget documents six separate and independent, yet interrelated substages:

1. Use of early reflexes
2. Primary circular reactions
3. Secondary circular reactions
4. Coordination of secondary schemes
5. Tertiary circular reactions
6. Symbolic representation

Through an examination of these individual substages, one can see how the child develops from a relatively passive organism that acts without any systematic goal into a thinking being who shows the beginning elements of intelligence. The last stage (18 to 24 months) is especially important; there is a major breakthrough in the child's ability to understand relationships between objects and the activities associated with the objects without direct experience or experimentation.

—Neil J. Salkind

SEPARATION ANXIETY DISORDER

Separation anxiety (SA) is nervousness or distress about being separated, or becoming separated, from the home or from an important person (e.g., mother, father) in the child's life. The anxiety experienced by the child impairs his or her ability to function in important areas of life (e.g., school and social settings). To make a diagnosis of separation anxiety, the child must be under 18 years of age at the onset of anxiety and the problem must exist for at least four weeks. The anxiety experienced by the child must be in excess of what is expected for the child's age. For example, it is normal (developmentally) for toddlers to cry or become upset when separated from their mother or father, but children, ages 5 years and older, should be able to separate from their parents for short periods of time (e.g., attending school).

Children with SA are reluctant to attend camp, school, or even sleep over at a friend's house. According to the *Diagnostic and Statistical Manual of Mental Disorders, Fourth Edition-Text Revision (DSM-IV-TR)* (American Psychological Association [APA], 2000), children age six years who are diagnosed with "Early Onset Separation Anxiety" may exhibit noncompliance, aggression, or anger when separation from significant adults is forced. For some SA children, the prospect of being apart from parents at night may result in an insistence that someone stay with them until they fall asleep, demands to sleep with the parents, or nightmares about being lost or abandoned. Physical complaints or arousal such as shortness of breath, heart palpitations, or sweating may accompany an impending separation. When away from home or parents, these children frequently fear that something bad will happen to their parents (i.e., illness, injury or death). As a result, children with SA frequently call home and harbor reunion fantasies.

PREVALENCE, ONSET, AND ASSOCIATED FEATURES

Prevalence estimates for SA are around 4% of the general population of children and adolescents. Younger children (especially females) are more at risk; in fact, SA is rare in late adolescence (*DSM-IV-TR*, 2000). SA seems to occur more often in close families and in children of parents (especially mothers) that experienced SA as a child or presently have an existing panic disorder.

Life stressors such as moving, changing schools, divorce, or the death of a loved one or animal can trigger SA in children; and they may result in the child perseverating on the possibility of accidents, death, or calamities that could happen while away from home or parents.

INTERVENTIONS

Few studies have investigated the effects of specific interventions for children with SA. Silverman and Dick-Niederhauser (2004) argue that treatments that work for other anxiety disorders may be equally effective for SA. Of the few studies that have assessed the effectiveness of interventions for SA children only, cognitive behavior therapy (CBT) seems to be the most efficacious (Silverman & Dick-Niederhauser, 2004). In CBT, the treatment uses principles of learning to help the child understand, monitor, and change behaviors, thoughts, or environmental events and to learn new ways to respond to the internal or external stimuli that trigger anxious responses.

There are many versions of CBT. For children with SA, a promising type of CBT involves exposure-based treatment. In exposure-based CBT, the emphasis is on teaching the child to remain relaxed, calm, and controlled while at the same time slowly removing (fading) the parent or other source of dependence from the child's presence. By rewarding the child for coping with thoughts and behaviors experienced through the fading process, the child learns the steps to take to cope with life events independently. This type of treatment has shown the most promise for children with SA.

In addition to CBT, treatments directed toward the family system are recommended. Family-based interventions that focus on altering the level of attachment between the parent and child are seen as critical for stable change to take place. While the best approach to reducing SA symptoms is unknown at this time, it is likely that broad-based approaches that include the family, school, and the child have the most promise for lasting change.

THE SCHOOL PSYCHOLOGIST AND SEPARATION ANXIETY

Unfortunately, SA frequently goes unrecognized in the schools (except in severe cases) because of the internalizing nature of the disorder (i.e., anxious thoughts, physiological reactions). Because SA is frequently difficult to detect, teachers may not be aware of students that have poor or nonexistent social lives, feel alienated, or simply miss their parents. For these reasons, school psychologists and educators must recognize the problem and act proactively to screen, evaluate, and offer programs that will assist children with SA and other anxiety-related disorders to become independent and fully functioning citizens.

Prevention programs designed to reduce the occurrence of SA may be targeted toward the parents of toddlers and preschool children in the school's enrollment area in an effort to help the parents provide activities (e.g., preschool, activities programs) and guidance to help their child learn to operate more independently. The school psychologist may be available during kindergarten screening to assist parents to prepare their child for school.

In persistent cases of SA, the school psychologist may offer CBT interventions in the school to help remediate the problem. In more severe cases, the parent and child may be referred to a community psychiatrist or psychologist for more intensive therapy or medication. At this time, no medications have been conclusively identified to be of value in the treatment of SA.

—Steven W. Lee

See also *DSM-IV*; Parenting; Psychopathology in Children; School Refusal

REFERENCES AND FURTHER READING

American Psychiatric Association. (2000). *Diagnostic and statistical manual of mental disorders* (4th ed., text rev.). Washington, DC: Author.

Silverman, W. K., & Dick-Niederhauser, A. (2004). Separation anxiety disorder. In T. L. Morris & J. S. March (Eds.), *Anxiety disorders in children and adolescents* (pp. 164–188). New York: Guilford.

SHAPING. *See* Behavior; Behavioral Concepts and Applications

SHYNESS

Shyness refers to anxiety, discomfort or inhibition experienced within the context of social settings or interpersonal interactions. Researcher Phillip Zimbardo (1977) estimated that 40% of Americans are shy, and has suggested that a large percentage (80%) of the population has experienced some form of shyness at some point in their lives. In most cases, shyness may reflect a normal emotional response elicited by a particular circumstance or situation. However, for some individuals shyness is characterized as an enduring trait in which anxiety and discomfort are experienced consistently across a wide variety of social settings and interpersonal interactions.

Arnold Buss (1986) developed an influential theory in which he describes two types of shyness: a fearful shyness, which develops around the age of seven months, and a self-conscious shyness that emerges in early childhood. Buss argues that the two forms develop independently, and the conditions that elicit them are very different. Fearful shyness first appears shortly after infants have developed secure attachments to caregivers and is manifested in terms of stranger wariness. This form of shyness, elicited by social novelty, generally continues through the first year and then gradually declines by the end of the second year. For some individuals, however, this type of shyness may persist throughout life, although older children and adults may become better skilled at masking their fears. Buss argues that similar to the basic emotion of fear, this form of shyness is associated with autonomic arousal and may include symptoms such as, accelerated heart rates and increased blood pressure. Jerome Kagan (2000) has focused on the physiological basis of such shyness and perceives social inhibition as a temperamental characteristic that is relatively stable throughout early childhood.

Kagan and his colleagues at Harvard University found physiological differences between sociable and shy babies as early as two months of age. Based on their findings, it is estimated that approximately 15% to 20% of newborns are biologically predisposed to be quiet, vigilant, and inhibited within novel situations. In response to novel stimuli, such as a moving mobile, inhibited infants demonstrate more physiological arousal manifested in terms of increased heart rates, jerky movements of the legs and arms, excessive fussiness, crying, and distress. Accelerated heart rates during the fetal period have also been linked to inhibition or shyness during infancy and childhood. Environmental factors, however, also play a role as approximately 25% of the time a physiological predisposition for shyness does not develop into shyness. Kagan suggests that a physiologically reactive temperament may be aggravated by stressful environmental factors such as inconsistent or unreliable parenting, family conflict, excessive criticism, or stressful school environments.

Just as the development of fear shyness is tied to the normal development of stranger wariness, the origin of self-conscious shyness is also tied to normal developmental processes. The cognitive abilities associated with public self-awareness develop between four and five years of age. Public self-awareness is a prerequisite to experiencing the emotions of embarrassment or self-consciousness. Self-conscious shyness is elicited by feeling exposed to the scrutiny of others and involves concern with how one is evaluated by peers. Self-conscious shyness is also associated with preoccupation or negative evaluations of one's own thoughts and behaviors. The anxiety stemming from this preoccupation may make it difficult to tune in to what others are saying and may interfere with a child's ability to communicate effectively.

According to Mary Ann Evans (2000), children who are shy tend to take longer to make their first comment, make fewer spontaneous comments, and spend less time speaking to adults and other children. Shy children also speak less frequently when arriving at school, during classroom discussions, and during school recess. In some cases the anxiety associated with school entry may result in selective mutism in children who are very shy.

Shyness may also limit children's opportunities to develop close friendships, which may, in turn, have negative effects on their social–emotional development. Jeffrey Parker and Steven Asher (1987) reported that children who have friends are more socially competent, happier, and less lonely. Close friendships, according to Gary Ladd (1987), contribute to children's emotional development by providing social support during potentially stressful events, such as the transition from preschool to kindergarten or their parents' divorce. In addition to interfering with children's social and emotional development, shyness may contribute to learning difficulties in the classroom. According to Zimbardo, children who are shy are more reluctant to ask questions, or ask for help in school. Social anxiety may make it difficult for children to think clearly and communicate effectively. Because participation in discussions and social interactions are important for the attainment of learning objectives, children who are shy may be at risk for lower academic achievement. Some research suggests that, on average, shy children are less verbally competent compared to their peers.

Unfortunately, shy children also appear to be viewed less favorably by teachers compared to children who are more outgoing. In one study, Evans and colleagues found that teachers gave lower evaluations to inhibited children in several areas including mathematics, reading comprehension, written expression, decision making and problem solving. Other research has found that teachers estimate higher intelligence quotient (IQ) scores for children who more easily plunge into new situations compared to those who are more hesitant, even when the two groups of children are equivalent in terms of measured intelligence.

CONCLUSION

For most individuals, shyness reflects a normal emotional response that occurs occasionally within in the context of certain situations. However, for some individuals shyness can be characterized as an enduring trait in which increased levels of anxiety and discomfort are experienced regularly across a wide variety of social settings and interpersonal interactions. Two independent types of shyness have been described, and the origins of each have been tied to normal developmental processes. Fearful shyness, elicited by social novelty, develops beginning in infancy and in most cases gradually disappears around the age of two years. Self-conscious shyness, elicited by embarrassment or social scrutiny, first emerges during early childhood. Although the two types of shyness are independent, they may coexist. Both physiological and environmental factors appear to contribute to the degree to which children experience shyness, which, in turn, may influence their social–emotional development and academic performance.

—*Brenda L. Lundy*

See also Communication Disorders; Defense Mechanisms; Fears; Friendships; School Refusal; Selective Mutism; Social Skills

REFERENCES AND FURTHER READING

Buss, A. H. (1986). A theory of shyness. In W. H. Jones, J. M. Cheek, & S. R. Briggs (Eds.), *Shyness: Perspectives on research and treatment* (pp. 39–46). New York: Plenum.

Evans, M. A. (2000). Shyness in the classroom and home. In W. R. Crozier (Ed.), *Shyness: Development, consolidation and change.* New York: Routledge.

Kagan, J. (2000). Inhibited and uninhibited temperaments: Recent developments. In W. R. Crozier (Ed.), *Shyness: Development, consolidation, and change.* New York: Routledge.

Ladd, G. W., & Price, J. M. (1987). Predicting children's social and school adjustment following the transition from preschool to kindergarten. *Child Development, 58,* 1168–1189.

Parker, J. G., & Asher, S. R. (1987). Peer relations and later personal adjustment: Are low-accepted children at risk? *Psychological Bulletin, 102,* 357–389.

Zimbardo, P. (1977). *Shyness: What is it, what to do about it.* New York: Symphony.

SINGLE-CASE EXPERIMENTAL DESIGN

Single-case experimental design (also known as time-series design) is a research methodology characterized by repeated assessment of a particular phenomenon (often a behavior) over time, and generally is used to evaluate interventions. There are three general types of single-case experimental designs, which differ according to their structure and purpose: within-series, between-series, and combined-series. Overall, single-case experimental designs offer an alternative to group designs in that they are particularly appropriate for, although not limited to, comprehensively evaluating interventions for individual clients. Because the client is repeatedly assessed across time, the single-case experimental design allows for investigation of client variability (i.e., changes) in response to treatment. Usually, this type of comprehensive information is unobtainable in group designs.

TYPES OF SINGLE-CASE EXPERIMENTAL DESIGNS

Within-Series Designs

The within-series designs are the most commonly used single-case experimental designs and are characterized by the evaluation of data points across time and within phases or conditions (e.g., treatment vs. no-treatment conditions). Specifically, data are gathered over time and grouped into phases, with each phase consisting of a certain number of consecutive data points. Changes are then assessed as they occur across time. Although there are a number of within-series designs (e.g., simple phase-change, changing-criterion, parametric, and periodic interventions), the simple phase-change design and the changing-criterion design are the most common.

The most basic form of the simple phase-change design is the A/B design in which A and B represent different phases—A represents a baseline phase (no treatment) and B represents an intervention phase (treatment). The simple phase-change design can be extended to include replication (e.g., A/B/A/B) and the investigation of additional interventions (e.g., A/B/A/ C/A or A/B/A/C/B+C). Intervention effects within the simple-phase change design are evaluated by investigating patterns of response across time and within phases.

The changing-criterion design is another example of a within-series design. It also typically consists of two phases: a baseline phase and an intervention phase. The intervention phase is characterized by systematic changes in the required level of performance in response to the dependent variable (the variable that is expected to change as a result of the intervention/ independent variable). Intervention effects are evaluated by the dependent variable's response to the preset criteria. As an example of a changing-criterion design, consider a student with selective mutism, an anxiety-based disorder characterized by the absence of speaking in particular social situations. The behavior of interest could be the number of times the child speaks to the teacher during class. Whereas the initial criterion could be one time per day, the subsequent criterion would consistently increase according to the student's performance and expected changes. The confidence by which one can draw conclusions about the effects of the intervention can be improved by scheduling a period of time when the criterion is not changed and demonstrating that the behavior did not change during the scheduled criterion. Moreover, the researcher can schedule an intervention withdrawal and replication, a procedure characteristic of the simple phase-change variation of a within-series design.

The parametric and periodic intervention designs are less common forms of the within-series designs. Briefly, the parametric intervention design involves varying one treatment (e.g., by intensity) and monitoring the effects of the variations. The periodic intervention design takes into account that treatments are not always present outside of scheduled treatment sessions. As such, if it is not feasible for a treatment to be implemented consistently in applied settings, the periodic intervention design allows for the implementation of a treatment and the monitoring of effects as frequently as treatment sessions.

Between-Series Designs

Similar to the within-series designs, between-series designs are structured by phases and across time, but the primary purpose is the comparison of two or more conditions (i.e., baseline compared to intervention or two or more interventions). The two types of between-series designs are the alternating-interventions design and simultaneous-interventions design. The alternating-interventions design is characterized by rapid and random or semirandom shifts between two or more interventions. In particular, different interventions (e.g., two procedures for teaching spelling) are alternated as often as necessary to capture meaningful measurement of the behavior of interest. Although a baseline condition is useful in this design, it is not necessary to establish that the observed effects are related to the intervention(s). Based on client response to the different interventions, effects are evaluated through the examination of intervention divergence and overlap. For example, if the data points recorded

for one intervention overlap minimally (e.g., 10%–20%) with the data points recorded for the second intervention, then differences between the interventions are likely more meaningful.

The simultaneous-interventions design is also a type of between-series design but is unique in that, following a baseline phase, all interventions are made available at the same time. However, clients are not necessarily exposed to all treatments equally. For example, a student may be exposed to praise, ignoring, and punishment in the classroom throughout the day. By using a simultaneous-interventions design, the student's "preference" for type of behavior management could be revealed. Overall, although the design can be useful in illuminating client preference for certain interventions, application of the simultaneous-interventions design has been limited.

Combined-Series Designs

The combined-series designs allow for comparisons within and between series. That is, participant variability is evaluated over time, as well as in response to different conditions. Similar to the within-series designs, there are several types of combined-series designs (e.g., multiple baseline, crossover, and constant-series control designs), with the multiple baseline design being the most common. The multiple baseline design's structure is a simple phase-change design (A/B series) in which the intervention phase is repeated across participants, settings, or behaviors. Ideally, the intervention phase is replicated across three different participants, settings, or behaviors; and interventions are implemented sequentially after changes are noted in the first A/B series. For example, if disruptive behavior is the behavior of concern, and the treatment is a behavior management plan, the behavior management plan could be implemented in an English class, and once improvements are observed, the behavior management plan could then begin in a Math class, and so on. Figure 1 gives an example of a multiple baseline design across participants, where the treatment is a reading intervention and the dependent variable is the number of words read correctly.

ANALYSES

Analysis of data is important so that one can understand the effects of the intervention(s) implemented in single-case experimental designs. In contrast to group designs, data in single-case experimental designs are

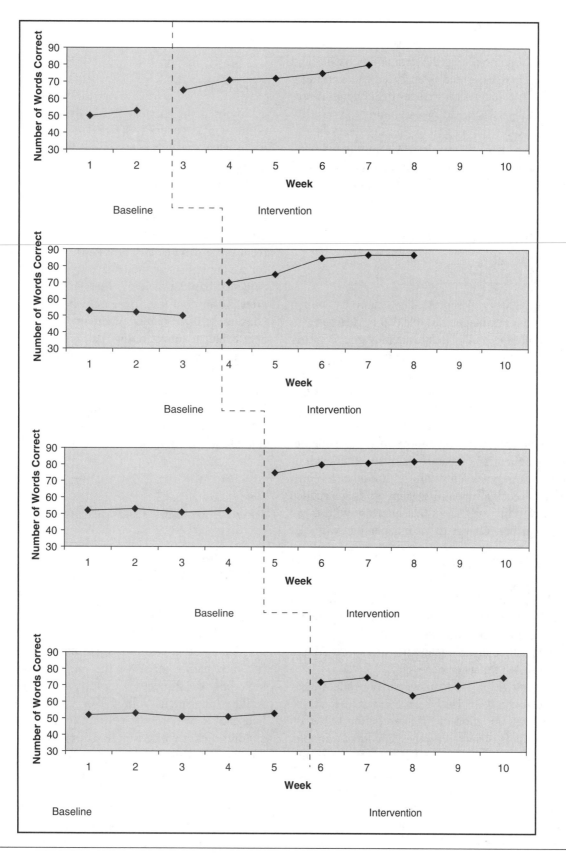

Figure 1   A Multiple-Baseline Research Design Across Participants Using "Number of Words Read Correctly" to Evaluate Reading Intervention

generally analyzed by visual inspection—that is, by assessing level, trend, and variability. Changes in level are assessed by comparing the data points before and after phase changes. Trend is analyzed by examining the slope of the data points to determine overall direction. Variability is assessed by examining the stability of the data points before and during the intervention. Although statistical analyses have not commonly been used to analyze data from single-case experimental designs, some statistical analyses are appropriate for these designs. In particular, nonparametric tests (tests used when assumptions of parametric tests are violated) can be appropriate for analyses.

INTERNAL VALIDITY

Internal validity describes the extent by which changes in the dependent variable can be attributed to the manipulation of the independent variable rather than other variables. Typically, the independent variable in single-case experimental designs is an intervention. Given that single-case experimental designs are fundamentally different from group designs, internal validity must be established in different ways. The fundamental procedure for establishing experimental control is replication, a feature that is used in each of the three design types. There are several other features of single-case experimental designs that can reduce threats to validity, or factors that interfere with one's ability to attribute change to the independent variable:

- Repeated assessment of the dependent variable occurs across phases of the experiment.
- Client variability is assessed over time. In addition, elements such as the independent and dependent variables and setting, clinician, and participant characteristics are specified and controlled for when necessary.
- Design flexibility to change the dependent measures is built in. That is, designs can be altered after the initiation of an intervention based on the effects observed on the dependent variable. For example, if sequential effects (effects resulting from the ordering of the conditions) are noted in an alternating-treatments design, the conditions can be reordered to strengthen the design and reduce this threat to validity.
- When possible, randomization can be used to structure the design to reduce threats to internal validity. Randomization refers to the random

assignment of treatments to observations/occasions.

APPLICATIONS

Although the application of single-case experimental designs is generally limited to research, there are some ways that they may be useful to psychologists in practice. First, as consumers of research, psychologists can use research findings from single-case experimental designs to inform their practice. In particular, because single-case experimental designs are often implemented in intervention studies, results from these designs can provide valuable information for psychologists as they strive to develop/implement evidence-based practices, that is, practices that are effective in controlled research. In addition to being consumers of research, practicing psychologists can also evaluate interventions using features of single-case experimental designs. For example, in using a simple phase-change design, a psychologist could first gather baseline data for the behavior of concern, then implement an intervention to address the behavior, and possibly replicate the baseline and intervention phases to strengthen the validity.

—*Gina C. Herrera and
Thomas R. Kratochwill*

See also Evidence-Based Interventions; Research

SINGLE-PARENT FAMILIES

As elevations in the rates of divorce and non-marital childbearing have altered the social landscape, the single-parent family is increasingly being blamed for germinating many of the nation's social issues, including delinquency, adolescent pregnancy, and welfare dependency. In 2000, 28% of all family households were single-parent families, and 84% of children living with a single parent resided with their mother (U.S. Bureau of the Census, 2000). Considering the implications for single parenting more broadly, it is estimated that 50% of children born in the 1980s and 1990s will reside in a one-parent situation during some period prior to reaching adulthood. These national demographics underscore the importance of understanding the effects of single-parent life on educational, social, and behavioral outcomes for children.

CHARACTERISTICS OF SINGLE-PARENT FAMILIES

The generally accepted definition of a single-parent home is a household in which one biological or adoptive parent raises at least one child under 18 years of age without the presence of a second adult. However, this general definition of single parenthood does not address the diversity in family form and basis. Considerable variations in a single-parent family exist, including the (Jones & Unger, 2000):

- Pathway that led to this status (i.e., never married, separated, divorced, or widowed)
- Household composition (e.g., multigenerational, cohabiting, or no additional adults present)
- Degree of support from family, friends, and absent parent
- Encompassing life conditions (e.g., economic, medical, psychological, and neighborhood)

In addition, ethnic diversity emerges as an especially important factor to consider in the incidence of single-parent homes. African American children are most likely to live in a single mother-child family (53% in 2000) compared to Hispanic (28%) and European American (21%) children. These differences reflect the heightened prevalence of nonmarital childbirth, higher rates of divorce, and lower remarriage rates among African American women compared with European American women (U.S. Bureau of Census, 2000). However, these statistics are misleading, as in the aggregate, the majority of children who reside with single parents were European American. Single-parent homes also differ in ethnic and cultural diversity regarding the basis for single parenthood.

Most European American children will reside in a postdivorce, single-parent home; however, African American children with single parents come from homes where their mother was never married. Racial differences also are apparent with regard to the head of the household in single-parent homes, with a significant percentage of African American children being raised by a grandparent alone and neither parent present. The dramatic increase in the prevalence of single fatherhood (percentage of single fathers increasing 25% from 1995 to 1998) is primarily among European American fathers (Lamb, 1999; U.S. Bureau of the Census, 2000).

Various social and psychological issues surround these various forms of single-parent families, as well as economic conditions. Economic destitution is a grave problem for many single-parent households, as 28% of single parents live below the poverty line (U.S. Bureau of the Census, 2000). Single mothers have the lowest annual median income for any family form (Jones & Unger, 2000), and adolescent single parenthood is particularly linked to notable economic disadvantage. Recent estimates suggest that nearly 70% of adolescent mothers and their children live in poverty; only 2% of adolescent mothers eventually complete college (Stoiber, 1997; U.S. Bureau of the Census, 2000). Additional economic ramifications include that single parents are more likely to reside in rental housing units located in unsafe neighborhoods and they do not have health insurance for either themselves or their children. Researchers surmise that single mothers are at a greater risk of facing financial hardships because of lower educational attainment, less employment and earnings, little to nonexistent child support, and meager public assistance (Stoiber & colleagues, 1998). Although single fathers endure economic adversities, they are less likely to be poor and more likely to be employed compared to single mothers.

ECOLOGICAL RISK AND RESILIENCY MODEL

Recent studies indicate that children in single-parent households are more likely to be raised in a high-risk environment. In particular, children of adolescent parents may represent a group of youngsters most seriously predisposed to serious social, developmental, and academic problems. Risk factors such as limited social and economic support, when fused with reduced parenting capacity, can impact negatively on the development of children of adolescent mothers. Rather than regarding children from single-parent homes, including those of adolescent mothers, as uniformly at risk for negative developmental outcomes, the ecological risk and resiliency model stresses individual differences in coping and adjustment (Stoiber & colleagues, 1998). The heterogeneity of risk and resilience factors surrounding lone-caregiver households is thought to influence children's school-related development and outcomes in diverse ways. More specifically, a sociocultural, ecological approach illuminates contextual processes associated with parental psychological functioning and child coping. Various dispositional characteristics and situational factors can influence whether single parents and their children either surmount or succumb to adversities. Moreover, the risk and resiliency model avoids "pathologizing" single caregivers and facilitates the examination of competencies that foster positive family functioning and adjustment.

FAMILY STRUCTURE AND CHILD DEVELOPMENTAL OUTCOMES

Economic level emerges as a notable factor both for young children and adolescents in their development and adjustment within a single-parent family. A recent review by Murry and colleagues (2001) indicates small differences in social–emotional and academic functioning between preschool- and elementary-age children from single-mother versus two-parent families. Specifically, children residing in lone-mother households exhibited slight elevations in reported behavioral problems and poor conflict management techniques, as well as reductions in social skills and academic achievement compared to youth from two-parent families. However, when income level was controlled, such differences dissipated.

Investigations of adolescents from divergent family forms revealed that superficially adolescents from single-mother households appeared to:

- Engage in more risk-taking behaviors (e.g., illegal behavior, substance use, sexual activity)
- Manifest greater levels of social–emotional difficulties (e.g., depression, aggression)
- Demonstrate inadequate social skills and academic performance compared to youth from married couples

Similar to the findings with younger children, however, when income level and family process variables were taken into account such differences diminished.

Taken together, these results indicate that single motherhood does not necessarily lead to negative academic and social–emotional outcomes for a child. Rather, economic destitution appears to have deleterious effects on children's adjustment in single-parent homes. In fact, McLanahan (1999) estimated that as much as half of the disadvantage associated with residing with a lone caregiver was the result of financial insecurity. As such, uncovering the processes involved in single parenting, poverty, and child development is essential for constructing efficacious interventions to insulate children from the effects of economic adversity.

FAMILY FACTORS AND YOUTH WELL-BEING

The findings thus far suggest that economic destitution is a significant contributor to the difficulties demonstrated by children raised in single-parent homes. Murry and colleagues (2001) and Kleist (1999) analyzed the extant research that has attempted to disentangle the relationship between poverty and child developmental outcomes in single-mother households. Taken as a whole, these findings suggest that financial strain influenced children's adaptive development indirectly through its pernicious grip on maternal psychological functioning and parenting quality. Specifically, the results reveal that a single mother's educational attainment is associated positively with better economic conditions (i.e., higher income level and less financial strain), which, in turn, foster parental involvement (e.g., spending time with children and effective supervision) and supportive, cognitively stimulating (e.g., reading books) parenting practices. Such positive parenting practices were associated with greater cognitive skills and low levels of behavioral problems in children. Conversely, financial strain in single mothers is associated with depressive symptoms, less maternal self-confidence, and poor parenting quality (i.e., punitive, aggravated, unsupervised, and nonstimulating caregiving), which, in turn, predicts heightened levels of child behavioral difficulties and academic problems. As such, it appears that poverty and associated family processes, rather than family structure, are vital factors for understanding child risk and outcomes associated with single parenting.

Children of a particular subgroup of lone caregiving—those born to adolescent, single mothers–are considered especially at risk for developing social–emotional and coping problems as compared with other children. Although not all children of adolescent mothers display problems in development, Stoiber and colleagues (1998) observed less competent coping behaviors (i.e., poorer self-regulation, greater irritability, negative or sad affect, and poorer social engagement and adapting to situations) for children of adolescent mothers, especially when the adolescent mothers seemed to experience heightened levels of distress. Stoiber also found that various protective factors appeared to promote positive coping skills in children of adolescent mothers. In particular, adolescent mothers who have positive and realistic expectations about their children and who demonstrate responsive parenting behaviors (e.g., positive verbal interactions, behavioral involvement, and monitoring) appear to have children who fare better than other children of adolescent mothers.

Marital dissolution is the largest single contributor to the increasing number of single-parent households, especially for European Americans. Unfortunately, the effects of divorce are often difficult to disentangle from other single-parent issues. The majority of post-divorce single-parent homes are headed by mothers, and research indicates particular age and sex differences in child adjustment. In general, both boys and girls during the first two years after the divorce demonstrate increases in internalizing and externalizing behaviors. Whereas by two years, the difficulties for girls seem to dissipate, higher rates of behavior problems and lower levels of academic achievement tend to continue for boys. The more negative outcomes for boys in single-mother divorce homes appear, at least in part, to be related to parenting style. In single-mother-headed homes, the interaction between parents and young boys tends to be more coercive and marked by nagging, inconsistency in rules, and escalating conflicts.

Although during the adolescent years girls typically continue to fare better than boys in academic performance, both male and female adolescents living in single/divorce homes engage in higher levels of risk-taking behaviors and conflictual exchanges, assume more independence, and are less likely to be supervised and monitored by an adult compared with children in two-parent families. Because parental monitoring is a key factor in predicting adolescent difficulties across family structure, single mothers' lack of active monitoring presents notable risks. For example, adolescents living in single-mother homes, particularly adolescent males, were found to be three times more likely to not complete high school compared to adolescents in two-biological-parent families, despite similar levels of school achievement. Although the reasons for school dropout are complex, it appears to be more related to support and coping difficulties than cognitive deficiencies for adolescents in single-mother homes.

Social support is also hypothesized to be a salient protective factor that diffuses the stress associated with economic hardship on maternal psychological functioning, thus facilitating adaptive child development. A series of studies have assessed the relationship between social support, maternal depression, stress, and children's behavioral problems among low-income, African American single mothers and their children (see, for example, McGroder, 2000). Greater financial strain and instrumental support (e.g., monetary and child care assistance) in conjunction with lower levels of emotional support and paternal involvement predicted elevated levels of maternal depression and stress. Such maternal difficulties were positively associated with increased physical punishment and child-challenging behavior (Jones & Unger, 2000). These results suggest that increases in social support may reduce the financial strain on mothers and, by extension, improve child outcomes.

CLINICAL AND SCHOOL PSYCHOLOGY PRACTICE IMPLICATIONS

As the challenges confronting single parents are numerous, several researchers in the field recommend a comprehensive, competency-based approach to intervention. Rather than a focus on remediating a single caregiver's "deficits," a normative, nondeficit approach aimed at enhancing the skills of single parents (who, on average, may be more permissive and less involved in their child's schooling) is suggested. Specifically, it is important for clinicians to be aware of the effects of limited adult resources within single-parent households, and thus, to provide single parents with the help and support needed to promote resiliency and adaptive child developmental outcomes. Approaching single-parent families within a normative stress and coping framework also facilitates moving the focus of prevention and intervention from altering a "deviant family structure" to enhancing coping ability, optimizing parenting resources, and clarifying critical family roles and responsibilities regarding the child. A competency-based approach does not preclude the need to be cognizant of the stresses involved in being a single parent, including economic strain, child care and health insurance issues, depression, and other life-transition circumstances. Therefore, psychologists must also address these multiple issues. Clinicians should implement evidence-based practices by drawing upon prevention and intervention approaches that reduce conduct problems, depression, and stress-related trauma. Effective prevention and intervention programs incorporate three important components (Greenberg & colleagues, 1999):

1. Build cognitive and behavioral skills in both the parent and child that are protective.

2. Help families become better attuned to emotional regulation and potential stressors.

3. Improve relationships and social functioning of children with parent(s) and peers.

The most efficacious interventions are those that integrate systems of mental health into systems of education and child care. Effective approaches also assist in attaining resources at the individual (e.g., parent and/or child therapy, educational/employment opportunities/job training), the family (e.g., parent-child interaction interventions, paternal involvement), and the community (e.g., affordable child and health care) levels. Successful provision of these comprehensive services requires collaboration among psychologists, social workers, and community organizers.

School psychologists are urged to engage in consultation with educational personnel regarding best practices in instruction and behavioral management. Brody and colleagues (2002) reported that positive classroom processes (i.e., high levels of organization, rule clarity, and student involvement) served a protection function that contributed to children's adjustment and self-regulation. In addition, school psychologists are encouraged to follow systematic procedures for incorporating evidence-based practices into their service delivery for children and families as provided in *Outcomes: Planning, Monitoring, Evaluating* (*Outcomes: PME*) (Stoiber & Kratochwill, 2002). *Outcomes: PME* also includes a Social Competence Goal Planner for establishing essential goals and priorities related to emotion regulation and self-control skills; social awareness and group participation/cooperation skills; and responsible social decision making and life choices. The most vital role for school psychologists is the promotion of healthy maturation for all children within the school, family, and community environments.

SUMMARY

Taken as a whole, these findings suggest that single parenthood by itself does not necessarily constitute a risk factor for children's development. However, single parents confront numerous obstacles that are less frequently encountered by two-parent families, including financial hardships, inadequate child care, and subsequent depression. Although less is known about single-father-headed households, when such stresses surpassed resources in single-mother households, adverse child outcomes were evidenced. As such, it is imperative for school psychologists to collaborate with other professionals in assisting single parents in surmounting such risks and strengthening protecting factors, thereby promoting caregivers' and children's positive adjustment.

—*Karen C. Stoiber and Michelle A. Miller*

See also Abuse and Neglect; Divorce Adjustment; Dropouts; Friendships; Parenting; Race, Ethnicity, Class, and Gender; Resilience and Protective Factors

REFERENCES AND FURTHER READING

Brody, G. H., Dorsey, S., Forehand, R., & Armistead, L. (2002). Unique and protective contributions of parenting and classroom processes to the adjustment of African American children living in single-parent families. *Child Development, 73,* 274–286.

Greenberg, M. T., Domitrovich, C., & Bumbarger, B. (1999). *Preventing mental disorders in school-aged children: A review of the effectiveness of prevention programs.* Report submitted to The Center for Mental Health Services (SaMHSA), Prevention Research Center, Pennsylvania State University.

Jones, C. W., & Unger, D. G. (2000). Diverse adaptations of single-parent, low-income families with young children: Implications for community-based prevention and intervention. *Journal of Prevention and Intervention in the Community, 20,* 5–23.

Kleist, D. M. (1999). Single-parent families: A difference that makes a difference? *The Family Journal: Counseling and Therapy for Couples and Families, 7,* 373–378.

Lamb, M. E. (Ed.). (1999). *Parenting and child development in "nontraditional" families.* Mahwah, NJ: Erlbaum.

McGroder, S. M. (2000). Parenting among low-income, African American single mothers with preschool-age children: Patterns, predictors, and developmental correlates. *Child Development, 71,* 752–771.

McLanahan, S. S. (1999). Father absence and the welfare of children. In E. Mavis Hetherington (Ed.), *Coping with divorce, single parenting, and remarriage: A risk and resiliency perspective* (pp. 117–145). Mahwah, NJ: Erlbaum.

Murry, V. M., Bynum, M. S., Brody, G. H., Willert, A., & Stephens, D. (2001). African American single mothers and children in context: A review of studies on risk and resilience. *Clinical Child and Family Psychology Review, 4,* 133–155.

Stoiber, K. C. (1997). Adolescent pregnancy and parenting. In G. G. Bear, K. M. Minke, & A. Thomas (Eds.), *Children's needs II: Development, problems, and alternatives.* Bethesda, MD: National Association of School Psychologists.

Stoiber, K. C., Anderson, A. J., & Schowalter, D. (1998). Group prevention and intervention with pregnant and parenting adolescents. In K. C. Stoiber & T. R. Kratochwill (Eds.), *Handbook of group intervention with children and families* (pp. 280–306). Boston, MA: Allyn & Bacon.

Stoiber, K. C., & Kratochwill, T. R. (2002). *Outcomes: Planning, monitoring, evaluating.* San Antonio: The Psychological Corporation.

U.S. Bureau of the Census (2000). *Current population survey.* Available online at http://www.census.gov

SMOKING (TEENAGE)

While smoking among U.S. adults has steadily declined since the Surgeon General's Report on Smoking and Health in 1964, tobacco use among adolescents has followed a roller coaster pattern. The Monitoring the Future National Survey (Johnston & colleagues, 2001) found that smoking among U.S. high school seniors peaked at 39% in 1976, dropped to 29% in 1981, resurged to 37% in 1997, and then declined to 31% in 2000. Cigarettes are not the only source of tobacco use for teenagers, however. The Centers for Disease Control and Prevention (CDC) (2000) reported that in 1999, 40.2% of high school students admitted using cigarettes, chewing tobacco, snuff, and/or cigars. This translates to 4.5 million teen tobacco users. Who are these teen tobacco users? CDC researchers found that:

- Around 35% of high school students smoked cigarettes.
- White (39%) and Hispanic (33%) students smoked more than African American (20%) students.
- High school dropouts (38%) were more likely to smoke.
- White male high school students (19%) used smokeless tobacco more often than Hispanic (6%) or African American (3%) students.
- Males were more likely to use smokeless tobacco or cigars than females.
- Students planning to go to college and students with college-educated parents were less likely to smoke.

- States' smoking rates varied from 11.9% in Utah to 43.6% in South Dakota.
- States' smokeless tobacco rates ranged from 3.8% in Hawaii to 29.8% in Montana.

NEGATIVE EFFECTS OF TOBACCO USE

As early as 1963, tobacco industry officials privately recognized that nicotine was addictive (Glantz & colleagues, 1996). On average, a cigarette puts 1 mg of poisonous nicotine into a smoker's blood—a thimbleful of nicotine, a 60-mg dose, would be fatal to adults. Researchers have found that the addictive power of nicotine can produce withdrawal-symptom-like cravings in teen smokers in a matter of weeks. Further, teens frequently underestimate how long and the amount they will smoke. Smoking a pack-a-day costs approximately $1,000 annually. The average smoker spends at least $3,300 per year on cigarettes.

Teens must consider both short-term and long-term outcomes of being hooked on nicotine. Tobacco smells cling to smokers—hands, clothes, hair—and many others strongly dislike the odor. Smokers develop bad breath and frequent coughs. Besides bad breath, smokers experience shortness of breath from reduced oxygen in the blood; the reason for this is printed in the Surgeon General's Warning on cigarette packs and ads: Cigarette smoke contains carbon monoxide.

Teens face additional risks. Smoking while driving distracts the driver and significantly accelerates the odds of having an accident. Also, for teens under 18 years of age, it is illegal to buy cigarettes. Depending on local statutes, teens risk probation, fines, or community service.

Smoking is considered a gateway drug. Researchers have found that teen smokers are more likely to use illegal substances, sell drugs, drink alcohol, quit school, or get pregnant by 12th grade than nonsmokers.

More long-term consequences are printed in the Surgeon General's Warning: Smoking can cause heart disease and cancer. The World Health Organization (1999) claims that smoking will eventually cause the demise of 500 million people currently alive. Smoking increases hardening of the arteries and heightens the risks for blood clotting, chest pains, and heart attacks. In 2002, smoking was linked to at least 30% of all cancer deaths. Smoking triggers the majority (87%) of lung cancer. Risks for lung cancer are 22 times higher for male smokers and 12 times higher for female smokers than nonsmokers. Smoking causes 47% of bladder cancer in men and 37% in women and puts kidneys at risk for cancer. Smoking increases risks for emphysema, peptic ulcers, and osteoporosis.

Smoking during pregnancy may result in fetal injury, premature birth, and low-birth-weight infants, warns the Surgeon General. Moreover, smoking heightens the risks for sudden death syndrome and otitis media. Smokers have lower fertility rates, more spontaneous abortions, and earlier menopause. Smokers are significantly more likely to lose teeth, develop cataracts and hearing losses, and to snore than nonsmokers.

Secondhand smoke, the third most preventable cause of death, causes 3,000 lung cancer deaths and 35,000 to 62,000 heart disease deaths annually. Secondhand smoke adversely affects children's cholesterol level. Besides heightening the odds of children getting meningitis, secondhand smoke also increases the frequency of asthma and snoring in children.

Smoking is a major cause of fire deaths and property damage globally. Overwhelming evidence documents the life-threatening impact of tobacco use.

PREVENTION STRATEGIES

Families, schools, and communities need to implement a balance of prevention and tobacco cessation programs. First, parents must endorse a tobacco-free lifestyle, even if they smoke. Authoritative parenting, characterized by parental warmth, firm limits, and autonomy to pursue ideas, is a protective factor against smoking. Tobacco-free friends, especially best friends, also help youngsters to internalize a tobacco-free norm.

Schools should implement effective strategies including tobacco-free policies, research-based prevention programs, stop-smoking programs, and strong extracurricular programs. Educators typically use one of three types of prevention programs: factual lectures like Drug Abuse Resistance Education (DARE), affective curriculum that enhances self-esteem, and social behavioral skills such as LifeSkills Training (LST) (Botvin, 1999). However, research shows that these prevention programs are not equally effective.

In analyzing drug prevention efforts, Cuijpers (2002) concluded that effective programs:

- Encouraged interactions among participants instead of lecturing

- Inoculated attitudes by students practicing rebuttals in the classroom to social pressures to smoke and use drugs
- Focused on social norms and public commitment not to use substances
- Gained community support from families and mass media while using community resources to combat drug use
- Used peer leaders as facilitators

Effective programs must also be developmentally appropriate for students from kindergarten to 12th grade.

Researchers have found that interactive programs cut tobacco use by 21%, while noninteractive ones yielded only a 4% reduction. Longitudinal data showed that DARE did not deter tobacco use. In contrast, when Botvin (1999) focused on teaching the behavioral skills in identifying and resisting peer influences, smoking rates were cut by 30% to 75%.

In addition, the availability and implementation of effective programs during the critical years of smoking initiation (ages 11 to 15 years) have the potential for delaying or reducing smoking. Approximately 25% of high school students reported smoking their first cigarette before their 13th birthday (CDC, 2000). CDC identified LST (Botvin, 1999) as effective in reducing tobacco use in middle school youths.

Finally, communities can contribute by enforcing laws banning tobacco to those younger than 18 years old. Raising taxes on cigarettes effectively reduces teenage smoking. States also need to invest more of their tobacco settlement money in prevention. In 2001, the average state spent about 6% of their tobacco settlement money on prevention with tobacco-producing states spending less than nontobacco-producing states.

—Albert F. Hodapp and Joan B. Hodapp

See also DARE Program; Self-Concept and Efficacy; Substance Abuse

REFERENCES AND FURTHER READING

Botvin, G. J. (1999). Prevention in schools. In R. T. Ammerman, P. J. Ott, & R. E. Tarter (Eds), *Prevention and societal impact of drug and alcohol abuse*. Mahwah, NJ: Erlbaum.

Centers for Disease Control and Prevention. (2000). Youth risk behavior-surveillance-United States 1999. *Morbidity and Mortality Weekly Report, 49*, SS–5.

Cuijpers, P. (2002). Effective ingredients of school-based drug prevention programs: A systematic review. *Addictive Behaviors, 27,* 1009–1023.

Glantz, S. A., Slade, J., Bero, L. A., Hanauer, P., & Barnes, D. E. (1996). *The cigarette papers.* Berkeley, CA: University of California Press.

Johnston, L. D., O'Malley, P. M., & Bachman, J. G. (2001). *Monitoring the future national results on adolescent drug abuse: 1975–2000. Volume 1: Secondary school students.* Bethesda, MD: National Institute on Drug Abuse.

World Health Organization. (1999). *The world health report 1999: Making a difference.* Geneva, Switzerland: Author.

SOCIAL REINFORCEMENT. *See* APPLIED BEHAVIOR ANALYSIS; BEHAVIOR; BEHAVIORAL CONCEPTS AND APPLICATIONS

SOCIAL SKILLS

Social skills are generally defined as socially accepted behaviors that result in desirable social outcomes. Although there is no specific agreed-upon definition, social skills most often are conceptualized as learned behaviors that:

- Are comprised of discrete verbal and nonverbal behaviors
- Require effective responsiveness to social situations
- Are influenced by the social environment

For example, saying "Hello" and shaking hands when meeting someone are learned verbal and nonverbal behaviors that are demonstrated in reaction to meeting a new person. However, this response may not be appropriate in another culture. Therefore, the social skills involved in greeting someone require responsiveness to the social environment.

There are five major domains of social skills that emerge from the research on social behaviors:

1. Cooperation involves behaviors such as helping others, sharing, and complying with the rules.

2. Assertion involves behaviors such as initiating social interactions (e.g., asking to enter a game) and responding assertively to others (e.g., responding appropriately to peer pressure).

3. Self-control involves behaviors such as managing anger in conflict situations and receiving criticism or feedback from others.

4. Peer relationships involve behaviors such as empathizing, complimenting or praising peers, and getting along with peers.

5. Academic social skills involve behaviors such as taking responsibility for completing assignments and completing academic tasks independently.

Social skills are further conceptualized as being part of a broader area of behavior called social competence. Whereas social skills are comprised of learned behaviors that facilitate social interactions and relationships; social competence involves multiple dimensions of functioning such as emotional adjustment, communication skills, and cognitive abilities. Social competence is further viewed as a summary term that reflects the social judgments and evaluations of others about the quality of an individual's overall social behavior.

Understanding children's and adolescents' social skills is important for several reasons. From a developmental standpoint, it is important to understand how children develop social skills as they mature. Social skills are necessary for the establishment of friendships and for interacting in the social world, including the school setting. Therefore, the establishment of positive peer relations and social interactions are important for children's social development. In research, the identification of the development of social skill strengths can aid one's understanding of the behaviors of socially successful children. These behaviors can, in turn, be used to understand children's and adolescents' social skill deficits and can aid in the design and study of social skills assessments and interventions. Children with social skills deficits often experience poor peer and adult relationships and often experience negative social and emotional consequences that can continue throughout adulthood. These negative consequences can include low academic achievement, depression, anxiety, low self-esteem, poor self-concept, social withdrawal, fewer positive employment opportunities, and antisocial behaviors such as aggression and criminality. Children with poor social skills also are at risk for becoming victims of bullying and other aggressive behaviors. Researchers have estimated that at least 10% of children experience negative peer relationships.

Therefore, a large number of children with poor social relationships are at risk for developing behavioral and emotional difficulties. Children with disabilities often have social skills deficits that put them at heightened risk.

ASSESSMENT OF SOCIAL SKILLS

The purposes of social skills assessments are to:

- Identify and classify social skill strengths and deficits
- Identify target behaviors for intervention
- Provide data on environmental influences on social skill development
- Provide data for intervention and monitoring progress

An important issue in the assessment of social skills is the determination of whether a child has a social skill acquisition or performance deficit. An acquisition deficit is one in which the child has not acquired the knowledge or ability to perform a social skill. For example, a child may not ask to play in a game because he or she does not know how to ask appropriately. A performance deficit is one in which the child has the knowledge and ability to perform a social skill, but the child does not consistently perform the skill in desired situations. Another important issue in social skills assessment is determining whether a child exhibits problematic behaviors that interfere with his or her ability to engage in appropriate social behaviors. For example, a child may know how to ask to join a game, but has heightened levels of social anxiety that interfere with his or her ability to ask. There are various potential interfering behaviors, including anxiety, impulsivity, or aggressive behavior.

There are a variety of methods that are used in the assessment of social skills. Rating scales represent one of the most frequently used measures. The majority of social skills rating scales are designed for gathering data on the frequency of occurrence of specific social skills. For example, a rating scale may contain items such as "Appropriately invites friends to play" or "Controls temper in conflicts with adults," which are rated on a frequency scale (e.g., Never, Sometimes, Always). Depending on the measure, ratings can be gathered from parents or parent surrogates, teachers, and, when appropriate, the children themselves. Gathering data from these multiple sources can assist

understanding of different perspectives regarding a child's social skills across home and school settings.

Observation methods are used to gather information about a child's social skills in natural settings such as in the classroom, in the cafeteria, and on the playground. Observation methods can be highly structured so that defined behaviors are measured for frequency of occurrence or measured for occurrence during specified time periods or intervals. For example, a child's play behavior may be observed during recess by a school psychologist who records every 30 seconds whether the child was playing alone or with others. Other observation methods are less structured and rely on a narrative approach for describing a child's social interactions. Observation methods often include a focus on the environmental variables that may increase or decrease a child's social skills, such as the reactions of peers and adults to a child's attempts to initiate a conversation. Observations also can be conducted in what is known as analogue assessment, which involves having a child role-play social scenarios and observing his or her performance.

Interview methods are used to gather information about a child's social skills strengths and weaknesses and to aid in the identification of specific skill deficits for intervention. Interviews can be conducted with children, parents (or parent surrogates), and teachers; and the information obtained from these interviews can be used separately or conjointly with information obtained from other sources. Interviews can be structured, with a focus on the identification and treatment of specific social skills, or they can be less structured, with a greater emphasis on feelings and perceptions about a child's social skills.

Sociometric methods focus on the assessment of a child's relationships in regard to popularity, peer acceptance, peer rejection, and reputation. Most sociometric assessment methods obtain information on social relationships by assessing children's positive and negative social perceptions of one another. There are a variety of sociometric assessment techniques. The most widely used technique is peer nominations, in which children in a social group or school classroom anonymously identify social preferences for their classmates. Peer ratings are conducted by providing a list of children's names in the social group or classroom along with a rating of items of social acceptance. In contrast to peer nominations and rankings, sociometric rankings are completed by an adult(s), most often the classroom teacher. The use of sociometric procedures has declined, most likely because of the advancement of social behavior rating scales and ethical concerns about the use of sociometric methods.

For the purposes of intervention, assessment methods often are combined in a comprehensive social skills assessment that may include rating scales, observations, and interviews. Using multiple methods of assessment is considered best practice because it increases the likelihood that the behaviors targeted for intervention are valid and that specific social skills deficits are clearly defined. It is also important to use multiple assessment methods to monitor a child's progress and to assess the effectiveness of the intervention.

SOCIAL SKILLS INTERVENTIONS

There are several types of interventions for social skills problems or deficits. Most social skills interventions (also known as social skills training) focus on increasing positive social behaviors and using nonaversive methods to improve a child's skills. The decision to use a particular intervention depends on a variety of factors, including:

- The environmental situations that surround a particular social skill
- The severity of the social skill deficits
- Whether the problems are acquisition or performance deficits or a combination of both
- Whether interfering behaviors are present

In many cases, a combination of interventions may be used to meet the needs of the child who receives the social skills intervention or training.

Behavioral intervention methods focus on observable behavior and the antecedent and consequent events that surround behavior. Antecedent events occur before a behavior and act as a stimulus that controls whether a particular social skill is initiated. Antecedent control interventions are used to modify social skills through cueing or prompting, such as a teacher reminding a student to play nicely at recess or having a peer initiate a conversation with a socially withdrawn child. Antecedent control interventions also include altering the setting in which a behavior occurs, such as changing seating arrangements or providing socially interactive games in the classroom or at home. Consequent events occur after a behavior and act to increase or decrease the likelihood that a behavior will occur. When a behavior is increased in

response to a consequence, it is referred to as reinforcement, whereas decreasing a behavior in response to a consequence is referred to as punishment. For example, tangible rewards, praise, and increased positive social interactions that occur after a social skill is exhibited may reinforce the occurrence of the behavior; whereas being teased or ignored by peers may punish the occurrence of a skill.

Cognitive behavior therapy intervention methods focus on changing an individual's internal cognitions (thoughts) coupled with behavioral intervention methods to increase self-regulation of behavior and problem-solving abilities. Two of the most frequently used cognitive–behavioral social skills intervention procedures are coaching and social problem solving. Coaching is a direct instruction technique that involves a coach (e.g., school psychologist, counselor, teacher, or parent) who provides the child with specific steps for enacting a social skill, rehearses the skill with the child, and then provides specific feedback to correct and to reinforce the child's performance. Social problem-solving interventions focus on teaching children the process of solving social or interpersonal problems. There are a variety of related social problem-solving methods that use a similar sequence of steps to train children with social skills difficulties. The basic steps are:

- Recognize and define when a problem exists.
- Generate alternative strategies for reacting to the problem.
- Consider the consequences for each alternative reaction.
- Choose the most adaptive strategy.
- Specify the steps required to implement the strategy.
- Evaluate the strategy and reinforce effective solutions.

Social learning intervention methods are based on social learning theory. According to the theory, social behaviors are acquired through observational learning and through reinforcement. A major component of social learning theory is modeling, where behaviors are learned by observing the behavior of others such as parents and peers. Models can have positive or negative influences on a child's behavior. For example, if a child observes her teacher often counting to 10 to get his anger under control, the child may use the same strategy to deal with her own anger. Alternatively, if a child observes his teacher often yelling when she is angry, the child may learn to use yelling when he is angry or frustrated. When used as a social skills intervention, modeling involves three major components:

1. Skill instruction, in which the need for the social skill and the steps to enact the skill are presented

2. Modeling, in which a social skills trainer models the skill

3. Skill performance, in which the child practices the skill in a role-play situation and receives feedback.

Peer and classroom-wide intervention methods focus on providing group intervention and support in natural settings. Peer-based interventions may include structured peer contact, in which children with social skills deficits are placed in a small group with peers who have social skills strengths. The group then engages in a cooperative, interactive learning situation that is oriented toward some goal or outcome, such as an in-class project. Peer-initiated contact is an intervention in which peers with strong social skills are enlisted to initiate social interactions with children who have social skills deficits. On a larger group level, classroom-wide (and sometimes schoolwide) interventions are used as both a preventive method and to increase children's social skills. Most classroom-wide interventions use some combination of the interventions already outlined in this article.

For an intervention to be judged successful, the child or adolescent who receives social skills training should be able to demonstrate those skills in the natural environment. Many social skills interventions take place in settings removed from the multiple environments in which social skills may be exhibited. For example, a child who learns new social skills in a school psychologist's office may not demonstrate the skills on the playground or in the classroom. When a behavior is demonstrated in natural environments beyond the training situation, it is known as generalization of the behavior. Methods for facilitating the generalization of social skills interventions include teaching social skills that are likely to be reinforced in natural environments and providing for the practice of the skills in multiple contexts and environments.

—*R. T. Busse*

See also Classroom Climate; Egocentrism; Friendships; Peer Pressure; Shyness; Study Skills

REFERENCES AND FURTHER READING

Elliott, S. N., & Busse, R. T. (1991). Social skills assessment and intervention with children and adolescents. *School Psychology International, 12,* 63–83.

Gresham, F. M. (2002). Best practices in social skills training. In A. Thomas & J. Grimes (Eds.), *Best practices in school psychology IV* (pp. 1029–1040). Bethesda, MD: National Association of School Psychologists.

Merrell, K. W. (1999). *Behavioral, social, and emotional assessment of children and adolescents.* Mahwah, NJ: Erlbaum.

Sheridan, S. M., & Walker, D. (1999). Social skills in context: Considerations for assessment, intervention, and generalization. In C. R. Reynolds & T. B. Gutkin (Eds.), *The handbook of school psychology* (3rd ed., pp. 686–708). New York: John Wiley.

SOCIAL VALIDITY. *See* BEHAVIORAL CONCEPTS AND APPLICATIONS; BEHAVIORAL MOMENTUM; GENERALIZATION; KEYSTONE BEHAVIOR

SOCIAL WORKERS (SCHOOL)

Social work is the professional activity of helping individuals, groups, and communities improve their overall social functioning and working toward influencing environmental social conditions that will aid is reaching this goal. Social workers help people gain access to resources; provide counseling to individuals, groups, and families; work to enhance social and health services; and advocate for the individuals they serve (National Association of Social Workers [NASW], 1973). Social workers are committed to helping individuals obtain ultimate functioning in their environment and have expertise in human behavior and development; social, community, and cultural organizations; and the interactions that take place between these factors (Barker, 1999).

ROLE AND FUNCTION

School social work is a specialized area of social work practice. School social workers help students make successful school adjustments to enhance their ability to learn in their educational environment. They work with other school personnel and local social service agencies to help students overcome or cope with physical, emotional, or economic difficulties, as well as address social and behavioral problems that may be influencing their ability to perform well in school. School social workers often provide individual and group counseling, consult with teachers, participate on educational teams, facilitate communication and change for the benefit of their students, and advocate for students' needs (NASW, 1973). In promoting enhanced school adjustment and functioning for students, school social workers help the school, family, and community coordinate their efforts for the benefit of those they serve in the school. They facilitate collaboration of all systems by providing the best services available to meet student needs. School social workers often assist in working with parents and the community for the purposes of promoting a better understanding of the school's practices, policies, and philosophies. Most school social workers have a master's degree in Social Work (MSW), and many are often certified or licensed according to the NASW Standards for School Social Work Services (Barker, 1999).

COMPARISON TO SCHOOL PSYCHOLOGISTS

The roles of school social workers may overlap with the professional roles of school psychologists. According to Fagan and Wise (2000), a school psychologist is a professional psychological practitioner who applies a psychological perspective when working with the difficulties of students and educators in a school. Like school social workers, school psychologists are often employed by school districts and serve on educational teams to help students succeed academically, socially, and emotionally. Both school social workers and school psychologists work directly and indirectly with children, teachers, parents, and the community to meet the needs of students and promote learning (Fagan & Wise, 2000). Social workers and school psychologists are trained to work at the individual level as well as the systems level. Each of these professionals may engage in counseling, consultation, assessment, and various intervention activities.

Despite these similarities, there are differences in their training and practice. Unlike school social workers, school psychologists have extensive training in both education and psychology, including expertise in providing both direct and indirect comprehensive psychological services (Fagan & Wise, 2000). School psychologists have a master's, specialist, or a doctoral

degree in school psychology. To practice school psychology, school psychologists must be certified or licensed in the state of employment. School psychologists are trained to provide a wide range of services including psychoeducational assessment, intervention, prevention, and mental health promotion. The expertise of social workers centers on understanding human development and behavior within the social environment, psychosocial assessment, casework, and social services; school psychologists' expertise lies in their training as psychoeducational consultants. They have an understanding of the learning environment as well as the cognitive, affective, social, and behavioral factors that may be influencing students' abilities to learn. When working to meet the needs of children, school psychologists consider the developmental levels and processes of children within the context of their environment; thus school psychologists take into consideration all factors that could be influencing a student's performance and functioning (Commission for the Recognition of Specialties and Proficiencies in Professional Psychology, 1998).

Both school social workers and school psychologists work to promote student functioning in a positive learning environment. Each profession is founded upon different training and expertise; however, their professional activities center on improving the academic, social, and emotional needs of children so that they can appropriately benefit from their educational program. The roles and functions of school social workers and school psychologists may coincide in some circumstances, but the defining boundaries are ultimately established by other factors, including the specific district of employment, the needs of the school, and the preferences of the professional.

—*Karen Rogers*

REFERENCES AND FURTHER READING

Barker, R. (Ed.). (1999). *The social work dictionary.* Washington, DC: National Association of Social Workers.

Commission for the Recognition of Specialties and Proficiencies in Professional Psychology. (1998). *Archival description of the specialty.* Washington, DC: Education Directorate.

Fagan, T., & Wise, P. (2000). *School psychology: Past, present, and future* (2nd ed.). Bethesda, MD: The National Association of School Psychologists.

National Association of Social Workers. (1973). *Standards for social service manpower.* Washington, DC: Author.

SOCIAL–EMOTIONAL ASSESSMENT

Social–emotional assessment is an essential part of the psychological and educational evaluation process. The term *social–emotional assessment* includes, but is not limited to, peer relations, affect, emotional resilience (e.g., the ability to recover from emotional setbacks), social withdrawal, social competence, antisocial behavior, and social status. Social–emotional assessment also involves the methods and procedures to measure these constructs. It is an important part of the process of identifying, understanding, and responding to the various problems and challenges that children and adolescents face.

FOUNDATIONS OF ASSESSMENT

First and foremost, assessment should be part of a problem-solving process. In such a process, the first issue to consider is "what is the question" that the assessment is supposed to answer. The initial phases of the assessment should be focused on clarifying the problem and developing a clear notion of the purpose of the assessment. The next phases of this problem-solving approach to assessment involve selecting tools for collecting assessment data, and then implementing those procedures. Next, the obtained data are analyzed with particular attention to how the data may help to answer the assessment question. Finally, the assessment information may be used to help guide the development of potential interventions and the evaluation of such interventions. When conducted in this manner, social–emotional assessment becomes a more comprehensive and useful process than simply administering a series of tests and then interpreting the results for diagnostic purposes.

ASSESSMENT TECHNIQUES

Direct behavioral observation is an essential tool for assessing many behavioral, social, and emotional problems of children and adolescents. Direct observation is a procedure where an observer defines the behaviors of interest, then systematically observes and records the target behaviors. This method allows the observer to gather practical information about an individual's behavior, as it occurs in an interactive environment. Gathering this information is more likely to provide understanding of the conditions that bring about and maintain behaviors of interest, including both problem and desirable behaviors. The preferred type of observation is to assess individuals in their natural day-to-day environment (e.g., playground, classroom).

There are two other types of observations commonly used for assessment. The first is to replicate the conditions of the natural environment under a more structured and controlled setting (e.g., clinic), while the second type is to train individuals to observe and record their own behavior during daily activities. There are several ways that observed behavior may be recorded. The foremost advantage of any direct behavioral observation is the ability to identify features in an environment that influences the occurrence and nonoccurrence of behavior in an attempt to explain the reason for the behavior. One challenge with direct behavioral observation is to ensure that an observer does not influence the behavior of the child or adolescent being observed.

Behavior rating scales provide another assessment method useful for planning and implementing interventions. Rating scales provide a standardized format for the development of summary judgments about child and adolescent behaviors by an informant. The informant is typically an adult (e.g., parent, teacher) who knows the child or adolescent well enough to provide information about specified behaviors. Behavior rating scales measure perceptions of behavior as opposed to providing a firsthand measure of the existence of the behavior. Examples of common behavior rating scales for children and adolescents include the Behavior Assessment System for Children (Reynolds & Kamphaus, 1992), Child Behavior Checklist (Achenbach, 1991), and the Conners' Rating Scales (Conners, 1997). Rating scales allow informants to indicate whether a specific symptom is present or absent in an individual and to estimate to what degree the symptom is present. For example, a common three-point rating system allows the rater to score a specific behavior descriptor such as "sad or depressed" from 0 to 2, with:

- 0 indicating the symptom is "never present"
- 1 indicating the symptom is "sometimes present"
- 2 indicating the symptom is "frequently present"

Rating scales are generally reliable and valid tools because they allow the informant to differentially weight each specified symptom based on a numerical value and frequency or intensity description. Weighing each of the specified behavior characteristics allows a more precise measurement of how frequent or intense the behavior is believed to be by the informant. Rating scales are best used for early screening of children and adolescents who have the potential for developing more severe problems. Behavior rating scales are also useful to assess progress during and after interventions. One major challenge in using behavior rating scales is the possibility of subjective responses from the raters, which may not be an accurate measure of the individual being assessed.

As part of an assessment battery, interviewing is a technique that may be an essential part of helping to understand and address the concerns of the child or adolescent. Although interviews may appear to resemble a typical conversation, they are driven by specific goals related to obtaining relevant information that may be used in making decisions. Interviews are, therefore, very structured and are usually "controlled" by the interviewer through initiating interchanges and posing questions with a clear direction on a particular topic. An advantage of interviewing is the flexibility provided during the course of the assessment. The clinician has the opportunity to shorten or lengthen the interview, to change directions when needed, and to focus on specific aspects of the child or adolescent thoughts, behaviors, or emotions that emerge as being important at the time. To obtain reliable and relevant information from the child or adolescent during an interview, the interviewer must have sufficient knowledge of child development and methods of making the interview appropriate to the interviewee. The interviewer can help determine the extent and quality of the self-reported information by providing an atmosphere that portrays an accurate understanding of the expressed concerns. It is important to show positive regard for the child or adolescent so that he or she feels safe and comfortable around the interviewer. Also, the interviewer must possess a keen eye and insight to detect both the nonverbal and verbal messages or signals that the child or adolescent sends out. Before conducting an interview, it is useful to obtain background information from parents and/or teachers to help guide the focus of the interview.

Objective self-report tests are assessment tools in which a children or adolescents respond to standardized questions about their own social–emotional behavior. Their responses are compared to those of a normative group, where each possible response is associated with a predetermined score, leaving no room for individual judgments in the scoring process. Self-report tests are useful for screening purposes and for making decisions about additional forms of assessment that may be needed. Examples of self-report tests include the Minnesota Multiphasic Personality Inventory-Adolescent (Butcher & colleagues, 1992), Personality Inventory for Youth (Lacher & Gruber, 1995), and Internalizing Symptoms Scale for Children (Merrell & Walters, 1998).

Projective-expressive techniques are assessment tools that use ambiguous tasks or stimuli (e.g., storytelling, drawings, and sentence completions) to detect underlying personality processes and social–emotional functioning. For example, a child may be asked to draw a picture of a person, and the evaluator uses this drawing as the basis for making inferences about the child's social–emotional functioning. Despite being among the more popular forms of social–emotional assessment, there are many concerns of misuse and weak technical properties that make the information obtained in this manner questionable. When compared to other forms of assessment, projective-expressive techniques are best used to help encourage communication and connection with children and adolescents, who often find the activities to be fun and nonthreatening. This form of assessment should not be used as a primary diagnostic tool.

An additional social–emotional assessment method is sociometric techniques, which involve directly gathering information within a peer group (e.g., classroom) concerning the social interactions within that group. Social status, popularity, and social acceptance or rejection are some of the common ideas assessed with sociometric procedures. Sociometric procedures involve asking children to list the other children within their group who they would most like to work or play with (or in some cases, who they would least like to work or play with). Despite many strengths, sociometric procedures are not commonly used because of concerns regarding the use of negative criteria in evaluating individuals and the fear of children comparing their responses and then alienating other children.

THE ROLE OF SCHOOL PSYCHOLOGISTS

School psychologists typically use social–emotional assessments as part of an information-gathering process to determine eligibility for special education services; provide early screening for potential problems; or to plan social, behavioral, or emotional interventions. Assessment is also used to monitor and evaluate interventions plans to determine their effectiveness. As the diversity of the American population continues to increase, school psychologists will be increasingly challenged to implement and integrate assessments that are sensitive to culture, ethnicity, and other forms of diversity. This sensitivity is crucial for obtaining accurate information as culture and other forms of diversity undoubtedly shape an individual's interpersonal communication style, behavioral characteristics, and perceptions.

CONCLUSION

The past two decades have brought about significant advances in the area of social–emotional assessment of children and adolescents. New technologies have been employed for developing more refined and accurate methods and models of assessment. A recommended best practice for school psychologists in social–emotional assessment of children and adolescents is to obtain information through the use of different methods, sources, and settings. Specifically, it is recommended that any comprehensive social–emotional assessment include information gathered from multiple settings, use multiple assessment methods, and include multiple sources or informants. Such a broad-based assessment design will help to minimize error, assist in identifying the core concerns of interest, and help link assessment findings to effective interventions.

—*Kenneth W. Merrell*
and Duane M. Isava

See also Behavioral Assessment; Interviewing; Projective Testing; Psychopathology in Children; Social Skills

REFERENCES AND FURTHER READING

Achenbach, T. M. (1991). *Integrative guide to the 1991 CBCL/ 4–18, YSR, and TRF Profiles.* Burlington, VT: University of Vermont, Department of Psychiatry.

Butcher, J. N., Williams, C. L., Graham, J. R., Archer, R., Tellegen, A., Ben-Porath, Y. S., et al. (1992). *Minnesota Multiphasic Personality Inventory-Adolescent (MMPI-A): Manual for administration, scoring, and interpretation.* Minneapolis, MN: University of Minnesota.

Conners, C. K. (1997). *Conners' rating scales revised.* North Tonawanda, NY: Multi-Health Systems.

Kamphaus, R. W., & Frick, P. J. (2001). *Clinical assessment of child and adolescent personality and behavior* (2nd ed.). Boston: Allyn & Bacon/Longman.

Lacher, D., & Gruber, C. P. (1995). *Personality Inventory for Youth (PIY) manual: Technical guide.* Los Angeles: Western Psychological Services.

Merrell, K. W. (2003). *Behavioral, social, and emotional assessment of children and adolescents* (2nd ed.). Mahwah, NJ: Erlbaum.

Merrell, K. W., & Walters, A. S. (1998). *Internalizing symptoms scale for children.* Austin, TX: Pro-Ed.

Reynolds, C. R., & Kamphaus, R. W. (1992). *Behavior assessment system for children: Manual.* Circle Pines, MN: American Guidance.

Sattler, J. M. (1998). *Clinical and forensic interviewing of children and families: Guidelines for the mental health, education, pediatric, and child maltreatment fields.* La Mesa, CA: Jerome M. Sattler.

Sattler, J. M. (2002). *Assessment of children: Behavioral and clinical applications* (4th ed.). La Mesa, CA: Jerome M. Sattler.

Shapiro, E. S., & Kratochwill, T. R. (2002). *Behavioral assessment in schools: Theory, research, and clinical applications* (2nd ed.). New York: Guilford.

SOCIOECONOMIC STATUS

Socioeconomic status (SES), a multidimensional social standing relevant to one's society, is comprised of interrelated factors, including income, wealth, occupation, education, political attitude, political power, tastes, cliques, prestige, and material comfort. The levels of socioeconomic status are on a continuum with unclear divisions. The five most common levels are upper class, upper-middle class, lower-middle class, working class, and lower class. Upper-class individuals tend to have very high incomes, prestigious occupations, and high levels of education (e.g., professional or graduate degrees). Upper-middle-class individuals tend to have high incomes, professional occupations, and college degrees. Lower-middle-class individuals usually have modest incomes, semiprofessional occupations, and little or no college education. Working-class individuals have low incomes, tend to work in skilled labor occupations, and some have not completed their high school education. Lower-class individuals have little income and a poor education. Understanding socioeconomic status and its influence is important for educators and psychologists. For example, low socioeconomic status often puts students at risk for academic, social–emotional, and behavior difficulties.

Understanding socioeconomic status and its influence offers insight into a child or adolescent's life, providing a greater understanding of behaviors, values, manners, and more.

—*Tonya N. Davis*

See also Race, Ethnicity, Class, and Gender; Single-Parent Families

SOCIOMETRIC ASSESSMENT

Sociometric assessment is the measurement of interpersonal relationships in a social group. Sociometric measurement or assessment methods provide information about an individual's social status, which is their social standing within a group. School-based sociometric assessment focuses on a child's relationships with peers. Most sociometric assessment methods derive information on social relationships by assessing children's positive and negative social perceptions of one another. Researchers have found that sociometric assessment can be useful in identifying children's social standing and predicting children's positive or negative social outcomes.

Measuring and understanding a child's social status is important for several reasons. The establishment of friendships and positive social interactions are important for children's social development. Children with poor peer relationships often experience negative social and emotional consequences that can continue throughout adulthood. These negative consequences can include depression, anxiety, low self-esteem, poor self-concept, social withdrawal, and antisocial behaviors such as aggression and criminality. Researchers have estimated that at least 1 in 10 children experience negative peer relationships. Therefore, a large number of children with poor social relationships may be at risk for developing behavioral and emotional difficulties.

Sociometric assessment methods were introduced in the 1930s. In the 1950s, several books were published on the topic of sociometrics, and sociometric measurements often were part of research and school-based assessments of children's social relationships. The use of sociometric procedures declined in the following decades with the advancement of social behavior rating scales and ethical concerns related to the use of sociometric methods.

There are a variety of sociometric assessment techniques. The most widely used is peer nominations, in which children in a social group or school classroom anonymously identify social preferences for their classmates. For example, children may be asked to provide a list of three classmates with whom they would most like to play and three with whom they would least like to play. Another peer nomination technique is to provide a list of names of the children in a classroom along with social acceptance items (e.g., "Who do you like to play with?" "Who is most likely to be alone during recess?" "Who gets into trouble the most?"). The children are asked to place an 'X' next to the name of one to three classmates who they perceive best fits the item description (Figure 1). An alternative for early readers is to use photographs rather than a list of names and to read the items aloud in either an individual or group classroom setting. In either method, the numbers of nominations are summed for each child, and the results are used to identify children who are positively and negatively perceived by their peers.

Other sociometric techniques can be described as peer ratings and sociometric rankings. Peer ratings are conducted by providing a list of children's names in the social group or classroom along with a rating for social acceptance items. The ratings methods that are used may vary, typically ranging from three to five responses (e.g., Agree, Neutral, Disagree). In contrast to peer nominations and ratings, sociometric rankings are completed by an adult(s), most often the classroom teacher.

The applications of sociometric assessment methods have resulted in controversy and ethical concerns regarding their use. These concerns center on the use of negative nominations and the possibility that children will compare responses, which may result in negative social and emotional consequences for children who are not positively perceived by their peers. These concerns have contributed to the decline in the use of sociometric assessment methods, particularly in school settings. However, researchers have found no evidence that negative consequences occur. Therefore, sociometric assessment continues to be used as a research tool for understanding children's social relationships.

—*R. T. Busse*

See also Behavior Intervention; Self-Concept and Efficacy; Social–Emotional Assessment

Place an X under the name of one classmate in answer to each question below	Alan	Bert	Cara	Dian	Edye	Faid	Geri	Hans	Inga	Jose	Kobi	Lian	Marc	Otto	Paul
Who would you most like to play with?	X														
Who would you least like to play with?												X			
Who gets in trouble the most?				X											
Who is most likely to be alone during recess?															X
Who gets along best with others?	X														

Figure 1   Hypothetical Example of a Peer Nomination Technique

REFERENCES AND FURTHER READING

McConnell, S. R., & Odom, S. L. (1986). Sociometrics: Peer-referenced measures and the assessment of social competence. In P. Strain, M. J. Guralnick, & H. M. Walker (Eds.), *Children's social behavior: Development, assessment, and modification* (pp. 215–284). New York: Academic.

Merrell, K. W. (1999). *Behavioral, social, and emotional assessment of children and adolescents.* Mahwah, NJ: Erlbaum.

SOMATOFORM DISORDERS

Soma and *somato* are both Greek words that mean body. Disorder means an ailment in the body. Thus, a somatoform disorder is a physical illness or illness in the body. Somatoform disorders vary by type and frequency of occurrence among school-age children. Depending on the type of disorder and age and gender of the person, prevalence rates range from less than 1% to 15%. Somatoform disorders rarely begin before age six years, and usually begin in late childhood and early adolescence.

According to the *Diagnostic and Statistical Manual of Mental Disorders-Fourth Edition (DSM-IV)*, somatoform disorders include (American Psychiatric Association, 1994):

- Somatization disorder
- Undifferentiated somatoform disorder
- Conversion disorder
- Pain disorder
- Hypochondriasis
- Body dysmorphic disorder

All the somatoform disorders result in significant problems at school, home, or in other social situations.

In somatization disorder, pain or other medical symptoms are not explained by a medical problem. For example, when a child's arm is broken, the swelling and pain that result are explained by the injury. However, a child with a somatization disorder will complain about physical pains such as stomachaches and headaches, but a medical doctor is unable to find a cause for the pain. A child may also experience backaches, dizziness, fatigue, and muscle aches. More pain is seen in a somatization disorder than an undifferentiated somatoform disorder. Both disorders may last for long periods of time. The physical symptoms are real to the child and typically result in medical treatment, or the continuous complaints cause problems in school and at home. For example, a child with these types of somatoform disorders may spend an excessive amount of time in the nurse's office and miss important academic learning time.

Conversion disorders may include a variety of medical symptoms that are related to psychological factors. Generally, a stressful situation is linked to the onset of this disorder. The symptoms of a conversion disorder may result in "secondary gains" (American Psychiatric Association, 1994). Secondary gains refer to benefits the individual receives or obtains, such as attention from a teacher or parent or a reduction in work requirements and other responsibilities, as a result of the physical complaints.

Severe body pain in one or more places for any length of time is typical of a pain disorder. Pain that lasts less than six months is considered acute; if it lasts more than six months, it is considered chronic. The pain symptoms are significantly linked to psychological factors and the severity of the pain leads the individual to seek medical care. According to the *DSM-IV*, the pain in this disorder becomes the focus of the sufferer's life (American Psychiatric Association, 1994).

Fear of having a disease is known as hypochondriasis. A person may experience pain and mistakenly think that the symptom is caused by a disease, despite a doctor's reassurance. Although hypochondriasis may start at any age, generally it begins in early adulthood and lasts for at least six months.

Concern about real or imagined body flaws is typical of those with body dysmorphic disorder. Types of defects include skin tone, facial hair, nose size, and shape of different body parts. Typically, the individual has excessive thoughts about the real or imagined body flaw, and these lead to unnecessary searches for medical cures to correct the defect. This disorder does not occur typically before adolescence and may result in dropping out of school. The adolescent's thoughts are centered on the flaw and not focused on learning resulting in a refusal to attend school.

Somatoform disorders are serious psychiatric disorders that result in frustration and distress for the individuals who are diagnosed, their families, and their medical providers. In a school setting, individuals with somatic symptoms may not be immediately recognized as having problems. However, a child with these symptoms may experience social–emotional problems and may be frequently absent from school. Treatments for the different types of somatoform disorders vary and include medication, cognitive behavior therapy, relaxation techniques, and modifications in the environment. It is important to consult with a physician and undergo a comprehensive medical examination to determine if medical treatment is necessary. Additionally, these disorders may be related to underlying psychological or environmental problems and are best treated by using a combination of medical and psychological interventions or techniques.

—*Laura A. Webber*

See also DSM-IV; Psychopathology in Children

REFERENCES AND FURTHER READING

American Psychiatric Association. (1994). *The diagnostic and statistical manual of mental disorders* (4th ed.). Washington, DC: Author.

Campo, J. V., & Fritsch, S. L. (1994). Somatization in children and adolescents. *Journal of the American Academy of Child and Adolescent Psychiatry, 33*(9), 1223–1236.

Egger, H. L., Costello, E. J., Erkali, A., & Angold, A. (1999). Somatic complaints and psychopathology in children and adolescents: Stomach aches, musculoskeletal pains, and headaches. *Journal of the American Academy of Child and Adolescent Psychiatry, 38*(7), 852–861.

Siegel, L. J. (1998). Somatic disorders. In R. J. Morris & T. R. Kratochwill (Eds.), *The practice of child therapy* (pp. 231–270). Boston: Allyn & Bacon.

Starfield, B., Gross, E., & Wood, M. (1980). Psychosocial and psychosomatic diagnoses in primary care of children. *Pediatrics, 66,* 159–166.

SPECIAL EDUCATION

Special education refers to the education—including instructional methods, curricular materials, and teachers—provided to students who have disabilities. Special education does not happen only in certain places. Instead, it is a collection of services that can take place in classrooms, resource rooms, special classes, or even outside of schools. In the United States, special education is defined and regulated by an important federal law, the Individuals With Disabilities Education Act (IDEA), which was reauthorized in 1997. Another reauthorization of this act took effect in 2004 (the Individuals with Disabilities Improvement Act; P. L. 108–446).

BRIEF HISTORY OF SPECIAL EDUCATION IN THE UNITED STATES

In the 19th century, the federal government created special schools for children who were mentally ill, blind, or deaf. Little progress in special education occurred until the 20th century when the return of disabled veterans from World Wars I and II brought the existence and needs of people with disabilities into the public eye. In 1954 the Supreme Court decision in *Brown v. Board of Education* made racial segregation in schools illegal. This set the stage for the Civil Rights Movement and recognition of the need to protect the civil rights of other groups who had suffered discrimination, including individuals with disabilities. It is now estimated that at the time of the Brown case half of children with disabilities did not receive appropriate educational services, including those in general education programs whose disabilities were undetected. One million children with disabilities had been entirely excluded from the public school system because of their disabilities, including children with problem behavior, mental retardation, and severe multiple disabilities.

The rights of children with disabilities to an education in the public schools were initially recognized in federal legislation in 1966 and 1970 that was intended to spur the states to develop special education programs and train teachers. During the early 1970s, two important civil action court cases helped to define the scope of educational services for students with disabilities. These were *Pennsylvania Association for Retarded Children (PARC) v. Commonwealth of Pennsylvania* and *Mills v. D.C. Board of Education.* In these cases, the courts ruled that a free public education was the right of students with mental retardation and other disabilities. The schools involved in these decisions recognized that students with disabilities, including mental retardation, could be educated and trained to higher levels of self-sufficiency. They objected to the difficulty and cost of providing such an education.

In 1975, as a result of these court decisions and dissatisfaction with the progress made by the individual states, the United States Congress passed the previously mentioned IDEA (Public Law 94–142), which was the first comprehensive federal legislation to describe the procedures for identifying and educating students with disabilities. IDEA requires that a free and appropriate public education (FAPE) be made available to all children with disabilities from the ages of 3 to 21 years, including special education and related services such as transportation or counseling.

The IDEA, together with section 504 of the Rehabilitation Act of 1973 and the 1990 Americans With Disabilities Act (ADA), provides a powerful set of guidelines and regulations to ensure that students with disabilities obtain access to and benefit from a public education. Section 504 and ADA are civil rights laws that prohibit discrimination and maintain access to businesses, public places, and job opportunities for all people with disabilities, including children and adolescents in schools. However, it is the IDEA that defines special education and related services throughout the United States. Because of this, the following discussion of special education will often refer directly to the definitions, guidelines, and regulations of the IDEA.

LOCATING AND IDENTIFYING ELIGIBLE STUDENTS

The IDEA requires that states locate and identify all children with disabilities. For preschoolers three to five years old, this is accomplished through screenings, advertised and available free to the public, with referral

and evaluation procedures when necessary. For children in school who have learning or behavior problems, interventions are tried in the general classroom to see if they help the child. These interventions are known as general education interventions because they occur within general education settings. Many children benefit from different teaching techniques or specific activities or strategies to improve the area of difficulty. Other general education interventions include extra instruction in an area of academic weakness. Early attention to academic difficulties in general education may prevent the need for special education services for many children. The IDEA states a preference for providing help to children through general education in order to avoid unnecessary labeling of children as disabled.

In some cases when these interventions are not successful, an initial evaluation may be recommended to determine if the child has a disability and needs special education. The evaluation includes various tests and assessments administered by appropriately trained professionals, including school psychologists, and is designed to identify all areas of suspected disability. The 1997 amendments to IDEA list the following 10 types of disability:

1. Mental retardation
2. Hearing impairments, including deafness
3. Speech or language impairments
4. Visual impairments, including blindness
5. Serious emotional disturbance
6. Orthopedic impairments
7. Autism
8. Traumatic brain injury
9. Other health impairments
10. Specific learning disabilities

In addition, a noncategorical definition of developmental delay is available for children from ages three to nine years who show delays in physical, cognitive, communication, social/emotional, or adaptive development. The results of an initial evaluation, if conducted, are used to determine whether the child meets the criteria for one or more of the eligible disability categories. If the child is found to have a disability and requires special education, an Individualized Education Plan (IEP) is prepared.

THE INDIVIDUALIZED EDUCATION PLAN

The IEP is written by a team consisting of parents, general education teacher, special education teacher, school district administrator, evaluation expert, the child with a disability (when appropriate), and other individuals or related service personnel (nurse, speech-language pathologist, occupational therapist, etc.) as necessary. The child's strengths, the parents' concerns for their child's education, and recent evaluation results are all considered during IEP preparation. The IEP describes the student's present levels of educational performance based on existing information and the results of current evaluations. These performance levels are used to define the subsequent learning objectives in the areas of disability where the student's educational needs differ from those of nondisabled peers. The IEP must also describe how the disability affects the child's involvement and progress in the general education curriculum.

The special education program for the child, as defined in the IEP, consists of annual goals that address the child's educational needs as a result of the identified disability. These goals define what the child will learn and do in any area where special teaching is needed, including academics, social and communication skills, self-help skills, motor skills, and/or behavior, and who will teach those skills. Progress toward annual goals is to be periodically measured and reported to parents, usually at the same times that progress in general education is indicated on report cards.

A range of related services, such as transportation, psychological services or counseling, speech-language therapy, audiology, or social work services, may be required to enable the student with a disability to benefit from special education. The IEP must explain the extent to which the child is to be educated apart from nondisabled children in a general classroom. The anticipated frequency, duration, and location of all services must be specified, along with a statement of how the child's progress will be monitored and reported to parents. Beginning at age 14 years, transition services must be considered to assist students with disabilities in preparing for postsecondary education, vocational training, and employment.

SPECIAL EDUCATION SERVICES

Special education services may include indirect services such as consultation for the general education teacher or having a special education teacher come into the classroom for part of the day to provide individualized teaching. These services help the classroom teacher learn to address the student's special needs and keep the student in the general educational classroom so that he or she does not miss classroom instruction or activities. Another option for keeping the student in the general class is to provide a paraprofessional to assist the teacher and the student. A paraprofessional is not a teacher but is trained to work with students with special needs. The nature of a student's disability and level of need might require the assistance of a paraprofessional for consistent support and to increase the adult-to-student ratio in the classroom. Because there are frequently several children with different needs in one classroom, a teacher might receive some combination of these supports.

At the other extreme are completely segregated services provided full-time in special classrooms or schools. Students with severe or multiple disabilities, behavior problems, or medical needs are more likely to be educated in separate classrooms, apart from nondisabled peers, perhaps joining other students only at lunch or recess. Sometimes students do not attend their neighborhood schools but are transported to special schools or classes. This method of providing educational services is often less expensive than sending special education teachers to many different schools and classes. However, removing students with special needs from general education classrooms has the negative effects of segregation and lack of access to the general curriculum provided to their nondisabled peers.

Between these extremes are services that remove the student from the class for some academic subjects or for part of the school day, referred to as pullout programs or resource rooms. The length of time that a student is removed from the general classroom varies according to the needs of the student and the types of services that must be delivered in another setting. Examples of these services include speech or occupational therapy, small group or individual instruction that differs from the general curriculum, vocational training, community activities, mobility training for students with visual impairments, or adaptive physical education. In secondary schools, a student may go to a resource room for one or more class periods, attending other classes along with peers with and without disabilities.

Concerns about the academic progress of students in pullout programs have prompted researchers to study the achievement of special education students who spend time away from the general education classroom. Moody and colleagues (2000) evaluated elementary students who received reading instruction almost entirely in the resource room instead of in the general education classroom. Resource room teachers had large classes that spanned many reading levels and were mostly unable to provide intensive, individualized instruction. Students made little or no gains in reading achievement over an entire year, even though their special education program was designed to narrow the gap between their achievement and that of nondisabled students. In contrast, Rea and colleagues (2002) found that children with learning disabilities served in inclusive general education classrooms earned higher grades, did just as well on standardized achievement tests, and attended more days of school than the students served in pullout programs.

Results of research such as this, along with the efforts of advocacy groups for students with disabilities, have produced a legal preference for educating children in general classrooms. The IDEA states that learning needs should first be addressed in general education through prereferral interventions. If general education interventions are not effective and a child is identified as having a disability, a key issue in determining appropriate special education services is the requirement that services be offered in the least restrictive environment (LRE). LRE is presumed to be the general education classroom unless the IEP team can demonstrate that necessary and appropriate services for the student cannot be delivered in that environment. The LRE provision of the IDEA is intended to allow children with special needs the greatest possible access to the general education curriculum. This preference is based on the idea that schools and society should have high expectations that children with disabilities will be successful in school and prepared for postsecondary education or employment.

PROGRESS MONITORING

While a student is in a special education program, the special education teacher provides regular reports to parents on the child's progress toward the IEP goals. A new IEP is written every year to address the child's current performance and instructional needs. A reevaluation of the child takes place every three years. The purpose of the reevaluation is to determine whether the child continues to have a disability and needs special education services. These guidelines serve to ensure that the child's educational program is evaluated regularly and that it continues to be appropriate for the child.

Students with disabilities are required by the 1997 IDEA amendments to participate in all statewide and districtwide assessment programs. When students with disabilities cannot meaningfully participate in general assessments, an alternate assessment must be provided to assess their learning. The purpose of this regulation is so the academic achievement of all students will be measured and evaluated by districts and states. Schools and states must be accountable for the learning of all students, including students with disabilities. Before the 1997 amendments to the IDEA, students with disabilities were often exempted from large-scale assessments. Because they were not tested, no one knew if they had learned the material that was on the tests. These amendments, like the LRE provision, are intended to make sure that students with disabilities are learning the general curriculum content by including their scores when that content is assessed.

PROCEDURAL SAFEGUARDS

Several protections and safeguards are explicitly spelled out in the IDEA for children with disabilities and their parents. These include the use of nondiscriminatory evaluation materials and procedures. No single instrument or procedure may be used as the sole criterion for determining eligibility for special education services or an appropriate educational program. Records must be kept confidential and must be available for parents to inspect. Parents must be provided with a written summary of their rights in understandable language, preferably in their native language. Parents must be given prior written notice and are generally required to provide written consent for the evaluation and placement of their child and for subsequent changes in placement. Both parents and school districts may access due-process procedures at any stage of the special education process to resolve disagreements over evaluation and placement. Parents have the right to obtain an independent evaluation, to voluntary mediation, to a due-process hearing, and to further appeals to the state educational agency or the court system. School districts may obtain an evaluation or additional assessment in some cases and have the right to mediation and due-process review. Schools bear the responsibility for providing an appropriate educational plan. All of these procedures and safeguards are designed to protect the rights of students with disabilities and their families to a free appropriate public education.

Point Versus Counterpoint:
Full Inclusion or Continuum of Services

One of the contentious issues affecting implementation of the IDEA is disagreement over the location of services for students with disabilities. When special education is provided within a general education setting it is commonly referred to as inclusion, or inclusive, education. Full inclusion means providing all educational and related services to students with disabilities in general education or community environments with nondisabled peers. This issue has prompted heated debate by professionals, advocacy groups, and researchers. Advocacy groups for individuals with severe disabilities have called for inclusive practices for all students on civil rights grounds. Others prefer a continuum of services ranging from inclusion in general classes to pullout programs or segregated instruction. The Learning Disabilities Association of America (LDA) does not support "any policies that mandate the same placement, instruction, or treatment for all students with learning disabilities."

The case for full inclusion:

- Discrimination on the basis of disability is prohibited by the Constitution, the Rehabilitation Act, the Americans With Disabilities Act, and federal education laws.
- Students with disabilities deserve an equal educational opportunity to learn what all other students are expected to learn. The general classroom provides access to the general curriculum for all students.
- Parents and teachers have reported that including students with disabilities in general education improves their behavior, social competence, and independence (Turner & Traxler, 1995).
- Students with learning disabilities in inclusive classrooms learn and behave as well or better than students in pullout programs (Rea & colleagues, 2002).
- Instead of being bused to special classes, attending local schools fosters friendships with neighborhood peers.
- Inclusive education promotes the values of diversity, social justice, and belonging.
- Learning and working with students with disabilities increases empathy and self-confidence in nondisabled students.
- Inclusion teaches nondisabled students about the diversity of people with whom they will live and work as adults. The acceptance of persons with differences has future economic benefit when individuals with disabilities can become employed, productive members of a society that welcomes them.

The case for a continuum of services:

- The IDEA guarantees an education in the least restrictive environment that is appropriate for each student's individual needs.
- Students with learning differences may need access to alternate environments, instructional strategies, or materials that cannot or will not be provided in the general classroom environment.
- Research on inclusive practices has found that classroom teachers may be unprepared to teach students with disabilities. Successful programs offer a continuum of services in which teachers have choices about their teaching environment and receive adequate assistance for special needs students (Vaughn & Schumm, 1995).
- Just like nondisabled students, aggressive or violent students with disabilities should not be allowed to threaten the safety of others.
- Students with disabilities may divert the teacher's attention from other students who need assistance.
- Emotionally or medically fragile students may not be able to tolerate the general class environment. Segregated instruction offers greater protection for these students.
- Instruction for students with disabilities that differs greatly from that offered to other students may be distracting to other students and disruptive to the educational environment.
- Some instruction required by students with disabilities, such as self-care or speech therapy, is neither feasible nor appropriate in general classrooms.

THE ROLE OF SCHOOL PSYCHOLOGISTS

School psychologists are intimately involved in all aspects of special education, starting with the evaluation of students who are showing learning or behavior problems in their classrooms. School psychologists observe children in their classrooms and consult with teachers about instructional techniques or curricular adaptations. They help evaluate intellectual ability, academic achievement, social and adaptive skills, and behavior. School psychologists may interview teachers and parents in order to understand the factors that influence behavior and learning. They participate on student assistance teams and in planning and delivering general education interventions. They work closely with teachers who instruct students with special needs to determine whether the special education programs are beneficial. School psychologists also work with parents, explaining test results and special programs and providing information about how to help their child at home.

CURRENT ISSUES

An important provision was included in the 1997 amendments to the IDEA in response to concerns over violence, drugs, and weapons in schools. The consequences for students with disabilities differ somewhat from those for nondisabled students, who might immediately be suspended or expelled for dangerous acts on school grounds. Nonetheless, schools now have the power to take immediate disciplinary action for students with disabilities who threaten school safety and security. A student with a disability who brings drugs or weapons to school or engages in dangerous or violent behavior may be placed in an alternative interim educational setting, where special education services continue, or can be temporarily removed from school.

A second issue concerns the role of special education in the current school reform movement. Schools used to be evaluated and accredited on the basis of inputs such as the number of books in the library or the experience of the teachers. Within the last decade, educational outcomes such as student achievement have become the basis for evaluating educational practices. This movement found legislative voice in the Improving America's Schools Act of 1994, which addressed the achievement of economically disadvantaged students eligible for title I federal education

assistance. The 1997 IDEA amendments, with their required participation in large-scale assessment, provided parallel provisions for students with disabilities. Recently, the 2001 No Child Left Behind Act (NCLB) required all states to develop rigorous academic standards and assess all students on those standards, including the lower-achieving groups of students with limited English proficiency, disadvantaged economic status, and disabilities. A major issue in the outcomes-based education movement is the impact of high-stakes tests on students with disabilities. It remains to be seen whether students with disabilities will be able to meet these high standards through the improved education and testing procedures that are intended by NCLB.

Another facet of school reform concerns charter schools, which are experimental schools designed to take advantage of contemporary technology and creative teaching. Charter schools are often founded on the premise that innovative instruction will increase academic achievement for at-risk students, including those with disabilities or from low-income families. While charter schools hold much attraction for students and families who are dissatisfied with traditional schools, their educational promise has yet to be evaluated.

CONCLUSION

The history of special education largely evolved in the 20th century, and the basis for current special education practice is based on creation and interpretation of laws enacted to protect and advocate for the education of disabled persons. The process of identifying students who have disabilities and then planning and delivering special education services is complex. The field of special education is extremely broad and involves many professional fields, as well as a vast number of children, teachers, and parents. The current school reform movement and new federal laws increasing state requirements for quality education and assessment will undoubtedly have a huge impact on special education practices and outcomes in the United States.

—*Julia Shaftel*

See also Adaptive Behavior Assessment; Diagnosis and Labeling; Individuals With Disabilities Education Act; Individualized Education Plan; Learning Disabilities; Mental Retardation; Multidisciplinary Teams

REFERENCES AND FURTHER READING

Learning Disabilities Association of America. (2002). *Inclusion: Position paper of the Learning Disabilities Association of America.* Retrieved August 14, 2004, from http://www.ldanatl.org/positions/

Moody, S. W., Vaughn, S., Hughes, M. T., & Fischer, M. (2000). Reading instruction in the resource room: Set up for failure. *Exceptional Children, 66,* 305–316.

Palmaffy, T. (2001). The evolution of the federal role. In C. E. Finn, Jr., A. J. Rotherham, & C. R. Hokanson, Jr. (Eds.), *Rethinking special education for a new century* (pp. 1–21). Washington, DC: Thomas B. Fordham Foundation. Retrieved August 1, 2004, from http://www.ed-excellence.net/

Rea, P. J., McLaughlin, V. L., & Walther-Thomas, C. (2002). Outcomes for students with learning disabilities in inclusive and pullout programs. *Exceptional Children, 68,* 203–222.

TASH (formerly The Association for Persons with Severe Handicaps). (2002). *TASH resolution on inclusive quality education.* Retrieved July 27, 2004, from http://www.tash.org/resolutions/

Turnbull, A. P., Stowe, M., Wilcox, B., Turnbull, H. R., III, Turnbull, A. P. (2000). *Free appropriate public education: The law and children with disabilities.* Denver: Love.

Turner, N. D., & Traxler, M. (1995, April). *Observations of parents, teachers, and principals during the first year of implementation of inclusion in two Midwestern school districts.* Paper presented at the annual convention of the Council for Exceptional Children, Indianapolis, IN.

Vaughn, S., & Schumm, J. S. (1995). Responsible inclusion for students with learning disabilities. *Journal of Learning Disabilities, 28,* 264–290.

SPEECH IMPAIRMENTS. *See*
Communication Disorders; Developmental Milestones; Stuttering

SPELLING INTERVENTIONS AND STRATEGIES

Given the number of words in the English language, mastering spelling is a daunting and complex task. Yet, spelling is critical for enhancing word knowledge used in reading and for fluent and qualitative writing that provides effective communication. However, many students, particularly those with learning disabilities, are poor spellers. Computer spell checkers are one option for poor spellers even though up to 63% of errors can remain uncorrected. Hence, an emphasis on spelling as a structured curriculum area is reemerging in research, in the classroom, and in school psychologists' assessment and intervention practices.

Decades of research present a number of effective teaching options for spelling; however, there are two barriers to effective spelling practices in the classroom. First, teachers persistently use a simple but ineffective method that focuses on memorization of an optimal number of words with little emphasis on word concepts. Second, there is a lack of adequate teacher training in spelling development, systematic spelling patterns, or effective methods that promote word concepts or individualized strategies for poor spellers. One promising finding from a survey conducted by Traynelis-Yerek and Strong (1999) suggests that school districts are increasingly employing a wider variety of spelling approaches; however, few combine individualized spelling practices with developmental spelling or direct instruction.

Theories on the developmental stages of spelling have been the primary influence for change in spelling practices. Based on observations of children's spelling, Henderson and Templeton (1986) proposed five stages of spelling, which are represented in spelling production and types of errors as spelling skills increase (Table 1). Initially, theorists proposed that spelling stages developed by learning a sequence of tactics in an orderly manner, starting with the use of sound–letter associations (phonological processing), to rules on blending of letters and syllables within words (orthographic processing), to deriving word meaning from root words and their affixes (morphological processing). Instead, Trieman and Cassar (1997) reviewed a series of studies that demonstrated immature spellers primarily use phonological skills when generating words, but simple orthographic and morphemic aspects of spelling also contribute to early spelling attempts. However, exactly how the integration of the three skills evolves and changes to advanced spelling levels is not well understood.

Good spellers are those who are explicitly taught spelling skills corresponding with reading and writing experience. Three objectives of spelling programs are to obtain accurate spelling, retention of accurate spelling over time, and generalization of accurate spelling in writing. Basic teaching strategies that effectively achieve these objectives include:

Table 1   Developmental Stages of Spelling Knowledge as Proposed by Henderson and Templeton (1986)

Stage	Estimated Grade	Skill Development	Common Errors Observed as Knowledge Is Applied
Semiphonetic Stage (or early letter name)	Pre-K–2nd	Student spells words with initial and final consonants using sounds based on the letter name.	Student uses letter names as sounds and often does not does not separate words in writing. Example: Yru Ht for Why are you hot?
Phonetic Stage	1st-3rd	Student includes vowels with consonants in CVC words and understands letter-sound associations including letter blends.	Student uses mixture of letter names and CVC based on sounds. Fails to recognize silent vowels or blends. Example: bup for bump
Within Word Pattern Stage	1st-4th	Student understands patterns within syllables with blends, long vowels, and CVVC.	Student increases complex letter patterns within single syllable but may overgeneralize. Example: bate for bait; cote for coat
Syllable Juncture Stage	3rd-8th	Student becomes aware of prefixes, inflected endings (ed, ing), and the different spellings between junctures in syllables as the child understands that more than one syllable can make a word.	Student uses syllable patterns incorrectly. Example: skiping for skipping; biteing for biting
Derivational Constancy Stage	5th-8th	Student understands connections in meaning for root word spellings in polysyllabic words.	Student relies on spelling based on sound when unclear about vowel alternations used with root words. Example: compution for competition.

- Presenting and modeling
- Providing practice
- Giving feedback
- Reinforcing increased performance

A review on spelling instruction suggests that basic teaching strategies are effective for all students because similar developmental spelling patterns are observed with good and poor spellers. Nonetheless, poor spellers differ from good spellers in three ways. Poor spellers learn phonological, orthographic, and morphological skills at a slow rate; fail to retain accurate spelling over time; and fail to generalize skills when spelling unknown words. However, straightforward modifications of basic teaching steps by altering frequency, duration, intensity, or quantity of each step have enhanced spelling for poor spellers. The following sections discuss strategies for each of the basic teaching steps that enhance spelling performance for good and poor spellers, with specific parametric modifications for remediation.

SELECTING SPELLING SKILLS

To enhance generalization of spelling skills to unknown words, many spelling programs consist of a combination of high-frequency writing words with words consisting of predictable spelling patterns. Because of the different word concepts taught at each grade level, a critical step is determination of spelling instructional level. For example, students who are not progressing at grade level in spelling will more likely make greater gains in performance when taught at a lower grade level. These results suggest that spelling performance may be stalled because of an inability to learn advanced word concepts without firmly developed preliminary concepts. However, the relationship between amount of words with patterns, irregular words, and number of words presented each week needs to be further investigated.

PRESENTING SPELLING SKILLS

When presenting new spelling words to students, correct-your-own-test approaches have been found to be superior to traditional methods. During a correct-your-own-test procedure, students produce words on their own before getting assistance, but a spelling response is immediately followed by a corrective method for misspelled words. In this method, the student rewrites the error(s) prior to writing the correct version of the word. This approach leads to greater gains in spelling accuracy than modeling only the correct spelling. With older children, using proofreading marks on errors while comparing answers to a correct model increases spelling accuracy, retention, and generalization.

These approaches can be combined with explicit teaching of spelling rules to promote spelling accuracy with similar but untrained words. For example, rule-based strategies describing phonemic, orthographic, or morphological word patterns seem to result in greater improvements with untrained words when compared to traditional methods that focus only on word memorization.

PRACTICING SPELLING

Practicing spelling words effectively increases spelling accuracy and retention if practice is daily, given with self-correction procedures, and provided with feedback after a word is practiced. Based on Graham's (1999) review, there is more than one effective way to systematically implement these basic steps; however, using a cover-copy, self-correction approach was shown to increase spelling accuracy as well as retention and generalization. Moreover, this approach is effective for poor spellers at elementary, middle, and secondary grade levels and for students with mild disabilities. For efficiency, systematic practices have also been effectively implemented with peer tutors. Finally, recent research extended the positive effects of word sort practice with words that share spelling patterns on spelling accuracy, retention,

and generalization to untrained words to student with mild disabilities.

PROVIDING FEEDBACK AND REINFORCEMENT

In general, Graham's (1999) review of spelling studies suggests that increases in spelling accuracy, word retention, and generalization are obtained when feedback is presented immediately after students practice a word on a daily basis. Moreover, feedback is equally effective if provided from peers, teachers, public posting, and computers. Finally, numerous studies demonstrate that praise and/or token systems (contingent on group or individual performance) paired with goal setting positively reinforce increases in spelling accuracy and result in word retention and generalization.

In summary, spelling research indicates a wide range of individual responses to various modifications of basic teaching strategies for poor spellers. Interestingly, levels of phonological and orthographical skills are better predictors of learning in spelling and reading with intervention than intelligence quotient (IQ) scores. Thus, school psychologists who have knowledge about spelling development, systematic spelling patterns, and effective methods are empowered to effectively assess relevant spelling deficits and design instructional modifications for poor spellers with or without disabilities.

—Donna Gilbertson

See also Academic Achievement; Mastery Learning; Mathematics Interventions and Strategies; Reading Interventions and Strategies; Writing Interventions and Strategies; Written Language Assessment

REFERENCES AND FURTHER READING

Graham, S. (1999). Handwriting and spelling instruction for students with learning disabilities: A review. *Learning Disabilities Quarterly, 22,* 78–96.

Henderson, E. H., & Templeton, S. (1986). A developmental perspective of formal spelling instruction through alphabet, pattern, and meaning. *Elementary School Journal, 86*(3), 305–316.

Traynelis-Yerek, E., & Strong, M. (1999). Spelling practices in school districts and regions across the United States and state spelling standards. *Reading Horizons, 39,* 279–294.

Treiman, R., & Cassar, M. (1997). Spelling acquisition in English. In C. A. Perfetti, L. Rieben, & F. Micheal (Eds.), *Learning to spell: Research, theory, and practice across languages* (pp. 61–80). Mahwah, NJ: Erlbaum.

STANDARD DEVIATION

Standard deviation (SD) is the average distance of each score in a distribution from the mean. It is calculated by squaring the difference between each score and the mean, averaging those squared differences, and taking the square root of that average. Operating under an assumption of a normal distribution of scores, the mean and standard deviation can be used to make probability statements about the likelihood of the occurrence of any individual score and to estimate the proportion of a population that will perform above, below, or between given score levels. For example, approximately 5% of students will score above or below 1.96 standard deviations from the mean in a normal distribution. In measurement, the standard error of measurement is assumed to be the standard deviation of observed scores around a student's theoretical true score. In inferential statistics, the standard error of the mean is assumed to be the standard deviation of sample means around the population mean.

—*Bruce Frey*

See also Grade Equivalent Scores; Percentile Ranks; Standard Error of Measurement; Stanines

STANDARD ERROR OF MEASUREMENT

The standard error of measurement (SEM) is the standard deviation of observed scores around a true score. Under classical test theory, an observed score is the score a student actually receives and a true score is the score one would receive if no random errors affected the score. The standard error is calculated by subtracting a scale's estimate of internal reliability from 1 and multiplying the square root of that difference by the observed scores' standard deviation—higher internal reliability estimates result in smaller standard errors of measurement. Because observed scores are assumed to be normally distributed around true scores, the standard error of measurement can be used as a standard deviation to compute confidence intervals to estimate a student's true score. For example, by multiplying the standard error of measurement by 1.96, one creates the limits above and below an observed score within which a student's true score is 95% likely to fall.

—*Bruce Frey*

See also Grade Equivalent Scores; Percentile Ranks; Standard Deviation; Stanines

STANDARD SCORE

A standard score is an individual score that has been transformed into a number that shows a person's relative status in a distribution of means. To convert an individual score to a standard score, the distance (deviation) of the individual score from its mean (i.e., the average score of the distribution) is computed, and that distance is converted into the number of standard deviations (i.e., the square root of the average squared distance of a set of scores from their mean) that score falls above or below the mean.

Although many different kinds of standard scores have been developed, the ones used most frequently are called Z-scores and T-scores. If the length of an imaginary yardstick is used to define a standard deviation, then that yardstick can be used to measure the distance between the group mean and the individual score being considered. For Z-scores, the mean is fixed at zero and the yardstick's length (i.e., the standard deviation) is set at 1.0. For example, a person whose Z-score is −1.5 would indicate that this individual scored 1.5 standard deviations below the mean. A T-score is a converted Z-score and has a mean of 50 (i.e., the average) and a standard deviation of 10. Suppose a school psychologist has been asked to evaluate the aggressive behavior of a kindergarten student. He or she asks the student's teacher to complete a behavior rating scale, a measure used to assess one or more student behaviors, and finds the student's aggressive behavior score to be a 70, which is two standard deviations above the average score for this instrument. The school psychologist would then know that this child exhibits much higher levels of aggressive behavior than his or her peers.

—*Vicki Peyton*

See also Grade Equivalent Scores; Percentile Ranks; Standard Deviation

STANINES

Stanines are a type of norm-referenced score transformation. The term *stanine* is an abbreviation for standard nines. Stanines range from 1 (the lowest 4% of the distribution) to 9 (the highest 4% of the distribution), and each stanine represents a score interval rather than a score point in the normal distribution. The stanine distribution is centered on the stanine of 5, which includes the range of percentile ranks between the 40 and 59. To interpret stanine scores, one needs to know the percentage of scores included in the interval for each stanine reported. Because stanine scores are normalized standard scores, it is possible to compare scores from diverse sets of data. For example, a student who earns a stanine of 8 on an ability measure and a composite stanine score of 5 on an achievement measure could be said to be achieving at a level well below his or her ability.

—*Nona Tollefson*

See also Grade Equivalent Scores; Percentile Ranks; Standard Deviation; Standard Error of Measurement

STATEWIDE TESTS

Statewide tests are designed to measure academic content standards, which are the important facts, ideas, and concepts that students should know at each grade level. Most states have written standards in academic subjects such as reading, writing, mathematics, science, and social studies. In January 2002, President George W. Bush signed the No Child Left Behind Act (NCLB). Starting in the 2005–2006 school year, states will be required to test students in reading and math at every grade level from 3rd to 8th and once in the 10th to 12th grades.

WHAT IS THE PURPOSE OF STATEWIDE TESTS?

Statewide tests are used for educational planning, to evaluate instructional programs, and to measure student progress. They are also used for accountability, to make sure schools are delivering on their promise to teach students what they need to know. When students are held accountable for test results, they may need to earn certain scores in order to move to the next grade or to graduate from high school. If they do not pass the test, they may be required to attend summer school or they may be denied a high school diploma. When teachers and schools are held accountable for test results, financial rewards or school recognition may be earned for high scores. When schools fail to show sufficient progress on the state's academic content standards, they may be subject to penalties, such as losing their accreditation, or teachers and principals may lose their jobs. When important outcomes, such as high school graduation or school accreditation, depend on test scores, the tests are referred to as high-stakes tests. Tests can have high stakes for students, for teachers, and for entire schools and school districts.

WHAT DO STATEWIDE TESTS MEASURE?

The NCLB Act requires statewide tests to measure academic content standards that apply to all schools and all students. These standards must be challenging and encourage the teaching of advanced skills. To measure these standards, tests must be aligned, which means that they correspond to the standards. If the tests do not match what students are taught, they will not measure what students are learning and will not be sensitive to growth in student knowledge.

WHICH STUDENTS ARE TESTED?

The NCLB Act calls for all children to be included in testing. This law follows the lead of the Individuals With Disabilities Education Act of 1997, which requires that all children with disabilities be tested, no matter how severe their disabilities. Previously some of these children were exempted from testing. However, when students are excluded from testing, there is no way to know if they are making progress.

A similar argument holds for students with limited knowledge of English. They may be exempted from testing in English for a specified period of time, but after that they must be included. This way, schools are responsible for teaching them English as well as important subject material.

DO ALL STUDENTS TAKE THE SAME TESTS?

For students with disabilities who cannot take the regular tests, an alternate assessment must be provided to measure their learning. Alternate assessments can take many forms and they vary from state to state. For other children, accommodations are necessary in order for the tests to be fair. For example, glasses are an accommodation for children who do not see well. Some Children who have problems paying attention to task might need extra time or require a quiet setting in order to concentrate.

While research on how these accommodations affect test scores is currently underway, it is generally agreed that some changes in how the test is presented or in how the student takes the test are reasonable for students who need them, as long as they do not change what the test is actually measuring. An example would be reading science or mathematics questions aloud when the test is measuring science knowledge or computation, not reading skill. Other changes (called modifications) that may alter what is being measured are more controversial but may still be needed for certain students. Modifications may include using calculators to do mathematics problems or taking the test in a language other than English.

WHAT ARE THE TESTS LIKE?

Statewide achievement test items can take two basic forms, constructed response and selected response. Constructed response items, also called performance items, are those for which the student must perform a task, such as writing an essay or working a mathematics problem. They are scored by raters who use a rubric, or scoring system, to assign points to the student's answer depending on how well the student responded. The benefit of this type of item is that students perform the kinds of tasks they do in school or in real life, which may provide a better opportunity for them to demonstrate what they know. However, these items can be answered in many different ways, making them difficult to score. Furthermore, because these items take longer for students to answer, the test may not cover as much content.

Selected response items are traditional multiple-choice or true-false items, also called objective items. These items sometimes place fewer demands on the student's knowledge because the student only has to recognize the correct answer, not produce it. The benefit of this kind of item is that it is easier, quicker, and less expensive to score. Objective tests can include many more questions, thus sampling more

content in a subject area. The illustration on page 533 gives examples of items from statewide tests.

HOW ARE TEST RESULTS REPORTED?

Under the NCLB Act, states must assign students to performance categories based upon their scores. Students of all ages and grades, taking different tests, will be assigned to categories based on how their test scores compare to others who took the same test. The test scores, or performance categories, will be published separately for different groups of students. Results for students with disabilities, students who are learning English, students from low-income families, males, females, and major racial and ethnic groups must be published both separately and together and made available to the public.

Statewide tests have become an important part of education and will play an even larger role as the NCLB Act takes effect. States are required to define appropriate academic content standards, develop tests that measure those standards accurately and fairly, and ensure that all students master challenging academic content.

Julia Shaftel

See also Academic Achievement; Authentic Assessment; Criterion-Referenced Assessment; Curriculum-Based Assessment; Grade Equivalent Scores; No Child Left Behind Act of 2001, The; Normal Distribution; Norm-Referenced Tests; Percentile Ranks; Performance-Based Assessment

REFERENCES AND FURTHER READING

American Educational Research Association. (2000). *AERA position statement concerning high-stakes testing in PreK-12 education.* Retrieved April 4, 2004, from http://www.aera.net/about/

National Association of School Psychologists. Available online at http://www.nasponline.org

National Association of School Psychologists. (2002). *Large-scale assessments and high stakes decisions: Facts, cautions, and guidelines.* Bethesda, MD: Author. Available online at http://www.naspcenter.org/factsheets/

National Center on Educational Outcomes, University of Minnesota. Retrieved March 28, 2004, from http://www.coled.umn.edu/NCEO.

Within our reach: Higher student achievement (2002, May). *SEDLETTER 142.* Austin, TX: Southwest Educational Development Laboratory. Available from http://www.sedl.org/resources/.

Sample Constructed Response Items

Biology

The students in Mrs. Anton's biology class planted two 3-inch bean plant seedlings in pots of the same size. One seedling was planted in potting soil and the other seedling was planted in sand. The same amount of liquid was given to each plant at the same time each day. One seedling was given cherry soda and the other seedling was given plain water. After six weeks, students recorded the height of the plants and counted the number of leaves to determine which plant grew more.

What is wrong with this investigation? Identify and describe all problems.

Geography

Label each of the following directly on your map of Northern Africa and the Middle East.

1. The Nile River
2. Israel
3. Saudi Arabia
4. The Sahara Desert
5. The Suez Canal
6. Iraq
7. Libya
8. Jordan

Sample Selected Response Items

Language Arts

Which dictionary definition describes the word ring as it is used in the following sentence?

Detective Hugh Jamison uncovered the false claims filed by the ring of dishonest insurance clerks.

a. a circular band, usually of precious metal, worn on a finger as an ornament or a token of marriage or betrothal
b. a roped enclosure for boxing or wrestling
c. a combination of traders, bookmakers, spies, politicians, etc., acting together for the control of operations or profit
d. a thin band or disk of particles around a planet
e. a group of atoms each bonded to two others in a closed sequence
f. to make or draw a circle around

(Excerpted from *Oxford Dictionary and Thesaurus, American Edition* (1996). New York: Oxford University Press, p. 1300.)

Algebra

1. What is the value of the expression $5x^2 - 3(x + 2)$ when $x = 3$?
   a. 15
   b. 30
   c. 34
   d. 38

Point Versus Counterpoint: High-Stakes Assessments

The case for:
- Academic content standards are the foundation of standards-based education and assessment. Standards communicate clear, high educational expectations for students. Teachers, students, and taxpayers are all made aware of the goals toward which the schools are working and agree on the purposes of instruction and assessment. These principles apply whether tests have high stakes or not.
- According to the Southwest Educational Development Laboratory, students make better progress toward learning the standards when both classroom instruction and statewide tests are aligned with academic content standards.
- High academic content standards increase access to the general curriculum and improve instruction for everyone, according to the National Center on Educational Outcomes. Minority students, students from disadvantaged backgrounds, and students with disabilities or limited English proficiency frequently suffer from low academic expectations that are raised when all students are included in assessment.
- Results of assessments aligned with standards can be used to identify strengths and weaknesses in curriculum and instruction and guide staff development planning. Groups of students who are not benefiting from instruction can be targeted for better teaching and increased effort.
- High-stakes tests have meaningful consequences for performance that promote greater effort from teachers and students.

The case against:
- The risks of high-stakes assessments may outweigh the benefits when the outcomes of testing programs become more important than the processes they are intended to evaluate. Using test scores for rewards and sanctions can result in a narrowing of the curriculum, where the only things taught are what will be on the test. No test can cover all of a subject area, so achievement tests sample from different parts of the curriculum. Teachers may leave out important ideas if tests are used to determine whether they retain their jobs or earn bonuses.
- Similarly, reliance on test scores for educational decision making may result in an overemphasis on basic skills. Schools may stress only the subjects to be tested, usually math and reading, to the detriment of art, music, health, physical education, and the social sciences.
- Undesirable outcomes, such as increased dropout rates, may occur when assessments have high stakes for students. According to the National Association of School Psychologists, research shows that failing a grade does not improve achievement but does increase the likelihood that students will later drop out.
- The National Association of School Psychologists and the American Educational Research Association warn that major decisions for students, such as passing to the next grade or graduating from high school, should never be made on the basis of a single test score. Scores are affected by many factors other than content knowledge, such as the quality of instruction and the alignment of the test with standards. Because of measurement error, a student scoring just below the passing score may have virtually the same knowledge and achievement as another student who scored only one or two points higher.
- High-quality assessments are expensive to create and administer. Immense technical expertise is required to create large-scale assessments that evaluate all students fairly. Sufficient resources must be allocated if tests are to be meaningful and valid measures of educational progress. Otherwise results will be misleading and potentially harmful to schools and students.

STUDENT IMPROVEMENT TEAMS

Student improvement teams (SITs) are school-based teams that use a problem-solving process and the collective expertise of educators and families to assist students who are having difficulty, either academically or behaviorally. The role of the student improvement team is to facilitate a problem-solving process that results in the creation of a plan that will adequately address these academic or behavioral concern(s). Over the last decade, these teams have become instrumental in facilitating understanding of what is needed for any child to be successful in the educational setting.

In contrast to multidisciplinary teams, SIT teams use a systemic problem-solving process that fulfills state and federal requirements to intervene on behalf of students that are beginning to exhibit classroom problems but have not been identified as having an educational handicap. The SIT process can be used to meet:

- State requirements for a Student Improvement Plan when a student does not demonstrate continuous progress on state assessments
- District requirements for responding to students identified as "at risk"
- State requirements for students who are suspected of having a disability under section 504 of the Rehabilitation Act of 1973 or special education regulations

The alignment of a problem-solving process to meet several responsibilities is one step toward eliminating a categorically driven approach to meeting student needs and more effectively using limited resources.

THE PROBLEM-SOLVING PROCESS

Problem solving is a systematic process that enables teams to collect, understand, and analyze data to develop, implement, and monitor interventions for effectiveness (Tilly, 2002). The generic components of a problem-solving process include:

- Asset identification
- Problem identification
- Problem analysis
- Intervention generation and selection
- Goal setting and progress monitoring
- Evaluation of effectiveness

Each of these components is described in the following sections. To increase the likelihood that plans will improve student outcomes, teams are encouraged to monitor the degree to which they follow the problem-solving process in team meetings (Flugum & Reschly, 1993; Upah & Tilly, 2002).

Asset Identification

The purpose of identifying assets is to recognize student academic and social strengths. Assets include internal strengths (e.g., responsible, strong math skills, able to resist peer pressure, many friends) and external strengths (e.g., involved parents, opportunities to participate in community activities, caring neighborhood). The importance of identifying assets is realized when the team selects interventions. If the team is considering two interventions that both seem powerful and one is more closely aligned with a strength of the student, the team can use the information to assist in the selection decision. It is important that the team understand the function of identifying assets. When the team moves from identifying assets as a nice way to start a meeting, to mining for strengths as a way to increase the probability that the resulting interventions will work, it is extending to a higher intent of the problem-solving process.

Problem Identification

Teams frequently encounter students presenting multiple problems. While multiple concerns should be noted, the team must select no more than two concerns to be targeted on an improvement plan so that the plan is manageable to implement and not too overwhelming for the student or the teacher. The team needs to determine where to start the problem identification process by considering:

- Which problem has the highest educational priority
- When improved, whether the change will have a positive impact on learning and behavior
- Which academic or behavior problem could be the most easily improved and serve to build momentum for subsequent intervention efforts (i.e., using the success of one intervention to make addressing more difficult concerns more acceptable)

Once selected, problem identification consists of three components, which are determined and described in clear behavioral terms: (1) student current performance, (2) peer comparison or established standard, and (3) lessons learned from previous intervention efforts or observations.

The team needs to have a clear and complete picture of the student's current performance in the area of concern. To obtain this information the team will frequently collect objective information, by using technical indicators of student performance and progress, and a classroom observation that can provide a description of the student's level of performance in relation to the general education curriculum. For example, if the concern being addressed is how often the student follows teacher directions, observational data collected by a skilled observer would summarize the percentage of intervals the student was observed to be following directions in a particular time period. A brief description as to what the student was doing when he or she was not following directions and what factors appeared to increase the likelihood that the student would follow directions would be summarized. These data provide the team with a sense of the magnitude of the problem and the factors that trigger or maintain it.

A peer comparison or established standard is essential for putting the student's current performance in perspective. An established standard may be used when there are known and clear standards for acceptable behavior. For example, if the school district had a policy that allows for no more than three consecutive unexcused absences, the team would be using this standard to compare and understand the magnitude of the student's attendance problem.

Peer comparison data provide a way to understand the student's performance in comparison to what is "typical" in the classroom or school. These data often include comparisons made using achievement testing results or standardized observation tools. For example, the observer collecting data on following directions would watch both the target student and a peer comparison student. By comparing the resulting data, the team could discern the magnitude of the concern by having a sense of how the student compares to peers with regard to following teacher directions.

Teachers are frequently required to document what they have tried, for how long, and the effectiveness of the interventions prior to beginning the student improvement team's problem-solving process. Beyond a description of "what" has been done, the team needs to hear what has been learned about the student as a result of what has been done. To do this, the teacher provides a summary of what appears to work and what does not work with the student in relation to instruction, curriculum, environment, and the learner.

Other data to be considered by the team include observations or interviews with the student or teacher that seek to provide clues as to what could be contributing to, or causing, the problematic behavior (Doggett & colleagues, 2001). For example, the teacher may be asked to consider why he or she thinks the student is not following directions and asked to identify when the behavior occurs most, occurs least, and what differences in the instruction, curriculum, and environment may account for such differences.

During the summary of this information, the role of the team is to listen for clues as to what is causing or contributing to the problem at hand. Based on the summary of the student's current performance, how that performance compares to peers or a standard, and what has been learned from past intervention efforts and observations, the team is in a good position to move into the next phase of the problem-solving process, problem analysis.

Problem Analysis

In problem analysis, the team interprets the data shared during problem identification and generates hypotheses about the factors that are contributing to the problem. Depending on the data collected during problem identification and the concern at hand, this part of the problem-solving process might be very straightforward. For example, if the data shared during problem identification indicated that the student was observed to be trying to get his or her neighbors attention while the teacher was giving directions, the team may conclude that the student is not following teacher directions because the teacher did not have the student's complete attention prior to giving them. This component of developing possible causes for the problem is the key to intervention plan development. The significance of problem analysis is that determination of the factors that most contribute to the problem results in consideration of interventions that are directly linked to the selected probable cause.

To make use of the varied expertise and perspectives around the table, the team must pose several probable causes before selecting one or two to focus intervention efforts around. The team facilitator leads this by stating, "We think (insert concern) is occurring because . . .," and the team should consider potential contributing factors related to instruction, curriculum, environment, and the learner. After listening to the data provided during problem identification, team members may have different interpretations of what it means. After posing several possible causes, the team agrees (by consensus) on one or two of them that make the most sense and are most supported by the data collected to date. These one or two causes will be used when moving to the next component in the process.

Intervention Generation and Selection

Once the team develops and agrees upon a hypothesis for the reason(s) the student is having problems, intervention plans are generated related to that hypothesis. For effective intervention generation, the team usually engages in brainstorming sessions to spawn ideas. In brainstorming, no suggested ideas are criticized; the goal is to get a large number of possible solutions. Once ideas for interventions are generated, effective teams allow the person who will be the primary implementer (usually the teacher) to select the intervention that he or she believes will have the highest probability of success, is the easiest to manage, and has adequate supports to carry out the intervention plan. As stated in the asset identification component, considering the student's strengths when selecting the intervention of choice can be powerful. Allowing the referring teacher to select the intervention to be used increases ownership of the plan and increases the likelihood that the teacher will carry out the plan consistently.

Goal Setting and Progress Monitoring

An intervention plan isn't complete until the team determines a goal against which to measure the success or failure of the plan. When determining a goal, the team should first consider the data and information obtained during problem identification. Setting ambitious yet realistic and obtainable goals within a specified time frame provides a reference for evaluating intervention effectiveness. The time frame should be individually determined based on the student, the intervention, and what is known about learning and changing behavior. The team needs to allow enough time to give the intervention plan a chance to work.

The benefits of systematically monitoring student progress are well documented (Fuchs & Fuchs, 1986;

Stecker & Fuchs, 2000). When student progress is systematically monitored, teachers are more effective and efficient with instructional design and decision making, and student performance improves (Fuchs & Fuchs, 1986). The team must define a measurement strategy that includes frequent checks on student progress (i.e., at least biweekly) and that is sensitive to small increments of progress. Another aspect of monitoring is integrity checks. Integrity checks involve monitoring the consistency with which the planned intervention has been implemented. Simple checklists or direct observations of the teacher's implementation of the plan give the team information to determine the effectiveness (or ineffectiveness) of the intervention.

Evaluation of Effectiveness

The evaluative decision is based on implementation integrity (i.e., how consistently the intervention was implemented by the teacher, other staff, or family) and student progress. The team is required to review both graphed data and teacher/student/family perception of progress to determine growth. Decisions are made to maintain, change, or modify the plan based on the data. Adequacy of student progress is determined by comparing the student's progress over time to the aimline established during goal setting. There is not a universal rule for determining acceptability of progress, so teams make judgments based on the student's progress toward the goal and researched findings regarding acceptable rates of progress. If progress is adequate, the team determines whether the intervention can be sustained with current resources, whether the intervention or supports can be faded out, and whether the frequency of monitoring can be reduced. If student progress is not adequate, the team determines where to reenter the problem-solving process (e.g., problem identification, problem analysis).

Based on the student's response to the interventions, the team may suspect the student has a disability if:

- The interventions put in place are focused and powerful, but they do not result in the desired impact on student performance.
- The interventions result in improved performance, but the resources to continue such interventions are beyond what can be expected from general education.

If the team suspects a disability, the problem-solving process should continue as part of the initial evaluation for special education required by the Individuals With Disabilities Education Act of 1997 (IDEA) (Tilly & colleagues, 1998).

TEAM ORGANIZATION

Everyone should be considered part of the problem-solving community. The team designated as the student improvement team merely serves as the core team that facilitates the process for a student's plan. Strong collaborative planning is accomplished by using a team of, typically, six to eight people, which represent the expertise throughout the building. While the problem-solving process can be used in various scenarios, the use of a multidisciplinary team offers varied perspectives and expertise, resulting in an increase of successful plans. Team planning is enhanced by having a team of people who are committed to the problem-solving process and who make it a priority to understand the various resources available in the community, the district, and the school.

ROLE OF THE SCHOOL PSYCHOLOGIST

School psychologists have demonstrated critical skills that help in the creation, implementation, and evaluation of an SIT. When creating a team, school psychologists often can consider different levels within a system and make recommendations about team membership, linkages to different district requirements, and procedures that will serve to meaningfully involve students and families. During the implementation of the SIT process, school psychologists offer a perspective that encompasses a rich knowledge base regarding effective instruction and development of cognitive and academic skills, data-based decision making at building and district levels, and working across various related agencies such as mental health.

Calls for shifting the role of the school psychologist away from primarily the gatekeeper to special education has been longstanding in the school psychology literature (Ysseldyke & colleagues, 1997). Remaining a central player in the special education evaluation process can be accomplished—without being a gatekeeper—through offering skills and services during the problem-solving process. The intent of the participation shifts to developing a plan that demonstrates improved student outcomes, rather than determining if "enough" has been tried, or if the problem is of such demonstrated severity that it warrants a special education evaluation. Further, during the determination of eligibility for special education, the school psychologist focuses on assessment data that leads to intervention and demonstrated responsiveness to the intervention that will guide the overall question as to need and eligibility.

The new century brought with it a growing momentum in the field of school psychology, and the field of education as a whole. To make the underlying philosophy, "all children can and will learn" a reality, schools must be willing to implement a problem-solving process, like SIT, that will meet the needs of all students, families, and staff. It results in a true paradigm shift, from recognizing that a student needs help, to describing what instructional, curricular, or environmental modifications are effective for an individual student. This shift aligns the actions of the system with the goals of public education.

—*Dawn D. Miller*
and Kelli E. Mather

See also Multidisciplinary Teams

REFERENCES AND FURTHER READING

Doggett, R. A., Edwards, R. P., Moore, J. W., Tingstrom, D. H., & Wilczynski, S. M. (2001). An approach to functional assessment in general education classroom settings. *School Psychology Review, 30*(3), 313–328.

Flugum, K. R., & Reschly, D. J. (1993). Pre-referral interventions: Quality indices and outcomes. *Journal of School Psychology, 32,* 1–14.

Fuchs, L. S., & Fuchs, D. (1986). Effects of systematic formative evaluations: A meta-analysis. *Exceptional Children, 53,* 199–208.

Individuals With Disabilities Education Act. (1997). 20 U.S.C. Sections 1401–1485.

Stecker, P. M., & Fuchs, L. S. (2000). Effecting superior achievement using curriculum-based measurement: The importance of individual progress monitoring. *Learning Disability Research and Practice, 15,* 128–134.

Tilly, W. D. (2002). Best practices in school psychology as a problem-solving enterprise. In A. Thomas & J. Grimes (Eds.), *Best practices in school psychology-IV.* Bethesda, MD: National Association of School Psychologists.

Tilly, W. D., Reschly, D. J., & Grimes, J. P. (1998). Disability determination in problem solving systems: Conceptual foundations and critical components. In D. J. Reschly,

W. D. Tilly, & J. P. Grimes (Eds.), *Functional and noncategorical identification and intervention in special education* (pp. 221–254). Des Moines: Iowa Department of Education.

Upah, K. R. F., & Tilly, W. D. (2002). Best practices in designing, implementing, and evaluating quality interventions. In A. Thomas & J. Grimes (Eds.), *Best practices in school psychology-IV.* Bethesda, MD: National Association of School Psychologists.

Ysseldyke, J. E., Dawson, P., Lehr, C., Reschly, D., Reynolds, M., & Telzrow, C. (1997). *School psychology: A blueprint for training and practice II.* Bethesda, MD: National Association of School Psychologists.

STUDY SKILLS

Study skills are the processes individuals use to digest and learn information. Although the term is typically used to characterize student learning in school, study skills are used by individuals across the life span who may be engaged in study activities ranging from the acquisition of a driver's license to completing a continuing education class associated with a job or career.

In a basic way, study skills are critical for maximizing learning. Just as an automobile mechanic must possess specific tools to tune an automobile engine, so study skills are the tools of learning. Unfortunately, from elementary school through college, many students do not know or possess a solid knowledge of effective study skills and strategies. Poor study skills can lead to an array of negative consequences. Students that drop out of school, for example, produce enormous costs for society and many will never realize their potential.

EFFECTIVE STUDYING

There is no doubt that effective study skills can transform learning. Still, what are the most effective study habits? What is the most efficient way to study? Psychologists interested in the learning process—school psychologists, cognitive psychologists, and educational psychologists—have defined how people learn and how to get the most from their study time. Hettich (1995) suggests that time management skills, memory techniques, and note-taking strategies are critical for maximal learning. Sedita (1995) notes that, while not a panacea for all academic difficulties, study skills (and the learning of study skills) can improve educational experiences for both students and educators.

The fundamental task of primary school is to teach children to read. Subsequently, from elementary school forward, people read to learn. After learning to read, people need to learn effective study skills. The first step to doing this is for an individual to identify his or her most effective learning style. Petch (1991) indicates that while there is not a right or wrong way to learn, students who learn best use tools that complement their particular learning styles. For example, auditory learners should use tape recorders, reading aloud, discussions, and debates to increase their knowledge. Visual learners should focus on note taking, charts, note cards, and visual activities; and kinesthetic learners need to employ tactile approaches such as typing, calculators, writing, and other such activities.

How do people determine their preferred learning method? Skillful, observant, teachers can often help students identify and learn to accommodate to their most natural and strongest learning modality. Another source of information is a psychoeducational evaluation, which is often part of an evaluative process completed by a school psychologist and which may involve a battery of psychological assessment tools. When used by a skilled and appropriately trained examiner, cognitive assessment instruments, achievement tests, and processing instruments can help identify cognitive strengths and weaknesses, and provide remarkable insights into individual learning preferences. Educators can request that the school psychologist collaborate with their instructional curriculum through the administration of learning style indicators to entire classes of students, thus larger numbers of students learn their preferred learning styles. To this end instruments such as the Myers-Briggs Type Indicator (Myers & McCaulley, 1985) and Gregorc Style Delineator (Gregorc, 1982) represent a brief glimpse into the types of tools that often can be used with entire classes of students.

Students may also adopt multisensory approaches, which effectively blend auditory, visual, and kinesthetic approaches that can help them more effectively study and learn.

Unfortunately, despite the fact that study skills are critical to maximal learning, too few teachers and schools actually assess study skills and teach effective instruction in this domain. Students more typically complain to teachers about studying long hours for particular examinations, while often claiming relative ignorance for any rationale about a low grade. In truth, some students study without adequate attentional focus, others memorize concepts without translating terms to broad concepts, and others read without knowing how to maximize recall. The most effective students, however, use specific study strategies.

STUDY STRATEGIES

Nwafor (2001) suggests that effective study strategies must include:

- Identification of important information
- Note taking
- Retrieval of relevant prior knowledge
- Organization of key information
- Elaboration of new ideas
- Summarization of new knowledge
- Monitoring of comprehension

Without qualification, the more students learn about study skills, the more effective is the teaching/learning partnership (Perkins, 1995). However, building a workable conceptual framework around study skills remains on the periphery. It is clear that students who make classroom study material personally meaningful, who use repetition to obtain memory storage, and who link new knowledge with previous knowledge are more successful on classroom examinations. These three points alone are key to student learning:

1. New knowledge must be personally meaningful.

2. Repetition facilitates memory storage.

3. Linking new knowledge with old knowledge results in learning.

Still, students typically internalize poor study skills and sometimes believe that memorization is the only way to learn. To effectively learn, however, students must:

- Learn that sophisticated study skills and learning strategies can only be used if students have a knowledge base to which new material can be related
- Understand that study skills are truly useful and the reasons the skills are useful
- Understand that study skills are multifaceted and must incorporate multiple elements
- Understand that when properly applied, effective study skills can produce documented gains in educational outcomes

- Understand that just as learning any new skill takes practice, whether it is learning to ski or throwing free throws in basketball, so too, learning study skills takes lots and lots of practice

Ormrod, in two classic texts (1990, 2000) highlights seven key elements that characterize effective study techniques:

1. *Learning to Select Important Information:* Students are continually confronted with a barrage of information. Typically, students are confronted with more information even in a single class than can be easily accommodated in working memory. Unfortunately, students do not typically know what is important to select and to learn. Students must learn to identify key points.

2. *Learning to Summarize Information:* Summarizing is an effective way to review major points taught in classes and to group and organize general points. Summarizing helps with repetition, serves as a key review, and helps transfer new information into long-term memory. Students must learn to effectively summarize the overall major points.

3. *Learning to Organize Information:* Students typically do not know how to effectively organize classroom learning or how to organize the material. Listing facts is not organizing information. Organization is critical as it helps "chunk" new information into usable blocks of material, which can be more easily processed. To maximally learn, material needs to be effectively organized and grouped around central concepts.

4. *Learning to Take Effective Notes in Classes:* Students vary from writing virtually every facet spoken in lectures to writing virtually nothing. On the other hand, given that a relationship has been demonstrated between note taking and academic performance (Hale, 1983), effective note-taking strategies are important. Students must learn to tie notes to instructional objectives, summarize main ideas, and include details to link main themes with overall knowledge.

5. *Learning to Underline Appropriately:* Students commonly use highlighters or underline various components in textbooks. Given that underlining

can be more time efficient than outlining an entire text, students should learn to underline main ideas and supportive details underscoring major themes. They should also use underlining as a focusing tool. Simply underlining entire texts is not helpful; students must learn how to underline and use highlighters most effectively.

6. *Learning to Construct Questions:* Students who study effectively turn individual headings into questions to focus their attention. Clearly, turning each heading into a question can facilitate processing and encoding. Have you ever completed reading a section in a book only to realize you cannot recall virtually anything you have read? Try turning each heading into a question. Turning headings into questions can help facilitate learning.

7. *Learning to Facilitate Elaborative Processing:* Elaboration is a process where new information is attached to previously learned material to facilitate a relationship. What is the meaning behind a particular section or paragraph? What is the meaning behind a certain section in a text? What is the relevant point the author is attempting to emphasize? Can the material be related to a particular application in the reader's life?

Smith (2000) outlines a four-step approach to organize learning called the PARS Approach:

1. Purpose: Why are you reading?

2. Ask: Ask questions related to the purpose.

3. Read: Find answers to those questions.

4. Summarize: Record information in your own words.

Another approach to learning that is taught to students of all ages is the five-step SQ3R approach. This approach is especially helpful for students with difficulties in reading comprehension or for those who have trouble dissecting and analyzing written text.

1. *Survey.* Start by quickly surveying or scanning the text. Briefly look over the title and the body of the text in order to ascertain the main points, paying special attention to pictures, italicized words and phrases, questions, and first and last sentences in a paragraph.

2. *Question.* Question yourself as you survey. For example, if reading an article titled "How To Make a Pie," ask yourself questions as you go through the text. Some questions may be: What type of pies can be made? What ingredients are needed? How long does it need to bake? Within each question, ask more questions. What happens if the oven is too hot? What if one bakes it too long or not long enough? This adds a second level of processing to information gathering, and by asking your own questions, the answers that you come up with are processed in your own words, making understanding and retention easier.

3. *Read.* As you read, read to answer your questions, and answer your questions in your own words. It may be helpful to write down your questions before you start reading and write down the answers to each question as you learn. In essence this allows for translating sometimes technical information into easily understandable material.

4. *Recite.* Recite questions and answers out loud. Recitation helps anchor the material and strengthens the use of auditory learning.

5. *Review.* Effective learners continually review previously learned material. To maximally learn, review the notes on the reading within 24 hours. Then, review the material at another time, approximately one week later. Finally, review monthly until the examination.

MODELS FOR TEACHING AND LEARNING STUDY SKILLS

A University-Based Model

Study skills can be learned in diverse ways. Tuckman (2001) details a *Strategies for Achievement Approach* taught as a complete course at The Ohio State University. With a thorough curriculum and textbook developed to teach study skills to college students, the program was based on achievement-motivation research and draws from contemporary research in educational psychology.

The approach teaches four specific achievement strategies:

1. *Take Reasonable Risks:* Students must set challenging but attainable goals; students must break goals into smaller, workable pieces.

2. *Take Responsibility for Outcomes:* Students must believe in their abilities and must develop a specific study plan.

3. *Search the Environment for Information:* Students must learn to ask questions, and must see what they learn.

4. *Use Feedback:* Students must monitor self-action, and they must provide individual instructions to themselves.

The model covers four specific cognitive components: learning from lectures, learning from textbooks, preparing for examinations, and preparing speeches and papers. While initially developed as a traditional classroom curriculum, The Ohio State University course has shown impressive gains in grade point average.

A Self-Study Guide

Loulou (1995) has developed a unique guide, *How to Study for and Take College Tests* for the U.S. Department of Education's Office of Educational Research and Improvement. Offering a plan to assist students to prepare and study for tests, the guide reviews strategies for multiple-choice, essay, and other assorted examinations. In addition, time management, organization, and planning strategies are examined.

The curriculum has applicability for college students and could be invaluable for secondary school students as well. It offers a workable, down-to-earth model; for example, some of the simple, succinct guidelines are:

- Use organization, planning, and time management to maximize success.
- Read assignments, listen in class, and take notes.
- Reread assignments, highlight key points, and review.
- Review, review, review (daily and weekly).
- Look for false answers on multiple-choice tests.
- Look for key words on tests.
- Write formulas to review.
- Place tabs on key sections.
- Number notes.
- Use flash cards for definitions.

STRATEGIES FOR DISTANCE EDUCATION

Pilcher and Miller (2000) note that not all students learn in the context of traditional classrooms—more

than 750,000 students annually learn through distance education coursework. They have carefully analyzed the available research on distance learning and cognitive strategies, and note that note-taking is a prominent tactic to maximize learning, with metacognitive strategies including planning, monitoring, and self-regulation. Each metacognitive strategy is described below:

- *Planning:* Students need to set goals, learn to skim material, and use questions to maximize learning. Successful students skim chapters BEFORE reading the material, while unsuccessful students do not use skimming.
- *Monitoring:* Students must learn to monitor their own learning. In general, monitoring improves acquisition, generalization, and transfer of knowledge and distinguishes successful from less successful learners. Monitoring can include self-testing.
- *Self-Regulation:* Students need to develop self-regulatory strategies such as learning to modulate their reading rate. Self-regulatory strategies also include reviewing strategies and test-taking skills.

In addition to specific cognitive study skills, effective students have a:

- Study schedule with specific study times
- Daily and/or weekly study pattern
- Setting conducive to study
- Quiet and organized study location
- Persistent attitude to study regularly
- Pattern of self-talk to reinforce studying
- Support network to reinforce studying
- Relationship with an instructor to reinforce learning
- Pattern of note-taking, skimming, and self-testing

CONCLUSION

Students who use study skills experience greater academic successes—research shows a definitive relationship between study habits and academic success at both high school and college levels. At the same time, large numbers of students do not know or use effective study skills. Conceptually, it is ironic that while study skills are key to maximizing learning, study skills are not routinely taught in the educational environment. That is, while children are effectively taught to read in the primary grades, few students learn that while we subsequently read to learn—from the primary grades forward—we must also learn effective study strategies to master learning and development.

Can study skills enhance educational outcomes? The answer is an unequivocal yes. The only question is how to teach students the specific tools to reach their learning goals.

—*Tony D. Crespi and Richard P. Bieu*

See also Academic Achievement; Homework; Learning Styles; Mathematics Interventions and Strategies; Reading Interventions and Strategies; Writing Interventions and Strategies

REFERENCES AND FURTHER READING

Gregorc, A. F. (1982). *Gregorc style delineator. Developmental, technical, and administration manual.* Columbia, CT: Author.

Hale, G. A. (1983). Students' predictions of prose forgetting and the effects of study strategies. *Journal of Educational Psychology, 75,* 708–715.

Hettich, P. I. (1998). *Learning skills for college and career.* Pacific Grove, CA; Brooks-Cole.

Loulou, D. (1995). *How to study for and take college tests* (Report No. NLE97–2527). Washington, DC: Office of Educational Research and Improvement.

Myers, I. B., & McCaulley, M. H. (1985). *Manual: A guide to the development and use of the Myers-Briggs type indicator.* Palo Alto, CA: Consulting Psychological Press.

Nwafor, B. E. (2001). *Metacognition and effective study strategies among African-American college and university students.* Paper presented at the Annual National Conference of the National Association of African American Studies and the National Association of Hispanic and Latino Studies, Houston, TX.

Ormrod, J. E. (1990). *Human learning: Theories, principles, and educational Applications.* Columbus, OH: Merrill.

Ormrod, J. E. (2000). *Educational psychology.* Columbus, OH: Merrill.

Perkins, D. N. (1995). *Outsmarting IQ: The emerging science of learnable intelligence.* New York: Free Press.

Petch, B. (1991). *Modifying curriculum.* (Available from Quality Training Specialists, Box 96, Climax Springs, MO 65324).

Pilcher, C., & Miller, G. (2000). Learning strategies for distance education students. *Journal of Agricultural Education, 41,* 60–68.

Schau, C. G., & Scott, K. P. (1984). Impact of gender characteristics of instructional materials: An integration of the research literature. *Journal of Educational Psychology, 76,* 183–193.

Sedita, J. (1995, March). *A call for more study skills instruction.* Paper presented at The International Conference of the Learning Disabilities Association, Orlando, FL.

Smith, C. B. (2000). *Reading to learn: How to study as you read.* Bloomington, IN: ERIC Clearing House on Reading, English, and Communication. (ERIC Document Reproduction Service No. ED437610).

Tuckman, B. W. (2001). *The strategies for achievement approach (stACH) for teaching "study skills."* Paper presented at the Annual Meeting of the American Research Association, Seattle, WA.

Weiten, W., & Lloyd, M. A. (2000). *Psychology Applied to Modern Life* (6th ed.). Belmont, CA: Wadsworth/Thomson.

STUTTERING

Stuttering is defined as dysfluencies in speech including whole- and part-word repetitions, sound and syllable prolongations, and silent or audible blocking (i.e., inability to move lips and/or vocal folds to produce meaningful sounds). Fluent speakers exhibit 3% or less stuttered syllables (Caron & Ladouceur, 1989); therefore, a diagnosis of stuttering would not be appropriate unless the individual exceeds this level. Specifically, the formal diagnosis is based on an evaluation of oral reading and/or speaking that includes the determination of the percentage of stuttered words or syllables, the average duration of the stuttered events, and evidence of nonspeech sounds and physical concomitants such as facial grimaces, head movements, and movements of the extremities (Bray & Kehle, 1996).

The prevalence rate for stuttering is approximately 1% of the population, and males are diagnosed at a rate three times greater than females (American Psychiatric Association, 2000). Approximately 66% of all onsets of stuttering begin gradually during the preschool years and correspond with children beginning to use complete sentences in their speech (Karniol, 1995). Further, although the reasons are not completely understood, more than half of the children diagnosed in early childhood recover without intervention (Onslow & colleagues, 1994). In addition, the recovery rate is higher for females, again suggesting that stuttering is probably gender-linked (Ardila, 1994).

Determination of the causes of stuttering has been difficult. Tenable explanations include genetic factors, emotional states, cognitive and linguistic processes, learning factors, speech motor deficits, and neurological abnormalities. Effective intervention strategies that can be employed by school psychologists within the school setting include successive approximation, self-monitoring, and self-modeling. In addition, speech pathologists may employ interventions based on techniques that reduce speech rate such as prolonging words or sounds, continuous vocalization, and breath management. Finally, pharmacological agents are also beneficial. Although all of these techniques, to some degree, are effective in reducing stuttering (Ingham & Andrews, 1973), with the possible exception of self-modeling, they tend not to result in lasting changes beyond a year (Bray & Kehle, 1996, 1998a, 2001).

Self-modeling is defined as the attitudinal and behavioral gains made as a result of several spaced viewings of oneself on edited videotapes that depict fluent speech. Self-modeling is derived from research on observational learning. The extent to which a child identifies with the model determines whether or not that child chooses to imitate the model. Self-modeling maximizes the degree of observer identification. In concert with social learning theory, changes in fluency that result from observing oneself speaking fluently may influence cognitive processes such that these cognitions become consistent with the newly acquired observed behaviors. For example, in addition to acquiring more fluent speech as a result of modeling oneself, feelings of self-efficacy may also be promoted.

In summary, the primary role of the school psychologist, in collaboration with the speech-language pathologist, would be to design, implement, and evaluate treatment programs for stuttering. It is important to note that stuttering is associated with academic and social deficits, anxiety, depression, and other emotional problems; it, therefore, should be considered in the assessment process (Bray & colleagues, 2002). Although behavioral, cognitive–behavioral, and prolonged speech interventions appear to be effective, self-modeling is probably the most enduring (Bray & Kehle, 1998b). However, self-modeling requires considerable expertise, time, and relatively expensive equipment.

—*Melissa A. Bray,*
Thomas J. Kehle, and Lea A. Theodore

See also Communication Disorders; *DSM-IV*

REFERENCES AND FURTHER READING

American Psychiatric Association. (2000). *Diagnostic and statistical manual of mental disorders* (4th ed., text rev.). Washington, DC: Author.

Ardila, A. (1994). An epidemiological study of stuttering. *Journal of Communication Disorders, 27,* 37–48.

Bray, M. A., & Kehle, T. J. (1996). Self-modeling as an intervention for stuttering. *School Psychology Review, 25,* 359–370.

Bray, M. A., & Kehle, T. J. (1998a). Self-modeling as an intervention for stuttering. *School Psychology Review, 27,* 587–598.

Bray, M. A., & Kehle, T. J. (1998b). Stuttering: Etiology, assessment, and treatments. In L. Phelps (Ed.), *Health-related disorders in children and adolescents* (pp. 629–635). Washington, DC: American Psychological Association.

Bray, M. A., & Kehle, T. J. (2001). Long-term effects of self-modeling as an intervention for stuttering. *School Psychology Review, 30,* 131–137.

Bray, M. A., Kehle, T. J., & Theodore, L. A. (2002). Best practices in planning interventions for students with communication and language problems. In A. Thomas & J. Grimes (Eds.), *Best practices in school psychology IV* (Vol. 2, pp. 1513–1521). Silver Springs, MD: National Association of School Psychologists.

Caron, C., & Ladouceur, R. (1989). Multidimensional behavioral treatment for child stutterers. *Behavior Modification, 13,* 206–215.

Ingham, R. J., & Andrews, G. (1973). Details of a token economy stuttering therapy programme for adults. *Australian Journal of Fluency Disorders, 1,* 13–20.

Karniol, R. (1995). Stuttering, language, and cognition: A review and a model of stuttering as suprasegmental sentence plan alignment (SPA). *Psychological Bulletin, 117,* 104–124.

Onslow, M., Andrews, C., & Lincoln, M. (1994). A control/experimental trial of an operant treatment for early stuttering. *Journal of Speech and Hearing Research, 37,* 1244–1259.

SUBSTANCE ABUSE

Substance use refers to ingesting drugs by swallowing, smoking, inhaling, or injecting. Misuse refers to the use of drugs for other than intended purposes, such as recreational use of prescription medication or drugs used in greater amounts or more frequently than recommended. Abuse refers to the "accumulation of negative consequences resulting from drug misuse" (American Psychiatric Association, 1994). The *Diagnostic and Statistical Manual of Mental Disorders* (1994) defines drug abuse as a disorder characterized by significant impairment or distress resulting from recurrent drug use. Indicators of abuse include interference with roles and responsibilities (e.g., interference with job performance), impairment of interpersonal relationships, risk taking related to recurrent drug use (e.g., driving while intoxicated), and drug-related legal problems (e.g., drug arrests, driving under the influence [DUI]). In other words, the distinction between drug use and abuse depends on the degree of perceived impairment in everyday functioning and/or the associated risks to health and well-being. The degree to which a substance is considered to be abused is shaped and influenced by cultural beliefs, social norms, specific setting, and social context.

INCIDENCE OF DRUG USE AND ABUSE

According to the latest press release of Monitoring the Future's national, annual survey on adolescent drug use (Johnston & colleagues, 2003), alcohol, cigarettes, and marijuana are the leading substances used by adolescents in the United States. Alcohol is the substance most cited by 8th, 10th, and 12th graders; 46%, 66%, and 77%, respectively, report lifetime use (i.e., having ever used). Tobacco is the second most commonly reported substance; lifetime prevalence for adolescents has declined significantly but is increasing again with heavy marketing to this age group. Despite similar declines in use since the mid-to-late 1990s, marijuana is still the leading illicit drug cited by adolescents, with 18% of 8th graders, 36% of 10th graders, and 46% of 12th graders reporting lifetime use. Rates of ecstasy use rose steadily among adolescents through the mid-1990s and reached peak rates in 2001, with 5%, 8%, and 12% of 8th, 10th, and 12th graders, respectively, reporting lifetime use. However, since 2001 annual rates among 10th and 12th graders have declined by nearly half.

Use of other so-called *club drugs* (Rohypnol, GHB [gamma hydroxybutyrate], ketamine) have remained relatively stable at less than or equal to 2% reported annual use for all three grade levels. Since 2001, misuse (use without prescription) of two prescription narcotic drugs, OxyContin and Vicodin, has increased, with 2003 annual prevalence rates ranging from 1.7% for 8th graders to 4.5% for 12th graders for OxyContin use, and 2.8% for 8th graders to 10.5% for 12th graders for Vicodin. Following marijuana, Vicodin is the second most frequently reported drug among seniors in high school. Since 1998, rates of tranquilizer use among 12th graders have increased somewhat from 8.5% to 10.2%, while lifetime rates of hallucinogens have decreased from 14.1% to 10.6%.

Drug trends among subgroups obtained from a Monitoring the Future study, 1975–2002 showed that white students reported the highest drug use, followed by Latinos, over time and by grade, while African American students are consistently lower in all drug use across all grades. By 12th grade, gender differences that appeared in 10th grade increased, with males reporting more use than females for all drugs and most time points. Other factors influencing greater reported use are no college plans and density of residential area (Johnston & colleagues, 2003). It is critical for drug prevention program planners to monitor drug use rates over time as popularity of specific substances may change. In addition, it is important to attend to variations in drug use, misuse, or abuse across age, gender, ethnicity, community, and socioeconomic status.

DRUG PREVENTION AND INTERVENTION PROGRAMMING

Drug prevention programs for the school-age population (pre-K–12th grade) should prevent all forms of drug abuse (National Institute on Drug Abuse, 2003). Prevention of drug abuse in multiple settings calls for consistency of messages and approaches. Prevention of substance abuse can be organized along dimensions including target population, ecological focus, terms of delivery, and program exposure.

Target Population

The target population for drug prevention programs can be universal (all students regardless of risk), selective (students who are believed to be at high risk for drug use), and indicated (students already known to be using drugs). Program strategies and content will vary according to level of risk, need, and school setting. For example, universal programs emphasize drug education, life skills, improved school attachment, and peer resistance skills. Selective programs emphasize affective management, motivational factors, decision making, and communication skills, as well as the development of alternative peer networks. Indicated programs may include these factors plus drug counseling (National Institute on Drug Abuse, 2003). Although it is generally assumed that universal prevention programs will be less effective for students at risk of or already involved in drug use, there is some evidence to suggest that they have an effect on all students, regardless of risk exposure (Mackinnon & colleagues, 1988).

Ecological Focus

Drug prevention programs can be organized along an ecological continuum, with focus on the individual and/or family, school, and community contexts. Individually oriented programs focus on psychological factors such as self-esteem. Family-oriented programs address socialization practices, structure and supervision, and parenting skills as critical factors in reducing likelihood of drug use. Family strengthening programs that emphasize parenting skills and parent involvement in schools have shown efficacy in reducing student drug use. Because peer influence is widely recognized as a major contributor to initiation and persistence of drug use, many school-based programs focus on deflecting peer influence through resistance skills (Botvin & colleagues, 1995). School performance and attachment are also considered important contributors to risk of drug use (Hawkins & colleagues, 1992). Thus some researchers argue that prevention programs should concentrate on improving school performance and school acceptability. Most school-based programs have focused on changing the individual. Only a handful address needed changes in school policies, procedures, and practices designed to improve school desirability for high-risk youths. Although few school-based efforts have included either group or whole school multilevel interventions designed to change youth culture, such interventions are necessary to prevent drug use over time. Furthermore, despite significant evidence that school-age children are exposed to drug use in community settings (e.g., on the way home, in after-school parties, or in interventions), attention to these settings is missing in school-related intervention studies.

Terms of Delivery

Terms of delivery—the manner in which an intervention is delivered—constitutes a third way of considering interventions with school-age children. Interventions can be delivered didactically (information to students or exchanges between students and instructors) or interactively (exchanges between students and instructor). A third way of delivering an intervention is in terms of systems change or structural changes in educational settings. Meta-analyses suggest that interventions in the first domain (those concentrating on information delivery and student-teacher interaction) have less effect than interactive interventions where groups of students are engaged with each other and teachers (Tobler & colleagues, 2000). Whole-school structural interventions involving policy changes or organized students against substance abuse are rare.

Program Exposure

Interventions with consistent messages across multiple components and levels are more effective over time than single-component interventions. In addition, research shows that higher intensity, longer duration, and continuity of exposure to a program results in better outcomes (National Institute on Drug Abuse, 2003). Critical to effective program delivery is consistency or fidelity of implementation. Fidelity is strongest but sustainability weakest when trained researchers or interventionists administer a program. Fidelity declines when school personnel rather than intervention researchers administer a program. However, decline can be mediated by high levels of acceptability, satisfaction, congruency of instructional method with the curriculum, and sufficient training. Programs should take into consideration protective as well as risk factors, emphasizing known strengths along with reducing known risks (Hawkins & colleagues, 1992). Major influences will vary across a number of different dimensions including developmental period, urban-versus-rural context, and factors such as acculturation and ethnicity. Thus, risks and protective factors may be theoretically identified, but also should be locally identified by students, teachers, and other members of the school community; and programs should be tailored to fit local needs.

Students have reported alcohol and drug use in and around urban, suburban, and rural schools. Drugs may be sold by adults outside schools or internally through student dealers, especially at the high school level. It is important for school personnel to monitor and observe for signs of these exchanges, to confront and refer students, and remove adult distributors, with police assistance if necessary.

DRUG TREATMENT

Drug treatment for school-age students addresses experimentation, problem use, and habitual use.

Experimental use may be associated with family problems, including various forms of abuse, or mental health problems such as depression or attention deficit hyperactivity disorder (ADHD). These should be addressed through assessment and case management, if available, or referral. Both problem and habitual drug use (or addiction) generally require referrals to comprehensive programs that include behavioral therapy, family involvement, remediation programs to improve school performance, and attachment and other mental health interventions, as needed. Programs should address the needs of children and their families, taking into consideration such factors as age, race, culture, sexual orientation, gender, peer relations and networks, intimate relationships and pregnancy, personal and family financial situations, and exposure to violence or abuse.

ROLE OF SCHOOL PSYCHOLOGISTS

The involvement of school psychologists in drug prevention and intervention is consistent with recent calls to participate more actively in comprehensive health and mental health care and prevention. Activities appropriate to the knowledge and expertise of school psychologists include:

- Monitoring of drug-related attitudes, beliefs, norms, and practices through school- and district-wide survey and qualitative research
- Establishing multistage screening programs to identify students at risk for drug abuse and those in need of treatment
- Conducting educational programs for school administrators, teachers, and parents
- Assisting schools and districts in the selection, development, and implementation of appropriate drug prevention and intervention programs for students
- Participating in or conducting evaluations of school-based drug prevention and intervention programs
- Collaborating with community-based professionals to establish referral networks in the community for inpatient and outpatient drug treatment, and facilitating student transition from inpatient drug treatment facilities to school and home

—*Jean J. Schensul, Bonnie K. Nastasi,*
and Helena de Moura Castro

See also DARE Program; HIV/AIDS; Resilience and Protective Factors; Smoking (Teenage)

REFERENCES AND FURTHER READING

American Psychiatric Association (1994). *Diagnostic and statistical manual of mental disorders* (4th ed.). Washington, DC: Author.

Botvin, G. J., Baker, E., Dusenbury, L., Botvin, E. M., & Diaz, T. (1995). Long-term follow-up results of a randomized drug abuse prevention trial in a white, middle-class population. *Journal of the American Medical Association, 273*(14), 1106–1112.

Hawkins, J. D., Catalano, R. F., & Miller, J. Y. (1992). Risk and protective factors for alcohol and other drug problems in adolescence and early adulthood: Implications for substance abuse prevention. *Psychological Bulletin, 112*(1), 64–105.

Johnston, L. D., O'Malley, P. M., & Bachman, J. G. (2003). *Monitoring the future: National survey results on drug use, 1975–2002. Volume 1: Secondary school students.* (NIH Publication No. 03–5375). Bethesda, MD: National Institute on Drug Abuse.

Mackinnon, D. P., Webber, M. D., & Penz, M. A. (1988). How do school-based drug prevention programs work and for whom. *Drugs and Society, 3,* 125–143.

National Institute on Drug Abuse. (2003). *Preventing drug use among children and adolescents: A research-based guide for parents, educators, and community leaders* (2nd ed.). Rockville, MD: U.S. Department of Health and Human Services, National Institutes of Health.

Tobler, N. S., Roona, M. R., Ochshorn, P., Marshall, D. G., Streke, A. V., & Stackpole, K. M. (2000). School-based adolescent drug prevention programs: 1998 meta-analysis. *Journal of Primary Prevention, 20*(4), 275–336.

SUICIDE

The issue of suicide and suicidal behavior in children and adolescents is a significant mental health issue. Using the most current data from 2001, suicide is currently the third leading cause of death in the United States for youths between the ages of 10 and 19 (after automobile accidents and homicide); and in some states suicide is ranked second with homicide ranked third as the leading cause of death in 15- to 19-year-old adolescents.

Suicide, however, is only one behavior among a spectrum of behaviors that represent the suicidal behavior continuum (Reynolds & Mazza, 1994). The suicidal behavior continuum consists of suicidal

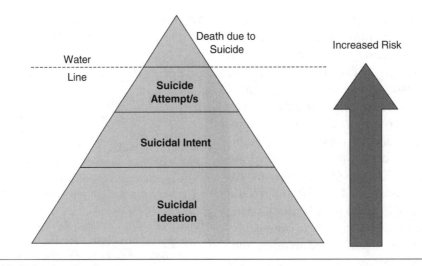

Figure 1   Suicide Behavior Continuum

ideation, suicidal intent, suicide attempt(s), and death caused by suicide, with suicidal ideation at the beginning of the continuum and suicide itself at the other end. Unfortunately, much of the attention regarding child and adolescent suicide focuses only on suicide itself, which is the rarest, missing the other more prevalent, but less lethal behaviors (Anderson, 2002). In fact, according to the Youth Risk Behavior Survey (YRBS) conducted by the Centers for Disease Control and Prevention (CDC) (2004) during the year 2003, 16.9% of high school students stated they had thought seriously of attempting suicide, 16.5% made a plan to attempt suicide, 8.5% actually attempted suicide, and 2.9% made a serious attempt that required medical attention. The analogy of an iceberg works well to represent the suicidal behavior continuum, with suicide being the tip of the iceberg and above the water, while the other behaviors are below the water but represent a greater proportion of the suicidal spectrum (Figure 1).

DESCRIPTIVE INFORMATION

The suicide rate for adolescents from 1955 to 1994 more than tripled to a rate of 11.2 per 100,000, but the rate has declined over the past 10 years and currently stands at 7.9 per 100,000 (National Center of Health Statistics [NCHS], 2003). Although the suicide rate for middle school students, ages 10 to 14 years, is significantly lower compared to high school age adolescents, it has continued to increase and is currently 1.3 per 100,000. According to the NCHS, the 10- to 14-year-old adolescents' suicide rate increased 109% from 1980 to 1997 compared to 11% for youths 15 to 19 years old during the same period (NCHS, 2003).

Gender Differences

There are important gender differences in adolescent suicidal behavior. Females attempt suicide approximately two to three times more often than males (CDC, 2004; Reynolds & Mazza, 1993). According to the recent YRBS data, incidence rate of suicide attempts for females was 11.5% compared to 5.2% for males, a 2:1 ratio. Similarly, Reynolds and Mazza, who sampled more than 3,400 adolescents across eight states, also reported a 2:1 female-to-male attempt ratio.

In examining suicidal ideation, defined as "the thoughts and cognitions about taking one's life as well as thoughts specific to the act of suicide" (Reynolds & Mazza, 1994, p. 533), females are more likely to be thinking about suicide than males (CDC, 2004; Reynolds, 1988). The YRBS data showed that approximately 23% of high school females had seriously thought about attempting suicide during 2003 compared to 14% of males. Using the Suicidal Ideation Questionnaire (Reynolds, 1988), Mazza and Reynolds identified 16% of females in their sample who scored above the clinical cutoff score, compared to 7% of males.

When examining gender differences regarding death caused by suicide, the ratio flips, with males committing suicide five times more often than females (Anderson, 2002; NCHS, 2003). There are two important factors that may contribute to this large discrepancy; first, males tend to use more lethal means to attempt suicide than females, which then are more likely to result in death. Second, males tend to be more involved in substance abuse than females, which research shows is associated with suicidal behavior.

Ethnicity

Suicide among youth is more common among whites than African Americans; however, the lowest rates are found among Asian/Pacific Islanders, while the highest rates are among Native Americans (Anderson, 2002). The high rate among Native Americans has been attributed to several different factors, including social isolation and low integration, high prevalence of firearms, and alcohol and/or drug use. The gap between the rates for whites and African Americans has been narrowing over the past two decades, largely because of the significant increase in suicides among male African Americans.

Methods

The methods used by children and adolescents to attempt suicide tend to be of low lethality. This fortunately allows them to change their minds and to seek immediate help. For example, taking pills allows time for the youth to regurgitate them or for a friend or parent to take the youth to the hospital. The two most common suicide attempt methods for male and female adolescents are taking pills, 22.5% and 45.1%, respectively, and cutting the wrists, 18.6% and 30.4%, respectively.

In contrast to unsuccessful suicide attempts, guns are the most frequently used method for both male and female adolescents who actually commit suicide. Guns are of high lethality and allow very little time for rescue. One societal myth surrounding suicide is that female adolescents most often commit suicide by pills or cutting their wrists; however, it is guns that are the leading cause of the suicide death in female adolescents. There is substantial evidence from other countries that restricting access to lethal means, such as guns, is an effective strategy for suicide prevention (U.S. Surgeon General, 2001).

WARNING SIGNS AND RISK FACTORS

There are a significant number of warning signs and risk factors related to suicide and suicidal behavior. Research that has investigated these risk factors has focused on two populations: those who have made a suicide attempt and those who have committed suicide. The method of "psychological autopsies" is used to collect information on the deceased by interviewing friends and family members about the psychological well-being of the person who committed suicide. Results from these studies have identified psychopathology, prior suicidal behavior, social isolation, family history of suicidal behavior and/or psychopathology, and stressful life events (including physical and sexual abuse and relationship problems), to name just a few.

A history of past suicidal behavior, especially a prior suicide attempt, is an important warning sign and one of the best predictors of those who have committed suicide or who will engage in future suicidal behavior. Groholt and colleagues (1997) found that between 25% and 33% of youths who died by suicide had made a prior attempt. A history of a prior suicide attempt is more predictive of suicide for boys than for girls.

Psychopathology is another important risk factor commonly found in youths who have engaged in suicidal behavior or have committed suicide. Psychological autopsies have reported that more than 90% of youths who died by suicide had at least one psychiatric disorder, such as depression, anxiety, substance abuse, conduct disorder, and borderline personality disorder. In fact, most adolescents who have committed suicide had multiple psychiatric disorders occurring simultaneously (comorbidity). The most common psychopathology linked to suicidal behavior is depression, with approximately 50% to 66% of those who committed suicide experiencing some type of depressive disorder. The psychopathology profile of an adolescent who attempts suicide looks very similar to those who die by suicide, with depression being the most common psychiatric disorder. Also, hopelessness, which is not a separate diagnosis, plays an important role regarding suicidal behavior in adolescents.

A third risk factor is impaired social and family relationships, which includes peer and parent-child relationships. Research shows that social support by peers and parents acts as a protective factor and reduces the likelihood of adolescents engaging in suicidal behavior. Peer relationships become increasingly important in high school as adolescents begin to use peer support more, while decreasing their dependence on parental support.

A fourth risk factor is family history of suicide and/or psychopathology. Research findings from the cited studies show that a family history of suicidal behavior significantly increases the likelihood of a youth dying by suicide or attempting suicide. Even when there is no family history of suicidal behavior, youths are at increased risk for suicidal behavior if the parents suffer from psychiatric illnesses.

One last risk factor is stressful life events that occur to the adolescent or to the family, including parents' divorce, breakup of a romantic relationship, legal or disciplinary actions, academic failure, and death of a loved one. In addition, adolescents who experience physical and/or sexual abuse are at an increased risk of engaging in suicidal behavior. Physical and sexual abuse are often accompanied by other related risk factors that increase adolescent suicidal behavior, and, thus, more research in this area is needed to account for the unique contribution of each risk factor.

MYTHS

One of the biggest myths surrounding child and adolescent suicidal behavior is the belief that talking about suicide will only put ideas of suicide into youths' minds (Reynolds, 1988). Unfortunately, this myth is held by many adults, including school administrators, and prevents the opportunity for children and adolescents to talk to someone about suicide. The issues of suicidal behavior are often on the minds of youngsters, and chances are many students know of someone who has died by suicide. Talking about suicide and suicidal behavior provides a bridge of communication to a difficult subject and allows students to talk about their feelings, their beliefs, and sometimes their misconceptions. Given the lethality of the behavior, it is more effective to take a proactive approach regarding suicidal behavior and identify those who are at risk rather than a passive approach and hope for the best. The U.S. Surgeon General (2001) stated in his National Strategy for Suicide Prevention that proactive identification through suicide-risk screening should be a primary care strategy.

A second myth regarding child and adolescent suicidal behavior is that children and adolescents leave suicide notes (Garfinkel & colleagues, 1982). In a research study of 505 youth seen in a hospital setting for suicide attempts, Garfinkel and colleagues (1982) reported that only approximately 5% of children and

adolescents wrote a suicide note. There may be several explanations for why youths do not write suicide notes; however, the primary reason according to the adolescents themselves is that they do not want their parents to find out what they were/are thinking. From their viewpoint, adolescents often do not want their parents interfering in their lives, and by writing a suicide note the likelihood that parents will get involved strongly increases. It is important to remember that most youth suicide attempts do not result in death.

Another myth regarding suicidal behavior among youth is that those who attempt suicide get medical treatment (Smith & Crawford, 1986). Unfortunately, similar to the issue of suicide notes, most do not communicate their suicidal actions to their parents or peers. Smith and Crawford (1986), in a sample of 313 adolescents, found that only 12% of those who had made a suicide attempt received medical treatment. Given that many adolescents are not old enough to drive nor are their peers, the only way they would receive medical treatment is by telling an older sibling or parent, an approach that most adolescents do not take.

The last myth is that parents know their child is suicidal (Kashani & colleagues, 1989). Unfortunately, like several of the other myths, adolescents do not communicate their suicidal thinking or behavior to their parents. Kashani and colleagues, who conducted a study with suicidal children and adolescents, reported that 86% of parents were unaware of their child's suicidal behavior, including suicide attempts. Thus, relying on parent's awareness or evaluation of their child's mental health, especially in the area of suicidal behavior, is not an effective means for identifying youth who are at risk for suicide.

SUICIDE PREVENTION AND INTERVENTION PROGRAMS

There are many different types of suicide prevention and intervention programs that take place in a variety of settings such as schools, community, hospitals, and at home. Although it is beyond the scope of this entry to go into detail regarding the effectiveness of each type of program, a cursory review of the different types of programs follows.

The most common suicide prevention and intervention programs are school-based programs that emphasize skills training, increased knowledge about suicide, changes in attitudes, and help-seeking behavior. The effectiveness of these programs is not universal; while some programs are effective in enhancing student knowledge about suicide and changing their attitudes, many do not evaluate changes in actual suicidal behavior (Mazza, 1997). More recently, revised programs have reported significant gains in enhancing knowledge and attitude change regarding suicide and, more importantly, have resulted in a reduction in suicidal behavior (Kalafat & Ryerson, 1999). These effective, revised programs are quite comprehensive and use a community approach that involves parents, teachers, school staff, bus drivers, and community resources; the message being that suicide prevention is a community issue not just a school problem. Guo and Harstall (2002), who recently evaluated 10 school-based suicide prevention programs, cautioned that there are great differences among programs in their duration, frequency, delivery, and evaluation components, so generalizations across programs should not be made.

Community-based suicide prevention programs often include crisis centers, hotlines, and media education guidelines. Although the overall rate of adolescents using community hotlines is low, Beautrais and colleagues (1998) found that approximately 15% of suicidal youths have used them. However, there is limited information regarding the effectiveness of crisis hotlines for adolescents who engage in suicidal behavior, and further research is needed.

Media education guidelines are another way to help reduce suicidal behavior, especially suicide contagion or copycat suicides, and also to help educate the public about the warning signs, risk factors, and resources available in the community that provide services to suicidal youth. Guidelines for media in covering a suicide death are available at the Web sites of the American Association of Suicidology and the American Foundation for Suicide Prevention. These guidelines are used to help reduce romanticizing suicide and reduce the likelihood of contagion suicides. Examples of these guidelines are:

- Avoid front-page coverage.
- Minimize description of method.
- Avoid use of pictures.
- Avoid describing the suicide as unexplainable.

WHAT YOU CAN DO

One does not need to be a suicidologist or have special training in the area of suicidology to make a difference to a child or adolescent who is suicidal.

However, it is important to know your own limitations and to keep in mind that getting the suicidal youth to an adult who is trained to deal with these types of issues needs to be the ultimate goal. There are three important steps anyone can use in talking to someone who is suicidal (Washington State Youth Suicide Prevention Program, 2004):

1. Show you care: "I am concerned about you and how you are feeling."

2. Ask the question: "Are you thinking about suicide?" or "Are you thinking about killing yourself?"

3. Get help from an adult: "I know where we can get help."

The first step, show you care, is designed to show the child or adolescent that you care and are willing to listen to his or her problems. It is important in this step not to make any judgments or dismiss the intensity of the feelings that the youth is experiencing. Avoid statements such as "everything will be better soon," "that is not a big problem," and "you have so much going for you."

The second step seems to be the hardest for adults. This step involves asking a direct question to the youth regarding if they are thinking about suicide. Although many adults feel like it is too abrasive or personal, this question is very appropriate. If the child or adolescent answers no, then keep listening to determine the central issues; however, if he or she says yes, then don't panic and continue to listen with the goal of getting help, which is step three.

Step three is getting the youth connected to the right resources or to an adult that can get him or her to the right resources. This may be a school psychologist, counselor, school nurse, clinical psychologist, or psychiatrist. It is important that you facilitate the transition and provide information to the adult resource, so the youth does not feel like he or she was passed off to someone else. In addition, it is important that a caring adult in each of the school, home, and community environments be in close contact with each other to make sure the youth is safe and being monitored. These three steps are important to remember and may help you be an active person in talking and listening to someone who is at risk for suicidal behavior.

—James J. Mazza

See also Crisis Intervention; Death and Bereavement; Depression; Learned Helplessness; Prevention; Psychopathology in Children

REFERENCES AND FURTHER READING

Anderson, R. N. (2002). *Deaths: Leading causes for 2000.* National Vital Statistics Reports (Vol. 50, no. 16). Hyattsville, MD: National Center for Health Statistics.

Beautrais, A. L., Joyce, P. R., & Mulder, R. T. (1998). Psychiatric contacts among youth aged 13 through 24 years who have made serious suicide attempts. *Journal of the American Academy of Child and Adolescent Psychiatry, 37,* 504–511.

Centers for Disease Control and Prevention. (2004). Youth Risk Behavior Surveillance-United States, 2003. *Mortality and Morbidity Weekly Review, CDC Surveillance Summaries, 53,* 1–96.

Garfinkel, B. D., Froese, A., & Hood, J. (1982). Suicide attempts in children and adolescents. *American Journal of Psychiatry, 139,* 1257–1261.

Groholt, B., Ekeberg, O., Wichstrom, L., & Haldorsen, T. (1997). Youth suicide in Norway, 1990–1992: A comparison between children and adolescents completing suicide and age- and gender-matched controls. *Suicide and Life-Threatening Behaviors, 27,* 250–263.

Guo, B., & Harstall C. (2002). *Efficacy of suicide prevention programs for children and youth.* Edmonton, Alberta, Canada: Alberta Heritage Foundation for Medical Research.

Kalafat, J., & Ryerson, D. M. (1999). The implementation and institutionalization of a school-based youth suicide prevention program. *Journal of Primary Prevention, 19,* 157–175.

Kashani, J. H., Goddard, P., & Reid, J. C. (1989). Correlates of suicidal ideation in a community sample of children and adolescents. *Journal of the American Academy of Child and Adolescent Psychiatry, 28,* 912–917.

Mazza, J. J. (1997). School-based suicide prevention programs: Are they effective? *School Psychology Review, 26,* 382–396.

National Center for Health Statistics. (2003). *Historical tables for 1979–1998.* Retrieved May 31, 2004, from http://www.cdc.gov/nchs/data/statab/gm290-98.pdf

Reynolds, W. M. (1988). *Suicidal ideation questionnaire: Professional manual.* Odessa, FL: Psychological Assessment Resources.

Reynolds, W. M., & Mazza, J. J. (1993). *Suicidal behavior in adolescents. I. Suicide attempts in school-based youngsters.* Unpublished manuscript.

Reynolds, W. M., & Mazza, J. J. (1994). Suicide and suicidal behavior. In W. M. Reynolds & H. F. Johnston (Eds.), *Handbook of depression in children and adolescents* (pp. 520–580). New York: Plenum.

Smith, K. & Crawford, S. (1986). Suicidal behavior among "normal" high school students. *Suicide and Life-Threatening Behavior, 16,* 313–325.

U.S. Surgeon General. (2001). *National strategy for suicide prevention: Goals and objectives for action.* Rockville, MD: U.S. Department of Health and Human Services.

Washington State Suicide Prevention Program. (2004, June). Available online at http://www.yspp.org/

SUMMATIVE EVALUATION

Summative evaluation is used to assess outcomes at the end of a unit of instruction, a grading period, or a school year. Summative evaluation in classrooms is associated with assigning grades and making decisions about promotion to the next level of instruction. Licensure and certification examinations are also forms of summative evaluation. The objective of summative evaluation is to make a judgment about the degree to which the instructional outcomes have been achieved. In program evaluation, summative evaluation occurs when program evaluators make judgments about whether the goals of the program have been realized. Summative evaluation, unlike formative evaluation, is a one-time event, and the summative decision is rarely changed. For example, it is rare for students to persuade teachers 'to give them a second or third chance to pass a test or submit a project' and to change their course grades based on their second efforts.

—*Nona Tollefson*

See also Communication Disorders; *DSM-IV*

SUPERVISION IN SCHOOL PSYCHOLOGY

Effective supervision in school psychology results in continued improvement in psychological services for children, youths, parents, teachers, and school systems. It includes both administrative and professional/clinical supervision.

Administrative supervision focuses on personnel issues; logistics of service delivery; and legal, contractual, and organizational practices. It addresses the performance of job duties in accordance with conditions of employment and assigned responsibilities and is primarily concerned with employer satisfaction rather than discipline-specific professional skills. Administrative supervision may be carried out by individuals trained in administration. Training as a school psychologist is beneficial but not essential.

Professional/clinical supervision focuses on promoting professional growth and exemplary practice. It requires specific training in school psychology and can only be provided by a skilled, licensed/certified school psychologist with at least three years experience as a school psychologist. Professional/clinical supervisors are responsible for:

- Supporting practices consistent with professional and ethical standards
- Promoting ongoing professional development to improve and update skills
- Conducting personnel evaluations that are consistent with specific professional standards

They assure high-quality services that support the educational attainment of children and youths.

FREQUENCY AND DURATION OF SUPERVISION

All school psychologists benefit from capable administrative and professional/clinical supervision regardless of work setting and degree of experience. Novice and advanced beginners require frequent, direct clinical/professional supervision to enhance skill development and ensure appropriate practice. Interns and first-year school psychologists should receive at least two hours of professional/clinical supervision per week. Collaborative work is a common and effective supervisory technique at this level. Thereafter, professional/clinical supervision should continue to be available to:

- Assure ongoing professional development
- Help maintain objectivity and deal with client resistance
- Foster appropriate methods of child advocacy
- Continually upgrade skills

Regardless of years of experience, school psychologists require more intense professional/clinical supervision whenever they enter situations in which they have no previous experience, either in terms of the population with which they are working or the procedures and/or tools used. Peer supervision is a common and effective supervisory technique at this level.

Experienced school psychologists are themselves likely to supervise interns or other school psychologists, which requires development of their own supervisory skills. At this level, supervision focuses on "metasupervision" (supervision of supervision) and addresses the conceptual, interpersonal, and technical skills required in supervision.

SUPERVISION TECHNIQUES

Supervisors of school psychologists adjust their supervisory strategies according to the skill level of the supervisee. Professional/clinical supervision techniques differ on a number of variables:

- The supervisor's ability to intervene and assist the supervisee and student
- The reliance on technology
- The amount of the supervisor's time required
- The level of supervisee skill required
- The intrusion on the student

Novices require direct and more intrusive techniques, supplemented by indirect techniques. Direct techniques include modeling, role-playing, direct observation, and collaborative work. Indirect techniques include instruction, readings, reviewing audiotapes, and reviewing psychological reports and case process notes.

SUPERVISION STRUCTURES

All supervision techniques may be used within the traditional one-on-one supervisory relationship. Most of them can also be used in alternative supervisory relationships, including peer mentoring, peer coaching, peer supervision, video conferencing, telephone contact, and Internet conferencing.

Supervision of school psychologists is most effective when the supervisor is employed by the same school district as the supervisee because familiarity with school district personnel and policies is a substantial advantage. However, not all service units have access to full-time school psychologist supervisors to provide professional/clinical supervision; in this case, alternative models such as part-time supervisors, collaboration among school districts, peer supervision networks across and within districts, and online supervision can be effectively employed.

PERSONNEL EVALUATION

Effective school psychology supervision includes personnel evaluations that improve practice. Appropriate summative outcome and formative process evaluations of school psychology service delivery require the collaboration of professional/clinical supervisors with administrative supervisors.

TRAINING AND EVALUATION OF SUPERVISORS

Supervisors of school psychologists have found formal training in supervision via coursework, workshops, and formal metasupervisory relationships very helpful. Informal training through peer supervisory support groups and through self-applying supervisory techniques (i.e., taping and analyzing supervisory sessions) is also very helpful.

Supervision programs and supervisors should be assessed regularly to ensure that accessible supervision, constructive feedback, and effective support is being provided for supervisees. These evaluations are most effective when they include evaluative information from multiple sources including supervisees, administrators, and the supervisors themselves.

—*Virginia Smith Harvey*

See also School Psychologist

REFERENCES AND FURTHER READING

Harvey, V., & Struzziero, J. (2000). *Effective supervision in school psychology.* Bethesda, MD: National Association of School Psychologists.

Haynes, R., Cory, C., & Moulton, P. (2003). *Professional supervision in the helping professions: A practical guide.* Pacific Grove, CA: Brooks/Cole.

Mead, D. (1990). *Effective supervision: A task-oriented model for the developing professions.* New York: Bruner/Mazel.

National Association of School Psychologists. (2000). *Standards for training and field placement programs in school psychology standards for the credentialing of school psychologists.* Bethesda, MD: Author.

Stoltenberg, C. D., McNeill, B., & Delworth, U. (1998). *IDM supervision: An integrated developmental model for counselors and therapists.* San Francisco: Jossey-Bass.

Todd, T. C., & Storm, C. L. (1997). *The complete systemic supervisor.* Boston: Allyn & Bacon.

SUSPENSION

Suspension is a disciplinary action that involves removal of a student from his or her usual classroom placement for a period not to exceed 10 consecutive school days. Specific definitions and criteria for determining when suspension is warranted vary from state to state and within individual school districts within each state. There are two primary forms of suspension, out-of-school suspension (OSS) and in-school suspension (ISS). In most school districts, OSS prohibits a student from attending school for a maximum of 10 days at a time (with no provision of instructional services), while in-school suspension involves having the student attend an alternative setting (e.g., an in-school suspension

classroom, an off-campus alternative-to-suspension site) for a minimum of 1 day (with no interruption of instructional services).

Suspension has been widely used in the United States since the 1930s. The use of suspension (and other exclusionary strategies such as expulsion) grew out of an early 20th-century school discipline paradigm shift away from threats, punishment, and harsh discipline in managing students' behavior; and toward more democratic ideals and strategies. Frequent use of harsh punitive strategies (e.g., paddling) decreased, and educators began to use behavioral strategies such as time-out for minor behavioral infractions, and suspension and expulsion for more serious or chronic behavioral infractions.

The use of suspension as an effective means for managing students' behavior has been questioned. One of the first large-scale reports documenting problems with suspension was published in 1975 by the Children's Defense Fund. Among the problems noted with out-of-school suspension in this report were:

- Missed instruction (often by students who need it the most)
- Labeling of suspended students as troublemakers
- Failure to provide assistance to deal with problems underlying students' misbehavior
- Over-representation of minority students among those suspended

Nonetheless, more than 25 years after the Children's Defense Fund report was published, out-of-school suspension continues to be one of the most commonly administered forms of discipline in the United States (Skiba, 2000). Importantly, minority students continue to be grossly over-represented when rates of suspension are compared (Raffaele Mendez and colleagues, 2002). Additionally, it has been noted that suspension may be used by students as an escape from the school environment. Many students who are suspended repeatedly experience school failure and eventually drop out of school.

Recent research shows that more than 3.1 million students nationwide (or 6.84% of the total student population) were suspended in 1997. Proportionally, the highest rates of suspension occur at the middle school and early high school levels, rising steadily from seventh through eighth grades and peaking in ninth grade. It is important to note that, contrary to popular belief, most out-of-school suspensions across the United States are for minor infractions of school rules rather than for dangerous or violent acts. One recent study of more than 100 secondary administrators found that the most common reasons for suspension were defiance of school authority, not reporting to after-school detention or Saturday school, and class disruption. More serious infractions such as weapons possession and narcotics possession typically make up a very small percentage of all infractions resulting in suspension (Raffaele Mendez, 2000; Skiba, 2000).

Under current Individuals With Disabilities Education Act (IDEA) law, there are certain procedural safeguards that school officials must consider in deciding whether to suspend a student who receives special education services. In most cases, students with disabilities are subject to the same disciplinary code that applies to all other students. However, when a student with a disability (either suspected or confirmed) is suspended for more than 10 days (cumulatively within one school year), a functional behavioral assessment and a manifestation determination must be conducted. The purpose of the functional behavioral assessment is to gather information so that the reasons for the student's problem behavior can be better understood. The manifestation determination is conducted to ascertain whether the student's problem behavior is a direct result of his or her disability. If the behavior is not determined to be a manifestation of the disability, then the child may be subject to the school's regular discipline code (although the student must continue to receive appropriate services and supports during the time of school exclusion). However, if the behavior is a manifestation of the disability, then options other than suspension or expulsion must be employed. These may include changes to the student's Individualized Education Plan (IEP) or a change in placement (with parent approval). These procedural safeguards were included in the 1997 amendments to IDEA to help ensure that children with disabilities were not arbitrarily removed from their parent-approved placement without parent consent and that they continued to receive a free and appropriate public education in the least restrictive environment.

Although there are many problems associated with the use of suspension, it can be difficult to find viable alternatives. It is commonly perceived that suspension is necessary to maintain the health and safety of staff and students and to reinforce the authority of those who are responsible for order and control in schools. Administrators also may use suspension to attempt to force the involvement of parents who have not responded to other attempts by the school to gain their assistance (Children's Defense Fund, 1975; Raffaele Mendez, 2000).

Most professional educational groups (e.g., National Association of School Psychologists) are not opposed to the use of suspension for particularly serious infractions of school rules (e.g., weapons possession), but they also recognize that suspension alone is not likely to result in a significant change in behavior for many students. This conclusion is supported by research showing that many children who are suspended once receive multiple suspensions during a school year (Costenbader & Markson, 1994; Skiba, 2000).

Suspension is best conceptualized as a disciplinary strategy that may be needed to intervene quickly and efficiently when student behavior presents a danger to oneself or others. However, it must be recognized that suspension is a temporary response to what is—in many cases—a larger problem that requires additional intervention. Best practices in the use of suspension begin with the recognition that school suspension is linked to the larger behavior management system of a school. Where there is little primary prevention related to disruptive classroom behavior, there is likely to be higher suspension rates (Raffaele Mendez and colleagues, 2002). Therefore, the effective use of suspension begins first and foremost with establishing a school environment that teaches, promotes, and facilitates appropriate, prosocial behavior. Such an approach to prevention should be grounded in an ecological perspective that considers:

- Students' developmental needs, challenges, and competencies
- Educators' needs for training and support
- The critical partnerships between schools, families, and communities in supporting the education and development of children and youth

In cases where removal of the student from the school environment is necessary to protect the safety of students, staff, and/or the child being disciplined, there should be procedures in place for following up with additional intervention efforts. In particular, for students with chronic rule infractions, it is recommended that educators use functional assessment strategies to determine the reasons behind students' misbehavior, regardless of whether the student has been identified as having a disability or not. Suspension alone is unlikely to significantly reduce misbehavior, especially among students who do not find the school environment to be particularly reinforcing.

—*Linda M. Raffaele Mendez*

See also Aggression in Schools; Behavior Intervention; Corporal Punishment; Discipline; Expulsion; Individuals With Disabilities Education Act; Manifestation Determination; Problem Solving; Special Education; Violence in Schools

REFERENCES AND FURTHER READING

Children's Defense Fund. (1975). *Out-of-school suspensions: Are they helping children?* Cambridge, MA: Author.

Costenbader, V. K., & Markson, S. (1994). School suspension: A survey of current policies and practices. *NASSP Bulletin, 78,* 103–107.

Raffaele Mendez, L. M. (2000, February). *An analysis of out-of-school suspensions in Hillsborough County.* Tampa, FL: The Children's Board of Hillsborough County.

Raffaele Mendez, L. M., Knoff, H. M., & Ferron, J. M. (2002). School demographic variables and out-of-school suspension rates: A quantitative and qualitative analysis of a large, ethnically diverse school district. *Psychology in the Schools, 30*(3), 259–277.

Skiba, R. J. (2000). *Zero tolerance, zero evidence: An analysis of school disciplinary practice* (Policy Research Rep. No. SRS2). Bloomington, IN: Indiana Education Policy Center.

T

TARGET BEHAVIOR. *See* APPLIED BEHAVIOR ANALYSIS; BEHAVIOR; BEHAVIOR INTERVENTION; BEHAVIORAL ASSESSMENT

TASK ANALYSIS

Task analysis is the process of breaking down a specific, complex behavior into small components in order for that behavior to be learned and then performed automatically on a regular basis. Typically, a task analysis is performed when a specific behavior is being taught to a student. School psychologists and other clinicians often complete a task analysis to teach new behaviors or to increase the frequency of present behaviors in children's and adults' repertoires. An analysis of behavior includes identifying the need for improvement of a specific target behavior as well as recognizing the social significance and function that the behavior plays in the individual's life. Once the behavior is identified, the clinician typically performs a task analysis to determine the steps that will need to be implemented for this new behavior to be learned and to increase the frequency of the behavior. Breaking down a complex behavior into a specific behavioral sequence makes it easier for the behavior to be learned and for the behavior to become part of the individual's everyday routine.

Antecedent-behavior-consequence (A-B-C) and latticing are two different types of task analysis. A-B-C task analysis includes observing the specific target behavior in the environment and identifying events that occur before, during, and after the target behavior is emitted. By examining the specific target behavior in the environment, the clinician is able to determine if any causal relationship exists between the environment and the specific target behavior. On the other hand, latticing includes listing the steps needed to perform the target behavior and the skill component that coincides with each step. For instance, brushing your teeth contains several different steps within it that must be completed for you to successfully brush your teeth.

A task analysis should include the specific step-by-step instructions needed to perform the target behavior as well as the type of instructional strategy that will be used to teach the different steps of the behavior (Gold, 1976). The type of instructional strategy should be determined by how the individual learns best. For instance, one step might be taught through modeling or through guided instruction, while another step of the behavioral sequence could be taught through reading literature on that specific topic.

A task analysis can be performed easily within the school setting. Teachers and school personnel can teach students to perform specific behaviors by breaking down the behavioral sequence into steps that the student can follow easily. For the task analysis to be effective, the clinician must identify the target behavior that is in need of improvement and break that specific behavior into small components so that no step is omitted. For instance, if the student needs to improve his or her participation in class, the teacher could break the task down into small components to be learned. The first step might be to think of something to add to the conversation, followed by raising your hand, and then waiting to be acknowledged by the teacher. When these steps are reinforced by the teacher, the student may respond by regularly continuing to participate in the classroom discussions.

—*Holly Yager*

See also Applied Behavior Analysis; Behavioral Assessment; Behavioral Concepts and Applications; Learning; Performance-Based Assessment

REFERENCES AND FURTHER READING

Cooper, J. O., Heron, T. E., & Heward, W. L. (1987). (Eds.). *Applied behavior analysis.* Englewood Cliffs, NJ: Prentice Hall.

Gold, M. (1976). Task analysis of a complex assembly task by the retarded blind. *Exceptional Children, 43*(2), 78–84.

Ninness, H. A. C., & Glenn, S. S. (1988). *Applied behavior analysis and school psychology: A research guide to principles and procedures.* New York: Greenwood.

TEACHING. *See* Discipline; High School; Learning; Middle School; Multicultural Education; Parent-Teacher Conferences; Resource Rooms; Special Education; Teacher-Student Relationships

---

TEACHER-STUDENT RELATIONSHIPS

The key elements of a quality relationship between teachers and students are composed of four broad factors. The first factor concerns features of the individuals involved in the relationship (e.g., gender, age, temperament, self-perceptions). The second component involves each individual's understanding of the relationship (e.g., how teachers and students view their own roles and the role of the other in this dyadic system). A third salient component includes the processes through which the two participants exchange information. Information exchange establishes and maintains a feedback loop between teacher and student, providing both individuals with verbal and nonverbal cues about the status and needs of each partner. The fourth component includes external factors that influence both teachers and students, including school-level variables such as discipline policies, schoolwide and classroom climate, class size, and organization of the school day.

It is important to note that although both participants in teacher-student relationships influence the quality of the relationship they form, the degree of responsibility for shared interactions is asymmetrical. The bulk of the responsibility for determining the quality of the relationship falls on the teacher in the early elementary school years; however, there is a shift toward shared responsibility as the child moves to middle and high school.

Research indicates two overlapping but distinct aspects of the teacher-student relationship: conflict and closeness. Although both aspects have been related to children's social and academic development, there are indications that conflict in relationships is more closely associated with child outcomes than is closeness. In early elementary school, teachers' reports of the quality of their relationships with students is relatively high (i.e., marked by low levels of conflict and high levels of closeness). Initial research has shown a trend toward relationships becoming less intense (in both conflict and closeness) as children move from preschool through the early elementary school grades. Furthermore, relationships that children develop with different teachers across their early school experiences are moderately stable, but demonstrate enough variability to indicate that each new teacher represents a new relational opportunity for students.

There is a clear association between the quality of the relationship and students' concurrent and future behavior, and academic achievement. Specifically, high closeness/low conflict teacher-student relationships in preschool and early elementary school are linked with positive peer relationships, higher levels of social competence, and better performance on tests of academic skills. This association between relational quality and children's outcomes is unique; that is, it is independent of the teacher's view of children's behavior problems, or children's cognitive ability, or prior levels of children's skills. Although the bulk of research on teacher-student relationships has been conducted with early elementary-age children, middle school students have also been shown to benefit from close, supportive relationships with teachers. Less research has been conducted on high school students, but it has been suggested that supportive relationships with teachers may be particularly salient for students at transition points, such as the transition from elementary to middle school or middle to high school. Supportive relationships between teachers and older students may be key features of the processes that link middle and high school students to the goals and benefits of schooling.

Teacher characteristics, including educational and teaching experiences, are not consistently linked with the quality of relationships that they share with their students. However, both gender and ethnic similarities are related to the quality of the relationship between teachers and students. Specifically, matches between teachers and students in ethnicity and in gender are associated with less conflict and more closeness in their relationship. The social and psychological mechanisms that underlie this association have yet to be identified.

Given the preponderance of evidence indicating that teacher-student relationships have the potential to be powerful, positive influences on children's social and academic development, school psychologists and other school personnel may consider harnessing this resource for use in both wellness enhancement and targeted intervention efforts. To maximize this potential resource for all school-age children, school personnel should consider factors at the four levels previously reviewed (i.e., individual characteristics, understanding of the relationship, communication processes, and external influences). The influence of overall school climate and schoolwide regulation of the type and amount of contact students and teachers have with one another should not be underestimated. Programs such as Students, Teachers, and Relationship Support (STARS; Pianta & Hamre, 2002) are available to guide interventions specifically targeting student-teacher interactions.

—*Megan W. Stuhlman and Robert C. Pianta*

See also Academic Achievement

REFERENCES AND FURTHER READING

Battistich, V., Solomon, D., Watson, M., & Schaps, E. (1997). Caring school communities. *Educational Psychologist, 32*(3), 137–151.

Birch, S. H., & Ladd, G. W. (1997). The teacher-child relationship and children's early school adjustment. *Journal of School Psychology, 35,* 61–79.

Pianta, R. C. (1999). *Enhancing relationships between children and teachers.* Washington, DC: American Psychological Association.

Pianta, R. C., & Hamre, B. (2002). *Students, Teachers, and Relationship Support: STARS.* Odessa, FL: Psychological Assessment Resources.

Wentzel, K. (1998). Social relationships and motivation in middle school: The role of parents, teachers, and peers. *Journal of Educational Psychology, 90*(2), 202–209.

TEEN PREGNANCY

Adolescent pregnancy is viewed as one of the major challenges to American society. This entry (a) describes factors contributing to teen pregnancy, (b) provides prevalence rates, (c) compares prevalence rates in the United States to other countries, and (d) reviews implications of teen pregnancy. In addition, a description of research-based components of teen pregnancy prevention programs is reviewed.

CONTRIBUTING FACTORS

Adolescence is generally conceptualized as the developmental period ranging from 13 to 19 years of age. Approximately 25% of sexually active individuals in the United States are adolescents. According to the Alan Guttmacher Institute (AGI) (2004), most teenagers become sexually active by their late teens. Sexual activity during this developmental time is linked to a number of risks; one of the most far-reaching is teen pregnancy. During adolescence many factors affect the youth's decision to engage in sexual activity. There appear to be two broad categories of factors that contribute to teen pregnancy: (a) dispositional characteristics, and (b) situational factors.

Dispositional factors generally refer to the adolescent's orientation or approach to thinking and behaving. When compared to adults, adolescents are more prone to risk-taking behavior as they usually have less reflective thinking dispositions and less developed decision-making competencies. Adolescents who have naïve dispositions about pregnancy (i.e., believe they will not become pregnant or contract a sexually transmitted disease) are also less likely to grasp the probable consequences of their actions. In addition, adolescents who tend to become pregnant often lack specific academic motivation and realistic career orientations. They hold unrealistic expectations as to what they need to do to achieve academically and to attain educational goals. Another dispositional quality of girls who become pregnant as teens is that they view pregnancy (and subsequent parenting) as a means toward establishing independence.

Situational factors refer to educational, family, and economic conditions that may promote or lead to whether the adolescent engages in sexual activity or becomes pregnant. Poverty is the primary situational condition related to adolescent childbearing. Race and ethnicity also emerge as critical situational factors related to the incidence of adolescent pregnancy and parenting. Although pregnancy rates fluctuate from year to year, the number of teens per 1,000 who become pregnant is approximately double for African American and Hispanic American girls ages 15 to 19 years compared to European Americans (AGI, 2004). African Americans appear to be at greater risk even when controlling for socioeconomic level because they:

- Attain menarche and hormonal fertility at an earlier age
- Experience sexual activity at an earlier age
- Are less likely to use contraceptives or to use them effectively

Nonetheless, the relation between ethnicity and adolescent pregnancy needs to be better understood. Educational disadvantage, peer group influence, school failure, and school dropout are additional factors that place an adolescent at risk for early pregnancy. For example, the adolescent pregnancy rates are disproportionately higher in schools having high dropout rates and in families with lower educational levels (AGI, 2004).

PREVALENCE RATES

Based on reports from AGI, more than 800,000 to 900,000 adolescents become pregnant each year, with more than half of those pregnancies leading to adolescent parenthood (AGI, 1994, 2004). For example, in the year 2000, 33% of pregnancies among 15- to 19-year-old girls ended in abortion. However, teen pregnancy rates and abortion rates vary considerably by ethnicity and by state. Among U.S. adolescent girls, 15% of all African American girls, 14% of Hispanic Americans, and 7% of European Americans become pregnant (AGI, 2004). The disproportionately higher incidence of adolescent pregnancy for young women of color is even more dramatic at younger ages. In 1997, 1.1 per 1,000 European American females younger than 15 years of age became pregnant compared to 3.9 per 1,000 Hispanic girls and 7.7 per 1,000 African American girls. Overall in 1995, 14% of all sexually experienced males 15 to 19 years were

involved in a pregnancy. In terms of ethnic ratios, this included 10%, 19%, and 22% of sexually experienced European American, Hispanic American, and African America males, respectively.

The highest teen pregnancy rates occur in the District of Columbia (128 per 1,000) and Nevada (113 per 1,000); North Dakota has the lowest rate (42 pregnancies per 1,000). Abortion rates are highest in New Jersey, New York, Massachusetts, and the District of Columbia where 50% to 60% of teen pregnancies were ended with an abortion. In contrast, only 13% to 16% of pregnancies among teens in Kentucky, Utah, Louisiana, Arkansas, and South Dakota ended in abortion (AGI, 2004). Nationwide the rate of pregnancy, birth, and abortion among U.S. teenagers has followed a downward trend since peaking in 1990.

Although pregnancy rates among adolescents have declined, the United States continues to have the highest adolescent pregnancy rates among industrialized countries. For example, whereas in 1996, the pregnancy rate for females ages 15 to 19 years in the United States was 83.6 per 1,000 it was considerably lower in other Western countries (France, 20.2 per 1,000; Sweden, 25.0 per 1,000; Canada, 45.7 per 1,000; and Great Britain, 46.7 per 1,000) (Population Resource Center, 2004). Thus, even those states with the lowest rates of teen pregnancy in the United States have rates higher than most other countries in the Western world. Effective forms and more use of contraceptives by adolescents in other industrialized countries appear to account for the lower rates in these countries.

IMPLICATIONS AND CONSEQUENCES

The incidence of adolescent pregnancy in the United States becomes most disturbing when the serious, and often irreversible, developmental and health consequences are considered. Of the approximately one million teenage pregnancies, nearly 80% of adolescent pregnancies are reported to be unintentional, with more than 40% resulting in unintended births. Intended or not, the outcomes for an adolescent who becomes pregnant can be deleterious. When compared to their same-age peers, pregnant teens are more likely to (Annie E. Casey Foundation, 1998; Coley & Chase-Lansdale, 1998):

- Drop out of high school
- Live in poverty and rely on public welfare
- Experience higher levels of psychological distress (i.e., depression and anxiety)

Not surprisingly, grim child outcomes also are associated with adolescent parenthood as these children often have low-birth weights; experience heath, coping, and developmental problems; and are more likely to be poor, abused, and/or neglected (Annie E. Casey Foundation, 1998).

One of the most serious consequences of early sexual activity is the increased risk of exposure to sexually transmitted diseases (STDs). Adolescents are at higher risk for contracting STDs than older sexually active adults because their cervix has not completely developed and because they have fewer protective STD antibodies. For example, sexually active adolescents ages 15 to 19 years have the highest level of gonorrhea than any other 5-year age group between 20 and 40 years. Another reason for higher levels of STDs in adolescents is that they are less likely to use barrier contraceptives such as condoms. Of the 40% of adolescents in the United States who are sexually active, approximately 60% report using condoms (Center for Disease Control [CDC], 2004). Drug and alcohol use (approximately 25% of all adolescents engaged in alcohol or drug use before having sexual intercourse) and unrealistic perceptions of STD risk decreases the likelihood that an adolescent will use contraceptives. The consequences of STDs can be devastating, including:

- Infertility
- Cancer
- HIV infection
- AIDS
- Death

In 1998, HIV was the ninth leading cause of death among youth ages 15 to 24 in the United States.

Teen pregnancy also has serious economic ramifications, as it poses substantial financial burdens to society. The cost of adolescent parenthood to public taxpayers increases each year because of medical costs rising at exponential levels. Estimates suggest that more than 50% of the federal budget for welfare aid goes to families begun by women who were adolescents when they first gave birth. Overall the financial cost of teen pregnancy in the United States is estimated at more than $7 billion annually in public assistance, child health care, foster care, lost tax revenues, and involvement with the criminal justice system (Annie E. Casey Foundation, 1998).

INTERVENTIONS THAT WORK

In view of the serious consequences of early sexual activity and teen pregnancy, the need for explicit prevention and intervention efforts is clear. A prevention or intervention is a specific activity (or set of related strategies) with an intended outcome such as reducing teen pregnancy. For an intervention to have the desired characteristic of scientific soundness (i.e., demonstrates it produces intended results, or works), it should have a distinct process and outcome goals as well as corresponding procedures or steps for implementation (Stoiber & Kratochwill, 2002).

As the most prominent public institution having the potential to influence teen pregnancy rates, schools play a critical role. However, schools face difficult choices in determining the best way to systematically address the issues surrounding adolescent sexual development and activity. The intervention approach implemented in a school should reflect the values and priorities of the surrounding community and the needs of the adolescents. As nearly half of all high school students in 2003 (47%) report having had sexual intercourse, it is crucial for schools to address the issue of teen pregnancy. Although some teens learn about sexuality from their family or church, a much greater portion of adolescents receive sex education through their school. As the effectiveness of any particular prevention or intervention strategy likely depends upon specific contexts and conditions surrounding a particular adolescent, it is difficult to discern which interventions have the most scientific evidence of effectiveness (i.e., evidence-based interventions). No single approach works for all teens in all schools.

The most effective programs appear to be those that are comprehensive and incorporate multiple components, which focus on:

- Increasing reproductive knowledge
- Improving social assertion and decision-making skills
- Promoting avoidance of risky behavior
- Developing long-term goals and career options

Based on a review of successful pregnancy prevention programs, several important key features or program components emerge as important:

- Consider early prevention and intervention before sexual behaviors are established. Once adolescents have initiated sexual activity it is very difficult to alter this behavior. Because of the young age at which adolescents may initiate sexual activity, systematic programs should begin prior to the onset of adolescence.

- Incorporate a focus on delaying sexual behavior and on providing information on how sexually active teens can protect themselves.
- Combine education with active learning and behavioral skills training (e.g., correct condom use, social assertion, risk recognition, problem solving under peer pressure).
- Incorporate interpersonal and communication training, including negotiation and refusal.
- Provide sexually active youth access to contraceptives and focus on contraceptive options.
- Provide outreach efforts through community-based programs to the most vulnerable of youths such as homeless or runaway youth, juvenile offenders, and school dropouts.
- Address sexual activity within a comprehensive prevention model that recognizes the coexistence of alcohol and drug use when many adolescents engage in sexual activity.
- Encourage self-evaluation of potential dispositions as adolescents usually make their decisions about sex in social situations, when decision making may be faulty, where time is limited, and when they are sexually aroused.
- Involve parents to participate in the selection and development of intervention programs as well as in their implementation.

As the contributive factors leading to adolescent pregnancy tend to be broad and complex, multimethod intervention strategies are needed to respond to individual risk conditions. The overwhelming societal consequences of adolescent pregnancy further call for continued evaluation of strategies and programs to ensure effective adolescent pregnancy prevention. Effective pregnancy prevention programs require the concerted commitments of educators, school psychologists, and other mental health workers. Efforts at reducing teen pregnancy depend on sound program design, home-school-community coordination, and high-quality monitoring and implementation of proven programs and prevention strategies.

—*Karen C. Stoiber*

See also Counseling; Dropouts; Parenting; Peer Pressure; Single-Parent Families

REFERENCES AND FURTHER READING

Alan Guttmacher Institute. (1994). *Sex and America's teenagers.* New York: Author.

Alan Guttmacher Institute. (2004). *U.S. teenage pregnancy statistics.* Retrieved August 24, 2004, from http://www.guttmacher.org

Annie E. Casey Foundation. (1998). *When teens have sex: Issues and trends.* Baltimore, MD: Author.

Centers for Disease Control. (2004). *Despite improvements, many high school students still engaging in risky health behaviors.* Retrieved August 26, 2004, from http://www.cdc.gov/

Coley, R. L., & Chase-Lansdale, P. L. (1998). Adolescent pregnancy and parenthood: Recent evidence and future directions. *American Psychologist, 53,* 152–166.

Population Resource Center. (2004). *Adolescent pregnancy and childbearing in the U.S.* Retrieved June 29, 2004, from http://www.prcdc.org/summaries/teenpreg/teenpreg.html

Stoiber, K. C., & Kratochwill, T. R. (2002). *Outcomes: Planning, monitoring, evaluating.* San Antonio, TX: Psychological Corporation.

TELEVISION. *See* MEDIA AND CHILDREN

THEORIES OF HUMAN DEVELOPMENT

Theories of human development are attempts at explaining the complexities of change that occurs over a life span, from conception through death. Each tends to represent a different worldview and is based on different fundamental assumptions about the developmental process and can usually be placed into one of the following four categories:

1. Biological models

2. Psychoanalytic models

3. Behavioral models

4. Cognitive–developmental models

THE MATURATIONAL AND BIOLOGICAL MODELS

Arnold Gesell, the foremost maturationalist in developmental psychology, represents a unique approach to the study of human development. As a physician,

Gesell believed that the sequence of development is determined by the biological and evolutionary history of the species. In other words, development of the organism is essentially under the control of biological systems and the process of maturation. Although the environment is of some importance, it acts only in a supportive role and does not provide any impetus for change.

While working with G. Stanley Hall within the tradition of the Darwinian influence that was very popular during the 1920s, Gesell applied the tenets of recapitulation theory to the study of individual development, or ontogenesis. Recapitulation theory states that the development of the species is reflected in the development of the individual. In other words, the child progresses through a series of stages that recount the developmental sequence that characterized the species.

Gesell believed that the most important influences on the growth and development of the human organism were biological directives. He summarized this theory in five distinct principles of development, which he later applied to behavior. All these principles assume that the formation of structures is necessary before any event outside the organism can have an influence on development. Interestingly, the notion that "function follows structure" was pursued not only by Gesell, but, later on, designers, architects, and engineers also found a great deal of truth in this idea.

Gesell also believed that behavior at different stages of development has different degrees of balance or stability. For example, at two years of age, the child's behavior might be characterized by a groping for some type of stability (the so-called "terrible twos"). Shortly thereafter, however, the child's behavior becomes smooth and consolidated. Gesell believed that development is cyclical in nature, swinging from one extreme to another, and that by means of these swings, the child develops and uses new structures.

Because he placed such a strong emphasis on the importance of biological processes, the majority of Gesell's work and that of his colleagues focused on biological systems as a beginning point to understanding development. Through Gesell's use of cinematic (moving picture) records, stop-action analysis provided the foundation for his extensive descriptions of "normal" development. This technique allowed Gesell to examine the frame-by-frame progression of certain motor tasks from their earliest reflex stage at birth through a system of fully developed and integrated behaviors. For example, his detailed analysis of walking provided the first graphic record of the sequence this complex behavior follows.

Gesell also made significant contributions with the development of the co-twin method for comparing the relative effects of heredity (nature) and environment (nurture) on development. One identical twin would receive specific training in some skill (such as stair climbing), and the other twin would receive no training in the skill. The rationale for this strategy was that because the children had an identical genetic makeup, any difference in stair-climbing ability must be the result of training. This is the basic paradigm that Gesell used to question some very interesting and controversial statements about the nature of intelligence.

Unquestionably, Gesell's greatest contribution is understanding the development of the "normal" child. His detailed cinematic records, their analyses, and their translation into books for the popular press have influenced child-rearing patterns in this country as much as that of the famous Dr. Spock (who incorporated many of Gesell's principles into his philosophy).

Gesell's ideas and theoretical approach never entered the mainstream of current thought about developmental psychology. Perhaps this is because much of his work was seen as too biological in nature and not sufficiently theoretical. Both from a historical and applied perspective, however, his contribution was and still is an outstanding one.

Over the last few years, there has been a heightened interest in other maturational approaches, most notably ethnology and sociobiology. These views, even more than Gesell's, emphasize the importance of biological and evolutionary principles as determinants of behavior.

THE PSYCHOANALYTIC MODEL

The psychoanalytic model, developed initially by Sigmund Freud, presents a view of development that is revolutionary in both its content and its implications for the nature of development. The basic assumption of this model is that development consists of dynamic, structural, and sequential components, each influenced by a continuously renewed need for the gratification of basic instincts. How psychic energy (or the energy of life, as it is sometimes called) is channeled through these different components constitutes the basis of the developmental process and individual differences.

The dynamic or economic component of Freud's tripartite system characterizes the human mind, or psyche, as a fluid, energized system that can transfer energy from one part to the other where and when needed. The structural or topographical component of the theory describes the three separate, yet interdependent psychological structures (and the way they regulate behavior) called the:

1. Id (unconscious structure that represents forces requiring immediate gratification)

2. Ego (an element of personality that mediates between the id and the outside world)

3. Superego (an element of personality that promotes the ideal view of the world and conscience)

Finally, the sequential or stage component emphasizes a progression from one stage of development to the next, focusing on different zones of bodily sensitivity (such as the mouth) and accompanying psychological and social conflicts.

It is difficult to identify the philosophical roots of psychoanalytic theory, because most psychoanalytic theorists would consider their roots to be in embryology, the biological study of the embryo from conception until the organism can survive on its own. This identification with a biological model has a great deal to do with Freud's training as a physician, his work in neuroanatomy, and his belief that biological needs play a paramount role in development. Some people believe that the philosophical tradition of preformationism (which in its extreme holds that all attitudes and characteristics are formed at birth and only expand in size) is basic to the psychoanalytic model, but this may be untrue. The preformationists stress the lack of malleability of the developing individual, while the psychoanalytic model describes a flexible character for the individual and the potential for change.

Freudian theory places an important emphasis on the resolution of conflicts that have their origin at an unconscious level. It states that the origin of these conflicts are biological and passed on from generation to generation. Development (and the development of individual differences) is an ongoing process of resolving these conflicts.

If the roots of behavior are located in the unconscious, how can they be accessible to study? Through a series of historical accidents, Freud was introduced to hypnotism as a method of treatment. This technique, in turn, gave birth to his now-famous method called free association, in which individuals are encouraged to freely associate anything that comes to mind in response to certain words or phrases. Freud believed that such an exposition of underlying needs and fears was the key to understanding a typical behavior. This method is a highly subjective way to collect information, and a large part of the criticism leveled against Freud and many of his followers was directed at this practice. The theory itself, however, is based on abstract and subjective judgments, and the fact that the behaviors under study are not easily amenable to scientific verification has caused controversy for years. However, the richness and diversity that Freud brought to a previously stagnant conception of development started a tradition that is healthy and strong even today. Perhaps Freud's most significant accomplishment was the first documentation and systematic organization of a theory of development.

The major impact of the psychoanalytic model and the work of such theorists as Freud and Erik Erikson have undoubtedly been in the study of personality and the treatment of emotional and social disorders. Erikson, unlike Freud, focused mainly on the social rather than the sexual dimension of behavior (hence the psychosocial nature of this approach). The impact and significance of both men's contributions cannot be overstated.

THE BEHAVIORAL MODEL

The behavioral model characterizes a movement that is peculiar to American psychology and distinct from any other theoretical model. The behavioral perspective views development as a function of learning and one that proceeds according to certain laws or principles of learning. Most important, it places the major impetus for growth and development outside of the individual and in the environment, rather than within the organism itself.

The importance placed on the environment varies with specific theories within this general model, but, in all cases, the organism is seen as reactive instead of active.

Within almost every behavioral theory, the assumption is incorporated that behavior is a function of its consequences. If the consequences of a behavior (e.g., studying) are good (e.g., high grades), studying is likely to continue in the future. If they are not good (e.g., losing privileges), the behavior (e.g., staying out past curfew) will change, perhaps to an earlier hour or to not going out at all on weekday nights.

The behavioral model makes the laws of learning and the influence of the environment paramount in the developmental process. Through such processes as classical conditioning and imitation, individuals learn what behaviors are most appropriate and lead to adaptive outcomes. Given that this model views development as a learned phenomenon, behaviors can be broken down into their basic elements. This leads people to view the behavioral model perhaps as being "reductionistic."

The behavioral perspective views the newborn child as naïve and unlearned. John Locke's notion of *tabula rasa* best exemplifies the philosophical roots of the behavioral tradition. Tabula rasa means "blank slate"—the newborn child as a blank page waiting to be written on, with only the most fundamental biological reflexes (e.g., sucking) operative at birth. The organism is malleable, and behavior develops and changes as a result of events or experiences. This is a more open view than the maturationist and psychoanalytic perspectives, because it sees human potential as unlimited by internal factors. Sometimes, however, biological endowment (an internal factor) can limit developmental outcomes, as in the case of genetic diseases or familial retardation. But even in the case of the severely retarded child, a restructuring of the environment can greatly affect basic competencies and caretaking functions such as eating and toilet training.

Given that the emphasis within the behavioral perspective is placed on events that originate in the environment and their effect on the organism, it is no surprise that the variable of primary interest to the behaviorist is the frequency or number of times a behavior occurs. For example, if one is interested in studying an aspect of sibling interaction, behaviors are explicitly defined, or operationalized, and must be objective enough to be reliably measured. Such constructs as "nice feelings" would not meet such criteria, but the "number of times brother touches friend" would.

Using frequency of behavior, the traditional way of studying development is to examine what effect certain environmental events have on behavior. This is most often done by identifying and observing those events in the environment that control behavior and then, if necessary, manipulating these events to see if the behavior under observation changes. For example, if a child's speech is delayed, the psychologist might want to observe what the events are that surround the child's verbalizations when left to run their course. Some intervention wherein the parents are encouraged to respond more directly might be suggested, and then additional observation might be done to see if there is any change. This type of design is frequently used in the area of behavior analysis. It illustrates the way in which the effects of certain contingencies can be isolated and identified.

Most interesting, however (given the behaviorists' deemphasis of biological age or stages of development), is the viewpoint that the sequence of experience is the critical factor in development; when discussing developmental status, experience—and not age—is the important factor. Although age and experience are somewhat related, age should not be thought of as a determinant (or cause) of behavior but only a correlate (i.e., a simultaneous outcome).

A more recently popular approach (within the last 50 years or so) to understanding development is through social learning theory and the work of such people as Robert Sears and Albert Bandura. A social learning theory approach is very much based on the same assumptions of the more traditional behavioral approach. A major difference, however, is that the social learning theory model incorporates such ideas as vicarious, or indirect, reinforcement. Here the individual does not need to directly experience something to actually learn it. This approach still reflects the importance of the environment, while at the same time suggests that individual differences contribute something as well.

The most significant impact this model has had is on the systematic analysis of behavior, on the treatment and management of deviant behaviors, and in educational applications such as programmed instruction.

THE COGNITIVE–DEVELOPMENTAL MODEL

The cognitive–developmental model of human development stresses the individual's active—rather than reactive—role in the developmental process. The basic assumptions of the model are that:

- Development occurs in a series of qualitatively distinct stages.
- These stages always follow the same sequence, but do not necessarily occur at the same times for all individuals.

- These stages are hierarchically organized such that a later stage subsumes the characteristics of an earlier one.

Another characteristic of the cognitive–developmental model that sets it apart from other theoretical models is the presence of psychological structures and the way in which changes in these underlying structures are reflected in overt changes in behavior. The form these changes take depends on the individual's developmental level. Many people categorize the cognitive–developmental perspective as an "interactionist" model because it encourages one to view development as an interaction between the organism and the environment.

The philosophical roots of this perspective are found in the predeterminist approach, which views development as a "process of qualitative differentiation or evolution of form." Jean-Jacques Rousseau, the noted 18th century French philosopher, wrote that development consists of a sequence of orderly stages that are internally regulated, and that the individual is transformed from one into the other. Although Rousseau believed that the child is innately good (and most of the early predeterminists believed that the environment plays a very limited role), modern cognitive–developmental theorists would not tacitly accept such a broad assumption.

Although the environment is decisive in determining the content of these stages, the important biological or organismic contribution is the development of structures within which this content can operate. For example, all human beings are born with some innate capacity to develop language and to imitate behavior. Human beings are not, however, born with a capacity to speak a specific language, or even to imitate a particular behavior. Children born in the United States of French-speaking parents would certainly not be expected to speak French, or any other language, without exposure to that language. Within the organismic model, the capacity for development emerges as part of the developmental process. Although the environment is an important and influential factor, the biological contribution is far more important because it is the impetus for further growth and development. The sequence and process of development are predetermined, but the actual content of behavior within these stages is not.

Of primary interest to the cognitive–developmental psychologist is the sequence of stages and the process of transition from one stage to the next. It is for this reason that the set of stage-related behaviors and their correlates across such dimensions as cognitive or social development have been the focus of study. For example, a psychologist might be interested in examining how children of different ages (and presumably different developmental stages) solve a similar type of problem. After observing many children of different ages, the psychologist can then postulate the existence of different types of underlying structures responsible for the strategies children use.

A great deal of Jean Piaget's work was directed at a better understanding of the thinking process that children at different developmental levels use to solve problems. In fact, much of the Piagetian tradition emphasizes that these different ways of solving problems reflect, in general, different ways of seeing the world.

Considering the cognitive–developmental psychologist's interest in the concept and use of stages, it is not surprising that the primary method used to study behavior is through the presentation of problems that emphasize differences in structural organization. The infant might depend on purely sensory information (e.g., touch or smell) to distinguish between different classes of objects, yet the older child might place a group of objects in categories based on more abstract criteria, such as "these are all toys, and these are food." The "how" of development is seen to be reflected in the strategies that children use at qualitatively different developmental levels to solve certain types of problems. More important, however, psychologists focus their attention on *why* these differences are present. Such studies have resulted in a model that hypothesizes that different underlying structures are operative at different stages.

Undoubtedly, the cognitive–developmental theorist has had the greatest impact in the different areas of education. Because much of the research conducted over the past 50 years by these theorists has focused on the general area of "thinking," this may be no surprise. Basically, the educational philosophy and practices that have resulted from this theoretical perspective have emphasized the unique contribution that children make to their own learning through discovery and experience. The child is allowed to explore within an environment that is challenging enough to facilitate development within the child's current stage of development, and one that is not boring.

—*Neil J. Salkind*

See also Defense Mechanisms; Learning; Learning Styles; Self-Concept and Efficacy

REFERENCES AND FURTHER READING

Bandura, A., Ross, D., & Ross, S. A. (1961). Transmission of aggression through imitation of aggressive modes. *Journal of Abnormal and Social Psychology, 3,* 575–582.

Erikson, E. (1950). *Childhood and society.* New York: Norton.

Erikson, E. (1968). *Identity: Youth and crisis.* New York: Norton.

Freud, S. (1933). *New introductory lectures on psychoanalysis.* New York: Norton.

Piaget, J. (1952). *The origins of intelligence in children.* New York: International Universities Press.

Skinner, B. F. (1948, 1976). *Walden two.* New York: Macmillan.

TIME ON TASK

Time on task (also referred to as engaged learning time) refers to the amount of time a learner is actively engaged in the task at hand. According to Savage (1991), it is the time students actually spend thinking about, acting on, or working with classroom assignments and tasks. Borich and Tombari (1997) reported that high time on task contributes to academic achievement. It has been suggested that time on task is more important to such achievement than the length of the school day or year.

Despite the importance of high time on task, it is potentially harmful to emphasize these behaviors to the exclusion of all other considerations. Some important classroom tasks, which require creativity and uncertainty, produce lower levels of on-task behavior than do simple clerical type tasks. Obviously, it would be counterproductive to exclude such activities from the curriculum.

Low time on task has been suggested by Barkley (1990) to be one of the most consistent school behavior problems displayed by children with attention deficit hyperactivity disorder. However, it is important to acknowledge that low time on task is associated with a number of other classroom challenges. For example, Brock (1998a) reports that developmental immaturity, learning disabilities, intellectual precocity, environmental stress, poor achievement motivation, and psychopathology are all potential causes of off-task behavior.

Behavioral assessment (or classroom observation) of time on task typically employs interval behavior-recording techniques. Whole-interval and momentary time sampling techniques are most appropriate for assessing on-task and in-seat classroom behaviors. Whole-interval procedures involve dividing the observational period into equal time intervals (e.g., 15 seconds) and then counting the intervals during which on-task behavior was displayed throughout. Momentary procedures also involve dividing the observational period into equal time intervals. However, on-task behavior is counted only if it is displayed at the moment each interval ends. Brock (1998a) recommends that when observing on-task behavior it is best to do so during a time when it is clear whether or not the student is on task (e.g., during an independent seat work writing activity).

A prerequisite to improving a classroom's on-task behavior is the establishment of a consistent classroom routine. Such a routine can help to ensure that the time allocated for instruction is maximized. This, in turn, increases the opportunity for students to be engaged in learning tasks. Additional strategies for maximizing on-task behavior suggested Brock (1998b) include:

- Presentation of engaging lessons that involve active (as opposed to passive) participation and use novel, interesting, highly motivating materials
- Use of external visual and auditory cues (e.g., posted classroom rules and verbal reminders) that prompt on-task behavior and clearly signal transitions from one activity to the next
- Self-monitoring strategies that require students to monitor and record their on-task behavior
- Contingency management strategies, which make the provision of reward or reinforcement contingent upon on-task behaviors
- Peer tutoring
- Ensuring that children are held accountable for their work by promptly checking the product of their efforts
- Group alerting or questioning strategies that result in students believing that everyone in a classroom has an equal probability of being called on by the teacher
- Physical proximity to the teacher
- Maintaining eye contact between individual students and the teacher

—*Stephen E. Brock*

See also Attention Deficit Hyperactivity Disorder; Behavioral Assessment; Classroom Observation

REFERENCES AND FURTHER READING

Barkley, R. A. (1990). *Attention deficit hyperactivity disorder: A handbook for diagnosis and treatment.* New York: Guilford.

Borich, G. D., & Tombari, M. L. (1997). *Educational psychology: A contemporary approach* (2nd ed.). New York: Longman.

Brock, S. E. (1998a). Appearances can be deceiving: Causes of "ADHD-like" behaviors. *CASP Today: A Quarterly Magazine of the California Association of School Psychologists, 47*(3), 25–27.

Brock, S. E. (1998b). Time on-task: A strategy for teachers. In A. S. Canter & S. A. Carroll (Eds.), *Helping children at home and school: Handouts from your school psychologist* (pp. 217–218). Bethesda, MD: National Association of School Psychologists.

Savage, T. V. (1991). *Discipline for self-control.* Englewood Cliffs, NJ: Prentice Hall.

TIME-OUT

Time-out (TO) is the most commonly used procedure of child disciplinary tactic in the United States. TO, the abbreviation for time-out from positive reinforcement, was first tested with laboratory animals in the 1950s (Ferster, 1958) and subsequently widely used for treatment of child misbehavior, the successes of which have been reported regularly since the early 1960s (Wolf & colleagues, 1964). The laboratory version typically involved limiting animal access to motivating activities such as eating or drinking. The child version involved limiting the child's access to preferred experiences, especially social interaction and all forms of entertainment. In both versions, TO regularly produced a remarkable effect, a dramatic reduction in the behaviors for which it was used as a consequence. Numerous replications of this effect, coupled with the fact that TO proved to be much more socially acceptable than corporal punishment, resulted in widespread dissemination of TO as a child disciplinary tactic. At present, a professional or popular book on child management techniques that does not include a section on TO would be hard to find.

UNDERLYING PROCESSES OF TIME-OUT

The fundamental process underlying the utility of TO involves an aspect of how children learn. Research on learning by the most eminent behavioral scientists of the 20th century shows that child learning largely occurs as result of the experiences that result from what children do. TO is used to deter children from certain types of behavior. Research on learning shows that when children do something that leads to unpleasant experiences such as being scolded, punished, or penalized (i.e., put in TO), they are less likely to repeat what they have done. For children to readily learn deterrence, two fundamental components are necessary, repetition and experiential contrast. The number of repetitions needed for learning to occur is governed by the amount of contrast between the child's experience that precedes and that follows things they do. For example, early in life children are at risk for being burned by open flame (e.g., from a candle) because it is inherently beautiful and they are inclined to touch it. One touch, however, generates such an extraordinary amount of unpleasant experiential contrast that it generates a virtual lifetime of caution around open flame. That is, virtually no repetition is needed for learning the connection. Conversely, numerous repetitions can be necessary to learn a connection between ignoring a parent's commands and unpleasant outcomes because many parents apply consequences inconsistently (Friman & Blum, 2003).

In sum, child learning occurs as a result of repetition followed by experiential contrast. Using TO effectively merely involves exploiting this salient fact of child learning. Specifically, an effective TO involves establishing an unpleasant experience that contrasts sharply with the child's experience prior to the TO. Ensuring the right level of contrast requires use of the companion procedure, time-in (TI).

TI can be thought of as the functional opposite of TO. TO is an experientially unpleasant event used as a consequence for misbehavior and TI involves experientially pleasant events that occur in the absence of misbehavior. There are many ways to establish TI, the most common of which involve:

- Increases in physical affection from parents
- Special time with parents and/or teachers
- Praise and appreciation from parents and/or teachers
- Opportunities to succeed in the eyes of peers
- Opportunities to meaningfully contribute to events in the family, classroom, school, church, and community

CONTRAINDICATIONS

Although TO appears to be a safe and effective means of treating a broad range of child behavior problems, its use is unwise in some circumstances.

Chief among them are those involving the possibility of self-harm or the probability of excessive stimulation if children are left unattended. TO is also not appropriate for children whose lives are impoverished in terms of human contact, marked by neglect, abuse, or inappropriate out-of-home placement, or who are ill. Additionally, TO is not appropriate for children whose misbehavior is motivated primarily by social avoidance. TO can be useful to establish a "cooling off" period for older children (i.e., older than seven years) faced with disciplinary action, but probably should not be the only disciplinary method employed.

WHERE SHOULD TIME-OUT BE LOCATED?

TO is a condition, not a location. Thus, although a barren locked room can provide TO, it is entirely unnecessary and usually inhumane to use one for that purpose. The key components of TO are major reductions in children's access to preferred events. Typically, the most preferred events in a child's life are social contact with others and engagement with entertaining objects (e.g., toys, games, television), and thus these are the preferred events to which access is curtailed in TO. Confining children to their room at home or in a hallway at school can accomplish these goals but so too can confining them to a seated position in a variety of places available in the home or classroom or on outings or the playground. Relying solely on bedrooms can inconvenience parents (e.g., when bedrooms are on a different floor than the location of the infraction).

HOW TO INITIATE A TIME-OUT

Immediately following a misbehavior the caregiver should very briefly specify the problem and say that time-out is going to occur as a result. Generally it is best to take children to TO rather than instruct them to go. Failure to follow instructions is one of the most typical reasons for using a TO and thus relying on instructions can exacerbate the problem.

WHAT BEHAVIORS SHOULD LEAD TO TIME-OUT?

At home, TO should be used for any behaviors that parents feel are unacceptable, or more generally, for any instance where the parents may be tempted to raise their hand or voice to their child. At school, TO should be used to back up less disruptive procedures such as reprimands or board-based critical feedback. To make matters simpler, unacceptable child behaviors can be divided into three categories:

1. Dangerous
2. Defiant
3. Disruptive

As a general rule, TO may best be used for dangerous and/or defiant behavior. Because disruption is an inevitable dimension of child behavior, however, much of it can be ignored at home, but it will often need to be targeted at school.

HOW LONG SHOULD A CHILD BE IN TIME-OUT?

Generally, exit from TO should be the result of child behavior, not the passage of time. Departure from TO is typically a highly preferred event and thus it has power to strengthen the behavior preceding it. Therefore, departure is allowed when the child exhibits quiet and composed behavior (i.e., crying, pleading, and bargaining have stopped) for as long as (but no longer than) one minute for every year of the child's age.

HOW SHOULD MISBEHAVIOR IN TIME-OUT BE ADDRESSED?

The two most common types of misbehavior that occur in TO are excessive protest and premature departure. Most experts agree that protests should be ignored, regardless of their content and that premature departures be met nonverbally by a dispassionate parent or teacher who merely physically returns the child to TO. However, protests and departures can be highly disruptive, especially in school settings, and thus a backup procedure is sometimes used (e.g., bedroom at home, hallway or office at school).

WHAT SHOULD BE DONE AFTER TIME-OUT?

Contrary to common practice, it is unnecessary and usually unproductive to lecture children about the misbehavior that led to TO (Blum & colleagues, 1995). Messages about the misbehavior are helpful but only when delivered in a brief and clear form, one more like labeling the problem than lecturing about it. More powerful than a retrospective lecture is an opportunity to practice appropriate alternatives to the misbehavior. A typical example involves the provision of several simple commands followed by praise and appreciation for child compliance or a return to TO for noncompliance. Additionally, if defiance or noncompliance led to TO, related commands should begin the practice session.

HOW SHOULD THE EFFECTIVENESS OF TIME-OUT BE MEASURED?

The most typical and effective method for measuring the effectiveness of TO is to document behavior problems prior to and following its use. The documentation can involve direct observation of specific behaviors or the completion of behavior problem checklists or scales.

CONCLUSION

Children learn through repetition with experiential contrast and thus good discipline will provide detectable contrast. TO serves this purpose very well if three conditions are met:

1. Sources of social interaction and preferred child experiences are minimized during TO.

2. The child's inappropriate attempts to terminate TO are ignored outright.

3. The child's environment before TO is imposed is generally interesting and fun.

In other words, an effective TO is devoid of social interaction and other forms of preferred interaction and occurs in a context called TI.

—*Patrick C. Friman*

See also Applied Behavior Analysis; Behavior Intervention; Classroom Climate; Intervention

REFERENCES AND FURTHER READING

Blum, N., Williams, G., Friman, P., & Christophersen, E. (1995). Disciplining young children: The role of reason. *Pediatrics, 96,* 336–341.

Ferster, C. (1958). Control of behavior in chimpanzees and pigeons by time-out from positive reinforcement. *Psychological Monographs, 72,* (8, Whole No. 461).

Friman, P. C., & Blum, N. J. (2003). Primary care behavioral pediatrics. In M. Hersen & W Sledge, (Eds.), *Encyclopedia of psychotherapy* (pp 379–399). New York: Academic.

Wolf, M., Risley, T., & Mees, H. (1964). Application of operant conditioning procedures to the behavior problems of an autistic child. *Behavior Research & Therapy, 1,* 305–312.

TOKEN ECONOMY

A token economy is a system that provides teachers with efficient ways to reinforce appropriate student behavior frequently and immediately without disruption to the classroom or school routine. Token economies have been effective in changing school behavior such as homework completion, noncompliance, aggression, tardies, talkouts, and completing functional skills routines such as food preparation. They are implemented similar to the way our monetary system is run. Students are given tokens for engaging in expected behavior (e.g., completing work, keeping hands and feet to self, using appropriate language, etc.) similar to the way individuals in our society are paid to complete work. These tokens can then be later exchanged for items the student desires such as free time, a piece of candy, extra recess, or other small rewards such as pencils or erasers.

DEVELOPING AND IMPLEMENTING A TOKEN ECONOMY

Developing and implementing a token economy system involves the following five steps. First, the behavior targeted for change should be well-defined in positive and observable terms. For example, if a student is noncompliant this could be further defined as "not following directions first time asked within 10 seconds." In the second step, teachers decide what will be used as tokens. Tokens can be anything from points on a point card, fake money, poker chips, or marbles. The goal is for the tokens to be easy for the teacher to dispense and difficult for the students to copy or counterfeit. The third step in implementing a token economy is to develop a reinforcer menu (reinforcers included on the menu are sometimes referred to as "backup reinforcers"), which involves listing items students would like to earn and setting prices for those items. When setting the price of each item, teachers should take into account the amount of effort the student must engage in to earn the item, how much the student desires the item, the amount of time it takes to deliver the item, and whether the item costs money. Figure 1 contains a sample reinforcer menu.

Mark	Number of Tokens
Swing chair	5 tokens
Computer (10 minutes)	10 tokens
Treat box	15 tokens
Rain stick	5 tokens
Trip to Burger King	50 tokens

Figure 1   Sample Reinforcer Menu for Mark—A Student With a Severe Disability

The fourth step involves determining when and how frequently tokens will be administered. Initially, tokens should be delivered immediately following the desired behavior, but over time teachers will need to reward behavior on a more intermittent basis. Teachers should always deliver tokens with social praise (e.g., "good job completing your assignment") so that over time the tokens can be faded and more natural forms of reinforcement can serve as the reward. The fifth step in developing a token economy involves determining when students will be allowed to exchange their tokens for items on the reinforcer menu. Students who are younger, have severe disabilities, or who have emotional and behavior disabilities may need to exchange tokens more frequently (e.g., hourly or daily) than students with mild or no disabilities (who might exchange tokens daily or weekly).

EXAMPLE OF A TOKEN ECONOMY

Token economies can be implemented with an individual student, classroom, or entire school. For example, at the individual student level, a teacher decides to implement a token economy with Donita, a third-grade student with a learning disability in reading, to increase her rate of work completion and the amount of time spent reading independently. Donita receives tokens for completing reading comprehension problems with 90% accuracy or better, and for each five minutes spent reading out loud with audio tapes. Figure 2 provides a sample reinforcer menu for Donita.

Donita	Number of Tokens
Get a 2-minute head start out to the bus	5 tokens
10 minutes computer time	5 tokens
10 minutes extra recess time	20 tokens
Walk to candy machines	7 tokens
Be the scorekeeper in volleyball	15 tokens

Figure 2   Sample Reinforcer Menu for Donita

At the school level, an elementary school may develop schoolwide expectations (e.g., Be Safe, Be Respectful, Be Responsible) and students would receive tokens (i.e, "WOW bucks") for following the expectations. These tokens can be exchanged for a piece of licorice, free gym time, or saved up for a quarterly drawing for prizes.

—*Leanne S. Hawken and Melissa Aubrey-Harper*

See also Behavior; Behavior Intervention; Self-Management

REFERENCES AND FURTHER READING

Boegli, R. G., & Wasik, B. H., (1978). Use of token economy system to intervene on a schoolwide level. *Psychology in the Schools, 15*(1), 72–78.

Higgins, J. W., Williams, R. L., & McLaughlin, T. F. (2001). The effects of a token economy employing instructional consequences for a third-grade student with learning disabilities: A data based case study. *Education and Treatment of Children, 24*(1) 99–106.

Kadzin, A. E., & Bootzin, R. R. (1972). The token economy: An evaluative review. *Journal of Applied Behavior Analysis, 5*(3), 343–372.

TOURETTE'S SYNDROME

Tourette's syndrome (TS) is a neuropsychiatric disorder of childhood characterized by motor and vocal tics that have been present for at least one year. Tics are defined as sudden, repetitive, stereotypic movements and vocalizations that are classified as simple (those that are rapid and appear to have no purpose) or complex (those that are slower, more orchestrated, and appear as if they do have some purpose). Common motor tics include eye blinking, facial grimacing, neck and shoulder movements, and tensing of muscles of the abdomen and limbs. Common vocal tics include sniffing, snorting, and throat clearing. In some cases, syllables, words, and phrases are repeated. Contrary to popular belief, only approximately 10% of individuals with TS have coprolalia (i.e., swearing).

The onset of tics is generally around the ages of five to seven years. Initial tics are simple in form and may gradually progress in complexity. In fact, it is unusual to have complex tics without having simple tics, either concurrently or in the past. Motor tics usually precede vocal tics, beginning in the facial area and progressing from the head downward. However, not everyone with TS has this presentation. In relatively mild cases of TS, the individual may have only some facial tics and simple vocal tics that do not progress in severity or complexity. Tics tend to occur in bouts and tend to wax and wane over time. Between the ages of 9 and 12 years, tics peak in frequency, intensity, and complexity, with occasional periods of significant exacerbation of symptoms. For most children, tics begin to subside in adolescence; approximately 65% of affected children will no longer have tics in adulthood.

Many tics are preceded by a "premonitory urge" to make the tic, in much the same way people experience an urge before a sneeze. Other tics, particularly simple tics such as eye blinking, just happen without warning, as with a hiccup. Also, the urges may be more generalized and experienced as a feeling of inner tension, which is considered more bothersome than the tic itself. One of the most troublesome aspects of TS has to do with the idea of volitional behavior. Because tics can sometimes be suppressed, people may believe that a child should be able to control the tic behavior at all times. Understanding that a tic is a response to an irresistible urge may help people to appreciate that, although the tic itself may be somewhat voluntary, the urge is not and the presence of the urge without being able to respond to it can create intolerable tension.

In school, the most interfering aspect of tics may be the energy a child exerts to stifle the tics, making the child appear as if he or she is not paying attention. Hence, it is important to determine the primary cause of inattention, as this has specific treatment implications, both pharmacologically and behaviorally. Children with TS also have visual–motor integration problems that may impact their school performance, particularly in the area of handwriting. Finally, the tics themselves may cause significant impairment in academic functioning. Eye-rolling tics can interfere with

reading, and arm and hand tics can interfere with writing. Vocal tics can be disruptive to the child experiencing them and to teachers and classmates.

—*Diane B. Findley*

See also Psychotropic Medications

REFERENCES AND FURTHER READING

Leckman, J. F., & Cohen, D. J. (Eds.). (1999). *Tourette's syndrome—Tics, obsessions, compulsions: Developmental psychopathology and clinical care*. New York: Wiley.

Wood, D. W., & Miltenberger, R. G. (Eds.). (2001). *Tic disorders, trichotillomania, and other repetitive behavior disorders: Behavioral approaches to analysis and treatment*. Boston: Kluwer.

TRAUMATIC BRAIN INJURY

In 1998, the National Institutes of Health (NIH) released a Consensus Statement that broadly defines traumatic brain injury (TBI) as a brain injury from an externally inflicted trauma (i.e., car accident, physical abuse) that may result in significant impairment of an individual's physical, cognitive, and psychosocial functioning. The NIH Consensus Statement noted that while TBI could result in physical impairment, generally the more significant and/or problematic sequelae involved the person's cognition, emotional functioning, and behavior.

Reid and colleagues (2001) noted that approximately 75 to 200 of every 100,000 children will sustain a TBI in the United States each year, with a male-to-female ratio of nearly 2:1. The incidence of TBI also increases significantly in people who are 15 to 24 years of age, particularly for males. These figures, coupled with the fact that approximately 75% to 80% of all head injuries are mild in nature and thus may go unreported, suggest that TBI in school-age children and adolescents is a major educational problem. Even with the high potential underestimation of occurrence, TBIs represent the most frequent neurological conditions that result in hospitalization of children and adolescents under 19 years of age, and they are the leading cause of death or permanent disability in children and adolescents.

Until legislative changes were initiated in the early 1990s, these children were not typically identified as needing special education and related services (e.g., detailed assessment, intervention); however, some school systems accommodated students who sustained moderate or severe head injuries under exceptional children classifications (e.g., learning disabled, mental retardation, multiply handicapped). Even with current legislative mandates acknowledging TBI as a special education classification, the range of outcomes following a TBI will vary, in large part secondary to the severity of the injury.

PSYCHOEDUCATIONAL OUTCOMES

Students typically show a decline in the level of intellectual performance following a TBI. For the most severely injured children, scores on the Wechsler Intelligence Scale for Children (Wechsler, 1974) are lower on the performance scale than on the verbal scale. This pattern of results is likely because of the dependence of many of the verbal scale's subtests on "old learning" (with the exception of tasks that require the use of numbers, which are more dependent upon speedy accuracy, problem solving, and novel learning). Further, it is unlikely that intelligence quotient (IQ) scores return to preinjury levels for children sustaining severe brain injuries, with evidence indicating that only a partial recovery of intellectual abilities is typically possible.

Academic problems following TBI at all severity levels have covered the gamut. In addition to specific problems in reading, writing, and arithmetic, there appears to be an increased need for special education programs, a tendency to return to a lower grade placement, and failure to return to school. Difficulties learning new or novel materials, problems with higher-order cognition (e.g., generalization, abstraction, organization, planning, strategy generation), slowed information processing speed, and overall reduced independent work efforts all can affect an individual's classroom or vocational performance in a negative fashion. It is important that all of these difficulties be taken into account when evaluating a TBI survivor's return to the formal academic setting.

NEUROPSYCHOLOGICAL OUTCOMES

Nearly every major neuropsychological domain has been reported as being impaired following different types of TBI. In a review of the pediatric TBI literature, Hooper (1998) noted problems in areas of gross- and fine-motor skills, attention-to-task, language skills, visual–spatial, memory, and executive functions. These deficits can be manifest as either mild, moderate, or severe, depending on the nature of the TBI, and they have been reported to persist to varying degrees well after the injury. Indeed, neuropsychological function or dysfunction has been predictive of which children required special education services two years postinjury. Hooper (2003) has noted that it is critical for school psychologists to be knowledgeable of neuropsychological assessment procedures in order to guide evaluation and treatment processes.

PSYCHOSOCIAL OUTCOMES

TBI can be associated with an increased vulnerability for the emergence of a psychiatric disorder, particularly in moderate and severe TBIs. These problems can manifest as denial of the injury and lack of concern for the injury in young children, and significant deterioration in self-concept and depression in older children and adolescents. Even in the instance of a mild TBI, behavior problems and accompanying changes in temperament (e.g., increased irritability) have been described; however, mild TBI does not appear to be associated with an increased risk for psychiatric disturbance.

For children and adolescents sustaining a severe TBI, rates of poor social adjustment have ranged from 25% at one year postinjury to more than 50% at three to five years postinjury. Significant declines in adaptive behavior at one year postinjury also have been noted. Butler and colleagues (1997) also have presented an emergent psychosocial typology in pediatric closed head injuries. Specific subtypes—normal, cognitive deficient, somatic, mild anxiety, antisocial behavior, and social isolation—have been proposed. This typology is awaiting further validation, but should prove useful in addressing possible treatment options.

FAMILY OUTCOMES

Given the psychosocial as well as the neurocognitive changes that can be observed in individuals who have sustained a TBI, it stands to reason that the larger family system is vulnerable as well. Martin (1990) reported that variables such as family support systems, family communication, extracurricular involvement of the family system (e.g., church), and availability of appropriate services and trained personnel were crucial to assisting families in coping with the injured individual. Issues pertinent to increased dependency, financial difficulties secondary to costs of rehabilitation and medical needs, and increased family stress (perhaps related to parental or spousal guilt following an injury) all serve to disrupt the family system. Wade and colleagues (1996) also noted that preinjury family status on such variables as communication, problem solving, role flexibility, and stress can be predictive of family functioning postinjury.

EDUCATIONAL PLANNING

Educational planning for individuals with TBI should be tailored to the specific strengths and weaknesses of each person. While this may seem a bit trite, this adage becomes extremely critical when working with these individuals. In particular, individuals in an acute phase of recovery may be showing frequent changes, and assessment-treatment linkages will need to be dynamic and reviewed on a regular basis (e.g., Individualized Education Plans should be written for shorter periods of time). The range of educational interventions for individuals with TBI is quite broad, with many different kinds of strategies being applicable to this population.

Telzrow (1991) asserted that the process of educational consultation and programming should begin before the student returns to the formal educational setting—perhaps even at the time of the injury—so as to promote communication between the family and the school, and to facilitate planning for the student's reentry. The initial consultation not only might entail performing a comprehensive assessment to determine current neurologically related behavioral deficits from the injury, but it also may require understanding the nature of the individual's injuries and his or her current medical status. This will increase the need for clear communication between the hospital or rehabilitation facility, the family, and the school. Furthermore, placement decisions should consider the full range of services available in a school system—including summer school programming and year-round schooling—in order to address the student's pending educational needs (e.g., maintenance and generalization of information).

It is also important for the practitioner to become familiar with specific teaching strategies that might be helpful with these students. While many of these strategies may not appear to be different from what is used in regular and special education settings, their use with individuals with TBI may be crucial with respect to learning, prevocational adaptation, and general school readjustment. For example, the practices that have been deemed important in the instructional process of students with TBI involve direct instructional techniques such as:

- Repetition and practice
- Cueing
- Modeling
- Instructional pacing
- Decreased use of time limits
- Immediate feedback regarding the individual's performance

Lastly, it is critical to note that one educational strategy for addressing TBI is prevention. By advocating for primary prevention venues such as those addressing bicycle and motorcycle helmets, child-restraint systems, child abuse, and drinking-and-driving laws, perhaps some of these injuries could be prevented.

—*Stephen R. Hooper*

See also Communication Disorders; Individuals With Disabilities Education Act; Intelligence; Learning; Memory; Neuropsychological Assessment; Perseveration; Problem Solving

REFERENCES AND FURTHER READING

Butler, K., Rourke, B. P., Fuerst, D. R., & Fisk, J. L. (1997). A typology of psychosocial functioning in pediatric closed-head injury. *Child Neuropsychology, 3*, 98–133.

Hooper, S. R. (1998). Individuals with traumatic brain injury. In A. S. Bellack & M. Hersen (Eds.), *Comprehensive clinical psychology* (pp. 137–153). New York: Pergamon.

Hooper, S. R. (2003). School psychology and traumatic brain injury: A programmatic approach to training. *Brain Injury Source, 7,* 28–31.

Martin, D. A. (1990). Family issues in traumatic brain injury. In E. D. Bigler (Ed.), *Traumatic brain injury: Mechanisms of damage, assessment, intervention, and outcome* (pp. 381-394). Austin, TX: Pro-Ed.

Rehabilitation of Persons with Traumatic Brain Injury. (1998). *NIH Consensus Statement, 16,* 1–41.

Reid, S. R., Roesler, J. S., Gaichas, A. M., & Tsai, A. K. (2001). The epidemiology of pediatric traumatic brain injury in Minnesota. *Archives of Pediatric and Adolescent Medicine. 155,* 784–789.

Telzrow, C. (1991). The school psychologist's perspective on testing students with traumatic brain injury. *Journal of Head Trauma Rehabilitation, 6,* 23-34.

Wade, S. L., Taylor, H. G., Drotar, D., Stancin, T., & Yeates, K. O. (1996). Childhood traumatic brain injury: Initial impact on the family. *Journal of Learning Disabilities, 29,* 652–661.

Wechsler, D. (1974). *The Wechsler Intelligence Scale for Children-Revised.* New York: Psychological Corporation.

TUTORING

Tutoring is a common instructional strategy used throughout schools, universities, and communities to enhance academic performance. Typically in tutoring, a more advanced individual (tutor) teaches an individual with less advanced skill (tutee) the necessary skills to master an academic task. The tutor typically works one-to-one with a tutee on skills that are deficient (e.g., reading, math, writing, or study skills). Through tutoring the tutee is provided an opportunity for individualized instruction in which he or she is able to practice and receive immediate feedback in the identified area(s) of need.

Tutoring programs may include strategic and/or instructional approaches. When using the strategic tutoring approach, the tutor teaches the tutee strategies needed to independently complete an academic task (e.g., strategies to write a research report). Instructional tutoring is a cooperative learning strategy in which the tutor teaches the tutee skills to complete a task. Unlike strategic tutors, instructional tutors are more content-based, which means that these tutors rely heavily on their knowledge of the subject matter to teach skills. Strategic tutoring is usually seen in schools, college and university settings, and agencies that employ professional tutors. Instructional tutoring is seen in schools that might use volunteer tutors and/or high-achieving students. Community-based tutoring involves volunteers or employed tutors from agencies outside of schools to provide academic remediation services to students. These tutors may offer their services in the form of after-school programs at a community organization (e.g., YMCA) or from within the school.

The most effective types of instructional tutoring formats used in schools are Classwide Peer Tutoring (CWPT) and Reciprocal Peer Tutoring (RPT). CWPT is an effective format for teaching at-risk students. CWPT involves pairing students within the classroom to carry out the tutoring process. The teacher serves as a supervisor of the process to ensure appropriate outcomes. RPT is cited as an effective tutoring format for students with mathematical deficiencies. Unlike CWPT, in RPT each student in the pair has an opportunity to assume the role of the tutor and the tutee during the tutoring process. This method is said to enhance the learning process for both students.

Tutoring is beneficial for students' academic success. Studies have shown that CWPT can help prevent school failure and that RPT has positive effects on mathematic achievement as well as student behavior.

—*Patricia Smith*

See also Classwide Peer Tutoring; Mentoring; Peer Tutoring

U

U.S. DEPARTMENT OF EDUCATION

The U.S. Department of Education is an agency within the federal government whose mission is to assure equal access to educational opportunity, improve the quality of education, encourage public involvement in education, and promote educational research (Department of Education Organization Act, 1979). In accordance with the 10th Amendment to the U.S. Constitution, the primary responsibility for American education rests not with the federal government, but with the individual states (Jacob & Hartshorne, 2003). State governments, in turn, typically delegate responsibility for the daily operation of schools to local educational agencies, such as school boards and county offices of education. Thus, schools are built, curricula are established, and graduation requirements are set under the authority of state and local government. In comparison to these broad powers, the role of the federal government in American education is decidedly limited. Nevertheless, the federal government wields enormous power in shaping educational policy through federal legislation, including antidiscrimination legislation and targeted federal funding, which is administered by the U.S. Department of Education.

Founded in 1876, the U.S. Department of Education (originally titled the Office of Education) was established to provide information and support to states in developing successful school systems. The department's scope expanded considerably with the passage of the Second Morrill Act in 1890, which included support for the newly emerging program of land-grant colleges and universities. During the first half of the 20th century, job-focused vocational education became a popular target for federal dollars (Smith-Hughes Act, 1917; George-Barden Act, 1947), providing courses in agriculture, industry, and home economics to high school students across the nation. Federal spending expanded further following World War II when approximately eight million veterans attended college under the "GI Bill of Rights." Officially known as the Servicemen's Readjustment Act of 1944, this legislation provided, among other benefits, books, tuition, educational supplies, and counseling to veterans wishing to continue their education after returning from military service (Schugurensky; U.S. Department of Education).

Triggered by the Soviet Union's launch of Sputnik, the National Defense Education Act of 1958 was the first in a series of comprehensive federal laws that greatly affected public education in the following years. Broad antidiscrimination and antipoverty legislation was enacted in the 1960s and 1970s, promoting equal access to education irrespective of race, gender, disability, or income level (title VI, Civil Rights Act, 1964; title I, Elementary and Secondary Education Act, 1965; title IX, Education Amendments Act, 1972; section 504, Rehabilitation Act, 1973). However, it was not until 1980, under Public Law 96–88, that the Department of Education received formal recognition as a U.S. cabinet-level agency service (U.S. Department of Education).

At present, the department includes the cabinet-level secretary of education, a deputy secretary, and an undersecretary of education. In addition to a number of administrative offices, the department has the following eight major program offices, each of which is responsible for a specific domain of federal support to education:

1. The Office of Elementary and Secondary Education (OESE) provides financial assistance through formula and discretionary grants for preschool through secondary schooling.

2. The Office of Special Education and Rehabilitative Services (OSERS) assists in the education of children and adults with disabilities and supports competitive grants for disability research.

3. The Office of Civil Rights (OCR) enforces antidiscrimination laws.

4. The Office of English Language Acquisition, Language Enhancement, and Academic Achievement for Limited English Proficient Students (OELA) supports educational programs for students with limited language skills in English.

5. The Office of Vocational and Adult Education (OVAE) provides assistance for adult education programs in basic skills as preparation for employment.

6. The Office of Postsecondary Education (OPE) provides grants, loans, and jobs to economically disadvantaged students wishing to extend their education beyond high school.

7. The Office of Educational Research and Improvement (OERI) collects, analyzes, and disseminates statistical information about the American education system, providing a kind of "report card" of its performance in educating our children.

8. The Office of Federal Student Aid (OFSA) administers student loan and grant programs funded by the federal government.

Through legislation, policy, and targeted funding, the federal government has come to play a vital role in shaping American education. Of the $40.7 billion spent on schooling by the U.S. Department of Education in the year 2000, approximately $16.1 billion went directly to school districts, primarily through formula-based grant programs; $7.4 billion went to postsecondary institutions; $6.7 billion went to college students; $4.8 billion went to state education agencies, and approximately $5.7 billion was used to subsidize student loans (National Center for Education Statistics, 2001).

—*Mary P. diSibio*

See also Individuals With Disabilities Education Act; Special Education

REFERENCES AND FURTHER READING

Jacob, S., & Hartshorne, T. S. (2003). *Ethics and law for school psychologists* (4th ed.). Hoboken, NJ: John Wiley.

National Center for Education Statistics, U.S. Department of Education Budget Office. (2001). *Digest of education statistics 2000.* Retrieved September 5, 2002, from http://nces.ed.gov/pubs2001digest/ch4.html

Schugurensky, D. (n.d.). *History of education: Selected moments of the 20th century.* Retrieved July 23, 2004, from University of Toronto, Ontario Institute for Studies in Education at http://fcis.oise.utoronto.ca / . . . l_schugurensky/assignmentl/1944gibill.html

U.S. Department of Education. (n.d.). *Mission.* Retrieved July 23, 2004, from http://ed.gov/about/overview/mission/mission.html

U.S. Department of Education. (n.d.). *The federal role in education.* Retrieved September 5, 2002, from http://www.ed.gov/offices/OUS/fedrole.html

U.S. Department of Education Web site. (n.d.) Available online at http://www.ed.gov/index.jhtml

V

VALIDITY

Validity is the meaning, or value, of assessment results or test scores. Whereas reliability refers to the precision of a test or assessment outcome, validity refers to the meaning of the test or assessment outcome. Historically, school psychologists have considered tests to have three forms of validity: content, construct, and criterion (American Education Research Association, American Psychological Association, & National Council on Measurement in Education, 1985). Content validity (sometimes known as face validity) refers to examination of test content to establish its meaning. For example, the validity of most academic achievement tests is determined by their content (e.g., mathematics items create a mathematics test). Construct validity refers to the relationship the test has with other variables as an approach to establish meaning. For example, the fact that raw scores on intelligence tests increase with age suggests that the test measures a phenomenon (e.g., cognitive ability) that increases with age. Criterion validity refers to the relationship of the test to other socially valued criteria. For example, the relationship between college entrance exams and college students' grade point averages provides evidence of criterion-related validity.

However, recent advances in research and practice, reflected in the current edition of the joint testing standards (American Education Research Association, American Psychological Association, & National Council on Measurement in Education, 1999), provide broader standards to guide school psychologists'

evaluation of test and assessment validity. The current *Standards* replace three forms of validity with the notion that validity is a unitary construct. Meaning, or validity, of a test or assessment should be judged according to five sources of evidence, which are:

1. *Content evidence* is the same as content validity discussed in the preceding paragraph.

2. *Response processes* refers to evidence showing that examinees use targeted psychological processes (e.g., specific cognitive abilities, emotional traits) when responding to a test or assessment, and not other, unintended processes that compromise the meaning of test results. For example, dynamic magnetic resonance imaging (MRI) showing increased neural activity in the brain's frontal lobes while completing a puzzle suggests the puzzle item taps the planning processes.

3. *Internal structure* refers to the way components of a test or assessment relate to other components. For example, intelligence test batteries present factor analytic evidence to show tests purporting to measure the same trait (e.g., fluid reasoning) are more related to each other than to other tests.

4. *Relations to other variables* refers to the relationship of the test to measures that are not part of the test. This includes construct and criterion evidence mentioned in the previous paragraph (e.g., the relationship between raw test scores and age, or test scores and performance, in school or work settings).

5. *Test consequences* refers to how the test brings about intended (e.g., improved planning for educational or psychological interventions) and unintended (e.g., diminished expectations because of labeling) consequences for test takers.

Test developers should provide evidence in the five domains that is relevant to the claims they make for the test, and test users (e.g., school psychologists) should review this evidence to evaluate the degree to which test scores mean what developers say they mean. Careful examination of test claims and supporting evidence suggests claims often exceed the evidence offered to support them. For example, developers of the intelligence tests generally provide strong evidence supporting test content, internal structure, and relations to other variables, yet they do not provide evidence relevant to response processes or test consequences (Braden & Niebling, in press). Intelligence test critics note these tests lack "treatment utility," or evidence that the test results improve interventions and outcomes for students. However, consequential validity evidence is limited for all forms of school psychology assessment, not just intelligence tests. The new *standards* challenge test developers and test users (e.g., school psychologists) to expand the breadth and depth of evidence that define the validity, or meaning, of test scores and assessment results.

—*Jeffery P. Braden*

See also Reliability

REFERENCES AND FURTHER READING

American Educational Research Association, American Psychological Association, & National Council on Measurement in Education. (1985). *Standards for educational and psychological testing* (2nd ed.). Washington, DC: American Psychological Association.

American Educational Research Association, American Psychological Association, & National Council on Measurement in Education. (1999). *Standards for educational and psychological testing* (3rd ed.). Washington, DC: American Educational Research Association.

Braden, J. P., & Niebling, B. C. (in press). Evaluating the validity evidence for intelligence tests using the joint test standards. In D. P. Flanagan & P. L. Harrison (Eds.). *Contemporary intellectual assessment: Theories, tests, and issues* (2nd ed.). New York: Guilford.

VERBAL PRAISE

"Claire, you wrote an excellent paper about the life cycle of butterflies! I especially liked the way you vividly described the butterfly emerging from its chrysalis." This is an example of verbal praise. Brophy (1981) defined verbal praise as statements communicating the value of student work or behavior by expressing approval.

Verbal praise is a component in an effective behavioral intervention. However, Brophy (1981) found that teachers infrequently praise good work and rarely praise good behavior. In fact, teachers praised good conduct once every 2 to 10 hours. First grade teachers only praised approximately 11% of their students' correct responses during reading.

Jones and Jones (2001) and Brophy (1981) reported that boys are given more praise than girls. Several studies have found that teachers praise high-achieving students more often than low-achieving students. Teachers praise difficult-to-manage students less frequently than their typical peers.

Good and Brophy (1987) found that teachers often use vague terms like "good" or "super" to describe a student's work. Teachers also appear to be responding spontaneously to students' achievements rather than systematically using verbal praise to reward behavior. In order for praise to be effective, teachers must know how and when to praise, and to use it descriptively.

Jones and Jones (2001) suggest several ways teachers can improve their verbal praise, resulting in students taking credit for their achievements. First, verbal praise needs to be contingent. It must immediately follow the desired behaviors. Second, verbal praise must specifically describe the behavior that is being reinforced. Third, the praise needs to be credible. When giving praise the teacher should consider the student and the situation.

Good and Brophy (1987) note that verbal praise should also help students attribute their success to effort and ability. Teachers can accomplish this goal by praising students' learning gains or skill mastery. This verbal praise will support students in developing intrinsic motivation for schoolwork rather than extrinsic motivation to please the teacher.

Hanson (2000) reported that teachers' verbal praise is recognized as a vital component in the development of student motivation to learn. Jones and Jones (2001) indicate that a teacher's praise appears to be important in supporting a student's positive feelings about school and learning. Researchers found that in classrooms where teachers' statements were positive at least 70% of the time, between 70% and 100% of the students reported that they liked school.

Sutherland (2000) noted that contingent teacher praise increased the number of words students read per minute and decreased the number of errors per minute. Contingent teacher praise also increased students' on-task rates from 56% to 85%.

—*Laure Wiethoff*

See also Behavior Intervention; Intervention; Motivation

REFERENCES AND FURTHER READING

Brophy, J. (1981). Teacher praise: A functional analysis. *Review of Educational Research, 51,* 5–32.

Good, T., & Brophy, J. (1987). *Looking in classrooms* (4th ed.). New York: Harper & Row.

Hanson, D. (2000). Impact of verbal praise on college students' time spent on homework. *The Journal of Educational Research, 93*(6), 384–389.

Jones, V., & Jones, L. (2001). *Comprehensive classroom management: Creating communities of support and solving problems.* Boston: Allyn & Bacon.

Sutherland, K. (2000). Promoting positive interactions between teachers and students with emotional/behavioral disorders. *Preventing School Failure, 44*(3), 110–115.

VIOLENCE IN SCHOOLS

Massive news media attention to a series of school shootings in the late 1990s radically altered public attitudes toward schools and transformed school safety policies and practices. Each tragic shooting seemed more horrific than the last, beginning in 1997 when a 16-year-old boy in Pearl, Mississippi, shot and killed a former girlfriend and another student while at school. One month later, a 14-year-old boy in Paducah, Kentucky, fired into a morning prayer group at his high school, killing three girls. A few months later in Jonesboro, Arkansas, two boys ages 11 and 13, lured elementary school children outside with a false fire alarm, then opened fire, killing four students and a teacher. Other shootings followed, and their occurrence in small, seemingly nonviolent communities stimulated fears that an epidemic of school violence was sweeping the nation.

Concern reached panic levels in the spring of 1999 when two heavily armed boys at Columbine High School in Littleton, Colorado, systematically executed 12 students and a teacher before killing themselves, as police converged on the scene. Live, nationwide media coverage of the Columbine and other school shootings bombarded the public with powerful images of terrified teenagers fleeing from school, bloody students receiving emergency medical treatment, and anguished parents desperate for information about the fate of their children. Follow-up coverage repeatedly emphasized the brutal, tragic nature of the shootings, the seemingly callous character of the killers, and the great pain and distress experienced by traumatized survivors as well as bereaved classmates and family members of the victims. It is not surprising that a Gallup Poll (1999) taken after the Columbine shooting revealed that 74% of parents in the United States believed that a school shooting was somewhat or very likely to occur in their community.

News attention to school shootings also stimulated many juveniles to engage in copycat behavior such as drawing up hit lists of students they disliked and telephoning schools with false bomb threats. Some students, like the two boys at Columbine High School who recorded their plans and aspirations on videotape before their crime, were stimulated by the news accounts of school shootings to carry out their own acts of violence with hopes of gaining similar publicity. In other cases, law enforcement officials wrestled with the difficult task of distinguishing fanciful talk about committing a school shooting from actual plans made by groups of alienated students.

Ironically, violent crime by juveniles, including shootings at school, actually declined substantially after peaking in the early 1990s, according to the Federal Bureau of Investigation's (FBI) annual *Uniform Crime Reports* (FBI, 1993–2002) and multiple studies summarized in the U.S. Department of Education's annual *Indicators of School Crime and Safety.* FBI statistics indicated that the number of youths arrested for murder in the United States dropped dramatically each year from more than 3,200 in 1993 to fewer than 900 by 2000 (FBI, 1993–2002). According to the National School Safety Center (2003), student-perpetrated homicides at school dropped from 42 fatalities in 1993 to just 5 in 2000. Among researchers, there was no question that school crime and violence were declining, even at a time when public opinion, news commentaries, and political rhetoric declared otherwise. Moreover, the 2001 report on youth violence by the U.S. Surgeon General observed that students were much less likely to be victims of violence at school than outside of school, and that fewer than 1% of homicides of school-age youths took place at school.

Nevertheless, the high-profile, tragic school shootings compelled school authorities nationwide to review school safety policies and to seek new practices for preventing student acts of violence. In 1998, the White House convened a conference on school safety and the U.S. Department of Education and Department of Justice sent a series of publications on school safety to every public school in the nation. The FBI and even the Secret Service undertook independent studies of school shootings and issued extensive recommendations for improved school safety (Fein & colleagues, 2002; O'Toole, 2000).

On state and local levels, authorities placed more police officers in schools, instituted new security procedures, and enacted more stringent discipline codes. "Zero tolerance" became a catchphrase strategy for highly punitive, inflexible school discipline policies. A common zero tolerance practice is that schools apply the same strict consequences to all students who commit a disciplinary infraction. Prompted by the Gun-Free Schools Act of 1994, schools began to expel, for one year, any student who brought a firearm to school. Over time, zero tolerance expanded to include other forms of weapons and many schools included objects that looked like weapons such as toy guns, or even objects that might be used as weapons such as plastic utensils and nail clippers.

Some school divisions were criticized, and in some cases sued, for what appeared to be excessively harsh zero tolerance practices. For example, a lawsuit supported by The Rutherford Institute contended that a school wrongfully suspended four kindergarten students for using their fingers as guns while playing cops and robbers during recess. In an article published in *Phi Delta Kappan* entitled "The Dark Side of Zero Tolerance," Skiba and Peterson (1999) identified the case of a 5-year-old boy who was suspended from school for finding a razor blade on the ground and turning it over to his teacher. In 2001, the American Bar Association passed a resolution condemning zero tolerance policies.

VIOLENT CRIME IN SCHOOLS

Intense concern with the specter of homicide may detract attention from more common, albeit, less extreme forms of violence at school. The National Academy of Sciences Panel on the Understanding and Control of Violent Behavior defined violence as "behaviors by individuals that intentionally threaten, attempt, or inflict physical harm on others" (Reiss & Roth, 1993, p.2). The U.S. Department of Education's 2001 *Indicators of School Crime and Safety* reported that approximately 186,000 violent crimes were committed in schools nationwide during the 1996–1997 school year. This included 8.7 physical attacks or fights without a weapon, 0.3 robberies, and 0.2 rapes or sexual batteries per 1,000 middle school (grades 6-8) students, as well as 8.0 physical attacks or fights without a weapon, 0.4 robberies, and 0.2 rapes or sexual batteries per 1,000 high school (grades 9-12) students. In addition, 36% of male students and 14% of female students admitted that they were involved in a fight within the past 12 months.

Official crime statistics do not include other common forms of violence. For example, bullying is increasingly recognized as a pervasive problem in American schools, as it is in European schools, according to widely cited studies by Norwegian researcher Dan Olweus (1993). Bullying can range from verbal threats of injury to physical assault and can also include harassment, teasing, and social rejection or isolation. Understandably, estimates of the frequency of bullying vary widely according to definition; however, Nansel and colleagues (2001) provided some troubling findings from the World Health Organization's Health Behavior in School-Aged Children survey. The study reported that 8.4% of a sample of more than 15,000 students in grades 6 through 10 reported being victims of frequent bullying (once per week or more), with 29.9% stating that they were involved in moderate or frequent bullying, either as a bully, a victim of bullying, or both. These findings suggest that in the United States there are approximately 5.7 million students in grades 6 to 10 who are involved in bullying, including 1.6 million who are victims of frequent bullying.

Unfortunately, bullying may be so commonplace that parents and educators have come to regard it as a natural and inevitable childhood experience. Parents may advise children simply to ignore those who bully them or to fight back; these two strategies are unlikely to be effective and often leave the victim feeling unsupported. While many students are able to tolerate some degree of bullying and teasing, studies have found that chronic victimization by bullies has a lasting, negative impact on a student's emotional adjustment and academic success and in extreme cases may lead to suicide.

Sexual harassment is another commonplace problem in schools that in many cases can be regarded as a form of violence. Some surveys indicate that as many as 83% of female students and 79% of male students reported that they were victims of sexual harassment to some degree. As defined by the U.S. Equal Opportunity Employment Commission (2002), sexual harassment is "unwelcome sexual advances, requests for favors, and other verbal and physical contact of a sexual nature" (p. 1). In 1999, the U.S. Supreme Court ruled in *Davis v. Monroe County Board of Education* that schools that receive federal funds could be held liable for sexual harassment inflicted on students by their peers, if school authorities were aware of the harassment and were deliberately indifferent to it, and if the harassment was serious enough to affect the student's access to educational opportunities and benefits. Under this opinion, sexual harassment does not include less severe incidents of teasing or name-calling that involve sexual or gender-based references.

MODEL OF YOUTH VIOLENCE

Most experts subscribe to a complex model of youth violence encompassing individual, family, social, and cultural factors. According to the U.S. Surgeon General (2001) report, the strongest behavioral risk factors for children are early involvement in serious but not necessarily violent criminal behavior, substance use, and physical aggression. Male children from socioeconomically disadvantaged backgrounds are also at increased risk, as are children whose parents have a history of antisocial or criminal behavior. During adolescence, peer influences become increasingly important and may overshadow family influences. Students with weak ties to conventional peers and relationships with antisocial or delinquent peers are at greater risk for violent behavior.

There is overwhelming evidence in support of a causal relationship between viewing violence in the media and engaging in violent behavior. In 2000, six major professional organizations including the American Psychological Association, American Academy of Pediatrics, and American Medical Association, issued a joint statement unequivocally concluding that exposure to media violence is harmful to children based on results from more than 1,000 studies. Although no researchers claim that media violence is a necessary or sufficient cause of violence, studies show that children who regularly watch violent television shows and movies tend to display increased aggressive behavior and tend to hold attitudes more accepting of violence than their peers.

Bushman and Anderson (2001) noted that the public is often misinformed about the status of the scientific evidence on media violence. Bushman and Anderson (2001) documented ways in which media accounts of scientific studies failed to reflect the growing body of evidence and increasing scientific certainty that media violence has a deleterious effect on children. The authors also showed that the correlation between violent media and aggression is equal to or stronger than many other widely agreed upon medical findings, such as the finding that smoking leads to lung cancer or that calcium consumption leads to increased bone mass. Although defenders of the entertainment industry sometimes argue that media violence is simply a reflection of violence in the world, studies demonstrate that television shows and movies tend to present an unrealistically high rate of violence and to portray unrealistically positive consequences of violence. There is a more recent body of research accumulating evidence that video games also can influence aggressive behavior (Anderson & Bushman, 2001). For example, repeated exposure to violent video games is related to aggression-related thoughts and feelings, and decreases prosocial behavior.

BEST PRACTICES IN ASSESSMENT AND INTERVENTION

There are several approaches schools can use to assess the prevalence and severity of violence within the school and increase more appropriate behavior from their students (Larson & colleagues, 2001). These strategies are both student focused and schoolwide. Careful, comprehensive assessment can play an important role in reducing student aggression and maintaining a healthy school environment.

Schoolwide Assessment

The use of student surveys can provide important information in the assessment of violence in schools. School officials can use standard surveys to measure student involvement in bullying and other forms of peer aggression, drug use or other high-risk behavior, and attitudes toward aggression. Peer nomination procedures can be particularly useful in identifying students who are victims of chronic bullying. Surveys that include the question, "Please write the names of up to three students whom you know to be bullied frequently" will identify victims of bullying who were not previously known to school officials.

Despite the advantages of efficiency and quantity of data, surveys have well-known limitations (Cornell & Loper, 1998). School districts must use careful administration procedures to increase the likelihood that students will provide meaningful information. Those who administer the survey should follow a standard protocol that encourages compliance and accurate reporting. Schools should avoid the use of homegrown instruments lacking evidence of reliability and validity. Completed surveys must be screened for invalid responses and abnormal answer patterns, such as all "yes" or all "no" response sets. Validity items (e.g., "I am telling the truth on this survey.") may be useful in identifying surveys that should be excluded from consideration. Users must be mindful not to interpret small, statistically insignificant differences and to recognize that group differences may not be taken at face value; for example, race differences may reflect socioeconomic differences.

Individual Threat Assessment

Practitioners are advised to exercise caution in assessing individuals for the purpose of predicting violence. Mulvey and Cauffman (2002) cautioned that because serious violent behavior in schools is rare, accurate predictions are nearly impossible. Moreover, clinicians should pay greater attention to the social context and circumstances that precipitate violence, as opposed to individual personality traits.

Studies of school shootings by the FBI and the Secret Service strongly oppose efforts to develop profiles or trait markers for student violence (Fein & colleagues, 2002; O'Toole, 2000). There is no test scale, profile, or set of individual characteristics that can accurately identify a violent student. Instead, mental health clinicians are advised to adopt a threat assessment approach (Cornell & Sheras, in press). The U.S. Department of Education has recommended that all schools use multidisciplinary threat assessment teams in response to student threats of violence (Fein & colleagues, 2002). Threat assessment involves the collection of information from multiple sources, including interviews with students, parents, and teachers, as part

of a careful, fact-based investigation to determine if a youth is on a behavioral pathway that leads toward violence. From this perspective, it is far more important to determine if a student has made specific threats of violence, is involved in a conflict or dispute with others, and has engaged in behavior that prepares for violence, such as obtaining a weapon. It is also critically important to determine whether the youth has a history of aggressive behavior and has been encouraged to engage in violence by peers or other role models. The clinician's role in contributing to a school-based threat assessment is to identify risk as well as protective factors for violence rather than to make bottom-line predictions. It is especially relevant for the clinician to determine if the student has mental health needs such as depression, anger control problems, or psychosis, which should be treated as part of a risk reduction strategy (Cornell & Sheras, in press).

Schoolwide Interventions

Nearly all approaches to school violence reduction emphasize the value of schoolwide efforts to improve school climate. Effective programs require the support and commitment of the school faculty. Many well-intentioned programs falter because they rely too heavily on the time, energy, and commitment of just a few staff members. All efforts at violence reduction should be reflected in a clear code of conduct and a school atmosphere that values and reinforces positive, prosocial behavior. It is important for all school staff members to understand and implement principles of positive behavior management. There is research evidence that school-based programs can teach students how to mediate or resolve conflicts, and how to solve interpersonal problems and improve social competence (Cornell, in press). Schoolwide bullying programs can reduce student victimization, although such programs may take a year or more to yield results.

Law Enforcement Partnerships

School Resource Officers (SROs) have emerged in a new area of law enforcement specialization and are increasingly an integral part of our school systems nationwide. The National Association of School Resource Officers (NASROs) is the largest school-based police organization and had a reported membership of more than 9,000 SROs in 2002. While many schools continue to hire security guards to monitor hallways and intervene in student conflicts, the SRO can serve a much greater role within the school as a practitioner of community-oriented policing. The SRO can become an active participant in the assessment and development of security policies and crisis plans. The SRO can provide some direct services to students by providing supervision, informally counseling students about behaviors that could lead to legal infractions, and instructing classes on legal requirements and law enforcement. The SRO can also develop networks for both staff and students to report threats of violence and participate in other crime prevention activities.

The U.S. Department of Education's Office of Safe and Drug-Free Schools has mandated that schools rely on scientifically valid, evidence-based programs and conduct evaluations of the effectiveness of their implementation. Fortunately, schools have many viable programs from which to choose. School-based violence prevention efforts are effective, according to an empirical review of 44 different interventions for aggressive students (Mytton & colleagues, 2002). Additional research is needed to document the effectiveness of new approaches such as threat assessment and the school resource officer movement.

Although a series of school shootings and the resulting media coverage contributed to a sentiment that schools were unsafe, numerous studies provide evidence that, in general, schools are secure and children are at greater risk of being victims of a serious violent act in the community or the home than at school. However, some forms of violence such as bullying and sexual harassment are quite common. School systems can implement assessment and intervention strategies geared toward violence reduction, both at the student and staff levels. Instead of relying on zero tolerance policies and profiling, schools should adopt a risk assessment model, using schoolwide surveys to assess the level of violence in the school, implementing empirically validated violence reduction programs, and building partnerships with law enforcement agencies through the use of SROs.

—*Dewey G. Cornell and Sebastian G. Kaplan*

See also Aggression in Schools; Bullying and Victimization; Corporal Punishment; Counseling; Crisis Intervention; Early Intervention; Gangs; Harassment; Media and Children; Peer Mediation; Posttraumatic Stress Disorder; Prevention

REFERENCES AND FURTHER READING

Anderson, C. A., & Bushman, B. J. (2001). Effects of violent video games on aggressive behavior, aggressive cognition, aggressive affect, physiological arousal, and prosocial behavior: A meta-analytic review of the scientific literature. *Psychological Science, 12,* 353–359.

Bushman, B. J., & Anderson, C. A. (2001). Media violence and the American public: Scientific facts versus media misinformation. *American Psychologist, 56,* 477–489.

Cornell, D. (in press). School violence: Fears versus facts. In K. Heilbrun, N. Goldstein, & R. Redding (Eds.), *Juvenile delinquency: Prevention, assessment, and intervention.* New York: Oxford University Press.

Cornell, D. G., & Loper, A. B. (1998). Assessment of violence and other high-risk behaviors with a school survey. *School Psychology Review, 27,* 317–330.

Cornell, D., & Sheras, P. (in press). *Guidelines for responding to student threats of violence.* Longmont, CO: Sopris West.

Federal Bureau of Investigation. (1993–2002). *Uniform crime reports: Crime in the United States.* Washington, DC: U.S. Government Printing Office.

Fein, R. A., Vossekuil, F., Pollack, W. S., Borum, R., Modzeleski, W., Reddy, M. (2002). *Threat assessment in schools: A guide to managing threatening situations and to creating safe school climates.* Washington, DC: U.S. Secret Service and U.S. Department of Education.

Gallup Organization. (1999). *School violence still a worry for American parents.* Retrieved July 1, 2002, from http://www.gallup.com/poll/content/login.aspx?ci=3613

Kaufman, P., Chen, X., Choy, S. P., Peter, K., Ruddy, S. A., Miller, A. K., et al. (2001). *Indicators of school crime safety, 2001.* Washington, DC: U.S. Departments of Education and Justice.

Larson, J., Smith, D. C., & Furlong, M. J. (2001). Best practices in school violence prevention. In A. Thomas & J. Grimes (Eds.), *Best practices in School Psychology-IV* (pp. 1081–1097). Washington, DC: National Association of School Psychologists.

Mulvey, E. P., & Cauffman, E. (2001). The inherent limits of predicting school violence. *American Psychologist, 56,* 797–802.

Mytton, J. A., DiGuiseppi, C., Gough, D. A., Taylor, R. S., & Logan, S. (2002). School-based violence prevention programs: Systematic review of secondary prevention trials. *Archives of Pediatrics and Adolescent Medicine, 156,* 752–762.

Nansel, T. R., Overpeck, M., Pilla, R. S., Ruan, J., Simons-Morton, B., & Scheidt, P. (2001). Bullying behaviors among U.S. youth, prevalence and association with psychosocial adjustment. *The Journal of the American Medical Association, 285,* 2094–2100.

National School Safety Center. (2003). *School associated violent deaths.* Westlake Village, CA.. Retrieved January 29, 2003, from http://www.nssc1.org/savd/savd.pdf

Olweus, D. (1993). *Bullying at school: What we know and what we can do.* Cambridge, MA: Blackwell.

O'Toole, M. (2000). *The school shooter: A threat assessment perspective.* Quantico, VA: National Center for the Analysis of Violent Crime, Federal Bureau of Investigation. Retrieved January 29, 2003, from http://www.fbi.gov/publications/school/school2.pdf

Reiss, A. J., & Roth, J. A. (1993). *Understanding & preventing violence.* Washington, DC: National Academy Press.

Skiba, R. & Peterson, R. (1999, March). The dark side of zero tolerance: Can punishment lead to safe schools? *Phi Delta Kappan, 80,* 372–376, 381–382.

U.S. Equal Employment Opportunity Commission. (2002). *Facts about sexual harassment.* Retrieved August 18, 2004, from http://www.eeoc.gov/facts/fs-sex.html

U.S. Surgeon General. (2001). *Youth violence: A report of the Surgeon General.* Rockville, MD: U.S. Department of Health and Human Services.

W

WRITING INTERVENTIONS AND STRATEGIES

Good writing is essential to children's success in school. Writing is the major means by which students demonstrate their academic knowledge, and the primary instrument that teachers use to evaluate scholastic performance (Graham & Harris, 2002). It is used as a tool for gathering, remembering, and sharing subject matter. It serves as an instrument for exploring and refining ideas about topics, allowing children to form new insights and more complex understandings. Writing also provides a medium through which children can explore their interests, feelings, and experiences as well as a mechanism for artistic self-expression.

Despite its importance, many children have difficulty mastering this basic skill. On the most recent National Assessment of Educational Progress (Greenwald & colleagues, 1999), only approximately 25% of the students in grades 4, 8, and 12 were classified as competent writers at their perspective grade levels. Although children's writing development is a complex process, it depends in large part on the methods and strategies used to teach it. In an effective writing program, teachers use a variety of instructional procedures to shape and transform students' writing knowledge, skills, wills, and self-regulation (Graham & Harris, 2002; Scardamalia & Bereiter, 1986).

The most essential element in teaching writing is to provide exemplary writing instruction right from the start, beginning in first grade and continuing through high school (Graham & Harris, 2002). Such instruction maximizes the writing development of children in general and minimizes the number of students who experience difficulty learning to write. Although quality writing instruction differs somewhat from grade to grade, there are a number of instructional features that should be emphasized (Table 1). The information in Table 1 is based on an analysis of the practices of highly effective writing teachers (Wray & colleagues, 2000), outcomes of experimental treatment studies (Hillocks, 1986), and clinical experience (Scott, 1989).

Another critical element in developing an effective writing program is to adapt instruction so that it is responsive to individual students' needs. Such adaptations are a regular part of the practices of highly effective teachers. Pressley and colleagues (1996), for example, found that outstanding literacy teachers provided qualitatively similar instruction for all students, but that children experiencing difficulty received extra teacher support.

There are a variety of adaptations that teachers can make to support struggling writers. In a nationwide survey involving primary grade teachers, for instance, Graham and colleagues (in press) found that children experiencing writing difficulties were often provided extra one-on-one help, including individual assistance from the teacher, adult tutors, or older and same-age peers (including collaborative planning, writing, and revising with a peer). Teachers also made adjustments for handwriting and spelling difficulties. In spelling, for instance, teachers created personalized spelling lists for weaker writers, directly helped them spell unknown words, and employed word banks and other aids to facilitate correct spelling. Other teachers, in contrast, sought to bypass transcription difficulties by allowing struggling writers to dictate their compositions or write with a keyboard (e.g., Alpha Smart).

The surveyed teachers further adjusted their instruction by providing additional support for the thinking and creative processes involved in writing. To illustrate, teachers facilitated the planning of weaker writers by having them talk out their ideas in advance of writing, draw what they planned to write about, or use webs or graphic organizers to generate and sequence ideas.

Revising efforts were supported through the use of revising checklists, or by the teacher or a peer directly helping the child revise. Finally, teachers indicated that they devoted extra time to teaching and reteaching specific writing skills to struggling writers, providing mini-lessons responsive to their needs, and conferencing with them about their writing.

Even when regular classroom teachers develop exemplary writing programs and tailor their instruction to meet the needs of individual students, some students, especially those with special needs, need additional support. This is likely to involve extra and intensive instruction in one or more of the following areas (Graham & Harris, 2002):

- Handwriting
- Spelling
- Sentence construction
- Planning or revising

To illustrate, Graham and colleagues (2000) provided seven hours of individualized handwriting instruction to first grade children who had slow handwriting and generally poor writing skills. Three times a week, each child met with a tutor for a 15-minute lesson. Each lesson involved the following four activities:

1. The student practices naming and identifying the letters of the alphabet.

2. Three lower-case letters, sharing common formational characteristics (e.g., *l*, *i*, and *t*) are introduced, and the child practices each letter by tracing it three times, writing it three times inside an outline of the letter, copying it three times, and circling the best formed letter. Three lessons are devoted to mastering each letter set, with the second and third sessions primarily involving letter practice in the context of single words (e.g., "lit") or hinky-pinks (e.g., "itty-bitty").

3. The child copies a short sentence quickly and accurately for a period of three minutes. The sentence contains multiple instances of the letters being taught in that lesson (e.g., L*i*tt*l*e k*i*ds *li*ke *t*o ge*t* le*t*ters.). The number of letters written by the child is recorded on a chart, and, during the next two lessons, students try to beat their previous score by writing at least three more letters during the specified time period.

4. The student is taught how to write one of the letters from the lesson in an unusual way (e.g., as long and tall or short and fat) or use it as part of a picture (e.g., turning an *i* into a butterfly).

Children who received this extra handwriting instruction became quicker and improved their handwriting skills more than peers assigned to a group receiving phonological awareness instruction. Even more important, they exhibited greater gains in their ability to craft sentences and generate text when writing a story.

Similarly, the planning and revising of struggling writers can be improved with extra, intensive instruction (Graham & Harris, 2003). Harris and colleagues (2003), for example, provided additional instruction on how to plan and write stories and persuasive essays to the weakest writers in 12 second-grade classrooms. Pairs of students would meet with an instructor three times a week for 20 minutes during each session. In these sessions, the students were taught a strategy for generating and organizing possible ideas for their composition in advance of writing. For story writing, students brainstormed ideas for common story elements (i.e., characters, setting, characters' goals, etc.). With persuasive writing, they generated ideas for the most basic elements of an argument (i.e., premise, supporting reasons, examples, and conclusion). Students were further taught how to organize their ideas by numbering which would come first, second, third, and so on. This extra instruction had a positive effect on these children's writing, as their stories and persuasive essays became longer, more complete, and qualitatively better. Instructional effects also generalized to two uninstructed genres, narrative and informational writing.

There are at least two ways in which school psychologists can play a role in developing and implementing writing interventions (Troia & Graham, in press). First, they can recommend and model best

Table 1   Features of Effective Writing Instruction

Students Write Daily

- Students write daily and work on a wide range of writing tasks for multiple audiences, including writing at home.
- Students use writing as a tool to explore, organize, and express their thoughts across the curriculum.

The Writing Environment Is a Pleasant, Supportive, and Motivating Place

- Teacher develops a literate classroom environment where students' written work is prominently displayed, and the room is packed with writing and reading material.
- Teacher holds individual conferences with students about their current writing efforts, helping them establish goals or criteria to guide their writing and revising efforts.
- Teacher motivates students to write by setting an exciting mood, creating a risk-free environment, allowing students to select their own writing topics or modify teacher assignments, developing assigned topics compatible with students' interests, reinforcing children's accomplishments, specifying the goal for each lesson, and promoting an "I can do" attitude.
- Students help each other plan, draft, revise, edit, and/or publish their written work.
- Students share their work with each other, receiving praise and critical feedback on their efforts.
- Teacher conducts periodic conferences with parents, soliciting their advice and communicating the goals of the program as well as their child's progress as a writer.

Important Writing Skills Are Taught

- Teacher provides instruction on a broad range of skills, including phonological awareness, handwriting, spelling, writing conventions, and sentence construction.
- Teacher provides follow-up instruction to ensure mastery of writing skills.

Strategic Writing Behavior Is Promoted

- Teacher establishes a writing routine where students are encouraged to think, reflect, and revise.
- Teacher models the processes involved in writing.
- Teacher directly teaches students strategies for planning and revising text.
- Teacher provides follow-up instruction to ensure maintenance and generalization of target planning and revising strategies.
- Students are provided with frequent opportunities to self-regulate their behavior during writing, including working independently, arranging their own space, and seeking help from others.

Knowledge About the Functions and Structure of Writing Are Taught

- Teacher uses reading to illustrate the attributes of good writing and specific tools used by skilled writers.
- Teacher provides instruction on the functions of writing and the structure of different genres.

practices in writing instruction. Many teachers are not familiar with how to best teach writing, and look to experts, such as school psychologists, for guidance. Second, as the examples given previously illustrate, many struggling writers benefit from extra, specialized instruction. School psychologists should not only be involved in identifying opportunities for obtaining such instruction, but should provide it as well.

—Steve Graham

See also Academic Achievement; Cooperative Learning; Grades; Homework; Learning; Learning Styles

REFERENCES AND FURTHER READING

Graham, S., & Harris, K. R. (2002). Prevention and intervention for struggling writers. In M. Shinn, H. Walker, & G. Stoner (Eds.), *Interventions for academic and behavior problems II: Preventive and remedial approaches* (pp. 589–610). Bethesda, MD: National Association of School Psychologists.

Graham, S., & Harris, K. R. (2003). Students with learning disabilities and the process of writing: A meta-analysis of SRSD studies. In L. Swanson, K. R. Harris, & S. Graham (Eds.), *Handbook of research on learning disabilities* (pp. 323–344). New York: Guilford.

Graham, S., Harris, K. R., & Fink, B. (2000). Is handwriting causally related to learning to write? Treatment of handwriting problems in beginning writers. *Journal of Educational Psychology, 92,* 620–633.

Graham, S., Harris, K. R., Fink, B., & MacArthur, C. (in press). Primary grade teachers' instructional adaptations for struggling writers: A national survey. *Journal of Educational Psychology.*

Graham, S., Harris, K. R., & MacArthur, C. (in press). Writing instruction. In B. Wong (Ed.), *Learning about learning disabilities* (Vol. 3). Orlando, FL: Academic Press.

Greenwald, E. A., Persky, H. R., Campbell, J. R., & Mazzeo, J. (1999). *NAEP 1998 writing report card for the nation and the states.* Washington, DC: National Center for Education Statistics, U.S. Department of Education.

Harris, K. R., Graham, S., & Mason, L. H. (2003). Self-regulated strategy development in the classroom: Part of a balanced approach to writing instruction for students with disabilities. *Focus on Exceptional Children, 35*(7), 1–16.

Hillocks, G. (1986). *Research on written composition: New directions for teaching.* Urbana, IL: National Conference on Research in English.

Pressley, M., Wharton-McDonald, R., Rankin, J., Mistretta, J., & Yokoi, L. (1996). The nature of outstanding primary-grades literacy instruction. In E. McIntyre & M. Pressley (Eds.), *Balanced instruction: Strategies and skills in whole language* (pp. 251–276). Norwood, MA: Christopher-Gordon.

Scardamalia, M., & Bereiter, C. (1986). Written composition. In M. Wittrock (Ed.), *Handbook of research on teaching* (3rd ed., pp. 778–803). New York: Macmillan.

Scott, C. (1989). Problem writers: Nature, assessment, and intervention. In A. Kamhi & H. Catts (Eds.), *Reading disabilities: A developmental language perspective* (pp. 303–344). Boston: Allyn & Bacon.

Troia, G., & Graham, S. (in press). Effective writing instruction across the grades: What every educational consultant should know. *Journal of Educational and Psychological Consultation.*

Wray, D., Medwell, J., Fox, R., & Poulson, L. (2000). The teaching practices of effective teachers of literacy. *Educational Review, 52,* 75–84.

WRITTEN LANGUAGE ASSESSMENT

Writing is the expression of ideas and feelings through the use of written symbols. Over the years, the rapid integration of technology into home and school environments has challenged traditional definitions of writing. Voice-activated software blurs the boundaries between oral and written language. While the mediating tools for writing are changing, the process of coding experiences into symbols (words) to provide meaning continues to be central to written expression. The writer remains the essential catalyst. Critical to evaluating a student's writing abilities is an understanding of the writer's background experiences (school and home), as well as emotional, cognitive, and linguistic abilities.

A growing number of students in our school systems are experiencing difficulty with written expression. The etiology of these problems is certainly not singular and often is the result of a mixture of factors. The source of underachievement in written expression for some students rests with thinking or oral language abilities. Learning to organize experiences or transforming ideas to oral language is the key instructional goal for such individuals (e.g., language or attention deficit hyperactivity disorder). Other students are fluent in developing ideas and demonstrate adequate oral language abilities. However, the breakdown for these students might be in the coding of oral language into written symbols (e.g., dyslexia). Students demonstrating significant social cognition problems (e.g., autism, Asperger's disorder) encounter problems with a sense of audience. Motivational or anxiety problems surrounding the process of writing can interfere with fluency and quality of text for any student. In addition, students coming from different cultures, as well as those for whom English is their second language can struggle with aspects of writing. Writing is much more than just spelling and handwriting, yet it is often ". . . taught [and assessed] as a motor skill and not as a complex cultural activity" (Vygotksy, 1978, p. 34).

WHAT ARE YOU MEASURING?

A key to any assessment of writing is an understanding of the influence of the task demands, the tools used for responding, and the topic. Before critical decisions are formed related to a student's potential and/or ability, this information should be put into proper perspective. Often discrepant performance across measures purporting to evaluate a specific writing skill (e.g., spelling) is not the result of a student's motivation or the psychometrics of a measure. The task, the topic, or the tool demands may be very different across two measures of a single skill.

Task

Two essential aspects of a task that should be considered are the modality and degree of structure. It is important to recognize that modalities are not the same as cognitive processes (e.g., memory, executive functioning, attention). Modalities represent the sensory channels through which information is perceived. Modality representation cannot be isolated from the nature of the task. The four modalities commonly represented across writing measures are:

1. Auditory, representing information heard or spoken

2. Visual, representing information seen or written

3. Haptic, involving touch (tracing or feeling an object)

4. Motor, dealing with movement

An examiner should consider the input and output modalities of a task. For instance, a spelling task might be dictated to a writer (auditory–verbal), but the output requires writing the correct word (motor–verbal). In addition, the information presented can be either verbal (spoken or written) or nonverbal (pictures, environmental sounds).

Consideration of the degree of structure that a task requires from a writer is also relevant to decision making. Evaluators often see the importance of this factor when they report a student's performance was in the average range on a specific writing test. The regular classroom teacher reports disbelief because in the classroom the student's writing performance is seriously impaired. Often this discrepancy can be traced to the difference in structure between the test and the classroom requirements.

Structure is best understood by considering two aspects, prompts and response types. Prompts are cues provided in the presentation of the task. For instance, a writer could be given a single picture, series of pictures, story starter, or a written topic. Writing from a series of pictures is the most structured, while a written topic is the least structured writing task. During an evaluation of writing, one would want to collect information on the writing skill being assessed across varying levels of structure by collecting test and classroom products.

Topic

In addition to considering modality and structure, the evaluator should give careful consideration to the background knowledge and motivation a student brings to the writing task. If a writer possesses information about a topic, the quality and fluency of the writing will often be positively influenced. Therefore, a student should always be given a choice of writing topics during an evaluation of their performance. When using story starters or picture stimuli, there should be several to choose from that include age-appropriate themes and culture-appropriate experiences. Such writing samples could be collected in the regular classroom and brought to the decision-making process. In addition, Britton and colleagues (1975) produced a seminal study that demonstrated students need experience communicating in writing directly to different audiences. They provided evidence that the student "must have a lively representation of this audience in mind—or, if he does not, he will fail in his intent" (p. 59). These different audiences might include student-to-teacher, student-to-student, student-to-trusted friend, student-to-examiner, or student-to-unknown audience. Often writers produce more elaborate and better organized text when they feel comfortable with the audience. Unfortunately, many writing experiences students are provided in schools focus on the student writing to the evaluator, shaping writer's perspective on the function of writing.

The writing task provides an opportunity for an evaluator to observe a student's ability to use writing for different functions. One function of writing is test-taking, such as fill-in-the-blank, short answer, copying, dictation, and translation. The demand on planning and organization is far less on such tasks. Informational uses of writing, such as note-taking, reports, and summaries, are a second function of school writing. More emphasis of this function is on planning, organizing, and transcribing abilities. Few opportunities are provided for students to demonstrate their abilities with imaginative (e.g., stories, poems, plays) or personal (e.g., diary, journal, and notes to friends) writing. Each function of writing should be examined by an evaluator to determine if errors (e.g., spelling) detected on one function are consistent across the others.

Tools

Whatever the area of writing under examination, an evaluator should provide an opportunity for a student to express his or her ideas using different writing tools (e.g., pencil, paper, computer, voice-activated software). The use of computers for enhancing writing competencies has increased dramatically over the last decade (Becker, 1999). Researchers have documented that writing with a computer can increase the fluency, editing, and quality of writing for a majority of students (Russell, Goldberg, & colleagues, 2003). For students with significant orthographic and motor disorders, the use of portable and affordable writing devices, such as Alpha Smarts, Dream Writers, and eMates, provide an access to learning never available to such individuals.

INTEGRATED ASSESSMENT PROCESS

Informal and criterion- and norm-based assessment tools are all part of an integrated assessment of writing. Information gathered from all three sources adds depth and validity to diagnostic decision making, avoiding the tendency to rely on only one perspective. A great deal of diagnostic information can be collected from the regular classroom teacher. Each of the sources (e.g., informal and criterion- and norm-referenced) provides answers to different questions related to a student's access to services or program planning. In addition, clinical judgment requires the interpretation of more than just scores. How a student arrives at a response or the type of error produced is invaluable information. As Shaugnessy (1977) discussed, error-laden work must be viewed in light of its intentional structures as evidence of systematic, rule-governed behavior.

Diagnostic Norm-Referenced Assessment in Written Expression

Diagnostic standardized achievement tests in written language are typically designed to provide a broad estimate of written language achievement. Unlike standardized group testing, they are administered individually to a student. The intent of such tests is to compare a student's functioning to that of their peer group. Such information is useful in documenting a writer's progress through the school grades, providing a great deal of inter- and intra-achievement comparisons. Table 1 includes an analysis of several commonly used diagnostic achievement tests with written expression sections. Two types of writing formats commonly seen on such measures are contrived or spontaneous tasks. Contrived formats measure skills such as capitalization, punctuation, spelling, syntax, or word usage in isolation from the general written product. Spontaneous formats ask the student to produce a writing sample from a specific topic and function. The different aspects (e.g., spelling, organization, ideation) of writing are measured through the production of written text.

Criterion-Referenced Measures

Criterion-referenced measures (CRMs) can contribute significantly to a student's program planning by providing a description of proficiency with tasks of average difficulty for their peers. Criterion measures can be standardized (*WJ III Relative Proficiency Index,* Mather & Wendling, 2003) or nonstandardized. However, as with norm-referenced measures, the evaluator must consider the task (structure and modality), the topic, and the tools (e.g., pen or computer) allowed for writing production.

Informal Measures

Informal measures are critical to an assessment of written expression. Luria (1980) describes three informal task formats for assessing writing: copying, dictation, and spontaneous. These different tasks allow the evaluator to examine different cognitive and linguistic processes required of an individual during the process of writing. Luria suggests that a writer be given different types of copying tasks (e.g., letters, single words, sentences, paragraphs). Spelling, sentence structure, and organizational deficits can be noted as the task demands increase the need for integration of cognitive and linguistic processes. The ability to complete a dictation task requires the individual to integrate phonological (sound awareness), orthography (sound/symbol awareness), and word and sentence structure. Again, varying the type of task demands, such as dictating individual letters, words, sentences, and paragraphs, is important. To distinguish between linguistic and motor disorders, the evaluator might vary the student's response by the use of anagrams (blocks with single letters written on them). A spontaneous writing sample requires that the student write either a sentence, paragraph, or story on a specific topic. Ideally, the evaluator should collect writing samples of a student's written expression across different audiences, genre, and topics in timed and untimed situations.

AREAS OF WRITTEN LANGUAGE IMPORTANT TO MEASURE

Assessing written language requires understanding the different areas of written expression and the abilities most necessary to complete task demands. No single norm- or criterion-referenced measure is capable of providing an evaluator with the information necessary

Table 1   Select Norm-Referenced Measures of Written Expression

Test	Author(s)	Publisher & Date	Age Span	Word: Spelling	Word: Word or Sentence Meaning	Contrived Syntax: Identification	Contrived Syntax: Sentence Combining	Contrived Syntax: Cloze	Contrived Syntax: Dictation	Contrived Syntax: Sentence Building	Genre: Narrative	Genre: Expository	Genre: Other	Time: Timed Writing	Spont. Prompt: Series of Pictures	Spont. Prompt: Single Picture	Spont. Prompt: Written Topic	Spont. Prompt: Story Starter	Spont. Scoring: Conventions	Spont. Scoring: Syntax Usage	Spont. Scoring: Text Structure
Illinois Test of Psycholinguistic Abilities-3	Hammill, D. D., Mather, N., & Roberts, R.	PRO-ED, 2001	5–12	✓	✓																
Written Language Scales of the Oral and Written Language Scales (OWLS)	Carrow-Wolfolk, E.	AGS, 1996	5–21				✓						Mixed				✓	✓	✓	✓	
Kauffman Test of Educational Achievement II	Kaufmann, A. S., & Kaufmann, N. L.	AGS	4.5–25	✓			✓	✓			✓				✓		✓		✓	✓	✓
Peabody Individual Achievement Test-R/NU	Markwardt, F.	AGS	5–22	✓							✓					✓					

(Continued)

Table 1 (Continued)

Test	Author(s)	Publisher & Date	Age Span	Word & Sentence Level							Text Level										
				Word		Contrived Syntax					Genre			Time	Spontaneous Prompt				Spontaneous Scoring		
				Spelling	Word or Sentence Meaning	Identification	Sentence Combining	Cloze	Dictation	Sentence Building	Narrative	Expository	Other	Timed Writing	Series of Pictures	Single Picture	Written Topic	Story Starter	Conventions	Syntax Usage	Text Structure
Test of Early Written Language-2	Hresko, W.P., Herron, S.R., & Peak, P.K.	PRO-ED, 1996	3-7-11	✓	✓	✓	✓		✓					✓					✓	✓	✓
Test of Written Language-3	Hammill, B & Larson, S.C.	Pro-Ed 1996		✓	✓	✓					✓					✓			✓	✓	✓
Wechsler Individual Achievement Test-II		Psychological Corporation, 2001	4-80	✓									✓						✓	✓	✓
Woodcock-Johnson III, Tests of Achievement	Woodcock, R.W., McGrew, K.S., & Mather, N.	Riverside, 2001	2-90	✓	✓	✓							Mixed					✓	✓	✓	✓

to investigate all of these areas. A diagnostician's knowledge of written expression in combination with an integrated assessment battery (e.g., informal and criterion- and norm-referenced) is critical to decision making. The areas of written language essential to an integrated assessment include spelling, syntax, text organization, and handwriting.

Spelling

As with all areas of writing, spelling strategies change as a function of general and academic knowledge. Key to understanding the source of a spelling problem is the assessment of a student's phonological and orthographic awareness. A significant amount of research has highlighted the important link of these linguistic processes to the ability to decode and encode words (Gregg & colleagues, in press). Phonological awareness is the "ability to recognize that words are composed of discrete segments of speech sounds" (Mather & Goldstein, 2001, p. 178). Rhyming (cat, fat), blending (c-a-t = cat), phoneme counting (cat = three sounds), phoneme deletion (say policeman without saying man), and phoneme manipulation (change /d/ in dip to /s/) are commonly used tasks to measure phonological awareness (Mather & Gregg, 2003). Orthographic awareness has received less attention in the research (Gregg & colleagues, in press), yet it is critical to success in the ability to spell. Orthographic awareness is the ability to recognize and produce symbols (e.g., numbers, letters, words). Tasks requiring students to visually scan letters and words, recall patterns of letters that were presented orally, and recognize and reproduce homonym patterns are all excellent methods to assess orthographic awareness. The Process Assessment of the Learner (PAL) (Berninger, 1999), a criterion-referenced measure, and the Illinois Test of Psycholinguistic Abilities-2 (ITPA-2) (Hammill & colleagues, 2001), a norm-referenced measure, are two excellent assessment tools providing phonological and orthographic awareness tasks.

Task format and content are very important to observe when measuring spelling abilities. First, a student should always be presented both real and pseudo words (i.e., nonsense words) to spell. The use of nonsense words allows for an examination of the influence of phonological awareness abilities. In addition, the spelling assessment process should include both recall and recognition of single words. A student's ability to correctly identify (recognize) the correct spelling of words (Peabody Individual Achievement Test–Revised-Normative Update [PIAT-R/NU]) requires processes that are different than a recall spelling task. On recall tasks, a student must remember the spelling words from memory and either spell it out loud or produce it in written form (Wide Range Achievement Test 3 [WRAT 3]). In addition, it is critical that an evaluator consider the time it took a student to write a spelling word. Therefore, both accuracy and fluency are important factors to consider.

In addition, the evaluator should consider obtaining informal information from the classroom related to the student's ability to spell words copied from the board or their textbook. Finally, spelling should be analyzed in the spontaneous creation of text. At times, a student can perform spelling tasks better if words are presented in isolation. Yet when trying to create text spontaneously, spelling patterns will be identified. Table 2 provides information related to several commonly used diagnostic norm-referenced spelling measures.

Handwriting

Many factors can influence a student's ability to produce legible text. These factors include experience with specific tools, motivation, orthographic awareness, and motor coordination. It is suggested that any evaluation of handwriting begin with administration of a measure such as the PAL (Berninger, 1999). Therefore, an evaluator must rely more heavily on informal indices. Handwriting should be measured using recall, copy, and spontaneous writing tasks. Error patterns can be observed across letter formation, letter size, proportion, spacing, line quality, slant, and rate of letter formation. More than an emphasis on letter perfect formation, an evaluator would want to observe whether a student can identify letters by name, draw nonverbal figures, trace letters, copy letters, write letters from oral dictation, and translate cursive or manuscript and capital or small letters.

Syntax

A student's ability to understand and use the rules of written language that govern punctuation and capitalization usage, word form, and sentence structure are critical for communicating ideas into written language. The assessment of written syntax should include task formats of both receptive (identification) and expressive (production) language. Three commonly used tasks to measure syntax include identification, sentence

Table 2 Select Norm-Referenced Achievement Measures Providing Spelling Measures

Test	Subtest(s)	Author(s)	Publisher & Date	Task Modality — Input: Auditory	Visual	Haptic	Motor	Output: Auditory	Visual	Haptic	Motor	Task Content — Real Words	Pseudo Words	Recognition	Recall	Rate	Age Range (In Years and Months)
Illinois Test of Psycholinguistic Abilities-3	Sight spelling	Hammill, D., Mather, N., & Roberts, R.	Pro-Ed, 2001	✓	✓			✓	✓		✓	✓			✓		5–0 to 12–11
	Sound spelling			✓				✓	✓		✓		✓		✓		
Process Assessment of the Learner (PAL)*	Alphabet writing	Berninger, V. W.	Psychological Corporation, 1999	✓				✓	✓		✓	✓			✓		5–0 to 13–11
	Receptive coding			✓	✓				✓		✓		✓	✓			
	Expressive coding			✓	✓				✓		✓	✓	✓			✓	
	Word choice			✓					✓		✓	✓	✓	✓		✓	
	Copying			✓	✓				✓		✓				✓		
Peabody Individual Achievement Test-R/NU	Spelling	Markwardt, F. C., Jr.	American Guidance Service, 1989	✓					✓			✓		✓			5–0 to 18–11
Test of Early Written Language-2	Spelling (#'s 24, 26–29, 34, 37, 42, 48, 53, 55)	Hresko, W., Herron, S., & Peak, P.	Pro-Ed, 1996	✓					✓		✓	✓			✓		3–0 to 10–11
Test of Written Language-3	Spelling	Hammill, D., & Larsen, S.	Pro-Ed, 1996	✓					✓		✓	✓			✓		7–0 to 17–11

(Continued)

Table 2 (Continued)

Test	Subtest(s)	Author(s)	Publisher & Date	Input: Auditory	Input: Visual	Input: Haptic	Input: Motor	Output: Auditory	Output: Visual	Output: Haptic	Output: Motor	Real Words	Pseudo Words	Recognition	Recall	Rate	Age Range (In Years and Months)
Test of Written Spelling-4		Hammill, D., & Larsen, S. Moats, L.	Pro-Ed, 1999	✓					✓		✓	✓			✓		6–0 to 18–11
Weschler Individual Achievement Test-II	Spelling	Wechsler, D.	Psychological Corporation, 2001	✓					✓		✓	✓			✓		5–0 to 19–11
	Written expression (mechanics)			✓					✓		✓	✓				✓	
Wide Range Achievement Test-3	Spelling/written encoding	Wilkinson, G. S.	Western Psychological Services, 1993	✓					✓		✓	✓	✓			✓	5–0 to 75–0
Woodcock-Johnson III, Tests of Achievement	Spelling	Woodcock, R., McGrew, K., & Mather, N.	Riverside Publishing, 2001	✓					✓		✓				✓		
	Spelling of sounds			✓					✓		✓		✓		✓		

*The PAL is a criterion-referenced measure

combining, and spontaneous writing tasks. Identification tasks such as multiple choice or editing tasks for word usage, punctuation, and style are commonly used formats.

Text Organization

The ability to organize ideas in written language and arrange them to create an organizational framework involves many linguistic and cognitive abilities. Writers' cognitive, linguistic, and reading abilities have a significant influence on the creation of different organizational patterns of text (Applebee, 1978; Gregg, 2004; Vygotsky, 1978). The two most commonly used genres in the schools are narrative and expository writing. Narrative is used in the early grades, but its influence is felt much less as students advance. The results of writing assessments that evaluate text organization using only narrative genre cannot be generalized to a student's ability with expository text.

Professionals and students participating in the assessment of written language are integral to the integrated assessment process. Informal and criterion- and norm-referenced measures are simply the tools to investigate a writer's abilities. It is the collaboration of teachers, psychologists, and students working together that is the key to the success of program planning and positive outcomes. Each party brings an equal wealth of information, observations, feelings, and experience to contribute to solutions.

—*Noel Gregg and Jennifer Hartwig*

See also Academic Achievement; Authentic Assessment; Behavioral Assessment; Communication Disorders; Criterion-Referenced Assessment; Learning Disabilities; Writing Intervention and Strategies

REFERENCES AND FURTHER READING

Applebee, A. N. (1978). *The child's concept of a story.* Chicago: University of Chicago Press.

Becker, H. J. (1999). *Internet use by teachers: Conditions of professional use and teacher-directed student use. Teaching, learning, and computing, 1998 national survey* (Report No.1). Irvine, CA: Center for Research on Information Technology and Organizations.

Berninger, V. W. (1999). *Manual for the process assessment of the learner (PAL): Test battery for reading and writing.* San Antonio, TX: Psychological Corporation.

Britton, J., Burgess, T., Martin, N., McLeod, A., & Rosen, H. (1975). *The development of writing abilities* (pp. 11–18). London: Macmillan.

Carrow-Woolfolk, E. (1996). *Manual for written expression scales.* Circle Pines, MN: American Guidance Services.

Gregg, N. (2004, March). *Orthography or what?* Paper presented at the International Conference of the Learning Disabilities Association, Atlanta, GA.

Gregg, N., Bandalos, D., Coleman, C., Davis, M., Robinson, K., & Blake, J. (in press). Dimensionality of phonological and orthographic awareness tasks for college students with and without dyslexia and attention deficit hyperactivity. *Journal of Developmental Neuropsychology.*

Hammill, D., & Larsen, S. (1996). *Manual for the test of written language* (3rd ed.) (TOWL-3). Austin, TX: Pro-Ed.

Hammill, D., Mather, N., & Roberts, R. (2001). *Manual for the revised Illinois test of psycholinguistic abilities -2* (ITPA-2). Austin, TX: Pro-Ed.

Hresko, W., Herron, S., & Peak, P. (1996). *Manual for the test of early written language* (TEWL-2). Austin, TX: Pro-Ed.

Kaufman, A., & Kaufman, N. (2004). *Manual for the Kaufman tests of educational achievement-2,* Circle Pines, MN: American Guidance.

Larsen, S., Hammill, D., & Moats, L. (1999). *Manual for the test of written spelling (TWS-4).* Austin, TX: Pro-Ed.

Luria, A. R. (1980). *Higher cortical functions in man.* New York: Basic Books.

Markwardt, F. C., Jr., (1989). *Manual for the Peabody individual achievement test-revised (PIAT-R/NU).* Circle Pines, MN: American Guidance Service.

Mather, N., & Goldstein, S. (2001). *Learning disabilities and challenging behaviors: A guide to intervention and classroom management.* Baltimore: Paul H. Brookes.

Mather, N., & Gregg, N. (2003). "I can rite": Informal assessment of written language. In S. Vaughn & K. L. Briggs (Eds.). *Reading in the classroom: Systems for the observation of teaching and learning* (pp. 179–220). Baltimore: Paul H. Brookes.

Mather, N., & Wendling, B. J. (2003). Instructional implications from the Woodcock-Johnson III. In F. A. Schrank & D. P. Flanagan (Eds.), *WJ III clinical use and interpretation: Scientist-practitioner perspectives* (pp. 93–124). Boston: Academic.

Russell, M., Goldberg, A., & O'Connor, K. (2003). *Computer-based testing and validity: A look back and into the future.* Retrieved March 16, 2004, from http://www.intasc.org

Shaugnessy, M. F. (1977). *Errors and expectations: A guide for the teacher of basic writing.* New York: Oxford University Press.

Vygotsky, L. V. (1978). *Mind and society: The development of higher psychological processes.* Cambridge, MA: Harvard University Press.

Wechsler, D. (2001). *Manual for the Wechsler individual achievement test* (2nd ed.) (WIAT-II). San Antonio, TX: Psychological Corporation.

Wilkinson, G. S. (1993). *Manual for the wide range achievement test* (3rd ed.) *(WRAT 3).* Los Angeles: Western Psychological Services.

Woodcock, R., McGrew, K. & Mather, N. (2001). *Manual for the Woodcock-Johnson tests of achievement* (3rd ed.). Itasca, IL: Riverside.

Z

ZERO TOLERANCE

Zero tolerance is a disciplinary orientation emphasizing immediate and often severe punishment, typically out-of-school suspension and expulsion, as a method of maintaining school order. Growing out of 1980s drug policies, the zero-tolerance approach has been highly controversial. Proponents argue that schools need a no-nonsense approach in the face of increasing school violence, while critics point to seemingly trivial applications of the policy and civil rights violations. Evidence, however, does not support the effectiveness of out-of-school suspension and expulsion. Available research raises a number of serious concerns about zero tolerance, including inconsistent application, disproportional effect on minorities, and a host of negative school outcomes that appear to be associated with the approach.

HISTORY, DEFINITION, AND APPLICATION

Zero tolerance grew out of the 1980s drug enforcement policies that mandated severe and certain penalties for any drug infraction, regardless of its seriousness. The term caught on as a disciplinary approach in school districts across the country and eventually became ensconced in federal law in the Gun-Free Schools Act. While the act mandates a one-calendar-year expulsion for possession of a firearm on school property, many school districts have extended the application of zero tolerance for a range of other school misbehaviors.

The extent of usage of zero tolerance is unclear and probably depends upon definition, which is also at issue; although the term *zero tolerance* is widely used, there is no single widely accepted definition. The National Center on Educational Statistics, which defines zero tolerance as a policy that mandates predetermined consequences or punishments for specified offenses, estimates that up to of 80% or 90% of the nation's schools employ zero-tolerance policies (Heaviside & colleagues, 1998). That definition of zero tolerance may be overly broad; however, one would expect that there are few schools in America that do not mandate some predetermined consequences for specific behaviors. A more limited definition of zero tolerance is a disciplinary policy "intended primarily as a method of sending a message that certain behaviors will not be tolerated, by punishing all offenses severely, no matter how minor" (Skiba & Peterson, 1999).

ZERO TOLERANCE: PRO AND CON

Proponents contend that, in the face of escalating school violence and disruption, the firm and resolute message provided by zero tolerance is needed to maintain school discipline. They argue that swift and certain punishments of zero tolerance are ultimately more fair and will eliminate racial imbalance in school discipline. Most importantly, they believe that removing troublemakers will produce a school climate that is free from disruption for those students that remain, and that observation of school punishments will deter others from disruption and violence.

Critics of the approach have tended to focus on the threats to individual liberties and fairness posed by a one-size-fits-all model. They point out that suspension and expulsion remove students from the opportunity to learn, and that many of those removed by strict zero-tolerance policies do not pose serious threats to school safety, but are often good students with no prior history of disruption. Finally, they note that continued racial disparities in suspension and expulsion put students of color at disproportionate risk for contact with the juvenile justice system, creating what has been termed a *school-to-prison pipeline*.

EVIDENCE FOR ZERO TOLERANCE

After 15 years of operation in our nation's schools, there has yet to be any evidence that zero-tolerance suspensions and expulsions have led to improvements in school climate or student behavior. Rather, research has found dramatic inconsistency in the application of suspension and expulsion across schools and school districts, and such inconsistency is more a result of school and teacher characteristics than student behavior or attitudes. Racial disparities in school discipline continue to increase, and some data suggest that, as the use of suspension and expulsion increases, so does minority over-representation in school discipline. Finally, outcome data for suspension and expulsion raise serious concerns: rather than improving student behavior, out-of-school suspension and expulsion have been found to be associated with more negative school climate characteristics, a higher rate of future misbehavior, lower average academic achievement, and higher school dropout rates.

SUMMARY

Since its inception, the disciplinary philosophy and practice of zero tolerance have created considerable controversy in education, pitting fears about increasing school safety against civil rights concerns. There is, however, no evidence that school suspension and expulsion contribute to safe and productive learning climates, and a good deal of evidence that they may be associated with racial disparity and negative school outcomes. In the face of federal mandates (e.g., No Child Left Behind Act of 2001) that educational interventions be evidence-based, one can only hope that researchers and practitioners will continue to develop and implement sound alternative disciplinary strategies that can maintain school safety without removing students from the opportunity to learn.

—*Russell J. Skiba*

See also Expulsion; Gangs; Substance Abuse; Suspension; Violence in Schools

REFERENCES AND FURTHER READING

Heaviside, S., Rowand, C., Williams, C., & Farris, E. (1998). *Violence and discipline problems in U.S. Public Schools: 1996–1997* (NCES 98–030). Washington, DC: U.S. Department of Education, National Center for Education Statistics.

Skiba, R. J., & Peterson, R. L. (1999). The dark side of zero tolerance: Can punishment lead to safe schools? *Phi Delta Kappan, 80,* 372–376, 381–382.

Index

A

AAMR. *See* American Association of Mental Retardation
Aaron, P. G., 432, 433, 438, 439, 444
AAS (American Association of Suicidology), 131, 551
AASP (American Academy of School Psychology), 20
AAUW (American Association of University Women), 221, 234
ABA. *See* Applied behavior analysis
ABES (Adaptive Behavior Evaluation Scale), 14*table,* 15
Ability grouping
  and achievement, 2
  advantages *vs.* disadvantages of, 1
  between-class groupings, 1
  and classroom instruction, 2–3
  and equity, 3
  "Joplin Plan" concept, 2
  quality of instruction issues, 2–3
  rate of instruction issues, 2
  types, prevalence of, 1–2
  within-class groupings, 1
  See also Academic achievement; Classroom climate;
    Cooperative learning; Grades; Learning; Mastery learning;
    Mathematics interventions and strategies; Reading
    interventions and strategies; Spelling interventions and
    strategies; Writing interventions and strategies
Abortion rates, 560
About Head Start, 403
ABPP. *See* American Board of Professional Psychology
Abrahams, N., 6
Abrego, P. J., 124
Abshier, D. W., 81, 362
ABSP (American Board of School Psychology), 20
Abuse and neglect
  aggressive behavior, 19
  definitions regarding, 4
  depression, 156
  eating disorders, 185
  identification of, 5–6, 5*table*
  parent, school psychologist collaboration, 374
  physical *vs.* sexual abuse, 4
  prevalence of, 3–4
  prevention programs, 7
  reporting maltreatment, 6
  risk factors for, 4–5
  working with maltreated children, 7
  See also Bullying and victimization; Confidentiality; Crisis
    intervention; Ethical issues in school psychology;
    Prevention; Resilience and protective factors
Academic achievement
  accountability, 11

changing educational practice, 11
constructed response test format, 9
criterion-referenced tests, 10
defined, 8
focusing public attention, 11
formative assessment, 10
grade retention and, 466
individual-referenced tests, 10
item format, 8–9
latchkey children, 281
norm-referenced tests, 9–10
purposes of, 10–11
selected response test format, 8–9
summary regarding, 11–12
summative assessment, 10
test referents, 9–10
See also Bias in testing; Criterion-referenced assessment; Grades;
    Learning disabilities (LDs); Mental retardation (MR);
    Norm-referenced testing; Normal distribution; Performance-
    based assessment (PA); Written language assessment
Academic Competence Evaluation Scales, 334
Accommodation, 12
Achenbach, Thomas M., 57, 160, 274, 275*table,* 277, 414,
    415*fig.,* 416, 516
*Achenbach System of Empirically Based Assessment
  (ASEBA),* 277
Achievement gap, 350–351
Acquired immune deficiency syndrome (AIDS). *See* HIV/AIDS
ACT (American College Testing) Program, 9
Activity-centered learning styles, 295
ADA (Americans with Disabilities Act), 72–73
Adams, G. B., 358
Adams, Jane, 326
Adams, M. J., 439
Adamson, R. J., 380
Adaptive behavior assessment, 13–14
  AAMR definition of, 12–13
  case example, 15
  direct assessment, 13
  DSM-IV-TR definition of, 12, 13
  indirect assessment, 13
  instruments, 14–15, 14*table*
  mental retardation diagnosis, 12
  norm *vs.* criterion-referenced instruments, 14, 14*table*
  summary, 15
  See also Autism spectrum disorders; Individualized Education
    Plan (IEP); Individuals With Disabilities Education Act
    (IDEA); Least restrictive environment (LRE); Mental
    retardation (MR); Traumatic brain injury (TBI)

Adaptive Behavior Evaluation Scale (ABES), 14*table,* 15
Adelman, H. S., 213
Adelman, H. W., 90
ADHD. *See* Attention deficit hyperactivity disorder
Adjustment disorder, 16–17
   acute *vs.* chronic, 16
   DSM-IV-TR definition of, 16
   duration and degree, 16
   subtypes, 16
   treatment, 17
Adulthood stage of psychosocial development, 190
Affective outcomes, of homeschooling, 247
African Americans
   bias in testing of, 68
   Black English *vs.* Standard English, 436
   gang membership, 220
   Head Start, 238
   obesity rates, 355
   retention rates, 465
   single-parent families, 505, 507
   substance abuse, 545
   suicide rates, 549
   teen pregnancy, 560
   teenage smoking, 509
   See also Class; Ethnicity; Gender; Multicultural
      education; Race, ethnicity, class and gender
Aggression in schools
   aggression subtypes, 17–18
   biological, psychobiological factors, 18
   bipolar disorder, 71
   cognitive-behavioral interventions, 97
   conduct disorder and, 107, 108
   corporal punishment and, 121
   ecological theories of, 19
   etiology of, 18–19
   expulsion, 199
   friendships of children, 211
   gender differences, 18
   learning/cognitive theories of, 18–19
   long-term effects of, 19
   peer relationships and, 519
   physical *vs.* indirect types of, 18
   prevention programs, 19
   projection defense mechanism, 155
   reactive *vs.* proactive type of, 17
   relational aggression, 18
   social aggression, 18
   TV violence and, 311–312
   See also Abuse and neglect; Bullying and victimization;
      Conduct disorder (CD); Discipline; Gangs; Theories of
      human development; Violence in schools
Aggressor effect, of TV violence, 311
Ahn, H., 126
AIDS. *See* HIV/AIDS
Akbar, N., 430
Alan Guttmacher Institute, 559, 560
Albanese, A. L., 252, 253
Albano, W., 358
Alberto, P., 51, 61*table,* 62*table,* 63*table,* 64*table,*
   65*table,* 66*table*
Albin, R. W., 26

Alcohol-related birth defects (ARBDs), 209
Alcohol-related neurodevelopmental disorder (ARND), 209
Aldridge, J. D., 163
Alexander, M. D., 109
Alexander, P. A., 8
Alfonso, Vincent C., 457
Allen, C., 325
Allen, J. G., 393
Allen, K. D., 39, 42
Allen, L. D., 395
Alpert, N. M., 357
Alpert-Gillis, L. J., 172
Alpha-adrenergic psychotropic medications, 423
Alsaker, F. D., 423, 424
Alsobrook, J. P., 357
Alstaugh, J. L., 328
Alt, M. N., 174
Alternating-interventions experimental design, 502
Altschuld, J. W., 365
Alvermann, D. E., 431
Aman, M., 420, 421, 422
Amaral, D., 209
American Academy of Pediatrics, 121, 122, 583
American Academy of School Psychology (AASP), 20, 216
American Association for Employment in Education, 476
American Association of Mental Deficiency, 14*table*
American Association of Mental Retardation (AAMR), 12–13
   adaptive behavior assessment, 12–13
   mental retardation, defined, 317–319
American Association of Suicidology (AAS), 131, 551
American Association of University Women
      (AAUW), 221, 234, 235
American Board of Examiners in Professional Psychology.
      See American Board of Professional Psychology
American Board of Professional Psychology (ABPP)
   certification process, 20–21
   credentialing areas, 20
   neuropsychological specialty status, 348–349
   structure of, 20
   See also American Psychological Association (APA);
      National Association of School Psychologists (NASP);
      School psychologist
American Board of School Psychology (ABSP), 20
American Cancer Society, 77, 78
American College Testing Program (ACT), 9
American Educational Research Association
   academic achievement, 8
   high-stakes assessments, 534
   test validity, 579
American Evaluation Association, 410
American Foundation for Suicide Prevention, 551
American Medical Association, 583
American Montessori Society, 403
American Psychiatric Association, 12, 16, 32, 33, 107, 108,
   160, 183, 359, 382, 392, 413, 431, 520, 521, 543, 544
   CDSPP and, 122–123
   DSM-IV-TR and, 175–177, 177
   mental retardation, defined, 318
   OCD defined, 357
   self-injurious behavior defined, 492
   structured diagnostic interviews, 274

American Psychological Association (APA), 21–22, 109, 140, 191, 192, 197, 498
  academic achievement, 8
  CRSPP, 348
  directorates and offices of, 21, 21*table*
  Division of School Psychology (Division 16), 169, 170*table,* 456, 475
  divisions of, 21, 22*table,* 348
  Ethics Code, committee, 21, 191–192, 195
  Futures Conference, 216
  International School Psychology Committee, 272
  media violence, 313, 583
  NASP and, 345, 347
  Psychology: Careers for the Twenty-First Century, 82
  salary information, 477
  school psychologist accreditation, 82
  School Psychology Journal, 456
  test validity, 579
  See also Division of School Psychologists (Division 16, APA); National Association of School Psychologists (NASP)
Americans with Disabilities Act (ADA)
  autism and, 42
  children with cancer, 79
  students with disabilities, 72–73, 261, 522
  See also Individuals With Disabilities Education Act (IDEA)
Ames, C. A., 333
Ames, Louise B., 563
Amir, R. E., 40
Anastasi, A., 413
Anastopoulos, A. D., 33
Anderman, E. M., 87, 334
Anderman, L., 334
Anderson, A. J., 505, 506
Anderson, C. A., 583
Anderson, D. R., 310
Anderson, G. E., 466
Anderson, J., 47
Anderson, R. N., 548, 549
Andrasik, F., 69
Andrews, C., 543
Andrews, G., 544
Anecdotal recording technique, of classroom management, 91
Angel Unaware (Rogers), 320
Anger control training, cognitive-behavioral modification, 97
Anger Coping Program, 54
Annie E. Casey Foundation, 560, 561
Anorexia nervosa
  DSM diagnostic criteria, 183
  health consequences of, 184
  restricting *vs.* binge eating-purging type, 183
ANS (autonomic nervous system), 69
Antecedent. *See* Antecedent-behavior-consequence (A-B-C) observations of behavior assessment; Behavior
Antecedent-behavior-consequence (A-B-C) observations of behavior assessment, 56, 59–60
  applied behavior analysis, 50
  classroom observation technique, 91
Antecedent stimulus, 62*table*
Antecedent terms and teaching procedures, 62–63*table*
Anticonvulsant psychotropic medications, 423
Antidepressant medications, 157

Antidepressant psychotropic medications, 422
Antipsychotic psychotropic medications, 422
Anxiety disorders
  bullying, 235
  cognitive-behavioral interventions, 97
  conduct disorder and, 108
  corporal punishment and, 121
  depression and, 155
  divorce adjustment, 170
  gender factors, 222
  peer relationships and, 519
  psychotropic medications for, 421, 422
  PTSD and, 34
  selective mutism, 490
  shyness, 500
  See also Generalized anxiety disorder (GAD)
Anxiety hierarchy, fear reduction technique, 208
Anxiolytic psychotropic medications, 422–423
APA. *See* American Psychological Association
Appetite effect, of TV violence, 312
APPIC (Association of Psychology Postdoctoral and Internship Centers), 122
Applebee, A. N., 599
Applied behavior analysis (ABA), 61*table*
  of ADHD, 93
  Asperger's disorder, 40
  autism, 39
  behavior and events relationship, 23–24
  behavior antecedents and consequences, 50
  behavioral excesses *vs.* deficits, 23
  classroom observation technique, 93
  descriptive *vs.* functional analysis, 26
  differential reinforcement process, 24
  extinction behavior process, 24
  functional behavioral assessment, 25–27, 214
  operational definition for behavior measurement, 23
  positive behavior analysis and, 390, 392
  positive *vs.* negative reinforcement, 24
  selective mutism, 490
  shaping procedure, 25
  single-case experimental design, 26
  stimulus control procedure, 25
  token economy procedure, 25
  withdrawal design, 26–27, 27*fig.*
  See also Behavior; Behavior intervention; Behavioral assessment; Cognitive-behavioral modification; Consultation: behavioral (BC)
Applied professional ethics, defined, 191
Applying Psychology to the Schools book series (APA), 169
Approaches to Studying Inventory (ASI), 295
Aptitude-treatment interactions (ATIs) learning theory, 294
ARBDs (alcohol-related birth defects), 209
Arbolino, L. A., 329
Archer, R., 517
Ardila, A., 543
Armelagos, G. J., 429
Armistead, L., 508
Armstrong, D. M., 47
Armstrong, F. D., 78
ARND (Alcohol-related neurodevelopmental disorder), 209
Arnold, W. R., 303

Arra, C., 439
Arredondo, P., 140
ASEBA (Achenbach System of Empirically Based Assessment), 277
Ash, M. J., 72
Asher, S., 500
ASI (Approaches to Studying Inventory), 295
Asian Americans
　gang membership, 220
　Head Start, 238
　See also Class; Ethnicity; Gender; Multicultural education; Race, ethnicity, class and gender
Asperger's disorder
　diagnostic criteria, 39–40
　etiology of, 40
　treatment, 40
　See also Autism spectrum disorders; Facilitated communication
ASPPB (Association of State and Provincial Psychology Boards), 478
Assessment. *See* Academic achievement; Adaptive behavior assessment; Antecedent-behavior-consequence (A-B-C) observations of behavior assessment; Authentic assessment; Behavioral assessment; Career assessment; Criterion-referenced assessment; Cross-cultural assessment; Curriculum-based assessment; Functional behavioral assessment (FBA); Infant assessment; Motor assessment; Neuropsychological assessment; Norm-referenced testing; Performance-based assessment (PA); Personality assessment; Portfolio assessment; Preschool assessment; Reliability; Responsiveness to intervention (RTI) learning disabilities assessment method; Retention; Social-emotional assessment; Sociometric assessment; Standard error of measurement; Statewide tests; Written language assessment
Association Montessori Internationale (AMI), 330
Association of Psychology Postdoctoral and Internship Centers (APPIC), 122
Association of State and Provincial Psychology Boards (ASPPB), 478
Asthma, 27–28
　academic performance and, 28
　psychological interventions, 28
Ataxic cerebral palsy, 83
Athetoid cerebral palsy, 83
ATIs (aptitude-treatment interactions) learning theory, 294
Atkins v. Virginia, 320
Atlas, R. S., 74
Attachment disorders, 431–432
　See also Reactive attachment disorder (RAD) of infancy and early childhood
Attempted suicide. *See* Suicide, attempted suicide
Attention
　ADHD and, 31
　attended *vs.* unattended input, 28–29, 30
　challenges in, 31
　development of, 30–31
　divided, alternating attention, 29–30
　inhibition and filtering, 30
　learning and memory, 31
　model of, 29

vs. perception, 28
selective, sustained attention, 29, 30–31
types of, 29–30
working memory, 30
See also Attention deficit hyperactivity disorder (ADHD); Time on task
Attention deficit hyperactivity disorder (ADHD), 32–35
　academic problems, 33
　assessment of, 33–34, 92–93
　attention, impulse control, activity level, 31
　biofeedback used in, 71
　bipolar disorder, 71
　causes of, 33, 196
　vs. central auditory processing disorder, 101
　classroom observation assessment of, 92–93
　classwide peer tutoring and, 94
　cognitive problems, 33
　Combined Type, 32
　comorbid disorders, 33
　conduct disorder and, 108
　conjoint behavioral consultation intervention, 113
　depression and, 156
　divorce adjustment, 170
　DSM-IV-TR definition of, 32–35, 413–414
　environmental, task modifications, 34
　expulsion and, 199
　friendships of children, 211
　gender factors, 33, 222
　home-school notes strategy, 35
　Hyperactive-Impulsive Type, 32
　Inattentive Type, 32
　learning disorder comorbidity, 102
　ODD with, 360
　parent training, 34–35
　peer strategies, 35
　prevalence of, 32–33
　psychotropic medications for, 420, 421, 422
　PTSD and, 34
　self-monitoring techniques, 35
　social problems, 33
　social skills training, 35
　substance abuse, 547
　time on task and, 567
　treatment strategies, 34–35
　See also Attention; Behavior intervention; Conduct disorder (CD); Diagnosis and labeling; Individuals With Disabilities Education Act (IDEA); Learning disabilities (LDs); Psychotropic medications
Attribution retraining procedure, cognitive-behavioral modification, 97
Aubey, L. W., 311
Aubrey-Harper, M., 571
Austin, G., 236
Austin, J. T., 365
Authentic assessment, 35–37
　examples of, 36*table*
　limitations of, 36–37
　procedural knowledge measurement, 36
　skills *vs.* traits measurement, 36
　student progress measurement, 36

See also Academic achievement; Criterion-referenced assessment; Curriculum-based assessment (CBA); Outcomes-based assessment; Performance-based assessment (PA); Portfolio assessment
Autism Society of America, Inc., 202
Autism spectrum disorders
    Asperger's disorder, 37, 39–40
    autism, 37–39, 45
    autism, myths and facts, 38*table*
    childhood disintegrative disorder, 37, 41–42
    classwide peer tutoring and, 94
    diagnosis, 38–39
    echolalia and, 186
    etiology, 38
    facilitated communication and, 202
    gender factors, 37
    IDEA category, 262, 264*table*
    interventions, 39
    pervasive developmental disorder - not otherwise specified, 37, 42
    prevalence of, 37
    psychotropic medications for, 420–421
    vs. reactive attachment disorder, 431
    Rett's disorder, 37, 40–41
    self-injurious behavior, 493
    summary regarding, 42
    See also Echolalia; Etiology; Preschool assessment; Self-management; Social skills
Autogenics, of biofeedback, 70
Automatic reinforcement, defined, 64*table*
Autonomic nervous system (ANS), 69
Autonomy concept, of psychosocial development, 189
Aversive stimulus, 62*table*
    See also Behavior; Functional behavioral assessment
Avoidance, 64*table*
    See also Behavior; Behavioral assessment; Functional behavioral assessment
Azrin, N. H., 47, 64*table*

B
Bachman, J. G., 509, 545
Backward chaining instructional procedure, 63*table*
Baddeley, A. D., 315
Baer, D. B., 12, 23
Baer, D. M., 66*table,* 214
Baer, L., 357
BAG (behavioral assessment grid) of behavior assessment, 55
Baglio, C., 39
Bagwell, C. L., 211
Bailey, D., 265
Bainter, T. R., 330
Baker, D. B., 324
Baker, E., 546
Baker, J., 152
Ballantine, H. T., 192
Balmer, L., 152
Balter, L., 374
Bambara, L., 382
Bander, K., 312
Bandura, Albert, 18, 332, 444, 490, 565

Banks, C. A. M., 338–339, 339*table,* 340*table*
Banks, J. A., 338–339, 339*table,* 340*table*
Baraker, R., 514
Barbetta, P. M., 94
Barker, R. G., 113, 514, 515
Barkley, R. A., 33, 360, 361, 567
Barnett, D., 279
Barrett, R. P., 494
Barrish, H., 53
Barry, T. D., 200
Bartini, M., 73, 74
BASC (Behavior Assessment System for Children), 99, 516
Baseline in experimental design, 65*table*
Bass, G. M., 135
Bateman, B. D., 255
Battiato, A. C., 253
Battistich, V., 406
Bauer, A. M., 370, 372
Bauer, D. H., 207
Bauman, K. E., 493
Baumeister, A. A., 492
Baumrind, D., 367, 373
Bayley Scales of Infant Development-II, 265, 336, 400
BBBS (Big Brothers Big Sisters) program, 325, 326
BC. *See* Consultation: behavioral (BC)
BD. *See* Bipolar disorder (BD) (childhood onset)
BDI (Beck Depression Inventory), 156
Bear, G. G., 165, 166, 168
Bearman, P. S., 130
Beatty, K, 495
Beautrais, A. L., 551
Beck, Aaron, 125
Beck Depression Inventory (BDI), 156
Becker, H. J., 591
Beckner, V., 224
Bedwetting. *See* Enuresis
Beebe, A., 265, 273
Beeler, T., 439
Beery, K. E., 401
Beery, N. A., 401
Behavior
    abuse and neglect characteristics, 5, 5*table*
    behavioral definitions, 46
    biological and environmental factors of, 45–46
    frequency, duration measurement, 46
    graphing data, 46
    interval systems, 46
    measurement, analysis of, 46
    observable *vs.* unobservable, 45
    origins of, 45–46
    traumatic events and, 45–46
    See also Adaptive behavior assessment; Applied behavior analysis (ABA); Behavior contracting; Behavior intervention; Behavioral assessment; Behavioral concepts and applications; Cognitive-behavioral modification; Functional behavioral assessment (FBA); Premack Principle; Self-injurious behavior
Behavior analysis. *See* Applied behavior analysis
Behavior Assessment System for Children (BASC), 99, 516
Behavior contracting
    bonus clause, 47

effectiveness of, 47
explanation of, 46–47, 53
formalization feature of, 47, 48*fig.,* 53
limitations of, 47–48
negotiation feature, 47
penalty clause, 47
reward motivator, 47
specificity of terms, 47
See also Behavior; Behavior intervention; Self-management
Behavior intervention
anger management programs, 54
Behavior Intervention Case Managers, 49
behavioral contracting, 53
BEST aversive consequences system, 52–53
biological/neurological theory of, 51
communication methods intervention, 52
conflict management, 54
contingency-based interventions, 52–53
ecobehavioral theory of, 50, 51
encopresis, 188
functional behavioral assessment, 49, 52
importance of, 49
medical/biochemical interventions, 54
obesity in children, 356
parent training programs, 368–369
Positive Behavioral Intervention, 49, 52
prevention intervention, 51–52
primary, secondary, tertiary levels of, 50
psychodynamic theory of, 50–51
research trends regarding, 457
self-injurious behavior, 494
social competency training interventions, 53–54
social skills training, 54, 289, 513
state, federal laws, 49
structured positive reinforcement interventions, 53
See also Adaptive behavior assessment; Behavioral assessment; Cognitive-behavioral modification; Consultation: behavioral (BC); Functional behavioral assessment (FBA)
Behavioral assessment
A-B-C observations, 56, 59–60
anecdotal observations, 56
behavioral assessment grid (BAG), 55
behavioral consultation model, 57
components of, 55–56
conjoint behavioral consultation process, 57
continuous recording procedures, 56
defined, 55
direct *vs.* indirect techniques, 56–57
functional assessment, 57–58
indirect measures, advantages of, 57
interval recording systems, 56
multiple methods and informants, 55
naturalistic observation, 56
other informant rating scales, 57
permanent products method, 57
problem-solving model phases, 55
repeated measurements, 55
self-report measures, 57
situational-environmental variables, 55
systematic observational instruments, 56
time/event sampling procedures, 56

time on task, 567
See also Adaptive behavior assessment; Applied behavior analysis (ABA); Classroom observation; Functional behavioral analysis; Interviewing
Behavioral assessment grid (BAG) of behavior assessment, 55
Behavioral concepts and applications
A-B-C assessment, 56, 59–60
antecedent terms, teaching procedures, 62–63*table*
assessment approaches, 59–60
case example, 60, 66
design/intervention terms, 65–66*table*
environmental response, 59
functional analysis, 59–60
functional communication training (FCT), 61, 66
general terms and procedures, 61–62*table*
human development theory, 564–565
noncontingent reinforcement (NCR) schedule, 60
reductive strategy, 66
reductive techniques, 65*table*
reinforcement terms, teaching procedures, 63–64*table*
summary regarding, 66–67
treatment strategies, 60, 61–66*table,* 66
See also Behavior intervention; Behavioral assessment; Behavioral momentum technique; Consultation: behavioral (BC); Functional behavioral assessment (FBA); Least restrictive environment; Positive behavior support (PBS)
Behavioral momentum technique, 67
Behavioral theory of motivation, 331
Behavioral theory of psychotherapy, 418
Beichner, R. J., 102
Belle, D., 281
Ben-Avie, M., 370, 372
Ben-Porath, Y. S., 517
Benas, J. S., 356
Benavidez, D. A., 39
Bender, J., 282
Bender-Gestalt Test, 337
Benson, K., 126
Bentum, K., 432
Bereavement. *See* Death and bereavement
Bereiter, C., 587
Berg, C. Z., 357, 358
Bergan, J. R., 57, 111, 112
Bergman, R. L., 357, 358
Berk, L. E., 30
Berkson, G., 493
Berninger, V. W., 179, 596
Berry-Buktenica Developmental Test of Visual-Motor Integration, 401
Bersoff, D. N., 67, 68, 191, 192
BEST aversive consequences system, 52–53
Between-series designs, alternating-interventions design, 502
Between-series experimental designs, 502
Bias in testing
construct validity bias, 69
content validity bias, 68
criterion-related validity bias, 68
differential item functioning (DIE) statistical method, 68
vs. etiology of group differences, 67
item characteristic curves (ICCs), 68

item response theory (IRT) methods, 68
predictive validity for ability tests, 68
preschool assessment, 396
in psychological testing, 67–68
racial, ethnic, 67, 136–139, 261 *See also* Cross-cultural
    assessment
teacher expectations, 163
Bickley, P. G., 252
Bielick, S., 246
Bieu, R. P., 543
Big Brothers Big Sisters (BBBS) program, 325, 326
Biklen, D., 201, 202
Binet, Alfred, 123, 271, 317, 474
Binet-Simon Intelligence Scale, 454, 474
Binge eating, 184
Biofeedback
    autogenics, 70
    autonomic nervous system (ANS), 69
    breathing techniques, 70
    Cognitive Behavior Therapy (CBT), 70
    effectiveness of, 71
    general adaptation syndrome (GAS), 69
    modality types, 70*table*
    parasymathetic nervous system (PNS), 69
    Relaxation Training, 70
    sympathetic nervous system (SNS), 69
    video technology, 70
    See also Attention deficit hyperactivity disorder
        (ADHD); Behavior intervention; Generalized anxiety
        disorder (GAD); Self-management
Biological evolution learning theory, 285*fig.,* 286
Biological model, of human development theory, 562–563
Bipolar disorder (BD) (childhood onset), 71–72
    best practice intervention, 72
    depression, 72, 155–156
    differential diagnosis, 71–72
    prevalence of, 71
    psychopharmacological intervention, 72
    psychosocial interventions, 72
    school psychologist role, 72
    symptoms of, 71
    See also DSM-IV-TR; Individuals With Disabilities
        Education Act (IDEA); Personality assessment
Birch, L. L., 355, 356
Birmaher, B., 359, 360, 361
Blachman, B. A., 385, 386
Blackorby, J., 175
Blankenship, C. S., 163
Blatt, B., 320
Block, J. H., 305
Bloom, Benjamin, 305
Bloomquist, M. L., 17
Blum, N. J., 568, 569
Blumberg, J. J., 78
BMI (body mass index), 355
Board v. Rowley, 260
Bodfish, J. W., 493
Bodine, R., 54
Body dysmorphic disorder, 521
Body mass index (BMI), 355
Boehlert, M., 258, 492

Boelter, E., 67
Bonner, M., 115
Borich, G. D., 567
Borman, G. D., 242, 480
Born to Learn Curriculum: Prenatal to 3 Years
    (PAT program), 375
Borthwick-Duffy, S., 318
Borum, R., 127, 582, 584
Bosch, J. J., 493
Bose, J., 347
Bottomore, T., 430
Botvin, E. M., 546
Botvin, G. J., 510, 546
Boulware-Gooden, R., 443
Boutin, F., 296
Bowes, J. M., 153
Bowlby, J., 432
Boyatzis, R. E., 295
Boyer, E. L., 242
Bracey, G. W., 247
Bracken, B. A., 401
Bracken Test of Basic Concepts, 401
Braddock, D., 321
Braden, J. P., 380
Bradley, R. H., 372
Brain cancer, 78
Brammer, L. M., 124
Brand, S., 406
Branden, J. P., 580
Bray, M. A., 101, 543, 544
Brazelton Neonatal Behavioral Assessment Scale, 265–266
Braziel, P. M., 174
Breathing techniques, 70
Breese, G. R., 493
Breiter, H. C., 357
Brendgen, M., 211
Brian, P., 74
Britton, J., 591
Broadbent, D. A., 28
Brock, S., 129, 567
Brody, G. H., 506, 508
Bronfenbrenner, U., 113, 250
Brooks, D., 428
Brooks, F., 73, 74
Brophy, J., 331, 580
Brophy, J. E., 164
Broughman, S. P., 246
Browder, D. M., 13
Brown, D., 117, 140, 141
Brown, D. R., 362
Brown, M., 254
Brown, M. B., 188, 224
Brown, R., 420, 421, 422
Brown, R. T., 423
Brown, S., 242, 480
Brown, S. P., 140
Brown-Chidsey, R., 15
Brown v. Board of Education, 298, 321, 521
Browne, K. D., 5, 5*table*
Bruner, J., 265
Bruner, J. S., 286

Bryan, T., 252
Bryant, B. R., 318
Buck, Pearl S., 320
Buck v. Bell, 320
Bulemia
    vs. binge eating-purging anorexia type, 183–184
    compensatory behavior and, 184
    consequences of, 184
Bull, K. S., 163
Bullough, R. F., Jr., 241
Bullying and victimization
    conclusions regarding, 75
    corporal punishment and, 121
    defined, 73, 233
    direct *vs.* indirect, 73
    gender factors, 73, 222
    impact of involvement in, 73–74
    peer victimization, 73–74
    prevalence of, 73, 234, 235*table,* 582–583
    school-based interventions, 74–75
    Steps to Respect program, 75
    suicide ideation, 74
    whole school intervention approach, 74
    See also Aggression in schools; Behavior intervention;
        Corporal punishment (CP); Parenting, parents
Bumbarger, B., 508
Buntinx, W. H. E., 318
Burgess, T., 591
Burke, J. D., 359, 360, 361
Burns, N., 120
Burns, R. G., 305
Buros, Oscar Krisen, 75–76
Buros Mental Measurements Yearbook, 75–76, 76*timeline*
Burrell, N., 377
Bursztyn, A., 140, 338
Bush, George H., 480
Bush, George W., 326, 350, 531
Bushman, B. J., 583
Buss, A. H., 499
Busse, R. T., 473, 514, 519
Butcher, J. N., 517
Butler, K., 573
Bynum, M. S., 506
Bystander effect, of TV violence, 312

C
Cabello, B., 140, 142
Cabot, R. C., 324
Cairns, B. D., 107, 108
Cairns, R. B., 107, 108
Caisango, T., 102
Cajigas-Sagredo, N., 140
Calculator, S. N., 202
California Achievement Test (CAT), 10, 352
California Student Survey (CSS), 234, 236*table*
Callahan, C. M., 227
CALS (Checklist of Adaptive Living Skills), 14*table,* 15
Cameron, J., 331
Campbell, E. M., 318
Campbell, J. R., 587
Campbell, M., 178

Campbell Interest and Skills Survey, 81
Cancer
    brain and spinal cord cancers, 78
    educational implications, 78–79
    leukemia, 77–78
    long-term outcomes, 78
    prevalence of, 77
Canivez, G. L., 69
Canter, L., 53
Canter, M., 53
Cantor, J., 312
CAPD (central auditory processing disorder), 100
Caplan, G., 115–117, 128, 169
Caplan, R. B., 115–117
Carbo, M., 434–435
Career assessment
    in elementary school, 80
    explanation of, 79
    goals of, 80
    group *vs.* individual, 80
    in high school, 80, 81
    instruments of, 80–81
    methods of, 80
    in middle school, 80–81
    software/Internet programs, 80
    See also Behavioral assessment; Bias in testing; Criterion-
        referenced assessment; School psychologist
Career Awareness Inventory, 80
Careers in school psychology
    administrative, in-service education, research activities, 81–82
    intervention role, 81
    occupation demographics, 81
    occupational settings, 82
    personnel shortage, 82
    psychoeducational assessment role, 81
    resource material on, 82
    training, accreditation, 82
    See also American Psychological Association (APA);
        Division of School Psychologists (Division 16, APA);
        Licensing and certification in school psychology;
        National Association of School Psychologists (NASP);
        School psychologist
Carey, K. T., 385
Carlson, C., 207
Carlson, J. S., 177, 267
Carlton, M., 182
Carne, W. F., 446
Carnegie Council on Adolescent Development, 327
Caron, C., 543
Carpenter, P. A., 433
Carr, B., 342
Carroll, J. B., 269
Carroll, John, 305
CASEL (Collaborative for Academic, Social,
    and Emotional Learning), 164
Casey, K., 6
Cassar, M., 527
CAT (California Achievement Test), 10, 352
Catalano, R., 73
Catalano, R. F., 546
Cataldo, M. R., 493

Catania, C. A., 62*table,* 63*table,* 64*table,* 65*table*
Cattell, James, 474
Cattell, R. B., 269
Catterall, Calvin, 272
Catterello, A. N., 151
Cauffman, E., 584
Causal attribution concept, 332–333
CBA. *See* Curriculum-based assessment (CBA)
CBC. *See* Consultation: conjoint behavioral
CBCL (Child Behavior Checklist), 57, 516
CCPTP (Council of Counseling Psychology Training
    Programs), 122
CCTC (Council of Chairs of Training Councils), 123
CDI (Children's Depression Inventory), 156
CDM-R (Career Decision-Making System-Revised,
    Harrington-O'Shea), 80
CDP (Child Development Project) school reform program, 406
CEC (Council for Exceptional Children), 319
Center for Epidemiologic Studies Depression (CESD) Scale, 156
Center for Research on the Education of Students Placed
    At Risk (CRESPAR), 480
Center for Research on the Influences of Television on
    Children (CRITC), 310
Centers for Disease Control and Prevention (CDC),
    355, 509, 510, 548, 561
Central auditory processing disorder (CAPD), 100
Cerebral palsy
    ataxic type, 83
    athetoid type, 83
    body parts affected, 83
    description of, 83
    mental retardation, 83
    mixed type, 83
    pre-, peri- and postnatal factors, 83
    prevalence of, 83
    spastic type, 83
Cerny, J. A., 207
Certification. *See* Licensing and certification in
    school psychology
CESD (Center for Epidemiologic Studies
    Depression) Scale, 156
Chandler, K., 246
Changing-criterion experimental design, 501–502
Chansky, T. E., 357, 358
Chapman, C. D., 174
Character education, 82
    See also Media and children; Parenting, parents
Character Education Partnership, 164, 165
Charter schools
    advantages of, 85–86
    challenges faced by, 85
    charter issuance, 84
    conversion *vs.* newly created schools, 84
    definition, explanation of, 84
    disabled, at-risk students, 526
    disadvantages of, 86
    federal mandates, 85
    performance standards, 84, 86
    prevalence of, 84
    student populations, 85
    teacher recruitment, 85, 86

    See also Montessori schools; School reform;
        U.S. Department of Education
Chase-Lansdale, P. L., 560
Chattin-McNichols, J. P., 330
Cheating
    defined, 86
    environmental factors, 87
    high *vs.* low rewards, 87
    honor system, 87
    Kohlberg's model of moral reasoning and, 86–87
    prevalence of, 86
    teaching styles, 87
    understanding motivations to cheat, 87
    See also Grades; Peers, peer pressure; Study skills
Checklist of Adaptive Living Skills (CALS), 14*table,* 15
Cheema, I., 294
Cheslow, D., 358
Child Behavior Checklist (CBCL), 57, 383, 516
Child Development Project (CDP) school
    reform program, 406
Child maltreatment. *See* Abuse and neglect
Child Protective Services (CPS) reports, 3, 6
Child Study Movement, 474
The Child Who Never Grew (Buck), 320
Childhood disintegrative disorder
    assessment, treatment, 41–42
    diagnosis, 41
Children of Divorce Intervention Project
    program, 172
Children's Academic Intrinsic Motivation Inventory, 334
Children's Defense Fund, 403, 554, 555
Children's Depression Inventory (CDI), 156
Children's Personality Questionnaire, 383
Children's Yale-Brown Obsessive Compulsive Scale, 358
Chinlen, C., 296
Chizhik, A. W., 380
Christenson, S. L., 112, 250, 251, 471
Christiansen, E., 48
Christophersen, E., 569
Chromosomal mental retardations, 319*table*
Chunking memory technique, 316
CI. *See* Confidence interval
CIPP (Context, Inputs, Process, Product) program
    evaluation model, 411
Civil Rights Act of 1964, 22–23, 261, 577
Civil Rights Movement, 479
Cizek, G. J., 365
Clark, C., 238
Clark, D., 328
Clark, Elaine, 123
Clark, S., 328
Clarke, G. N., 97
Class
    ability grouping and, 3
    economic status and, 430
    No Child Left Behind Act of 2001, 350–351
    self=perception, identity formation, 430
    See also Multicultural education; Race,
        ethnicity, class and gender
Class size
    achievement advantages, 88

Class Size Reduction programs, 88
  defined, 87
  expenses increase, 88
  instruction *vs.* classroom management, 88
  vs. teacher-pupil ratio, 87
  See also Academic achievement; School reform (SR)
Class Size Reduction (CSR) programs, 88
Classical conditioning, 285*fig.*
  See also Behavior; Behavior intervention; Behavioral
    assessment; Conditioning: classical and operant
Classroom climate
  behavior and learning, 89–90
  conclusions regarding, 90
  definitions regarding, 89
  importance of, 89–90
  as learning environment, 88–89
  personal development dimension of, 89
  positive approach to, 90
  relationship dimension of, 89
  school psychologist role, 90
  system maintenance and change dimension of, 89
  See also Academic achievement; Discipline; Motivation
Classroom management. *See* Classroom climate;
    Classroom observation
Classroom observation
  A-B-C observation, 91
  ADHD assessment, 92–93
  anecdotal recording technique, 91
  applications of, 92–93
  duration recording technique, 91
  frequency count technique, 91
  intensity measurement technique, 91
  latency recording technique, 91
  momentary time sampling (MTS) technique, 92
  observation and recording techniques, 91–92
  yoked observation technique, 92
  See also Applied behavior analysis (ABA); Behavioral
    assessment; Time on task
Classwide peer tutoring (CWPT), 575
  Classwide Student Tutoring Teams (CSTT), 379
  components of, 93
  cooperative and competitive aspects of, 93–94
  description of, 93
  example of, 93–94, 94
  vs. individual peer tutoring, 94–95
  materials organization, 93
  pre- and posttests, 93
  research regarding, 94
  student pairing, 93
  students used as teachers concept, 93
  See also Classroom climate; Peer tutoring; Study skills
Claus, R. E., 193
Clay, M, 443
Clayton, R. C., 151
Clifton, R., 94
Clinical assessment interview, 273
Clinical Evaluation of Language Fundamentals-3, 99
Cloth, A., 262, 299
Club drugs, 545
Clustering memory technique, 316
Coding memory technique, 316

Coffman, D. M., 244
Cognition-centered learning styles, 294–295
Cognitive Behavior Therapy (CBT)
  biofeedback and, 70
  bipolar disorder, 72
  depression and, 156–157
  exposure-based CBT, 499
  generalized anxiety disorder and, 224–225
  for OCD, 358
  Rational Emotional Therapy, 125
  selective mutism, 490
  separation anxiety, 498–499
  social skills training, 513
  See also Behavior intervention; Cognitive-behavioral
    modification; Learning; Problem solving; Self-
    management; Study skills
Cognitive-behavioral family therapy, 206
Cognitive-behavioral modification
  anger control training, 97
  attribution retraining procedure, 97
  cognitive distortions and deficiencies, 96
  cognitive restructuring technique, 96
  contingent reinforcement procedure, 97
  explanation of, 95
  imagery procedures, 96
  modeling technique, 97
  rational-emotive therapy, 96–97
  relaxation technique, 96
  research review, 97–98
  role-play technique, 97
  self-instructional training, 95
  social problem-solving interventions, 96
  techniques, 96–97
  See also Behavior intervention; Cognitive-behavioral
    modification; Learning; Problem solving;
    Self-management; Study skills
Cognitive deficits
  mental retardation diagnosis, 12
  preschool assessment, 401
Cognitive developmental milestones, 158–159*table*
Cognitive developmental model, of human development
    theory, 565–566
Cognitive dissonance
  explanation of, 98
  reduction techniques, 98
Cognitive module of Component Model of Reading
  comprehension, 434
  constituents of, 433*table*
  decoding problems, 438–439
  decoding skills, 433, 436–437
  knowledge of words, 434
  remedial approach, 438–440
  sight-word reading, 433, 437, 439
  understanding passages, 434
  understanding sentences, 434
  word recognition, 433–434, 438–439
Cognitive Profile Assessment Instrument (CPAI), 296
Cognitive restructuring technique, cognitive-behavioral
    modification, 96
Cognitive theory of motivation, 332–333
Cohen, R. J., 353, 412, 413

Cohort dropout rate calculation formula, 173
Coie, J. D., 18
Coladarci, T., 174
Cole, C., 495, 496
Coleman, M., 37, 40, 41, 281
Coleman, T., 387
Coley, R. L., 560
Collaborative for Academic, Social, and Emotional
    Learning (CASEL), 165
Collins, H. W., 240, 241
Columbine High School shootings, 127, 132, 581
Combined-series experimental designs, 502, 503*fig.*
Comer, J. P., 370, 372
Commission for the Recognition of Specialties
    and Proficiencies in Professional Psychology
    (CRSPPP), 169, 348, 515
Commission on the Relation of School and College, 241
Committee for Children, 75
Communication disorders
    assessment of language, 99
    expressive *vs.* receptive impairments, 99
    hearing disorders, 101
    impact of, 98, 101
    language disorders, assessment of, 99
    language disorders, treatment of, 99–100
    language learning disability, 99
    phonological disorder, 100
    stuttering, 100
    summary regarding, 101
    voice disorders, 100–101
    See also Adaptive behavior assessment; Autism spectrum
        disorders; Echolalia; Facilitated communication (FC);
        Selective mutism (SM); Stuttering
Communication methods behavior intervention, 52
Comorbidity
    examples of, 102
    explanation of, 101
    See also DSM-IV-TR
Competitive learning, 117
Comprehension, 437, 438, 440
Comprehensive school reform (CSR). *See* School
    reform (SR)
Comprehensive School Reform Demonstration (CRSD), 480
Comprehensive School Reform Program (CSRP), 480
Compton, L. S., 39
Computer technology
    drill and practice courseware, 103
    hardware, 102–103
    instructional courseware applications, 103–104
    instructional games, 103
    Internet, World Wide Web applications, 103, 104–105
    LANs, 103
    personal digital assistants (PDAs), 102–103
    prevalence of in schools, 102
    problem-solving courseware, 103
    report writing and scoring, 104
    simulation courseware, 103
    software, 102
    See also Communication disorders; Learning; Study skills
Comuntizis-Page, G., 258
Conant, J. B., 241

Conditioning: classical and operant
    behavioral response component of, 106
    classical conditioning, 105
    conditioning procedures, 106
    definitions regarding, 105
    examples of, 106
    involuntary *vs.* voluntary learning, 106
    operant conditioning, 105–106
    pairing procedures component of, 106
    parent training programs, 368, 369
    Pavlov's dogs example, 105
    unconditioned stimuli and response, 105
    See also Behavior; Behavior intervention; Learning
Conduct disorder (CD)
    aggressive behavior, 107, 108
    assessment, treatment, 108
    behavior patterns of, 107
    biological predispositions, 107
    bipolar disorder, 71
    causes of, 107
    comorbid disorders, 108
    depression and, 108, 156
    DSM-IV-TR definition, 107, 414
    expulsion and, 199
    gender differences, 107–108
    parent training programs for, 369
    parenting skills, 107, 108
    peer context and, 107, 108
    school context, 107, 108
    school psychologist role, 108
    social aggression, girls, 108
    social contexts, 107
    See also Aggression in schools; Attention deficit hyperactivity
        disorder (ADHD); DSM-IV-TR; Gangs; Oppositional
        defiant disorder (ODD)
Conduct Problems Prevention Research Group (CPPRG), 108
Cone, J. D., 55
Confidence interval (CI)
    explanation of, 109
    See also Norm-referenced testing; Reliability;
        Standard Error of Measurement (SEM)
Confidentiality, 110
    abuse and neglect, 6, 7, 109
    as ethical standard, 109
    family counseling and, 207
    in full-service schools, 213
    harm to others, violence, 109–110
    IDEA and, 524
    Internet, World Wide Web and, 104–105
    privilege status, 110
    self-harm, 110
    sociometric assessment and, 519
    student psychological report, 446
    student trust *vs.* parental information, 110
    See also Ethical issues in school psychology; Interviewing
Conjoint behavioral consultation process of behavior
    assessment, 57
    See also Consultation: conjoint behavioral
Conners, C. K., 516
Conners' Rating Scales, 516
Connolly, J., 234

Conoley, C. W., 113
Conoley, J. C., 113, 184
Consequence
  defined, 63*table See also* Behavior
  See also Antecedent-behavior-consequence (A-B-C)
    observations of behavior
Construct test validity, 579
Constructivism
  learning theory, 287
  math instruction, 308
Consultation: behavioral (BC)
  behavioral theory and procedures, 111
  example of, 112
  meta-analysis method efficacy studies, 112
  problem-solving consultation and, 408
  problem-solving model stages, 111, 112
  research outcome data, 111
  voting method efficacy studies, 111–112
  See also Conjoint behavioral consultation process
    of behavior assessment; Consultation:
    Ecobehavioral; Consultation: Mental health;
    Cross-cultural consultation; Ethical issues in
    school psychology; Prevention
Consultation: conjoint behavioral (CBC)
  consultant, parent, teacher collaboration, 112–113
  defined, 112
  vs. ecobehavioral consultation, 112–113
  effectiveness of, 113
  home and school focus, 113
  problem-solving model of behavioral consultation, 112
  school-home notes, 473
  See also Consultation: behavioral (BC); Consultation:
    ecobehavioral; Cross-cultural consultation; Parenting,
    parents
Consultation: ecobehavioral, 113
  anticidents-setting events-consequences and, 114
  applications of, 114–115
  behavioral theory and, 113
  ecological theory and, 113
  example of, 114–115
  explanation of, 113
  human behavior viewed by, 114
  preschoolers, 404
  social and nonsocial factors, 114
  See also Consultation: behavioral (BC); Consultation: conjoint
    behavioral (CBC); Consultation: mental health;
    Cross-cultural consultation
Consultation: mental health (MHC)
  consultant/consultee relationship, 116
  consultee-centered administrative consultation, 116
  consultee-centered consultation, 116
  consultee difficulties, 116–117
  consultee lack of objective focus, 116–117
  explanation of, 115
  features of, 116
  origins of methodology, 115
  program-centered administrative consultation, 116
  when to use, 117
  See also Academic achievement; Cross-cultural
    consultation; Learning
Content test validity, 579

Context, Inputs, Process, Product (CIPP) program
    evaluation model, 411
Contingency
  contingency-based behavior interventions, 52–53
  contingency contracts, discipline, 166
  defined, 63*table*
  See also Applied behavior analysis (ABA); Behavior;
    Behavior intervention; Behavioral assessment
Contingent reinforcement procedure, cognitive-behavioral
    modification, 97
Continuous reinforcement (CR) schedule, 469, 471
Contracts. *See* Behavior contracting
Conventional stage of moral development, 280
Conversion disorder, 520
Cook, E., 407
Coolahan, K., 238
Cooney, B., 260, 315, 316
Cooney, J., 314
Cooper, H., 251, 252
Cooperative learning
  appropriate social skills element, 119
  classroom use example of, 118–119
  vs. competitive learning, 117
  cooperative base group learning, 118
  effects of, 119
  elements of, 119
  explanation of, 117
  formal cooperative learning, 118
  goals of, 119
  group processing element, 119
  individual accountability element, 119
  vs. individualistic learning, 117
  informal cooperative learning, 118
  positive interdependence element, 119
  promotive interaction element, 119
  research on, 119
  See also Ability grouping; Academic
    achievement; Learning
Corey, G., 124
Corey, M. S., 124
Cornell, D., 584
Corporal punishment (CP)
  alternatives to, 122
  defined, 120
  effects of, 121
  incidence of, 120–121
  legal issues, 121
  parental spanking, 120–121
  prevention techniques, 121–122
  state bans against, 120, 166
  See also Discipline; Due process
Corwyn, R. F., 372
Cosden, M., 7, 252, 253
Cosmer, James, 481
Costenbader, V. K., 555
Costigan, T. E., 19
Cottone, R. R., 193
Coulter, D. L., 318
Coulter, Ernest, 326
Council for Exceptional Children (CEC), 319, 346
Council of Chairs of Training Councils (CCTC), 123

Council of Chief State School Officers, 134
Council of Counseling Psychology Training
  Programs (CCPTP), 122
 growth of, 123
 mission of, 122–123
 See also American Psychological Association (APA);
    National Association of School Psychologists
    (NASP); School psychologist
Council of Directors of School Psychology
 formation of, 122
 Futures Conference, 216
 specialty guidelines, 169
Council of Directors of School Psychology
  Programs (CDSPP), 122
Council of University Directors of Clinical Psychology
  (CUDCP), 122
Counseling
 affective approaches, 125
 behavioral approaches, 125
 client-centered counseling approach, 123
 cognitive approaches, 125
 common factors of approaches to, 126
 vs. consultation, 124
 counseling effectiveness, 126
 counseling outcomes, 125–126
 counseling process, 125
 defined, 123
 developmental emphasis, 123
 eclectic approaches, 125
 goal-oriented counseling, 123
 historical foundations of, 123
 individual and group counseling, 123–124
 multicultural perspective on, 124
 psychometric movement, 123
 vs. psychotherapy, 124, 417
 systemic approaches, 125
 See also Behavior intervention; Cognitive-behavioral
    modification; Etiology; Psychotherapy; School
    psychologist; Substance abuse
Coutinho, M., 36
Cowen, E., 405, 406
CP. *See* Corporal punishment
CPAI (Cognitive Profile Assessment Instrument), 296
CPPRG (Conduct Problems Prevention Research Group), 108
CPS reports. *See* Child Protective Services (CPS) reports
CR (continuous reinforcement) schedule, 469
Craig, E. M., 318
Craig, W. M., 74, 234
Crawford, D., 54, 376
Crawford, S., 550
Crawford et al. v. *Honig,* 68
CRESPAR (Center for Research on the Education
  of Students Placed At Risk), 480
Crespi, T. D., 543
Crick, J. D., 18
Crisis intervention
 Columbine High School, 127, 132
 coping with death or tragedy, 129–130
 crisis planning, 128
 crisis team size and membership, 129
 crisis teams organization, 128–129

Israeli model of, 130
 national tragedies, 130–132, 132–133
 9/11/01 attacks, 128, 132, 133
 organizations dealing with, 127
 primary prevention level of, 128
 school psychologist role, 128
 secondary intervention level of, 128
 statistics on school crisis, 127–128
 suicide intervention, 130–132
 tertiary intervention level of, 128
 theoretical framework for, 128
 See also Aggression in schools; Bullying and victimization;
    Counseling; Death and bereavement; Depression;
    Suicide, attempted suicide; Violence in schools
CRITC (Center for Research on the Influences of
  Television on Children), 310
Criterion-referenced adaptive behavior instruments,
  14, 14*table,* 133
Criterion-referenced assessment
 of academic achievement, 10
 classroom applications, 134
 defining the domain, 135
 explanation of, 133
 mastery learning and, 305
 minimum competency, 135
 vs. norm-referenced testing assessment, 134
 purpose of, 135
 standards, 135, 136*table*
 state compulsory testing, 134–135
 statistical properties factor, 134
 of written language, 592
 See also Academic achievement; Norm-referenced
    testing; Reliability; Retention; Standard error of
    measurement; Statewide tests
Criterion test validity, 579
Cross-cultural assessment
 cultural loading, 136
 cultural loading, linguistic demands, 137
 cultural loading, test performance, 138
 culturally different, defined, 136
 culture, defined, 136
 culture *vs.* race or ethnicity, 138
 examiner and examinee cross-cultural dynamics, 138–139
 examiner/examinee cross-cultural dynamics, 136
 linguistic demands, 137
 norm-sample representation, 136, 137–138, 139
 psychometric-based cultural bias, 137, 139, 396
 summary regarding, 138–139
 test-taking strategies and, 138
 See also Academic achievement; Bias in testing; Class;
    Ethnicity; Gender, gender factors; Intelligence;
    Multicultural education; Race, ethnicity, class and
    gender; Reliability
Cross-cultural consultation
 case study research regarding, 142–143
 cultural values, effects of, 140–141
 Eurocentric sociopolitical value limitations, 140
 factors in, 140
 multicultural school consultation components, 140–141, 141
 Rogerio Pinto's model of, 140–141
 specific populations, contexts, 141–142

triadic relationships in, 141, 141*fig.*
See also Consultation: behavioral (BC); Consultation:
    conjoint behavioral (CBC); Consultation: ecobehavioral;
    Consultation: mental health; Ethnicity; Multicultural
    education; Race, ethnicity, class and gender
Crossley, Rosemary, 201, 202
Crosson-Tower, C., 5, 5*table,* 432
CRSD (Comprehensive School Reform Demonstration), 480
CRSPPP (Commission for the Recognition of Specialties and
    Proficiencies in Professional Psychology), 348
Cruise, T. K., 453
Crump, A. D., 378
Csikszentmihalyi, M., 332
CSR (Class Size Reduction) programs, 88
CSRP (Comprehensive School Reform Program), 480
CSS (California Student Survey), 234, 235*table,* 236*table*
CSTT (Classwide Student Tutoring Teams), 379
CUDCP (Council of University Directors of Clinical
    Psychology), 122
Cuijpers, P., 510
Culbert, T. P., 71
Culture. *See* Multicultural education
Cumine, V., 39
Cummings, J. A., 169, 216, 217
Cunningham, A. E., 311
Curriculum-based assessment (CBA), 143–144
    advantages, limitations of, 147
    defined, 143
    General Outcome Measurement model of, 144
    mastery measurement, limitations, 144
    models of, 143
    outcome measurement model, 144–146
    school psychology applications of, 146
    Specific Subskill Mastery Measurement model of, 143–144
    See also Academic achievement; Authentic assessment;
        Behavioral assessment; Norm-referenced testing;
        Performance-based assessment; Written language
        assessment
Curtis, J., 81
Curtis, M. J., 116, 361, 363, 476
CWPT (Classwide Peer Tutoring method), 378–379

D

Dahlgren, M., 443
Dalley, M. B ., 178
Daly, E. J., 25, 26, 27, 352
D'Amato, R., 50
Daniel R. R. v. State Board of Education, 298
DARE America Online, 150
DARE program
    advantages *vs.* disadvantages of, 150–151
    creation of, 149
    curriculum of, 149–150
    DARE America parent organization, 149
    mission of, 149
    New DARE program, 150
    parent training, and after-school program, 150
    police officer's role, 149
    teenage smoking, 510
    See also Prevention; Substance abuse
Daro, D., 6, 7

Darwin, Charles, 286
Davidman, L., 338
Davidman, P. T., 338
Davies, M., 357, 358
Davis, L. A., 321
Davis, T. N., 519
Davis, W. E., 174
Davison, G. C., 184, 185
Dawson, H., 94
Dawson, M., 217
DDD (Division on Developmental Disabilities), 319
de Moura Castro, H., 547
DEAL (Dignity through Education and Language
    Communication Centre, Australia), 201
Dean, R. S., 82
Death and bereavement
    bereavement, developmental perspective on, 152–153
    bereavement, very young children, 152
    bereavement process, factors of, 153
    death, developmental perspective on, 129, 152
    depression, 130, 153
    family counseling intervention, 205
    finality of death, 152
    friend's death, 153
    grief responses, 153
    interventions, 154
    parental death, 152–153
    Piaget's cognitive development states, 152
    school psychologist role, 153–154
    sibling death, 153
    tasks to be completed, 153
    See also Crisis intervention; Defense mechanisms;
        Fears; Parenting, parents
deBoer-Ott, S., 204
Deci, E. L., 331
Decoding
    assessment of, 433, 436–437
    defined, 154
    differential diagnosis, 438
    letter-sound relationship, 154
    remedial approach to, 438–439
    See also Reading interventions and strategies
Defense mechanisms
    examples of, 155
    explanation of, 154
    reality interpretations, 154–155
DeGaetano, G., 312
DeKlyen, M., 432
Delong, J. M., 253
Delquadri, J., 94, 378, 379
Deni, J., 254
Denial defense mechanism, 155
Deno, S. L., 143, 144
Denver Developmental Screening Test, 336
Department of Education Organization Act, 577
Depression
    anorexia and, 184
    antidepressant medications, 156
    bipolar disorder, 71, 72, 155–156
    bulimia and, 184
    bullying, 235

causes of, 155
cognitive-behavioral interventions, 97
cognitive therapy, 125
comorbidity of, 155, 156
conduct disorder and, 108, 156
corporal punishment and, 121
death, reaction to, 130, 153
divorce adjustment, 170
explanation of, 155
friendships of children, 211
gender factors, 155, 222
generalized anxiety disorder and, 224
interpersonal theory of, 125
learned helplessness, 283
ODD with, 360
parent, school psychologist collaboration, 374
peer relationships and, 519
psychotherapy, 157
psychotropic medications for, 422
PTSD and, 34
risk factors, 156
in school-age children, 155
school refusal, 485
statistics regarding, 155
suicide risk factor, 131, 157, 549
symptoms, 155, 156
treatment of, 156–157
types of, 155–156
See also Abuse and neglect; Attention deficit hyperactivity
    disorder (ADHD); Bipolar disorder (BD) (childhood
    onset); Bullying and victimization; Comorbidity;
    Conduct disorder (CD); Learned helplessness;
    Psychotherapy; Psychotropic medications; Shyness;
    Theories of human development
Deprivation, defined, 64*table*
DeRuyck, K. A., 159, 283
Descriptive functional behavioral analysis, 215
Dettmer, P., 370, 372
Deutsch, M., 117
Developmental delay, 266, 421
Developmental milestones
    cognitive milestones, 158–159*table,* 159
    fear and, 207
    genetic and environmental factors, 159
    importance of, 157, 159
    language milestones, 159
    physical milestones, 158–159*table,* 159
    sensorimotor stage of development, 498
    social milestones, 158–159*table,* 159
    See also Communication disorders; Early intervention (EA);
        Erikson's stages of psychosocial development; Infant
        assessment; Preschool assessment; Theories of human
        development
Developmental Test of Visual Perception-2, 337
Devries, D., 379
Diagnosis and labeling
    derogatory labels, 162–163
    diagnosis *vs.* label, 160
    DSM-IV-TR, 160–162, 161*table*
    empirically-based behavioral dimensions system, 160
    IDEA diagnostic categories, 160, 162, 162*table*

origins of, 160
Resistance to Intervention paradigm, 162
suspension and, 554
teacher expectations, 163
See also DSM-IV-TR; Individuals With Disabilities Education
    Act (IDEA); Reports (psychological); Special education
*Diagnostic and Statistical manual of Mental Disorders, Fourth
    Edition-Text Revision (DSM-IV-TR,* APA). *See DSM-IV-TR*
*Diagnostic Interview for Children and Adolescents, Version Four
    (DICA-IV),* 274–275
*Diagnostic Interview Schedule for Children, Version Four
    (DISC-IV),* 274
Diana v. *State Board of Education,* 68
Diaz, T., 546
DIBELS (Dynamic Indicators of Basic Early
    Literacy Skills), 164, 386
    See also Academic achievement; Early intervention (EA)
*DICA-IV (Diagnostic Interview for Children and Adolescents,
    Version Four),* 274
Dick-Niederhauser, A., 498, 499
Dietz, W. H., 356
Differential Ability Scales, 400
Differential reinforcement, 63*table*
    See also Behavior; Behavior intervention; Discipline
Dignity through Education and Language Communication
    Centre (DEAL, Australia), 201
DiGuiseppi, C., 585
D'Incau, B., 199
DiPerna, J. C., 334
*DISC-IV (Diagnostic Interview Schedule for
    Children, Version Four),* 274
Discipline
    alternative education program placement,
        167, 168, 199–200
    character education programs, 164
    classroom environment (physical) focus, 166
    contingency contract, 166
    corporal punishment, 166
    correcting misbehavior, 166–167
    dropouts and, 174
    effective classroom management, 165–166
    fair rules and consequences, 166
    functional behavioral assessment, 214–216
    gender factors, 221
    home-school relationship focus, 165
    IDEA and, 215–216, 260
    monitoring behavior, 166
    motivational learning, 165–166
    nonretentive encopresis and, 187–188
    positive behavior supports approach to, 166
    praise and reward techniques, 166
    predictable procedures and routines, 166
    prevention of misbehavior techniques, 165–166
    punishment, limitations of, 166–167
    self-discipline, development of, 164–165
    self-discipline *vs.* correcting behavior, 164
    serious and chronic behavior problems, 167–168
    social and emotional learning, 165
    social and moral problem-solving skills, 164–165, 167
    suspension, expulsion, 166–167
    zero tolerance policies, 167, 235, 582

See also Aggression in schools; Behavior intervention;
    Bullying and victimization; Classroom climate;
    Consultation: behavioral (BC); Corporal punishment
    (CP); Dropouts; Expulsion; Functional behavioral
    assessment; Harassment; Prevention; Social skills;
    Suspension; Violence in schools
DISCOVER (ACT) career assessment program, 80, 81
Discovery learning theory, 285*fig.*
Discriminative stimulus (SD), 62*table*
Dishion, T. J., 107, 108, 324
diSibio, M. P., 578
Displacement defense mechanism, 155
Distance education coursework, 542
Division of School Psychologists (Division 16, APA), 475
    Applying Psychology to the Schools book series, 169
    conferences, 169
    doctoral preparation level, 169, 475
    Evidence-Based Intervention Task Force, 169
    objectives of, 170*table*
    Professional School Psychology journal, 169
    specialty guidelines, 169
    timeline of, 170*table*
    See also American Psychological Association (APA); National
        Association of School Psychologists (NASP); School
        Psychologist
Division on Developmental Disabilities (DDD), 319
Divorce adjustment
    behavior problems, 170, 172
    defined, 170
    degree of disruption factor, 171
    divorce statistics, 170
    family focused intervention, 172, 205
    group therapy intervention, 172
    parental and parenting changes factor, 171
    predivorce family relationships and, 171
    preschoolers and adolescents, 171
    problems caused by, 171
    school-based interventions, 172
    school psychologist role, 172
    social systems factors and, 172
    See also Latchkey children; Parenting, parents; Resilience
        and protective factors; Single-parent families
Dodge, K. A., 18, 107
Doepka, K., 33
Doggert, R. A., 536
Dolan, L. J., 406
Dolezal, Danielle, 67
Doll, B., 458
Domitrovich, C., 508
Donaldson, G. A., 174
Donaldson, S. I., 411
Donnelly, D., 121
Dorsey, M. F., 493
Dorsey, S., 508
*Double Jeopardy: Addressing Gender Equity in Special
    Education* (Russo and Wehmeyer), 222
Down syndrome, 320, 322, 363
    See also Mental retardation
Downs, D. L., 209
Dozois, D. J. A., 161
Drasgow, E., 255, 256

Drew, C. J., 321
Dropouts
    cohort rate calculation formula, 173
    consequences of, 174–175
    dropout rates calculation, 173
    event rate calculation formula, 173
    explusion and, 199
    factors in, 174
    grade retention and, 466–467
    graduation rates, 174
    importance of issue, 173
    inaccurately reported data, 173
    prevention of, 175
    "pushouts" *vs.*, 174
    statistics regarding, 174
    status rate calculation formula, 173
    suspension and, 554
    teen pregnancy, 560
    See also Academic achievement; Ethnicity; Expulsion;
        Gender, gender factors; High school; Race, ethnicity,
        class and gender; Resilience and protective factors;
        Retention; School refusal; Self-concept and efficacy;
        Substance abuse; Suspension
Drotar, D., 574
Dryfoos, J., 213
DSM-IV-TR
    adaptive behavior, mental retardation measurement, 12, 13
    ADHD, 32, 413–414
    adjustment disorder, 16
    anorexia nervosa, 183–184
    Asperger's disorder, 39–40
    autism, 37
    Axes of, 160–161, 161*table,* 176
    binge eating, 184
    bulimia nervosa, 184
    child psychopathology, defined, 413–414
    childhood disintegrative disorder, 41
    communication, consultation facilitation, 176
    conduct disorder, 107, 414
    diagnostic codes focus of, 175, 274
    first, second, third editions of, 175–176
    generalized anxiety disorder, 224
    vs. IDEA, 162
    mental retardation, defined, 12, 318
    multiaxial assessment system, 176
    OCD diagnosis, 358
    ODD diagnosis, 359
    pedophilia defined, 376
    personality assessment, 382
    phonological disorder, 100
    PTSD defined, 392
    reactive attachment disorder, 431
    Rett's disorder, 40–41
    selective mutism, 489
    separation anxiety, 498
    somatoform disorders, 520, 521
    stuttering, fluency disorder, 100
    subjectivity of, 161
    See also Individuals With Disabilities Education Act (IDEA)
Dsylexia and the Life Course, 179, 180
Dubas, J. S., 424

DuBois, D. L., 325
Dubowitz, H., 4
Dudley, B., 377
Due process
  appeals, 178
  avoidance strategies, 178
  defined, 177
  mediation process of, 177
  participants in, 177
  school psychologist role, 178
  school systems application of, 177
  stages of, 177–178
  See also Confidentiality; Ethical issues in school
    psychology; Individuals With Disabilities Education
    Act (IDEA); Special education
Duff, A., 295
Dukes, R. I., 151
Dulcan, M., 274
Dunbar, S., 109
Dunlap, G., 382
Dunn, K., 295
Dunn, L. M., 401
Dunn, R., 295
DuPaul, G. J., 94
Dupuis, V. L., 240, 241
Duration recording technique, of classroom
    management, 91
Durlak, J., 406
Dusek, J. B., 329
Dusenbury, L., 546
Duskin Feldman, R., 491
Dweck, C. S., 333
Dyck, N., 370, 372
Dye, G. A., 372
Dynamic Indicators of Basic Early Literacy
    Skills (DIBELS), 386
  See also DIBELS
Dyslexia
  academic interventions, 179–180
  genetic factors, 179
  lifespan display of, 179
  neurological origins of, 179
  phonological disorders and, 179
  symptoms of, 178–179
  See also Reading interventions and strategies
Dysthemic disorder, 155, 156
Dzuiba-Leatherman, J., 7
D'Zurilla, T. J., 408

E
EA. *See* Early intervention
Eagle, J., 249
EAHCA (Education of All Handicapped Children
    Act), 259, 261, 265
Early Head Start program, 237, 403
Early intervention (EA)
  advantages *vs.* disadvantages of, 182–183
  benefits of, 181
  cultural factors, 181–182
  developmental focus of, 182
  effectiveness of, 182

federal legislation regarding, 181
multidisciplinary approach of, 181
parental/family context, 181–182
research trends regarding, 456–457
service provision systems of, 182
See also Autism spectrum disorders; Head Start
Eating disorders
  anorexia nervosa, 183–184
  binge eating, 184
  bulimia nervosa, 184
  child abuse and neglect factors, 185
  divorce adjustment, 170
  etiological factors, 184–185
  explanation of, 183
  family context, 185
  gender factors, 185, 222
  interventions, 185–186
  obesity risk factor, 356
  parent, school psychologist collaboration, 374
  personality factors, 185
  school psychologist role, 185–186
  See also Etiology; Parenting, parents; Prevention; Puberty
Ebbinghaus, H., 284, 285*fig.*
Eberlein, L., 193
Echolalia, 186
Eckstrom, R. B., 174
Ecological module of Component Model of Reading
  classroom environment, 436, 442
  constituents of, 433*table*
  dialect, 436, 442
  English as second language, 436, 442
  home environment, culture, parental involvement,
    435–436, 441–442
  peer influence, 436
  remedial approach, 441–442
Ecological risk and resiliency model, of single-parent
    families, 505–506
Ecstasy drug use, 545
Edgar, E., 174
Educate America Act, 480
Education for All Handicapped Children Act (EAHCA),
    162, 177, 259, 261, 265, 298, 303, 342, 404, 475
  See also Individualized education plan meeting; Individuals
    With Disabilities Education Act (IDEA); Special
    education
Education outcomes, of homeschooling, 247
Educational Testing Service (ETS), 80
Edward, J., 103
Edwards, R. P., 536
EEOA (Equal Educational Opportunities Act), 479
Effect size
  defined, 187
  measures of association, 187, 188
  standardized mean difference, 187–188
  See also Behavior intervention; Research in school
    psychology
Efthim, H. E., 305
Ego integrity concept, of psychosocial development, 190
Egocentrism
  self-other relations differentiating error, 187
  vs. selfishness, 187

Ehly, S. W., 478
Ehrhardt, K. E., 25
Ehrhardt-Padgett, G. N., 478
Ehri, L. C., 385
Eisner, E. W., 242
Eitel, P., 378
Ekeberg, O., 549
Elementary and Secondary Education Act (ESEA), 479, 577
Elkind, D., 187
Elliott, S., 54
Elliott, S. N., 334, 352, 473
Ellis, A., 96
Ellis, Albert, 125
Emerson, Ralph Waldo, 210
Emotional neglect, 4
Empowerment program evaluation model, 411
Encopresis
   defined, 187
   intentional, nonretentive type, 187–188
   interventions, 188
   social and behavioral problems with, 187
   See also DSM-IV-TR; Enuresis
Endriga, M. C., 432
Engaged learning time. *See* Time on task
Engelmann, Siegfried, 481
English as a second language (ESL), 436, 442, 531
Ennett, S. T., 151
Enuresis
   defined, 188
   gender factors, 188
   interventions, 188–189
   primary *vs.* secondary enuresis, 188
   psychotropic medications for, 421, 422
   See also DSM-IV-TR; Encopresis
EO (establishing operation), 62*table*
EPPP (Examination for the Professional
   Practice of Psychology), 301
Epstein, J. L., 249, 253, 370
Epstein, L. H., 356
Epstein, M. H., 252
Epstein, S. H., 251
Equal Educational Opportunities Act (EEOA), 479
Erb, T. O., 244
Erbacher, T. A., 122
Erchul, W. P., 115, 117, 169
Erikson, Erik, 189, 564
Erikson's stages of psychosocial development
   stage 1: oral-sensory; trust *vs.* distrust, 189
   stage 2: muscular-anal; autonomy *vs.* doubt, 189
   stage 3: locomotor-genetal; initiative *vs.* guilt, 189–190
   stage 4: latency; industry *vs.* inferiority, 190
   stage 5: puberty and adolescence; identity *vs.*
      role confusion, 190
   stage 6: young adulthood; intimacy *vs.* isolation, 190
   stage 7: adulthood; generativity *vs.* stagnation, 190
   stage 8: maturity; ego integrity *vs.* despair, 190
Eron, L. C., 311
Ervin, R. A., 25, 94
Escape
   negative reinforcement, 63*table*
   See also Behavior; Behavior intervention

ESEA (Elementary and Secondary Education Act), 479, 577
ESL. *See* English as a second language
Espelage, D. L., 235
Esquivel, G., 140
Establishing operation (EO), 62*table*
Ethical issues in school psychology
   APA's code of, 191–192
   applied professional ethics, defined, 191
   confidentiality, 109–110, 194
   consultation conflicts, 195
   ethical dilemmas, 193
   ethics, defined, 191
   ethics training, 192–193
   evidence-based interventions, 194
   federal and state laws and, 192
   informed consent, 194
   minimize harm, 194–195
   vs. morality, 191
   NASP's code of, 191, 192
   parental consent, 194
   privacy issue, 193–194
   problem-solving models, 193
   psychological research, 454
   sociometric assessment and, 519
   student psychological report, 446
   supervision of trainees issues, 195
   unethical conduct, 195
   welfare of the student issue, 194
   See also Confidentiality; Informed consent
Ethnicity
   ability grouping and, 3
   counseling, multicultural focus in, 124
   vs. culture, 138
   dropout rates, 174
   eating disorders and, 184
   examiner and examinee cross-cultural
      dynamics, 138–139
   gang membership, 220
   Head Start statistics, 238
   No Child Left Behind Act of 2001, 350–351
   parenting beliefs, values, 373
   substance abuse, 545
   suicide, 548–549
   suspension discrimination and, 554
   teacher-student relationships, 559
   teen pregnancy, 560
   zero tolerance policies, 601, 602
   See also Cross-cultural assessment; Cross-cultural
      consultation; Multicultural education; Race,
      ethnicity, class and gender
Etiology
   ADHD example, 196
   defined, 196
   See also Diagnosis and labeling
ETS. *See* Educational Testing Service
European Americans
   single-parent families, 505
   teen pregnancy, 560
Evaluation. *See* Reports (psychological)
Evans, M. A., 500
Event dropout rate calculation formula, 173

Everything You Need to Know About Peer Pressure (Feller), 378–379
Evidence-Based Intervention Task Force (APA, Division 16), 169
Evidence-based interventions (EBIs)
  advantages *vs.* disadvantages of, 198–199
  defined, 196
  evaluation criteria, 196, 197, 198
  parent training programs, 368
  Procedural and Coding Manual for, 197–198
  rationale, history of, 196–197
  school psychology relevance of, 196, 197, 198–199
  school *vs.* clinical settings, 197
  scientist-practitioner model, 197
  See also Comorbidity; Effect size; Research in school psychology
Examination for the Professional Practice of Psychology (EPPP), 301
Experimental functional behavioral analysis, 215
Experimental program evaluation model, 410–411
Experimentation learning method, 284–285, 285*fig.*
Expressive Vocabulary Test, 401
Expulsion
  alternative education programs, 199–200
  of disabled students, 526
  drop out rates and, 199
  gender factors, 199
  reasons for, 199
  risk factors, 199
  serious rules violation, 199
  zero tolerance policies, 199, 601–602
  See also Discipline; Due process; Individualized education plan; Manifestation determination; Special education; Suspension; Violence in schools
Extinction and recovery. *See* Applied behavior analysis (ABA); Behavior
Extinction reductive technique, 65*table*
Extrinsic motivation, 331
Eyberg, S. M., 368
Eysenck, H., 197

F

FAAB (Functional Assessment of Academic Behavior), (Ysseldyke and Christenson), 51–52
Face validity. *See* Validity
FACES (Family and Child Experiences Survey, Head Start), 238
Facilitated communication (FC)
  authorship issues, 202–203
  criticism of, 202–203
  explanation of, 201
  global apraxia, 201
  introduction of, 201–202
  scientific validation issues, 202
  See also Autism spectrum disorders; Communication disorders; Mental retardation
Fade-out effect, Head Start, 238, 239
Fading teaching procedure, 63*table*, 497
  See also Behavior; Behavior intervention
Fagan, T., 515
Fagan, T. K., 81, 82, 347, 404, 475
Fairbanks, L. D., 163

Family, families. *See* Family counseling; Parenting, parents; Single-parent families
Family and Child Experiences Survey (FACES, Head Start), 238
Family counseling
  cognitive-behavioral family therapy, 206
  confidentiality issues, 207
  explanation of, 204
  vs. individual counseling, 206
  multisystemic family therapy, 205, 206
  reasons for seeking, 205
  school psychologist role in, 206–207
  settings for, 205
  solution-focused therapy, 206
  strategic family therapy, 205–206
  structural family therapy, 205
  systems theory focus, 204–205
  See also Behavior intervention; Counseling; Divorce adjustment; Parenting, parents; Single-parent families
Family Educational Rights and Privacy Act (FERPA), 446
  See also Americans with Disabilities Act (ADA); Individuals With Disabilities Education Act (IDEA); Section 504, of the Rehabilitation Act of 1973; U.S. Department of Education
Family-focused therapy, 72
Family systems theory
  as cognitive counseling approach, 125
  selective mutism, 490
  separation anxiety, 499
Fantuzzo, J., 238
FAPE (free and appropriate public education),
  for disabled students, 255, 259, 261, 298, 321
  preschoolers, 396, 404
Farber, J. M., 494
Farley, S. E., 299
Farris, E., 601
FAS. *See* Fetal alcohol syndrome
Fashola, O. S., 483
Favazza, A., 406
Favell, J. E., 492
FBA. *See* Functional behavioral assessment
FC. *See* Facilitated communication
FCT (functional communication training), 61, 64*table*
Fear Survey Schedule for Children-Revised (FSSC-R), 207
Fearful shyness, 499–500, 501
Fears
  anxiety hierarchy intervention, 208
  cultural factors, 207
  developmental patterns of, 207
  empirical studies of, 207
  phobias and, 207–208
  relaxation technique intervention, 208
  systemic desensitization intervention, 208
  See also Behavior intervention; Bullying and victimization; Intervention; Posttraumatic stress disorder (PTSD); Resilience and protective factors; School refusal
Federal Bureau of Investigation, 581
Fehrmann, P. G., 311
Fein, R., 127, 584
Fein, R. A., 582

Feller, Robyn, 377–378
Felner, R., 406
Ferguson, C. J., 313
FERPA (Family Educational Rights and Privacy Act). *See*
    Americans with Disabilities Act (ADA); Individuals With
    Disabilities Education Act (IDEA); Section 504, of the
    Rehabilitation Act of 1973; U.S. Department of Education
Ferron, J. M., 554, 555
Ferster, C., 568
Festinger, L., 98
Fetal alcohol syndrome (FAS)
    alcohol-related birth defects, 209
    alcohol-related neurodevelopmental disorder, 209
    fetal alcohol effect, 209
    prevalence of, 209
    symptoms, 209
    See also Substance abuse
Fetterman, D., 411
Field trials program evaluation model, 410–411
Findley, D. B., 572
Findling, R. L., 72
Fine, E. M., 420
Fine, S., 211
Finger, M., 109
Fink, B., 587
Finkelhor, D., 3, 4, 7
Finn, P. J., 430
Fisch, S. M., 311
Fischer, M., 523
Fisher, J. O., 355, 356
Fisher, P., 274
Fisk, J. L., 573
Fister, S., 94
Fixed-interval (FI) reinforcement schedule, 470, 471
Fixed-ratio (FR) schedule of reinforcement, 470, 471
Flament, M. F., 357, 358
Flanagan, D. P., 137
Flanagan, R., 20, 21
Flannery-Schroeder, E. C., 224
Flatter, C. H., 282
Flavell, J. H., 315
Fleischmann, R. L., 358
Fleischner, J. E., 307
Fleming, S, 152
Fleweling, R. L., 151
Flojo, J. R., 310
Fluency disorder, 100
Flugum, K. R., 535
Fluid intelligence, 209
    See also Intelligence
Foley, R. M., 251, 252
Foorman, B., 439
Foote, R. C., 368
Fopiano, J. E., 249
Ford, L., 209
Fordham, S., 430
Forehand, R. L., 361, 368, 508
Forensic interview, 273
Forman, S. G., 96, 98
Formative evaluation, 209
    See also Grades; Retention; Summative evaluation

Forness, S. R., 299
Forward chaining instructional procedure, 62*table*
Fosier, N., 189
Fossey, R., 173
Foudin, L. L., 209
Fournier, C. J., 489
Fox, J. D., 163
Fox, R., 587
Fragile X syndrome (FXS)
    gender factors, 210
    mental retardation gene, 209–210
    symptoms, 210
Francis, J. M., 296
Francke, U., 40
Frank, J. D., 126
Franz, C., 402
Fraser, B. J., 89
Frede, E. C., 403
Free and appropriate public education (FAPE) for
        disabled students, 255, 259, 261, 298, 321, 522
    preschoolers, 396, 404
Freedman, M., 324
Freeland, J. T., 352
Freeman, K. E., 334
Freer, P., 113
Freiberg, H. J., 89
Frequency count technique, of classroom observation, 91
Fretz, B., 123, 124
Freud, Sigmund
    defense mechanisms, 155
    psychoanalytic model of human development
            theory, 563–564
    psychosocial development, 189
Frey, B., 530
Frick, P. J., 196, 360
Friedman, M. A., 356
Friendships
    characteristics of, 210
    defined, 210
    developmental course of, 211–212
    importance of, 210–211
    lack of friends, effect of, 210–211
    poor quality friendship development, 211
    school psychologist role, 212
    shyness, 500
    vs. social skills, 210
    social skills training, 212
    vs. social status, peer reputation, 210
    See also Aggression in schools; Cooperative learning; Middle
            School; Peers, peer pressure; Prevention; Retention;
            Shyness; Single-parent families; Social skills
Friman, P. C., 568, 569, 570
Frisbie, D., 109
Frisby, C. L., 296
Fristad, M. A., 153
Froese, A., 550
FSS. *See* Full-Service Schools (FSS)
FSSC-R (Fear Survey Schedule for Children-Revised), 207
Fuchs, D., 94, 144, 344, 379, 462, 537
Fuchs, L., 94
Fuchs, L. S., 143, 344, 379, 537

Fuerst, D. R., 573
Fugate, M., 88
Full-Service Schools (FSS)
   case managers, 213
   components of, 213
   disabled student needs, special education
        services, 213–214
   evaluation of, 213
   high-risk environment focus, 212
   implementation challenges, 213
   legal, ethical issues, 213
   physical, emotional, social, academic focuses, 212–213
   political controversy, 213
   school psychologist role, 214
   See also School reform
Function. *See* Functional behavioral assessment
Function-based treatment, 61*table*
Functional Assessment of Academic Behavior (FAAB),
   (Ysseldyke and Christenson), 51–52
Functional behavioral analysis, 61*table*
   See also Applied behavior analysis (ABA); Behavior
        intervention
Functional behavioral assessment (FBA), 25–27,
        49, 52, 57–58, 59, 61*table*
   descriptive analysis, 215
   discipline of students with disabilities, 214–216, 555
   educational implications, 215–216
   experimental analysis, 215
   functions of behavior, 214–215
   indirect assessment, 215
   manifestation determination and, 304
   positive, negative reinforcement, 214–215
   positive behavior support and, 390–391
   self-injurious behavior, 493–494
   steps in, 215
   See also Applied behavior analysis (ABA); Behavioral
        assessment; Expulsion; Individuals With Disabilities
        Education Act (IDEA); Manifestation determination;
        Suspension
Functional communication training (FCT), 61, 64*table*
Functional relationship, 61*table*
Fuqua, R. W., 64*table*
Furlong, M. J., 236, 583
Futrell, M. K., 102, 103, 104
Futures Conference
   long-term goal strategies, 216
   mission of, 216
   NASP and, 347
   sponsors of, 216
   themes of, 216
FXS. *See* Fragile X syndrome

G
Gable, R. A., 382
GAD. *See* Generalized anxiety disorder
Gaffney, J., 316
Gaichas, A. M., 572
Galloway, J., 408
Gallup Organization, 581
Galton, Sir Francis, 123, 474
Gamoran, A., 1, 2, 3

Gangs
   characteristics of, 219–220
   community risk factors, 220
   defined, 219
   ethnicity factors, 219
   family risk factors, 220
   gender factors, 219
   individual, peer risk factors, 220
   latchkey children, 281
   peer pressure, 379
   risk factors, 219–220
   violent behavior, 220
   See also Aggression in schools; Bullying and victimization;
        Ethnicity; Friendships; Gender, gender factors; High
        school; Middle school; Peers, peer pressure; Race,
        ethnicity, class and gender; Substance abuse; Violence
        in schools
Gansle, K. A., 161
Gardner, H., 268
Garfinkel, B. D., 550
Gartner, S., 260
GAS. *See* Goal Attainment Scaling
GAS (general adaptation syndrome), 69
Gates-McGinitie tests, 437
Gaudin, J., 4
Gay, A. S., 308
Gay, G., 342
Geary, D., 291
Gedye, A., 493
Geiger, B., 395
Geisert, P. G., 102, 103, 104
Geller, B., 72
Gelso, C., 123, 124
Gender, gender factors
   ADHD, 33
   aggression in school, 18, 221, 222
   Asperger's disorder, 39
   autism, 37
   bipolar disorder, 71
   bullying, 73, 222
   causes of, 357
   conduct disorder, 107–108
   cultural factors and, 221
   culture and social construct through language, 430
   depression, 155, 222
   disabilities and, 222
   divorce adjustment, 171, 507
   early high school, 241, 242
   eating disorders, 184, 185, 222
   enuresis, 188
   expulsion and, 199
   fragile X syndrome, 210
   gang membership, 219
   gender *vs.* gender equity, 221
   neurobehavioral disorder, 357
   OCD, 357
   ODD, 359
   puberty, 423–425
   reading difficulties, 435
   retention, 221, 465
   Rhett's disorder, 40

school failure and, 221–222
school success and, 221
sexual harassment, 234, 235*table*
social expectations, 221, 222, 430
stuttering, 543
substance abuse, 545
suicide, 548–549
teacher expectations, 221
teacher praise, 580
teenage smoking, 509
TV violence, school aggression, 312
See also Aggression in schools; Attention deficit
    hyperactivity disorder (ADHD); Bullying and
    victimization; Depression; Dropouts; Eating disorders;
    Ethnicity; Gangs; Harassment; Puberty; Race, ethnicity,
    class and gender; Social skills
General adaptation syndrome (GAS), 69
Generalization, 62*table*, 222
    maintenance generalization, 222
    multiple examples exposure, 223
    natural condition simulation, 223
    reinforcement, 223
    response generalization, 222
    stimulus generalization, 222
    student self-instruction, 223
    transfer of training effects, 222
    undesirable generalizations, 223
    See also Learning; Research in school psychology; Single-
        case experimental design
Generalized anxiety disorder (GAD)
    cognitive behavior therapy, 224–225
    comorbidity of, 224
    "Copy Cat" intervention program, 225
    interventions, 224–225
    learning obstructed by, 223–224
    pharmacological interventions, 224
    prevalence of, 224
    prevention program, 224
    school psychologist role, 224–225
    school refusal, 485
    symptoms, 223–224
    threat perception distortions, 224
    See also Counseling; DSM-IV-TR; Psychopathology in
        children; Separation anxiety (SA) disorder
Generativity concept, of psychosocial development, 190
Genetic factors
    developmental milestones and, 159
    dyslexia, 179
Genetic mental retardations, 319*table*
Gentile, J. R., 305, 306
Gersten, R., 310
Gesell, Arnold, 474, 562–563
Gestalt psychology, 285*fig.*, 286
Gettinger, M., 483
Ghaemi, S. N., 72
Gifted students
    debate regarding, 227
    defined, 225
    identification guidelines, 226
    prevalence of, 226
    school psychologist role, 226–227

See also Ability grouping; Academic achievement;
    Intelligence; Learning
Gil-Hernandez, D., 325
Gilberton, D., 529
Gillberg, C., 37, 40, 41
Gilligan, T. D., 273
Gillingham, A., 442
Ginsburg-Block, M., 379
Giroux, B., 107
Glaser, R., 134
Glass, G., 126
Global apraxia, 201
Glutting, J. J., 295
Goal Attainment Scaling (GAS)
    expected levels of progress, 228
    explanation of, 227–228, 228*fig.*
    multidisciplinary team approach, 229
    operationally defined goals, 228
    See also Behavior intervention; Criterion-referenced
        assessment
Goals 2000: Educate America Act, 480
Goddard, P., 550
Goertz, M. E., 174
Golan, M., 356
Gold, M., 558
Goldfield, G. S., 356
Goldfried, M. R., 408
Goldman-Fristoe Test of Articulation-2, 100
Goldstein, A., 54
Goldstein, A. B., 19
Goldstein, S., 596
Gonzalez, M., 72
Good, T., 580
The Good Behavior Game (Barrish, et. al.), 53
Goodlad, J. I., 242
Goodman, A. H., 429
Goodman, G., 324
Goodman, J., 95
Goodman, K., 439
Goodman, W., 357
Goodman, W. K., 358
Gordon, M., 33
Gore, P. A., Jr., 81
Gorin, S., 216, 217, 346, 347
The Gospel According to St. Matthew, 434
Gottfried, A. E., 334
Gough, D. A., 585
GPAs (grade point averages), 231
Graber, J. A., 424
Grabowecky, M., 30
Grade equivalent scores
    achievement test application, 229
    interpretation guidelines, 229
    norm-referenced, developmental scores, 229
    See also Academic achievement; Intelligence;
        Percentile ranks; Stanines
Grade point averages (GPAs), 231
Grade retention, dropouts and, 174
Grades
    academic placement, 230
    for advanced placement courses, 230

college level credit value, 230–231
grade point average, 230
quality of work, progress made, 230
10-point number/letter system, 230
See also Ability grouping; Academic achievement;
    Criterion-referenced assessment; Retention
Graduate Record Examination (GRE), 9
Graham, J. R., 517
Graham, S., 529, 587, 588, 589
Grant, C. A., 338, 339–342, 341*table*
GRE (Graduate Record Examination), 9
Greathouse, S., 252
Gredler, G. R., 404
Green, B. L., 393
Green, G., 39
Green, J., 53
Green, L. F., 296
Green, T. D., 342
Greenberg, M., 407, 508
Greenberg, M. T., 432
Greenfield, D. B., 238, 239, 240
Greenwald, E. A., 587
Greenwood, C. R., 94, 378, 379, 575
Greer v. Rome, 299
Gregg, N., 596, 599
Gregorc, A. F., 295, 539
Gregorc Style Delineator, personality learning style
    measure, 295, 539
Greif, J. L., 236
Gresham, F., 54
Gresham, F. K., 161, 162
Gresham, F. M., 55–56, 352
Grier, J. E. C., 81, 362, 476
Griesinger, T., 87
Grigorenko, E. L., 270, 272
Grimm, J., 360
Groholt, B., 549
Gronlund, N., 8
Gronlund, N. E., 134
Grooved Pegboard measure, 337
Grossman, J. B., 324
Grotpeter, J. K., 18
Gruber, C. P., 517
Gu, K., 406
Guadalupe v. *Tempe Elementary School District No. 3.,* 68
Guide to Recovery, 184
Guilford, J. P, 268
Gulley, S., 321
Gun-Free Schools Act of 1994, 582, 601
Guo, B., 551
Guralnick, M. J., 183
Gutkin, T. B., 113, 116, 328

H
Habit reversal treatment, 64*table*
Habituation reductive technique, 65*table*
Haeberli, F., 490
Haertel, E., 10–11
Hale, C., 377
Hale, G. A., 540
Hale, N. M., 87

Hall, G. Stanley, 474, 563
Hall, M., 53
Hall, R., 53
Hall, R. V., 94
Hallahan, D. P., 303
Halo effect, 233
    See also Bias in testing; Class; Ethnicity; Gender, gender
        factors; Race, ethnicity, class and gender; Reliability
Hamel, S., 105
Hammer, A. L., 295
Hammill, D., 596
Hamre, B., 559
Hanaway, L. K., 312
The Handbook of School Psychology-Third Edition, 457
Handicapped Children's Protection Act, 261
Handorsen, T., 549
Hanson, D., 580
Hanson, K., 360
Hanson, N. J., 141
Harassment
    bullying, 233, 234, 235
    bystander effect concept, 236
    effects of, 234–235
    gender factors, 234, 235*table,* 236*table*
    hostile environment harassment, 234
    prevalence of, 234
    prevention and intervention, 235–236
    quid pro quo harassment, 234
    sexual harassment, 233–234, 235
    types of, 234, 235*table,* 236*table*
    victimization, power imbalance, 233
    See also Bullying and victimization; Class; Ethnicity;
        Gender, gender factors; Multicultural education; Race,
        ethnicity, class and gender
Hardin, M. T., 358
Hardman, M. L., 321
Hardware, for computer technology applications, 102–103
Hare, V. C., 8
Harold, W., 245
Harper, G. F., 94, 379
Harrington-O'Shea Career Decision-Making
    System-Revised (CDM-R), 80
Harris, A. H., 344
Harris, K. R., 587, 588
Harrison, K. A., 46
Harrison, P. L., 1, 3, 216, 217
Harrison, R. J., 46
Harstall, C., 551
Hartlage, L. C., 349
Hartshorne, T. S., 192, 193, 259, 328, 577
Hartup, W. W., 211, 212
Hartwig, J., 599
Harvey, D., 362
Harvey, J. M., 272
Harvey, V. W., 554
Hatzishristou, C., 478
Hawken, L. S., 571
Hawkins, J. D., 546
Hawkins, W., 97
Hawley, K., 197
Haye, K. M., 358

Haynes, N. M., 370, 372
Haynie, D. L., 378
Head Start
   creation of, 237
   definitions regarding, 237
   demographics, families served, 237–238
   Early Head Start program, 237, 403
   eligibility requirements, 237
   "fade-out" effect, 238, 239
   Family and Child Experiences Survey
      (FACES), 238
   learning disabled children, 239–240
   preschool assessment, 396
   preschool development, 403
   program goals, 238
   research and evaluation, 238–239
   school psychologist role, 239–240
   speech or language impaired children, 240
   See also Early intervention (EA); Learning; Preschoolers;
      Resilience and protective factors; U.S. Department of
      Education
Health Maintenance Organizations. *See* HMOs
Hearing disorders, 101
Hearing impairment. *See* Otitis media
Heaviside, S., 601
Heeter, A., 84
Helping the Noncompliant Child (McMahon &
   Forehand) parent training program, 368
Hemp, R., 321
Henderson, E. H., 527, 528*table*
Henderson, K., 234
Henin, A., 224
Henley, A. M., 94
Heppner, P. P., 408
Herr, L. M., 428
Herra, C., 324
Herrera, G. C., 381, 504
Herring, R., 80
Herzog, E., 221
Hess, R., 140
Hess, R. S., 174
Hettich, P. I., 539
Heward, W., 47
Hewes, G. M., 242, 480
Hextall, I., 90
Hieronymus, A., 109
High school
   1600s, 240–241
   1700s-1800s, 241
   1900s, 241–242
   ability groupings, 241
   curriculum development, 241–243
   history of, 240–242
   National Education Association, 241
   No Child Left Behind initiative, 242
   reform goals, 242
   school psychologist role, 243–244
   special education, 243
   See also Career assessment; Dropouts
High stakes tests. *See* Bias in testing; Norm-referenced
   testing; Outcomes-based assessment

Hildreth, Gertrude, 475
Hill, C. L., 412
Hillocks, G., 587
Hillyard, S. A., 29
Hintze, J. M., 146
Hirschstein, M., 75
Hispanic Americans
   bias in testing of, 68
   eating disorders, 184
   gang membership, 220
   Head Start, 238
   obesity rates, 355
   retention rates, 465
   single-parent families, 505
   substance abuse, 545
   teen pregnancy, 560
   teen smoking, 509
   See also Class; Cross-cultural assessment;
      Cross-cultural consultation; Ethnicity; Gender, gender
      factors; Multicultural education; Race, ethnicity, class
      and gender
HIV/AIDS
   adolescent at-risk behaviors, 245
   prevalence of, 244–245
   primary prevention of, 245
   retrovirus, explained, 244
   teen pregnancy, 561
   transmission methods, 244
   See also Confidentiality; Death and bereavement;
      Resilience and protective factors
HMOs, 197
Hodapp, A. F., 510
Hodapp, J. B., 510
Hoff, K. E., 33, 497
Hohn, R., 98, 289
Holistic *vs.* analytic cognitive style, 294
Holland, J. L., 80
Holmes, C. T., 466
Holt, J., 53
Holton, J., 241
Holubec, E., 118
Home-school collaboration
   approach, attitude, atmosphere, action elements of, 251
   barriers to, 250
   benefits of, 250
   communication focus, 250
   community collaboration focus, 250
   decision making focus, 250
   ecological system theory and, 250
   education reform efforts and, 249
   home environment focus, 250
   Learning at home focus, 250
   No Child Left Behind policies of, 249
   school psychologist role, 250–251
   volunteering focus, 250
   See also Homework; Latchkey children;
      School-home notes; Single-parent families
Home School Legal Defense Association, 245
Homelessness
   McKiney-Veto Homeless Assistance Act, 249
   prevalence of, 248

vs. runaways *vs.* throwaways, 248
school, education services for, 248–249
transitionally homelessness, 248
See also Dropouts; Homework; School reform
Homeschooling
advantages of, 246
affective outcomes, 247
disadvantages of, 246
education outcomes, 247
prevalence of, 245–246
social outcomes, 247
trends in, 246
See also Career assessment; Dropouts
Homework
academic achievement and, 252
advantages *vs.* disadvantages of, 252
after school homework programs, 253
defined, 251
interventions, 252–253
latchkey children, 281
parental involvement, 251–253
purposes of, 251
school psychologist role, 253–254
See also Academic achievement; Grades; Learning;
    Motivation; School-home notes; Study skills
Hood, J., 550
Hook, C. L., 94
Hooper, S. R., 348, 573, 574
Hoover, H., 109
Hoover-Dempsey, K. V., 250, 253
Horn, J. L., 269
Horner, R. H., 26
Horton, C. B., 295
Hoskyn, M., 293
Hostile environment harassment, 234
How to Study for and Take College Tests (Loulou), 542
Howard, A. M., 212
Howard, L., 52
Howe, D., 432
Howell, K. W., 382
Hrduda, L. A., 334
Huberty, T. J., 301
Huefner, D. S., 256
Huerta-Macias, A., 138
Huesmann, L. R., 311
Hughes, C. M., 318
Hughes, III, P., 431
Hughes, J. M., 184
Hughes, M. T., 523
Human immunodeficiency virus (HIV). *See* HIV/AIDS
Humanistic theory of psychotherapy, 418
Hummel, D. L., 109
Humphries, T., 377
Hunley, S., 81, 362, 476
Hunt, G. H., 200
Huston, A. C., 310, 311
Hyman, I. A., 120–122
Hynd, G. W., 348
Hypnosis
defined, 254
education applications of, 254

myths regarding, 254
See also Ethical issues in school
    psychology; Psychotherapy
Hypochondriasis, 521
Hypomania. *See* Bipolar disorder (BD) (childhood onset)
Hyyon P., 438

I

ICD (International Classification of Diseases,
    WHO), 176
IDEA. *See* Individuals With Disabilities Education Act
Identity concept, of psychosocial development, 190
IEP (Individualized Education Program), 84
IFSP (Individualized Family Service Plan), 84
Ilg, Frances, 563
Illinois Test of Psycholinguistic Abilities-2, 596
Imagery procedures, cognitive-behavioral modification, 96
Imitation behavior, 64*table*
    See also Behavior; Theories of human development
Impact of Head Start on Children, Families and Communities:
    Head Start Synthesis Project (U.S. Dept. of Health and
        Human Services), 238
Impartial due process. *See* Due process
Impulse control
    biofeedback used in, 71
    divorce adjustment, 170
Impulsivity. *See* Attention deficit hyperactivity disorder
    (ADHD); Time on task
Incredible Years Parents Training Series (Webster-Stratton &
    Reid) parent training program, 369
Indicators of School Crime and Safety (U.S. Department of
    Education), 582
Indirect functional behavioral analysis, 215
Individual peer tutoring, 94–95
Individualistic learning, 117
Individualized Education Plan (IEP), 261
    accountability, 256
    annual goals focus, 523
    behavior intervention plan (BIP) and, 257
    children with cerebral palsy, 84
    disabled student disciple and, 303–305, 555
    free appropriate public education (FAPE) for disabled
        students, 255, 259, 298, 321, 396, 404
    IDEA and, 255–257, 259–260, 261, 522–523
    least restrictive environment plan and, 298
    legal challenges to, 260
    mainstreaming and, 303
    motor assessment, 337
    multidisciplinary teams, 342–343, 522–523
    parental involvement, 255–257, 522–523
    program strengths, 256
    program weaknesses, 256–257
    school psychologist role, 257
    special disability factors, 255
    support services, 523
    team members, 255–256
    traumatic brain injury and, 574
    See also Accommodation; Individualized Education Plan
        meeting; Individuals With Disabilities Education Act
        (IDEA); Program evaluation; Resource rooms; Special
        education

Individualized Education Plan meeting
documentation, 258
evaluation, 258
IEP team, 258
parental involvement, 258
processes in, 258
school psychologist role, 258
special education services, 257–258
See also Individualized Education Plan (IEP); Individuals
With Disabilities Education Act (IDEA); Least restrictive
environment; Multidisciplinary teams (MDTs); Special
education
Individualized Family Service Plan (IFSP), 84
Individuals With Disabilities Education Act (IDEA), 342
ADHD and, 33
assessment, 524, 538
autism and, 42
behavior interventions, 49
Child Find component, 259
children with cancer, 79
components of, 259
conclusions regarding, 260, 262
diagnosis, label using, 160, 162
disability categories, 260, 522
discipline of disabled students, 214–216, 260, 303–305, 555
DSM-IV-TR and, 162, 176
early intervention focus, 181
expelled students and, 168, 526
free appropriate public education, 259
functional behavioral assessment, 59, 214–216
fund allocation, 259
generalized anxiety disorder, 224
historic timeline of, 261, 475
impartial due process hearing, 177
inclusion *vs.* inclusive education, 525
Individualized Education Plan (IEP) and, 255–257, 259–260
least restrictive environment, 259, 299, 524, 525
mainstreaming and, 303
mediation process, 177
mental retardation, defined, 318
mental retardation services, 319, 321
multidisciplinary teams, 343
NASP and, 346
nondiscriminatory evaluation, 259
personality assessment and, 381, 382, 383
positive behavior support intervention, 392
preschool assessment, 396, 404
procedural safeguards, 524
projective testing, 412
reauthorization of, 260
Section 504, Rehabilitation Act of 1973, 486–487
seizure disorders, 489
Special Education Diagnostic Categories, 162*table*
state responsibility for education, 259, 260, 524
subjectivity of, 162
zero reject policy, 259
See also Diagnosis and labeling; Due process;
Individualized Education Plan (IEP); Individualized
Education Plan meeting; Least restrictive
environment; Multidisciplinary teams (MDTs);
Special education

Individuals With Disabilities Education Act (IDEA),
disability categories-Part B, 522
autism, 264*table*
category criteria, 264*table*
deaf-blindness, 262
deafness, 262
emotional disturbance, 263
hearing impairment, 263
mental retardation, 263
multiple disabilities, 263
orthopedic impairment, 263
other health impairment, 263
specific learning disability, 263
speech or language impairment, 263
traumatic brain injury, 263, 265
visual impairment, including blindness, 265
zero reject policy, 262
See also Diagnosis and labeling; Individuals With
Disabilities Education Act (IDEA); Learning disabilities;
Mental retardation; Psychopathology in children;
Traumatic brain injury
Industry concept, of psychosocial development, 190
Infant assessment
defined, 265
developmental delay concept, 266
federal legislation, 265
importance of, 265
multiple assessment methods, 266
neurobehavioral assessment, 266
nontraditional character of, 265–266
phases of, 266–267
school psychologist role, 266–267
See also Autism spectrum disorders; Cerebral palsy;
Communication disorders; Early intervention (EA);
Fetal alcohol syndrome (FAS); Fragile X syndrome
(FXS); Individuals With Disabilities Education Act
(IDEA); Motor assessment; Prevention
Informal measures of written language, 592
Information processing learning theory, 285*fig.,* 286–287,
287–288, 288*fig.*
Informed consent
ethical issue of, 194
protection of participants, 267
special education decision making, 267
written agreement, 267
Ingham, R. J., 544
Ingraham, C. L., 140, 142, 143, 342
Initiative concept, of psychosocial development, 189–190
Instrumental conditioning learning method, 284–285, 285*fig.*
Integrative Family Therapy Model (Lebow), of divorce
intervention, 172
Intelligence
biological, cognitive, motivation, behavioral foci, 267
contemporary measures of, 271–272
cultural factors, 270, 271
defining concepts, 267
fluid and crystallized theory of, 269
information processing models of, 285*fig.,* 268, 287–288,
288*table*
IQ tests, 269–271, 317, 454 *See also* IQ tests
measures of for school-age children, 270*table*

multiple intelligence theory, 268–269
norm- *vs.* growth-referenced tests of, 271–272
psychometric approach to, 268
theories of, 268–269
triarchic model of intelligence, giftedness, 268
See also Ability grouping; Bias in testing; Fluid intelligence;
    Mental age; Mental retardation; Neuropsychological
    assessment; Norm-referenced testing; Normal
    distribution; Psychometric G
Intensity measurement technique, of classroom observation, 91
Intentional encopresis, 187–188
Intermittent reinforcement, 469, 471
Internal consistency test reliability, 445
Internal structure evidence, of test validity, 579
Internalizing Symptoms Scale for Children, 517
International Classification of Diseases (ICD, WHO), 176
International Dyslexia Association, 178, 179
International Neuropsychological Society, 348
International School Psychology Association (ISPA)
    formation of, 272
    Futures Conference, 216
    objectives of, 272
    policy statements, 272
    See also American Psychological Association (APA); National
        Association of School Psychologists (NASP); School
        psychologist
International Year of the Child (UN), 272
Internet
    explanation of, 103
    school psychologist use of, 104–105
    school psychology research on, 456
    See also Computer technology; Media and children
Interpersonal psychotherapy (IPT), 157
Interpersonal theory, of depression, 125
Interrater test reliability, 445
Interval recording systems of behavioral assessment, 56
Interval schedules of reinforcement, 470, 471
Intervention
    defined, 273
    school psychologist role, 273
    See also Behavior intervention; Counseling; Crisis
        intervention; Individualized Education Plan (IEP);
        Psychotherapy; Psychotropic medications
Interviewing
    behavioral interviews with parents, teachers, 276, 276*table*
    clinical assessment interview, 273–274
    multimethod assessment, 276–277
    school psychologist, 276
    semistructured interview, 274, 275*table*
    social-emotional assessment, 517
    structured diagnostic interview, 274
    types of, 273
    unstructured interviews with parents, teachers, 274, 276
    See also Behavioral assessment; Counseling; Infant
        assessment; Personality assessment; Preschool
        assessment; Psychotherapy; Social-emotional assessment
Intimacy concept, of psychosocial development, 190
Intrinsic motivation, 331–332
Iowa Test of Basic Skills (ITBS), 10, 109
IPT (interpersonal psychotherapy), 157
IQ tests

vs. academic achievement tests, 270
    disability measurement, 269–270
    gifted, talented programs, 269
    history of, 454, 474
    learning disorders and, 290
    learning styles research and, 294
    mental age, 317
    mental retardation measurement, 270, 318
    racial, ethnic biases in, 68, 261, 319
    retention rates and, 465
    special education eligibility, 271
    success in school prediction, 269
    traumatic brain injury and, 573
    See also Fluid intelligence; Intelligence; Mental age; Mental
        retardation; Psychometric G
Irving Independent School District v. Tatro, 260
Isava, D. M., 518
Isolation defense mechanism, 155
ISPA. *See* International School Psychology Association
ITBS (Iowa Test of Basic Skills), 10, 109
Iwata, B. A., 395, 493, 494
Izard, C. E., 211

J

Jacklin, C., 221
Jackson, Y., 17
Jacob, S., 192, 193, 195, 577
Jacob-Timm, S., 259, 328
Jacobson, L., 163
Jaffe, M. D., 245
Jaklitsch, B., 248
Jarosewich, T, 412
Jarratt, K. P., 350
Jason, L. A., 312
Thomas Jefferson University Hospital, 184
Jenike, M. A., 357
Jensen, P. S., 416
Jenson, W. R., 47
Jimerson, S. R., 466, 468
Johanning, M. L., 395
Johansen, J. H., 240, 241
Johnson, D., 377
Johnson, D. W., 117–119
Johnson, J. A., 240, 241
Johnson, L. J., 163
Johnson, Lyndon B., 237, 479
Johnson, R., 377
Johnson, R. T., 117–119
Johnston, J. H., 328
Johnston, L. D., 509, 545
Johnstone, B. M., 151
Joint Committee on Standards for Educational Evaluation, 410
Jolivette, K., 53
Jones, C. W., 505, 507
Jones, J., 140
Jones, K. M., 216
Jones, K. P., 253
Jones, L., 580
Jones, M. L., 368, 492
Jones, V., 580
"Joplin Plan" concept, of ability grouping, 2

Joshi, R. M., 438, 443
Journal of School Psychology, 456
Joyce, P. R., 551
Joyner, E. T., 370, 372
Junger-Tas, J., 73
Jupitermedia Corporation, 102, 103
Just, R. M., 433

K
Kagan, J., 500
Kaiser Foundation, 313
Kajander, R. L., 71
Kalafat, J., 551
Kalat, J., 282
Kalikow, K., 357, 358
Kalyman, K., 483
Kamphaus, R. W., 196, 516
Kamps, D., 94
Kampwirth, T., 52, 54
Kane, M. B., 380
Kanna, E., 246, 247
Kanner, L., 37
Kantor, G. K., 120, 121
Kantor, J. R., 113
Kaplan, F., 320
Kaplan, S. G., 585
Karcher, M. J., 325
Karniol, R., 543
Karp, K. S., 307
Kashani, J. H., 550
Katsiyannis, A., 304–305
Kauffman, J. M., 303
Kaufman, P., 174
Kavale, K., 299
Kazdin, A. E., 369
Keenan, K., 107, 108
Kehle, T. J., 101, 543, 544
Keith, P. B., 252
Keith, T. Z., 252, 311
Keith-Spiegel, P., 193
Keller, F. S., 305
Kelly, M. L., 473
Kemp, S., 350
Kendall, P. C., 224, 225, 358
Kennedy, John F., 320
Kenny, M. C., 6
Ketterlin-Geller, L. R., 12
Keystone behaviors
    keystone variable, 279
    targets for behavioral change, 279
    See also Behavior intervention;
        Behavioral assessment
Khattri, N., 380
Kiekhaefer, A., 282, 377
Kincaid, D., 382
King, N. J., 206, 207
King, R., 358
King, S., 360
Kirby, E., 438
Kiresuk, T. J., 228
Kirk, U., 350
Kissel, R. C., 494

Kitson, J., 478
Klein, D. N., 71
Klein, H. W., 356
Kleist, D. M., 506
Kleist-Tesch, J. M., 245
Kline, C., 443
Kline, R. B., 186, 187
Klinger, E. E., 33
Knesting, K., 175
Knight, R. T., 30
Knoff, H. M., 384, 408, 554, 555
Knoster, T. P., 382
Knotek, S, 105, 390
Knox, P. L., 157
Knutson, J. F., 4
Knutson, N., 143, 144
Ko, S., 7
Kochenderfer, R., 246, 247
Koeppl, P. M., 191, 192
Koestner, R., 331
Kofka, K., 286
Kohlberg, Lawrence, 86
Kohlberg's stages of moral development
    Level 1: preconventional morality, 279–280
    Level 2: conventional morality, 280
    Level 3: postconventional morality, 280
    cheating and, 86–87
Kolb, D. A., 295
Koocher, G., 193
Koonce, D. A., 163
Korkman, M., 350
Korn, C., 338
Korol, M., 393
Kortering, L. J., 174
Kotchick, B. A., 360
Kotler, J., 310
Kotva, H., 433
Kovaleski, J., 382
Kraepelin, E., 160
Kramer, J. J., 352
Kranzler, J. H., 413
Kratochwill, T. R., 57, 111, 112, 117, 169, 196,
    197, 198, 490, 504, 508, 561
Krauss, M. W., 321
Kridel, C., 241
Kronick, R. F., 213
Kruk, R. S., 179
Kubick, R. J., Jr., 86, 352
Kuder Career Search, 81
Kulik, C. C., 1
Kulik, J. A., 1, 2
Kupfer, D. J., 72
Küpper, L., 258
Kurz, J., 313
Kusche, C., 407
Kushida, D., 140, 142
Kussmaul, Adolf, 489
Kutcher, R., 420, 421

L
La Greca, A. M., 184
La Rosa, A., 423

Labeling. *See* Diagnosis and labeling; Individuals With Disabilities Education Act (IDEA); Special education
Lacher, D., 517
Ladd, G., 500
Ladouceur, R., 543
Lagerspetz, K., 311
Lahey, B. B., 360
Lalley, J. P., 305
Lamb, A., 103, 104
Lamb, M. E., 505
Lambros, K. M., 55–56, 162
Lamorey, S., 281
Lamp-Parker, F., 238
Land, D., 234
Landau, S., 33, 212
Lane, K. L., 162
Lang, J., 445
Lange, J. S., 379
Language developmental milestones, 158–159*table*
Language learning disability, 99
    echolalia and, 186
    ODD with, 186
    otitis media and, 364
    preschool assessment, 401
Lapierre, Coady, 229
Larry P. v. *Riles,* 68
Larson, J., 54, 583
Lassman, K., 53
Latchkey children
    academic achievement, 281
    after school programs, 282
    emotional hardships, 281
    gender role changes, 281
    risk factors of, 281
    See also Fears; Parenting, parents
Latency recording technique, of classroom observation, 91
Latency stage of psychosocial development, 190
Lauber, M. O., 220
Law of Effect, 284–285
Law of Exercise, 285
Law of Readiness, 285–286
Lazarus, P., 127
LBS (Learning Behaviors Scale), 296
LDA (Learning Disabilities Association of America), 525
Leach, J., 39
Lead exposure
    effects of, 282
    prevention, intervention strategies, 282
Leal, D., 83
Learned helplessness
    defined, 283
    interventions, 283
    learning disability diagnosis, 283
    reading interventions, 434
    See also Bullying and victimization; Learning
Learning
    behavior changes, 284
    biological evolution theory, 285*fig.,* 286
    constructivism, 287
    cooperative *vs.* competitive *vs.* individual, 117
    experimentation, 284–285, 285*fig.*
    Gestalt psychology, 285*fig.,* 286

information processing theory, 285*fig.,* 286–288, 288*table*
    instructional practices to enhance, 287–288, 288*table*
    instrumental conditioning, 284–285, 285*fig.*
    observable products of, 283–284
    operant conditioning, 285*fig.,* 286, 287
    performance behavior, 284
    permanence of, 284
    reciprocal determinism, 444–445
    school psychologist implications, 288–289
    social learning theory, 285*fig.,* 286, 287
    vicarious learning, 445
    See also Ability grouping; Academic achievement; Cooperative learning; Curriculum-based assessment (CBA); Intelligence; Learning disabilities; Learning styles; Mastery learning; Mathematics interventions and strategies; Memory; Mental retardation; Motivation; Reading interventions and strategies; Retention; Spelling interventions and strategies; Study skills; Writing interventions and strategies
Learning Behaviors Scale (LBS), 296
Learning Disabilities Association of America (LDA), 525
Learning disabilities (LDs)
    ADD comorbidity, 102
    component level interventions, 292
    explicit strategy instruction intervention, 292
    friendships of children, 211
    gender factors, 222
    general intervention models, 291
    generalized anxiety disorder and, 225
    IDEA category, 263, 264*table*
    information conveyance tactics, 291–292
    IQ tests, 270
    LD field history, 290
    learned helplessness, 283
    math disabilities, 291
    mental information processing impairments, 289
    norm-referenced assessment of, 290
    phonologic skills intervention, 290
    reading disabilities, 290–291
    research on, 315–316
    shyness, 500
    study *vs.* assessment and treatment construct, 292–293
    word recognition measures, 290, 438–439
    See also Academic achievement; Intelligence; Learning; Learning styles; Mathematics interventions and strategies; Memory; Motivation; Reading interventions and strategies; Study skills; Writing interventions and strategies
Learning styles
    accommodating learning style, 295
    activity-centered styles, 295–296
    affective, 435
    Approaches to Studying Inventory, 295
    aptitude-treatment interactions, 294
    assimilating learning style, 295
    case for *vs.* against, 296–297
    cognition-centered styles, 294–295, 435
    Cognitive Profile Assessment Instrument (CPAI), 296
    cognitive skills strengths, weaknesses, 296
    converging learning style, 295
    diverging learning style, 295

environmental, instructional factors, 295
grasping *vs.* transforming experience modes, 295
history, definitions regarding, 294
integration of, 296
Learning Styles Inventory, 295, 539
personality-centered styles, 295
physiological, 435
psychological, 435
reading interventions, 434–435
study skills and, 539
styles *vs.* strategies *vs.* behaviors terms, 296
terms used with, 296
"thinking styles" concept, 295
See also Academic achievement; Learning
Least restrictive environment (LRE)
court cases, 299
court precedents, 298
explanation of, 298
federal legislation, 298
IDEA and, 259, 261, 524
IEP and, 298, 299
inclusion issue, 298, 299
mental retardation, 321
Resource Room concept, 460, 524
school psychologist role, 299
sociocultural classroom focus, 299
See also Due process; Functional behavioral assessment
(FBA); Individuals With Disabilities Education Act
(IDEA); Mainstreaming; Resource rooms; Special
education
Lebow, J., 172
Leckman, J. F., 357
Lee, A. L., 231
Lee, D, 409
Lee, S., 22
Lee, S. W., 71, 164, 225, 499
Leff, S. S., 19
Lehman, J. D., 103
Lehr, C. A., 471, 472
Lella, S. A., 139
Lenane, M., 358
Lentz, F. E., 56
Leonard, B. R., 94
Leonard, H. L., 357, 358
Letteri, C. A., 296
Leukemia
acute *vs.* chronic, 77
prevalence of, 78
Levin, Henry, 482
Levin, J. R., 316
Levine, M., 184
Lewinsohn, P. M., 71, 97
Lewis, L., 254
Lewis-Snyder, Gretchen, 199
Licensing and certification in school psychology
independent practice, 300–301
licensure *vs.* certification, 300
National School Psychology Certification System, 300
state departments of education authority, 300, 301
Lichtenberg, J. W., 157
Lieberman, R., 131

Lincoln, M., 543
Lindamood, C., 386
Lindamood, P., 386
Lindamood Auditory Conceptualization Test of phonemic
awareness, 386
Lindamood Phonemic Sequencing program, 386
Linden, M. A., 255
Lindsay, J. J., 252
Linebarger, D. L., 310
Linn, R., 8
Linn, R. L., 134
Lipsky, D., 260
Liu, D., 408
Local Area Network (LAN), computer application, 103
Lochman, J., 54
Lochman, J. E., 200
Locke, D. C., 140
Locke, John, 565
Locomotor-genetal stage of psychosocial
development, 189–190
Locus of control, learning and, 434
Loeber, R., 107, 108, 359, 360, 361
Logan, S., 585
Logan, T. K., 151
Long term memory (LTM), 287
Lopez, A. B., 584
Lopez, S. J., 126, 472
Loulou, D., 542
Loveless, T., 1, 2
Lowe, C., 186, 282
Lowe, P. A., 35, 67, 196, 217, 353, 413, 445
LTM (long term memory), 287
Lucas, C. P., 274
Luce, S. C., 39
Luckasson, R., 318
Luhr, M. E., 79, 491
Lundberg, I., 439
Lundy, B. L., 501
Luria, A., 221
Luria, A. R., 268, 591
Lustig, J. L., 172
Lynam, D. R., 151
Lynch, E. W., 141
Lyon, G. R., 179
Lyon, M. A., 458, 459
Lyons, E., 58

M
Maag, J. W., 304–305
Maccoby, E., 221
Maccow, G. C., 214
Macey, K., 72
Macfarlane, C., 322
Macias, S., 252, 253
Mackinnon, D. P., 546
Madan-Swain, A., 78
Maddan, N., 480
Madden, N. A., 406
Maehr, M. L., 334
Maguire, C., 324
Maguire, S., 213

Maheady, L., 94, 378, 379
Mahlios, M. C., 244
Mahony, P., 90
Maier, S. E., 209
Mainemeilis, C., 295
Mainstreaming, 301
  defined, 303
  IEP and, 303
  vs. inclusion, 303
  vs. least restrictive environment, 298
  See also Special education
Maintenance response, 63*table*
Major depressive disorder, 155
Mallette, B., 94, 379
Malott, R. W., 106
Malouf, D., 36
Maltreatment of children. *See* Abuse and neglect
Manheimer, M. A., 307
Mania. *See* Bipolar disorder (BD) (childhood onset)
Manic-depressive disorder. *See* Bipolar disorder
    (BD) (childhood onset)
Manier, K. L., 376
Manifestation determination
  concept explanation, 303
  data collection procedures, 304
  general procedures, 304
  medical model orientation, 304
  pattern of removal concept, 304
  socially constructed disability categories, 304–305
  See also Behavioral assessment; Diagnosis and labeling;
    Discipline; Expulsion; Individuals With Disabilities
    Education Act (IDEA); Special education; Suspension;
    Violence in schools
Mantagna, D., 94
Manz, P. H., 19
March, J. S., 357, 358
Marijuana use, 545
Markle, G. C., 328
Markson, S., 555
Marshall, D. G., 546
Marshall, L. H., 343
Marshall, M. L., 220
Martens, B. K., 25, 26, 117
Martin, C., 151
Martin, D. A., 573
Martin, G., 25, 105
Martin, J. E., 343
Martin, N., 591
Mash, E. J., 161
Massengill, D., 154, 387
Mastery learning
  instruction philosophy, 305
  mastery as endpoint of learning, 305–306
  norm- *vs.* criterion-referenced assessment, 305
  teaching and assessing methods, 305
  See also Classroom climate; Criterion-referenced assessment;
    Learning; Norm-referenced testing
Mastropieri, M. A., 316
Mathematics curriculum and instruction
  constructivism *vs.* behavioral theory, 307
  problem-solving and reasoning processes, 306–307

solving problems, 307
study of algebra, 306
study of geometry and measurement, 306
study of numbers, 306
study of statistics and probability, 306
using concrete materials, 307
using technology, 307–308
writing and reflecting, 308
See also Mathematics interventions and strategies
Mathematics interventions and strategies
  instructional methods reform, 308–309
  math learning disabilities, 291
  math proficiency elements, 309
  mediated verbal rehearsal technique, 309
  peer-assisted instruction, 309
  retrieval efficiency, 309–310
  school psychologist role, 310
  visual representation technique, 309
  See also Academic achievement; Cooperative learning;
    Homework; Learning; Learning styles; Mathematics
    curriculum and instruction
Mather, K. E., 538
Mather, N., 401, 591, 596
Mathes, P. G., 94, 379
Mathews, J. R., 39, 42
Mathot-Buckner, C., 94
Matson, J. L., 39
Matsumoto, D., 136
Matthews, K. M., 466
Mattie T. v. Holladay, 299
Maturity stage of psychosocial development, 190
Maurice, C., 39
Mazure, C., 358
Mazza, J. J., 547, 548, 551
Mazzeo, J., 587
MBTI (Myers-Briggs Type Indicator), 81
McCabe, P. C., 404
McCaul, E. J., 174
McCaulley, M. H., 295, 539
McClanahan, W. S., 324
McConaughy, S. H., 274, 275*table,* 277
McCord, J., 324
McCormick, J., 128, 129, 130, 131
McCoy, J. D., 12
McCurdy, M., 27, 106
McDermott, P. A., 160, 296
McDonnell, J., 94
McGimsey, J. F., 492
McGoey, K. E., 94
McGrew, K. S., 401
McGroder, S. M., 507
McKellar, N. A., 344
McKiney-Veto Homeless Assistance Act, 249
McLanahan, S. S., 506
McLaughlin, V. L., 524, 525
McLean, M., 265
McLeod, A., 591
McLoone, B., 316
Mcloughlin, C. S., 86, 352
McMahon, R. J., 361, 368
McMahon, T. J., 212, 213

McMillan, J. H., 388
McNally, R. J., 394
McPherson Shilling, L., 423
MDTs. *See* Multidisciplinary teams
Mead, J., 260
Measurement and Assessment in Teaching (Linn and Gronlund), 8
Measures of association, of effect size, 187, 188
Media and children
    advantages *vs.* disadvantages of media, 313
    behavior affected by, 311–312
    childhood obesity, 312
    elementary level, 311
    media varieties, 310
    media violence, 313
    parental controls, 312
    preschool level, 310–311
    secondary level, 311
    Sesame Street, 310–311, 313
    statistics regarding, 310
    TV education programs, 310–313
    TV supervision tips, 312–313
    TV violence, 311–312
    See also Aggression in schools; Computer technology;
        Homework; Latchkey children; Parenting, parents;
        Violence in schools
Mediation process, of due process, 177
Mediation Programs of conflict management, 54
Medlin, R. G., 247
Medway, F., 111, 112
Medway, F. J., 172
Medwell, J., 587
Mees, H., 568
Mehaffey, Kerry, 257
Mehrens, W. A., 36
Meichenbaum, D. H., 95, 496
Mellard, D. F., 464
Memory
    chunking technique, 316
    clustering technique, 316
    coding technique, 316
    control processes, 316
    critical to learning, 314
    information processing model, components of, 314–315
    information processing model, connectionist, 315
    long-term memory, 314, 315
    mediational processes, 315
    metacognition, 315, 316
    mnemonic strategies, 315, 316
    organizational strategies to improve, 316
    production deficiencies, 315–316
    research on, 315–316
    short-term memory, 314, 315
    working memory, 315
    See also Learning; Learning disabilities (LDs); Mastery
        learning; Mathematics interventions and strategies;
        Neuropsychological assessment; Reading interventions
        and strategies; Spelling interventions and strategies;
        Writing interventions and strategies
Mental age (MA)
    defined, 317
    lifetime changes in, 317

    See also Mental retardation; Social skills; Theories of human
        development
The Mental Measurements Yearbook (Buros), 75–76
Mental retardation (MR)
    cultural biased testing, 319, 396
    death penalty legislation, 320–321
    defined, 317–318
    deinstitutionalization, 298
    DSM-IV-TR defined, 12, 318
    education and service trends, 321–322
    educational services for students with, 319–320
    etiology of, 319, 319*table*
    FAPE, 255, 259, 261, 298, 321
    forced sterilization, 320
    fragile X syndrome, 209–210
    historical perspective on, 320–321
    IDEA category, 263, 264*table,* 318, 319, 321
    institutionalization practice, 320
    IQ tests, 270, 318
    least restrictive environment, 321
    medical provision, 321–322
    psychotropic medications for, 421
    self-determination skills, 321
    Special Olympics, 320
    state legislation, 320, 321
    Supports Intensity Scale, 318
    terminology debate, 318–319
    See also Academic achievement; Intelligence;
        Learning; Retention
MENTOR/National Mentoring Partnership, 325
Mentoring
    Big Brothers Big Sisters (BBBS) program, 325, 326
    community- *vs.* school-based programs, 323–324
    dropouts and, 175
    effective practices in, 325, 326*table*
    history of, 324
    natural- *vs.* program-based mentoring, 323
    research and literature regarding, 324–325
    school psychologist role, 325
    YMCA, YWCA, 325–326
    See also Intervention
Merrell, K. W., 160, 517, 518
Metabolic mental retardation, 319*table*
Metacognition, 315, 316
Metz, A. J., 81
Meyers, J., 140, 220, 478
MHC. *See* Consultation: mental health
Michael, J., 62*table*
Middle school
    effectiveness of, 327–328
    evolution, definition, purpose of, 327
    vs. junior high school, 327, 328*table*
    research on, 327–328
    school psychologist, 328–329
    transition issue, 328, 406
    See also Theories of human development
Midgley, C., 334
Milich, R., 151
Miller, D. D., 538
Miller, G., 542
Miller, J. G., 361

Miller, J. Y., 546
Miller, M. A., 199, 508
Miller, R., 186, 317
Million Adolescent Personality Inventory, 383
Millon, T., 160
Mills v. Board of Education, 298, 522
Miltenberger, R. G., 64*table,* 105
Minnesota Importance Questionnaire, 81
Minnesota Multiphasic Personality
    Inventory-Adolescents, 383, 517
Minor, M. W., 114
Mistretta, J., 587
Mitchell, M. C., 28
Mixed cerebral palsy type, 83
Mizerek, E. A., 251
Mnemonic memory strategies, 315, 316
Moats, L. C., 439
Mock, D., 462
Modeling technique, cognitive-behavioral
    modification, 97
Modzeleski, W., 127, 582, 584
Moffitt, T. E., 107
Momentary time sampling (MTS) technique, of
    classroom observation, 92
Mondin, G. W., 126
Monitoring the Future National Survey
    (Johnson, et. al.), 509, 545
Montessori schools
    research outcomes, 330
    skill areas, 330
    students responsible for own learning, 329–330, 403
    teacher role in, 330
    See also Class size; Learning; Motivation; Preschoolers
Mood disorders, 421
    See also Bipolar disorder (BD) (childhood onset)
Mood stabilizer psychotropic medications, 423
Moody, J., 130
Moody, M., 126
Moody, S. W., 523
Moore, J. W., 471, 536
Moos, R., 89
Moral development. *See* Kohlberg's stages of
    moral development
Morality, defined, 191
Morgan, D., 496
Morgan, P., 462
Morita, Y., 73
Morrison, G. M., 199, 252, 253, 254
Mortweet, S. L., 94
Mostow, A. J., 211
Motivation
    achievement goals, 333
    assessment of, 333–334
    behavioral approach to, 331
    causal attributions, 332–333, 334
    cognitive approach to, 332–333
    contexts of, 333
    extrinsic motivation, 331, 334
    intrinsic motivation, 331–332, 334
    motivation to learn, 330–331
    motivational interventions, 334–335

reading interventions, 434
school psychologist role, 333, 334–335
self-perceptions of competence, 332
See also Ability grouping; Behavior intervention;
    Cooperative learning; Dropouts; Homework; Learning;
    Self-management
Motor assessment
    fine motor skills evaluation, 336–337
    finger dexterity, 337
    frontal lobes, 335
    gross motor skills evaluation, 336
    gross *vs.* fine motor skills, 335, 337
    laterality, 336
    neuroanatomy, 335–337
    neuroanatomy and behavior relationship, 335
    occupational therapist intervention, 337
    parietal lobe, 335
    preschool assessment, 401
    visual-motor integration, 337
    See also Sensorimotor stage of development
Movies. *See* Media and children
Mulder, R. T., 551
Mulle, K., 357
Mullen Scales of Early Learning, 336
Mullins, Francis, 272
Mullis, C. B., 186
Mulrine, A., 81
Multicultural education
    Banks and Banks contributions, 338–339,
        339*table,* 340*table*
    Black English *vs.* Standard English, 436
    classification system of, 340–341, 341*table*
    content integration approaches, 338–339, 340*table*
    cultural diversity understanding, appreciation, 338
    culturally responsive teaching, 342
    dialect, 436, 442
    dimensions of, 338, 339*table*
    English as a second language, 436, 442
    equal learning opportunity, 338
    parent training programs, 369
    parenting beliefs, practices and, 373
    Sleeter and Grant contributions, 339–342, 341*table*
    statistics regarding, 338
    testing bias, 338
    See also Class; Cross-cultural assessment; Ethnicity; Gender,
        gender factors; Race, ethnicity, class and gender; School
        reform
Multidisciplinary teams (MDTs)
    collaboration focus, 343
    IDEA and, 343
    Individualized Education Plans (IEPs), 342–343
    preschool special education services, 404
    special education services planning, 342–344
    vs. student improvement teams (SITs), 534
    See also Diagnosis and labeling; Individualized Education
        Plan (IEP); Individuals With Disabilities Education Act
        (IDEA); Least restrictive environment; Reports
        (psychological); Special education; Student improvement
        teams
Multiple baseline experimental design, 502, 503*fig.*
Multiple disabilities, infant assessment, 266

Multisystemic family therapy, 205, 206
Mulvaney, M., 53
Mulvey, E. P., 584
Munson, S., 356
Murdock, T. B., 87
Murguia, A., 140, 142
Muris, P., 206, 207
Murphy, L. L., 76
Murphy, M., 97
Murry, V. M., 506
Muscular-anal stage of psychosocial development, 189
Myers, I. B., 295, 539
Myers, S., 83
Myers-Briggs Type Indicator (MBTI), personality
    learning style measure, 81, 295, 539
Myles, B. S., 204, 257
Mytton, J. A., 585

N
Nabors, L. A., 19
NAEP (National Assessment of Educational
    Progress), 10, 364
NAEYC (National Association for the Education
    of Young Children), 403
Nagle, Richard, 397, 404
Nagy, M. H., 152
Nansel, T. R., 73, 74, 234, 582
NASDE (National Association of State Directors of Special
    Education), 214
NASP. *See* National Association of School Psychologists
NASROs (National Association of School Resource Officers),
    584–585
Nastasi, B. K., 257, 547
Nathan, P., 360
Nathan, P. E., 197
A Nation at Risk report (Nat'l. Commission on
    Excellence in Education), 242, 362, 479
National Assessment of Educational Progress
    (NAEP), 10, 364, 587
National Assessment of Vocational Education (NAVE), 364
National Association for the Education of Young Children
    (NAEYC), 403–404
National Association of School Psychologists
    (NASP), 403, 404
  1969-1979, 345
  1980-1989, 345–346
  1990-1999, 346
  NASP today, 346–347
  APA, Div. of School Psychology, 345, 347
  APA/NASP Interorganizational Committee, 345, 347
  CDSPP and, 123
  crisis training, 127
  ethics codes, committees, 109, 191–192, 195, 346
  founding of, 345, 475
  Futures Conference, 216, 347
  governmental, professional relations, 346–347
  Governmental and Professional Relations
      Committee, 345, 346
  high-stakes assessments, 534
  historic timeline, 347*timeline*
  home-school collaboration, 249
    IDEA and, 346
    International School Psychology Committee, 272
    National Certification in School Psychology, 345, 476
    National Emergency Assistance Team, 127
    NCATE and, 345
    portfolio requirement, 390
    preschool assessment, 397
    publications, 346, 476
    retention policy, 397
    salary information, 477
    school psychologist accreditation, 82, 300
    School Psychology Review, 456
    specialty guidelines, 169
    suicide prevention, 131
    suspension and, 555
    training and practice guidelines, 476
National Association of School Resource
    Officers (NASROs), 584–585
National Association of Secondary School Principals, 131
National Association of Social Workers, 514
National Association of State Directors of Special Education
    (NASDE), 214
National Center for Health Statistics, 548, 549
National Center on Educational Outcomes, 534
National Center on Educational Statistics, 338, 578, 601
National Certification in School Psychology
    (NCSP), 345, 476
National Child Abuse and Neglect Data System
    (NCANDS), 3
National Commission on Excellence in
    Education, 242, 362, 479
National Council for Accreditation of Teacher
    Education (NCATE)
  NASP and, 346–347
  portfolio requirement, 390
  school psychologist accreditation, 82, 345, 476
National Council of Teachers of Mathematics, 308
National Council on Measurement in Education
  academic achievement, 8
  test validity, 579
National Defense Education Act (NDEA), 479, 577
National Dissemination Center for Children
    with Disabilities (NICHCY), 83
National Education Association (NEA), 241, 327
National Education Goals Panel, 249
National Emergency Assistance Team (NEAT), 127
National Gang Youth Survey, 219
National Institute of Mental Health (NIMH), 274
National Institute on Drug Abuse, 545, 546
National Middle School Association (NMSA), 327, 328
National Organization for Victim Assistance (NOVA), 127
National Reading Panel, 385, 386
National Research Council, 309
National School Psychology Certification System
    (NSPCS), 300–301
National School Safety Center, 581
Native Americans
  bias in testing of, 68
  eating disorders, 184
  Head Start, 238
  suicide rates, 549

See also Class; Cross-cultural assessment; Cross-cultural
consultation; Ethnicity; Gender, gender factors;
Multicultural education; Race, ethnicity,
class and gender
Naturalistic observation of behavioral assessment, 56
Nau, P. A., 494
NAVE (National Assessment of Vocational Education), 364
NCANDS (National Child Abuse and Neglect Data System), 3
NCATE. *See* National Council for Accreditation of Teacher
Education
NCLB. *See* No Child Left Behind Act of 2001 (NCLB)
NCR (noncontingent reinforcement) schedule, 60, 63*table*
NCSP (National Certification in School Psychology), 345, 476
NDEA (National Defense Education Act), 479, 577
NEA (National Education Association), 241
Neale, J. M., 184, 185
NEAT (National Emergency Assistance Team), 127
Negative reinforcement, defined, 64*table*
Neglect. *See* Abuse and neglect
Nemer, K. M., 380
Neuberger, W., 380
Neuropsychological assessment, 335–337
behavioral domains of, 349*table*
brain-behavior relationship study, 348
competency to conduct, 348–349
education setting applications, 349
strengths, weaknesses of, 350
traumatic brain injury, 573
See also Behavioral assessment; Bias in testing;
Communication disorders; Intelligence; Learning;
Reliability; Social-emotional assessment
Neville, H. A., 325
New Beginnings Program (Lusting, et. al.),
divorce intervention, 172
Newby, T. J., 103
Newcomb, A. F., 211
Newton, J. S., 26
Newton, K., 395
NICHCY (National Dissemination Center for
Children with Disabilities), 83
Nicholas, C., 239
Niebling, B. C., 580
NIH (National Institutes of Health), 572
NIMH (National Institute of Mental Health), 274
Nix, C., 377
No Child Left Behind Act of 2001 (NCLB), 85, 242, 249, 261
achievement gap focus, 350–351
disabled students and, 526, 531
funds allocation and, 480
noncompliance consequences, 351, 531
statewide tests, 531–532
themes, mandates of, 350, 480
zero tolerance policies, 602
See also Academic achievement; Individuals With
Disabilities Education Act (IDEA); School reform
Noam, G. G., 199
Noncontingent reinforcement (NCR) schedule, 60, 63*table*
Nonretentive encopresis, 187–188
Noonan, N., 406
Norm-referenced adaptive behavior instruments,
14, 14*table*, 290

Norm-referenced testing
of academic achievement, 9–10
advantages *vs.* disadvantages of, 352
explanation of, 352
functions of, 352
of intelligence, 271
mastery learning and, 305
normal curve, 353*fig.*
percentile ranks, 379–380
vs. portfolio assessment, 388
projective testing, 412–413
of spelling, 596, 597–598*table*
stanines, 531
of written language, 592, 593–595*table*
See also Bias in testing; Criterion-referenced assessment;
Grade equivalent scores; Normal distribution; Percentile
ranks; Reliability; Statewide tests
Normal distribution, 353, 353*fig.*
See also Percentile ranks; Standard deviation
Northup, J. A., 478
Norton, P., 104
NOVA (National Organization for Victim Assistance), 127
Novak, S. P., 151
NSPCS (National School Psychology Certification System),
300–301
Nunez, R., 248
Nunn, R. G., 64*table*
Nwafor, B. E., 540
Nye, B., 251, 252

O
Oakes, J., 1, 2, 3
Oakland, T., 273, 295
*Oberti v. Board of Education of the Borough
of Clementon School District,* 299
Obesity in children
behavior therapy, 356
body mass index (BMI), 355
consumption patterns, 355
health, psychological risk factors, 356
lifestyle exercise, 356
nutrition program intervention, 356
parental feeding habits, 355–356
school psychologist role, 356
sedentary lifestyle, 355
societal, genetic, behavioral factors, 355
statistics regarding, 355
See also Eating disorders; Pica; Prevention;
Self-management
Observation and recording techniques, of classroom
observation, 91–92
Obsessive-compulsive disorder (OCD)
common obsessions of, 358
comorbidity of, 358
diagnosis of, 358
impaired daily functioning, 357
psychotropic medications for, 422
school psychologist role, 358
SSRI treatment of, 421
statistics regarding, 357
treatment, 358

See also Comorbidity; Counseling; *DSM-IV-TR;*
    Interviewing; Psychopathology in children
Ochshorn, P., 546
O'Connor, T. G., 431
OCR (Office of Civil Rights), 234, 578
Oehler-Stinnet, J., 272
OELA (Office of English Language Acquisition), 578
OERI (Office of Educational Research and Improvement), 578
OESE (Office of Elementary and Secondary Education), 578
O'Farrell, S. L., 87
Office of Civil Rights (OCR), 234, 578
Office of Educational Research and Improvement (OERI), 578
Office of Elementary and Secondary Education (OESE), 578
Office of English Language Acquisition (OELA), 578
Office of Federal Student Aid (OFSA), 578
Office of Special Education and Rehabilitation Services
    (OSERS), 578
Office of Special Education Programs, 255
Office of Vocational and Adult Education (OVAE), 578
OFSA (Office of Federal Student Aid), 578
Oka, E. R., 335
Oliver, M. B., 313
Ollendick, T. H., 207, 208
Olmi, D. J., 58
Oltjenbruns, K. A., 153
Olumpia, D. E., 48
Olweus, D., 73, 74, 233, 234, 235, 582
O'Malley, P. M., 509, 545
O'Neill, R. E., 26
Online or Internet homeschooling method, 246
Onslow, M., 543
Operant behaviorism, 61*table*
    parent training programs, 368, 369
Operant conditioning, 285*fig.,* 287
    positive behavior support and, 390–391
    self-injurious behavior and, 492
    See also Behavior; Conditioning: classical and operant
Oppositional defiant disorder (ODD)
    causes of, 359–360
    comorbidity of, 360
    diagnosis of, 360
    disruptive behavior disorder, 359
    divorce adjustment, 170
    DSM-IV-TR diagnosis, 359
    encopresis and, 187
    gender factors, 359
    school psychologist role, 360
    selective mutism, 489, 490
    treatment for, 360–361
    See also Aggression in schools; Attention
        deficit hyperactivity disorder (ADHD); Counseling;
        Depression; *DSM-IV-TR;* Parenting, parents;
        Psychopathology in children
Oral-sensory stage of psychosocial development, 189
Organizational consultation and development
    collaborative skills, 362
    explanation of, 361
    facilitative role, 362–363
    problem-solving capacity focus, 362
    school psychologist role, 362
    systems theory, 361–362

See also Careers in school psychology; Consultation:
    behavioral (BC); Consultation: conjoint behavioral
    (CBC); Consultation: ecobehavioral; Consultation:
    mental health (MHC); Cross-cultural consultation;
    Ethical issues in school psychology; Evidence-based
    interventions (EBIs); Program evaluation; School
    psychologist; School reform
Orme, S. F., 111
Ormrod, J. E., 540
Ort, S. I., 358
Orthographic awareness, 596
Ortiz, S., 137, 139
Orton, S., 442
Orton-Gillingham approach, teaching children at risk, 442–443
OSERS (Office of Special Education and
    Rehabilitation Services), 578
O'Shaughnessy, T., 314, 315, 316
Oster-Granite, M. L., 493
Osterman, K. F., 333
Otitis media (OM)
    diagnosis, treatment, 363–364
    explanation of, 363
    incidence of, 363
    outcomes, 364
    self-injurious behavior, 493
O'Toole, M., 582
Outcomes-based assessment
    defined, 364
    high-stakes testing, advantages/disadvantages
        of, 364–365, 526
    outcomes *vs.* output, 364
    school proficiency tests and, 364
    school psychologist role, 365
    See also Academic achievement; Authentic assessment;
        Performance-based assessment; School reform
OVAE (Office of Vocational and Adult Education), 578
Overcorrection
    overcorrection reductive technique, 65*table*
    See also Behavior intervention; Conditioning:
        classical and operant
Overman, L. T., 242, 480
Overpeck, M., 73, 74, 234, 582

P

PA. *See* Performance-based assessment
Pace, G. M., 494
Paclawskyj, T., 39
Page, R. N., 1, 2, 3
Paige, L. Z., 486
Palomares, R., 216, 217
PALS (Peer-Assisted Learning Strategies), 379
Panichelli-Mindel, S. M., 224
Papalia, D. E., 491
Parametric and periodic intervention experimental
    designs, 502
Parasymathetic nervous system (PNS), 69
PARC (Pennsylvania Assn. for Retarded Children), 298
PARC (Pennsylvania Assn. for Retarded Children) v.
    Pennsylvania, 298
Parent-Child Interaction Therapy (PCIT, Foote & colleagues)
    parent training program, 368–369

Parent education (PE) and parent training (PT)
authoritative parenting, 367, 373
cultural diversity in, 369
Helping the Noncompliant Child (McMahon &
Forehand), 368
Incredible Years Parents Training Series
(Webster-Stratton & Reid), 369
Parent-Child Interaction Therapy (PCIT,
Foote & colleagues), 368–369
*Parent Management Training for Conduct
Disorder* (Kazdin), 369
PE programs, 367–368
PE programs, outcomes of, 368
PE programs, power differential in, 368
PE *vs.* PT, 367
PT programs, 368–369
PT programs, disruptive behavior focus, 368
school psychologist role, 374
See also Conditioning: classical and operant; Parenting,
parents; Theories of human development
Parent Management Training for Conduct Disorder
(Kazdin) parent training program, 369
Parent-teacher conferences
communication skills, 372
conversation-friendly environment, 371
expectations regarding, 370
growth areas focus, 371
information sharing, 371
rapport building, 372
reasons for, 370
school-home notes, 473
strengths focus, 371
suggestions for parents, 370–371
suggestions for teachers, 371–372
See also Grades; Homework; Individualized Education Plan
(IEP); School-home notes; Student improvement teams
Parenting, parents
academic achievement and, 373–374
authoritative parenting, 373
child abuse and neglect, 4–5
conduct disorder and, 107, 108
corporal punishment and, 121
cultural variations, 373
diagnostic interviews, 274–275
early intervention programs, 181–182
functions performed by, 372–373
homework and, 251–253
IDEA and, 524
IEP meeting, 258
impartial due process hearing, 177, 178
Individualized Education Plan and, 255–257
informed consent, 267
media regulation, 312
multidisciplinary team and, 343
parenting styles, 373–374
reading interventions, 435–436
retention rates, 465
school-home notes, 473
school psychologist role, 374
separation anxiety disorder, 484, 499
social-emotional development, 373–374

spanking, 120–121
suicidal students, 131
See also Abuse and neglect; Class; Divorce adjustment;
Ethnicity; Gender, gender factors; Homelessness;
Latchkey children; Media and children; Parent-teacher
conferences; Parents as teachers; Race, ethnicity, class
and gender; Resilience and protective factors; School
refusal; Single-parent families
Parents As Teachers (PAT) program
growth of, 374
outcome measures, 374–375
See also Head Start; Parenting, parents;
Single-parent families
Parents in Action on Special Education (PASE) v.
Joseph P. Hannon, 68
Parke, R. D., 311
Parker, J., 500
Parra, G. R., 325
Pasley, J. D., 242
PAT. *See* Parents As Teachers (PAT) program
PATHS (Promoting Alternative THinking Strategies)
curriculum program, 407
Patterns of Adaptive Learning Styles, 334
Patterson, G. R., 107, 108, 361
Patton, M. Q., 411
Pauls, D. L., 357
Pavlov, Ivan, 105
Payne, M., 430
PBS. *See* Positive behavior support (PBS)
PCIT (*Parent-Child Interaction Therapy,* Foote & colleagues)
parent training program, 368–369
PDAs (personal digital assistants), 102–103
PDD-NOS (pervasive developmental disorder - not otherwise
specified), 42
PE. *See* Parent education (PE) and parent training (PT)
Peabody Individual Achievement Test, 437, 596
Peabody Picture Vocabulary Test-Revised, 99, 401, 437
Peaceable Classroom of conflict management, 54
Pear, J., 25
Pedophilia
DSM-IV diagnosis, 376
incidence statistics, 376
treatment approaches, 376
Pedro-Carroll, J. L., 172
Peer-Assisted Learning Strategies (PALS), 379
Peer mediation
advantages, challenges, 377
aggression in school, 376–377
cadre *vs.* student body approach, 377
social skills training, 514
student empowerment, 377
See also Bullying and victimization; Discipline; Friendships;
Gangs; Mentoring; Peer tutoring; Peers, peer pressure;
Prevention; Problem solving; Violence in schools
Peer tutoring
active *vs.* passive learning, 378
Classwide Peer Tutoring, 378–379
Classwide Student Tutoring Teams, 379
Peer-Assisted Learning Strategies, 379
Reciprocal Peer Tutoring model, 378
Teams-Games-Tournaments Model, 379

See also Classroom climate; Classwide peer
        tutoring (CWPT); Study skills; Tutoring
Peers, peer pressure
    conduct disorder and, 107, 108
    gang behavior, 379
    peer strategies, ADHD, 35
    peer victimization, 73–74
    positive *vs.* negative, 379
    power of, 378
    reading difficulties, 436
    smoking, drinking, 379
    sociometric assessment and, 519
    teen pregnancy, 560
    See also Cheating; Classwide peer tutoring
        (CWPT); DARE program; Friendships; Peer
        mediation; Peer tutoring; Smoking (teenage); Social
        skills; Substance abuse
Peerson, S., 4, 7
Pellegrini, A. D., 73, 74
Pennington, B. F., 179
Pennsylvania Assn. for Retarded Children (PARC), 298, 321
*Pennsylvania Assn. for Retarded Children (PARC) vs.
        Commonwealth of Pennsylvania,* 522
Penz, M. A., 546
Pepler, D. J., 74, 234
Percentile ranks
    disadvantage of, 379
    explanation of, 378–379
    norm-referenced scoring, 379
    See also Academic achievement; Grade equivalent
        scores; Intelligence; Stanines
Perfect, M., 420
Perfetti, C. A., 385
Performance anxiety, 485
Performance-based assessment (PA)
    advantages, limitations of, 380
    standards-based assessment, 380
Perinatal, postnatal mental retardations, 319*table*
Perkins, D. N., 540
Permanent products method of behavioral assessment, 57
Perseveration
    behavior repetition, 381
    sensory stimulation, 381
Persky, H. R., 587
Personal digital assistants (PDAs), 102–103
Personality assessment
    applications of, 381
    causal *vs.* correlational identification, 384
    contexts of, 381–382
    data collection, 383–384
    DSM-IV-TR classification, 382
    emotional disturbance qualification, 383
    empirically based classification, 382
    functions of, 381
    hypotheses validation, 383
    IDEA and, 381, 382, 383
    of nonspecial education students, 381
    process *vs.* product, 384
    psychometric classification, 383
    school psychologist role, 383–384
    student skills, assists, 382

See also Applied behavior analysis (ABA); Behavioral
        assessment; Buros Mental Measurements Yearbook;
        Projective testing; Psychopathology in children; Social-
        emotional assessment; Theories of human development
Personality-centered learning styles, 295
Personality Inventory for Children and for Youth, 383, 517
Pervasive developmental disorder - not otherwise specified
        (PDD-NOS), 42
Peskin, H., 425
Petch, B., 539
Petersen, A. C., 424
Peterson, D. R., 160
Peterson, R., 582
Peterson, R. J., 601, 602
Petit, G. S., 107
Pettersson, H., 48
Pevsner, J., 40, 41
Peyton, V., 187, 530
Pfannenstiel, J., 375
Pfeiffer, S. I., 82
Phelps, L., 421, 422
Phelps, LeAdelle, 123
Phelps Kindergarten Readiness Scale-Second Edition, 401
Phenylketonuria (PKU)
    dietary compliance, 384–385
    outcomes of, 384
    screening procedure, 384
Phillips, B. N., 457
Phipps, J., 438
Phobias, 207–208
Phonemic awareness
    assessment, 385–386
    decoding skills improvement, 438–439
    development levels and, 385–386
    Elkonin box tool, 386
    interventions, 385–386
    Lindamood Phonemic Sequencing program, 386
    Orton-Gillingham approach to, 442–443
    vs. phonological awareness, 385
    reading ability and, 385, 387
    school psychologist role, 386–387
    spoken, written word bridge, 385
    theory and research, 385
    writing and spelling, 386, 596
    The Writing Road to Reading (Spalding), 443
    See also Academic achievement; Curriculum-based
        assessment (CBA); Early intervention (EA); Learning;
        Reading interventions and strategies
Phonemic Awareness in Young Children
        (Adams, et. al.), 438–439
Phonemic Awareness Inventory, 449
Phonological recording, 154, 179
Phonological speech disorder, 100
Physical abuse, 4, 5–6
Physical developmental milestones, 158–159*table*
Physical neglect, 4
Piacentini, J., 357, 358
Piaget, Jean, 12, 187, 498
Pianta, R. C., 407, 458, 559
Pica eating disorder, 387
Pierce, W. D., 331

Pilcher, C., 542
Pilla, R. S., 73, 74, 234, 582
Pitcher, G., 127, 128, 129
PKU. *See* Phenylketonuria
Play-based assessment. *See* Authentic assessment;
    Developmental milestones; Infant assessment
Play therapy, 404
PNS. *See* Parasymathetic nervous system
Poland, D., 129
Poland, S., 127–133
Poling, A., 25
Pollack, J. M., 174
Pollack, W. S., 582, 584
Polloway, E. A., 251, 252
Polya, G., 307
Pomeranz-Essley, A., 321
Poole, B. J., 102, 103
Popham, J. W., 134, 135
Population Resource Center, 560
Portfolio assessment
    augmentation use of, 389
    authentic assessment approach, 388
    characteristics, uses of, 388
    documentation portfolio, 388
    documentation use of, 389
    evaluation portfolio, 388
    limitations of, 388–389
    linkage use of, 389–390
    vs. norm-referenced assessment, 388
    professional training use of, 390
    regular education use of, 389
    showcase portfolio, 388
    student's work samples, 387–388
    See also Authentic assessment
Positive behavior support (PBS)
    applied behavior analysis and, 390, 392
    functional behavioral assessment focus, 390–391
    group support application, 391
    individual support application, 391
    operant conditioning learning theory and, 390
    school psychologist role, 392
    schoolwide support application, 391–392
    See also Applied behavior analysis (ABA); Classroom
        climate; Conditioning: classical and operant; Functional
        behavioral assessment (FBA)
Positive Behavioral Intervention, 49, 52
Positive reinforcement, 64*table*
    See also Applied behavior analysis (ABA); Behavior;
        Behavior intervention; Discipline; Functional
        behavioral assessment (FBA); Premack Principle;
        Verbal praise
Posner, M. I., 29
Postconventional stage of moral development, 280
Postreinforcement pause concept, 470, 471
Posttraumatic stress disorder (PTSD)
    arousal increase, 393
    bullying, 235
    comorbidity, 394
    corporal punishment and, 121
    prevalence of, 392
    reexperience of trauma, 393

reminders avoidance, 393
school psychologist role, 392–393, 394
symptoms duration, 393
trauma exposure, 393
treatment, 394
See also Abuse and neglect; Counseling; *DSM-IV-TR;* Fears;
    Psychopathology in children; Violence in schools
Pottebaum, S. M., 311
Poulin, F., 211, 324
Poulson, L., 587
Poverty, 4
    aggressive in schools, 19
    dropouts and, 175, 221–222
    fetal alcohol syndrome, 209
    No Child Left Behind Act of 2001, 350–351
    single-parent families, 505–508
    teen pregnancy, 560
Power, T., 421, 422
Power, T. J., 19
Powers, A. M. R., 86, 87
Powers, F. C., 86, 87
Powers, J. L., 248
Powers, K., 36, 37
Practice effects
    defined, 66*table*
    See also Behavior; Learning; Mastery learning
Prader-Willi syndrome (PWS)
    neuro-behavioral genetic disorder, 394
    symptoms of, 394–395
Prasse, D. P., 259, 298
Preconventional stage of moral development, 279–280
Premack, D., 395
Premack Principle
    behavior frequency focus, 395
    operant conditioning principle, 395
Prenatal mental retardations, 319*table*
Preschool assessment
    adaptive techniques, 399
    alternative testing methods, 400
    basic skills, tests, 401
    behavior, attention, tests, 401–402
    cognitive and learning ability, tests, 401
    controversy over, 397, 398–400
    defined, 305
    developmental inconsistencies, 398–399
    diagnosis purpose of, 398
    domains of assessment, 401–402
    federal mandates, 396
    fine, gross motor skill development, tests, 401
    goals of, 397
    Head Start, 396
    importance of, 396
    individual program planning, monitoring purpose of, 398
    instruments of assessment, 396–397
    language, speech development, tests, 401
    language skill deficiencies, 399
    methods of assessment, 400–401
    observation data, importance of, 399
    parental involvement, 400–401
    program evaluation purpose of, 398

reliability issues, 400
screening purpose of, 397–398
setting, environment changes, 399
standard procedure alteration, 399
traditional testing methods, 400
transition problems, 399–400
See also Intelligence; Special education; Theories
    of human development
Preschoolers
assessment, 404
child care options, 403
development domains, 402
ecological behavior management, 404
family counseling, 404
Federal legislation, 404
Head Start program, 403
Montessori program, 403
multidisciplinary teams, 404
NAEYC program accreditation, 403–404
play function, 402–403
play therapy, 404
school psychologist role, 404
special education services, 404
See also Early intervention (EA); Preschool assessment
Pressley, M., 316, 587
Prevention
competence enhancement approach, 405–406
outcome elimination, 405
primary prevention programs, 405, 406
risk and, 405–406
school transition programs, 406
secondary prevention programs, 405, 407
tertiary prevention programs, 405
See also Bullying and victimization; Cheating; DARE
    program; Discipline; Early intervention (EA); Gangs;
    Parents As Teachers (PAT) program; Peer mediation;
    Resilience and protective factors; Substance abuse;
    Violence in schools
Price, G. E., 295
Price, L. H., 358
Principles for Professional Ethics (NASP), 109
Principles of Psychologists and Code of Conduct (APA), 109
Problem solving
behavioral consultation, 408
defined, 407
problem solving appraisal, 408
problem solving consultation, 408
problem solving process model, 408
See also Consultation: behavioral (BC); Consultation:
    conjoint behavioral (CBC); Consultation:
    ecobehavioral; Early intervention (EA); Interviewing;
    Multidisciplinary teams (MDTs); School psychologist;
    Special education
Problem Solving Inventory (PSI), 408
Problem-solving model phases of behavioral
    assessment, 55
*Procedure and Coding Manual for Review of Evidence-Based
    Interventions* (Kratochwill & Stoiber), 197–198
Process Assessment of the Learner, 596
Process Curriculum conflict management, 54
Professional School Psychology journal, 169

Program evaluation
activities and outcomes, 408
Context, Inputs, Process, Product (CIPP) model, 411
design and methodology, 408–409
education program evaluation standards, 410
empowerment evaluation model, 411
evaluation process, 409–410
evaluation *vs.* research, 410
experimental or field trial models, 410–411
formative evaluation, 408
functions of, 408
models of, 410–411
principles of practice, 410
school psychologist role, 411–412
school reform effectiveness and, 411
in the schools, 411
summative evaluation, 408
theory-driven evaluation model, 411
utilization-focused evaluation model, 411
See also Formative evaluation; Special education;
    Summative evaluation
Progressive Education Association, 241
Project Fast Track school reform program, 407
Projection defense mechanism, 155
Projective testing
behavioral, emotional, social functioning assessment, 412
controversy regarding, 412–413
examples of, 412
open-ended stimuli use, 412
personality assessment, 412
social-emotional assessment, 517
See also Diagnosis and labeling; Personality assessment;
    Reliability; Social-emotional assessment; Validity
Promiscuity, 170
Promoting Alternative THinking Strategies (PATHS)
    curriculum program, 407
Protective factors. *See* Resilience and protective factors
Pryzwansky, W. B., 20, 117
PSC (problem-solving consultation), 408
PSI (Problem Solving Inventory), 408
Psychoanalytic model, of human development theory, 563–564
Psychoanalytic theory of psychotherapy, 417–418
Psychodynamic theory of behavior intervention, 50–51, 490
Psychological module of Component Model of Reading
constituents of, 433*table*
gender differences, 435, 441
learned helplessness, 434, 441
learning styles, 434–435, 441
locus of control, 434, 441
motivation and interest, 434, 441–442
remedial approach, 440–441
teacher expectations, 435
teacher/parent expectations, 441
Psychological reports. *See* Reports (psychological)
Psychological Service for School Problems (Hildreth), 475
Psychology in the Schools journal, 456
The Psychology of Sex Differences (Maccoby and Jacklin), 221
Psychometric *g*
cognitive ability, 413
IQ tests, 413
See also intelligence

Psychopathology in children
defined, 413
DSM-IV approach to, 413–414, 416
empirically based approach, 415*fig.*, 416
maladaptive deviance, 413
suicide risk factors, 549
treatment, 416
See also Aggression in schools; Autism spectrum disorders;
    Depression; *DSM-IV-TR;* Obsessive-compulsive disorder
    (OCD); Oppositional defiant disorder (ODD);
    Posttraumatic stress disorder (PTSD)
Psychosocial development, 573
See also Erikson's stages of psychosocial development
Psychotherapeutic interview, 273
Psychotherapy
behavioral therapy theory, 418
client factors, 416
components of, 416–417
vs. counseling, 124, 417
depression, 157
humanistic theory, 418
integrative approach to, 418
motivations to seek, 416
psychoanalytic theory, 417–418
school psychologist role, 419–420
school setting factors, 419
theoretical perspectives on, 417–418
therapist characteristics, 416
unique aspects for children, adolescents, 418–419
Psychotropic medications
ADHD, 420
affective and mood disorders, 421
alpha-adrenergic medications, 423
anticonvulsants, mood stabilizers, 423
antidepressants, 422
antipsychotics, 422
anxiolytics, 422–423
assessment of, 420
autism spectrum disorders, 420–421
children *vs.* adult distinctions, 420
enuresis, 421
legal issues, 423
mental retardation, developmental disabilities, 421
stimulants, 421–422
Tourette's syndrome, 421
See also Aggression in schools; Attention deficit hyperactivity
    disorder (ADHD); Autism spectrum disorders;
    Depression; Enuresis; Mental retardation (MR);
    Personality assessment; Social-emotional assessment;
    Substance abuse; Tourette's syndrome
Psyhometrics, 123
PT. *See* Parent education (PE) and parent training (PT)
PTSD. *See* Posttraumatic stress disorder
Puberty
gender differences, 423–425
genetic, environmental factors, 425
male, female changes of, 423–424
psychosocial development, 190
See also Friendships; Gangs; Social skills
Public Law (P.L.) 91-142, 177, 404
Public Law (P.L.) 94-142, 181, 396, 475, 522

Public Law (P.L.) 96-88, 577
Public Law (P.L.) 99-457, 396, 404
Public Law (P.L.) 102-119, 396
Public Law (P.L.) 105-17, 396
Pugh-Lilly, A. O., 325
Punishment. *See* Applied behavior analysis (ABA); Behavior;
    Behavior intervention; Discipline; Functional behavioral
    analysis
Punishment reductive technique, 65*table*
Purdue Pegboard measure, 337
Purpose, Ask, Read, Summarize (PARS) study approach, 541

Q
Qualitative research
case study strategy, 427
clinical research method, 428
ethnography method, 427
explanation of, 427
life history method, 427
models, methodologies, 427–428
participatory action research method, 427–428
vs. quantitative research, 427, 454
See also Research in school psychology
Quamma, J., 407
Quantitative research, 427, 454
Quay, H. C., 18, 160, 360
Quenk, N. L., 295
Quid pro quo harassment, 234
Quinn, M. M., 382
Quiroz, D. B., 97

R
Race, ethnicity, class and gender
ability grouping and, 3
class and economic status, 430
vs. culture, 138
culture as shared history, 429
European *vs.* Black psychology, 429
examiner and examinee cross-cultural
    dynamics, 138–139
gender as social construct through language, 430
gender bias, 430
No Child Left Behind Act of 2001, 350–351
parenting beliefs, values, 373
race, scientific *vs.* social construct, 429
race *vs.* ethnicity, 429
self-perceptions, identity structures, 430
single-parent families, 505
suicide, 548–549
suspension discrimination and, 554
teacher-student relationships, 559
teen pregnancy, 560
zero tolerance policies, 601, 602
See also Ability grouping; Americans with
    Disabilities Act (ADA); Bias in testing;
    Cross-cultural assessment; Ethnicity;
    Friendships; Gender, gender factors; Intelligence;
    Multicultural education; Resilience and
    protective factors
RAD. *See* Reactive attachment disorder (RAD)
    of infancy and early childhood

Radio/music. *See* Computer technology; Media and children
Rae, W. A., 364, 395, 489
Raffaele Mendez, L. M., 554, 555, 556
Rafferty, Y., 248
Raichle, M. E., 29
Raineri, G., 3
Rankin, J., 587
Rapoport, J. L., 357, 358
Rasavage, C., 495
Rasmussen, H. N., 126, 472
Rasmussen, S., 357, 358
Rathvon, N., 52, 53
Ratio schedule of reinforcement, 469–470, 471
Ratio strain of reinforcement schedules, 469
Rational Emotional Therapy, 125
Rational-emotive therapy, cognitive-behavioral
    modification, 96–97
Rationalization defense mechanism, 155
Rauch, S. L., 357
Ray, B. D., 247
Rayner, S., 294, 295, 296
Rea, P. J., 524, 525
Reaction formation defense mechanism, 155
Reactive attachment disorder (RAD) of infancy and
    early childhood
  vs. autism, 431
  gross pathological care, 431, 432
  inhibited *vs.* disinhibited types of, 431
  research studies, 431–432
  social relatedness disturbance, 431
  treatment, 432
  See also Autism spectrum disorders; *DSM-IV-TR;* Infant
    assessment; Mental retardation (MR); Preschoolers
Reading interventions and strategies
  ADHD, differential diagnosis, 438
  case example, 446–453
  children at risk, interventions for, 442–444
  cognitive module, 433–434, 433*table See also* Cognitive
    module of Component Model of Reading
  cognitive module, remedial approach, 438–440
  Component Model of, 433, 433*table*
  comprehension assessment, 437
  comprehension problems, differential diagnosis, 438
  comprehension problems, instructional strategies for, 438, 440
  decoding problems, differential diagnosis of, 438
  decoding problems, remedial approach, 438–439
  decoding skills, 433
  decoding skills, assessment of, 436–437
  ecological model, 435–436 *See also* Ecological module of
    Component Model of Reading
  ecological module, remedial approach, 441–442
  psychological module, 434–435 *See also* Psychological
    module of Component Model of Reading
  psychological module, remedial approach, 440–441
  reading learning disabilities, 290–291
  research trends regarding, 457
  spelling skills, 438
  spelling skills, improvement of, 439–440
  Success for All (SFA) program, 480–481
  vocabulary knowledge, assessment of, 437
  vocabulary knowledge, improvement of, 440

  See also Academic achievement; Cognitive module of
    Component Model of Reading; Cooperative
    learning; Ecological module of Component Model of
    Reading; Grades; Homework; Learning; Learning
    styles; Psychological module of Component
    Model of Reading
Reading Recovery (RR) program, 443–444
Reaney, J. B., 71
Reavis, H. K., 47
Recapitulation theory of human development, 563
Reciprocal determinism
  behavior, environment, personal interactions, 444
  school learning and, 444–445
  social learning theory, 445
  vicarious learning, 444
Reciprocal Peer Tutoring model (RPT), 378, 575
Recovery reductive technique, 65*table*
Reddy, M., 127, 582, 584
Reddy, S. S., 94
Reed, R. P., 253
Reeder, G. D., 214
Reeve, A., 318
Reeve, A. L., 380
Reflex. *See* Developmental milestones;
    Neuropsychological assessment
Rehabilitation Act of 1973, 22, 243, 577
  ADHD and, 33
  behavior interventions, 49
  bipolar disorder, 72
  children with cancer, 79
  student improvement teams, 536
  See also Section 504, of the Rehabilitation Act of 1973
Reich, W., 274
Reid, J. B., 107, 108
Reid, J. C., 550
Reid, M. J., 368
Reid, S. R., 572
Reimers, T. M., 311
Reis, S. M., 227
Reiss, A. J., 582
Relations to other variables evidence of test validity, 579
Relaxation technique
  cognitive-behavioral modification, 96
  fear reduction, 208
Relaxation Training, 70
Relaxed or eclectic homeschooling method, 246
Reliability of test scores
  defined, 445
  internal consistency reliability, 445
  interrater reliability, 445
  test-retest reliability, 445
  See also Bias in testing; Cross-cultural assessment; Ethical
    issues in school psychology; Norm-referenced testing;
    Statewide tests
Remley, C., 105
Renzulli, J. S., 227
Reports (psychological)
  assessment tools, 448
  background information, 446–448
  classroom observations, 448–449
  cognitive assessment, 449

components of, 446
ethical issues, 446
family history, 448
math assessment, 451
medical history, 447–448
personality and behavioral assessment, 451
psychometric summary sheet, 452–453*fig.*
purpose of, 445–446
reading assessment, 449–450
recommendations, 453
referral problem history, 448
school history, 446–447
social history, 448
spelling assessment, 450
summary, conclusions, 451, 452–453*fig.*, 453
testing observations, 449
visual-motor and achievement assessment, 449
written language, 450–451
See also Confidentiality; Ethical issues in school
psychology; Multidisciplinary teams (MDTs)
Repp, A. C., 494
Repression defense mechanism, 155
Resalel-Azrin, W., 47
Reschly, D. J., 67, 68, 81, 404, 535
Rescorla, L. A., 277, 414, 415*fig.*
Research in school psychology
basic *vs.* applied research, 454
data collection methods, 454
defined, 453–454
disorder-specific intervention focus, 457
domains in, 455
early intervention focus, 456–457
history of, 454
primary sources of, 456
quantitative *vs.* qualitative, 454
topics in, 455–456
trends, future directions in, 456–457
types of, 454
violence, violence prevention focus, 456
See also Careers in school psychology; Diagnosis and
labeling; Division of School Psychologists
(Division 16, APA)
Resilience and protective factors
contextual protective factors, 458–459
individual characteristic protective factors, 458
research directions in, 459
risk factors and, 457–458
risk negative outcomes, 458
school-based programs aiding, 459
See also Abuse and neglect; Attention deficit hyperactivity
disorder (ADHD); Divorce adjustment; Dropouts;
Learned helplessness; Self-concept and efficacy;
Self-injurious behavior; Violence in schools
Resistance to Intervention diagnostic paradigm, 162
Resource rooms, 460, 523–524
See also Least restrictive environment; Special education
Respondent conditioning, 105
Response cost reductive technique, 65*table*
See also Applied behavior analysis (ABA); Behavior
intervention; Behavioral assessment; Behavioral
concepts and applications

Response processes evidence of test validity, 579
Responsiveness to intervention (RTI) learning disabilities
assessment method
aptitude-achievement discrepancy formulas, 460–461
categorical *vs.* noncategorical placement, 462–463
classroom instruction assessment, 460, 461
common attributes of, 462–463
continuous process monitoring, 461
criticism of, 463–464
differentiated curriculum, 462
explanation of, 460–461
fidelity measures, 462
prevention focus, 463
progress monitoring, 462
research-based interventions, 461
school psychologist role, 464
tiers of interventions, 462
universal screening, 461
varied features, 462
See also Learning disabilities (LDs)
Retention
academic achievement and, 466
advantages *vs.* disadvantages of, 467
characteristics of retained students, 465
dropout rates and, 466–467
gender factors, 221, 465
inadvisability of, 397
ineffectiveness of, 465–466
IQ scores, 465
long-term outcomes and, 467–468
parental factors, 465
retention, defined, 465
self-concept, 465
social adjustment, behavior and, 465, 466
statistics regarding, 465
students' perspectives on, 468
See also Academic achievement; Friendships; Grades;
Race, ethnicity, class and gender; Special education
Retrovirus, 244
Rett's disorder
assessment of, 41
development stages of, 41
diagnosis of, 40–41
gender factors, 40
interventions, 41
prevalence factors, 40
Reynolds, C. L., 328
Reynolds, C. R., 67, 350, 516
Reynolds, W. M., 547, 548
Rhett's disorder. *See* Autism spectrum disorders
Rhoades, E. K., 245
Rhode, G., 496
Rhodes, J. E., 323, 325
Riccio, C., 72, 272, 350
Riccio, C. A., 350
Richards, M. M., 360
Richman, G. S., 493
Rickover, H. G., 241
Riddle, M. A., 358
Riding, R., 294, 295, 296
Ries, R. R., 135

Rigby, K., 74
Rimland, B., 202
Ringdahl, J., 67
Ringwalt, C. L., 151
Risk-factors. *See* Resilience and protective factors
Risley, T., 568
Risley, T. R., 23, 66*table,* 214
Rizzolo, M. C., 321
Roberts, M. C., 28, 405
Roberts, P. H., 344
Roberts, R., 596
Robertson, D. F., 427
Robins, L. N., 459
Robinson, B. E., 281
Robinson, C. D., 3
Robinson, E., 93
Robinson, S. L., 112, 497
Robinson, T. R., 255, 256
Roblyer, M. D., 103
Rock, D. A., 174
Rodriguez, O., 272
Roesler, J. S., 572
Rogers, Carl, 123
Rogers, Dale Evans, 320
Rogers, K., 515
Rogers, M. R., 140
Roid, G. H., 401
Role-play technique, cognitive-behavioral modification, 97
Rollings, J. P., 492
Roncker v. Walters, 299
Roodbeen, P. S., 257
Roona, M. R., 546
Roots and Wings school reform program, 406
Rosen, H., 591
Rosenfield, S, 143, 144
Rosenthal, E., 72, 491
Rosenthal, R., 163
Ross, C. M., 1
Ross, W. D., 191
Roth, J. A., 582
Rothlisberg, B., 50
Rotholz, D. A., 318
Rotter, Julian, 434
Rourke, B. P., 573
Rousseau, Jean-Jacques, 566
Rowand, C., 601
Rowland, B. H., 281
Roy-Carlson, L., 325
RPT (Reciprocal Peer Tutoring model), 378
RR (Reading Recovery) program, 443–444
RTI. *See* Responsiveness to intervention (RTI) learning
    disabilities assessment method
Ruan, J., 582
Ruan, W. J., 73, 74, 234
Ruenzel, D., 330
Ruiz-Primo, M. A., 380
Rumberger, R. W., 174
Russell, J. D., 103
Russell, M., 591
Russo, H., 222
Rutherford, R. B., 382

Rutter, M., 431, 458, 459
Ryan, R. M., 331
Ryerson, D. M., 551

S
SA. *See* Separation anxiety (SA) disorder
Sabella, R. A., 235
Sacca, M. K., 94, 379
Saedker, D., 221
Saedker, M., 221
Saentz, A. L., 67
Safer, D., 420
Saigh, P. A., 393
Sailor, W., 392
Sale, P., 343
Salkind, N. J., 190, 280, 498, 566
Salvia, J., 13, 35, 36, 137, 389
Sammons, M., 420, 421, 422
Sanchez, J., 140
Sanders, M., 53, 94
Sandler, H. M., 250
SAT (Scholastic Achievement Test), 9
Satiation, 64*table*
    See also Behavioral concepts and applications
Sattler, J. M., 12, 66*table,* 273, 352, 446
Saudargas, R. A., 56
Savage, C. R., 357
Savage, T. V., 567
Sawyer, M., 420, 421, 422
Sax, G., 317
Saylor, K. E., 378
Scafidi, E. C., 356
Scahill, L., 358
Scales of Independent Behavior, Revised (SIB-R), 14*table,* 15
SCANS (Secretary's Commission on Achieving Necessary
    Skills), 242
Scantlin, R., 310
Scardamalia, M., 587
Schab, F., 86, 87
Schallert, D. L., 8
Schaps, E., 406
Schedules of reinforcement
    conclusions regarding, 471
    continuous reinforcement, 469, 471
    fixed-interval schedule, 470, 471
    fixed-ratio schedule of reinforcement, 470, 471
    intermittent reinforcement, 469, 471
    interval schedules, 470, 471
    postreinforcement pause concept, 470, 471
    ratio schedules, 469–470, 471
    ratio strain concept, 469
    variable-interval schedule, 470, 471
    variable-ratio schedule, 470, 471
    See also Behavior; Behavior intervention;
        Generalization; Self-management
Scheidt, P., 73, 74, 234, 582
Schensul, J. J., 547
Schizophrenia
    bipolar disorder, 71
    echolalia and, 186
Schloss, P., 53

Schmitt, K. L., 310
Schneider, B., 211
Schnell, S. V., 17
Scholastic Achievement Test (SAT), 9
School-at-home schooling method, 246
School climate
  components of, 471
  negative climate outcomes, 471
  policies and practices implications, 471–472
  positive climate outcomes, 471
  positive climate programs and strategies, 472
  school psychologist role, 472
  See also Discipline; Dropouts; High school; Middle school;
    Multicultural education; School reform; Violence in
    schools
School counselors
  developmental stages focus, 472
  vs. school psychologist, 472
  standards-based program, 472
  See also Counseling
The School Entry Assessment Project, 375
School-home notes
  behaviors addressed by, 473
  daily report card, 473
  See also Consultation: conjoint behavioral (CBC);
    Intervention; Motivation; Parenting, parents
School psychologist
  behavioral consultation, 408
  behavioral interviews, 276
  bipolar disorder, 72
  classroom climate and, 90
  conduct disorder, 109
  crisis intervention, 109
  current trends in, 475–476
  death and bereavement, 153–154
  divorce adjustment, 172
  due process, 178
  earliest years, 473–474
  eating disorders and, 185–186
  encopresis interventions, 188
  evidence-based interventions, 196, 197, 198–199
  family counseling, 206–207
  federal legislation, 474–475
  friendships and, 212
  full-service school, 214
  future service needs, 478
  generalized anxiety disorder, 224
  Head Start, 239–240
  home-school collaboration, 250–251
  homework and, 253–254
  IDEA and, 260
  IEP meeting, 258
  Individualized Education Plan and, 257
  infant assessment, 266–267
  interventions and, 273
  job description, employment settings, 476
  job market supply and demand, 476–477
  lead exposure, 282
  learning theory and, 288–289
  least restrictive environment and, 299
  licensing and certification of, 300–301, 478, 515

math interventions, strategies, 310
mentoring, 325
middle school, 328–329
motivation *vs.* disability, 333, 334
motivational interventions, 334–335
motor assessment, 337
multidisciplinary teams, 342–343
obesity in children, 356
obsessive-compulsive disorder, 358
oppositional defiant disorder, 360
organizational consultation and development, 362
outcomes-based assessment, 365
parent collaboration, 374
peer pressure, 379
personality assessment, 381–384
phonemic awareness, 386–387
placement role, 474
portfolio assessment, 387–390
positive behavior support, 392
preschoolers, 404
problem-solving process, 408–409
professional development, 474–475
program evaluation, 411–412
PTSD, 394
responsiveness to intervention model, 464
salary and fringe benefits, 477–478
school climate, 472
school-home notes, 473
vs. school social worker, 515
secondary school roles and duties, 243–244
separation anxiety, 499
single-case experimental design applications, 504
single-parent families, 507–508
social-emotional assessment, 517–518
special education placement, 474, 538
spelling strategies, 529
standard scores, 530
student improvement teams (SITs), 538
stuttering, 544
substance abuse, 547
task analysis, 557–558
typical workday of, 477*fig.*
writing interventions, 588–589
See also American Psychological Association (APA); Careers
    in school psychology; Crisis intervention; Division of
    School Psychologists (Division 16, APA); Ethical issues
    in school psychology; Licensing and certification in
    school psychology; National Association of School
    Psychologists (NASP); Reports (psychological);
    Research in school psychology; Special education;
    Supervision in school psychology
School Psychology International journal, 456
School Psychology Quarterly journal, 456
School Psychology Review journal, 456
School reform (SR)
  Accelerated Schools (AS) model of, 482–483
  advantages *vs.* disadvantages of, 483
  Community for Learning (CFL) model of, 481–482
  components of, 478, 479*table*
  comprehensive school reform, defined, 478, 479*table*
  Direct Instruction (DI) model of, 481

High Schools That Work (HSTW) model of, 482
history of, 479–480
No Child Left Behind Act, 526
organizational consultation and development, 362
program evaluation, 411
School Development Program (SDP) model of, 481
special education curriculum, 526
student success variables, 480
Success for All (SFA) model of, 406, 480–481
See also Academic achievement; Charter schools; Discipline;
    No Child Left Behind Act of 2001 (NCLB); Outcomes-
    based assessment; Performance-based assessment (PA);
    Prevention; Special education; Statewide tests
School refusal
causes of, 484–485
diagnosis, treatment, 485–486
outcomes from, 484
separation anxiety disorder, 484
See also Cognitive-behavioral modification;
    Dropouts; Fears; Separation anxiety (SA) disorder
School-to-Work Opportunities Act, 261
School Transitional Environment Project (STEP), 406
Schowalter, D., 505, 506
Schroeder, S. R., 493
Schubert, W. H., 241
Schugurensky, D., 577
Schuhmann, E. M., 368
Schulte, A. C., 115, 117
Schumm, J. S., 525
Schunk, D. H., 491
Schwab-Stone, M. E., 274
Schwartz, J. E., 102
Schwartz, M. S., 69
SCICA. *See* Semistructured Clinical Interview
    for Children and Adolescents
Sciegaj, M., 321
Scott, C., 587
Scruggs, T. E., 316
SD. *See* Standard deviation (SD)
SD (systemic desensitization) phobia intervention, 208
SDRT (Stanford Diagnostic Reading Test), 437
Sears, Robert, 565
SECOS (State-Event Classroom Observation System) of
    behavioral assessment, 56
Secretary's Commission on Achieving Necessary Skills
    (SCANS), 242
Section 504, of the Rehabilitation Act of 1973, 522
antidiscrimination legislation, disabled students, 486
major life activity, defined, 487
physical or mental impairment, defined, 486
student improvement teams, 536
See also Due process; Individualized Education
    Plan (IEP); Individuals With Disabilities Education Act
    (IDEA); Special education
Sedita, J., 539
Sedney, M., 153
Seeley, J. R., 71, 97
Seizure disorders
absence seizures, 487–488
complex partial seizures, 487
educational implications, intervention, 488–489

generalized seizures, 487
myoclonic seizures, 488
partial seizures, 487
partial with secondary generalization seizures, 487
prevalence, etiology, 488
simple partial seizures, 487
tonic-clonic seizures, 488
treatment, 488
Selective mutism (SM)
anxiety and, 490
DSM-IV-TR diagnostic criteria, 489
interventions, 490
oppositional defiant behavior, 489, 490
prevalence of, 489
shyness, 500
trauma cause of, 490
See also Applied behavior analysis (ABA); Behavior
    intervention; Behavioral assessment; *DSM-IV-TR*
Selective serotonin reuptake inhibitors (SSRIs)
depression therapy, 157
selective mutism therapy, 490
Self-concept and efficacy
peer relationships and, 519
protective resilient factor of, 458
retention and, 465
school-home notes, 473
self-concept assessment, 491
self-concept components, 490
self-concept interventions, 491
self-efficacy, defined, 490
self-report measures of, 491
social-cognitive theory and, 490
See also Dropouts; Learning styles; Motivation;
    Personality assessment
Self-conscious shyness, 500, 501
Self-Directed Search Career Explorer, 81
Self-discipline, 164–165
Self-efficacy. *See* Self-concept and efficacy
Self-esteem. *See* Self-concept and efficacy
Self-fulfilling prophecy
positive *vs.* negative outcomes from, 491
teacher, parent expectations, 491–492
See also Dropouts
Self-injurious behavior
assessment of, 493–494
behavior therapy, 492
defined, 492
developmental cause of, 493
endorphin narcotic effect and, 493
forms of, 492
genetic disorder cause of, 493
motivational and biological hypotheses of, 492–493
negative reinforcement cause of, 492–493
positive reinforcement cause of, 492
self-stimulation cause of, 493
treatment of, 494
See also Abuse and neglect; Aggression; Behavior
    intervention; Mental retardation (MR); Traumatic
    brain injury
Self-instructional training, cognitive-behavioral
    modification, 95

Self-management
  advantages *vs.* disadvantages of, 496
  behavioral *vs.* cognitive strategies of, 494–495
  "cover, copy and compare" technique, 495, 529
  example of, 496–497
  phases of: baseline phase, 496–497
  phases of: teacher-directed phase, 497
  phases of: matching phase, 497
  phases of: fading and self-management phase, 497
  populations and behaviors, 496
  self-evaluation, 495
  self-instruction, 495–496
  self-monitoring, 495
  self-reinforcement, 495
  See also Applied behavior analysis (ABA); Behavior
       intervention; Social skills; Study skills
Seligman, M. E. P., 126
Selye, H., 69
Semistructured Clinical Interview for Children and
     Adolescents (SCICA), 57, 274, 275*table,* 277
Semrud-Clikeman, M., 31, 262, 299, 335, 337
Sensorimotor stage of development, 498
Separation anxiety (SA) disorder
  interventions, 498–499
  prevalence, onset, associated features, 498
  school psychologist role, 499
  school refusal and, 484
  See also DSM-IV-TR; Parenting, parents; Psychopathology
       in children; School refusal
Serious emotional disturbance (SED), 225
SERV (School Emergency Response to Violence), 127
Sesame Street, 310–311
Severe body pain disorder, 520–521
Sex education, 374
Sexson, S., 78
Sexton, T. L., 126
Sexual abuse, 4, 5–6
Sexual harassment
  defined, 233–234
  prevention, intervention, 236
  school liability for, 583
  See also Harassment
Sexually transmitted diseases (STDs), 561
SFA (Success for All) school reform program, 406
Shaffer, D., 274
Shaftel, J., 526, 532
Shank, M., 83
Shaping behavior technique, 63*table*
  See also Behavior; Behavioral concepts and applications
Shapiro, B., 83
Shapiro, E., 495, 496
Shapiro, E. S., 56, 143, 473
Sharkey, J. D., 87
Sharp, S., 74, 75
Shaugnessy, M. F., 591
Shavelson, R. J., 380
Shaywitz, B. A., 179
Shaywitz, S., 179
Shea, T. M., 370, 372
Sheeber, L. B., 97
Sheras, R., 584

Sherer, M. M., 472
Sheridan, S. M., 57, 111, 112, 250, 251, 408
Sherman, R. E., 229
Shim, M., 406
Shine, A. E., 209
Shinn, M. R., 143, 144, 145
Short, R. J., 216
Showstrom, E. L., 124
Shriver, Eunice, 320
Shriver, M. D., 39, 42
Shure, M. B., 96
Shyness
  fearful shyness, 499–500, 501
  generalized anxiety disorder and, 224
  self-conscious shyness, 500, 501
  teacher expectations, 500
  See also Communication disorders; Defense mechanisms;
       Fears; Friendships; School refusal; Selective mutism
       (SM); Social skills
SIB-R (Scales of Independent Behavior, Revised), 14*table,* 15
Siegel, L., 290
Siegel, M., 193
Siekierski, B. M., 364
Sight-word reading, 433, 437, 439
SIGI PLUS (Educational Testing Service) career assessment
     program, 80
Signs of Suicide (SOS) program, 131
Silver, C. H., 460
Silverman, W., 358, 498, 499
Simmons, D. C., 379
Simon, Theodore, 123, 317, 474
Simons-Mortin, B., 73, 74, 378, 582
Simons-Morton, B., 234
Simple phase-change experimental design, 501
Simpson, R. L., 204
Simultaneous-interventions experimental design, 502
Singh, K., 252
Singh, N. N., 494
Single-case experimental design, 65*table*
  applications, 504
  between-series designs, alternating-interventions design, 502
  between-series designs, simultaneous-interventions
       design, 502
  combined-series designs, multiple baseline design,
       502, 503*fig.*
  data analysis, 502, 504
  vs. group designs, 501
  internal validity, 504
  within-series designs, changing-criterion design, 501–502
  within-series designs, parametric and periodic
       intervention designs, 502
  within-series designs, simple phase-change design, 501
  See also Evidence-based interventions (EBIs); Research in
       school psychology
Single-parent families
  characteristics of, 505
  child development outcomes, 506
  defined, 505
  divorce factors, 507
  dropout rates, 507
  ecological risk and resiliency model of, 505–506

ethnic diversity factor, 505
national demographics regarding, 504
poverty, 505
school psychology implications, 507–508
social support, 507
youth well-being, 506–507
See also Abuse and neglect; Divorce adjustment;
    Dropouts; Friendships; Parenting, parents; Race,
    ethnicity, class and gender; Resilience and
    protective factors
Sipe, C. L., 324
Sizer, T., 242
Skiba, R. J., 199, 554, 555, 582, 601
Skinner, B. F., 50, 113, 286, 287, 390, 495
Skorupski, W. P., 428
Slaby, R. G., 311
Slap, G. B., 423
Slavin, R. E., 1, 2, 379, 406, 480, 483
Slee, P., 73, 74
Sleep disorders
    anorexia and, 184
    bulimia and, 184
    divorce adjustment, 170
Sleeter, C. E., 338, 339–342, 341*table*
Slifer, K. J., 493
Smith, B., 233
Smith, C. B., 541
Smith, D. C., 583
Smith, J. D., 319
Smith, K., 550
Smith, L. H., 227
Smith, M., 126
Smith, M. C., 358
Smith, N., 438
Smith, P., 73, 186, 575
Smith, P. K., 74, 75
Smith, S., 83
Smith, T., 39
Smith, T. E. C., 487
Smits, J. A., 224
Smoking (teenage)
    demographics, 509
    gateway drug, 509, 545
    negative effects of, 509–510
    prevention strategies, 510
    secondhand smoke, 510
    See also DARE program; Self-concept and efficacy;
        Substance abuse
Smotak, L., 184
Snell, J. L., 75
Snell, M. E., 13
Snider, L. A., 357, 358
SNS. *See* Sympathetic nervous system
Sobsey, D., 4
Social class. *See* Multicultural education
Social cognitive theory, self-efficacy and, 490
Social competency training behavior interventions, 53–54
Social developmental milestones, 158–159*table*
Social-emotional assessment
    behavior rating scales, 516–517
    behavioral observation technique, 516–517

importance of, 516
interviewing technique, 517
objective self-report tests, 517
phases of, 516
projective-expressive techniques, 517
school psychologist role, 517–518
sociometric techniques, 517
techniques, 516–517
See also Behavioral assessment; Interviewing; Projective
    testing; Psychopathology in children; Social skills
Social learning theory, 285*fig.*, 286, 287
    human development theory, 565
    reciprocal determinism, 444–445
    social skills training, 513–514
Social outcomes, of homeschooling, 247
Social problem-solving interventions, cognitive-behavioral
    modification, 96
Social reinforcement, 63*table*
    See also Applied behavior analysis (ABA); Behavior;
        Behavioral concepts and applications
Social skills, 289
    academic social skills, 511
    acquisition *vs.* performance deficit, 512
    assertion, 511
    assessment of, 512–513
    behavior interventions, 513
    cognitive behavior therapy, 513
    cooperation, 511
    defined, 511
    importance of, 511–512
    interventions, 513–514
    interview assessment, 512
    observation assessment, 512
    peer and classroom-wide intervention, 514
    peer relationships, 511
    rating scales assessment, 512
    self-control, 511
    social behavior research, 511
    social competence and, 511
    social environment factors, 511
    social learning intervention, 513–514
    sociometric assessment, 512–513
    See also Classroom climate; Egocentrism; Friendships;
        Peers, peer pressure; Shyness; Study skills
Social validity, 66*table*
    See also Behavioral concepts and applications; Behavioral
        momentum technique; Generalization; Keystone
        behaviors
Social workers (school)
    role and function, 514–515
    vs. school psychologists, 515
Society for the Study of School Psychology, 169, 216
Socioeconomic status (SES)
    at-risk behaviors and, 517
    interrelated factors of, 517
    levels of, 517
    See also Poverty; Race, ethnicity, class and
        gender; Single-parent families
Sociometric assessment
    controversy regarding, 519
    explanation of, 519

peer nomination technique, 519, 520*fig.*
peer ratings, 519
peer relationships, 519
social-emotional assessment, 517
social skills assessment, 512–513
social status importance, 519
See also Behavior intervention; Self-concept
and efficacy; Social-emotional assessment
Sociometric socio-emotional assessment
technique, 517
Software, for computer technology applications, 102
Solberg, M. E., 234, 235
Solomon, D., 406
Solomon, R. S., 191
Solution-focused family therapy, 206
Somatic disorders, 108
Somatization disorder, 520
Somatoform disorders
body dysmorphic disorder, 521
conversion disorder, 520
DSM-IV list of, 520
hypochondriasis, 521
prevalence of, 520
severe body pain, 520–521
somatization disorder, 520
treatment of, 521
See also Psychopathology in children
Sorrentino, J. M., 282
SOS (Signs of Suicide) program, 131
South, M., 471
Southam-Gerow, M., 224
Spalding, R., 443
Spastic cerebral palsy, 83
Special education
advantages *vs.* disadvantages of, 525
charter schools and, 526
child abuse and neglect, 4
classroom *vs.* outside services, 523–524
court cases, 68, 260, 298, 299, 320,
321, 521, 522
current issues, 526
disability types, 522
discipline of disabled students, 526
gender factors, 222
general education interventions, 522
high-stakes testing and, 526
history of, 521–522
IDEA and, 521, 522, 524
IEP and, 522–523
inclusion *vs.* inclusive education, 525
learned helplessness, 283
least restrictive environment, 524
location, identification of, 522
neuropsychological assessment, 349
procedural safeguards, 524
progress monitoring, 524
resource rooms, 523–524
school psychologist role, 526
school reform movement, 526
social-emotional assessment, 517–518
special education services, 523–524

See also Adaptive behavior assessment; Diagnosis and
labeling; Individualized Education Plan (IEP);
Individuals With Disabilities Education Act (IDEA);
Learning disabilities (LDs); Mental retardation (MR);
Multidisciplinary teams (MDTs)
Special Olympics, 320
*Specialty Guidelines for the Delivery of Services by School
Psychologists (American Psychologist),* 169
Speech or language impairment
Head Start, 240
IDEA and, 263
phonological speech disorder, 100
preschool assessment, 401
See also Communication disorders; Developmental
milestones; Language developmental milestones;
Language learning disability; Stuttering
Spelling interventions and strategies, 439–440
barriers to, 527
correct-your-own-test procedure, 529
developmental stages of spelling knowledge, 527, 528*table*
feedback and reinforcement, 529
importance of, 527
poor speller characteristics, 528
practicing spelling, 529
presenting spelling skills, 529
rule-based strategies, 529
selecting spelling skills, 528–529
written language assessment, 596
See also Academic achievement; Mastery learning;
Mathematics interventions and strategies; Reading
interventions and strategies; Writing interventions and
strategies; Written language assessment
Speltz, M., 432
Spies, R. A., 76
Spinal cord cancer, 78
Spinelli, G. G., 79
Spivack, G., 96
Sprague, J. R., 26
Sprick, R., 52
Squire, L. R., 31
SR. *See* School reform
SSF (Supplemental Security Income), 237
SSRIs. *See* Selective serotonin reuptake inhibitors
Stackpole, K. M., 546
Stage, S. A., 97
Stamp, M. R., 361
Stancin, T., 574
Standard deviation, of normal distribution, 353, 353*fig.*
Standard deviation (SD), 530
explanation of, 530
standard error of measurement, 530
See also Grade equivalent scores; Percentile ranks; Standard
error of measurement; Stanines
Standard error of measurement (SEM)
explanation of, 530
observed *vs.* true scores, 530
See also Grade equivalent scores; Percentile ranks;
Standard deviation (SD); Stanines
Standard scores
explanation of, 530
relative status in distribution of means, 530

Z- *vs.* T-scores, 530
  See also Grade equivalent scores; Percentile ranks;
      Standard deviation (SD)
Standardized mean difference, of effect size, 187–188
Stanford-Binet Intelligence Scale, 271*table,* 272, 400, 401, 474
Stanford Diagnostic Reading Test (SDRT), 437
Stanines, 531
  See also Grade equivalent scores; Percentile ranks; Standard
      deviation (SD); Standard error of measurement
      (SEM)
Stanley, M., 492
Stanovich, K. E., 311
STARS (Students Teachers and Relationship Support)
      program, 559
State-Event Classroom Observation System (SECOS)
      of behavioral assessment, 56
Statewide tests
  academic standards measured by, 531
  accommodations to, 531–532
  accountability, 531
  constructed *vs.* selected response tests, 531–532, 533
  disabled students measured by, 531
  explanation of tests, 532
  high-stakes assessments, 534
  No Child Left Behind Act, 531
  purpose of, 531
  results, 532
  See also Academic achievement; Authentic assessment;
      Criterion-referenced assessment; Curriculum-based
      assessment (CBA); Grade equivalent scores; No Child
      Left Behind Act of 2001 (NCLB); Norm-referenced
      testing; Normal distribution; Percentile ranks;
      Performance-based assessment (PA)
Status dropout rate calculation formula, 173
STDs (sexually transmitted diseases), 561
Stecker, P. M., 537
Steege, M. W., 15
Steele, R. C., 360
Stefkovich, J., 121
Stein, J. A., 151
Stein, N., 234
STEP (School Transitional Environment Project), 406
Stephens, D., 506
Stepich, D. A., 103
Steps to Respect bullying/peer relationship program, 75
Sterling, S. E., 172
Sterling-Turner, H. E., 112
Sternberg, R. J., 268, 270, 272, 296
Stevens, N., 211, 212
Stevenson, G., 39
Stimulant psychotropic medications, 421–422
Stimulus control, 62*table*
Stimulus-response-model, 61*table*
Stinnett, T. A., 163, 272
Stipek, D., 331
Stitch, F., 126
Stoiber, K. C., 117, 197, 199, 505, 506, 508, 561, 562
Stollar, S. A., 362
Storey, K., 26
Stott, D. H., 296
Stouthamer-Loeber, M., 107, 360

Strategic family therapy, 205–206
Strategies for Achievement Approach (Tuckman), 541–542
Straus, M. A., 120, 121
Strauss, S., 234, 236
Strein, W., 491
Streke, A. V., 546
Strong, M., 527
Strong Interest Inventory, 81
Struckman, A., 95
Structural family therapy, 205
Structured positive reinforcement behavior interventions, 53
Student improvement teams (SITs), 532
  asset identification, 535
  effectiveness evaluation, 537–538
  goal setting, progress monitoring, 537
  high-stakes assessments, 534
  intervention generation, selection, 537
  vs. multidisciplinary teams, 534
  peer comparisons, 536
  previous intervention outcomes, 536
  problem analysis, 536–537
  problem identification, 535–536
  problem-solving process, 535–538
  school psychologist role, 538
  student current performance, 536
  student interviews, 536
  team organization, 538
  See also Multidisciplinary teams (MDTs)
Student Styles Questionnaire, personality learning
      style measure, 295
Students Teachers and Relationship Support (STARS)
      program, 559
Study skills
  achievement-motivation model of, 541–542
  distance education strategies, 542
  effective studying, 539–540
  elaborative processing, 541
  information organization, 540
  information selection, 540
  information summarization, 540
  learning maximization, 539
  learning style identification, 539
  note taking, 540
  Purpose, Ask, Read, Summarize (PARS) approach, 541
  questions construction, 541
  self-study guide, 542
  study strategies, 540–541
  Survey, Question, Read, Recite, Review (SQ3R)
      approach, 541
  underlining, 540–541
  See also Academic achievement; Homework; Learning styles;
      Mathematics interventions and strategies; Reading
      interventions and strategies; Writing interventions and
      strategies
Stufflebeam, D. L., 411
Stuhlman, M. W., 559
Stuttering, 100
  causes of, 543
  defined, 543
  diagnosis criteria, 543
  gender factors, 543

interventions, 543–544
school psychologist role, 544
self-modeling, 544
See also Communication disorders
Sublimation defense mechanism, 155
Substance abuse
ADHD, 547
adjustment disorder, 16
club drugs, 545
conduct disorder and, 108
death, reaction to, 130
depression and, 155, 156
divorce adjustment, 170
drug treatment, 546–547
DSM-IV definition, 544
ecological focus, 546
ethnic demographics, 545
gender factors, 545
incidence of, 545
indicators of, 544–545
intervention target population, 545–546
intervention terms of delivery, 546
latchkey children, 281
parent, school psychologist collaboration, 374
prescription narcotic drugs, 545
program exposure, 546
PTSD and, 34
school psychologist role, 547
suicide risk factor, 131, 549
universal *vs.* selective *vs.* indicated targets, 545–546
use *vs.* abuse, 544–545
See also DARE program; HIV/AIDS; Resilience and
protective factors; Smoking (teenage)
Substitution defense mechanism, 155
Success for All (SFA) school reform program, 406
Sugrue, B., 380
Suicide, attempted suicide
adjustment disorder, 16
bullying, 74
community-based programs, 551
conduct disorder and, 108
corporal punishment and, 121
death, reaction to, 130
depression and, 131, 157, 549
developmental stages of understanding death, 129
ethnicity factors, 549
family history factors, 550
gender factors, 222, 548–549
immediate steps to take, 551
media education guidelines, 551
methods of, 549
myths regarding, 550
no-harm contracts, 130
parent awareness, 550
parental roles, 131
postvention guidelines, 131
prevention and intervention programs, 550–551
prior attempts, 549
psychological autopsy concept, 549
psychopathology risk factor, 549
risk factors, 131

risk levels, 130–131
school-based programs, 550–551
school shootings, 128
statistics regarding, 130
stressful life events factors, 550
substance abuse, 131, 549
suicide behavior continuum, 547–548, 548*fig.*
suicide notes, 550
warning signs, risk factors, 549–550
Yellow Ribbon group, of suicide survivors, 130
See also Crisis intervention; Death and bereavement;
depression; Learned helplessness; Prevention;
Psychopathology in children
Sullivan, P. M., 4, 408
Sullivan-Burstein, K., 252
Summative evaluation, 552
See also Communication disorders; *DSM-IV-TR*
Supervision in school psychology
administrative supervision, 552
collaboration, 553
frequency, duration of, 553
metasupervision concept, 553
personnel evaluation, 553
professional/clinical supervision, 552–553
structures of, 553
techniques of, 553
training, evaluation of supervisors, 553–554
See also School psychologist
Supplemental Security Income (SSF), 237
Supports Intensity Scale of mental retardation, 318
Survey, Question, Read, Recite, Review (SQ3R)
study approach, 541
Survey interview, 273
Suspension
criticism of, 554
disabled students and, 555
discipline of disabled students, 303–305
follow-up procedures, 556
gender factors, 221
IDEA law and, 555
out-of-school *vs.* in-school suspension, 554
prevention alternatives to, 555
zero tolerance policies, 601–602
See also Aggression in schools; Behavior intervention;
Corporal punishment (CP); Discipline; Expulsion;
Individuals With Disabilities Education Act (IDEA);
Problem solving; Special education; Violence in schools
Sutherland, K., 581
Sutton, N. T., 81, 362
Swanger, M., 106
Swanson, H. L., 292, 293, 314, 315, 316
Swearer, S. M., 235, 358
Swedo, S., 357, 358
Swerdlik, M. E., 353, 412, 413
Sympathetic nervous system (SNS), 69
Systemic desensitization (SD) phobia intervention, 208
Systems theory, on relationships patterns, 125

T
Taich, S., 121
Talbott, E., 108

Talbutt, L. C., 109
Tallent, N., 445, 446
TANF (Temporary Assistance to Needy Families), 237
Tanner, D., 241
Tanner, L., 241
Target behavior, 61*table*
    See also Applied behavior analysis (ABA); Behavior;
        Behavior assessment; Behavior intervention
Tarnofsky, M. B., 457
Tarver Behring, S., 140, 142
Task analysis
    anticedent-behavior-consequence type, 557
    complex behavior into behavioral sequence, 557
    latticing type, 557
    step-by-step instructions, 557–558
    See also Applied behavior analysis (ABA); Behavioral
        assessment; Behavioral concepts and applications;
        Learning; Performance-based assessment (PA)
Task Force on Evidence-Based Interventions in School
    Psychology (Kratochwill & Stoiber), 197
Task Force on Psychological Intervention Guidelines (APA), 197
Taton, J., 195
Taylor, H. G., 574
Taylor, L., 90, 213
Taylor, R. S., 585
TBI. *See* Traumatic brain injury
TCAs (tricyclic antidepressants), 157
Teacher-student relationships
    academic achievement and, 558–559
    communication processes, 558, 559
    conflict *vs.* closeness in, 558
    external influences, 558, 559
    gender, ethnic factors and, 559
    individual characteristics, 558, 559
    responsibility for, 558
    teacher characteristics and, 559
    understanding of the relationship, 558, 559
    See also Academic achievement
Teachers of Psychology in Secondary
    Schools (TOPSS), 21
Teaching. *See* Discipline; High school; Learning; Middle
    school; Multicultural education; Parent-teacher
    conferences; Resource rooms; Special education;
    Teacher-student relationships
Teams-Games-Tournaments Model (TGTM) of
    peer tutoring, 379
Teen pregnancy
    abortion rates, 560
    dispositional factors, 560
    HIV/AIDS and, 561
    implications, consequences of, 560–561
    multimethod intervention strategies, 561–562
    prevalence rates, 560
    risk factors, 559–560
    sexually transmitted diseases and, 561
    situational factors, 560
    taxpayer costs, 561
    See also Counseling; Dropouts; Parenting, parents;
        Peers, peer pressure; Single-parent families
Teeter, P. A., 30, 335
Teitelbaum, M. A., 154

Telch, M. J., 224
Television. *See* Media and children
Tellegen, A., 517
Telzrow, C. F., 273, 574
Temple, E. P., 33
Templeton, S., 527, 528*table*
Temporary Assistance to Needy Families (TANF), 237
Terepocki, M., 179
Terman, Lewis, 474
Terry, B., 94
Test consequences evidence of test validity, 579
Test for Auditory Comprehension of Language-Revised, 99
Test of Language Development, 99
Test of Visual-Motor Integration (VMI), 337
Test reliability. *See* Reliability of test scores
Test-retest reliability, 445
Tests in Print (Buros), 75–76
TGTM (Teams-Games-Tournaments Model) of
    peer tutoring, 379
Tharinger, D., 347, 420
Theodore, L. A., 101
Theories of human development
    behavioral model, 564–565
    cognitive-developmental model, 565–566
    embryology, 564
    environmental factors, 564–565
    ethnology, 563
    free association, 564
    Id, Ego, Superego structures and, 564
    interactionist cognitive development, 566
    maturational and biological models, 562–563
    preformation concept, 564
    psychoanalytic model, 563–564
    recapitulation theory, 564–565
    resolution of conflicts, 564
    social learning theory, 565
    sociobiology, 563
    See also Defense mechanisms; Learning; Learning
        styles; Self-concept and efficacy
Theory-driven evaluation model of program evaluation, 411
Think First anger management program, 54
Thinking styles, 294–295
Thomas, Alex, 169
Thompson, J. R., 318
Thorndike, E., 284–285, 285*fig.*
Thorson, N., 94
Thurston, L. P., 370, 372
Thurstone, L. L., 268
Tierney, Grossman, 324
Tilly, W. D., 382, 535
Time/event sampling procedures of behavioral
    assessment, 56
Time on task
    behavioral assessment, 567
    consistent classroom routine and, 567
    maximization strategies, 567
    momentary sampling technique, 567
    off-task behavior causes, 567
    whole-interval sampling technique, 567
    See also Attention deficit hyperactivity disorder (ADHD);
        Behavioral assessment; Classroom observation

Time-out reductive technique, 65*table*
Time-out (TO)
    behaviors leading to, 569
    contraindications to, 568–569
    evaluation of, 570
    experiential contrast component, 568
    initiation of, 569
    length of, 569
    locations for, 569
    misbehaviors during, 569
    popularity of, 568
    post time-out activity, 569–570
    repetition component, 568
    time-in and, 568
    underlying processes of, 568
    See also Applied behavior analysis (ABA); Behavior
        intervention; Classroom climate; Intervention
Time-series research design. *See* Single-case
    experimental design
Tindal, G., 12
Tingstrom, D. H., 471, 536
Tobler, N. S., 151, 546
Token economy
    behavior reinforcement, 570
    development, implementation, 570–571
    example of, 571
    sample reinforcer menus, 571*figs.*
    See also Behavior; Behavior intervention;
        Self-management
Toledano, S. R., 78
Tollefon, N., 531, 552
Tollefson, N., 209, 229, 380
Tombari, M. L, 567
Toporek, R., 140
TOPSS (Teachers of Psychology in
    Secondary Schools), 21
Tourette's syndrome (TS)
    echolalia and, 186
    motor, vocal tics, 571–572
    premonitory urge and, 572
    psychotropic medications for, 421
    self-injurious behavior, 493
    visual-motor integration problems, 572
    See also Psychotropic medications
Towbin, K. E., 358
Trainers of School Psychologists, 216
Trans, C. Q., 40
Trapani, J., 207
Traub, J., 478
Traudt, A., 473
Traumatic brain injury (TBI), 263, 264*table*
    defined, 572
    educational planning, 573–574
    family outcomes, 573–574
    IDEA category, 263, 264*table*
    incidence rates, 572
    lead exposure, 282
    neuropsychological outcomes, 573
    psychoeducational outcomes, 573
    psychosocial outcomes, 573
    special education services need, 572–573

See also Communication disorders; Individuals With
        Disabilities Education Act (IDEA); Intelligence;
        Learning; Memory; Neuropsychological assessment;
        Perseveration; Problem solving
Traxler, M., 525
Traynelis-Yerek, E., 527
Treatment, defined, 66*table*
Treatment integrity, defined, 66*table*
Treiman, R., 438
Treisman, A. M., 28
Tremblay, R., 211
Trentacosta, C. J., 211
Tricyclic antidepressants (TCAs), 157
Trieman, R., 527
Trivette, P. S., 252
Troia, G., 588
Trojan Suarez, E. A., 106
Troutman, A., 51, 61*table*, 62*table*, 63*table*,
        64*table*, 65*table*, 66*table*
Troutman, G. C., 252
Trust concept, of psychosocial development, 189
TS. *See* Tourette's syndrome
Tsai, A. K., 572
Tuckman, B. W., 541
Tunick, R. A., 179
Turco, T., 495
Turgeon, L., 211
Turnbull, A., 83
Turnbull, R., 83
Turner, J., 258
Turner, N. D., 525
Tutoring
    Classwide Peer Tutoring, 575
    instructional tutoring approach, 575
    Reciprocal Peer Tutoring, 575
    strategic tutoring approach, 575
Twyman, T., 12

U
Ullman, J. B., 151
Unger, D. G., 505, 507
Unit studies homeschooling method, 246
Unschooling homeschooling method, 246
Upah, K. R. F., 535
Updyke, F. J., 112
Urban Institute, 248
U.S. Bureau of the Census, 504, 505
U.S. Department of Agriculture (USDA), 355
U.S. Department of Education, 120, 199, 227, 263, 319, 327, 478
    antidiscrimination, antipoverty legislation, 577
    education policies, legislation, 577
    funding statistics, 578
    National Defense Education Act, 577
    No Child Left Behind Act of 2001, 351
    program offices of, 578
    Public Law 96-88, 577
    violence in schools, 581, 582, 584, 585
    See also Individuals With Disabilities Education
        Act (IDEA); Special education
U.S. Department of Health and Human Services,
    238, 355, 486–487

U.S. Department of Labor, 242
U.S. Environmental Protection Agency, 282
U.S. Equal Employment Opportunity Commission, 233, 583
U.S. General Accounting Office, 167
U.S. Surgeon General, 549, 550, 581, 583
Utilization-focused program evaluation model, 411
Utley, C. A., 94

V
Vacca, J., 267
Valas, H., 283
Validity
  construct validity, 579
  content validity, 579
  criterion validity, 579
  standards, sources of evidence, 579–580
  See also Reliability of test scores
Valle, M., 272
Van Den Veyver, I. B., 40
Van Kammen, W. B., 107
Vanderwood, M., 36
Variable-interval (VI) schedule of reinforcement, 470, 471
Variable-ratio (VR) schedule of reinforcement, 470, 471
Vartanian, L. R, 187, 425
Vaughn, S., 523, 525
Vebten-Mortenson, S., 150
Veltman, M. W. M., 5, 5*table*
Verbal praise
  of effort and ability, 580
  gender bias, 580
  improvement of, 580
  motivation to learn, 580–581
  value of student work, behavior, 580
  See also Behavior intervention; Intervention; Motivation
Verbal *vs.* imagery cognitive style, 294
Verhaalen, S. E., 245
Vernon, P. E., 268
Vess, S. M., 23
Vicarious learning, 445
Victim effect, of TV violence, 311
Victimization. *See* Bullying and victimization
Video technology, 70
Vineland Adaptive Behavior Scales, 40
Violence in schools
  behavioral risk factors, 583
  bullying, 582–583, 584, 585
  copycat behavior, 581
  expulsion, 199
  individual threat assessment, 584
  law enforcement partnerships, 584–585
  media violence and, 313, 583
  model of youth violence, 583
  research trends regarding, 456
  school safety procedures, 582
  school shootings, 128, 581
  schoolwide assessment, 583–584
  schoolwide interventions, 584
  sexual harassment, 583
  statistics regarding, 582
  violence, defined, 582
  violent crime, 582–583

zero tolerance discipline policies, 167, 199, 235, 582
  See also Aggression in schools; Bullying and victimization;
    Corporal punishment (CP); Counseling; Crisis
    intervention; Early intervention (EA); Gangs;
    Harassment; Media and children; Peer mediation;
    Posttraumatic stress disorder (PTSD); Prevention
Vitaro, F., 211
VMI (Test of Visual-Motor Integration), 337
Vocabulary skills, 401, 437, 440
Vogl, S., 377
Voice disorders, 100–101
Vollmer, T. R., 25, 26
Voltz, D. L., 307
von Bertalanffy, L., 113
Vossekuil, B., 127
Vossekuil, F., 582, 584
Vygotsky, L. V., 590, 599

W
W. K. Kellogg Foundation, 409
Waas, G. A., 358
Wacker, D. P., 67
Wade, S. L., 574
Walker, D., 94
Walker, J. M. T., 253
Walkowiak, J., 337
Walsh, D., 458
Walters, A. S., 517
Walthall, K., 110
Walther-Thomas, C., 524, 525
Wampold, B. E., 126
Wan, M., 40
Wang, Margaret, 481–482
War on Poverty, Johnson administration, 237
Warman, M., 224
Warren, K. R., 209
Washington State Youth Suicide Prevention Program, 551
Wasik, B. A., 406
Watson, J., 50
Watson, J. B., 113
Watson, M., 406
Watson, T. S., 113, 189
Webb, N. M., 380
Webber, L. A., 521
Webber, M. D., 546
Weber, M. J., 87
Webster, L., 432
Webster, R. E., 155, 376
Webster-Stratton, C., 361, 369
Wechsler Individual Achievement Test, 438
Wechsler Intelligence Scale for Children - 4th Edition
    (WISC-IV), 40, 99, 104, 271*table,* 272, 290, 572–573
Wehby, J., 53
Wehmeyer, M., 222
Weiner, B., 332
Weiss, I. R., 242
Weiss, L., 172
Weiss, R. V., 160
Weisz, J. R., 197, 416
Weizman, A., 356
Welch, M., 111

Weller, E. B., 153
Weller, N., 247
Weller, R. A., 153
Wellman, H. M., 30
Wells, A., 406
Wells, K., 54
Wells, N., 321
Wendkos Olds, S., 491
Wendling, B. J., 591
Wenning, K., 360
Werry, J., 420, 421, 422
Weschler Preschool and Primary Sale of
    Intelligence-Revised, 400, 401
West, J. R., 209
Westerfield, G., 87
Wharton-McDonald, R., 587
Wheeler, A. C., 210
Whipple, A. D., 466
Whiston, S. C., 126
Whitaker, A., 357, 358
Whitaker, J. D., 247
WHO. *See* World Health Organization
Wiburg, K. M., 104
Wichstrom, L., 549
Wide Range Achievement Test, 438, 596
Wide Range Interest-Opinion Test, 80
Wiethoff, L., 581
Wiggins, G. P., 388
Wilczynski, S. M., 536
Wiley, E. W., 380
Wilkinson, S., 3
Willert, A., 506
Williams, B. L., 349
Williams, C., 601
Williams, C. L., 517
Williams, G., 569
Williams, K. T., 401
Williamson, E. G., 123
Willis, G., 241
Willows, D. M., 179
Wilson, A., 429, 430
Wilson, M. S., 12, 221
Winchel, R. M., 492
WISC-IV. *See* Wechsler Intelligence Scale for
    Children - 4th Edition
Wise, J., 121
Wise, P., 515
Wise, P. S., 81, 347, 404
Wiseman, D. G., 200
Witaro, F., 211
Within-series experimental designs, 501–502
Witmer, Lightner, 454, 473–474
Witt, J. C., 25, 26, 352
Witteborg, K., 67
WM (working memory), 287
Woehr, S. M., 468
Wolber, G. J., 446
Wolchik, S. A., 172
Woldoroff, M. G., 29
Wolery, M., 265
Wolf, M. M., 23, 53, 66*table,* 214, 568

Wolpe, J., 207
Woodcock, R. W., 401
Woodcock-Johnson III Tests of Achievement, 104, 388, 400, 401
Woodcock-Johnson III Tests of Cognitive Ability, 400, 401
Woodcock Language Proficiency Battery-Revised, 437, 438
Woods, D. W., 64*table*
Woolfolk, A., 388
Working memory (WM), 287
World Health Organization (WHO), 176, 509, 582
World Wide Web
    explanation of, 103
    school psychologist use of, 104–105
Wray, D., 587
Wright, J., 310
Wright, J. C., 310
Writing interventions and strategies
    effective writing instruction, 587, 589*table*
    handwriting instruction, 588
    individual student needs, 587–588
    planning, revision, 588
    school psychologist role, 588–589
    writing importance, 587
    See also Academic achievement; Cooperative learning;
        Grades; Homework; Learning; Learning styles
The Writing Road to Reading (Spalding), 443
Written language assessment
    coding experience into symbols, 590
    criterion-referenced measures, 592
    degree of structure of task, 590–591
    diagnostic norm-referenced assessment, 592
    handwriting, 596
    informal measures, 592
    modality of task, 590–591
    narrative *vs.* expository, 599
    norm-referenced assessment, 592, 593–595*table,*
        596, 597–598*table*
    spelling, 596
    syntax, 596, 599
    task measurement, 590–591
    text organization, 599
    tools measurement, 591–592
    topic measurement, 591
    written expression difficulties, 590
    See also Academic achievement; Authentic assessment;
        Behavioral assessment; Communication disorders;
        Criterion-referenced assessment; Learning disabilities;
        Writing interventions and strategies
Wundt, W., 284, 285*fig.*
Wung, P., 107
Wurm, T., 282

Y
Yager, H., 559
Yeates, K. O., 574
Yell, M. L., 255, 256
YMCA, 325–326
Yoked observation technique, of classroom observation, 92
Yokoi, L., 587
Yopp, H., 385
Yopp-Singer Test of Phoneme Segmentation, 386
Young, C., 462

Young, R., 496
Young adulthood stage of psychosocial development, 190
Youth Gang Survey, 220
Youth Risk Behavior Survey (YRBS), 548
YRBS (Youth Risk Behavior Survey), 548
Ysseldyke, J. E., 13, 35, 36, 51, 137, 389
YWCA, 325–326

Z
Zametkin, A. J., 356
Zeanah, C. H., 431
Zenere, F., 130
Zero to Three, National Center for Infants, Toddlers,
    and Families, 265

Zero tolerance policies, 167, 199, 235, 582
    evidence for, 602
    history, definition, application, 601
    pro and con, 601–602
    racial disparities in, 601, 602
    See also Expulsion; Gangs; Substance abuse; Suspension;
        Violence in schools
Zhang, I., 296
Zimbardo, P., 499, 500
Zimmerman, R., 151
Zito, J. M., 420
Zoghbi, H. Y., 40
Zoon, C. K., 356